Main Cities of Europe 2008

Commitments

"This volume was created at the turn of the century and will last at least as long".

This foreword to the very first edition of the MICHELIN Guide, written in 1900, has become famous over the years and the Guide has lived up to the prediction. It is read across the world and the key to its popularity is the consistency of its commitment to its readers, which is based on the following promises.

THE MICHELIN GUIDE'S COMMITMENTS

Anonymous inspections: our inspectors make regular and anonymous visits to hotels and restaurants to gauge the quality of products and services offered to an ordinary customer. They settle their own bill and may then introduce themselves and ask for more information about the establishment. Our readers' comments are also a valuable source of information, which we can then follow up with another visit of our own.

Independence: Our choice of establishments is a completely independent one, made for the benefit of our readers alone. The decisions to be taken are discussed around the table by the inspectors and the editor. The most important awards are decided at a European level. Inclusion in the Guide is completely free of charge.

Selection and choice: The Guide offers a selection of the best hotels and restaurants in every category of comfort and price. This is only possible because all the inspectors rigorously apply the same methods.

Annual updates: All the practical information, the classifications and awards are revised and updated every single year to give the most reliable information possible.

Consistency: The criteria for the classifications are the same in every country covered by the Michelin Guide.

... and our aim: to do everything possible to make travel,holidays and eating out a pleasure, as part of Michelin's ongoing commitment to improving travel and mobility.

Dear Reader

Welcome to the 27th edition of the 'Main Cities of Europe' guide. This guide is aimed primarily at the international business traveller who regularly journeys throughout Europe but it is equally ideal for those wishing to discover the delights of some of Europe's most romantic and culturally stimulating cities for a weekend break or special occasion.

Entry in the Michelin Guide is completely free of charge and it continues to be compiled by our professionaly trained teams of full-time inspectors from across Europe who make their assessments anonymously in order to ensure complete impartiality and independence. Their mission is to check the quality and consistency of the amenities and services provided by the hotels and restaurants throughout the year and our listings are updated annually in order to ensure the most up-to-date information.

Most of the establishments featured have been hand-picked from our other national guides and therefore our European selection is, effectively, a best-of-the-best listing.

In addition to the user-friendly layout the guide contains key thematic words which succinctly convey the style of the establishment; practical and cultural information on each country and each city; suggestions on when to go, what to see and what to eat.

This year we have expanded the guide to include Cologne and Stuttgart in Germany and Cracow in Poland.

Thank you for your support and please continue to send us your comments. We hope you will enjoy travelling with the 'Main Cities of Europe' guide 2008.

Consult the Michelin Guide at
www.ViaMichelin.com
and write to us at:
themichelinguide-europe@uk.michelin.com

Contents

Contents

COUNTRIES

Classification & Awards

CATEGORIES OF COMFORT

The Michelin Guide selection lists the best hotels and restaurants in each category of comfort and price. The establishments we choose are classified according to their levels of comfort and, within each category, are listed in order of preference.

🏨🏨🏨🏨🏨	XXXXX	Luxury in the traditional style
🏨🏨🏨🏨	XXXX	Top class comfort
🏨🏨🏨	XXX	Very comfortable
🏨🏨	XX	Comfortable
🏨	X	Quite comfortable
	🍺	Traditional pubs serving good food
	🍷	Tapas bars
🏠		Other recommended accommodation
without rest.		This hotel has no restaurant
with rm		This restaurant also offers accommodation

THE AWARDS

To help you make the best choice, some exceptional establishments have been given an award in this year's Guide. They are marked ✿ or ☺ and **Rest**.

THE BEST CUISINE

Michelin stars are awarded to establishments serving cuisine, of whatever style, which is of the highest quality. The cuisine is judged on the quality of ingredients, the skill in their preparation, the combination of flavours, the levels of creativity, the value for money and the consistency of culinary standards.

✿✿✿ **Exceptional cuisine, worth a special journey**
One always eats extremely well here, sometimes superbly.

✿✿ **Excellent cooking, worth a detour**

✿ **A very good restaurant in its category**

RISING STARS

These establishments, listed in red, are the best in their present category. They have the potential to rise further, and already have an element of superior quality; as soon as they produce this quality consistently, and in all aspects of their cuisine, they will be hot tips for a higher award. We've highlighted these promising restaurants so you can try them for yourselves; we think they offer a foretaste of the gastronomy of the future.

GOOD FOOD AT MODERATE PRICES

Bib Gourmand

Establishments offering good quality cuisine at reasonable prices (the actual price limit varies from country to country according to the relative costs).

PLEASANT HOTELS AND RESTAURANTS

Symbols shown in red indicate particularly pleasant or restful establishments: the character of the building, its décor, the setting, the welcome and services offered may all contribute to this special appeal.

to **Pleasant hotels**

to **Pleasant restaurants**

OTHER SPECIAL FEATURES

As well as the categories and awards given to the establishment, Michelin inspectors also make special note of other criteria which can be important when choosing an establishment.

LOCATION

If you are looking for a particularly restful establishment, or one with a special view, look out for the following symbols:

Quiet hotel

Very quiet hotel

Interesting view

Exceptional view

WINE LIST

If you are looking for an establishment with a particularly interesting wine list, look out for the following symbol:

Particularly interesting wine list

This symbol might cover the list presented by a sommelier in a luxury restaurant or that of a simple restaurant where the owner has a passion for wine. The two lists will offer something exceptional but very different, so beware of comparing them by each other's standards.

Facilities & Services

30 rm	Number of rooms
A/C	Air conditioning (in all or part of the establishment)
	Establishment with areas reserved for non-smokers.
	Establishment at least partly accessible to those of restricted mobility
	Meals served in garden or on terrace
SAT	Satellite TV
	Wireless Internet access
Spa	Wellness centre: an extensive facility for relaxation and well-being
	Sauna – Exercise room
	Swimming pool: outdoor or indoor
	Garden
	Tennis court
	Equipped conference room
	Private dining rooms
P P	Valet parking – Garage – Car park, enclosed parking
	No dogs allowed (in all or part of the establishment)
May-October	Dates when open, as indicated by the hotelier
M	Nearest metro station

Prices

These prices are given in the currency of the country in question. Valid for 2008 the rates shown should only vary if the cost of living changes to any great extent.

SERVICE AND TAXES

Except in Greece, Hungary, Poland and Spain, prices shown are inclusive, that is to say service and V.A.T. included. In the U.K. and Ireland, s = service included. In Italy, when not included, a percentage for service is shown after the meal prices, eg. (16 %).

MEALS

Meals 40/56	Set meal prices
Carte	"à la carte" meal prices

HOTEL

86 rm 🚹 650/750	Lowest and highest price for a comfortable single
🚹🚹 750/890	and a best double room
☕ 60/120	Prices include breakfast

BREAKFAST

☕ 20	Price of breakfast (where not included in rate)

CREDIT CARDS

	Credit cards accepted by the establishment:
AE Ⓓ MC VISA	American Express – Diners Club – MasterCard – Visa

How to use this guide

PRACTICAL & TOURIST INFORMATION

Pages with practical information on every country and city: public transport, tourist information offices, main sites and attractions (museums, monuments, theatres, etc), with a directory of shop addresses and examples of local specialities to take home.

RESTAURANTS

XXXXX to X

The most pleasant: in red.

STARS

✿✿✿ Worth a special journey.

✿✿ Worth a detour.

✿ A very good restaurant.

Establishment named in red: "Rising Star".

RESTAURANTS & HOTELS

The country is indicated by the coloured strip down the side of the page: dark for restaurants, light for hotels.

HOTELS

(five house symbols) to (one house symbol)

The most pleasant: in red.

BIB GOURMAND ☺

Good food at moderate prices.

LOCATING THE ESTABLISHMENT

Location on the town plan, with principal sights.

LOCATION

The district, the map.

ADDRESS

All the information you need to make a reservation and find the establishment.

FACILITIES & SERVICES

See also p. 8.

DESCRIPTION OF THE ESTABLISHMENT

Atmosphere, style and character.

CLASSIFICATION BY DISTRICT

With the corresponding plan number.

PRICES

See also p. 9.

KEY WORDS

If you're looking for a specific type of establishment, look out for these words. They aim to encapsulate the key 'theme' of the hotel or restaurant – the type of cooking, style of establishment, décor or atmosphere – in no more than three words, guiding you quickly to the type of hotel or restaurant that you are looking for.

The Michelin Guide and Europe

Whether it be for business or pleasure, travellers throughout Europe know that they can rely on the Michelin Guide. For over a century, it has been their companion, first in France and then beyond the dotted borderlines printed on the Michelin maps.

Over the last hundred years, the boundaries of Europe have been extended and the circle of gold stars on the European flag has had to adjust in order to welcome other nations. The Michelin Guide has always kept abreast of these profound changes on the ground, in keeping with its goal and its motto: *serving the traveller*. Indeed, in its coverage of Europe, it has witnessed the history of the continent as it unfolded. Year after year, the guide's publication, or absence from the market, has reflected the great upheavals experienced during the 20th century, with its vicissitudes, crises, eras of prosperity and peace.

THE MICHELIN GUIDE: MULTILINGUAL AND INTERNATIONAL

Inspired by its success in France and encouraged by the development of the automobile industry throughout Europe, the Michelin Guide started to spread the concept to neighbouring countries: *Belgique* appeared in 1904 – the second volume in what would quickly become a true European-wide collection. The following year, a third guide – *Benelux* – was published. The collection began to adopt an approach which would include **tourist information**, with new sections covering sights and excursions not to be missed, in addition to the advice and practical information already in the guides. At the same time, the Michelin Guide collection started to espouse Michelin's international ambitions: every new title was published in the language(s) of the country, services and main facilities were indicated by **symbols** that everyone could understand, and several pages were devoted to **international regulations** useful for travellers. Consequently readers could refer to a page dedicated to «General European Traffic Rules», for example, with specific information regarding

which side of the road to drive on in every European country. It is interesting to note that, at the time, the Michelin Guide included Turkey as part of Europe, with information about traffic in that country.

MICHELIN TRAVELS ABROAD

The Michelin Guide began to expand throughout Europe and use other languages. In 1908 *The Michelin Guide to France* was published, an **adaptation in English** of the original French guide, and two years later two new titles were published: *Deutschland und Schweiz* and *España y Portugal*. The following year (1911) three more guides were published, expanding the collection still further: *British Isles, Alpes et Rhin*, and the exotic *Les pays du Soleil*, covering not only the Côte d'Azur, Corsica and Italy, but also North Africa and Egypt! And that same year, all of these guides were translated into English.

This unprecedented expansion marked the start of the company's desire to spread throughout Europe and North Africa. Proof of the successful formula of the Michelin Guides was summed up in an advertising poster of the era showing Bibendum – the Michelin Man – proudly demonstrating that the total number of copies of the Michelin guide collection, if piled up, would be equivalent to 60 times the height of St Paul's Cathedral in London!

Success was then interrupted in 1939, with the start of the **Second World War**. From 1940 to 1944, the absence of the guide revealed the torment which Europe was going through. When the guide finally reappeared, it was «*for official use only*», printed in Washington to accompany the officers of the Allied forces during the Normandy Landings.

FROM A EUROPEAN COLLECTION...

The 1950s brought new growth, with Michelin maps now covering all of Western Europe. But it was in the 1960s that the Michelin Guide collection really started to take on a **European dimension**, taking a step by step approach to expansion. In 1964, after a half century's absence, *Deutschland* reappeared (without the GDR and East Berlin), followed ten years later by *Great Britain & Ireland*. Meanwhile, the shorter *Paris* and *London* guides appeared on the shelves, based on information taken from the national guides, and revealing an interest in large **European capital cities**. In order to remain the indispensable companion for travellers throughout Europe, the guides would from then on follow the model of *France*: enhanced with more information, including a **rigorous selection of fine restaurants**.

...TO A GUIDE FOR EUROPE

Means of transport were becoming more and more diversified and journey times were shortening considerably, encouraging faster travel and trips made more often and over longer distances than ever before. Michelin needed to bring tourists and business travellers alike a guide which covered the relevant areas, and at the same time cross the borders of the new Europe to the north and to the east.

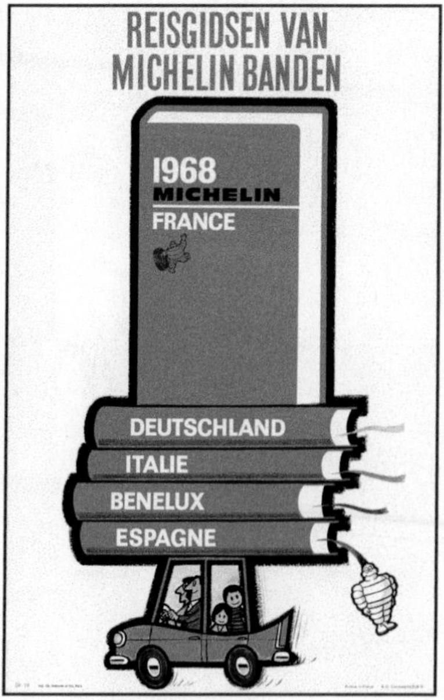

1982 saw the chance to do this. The first guide devoted to Europe was born of a **partnership** with *Times-Life Magazine* and appeared under the title *20 Cities/Villes EUROPE*. The guide was written in English and twenty thousands copies were published. The selection of establishments adopted for the guide took the best hotel and restaurant addresses in each category from the «country» guides, following the criteria guaranteeing **a constant level of quality**, above and beyond specific national considerations.

The huge success of this first edition led the company to repeat the experience. The following year, Copenhagen and Wien were included in the guide: until then, no guide existed which covered these cities, and the more global title *Main Cities of Europe* was adopted in 1984 with more than 50 towns and cities – some of them capitals, but also the other large influential cities in **20 countries**.

Who does not recognise the famous red cover of the Michelin Guide today? Since the beginning of the 20th century, the Guide has established itself throughout Europe thanks to quality, service and up-to-date selection. From Oslo to Athens, Lisbon to Budapest, the 23 titles in the collection (including the latest city guides to Los Angeles, Las Vegas and Tokyo) recommend over 25 000 hotels and 16 000 restaurants, including over 1 800 starred restaurants, and 1 200 town plans. With new introductions and practical information on every country and every town and city selected, the 2008 vintage of *Main Cities of EUROPE* offers you the very best. Happy reading and bon voyage with Michelin!

AUSTRIA

ÖSTERREICH

PROFILE

→ **Area:**
83 853 km² (32 376 sq mi).

→ **Population:**
8 150 000 inhabitants (est. 2005), density = 97 per km².

→ **Capital:**
Vienna (conurbation 1 892 000 inhabitants).

→ **Currency:**
Euro (€); rate of exchange: € 1 = US$ 1.46 (Dec 2007).

→ **Government:**
Parliamentary republic and federal state (since 1955). Member of European Union since 1995.

→ **Language:**
German.

→ **Specific public holidays:**
Epiphany (6 January); Corpus Christi (late May/June); National Day (26 October); Immaculate Conception (8 December); St. Stephen's Day (26 December).

→ **Local Time:**
GMT + 1 hour in winter and GMT + 2 hours in summer.

→ **Climate:**
Temperate continental with cold winters – high snow levels – and warm summers (Vienna: January: 0°C, July: 20°C).

→ **International dialling Code:**
00 43 followed by area code without initial 0 and then the local number.

→ **Emergency:**
Police: ✆ **133**; Medical Assistance: ✆ **144**; Fire Brigade: ✆ **122.**

→ **Electricity:**
220 volts AC, 50Hz; 2-pin round-shaped continental plugs

VIENNA

→ **Formalities**
Travellers from the European Union (EU), Switzerland, Iceland and the main countries of North and South America need a national identity card or passport (America: passport required) to visit Austria for less than three months (tourism or business purpose). For visitors from other countries a visa may be required, in addition to a passport, especially for those wishing to stay for longer than three months. We advise you to check with your embassy before travelling.

VIENNA
WIEN

Population: 1 573 000 (conurbation 1 892 000) – Altitude: 156m.

R. Mauritius/PHOTONONSTOP

Beethoven, Brahms, Mozart, Haydn, Strauss…not a bad list of former residents, by any stretch of the imagination. One and all, they succumbed to the opulent aura of Vienna, a city where an appreciation of the arts is as conspicuous as its famed big cream cakes. Sumptuous architecture and a refined air reflect the city's historical position as the seat of the powerful Habsburg dynasty and former epicentre of the Austro-Hungarian Empire. This is a city where the words rococo and baroque could have been invented.

Despite its grand image, Vienna is propelling itself into the twenty-first century with a handful of seriously innovative hotspots, most notably the MuseumsQuartier cultural complex, a stone's throw from the mighty Hofburg Imperial Palace. This is not a big city, although its vivid image gives that impression. The compact centre teems with elegant shops, fashionable coffee-houses and grand avenues, and the empire's awesome nineteenth-century remnants keep visitors' eyes fixed forever upwards.

LIVING THE CITY

Many towns and cities are defined by their ring roads, but Vienna can boast a truly upmarket version: the **Ringstrasse**, a showpiece boulevard that cradles the inner city and the riches that lie therein. Just outside here – to the southwest - are the districts of **Neubau** and **Spittelberg**, both of which have taken on a quirky, modernistic feel, exemplified by the outstanding **MuseumsQuartier**, and a buzzing coterie of hip galleries and bars. To the east of town in the Leopoldstadt quarter lies **Prater,** the green lung of Vienna, and home to some of the world's oldest merry-go-rounds. Further out, southwest of the city, lies the suburban area utterly enhanced by the grandeur of the Schönbrunn palace. Where in all this is the blue Danube? Surprisingly enough, the great river of waltzing legend plays less of a role than many other city waterways as it flows some way out to the northeast of the city. Of more 'strategic' relevance to visitors is the Danube Canal, which divides the centre from the northern and eastern suburbs.

PRACTICAL INFORMATION

ARRIVAL-DEPARTURE

Wien-Schwechat Airport is 19km from the city centre. The City Airport Express train to Wien Mitte takes 16min and leaves every 30min. A taxi will cost around €30 and take 30min.

TRANSPORT

The Vienna Card, which allows unlimited travel on the whole of the city's public transport network for 72hr and offers a discount to sights, cafes, restaurants and shops, can be bought from the Tourist Office, at your hotel or from ticket offices of the Vienna Transport Authority. You can also purchase Rover tickets for 24hr or 72hr. The city's buses, trams and metro are renowned for their excellent efficiency.

There are around eighty bus routes around the city. Night buses run every half-hour throughout the small hours. The trams run every five to ten minutes, and there are timetables at every stop. You can bet your Sachertorte on them arriving exactly on time!

This is not a drivers' city. With its profusion of one-way streets, tramways and difficult-to-find parking spots, Vienna is most definitely somewhere to discover by foot or by public transport.

EXPLORING VIENNA

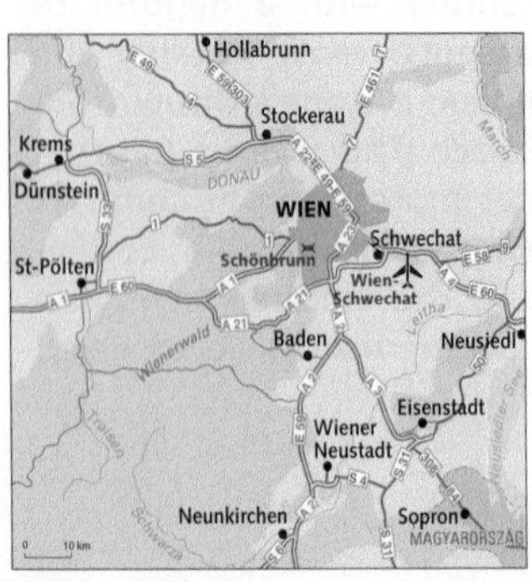

Take a ruling dynasty, give it six hundred years of power and influence, and what have you got? Answer: a city bursting with imperial pomp and palaces, a high-brow concoction set fair to impose and overawe. You've got Vienna. This is Europe's *grand dame*, where former royal palaces burst with treasure troves of art, white stallions trot daintily amongst visitors and classical concerts are performed in streets crammed with regal delights. The era of the Habsburgs came crashing to an uncomfortable end at the climax of World War I, but you only have to stroll around the old town, embraced by the Ringstrasse, to come face-to-face with its former glories. One location sums it all up: the **Hofburg**, or Imperial Palace. It dominates this famous area, and is a small town in itself, an immense palace complex with extensions and add-ons depending on the whim of successive Habsburg rulers. Two of the city's most famous institutions are based here: the **Vienna Boys' Choir** and the **Spanish Riding School**. You could spend all your time at the Hofburg, wandering around the Imperial Apartments, decked out with Biedermeier portraits and Bohemian crystal chandeliers, or following the melodramatic events of Empress Elisabeth's life in the Sisi Museum.

➜ TOWERING GLORY

In time, though, you'll more than likely want to stroll the quarter-mile north to Vienna's second great visitor magnet, **St Stephen's Cathedral**, towering over Stephansplatz Square. Its chevron style mosaic roof and skeletal spires are iconic landmarks, and its near-450ft. tower (completed in 1433) means it can be seen from all over the city. Climb its 343 steps and you can return the favour. Your bird's eye view will take in a whole holiday's worth of museums and galleries, so cherry-pick the best, and your footsteps will invariably lead you to the **Art History Museum** on Maria-Theresien Platz. It's stacked with centuries of Habsburg-acquired artistic gems: the Picture Gallery is hung with 16C and 17C masters such as Titian, Caravaggio and Rubens, and there are other superb collections, including those of Roman and Egyptian antiquity.

➜ QUIRKY QUARTIER

Anyone who knew Vienna before 2001 will wonder what's happened to the imperial stables, just over the road from the Art History Museum. These days, you won't see any horses, but you will find the impressively trendy **MuseumsQuartier.** This is now one of the biggest cultural complexes in the world, and its irresistible quirkiness draws visitors twenty-four hours a day (the courtyards and alleyways here never close; its cafés and bars think along much the same lines). The MQ is home to an awesome array of artists and art spaces, galleries and museums. Its defining attraction is a massive white cube – the Leopold Museum – which has five floors of 19C and 20C art, the highlights being Austria's 'dynamic duo' Klimt and Schiele: the latter's world-famous Reclining Woman is here.

Find your way out of the MQ, head east along the Ringstrasse, and before you can say Don Giovanni you're at the **Staatsoper**, or State Opera House. This is possibly the most cherished building of them all to locals, and has had a special place in Viennese hearts since t opened to the strains of Mozart in 1869. Designed in grandiose Italian Renaissance style, there's an invariable throng of people getting in line for their cheap standing-room tickets. If you can't make it to a concert here, then try the Musikverein further east. Also built in the 1860s, it matches the Opera House in terms of popularity, not least because its acoustics are second-to-none, its décor is sumptuous, and it's home to the globally renowned Vienna Philharmonic. When the play's the thing, the Viennese head back west along the Ringstrasse to the Burgtheater. You can't miss it: it's right opposite the grand neo-Gothic City Hall. Some go to the Burgtheater just to clap eyes on the sumptuously decorated staircases that define the place. Others go for the city's finest drama productions.

➜ BEL-EPOQUE

Just when you think this box of treasures has given up all its golden contents, along comes a palace that even outdoes the Hofburg. The **Belvedere** is southeast of the centre, and its two superb Baroque mansions, atop a sweeping garden, offer wonderful vistas of central Vienna. One of these imposing buildings (the grander of the two, the Upper Belvedere,) houses the wondrous Austrian Art Gallery, which boasts an impressive collection of works by Klimt, plus a notable selection by Schiele. Great paintings by Van Gogh and Monet are here, too. Not to be totally outdone, the Lower Belvedere showcases treasures with a medieval, baroque and Golden Age hue.

→ THE AVANT GARDE

To be honest, the area of Leopoldstadt, to the east of the city, isn't going to win any tourism awards. On the whole, it's pretty suburban, and pretty uninteresting, save for two shining lights. The Hundertwasserhaus, by the Danube Canal, is a fifty-apartment housing complex. In 1983, avant-garde architect Friedensreich Hundertwasser took it by the scruff of the neck and converted it into an eyeball-popping explosion of colour and wavy lines, a higgledy-piggledy jumble of textures that draws tourists united by one common denominator – the dropped jaw. Meanwhile, across the canal, the more conservative Prater is a traditional magnet for suburban dwellers and visiting hordes alike; this vast park has been welcoming all comers for nearly two hundred and fifty years. It's a vast place, with a funfair, tracts of woodland, a miniature railway and a planetarium. Its giant Ferris wheel lifts you above the skyline in rickety red gondolas, and on high you can see right across to St Stephen's Cathedral. If you love the aroma of candyfloss and the twinkling tinkle of the merry-go-round, then you might want to forget the more *fin-de-siècle* attractions of Vienna, and hang round the Prater instead.

One little quarter even the most devout Prater lover would not wish to miss out on lies just beyond the MuseumsQuartier. It's called Spittelberg, and it comprises half a dozen parallel, narrow cobbled streets that have retained their eighteenth-century appeal, a taste of Old Vienna beyond the Ringstrasse. There's a modern twist here: this charming district now has a new lease of life, enhanced by a string of bars, cafés and stylish art galleries, smartly entwined with the Baroque and Biedermeier houses that have been carefully restored to their former glory.

CALENDAR HIGHLIGHTS

Vienna's cultural highlights, not to anyone's great surprise, have a predominantly musical flavour, kicking off in January with the world-famous New Year's Day Concert at the Musikverein; almost as fancy are the balls which waltz through the city in deepest winter. Two of the more glitzy are the Practitioners' Ball (January) and the Opera Ball (February), when pink carnations and *The Blue Danube* are obligatory. Springtime is heralded with April's City Festival, and free musical concerts are the backbone here. A couple of cultural biggies hit town in June. The Vienna Festival is a huge event with music and theatrical highlights

VIENNA IN...

→ ONE DAY

A tram ride round the Ringstrasse (two and a half miles), St Stephen's Cathedral, a section of the Hofburg Palace, cream cakes at a smart café

→ TWO DAYS

MuseumsQuartier, Spittelberg, Hundertwasserhaus, Prater

→ THREE DAYS

A day at the Belvedere, a night at the opera

being shared out, while the Danube Island Festival is a three-day extravaganza of free concerts by bands from far and wide with the added allure of it all happening on the river's dinky islands. Later in the month and into July the vibe changes with the Vienna Jazz Festival, which spreads itself to hip venues across the city, while later in the summer the mood changes once again with KlangBogen, a chance to catch top opera and classical performers in a widely-renowned series of concerts. November brings the twenty-year-old festival Wien Modern, which succeeds in adding a cutting edge to contemporary classical music. It's not all batons, bass and big beats in this city – September's Literature Festival lasts for twenty four hours and features Austria's leading authors reading from their works non-stop around the clock – an "adventure in the head" - while the Viennale in October is Austria's biggest festival of film.

EATING OUT

Vienna is the spiritual home of the café ; the landing stage of Europe's first coffee bean (or so legend has it). Austrians drink nearly twice as much coffee as beer, astonishingly over a pint a day per head of population. A sweet tooth characterises the city: chunky mounds of glistening cream cakes enhance the window displays of most eateries. Is there a visitor to Vienna who hasn't succumbed to the sponge of the Sachertorte? Reflecting its empire days, the city's restaurants are many-pronged, so if you wish to eat your way around the globe, you shouldn't have a problem here. Viennese food is essentially the food of Bohemia, which means that meat has a strong presence on the plate. Beef, veal, pork, alongside potatoes, dumplings or cabbage, gives you pretty much the picture - be sure to try traditional boiled beef or the ubiquitous Wiener Schnitzel, deep-fried breaded veal. Also worth experiencing are the Heurigen, the traditional Austrian wine taverns which are found in Grinzing, Heiligenstadt, Neustift and Nussdorf. Elsewhere, there are snug cafés and sushi bars, tasty trattorias and tapas bars. MuseumsQuartier and Spittelberg are great places to head for to get good food and avoid the tourist centre scrum. If you want to eat on the hoof, the place to go is Naschmarkt, Vienna's best market, where the ethnic range of stalls spills over into the vibrant little restaurants dishing up everything from a plateful of noodles to a steaming, spicy curry. When it comes to tipping, if you're in the more relaxed, local pubs and wine taverns, just round up the bill, otherwise add on ten per cent.

→ UNDERGROUND SPY NETWORK

Much of cinema's iconic The Third Man was filmed in Vienna – and in particular, the sewers. Harry Lime spent an unforgettable period scurrying round beneath *strasse* level. He had a lot of sewer to choose from: there are about three thousand miles' worth in the city. About half can be walked, and you can sample them for yourself on various tours.

→ HOLIDAYING HAPSBURGS

Where did the Hapsburgs go for summer retreat? Answer: the grandiose **Schönbrunn Palace** three miles southwest of the centre. It's Austria's answer to Versailles, boasting a seventy foot high Palm House and a Hall of Mirrors where Mozart played. The whole complex is a symmetrical masterwork of 1500 rooms that in its day would have housed more than a thousand servants. Nowadays it welcomes over six and a half million visitors a year.

HISTORICAL CENTRE — Plan II

Imperial

Kärntner Ring 16 ✉ 1015 – Ⓜ Karlsplatz – ✆ (01) 50 11 00 – hotel.imperial@luxurycollection.com – Fax (01) 50 11 04 10 – www.luxurycollektion.com/imperial
138 rm – †355/1080 € ††355/1080 €, ☕ 37 € – 31 suites **E3**
Rest *Imperial* – *(dinner only) (booking advisable)* Carte 46/77 €
Rest *Café Imperial* – Carte 32/54 €
♦ Palace ♦ Grand Luxury ♦ Historic ♦
The noble grand hotel, built in 1873, enjoys a captivating historical setting, top-quality service and beautiful furnishings. The suites offer pure luxury. A restaurant with a refined and authentic atmosphere. The Café Imperial offers all the flair of a Viennese coffee house.

Palais Coburg

Coburgbastei 4 ✉ 1010 – Ⓜ Stubentor – ✆ (01) 51 81 80 – hotel.residenz@palais-coburg.com – Fax (01) 51 81 81 00 – www.palais-coburg.com **E2**
35 suites ☕ – †490/2140 € ††490/2140 €
Rest *Restaurant Coburg* – see below
Rest *WeinBistro* – *✆ (01) 51 81 88 70* – Carte 27/45 €
♦ Grand Luxury ♦ Historic ♦ Modern ♦
Here, guests are surrounded with elegance and spaciousness. A sumptuous interior lies behind the impressive facade of this Palais, built in 1840. WeinBistro: a pleasantly bright garden pavilion and wine bar.

Grand Hotel

Kärntner Ring 9 ✉ 1010 – Ⓜ Karlsplatz – ✆ (01) 51 58 00 – sales@grandhotelwien.com – Fax (01) 5 15 13 12 – www.grandhotelwien.com **E3**
205 rm – †340/440 € ††390/490 €, ☕ 30 € – 11 suites
Rest *Le Ciel* – *✆ (01) 5 15 80 91 00 (closed Sunday)* Menu 36 € (lunch)/60 € – Carte 47/71 €
Rest *Unkai* – *✆ (01) 5 15 80 91 10 (closed Monday lunch)* Menu 38/99 € – Carte 18/74 €
Rest *Grand Café* – *✆ (01) 5 15 80 91 20* – Menu 26 € – Carte 26/46 €
♦ Grand Luxury ♦ Classic ♦
A striking entryway welcomes you into this beautiful grand hotel full of historic flair and a classically elegant atmosphere. Le Ciel is an elegant restaurant on the 7th floor with a beautiful terrace. The Unkai features Japanese cuisine.

Sacher

Philharmonikerstr. 4 ✉ 1010 – Ⓜ Karlsplatz – ✆ (01) 51 45 60 – wien@sacher.com – Fax (01) 51 45 68 10 – www.sacher.com **D3**
152 rm – †385/650 € ††385/650 €, ☕ 30 € – 7 suites
Rest *Anna Sacher* – *(closed July - August and Monday)* Menu 62/94 € – Carte 38/77 €
Rest *Rote Bar* – Carte 33/72 €
♦ Grand Luxury ♦ Traditional ♦ Classic ♦
This Viennese institution, established in 1876, has style and elegance with first-class service and a beautiful recreational area. Suites with terrace and view of Vienna. Anna Sacher: classic and elegant. The Rote Bar is sumptuously bedecked in red velvet and serves delicious traditional cuisine.

Bristol

Kärntner Ring 1 ✉ 1015 – Ⓜ Karlsplatz – ✆ (01) 51 51 60 – hotel.bristol@luxurycollection.com – Fax (01) 51 51 65 50 – www.luxurycollection.com/bristol **D3**
140 rm – †235/550 € ††235/630 €, ☕ 33 € – 10 suites
Rest *Korso* – see below
Rest *Sirk* – *(closed 4 weeks July - August)* Carte 32/70 €
♦ Grand Luxury ♦ Traditional ♦ Classic ♦
A stylish hotel with professional service. The Prince of Wales suite is sumptuous and luxurious and features its own fitness and sauna rooms. Enjoy beautiful views over the State Opera House through the large windows of the Sirk restaurant.

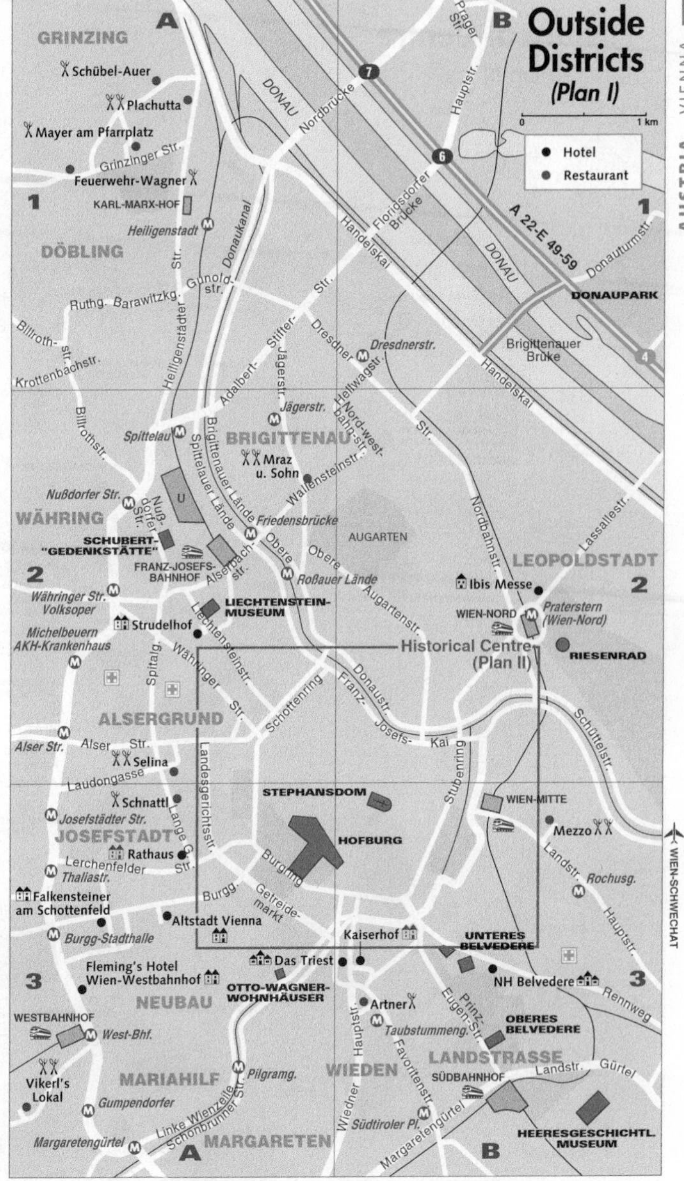
Outside Districts
(Plan I)
0
1 km
Hotel
Restaurant
A
B
1
2
3
GRINZING
Schübel-Auer
Plachutta
Mayer am Pfarrplatz
Grinzinger Str.
Feuerwehr-Wagner
KARL-MARX-HOF
Heiligenstadt
DÖBLING
Ruthg.
Barawitzkg.
Billroth-str.
Krottenbachstr.
Heiligenstädter Str.
Gunold-str.
Donaukanal
DONAU
Nordbrücke
Prager Str.
Hauptstr.
Floridsdorfer Brücke
Handelskai
A 22-E 49-59
Donauturmstr.
DONAUPARK
Brigittenauer Brüke
Adalbert-Stifter-Str.
Dresdner Str.
Dresdnerstr.
Jägerstr.
Hellwagstr.
Nord-west-bahn-str.
Spittelau
BRIGITTENAU
Mraz u. Sohn
Wallensteinstr.
Billrothstr.
Nußdorfer Str.
Nuß-dorfer Str.
WÄHRING
SCHUBERT-"GEDENKSTÄTTE"
FRANZ-JOSEFS-BAHNHOF
Alserbach-str.
Spittelauer Lände
Brigittenauer Lände
Friedensbrücke
Obere
Roßauer Lände
AUGARTEN
Nordbahnstr.
Lassallestr.
LEOPOLDSTADT
Ibis Messe
WIEN-NORD
Praterstern (Wien-Nord)
RIESENRAD
Währinger Str. Volksoper
LIECHTENSTEIN-MUSEUM
Strudelhof
Liechtensteinstr.
Augartenstr.
Michelbeuern AKH-Krankenhaus
Historical Centre (Plan II)
Spitalg.
Währinger Str.
Schottenring
Franz-Josefs-Kai
Donaustr.
ALSERGRUND
Schüttelstr.
Alser Str.
Selina
Laudongasse
Landesgerichtsstr.
Stubenring
STEPHANSDOM
Schnattl
Lange G.
WIEN-MITTE
Josefstädter Str.
JOSEFSTADT
HOFBURG
Mezzo
Rathaus
Burgring
Landstr.
Rochusg.
Lerchenfelder Str.
Thaliastr.
Hauptstr.
Falkensteiner am Schottenfeld
Burgg.
Getreide-markt
Altstadt Vienna
Kaiserhof
UNTERES BELVEDERE
Burgg-Stadthalle
Das Triest
Fleming's Hotel Wien-Westbahnhof
NH Belvedere
OTTO-WAGNER-WOHNHÄUSER
Rennweg
NEUBAU
Artner
Prinz-Eugen-Str.
WESTBAHNHOF
West-Bhf.
Taubstummeng.
OBERES BELVEDERE
Hauptstr.
Favoritenstr.
LANDSTRASSE
Vikerl's Lokal
MARIAHILF
Pilgramg.
WIEDEN
SÜDBAHNHOF
Landstr.
Gürtel
Gumpendorfer
Wiedner Hauptstr.
Südtiroler Pl.
Linke Wienzeile
Schönbrunner Str.
Margaretengürtel
MARGARETEN
HEERESGESCHICHTL. MUSEUM
WIEN-SCHWECHAT

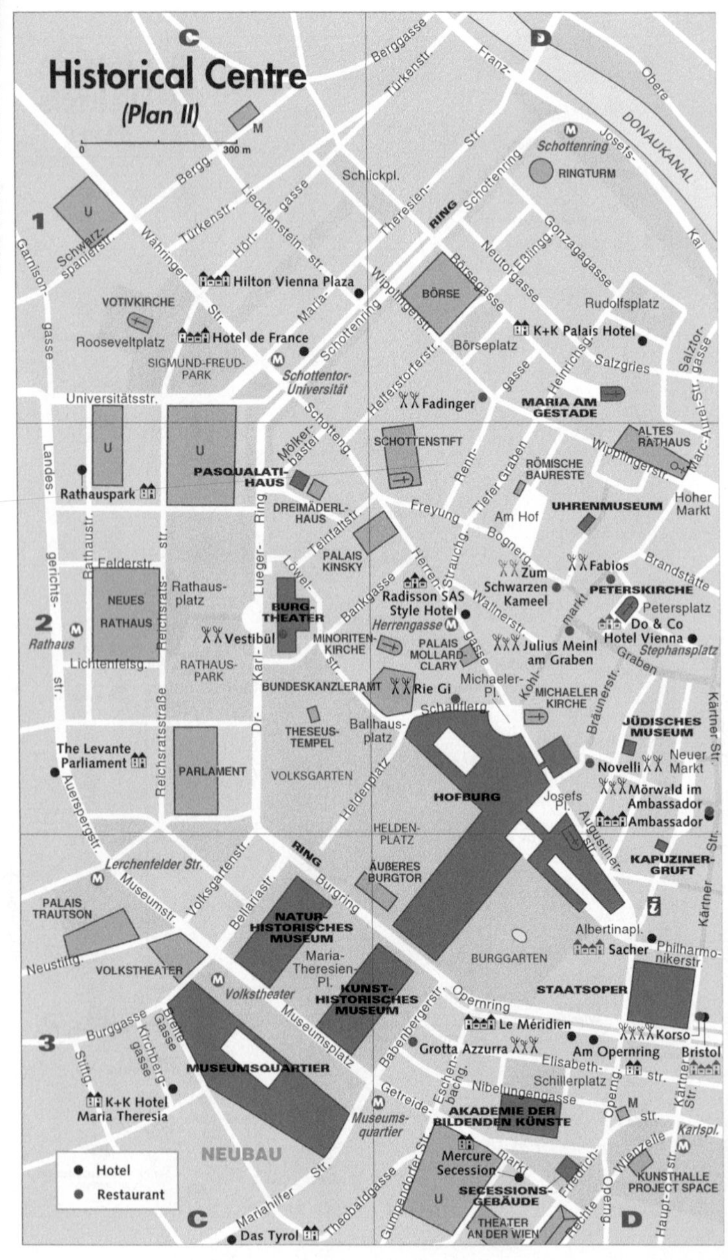
Historical Centre
(Plan II)
0
300 m
Hilton Vienna Plaza
Hotel de France
K+K Palais Hotel
Fadinger
Radisson SAS Style Hotel
Zum Schwarzen Kameel
Fabios
Do & Co Hotel Vienna
Julius Meinl am Graben
Vestibül
Rie Gi
Rathauspark
The Levante Parliament
Novelli
Mörwald im Ambassador
Ambassador
Sacher
Le Méridien
Korso
Am Opernring
Bristol
Grotta Azzurra
K+K Hotel Maria Theresia
Mercure Secession
Das Tyrol
VOTIVKIRCHE
BÖRSE
RINGTURM
MARIA AM GESTADE
ALTES RATHAUS
SCHOTTENSTIFT
RÖMISCHE BAURESTE
UHRENMUSEUM
PASQUALATI-HAUS
DREIMÄDERL-HAUS
PALAIS KINSKY
BURG-THEATER
NEUES RATHAUS
MINORITEN-KIRCHE
PALAIS MOLLARD-CLARY
PETERSKIRCHE
BUNDESKANZLERAMT
MICHAELER KIRCHE
JÜDISCHES MUSEUM
THESEUS-TEMPEL
PARLAMENT
VOLKSGARTEN
HOFBURG
HELDEN-PLATZ
ÄUßERES BURGTOR
KAPUZINER-GRUFT
PALAIS TRAUTSON
NATUR-HISTORISCHES MUSEUM
KUNST-HISTORISCHES MUSEUM
VOLKSTHEATER
BURGGARTEN
STAATSOPER
MUSEUMSQUARTIER
AKADEMIE DER BILDENDEN KÜNSTE
SECESSIONS-GEBÄUDE
THEATER AN DER WIEN
KUNSTHALLE PROJECT SPACE
NEUBAU
SIGMUND-FREUD-PARK
RATHAUS-PARK
Schottenring
Schottentor-Universität
Herrengasse
Stephansplatz
Rathaus
Lerchenfelder Str.
Volkstheater
Museumsquartier
Karlspl.
DONAUKANAL
RING
Hotel
Restaurant

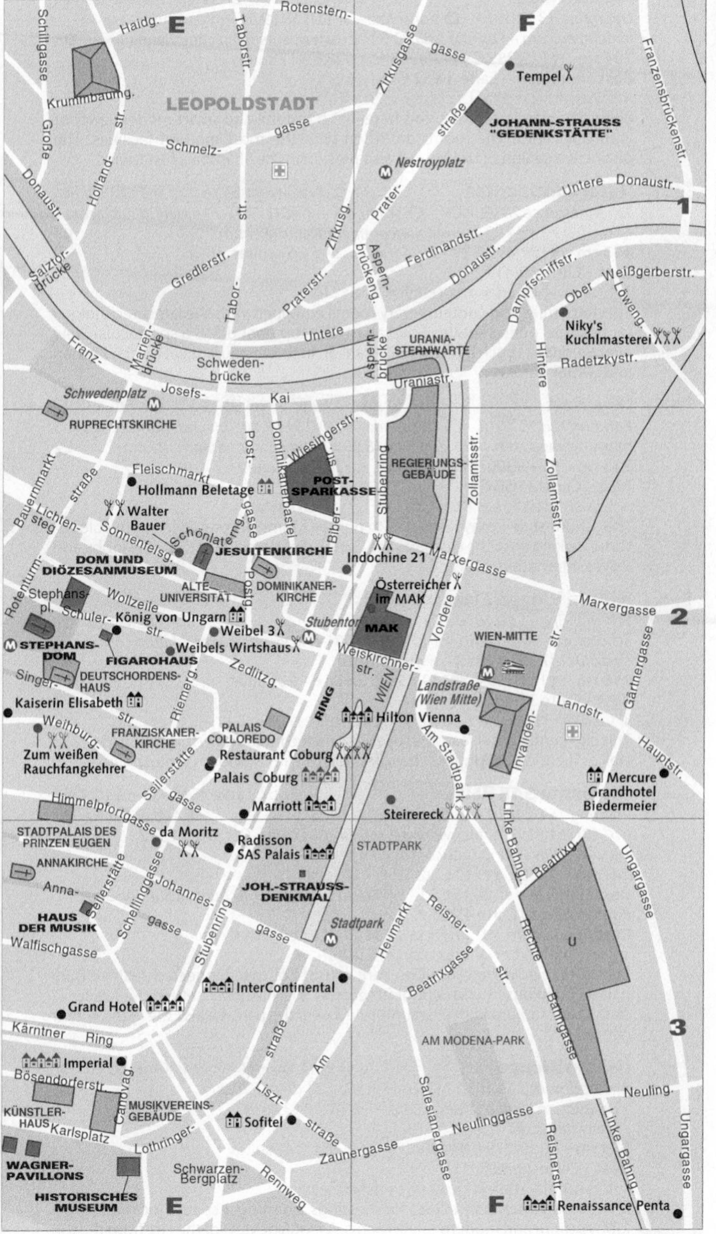
LEOPOLDSTADT
Tempel
JOHANN-STRAUSS "GEDENKSTÄTTE"
Nestroyplatz
Niky's Kuchlmasterei
URANIA-STERNWARTE
Schwedenplatz
RUPRECHTSKIRCHE
Hollmann Beletage
POST-SPARKASSE
REGIERUNGS-GEBÄUDE
Walter Bauer
JESUITENKIRCHE
DOM UND DIÖZESANMUSEUM
ALTE UNIVERSITÄT
DOMINIKANER-KIRCHE
Indochine 21
Österreicher im MAK
MAK
König von Ungarn
Weibel 3
Stubentor
STEPHANS-DOM
FIGAROHAUS
Weibels Wirtshaus
WIEN-MITTE
Landstraße (Wien Mitte)
DEUTSCHORDENS-HAUS
Kaiserin Elisabeth
Hilton Vienna
PALAIS COLLOREDO
FRANZISKANER-KIRCHE
Zum weißen Rauchfangkehrer
Restaurant Coburg
Palais Coburg
Mercure Grandhotel Biedermeier
Marriott
Steirereck
STADTPALAIS DES PRINZEN EUGEN
da Moritz
Radisson SAS Palais
STADTPARK
ANNAKIRCHE
JOH.-STRAUSS-DENKMAL
HAUS DER MUSIK
Stadtpark
InterContinental
Grand Hotel
AM MODENA-PARK
Imperial
KÜNSTLER-HAUS
MUSIKVEREINS-GEBÄUDE
Sofitel
WAGNER-PAVILLONS
HISTORISCHES MUSEUM
Renaissance Penta
Rotensterngasse
Haidg.
Taborstr.
Zirkusgasse
Franzensbrückenstr.
Schillgasse
Krummbaumg.
Große Donaustr.
Hollandstr.
Schmelzgasse
Praterstraße
Untere Donaustr.
Zirkusg.
Aspernbrückeng.
Ferdinandstr.
Donaustr.
Dampfschiffstr.
Ober Weißgerberstr.
Löweng.
Salztorbrücke
Gredlerstr.
Taborstr.
Praterstr.
Untere
Marienbrücke
Schwedenbrücke
Aspernbrücke
Hintere
Radetzkystr.
Franz-Josefs-Kai
Uraniastr.
Wiesingerstr.
Post-gasse
Dominikanerbastei
Biberstr.
Stubenring
Zollamtsstr.
Fleischmarkt
Bauernmarkt
Lichtensteg
Rotenturmstraße
Sonnenfelsg.
Schönlaterng.
Postg.
Marxergasse
Stephanspl.
Wollzeile
Schulerstr.
Vordere Zollamtsstr.
Gärtnergasse
Weiskirchnerstr.
Singerstr.
Zedlitzg.
Riemerg.
RING
WIEN
Landstr. Hauptstr.
Weihburg.
Invalidenstr.
Am Stadtpark
Seilerstätte
Himmelpfortgasse
Linke Bahng.
Beatrixg.
Ungargasse
Seilerstätte
Schellinggasse
Johannesgasse
Annagasse
Walfischgasse
Stubenring
Heumarkt
Reisnerstr.
Rechte Bahngasse
Beatrixgasse
Kärntner Ring
Bösendorferstr.
Canovag.
Karlsplatz
Lothringerstraße
Lisztstraße
Am Heumarkt
Salesianergasse
Neulinggasse
Neuling.
Zaunergasse
Reisnerstr.
Schwarzenbergplatz
Rennweg
E
F
1
2
3
U

Le Méridien

Opernring 13 ✉ 1010 – Ⓜ Karlsplatz – ✆ (01) 58 89 00 – info.vienna@lemeridien.com – Fax (01) 5 88 90 90 90 – www.lemeridien.com/vienna **D3**

294 rm – 175/285 € 175/285 €, ☕ 28 € – 17 suites

Rest *Shambala* – Carte 34/52 €

♦ Chain hotel ♦ Luxury ♦ Stylish ♦

Behind its classical facade, this hotel has a tasteful and smart modern interior with bold lines. The rooms are fitted with the most modern facilities. The distinctive design of the hotel is also present in the Shambala restaurant.

InterContinental

Johannesgasse 28 ✉ 1037 – Ⓜ Stadtpark – ✆ (01) 71 12 20 – vienna@ihg.com – Fax (01) 7 13 44 89 – www.intercontinental.com/vienna **E3**

453 rm – 189/499 € 189/499 €, ☕ 27 € – 61 suites

Rest – Carte 30/41 €

♦ Chain hotel ♦ Luxury ♦ Classic ♦

Spacious areas and contemporary rooms equipped with the latest technology for business guests set this hotel apart. The top floor offers a spectacular view over Vienna. A touch of the Mediterranean in this restaurant with open kitchen and winter garden.

Marriott

Parkring 12a ✉ 1010 – Ⓜ Stadtpark – ✆ (01) 51 51 80 – vienna.marriott.info@marriotthotels.com – Fax (01) 5 15 18 65 10 – www.viennamarriott.com **E2**

313 rm – 249/300 € 249/300 €, ☕ 24 € – 5 suites

Rest – Carte 26/56 €

♦ Chain hotel ♦ Luxury ♦ Functional ♦

The atrium-style lobby leads you to homey rooms decorated in warm colours, some looking onto the city park. The Garten-Café is inside of the hotel lobby and serves international cuisine.

Hilton Vienna Plaza

Schottenring 11 ✉ 1010 – Ⓜ Schottentor-Universität – ✆ (01) 31 39 00 – info.vienna-plaza@hilton.com – Fax (01) 31 39 02 20 09 – www.hilton.at **C1**

218 rm – 139/359 € 139/359 €, ☕ 26 € – 10 suites

Rest – Carte 31/46 €

♦ Chain hotel ♦ Luxury ♦ Functional ♦

This city-centre hotel features spacious and technologically functional rooms as well as luxurious designer suites. Restaurant with a modern atmosphere.

Radisson SAS Palais

Parkring 16 ✉ 1010 – Ⓜ Stadtpark – ✆ (01) 51 51 70 – sales.vienna@radissonsas.com – Fax (01) 5 12 22 16 – www.palais.vienna.radissonsas.com **E3**

247 rm – 260 € 260 €, ☕ 25 € – 10 suites

Rest *Le siècle* – *✆ (01) 5 15 17 34 40 (closed 16 July - 19 August, Sunday and Bank Holidays)* Carte 45/65 €

Rest *Palais Café* – *✆ (01) 5 15 17 34 70* – Carte 26/44 €

♦ Chain hotel ♦ Luxury ♦ Classic ♦

This hotel across from the City Park consists of two connected 19th-century palace buildings. Stylish appointments fit the historical setting. Le siècle : a classical restaurant with a beautiful view over the park. Palais Café in the winter garden.

Hilton Vienna

Am Stadtpark 3 ✉ 1030 – Ⓜ Landstraße – ✆ (01) 71 70 00 – reservation.vienna@hilton.com – Fax (01) 7 13 06 91 – www.hilton.de **F2**

579 rm – 139/279 € 139/279 €, ☕ 26 € – 41 suites

Rest – Carte 29/48 €

♦ Chain hotel ♦ Luxury ♦ Modern ♦

A large hotel perfectly suited for meetings, boasting a central location with a lobby atrium and modern guest rooms. A fantastic view of the city from the top floor. Restaurant features a contemporary style.

Hotel de France

Schottenring 3 ✉ 1010 – Ⓜ Schottentor-Universität – ✆ (01) 31 36 80 – defrance@austria-hotels.at – Fax (01) 3 19 59 69 – www.hoteldefrance.at **C1**

194 rm – 170/275 € 200/305 €, 25 €

Rest – Carte 19/49 €

♦ Luxury ♦ Classic ♦

The classic, elegant city hotel offers comfortable rooms with either modern or traditional design. The top floor has spacious, two-storey suites. No. 3 is the name of the brasserie-style restaurant.

Ambassador

Kärntner Str. 22 ✉ 1010 – Ⓜ Stephansdom – ✆ (01) 96 16 10 – office@ambassador.at – Fax (01) 5 13 29 99 – www.ambassador.at **D2**

86 rm – 240/439 € 304/550 €, 25 €

Rest *Mörwald im Ambassador* – see below

♦ Business ♦ Classic ♦

A successful combination of traditional and modern characterises the stylish, technically well-equipped rooms. The themed rooms are named after famous people.

Renaissance Penta

Ungargasse 60 ✉ 1030 – ✆ (01) 71 17 50 – renaissance.penta.vienna@renaissancehotels.com – Fax (01) 7 11 75 81 43 – www.renaissancehotels.com/viese **F3**

339 rm – 139/360 € 139/360 €, 21 €

Rest – Carte 16/35 €

♦ Chain hotel ♦ Functional ♦

Its history sets this former imperial military riding school apart. A tall arched ceiling and columns adorn the beautiful entryway. Functional rooms. Restaurant with an elegant atmosphere.

Do & Co Hotel Vienna

Stephansplatz 12 (6th floor) ✉ 1010 – Ⓜ Stephansplatz – ✆ (01) 2 41 88 – hotel@doco.com – Fax (01) 24 18 84 44 – www.doco.com **D2**

43 rm – 215/450 € 215/450 €, 25 €

Rest – Carte 32/52 €

♦ Business ♦ Design ♦

This hotel, opening on St. Stephen's Cathedral, showcases the most modern design. The rooms are tastefully and beautifully decorated. Eurasian cuisine is served from the open kitchen in the restaurant located on the 7th floor. Terrace with view of the cathedral.

Radisson SAS Style Hotel

Herrengasse 12 ✉ 1010 – Ⓜ Herrengasse – ✆ (01) 22 78 00 – info.style@radissonsas.com – Fax (01) 2 27 80 77 – www.style.vienna.radissonsas.com **D2**

78 rm – 260/300 € 260/315 €, 23 € – 6 suites

Rest *Sapori* – *(closed August, Sunday and Bank Holidays, July also Saturday lunch, Sunday)* Menu 35 € (lunch)/60 € – Carte 39/48 €

♦ Business ♦ Stylish ♦

Refined, modern interiors decorated in a simple, clean style surround you from the entryway rotunda to the elegant rooms of this former bank building. A former basement vault is home to the Sapori. Italian cuisine.

Das Triest

Wiedner Hauptstr. 12 ✉ 1040 – Ⓜ Karlsplatz – ✆ (01) 58 91 80 – office@dastriest.at – Fax (01) 5 89 18 18 – www.dastriest.at *Plan I* **B3**

72 rm – 210 € 270 € – 3 suites

Rest – *(closed 3 to 17 August and Saturday lunch, Sunday)* Menu 40 € – Carte 30/53 €

♦ Business ♦ Design ♦

The rooms, designed by Sir Terence Conran, have simple, clean lines and are equipped with the latest technology: functional, yet comfortable. Restaurant with a modern atmosphere and Italian cuisine.

NH Belvedere without rest
Rennweg 12a ✉ 1030 – ☎ (01) 2 06 11 – nhbelvedere@nh-hotels.com – Fax (01) 2 06 11 15 – www.nh-hotels.com Plan I **B3**
114 rm – 90/155 € 90/155 €, ☕ 15 €
◆ Chain hotel ◆ Modern ◆
A modern hotel in the classical building of the former State Printing Office. Impressive rooms, some with views of the Botanic Gardens, bistro with snacks.

The Levante Parliament
Auerspergstr. 9 ✉ 1080 – Ⓜ Rathaus – ☎ (01) 22 82 80 – parliament@thelevante.com – Fax (01) 2 28 28 28 – www.thelevante.com **C2**
70 rm ☕ – 130/220 € 155/286 €
Rest – *(closed Sunday)* Carte 26/45 €
◆ Townhouse ◆ Design ◆
Hidden behind the stone façade is this hotel with linear-modern design throughout. Glass art objects add interesting touches. Rooms with the most modern facilities. The minimalist hotel serves international cuisine.

Kaiserhof without rest
Frankenberggasse 10 ✉ 1040 – Ⓜ Karlsplatz – ☎ (01) 5 05 17 01 – wien@hotel-kaiserhof.at – Fax (01) 5 05 88 75 88 – www.hotel-kaiserhof.at Plan I **B3**
74 rm ☕ – 130/180 € 165/260 € – 3 suites
◆ Traditional ◆ Art Deco ◆
Guests receive friendly and attentive service in this beautifully furnished hotel built in 1896 – two floors are especially modern. Snack menu in the bar.

Fleming's Hotel Wien-Westbahnhof
Neubaugürtel 26 ✉ 1070 – Ⓜ West-Bahnhof – ☎ (01) 22 73 70 – wien@flemings-hotels.com – Fax (01) 2 27 37 99 99 – www.flemingshotels.com Plan I **A3**
146 rm ☕ – 125/175 € 145/211 € – 4 suites
Rest – Carte 20/36 €
◆ Business ◆ Modern ◆
This hotel is characterized by its location near the city centre and offers bright, modern style from the reception area to the beautifully furnished rooms. Restaurant with a brasserie-style atmosphere.

Hollmann Beletage
Köllnerhofgasse 6 ✉ 1010 – Ⓜ Schwedenplatz – ☎ (01) 9 61 19 60 – hotel@hollmann-beletage.at – Fax (01) 9 61 19 60 33 – www.hollmann-beletage.at **E2**
16 rm ☕ – 140/180 € 140/180 €
Rest – *(closed Sunday and Bank Holidays)* Menu 12 € (lunch)/49 € – Carte 26/43 €
◆ Townhouse ◆ Design ◆
This small hotel is an interesting establishment. Behind its townhouse facade are clean, modern interiors. Restaurant Hollmann Salon is located in "Heiligenkreuzerhof", opposite the hotel.

K+K Hotel Maria Theresia without rest
Kirchberggasse 6 ✉ 1070 – Ⓜ Volkstheater – ☎ (01) 5 21 23 – kk.maria.theresia@kuk.at – Fax (01) 5 21 23 70 – www.kkhotels.com **C3**
123 rm ☕ – 185/210 € 250/275 €
◆ Business ◆ Modern ◆
Located in the artists' quarter of Spittelberg, this hotel also has especially nice rooms with views of Vienna. The bar in the spacious lobby offers a small menu.

Kaiserin Elisabeth without rest
Weihburggasse 3 ✉ 1010 – Ⓜ Stephansplatz – ☎ (01) 51 52 60 – info@kaiserinelisabeth.at – Fax (01) 51 52 67 – www.kaiserinelisabeth.at **E2**
63 rm ☕ – 126/180 € 216/230 €
◆ Traditional ◆ Classic ◆
Both Mozart and Wagner were guests at this hotel near the Stephansdom, in operation since 1809. Elegant, dark timber furniture in a style from the end of the 19C.

Mercure Grandhotel Biedermeier without rest
Landstraßer Hauptstr. 28 (at Sünnhof) ✉ 1030 – Ⓜ Landstraße – ✆ (01) 71 67 10 – h5357@accor.com – Fax (01) 71 67 15 03 – www.mercure.com **F2**
201 rm – 156/205 € 184/233 €, 15 € – 12 suites
◆ Chain hotel ◆ Classic ◆
This hotel is located in a town house with a delightful arcade. All of the rooms are tastefully decorated with Biedermeier-style cherry-wood furniture.

König von Ungarn
Schulerstr. 10 ✉ 1010 – Ⓜ Stephansplatz – ✆ (01) 51 58 40 – hotel@kvu.at – Fax (01) 51 58 48 – www.kvu.at **E2**
33 rm – 145/165 € 208 €
Rest – *(dinner only)* Carte 24/36 €
◆ Traditional ◆ Classic ◆
Located behind the Stephansdom is this classically decorated 16C building, with lots of style and warm colours. Don't miss the attractive courtyard! The restaurant is located in a house that Mozart once lived in.

Das Tyrol without rest
Mariahilfer Str. 15 ✉ 1060 – Ⓜ Museumsquartier – ✆ (01) 5 87 54 15 – reception@das-tyrol.at – Fax (01) 58 75 41 59 – www.das-tyrol.at **C3**
30 rm – 109/209 € 149/259 €
◆ Family ◆ Modern ◆
This lovingly restored corner building is home to tastefully decorated rooms with modern furnishings. Paintings by Viennese artists adorn the walls.

Altstadt Vienna without rest
Kirchengasse 41 ✉ 1070 – Ⓜ Volkstheater – ✆ (01) 5 26 33 99 – hotel@altstadt.at – Fax (01) 5 23 49 01 – www.altstadt.at *Plan I* **A3**
42 rm – 109/149 € 129/189 € – 8 suites
◆ Traditional ◆ Stylish ◆
Each room in this patrician house has its own character. Well-appointed rooms with high ceilings, parquet, and select objets d'art.

Sofitel
Am Heumarkt 35 ✉ 1030 – Ⓜ Stadtpark – ✆ (01) 71 61 60 – h1276@accor.com – Fax (01) 71 61 68 44 – www.sofitel.com **E3**
211 rm – 116/297 € 141/297 €, 19 €
Rest – *(closed Saturday lunch, Sunday lunch and Bank Holidays lunch)* Carte 23/48 €
◆ Chain hotel ◆ Functional ◆
Elements of art nouveau and Gustav Klimt reproductions lend the rooms an agreeable ambience. Timeless natural wood and modern technical facilities. The Pullmann Bar is lovely. International and Viennese dishes are served in the restaurant.

Rathauspark without rest
Rathausstr. 17 ✉ 1010 – Ⓜ Rathaus – ✆ (01) 40 41 20 – rathauspark@austria-trend.at – Fax (01) 40 41 27 61 – www.austria-trend.at/rhw **C2**
117 rm – 200/300 € 240/350 €, 15 €
◆ Business ◆ Classic ◆
An attractive stuccoed entrance welcomes guests to this smart hotel from 1880. The mostly high-ceilinged rooms are decorated with modern elegance. An original lift.

Falkensteiner Am Schottenfeld without rest
Schottenfeldgasse 74 ✉ 1070 – Ⓜ Burgg-Stadthalle – ✆ (01) 5 26 51 81 – schottenfeld@falkensteiner.com – Fax (01) 52 65 18 11 60 – www.falkensteiner.com/schottenfeld *Plan I* **A3**
95 rm – 133/169 € 169/219 €
◆ Business ◆ Modern ◆
Modern interiors from the large lobby through to the pleasantly decorated rooms, with light furnishings and good facilities. The hotel is integrated into a row of houses.

K+K Palais Hotel without rest
Rudolfsplatz 11 ✉ 1010 – Ⓜ Schwedenplatz – ☎ (01) 5 33 13 53
– kk.palais.hotel@kuk.at – Fax (01) 5 33 13 53 70
– www.kkhotels.com **D1**
66 rm – 🛉180 € 🛉🛉240 €
◆ Traditional ◆ Functional ◆
Functional, yet homely rooms and warm breakfast room at this historic city villa. The Stephansdom and the underground are close by.

Rathaus without rest
Lange Gasse 13 ✉ 1080 – Ⓜ Rathaus – ☎ (01) 4 00 11 22
– office@hotel-rathaus-wien.at – Fax (01) 4 00 11 22 88
– www.hotel-rathaus-wien.at
closed 22 to 26 December Plan I **A3**
40 rm – 🛉118/138 € 🛉🛉148/198 €, 13 €
◆ Family ◆ Design ◆
This original city hotel, built in 1890, offers tasteful, modern design. Each room is named after Austrian wine-growers, after the motto "Wine Design."

Strudlhof without rest
Pasteurgasse 1 ✉ 1090 – Ⓜ Währinger Str.-Volksoper – ☎ (01) 3 19 25 22
– hotel@strudlhof.at – Fax (01) 31 92 52 28 00 – www.strudlhof.at Plan I **A2**
84 rm – 🛉142/149 € 🛉🛉189/209 €
◆ Business ◆ Functional ◆
This hotel offers technologically well equipped guest rooms. A stylish setting for your business function in this former palace.

Am Opernring without rest
Opernring 11 ✉ 1010 – Ⓜ Karlsplatz – ☎ (01) 5 87 55 18 – hotel@opernring.at
– Fax (01) 5 87 55 18 29 – www.opernring.at **D3**
35 rm – 🛉140/200 € 🛉🛉155/240 €
◆ Business ◆ Classic ◆
Opposite the State Opera House is this hotel with its pretty art nouveau façade. Spacious rooms combine homeliness with the functionality of modern hotels.

Mercure Secession without rest
Getreidemarkt 5 ✉ 1060
– Ⓜ Museumsquartier – ☎ (01) 5 88 38 – h3532@accor.com
– Fax (01) 58 83 82 12 – www.mercure.com **D3**
70 rm – 🛉99/165 € 🛉🛉122/206 €
◆ Chain hotel ◆ Functional ◆
Thanks to its central location, this residence is a great base for discovering the city. The rooms are homely and comfortable. Apartments also available.

Ibis Messe
Lassallestr. 7a ✉ 1020 – Ⓜ Praterstern – ☎ (01) 21 77 00 – h2736@accor.com
– Fax (01) 21 77 05 55 – www.ibishotels.com Plan I **B2**
166 rm – 🛉66 € 🛉🛉81 €, 9 €
Rest – Carte 16/25 €
◆ Chain hotel ◆ Functional ◆
Contemporary, functional rooms with light-coloured furnishings, close to the Prater park. Guests enjoy spacious desks and excellent modern technology.

Steirereck (Heinz Reitbauer Jun.)
Am Heumarkt 2 (at Stadtpark) ✉ 1030 – Ⓜ Stadtpark – ☎ (01) 7 13 31 68
– wien@steirereck.at – Fax (01) 71 33 16 82 – www.steirereck.at
closed Saturday - Sunday and Bank Holidays **F2**
Rest – *(booking advisable)* Menu 49 € (lunch)/98 € – Carte 47/85 €
Spec. Steinpilze mit Meeresfrüchtesalat und marinierter Gänseleber. Pogusch Lamm aus eigener Landwirtschaft. Reh mit Wald- und Wiesenaromaten.
◆ Inventive ◆ Design ◆
The elegant restaurant in the city park offers creative cuisine mainly using regional products. Typical Viennese pastries served in the renovated pavilion.

XXXX ✿

Restaurant Coburg – Hotel Palais Coburg

Coburgbastei 4 ✉ 1010 – Ⓜ Stubentor – ☎ (01) 51 81 88 00 – restaurant@palais-coburg.com – Fax (01) 51 81 88 18 – www.palais-coburg.com
closed Sunday - Monday **E2**
Rest – *(dinner only)* Menu 78/108 € – Carte 46/75 €
Spec. Kalbskutteln mit roten Rüben und Kaviar. Zanderfilet im Räucherpilzfond mit Gnocchetti. Lammrücken mit Senfjus und Spitzkraut.
◆ Classic ◆ Formal ◆
A beautiful, elegant atmosphere characterises this restaurant. Christian Petz's classical cuisine is complemented by a vast selection of approximately 5,000 wines.

XXXX

Korso – Hotel Bristol

Kärntner Ring 1 ✉ 1015 – Ⓜ Karlsplatz – ☎ (01) 51 51 65 46 – Fax (01) 51 51 65 75 – www.luxurycollection.com/bristol
closed August and Saturday lunch **D3**
Rest – Menu 48 € (lunch)/86 € – Carte 62/86 €
◆ Classic ◆ Formal ◆
Enjoy classical cuisine in a classical setting. An illuminated wall of onyx adorns the restaurant.

XXX

Mörwald im Ambassador

Kärntner Str. 22 (1st floor) ✉ 1010 – Ⓜ Stephansplatz – ☎ (01) 96 16 11 61 – ambassador@moerwald.at – Fax (01) 96 16 11 60 – www.moerwald.at
closed Sunday and Bank Holidays **D2**
Rest – *(booking advisable)* Menu 39 € (lunch)/125 € – Carte 52/74 €
◆ French ◆ Friendly ◆
The elegant restaurant featuring French cuisine is next to a beautiful atrium bar. The glass-front winter garden overlooks the Neuen Markt and opens in the summer.

XXX

Niky's Kuchlmasterei with rm

Obere Weissgerberstr. 6 ✉ 1030 – ☎ (01) 7 12 90 00 – office@kuchlmasterei.at – Fax (01) 7 12 90 00 16 – www.kuchlmasterei.at
closed Sunday and Bank Holidays except December **F1**
7 suites – †250 € ††250 €, ☕ 13 €
Rest – Menu 29 € (lunch)/52 € – Carte 35/58 €
◆ International ◆ Cosy ◆
Rich décor and original artwork set the tone in this unique restaurant. Beautiful terrace and large wine cellar. Individually decorated, exclusive suites.

XXX

Julius Meinl am Graben

Graben 19 (1st floor) ✉ 1010 – Ⓜ Stephansplatz – ☎ (01) 5 32 33 34 60 00 – restaurant@meinlamgraben.at – Fax (01) 5 32 33 34 12 90 – www.meinlamgraben.at
closed Sunday and Bank Holidays **D2**
Rest – *(booking essential)* Menu 34 € (lunch)/89 € (dinner) – Carte 48/70 €
◆ Classic ◆ Friendly ◆
In a gourmet shop rich in tradition you will find this popular restaurant with classical cuisine. The window seats provide a lovely view over the Graben and Pestsäule.

XXX

Grotta Azzurra

Babenbergerstr. 5 ✉ 1010 – Ⓜ Museumsquartier – ☎ (01) 5 86 10 44 – office@grotta-azzurra.at – Fax (01) 5 86 10 44 15 – www.grotta-azzura.at **D3**
Rest – Menu 70 € – Carte 32/49 €
◆ Italian ◆ Friendly ◆
Austria's oldest Italian restaurant has existed since the beginning of the '50s. Details such as high ceilings, beautiful candlesticks and artwork create a special atmosphere.

Mraz & Sohn

Wallensteinstr. 59 ✉ 1200 – Ⓜ Friedensbrücke – ☎ (01) 3 30 45 94 – Fax (01) 3 50 15 36 – www.mraz-sohn.at
closed 24 December - 6 January, 11 to 31 August and Saturday - Sunday, Bank Holidays Plan I **A2**
Rest – *(booking advisable)* Menu 38/89 € – Carte 47/57 €
Spec. Gänseleber mit Kirschen und Frenchtoast. Ox mit Knoblauchschnecken. Rösthaselnuss-Mousse.
♦ Inventive ♦ Fashionable ♦
The Mraz family attentively runs this lovely, uniquely designed restaurant. Creative cuisine is complemented by an interesting selection of wines.

Selina

Laudongasse 13 ✉ 1080 – Ⓜ Rathaus – ☎ (01) 4 05 64 04 – Fax (01) 4 08 04 59 – www.selina.at Plan I **A2**
Rest – Menu 49/68 € – Carte 21/43 €
♦ International ♦ Friendly ♦
In a modern, elegant setting with a southern touch, refined international and Mediterranean/Middle Eastern cuisine is served.

Novelli

Bräunerstr. 11 ✉ 1010 – Ⓜ Herrengasse – ☎ (01) 5 13 42 00 – novelli@haslauer.at – Fax (01) 51 34 20 01 – www.novelli.at
closed Sunday **D2**
Rest – *(booking advisable)* Menu 26 € (lunch) – Carte 33/54 €
♦ Mediterranean ♦ Trendy ♦
Italian cuisine is coupled with friendly service. Robust, warm colours lend a Mediterranean atmosphere to this modern restaurant.

Vestibül

Dr. Karl-Lueger-Ring 2 (at Burgtheater) ✉ 1010 – Ⓜ Herrengasse – ☎ (01) 5 32 49 99 – restaurant@vestibuel.at – Fax (01) 5 32 49 99 10 – www.vestibuel.at
closed Saturday lunch, Sunday and Bank Holidays, July - August also Saturday dinner **C2**
Rest – Menu 39 € – Carte 29/49 €
♦ Austrian ♦ Friendly ♦
In the side wing of the Burgtheater, this stylish restaurant, decorated in marble and stucco, offers delicious regional and Mediterranean dishes.

Walter Bauer

Sonnenfelsgasse 17 ✉ 1010 – Ⓜ Stubentor – ☎ (01) 5 12 98 71 – restaurant.walter.bauer@aon.at – Fax (01) 5 12 98 71
closed Holy week, 21 July - 15 August and Saturday - Monday lunch **E2**
Rest – *(booking advisable)* Menu 49/69 € – Carte 45/65 €
Spec. Steinbutt an der Gräte gebraten. Entrecôte mit Kräuterbutter und hausgemachten Pommes Frites. Crème brûlée mal drei.
♦ Inventive ♦ Cosy ♦
Hidden away in a small alleyway is this 14th century house in the old city. Enjoy modern cuisine under the beautiful vaulted ceiling.

Zum weißen Rauchfangkehrer

Weihburggasse 4 ✉ 1010 – Ⓜ Stephansplatz – ☎ (01) 5 12 34 71 – rauchfangkehrer@utanet.at – Fax (01) 5 12 34 71 28 – www.weisser-rauchfangkehrer.at
closed mid July - mid August and Sunday - Monday **E2**
Rest – *(dinner only) (booking advisable)* Carte 45/77 €
♦ Viennese cuisine ♦ Cosy ♦
A traditional inn with a comfortable atmosphere. Friendly service in cosy, beautifully decorated rooms with Viennese cuisine.

XX

Fabios

Tuchlauben 6 ⊠ 1010 – Ⓜ Stephansplatz – ✆ (01) 5 32 22 22 – fabios@fabios.at – Fax (01) 5 32 22 25 – www.fabios.at
closed Sunday **D2**
Rest – *(booking essential)* Carte 46/63 €
♦ Mediterranean ♦ Trendy ♦
The atmosphere in this modern restaurant is lively and cosmopolitan. The restaurant is located at the end of the pedestrian zone and serves creative Mediterranean cuisine.

XX

Indochine 21

Stubenring 18 ⊠ 1010 – Ⓜ Stubentor – ✆ (01) 5 13 76 60 – restaurant@indochine.at – Fax (01) 5 13 76 60 16 – www.indochine.at **E2**
Rest – Menu 27/90 € – Carte 38/67 €
♦ Fusion ♦ Fashionable ♦
A trendy city location, where a piece of colonial Indo-China is recreated. High-class fusion cooking, Asiatic with French accents.

XX

Zum Schwarzen Kameel

Bognergasse 5 ⊠ 1010 – Ⓜ Herrengasse – ✆ (01) 5 33 81 25 – info@kameel.at – Fax (01) 5 33 81 25 23 – www.kameel.at
closed Sunday and Bank Holidays **D2**
Rest – *(booking essential)* Menu 29 € (lunch)/64 € – Carte 34/59 €
♦ Austrian ♦ Friendly ♦
Near St. Stephen's Cathedral, this restaurant features art nouveau style with the charm of a Viennesse coffee house. Also a gourmet shop on the premises.

XX ✿

RieGi

Schauflergasse 6 ⊠ 1010 – Ⓜ Herrengasse – ✆ (01) 5 32 91 26 – world@barbaro.at – Fax (01) 5 32 91 26 20 – www.riegi.at
closed 1 week early January, end July - mid August, and Sunday - Monday, Bank Holidays **D2**
Rest – Menu 45/78 € – Carte 47/59 €
Spec. Jakobsmuschelravioli im Tomatensud mit Pesto. Warme Pastete vom Perlhuhn mit Gänseleber und Spargelgemüse. Geschmorte Lammschulter mit jungen Artischocken.
♦ International ♦ Friendly ♦
This modern, elegant restaurant near the Hofburg Imperial Palace features Mediterranean-influenced international cuisine under a lavishly illuminated sky ceiling.

XX

da moritz

Schellinggasse 6 ⊠ 1010 – Ⓜ Stubentor – ✆ (01) 5 12 44 44 – tisch@damoritz.at – Fax (01) 5 13 56 44 – www.damoritz.at
closed Sunday **E3**
Rest – Menu 15 € (lunch)/55 € – Carte 33/40 €
♦ Mediterranean ♦ Modern ♦ Trendy ♦
The restaurant boasts a great location and occupies two floors of a beautiful corner house. Dishes feature Mediterranean flavours.

XX

Mezzo

Esteplatz 6 ⊠ 1030 – Ⓜ Rochusgasse – ✆ (01) 7 15 51 48 – mezzo@mezzo.cc – Fax (01) 7 15 51 48 – www.mezzo.cc
closed 24 December - 7 January and Saturday - Sunday, Bank Holidays *Plan I* **B3**
Rest – Menu 27/59 € – Carte 27/42 €
♦ International ♦ Fashionable ♦
Pure and modern, with warm colours, this refined restaurant is in a townhouse at the edge of the city centre. International menu with Mediterranean and regional flavours.

Fadinger

Wipplingerstr. 29 ✉ 1010 – Ⓤ Schottentor-Universität – ✆ (01) 5 33 43 41 – restaurant@fadinger.at – Fax (01) 5 32 44 51 – www.fadinger.at
closed 11 to 17 August, Saturday lunch, Sunday and Bank Holidays **D1**
Rest – *(booking advisable)* Menu 20 € (lunch)/55 € (dinner) – Carte 26/50 €
◆ International ◆ Friendly ◆
The restaurant features a great location near the stock exchange and offers a bright and lively atmosphere. Delicious international and regional cuisine. Good selection of wines.

Österreicher im MAK

Stubenring 5 (at Museum MAK) ✉ 1010 – Ⓤ Stubentor – ✆ (01) 7 14 01 21 – office@oesterreicherimmak.at – Fax (01) 7 10 10 21 – www.oesterreicherimmak.at **F2**
Rest – Carte 20/37 €
◆ Austrian ◆ Trendy ◆
In the historical building of the Museum for Applied Arts, in a modern atmosphere with clean lines, regional dishes are served. Outdoor dining area.

Schnattl

Lange Gasse 40 ✉ 1080 – Ⓤ Rathaus – ✆ (01) 4 05 34 00 – Fax (01) 4 05 34 00
closed 2 weeks after Easter, 2 weeks end August and Saturday - Sunday, Bank Holidays *Plan I* **A3**
Rest – Menu 35/50 € – Carte 31/47 €
◆ International ◆ Cosy ◆
This small, well-presented restaurant with a simple but pleasant ambience is located on the edge of the inner city. The courtyard deck is particularly nice.

Weibels Wirtshaus

Kumpfgasse 2 ✉ 1010 – Ⓤ Stubentor – ✆ (01) 5 12 39 86 – Fax (01) 5 12 39 86 – www.weibel.at **E2**
Rest – *(booking advisable)* Menu 30/36 € – Carte 22/40 €
◆ Viennese cuisine ◆ Cosy ◆
This cosy, traditional restaurant is located in the city centre. Friendly service and Viennese cuisine are served in the restaurant as well as on the outdoor terrace.

Weibel 3

Riemergasse 1 ✉ 1010 – Ⓤ Stubentor – ✆ (01) 5 13 31 10 – Fax (01) 5 13 31 10 – www.weibel.at
closed Sunday - Monday and Bank Holidays **E2**
Rest – *(dinner only) (booking advisable)* Menu 48 € – Carte 32/45 €
◆ Spanish ◆ Rustic ◆
The small restaurant offers a cosy, tavern-like atmosphere, a menu featuring mainly Spanish cuisine and a comprehensive wine list.

Artner

Floragasse 6 ✉ 1040 – Ⓤ Taubstummengasse – ✆ (01) 5 03 50 33 – restaurant@artner.co.at – Fax (01) 5 03 50 34 – www.artner.co.at
closed Saturday lunch, Sunday and Bank Holidays lunch *Plan I* **B3**
Rest – Menu 30/50 € – Carte 25/45 €
◆ Regional ◆ Minimalist ◆
Smart lines and a modern style characterise the restaurant, where contemporary regional dishes with international flavours are served. Reasonably priced set lunch menu.

Tempel

Praterstr. 56 ✉ 1020 – Ⓤ Nestroyplatz – ✆ (01) 2 14 01 79 – restaurant.tempel@utanet.at – Fax (01) 2 14 01 79
closed 22 December - 7 January, 2 weeks August and Saturday lunch, Sunday - Monday **F1**
Rest – Menu 15 € (lunch)/39 € – Carte 23/32 €
◆ Regional ◆ Friendly ◆
This cosy, bistro-style restaurant in a courtyard offers regional cuisine with international influences and a reasonably priced lunchtime menu that changes daily. Beautiful terrace.

OUTER DISTRICTS Plan I

Landhaus Fuhrgassl-Huber without rest

Rathstr. 24 (by Krottenbachstr. A1) ✉ 1190 – ✆ (01) 4 40 30 33 – landhaus@fuhrgassl-huber.at – Fax (01) 4 40 27 14 – www.fuhrgassl-huber.at

38 rm – 85 € 135/138 €

◆ Family ◆ Cosy ◆

This family-run establishment offers homey, attractively furnished rooms in a country-house atmosphere. In the summer, enjoy breakfast in the lovely inner courtyard. Extensive buffet.

Vikerl's Lokal

Würffelgasse 4 ✉ 1150 – ✆ (01) 8 94 34 30 – office@vikerls.at – Fax (01) 8 94 34 30 – www.vikerls.at

closed 1 week early January, Holy week, 2 weeks August and Saturday lunch, Sunday dinner - Monday also June - August Saturday lunch, Sunday - Monday

Rest – *(booking advisable)* Menu 36/45 € – Carte 21/40 € **A3**

◆ Regional ◆ Friendly ◆ Traditional ◆

On the edge of the city centre is this restaurant made up of attractive rustic dining rooms. Regional cuisine is served with friendly service directed by the patron.

Plachutta

Heiligenstädter Str. 179 ✉ 1190 – ✆ (01) 3 70 41 25 – nussdorf@plachutta.at – Fax (01) 3 70 41 25 20 – www.plachutta.at **A1**

Rest – Carte 24/44 €

◆ Austrian ◆ Friendly ◆

This friendly establishment serves a variety of delicious beef dishes: hearty soups served in copper pots feature various gourmet cuts of meat.

Eckel

Sieveringer Str. 46 (by Billrothstr. A1) ✉ 1190 – ✆ (01) 3 20 32 18 – restaurant.eckel@aon.at – Fax (01) 3 20 66 60 – www.restauranteckel.at

closed 23 December - 21 January, 10 to 25 August and Sunday - Monday

Rest – Carte 27/48 €

◆ Regional ◆ Rustic ◆

This country house features beautiful rooms, some with wood panelling. Traditional cuisine served. Beautiful terrace.

Schübel-Auer

Kahlenberger Str. 22 (Döbling) ✉ 1190 – ✆ (01) 3 70 22 22 – daniela.somloi@schuebel-auer.at – Fax (01) 3 70 22 22 – www.schuebel-auer.at

closed 22 December - January, 16 to 24 April and Sunday - Monday **A1**

Rest – *(open from 4pm)* Menu 18 € (buffet)

◆ Buffet ◆ Cosy ◆

Built in 1642 as a wine-grower's house with mill, this traditional building was carefully renovated in 1972 and then lovingly furnished. Courtyard terrace.

Feuerwehr-Wagner

Grinzingerstr. 53 (Heiligenstadt) ✉ 1190 – ✆ (01) 3 20 24 42 – heuriger@feuerwehrwagner.at – Fax (01) 3 20 91 41 – www.feuerwehrwagner.at

Rest – *(open from 4pm)* Carte 15 € (buffet) **A1**

◆ Buffet ◆ Cosy ◆

This typical "Heurige" (traditional Austrian wine tavern) is greatly appreciated by regulars. Cosy, rustic décor with dark wood and simple tables. Particularly nice: the terraced garden.

Mayer am Pfarrplatz

Pfarrplatz 2 (Heiligenstadt) ✉ 1190 – ✆ (01) 3 70 12 87 – mayer@pfarrplatz.at – Fax (01) 3 70 47 14 – www.mayer.pfarrplatz.at

closed 20 December - 15 January **A1**

Rest – *(open from 4 pm Monday - Saturday)* Carte 19 € (buffet)

◆ Buffet ◆ Cosy ◆

A textbook "Heurige" (traditional Austrian wine tavern): rustic furnishings, traditional Viennese folk music, and an attractive courtyard terrace. Of note: Beethoven lived here in 1817!

AT THE AIRPORT

NH Vienna Airport

Hotelstr. 1 ✉ 1300 Wien – ✆ (01) 70 15 10 – nhviennaairport@nh-hotels.com – Fax (01) 7 01 51 95 71 – www.nh-hotels.com

500 rm – 🚹130/360 € 🚹🚹130/360 €, ☕ 19 €

Rest – Carte 26/56 €

♦ Chain hotel ♦ Functional ♦

In the hotel across from the arrival hall, guests are welcomed by a spacious, simple and elegant lobby and rooms decorated in a tasteful modern or classical style. This restaurant is characterised by clean lines and an open floor plan.

BELGIUM
BELGIQUE - BELGIË

PROFILE

→ **Area:**
30 513 km²
(11 781 sq mi)

→ **Population:**
10 710 000 inhabitants (est. 2005), nearly 55% Flemish, 33% Walloons and about 10% foreigners. Density = 351 per km².

→ **Capital:**
Brussels (1 018 804 inhabitants).

→ **Currency:**
Euro (€); rate of exchange: € 1 = US$ 1.46 (Dec 2007).

→ **Government:**
Constitutional parliamentary monarchy (since 1830) and a federal state (since 1994). Member of European Union since 1957 (one of the 6 founding countries).

→ **Languages:**
French (Wallonia), Flemish (Flanders), German (Eastern cantons); most Belgians also speak English.

→ **Specific public holidays:**
National Day (21 July), Armistice Day 1918 (11 November).

→ **Local Time:**
GMT + 1 hour in winter and GMT + 2 hours in summer.

→ **Climate:**
Temperate maritime with cool winters and mild summers (Brussels: January: 2°C, July: 18°C); more continental towards the Ardennes. Rainfall evenly distributed throughout the year.

→ **International dialling Code:**
00 32 followed by local number without the initial **0**. Electronic directories: www.skynet.be, www.belgacom.be

→ **Emergency:**
Police: ✆ **101**; Medical Assistance and Fire Brigade: ✆ **100**; Police or Medical Assistance from cellular phones : ✆ **112**.

→ **Electricity:**
220 volts AC, 50Hz; 2-pin round-shaped continental plugs.

→ **Formalities**
Travellers from the European Union (EU), Switzerland, Iceland and the main countries of North and South America need a national identity card or passport (America: passport required) to visit Belgium for less than three months (tourism or business purpose). For visitors from other countries a visa may be required, in addition to a passport, especially for those wishing to stay for longer than three months. We advise you to check with your embassy before travelling.

1697
SALVS GENERIS
EVERSIO
REIPVBLICAE

Brussels

BRUXELLES/BRUSSEL

Population: 1018804 – Altitude: approx 100m

Tips/PHOTONONSTOP

It's not every city where you can employ a 16C century map and accurately navigate your way around. Or where there are enough restaurants to dine somewhere new every day for five years. Or where you'll find a museum dedicated to the comic strip. But then every city is not Brussels. Unfortunately tagged a 'grey' capital because of its associations with the suited hordes of the European Union, those who've actually visited the place know it to be, by contrast, a buzzing town, the home of art nouveau, with a wonderful maze of medieval alleys and great places to eat.

It's warm and friendly, with a cosmopolitan outgoing feel, due in no small part to its turbulent history, which has seen it under frequent occupation. The idea of multiculturalism has long been part and parcel of life for the Bruxellois, who believe, generally speaking, that you shouldn't take things too seriously. They have a soft spot for street music and puppets, Tintin and majorettes. They do their laundry in communal places like the Wash Club, and have restaurants with names such as 'L'Idiot du Village' and 'Morte Subite' (Sudden Death). Not so grey, after all…

LIVING THE CITY

The area where all visitors wend is the area that historically belonged to the poorer elements of Brussels, the Lower Town, and in particular the **Grand Place**. Its northwest and southern quarters (Ste-Catherine and The Marolles) are of particular interest. To the east, higher up an escarpment, lies the Upper Town, which, literally and symbolically, has always had a penchant for looking down at its westerly neighbour. This is the traditional home of the aristocracy, and it encircles the landmark Parc de Bruxelles. Further east in the Upper Town is the **European Parliament** area, which is saved from itself by two rather lovely parks. Two suburbs of interest are St.Gilles, to the southwest, and Ixelles, to the southeast, where trendy bars and Art Nouveau are the order of the day.

PRACTICAL INFORMATION

ARRIVAL-DEPARTURE

Brussels-National Airport is 14km northeast of the city centre. Take the Airport City Express train which runs every 20min and takes 25min. A taxi will cost approximately €30. Eurostar trains run from Brussels-Midi, which is a 20min walk from the city centre or else take the Metro, Lines 4, 55 or 56.

TRANSPORT

Buses, trams and metro all run efficiently in Brussels. You can buy a single short distance ticket, or if you're in the city for a while, 5-10 journey cards and one-day travelcards. These are available from metro stations, travel authority (STIB/MIVB) offices, tourist information centres and newsagents.

Remember to stamp your ticket before each journey. Machines are on every metro station concourse and every tram or bus. The ticket is valid for an hour, and you can hop on and off all forms of public transport as often as you like. Roving inspectors impose heavy on-the-spot fines for anyone caught without a valid ticket.

EXPLORING BRUSSELS

Brussels is a rollicking city, living up to its Brueghelesque depictions, albeit

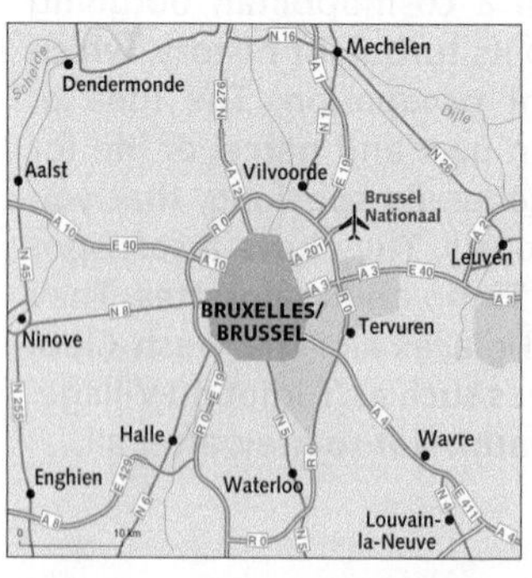

without the medieval accoutrements. It's somewhere that's fun just to wander around, buoyed up by frites and chocolate, two 'delicacies' which announce themselves practically every step of the way. There's no better place to get a feel for Brussels than at its Lower Town heart, the Grand Place, whose Baroque magnificence makes it the world's most uniformly satisfying square. The awesomely Gothic, 15C **Town Hall** engenders enough import to take up a whole side; powerful trade guilds took up the cudgels in the late 17C and created superbly harmonious buildings in Flemish Renaissance style to complete the magical whole. No wonder Victor Hugo famously described it as "La plus belle place du monde". Around and about the Grand Place is a mix of ancient cobbled lanes; most of the thoroughfares tumbling into the main hub have a time scale that ranges from the Middle Ages up to the 18C.

The **Lower Town** is at its most magical going northwest from the Grand Place. This is a cobweb of spidery lanes topped off by dinky squares. The one that draws most visitors is Place Ste Catherine: some come for its eponymous church with curvaceous Baroque belfry, but most are seduced by its fashionable aura, inspired by a plethora of great seafood restaurants. Around here are to be found an intriguing assemblage of late 19C bourgeois houses: they're a mix of the elegant and the run-down, giving the quarter its slightly battered charm. Just up the way from here is one of the city's finest churches, St-Jean-Baptiste-au-Beguinage, decked out in fanciful Flemish Baroque detail.

→ SOUTHERN COMFORT

If you're after a feel of old working class life, then head to the **Marolles** quarter at the southern extremity of the Lower Town. The former stronghold of Flemish weavers and craftsmen, it possesses its own (dying out) fruity dialect, the city's best daily flea market, and a neat collection of antique and suitably 21C interior design shops. Step a little way east from here, and you're on the ridge of the Upper Town, the posh side of the city with its pre-planned wide boulevards and squares. Those very same workmen from the Marolles would have crossed this 'border' to beaver away and create the elegant town houses which give the Place du Grand Sablon its abidingly popular air. Riding up the slope of the escarpment that slices Brussels in two, this is a wealthy and smart area where Art Nouveau meets grand Neoclassical. The trendy bars here act as a magnet for al fresco people-watchers in the summer months.

→ ART ATTACK

In spite of a history spanning over a thousand years, it's fair to say Brussels doesn't boast the best museum scene in Europe. There are certainly a good number of them, but only a few seem to have any great confidence in themselves; others lean towards the mundane. So make sure you choose a good one, and chief amongst these is the **Museum of Ancient Art**, allied to the Museum of Modern Art, near the Place Royale in the Upper Town. Together they make up the Musées Royaux des Beaux Arts. Pay your money, take your choice: will you settle for the finest collection of Flemish art in the world, with many Old Masters such as Rubens, Brueghel the Elder and van Dyck (Ancient), or will you shell out your euros on a comprehensive eight floors of 20C art featuring Magritte, Monet and Gauguin (Modern)? Either way you can't lose, but don't try to do justice to both in one day: you'll never manage it.

→ MUSIC TO YOUR EYES

The two-buses-together scenario applies to Brussels' museums. You've only just recovered from the glories of the Beaux Arts, when along comes another spellbinder, just across Place Royale. The Musical Instrument Museum is housed in a wonderful Art Nouveau building of glass and wrought-iron that was once home to the Old England company (whose name still adorns the eye-catching black façade). Inside, over three floors, the collection of instruments is breathtaking, having grown steadily from its humble nineteenth century origins. If it emits a sound, then it's probably here, from a medieval Cornemuse to a Tibetan temple trumpet, via every kind of international and European music making vessel imaginable. What's more, there's a top-floor restaurant which rewards you with superb views.

You don't have to travel much further to find somewhere to actually go and hear some music: the **Palais des Beaux-Arts** is Brussels' top cultural venue, with the city's largest classical music auditorium, home to the Belgian National Orchestra. If your taste is more operatic, then across in the Lower Town is the nineteenth century **La Monnaie**, one of the best opera venues in Europe. It has a rousing claim to fame: in 1830, a nationalistic aria sung here provoked the audience to take to the streets and rebel against their Dutch rulers, setting Belgium on its path to independence. Most productions here are sold out months in advance. Concertgoers remain as rapt as ever by the music, though these days they have a tendency to remain in their seats till the end.

→ PARKING FINE

It would appear that the life of the Bruxellois was so bound up in medieval urban intrigue and revelry that they forgot about the addition of parkland. Not quite true: there is the **Parc de Bruxelles** in the heart of the Upper Town, but it's often seen as little more than a quick shortcut to the metro rather than a green oasis to stop and linger. The best park in the city is way over to the east in Euroland: the **Parc du Cinquantenaire** has a grand arch based on the Arc de Triomphe, a fine collection of old cars housed in a palace, a renowned museum for decorative arts and ancient civilisations, and wonderful walks watched over by old elms and plane trees. Close by is another park worth a meander: Parc Leopold, which has a lake to sit by, and a lot of politicians to bypass.

Many people come to Brussels for a close encounter with **Art Nouveau**. This is the city where architecturally it all started, led by local architect Victor Horta in the late nineteenth century. In the 1890s, over two thousand new houses were built in the style. The bad news is that many have been demolished, or are in use as private houses or offices. The good news is that just about every Brussels street retains details of Art Nouveau, and Horta's house, down south on the borderline between Ixelles and St Gilles, is an absorbing museum containing many artefacts from his time spent there. Stick around these two southern suburbs for the best array of Art Nouveau buildings. Both are pretty hot, too, for their café and street life scenes. Ixelles, in particular, boasts an arty, bohemian feel – certainly enough for the likes of Marx, Dumas and Rodin, who all lived here awhile.

BRUSSELS IN...

→ ONE DAY

Grand Place, Place Ste Catherine, Musees Royaux des Beaux Arts, fish restaurant at Ste-Catherine

→ TWO DAYS

Marolles, Place du Grand Sablon, Musical Instrument Museum, concert at
Palais des Beaux-Arts or La Monnaie

→ THREE DAYS

Parc du Cinquantenaire, Horta's house, a tour of St Gilles and Ixelles

CALENDAR HIGHLIGHTS

Important festivals kick off early in the New Year in Brussels. Pleasingly, with the iffy weather outside, they take place indoors. January sees Europe's first big film festival of the year, the Brussels festival, and a month later the imposing Palais des Beaux-Arts hosts the engrossing Antiques Fair. At the same time, the city's comic strip heritage comes to the fore at the International Comic Strip and Cartoon Festival. And staying with the world of publishing, the Brussels Book Fair engrosses hundreds of visitors, also in February. March and April boasts a real highlight with Ars Musica, a well-renowned celebration of contemporary music. May's Kunsten Festival des Arts is a showcase for exciting new names in dance and theatre, while classical lovers feed their fixation at the Queen Elisabeth Music Contest, also in May, during which Europe's top student musicians gather to play. If you want to know what people got up to in Renaissance times, go to July's famed Ommegang, in which two thousand participants take to the Grand Place dressed as nobles, soldiers and jesters (book well in advance for this one). Don't book, but drive up to the Drive-In Movies, every July to September at Esplanade du Cinquantenaire: blockbusters are shown on weekend evenings. Back on the musical front, there are classical shows all over the city in the Brussels Summer Festival (July and August) and gyrating hips aplenty on the Place du Chatelain for the Fiesta Latina, also in August. September's Lucky Town Festival is a very cool event indeed, with trendy cafes hosting a range of concerts.

EATING OUT

As long as your appetite hasn't been sated at the chocolatiers, or you haven't had your hand in a cone full of frites from a street stall, then you'll relish the dining experience in Brussels: this is a city where it's almost impossible to eat badly. In fact, food is one of the best reasons for visiting. Some say that the EU decamped here en masse because of the wealth of fine restaurants. As long as you stay off the main tourist drag (ie, Rue des Bouchers) then you're guaranteed somewhere good to eat within a short strolling distance and that doesn't just mean Moules Frites, which is so popular that some restaurants serve it all year but it really should be enjoyed from August until March. There are lots of places to enjoy Belgian dishes such as lobster from Ostend, eels served with green herbs, and waterzooi (chicken or fish stew simmered in water and served with vegetables). Wherever you're eating, at whatever price range, food is invariably well cooked, often bursting with innovative touches, and served with pride, albeit mixed with a slice of self-deprecating Belgian humour. As a rule of thumb, the Lower Town has the best places to eat, with the Ste-Catherine quarter's fish and seafood establishments the pick of the bunch. You'll also find a mini Chinatown here. Because of the city's cosmopolitan character, there are dozens of international restaurants, ranging from the expected cluster of French and Italian dining spots, to the more unusual Moroccan, Tunisian and Congolese destinations. Belgium beers are famous the world over and come served in special glasses but it is not just found in the taverns; you can also discover a few dishes involving the use of beer.

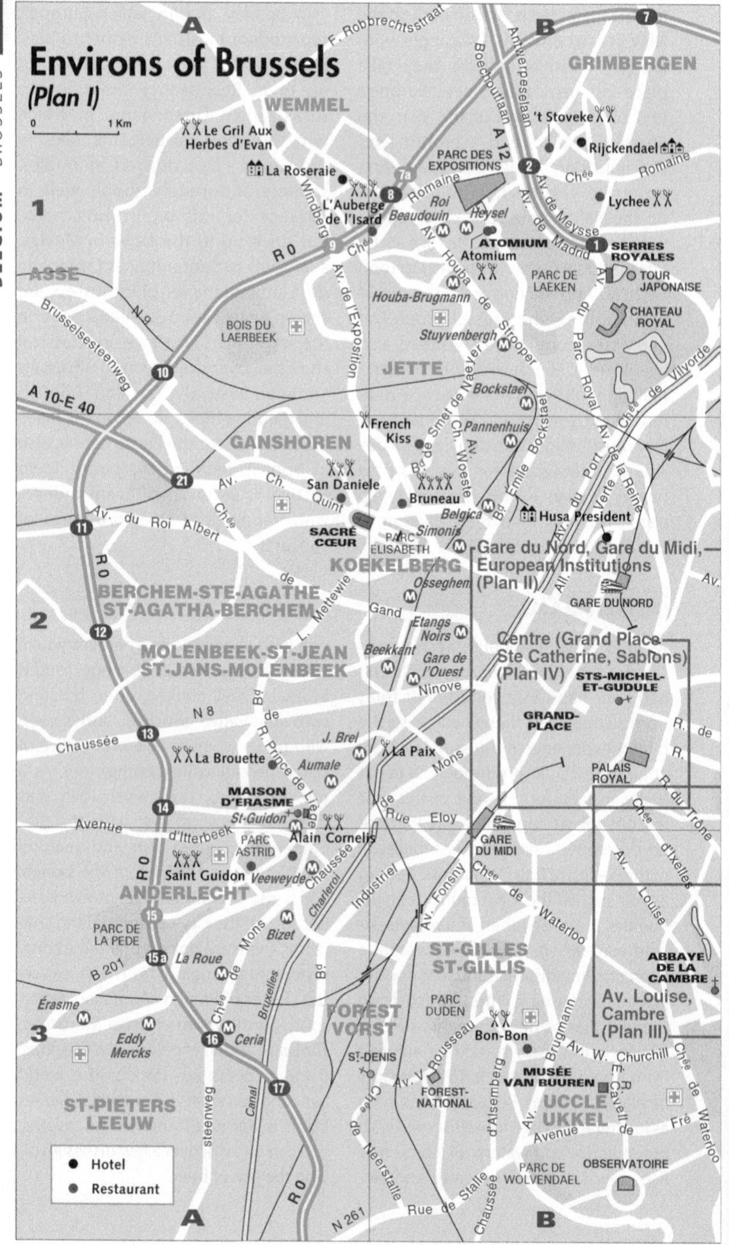

Environs of Brussels
(Plan I)
0 1 Km
Hotel
Restaurant
Gare du Nord, Gare du Midi, European Institutions (Plan II)
Centre (Grand Place Ste Catherine, Sablons) (Plan IV)
Av. Louise, Cambre (Plan III)
WEMMEL
GRIMBERGEN
ASSE
JETTE
GANSHOREN
KOEKELBERG
BERCHEM-STE-AGATHE
ST-AGATHA-BERCHEM
MOLENBEEK-ST-JEAN
ST-JANS-MOLENBEEK
ANDERLECHT
ST-GILLES
ST-GILLIS
FOREST
VORST
UCCLE
UKKEL
ST-PIETERS
LEEUW
Le Gril Aux Herbes d'Evan
La Roseraie
L'Auberge de l'Isard
't Stoveke
Rijckendael
Lychee
PARC DES EXPOSITIONS
ATOMIUM
SERRES ROYALES
TOUR JAPONAISE
CHATEAU ROYAL
PARC DE LAEKEN
BOIS DU LAERBEEK
French Kiss
San Daniele
Bruneau
Husa President
SACRÉ CŒUR
PARC ELISABETH
GARE DU NORD
STS-MICHEL-ET-GUDULE
GRAND-PLACE
PALAIS ROYAL
La Brouette
La Paix
MAISON D'ERASME
Alain Cornelis
PARC ASTRID
Saint Guidon
GARE DU MIDI
PARC DE LA PEDE
ABBAYE DE LA CAMBRE
PARC DUDEN
Bon-Bon
ST-DENIS
FOREST-NATIONAL
MUSÉE VAN BUUREN
PARC DE WOLVENDAEL
OBSERVATOIRE

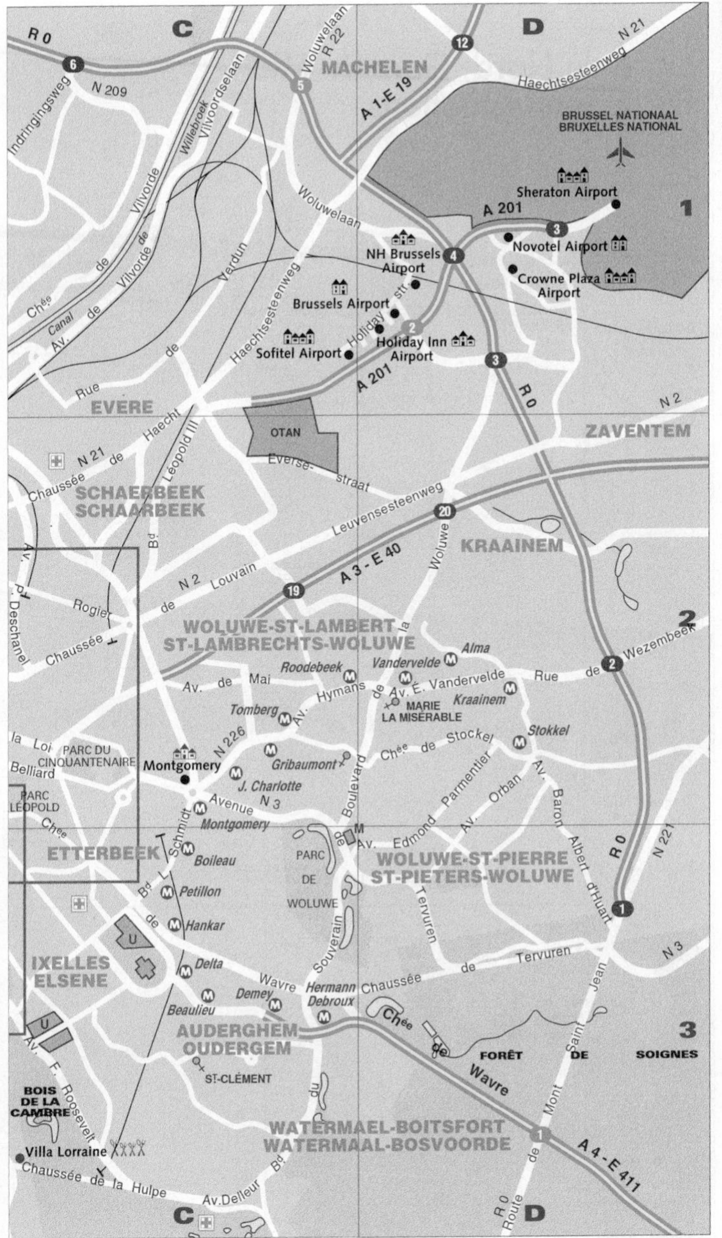
MACHELEN
BRUSSEL NATIONAAL
BRUXELLES NATIONAL
Sheraton Airport
Novotel Airport
Crowne Plaza Airport
NH Brussels Airport
Brussels Airport
Holiday Inn Airport
Sofitel Airport
EVERE
OTAN
ZAVENTEM
SCHAERBEEK
SCHAARBEEK
KRAAINEM
WOLUWE-ST-LAMBERT
ST-LAMBRECHTS-WOLUWE
Montgomery
PARC DU CINQUANTENAIRE
PARC LÉOPOLD
ETTERBEEK
PARC DE WOLUWE
WOLUWE-ST-PIERRE
ST-PIETERS-WOLUWE
IXELLES
ELSENE
AUDERGHEM
OUDERGEM
ST-CLÉMENT
FORÊT DE SOIGNES
BOIS DE LA CAMBRE
Villa Lorraine
WATERMAEL-BOITSFORT
WATERMAAL-BOSVOORDE
MARIE LA MISERABLE
A 201
A 1-E 19
A 3 - E 40
A 4 - E 411
R 0
N 21
N 2
N 3
N 209
N 226
N 221
Woluwelaan
Haechtsesteenweg
Leuvensesteenweg
Chaussée de Louvain
Chaussée de Haecht
Chaussée de Wavre
Chaussée de Tervuren
Chée de Stockel
Chaussée de la Hulpe
Rue de Wezembeek
Av. de Mai
Av. Hymans
Av. É. Vandervelde
Av. Edmond Parmentier
Av. Orban
Av. Baron Albert d'Huart
Av. de Tervuren
Boulevard de la Woluwe
Boulevard du Souverain
Bd. Léopold III
Bd. Schmidt
Av. F. Roosevelt
Av. Delleur
Route de Mont Saint Jean
Avenue Montgomery
Rue de Verdun
Av. de Vilvorde
Chée de Vilvorde
Canal de Willebroek
Vilvoordselaan
Indringingsweg
Eversestraat
Rogier
Av. P. Deschanel
Belliard
la Loi
Roodebeek
Vandervelde
Alma
Kraainem
Stokkel
Tomberg
Gribaumont
J. Charlotte
Montgomery
Boileau
Petillon
Hankar
Delta
Demey
Beaulieu
Hermann Debroux
C
D
1
2
3

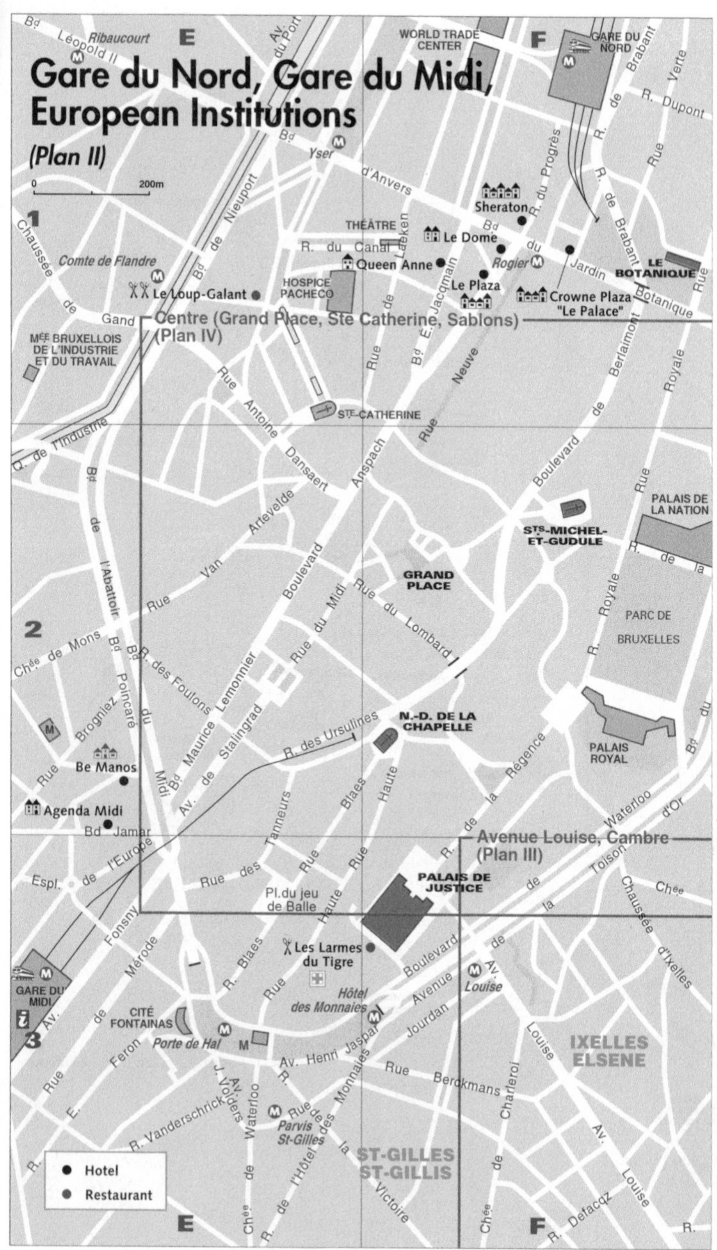
Gare du Nord, Gare du Midi, European Institutions
(Plan II)
0
200m
Centre (Grand Place, Ste Catherine, Sablons) (Plan IV)
Avenue Louise, Cambre (Plan III)
Sheraton
Le Dome
Queen Anne
Le Plaza
Crowne Plaza "Le Palace"
Le Loup-Galant
Be Manos
Agenda Midi
Les Larmes du Tigre
GARE DU NORD
GARE DU MIDI
WORLD TRADE CENTER
THÉÂTRE
HOSPICE PACHECO
LE BOTANIQUE
STE-CATHERINE
STS-MICHEL-ET-GUDULE
PALAIS DE LA NATION
GRAND PLACE
PARC DE BRUXELLES
N.-D. DE LA CHAPELLE
PALAIS ROYAL
PALAIS DE JUSTICE
MÉE BRUXELLOIS DE L'INDUSTRIE ET DU TRAVAIL
CITÉ FONTAINAS
Porte de Hal
Hôtel des Monnaies
Parvis St-Gilles
Comte de Flandre
Rogier
Yser
Louise
IXELLES ELSENE
ST-GILLES ST-GILLIS
Pl.du jeu de Balle
Hotel
Restaurant

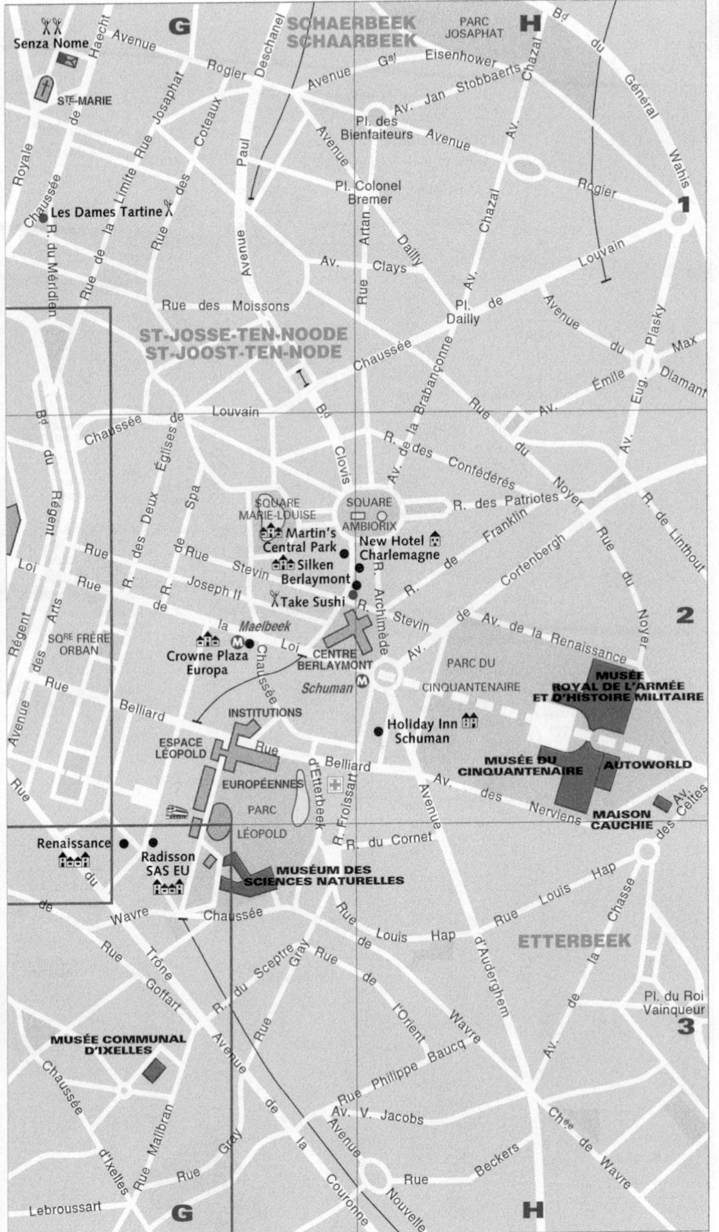
G
H
1
2
3
SCHAERBEEK
SCHAARBEEK
PARC JOSAPHAT
ST-JOSSE-TEN-NOODE
ST-JOOST-TEN-NODE
ETTERBEEK
Senza Nome
STE-MARIE
Les Dames Tartine
Martin's Central Park
New Hotel Charlemagne
Silken Berlaymont
Take Sushi
Crowne Plaza Europa
CENTRE BERLAYMONT
Schuman
SQUARE MARIE-LOUISE
SQUARE AMBIORIX
SQRE FRÈRE ORBAN
PARC DU CINQUANTENAIRE
MUSÉE ROYAL DE L'ARMÉE ET D'HISTOIRE MILITAIRE
MUSÉE DU CINQUANTENAIRE
AUTOWORLD
MAISON CAUCHIE
Holiday Inn Schuman
INSTITUTIONS EUROPÉENNES
ESPACE LÉOPOLD
PARC LÉOPOLD
MUSÉUM DES SCIENCES NATURELLES
Renaissance
Radisson SAS EU
MUSÉE COMMUNAL D'IXELLES
Pl. des Bienfaiteurs
Pl. Colonel Bremer
Pl. Dailly
Pl. du Roi Vainqueur
Bd du Général Wahis
Bd Clovis
Bd du Régent
Av. Gal Eisenhower
Av. Jan Stobbaerts
Av. Rogier
Rue Royale
Chaussée de Haecht
Chaussée de Louvain
Rue de la Loi
Rue Belliard
Rue Joseph II
Rue Stevin
Rue des Arts
Av. de la Renaissance
Av. de Cortenbergh
Av. des Nerviens
Av. des Celtes
Rue du Noyer
Rue de Linthout
Av. Émile Max
Av. Eug. Plasky
Diamant
Av. de la Brabançonne
R. des Confédérés
R. des Patriotes
R. Franklin
R. Archimède
Chaussée d'Etterbeek
R. Froissart
R. du Cornet
Rue Louis Hap
Av. de la Chasse
Av. d'Auderghem
Rue de l'Orient
Rue Gray
R. du Sceptre
Rue Philippe Baucq
Av. V. Jacobs
Rue Beckers
Chée de Wavre
Chaussée de Wavre
Rue du Trône
Rue Goffart
Avenue de la Couronne
Avenue Nouvelle
Chaussée d'Ixelles
Rue Malibran
Rue Lebroussart
Rue des Moissons
Rue Josaphat
Rue de la Limite
Rue des Coteaux
Avenue Paul Deschanel
Rue Artan
Av. Clays
Rue Dailly
Av. Chazal
R. du Méridien
Rue des Deux Églises
R. de Spa
Maelbeek
Avenue des Arts

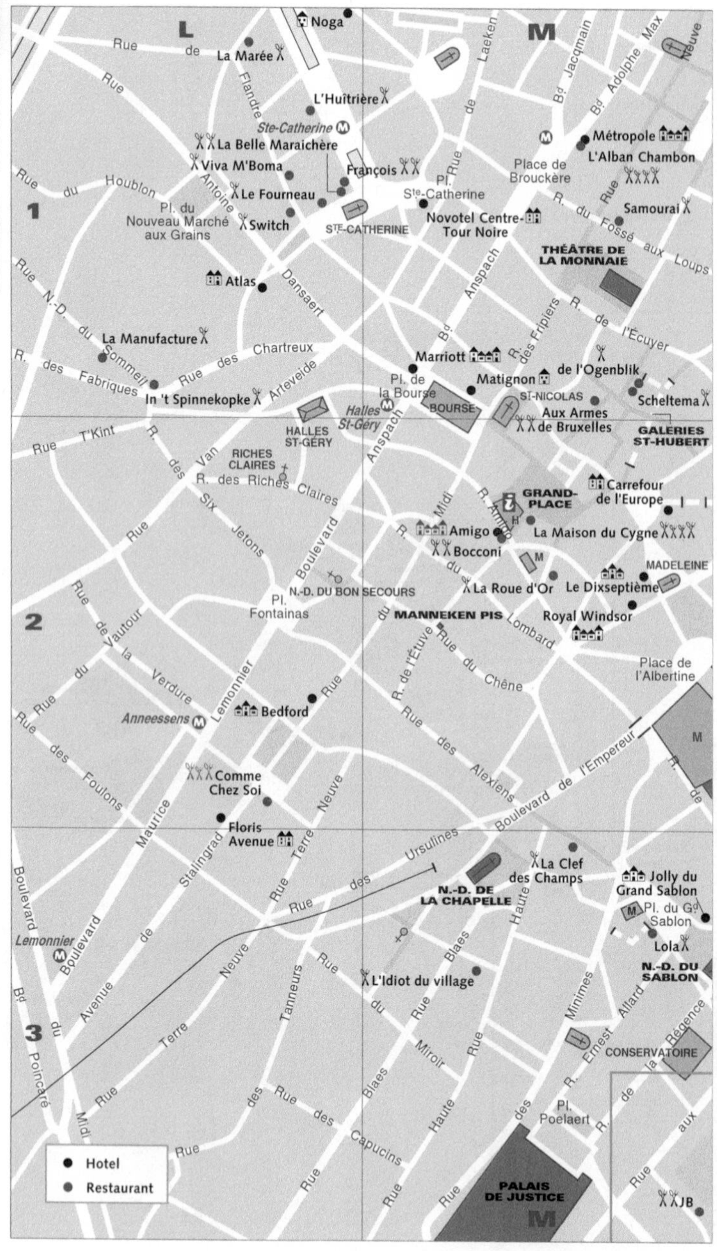

Noga
La Marée
L'Huîtrière
Ste-Catherine
La Belle Maraichère
Viva M'Boma
François
Le Fourneau
Switch
Atlas
La Manufacture
In 't Spinnekopke
Métropole
L'Alban Chambon
Samourai
Novotel Centre-Tour Noire
THÉÂTRE DE LA MONNAIE
Marriott
Matignon
de l'Ogenblik
Scheltema
Aux Armes de Bruxelles
GALERIES ST-HUBERT
BOURSE
HALLES ST-GÉRY
RICHES CLAIRES
Carrefour de l'Europe
GRAND-PLACE
Amigo
La Maison du Cygne
Bocconi
La Roue d'Or
Le Dixseptième
MADELEINE
Royal Windsor
MANNEKEN PIS
N.-D. DU BON SECOURS
Pl. Fontainas
Place de l'Albertine
Bedford
Anneessens
Comme Chez Soi
Floris Avenue
La Clef des Champs
N.-D. DE LA CHAPELLE
Jolly du Grand Sablon
Pl. du Gd Sablon
Lola
N.-D. DU SABLON
L'Idiot du village
CONSERVATOIRE
Pl. Poelaert
PALAIS DE JUSTICE
JB
Lemonnier
Hotel
Restaurant

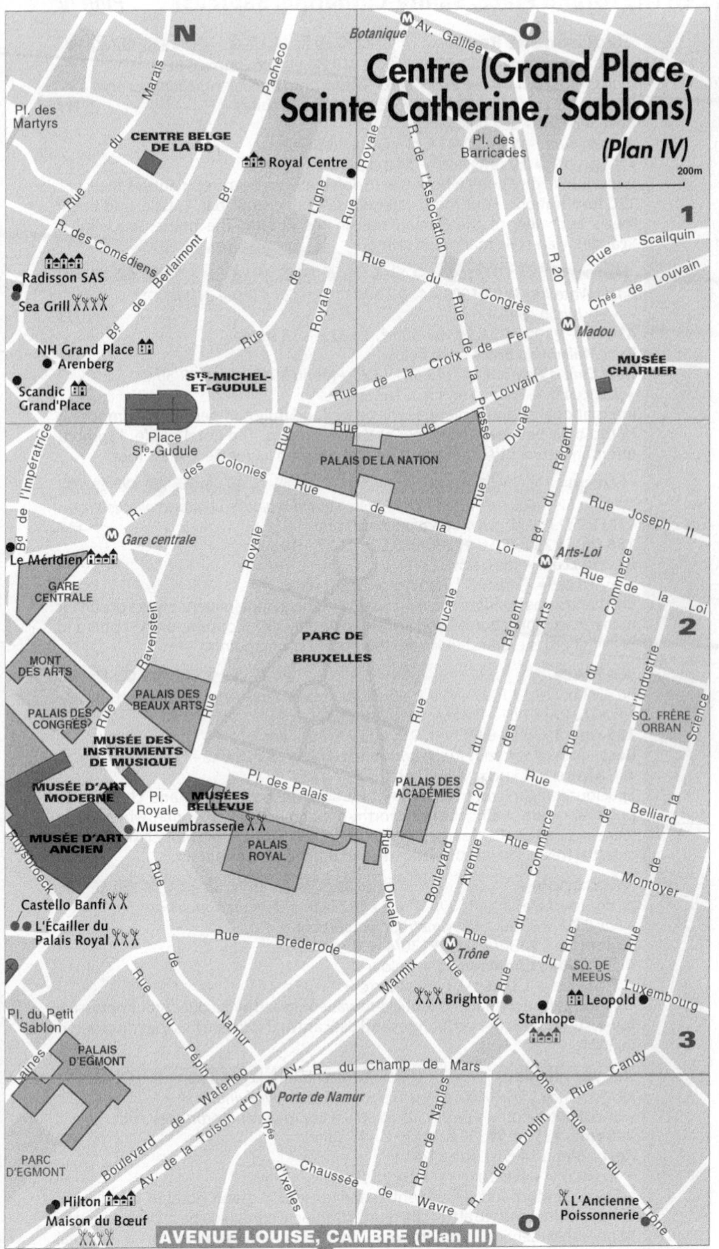
Centre (Grand Place, Sainte Catherine, Sablons)
(Plan IV)
0
200m
N
O
1
2
3
Botanique
Av. Galilée
Pl. des Martyrs
Rue du Marais
Pachéco
Pl. des Barricades
CENTRE BELGE DE LA BD
Royal Centre
R. de l'Association
Rue Royale
Rue de Ligne
Bd. de Berlaimont
R. des Comédiens
Radisson SAS
Sea Grill
Rue du Congrès
R 20
Rue Scailquin
Chée de Louvain
Madou
MUSÉE CHARLIER
NH Grand Place
Arenberg
Scandic Grand'Place
STS-MICHEL-ET-GUDULE
Rue de la Croix de Fer
Rue de la Presse
Rue de Louvain
Ducale
Bd. du Régent
Place Ste-Gudule
Bd. de l'Impératrice
R. des Colonies
PALAIS DE LA NATION
Rue de la Loi
Rue Joseph II
Gare centrale
Le Méridien
Arts-Loi
GARE CENTRALE
Rue Ravenstein
PARC DE BRUXELLES
Rue Ducale
Rue des Arts
Rue du Commerce
Rue de l'Industrie
MONT DES ARTS
PALAIS DES BEAUX ARTS
PALAIS DES CONGRÈS
SQ. FRÈRE ORBAN
Science
MUSÉE DES INSTRUMENTS DE MUSIQUE
MUSÉE D'ART MODERNE
Pl. des Palais
PALAIS DES ACADÉMIES
Rue Belliard
Pl. Royale
MUSÉES BELLEVUE
Museumbrasserie
MUSÉE D'ART ANCIEN
PALAIS ROYAL
Rue de la Montoyer
Ruysbroeck
Avenue R 20
Boulevard du Régent
Castello Banfi
L'Écailler du Palais Royal
Rue Brederode
Rue de Namur
Rue du Trône
Trône
Marmix
SQ. DE MEEÛS
Rue du Luxembourg
Brighton
Leopold
Stanhope
Pl. du Petit Sablon
Rue du Pépin
PALAIS D'EGMONT
R. du Champ de Mars
Rue Candy
Boulevard de Waterloo
Av. de la Toison d'Or
Porte de Namur
Chée d'Ixelles
Rue de Naples
R. de Dublin
PARC D'EGMONT
Chaussée de Wavre
Rue du Trône
Hilton
Maison du Bœuf
L'Ancienne Poissonnerie
AVENUE LOUISE, CAMBRE (Plan III)

BELGIUM - BRUSSELS

CENTRE (Grand Place, Sainte-Catherine, Sablons) *Plan IV*

Radisson SAS Royal

r. Fossé-aux-Loups 47 ✉ 1000 – ☎ 0 2 219 28 28 – info.brussels@radissonsas.com – Fax 0 2 219 62 62 – www.royal.brussels.radissonsas.com

271 rm – 115/475 € 115/475 €, ☕ 25 € – 10 suites **N1**

Rest *Sea Grill* – see below

Rest *Atrium* – Menu 22/41 € bi – Carte 38/56 €

♦ Luxury ♦ Business ♦ Modern ♦

A modern luxury hotel whose glass-roofed atrium bears remnants of the city's 12C fortifications. Four room categories. "Comic strip" bar. Classic, traditional meals and view of the Roman wall in the atrium. The house speciality is Scandinavian-style marinated salmon.

Hilton

< town, rest

bd de Waterloo 38 ✉ 1000 – ☎ 0 2 504 11 11 – Fax 0 2 504 21 11 – www.hilton.com **N3**

416 rm – 109/505 € 109/505 €, ☕ 32 € – 15 suites

Rest *Maison du Bœuf* – see below

Rest *Café d'Egmont* – ☎ *0 2 504 13 33* – Menu 35 € – Carte 38/59 €

♦ Luxury ♦ Business ♦ Classic ♦

International business clientele will be well and truly pampered in this imposing Hilton built between the upper and lower towns. The hotel's Café d'Egmont offers an intercontinental menu, served beneath its Art Deco glass roof.

Amigo

r. Amigo 1 ✉ 1000 – ☎ 0 2 547 47 47 – reservations.amigo@roccofortecollection.com – Fax 0 2 513 52 77 – www.roccofortehotels.com **M2**

156 rm – 250/750 € 280/800 €, ☕ 30 € – 18 suites

Rest *Bocconi* – see below

♦ Palace ♦ Grand Luxury ♦ Stylish ♦

This handsome building showing Spanish Renaissance influence was a prison for many years. Collection of works of art on display, chic, contemporary rooms and proximity to the Grand-Place are this hotel's strong points.

Le Plaza

bd A. Max 118 ✉ 1000 – ☎ 0 2 278 01 00 – reservations@leplaza-brussels.be – Fax 0 2 278 01 01 – www.leplaza-brussels.be Plan II **F1**

185 rm – 99/450 € 99/450 €, ☕ 27 € – 6 suites

Rest – *(closed Saturday lunch and Sunday)* Menu 30/50 € bi – Carte 43/74 €

♦ Palace ♦ Luxury ♦ Classic ♦

Spacious, elegant rooms, a superb Baroque lounge-theatre and classic-style public areas are among the noteworthy features of this 1930s hotel, whose plans were inspired by the Georges V Hotel in Paris. A wide cupola embellished with a celestial fresco crowns the intimate and refined bar-restaurant.

Métropole

pl. de Brouckère 31 ✉ 1000 – ☎ 0 2 217 23 00 – info@metropolehotel.be – Fax 0 2 218 02 20 – www.metropolehotel.com **M1**

284 rm ☕ – 130/419 € 130/449 € – 14 suites

Rest *L'Alban Chambon* – see below

♦ Palace ♦ Luxury ♦ Historic ♦

This 19C palace on place de Brouckère was eulogised by Jacques Brel. Impressive foyer, sumptuous period lounges and delicate Art Nouveau frescoes discovered in 2004.

Royal Windsor

rm

r. Duquesnoy 5 ✉ 1000 – ☎ 0 2 505 55 55 – resa.royalwindsor@warwickhotels.com – Fax 0 2 505 55 00 – www.royalwindsorbrussels.com

249 rm – 355 € 355 €, ☕ 26 € – 17 suites **M2**

Rest – Menu 14 € – Carte 31/41 €

♦ Luxury ♦ Business ♦ Stylish ♦

Luxury, comfort and refinement characterise this grand hotel in the historic centre, which tends to attract Belgium's fashion victims (you have been warned). Impeccable service. Contemporary bar-restaurant striving for a colonial ambience. Modern cuisine.

Marriott

r. A. Orts 7 (opposite the Stock Exchange) ✉ 1000 – ☎ 0 2 516 90 90 – Fax 0 2 516 90 99 – www.marriottbrussels.com **M1**

214 rm – †129/299 € ††129/299 €, ☕ 20 € – 4 suites

Rest – ☎ 0 2 516 91 00 *(closed Saturday lunch and Sunday)* Menu 13 € – Carte 36/75 €

♦ Chain hotel ♦ Business ♦ Functional ♦

Luxurious hotel situated in front of the Stock Exchange. Its imposing turn-of-the-century façade, interior public areas and rooms were given a facelift in 2002. Modern brasserie where the usual international fare is served with a contemporary touch. Kitchens and rotisserie opening onto the dining area.

Le Méridien

Carrefour de l'Europe 3 ✉ 1000 – ☎ 0 2 548 42 11 – info.brussels@lemeridien.com – Fax 0 2 548 40 80 – www.lemeridien.com/brussels **N2**

216 rm – †180/525 € ††210/550 €, ☕ 25 € – 8 suites

Rest *L'Épicerie* – *(closed mid July-mid August, Saturday lunch and Sunday dinner)* Menu 40 € – Carte 51/73 €

♦ Chain hotel ♦ Business ♦ Stylish ♦

The hotel's majestic neo-Classical façade stands opposite the Gare Centrale. Gleaming interior décor, with elegant bedrooms boasting the very latest in facilities. The restaurant menu is distinctly modern, and offers a cuisine inspired by the New World and its spices.

Le Dixseptième without rest

r. Madeleine 25 ✉ 1000 – ☎ 0 2 517 17 17 – info@ledixseptieme.be – Fax 0 2 502 64 24 – www.ledixseptieme.be **M2**

18 rm ☕ – †140/300 € ††160/400 € – 6 suites

♦ Family ♦ Luxury ♦ Stylish ♦

As its name indicates, this old town house dates from the 17C, when the Spanish Ambassador occupied its rooms. Elegant lounges and large bedrooms furnished with antiques from different periods.

Bedford

r. Midi 135 ✉ 1000 – ☎ 0 2 507 00 00 – info@hotelbedford.be – Fax 0 2 507 00 10 – www.hotelbedford.be **L2**

318 rm ☕ – †260/340 € ††300/380 € – 8 suites

Rest – *(15 July - 15 August dinner only)* Menu 36/56 € bi – Carte 37/51 €

♦ Traditional ♦ Business ♦ Classic ♦

Just a short walk from the Manneken Pis and 500m/550yd from the Grand-Place, this hotel houses major seminar facilities and well-appointed rooms. Franco-Belgian cuisine served in a large dining area with British-inspired décor.

Jolly du Grand Sablon

r. Bodenbroek 2 ✉ 1000 – ☎ 0 2 518 11 00 – jollyhotelsablon@jollyhotels.be – Fax 0 2 512 67 66 – www.jollyhotels.com **M3**

187 rm ☕ – †275/337 € ††305/367 € – 6 suites

Rest – *(closed August and Sunday)* Carte 26/42 €

♦ Chain hotel ♦ Business ♦ Stylish ♦

This Italian-owned hotel is located just a stone's throw from the city's prestigious royal museums. Spacious lobby area, well-appointed rooms, plus meeting rooms with all the facilities. The restaurant offers Italian cuisine, buffets and Sunday brunch accompanied by music.

Royal Centre without rest

r. Royale 160 ✉ 1000 – ☎ 0 2 219 00 65 – hotel@royalcentre.be – Fax 0 2 218 09 10 – www.royalcentre.be **N1**

73 rm ☕ – †340/450 € ††360/450 €

♦ Chain hotel ♦ Business ♦ Classic ♦

This hotel near to the EU institutions has a marble entrance hall and reception area, comfortable living room and contemporary-style rooms of varying sizes housed on eight floors.

Carrefour de l'Europe without rest
r. Marché-aux-Herbes 110 ✉ 1000
– ☎ 0 2 504 94 00 – info@carrefourhotel.be – Fax 0 2 504 95 00
– www.carrefourhotel.be **M2**
59 rm – 🚹99/290 € 🚹🚹99/310 € – 4 suites
◆ Traditional ◆ Business ◆ Functional ◆
This modern hotel on the Place d'Espagne with its statue of Don Quixote is in keeping with the harmony of the city's architecture. Bedrooms slightly on the drab side, but of a good standard nonetheless.

NH Grand Place Arenberg
r. Assaut 15 ✉ 1000 – ☎ 0 2 501 16 16 – nhgrandplace@nh-hotels.com
– Fax 0 2 501 18 18 – www.nh-hotels.com **N1**
155 rm – 🚹75/250 € 🚹🚹75/250 €, 19 €
Rest – *(closed Saturday and Sunday)* Menu 25 € – Carte 27/36 €
◆ Chain hotel ◆ Business ◆ Modern ◆
This hotel is well-placed for exploring the heart of the city around the Grand-Place. The modern bedrooms are functional yet welcoming, and typical of the NH chain. Contemporary-style restaurant serving international cuisine with modern overtones.

Scandic Grand'Place
r. Arenberg 18 ✉ 1000 – ☎ 0 2 548 18 11 – Fax 0 2 548 18 20
– www.scandic-hotels.com **N1**
100 rm – 🚹112/299 € 🚹🚹132/319 €
Rest – *(closed Saturday lunch and Sunday lunch)* Menu 10 €
– Carte 23/33 €
◆ Chain hotel ◆ Business ◆ Functional ◆
This new hotel close to the Grand-Place and accessible via the luxurious Galeries St-Hubert has public areas decorated with wood and an atrium giving onto rooms with a Scandinavian feel. A soberly-designed, yet welcoming and light modern brasserie.

Floris Avenue without rest
av. de Stalingrad 25 ✉ 1000 – ☎ 0 2 548 98 38 – reservations@florishotels.com
– Fax 0 2 513 48 22 – www.florishotels.com **L2**
47 rm – 🚹95/165 € 🚹🚹105/175 €
◆ Luxury ◆ Cosy ◆
A modernised mansion with a trendy lobby illuminated by wide bay windows, spacious, modern guestrooms, a bright, contemporary bar and attractive breakfast area.

Novotel Centre-Tour Noire
r. Vierge Noire 32 ✉ 1000 – ☎ 0 2 505 50 50
– h2122@accor.com – Fax 0 2 505 50 00 – www.novotel.com **M1**
217 rm – 🚹220/250 € 🚹🚹220/250 €, 15 €
Rest – Menu 30 € bi – Carte 26/38 €
◆ Chain hotel ◆ Business ◆ Functional ◆
This modern chain hotel is built around the remains of the city's first defensive walls, including a restored tower. Spacious guestrooms, seminar rooms, aqua centre, fitness centre and sauna. Contemporary-style brasserie.

Atlas without rest
r. Vieux Marché-aux- Grains 30 ✉ 1000 – ☎ 0 2 502 60 06 – info@atlas.be
– Fax 0 2 502 69 35 – www.atlas.be **L1**
88 rm – 🚹75/195 € 🚹🚹85/225 €
◆ Traditional ◆ Business ◆ Classic ◆
This 18C hotel (modernised inside) stands on a small square in a festive neighbourhood full of Belgian fashion boutiques. Most of the rooms look onto an inner courtyard.

Agenda Midi without rest
bd Jamar 11 ✉ 1060 – ✆ 0 2 520 00 10 – midi@hotel-agenda.com – Fax 0 2 520 00 20 – www.hotel-agenda.com Plan II **E2**
35 rm – 78/99 € 78/114 €
♦ Traditional ♦ Business ♦ Classic ♦
This hotel building is just a short distance from the Gare du Midi TGV railway station. Reliable accommodation at bargain prices. Breakfast buffet served in an inviting room decorated in warm tones.

Noga without rest
r. Béguinage 38 ✉ 1000 – ✆ 0 2 218 67 63 – info@nogahotel.com – Fax 0 2 218 16 03 – www.nogahotel.com **L1**
19 rm – 70/95 € 85/110 €
♦ Traditional ♦ Classic ♦
A friendly hotel in a fine townhouse in a quiet area of the city. A pleasant lounge, bar with a nautical decor, attractive rooms and a stairway decorated with portraits of Belgian royalty.

Queen Anne without rest
bd E. Jacqmain 110 ✉ 1000 – ✆ 0 2 217 16 00 – reservation@queen-anne.be – Fax 0 2 217 18 38 – www.queen-anne.be Plan II **F1**
60 rm – 60/250 € 65/250 €
♦ Traditional ♦ Family ♦ Minimalist ♦
This glass-fronted hotel is located on a main road. Ask for one of the small, recently refurbished rooms: sober, fresh and discreet designer features.

Matignon without rest
r. Bourse 10 ✉ 1000 – ✆ 0 2 511 08 88 – hotelmatignon@skynet.be – Fax 0 2 513 69 27 – www.hotelmatignon.be **M1**
37 rm – 85/105 € 105/150 €
♦ Traditional ♦ Family ♦ Classic ♦
This hotel next to the Stock Exchange has well-maintained rooms, including a dozen junior suites. Mainly popular with tourists.

Sea Grill – Hotel Radisson SAS Royal
r. Fossé-aux-Loups 47 ✉ 1000 – ✆ 0 2 217 92 25 – marc.meremans@radissonsas.com – Fax 0 2 227 31 27 – www.seagrill.be
closed 29 March-6 April, 1-4 May, 19 July-17 August, 25 October-2 November, 2-10 February, Saturday, Sunday and Bank Holidays **N1**
Rest – Menu 55 €, 100/220 € bi – Carte 91/225 €
Spec. Crabe royal cuit au gros sel d'algue et épices. Turbot rôti, béarnaise d'huîtres. Thon rouge et foie gras, jus des sucs au belota.
♦ Seafood ♦ Cosy ♦
A warm, Scandinavian-influenced ambience, ambitious fish-dominated menu, excellent wine cellar, plus a lounge offering a good choice of cigars. Impeccable, friendly service.

La Maison du Cygne
r. Charles Buls 2 ✉ 1000 – ✆ 0 2 511 82 44 – info@lamaisonducygne.be – Fax 0 2 514 31 48 – www.lamaisonducygne.be
closed 3 weeks August, Saturday lunch and Sunday **M2**
Rest – Menu 40/85 € – Carte 65/164 €
♦ French traditional ♦ Formal ♦
This 17C house on the Grand-Place was originally the headquarters of the Butchers' Guild. Varied classic menu and opulent décor popular with an international clientele.

Maison du Bœuf – Hotel Hilton
bd de Waterloo 38 (1st floor) ✉ 1000 – ✆ 0 2 504 11 11 – Fax 0 2 504 21 11 – www.hilton.com **N3**
Rest – Menu 39 €, 58/68 € – Carte 71/116 €
♦ French traditional ♦ Formal ♦
Chic, classical setting, appetising menu and the famous rib of beef carved at the table. Ask for a table with a view of the park.

XXXX ✿✿

Bruneau (Jean-Pierre Bruneau) (dinner) VISA MC AE D

av. Broustin 75 ✉ 1083 – ✆ 0 2 421 70 70 – restaurant_bruneau@skynet.be – Fax 0 2 425 97 26 – www.bruneau.be

closed 31 January-10 February, August, Tuesday, Wednesday and Thursday holidays Plan I **B2**

Rest – Menu 35 €, 95/150 € bi – Carte 80/191 €

Spec. Fond d'artichaut au moelleux de crabe royal, sorbet épicé à la tomate (April-January). Croustillant de langoustines et foie d'oie, parmentier aux lentilles du Puy. Blanc de coucou de Malines à la Kieff façon demi-deuil.

♦ Innovative ♦ Formal ♦

This renowned restaurant has achieved a perfect balance of innovation and tradition while at the same time maintaining its commitment to local products. Prestigious wine-list. Summer terrace.

XXXX

L'Alban Chambon – Hotel Métropole AC VISA MC AE D

pl. de Brouckère 31 ✉ 1000 – ✆ 0 2 217 23 00 – info@metropolehotel.be – Fax 0 2 218 02 20 – www.metropolehotel.com

closed 19 July-18 August, Saturday, Sunday and Bank Holidays **M1**

Rest – Menu 39/120 € – Carte 76/98 €

♦ French traditional ♦ Retro ♦

This restaurant is named after the architect who designed it. Light, classic cuisine served in a former ballroom embellished with period furniture.

XXX ✿✿

Comme Chez Soi AC VISA MC AE D

pl. Rouppe 23 ✉ 1000 – ✆ 0 2 512 29 21 – info@commechezsoi.be – Fax 0 2 511 80 52 – www.commechezsoi.be

closed 25 March, 6 July-4 August, 19 August, 28 October, 21 December-5 January, 5 February, Sunday, Monday and Wednesday lunch **L2**

Rest – *(booking essential)* Menu 68/175 € – Carte 79/286 €

Spec. Filet de bar poêlé et couteau de mer aux graines de fenouil et au vinaigre de vin. Noisettes d'agneau à la sauge, pâtes farcies à l'enveurrée de tomates confites, petits sautés de langues et ris. Croquant d'agrumes farcis aux fraises des bois, glace à la verveine.

♦ French traditional ♦ Retro ♦

A Brussels institution since 1926. Belle Époque atmosphere with a Horta-inspired decor. Classic specialities on a menu that changes regularly. The tables close to the kitchen are popular for business lunches and dinner.

XXX ✿

L'Écailler du Palais Royal (Richard Hahn) AC VISA AE D

r. Bodenbroek 18 ✉ 1000 – ✆ 0 2 512 87 51 – lecaillerdupalaisroyal@skynet.be – Fax 0 2 511 99 50 – www.lecaillerdupalaisroyal.be

closed August, Christmas-New Year, Sunday and Bank Holidays **N3**

Rest – Carte 63/129 €

Spec. Demi homard rôti, confit d'aubergine et mangue, émulsion à l'absinthe. Barbue à la moutarde. Eventail de bar et croustillant de pommes de terre, vinaigrette au jus de truffe.

♦ Seafood ♦ Cosy ♦

Cosy, smart oyster bar frequented by diplomats, politicians and business people. Comfortable benches, chairs and a bar counter on the ground floor; round tables upstairs.

XXX ✿

San Daniele (Franco Spinelli) AC VISA MC AE D

av. Charles-Quint 6 ✉ 1083 – ✆ 02 426 79 23 – Fax 02 426 92 14 – www.san-daniele.be

closed 2 weeks Easter, mid July-15 August, Sunday and Monday Plan I **A2**

Rest – Menu 65 € – Carte 49/90 €

Spec. Ravioli à l'encre de seiche, homard et courgettes, jus de crustacés. Rouget rôti au four, émulsion de palourdes. Semifreddo aux noisettes, crème façon cappuccino.

♦ Italian ♦ Friendly ♦

The warm, family welcome, extensive Italian menu and alluring choice of Transalpine wines continue to attract a loyal following.

XX

Aux Armes de Bruxelles

r. Bouchers 13 ✉ 1000 – ✆ 0 2 511 55 98 – arbrux@beon.be – Fax 0 2 514 33 81 – www.armesdebruxelles.be
closed July and Monday **M1**
Rest – *(open until 11 p.m.)* Menu 23 € bi, 32/46 € – Carte 30/40 €
♦ Traditional ♦ Brasserie ♦
A veritable Brussels institution at the heart of the historic centre, this family-run restaurant established in 1921 focuses resolutely on the country's culinary traditions. Rooms in contrasting styles.

XX

Museumbrasserie

pl. Royale 3 ✉ 1000 – ✆ 02 508 35 80 – info@museumfood.be – Fax 02 508 34 85 – www.museumfood.be **N2**
Rest – *(open until midnight)* Menu 25/35 € – Carte 40/64 €
♦ Traditional ♦ Design ♦
A hip brasserie housed within the city's Royal Museums of Fine Arts, where the cuisine reflects the commitment of the consultant chef Peter Goossens (Hof van Cleve) to Belgian culinary traditions. Design by Antoine Pinto.

XX

Bocconi – Hotel Amigo

r. Amigo 1 ✉ 1000 – ✆ 0 2 547 47 15 – bocconirestaurant@roccofortecollection.com – Fax 0 2 547 47 67 – www.ristorantebocconi.com
Rest – *(open until 11 p.m.)* Menu 34/50 € – Carte 47/58 € **M2**
♦ Italian ♦ Design ♦
This fine Italian restaurant is in a luxury hotel near the Grand-Place. Inside, the design is that of a modern brasserie. The cuisine features appetising Italian classics.

XX

François

quai aux Briques 2 ✉ 1000 – ✆ 0 2 511 60 89 – Fax 0 2 502 61 80 – www.restaurantfrancois.be
closed Sunday, Monday and day after Bank Holidays **L1**
Rest – Menu 25 €, 35/39 € – Carte 36/119 €
♦ Seafood ♦ Friendly ♦
Seafood restaurant and fishmonger run by the same family since the 1930s. The maritime interior is enlivened with nostalgic photos.

XX

La Belle Maraîchère

pl. Ste-Catherine 11 ✉ 1000 – ✆ 0 2 512 97 59 – Fax 0 2 513 76 91 – www.labellemaraichere.com
closed 3 weeks February, Wednesday and Thursday **L1**
Rest – Menu 33/52 € – Carte 35/88 €
♦ Seafood ♦ Family ♦
This convivial restaurant with a slightly dated charm is without a doubt one of the most reliably good-value eats in the neighbourhood. Tasty classic cuisine with a penchant for fish and seafood.

XX

Castello Banfi

r. Bodenbroek 12 ✉ 1000 – ✆ 0 2 512 87 94 – Fax 0 2 512 87 94
closed Easter week, last 3 weeks August, Christmas-early January, Sunday and Monday **N3**
Rest – Menu 29/55 € – Carte 39/84 €
♦ Italian ♦ Fashionable ♦
The menu at this gastronomic restaurant, hidden behind a 1729 façade, encompasses culinary and viticultural specialities from both France and Italy. The name refers to a large Tuscan wine estate.

XX

JB

r. Grand Cerf 24 ✉ 1000 – ✆ 0 2 512 04 84 – restaurantjb@tele2.be – Fax 0 2 511 79 30 – www.restaurantjb.be
closed Saturday lunch and Sunday **M3**
Rest – Menu 32 € bi/42 € bi – Carte 45/69 €
♦ Traditional ♦ Family ♦
This friendly, family-run restaurant serves traditional cuisine created by its owner-chef, who is an expert in sauces. Modern furniture, Venetian-glass chandeliers and yellow tones in the dining room.

Le Loup-Galant

quai aux Barques 4 ✉ 1000 – ✆ 0 2 219 99 98 – loupgalant@swing.be – Fax 0 2 219 99 98 – closed late December, Sunday and Monday Plan II **E1**

Rest – Menu 15 €, 30/55 € bi – Carte approx. 40 €

◆ Traditional ◆ Rustic ◆

You can spot this old house at one end of the Vismet thanks to its yellow walls and the gold statue of St Michel on the façade of the next house. Classic meals served in a rustic décor of chimney piece and exposed beams.

La Manufacture

r. Notre-Dame du Sommeil 12 ✉ 1000 – ✆ 0 2 502 25 25 – info@manufacture.be – Fax 0 2 502 27 15 – www.manufacture.be
closed Saturday lunch and Sunday **L1**

Rest – *(open until 11 p.m.)* Menu 14 €, 32/70 € bi – Carte 32/48 €

◆ Contemporary ◆ Brasserie ◆

Metal, wood, leather and granite have all been used to decorate this trendy brasserie occupying the workshop of a renowned leather manufacturer. Contemporary cuisine.

L'Huîtrière

quai aux Briques 20 ✉ 1000 – ✆ 02 512 08 66 – huitriere@skynet.be – Fax 02 512 12 81 – www.huitriere.eu **L1**

Rest – Menu 15 €, 25/44 € – Carte 40/68 €

◆ Seafood ◆ Inn ◆

Fish and seafood served amid a decor of wood panelling, stained glass and Bruegel-inspired frescos recalling the evocative charms of old Brussels. Lively atmosphere.

De l'Ogenblik

Galerie des Princes 1 ✉ 1000 – ✆ 0 2 511 61 51 – ogenblik@scarlet.be – Fax 0 2 513 41 58 – www.ogenblik.be
closed Sunday and Bank Holidays lunch **M1**

Rest – *(open until midnight)* Menu 51/70 € bi – Carte approx. 65 €

◆ Traditional ◆ Bistro ◆

This restaurant housed in an old café is known for its classic cuisine and bistro-style. Popular with the local business community. The same chef has worked here since 1975.

Samourai

r. Fossé-aux-Loups 28 ✉ 1000 – ✆ 0 2 217 56 39 – Fax 0 2 771 97 61 – www.restaurant-samourai.be
closed 15 July-15 August, Tuesday, Sunday lunch and Bank Holidays **M1**

Rest – Menu 22 €, 60/85 € – Carte 43/100 €

◆ Japanese ◆ Traditional ◆

A Japanese restaurant established more than 30 years ago near the Théâtre de la Monnaie. Authentic, varied menu. Rooms with Japanese décor on several floors.

La Roue d'Or

r. Chapeliers 26 ✉ 1000 – ✆ 0 2 514 25 54 – roue.dor@hotmail.com – Fax 0 2 512 30 81
closed 10 July-10 August **M2**

Rest – Menu 13 € – Carte 40/60 €

◆ Traditional ◆ Brasserie ◆

A typical old café with a convivial atmosphere where the culinary emphasis is on staple Belgian brasserie fare. Surrealist wall paintings in the genre of Magritte and a superb clock in the dining area.

Scheltema

r. Dominicains 7 ✉ 1000 – ✆ 0 2 512 20 84 – scheltema@skynet.be – Fax 0 2 512 44 82 – www.scheltema.be – closed Sunday **M1**

Rest – *(open until 11.30 p.m.)* Menu 18 €, 35/43 € – Carte 38/77 €

◆ Traditional ◆ Brasserie ◆

An attractive old brasserie in the Ilot Sacré district specialising in fish and seafood. Classic menu choices, inventive specials, a lively atmosphere and a pleasantly retro wood-inspired decor.

La Marée

AC VISA MC

r. Flandre 99 ✉ 1000 – ☎ 0 2 511 00 40 – Fax 0 2 511 86 19 – www.lamaree-sa.com
closed 1-21 July, 21 December-2 January, Sunday and Monday **L1**

Rest – Carte 22/61 €

♦ Seafood ♦ Family ♦

The friendly atmosphere and unpretentious cuisine and décor of this restaurant account for its popularity. Open kitchen, where the chef prepares freshly delivered fish and seafood.

Switch

VISA MC AE

r. Flandre 6 ✉ 1000 – ☎ 0 2 503 14 80 – info@restofood.be – Fax 0 2 502 58 78 – www.switchrestofood.be
closed 5-21 August, Sunday and Monday **L1**

Rest – Menu 13 €, 28/55 € bi – Carte 29/43 €

♦ Contemporary ♦ Bistro ♦

A modern bistro with the unique characteristic of allowing you to choose how you want your chosen dish cooked, including seasoning and accompanying vegetables.

Le Fourneau

AC VISA MC AE

pl. Ste-Catherine 8 ✉ 1000 – ☎ 0 2 513 10 02
closed 1-21 July, 24, 25 and 31 December, 1 January, Sunday and Monday

Rest – Carte 24/47 € **L1**

♦ Contemporary ♦ Trendy ♦

Fine cuisine from the Mediterranean served around a circular counter overlooking the kitchen area. Flexible choice, ranging from tapas portions to start to main courses priced according to weight. No reservations.

In 't Spinnekopke

AC VISA MC AE

pl. du Jardin aux Fleurs 1 ✉ 1000 – ☎ 0 2 511 86 95 – info@spinnekopke.be – Fax 0 2 513 24 97 – www.spinnekopke.be
closed Saturday lunch and Sunday **L1**

Rest – *(open until 11 p.m.)* Menu 14 € bi, 42 € bi/60 € bi – Carte 29/55 €

♦ Regional ♦ Bistro ♦

This charming, typical tavern is esteemed for its good bistro-style atmosphere and regional cuisine which does justice to the Belgian tradition.

Viva M'Boma

AC VISA MC

r. Flandre 17 ✉ 1000 – ☎ 0 2 512 15 93 – Fax 02 469 42 84
closed 31 July-18 August, 1-7 January, Sunday, Monday dinner, Tuesday dinner and Wednesday **L1**

Rest – Carte 23/32 €

♦ Regional ♦ Bistro ♦

This modern "canteen" serves typical Belgian dishes, which has also an adjoining delicatessen (tripe is a speciality). Tables are close together and the walls are decorated with tiles. Small hidden terrace.

Lola

AC VISA MC AE

pl. du Grand Sablon 33 ✉ 1000 – ☎ 0 2 514 24 60 – restaurant.lola@skynet.be – Fax 0 2 514 26 53 – www.restolola.be
closed 24 dinner, 25 and 31 December dinner - 1 January **M3**

Rest – *(open until 11.30 p.m.)* Carte 38/64 €

♦ Contemporary ♦ Trendy ♦

This convivial brasserie with its contemporary décor devotes its energies to the latest culinary trends. Choose between sitting on benches, chairs or at the bar.

La Clef des Champs

VISA MC AE

r. Rollebeek 23 ✉ 1000 – ☎ 0 2 512 11 93 – info@clefsdeschamps.be – Fax 0 2 502 42 32 – www.clefdeschamps.be
closed Sunday dinner and Monday **M3**

Rest – Menu 19 €, 32/58 € bi – Carte 41/50 €

♦ Regional ♦ Friendly ♦

Pleasant, family-run restaurant, completely renovated in 2006. Décor includes large mirrors, crystal chandeliers, white wall panelling, and stylish chairs with openwork backs.

L'Idiot du village

r. Notre Seigneur 19 ✉ 1000 – ☎ 0 2 502 55 82
closed 20 July-20 August, 23 December-3 January, Saturday and Sunday
Rest – *(open until 11 p.m.)* Menu 15 € – Carte 37/57 € **M3**
♦ Traditional ♦ Bistro ♦
Service with a smile, eclectic, pleasingly kitsch decor, a warm ambience, bistro-style cuisine with an original, modern touch, astute wine-list and friendly service.

Les Larmes du Tigre

r. Wynants 21 ✉ 1000 – ☎ 0 2 512 18 77 – larmesdutigre@skynet.be – Fax 0 2 502 10 03 – www.leslarmesdutigre.be
closed Saturday lunch *Plan II* **F3**
Rest – Menu 11/35 € – Carte 26/36 €
♦ Thai ♦ Exotic ♦
Thai cuisine has been served in this mansion close to the Palais de Justice for 20 years. Parasols adorn the ceiling. Sunday buffet (lunch and dinner).

QUARTIER LOUISE-CAMBRE *Plan III*

Conrad

av. Louise 71 ✉ 1050 – ☎ 0 2 542 42 42 – brusselsinfo@conradhotels.com – Fax 0 2 542 42 00 – www.conradhotels.com **J1**
254 rm – 199/595 € 224/620 €, 35 € – 15 suites
Rest *Café Wiltcher's* – Menu 40 € – Carte 53/93 €
♦ Grand Luxury ♦ Business ♦ Classic ♦
A modern upmarket hotel brilliantly arranged inside a mansion dating from 1918. Excellent bedrooms with classic furnishings; full range of seminar and leisure facilities, including a spa. Caters for large conferences. The café serves popular lunch buffets.

Bristol Stephanie

av. Louise 91 ✉ 1050 – ☎ 0 2 543 33 11 – hotel_bristol@bristol.be – Fax 0 2 538 03 07 – www.bristol.be **J1**
139 rm – 360/395 € 360/395 €, 27 € – 3 suites
Rest – *(closed 12 July-31 August, 20 December-6 January, Saturday and Sunday) (buffets)* Menu 19 €, 40/66 € bi – Carte 44/63 €
♦ Luxury ♦ Business ♦ Classic ♦
The very pleasant guestrooms of this luxury property occupy two interlinked buildings. Three superb suites adorned with typical Norwegian furniture. Contemporary dining in a Scandinavian-inspired ambience. Buffet options also available.

Le Châtelain

r. Châtelain 17 ✉ 1000 – ☎ 0 2 646 00 55 – info@le-chatelain.net – Fax 0 2 646 00 88 – www.le-chatelain.net **J2**
108 rm – 100/630 € 100/630 € – 2 suites
Rest – *(closed Saturday and Sunday lunch)* Carte 36/46 €
♦ Luxury ♦ Business ♦ Functional ♦
A new hotel with large, modern rooms featuring the very latest equipment and facilities. Superb reception area, well-equipped fitness room and a small garden. The restaurant offers a range of continental dishes, as well as Asian specialities.

Warwick Barsey

av. Louise 381 ✉ 1050 – ☎ 0 2 641 51 11 – res.warwickbarsey@warwickhotels.com – Fax 0 2 640 17 64 – www.warwickbrussels.com **K3**
94 rm – 280 € 280 €, 24 € – 5 suites
Rest – *(closed Sunday)* Carte approx. 40 €
♦ Luxury ♦ Business ♦ Stylish ♦
A characterful hotel near the Bois de la Cambre skilfully refurbished in a style inspired by the Second Empire. Elegant public areas and plush, well-appointed rooms. Personalised service. Neo-classical décor in the Jacques Garcia-designed restaurant-lounge.

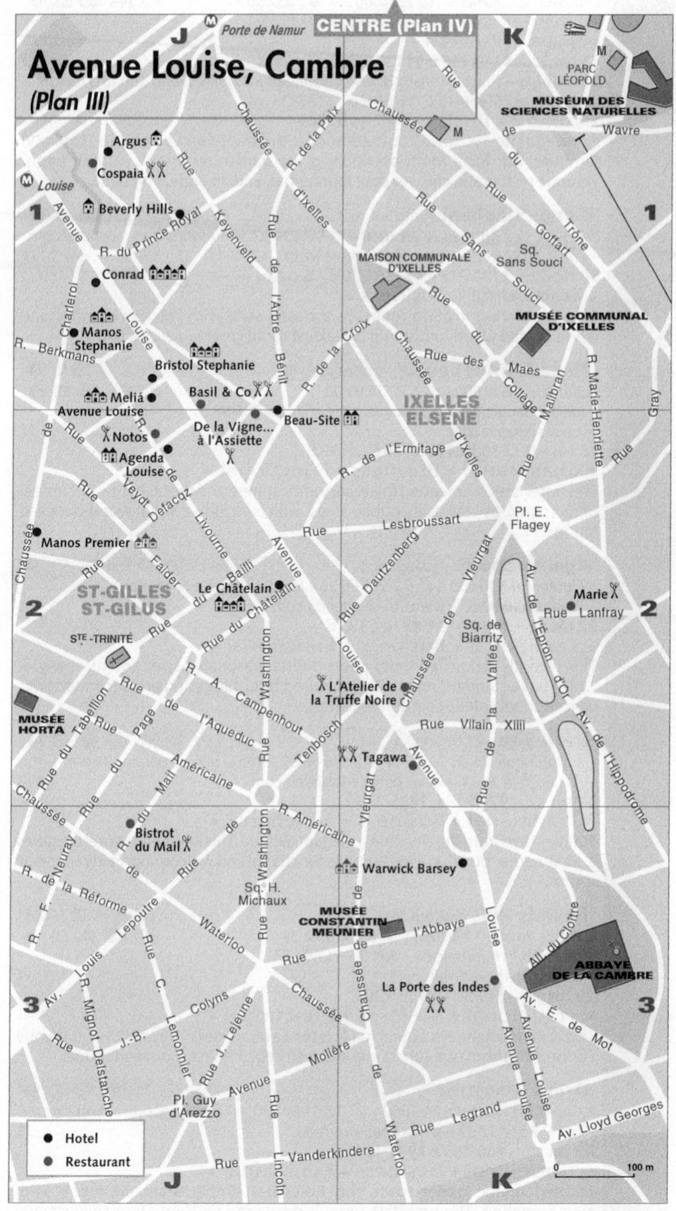
Avenue Louise, Cambre
(Plan III)
CENTRE (Plan IV)
Porte de Namur
Argus
Cospaia
Beverly Hills
Conrad
Manos Stephanie
Bristol Stephanie
Meliá Avenue Louise
Basil & Co
De la Vigne... à l'Assiette
Beau-Site
Notos
Agenda Louise
Manos Premier
Le Châtelain
Marie
L'Atelier de la Truffe Noire
Tagawa
Bistrot du Mail
Warwick Barsey
La Porte des Indes
MUSÉUM DES SCIENCES NATURELLES
PARC LÉOPOLD
MAISON COMMUNALE D'IXELLES
MUSÉE COMMUNAL D'IXELLES
IXELLES ELSENE
ST-GILLES ST-GILUS
STE-TRINITÉ
MUSÉE HORTA
MUSÉE CONSTANTIN MEUNIER
ABBAYE DE LA CAMBRE
Pl. E. Flagey
Sq. Sans Souci
Sq. de Biarritz
Sq. H. Michaux
Pl. Guy d'Arezzo
Hotel
Restaurant
100 m

Manos Premier (dinner)
chaussée de Charleroi 102 ✉ 1060 – ✆ 0 2 537 96 82 – manos@manoshotel.com – Fax 0 2 539 36 55 – www.manoshotel.com **J2**
45 rm – 110/295 € 120/320 € – 5 suites
Rest *Kolya* – *(closed Christmas - New Year, Saturday lunch and Sunday) (open until 11 p.m.)* Menu 15 €, 35/60 € bi
♦ Luxury ♦ Business ♦ Stylish ♦
A graceful late-19C town house adorned with sumptuous Louis XV and Louis XVI furniture. Ask for a room overlooking the garden. Authentic Turkish baths. Veranda restaurant, chic yet cosy lounge-bar, and an appealing patio.

Manos Stéphanie without rest
chaussée de Charleroi 28 ✉ 1060 – ✆ 0 2 539 02 50 – manos@manoshotel.com – Fax 0 2 537 57 29 – www.manoshotel.com **J1**
50 rm – 100/245 € 110/270 € – 5 suites
♦ Traditional ♦ Business ♦
A hotel offering inviting rooms in a classic style with modern touches and white-leaded wood furnishings. Breakfast room crowned with a cupola.

Meliá Avenue Louise without rest
r. Blanche 4 ✉ 1000 – ✆ 0 2 535 95 00 – melia.avenue.louise@solmelia.com – Fax 0 2 535 96 00 – www.solmelia.com **J1**
80 rm – 90/300 € 90/320 €, 22 €
♦ Chain hotel ♦ Business ♦ Functional ♦
This hotel is recommended for its cosy atmosphere and the elegantly British feel of its rooms, as well as its public areas, which include a snug, wood-panelled lounge.

Agenda Louise without rest
r. Florence 6 ✉ 1000 – ✆ 0 2 539 00 31 – louise@hotel-agenda.com – Fax 0 2 539 00 63 – www.hotel-agenda.com **J2**
37 rm – 138/170 € 144/170 €
♦ Traditional ♦ Business ♦ Functional ♦
This recently renovated hotel offers guests reasonably-sized rooms, many of which have standard mahogany-coloured furnishings and are decorated with warm-toned, colour-coordinated fabrics.

Beau-Site without rest
r. Longue Haie 76 ✉ 1050 – ✆ 0 2 640 88 89 – info@beausitebrussels.com – Fax 0 2 640 16 11 – www.beausitebrussels.com **J1-2**
38 rm – 70/219 € 75/239 €
♦ Traditional ♦ Business ♦ Functional ♦
100m/110yd from the city's most elegant avenue. This family-run hotel occupies a small corner building and is simple, functional and welcoming. Fairly spacious rooms.

Beverly Hills without rest
r. Prince Royal 71 ✉ 1050 – ✆ 0 2 513 22 22 – beverlyhills@infonie.be – Fax 0 2 513 87 77 – www.hotelbeverlyhills.be **J1**
28 rm – 49/99 € 69/139 €
♦ Traditional ♦ Business ♦ Functional ♦
This hotel is situated in a quiet road close to avenue de la Toison d'Or and avenue Louise. The rooms are functional and well kept. Fitness room and sauna.

Argus without rest
r. Capitaine Crespel 6 ✉ 1050 – ✆ 0 2 514 07 70 – reception@boisel-argus.be – Fax 0 2 514 12 22 – www.hotel-argus.be **J1**
42 rm – 60/165 € 70/165 €
♦ Traditional ♦ Business ♦ Functional ♦
Located in the upper town, this hotel has simple, standard rooms with soundproofing. The breakfast room is decorated with Art Deco-style stained glass. Good value for money.

Villa Lorraine

av. du Vivier d'Oie 75 ✉ 1000 – ✆ 0 2 374 31 63 – info@villalorraine.be – Fax 0 2 372 01 95 – www.villalorraine.be

closed 7-28 July and Sunday — *Plan I* **C3**

Rest – Menu 45 €, 85/150 € bi – Carte 66/165 €

◆ French traditional ◆ Formal ◆

A fine restaurant established in 1953 on the edge of the Bois de la Cambre woods. Classic setting and a prestigious wine cellar. Gorgeous terrace in the shade of a chestnut tree.

Basil & Co

av. Louise 156 ✉ 1050 – ✆ 0 2 642 22 22 – louise@basil-co.be – Fax 0 2 642 22 25 – www.basil-co.be

closed first week Easter, first 3 weeks August, week after Christmas and Sunday

Rest – Menu 35 € – Carte 38/67 € **J1**

◆ Inventive ◆ Formal ◆

A change of style for this attractive private mansion with its new trendy décor and contemporary cuisine. Good choice of dishes, lunch menu and wines by the glass.

Cospaia

(lunch)

r. Capitaine Crespel 1 ✉ 1050 – ✆ 02 513 03 03 – info@cospaia.be – Fax 02 513 45 72 – www.cospaia.com – closed Sunday lunch **J1**

Rest – Menu 20 € – Carte 45/57 €

◆ Contemporary ◆ Fashionable ◆

On the corner of a swish shopping centre, this very trendy restaurant is making a name for itself through its fine cuisine and contemporary and elegant décor by Marcel Wolterinck.

Tagawa

av. Louise 279 ✉ 1050 – ✆ 0 2 640 50 95 – o.tagawa@scarlet.be – Fax 0 2 648 41 36

closed 26 December-3 January, 13-19 August, Saturday lunch and Sunday

Rest – Menu 12 €, 38/90 € – Carte 29/66 € **K2**

◆ Japanese ◆ Minimalist ◆

This simply furnished Japanese restaurant is worth tracking down inside one of the city's shopping galleries. Minimalist dining room, private lounge with traditional Japanese tatami mats, and kimono-clad waitresses. Private parking.

La Porte des Indes

av. Louise 455 ✉ 1050 – ✆ 0 2 647 86 51 – brussels@laportedesindes.com – Fax 0 2 375 44 68 – www.laportedesindes.com

closed Sunday lunch **K3**

Rest – Menu 17 €, 43/58 € – Carte 31/60 €

◆ Indian ◆ Exotic ◆

If your taste-buds fancy a change, head for La Porte des Indes, with its exotic, deliciously flavoured cuisine. The restaurant interior is decorated with Indian antiques.

L'Atelier de la Truffe Noire

av. Louise 300 ✉ 1050 – ✆ 0 2 640 54 55 – luigi.ciciriello@truffenoire.com – Fax 0 2 648 11 44 – www.atelier.truffenoire.com

closed 1 week Easter, first 2 weeks August, first week January, Sunday and Monday dinner **K2**

Rest – *(open until 11 p.m.)* Carte 30/108 €

◆ Traditional ◆ Fashionable ◆

A modern bistro whose originality and success lie in its fast service and truffle-based gourmet menu. Varied à la carte dishes showing Italian influence. Small terrace.

Notos

r. Livourne 154 ✉ 1000 – ✆ 02 513 29 59 – info@notos.be – www.notos.be

closed 3 weeks August, Saturday lunch, Sunday and Monday **J2**

Rest – *(open until 11 p.m.)* Menu 18 €, 35/50 € – Carte 36/52 €

◆ Greek ◆ Trendy ◆

A "new generation" Greek restaurant giving new life to a former garage. Refined, contemporary setting for traditional dishes created with a modern slant, accompanied by excellent Greek wines.

Marie

r. Alphonse De Witte 40 ✉ 1050 – ✆ 02 644 30 31 – Fax 02 644 27 37
closed 20 July-19 August, 21 December-6 January, Saturday lunch, Sunday and Monday **K2**
Rest – Menu 17/58 € – Carte 47/58 €
Spec. Brandade de morue à l'huile d'olive, concassée de tomates et coulis de poivrons. Filet de turbot poêlé, crème émulsionnée aux moules de bouchot et crevettes grises (June-September). Filet de biche rôti, sauce poivrade et cannelloni aux champignons des bois (October-February).
♦ French traditional ♦ Bistro ♦
This pleasant gourmet bistro serves a traditional type cuisine and offers a wide variety of wines, many of which are available by the glass.

Bistrot du Mail

r. Mail 81 ✉ 1050 – ✆ 02 539 06 97 – contact@bistrodumail.be – www.bistrodumail.be
closed 15 July-15 August, Saturday lunch, Sunday and Monday **J3**
Rest – Menu 15 €, 38/50 € – Carte 48/64 €
Spec. Langoustines rôties au gingembre, melon et pois frais. Pigeon rôti à la sauge, laitue braisée aux petits légumes. Sablé breton et pommes caramélisées, glace au sirop d'érable.
♦ Contemporary ♦ Bistro ♦
A popular address for serious food-lovers who come here to enjoy the personalised cuisine and refined décor. Large bay windows, grey and aubergine walls, and modern canvases. Friendly and attentive service. Valet parking.

De la Vigne... à l'Assiette

r. Longue Haie 51 ✉ 1000 – ✆ 0 2 647 68 03 – Fax 0 2 647 68 03 closed 24 December-3 January, Saturday lunch, Sunday and Monday **J2**
Rest – Menu 14 €, 21/35 € – Carte 37/49 €
♦ Contemporary ♦ Bistro ♦
Copious portions and innovative cuisine at this "gastro-bistro", which has a good selection of reasonably priced wines from around the world and knowledgeable staff.

EUROPEAN INSTITUTIONS *Plan II*

Stanhope

square de Meeûs 4 ✉ 1000 – ✆ 0 2 506 90 12 – brighton@stanhope.be – Fax 0 2 512 17 08 – www.stanhope.be *Plan IV* **O3**
99 rm – †95/250 € ††120/250 €, ☕ 25 € – 9 suites
Rest Brighton – see below
♦ Grand Luxury ♦ Traditional ♦ Stylish ♦
Relive the splendour of the Victorian era in this town house with a distinctly British feel. Choose from a variety of room categories: the suites and split-level rooms are superb.

Renaissance

r. Parnasse 19 ✉ 1050 – ✆ 0 2 505 29 29 – renaissance.brussels@renaissancehotels.com – Fax 0 2 505 25 55 – www.renaissancebrussels.com **G3**
256 rm – †79/389 € ††79/389 €, ☕ 20 € – 6 suites
Rest – *(closed Saturday lunch, Sunday lunch and Bank Holidays lunch)* Menu 21 € – Carte 29/50 €
♦ Chain hotel ♦ Business ♦ Modern ♦
This hotel enjoys a good location on the edge of the European institutions district. Modern, well-appointed rooms, excellent business, conference and leisure facilities, plus a full range of hotel services. The brasserie offers a traditional choice, including a lunch menu served over three sittings.

Radisson SAS EU

r. Idalie 35 ✉ 1050 – ✆ 0 2 626 81 11 – info.brusseleu@radissonsas.com – Fax 0 2 626 81 12 – www.brussels.eu.radissonsas.com **G3**

145 rm – †95/800 € ††95/800 €, ☕ 25 € – 4 suites

Rest – *(closed Saturday lunch and Sunday lunch)* Carte 36/56 €

♦ Chain hotel ♦ Business ♦ Stylish ♦

A new ultra-modern palace hotel offering three room categories labelled "Fresh", "Chic" and "Fashion". Popular with business clients and staff from the European parliament. A fusion of classic/contemporary dishes served to a trendy decorative backdrop, either at individual tables or at the large designer counter.

Montgomery

av. de Tervuren 134 ✉ 1150 – ✆ 0 2 741 85 11 – reservations@eurostarsmontgomery.com – Fax 0 2 741 85 00 – www.eurostarshotels.com

61 rm – †210/360 € ††210/360 €, ☕ 20 € – 2 suites *Plan I* **C2**

Rest – Menu 25 € – Carte 25/46 €

♦ Luxury ♦ Business ♦ Stylish ♦

An elegant, discreet hotel with theme-based rooms (Asian, nautical or romantic décor), lovely penthouses, lounge-library, fitness room and sauna. Attentive service. The cuisine in the snug restaurant will find favour with aficionados of modern cuisine.

Crowne Plaza Europa

r. Loi 107 ✉ 1040 – ✆ 0 2 230 13 33 – info@europahotelbrussels.com – Fax 0 2 230 03 26 – www.europahotelbrussels.com **G2**

238 rm – †260/380 € ††260/380 €, ☕ 25 € – 2 suites

Rest *The Gallery* – *(closed Saturday lunch and Sunday lunch) (buffets)* Menu 19 € – Carte 26/56 €

♦ Chain hotel ♦ Business ♦ Functional ♦

A twelve-storey hotel, located a few steps from the main European institutions. Comfortable rooms, modern lobby, business centre and full conference facilities. The Gallery offers a choice of classic and contemporary cuisine as well as buffets.

Silken Berlaymont

bd Charlemagne 11 ✉ 1000 – ✆ 0 2 231 09 09 – hotel.berlaymont@hoteles-silken.com – Fax 0 2 230 33 71 – www.hotelsilkenberlaymont.com

212 rm – †89/325 € ††89/325 €, ☕ 25 € – 2 suites **G2**

Rest *L'Objectif* – Menu 20 € – Carte 33/53 €

♦ Design ♦ Business ♦ Functional ♦

This newly built chain hotel comprises two modern, inter-connected buildings with fresh, well-kept contemporary rooms. The interior décor follows a theme of contemporary photography. The menu is varied and the appetisers original.

Martin's Central Park

bd Charlemagne 80 ✉ 1000 – ✆ 0 2 230 85 55 – mcp@martinshotels.com – Fax 0 2 230 56 35 – www.martinshotels.com

97 rm ☕ – †210/330 € ††240/360 € – 3 suites **G2**

Rest – *(closed Saturday lunch, Sunday lunch and Bank Holidays)* Menu 16/29 € – Carte 38/45 €

♦ Luxury ♦ Business ♦ Design ♦

A modern hotel building near the Berlaymont building offering three room categories and good seminar and business facilities. Stylish public rooms adorned with photos of show-biz celebrities. Contemporary brasserie, lounge-bar and courtyard terrace.

Leopold

r. Luxembourg 35 ✉ 1050 – ✆ 0 2 511 18 28 – reservations@hotel-leopold.be – Fax 0 2 514 19 39 – www.hotel-leopold.be *Plan IV* **O3**

111 rm ☕ – †150/230 € ††170/420 €

Rest *Salon Les Anges* – *(closed Saturday lunch and Sunday) (dinner only in July-August)* Menu 35 € – Carte 52/61 €

♦ Traditional ♦ Business ♦ Classic ♦

This continually expanding and improving hotel boasts well-appointed bedrooms, smart public areas and a winter garden where breakfast is served. A classic menu is on offer in the hushed Salon Les Anges restaurant; a variety of dishes served in the relaxed brasserie.

Holiday Inn Schuman
r. Breydel 20 ✉ 1040 – ✆ 0 2 280 40 00 – hotel@holiday-inn-brussels-schuman.com – Fax 0 2 282 10 70 – www.holiday-inn.com/brusselsschuman **H2**
57 rm – †50/450 € ††60/460 €, ☕ 21 € – 2 suites
Rest – *(residents only)*
♦ Chain hotel ♦ Business ♦ Functional ♦
Hotel named after a renowned pro-European politician, who would surely have appreciated this hotel offering rooms with a high level of comfort, perfect for those on European business.

New Hotel Charlemagne
bd Charlemagne 25 ✉ 1000 – ✆ 0 2 230 21 35 – brusselscharlemagne@new-hotel.be – Fax 0 2 230 25 10 – www.new-hotel.com **H2**
68 rm – †59/260 € ††59/360 €, ☕ 21 €
Rest – *(residents only)*
♦ Traditional ♦ Business ♦ Functional ♦
This practical small hotel between Square Ambiorix and the Centre Berlaymont is popular with EU staff. Reception, lounge-bar and breakfast room on the same floor.

Brighton – Hotel Stanhope
r. Commerce 9 ✉ 1000 – ✆ 0 2 506 90 35 – brighton@stanhope.be – Fax 0 2 512 17 08 – www.stanhope.be
closed 7-13 April, 14 July-August, 1-9 January, Saturday and Sunday *Plan IV* **O3**
Rest – Menu 40/55 € bi – Carte 58/87 €
♦ Traditional ♦ Formal ♦
An elegant hotel whose dining room with a refined English-style décor is inspired by Brighton's Royal Pavilion. Pleasant patio with a terrace open in fine weather.

L'Ancienne Poissonnerie
r. Trône 65 ✉ 1050 – ✆ 02 502 75 05
closed August, Saturday lunch and Sunday *Plan IV* **G3**
Rest – Carte 35/48 €
♦ Italian ♦ Bistro ♦
This former Art Nouveau fishmonger's has been transformed into a contemporary Italian restaurant. Simple table settings, charming service, and a relaxed and friendly atmosphere.

Take Sushi
bd Charlemagne 21 ✉ 1000 – ✆ 0 2 230 56 27 – Fax 0 2 231 10 44
closed Saturday and Sunday lunch **G2**
Rest – Menu 15 €, 23/56 € bi – Carte 30/50 €
♦ Japanese ♦ Traditional ♦
This corner of Japan has existed at the heart of the city's European institutions district for more than 20 years. Japanese décor, background music and small garden. Sushi bar and fixed menus.

GARE DU NORD *Plan II*

Sheraton
pl. Rogier 3 ✉ 1210 – ✆ 0 2 224 31 11 – reservations.brussels@sheraton.com – Fax 0 2 224 34 56 – www.sheraton.com **F1**
486 rm – †115/375 € ††115/375 €, ☕ 25 € – 22 suites
Rest – *(buffets)* Menu 31 €, 30/55 € bi – Carte 40/66 €
♦ Grand Luxury ♦ Business ♦ Modern ♦
With its full range of facilities, the imposing Sheraton has won over a business clientele, international travellers and conference-goers. Spacious standard rooms, plus club rooms and numerous suites. Attractive contemporary bar. Classic, traditional meals in the dining area facing the place Rogier. Lunch buffet.

Crowne Plaza "Le Palace"
r. Gineste 3 ✉ 1210 – ☎ 0 2 203 62 00 – info@cpbxl.be – Fax 0 2 203 55 55 – www.crowneplazabrussels.com **F1**
353 rm – †125/350 € ††125/350 €, ☕ 26 € – 1 suite
Rest – *(closed lunch Saturday and Sunday)* Menu 18/35 € – Carte approx. 45 €
♦ Chain hotel ♦ Business ♦ Functional ♦
A Belle Époque-style palace which celebrates its centenary in 2008. Opulent yet cosy public areas, a brand-new bar, neo-retro-style guestrooms and new suites. Cosmopolitan cuisine to a backdrop of chic, trendy décor.

Husa President
bd du Roi Albert II 44 ✉ 1000 – ☎ 0 2 203 20 20 – info.president@husa.es – Fax 0 2 203 24 40 – www.husa.es *Plan I* **B2**
281 rm – †75/120 € ††80/150 €, ☕ 20 € – 16 suites
Rest – *(closed Sunday)* Menu 21 € – Carte 31/50 €
♦ Traditional ♦ Business ♦ Functional ♦
An imposing hotel at one end of Brussels' "Manhattan", close to the Gare du Nord (North Station) and the World Trade Center. The public areas are spacious and the rooms very comfortable. The relaxed restaurant's classic menu includes several fixed options and good daily suggestions.

Le Dome (annex Le Dome II)
bd du Jardin Botanique 12 ✉ 1000 – ☎ 0 2 218 06 80 – dome@skypro.be – Fax 0 2 218 41 12 – www.hotel-le-dome.be **F1**
125 rm ☕ – †84/218 € ††98/350 €
Rest – Menu 16 € – Carte 24/52 €
♦ Traditional ♦ Business ♦ Retro ♦
The dome crowning the 1900s-style façade overlooks the lively place Rogier. Art Nouveau-inspired decor in the hotel's public areas and rooms. A modern brasserie with mezzanine serving traditional Belgian fare, including salads and snacks.

Senza Nome (Giovani Bruno)
r. Royale Ste-Marie 22 ✉ 1030 – ☎ 02 223 16 17 – senzanome@skynet.be – Fax 02 223 16 17 – www.senzanome.be
closed 21 July-mid August, Christmas-New Year, Saturday lunch and Sunday
Rest – Menu 55 € – Carte 44/62 € **G1**
Spec. Spaghetti à l'huile aromatisée à l'ail pimenté, coulis de tomates et encre de seiche. Carpaccio de bœuf et duo de mostarda, coulis de roquette. Tagliata de thon, émulsion d'huile d'olive, vinaigre balsamique, copeaux de parmesan.
♦ Italian ♦ Family ♦
A Sicilian-influenced menu, excellent choice of daily specials, an extensive Italian wine list plus a knowledgeable owner. Popular with politicians and government officials.

Les Dames Tartine
chaussée de Haecht 58 ✉ 1210 – ☎ 02 218 45 49 – Fax 02 218 45 49
closed first 3 weeks August, Saturday lunch, Sunday and Monday **G1**
Rest – Menu 19 €, 33/45 € – Carte 38/48 €
♦ Traditional ♦ Retro ♦
Two "Dames Tartine" are at the helm of this charming, small restaurant that remains loyal to its past. Customers sit at sewing machine tables, surrounded by paintings of the owner's ancestors.

GARE DU MIDI *Plan I*

Be Manos (lunch)
square de l'Aviation 23 ✉ 1070 – ☎ 02 520 65 65 – stay@bemanos.com – Fax 02 520 67 67 – www.bemanos.be **E2**
59 rm ☕ – †275/370 € ††315/410 € – 1 suite
Rest *Be Lella* – *(closed weekends) (lunch only)* Menu 17 € – Carte 29/51 €
♦ Luxury ♦ Design ♦
A new designer hotel opened in a trendy district of Anderlecht in 2007. Ultra-fashionable lounges and guestrooms decorated in black and white tones. Very trendy restaurant serving a range of Brussels and Belgian specialities. Spa.

XXX

Saint Guidon

av. Théo Verbeeck 2 (1st floor, in the R.S.C. Anderlecht football stadium) ✉ 1070 – ✆ 0 2 520 55 36 – saint-guidon@skynet.be – Fax 0 2 523 38 27 – www.saint-guidon.be
closed 20 June-21 July, 22 December-2 January, Saturday, Sunday and at home matches **A3**
Rest – *(lunch only)* Menu 32/57 € bi – Carte 53/95 €
♦ Contemporary ♦ Formal ♦
This smart restaurant is situated on the second floor of Anderlecht's football stadium. The fine traditional cuisine and excellent service make it a popular venue.

XX ✿

Bon-Bon (Christophe Hardiquest)

r. Carmélites 93 ✉ 1180 – ✆ 02 346 66 15 – www.bon-bon.be
closed 1-7 January, 21 July-15 August, Saturday lunch, Sunday and Monday *Plan I* **B3**
Rest – *(booking essential)* Menu 40 €, 65/85 € – Carte 52/90 €
Spec. Tomate farcie au fois gras grillé, poudre d'agrume. Canard grillé à la gastrique noire, pommes sarladaises. Paupiette d'aile de raie aux moules de bouchot et concombre.
♦ Contemporary ♦ Bistro ♦
A backdrop of wall panelling, wood flooring, mirrors and grey velvet for modern cuisine prepared exclusively with ingredients of certified origin, that are often obscure.

XX

Alain Cornelis

av. Paul Janson 82 ✉ 1070 – ✆ 0 2 523 20 83 – alaincornelis@skynet.be – Fax 0 2 523 20 83 – www.alaincornelis.be
closed 1 week Easter, first 2 weeks August, late December, Wednesday dinner, Saturday lunch, Sunday and Bank Holidays **A3**
Rest – Menu 30/65 € bi – Carte 30/44 €
♦ Traditional ♦ Friendly ♦
A classically bourgeois restaurant with a traditional menu, décor and ambience. The terrace to the rear is embellished with a small garden. Fixed menus and à la carte selection.

XX

La Brouette

bd Prince de Liège 61 ✉ 1070 – ✆ 0 2 522 51 69 – info@labrouette.be – Fax 0 2 522 51 69 – www.labrouette.be
closed 21 July-15 August, Carnival week, Saturday lunch, Sunday dinner and Monday **A2**
Rest – Menu 25 €, 35/65 € bi – Carte approx. 45 €
♦ Contemporary ♦ Design ♦
This restaurant's grey and burgundy interior gives it a modern feel. The art photos displayed on the walls were taken by the owner, who is also the sommelier. The "Brouette" menu is highly recommended.

X

La Paix

r. Ropsy-Chaudron 49 (opposite the slaughterhouse) ✉ 1070 – ✆ 02 523 09 58 – restaurantlapaix@skynet.be – Fax 02 520 10 39 – www.lapaix1892.com
closed last 3 weeks July, Saturday and Sunday *Plan I* **B2**
Rest – *(lunch only except Friday)* Carte 35/60 €
♦ French traditional ♦ Brasserie ♦
This former wholesale butchers' café is now the domain of a French chef who has reinvented and adopted a fresh approach to traditional bistro cuisine amid a typically Brussels setting and ambience. Wood panelling, high ceilings and a kitchen visible to diners.

Rijckendael

J. Van Elewijckstraat 35 ✉ 1853 Strombeek-Bever – ✆ 0 2 267 41 24 – restaurant.rijckendael@vhv-hotels.be – Fax 0 2 267 94 01 – www.rijckendael.be

49 rm – 95/185 € 95/185 € **B1**

Rest – *(closed last 3 weeks July-first week August and Sunday dinner)* Menu 23 €, 38/70 € bi – Carte 36/66 €

♦ Inn ♦ Classic ♦

This hotel of modern design is located in a residential area a short walk from the Atomium and Heysel stadium. Well-appointed rooms. Private car park. Restaurant with a rustic feel housed in a small former farmhouse (1857). Classic, traditional meals.

La Roseraie

Limburg Stirumlaan 213 ✉ 1780 Wemmel – ✆ 0 2 456 99 10 – hotel@laroseraie.be – Fax 0 2 460 83 20 – www.laroseraie.be **A1**

8 rm – 107/125 € 130/180 €

Rest – *(closed Saturday lunch, Sunday dinner and Monday)* Menu 25 €, 30/65 € bi – Carte 43/56 €

♦ Family ♦ Personalised ♦

A warm welcome awaits you at this 1930s villa transformed into a family-run hotel offering impeccably maintained rooms decorated along different themes: African, Japanese, Roman etc. Traditionally furnished dining room with a piano which is home to lobsters!

L'Auberge de l'Isard

Romeinsesteenweg 964 ✉ 1780 Wemmel – ✆ 02 479 85 64 – info-reservation@isard.be – Fax 02 479 16 49 – www.isard.be

closed 1 week Easter, late July-mid August, Sunday dinner, Monday and Thursday dinner **B1**

Rest – Menu 25 €, 35/95 € bi – Carte 51/70 €

♦ Contemporary ♦ Formal ♦

An auberge with a good local reputation near the ring road and Heysel stadium. Refined dining room in beige and grey tones with leather chairs. Summer restaurant on the lawn.

't Stoveke

Jetsestraat 52 ✉ 1853 Strombeek-Bever – ✆ 0 2 267 67 25 – info@tstoveke.be – www.tstoveke.be

closed September, 26 December-3 January, Tuesday, Wednesday and Saturday lunch

Rest – Menu 30/50 € – Carte 40/48 € **B1**

♦ Contemporary ♦ Family ♦

A house modernised inside and out in a residential district close to the Heysel stadium. Discreet terrace embellished with blue stone tiling and teak furniture. A choice of traditional and contemporary dishes.

Le Gril aux Herbes d'Evan

Brusselsesteenweg 21 ✉ 1780 Wemmel – ✆ 0 2 460 52 39 – evant@skynet.be – Fax 0 2 461 19 12

closed 24 December-1 January, Monday in July-August, Saturday lunch and Sunday **A1**

Rest – Menu 35 €, 50/90 € bi – Carte 65/129 €

♦ Traditional ♦ Fashionable ♦

This small villa perched on a hilltop has a terrace and a large garden. Classic cuisine and a wine-list that does justice to the reputation of French vineyards.

Lychee

r. De Wand 118 ✉ 1020 – ✆ 0 2 268 19 14 – Fax 0 2 268 19 14

closed Monday **B1**

Rest – *(open until 11 p.m.)* Menu 9 €, 25/35 € – Carte 18/40 €

♦ Chinese ♦ Exotic ♦

This Chinese restaurant between the Chinese Pavilion and the Roman road has been serving its Cantonese dishes for more than 25 years. A wide choice of fixed menus and a very reasonably-priced lunch.

Atomium town,

square de l'Atomium ✉ *1020* – ✆ *02 479 58 50*
– restaurant@belgiumtaste.com – Fax 02 479 68 78
– www.belgiumtaste.com
closed 22 July-7 August **B1**

Rest – *(open until 11 p.m.) (lunch buffet only)* Menu 20 €, 30/100 € bi – Carte 41/82 €

♦ Contemporary ♦ Retro ♦

This restaurant has taken up residence in the symbolic monument from the 1958 World Expo, which was renovated in 2006. Buffet dining at lunchtime, with à la carte in the evening. Make sure you book a table near the windows!

French Kiss

r. Léopold 1er 470 ✉ *1090* – ✆ *02 425 22 93 – www.restaurantfrenchkiss.be*
closed 21 July-15 August and Monday **B2**

Rest – Menu 19/29 € – Carte 29/56 €

♦ Traditional ♦ Family ♦

A pleasant restaurant renowned for its fine grilled dishes and its esteemed selection of wines. The dining room has a low ceiling and brick walls that are brightened by multicoloured drapes.

AIRPORT & NATO *Plan I*

Sheraton Airport

at airport (North-East by A 201) ✉ *1930 Zaventem* – ✆ *0 2 710 80 00*
– reservations.brussels@sheraton.com – Fax 0 2 710 80 80
– www.sheraton.com/brusselsairport **D1**

292 rm – †115/495 € ††115/495 €, ☕ 25 € – 2 suites

Rest *Concorde* – *(closed Saturday)* Menu 55 € bi/40 € – Carte 44/64 €

♦ Chain hotel ♦ Business ♦ Modern ♦

The closest luxury hotel to the airport, offering comfort and numerous services, this is a popular choice with business customers from around the world. Contemporary international à la carte menu at the Concorde, which shares a vast atrium with a bar serving buffets.

Crowne Plaza Airport

Da Vincilaan 4 ✉ *1831 Diegem*
– ✆ *0 2 416 33 33 – cpbrusselsairport@whgev.com – Fax 0 2 416 33 44*
– www.crowneplaza.com/cpbrusselsarpt **D1**

311 rm – †355 € ††355 €, ☕ 21 € – 4 suites

Rest – *(closed Friday dinner, Saturday, Sunday lunch and Bank Holidays) (open until 11 p.m.)* Menu 23 € – Carte 34/67 €

♦ Chain hotel ♦ Business ♦ Functional ♦

Part of the Crowne Plaza chain, this hotel is located in a business park close to the airport. Central atrium, comfortable, well-equipped rooms as well as good conference facilities and neat gardens. The restaurant offers a choice of contemporary dishes including a buffet lunch option.

Sofitel Airport

Bessenveldstraat 15 ✉ *1831 Diegem* – ✆ *0 2 713 66 66 – h0548@accor.com*
– Fax 0 2 721 43 45 – www.sofitel-brussels-airport.com **C1**

125 rm – †120 € ††120/430 €, ☕ 23 €

Rest *La Pléiade* – *(closed 20 July-24 August, Friday dinner, Saturday and Sunday lunch)* Carte approx. 50 €

♦ Chain hotel ♦ Business ♦ Functional ♦

A top-of-the-range chain hotel alongside a motorway 4km/2.5mi from Zaventem airport with quiet, inviting rooms, seven meeting rooms and some leisure facilities. Friendly bar and a restaurant decked out like a luxury brasserie.

NH Brussels Airport

De Kleetlaan 14 ⊠ 1831 Diegem – ✆ 0 2 203 92 52
– nhbrusselsairport@nh-hotels.com – Fax 0 2 203 92 53
– www.nh-hotels.com **D1**

234 rm – 90/189 € 90/189 €

Rest – *(closed 20 July-20 August, Friday dinner, Saturday and Sunday) (open until 11 p.m.) (buffets)* Menu 15/30 € – Carte 34/54 €

♦ Chain hotel ♦ Business ♦ Functional ♦

A distinctly modern-looking business hotel in the business district close to the airport. Rooms well soundproofed against the nearby railway. Contemporary-style lounge bar and restaurant serving cuisine from around the world as well as fixed buffet menus.

Holiday Inn Airport

Holidaystraat 7 ⊠ 1831 Diegem – ✆ 0 2 720 58 65
– hibrusselsairport@ichotelsgroup.com – Fax 0 2 720 41 45
– www.benelux.ichotelsgroup.com **D1**

310 rm – 230 € 230 €, 21 €

Rest – *(closed Bank Holidays)* Menu 22 € – Carte 33/42 €

♦ Chain hotel ♦ Business ♦ Functional ♦

A 1970s hotel close to the airport. The rooms are due an overhaul. Comprehensive range of facilities for business or for pleasure. International cuisine is served at the restaurant on the first floor, and simple meals and snacks at the bar downstairs.

Novotel Airport

Da Vincilaan 25 ⊠ 1831 Diegem – ✆ 0 2 725 30 50 – h0467@accor.com
– Fax 0 2 721 39 58 – www.accorhotels.com/be **D1**

209 rm – 90/225 € 96/231 €, 15 €

Rest – Carte 25/44 €

♦ Chain hotel ♦ Business ♦ Functional ♦

Ideal for those with an early flight to catch. No surprises in the identical bedrooms, which conform to the Novotel's usual criteria. Seminar rooms and outdoor pool.

Brussels Airport

Berkenlaan 4 ⊠ 1831 Diegem – ✆ 0 2 721 77 77
– brusselsairport.reservations@thonhotel.be – Fax 0 2 721 55 96
– www.thonhotelbrussels.be/brusselsairport **D1**

100 rm – 80/175 € 80/215 €, 16 €

Rest – *(closed 28 July-10 August, Saturday and Sunday)* Menu 25 €, 30/50 € bi – Carte 33/44 €

♦ Chain hotel ♦ Business ♦ Functional ♦

The delightful rooms are well-maintained and spotlessly clean. Modern décor in the restaurant, where the emphasis is on conventional dishes. A haven of peace and quiet for stopover or transit passengers.

De Troubadour

ANTWERP

ANVERS – ANTWERPEN

Population (est.2004): 455 300 – Altitude: sea level

A. Kouprianoff/www.tourismebelgique.com

Antwerp calls itself the pocketsize metropolis, and with good reason. Although it's Belgium's second-largest port with a population of half a million, it still retains a compact intimacy, defined by bustling squares and narrow streets. It's a place with many facets, not least its marked link to Rubens and the diamond trade; in recent years it's become a fashion hotspot due to the success of the renowned design collective The Antwerp Six in the 1990s.

The city's centre teems with ornate gabled guildhouses. In summer, open-air cafés line the area beneath the towering cathedral, giving the place a festive, almost bohemian air. It's a fantastic place to shop; besides the clothing boutiques, there are antiques emporiums and diamond stores that can't help but entice the eye. That's to say nothing of the chocolate shops, whose window displays are a visitor attraction in themselves. Bold regeneration projects have transformed the skyline over the last decade, and the waterfront has undergone a big change with its decrepit warehouses starting a new life as ritzy storerooms of twenty-first century commerce. Nightlife here is the best in Belgium, while the beer is savoured with a cellar bar reverence, a satisfied sniff and a glorious gargle, the way others in Europe might treat a vintage wine.

LIVING THE CITY

Antwerp lies on the east bank of the **River Scheldt**. The **Old Town** is defined by **Grote Markt** and **Groenplaats,** and slightly further east, The **Meir** shopping street. These are a kind of dividing line between Antwerp's north and south. The city can be defined as an island, cut off from the suburbs by a ring road. North of the centre is **Het Eilandje**, the hip former warehouse area. To the east is the **Diamond District** and the main **railway station**. Antique and bric-a-brac shops are in abundance in the 'designer heart' **Het Zuid** south of the centre. This is also where you'll find the best museums and art galleries. The smart suburb of **Zurenborg** is to the southeast.

PRACTICAL INFORMATION

ARRIVAL-DEPARTURE

If arriving at Brussels (Zaventem) Airport take the SN Brussels Airlines shuttle bus to Central Station which runs on the hour and takes 45min. Antwerpen-Deurne Airport is 7km from the city - take bus number 16 to Pelikaanstraat. International and inter-city trains both stop at Antwerpen-Central and Antwerpen-Berchem stations.

TRANSPORT

Antwerp has an efficient network of trams, buses and premetro, which is a tram that runs underground at some stage of the journey. Invest in a Dagpas Stad – a city day pass – which gives unlimited travel on the whole of the city's public transport system; it's obtainable on board buses and trams and from De Lijn kiosks.

On many occasions you'll find it quicker to walk around, for this is a compact city made for pedestrians. Or if you want to get about by bike, head into the Tourism Antwerp in Grote Markt for more information.

EXPLORING ANTWERP

Antwerp is a feast for the eyes. It can give you medieval character, Gothic splendour and scintillating fashion creations in a single three- hundred-and-sixty degree visual sweep. Although steeped in modern folklore due to the exploits of its now legendary designers-with-attitude, Antwerp is essentially a fine old Flanders town, living easily with its old age. Stroll just off the central Grote Markt to get a feel for its ancient bones. Off the adjacent **Oude Koornmarkt** you'll find **Vlaeykensgang**, a baffling maze of alleys that date back to the 16C. There's a little square here that allows you to wallow in the atmosphere of bygone times. Take a deep breath and head back out into the full glare of tourist heaven – Grote Markt is the heart of the Old Centre, and the home of Antwerp's finest sixteenth century architecture, including the awesome town hall and a selection of wonderfully impressive guildhouses. Gaze at the iconic **Brabo Fountain** in the middle of the square and you gaze at the very epicentre of the city.

MAKING ITS MARKT

Grote Markt's great Gothic cathedral, **Onze Lieve Vrouwekathedraal** (Our Lady's Cathedral) holds two titles of distinction: it's the largest Gothic church in the Low Countries, and the most popular visitor attraction in Flanders. Nearly five hundred years old, its intricate spire dominates the skyline, but its greatest treasures await within. Despite the beautiful nooks, crannies, altars and aisles, all eyes inevitably fall on four paintings by Rubens, including two spectacular triptychs. There's another fine church nearby: **Carolus Borromeuskerk** took six years to build in the early 17C and the result is a fabulously ornate baroque confection: it would have been even more spectacular if thirty nine ceiling paintings by Rubens hadn't been destroyed in a fire in 1718. Confound your disappointment by heading into the church's beautiful square. It's called **Hendrik Conscienceplein** , and rivals Grote Markt for the old town's top plaudits. Stop here for a drink at one of its smart cafés.

RUBENS QUEUE

No apologies for bringing up the name of Antwerp's most famous son again. **Rubens' House** is situated just off the Meir shopping street. It's easy to find, just attach yourself to the queues of tourists waiting at the front door. This is where almost all of his great works were produced; its collections are on an intimate scale, with only ten paintings by Rubens to see, but the house gives you a vivid picture of his personality and his daily life. He would have approved of the **Royal Museum of Fine Arts** (way down south of the centre), not least because it devotes two of its large rooms to his paintings. There are over seven thousand works here, making it one of the most important collections in Europe. You'll also find Van Eyck, Magritte, Breughel the Younger and Memling in an eclectic array of highlights. Unlike Rubens' House, the light and airy rooms allow you some welcome space to manoeuvre. What if your tastes are more up-to-date? Well, for a modern hit, head west a little way to the river where you'll find the **Museum of Contemporary Art**, an old grain silo converted into a happening space of post-1970 artworks, grungy and cutting-edge pieces with a decent place to squat. This is a modernist's heaven but, for the most dynamic gallery in Antwerp, you have to retrace your steps and head back towards the centre. Only five years old, **MoMu** chronicles the history of fashion in what is now one of Europe's leading design cities. Its permanent collection is fascinating, but what really draw the crowds are the hip and happening temporary exhibits, a fitting tribute to the Antwerp 6, whose exploits took the fashion world by storm twenty years ago. To enhance the modish experience, you can dine in a seriously snazzy brasserie and flick through the coolest pages in the zeitgeist in the glossily smart bookshop.

SMART STRAAT-EGY

MoMu is flush in the heart of Het Zuid, the neighbourhood just south of the old centre. Twenty years ago, this was a rundown quarter with art nouveau buildings that had pretty much gone to seed. Largely as a result of the fashion industry waving its magic wand over the area, it's now the most glamorous address in town; smart boutiques and chic dressers meet at every turn. Two of the city's best shopping streets run parallel here. **Nationalestraat** is a wide nineteenth-century boulevard of designer stores (a more discerning address than the nearby mainstream Meir), while a short stroll to its west is **Kloosterstraat**, the antiques street of Antwerp. Rummage through the bizarre artefacts tumbling onto the pavement, and you'll sooner or later find something truly out of this world. That's the theory, and often enough it bears fruit (or something a little more exotic).

To get a feel for the city's nicely weighted schizophrenia (the old town balanced by the new 'hipdom'), take a hike to two of its suburbs. Zurenborg is a village-like quarter in the 'far' southeast of Antwerp, by the railway line leading up towards the station. The wealthy merchant classes built it up, and today it's where the city's moneyed bohemians and artists live. There are sumptuous belle-epoque buildings here; the most interesting walk is up and down the seven avenues that fan out from **Draakplaats Tramplein**, where you can take in the fine – not to say eccentic – art nouveau buildings. Right up the other end of town is Het Eilandje, a one-time collection of mangy warehouses and storage facilities that the world steered clear of. Nowadays it's alive with quirky shops, cafes and offices; notable names have moved in, including Antwerp 6 fashion guru Dries Van Noten, whose workshop and office is based in a local warehouse.

ROCK SOLID

Another aspect of the city is the area around the mighty Centraal station, a terminus that ranks as one of Europe's finest, with its sweeping staircases and vaulted dome. It's relevant that the station displays a wealth of gold gilt, because this is also the **Diamond District**, a grungy kind of area after dark, but during the day the centre of the city's historic diamond industry, where many billions of euros' worth of shiny things are handled each year. If the sight of all those sparklers proves too much, take a pew at the nearby triangular shaped **Stadspark**, Antwerp's largest green space, where you can watch the cosmopolitan mix that for many decades has defined the area. Take a deep breath, then head back to that diamond shop to double-check the price of that rock…

CALENDAR HIGHLIGHTS

Laundry Day only comes once a year in Antwerp, but the hip Het Eilandje area cleans up when it happens early every September. This is the coolest event of the year, bringing in forty thousand revellers who dance to the various DJs at outdoor stages in the area. Why Laundry Day? Well, the first one in the mid-1990s was held at a weekend, when Belgians traditionally hang their washing out to dry…Later in the month, it's the turn of architecture addicts to hit the streets for Open Monument Day, when various historic buildings, usually closed to the public, open their doors for a day. The city is well known for its antiques, and in March this reputation comes to the fore when twenty thousand visitors head to the Bouwcentrum for the Eurantica Antwerp Antiques Festival, a grand fair with paintings,

ANTWERP IN…

➜ ONE DAY
Grote Kerk, Our Lady's Cathedral, MoMu, Het Zuid

➜ TWO DAYS
Rubens' House, Royal Museum of Fine Arts, a stroll across to the Left Bank via the Sint-Anna tunnel

➜ THREE DAYS
Het Eilandje, a river trip, Kloosterstraat, Nationalestraat

jewellery, furniture and objets d'art up for grabs. May brings out revellers for five weeks of ghost trains and roller-coasters at the Sinksefoor funfair, which takes over a capacious square in southern Antwerp. The free carillon concerts on Monday nights between May and September have become hugely popular.The Groenplaats is heaving in June with ale quaffers for Beer Passion Weekend, with over 150 tipples on offer. You can lie on Antwerp Beach through the summer – a long stretch of sand in the dock area south of the centre boasting terraces with comfy sun-loungers - or, in July, you might prefer classical music at the Festival of Flanders (at venues across the city), or the International Summer Festival, which has street theatre, open-air cinema and jazz concerts happening on various city squares. Antwerp wouldn't be Antwerp without Rubens, and the Rubens Market in August sees Grote Markt's traders donning their best sixteenth century garb in honour of the great man.

EATING OUT

With Antwerp being Europe's second-largest commercial port, it's no surprise that fish and seafood play a big part in the local diet. The menus of Flanders are heavily influenced by proximity to the North Sea, lush meadows and canals swarming with eels. But the eating culture in Antwerp offers a lot more than crustacean flavours. With its centuries old connection to more exotic climes, there's no shortage of fragrant spices such as cinnamon finding their way regularly into local dishes: check out the rich stews so beloved by the locals. Having such a high ratio of trend-setting types flitting around, there's always a good chance of finding a restaurant devoted to the latest in food fads. If you want to eat with the chic, hang around the Het Eilandje dockside or the rejuvenated ancient warehouses south of Grote Markt. For early risers, grand cafés are a popular port of call here. They're open nice and early in the morning, and are ideal for a slow coffee and trawl through the papers. Overall, though, the city boasts the same tempting Belgian gastronomic specialities as Brussels (eg, stewed eel in chervil sauce, mussels in various sauces, dishes with rabbit, beef stew and chicory), the focus in Antwerp is more on contemporary cuisine, matched with up-to-date décor. Don't miss out on the local chocolate, shaped like a hand in keeping with the local legend which tells of a Roman soldier who cut off the hand of a giant and threw it in the river, and in the process gave the city its name: Hand werpen, meaning 'to throw a hand'. And make sure you try your hand at the local beer: Antwerp's Konings brewery serves the popular keuninkske, served in a glass shaped like an open bowl.

→ SCHELDT SHOCKED

The best view of Antwerp's dramatic skyline is from the west bank of the Scheldt. Firstly, stroll through the listed Sint-Anna tunnel with its lovely art deco interior, and, at the other side, go 'wow' as you take in the superb panoramic view of the city from the Left Bank.

The river has always been Antwerp's lifeline, and you can make the most of it on fifty-minute river cruises, which depart from Steenplein on a regular basis in the afternoons. The trip offers up a taste of the city's maritime history; you'll also get a good look at modern riverside landmarks such as the unmistakable Palace of Justice, an iconic twenty-first century building that resembles a white-sailed ship – fittingly, in a city whose port has been its fortune.

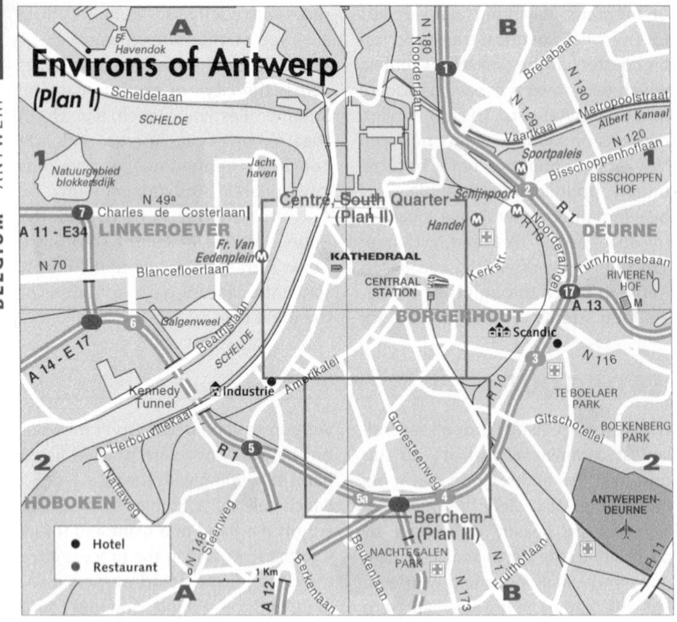

CENTRE (Old Town and Main Station) *Plan II*

Hilton

Groenplaats – ✆ 0 3 204 12 12 – sales-antwerp@hilton.com – Fax 0 3 204 12 13 – www.hilton.com **D2**

199 rm – 149/369 € 149/369 €, 25 €
12 suites
Rest ***Terrace-Café*** – Menu 30/45 € – Carte 29/41 €

♦ Chain hotel ♦ Luxury ♦ Stylish ♦

This luxury hotel occupies a fine early-20C building which started life as a department store. Large, well-appointed rooms, plus pleasant public areas. Views of the cathedral and lively Groenplaats from the Terrace Café with its comprehensive menu.

Park Plaza Astrid

Koningin Astridplein 7 ✉ 2018 – ✆ 0 3 203 12 34 – appres@pphe.com – Fax 0 3 203 12 51 – www.parkplazaantwerp.com **F2**

225 rm – 129/179 € 149/199 €, 20 €
3 suites
Rest – Menu 30 € – Carte 28/48 €

♦ Chain hotel ♦ Luxury ♦ Design ♦

A modernised hotel with its original architecture situated on a busy square near the railway station. Renovated public areas and spacious, attractive and cosily refurbished guestrooms. Bright restaurant serving contemporary recipes in a trendy canteen-style dining room with parquet flooring and city views.

Radisson SAS Park Lane

Van Eycklei 34 ✉ 2018 – ✆ 0 3 285 85 85 – guest.antwerp@radissonsas.com – Fax 0 3 285 85 86 – www.radissonsas.com

E3

160 rm – †138/210 € ††138/210 €, ☕ 24 € – 14 suites

Rest – Menu 24/35 € – Carte 36/54 €

◆ Chain hotel ◆ Business ◆ Stylish ◆

This luxury hotel is located on a main road opposite a public park. Two types of well-appointed guestrooms, plus suites, and tailored facilities and services for its mainly business clientele. Winter garden-style dining room crowned by a glass roof. Adjoining bar.

De Witte Lelie without rest

Keizerstraat 16 – ✆ 0 3 226 19 66 – hotel@dewittelelie.be – Fax 0 3 234 00 19 – www.dewittelelie.be

closed 18 December-6 January

D1

7 rm ☕ – †205/425 € ††280/520 € – 3 suites

◆ Luxury ◆ Stylish ◆

Quiet and full of charm, this small "grand hotel" is spread across several 17C houses. Cosy, elegantly decorated rooms, in addition to an inviting patio.

't Sandt without rest

Het Zand 17 – ✆ 0 3 232 93 90 – reservations@hotel-sandt.be – Fax 0 3 232 56 13 – www.hotel-sandt.be

C2

27 rm ☕ – †145/275 € ††165/295 € – 2 suites

◆ Luxury ◆ Stylish ◆

The fine Rococo façade of this impressive 19C residence contrasts starkly with the sober, contemporary décor of its interior. Delightful, Italianate winter garden and roomy, elegant guest accommodation.

Theater

Arenbergstraat 30 – ✆ 0 3 203 54 10 – info@theater-hotel.be – Fax 0 3 233 88 58 – www.vhv-hotels.be

E2

122 rm – †110/220 € ††130/240 €, ☕ 20 € – 5 suites

Rest – *(closed 18 July-17 August, 19 December-1 January, Saturday, Sunday and Bank Holidays)* Menu 17 € – Carte 33/45 €

◆ Business ◆ Classic ◆

A modern, comfortable hotel with an ideal location at the heart of the old city, just a short distance from the Bourla theatre and Rubens' house. Spacious bedrooms decorated either in contemporary or typically "British" style. Comfortable lounge. Formal atmosphere in the restaurant, which has a varied menu of fusion cuisine and traditional dishes.

Rubens without rest

Oude Beurs 29 – ✆ 0 3 222 48 48 – hotel.rubens@glo.be – Fax 03 225 19 40 – www.hotelrubensantwerp.be

D1

35 rm ☕ – †145/255 € ††150/255 € – 1 suite

◆ Traditional ◆ Classic ◆

A quiet and friendly renovated hotel near the Grand-Place and cathedral. The best rooms overlook the inner courtyard, which is flower-decked in summer.

Hyllit without rest

De Keyserlei 28 (access by Appelmansstraat) ✉ 2018 – ✆ 0 3 202 68 00 – info@hyllithotel.be – Fax 0 3 202 68 90 – www.hyllithotel.be

E2

123 rm – †100/205 € ††125/230 €, ☕ 17 € – 4 suites

◆ Business ◆ Modern ◆

This modern hotel has an intimate lounge-bar, spacious bedrooms and contemporary-style suites, and an attractive pool with Roman décor. Good view of Antwerp's rooftops from the breakfast room.

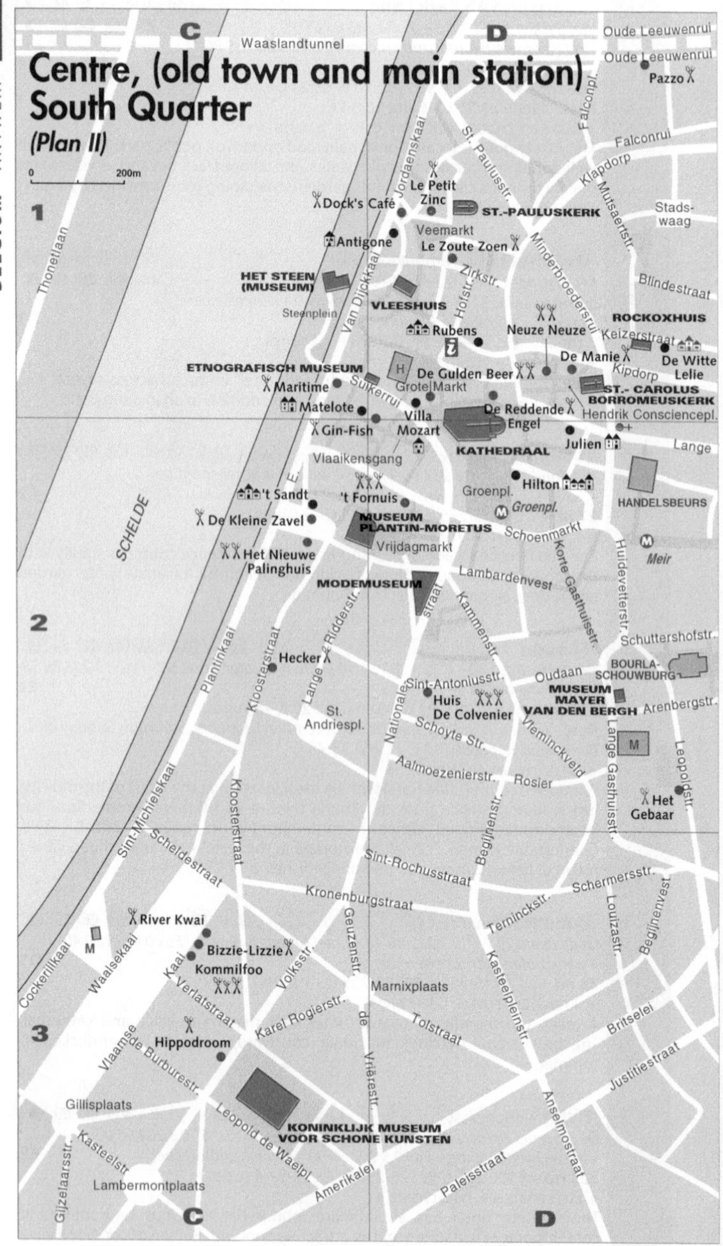
Centre, (old town and main station)
South Quarter
(Plan II)
0 200m
C
D
1
2
3
Waaslandtunnel
Oude Leeuwenrui
Pazzo
Falconpl.
Falconrui
Klapdorp
Mutsaertstr.
Stadswaag
Blindestraat
ROCKOXHUIS
Keizerstraat
De Witte Lelie
De Manie
Kipdorp
ST.- CAROLUS BORROMEUSKERK
Hendrik Consciencepl.
Lange
Julien
HANDELSBEURS
Meir
Hilton
Groenpl.
Groenpl.
Schoenmarkt
Korte Gasthuisstr.
Huidevetterstr.
Schuttershofstr.
BOURLA-SCHOUWBURG
Oudaan
MUSEUM MAYER VAN DEN BERGH
Arenbergstr.
Lange Gasthuisstr.
Leopoldstr.
Het Gebaar
Rosier
Vleminckveld
St. Paulusstr.
Le Petit Zinc
ST.-PAULUSKERK
Veemarkt
Le Zoute Zoen
Minderbroedersrui
Zirkstr.
Hofstr.
Neuze Neuze
Rubens
VLEESHUIS
Jordaenskaai
Dock's Café
Antigone
HET STEEN (MUSEUM)
Steenplein
Van Dijckkaai
ETNOGRAFISCH MUSEUM
Maritime
Matelote
Suikerrui
De Gulden Beer
Grote Markt
De Reddende Engel
Villa Mozart
Gin-Fish
KATHEDRAAL
Vlaaikensgang
't Fornuis
't Sandt
De Kleine Zavel
MUSEUM PLANTIN-MORETUS
Vrijdagmarkt
Het Nieuwe Palinghuis
MODEMUSEUM
Lambardenvest
Kammenstr.
Nationalestraat
SCHELDE
Thonetlaan
Plantinkaai
Kloosterstraat
Hecker
Lange Ridderstr.
St. Andriespl.
Sint-Antoniusstr.
Huis De Colvenier
Schoyte Str.
Aalmoezenierstr.
Begijnenstr.
Sint-Michielskaai
Scheldestraat
Sint-Rochusstraat
Kronenburgstraat
Schermersstr.
Ternickstr.
Louizastr.
Begijnenvest
River Kwai
Bizzie-Lizzie
Kommilfoo
Waalsekaai
Cockerillkaai
Kaai
Verlatstraat
Volksstr.
Geuzenstr.
Marnixplaats
Karel Rogierstr.
de Vrièrestr.
Tolstraat
Kasteelpleinstr.
Britselei
Justitiestraat
Hippodroom
Vlaamse
de Burburestr.
Gillisplaats
Leopold de Waelpl.
KONINKLIJK MUSEUM VOOR SCHONE KUNSTEN
Anselmostraat
Kasteelstr.
Gijzelaarsstr.
Lambermontplaats
Amerikalei
Paleisstraat
M

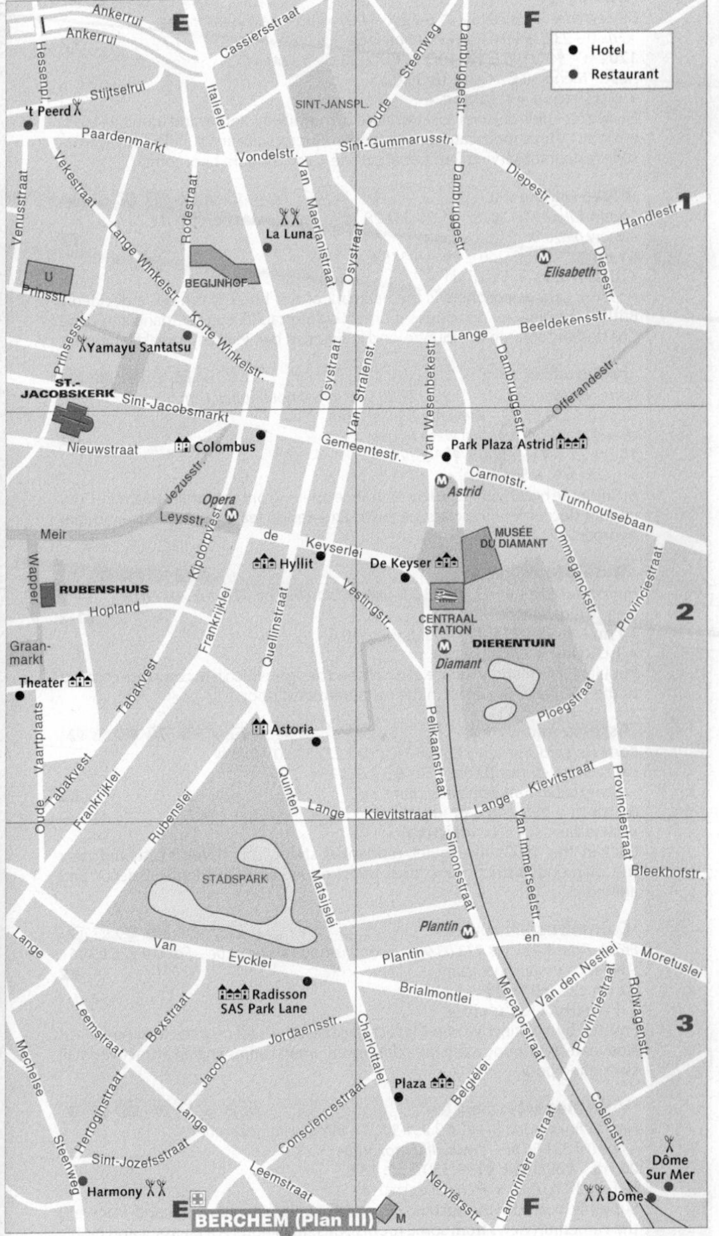
Hotel
Restaurant
E
F
1
2
3
Ankerrui
Cassiersstraat
Hessenpl.
Stijtselrui
't Peerd
Paardenmarkt
Italielei
SINT-JANSPL.
Oude Steenweg
Dambruggestr.
Vondelstr.
Sint-Gummarusstr.
Diepestr.
Vekestraat
Venusstraat
Rodestraat
Van Maerlanstraat
La Luna
Osystraat
Handlestr.
Lange Winkelstr.
BEGIJNHOF
Elisabeth
Prinsstr.
Korte Winkelstr.
Lange Beeldekensstr.
Prinsesstr.
Yamayu Santatsu
Van Stralenst.
Van Wesenbekestr.
Otterandestr.
ST.-JACOBSKERK
Sint-Jacobsmarkt
Nieuwstraat
Colombus
Gemeentestr.
Park Plaza Astrid
Carnotstr.
Astrid
Turnhoutsebaan
Jezusstr.
Opera
Leysstr.
Meir
de Keyserlei
Kipdorpvest
MUSÉE DU DIAMANT
Hyllit
De Keyser
Wapper
RUBENSHUIS
Vestingstr.
Ommeganckstr.
Provinciestraat
Hopland
Frankrijklei
Quellinstraat
CENTRAAL STATION
DIERENTUIN
Diamant
Graanmarkt
Theater
Tabakvest
Ploegstraat
Astoria
Pelikaanstraat
Oude Vaartplaats
Kievitstraat
Lange Kievitstraat
Quinten Matsijslei
Rubenslei
Simonsstraat
Van Immerseelstr.
Bleekhofstr.
STADSPARK
Plantin
Plantin en Moretuslei
Lange Leemstraat
Van Eycklei
Brialmontlei
Van den Nestlei
Radisson SAS Park Lane
Bexstraat
Jordaensstr.
Charlottalei
Mercatorstraat
Rolwagenstr.
Mechelse Steenweg
Jacob
Hertoginstraat
Plaza
Belgiëlei
Coslenstr.
Conscienceestraat
Sint-Jozefsstraat
Lamorinière straat
Dôme Sur Mer
Harmony
Nerviërsstr.
Dôme
BERCHEM (Plan III)
M

De Keyser

De Keyserlei 66 ✉ 2018 – ✆ 0 3 206 74 60 – info@dekeyserhotel.be – Fax 0 3 232 39 70 – www.vhv-hotels.be **F2**

120 rm – 🚹90/195 € 🚹🚹110/215 €, ☕ 20 € – 3 suites

Rest – Menu 30 € – Carte 18/30 €

◆ Business ◆ Classic ◆

Easily accessible and well located close to the railway station and tramline. Modern lobby. Three room categories (standard, junior suite and suite) and a taverna-style restaurant serving traditional cuisine. Cosy, modern bedrooms.

Plaza without rest

Charlottalei 49 ✉ 2018 – ✆ 0 3 287 28 70 – book@plaza.be – Fax 0 3 287 28 71 – www.plaza.be **F3**

81 rm ☕ – 🚹116/260 € 🚹🚹116/315 €

◆ Business ◆ Stylish ◆

A warm, cosy atmosphere is the hallmark of this hotel which has a decidedly British ambience. Spacious rooms, comfortable suites, panelling and Chesterfield sofas in the lounge, and a Victorian bar. Pleasant breakfast room.

Julien without rest

Korte Nieuwstraat 24 – ✆ 0 3 229 06 00 – info@hotel-julien.com – Fax 0 3 233 35 70 – www.hotel-julien.com

closed last week July-first week August **D2**

11 rm ☕ – 🚹165/260 € 🚹🚹165/260 €

◆ Luxury ◆ Stylish ◆

An intimate hotel with a carriage entrance opening onto a tramlined street. Cosy interior décor blending classical, rustic and design features. Attractive modern bedrooms.

Matelote without rest

Haarstraat 11a – ✆ 03 201 88 00 – info@matelote.be – Fax 03 201 88 08 – www.matelote.be **C1-2**

10 rm – 🚹115/225 € 🚹🚹115/225 €, ☕ 10 €

◆ Luxury ◆ Modern ◆

Popular for its friendly service and polished design, which is in complete contrast to the 16C walls. Breakfast in the restaurant next door.

Astoria without rest

Korte Herentalsestraat 5 ✉ 2018 – ✆ 0 3 227 31 30 – info@carltonhotel-antwerp.com – Fax 0 3 227 31 34 – www.tulipinnantwerpastoriahotel.be **E2**

66 rm ☕ – 🚹95/140 € 🚹🚹108/165 €

◆ Business ◆ Functional ◆

Built in the 1990s in a quiet residential street, this hotel is situated near the diamond district. Functional guestrooms, all with identical décor and amenities.

Colombus without rest

Frankrijklei 4 – ✆ 0 3 233 03 90 – colombushotel@skynet.be – Fax 0 3 226 09 46 – www.columbushotel.com **E2**

32 rm ☕ – 🚹97 € 🚹🚹117 €

◆ Family ◆ Classic ◆

Fronted by a distinctive neo-Classical façade, this hotel near the Meir has an Art Nouveau-style lounge and breakfast room, smart rooms and an attractive small swimming pool.

Villa Mozart without rest

Handschoenmarkt 3 – ✆ 0 3 231 30 31 – info@villamozart.be – Fax 0 3 231 56 85 – www.villa-mozart.be **D1**

25 rm – 🚹89/139 € 🚹🚹99/350 €, ☕ 13 €

◆ Traditional ◆ Functional ◆

Superbly located in the bustling heart of Antwerp between the Grand-Place and the cathedral (views from some rooms), this small hotel is a pleasant and highly practical option. Traditionally furnished rooms.

Antigone without rest

Jordaenskaai 11 – ✆ 0 3 231 66 77 – info@antigonehotel.be – Fax 0 3 231 37 74 – www.antigonehotel.be **D1**

21 rm – †75/95 € ††85/140 €

♦ Traditional ♦ Functional ♦

Occupying a corner house near the River Schelde and Steen Museum, this hotel has a smart restored façade brightened by blue canopies. Functional, contemporary-style rooms which offer good value for money.

't Fornuis (Johan Segers)

Reyndersstraat 24 – ✆ 0 3 233 62 70 – fornuis@skynet.be – Fax 0 3 233 99 03

closed 21 July-15 August, Christmas-New Year, Saturday and Sunday **D2**

Rest – *(booking essential)* Carte 65/95 €

Spec. Carpaccio de langue de veau, sauce à la cervelle. Anguille fumée et son jus aux haricots blancs. "Cube roll cut" de bœuf wagyu persillé.

♦ Traditional ♦ Rustic ♦

This restaurant, occupying an old residence, offers fine traditional cuisine and a good selection of wine. Rustic dining room upstairs and exhibition of small stoves downstairs. No menu - the chef himself comes to your table with details of the day's offerings.

Huis De Colvenier

Sint-Antoniusstraat 8 – ✆ 0 3 226 65 73 – info@colvenier.be – Fax 0 3 227 13 14 – www.colvenier.be

closed carnival week, August, Saturday lunch, Sunday and Monday **D2**

Rest – Menu 50 €, 60/100 € bi

♦ Traditional ♦ Retro ♦

This restaurant is housed in an elegant townhouse dating from 1879. Dine in the chic traditional dining room or under a modern glass roof. Sophisticated menu, the details of which are given at your table by the chef. Fine wine list.

Neuze Neuze

Wijngaardstraat 19 – ✆ 0 3 232 27 97 – neuzeneuze@telenet.be – Fax 0 3 225 27 38 – www.neuzeneuze.be

closed 2 weeks August, 1 week February, Wednesday lunch, Saturday lunch, Sunday and Bank Holidays **D1**

Rest – Menu 25 €, 53/83 € bi – Carte 48/90 €

♦ Contemporary ♦ Retro ♦

Comprising five small houses dating from the 16C, this intimate restaurant is ideal for business meetings or a romantic meal for two. Traditional cuisine with a contemporary twist and friendly service.

La Luna

Italiëlei 177 – ✆ 0 3 232 23 44 – info@laluna.be – Fax 0 3 232 24 41 – www.laluna.be

closed 28 July-14 August, Christmas-New Year, Saturday lunch, Sunday and Monday **E1**

Rest – Carte 40/67 €

♦ Contemporary ♦ Design ♦

Refined setting with a lunar design by Jean De Meulder (1996), delicious cuisine featuring French, Italian and Japanese influences, and a good selection of wines.

De Gulden Beer

Grote Markt 14 – ✆ 0 3 226 08 41 – Fax 0 3 232 52 09

closed Wednesday **D1**

Rest – Menu 25 €, 40/90 € bi – Carte 37/72 €

♦ Italian ♦ Formal ♦

This old house with its crow-step gables stands on the Grand-Place. Authentic Italian menu and pleasant views from the terrace and the bay windows on the first floor.

XX

Harmony

Mechelsesteenweg 169 ✉ 2018 – ☏ 0 3 239 70 05 – info@diningroomharmony.com – Fax 0 2 343 48 61 – www.diningroomharmony.com
closed 21 July-9 August, 22 December-8 January, Wednesday and Saturday lunch **E3**

Rest – Menu 23/50 € – Carte 42/69 €

♦ Contemporary ♦ Retro ♦

The contemporary cuisine on offer here is in harmony with the décor of modern filtered lighting, fluted Art Deco pilasters, Lloyd Loom chairs and parquet floor. Valet-parking.

XX

Het Nieuwe Palinghuis

Sint-Jansvliet 14 – ☏ 0 3 231 74 45 – hetnieuwepalinghuis@skynet.be – Fax 0 3 231 50 53 – www.hetnieuwepalinghuis.be
closed June, 1-20 January, Monday and Tuesday **C2**

Rest – Menu 37/110 € – Carte 42/87 €

♦ Seafood ♦ Formal ♦

Eel takes pride of place in this fish and seafood restaurant, whose dining room is adorned with nostalgic images of the sea. Close to the pedestrian subway which runs under the River Schelde.

XX

Dôme (Julien Burlat)

Grote Hondstraat 2 ✉ 2018 – ☏ 0 3 239 90 03 – info@domeweb.be – Fax 0 3 239 93 90 – www.domeweb.be
closed 2 weeks August, 25 December-6 January, Saturday lunch, Sunday and Monday **F3**

Rest – Menu 35/65 € – Carte 57/77 €

Spec. Terrine de foie gras aux artichauts, rhubarbe et orange amère. Pigeon, pommes de terre rattes au lard, légumes de saison. Tarte au chocolat.

♦ Contemporary ♦ Formal ♦

Ambitious contemporary cuisine is served in this restaurant with an impressive 19C neo-Baroque dome and circular dining area. Popular surprise menu. Excellent sommelier.

X

De Manie

H. Conscienceplein 3 – ☏ 0 3 232 64 38 – demanie@euphonynet.be – Fax 0 3 232 64 38
closed 13 August-1 September, Wednesday, Sunday lunch in school holidays and Sunday dinner **D1**

Rest – Menu 28/78 € bi – Carte 47/61 €

♦ Contemporary ♦ Formal ♦

On a picturesque square by the St-Charles-Borromée Baroque church, this pleasant restaurant is fronted by a summer terrace. Mezzanine level indoors.

X

Dock's Café

Jordaenskaai 7 – ☏ 0 3 226 63 30 – info@docks.be – Fax 0 3 226 65 72 – www.docks.be
closed Sunday **D1**

Rest – *(open until 11 p.m.)* Menu 15 €, 24/40 € – Carte 22/91 €

♦ Brasserie ♦ Trendy ♦

A sense of travel pervades this seafood bar-cum-brasserie with its futurist, maritime décor. Dining room with mezzanine and neo-Baroque staircase. Reservation recommended.

X

De Kleine Zavel

Stoofstraat 2 – ☏ 0 3 231 96 91 – info@kleinezavel.be – Fax 0 3 231 79 01 – www.kleinezavel.be
closed Saturday lunch **C2**

Rest – Menu 29 €, 43/82 € bi – Carte 45/62 €

♦ Brasserie ♦ Bistro ♦

A warm, friendly restaurant with floorboards, bare tables, and an old bar. Classical or bistro-style dishes with daily suggestions and a good-value lunch.

De Reddende Engel

Torfbrug 3 – 0 3 233 66 30 – de.reddende.engel@telenet.be – Fax 0 3 233 73 79 – www.de-reddende-engel.be
closed mid August-mid September, Tuesday, Wednesday and Saturday lunch
Rest – Menu 26/49 € bi – Carte 30/52 € **D1**

♦ Traditional ♦ Rustic ♦

A 17C house close to the cathedral is the setting for this friendly, rustic restaurant serving classic French cuisine including bouillabaisse and cassoulet.

Le Petit Zinc (Philippe Grootaert)

Veemarkt 9 – 0 3 213 19 08 – philippe.grootaert@pandora.be – Fax 0 3 288 80 45 – www.pzinc.be
closed 1 week Easter, 16-31 August, Saturday and Sunday **D1**
Rest – Menu 20 €, 34/68 € – Carte 64/109 €
Spec. Huîtres tièdes, vinaigrette aux lardons et lentilles. Darne de turbot en croûte de gros sel. Confit d'épaule d'agneau, jardinière de légumes.

♦ Traditional ♦ Bistro ♦

A convivial local bistro with closely packed small tables, slate menus featuring tasty, traditional dishes, and attentive service.

Le Zoute Zoen

Zirkstraat 17 – 0 3 226 92 20 – lezoutezoen@telenet.be – Fax 0 3 231 01 30
closed Monday and Saturday lunch **D1**
Rest – Menu 18 €, 27/65 € bi – Carte 30/48 €

♦ Contemporary ♦ Bistro ♦

The menu in this cosy, intimate "gastro-bistro" offers unique value for money in Antwerp. A range of copious contemporary dishes served by efficient, friendly staff.

Gin-Fish (Didier Garnich)

Haarstraat 9 – 0 3 231 32 07 – Fax 0 3 231 08 13
closed June, 1-15 January, Sunday and Monday **D1-2**
Rest – *(dinner only) (booking essential)* Menu 60/75 € bi
Spec. Préparations avec la marée du jour. Glace tournée minute.

♦ Seafood ♦ Trendy ♦

Good seafood dishes prepared before you, behind the counter where guests dine. As the chef is working in full view, he errs on the side of caution by offering only one fixed menu. Lovely staff.

Het Gebaar

Leopoldstraat 24 – 0 3 232 37 10 – hetgebaar@pandora.be – Fax 0 3 293 72 32 – www.hetgebaar.be
closed Sunday and Monday **D2**
Rest – *(lunch only)* Carte approx. 40 €

♦ Innovative ♦ Cosy ♦

A welcoming restaurant occupying a cottage-style old house alongside the "Parc Botanique". Inventive "molecular"-influenced cuisine, as well as sumptuous desserts.

Maritime

Suikerrui 4 – 0 3 233 07 58 – restaurant.maritime@pandora.be – www.maritime.be
closed Wednesday and Thursday **C1**
Rest – Carte 35/60 €

♦ Seafood ♦ Family ♦

Fish and seafood reign supreme here with some of the city's best mussels and eel in season. Colourful décor of bright red tablecloths, a good choice of Burgundies and attentive service from the owner and his son.

Hecker

Kloosterstraat 13 – 0 3 234 38 34 – info@hecker.be – Fax 0 2 343 48 61 – www.hecker.be
closed 21 July-9 August, 22 December-8 January, Monday lunch and Wednesday
Rest – Menu 17/48 € – Carte 38/52 € **C2**

♦ Contemporary ♦ Wine bar ♦

This modern bistro adjoins one of the many antique shops in this district. Contemporary menu, wine-bar ambience and a good choice of wines from around the world.

Pazzo

Oude Leeuwenrui 12 – ✆ 0 3 232 86 82 – pazzo@skynet.be – Fax 0 3 232 79 34 – www.pazzo.be
closed mid July-mid August, Christmas, New Year, Saturday, Sunday and Bank Holidays **D1**
Rest – *(open until 11 p.m.)* Menu 20 € – Carte 32/51 €
◆ Contemporary ◆ Trendy ◆
A lively dockside restaurant occupying a former warehouse converted into a modern brasserie, where the emphasis is on Mediterranean and Asian cuisine. Knowledgeable sommelier, who is also the owner.

Dôme Sur Mer

Arendstraat 1 ✉ 2018 – ✆ 0 3 281 74 33 – info@domeweb.be – Fax 0 3 239 93 90 – www.domeweb.be
closed 2 weeks September, 24 December-5 January, Saturday lunch, Sunday and Monday **F3**
Rest – *(open until midnight)* Carte 28/75 €
◆ Seafood ◆ Brasserie ◆
This grand residence has been transformed into an "über-trendy" seafood brasserie with designer décor of bright white set off by the blue of a row of aquariums containing goldfish.

't Peerd

Paardenmarkt 53 – ✆ 0 3 231 98 25 – resto_t_peerd@yahoo.com – Fax 0 3 231 59 40 – www.tpeerd.be
closed 2 weeks Easter, 2 weeks September, Tuesday and Wednesday **E1**
Rest – Menu 39 € – Carte 49/75 €
◆ Traditional ◆ Rustic ◆
This small rustic-style restaurant is embellished with equestrian décor, providing a hint of the house specialities. Run by the same owner since 1970, the restaurant has a local ambience and focuses on traditional cuisine.

Yamayu Santatsu

Ossenmarkt 19 – ✆ 0 3 234 09 49 – Fax 0 3 234 09 49
closed Sunday lunch and Monday **E1**
Rest – Menu 15 €, 47/53 € – Carte 25/54 €
◆ Japanese ◆ Minimalist ◆
This lively, authentic Japanese restaurant serves quality produce and has an extensive choice of dishes, including four different menus. Sushi prepared at the bar.

SOUTH QUARTER AND BERCHEM *Plan III*

Crowne Plaza

G. Legrellelaan 10 ✉ 2020 – ✆ 0 3 259 75 00 – www.crowneplaza.be **G1**
256 rm – 124/235 € 124/235 €, 21 € – 6 suites
Rest – *(dinner only in July-August)* Menu 20 € – Carte 33/62 €
◆ Business ◆ Functional ◆
This hotel-cum-conference centre is situated close to the ring-road and to one of the main roads heading into the city centre. Facilities include a fitness centre, sauna and indoor pool. There are also plans for a new restaurant. Ask for one of the refurbished rooms.

Firean

Karel Oomsstraat 6 ✉ 2018 – ✆ 0 3 237 02 60 – info@hotelfirean.com – Fax 0 3 238 11 68 – www.hotelfirean.com
closed 29 July-20 August and 23 December-8 January **G1**
12 rm – 143/180 € 167/235 €
Rest *Minerva* – see below
◆ Luxury ◆ Stylish ◆
A charming hotel with a patio occupying an Art Deco residence dating from 1929. Period-style public areas, rooms decorated with stylish antique furniture and attentive service.

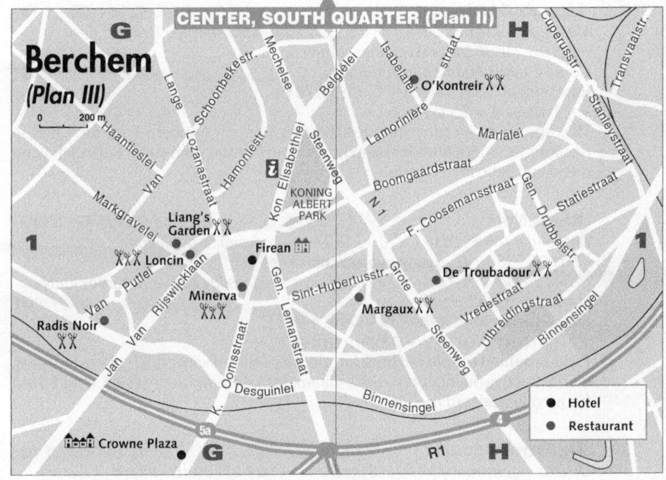

Industrie without rest

Emiel Banningstraat 52 – 0 3 238 66 00 – sleep@hotelindustrie.be – www.hotelindustrie.be Plan I **A2**

13 rm – 55/67 € 67/80 €

◆ Traditional ◆ Classic ◆

A charming small hotel occupying two mansions close to two of the city's finest museums and to the new and unusual Law Courts.

Minerva – Hotel Firean

Karel Oomsstraat 36 ✉ 2018 – 0 3 216 00 55 – restaurantminerva@skynet.be – Fax 0 3 216 00 55 – www.hotelfirean.com

closed 29 July-20 August, 23 December-8 January, Sunday and Monday **G1**

Rest – Menu 35 € – Carte 51/92 €

◆ Traditional ◆ Cosy ◆

Chic restaurant named after a pre-war brand of Belgian car, set in a garage complete with mechanic's pit (covered by a glass panel). Classical cuisine.

Kommilfoo

Vlaamse Kaai 17 – 0 3 237 30 00 – kommilfoo@resto.be – Fax 0 3 237 30 00

closed 1-15 July, Saturday lunch, Sunday and Monday Plan II **C3**

Rest – Menu 33 €, 48/80 € – Carte 45/77 €

◆ Innovative ◆ Cosy ◆

This former warehouse has been transformed into a restaurant ("kommilfoo" or "comme il faut" in French) with a modern dining room furnished with Lloyd Loom chairs. Inventive head chef.

Loncin

Markgravelei 127 ✉ 2018 – 0 3 248 29 89 – info@loncinrestaurant.be – Fax 0 3 248 38 66 – www.loncinrestaurant.be

closed 2 weeks February, 2 weeks July, Saturday lunch and Sunday **G1**

Rest – Menu 38 €, 50/105 € bi – Carte 47/108 €

◆ Contemporary ◆ Formal ◆

Housed in a building dating from 1900, this elegant restaurant serves traditional cuisine, including game during the hunting season. Extensive wine list featuring a good choice of half-bottles.

XX **Liang's Garden**

Markgravelei 141 ✉ 2018 – ✆ 0 3 237 22 22 – liangsgarden@skynet.be – Fax 0 3 248 38 34 – www.liangsgarden.be
closed 7 July-3 August and Sunday **G1**
Rest – Menu 25 €, 45/70 € – Carte 31/78 €
◆ Chinese ◆ Exotic ◆
This spacious, elegant mansion houses one of Antwerp's oldest Chinese restaurants. Specialities include dishes from Canton (dim sum), Beijing (Peking duck) and Szechuan (fondue).

XX **Radis Noir**

Desguinlei 186 ✉ 2018 – ✆ 0 3 238 37 70 – radisnoir@skynet.be – Fax 0 3 238 39 07 – www.radisnoir.be
closed 24 March-2 April, 21 July-13 August, Wednesday dinner, Saturday lunch, Sunday and Bank Holidays **G1**
Rest – Menu 30 €, 50/84 € bi – Carte 49/93 €
◆ Contemporary ◆ Minimalist ◆
Hidden behind the old red brick façade, modernised with panels of frosted glass, is an attractive dining room with a minimalist, contemporary design. Limited but frequently updated menu.

XX **De Troubadour**

Driekoningenstraat 72 ✉ 2600 Berchem – ✆ 0 3 239 39 16 – info@detroubadour.be – Fax 0 3 230 82 71 – www.detroubadour.be
closed 3 first weeks August, Sunday and Monday **H1**
Rest – Menu 25/33 € – Carte 33/44 €
◆ Contemporary ◆ Trendy ◆
A modern, cosy restaurant where the charismatic owner ensures a warm and friendly atmosphere. Creative classic dishes and good menu choices described at your table. Ask about parking when you book.

XX **Margaux**

Terlinckstraat 2 ✉ 2600 Berchem – ✆ 0 3 230 55 99 – info@restaurant.margaux.be – Fax 0 3 230 40 71 – www.restaurant-margaux.be
closed Saturday lunch and Sunday **H1**
Rest – Menu 31 €, 35/55 € – Carte 35/58 €
◆ Contemporary ◆ Brasserie ◆
This old house in a residential district has been renovated in the style of a cosy bistro. In summer, enjoy the courtyard terrace with its teak furniture and trimmed box hedges.

XX **O'Kontreir**

Isabellalei 145 ✉ 2018 – ✆ 0 3 281 39 76 – info@okontreir.com – Fax 0 3 237 92 06 – www.okontreir.com
closed 27 July-14 August, 24 December-2 January, Saturday lunch, Sunday lunch, Monday and Tuesday **H1**
Rest – Menu 25/45 € – Carte 35/62 €
◆ Contemporary ◆ Trendy ◆
An emphasis on creative, contemporary and well-presented dishes in a distinctly fashionable lounge-style setting with a contrasting black and white décor in the city's Jewish quarter. Dining room and mezzanine.

X **Hippodroom**

Leopold de Waelplaats 10 – ✆ 03 248 52 52 – resto@hippodroom.be – Fax 03 238 71 67 – www.hippodroom.be
closed Saturday lunch and Sunday Plan II **C3**
Rest – *(open until 11 p.m.)* Menu 20 € – Carte 36/59 €
◆ Brasserie ◆ Trendy ◆
A modern brasserie occupying a mansion next to the city's Fine Arts Museum, understandably popular with customers from the world of the arts. Globetrotting menu. Terraces to the front and rear.

Bizzie-Lizzie

Vlaamse Kaai 16 – 03 238 61 97 – info@bizzielizzie.com – Fax 03 248 30 64 – www.bizzielizzie.com

closed Saturday lunch and Sunday Plan II **C3**

Rest – Menu 22 € – Carte 33/47 €

♦ Brasserie ♦

A Flemish house converted into a contemporary brasserie with a rustic touch. Dining rooms on various levels, where diners can enjoy a small choice of dishes enlivened with the occasional exotic flourish. International wine list and knowledgeable sommelier.

River Kwai

Vlaamse Kaai 14 – 03 237 46 51 – kwai@telenet.be

closed last 2 weeks June, Wednesday and lunch Saturday and Sunday Plan II **C3**

Rest – Menu 15/45 € – Carte 28/46 €

♦ Thai ♦ Exotic ♦

This building dating back to 1906 is now home to a Thai restaurant with an exotic, neo-colonial-style décor. Dining rooms one above the other, plus a small enclosed urban terrace.

AT THE AIRPORT *Plan I*

Scandic

Luitenant Lippenslaan 66 ✉ 2140 Borgerhout – 0 3 235 91 91 – info-antwerp@scandic-hotels.com – Fax 0 3 235 08 96 – www.scandic-hotels.com **B2**

200 rm – †88/182 € ††106/200 € – 4 suites

Rest – Menu 33 € – Carte 30/46 €

♦ Chain hotel ♦ Functional ♦

A chain hotel with a good location along the ring road, close to a railway station, the Zilvercentrum (museum) and a golf course. Well-appointed guestrooms, plus meeting rooms, swimming pool, sauna and fitness centre. Somewhat formal brasserie with an attractive teak terrace.

CZECH REPUBLIC

ČESKÁ REPUBLIKA

PROFILE

→ **Area:**
78 864 km² (30 449 sq mi).

→ **Population:**
10 241 000 inhabitants (est. 2005), density = 130 per km².

→ **Capital:**
Prague (population 1 141 000 inhabitants).

→ **Currency:**
Czech crown (Kč); rate of exchange: CZK 100 = € 3.82 = US$ 5.56 (Dec 2007).

→ **Government:**
Parliamentary republic (since 1993). Member of European Union since 2004.

→ **Language:**
Czech; also German and English.

→ **Specific public holidays:**
Liberation Day (8 May); St. Cyril and St. Methodius Day (5 July); Martyrdom of Jean Hus (6 July); Czech Statehood Day (28 September); Independence Day (28 October); Freedom and Democracy Day (17 November); Boxing Day (26 December).

→ **Local Time:**
GMT + 1 hour in winter and GMT + 2 hours in summer.

→ **Climate:**
Temperate continental with cold winters and warm summers (Prague: January: 0°C, July: 20°C).

→ **International Dialling Code:**
00 420 followed by area code (Prague: 2), and then the local number.

→ **Emergency:**
Police: ✆ **158**; Ambulance: ✆ **155**; Fire Brigade: ✆ **150**.

→ **Electricity:**
220 volts AC, 50Hz; 2-pin round-shaped continental plugs.

→ **Formalities**
Travellers from the European Union (EU), Switzerland, Iceland and the main countries of North and South America need a national identity card or passport (America: passport required) to visit Czech Republic for less than three months (tourism or business purpose). For visitors from other countries a visa may be required, in addition to a passport, especially for those wishing to stay for longer than three months. We advise you to check with your embassy before travelling.

Prague
PRAHA

Population: 1 141 000 – Altitude: 250m

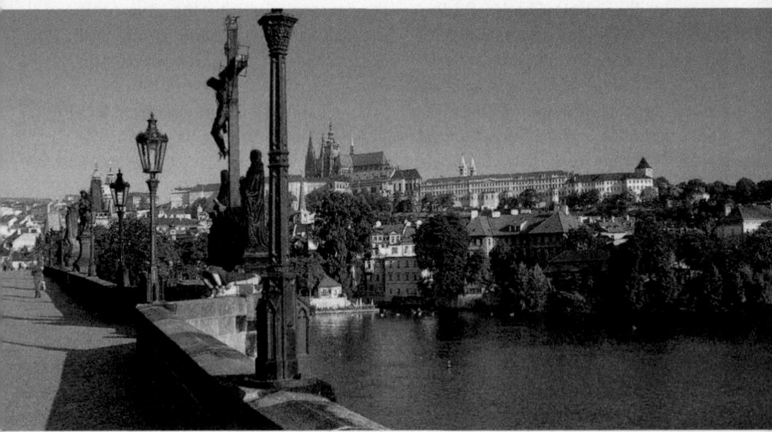

Siméone/PHOTONONSTOP

The most important thing to remember about Prague is that its history stretches back to the Dark Ages. In the ninth century a princely seat comprising a simple walled-in compound was built where today stands the castle. In the tenth century the first bridge over the Vltava arrived. By the thirteenth century the enchanting cobbled alleyways below the castle were complete. Wherever you tread here, the musty scent of the past travels with you. But Prague has come of age and in many ways it's had to. It now receives ten times as many visitors as it did 20 years ago, and that figure could jump to double again (15 million) by 2010. Europe's most perfectly preserved capital now proffers consumer choice as well as medieval marvels. Its state-of-the-art shopping malls and pulsing nightlife bear testament to its popularity with tourists, the iron glove of communism long since having given way to the silk purse of western consumerism. These days there are practically two versions of Prague - the lively, youthful version which has spawned the unfortunate, headline grabbing epithet of 'stag party central', and the sedate, enchanting version most people have succumbed to, the 'city of a hundred spires', where cathedrals, churches, chapels and monasteries – exuberant and extraordinary - prod the skyline. And this is the city, prosperous, cosmopolitan and orderly, where music of all shades seeps into your senses.

LIVING THE CITY

The four main zones of Prague were originally independent towns in their own right. The river Vltava winds its way through their heart, and they're linked by the iconic Charles Bridge, possibly the most charismatic of Europe's spans. On the west side lie Hradèany, the castle quarter, built on a rock spur commanding the river bend, and Malá Strana, Prague's most perfectly preserved district at the bottom of the castle hill. Over the river are Staré Město, the old town with its vibrant medieval square and outer boulevards, and Nové Město, the new town, which is the city's commercial heart extending south and east of the old town. It's where you find Wenceslas Square and it's where Prague's suited and booted new execs hang out and the young things go to party.

PRACTICAL INFORMATION

ARRIVAL-DEPARTURE

Ruzyně (Prague Airport) is 20km west of the city. Take a taxi displaying 'Airport Cars' sign ; this should cost around CZK650. The shuttle bus leaves every 30min. International trains stops at Hlavni nádraží.

TRANSPORT

Trams and buses are frequent in Prague and run from early morning to past midnight. There's also a 49-station Metro comprising three lines and covering much of the city. All three are invariably cheap.

Be wary of taxis. Although regulations specify rates, it's not uncommon to be grossly overcharged. Always use a designated rank, and avoid flagging down a cab anywhere.

If you think you'll be public transport hopping on a pretty regular basis, then buy a short-term season pass that allows unlimited travel on bus, tram, metro and Petrin funicular.

EXPLORING PRAGUE

No other capital in Europe can match Prague's enviable mix of Medieval, Gothic, Baroque and art nouveau. It creates a heady fairytale patchwork set off by glinting spring sunshine

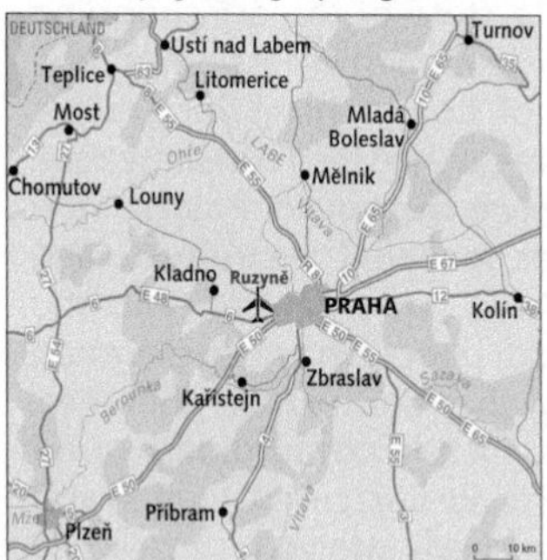

or a pure blanket of winter snow. The city's laid-back citizens sit in their gloomily atmospheric pubs and relax with a beer, leaving the hard work to the tourists. Outside, many of those are trying to decide just how to fit the jigsaw pieces together...museums, art galleries, churches, synagogues, a chamber concert in an ornate chapel. Or perhaps they're trying to find their way around the labyrinthine web of lanes and passageways that may link those very tourist landmarks.

→ YOU'LL BE A-MAZED

If you're all set to 'do' Staré Město or Malá Strana, be prepared to lose yourself in a maze of crooked streets and narrow alleyways; don't be afraid to peek down passageways and slip into secret courtyards hemmed in by old-style dwellings. The real itch of Prague is feeling you haven't discovered it until it's concocted a way of getting you lost. As confused as you may be, you can take heart in the knowledge that before too long you'll end up by the Vltava or catch sight of a recognizable landmark. If it all gets a little bit too claustrophobic, you can take refuge in the Nové Město. Here the medieval town planner has taken pity on the confused visitor and the streets and squares are logically laid out, as typified by the broad boulevard of **Wenceslas Square**.

To get a real perspective on the city, everyone – and we mean everyone – takes a stroll over the **Charles Bridge** (completed in 1402) with its various bronze saints staring down implacably on the never-ending shuffle of passers-by. At each end is a tower, open to visitors, both offering superb views from their roofs. This merely whets the appetite for the climb up to **Prague Castle**, with its commanding cliff-top outlook. Its scale is breathtaking; quite simply, it's the biggest ancient castle in the world. So big that within its third courtyard stands the immense Gothic structure that is **St Vitus Cathedral,** complete with massive main tower, scintillating rose window, spectacular stained-glass windows, and a chapel to St Wenceslas that glitters with gold, silver and semi-precious stones. There are other jewels in the Castle's crown, such as the Royal Garden, the Old Royal Palace and the Summer Palace, while close by are the smart boutiques of the tiny, magical Golden Lane, where Franz Kafka, at number 22, wrote much of his work. There's so much to take in around here that it might be worth doing it in more than one visit.

→ THROUGH TICK AND TYN

If you just love the warm glow of big crowds, then cross the river for another fix. This time the masses gather every hour in Staré Město's Old Town Square beneath the Orloj, or **Astronomical Clock,** which has three hands to show the position of the sun, moon and stars. On the hour, with the crowds in tow, carved figures do a turn, death wags his hourglass, and a cockerel crows to bring the drama to its conclusion. There are other great charms to the historical square (aside from the ubiquitous restaurants and bars to rest weary feet); every hue and nuance of architectural style vies for attention in the shape of the rococo Kinsky Palace, the Gothic/Baroque House of the Stone Bell, the Renaissance façade of Storch House, and the dramatic twin spires signalling the great Gothic landmark of the Church of Our Lady Before Tyn. Here, inside the richly adorned interior, search out the tomb of Tycho Brahe, Renaissance astronomer, who lost the tip of his nose in a duel, had it replaced in gold and silver, and died when his bladder burst after an excess of beer and wine. He might have appreciated the Municipal House, an art nouveau masterpiece close to Old Town Square where you can wine and dine in luxuriously refined surroundings. It's a great place for concerts, too.

To the north of Staré Město is Josefov, the Jewish quarter, where the Old Jewish Cemetery is a fascinating place to visit. Hemmed in by buildings and high walls, there was only so much space for the 12,000 tombstones, and these topple across each other in chaotic disarray. The synagogues of the area remain, some used as museums outlining the long history of Jews in Prague, others as places of worship. The Old-New Synagogue, near the cemetery, is one of Europe's oldest functioning synagogues, and boasts an eye-catching high brick gable and an atmospheric feel. Josefov is a rather small area that does get packed, so a good time to go along is early in the day.

→ GRAND NATIONAL

At the other end of town, at the southern end of Wenceslas Square, looms the brooding bulk of another great Prague institution, **the National Museum.** With its vast natural history and archaeology collections, it's a city institution, but some may find the most intriguing aspect of the place its cavernous atrium and grand staircases (incidentally, there are many quirky museums in Prague, devoted to the likes of spiders and scorpions, medieval torture and Barbie). The National Museum is a towering experience under a big roof, and you can get a similar kind of awesome hit at **the National Theatre**, south of Charles Bridge by the river, an opulent home of opera, ballet and theatre, full of lavish decorations from the country's top nineteenth century artistic talents.

To appreciate a complete contrast, head back over the river to **Petrin Hill,** which towers gloriously over Malá Strana's dappled squares and aristocratic palaces. It offers great vistas over the city, and features lots of leafy trails that criss-cross the surface. Sitting atop of it all is Prague's mini Eiffel Tower, the Petrin Tower, gifting you more stunning views. Heading back down to river level, you might be surprised to find the John Lennon Wall, painted after his murder in 1980, covered in graffiti, slightly tatty and peeling, but preserved as a totem to free expression.

However hard-wired to the newly opened-up, globalized world Prague aspires to be, it'll surely never lose its magical medieval appeal. It's at its best in the winter with damp mists swirling off the river, and the crowds mysteriously evaporated. In November or February, you can walk unsullied across Charles Bridge and appreciate this stunning city at its best.

CALENDAR HIGHLIGHTS

There's an English language paper in the city, **The Prague Post**, which is particularly good for listing details of what's on where. And there are so many people handing out leaflets announcing recitals and concerts that your hand will soon start to feel like a mini JCB. Many of these events are worth looking into, so don't just stuff that bit of paper away in your pocket. The Prague Spring Festival, which takes place in May and offers a scintillating variety of classical concerts at many venues, is internationally lauded, but there's also an Autumn Festival in September, and a Winter

PRAGUE IN...

→ ONE DAY

Old Town Square, the astronomical clock, Charles Bridge, Prague Castle, take it all in on Petrin Hill

→ TWO DAYS

Josefov, the National Theatre, Golden Lane

→ THREE DAYS

Wenceslas Square and the National Museum, across the bridge for a detailed look round Malá Strana

Festival in January, so...if you miss one, remember there'll be another along soon. Fans of gipsy roots music have a treat every May, with the World Roma Festival, which, as well as gipsy music, features films and theatre shows in various locations. Dance Prague, every June, is another highlight of the cultural year, while, without employing a trace of the city's trademark irony, June the third is devoted to the death of Kafka, with admirers flocking to his burial place. December is a good time to be in Old Town Square, with its huge Christmas tree and surrounding markets selling all manner of things you might not really want. On New Year's Eve, the square is a manic place to be, and the fireworks over the castle are something else.

EATING OUT

Prague was and still is to an extent famous for its infinite variety of dumplings. These were the glutinous staple that saw locals through the long years of stark Communist rule. It's still as easy as bumping into another tourist on Charles Bridge to get the favoured local nosh: pork, pickled cabbage and dumplings. You can also mix the likes of schnitzel, beer and ginger cake for a ridiculously cheap outlay. But since '89's Velvet Revolution, Prague has undergone a bit of a foodie revolution, and the heavy traditional cuisine is now served, in the better establishments, with a creative flair and international approach. Global menus are now common currency here. Less palatably, the city has earned a reputation for rather straight-faced and indifferent service: lots of restaurants include a tip in your final bill, so check closely to make sure you don't tip twice. It's worth remembering that lunch is the main meal of the Czech day, and many restaurants have shut up shop well before midnight.

Czechs consume more beer than anyone else in the world, and there are some excellent microbrewery tipples to be had. In Staré Město there's a very popular establishment, with an amazing selection of beers, conveniently called Alcohol Bar. Harder to find in the city, but well worth the effort, are the brilliant flea markets, which set up their stalls depending on the time of year. A good place to check out details is the Globe English language bookstore by the Vltava near the National Theatre. Everyone knows everything there, and the coffee's good too!

→ RISING DAMP

The floods of 2002 were a wake-up call to locals that the Vltava is no respecter of the tourist trade. The costs reached some 70 billion crowns in structural damage and loss of visitors. Although buildings were smartly renovated in good time, the city has learnt its lesson and the authorities have built a new flood wall and early warning system in case the river decides to put them to the test again.

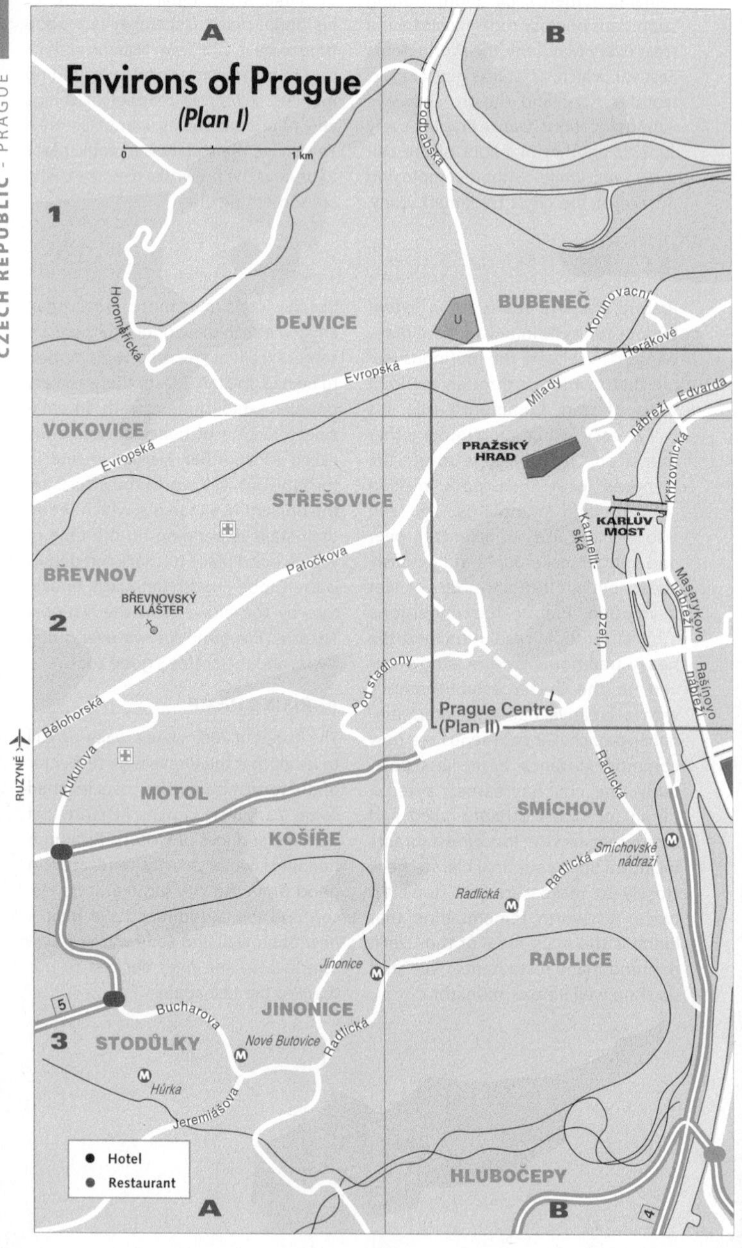
Environs of Prague
(Plan I)
0
1 km
A
B
1
2
3
Podbabská
BUBENEČ
Korunovační
DEJVICE
U
Horomeřická
Evropská
Horákové
Milady
Edvarda
nábřeží
VOKOVICE
Evropská
PRAŽSKÝ HRAD
Křižovnická
STŘEŠOVICE
KARLŮV MOST
Karmelit-ská
Patočkova
BŘEVNOV
BŘEVNOVSKÝ KLÁŠTER
Masarykovo nábřeží
Újezd
Pod stadiony
Rašínovo nábřeží
Bělohorská
Prague Centre (Plan II)
RUZYNĚ
Kukulova
MOTOL
Radlická
SMÍCHOV
KOŠÍŘE
Smíchovské nádraží
Radlická
Radlická
RADLICE
Jinonice
5
Bucharova
JINONICE
Radlická
STODŮLKY
Nové Butovice
Hůrka
Jeremiášova
Hotel
Restaurant
HLUBOČEPY
A
B
4

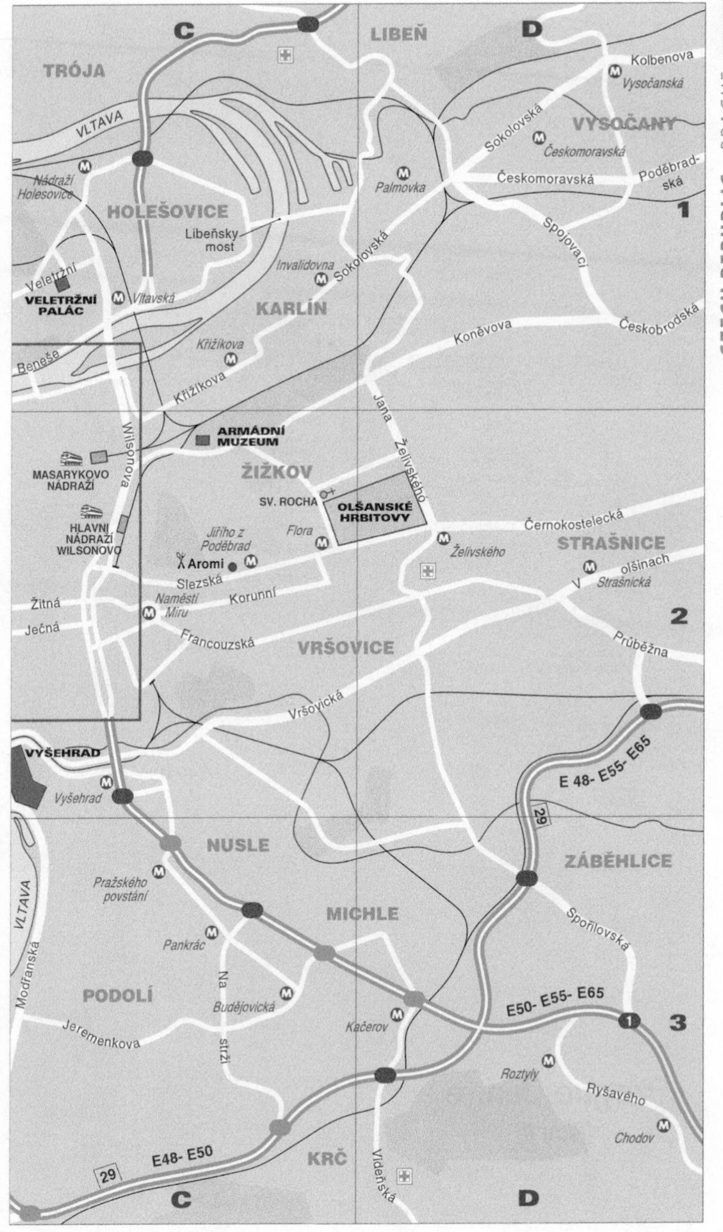

C
D
LIBEŇ
TRÓJA
Kolbenova
Vysočanská
VLTAVA
VYSOČANY
Sokolovská
Českomoravská
Nádraží Holesovice
Palmovka
Českomoravská
Poděbradská
1
HOLEŠOVICE
Libeňsky most
Sokolovská
Spojovací
Invalidovna
Veletržní
VELETRŽNÍ PALÁC
Vltavská
KARLÍN
Českobrodská
Koněvova
Křižíkova
Beneše
Křižíkova
Jana Želivského
Wilsonova
ARMÁDNÍ MUZEUM
MASARYKOVO NÁDRAŽÍ
ŽIŽKOV
SV. ROCHA
OLŠANSKÉ HRBITOVY
HLAVNÍ NÁDRAŽÍ WILSONOVO
Jiřího z Poděbrad
Flora
Černokostelecká
Želivského
STRAŠNICE
Aromi
Slezská
V olšinach
Strašnická
Žitná
Náměstí Míru
Korunní
2
Ječná
Francouzská
VRŠOVICE
Průběžna
Vršovická
VYŠEHRAD
E 48- E55- E65
Vyšehrad
29
NUSLE
ZÁBĚHLICE
Pražského povstání
VLTAVA
MICHLE
Spořilovská
Pankrác
Na strži
PODOLÍ
Budějovická
E50- E55- E65
Modřanská
Kačerov
1
3
Jeremenkova
Roztyly
Ryšavého
Chodov
KRČ
Vídeňská
E48- E50
29
C
D

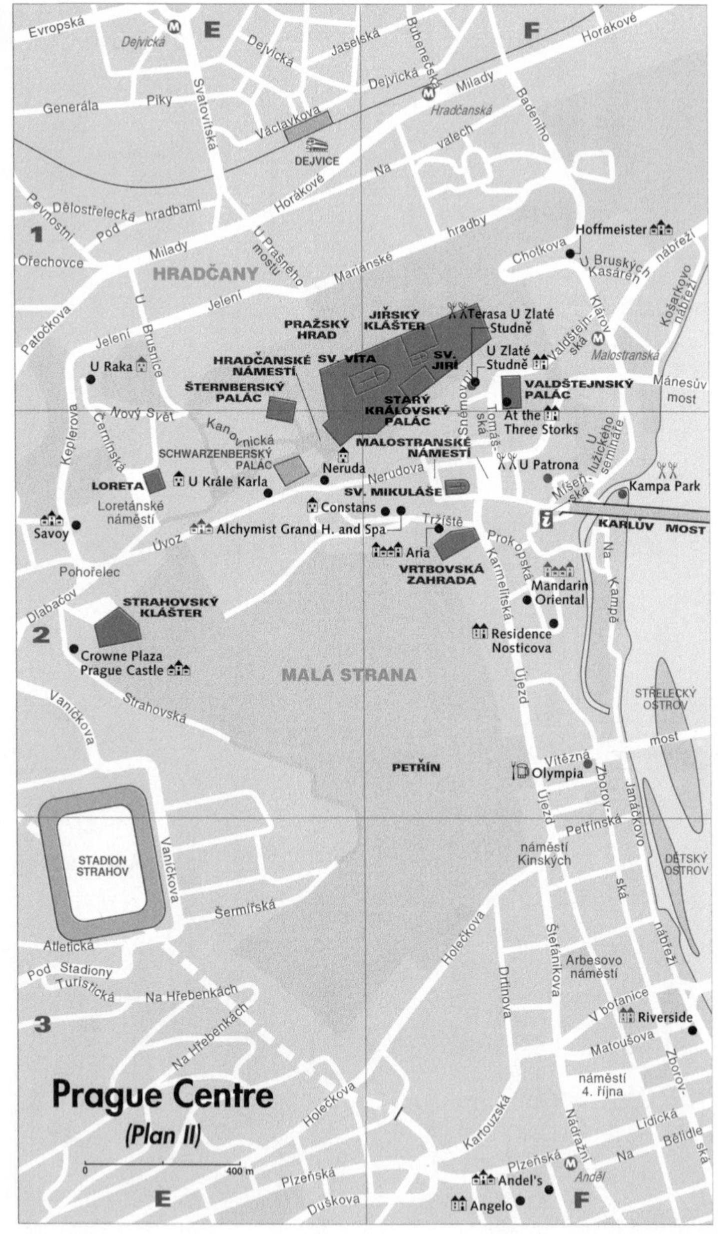
Prague Centre
(Plan II)
HRADČANY
MALÁ STRANA
PETŘÍN
PRAŽSKÝ HRAD
JIŘSKÝ KLÁŠTER
HRADČANSKÉ NÁMĚSTÍ
SV. VÍTA
SV. JIŘÍ
ŠTERNBERSKÝ PALÁC
STARÝ KRÁLOVSKÝ PALÁC
SCHWARZENBERSKÝ PALÁC
MALOSTRANSKÉ NÁMĚSTÍ
SV. MIKULÁŠE
VALDŠTEJNSKÝ PALÁC
LORETA
VRTBOVSKÁ ZAHRADA
STRAHOVSKÝ KLÁŠTER
KARLŮV MOST
STADION STRAHOV
STŘELECKÝ OSTROV
DĚTSKÝ OSTROV
DEJVICE
Hoffmeister
Terasa U Zlaté Studně
U Zlaté Studně
At the Three Storks
U Patrona
Kampa Park
U Raka
U Krále Karla
Neruda
Constans
Alchymist Grand H. and Spa
Aria
Savoy
Mandarin Oriental
Residence Nosticova
Crowne Plaza Prague Castle
Olympia
Riverside
Andel's
Angelo
Evropská
Dejvická
Jaselská
Bubenečská
Horákové
Milady
Hradčanská
Generála
Piky
Svatovítská
Václavkova
Badeniho
Na valech
Dělostřelecká
Pevnostní
Pod hradbami
Ořechovce
U Prašného mostu
Mariánské hradby
Chotkova
U Bruských Kasáren
nábřeží
Kosarkovo nábřeží
Jelení
Patočkova
U Brusnice
Klárov
Valdštejnská
Malostranská
Mánesův most
Nový Svět
Kanovnická
Keplerova
Černínská
Sněmovní
Tomášská
U lužického semináře
Nerudova
Míšeňská
Loretánské náměstí
Úvoz
Tržiště
Prokopská
Karmelitská
Na Kampě
Pohořelec
Dlabačov
Vaníčkova
Strahovská
Újezd
most
Vítězná
Zborovská
Janáčkovo nábřeží
Petřínská
náměstí Kinských
Šermířská
Atletická
Pod Stadiony
Turistická
Na Hřebenkách
Holečkova
Štefánikova
Drtinova
Arbesovo náměstí
V botanice
Matoušova
náměstí 14. října
Kartouzská
Nádražní
Lidická
Na Bělidle
Plzeňská
Anděl
Duškova
E
F
1
2
3
0
400 m

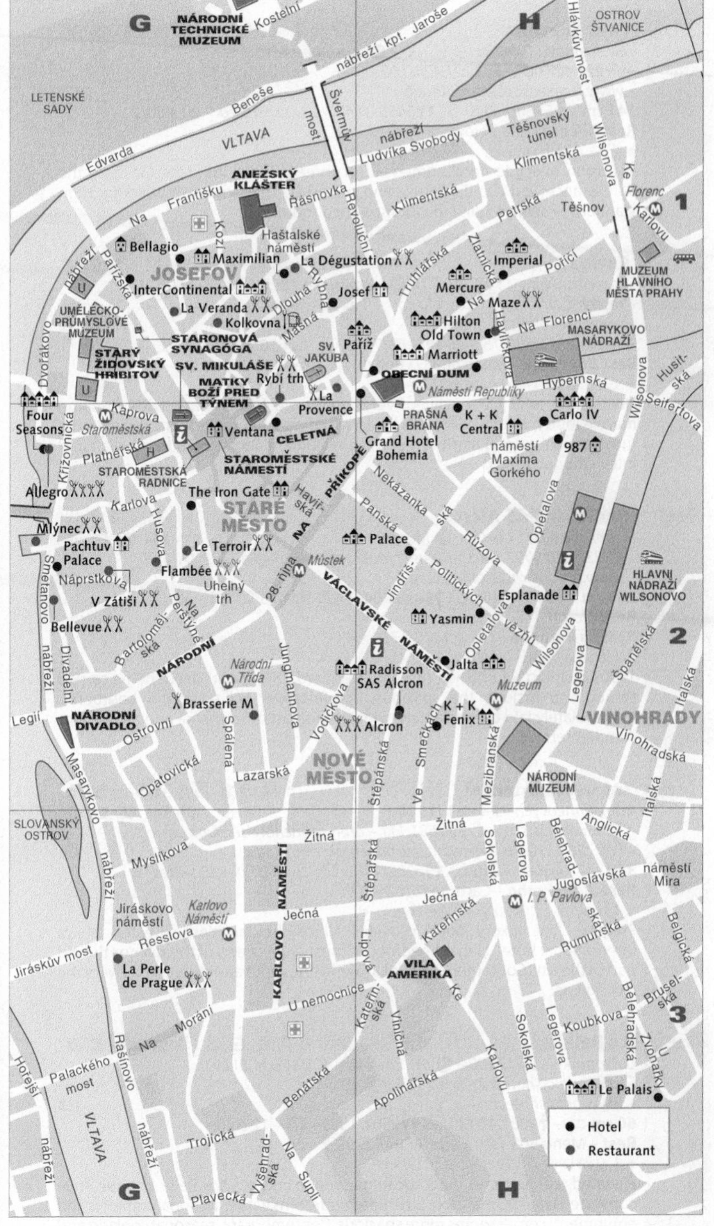

Hotel
Restaurant

ON THE RIGHT BANK *Plan II*

Four Seasons

Veleslavínova 1098/2a ✉ 110 00 – Ⓜ Staroměstská
– ✆ 221 427 000 – Fax 221 426 0 00
– www.fourseasons.com/prague **G2**
141 rm – 5760/10300 CZK 6455/11400 CZK, 910 CZK – 20 suites
Rest *Allegro* – see below
♦ Grand Luxury ♦ Modern ♦
Imposing riverside hotel composed of three 3 buildings - the Classical, the Renaissance and the Baroque - and united by modern main building. High standard of service. Luxuriously appointed rooms.

Carlo IV

Senovážné Nám. 13 ✉ 110 00 – Ⓜ Náměsti Republiky – ✆ 224 593 111
– reservation@carloiv.boscolo.com – Fax 224 593 0 00
– www.boscolohotels.com **H2**
150 rm – 5968/7785 CZK 5968/7785 CZK, 650 CZK – 2 suites
Rest *Box Block* – Menu 560 CZK (lunch) – Carte 1350/1550 CZK
♦ Grand Luxury ♦ Stylish ♦
Unabashed luxury personified: very impressive former bank with stunning marble lobby, ornate ceiling and pillars. Bedrooms in the original building the most spacious and luxurious. A stylish restaurant serving modern Italian and international dishes.

Radisson SAS Alcron

Štěpánská 40 ✉ 110 00 – Ⓜ Muzeum
– ✆ 222 820 000 – sales.prague@radissonsas.com – Fax 222 820 1 00
– www.prague.radissonsas.com **H2**
200 rm – 4385/6461 CZK 4385/6461 CZK, 623 CZK – 6 suites
Rest *Alcron* – see below
Rest *La Rotonde* – Carte 1270/1330 CZK
♦ Luxury ♦ Business ♦ Modern ♦
1930s building refurbished to a high standard. Original art deco theme carried through to include the spacious, comfortable, well-equipped bedrooms. Immaculately laid out restaurant with a stylish art deco theme and an outdoor summer terrace.

Inter-Continental

Nám. Curieových 43-45 ✉ 110 00
– Ⓜ Staroměstská – ✆ 296 631 111 – prague@ichotelsgroup.com
– Fax 226 631 2 16 – www.intercontinental.com/prague **G1**
349 rm – 5683/7240 CZK 6202/7785 CZK, 670 CZK – 23 suites
Rest *Zlata Praha* – Carte 1175/2240 CZK
♦ Grand Luxury ♦ Modern ♦
Prague's first luxury hotel provides all of the facilities expected of an international hotel. Elegant bedrooms, most enjoy views of the river or the old part of the city. Contemporary cooking with fine wines and stunning views of the city skyline.

Le Palais

U Zvonařky 1 ✉ 120 00 – Ⓜ I. P. Pavlova – ✆ 234 634 111
– info@palaishotel.cz – Fax 234 634 6 35
– www.palaishotel.cz **H3**
60 rm – 9082/10120 CZK 9601/13234 CZK – 12 suites
Rest – Menu 908 CZK – Carte 1116/1220 CZK
♦ Luxury ♦ Classic ♦
Elevated, affluent and quiet location overlooking city for Belle Epoque style converted late 19C mansion. Luxurious bedrooms with traditional comforts and equipment; corner rooms more spacious. Contemporary, seasonal cooking and attentive service in Le Papillon; delightful outlook from terrace.

Marriott

V Celnici 8 ✉ 110 00 – Ⓜ Námësti Republiky – ✆ 222 888 888 – prague.marriott@marriott.cz – Fax 222 888 8 89 – www.marriott.com

258 rm – 6100/7800 CZK 6100/7800 CZK, ☕ 670 CZK – 35 suites **H1**

Rest – Carte 730/1205 CZK

♦ Business ♦ Classic ♦

International hotel boasting first-class conference and leisure facilities. Committed service and modern, smart bedrooms with all the latest mod cons. Brasserie offers a wide selection of cuisine from American, French to traditional Czech.

Hilton Old Town

V Celnici 7 ✉ 111 21 – Ⓜ Námësti Republiky – ✆ 221 822 100 – renaissance.prague@renaissance.cz – Fax 221 822 2 00 – www.renaissancehotels.com **H1**

302 rm ☕ – 3642/7828 CZK 3642/7828 CZK – 3 suites

Rest *Maze* – see below

Rest *Seven* – Carte 800/1720 CZK

Rest *U Korbele* – ✆ *221 822 433* – Carte 460/1140 CZK

♦ Business ♦ Modern ♦

Located in the heart of the city, this hotel has recently been fully refurbished and boasts an art deco style lobby with white marble and gold décor. Modern, functional bedrooms. Seven specialises in grills and seafood. Czech specialities in casual, relaxing U Korbele.

Palace

Panská 12 ✉ 111 21 – Ⓜ Můstek – ✆ 224 093 111 – info@palacehotel.cz – Fax 224 221 2 40 – www.palacehotel.cz **H2**

122 rm ☕ – 8563 CZK 9082 CZK – 2 suites

Rest *Gourmet Club* – Carte 1427/1557 CZK

♦ Traditional ♦ Classic ♦

Original Viennese art nouveau style façade dating back to 1909. Elegant interior; bedrooms combine period furniture with modern facilities and services. Classic club ambience and fine dining off broad global menu.

Paříž

U obecniho domu 1 ✉ 110 00 – Ⓜ Námësti Republiky – ✆ 222 195 195 – booking@hotel-pariz.cz – Fax 224 225 4 75 – www.hotel-pariz.cz **H1**

83 rm – 9082 CZK 9082 CZK, ☕ 600 CZK – 3 suites

Rest *Sarah Bernhardt* – Menu 778 CZK

♦ Traditional ♦ Classic ♦

Culturally and historically, a landmark famed for its neo-gothic, art nouveau architecture. Original staircase with preserved window panels. Sound-proofed rooms; corner rooms are larger. Fine example of art nouveau in Sarah Bernhardt restaurant.

Grand Hotel Bohemia

Králodvorská 4 ✉ 110 00 – Ⓜ Námësti Republiky – ✆ 234 608 111 – office@grandhotelbohemia.cz – Fax 222 329 5 45 – www.grandhotelbohemia.cz **H1**

78 rm – 5880/7560 CZK 7000/9520 CZK, ☕ 560 CZK

Rest – Menu 990 CZK – Carte 850/1540 CZK

♦ Traditional ♦ Classic ♦

Classic 1920s hotel, in an ideal location for tourists, with a splendid neo-Baroque ballroom. Comfortable bedrooms are generously proportioned and service professional. Large, classic restaurant with a menu of Czech/international dishes.

Jalta

Václavské Nám. 45 ✉ 110 00 – Ⓜ Muzeum – ✆ 222 822 111 – booking@hoteljalta.com – Fax 222 822 8 33 – www.hoteljalta.com **H2**

89 rm ☕ – 4480/6480 CZK 4480/6480 CZK – 5 suites

Rest *Hot* – Carte 575/875 CZK

♦ Traditional ♦ Stylish ♦

Hotel with classic 1950s façade overlooking Wenceslas Square, celebrating its 50th anniversary this year. Spacious, modern, well equipped bedrooms with art deco styling and furniture. Stylish modern restaurant offering steaks and pasta.

Mercure

Na Poříčí 7 ✉ 110 00 – Ⓜ Náměsti Republiky – ✆ 221 800 800 – h3440@accor.com – Fax 221 800 8 01 – www.accorhotels.com **H1**

173 rm – †4022/5449 CZK ††4022/5449 CZK, ☕ 415 CZK – 1 suite

Rest *Felice* – *(Closed Saturday and Sunday lunch)* Carte 685/1250 CZK

◆ Business ◆ Functional ◆

Modern hotel behind ornate 19C façade: many original features remain. Kafka worked here for seven years when it was insurance offices. Ask for a more spacious deluxe room. Restaurant named after one of Kafka's lovers: modern Parisian brasserie; pleasant terrace.

Imperial

Na Poříčí 15 ✉ 110 00 – Ⓜ Náměsti Republiky – ✆ 246 011 600 – info@hotel-imperial.cz – Fax 246 011 6 70 – www.hotel-imperial.cz

Closed 20-26 September *Plan 2* **H1**

126 rm – †3893/5450 CZK ††3893/9083 CZK, ☕ 519 CZK

Rest – Menu 250 CZK (lunch) – Carte 350/545 CZK

◆ Business ◆ Retro ◆

Newly restored hotel, originally built in 1914, featuring fine ceramic mosaics in an art deco style. Dark wood bedrooms combine retro styling with modern comforts. Popular, open plan restaurant serving seasonal menu, with a remarkable backdrop of colourfully tiled pillars and walls.

Pachtuv Palace without rest

Karolíny Světlé 34 ✉ 110 00 – Ⓜ Staroměstská – ✆ 234 705 111 – reception@pachtuvpalace.com – Fax 234 705 1 12 – www.mamaisonresidences.com **G2**

18 rm – †9471 CZK ††11028 CZK – 32 suites – †12326 CZK ††19851 CZK, ☕ 650 CZK

◆ Traditional ◆ Cosy ◆

17C residence with commanding views over the city. Large and luxurious bedrooms and suites blend antique furniture with modern accessories. Relaxing courtyard terrace.

Josef without rest

Rybná 20 ✉ 110 00 – Ⓜ Náměsti Republiky – ✆ 221 700 901 – reservation@hoteljosef.com – Fax 221 700 9 99 – www.hoteljosef.com **G1**

109 rm ☕ – †3866/5812 CZK ††5890/10328 CZK

◆ Townhouse ◆ Design ◆

Stylish boutique hotel with light glass lobby, bar and breakfast room. Design-led bedrooms; deluxe rooms have ultra modern glass bathrooms.

Yasmin

Politických vězňu 12/913 ✉ 110 00 – Ⓜ Muzeum – ✆ 234 100 100 – info@hotel-yasmin.cz – Fax 234 110 1 01 – www.hotel-yasmin.cz **F2**

198 rm ☕ – †55600/65780 CZK ††55600/75900 CZK

Rest – Carte 307/617 CZK

◆ Business ◆ Modern ◆

Modern and design-led centrally located hotel. Stylish lobby leads into winter garden and cool lounge. Modular bedrooms in soft shades of sage with black-tiled bathrooms. Colourful and casual dining room with vast Asian menu specialising in noodles.

Maximilian without rest

Haštalská 14 ✉ 110 00 – Ⓜ Náměsti Republiky – ✆ 225 303 111 – reservations@maximilianhotel.com – Fax 225 303 1 10 – www.maximilianhotel.com **G1**

70 rm ☕ – †4015/4540 CZK ††4933/5458 CZK – 1 suite

◆ Business ◆ Modern ◆

Converted apartment block in quiet area near St Agnes Convent. Designer boutique style prevails. Glass and steel breakfast room. Basement Thai massage spa. Contemporary rooms.

Ventana without rest
Celetná 7 ✉ 110 00 – Ⓜ Náměsti Republiky – ☎ 221 776 600 – booking@ventana-hotel.cz – Fax 221 776 6 03 – www.ventana-hotel-cz *Plan 2* **G2**
19 rm – ♦4282/7655 CZK ♦♦6617/8953 CZK – 10 suites
♦ Traditional ♦ Classic ♦
Tranquil hotel near the Old Town market, featuring art deco style lobby. Spacious, well-equipped bedrooms in modern, muted hues; loft rooms on top floor have separate lounge.

K + K Central
Hybernská 10 ✉ 110 00 – Ⓜ Náměsti Republiky – ☎ 225 022 000 – hotel.central@kkhotels.cz – Fax 222 022 9 99 – www.kkhotels.com/central **H2**
126 rm – ♦7136 CZK ♦♦7655 CZK – 1 suite
Rest – *(in bar)* Carte 600/1110 CZK
♦ Business ♦ Modern ♦
Beautifully restored hotel with elegant art nouveau façade; interior is blend of ultra modern and period décor. Glass and steel breakfast gallery in old theatre. Modish rooms. Light dishes in bar/restaurant.

The Iron Gate
Michalská 19 ✉ 110 00 – Ⓜ Staroměstská – ☎ 225 777 777 – hotel@irongate.cz – Fax 225 777 7 78 – www.irongate.cz **G2**
13 rm – ♦5600/7000 CZK ♦♦7000/8400 CZK – **30 suites** – ♦9800/25200 CZK, 467 CZK
Rest *Khajuraho* – Carte 750/1350 CZK
♦ Traditional ♦ Classic ♦
Hidden away in Old Town's cobbled street maze. 14C origins; attractive central courtyard. Large rooms with antique furniture or painted beams; some duplex suites. Khajuraho in basement for Indian cuisine.

Esplanade
Washingtonova 1600-19 ✉ 110 00 – Ⓜ Muzeum – ☎ 224 501 111 – esplanade@esplanade.cz – Fax 224 229 3 06 – www.esplanade.cz **H2**
74 rm – ♦2725/3607 CZK ♦♦3347/4385 CZK
Rest – Menu 570 CZK (dinner) – Carte 571/830 CZK
♦ Traditional ♦ Classic ♦
Charming and atmospheric; this art nouveau building is something of an architectural gem. Original features abound; bedrooms enjoy style and a timeless elegance. International menu offered in friendly surroundings.

K + K Fenix
Ve Smečkách 30 ✉ 110 00 – Ⓜ Muzeum – ☎ 225 012 222 – hotel.fenix@kkhotels.cz – Fax 222 212 1 41 – www.kkhotels.com **H2**
128 rm – ♦6954 CZK ♦♦7474 CZK
Rest – *(in bar)* Carte 450/840 CZK
♦ Business ♦ Modern ♦
Located off Wenceslas Square; up to date interior behind a classic façade. Bedrooms vary in size and shape but all are smart, clean and comfortable. Simple bathrooms. Light dishes in lounge bar.

Bellagio
U Milosrdných 2 ✉ 110 00 – Ⓜ Staroměstská – ☎ 221 778 999 – info@bellagiohotel.cz – Fax 221 778 9 00 – www.bellagiohotel.cz **G1**
46 rm – ♦3347/6461 CZK ♦♦5164/6876 CZK, 380 CZK – 1 suite
Rest *Isabella* – *(dinner only)* Carte 675/1225 CZK
♦ Business ♦ Stylish ♦
Quiet, converted apartment block near the river. Basement vaulted bar/breakfast room. Airy, attractive bedrooms, well equipped in warm colours. Impressive bathrooms. Restaurant is Mediterranean style.

987 without rest

Senovážné 15 ✉ 110 00 – Ⓜ Náměsti Republiky – ☎ 255 737 200 – reservations@987praguehotel.com – Fax 222 210 3 69 – www.designhotelscollection.com Plan 2 **H2**

80 rm – †3374/4671 CZK ††3893/5190 CZK, ☕ 389 CZK – 3 suites

◆ Traditional ◆ Modern ◆

Well located, value-for-money hotel with cosy atmosphere and well-equipped, comfortable bedrooms, featuring modern design and furnishings. Colourful ground floor breakfast room.

Allegro – at Four Seasons H.

Veleslavínova 1098/2a ✉ 110 00 – Ⓜ Staroměstská – ☎ 221 426 880 – Fax 221 426 0 00 – www.fourseasons.com/prague **G2**

Rest – Menu 1330 CZK (lunch) – Carte 1690/2415 CZK

Spec. Yellowfin tuna caramelised with ginger, sour tomato sorbet. Suckling pig with horseradish mashed potato and liquorice jus. Vanilla and pear Tatin with ice cream.

◆ Italian ◆ Formal ◆

Elegant, luxurious restaurant overlooking river. Talented Italian chef creates innovative, harmoniously-balanced Italian dishes using prime quality ingredients; popular set menus include selected wines by the glass.

Alcron – at Radisson SAS Alcron H.

Štěpánská 40 ✉ 110 00 – Ⓜ Muzeum – ☎ 222 820 038 – sales.prague@radissonsas.com – Fax 222 820 1 00 – www.alcron.cz

Closed Sunday **H2**

Rest – *(booking essential) (dinner only)* Carte 1660/2154 CZK

◆ Seafood ◆ Design ◆

An Art Deco mural after de Lempicka dominates this intimate, semi-circular restaurant. Creative and classic seafood served by friendly, professional staff.

Flambée

Husova 5 ✉ 110 00 – Ⓜ Můstek – ☎ 224 248 512 – flambee@flambee.cz – Fax 224 248 5 13 – www.flambee.cz **G2**

Rest – Carte 1220/2024 CZK

Rest *Cafe Bistro 'F'* – *☎ 224 401 236* – Menu 255/615 CZK – Carte 225/475 CZK

◆ Traditional ◆ Formal ◆

Elegant fine dining in established cellar restaurant dating from 11C. Well-judged classics prepared using quality produce; flambéed food a speciality. Formal yet friendly service. Cafe Bistro 'F' - above the restaurant - is a little modern eatery serving simpler international dishes.

La Perle de Prague ≤ Prague,

Dancing House (7th floor), Rašínovo Nábřeží 80 ✉ 120 00 – Ⓜ Karlovo Náměstí – ☎ 219 841 60 – info@laperle.cz – Fax 219 841 79 – www.laperle.cz

Closed Sunday and lunch Monday **G3**

Rest – Menu 1000 CZK (lunch) – Carte 920/1640 CZK

◆ French ◆ Fashionable ◆

Eye-catching riverside building: seventh floor restaurant has simply stunning views of city, river and castle. Comfortable, strikingly modern décor. French-inspired menu.

Maze – at Hilton Old Town

V Celnici 7 ✉ 111 21 – Ⓜ Náměsti Republiky – ☎ 221 822 100 – mazeprague@gordonramsay.com – Fax 221 822 2 00 – www.gordonramsay.com Plan 2 **H1**

Rest – Menu 707 CZK (lunch) – Carte 1309/1361 CZK

◆ French ◆ Brasserie ◆

Modelled on Gordon Ramsay's eponymous London restaurant, offering a number of small dishes alongside the à la carte menu. Classic French cooking. Elegant setting, with art deco styling.

XX **Bellevue**

Smetanovo Nábřeží 18 ✉ 110 00 – Ⓜ Staroměstská – ✆ 222 221 443 – bellevue@zatisigroup.cz – Fax 222 220 4 53 – www.zatisigroup.cz **G2**

Rest – Carte 870/1770 CZK

◆ Traditional ◆ Formal ◆

Refurbished restaurant in elegant 19C building, affording views of river and royal palace. Contemporary styling in pastel shades; dine on international cuisine as the nightly piano plays.

XX **La Degustation**

Haštalská 18 ✉ 110 00 – Ⓜ Náměsti Republiky – ✆ 222 311 234 – www.ledegustation.cz

Closed Sunday and Christmas *Plan 2* **G1**

Rest – *(dinner only)* Menu 945/2450 CZK

◆ Modern ◆ Intimate ◆

Modern L-shaped restaurant with dark wood interior and intimate atmosphere. Talented kitchen produces innovative, flavourful cooking; regularly changing menus include 3 tasting menus which reflect the best produce available.

XX **Le Terroir**

Vejvodova 1 ✉ 110 00 – Ⓜ Můstek – ✆ 222 220 260 – rezervace@leterroir.cz – Fax 222 220 2 60 – www.leterroir.cz

Closed Sunday and Monday **G2**

Rest – Menu 1090 CZK – Carte 1160/1390 CZK

◆ Innovative ◆ Rustic ◆

Cobbled courtyard and steps descending past wine store to atmospheric vaulted 10C cellar. Personally run; superb wine list. Good value, accomplished, Pan-European cooking.

XX **La Veranda**

Elišky Krásnohorské 2 ✉ 110 00 – Ⓜ Staroměstská – ✆ 224 814 733 – office@laveranda.cz – Fax 224 814 5 96 – www.laveranda.cz **G1**

Rest – Menu 265 CZK (lunch) – Carte 555/1100 CZK

◆ Innovative ◆ Design ◆

Charming restaurant in the old Jewish district; with stylish, contemporary décor in the sunny colours of the Mediterranean. Well-prepared, flavoursome modern cooking.

XX **V Zátiši**

Liliová 1, Betlémské Nám. ✉ 110 00 – Ⓜ Můstek – ✆ 222 221 155 – vzatisi@zatisigroup.cz – Fax 222 220 6 29 – www.zatisigroup.cz

Closed 24 December and lunch 31 December and 1 January **G2**

Rest – *(booking essential at dinner)* Menu 795/995 CZK – Carte 785/1485 CZK

◆ Modern ◆ Cosy ◆

Well run, slick and dependable restaurant offering modern, well-priced cuisine within a range of four rooms which are intimate in places, and more stylish in others. Traditional Czech dishes; Asian influences.

XX **Mlýnec**

Novotného Lávka 9 ✉ 110 00 – Ⓜ Staroměstská – ✆ 221 082 208 – mlynec@zatisigroup.cz – Fax 221 082 3 91 – www.zatisigroup.cz

Closed 24 December **G2**

Rest – Menu 495 CZK – Carte 835/1435 CZK

◆ Contemporary ◆ Retro ◆

Spacious and contemporary; popular with tourists because of setting. Modern dishes combined with Czech classics. Terrace views of Charles Bridge on fine summer evenings.

XX **Rybí trh**

Týnský dvůr 5 ✉ 110 00 – Ⓜ Náměsti Republiky – ✆ 602 295 911 – info@rybitrh.cz – Fax 224 895 4 49 – www.rybitrh.cz **G1**

Rest – Carte 730/2280 CZK

◆ Seafood ◆ Friendly ◆

Modern restaurant which lives up to its name - Fish Market - with fresh seafood on crushed ice before open-plan kitchen; fish tanks and adjacent wine shop. Creative, contemporary cooking.

CZECH REPUBLIC - PRAGUE

Aromi

Mánesova 78/1442 ✉ 120 00 – Ⓜ Jiřiho z Poděbrad – ✆ 222 713 222 – info@aromi.cz – Fax 222 713 4 44 – www.aromi.cz

Closed Christmas **C2**

Rest – *(booking essential at dinner)* Menu 145 CZK (lunch) – Carte 605/1090 CZK

◆ Italian ◆ Rustic ◆

Buzzy neighbourhood restaurant boasts spacious, rustic interior with big, chunky wood tables and open kitchen. Great value, authentic Italian dishes and quality wine list.

Brasserie M

Vladislavova 17 ✉ 110 00 – Ⓜ Národni Třída – ✆ 224 054 070 – info@brasseriem.cz – Fax 224 054 4 40 – www.brasseriem.cz

Closed Christmas and Sunday **G2**

Rest – Menu 185/270 CZK – Carte 1533/4758 CZK

◆ French ◆ Bistro ◆

Central but away from touristy main streets. Big, high-ceilinged room with dominant open-plan kitchen and French accent to décor. Well-priced Gallic favourites on menu too.

La Provence

Štupartská 9 ✉ 110 00 Praha – Ⓜ Náměsti Republiky – ✆ 296 826 155 – kontakt@laprovence.cz – Fax 224 819 5 70 – www.kampagroup.com **G1**

Rest – Carte 623/1168 CZK

◆ French ◆ Brasserie ◆

Ground floor is in classic French brasserie style with etched mirrors, tile mosaics and Gallic scenes. More intimate basement room with Mediterranean feel and menu to match.

Kolkovna

V Kolkovně 8 ✉ 110 00 – Ⓜ Staroměstská – ✆ 224 819 701 – info@kolkovna.cz – Fax 224 819 7 00 – www.kolkovna.cz **G1**

Rest – Menu 250/400 CZK – Carte 279/655 CZK

◆ Traditional ◆ Inn ◆

Atmospheric Czech Pilsner Urquell bar/restaurant: old pictures, tools and advertisements line green walls under vaulted ceilings. Huge traditional dishes and excellent beers.

ON THE LEFT BANK

Plan II

Mandarin Oriental

Nebovidská 459/1 ✉ 118 00 – Ⓜ Malostranská – ✆ 233 088 888 – moprg-reservations@mohg.com – Fax 233 088 6 68 – www.mandarinoriental.com **F2**

77 rm – †10380 CZK ††18165 CZK, ☕ 650 CZK – 22 suites

Rest *Essensia* – Menu 688 CZK (lunch) – Carte 773/1079 CZK

◆ Luxury ◆ Stylish ◆

Housed within a 14C monastery, the hotel opened in 2006 and is more boutique in style than most in this group. Spa within the former chapel. Luxurious and sleek bedrooms. Vaulted, chic dining room with contemporary lighting; menu a blend of European and Asian.

Aria

Tržiště 9 ✉ 118 00 – Ⓜ Malostranská – ✆ 225 334 111 – stay@aria.cz – Fax 225 334 6 66 – www.aria.cz **F2**

43 rm ☕ – †5709/8044 CZK ††5709/8094 CZK – 9 suites

Rest *Coda* – Menu 519 CZK (lunch) – Carte 1038/1557 CZK

◆ Luxury ◆ Design ◆

Stylishly overlooking lovely castle gardens; boasts strong music orientation, including library and rooms themed individually to different music genres. Personable service. Choose from the international menu in intimate Coda or eat on the stunning summer rooftop terrace.

Alchymist Grand H. and Spa

Tržiště 19 ✉ 118 00 – Ⓜ Malostranská
– ✆ 257 286 011 – info@alchymisthotel.com – Fax 257 286 0 17
– www.alchymisthotel.com **F2**
38 rm – 🚹8174/9082 CZK 🚹🚹8174/9082 CZK, ☕ 519 CZK – 9 suites
Rest *Aquarius* – Carte 1427/2076 CZK
◆ Luxury ◆ Classic ◆
Four 15C Renaissance and Baroque houses on UNESCO street, sympathetically restored and offering sumptuous style. Beautiful spa; enchanting rooms with 16C-19C artefacts. Formal restaurant and café opening onto a courtyard; contemporary cuisine.

Savoy

Keplerova 11 ✉ 118 00 – ✆ 224 302 430 – info@savoyhotel.cz
– Fax 224 302 1 28 – www.savoyhotel.cz **E2**
60 rm ☕ – 🚹5190/7006 CZK 🚹🚹5709/7525 CZK – 1 suite
Rest *Hradčany* – Menu 600 CZK – Carte 1246/1220 CZK
◆ Luxury ◆ Classic ◆
Timeless charm; popular with statesmen. Strength lies in its classically styled bedrooms, which are spacious, tasteful, well equipped and benefit from high levels of service. Bright formal dining room with glass ceiling and distant city view.

Crowne Plaza Prague Castle

Strahovská 128 ✉ 118 00 – ✆ 226 080 000
– cp.castle@keyhotels.cz – Fax 226 080 2 00 – www.crowne plaza.com *Plan 2* **E2**
135 rm – 🚹3893/4930 CZK 🚹🚹4931/5969 CZK, ☕ 519 CZK – 3 suites
Rest – Carte 895/1349 CZK
◆ Business ◆ Historic ◆
Comfortable hotel in unique location next to the castle, within the site of the Strahov Monastery. Bedrooms in the old building, which dates from the 16C, are the more spacious. International dishes served in restaurant.

Andel's

Stroupeznického 21 ✉ 150 00 – Ⓜ Anděl – ✆ 296 889 688
– info@andelshotel.com – Fax 296 889 9 99 – www.andelshotel.com **F3**
257 rm ☕ – 🚹3269 CZK 🚹🚹3788 CZK – 33 suites
Rest *Oscar's* – Carte 540/635 CZK
Rest *Nagoya* – *✆ 251 511 724 (closed Sunday) (dinner only)* Menu 500 CZK – Carte 500/1500 CZK
◆ Business ◆ Modern ◆
Stylish modern hotel with distinctively minimalist appeal; luxurious apartments in adjacent block. Conference and fitness centres. Well-equipped rooms with all mod cons. Informal dining in Oscar's brasserie; simple international menu. Nagoya offers traditional Japanese dishes.

Hoffmeister

Pod Bruskou 7 ✉ 118 00 – Ⓜ Malostranská – ✆ 251 017 111
– hotel@hoffmeister.cz – Fax 251 017 1 20 – www.hoffmeister.cz **F1**
43 rm ☕ – 🚹4152/5449 CZK 🚹🚹4671/6747 CZK – 5 suites
Rest *Ada* – Carte 934/1505 CZK
◆ Traditional ◆ Classic ◆
Unprepossessing façade but inside full of artworks by Adolf Hoffmeister; son owns hotel. Eclectic range of classically decorated bedrooms plus 15C steam room. Elegant restaurant with original Adolf Hoffmeister cartoons. Attentive service; classical French cooking.

Riverside without rest

Janáčkovo Nábřeži 15 ✉ 150 00 – Ⓜ Anděl – ✆ 225 994 611 – reservation@riversideprague.com – Fax 225 994 6 22 – www.riversideprague.com **F3**
42 rm ☕ – 🚹4022/5839 CZK 🚹🚹4022/5839 CZK – 3 suites
◆ Business ◆ Modern ◆
An early 20C riverside façade conceals relaxing modern hotel with castle view. Efficient service. Very well-appointed bedrooms with luxurious bathrooms; many with views.

U Zlaté Studně

U Zlaté Studně 166/4 ✉ 118 00 – Ⓜ Malostranská – ✆ 257 011 213
– hotel@goldenwell.cz – Fax 257 533 3 20
– www.goldenwell.cz **F1**
17 rm – †4541/6358 CZK ††5320/7006 CZK, ☕ 311 CZK – 2 suites
Rest ***Terasa U Zlaté Studně*** – see below
♦ Historic ♦ Classic ♦

16C Renaissance building in quiet spot between the castle and Ladeburg Gardens. Inviting bedrooms - most boasting city views - are richly furnished but uncluttered.

At The Three Storks

Tomášská 20 ✉ 118 00 – Ⓜ Malostranská – ✆ 257 210 779
– utricapu@ok.cz – Fax 257 212 9 67 – www.utricapu.cz **F1**
20 rm ☕ – †3348/6098 CZK ††4126/7266 CZK
Rest – Carte 700/940 CZK
♦ Townhouse ♦ Modern ♦

Renovated 17C house with white 19C façade. Modern lobby bar and panoramic lift. Choice between superior and deluxe bedrooms; the latter are more spacious; all have luxury bathrooms. Modern restaurant with clean, bright interior, serving international and Czech dishes.

Residence Nosticova

Nosticova 1, Malá Strana ✉ 118 00 – Ⓜ Malostranská – ✆ 257 312 513
– info@nosticova.com – Fax 257 312 5 17
– www.nosticova.com **F2**
8 rm – †7280/8680 CZK ††7420/8820 CZK, ☕ 400 CZK – 5 suites
Rest ***Alchymist*** – *✆ 257 312 518* – Menu 1050/1250 CZK – Carte 945/1495 CZK
♦ Townhouse ♦ Classic ♦

Tastefully refurbished 17C town house in a quiet, cobbled side street near the river. Stylish suites - all with their own kitchen - combine modern and antique furnishings and works of art. Mediterranean cuisine served in flamboyantly-styled restaurant.

Angelo without rest

Radlicka 1g ✉ 150 00 – Ⓜ Anděl – ✆ 234 801 111
– info@angelohotel.com – Fax 234 809 9 98
– www.angelohotel.com **F3**
168 rm ☕ – †6617 CZK ††6617 CZK
♦ Business ♦ Modern ♦

Behind its sister hotel, Andel's, this is a colourfully decorated and relaxed hotel. Spacious bedrooms, with showers and large beds; Executive rooms on the top two floors.

U Raka without rest

Černínská 10 ✉ 118 00 – ✆ 220 511 100 – info@romantikhotel-uraka.cz
– Fax 233 358 0 41 – www.romantikhotel-uraka.cz **E1**
6 rm ☕ – †3200/4350 CZK ††4350/6700 CZK
♦ Family ♦ Cosy ♦

Tucked away, two timbered cottages in a rustic Czech style creating a charming little hotel. Cosy, comfy and inviting. Clean-lined rooms in warm brick and wood. Friendly welcome.

U Krále Karla without rest

Úvoz 4 ✉ 118 00 – ✆ 257 531 211 – ukrale@iol.cz – Fax 257 533 5 91
– www.romantichotels.cz **E2**
19 rm ☕ – †3400/5000 CZK ††3900/7500 CZK
♦ Historic ♦ Classic ♦

Below the castle: rebuilt in 1639 into a Baroque house; the style of furniture endures. Bags of character: every bedroom features stained glass and a stencilled wood ceiling.

Neruda

Nerudova 44 ✉ 118 00 – ☎ 257 535 557 – info@hotelneruda.cz – Fax 257 531 4 92 – www.hotelneruda.eu **E2**

42 rm – 3893/4905 CZK 5164/7785 CZK

Rest – Menu 649 CZK

◆ Modern ◆

Castle dominates views from rooftop terrace. Modern style complements 14C ceiling and architecture; poet Neruda's quotes decorate walls. Spacious, well sound-proofed rooms. Simple but attractive café/restaurant offering popular dishes.

Constans

Břetislavova 309 ✉ 110 00 – Ⓜ Malostranská – ☎ 246 020 000 – reservation@hotelconstans.cz – Fax 246 020 1 66 – www.hotelconstans.cz **F2**

31 rm – 2855/6228 CZK 3374/6747 CZK

Rest – Carte 960/1557 CZK

◆ Townhouse ◆ Classic ◆

Three converted townhouses transformed by recent renovation, situated in quiet street. Very spacious bedrooms with period furniture and well equipped, marble bathrooms. International cuisine served in traditional restaurant.

Kampa Park

< Charles Bridge,

Na Kampě 8b, Malá Strana ✉ 118 00 – Ⓜ Malostranská – ☎ 296 826 102 – kontakt@kampapark.com – Fax 257 533 2 23 – www.kampagroup.com **F2**

Rest – *(booking essential at dinner)* Carte 1246/1713 CZK

◆ Modern ◆ Fashionable ◆

Celebrity heavy; stunningly located at water's edge by Charles Bridge. Capacious, contemporary interior; heated terraces: good view likely. Modern global menus.

Terasa U Zlaté Studně – at U Zlaté Studně H.

< Prague,

U Zlaté Studně 4 ✉ 118 00 – Ⓜ Malostranská – ☎ 257 011 213 – restaurant@zlatestudne.cz – Fax 257 533 3 20 – www.terasauzlatestudne.cz **F1**

Rest – Carte 1340/1690 CZK

◆ Modern ◆ Design ◆

Beautiful skyline views from a clean-lined top-floor restaurant and terrace, reached by its own lift. Affable staff; full-flavoured modern dishes.

U Patrona

Dražického Nám. 4 ✉ 118 00 – Ⓜ Malostranská – ☎ 257 530 725 – upatrona@upatrona.cz – Fax 257 530 7 23 – www.upatrona.cz **F2**

Rest – Carte 970/1370 CZK

◆ Traditional ◆ Cosy ◆

Charming period house near Charles Bridge. Elegant ground floor restaurant or larger upstairs room with window into kitchen. French-influenced classics and Czech specialities.

Olympia

Vítězná 7 ✉ 110 00 – Ⓜ Národni Třída – ☎ 251 511 080 – info@olympia-restaurant.cz – Fax 251 511 0 79 – www.olympia-restaurant.cz **F2**

Rest – Carte 350/605 CZK

◆ Traditional ◆ Inn ◆

The menu of Czech specialities is a carnivore's delight, with generous portions and assured flavours. A relaxed and easy-going pub atmosphere pervades this converted bank.

DENMARK

DANMARK

PROFILE

→ **Area:**
43 069 km² (16 629 sq mi) excluding the Faroe Islands and Greenland.

→ **Population:**
5 432 000 inhabitants (est. 2005), density = 126 per km².

→ **Capital:**
Copenhagen (conurbation 1 426 000 inhabitants).

→ **Currency:**
Danish Krone (DKK) divided into 100 øre; rate of exchange: DKK 1 = € 0.13 = US$ 0.19 (Nov 2006).

→ **Government:**
Constitutional parliamentary (single chamber) monarchy (since 1849). Member of European Union since 1973.

→ **Languages:**
Danish; many Danes also understand and speak English.

→ **Specific public holidays:**
Maundy Thursday (the day before Good Friday); Good Friday (Friday before Easter); Prayer Day (4th Friday after Easter); Constitution Day (5 June); Boxing Day (26 December).

→ **Local Time:**
GMT + 1 hour in winter and 2 GMT + 2 hours in summer.

→ **Climate:**
Temperate northern maritime with cold winters and mild summers Copenhagn: January: 1°C, July: 18°C).

→ **International dialling Code:**
00 45 followed by full local number. Directory Enquiries: ✆ **118**; International Directory Enquiries: ✆ **113**.

→ **Emergency:**
Dial ✆ **112** for Police, Ambulance and Fire Brigade.

→ **Electricity:**
220 volts AC, 50Hz; 2-pin round-shaped continental plugs.

→ **Formalities**
Travellers from the European Union (EU), Switzerland, Norway, Iceland and

the main countries of North and South America need a national identity card or passport (America: passport required) to visit Denmark for less than three months (tourism or business purpose). For visitors from other countries a visa may be required, in addition to a passport, especially for those wishing to stay for longer than three months. If you plan to visit Greenland or Faroe Islands while in Denmark, you must purchase a visa in advance in your own country. We advise you to check with your embassy before travelling.

COPENHAGEN

KØBENHAVN

Population: 514 000 (conurbation 1 426 000) Altitude: approx 13m above sea level

Mauritius/PHOTONONSTOP

You have to go right over to the far eastern coast of Denmark to find Copenhagen. It stares straight across the Öresund Straight at Sweden, as though anxious to leave its own shores. They've even built a bridge connecting it to Malmö on the other side. But once you've idled away some time in the Danish capital, you'll wonder why anyone might ever want to leave. This bright, sleek city has a nicely digestible, compact feel and is an easy place to discover on foot. It's a laid-back, hassle-free city generally free from threatening behaviour, and there are lots of elegant, smartly designed buildings to look at. The people fall pretty much into that category, too.

Though Denmark is one of the richest countries in the world, the citizens of Copenhagen are not given to brashness; if anything, they get embarrassed by what they call their provincialism, at being way out on the margins of Europe. But at the same time, they have an infectious enthusiasm for the arts and a world-renowned appreciation of design. Ingest this alongside a good cup of coffee, an open fire and sleek, cosy surroundings, and you'll be partaking of Danish hygge, a word much prized by locals loosely translated as 'warm conviviality'. To the list can now be added good food: fresh regional ingredients have revolutionized the menus of Copenhagen's hip restaurants.

LIVING THE CITY

Some cities overwhelm you, and give the impression that there's too much of them to take in. Not Copenhagen. Most of its key sights are neatly compressed within its central **Slotsholmen** 'island', an area that enjoyed its first golden age in the early seventeenth century in the reign of Christian IV, when it became a harbour of great consequence. It has canals on three sides and opposite the harbour is the area of **Christianshavn**, home of the legendary freewheeling 'free-town' community of Christiania. Further up from the centre are **Nyhavn**, the much-photographed canalside with brightly coloured buildings where the sightseeing cruises leave from, and the elegant **Frederiksstaden**, whose wide streets contain palaces and museums. West of centre is where Copenhageners love to hang out: the **Tivoli Gardens**, a kind of magical fairyland. Slightly more down-to-earth are the western suburbs of Vesterbro and Nørrebro, which were run-down areas given a street credible spit and polish for the 21st century.

PRACTICAL INFORMATION

ARRIVAL-DEPARTURE

Copenhagen Airport is located in Kastrup, 9km southeast of the city. The new extension to the metro allows you to now travel to the centre in 15min. A taxi, meanwhile, will cost about Kr200 and take 25min.

TRANSPORT

If you wish to dart about the city by rail, the metro – opened only in 2002 – is a triumph of sleek, smooth, beautifully detailed efficiency.

Want to see as much of Copenhagen as possible without continually digging into your pocket for cash? Get a Copenhagen Card, which gives free entry to all museums and galleries, as well as free bus, train and metro travel. Get one from the main tourist office just across the road from the central railway station.

It's not every day you're offered a free city bike ride but brightly painted bicycles, lined up in racks, are available for the deposit of a Dkr20 coin. The coin releases a cycle from a stand for an unlimited period and is retrieved when the cycle is returned to any of the 150 stands in the city. It takes about two hours to circumnavigate the major attractions.

It's possible to see the city...by kayak. Kajak Ole (that's Ole's Kayaks) can get you paddling round the central harbour area for a very different perspective. No previous experience is necessary, and it beats taking a crowded bus.

EXPLORING COPENHAGEN

The medieval centre of Copenhagen is a walker's paradise, compounded by the fact that the longest shopping street in Europe, **Strøget**, is these days pedestrianised. (It's actually a collective name for five streets running from east to west, in case you're looking for Strøget on a map). Some of the world's top retail names are squashed into its eastern end, while for half a mile further west run fountains, churches, squares and cafés (and a wealth of shops, of course). The cluster of grand brand names gives a clue to Copenhagen's love affair with design and style. Turn any corner in the central area and you'll find an elegant 17C building rubbing shoulders with a sleek example from the modern age.

The city's royal history stretches back for a millennium, and the rich architectural legacy is seen in its castles, museums and palaces. These merge so well with the new buildings around them that you might well think they were made for each other. The city presents a user-friendly modern ambience with its extensive waterfronts, quirky little shops and hundreds of cafés, but it also boasts world class art collections, museums, and impressive parks, gardens and lakes, all of which bear the mark of an earlier time. A design footprint of impeccable taste remains a pedestrian's constant companion. Even the airport has smart wooden floors and a clean, fresh charm about it.

→ DESIGNED TO PLEASE

The place to go to find out what's causing the latest aesthetic stir is the **Danish Design Centre** just south of Tivoli on the splendidly named Hans Christian Andersens Boulevard. It's a beautiful, five-storey, smoked-glass building opened in 2000 that houses temporary exhibitions and interactive installations. And it's right opposite one of Copenhagen's crown jewels, the nineteenth century **Ny Carlsberg Glyptotek**, which contains a superb art collection including world-renowned French Impressionist paintings housed in a graceful modern extension. To complete a stylish trio, all within the space of half a mile, head to the waterfront to take in the **Black Diamond**, a dramatic name for a radical building. Not yet a decade old, it's the extension to the old Royal Library, and the clash of styles is breathtaking. So is the Black Diamond's reflective surface (made up of glass, silk concrete, sandstone, maple and granite) which changes colour moment by moment as it ripples against the water and sky.

The most recent of the modernist eye-catchers to turn heads is over the canal on Dock Island: the colossal **Opera House** was opened in 2005 and its knife-edge roof abuts the water, leaning across towards the rococo royal palaces on the other side (a fact that horrified some locals at the time). It's nine floors high, on a scale with the Met in New York, and is seen as a kind of gargantuan twin of The Black Diamond. Until recently, Copenhagen was an almost exclusively low-rise city, but these two big, bold intruders have certainly stirred up the cool, calm Danish waters.

→ TIVOLI OR NOT TIVOLI...

For a more traditional experience, it's hard to beat the **National Gallery** (in a lovely park setting in the northern area of Rosenborg), with its superb collection of Matisse paintings, or the National Museum in the heart of town. This imposing centerpiece is housed in a gorgeous one-time royal palace, and boasts some of the finest rooms in the city. It also lays claim to the most extensive collection of Danish artefacts in the world. Star turn must be the 3,500 year-old Sun Chariot unearthed by a Sjaelland farmer in 1902; it's exquisite to look at, still bearing some of its gold leaf. Walk a few blocks down from here and you come to that city icon so traditional that it would make even the Sun Chariot feel like a new cart on the block: the **Tivoli Gardens** seem to have been around forever (they actually opened in 1843) and, judging by admission figures, it seems the whole of Scandinavia has been taken for a ride here. There are roller-coasters, open air shows, troubadours, jugglers, orchestras, parades, ice-cream and beer stands. At night Tivoli turns into a fairyland with over 100,000 lights illuminating the sky as the Demon rollercoaster whirls through the air and fireworks crackle heavenwards. The whole smorgasbord of innocent delights might not be to everyone's taste, considering the refined air of the rest of Copenhagen, but in the end even the biggest cynic is usually won over by the relentlessly magical atmosphere. And if you really can't stand all the showground stuff, you can at least admire the lovely lake, gushing fountains and eye-catching flowerbeds.

→ THE ROYAL FAMILIARITY

It might seem strange to visitors that egalitarian Denmark stands fast behind a monarchy, but the Danes love their populist, chain-smoking Queen Margrethe II, and tourists love to visit where she lives, **Amalienborg Palace,** in the posh Frederiksstaden part of town. Its four palaces stand around a rather grand cobbled square, and when Margrethe is in, a flag flies from the roof. There's a rumour that if they sing loud enough from the new Opera House opposite, the production can be enjoyed from the royal apartments. At the diametrically opposite end of the tourist radar scan, but no less a tourist attraction, is the free state of **Christiania**, an eastern section of Christianshavn that until 1971 was a military camp. When it was abandoned, hundreds of hippies moved in and attracted hundreds more from around Denmark. Their concepts of recycling, solar and wind power have over time become mainstream, and the government has allowed the 'free state' to continue as a social experiment. With three quarters of a million tourists coming to visit a year, an odd 'human zoo' ambience can prevail.

These days, the edgier parts of town are to the west – **Vesterbro** and **Nørrebro.** They offer a couple of interesting alternatives to the city centre for those wanting a taste of how Copenhageners live. Vesterbro was a rough quarter sprawling from the Central station, but regeneration has given it a creative boost, with a younger, racially mixed population running bohemian cafés, trendy clothes emporiums and independent design shops. Nørrebro's deep, dark working-class streets were fashioned in the mid-19th century, and the 1970s and 80s saw a wave of Muslim immigrants come into the area. These days it's home to vinyl stores, junk shops, coffee dens and middle-class teenagers drawn by its ethnic appeal.

COPENHAGEN IN…

→ ONE DAY

Walk along Strøget, visit The National Museum, Ny Carlsberg Glyptotek, Black Diamond on waterfront; sit at Nyhavn and watch the boats go by.

→ TWO DAYS

Spend most of the day in Tivoli Gardens; head on across to the trendy Vesterbro; take in the Opera House and Christiania

→ THREE DAYS

The royal palaces at Frederiksstaden; a train ride along the Danish coastline

CALENDAR HIGHLIGHTS

Spring and summer are the times to visit Copenhagen for its festivals (deepest winter is a time of hibernation in Denmark). You can get your bearings at the May Day Festival when brass bands and marchers descend on Faelled Park (in the shadow of the national stadium in Osterbro) for much food, drink and music. There's more beer to be consumed at the Copenhagen Beer Festival, also in May: you don't just have to put up with Carlsberg here but can enjoy the offerings from microbreweries too. Dance it all off at the Latin American Festival, in venues around the city centre in May, when rhythms from Cuba and Brazil typically include salsa, samba and tango. June kicks off with the Whitsun Carnival in Faelled Park, while lagers are to the fore again at the St Hans Eve Festival, in the same park and along the northern beaches near the city, as locals celebrate the longest day of the year. Northern Europe's largest music festival, a four-day rock jaunt at Roskilde, is a 25-minute train journey away from the capital in June, while jazz lovers can gorge themselves with 600 concerts as the Jazz Festival takes over the city in July. The more sophisticated Ballet Festival, featuring the Royal Danish Ballet, is in August, and pre-1971 Bentleys, Bugattis and Alfa Romeos make their own kind of music at the Copenhagen Historic Grand Prix in the same month. Finally, if you go to see the Little Mermaid while you're in the city, try the 32 August – that was the date in 1913 she was placed in her location at the harbour, so they call it her birthday.

EATING OUT

Copenhagen's reputation for its food just keeps getting bigger and bigger. The city's dining establishments manage to marry Danish dining traditions such as herring or frikkadeller meatballs with global influences to impressive effect. So impressive that in recent times the city has earned itself more Michelin stars, for its crisp and precise cooking, than any other in Scandinavia. Top- and bottom-end restaurants and cafés – those most expensive and those most cheap - are pretty well catered for but the trick is to find one that fits the mid-range, so be warned: you could use up much energy trying to locate a smart restaurant with reasonable prices. Many good restaurants blend French methods and dishes with fresh regional ingredients and innovative touches and there is a trend towards fixed price, no choice menus involving several courses. Danes love their coffee and drink more of it per capita than anywhere else; you're guaranteed a good, strong cup all around the city. There's no need to tip, as it should be included in the cost of the meal. Danes, though, have a very good reputation as cheerful, helpful waiting staff, so you might feel like adding a bit extra.

→ ROUND AND ROUND WE GO

You don't have to go to the top of Black Diamond or the Opera House to get a view over the city. The **Rundetårn** (Round Tower), just off Strøget, is Europe's oldest working observatory, and from the top of its long spiral staircase you get a fine vista of Copenhagen's low-rise symmetry.

→ FALLEN LADY

She may be a tourist attraction, but locals aren't that keen on The **Little Mermaid**. In her near century long residence along the Langelinie docks she's been painted red, had her head hacked off and arm lopped off – and then, in 2003, she was actually bombed into the water! Are residents trying to tell us something?

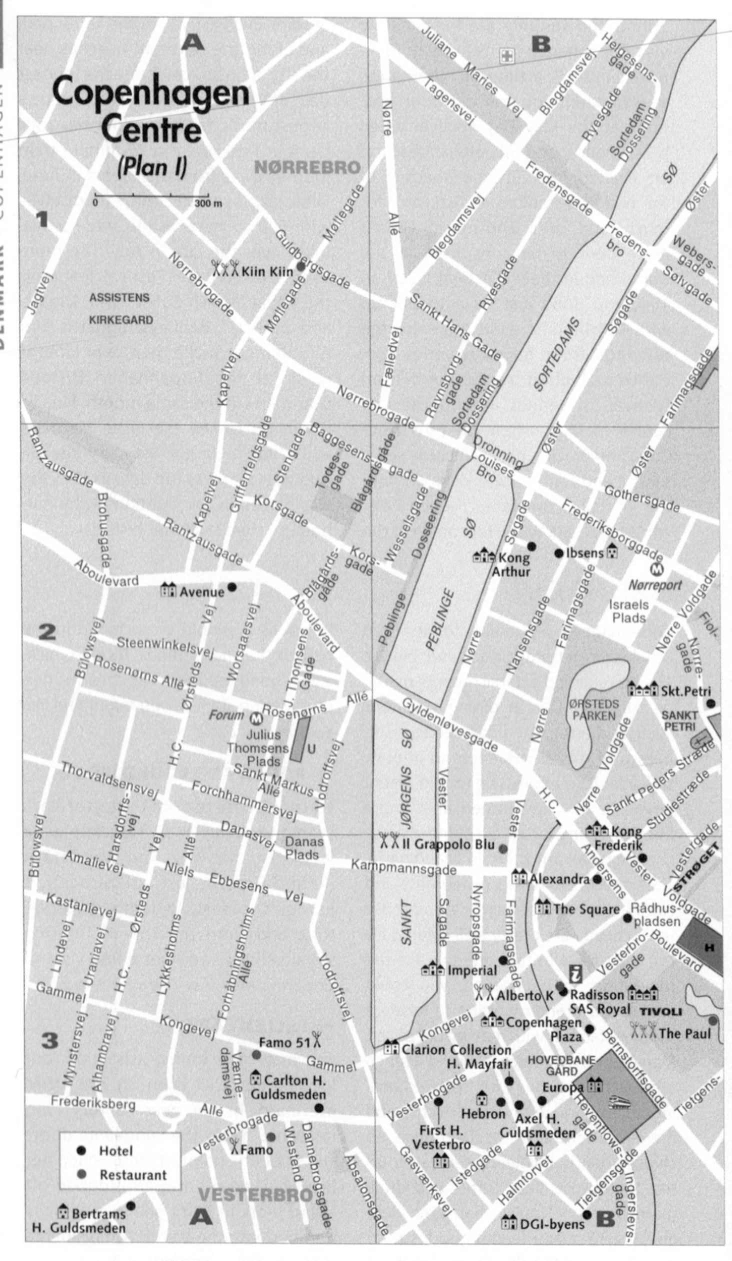
Copenhagen Centre
(Plan I)
0
300 m
A
B
1
2
3
NØRREBRO
VESTERBRO
ASSISTENS KIRKEGARD
SØ
SORTEDAMS
PEBLINGE
SANKT JØRGENS SØ
ØRSTEDS PARKEN
SANKT PETRI
TIVOLI
STRØGET
HOVEDBANE GÅRD
Kiin Kiin
Avenue
Kong Arthur
Ibsens
Nørreport
Israels Plads
Skt.Petri
Forum
Julius Thomsens Plads
Kong Frederik
Il Grappolo Blu
Danas Plads
Alexandra
The Square
Rådhus-pladsen
Imperial
Alberto K
Radisson SAS Royal
Copenhagen Plaza
The Paul
Clarion Collection H. Mayfair
Famo 51
Carlton H. Guldsmeden
Europa
Hebron
Axel H. Guldsmeden
First H. Vesterbro
Famo
DGI-byens
Bertrams H. Guldsmeden
Hotel
Restaurant
Jagtvej
Nørrebrogade
Guldbergsgade
Møllegade
Kapelvej
Fælledvej
Nørre Allé
Juliane Maries Vej
Tagensvej
Blegdamsvej
Helgesensgade
Ryesgade
Sortedam Dossering
Fredensgade
Fredens bro
Webersgade
Sølvgade
Øster Søgade
Sankt Hans Gade
Ravnsborggade
Farimagsgade
Rantzausgade
Brohusgade
Griffenfeldsgade
Stengade
Baggesensgade
Todesgade
Blågårdsgade
Korsgade
Wesselsgade
Peblinge Dossering
Dronning Louises Bro
Gothersgade
Frederiksborggade
Nørre Søgade
Aboulevard
Steenwinkelsvej
Worsaaesvej
J. Thomsens Gade
Bülowsvej
Rosenørns Allé
H.C. Ørsteds Vej
Nansensgade
Nørre Voldgade
Fiolstræde
Nørregade
Gyldenløvesgade
Sankt Markus Allé
Vodroffsvej
Thorvaldsensvej
Forchhammersvej
Sankt Peders Stræde
Studiestræde
H.C. Andersens Boulevard
Harsdorffsvej
Danasvej
Vester Søgade
Vester Farimagsgade
Vestergade
Vester Voldgade
Amalievej
Niels Ebbesens Vej
Kampmannsgade
Nyropsgade
Kastanievej
Lindevej
Uraniavej
Lykkesholms Allé
Forhåbningsholms Allé
Vesterbrogade
Gammel Kongevej
Mynstersvej
Alhambravej
Værnedamsvej
Bernstorffsgade
Tietgensgade
Reventlowsgade
Frederiksberg Allé
Dannebrogsgade
Westend
Absalonsgade
Gasværksvej
Istedgade
Halmtorvet
Ingerslevsgade

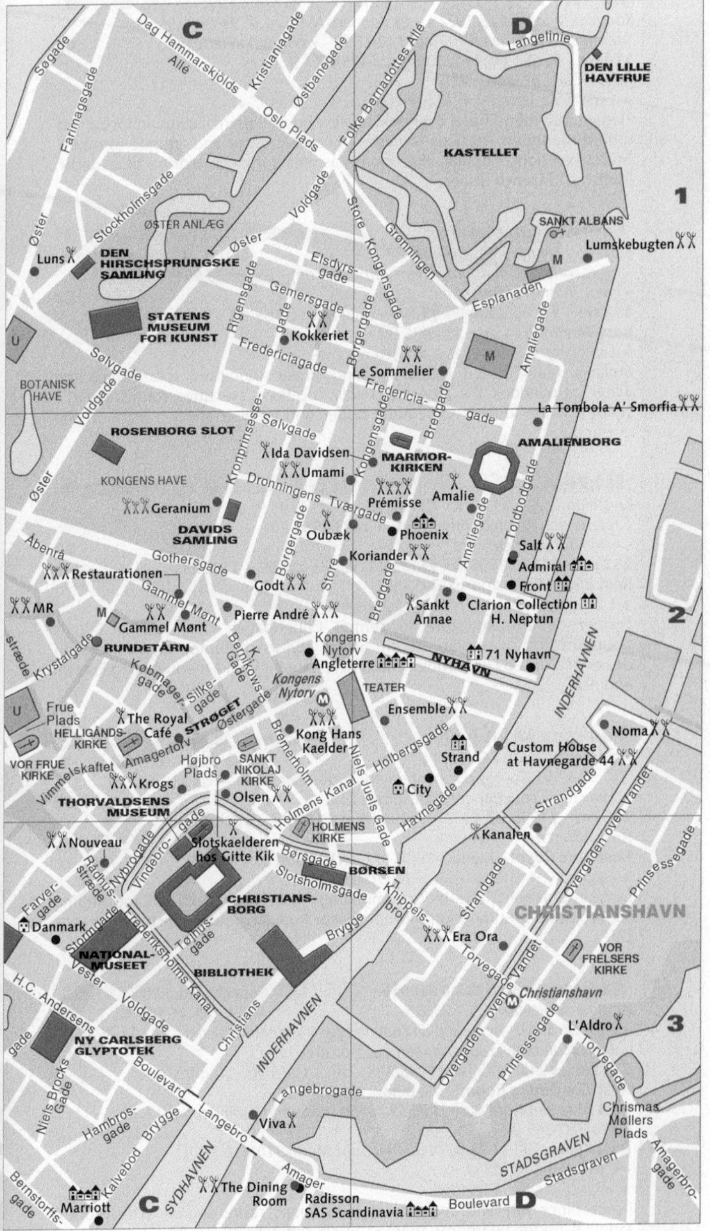

C
D
Dag Hammarskjölds Allé
Kristianiagade
Østbanegade
Folke Bernadottes Allé
Langelinie
DEN LILLE HAVFRUE
KASTELLET
Søgade
Farimagsgade
Oslo Plads
Stockholmsgade
Voldgade
Store Kongensgade
Grønningen
1
SANKT ALBANS
Lumskebugten
ØSTER ANLÆG
Øster
Luns
DEN HIRSCHSPRUNGSKE SAMLING
Elsdyrsgade
Gemersgade
Esplanaden
STATENS MUSEUM FOR KUNST
Rigensgade
Kokkeriet
Fredericiagade
Borgergade
Le Sommelier
Amaliegade
Sølvgade
BOTANISK HAVE
La Tombola A' Smorfia
ROSENBORG SLOT
Kronprinsessegade
Ida Davidsen
MARMORKIRKEN
AMALIENBORG
Umami
KONGENS HAVE
Dronningens Tværgade
Prémisse
Amalie
Geranium
DAVIDS SAMLING
Oubæk
Phoenix
Toldbodgade
Salt
Admiral
Front
Abenrå
Gothersgade
Koriander
Restaurationen
Godt
Sankt Annae
Clarion Collection H. Neptun
MR
Gammel Mønt
Pierre André
2
RUNDETÅRN
Krystalgade
Købmagergade
Kongens Nytorv
Angleterre
NYHAVN
71 Nyhavn
INDERHAVNEN
Silkegade
Kongens Nytorv
TEATER
Frue Plads
The Royal Café
STRØGET
Østergade
Ensemble
Noma
HELLIGÅNDSKIRKE
Kong Hans Kaelder
Strand
Custom House at Havnegarde 44
VOR FRUE KIRKE
Amagertorv
Højbro Plads
SANKT NIKOLAJ KIRKE
Bremerholm
Holbergsgade
Vimmelskaftet
Krogs
City
THORVALDSENS MUSEUM
Olsen
Holmens Kanal
Niels Juels Gade
Havnegade
Strandgade
HOLMENS KIRKE
Kanalen
Nouveau
Slotskaelderen hos Gitte Kik
Børsgade
BØRSEN
Overgaden oven Vandet
Prinsessegade
Rådhusstræde
Nybrogade
Vindebrogade
Slotsholmsgade
Knippelsbro
Farvergade
CHRISTIANSBORG
CHRISTIANSHAVN
Danmark
Frederiksholms Kanal
Tøjhusgade
Brygge
Era Ora
VOR FRELSERS KIRKE
NATIONALMUSEET
BIBLIOTHEK
Torvegade
Vester Voldgade
Christianshavn
H.C. Andersens
INDERHAVNEN
Christians
L'Aldro
3
NY CARLSBERG GLYPTOTEK
Boulevard
Langebrogade
Niels Brocks Gade
Hambrosgade
Langebro
Viva
Chrismas Møllers Plads
STADSGRAVEN
Stadsgraven
Amagerbrogade
Kalvebod Brygge
Amager
Bernstorffsgade
SYDHAVNEN
The Dining Room
Radisson SAS Scandinavia
Boulevard
Marriott

Angleterre

Kongens Nytorv 34 ✉ 1022 K – Ⓜ Kongens Nytorv – ✆ 33 12 00 95 – remmen@remmen.dk – Fax 33 12 11 18 – www.dangleterre.dk **C2**

114 rm – 🚹2650 DKK 🚹🚹4250 DKK, ☕ 175 DKK – 9 suites

Rest – Carte 605/685 DKK

♦ Grand Luxury ♦ Traditional ♦ Classic ♦

Elegant 18C grand hotel overlooking New Royal Square. Luxury in lobby sets tone throughout. Spacious rooms enjoy classic décor and antique furniture. Grand ballroom. Popular afternoon teas. Restaurant in marine blue décor; Danish and French dishes.

Copenhagen Marriott

Kalvebod Brygge 5 ✉ 1560 – ✆ 88 33 99 00 – mhrs.cphdk.reservations@marriotthotels.com – Fax 88 33 99 99 – www.marriott.com/cphdk **C3**

392 rm – 🚹2000/2900 DKK 🚹🚹2000/2900 DKK, ☕ 165 DKK – 9 suites

Rest *Terraneo* – Carte 285/425 DKK

♦ Luxury ♦ Business ♦ Modern ♦

Striking, glass-fronted hotel, its handsomely appointed rooms face the water or overlook the city and Tivoli. Top-floor executive rooms share a stylish private lounge. Lunchtime buffet and Mediterranean cuisine in the evening.

Skt.Petri

Krystalgade 22 ✉ 1172 K – Ⓜ Nørreport – ✆ 33 45 91 00 – reservation@hotelsktpetri.com – Fax 33 45 91 10 – www.hotelsktpetri.com **B2**

257 rm – 🚹1195/1995 DKK 🚹🚹1395/2195 DKK, ☕ DKK – 11 suites

Rest *Bleu* – Carte approx. 295 DKK

♦ Luxury ♦ Business ♦ Design ♦

Former department store in central Copenhagen near old St Peter's Church. Large open-plan atrium. Bright, stylish contemporary rooms with design features by Per Arnoldi. Modern restaurant with a menu mixing Europe and Asia.

Radisson SAS Royal

< Copenhagen,

Hammerichsgade 1 ✉ 1611 V – ✆ 33 42 60 00 – royal.copenhagen@radissonsas.com – Fax 33 42 61 00 – www.royal.copenhagen.radissonsas.com **B3**

258 rm – 🚹1995 DKK 🚹🚹1495/1995 DKK, ☕ 165 DKK – 2 suites

Rest *Alberto K* – see below

Rest *Café Royal* – Menu 345 DKK (dinner) – Carte 395/463 DKK

♦ Luxury ♦ Business ♦ Modern ♦

Large international hotel block dominating the skyline west of Tivoli and offering superb views. Scandinavian bedroom décor. Popular ground floor brasserie style café.

Radisson SAS Scandinavia

< Copenhagen,

Amager Boulevard 70 ✉ 2300 S – ✆ 33 96 50 00 – scandinavia.copenhagen@radissonsas.com – Fax 33 96 55 55 – www.scandinavia.copenhagen.radissonsas.com **C3**

538 rm – 🚹945/1895 DKK 🚹🚹945/1895 DKK, ☕ 175 DKK – 4 suites

Rest *The Dining Room* – see below

Rest *Blue Elephant* – *✆ 33 96 59 70 (Closed Sunday) (dinner only)* Carte 220/545 DKK

Rest *Kyoto* – *✆ 33 32 16 74 (dinner only)* Menu 310/410 DKK – Carte 250/390 DKK

♦ Business ♦ Classic ♦

Tower block hotel with spectacular views. Shops, casino and bar in busy lobby. Original bright bedrooms themed in six different styles. Blue Elephant for authentic Thai cuisine. Kyoto for Japanese menu.

Imperial

Vester Farimagsgade 9 ✉ 1606 V – ✆ 33 12 80 00 – imperialhotel@arp-hansen.dk – Fax 33 93 80 03 – www.imperialhotel.dk **B3**

239 rm – 1265/2155 DKK 1410/2155 DKK, 135 DKK – 1 suite

Rest *The Grill Room* – *(Closed Sunday, July and Bank Holidays) (dinner only)* Carte 350/555 DKK

Rest *Imperial Brasserie* – *✆ 33 43 20 83* – Menu 290 DKK – Carte 355/440 DKK

◆ Traditional ◆ Classic ◆

Large mid 20C hotel, renovated in 2006, on a wide city thoroughfare. Well serviced rooms range in size and are comfortable, stylish and elegantly decorated. The Grill Room boasts resident pianist. Less formal dining in ground floor Brasserie.

Copenhagen Plaza

Bernstorffsgade 4 ✉ 1577 V – ✆ 33 14 92 62 – copenhagenplaza@profilhotels.dk – Fax 33 93 93 62 – www.profilhotels.dk **B3**

87 rm – 1299/2600 DKK 1299/2800 DKK, DKK – 6 suites

Rest *Flora Danica* – *(dinner only)* Menu 285 DKK – Carte approx. 265 DKK

◆ Traditional ◆ Cosy ◆

Venerable hotel commissioned in the early 20C by King Frederik VIII and overlooking Tivoli Gardens. Classically styled, cosy rooms and an atmospheric library bar. A modern, welcoming brasserie with a French-based menu.

Admiral

Toldbodgade 24-28 ✉ 1253 – Ⓜ Kongens Nytorv – ✆ 33 74 14 14 – admiral@admiralhotel.dk – Fax 33 74 14 16 – www.admiralhotel.dk **D2**

366 rm – 1315/1715 DKK 1660/2720 DKK, 120 DKK

Rest *Salt* – see below

◆ Business ◆ Modern ◆

Converted 18C dockside warehouse with some rooms facing passing liners. Maritime theme throughout. Compact bedrooms complement the rustic charm.

Kong Arthur

Nørre Søgade 11 ✉ 1370 K – Ⓜ Nørreport – ✆ 33 11 12 12 – hotel@kongarthur.dk – Fax 33 32 61 30 – www.kongarthur.dk **B2**

117 rm – 1110/1740 DKK 1320/2190 DKK, 125 DKK

Rest *Sticks 'n' Sushi* – *✆ 33 11 14 07* – Menu 168/265 DKK

◆ Traditional ◆ Family ◆ Classic ◆

Pleasant family run hotel on elegant late 19C residential avenue by Peblinge lake. Bedrooms divided between three different buildings. Sticks 'n' Sushi for Japanese dishes.

Kong Frederik

Vester Voldgade 25 ✉ 1552 V – ✆ 33 12 59 02 – remmen@remmen.dk – Fax 33 93 59 01 – www.remmen.dk

Closed Christmas and New Year **B3**

108 rm – 1090/1510 DKK 1510/1930 DKK, 135 DKK – 2 suites

Rest *Le Coq Rouge* – *✆ 33 42 48 48* – Menu 395 DKK (dinner) – Carte 340/445 DKK

◆ Traditional ◆ Classic ◆

Classic elegant old building in good location. Traditional style décor with dark wood panelling. Comfortable rooms with old-fashioned furniture. Atrium style banquet hall. Wood-panelled, atmospheric brasserie offering traditional Danish cooking.

Phoenix

Bredgade 37 ✉ 1260 K – Ⓜ Kongens Nytorv – ✆ 33 95 95 00 – phoenixcopenhagen@arp-hansen.dk – Fax 33 33 98 33 – www.phoenixcopenhagen.dk **D2**

210 rm – 1775/2130 DKK 2825 DKK, 135 DKK – 3 suites

Rest *Von Plessen* – *(Closed Sunday and Monday) (dinner only)* Menu 368 DKK

◆ Traditional ◆ Classic ◆

Parts of this elegant hotel, located in the lively modern art and antiques district, date from the 17C. It features a grand marbled lobby and comfortable high ceilinged rooms. Elegant basement dining room with discreet décor in neutral tones.

Island

Kalvebod Brygge 53 ✉ 1560 – ✆ 33 38 96 00 – copenhagenisland@arp-hansen.dk – Fax 33 38 96 01 – www.copenhagenisland.dk

326 rm – †895/2025 DKK ††1535/3715 DKK, ☕ 135 DKK

Rest *The Harbour* – Menu 330 DKK (dinner) – Carte 294/474 DKK

♦ Business ♦ Design ♦

A gleaming glass and steel structure on a man-made island in the harbour. Vast atrium with suspended walkways. Well-equipped bedrooms, some with balconies. Stylish multi-levelled lounge bar and restaurant with menu for all tastes.

The Square without rest

Rådhuspladsen 14 ✉ 1550 V – ✆ 33 38 12 00 – thesquare@arp-hansen.dk – Fax 33 38 12 01 – www.thesquare.dk **B3**

267 rm – †1740/1990 DKK ††2640/3940 DKK, ☕ 95 DKK

♦ Business ♦ Design ♦

Ideally located hotel in Town Hall Square. Breakfast room on 6th floor with view of city roofs. Good sized modern bedrooms with square theme in décor and fabrics.

Front

Sankt Annae Plads 21 ✉ 1022 K – Ⓜ Kongens Nytorv – ✆ 33 13 34 00 – info@front.dk – Fax 33 11 77 07 – www.front.dk **D2**

132 rm – †1680/1920 DKK ††2950/4920 DKK, ☕ 155 DKK

Rest – Carte 165/195 DKK

♦ Business ♦ Stylish ♦

Behind the understated façade lies a thoroughly modern and stylish hotel. All bedrooms boast plenty of mod cons and the best views are over the dockside. Equally stylish restaurant with a contemporary menu to match.

Strand without rest

Havnegade 37 ✉ 1058 K – Ⓜ Kongens Nytorv – ✆ 33 48 99 00 – copenhagenstrand@arp-hansen.dk – Fax 33 48 99 01 – www.copenhagenstrand.dk **D2**

172 rm – †1540/1730 DKK ††1730 DKK, ☕ 95 DKK – 2 suites

♦ Business ♦ Modern ♦

Modern warehouse conversion on waterfront and a useful central location. Comfortable and well kept bedrooms with dark wood furniture and bright colours.

Avenue without rest

Åboulevard 29, Frederiksberg C ✉ 1960 – Ⓜ Forum – ✆ 35 37 31 11 – info@avenuehotel.dk – Fax 35 37 31 33 – www.avenuehotel.dk

Closed 22 December-2 January **A2**

68 rm ☕ – †975/1275 DKK ††1175/1475 DKK

♦ Business ♦ Design ♦

Restored and refurbished in 2005, the hotel is housed within a building dating from 1898. The smart bedrooms are bright and crisp in style, well equipped and comfortable.

First H. Vesterbro

Vesterbrogade 23-29 ✉ 1620 V – ✆ 33 78 80 00 – reception.copenhagen@firsthotels.dk – Fax 33 78 80 80 – www.firsthotels.com **B3**

399 rm – †1745 DKK ††1145/1945 DKK, ☕ DKK

Rest – *(Closed Sunday) (dinner only)* Carte 80/200 DKK

♦ Business ♦ Modern ♦

Large modern hotel with metal and glass façade on busy avenue. All bedrooms have good modern facilities in a contemporary style; superior rooms are larger. Informal dining in front bar from international menu.

71 Nyhavn

Nyhavn 71 ✉ 1051 K – Ⓜ Kongens Nytorv – ✆ 33 43 62 00 – 71nyhavnhotel@arp-hansen.dk – Fax 33 43 62 01 – www.71nyhavnhotel.dk **D2**

142 rm – 🚹1285/2030 DKK 🚹🚹1850/2485 DKK, ☕ 135 DKK – 8 suites

Rest *Pakhus Kaelder* – *(Closed Sunday and Bank Holidays)* Menu 345 DKK

♦ Business ♦ Stylish ♦

Charming converted warehouse by the canal. Interior features low ceilings with wooden beams throughout. Compact comfortable bedrooms, many with views of passing ships. Cellar restaurant with low wood-beamed ceiling. Interesting, seasonal menus.

Axel H. Guldsmeden

Helgolandsgade 11 ✉ 1653 K – ✆ 33313266 – www.hotelguldsmeden.com **B3**

128 rm ☕ – 🚹1050/1995 DKK 🚹🚹1615/1995 DKK

Rest – *(Residents only)*

♦ Business ♦ Design ♦

Stylish new hotel near central station, with open plan lounge and bar. Up-to-date, comfortable bedrooms decorated in a Balinese style; most with four poster beds, some with balconies. Restaurant and open plan kitchen, where the focus is on organic produce.

Alexandra

H.C. Andersens Boulevard 8 ✉ 1553 V – ✆ 33 74 44 44 – reservations@hotel-alexandra.dk – Fax 33 74 44 88 – www.hotel-alexandra.dk

Closed 24-27 December **B3**

61 rm ☕ – 🚹1225/1625 DKK 🚹🚹1425/2125 DKK

Rest *Mühlhausen* – *✆ 33 74 44 66 (Closed Sunday lunch)* Menu 500 DKK – Carte 295/440 DKK

♦ Traditional ♦ Classic ♦

Classic 19C hotel conveniently located for city centre. Some special design rooms feature Danish style furniture and fittings and an original painting in each. Banquettes and crisp linen in a stylish brasserie with a Mediterranean tone.

Clarion Collection H. Neptun

Sankt Annae Plads 18-20 ✉ 1250 K – Ⓜ Kongens Nytorv – ✆ 33 96 20 00 – cc.neptun@choice.dk – Fax 33 96 20 66 – www.choicehotels.dk

Closed 22 December-3 January **D2**

133 rm ☕ – 🚹895/2395 DKK 🚹🚹995/2995 DKK

Rest *Gendarmen* – *✆ 33 93 66 55 (closed Sunday) (dinner only)* Carte 385/470 DKK

♦ Business ♦ Functional ♦

Converted from two characterful neighbouring houses in the popular Nyhavn district. Rooms are fitted with light wood furniture and offer good range of facilities. Rustic restaurant with traditional Danish menu; courtyard breakfast room.

Europa without rest

Colbjørnsensgade 5-11 ✉ 1652 V – ✆ 33 21 33 33 – co.europa@choice.dk – Fax 33 31 33 99 – www.choicehotels.dk **B3**

230 rm – 🚹695/1895 DKK 🚹🚹745/3100 DKK, ☕ 95 DKK

♦ Chain hotel ♦ Modern ♦

Centrally located chain hotel fully renovated in 2002. Bedrooms are compact but tidy and decorated in a bright Nordic style. Comfortable breakfast room.

DGI-byen

Tietgensgade 65 ✉ 1704 V – ✆ 33 29 80 00 – info@dgi-byen.dk – Fax 33 29 80 80 – www.dgi-byen.dk

Closed 22-27 December **B3**

104 rm ☕ – 🚹1395/1495 DKK 🚹🚹1595 DKK

Rest *Vestauranten* – *✆ 33 29 80 30* – Menu 150/295 DKK

♦ Business ♦ Functional ♦

Turn of millennium hotel, part of huge, modern leisure complex with all the equipment. Minimalist bedrooms with simple, clean style and up-to-date facilities. Bright restaurant in original building offering a varied menu; pleasant terrace.

Clarion Collection H. Mayfair without rest
Helgolandsgade 3 ✉ 1653 V – ✆ 70 12 17 00
– cc.mayfair@choice.dk – Fax 33 23 96 86 – www.choicehotels.dk
Closed 22 December-3 January **B3**
99 rm – 695/1995 DKK 995/2396 DKK – 3 suites
◆ Business ◆ Functional ◆
Large well run hotel usefully located near station. Interior décor and furniture in classic English style. Neat rooms, well equipped with mod cons. Relaxing bar.

City without rest
Peder Skrams Gade 24 ✉ 1054 K – Ⓜ Kongens Nytorv – ✆ 33 13 06 66
– hotelcity@hotelcity.dk – Fax 33 13 06 67 – www.hotelcity.dk **D2**
81 rm – 1050/1350 DKK 1550 DKK
◆ Business ◆ Functional ◆
Usefully positioned, functional hotel between the city centre and docks. Simple and tidy Danish style interior décor with appropriate room facilities.

Danmark without rest
Vester Voldgade 89 ✉ 1552 V – ✆ 33 11 48 06 – hotel@hotel-danmark.dk
– Fax 33 14 36 30 – www.hotel-danmark.dk **C3**
88 rm – 1130/1290 DKK 1320/2100 DKK, 75 DKK
◆ Business ◆ Classic ◆
Centrally located close to Tivoli Gardens, offers well kept functional rooms with traditional Scandinavian style décor. Newer rooms in older building are the best.

Bertrams H. Guldsmeden
Vesterbrogade 107 ✉ 1620 V – ✆ 33 25 04 05 – bertrams@hotelguldsmeden.dk
– Fax 33 25 04 02 – www.hotelguldsmeden.dk **A3**
47 rm – 995/1495 DKK 1295/1795 DKK, 100 DKK
Rest – *(Closed Sunday) (dinner only)* Menu 225 DKK
◆ Family ◆ Personalised ◆
Opened in 2006 and sister hotel to Guldsmeden. It shares the same bright décor with most bedrooms looking out onto a courtyard. Four poster beds and balconies also available. Organic breakfasts and a warm, café style restaurant with set menu.

Ibsens
Vendersgade 23 ✉ 1363 K – Ⓜ Nørreport – ✆ 33 13 19 13
– hotel@ibsenshotel.dk – Fax 33 13 19 16 – www.ibsenshotel.dk **B2**
118 rm – 990/1240 DKK 1310/2400 DKK
Rest *La Rocca* – Menu 365 DKK
Rest *Pintxos* – Menu 168/265 DKK
◆ Business ◆ Classic ◆
Large characterful converted apartment block next to sister hotel Kong Arthur. Variety of neat rooms with good facilities. Superior top floor bedrooms. Modern La Rocca for formal Italian dining. Pintxos offers authentic Spanish tapas dinner menu.

Carlton H. Guldsmeden without rest
Vesterbrogade 66 ✉ 1620 V – ✆ 33 22 15 00 – carlton@hotelguldsmeden.dk
– Fax 33 22 15 55 – www.hotelguldsmeden.dk **A3**
64 rm – 995/1295 DKK 1195/1795 DKK
◆ Family ◆ Personalised ◆
Family owned hotel. Indonesian and Mexican furniture in rooms; most have four posters; some have balconies; those in annex are quieter. Cycles for hire. Extensive organic breakfasts.

Hebron without rest
Helgolandsgade 4 ✉ 1653 V – ✆ 33 31 69 06 – info@hebron.dk
– Fax 33 31 90 67 – www.hebron.dk – Closed Christmas **B3**
93 rm – 950/1150 DKK 1250/1550 DKK – 6 suites
◆ Traditional ◆ Functional ◆
When it opened in 1900 it was one of the biggest hotels in the city and some of the original features remain. Simple, clean and uncluttered bedrooms.

XXXX

Prémisse

Dronningens Tvaergade 2 ✉ 1302 K – Ⓜ Kongens Nytorv – ☎ 33 11 11 45 – mail@premisse.dk – Fax 33 11 11 68 – www.premisse.dk

Closed July, Easter, 23 December-3 January and Sunday **D2**

Rest – *(dinner only and Saturday lunch)* Menu 850 DKK – Carte 760/1000 DKK

♦ Innovative ♦ Formal ♦

17C vaulted cellar restaurant further enhanced by stylish, modern décor. Wine cellar on view. Open-plan kitchen serving uncompromisingly adventurous menu with original flavours.

XXX ✿

Geranium (Søren Ledet/Rasmus Kofoed)

Kronprinsessegade 13 ✉ 1306 K – ☎ 33 11 13 04 – info@restaurantgeranium.dk – www.restaurantgeranium.dk

Closed 22 December-15 January, Saturday lunch, Sunday and Monday **C2**

Rest – *(booking essential) (set menu only)* Menu 428/838 DKK

Spec. Smoked cream cheese with cod cheeks and caviar. Free range pork with watercress and wild mushrooms. Elderflower jelly, chocolate foam and frozen elderflower juice.

♦ Innovative ♦ Design ♦

Delightfully located in 19C summer house in the King's Garden; passionate kitchen produces flavourful, original dishes made from organic, bio-dynamic ingredients. 100 % organic wine list.

XXX ✿

Kong Hans Kaelder

Vingårdsstraede 6 ✉ 1070 K – Ⓜ Kongens Nytorv – ☎ 33 11 68 68 – kontakt@konghans.dk – Fax 33 32 67 68 – www.konghans.dk

Closed 3 weeks July, Easter, Christmas and Bank Holidays **C2**

Rest – *(booking essential) (dinner only)* Carte 855/865 DKK

Spec. Roast langoustines with brown butter vinaigrette and seaberries. Fillet of Danish beef with mead and oxtail sauce. Valrhona chocolate with seasonal fruit and berries.

♦ Modern ♦ Formal ♦

Discreetly located side street restaurant in vaulted Gothic cellar with wood flooring. Fine dining experience; classically based cooking. Friendly and dedicated service.

XXX ✿

Formel B (Rune Jochumsen/Kristian Møller)

Vesterbrogade 182-184, Frederiksberg (via Vesterbrogade) ✉ 1800 C – ☎ 33 25 10 66 – info@formel-b.dk – www.formel-b.dk

Closed 13-29 July, 23-26 December, first week January and Sunday

Rest – *(booking essential) (dinner only)* Menu 800 DKK

Spec. Langoustines with baby vegetables and pickled green tomato. Fillet of beef with foie gras and truffle sauce. Vanilla poached pear with chocolate soufflé and sorbet.

♦ Innovative ♦ Design ♦

Sleek, intimate restaurant dominated by open plan kitchen. Young, dynamic team serve precisely crafted, classically based cooking which uses top quality ingredients. Well chosen wines and beautiful china.

XXX

Restaurationen

Møntergade 19 ✉ 1116 K – Ⓜ Kongens Nytorv – ☎ 33 14 94 95 – Fax 33 14 85 30 – www.restaurationen.com

Closed July-August, 22 December-8 January, Easter, Sunday, Monday and Bank Holidays **C2**

Rest – *(booking essential) (dinner only)(set menu only)* Menu 700 DKK

♦ Classic ♦ Friendly ♦

A long standing and personally run restaurant. Accomplished classically based Danish cooking using well sourced ingredients, accompanied by a comprehensive wine list.

XXX

Pierre André

VISA MC AE

Ny Østergade 21 ✉ 1101 K – Ⓜ Kongens Nytorv – ✆ 33 16 17 19 – Fax 33 16 17 72 – www.pierreandre.dk

Closed 3 weeks summer, Easter, Christmas-New Year, Sunday, Monday, Saturday lunch and Bank Holidays **C2**

Rest – *(booking essential)* Menu 395/820 DKK – Carte 545/675 DKK

♦ French ♦ Formal ♦

Elegant, comfortable dining room with stylish décor in an attractive old building. Full-flavoured cuisine on a classical French base. Efficient and attentive service.

XXX

Krogs

AC VISA MC AE

Gammel Strand 38 ✉ 1201 K – ✆ 33 15 89 15 – krogs@krogs.dk – Fax 33 15 83 19 – www.krogs.dk

Closed 22 December-1 January and Sunday **C2**

Rest – *(booking essential) (dinner only)* Menu 750 DKK – Carte 695/2250 DKK

♦ Seafood ♦ Formal ♦

Characterful 18C house pleasantly located by canal. Classic room with high ceiling, well lit through large end window. Formal service; seafood dishes attractively presented.

XXX ✿

Kiin Kiin (Lertchai Treetawatchaiwong)

AC VISA MC AE

Guldbergsgade 21 ✉ 2200 – ✆ 35 35 75 55 – kiin@kiin.dk – Fax 35 35 75 59 – www.kiin.dk

Closed Christmas and Sunday **A1**

Rest – *(booking essential) (dinner only) (set menu only)* Menu 650 DKK

Spec. Frozen red curry with lobster and fresh coriander seeds. Quail in coconut with holy basil and crisp onions. Passion fruit with lemongrass and pandanus leaves.

♦ Thai ♦ Exotic ♦

Thai design and furnishings in comfortable, semi-basement sitting room; spacious first floor dining room - table 9 would suit romantics. Precise, authentic modern Thai cooking with delicate, balanced flavours.

XXX ✿

Era Ora

VISA MC AE

Overgaden neden Vandet 33B ✉ 1414 K – Ⓜ Christianshavn – ✆ 32 54 06 93 – era-ora@era-ora.dk – Fax 32 96 02 09 – www.era-ora.dk

Closed 24-26 December, 1 January and Sunday **D3**

Rest – *(booking essential at dinner) (set menu only)* Menu 325/780 DKK

Spec. Antipasti. Veal with eggplant, caper and parsley sauce. Lemon and white chocolate ganache with dark chocolate mousse and sharon fruit sauce.

♦ Italian ♦ Formal ♦

Discreetly located, stylish canalside restaurant serving precise, well conceived Italian cooking, with wines expertly chosen to complement the food. Professional, formal service.

XX ✿

Ensemble (Martin Schou)

VISA MC AE

Tordenskjoldsgade 11 ✉ 1055 K – Ⓜ Kongens Nytorv – ✆ 33 11 33 52 – kontakt@restaurantensemble.dk – Fax 33 11 33 92 – www.restaurantensemble.dk

Closed July, 2 weeks Christmas, Easter, Sunday and Monday **D2**

Rest – *set menu only (dinner only)* Menu 450/700 DKK

Spec. Oysters with breadcrumbs, Ventrèche bacon and parsley. Pigeon with chips, butternut squash and béarnaise sauce. Salt caramel with marjoram gel and fresh English liquorice.

♦ Modern ♦ Formal ♦

Whites, greys and ultra bright lighting add to clean, fresh feel. Open-plan kitchen serves 6 course set menu; well crafted, original dishes make use of good quality ingredients. Formal service.

XX ✿✿ **Noma** (Rene Redzepi)

Strandgade 93 ✉ 1401 K – Ⓜ Christianshavn – ✆ 32 96 32 97 – noma@noma.dk – www.noma.dk

Closed 3 weeks July, 23-26 December, Easter Monday, Sunday and lunch Monday and Saturday **D2**

Rest – Menu 350/675 DKK – Carte 675/950 DKK

Spec. King crab and leeks with mussel stock. Musk ox with milk skin and unripe elderberries. Garden sorrel and glazed sheep's milk mousse.

♦ Innovative ♦ Design ♦

Splendidly innovative, stimulating cuisine which tests the culinary boundaries and utilises quality ingredients from the Nordic countries. Stylish interior has a charming rustic simplicity.

XX ✿ **MR** (Mads Refslund)

Kultorvet 5 ✉ 1175 K – ✆ 33 91 09 49 – mr@mr-restaurant.dk – www.mr-restaurant.dk

Closed 20 December-3 January, 1 week Easter and Sunday **C2**

Rest – *(booking essential) (dinner only)* Menu 600 DKK – Carte approx. 815 DKK

Spec. Langoustines in milk skin, aroma of smoke and woodruff. Lamb sweetbread, sea snails and fiddlehead fern. Olive oil jelly with roast bread and citrus.

♦ Modern ♦ Fashionable ♦

18C three-storey town house on paved square. Stylish ground floor lounge with squashy sofas. First floor restaurant serves accomplished, innovative dishes. Knowledgeable service.

XX **Koriander**

Store Kongensgade 34 ✉ 1264 K – Ⓜ Kongens Nytorv – ✆ 33 15 03 15 – mail@restaurantkoriander.dk – www.restaurantkoriander.dk

Closed 24 to 27 December **C2**

Rest – *(dinner only)* Carte 630/835 DKK

♦ Indian ♦ Exotic ♦

Charming both without and within: ornate décor that includes eye-catching lampshades, swags and curtains. Contemporary Indian cooking with subtle French influences.

XX **Kokkeriet**

Kronprinsessegade 64 ✉ 1306 K – ✆ 33 15 27 77 – info@kokkeriet.dk – Fax 33 15 27 75 – www.kokkeriet.dk

Closed Easter, 12-18 February, 22 July-11 August, 14-20 October, 23-26 & 31 December, Sunday and Monday **C1**

Rest – *(dinner only)* Menu 650 DKK – Carte 600/950 DKK

♦ Modern ♦ Neighbourhood ♦

Smart, intimate restaurant with neighbourhood feel and stylish furnishings. Inventive modern menu offering 5-7 courses with wine to match. Enthusiastic service.

XX **Nouveau**

Magstræde 16 ✉ 1204 K – ✆ 33 16 12 92 – mail@restaurantnouveau.dk – www.restaurantnouveau.dk

Closed 22 December-5 January 3 weeks July, Sunday and Bank Holidays **C3**

Rest – *(dinner only)* Menu 650 DKK – Carte approx. 570 DKK

♦ Innovative ♦ Rustic ♦

Simply furnished three-storey 18C house. Experienced chef has a sure touch and an understated style, creating original, well balanced dishes from top quality ingredients.

XX **Godt**

Gothersgade 38 ✉ 1123 K – Ⓜ Kongens Nytorv – ✆ 33 15 21 22 – restaurant.godt@get2net.dk – www.restaurant-godt.dk

Closed 12-18 February, 18-24 March, 1 July-4 August, 14-19 October, 23 December-5 January, Sunday, Monday and Bank Holidays **C2**

Rest – *((dinner only)(set menu only)* Menu 480/640 DKK

♦ Classic ♦ Design ♦

Small, stylish modern two floor restaurant with grey décor, ceiling fans and old WWII shells as candle holders. Personally run. Classic fare in three, four or five courses.

XX **The Dining Room** – at Radisson SAS Scandinavia H.
25th Floor, ≤ Copenhagen, ⇄ P VISA MC AE D
Amager Boulevard 70 ✉ 2300 S – ✆ 33 96 58 58 – info@thediningroom.dk
– Fax 33 96 55 00 – www.thediningroom.dk
Closed Sunday and Monday **C3**
Rest – *(dinner only)* Carte 345/475 DKK
♦ Modern ♦ Design ♦
Situated on the 25th floor of the hotel but run independently and providing diners with wonderful panoramic views of the city. Original and modern menu.

XX **Umami** AC VISA MC AE D
Store Kongensgade 59 ✉ 1264 – Ⓜ Kongens Nytorv – ✆ 33 38 75 00
– mail@restaurantumami.dk – Fax 33 38 75 15 – www.restaurantumami.dk
Closed 23 December-3 January **C-D2**
Rest – *(dinner only)* Menu 525/850 DKK – Carte 310/490 DKK
♦ Japanese ♦ Fashionable ♦
Elegant and contemporary with stylish wood tables and eating options on two floors: sushi bar, ancillary dining area or spacious main dining room. Modern Japanese dishes.

XX **Custom House at Havnegade 44** ≤ Harbour and
Havnegade 44 Christianshavn, AC ⇄ VISA MC AE D
✉ 1058 – Ⓜ Kongens Nytorv – ✆ 33 31 01 03 – info@customhouse.dk
– Fax 33 31 01 29 – www.customhouse.dk **D2**
Rest *Bacino* – Menu 311/577 DKK – Carte 255/544 DKK
Rest *Ebisu* – Menu 177/611 DKK – Carte 277/511 DKK
Rest *Bar and Grill* – Carte 244/866 DKK
♦ Modern ♦ Design ♦
Converted quayside customs building with harbour views and a choice of three restaurants. Bacino for Italian food. Ebisu is the first floor Japanese with a sushi counter. The busy Bar and Grill on the ground floor is the most informal.

XX **Alberto K** – at Radisson SAS Royal H. ≤ Copenhagen, AC
Hammerichsgade 1 ✉ 1611 V – ✆ 33 42 60 00 P VISA MC AE D
– copenhagen@radissonsas.com – Fax 33 42 61 00 **B3**
Rest – *(dinner only)* Menu 555/695 DKK
♦ Italian influences ♦ Design ♦
Italian-influenced cuisine and terrific views are the attractions at this restaurant on the 20th floor of the Radisson SAS Royal Hotel. Open kitchen and a modern design; friendly service.

XX **Il Grappolo Blu** VISA MC AE D
Vester Farimagsgade 35 ✉ 1606 V – ✆ 33 11 57 20 – ilgrappoloblu@ilgrappoloblu.com – Fax 33 12 57 20 – www.ilgrappoloblu.com
Closed July, Easter, Christmas-New Year, Sunday, Monday and Bank Holidays **B3**
Rest – *(dinner only) (set menu only)* Menu 320/680 DKK
♦ Italian ♦ Friendly ♦
Behind the unpromising façade lies this friendly restaurant, personally run by the owner. Ornate wood panelling and carving. Authentic Italian dishes that just keep on coming.

XX **Frederiks Have** VISA MC AE D
Smallegade 41/Virgina Vej (West : 1 1/2 km via Gammel Kongevej)
✉ 2000 Frederiksberg – Ⓜ Frederiksberg – ✆ 38 88 33 35 – info@frederikshave.dk – Fax 38 88 33 37 – www.frederikshave.dk
Closed 22 December-7 January, Easter and Sunday
Rest – Menu 235/328 DKK – Carte 390/473 DKK
♦ Modern ♦ Neighbourhood ♦
Established restaurant in leafy residential district. Homely ambience and delightful terrace. Monthly menus offer traditional and modern Danish cooking.

XX

Gammel Mønt

Gammel Mønt 41 ✉ 1117 K – Ⓜ Kongens Nytorv – ✆ 33 15 10 60 – info@gammel-moent.dk – Fax 33 15 10 60 – www.gammel-moent.dk
closed Easter, 22 June-15 August, 22 December-8 January, Saturday, Sunday and Bank Holidays **C2**
Rest – *(lunch only)* Menu 275/650 DKK – Carte 245/495 DKK
♦ Traditional ♦ Cosy ♦
Half-timbered house from 1732 with striking red façade in smart commercial district. Traditional cuisine with seasonal variations and interesting range of herring dishes.

XX

Le Sommelier

Bredgade 63-65 ✉ 1260 K – ✆ 33 11 45 15 – mail@lesommelier.dk – Fax 33 11 59 79 – www.lesommelier.dk
Closed Saturday and Sunday **D1**
Rest – Menu 385 DKK – Carte 355/490 DKK
♦ French ♦ Brasserie ♦
Popular brasserie in the heart of the old town. The owners' passion for wine shows in posters, memorabilia and a good "by glass" list. Classic French cooking.

XX

Salt – at Admiral H.

Toldbodgade 24-28 ✉ 1253 – Ⓜ Kongens Nytorv – ✆ 33 74 14 44 – info@saltrestaurant.dk – Fax 33 74 14 16 **D2**
Rest – Menu 360 DKK
♦ Modern ♦ Design ♦
Conran-designed restaurant in 18C warehouse; outdoor summer tables. Only sea salt is used. Danish buffet and modern à la carte at midday; more extensive modern dinner menu.

XX

LaTombola A'Smorfia

Toldbodgade 55 ✉ 1253 – ✆ 33 14 57 20 – info@latombola.dk – Fax 33 15 57 20 – www.latombola.dk
Closed Christmas-New Year, Easter, Sunday and lunch November-May **D2**
Rest – Menu 353 DKK (lunch) – Carte dinner 413/438 DKK
♦ Italian ♦ Brasserie ♦
Spacious and airy Italian brasserie, sister to Il Grappolo Blu. Decorated with tombola-themed numbers, with the chance to win your meal for free! Daily changing dishes with Neapolitan specialities.

XX

Lumskebugten

Esplanaden 21 ✉ 1263 K – ✆ 33 15 60 29 – Fax 33 32 87 18 – www.lumskebugten.dk
Closed 22 December-2 January, Sunday and Saturday lunch **D1**
Rest – Menu 425 DKK (dinner) – Carte 375/605 DKK
♦ Traditional ♦ Cosy ♦
Mid 19C café-pavilion near quayside and Little Mermaid. Interesting 19C maritime memorabilia and old paintings. Good traditional cuisine. Possibility of dining on boat.

XX

Olsen

Ved Stranden 18 ✉ 1061 – ✆ 33 14 64 00 – Fax 33 14 64 01 – www.restaurantolsen.com
Closed Sunday **C2**
Rest – *(dinner only)* Menu 395 DKK – Carte 405/475 DKK
♦ Modern ♦ Fashionable ♦
Centrally located restaurant boasts relaxing, though buzzy, vibe with terrace and canal views. Intimate, popular bar. Tightly packed dining tables: the place to be seen! Interesting seasonal menus with a Norwegian base.

Kanalen

VISA AE

Christianshavn-Wilders Plads 1-3 ✉ 1403 K – Ⓜ Christianshavn – ☎ 32 95 13 30 – info@restaurant-kanalen.dk – Fax 32 95 13 38 – www.restaurant-kanalen.dk

Closed 23-30 December, Sunday and Bank Holidays **D3**

Rest – *(booking essential) (set menu only at dinner)* Menu 290/360 DKK – Carte 360/538 DKK

♦ Modern ♦ Friendly ♦

Delightfully located former Harbour Police office on canalside. Simple elegant décor, informal yet personally run. Well balanced menu of modern Danish cooking.

Famo 51

VISA

Gammel Kongevej 51 ✉ 1610 – ☎ 33 22 22 50 – famo@mail.tele.dk – www.osteriafamo.dk

Closed July, Easter, Christmas and Sunday **A3**

Rest – *(booking essential) (dinner only)* Menu 400 DKK

♦ Italian ♦ Neighbourhood ♦

Relaxed restaurant with unostentatious interior and intimate two-tabled cellar. 10 course daily-changing menu of rustic Italian cooking; with fresh, unfussy flavours - each course a surprise.

Oubaek

VISA AE

Store Kongensgade 52 ✉ 1264 – Ⓜ Kongens Nytorv – ☎ 33 32 32 09 – rasmus-oubaek@mail.dk – www.rasmusoubaek.dk

Closed 18 July-5 August, 20 December-6 January, Easter, Saturday and Sunday **C-D2**

Rest – Menu 225 DKK (lunch) – Carte 300/380 DKK

♦ Classic ♦ Bistro ♦

Unpretentious restaurant with tables on mezzanine level above kitchen. Offers carefully prepared, classic and familiar bistro dishes at a competitive price. Informal and friendly service.

Famo

VISA

Saxogade 3 ✉ 1662 – ☎ 33 23 22 50 – famo@mail.tele.dk – www.osteriafamo.dk

Closed July, Easter, Christmas and Monday **A3**

Rest – *(booking essential) (dinner only)(set menu only)* Menu 350 DKK

♦ Italian ♦ Bistro ♦

Simple, personally run Italian eatery that feels like an osteria; opened in 2005. No written menus: owners propose the day's good value, authentic regional dishes. Chatty, attentive service completes the picture.

M/S Amerika

VISA AE

Dampfaergevej 8 (Pakhus 12, Amerikakaj) (via Folke Bernadottes Allée) ✉ 2100 K – ☎ 35 26 90 30 – info@msamerika.dk – Fax 35 26 91 30 – www.msamerika.dk

Closed 24 December-2 January, Sunday and Bank Holidays

Rest – Menu 275/345 DKK – Carte 350/458 DKK

♦ Modern ♦ Brasserie ♦

Characterful 19C former warehouse in attractive quayside location with popular summer terrace. Lunch quite simple and traditional; more contemporary at dinner.

Fiasco

VISA AE

Gammel Kongevej 176, Frederiksberg (via Gammel Kongevej) ✉ 1850 C – ☎ 33 31 74 87 – fiasco@tiscali.dk – Fax 33 31 74 87

Closed July, Christmas-New Year, Sunday and Monday

Rest – *(dinner only) (set menu only)* Menu 275/335 DKK

♦ Italian ♦ Friendly ♦

Modern Italian restaurant to the west of the city centre. Bright room with fresh feel and large picture windows. Friendly young owners. Carefully prepared, authentic cuisine.

L'Altro

Torvegade 62 ✉ 1400 K – Ⓜ Christianshavn – ✆ 32 54 54 06 – laltro@laltro.dk – Fax 32 54 54 06 – www.laltro.dk

Closed 24-26 December, 1 January and Sunday **D3**

Rest – *(booking essential) (dinner only) (set menu only)* Menu 298/420 DKK

♦ Italian ♦ Intimate ♦

Little sister to Era Ora, well priced Tuscan and Umbrian home cooking is the feature here. Divided between the ground floor and a characterful wine cellar basement.

Viva

Langebrogade Kaj 570 ✉ 1411 K – Ⓜ Christianshavn – ✆ 27 25 05 05 – viva@restaurantviva.dk – www.restaurantviva.dk

Closed 22 December-3 January **C3**

Rest – Menu 265/345 DKK – Carte 295/405 DKK

♦ Modern ♦ Minimalist ♦

Converted German tug boat moored on the river; stylish minimalist interior and top deck terrace. Eclectic menu with strong Danish note at lunch.

Luns

Øster Farimagsgade 12 ✉ 2100 – ✆ 35 26 33 35 – www.restaurantluns.dk

Closed July-August, Easter,Christmas, Sunday-Tuesday and Bank Holidays **C1**

Rest – *(booking essential) (dinner only)* Carte 250/275 DKK

♦ Home cooking ♦ Rustic ♦

Opened in 2005: simple rustic neighbourhood eatery that's quickly become locally renowned. Owner cooks and serves set menus of good value rural French fare. You can eat from two to five courses in totally relaxed surroundings.

IN TIVOLI

The Paul (Paul Cunningham)

Vesterbrogade 3 ✉ 1630 K – ✆ 33 75 07 75 – info@thepaul.dk – Fax 33 75 07 76 – www.thepaul.dk

Closed mid September-mid November, Christmas Eve-mid April and Sunday **B3**

Rest – *(set menu only)* Menu 450/800 DKK

Spec. Danish turbot with celeriac, truffle and woodland herbs. Langoustine and grilled rabbit with fennel aïoli and apple. Roast mandarin consommé and olive oil sorbet.

♦ Innovative ♦ Elegant ♦

Elegant glass-domed 20C structure by the lake in Tivoli Gardens. Open-plan kitchen with chef's table. Set menus make excellent use of Danish produce; original and precise cooking, attentive service.

SMØRREBRØD *The following list of simpler restaurants and cafés/bars specialise in Danish open sandwiches and are generally open from 10.00am to 4.00pm.*

The Royal Cafe

Amagertorv 6 ✉ 1160 K – ✆ 38 14 95 27 – www.theroyalcafe.dk **C2**

Rest – *(lunch only)* Menu 120 DKK

♦ Modern ♦ Fashionable ♦

Part of the world renowned china shop, The Royal Copenhagen, this narrow, quirkily-designed 'café' has become the place to be, taking smørrebrød into the 21C; crossing them with sushi to create intricate 'smushies'.

Amalie
VISA MC AE

Amaliegade 11 ✉ 1256 K – Ⓜ Kongens Nytorv – ✆ 33 12 88 10 – jjmaltesen@mail.dk – Fax 33 12 88 10
Closed July, Easter, Christmas-New Year, Sunday and Bank Holidays **D2**
Rest – *(booking essential) (lunch only)* Menu 198 DKK – Carte 196/280 DKK
◆ Traditional ◆ Friendly ◆
Located in a pretty 18C town house. Wood panelled walls and a clean, uncluttered style. Helpful service and ideal for those looking for an authentic, traditional Danish lunch.

Slotskælderen hos Gitte Kik
VISA MC AE

Fortunstræ 4 ✉ 1065 K – ✆ 33 11 15 37
Closed July, Sunday, Monday and Bank Holidays **C2**
Rest – *(booking essential) (lunch only)* Carte 45/90 DKK
◆ Traditional ◆ Family ◆
Serving authentic homemade smørrebrød, this restaurant is the benchmark for this style of Danish cuisine; its walls filled with family portraits and cityscapes. Choose your dishes at the counter - 3 should suffice.

Sankt Annae
VISA MC AE

Sankt Annae Plads 12 ✉ 1250 K – Ⓜ Kongens Nytorv – ✆ 33 12 54 97 – Fax 33 15 16 61 – www.restaurantsanktannae.dk **D2**
Rest – *(lunch only)* Carte 150/250 DKK
◆ Traditional ◆ Friendly ◆
Pretty terraced building in popular part of town. Simple décor with a rustic feel and counter next to kitchen. Typical menu of smørrebrød. Service prompt and efficient.

Ida Davidsen
VISA MC AE

Store Kongensgade 70 ✉ 1264 K – Ⓜ Kongens Nytorv – ✆ 33 91 36 55 – reservation@idadavidsen.dk – Fax 33 11 36 55 – www.idadavidsen.dk
Closed 1 July-4 August, 22 December-11 January, 20-24 March Saturday, Sunday and Bank Holidays **D2**
Rest – *(lunch only)* Carte 165/185 DKK
◆ Traditional ◆ Family ◆
Family run for five generations, this open sandwich bar on a busy city-centre street is almost a household name in Denmark. Offers a full range of typical smørrebrød.

ENVIRONS OF COPENHAGEN

at Nordhavn North : 3 km by Østbanegade and Road 2

Bo Bech at Paustian
A/C P VISA MC AE

Kalkbraenderiløbskaj 2 ✉ 2100 – ✆ 39 18 55 01 – mail@bobech.net – www.bobech.net – closed 3 weeks July, 23 December-13 January and Sunday
Rest – Menu 375 DKK (lunch) – Carte 575/790 DKK
Spec. Avocado wafers, lightly salted caviar. Neglected roots with black lobster. Imaginary landscapes of white chocolate.
◆ Innovative ◆ Design ◆
Located on a redeveloped marina, this stylish, spacious restaurant serves 3 set menus and an à la carte; choose The Alchemist to fully appreciate the chef's original repertoire and techniques.

at Hellerup North : 7.5 km by Østbanegade and Road 2 - ✉ 2900 Hellerup

Hellerup Parkhotel
rm P VISA MC AE

Strandvejen 203 ✉ 2900 – ✆ 39 62 40 44 – info@hellerupparkhotel.dk – Fax 39 45 15 90 – www.hellerupparkhotel.dk
Closed 22 December-2 January
71 rm – †1235/1430 DKK ††1535/1825 DKK, ☐ 130 DKK
Rest *Saison* – see below
Rest *Wine & Dine* – *✆ 39 62 27 67 (dinner only)* Carte 250/455 DKK
◆ Business ◆ Classic ◆
Attractive classic hotel located in affluent suburb north of the city. Rooms vary in size and colour décor but offer same good standard of facilities and level of comfort. Popular local Italian restaurant on side of hotel with terrace.

Saison

Strandvejen 203 ✉ 2900 – ☎ 39 62 21 40 – saison@saison.dk – Fax 39 62 20 30 – www.saison.dk

Closed 3 weeks in summer and Sunday

Rest – Menu 335/405 DKK – Carte 475/580 DKK

♦ Modern ♦ Friendly ♦

Run separately from the hotel in which it is located. Enjoys a bright and airy feel with high ceiling and large windows. Carefully prepared cooking using quality ingredients.

at Skovshoved North : 10 km by Østbanegade and Road 2

Skovshoved

Strandvejen 267 ✉ 2920 K Charlottenlund – ☎ 39 64 00 28 – reception@skovshovedhotel.com – Fax 39 64 06 72 – www.skovshovedhotel.com

Closed 24-26 December

20 rm – †1300/1500 DKK ††1700 DKK, ☕ 135 DKK – 2 suites

Rest – Menu 325/385 DKK – Carte 405/685 DKK

♦ Inn ♦ Cosy ♦

Set in a charming village, this inn dates from the 1660's and was fully refurbished in 2003. Cosy bedrooms, most with balconies looking out to sea. Welcoming atmosphere. Warm and inviting restaurant with pleasant terrace and a classic menu.

at Søllerød North : 20 km by Tagensvej (take the train to Holte then taxi) - ✉ 2840 Holte

Søllerød Kro

Søllerødvej 35 ✉ 2840 K – ☎ 45 80 25 05 – mail@soelleroed-kro.dk – Fax 45 80 22 70 – www.soelleroed-kro.dk

Closed 3 weeks July, 1 week February, Easter, 24 December-1 January and Monday

Rest – Menu 350/575 DKK – Carte 640/1075 DKK

Spec. Baerii caviar "en surprise". Lobster with morels and white asparagus. Strawberries with Tahitian vanilla and verbena.

♦ Modern ♦ Inn ♦

Characterful 17C thatched inn with delightful courtyard terrace and stylish Danish rustic-bourgeois décor. Classical French cooking with mild Danish influences; luxury ingredients abound.

at Kastrup Airport Southeast : 10 km by Amager Boulevard

Hilton Copenhagen Airport

Ellehammersvej 20, Kastrup ✉ 2770 – ☎ 32 50 15 01 – res_copenhagen-airport@hilton.com – Fax 32 52 85 28 – www.hilton.com

381 rm – †2395 DKK ††1295/2395 DKK, ☕ 185 DKK – 1 suite

Rest *Hamlet* – Carte 378/525 DKK

Rest *Horizon* – ☎ 32 44 53 53 – Carte 378/525 DKK

♦ Business ♦ Modern ♦

Glass walkway leads from arrivals to this smart business hotel. Bright bedrooms with light, contemporary Scandinavian furnishings and modern facilities. Hamlet is a formal open-plan restaurant with eclectic menu. Relaxed dining in Horizon beneath vast atrium.

Quality Airport H. Dan

rest rm

Kastruplundgade 15, Kastrup (North : 2 ½ km by coastal rd) ✉ 2770 – ☎ 32 51 14 00 – q.dan@choice.dk – Fax 32 51 37 01 – www.choicehotels.dk

227 rm – †1895/2095 DKK ††1895/2095 DKK, ☕ 95 DKK – 1 suite

Rest – *(buffet dinner only)* Menu 98 DKK

♦ Business ♦ Functional ♦

Airport hotel not far from beach and countryside, popular with business travellers. All rooms with modern facilities; some with views of canal. Traditional Danish cuisine in the restaurant.

FINLAND
SUOMI

PROFILE

→ **Area:**
338 145 km²
(130 558 sq mi).

→ **Population:**
5 225 000 inhabitants (est. 2005), density = 15 per km².

→ **Capital:**
Helsinki (conurbation 1 151 000 inhabitants).

→ **Currency:**
Euro (€); rate of exchange: € 1 = US$ 1.46 (Dec 2007).

→ **Government:**
Parliamentary republic (since 1917). Member of European Union since 1995.

→ **Languages:**
Finnish (a Finno-Ugric language related to Estonian) spoken by 92% of Finns, Swedish (6%) and Sami (some 7 000 native speakers). English is widely spoken.

→ **Specific public holidays:**
Epiphany (6 January); Good Friday (Friday before Easter); Midsummer's Eve Day (mid June); Independence Day (6 December); Boxing Day (26 December).

→ **Local time:**
GMT + 2 hours in winter and GMT + 3 hours in summer.

→ **Climate:**
Temperate continental with very cold winters and mild summers (Helsinki: January: -7°C, July: 17°C). Midnight sun: the sun never sets for several weeks around Midsummer in the north. Snow settles in early December to April in the south and centre of the country. Northern Lights *(Aurora Borealis)* visible in the north on clear, dark nights; highest frequency in Feb-Mar and Sep-Oct.

→ **International dialling Code:**
00 358 followed by area code (Helsinki: 9) and then the local number.

→ **Emergency:**
Fire Brigade, Ambulance, Police: ✆ **112**.

→ **Electricity:**
220 volts AC, 50Hz; 2-pin round-shaped continental plugs.

→ **Formalities**
Travellers from the European Union (EU), Switzerland, Iceland and the main countries of North and South America need a national identity card or passport (America: passport required) to visit Finland for less than three months (tourism or business purpose). For visitors from other countries a visa may be required, in addition to a passport, especially for those wishing to stay for longer than three months. If you plan to visit Russia while in Finland, you must purchase an appropriate visa in advance in your own country. We advise you to check with your embassy before travelling.

Helsinki

Helsingfors

Population; 583 000 (conurbation 1 151 000) – Altitude: sea level

www.visitfinland.com

Cool, clean and chic, the 'Daughter of the Baltic' sits prettily on a peninsula, jutting out between the landmasses of its historical overlords, Sweden and Russia. Surrounded on three sides by water, Helsinki is a busy port, but that only tells a small part of the story: forests grow in abundance around here and trees reach down to the lapping shores. This is a striking city to look at: it was rebuilt in the nineteenth century after fire, and many of the buildings have a handsome neoclassical or art nouveau façade. Shoppers can browse the picturesque outdoor food and tourist markets stretching along the main harbour, where island-hopping ferries ply their trade.

Wherever you are here, you get the feeling of man and nature thinking pretty much along the same lines. In a country with over 200,000 lakes it would be pretty hard to escape a green sensibility, and the Finnish capital has made sure that concrete and stone have never taken priority over its distinctive features of trees, water and open space. There are bridges at every turn connecting the city's varied array of small islands, and a ten kilometre strip of parkland acts as a spine running vertically up from the centre. Renowned as a city of cool, it's somewhere that also revels in a hot nightlife and even hotter saunas – this is where they were invented. And if your blast of dry heat has left you wanting a refreshing dip, there's always a freezing lake close at hand.

LIVING THE CITY

The harbour is the hub of Helsinki. Arrive by boat and **Senate Square,** identified by the proud lines of its Lutheran cathedral, beckons in the background. To your east juts the headland of **Katajanokka,** while moving away from the harbour the city centre continues to the northwest, pierced by the elongated **Mannerheimintie** shopping street. To the east as you proceed along this thoroughfare is **Töölönlahti Bay**, the southern-most tip of **Central Park's** gloriously green spine. To the west is **Sibelius Park**, named after Finland's greatest composer. Helsinki sits in an archipelago and islands around it include **Suomenlinna** to the south, which houses an eighteenth century sea fortress, now a UNESCO World Heritage site.

PRACTICAL INFORMATION

ARRIVAL-DEPARTURE

Helsinki-Vantaa Airport is 19km north of the city. By taxi it'll cost around €30 and take 20-30min. There are also buses to Central Bus Station which will take 40min.

TRANSPORT

Getting across Helsinki is fast and easy: trams and buses whizz you round efficiently. A single ticket is cheap and good for any transfers you make within an hour: buy them from the driver, ticket machines, kiosks, metro stations or ferry terminal.

If you expect to use public transport often, it might be worth buying a tourist ticket, valid for one, three or five days and available from railway station, ticket machines or tourist office.

The Helsinki Card is another good option: it's valid for one, two or three days with a sliding scale of prices, and allows you unlimited transport plus free admission to museums and attractions.

There are regular ferries from the harbour to Suomenlinna; they sail a little less frequently to the other main islands.

EXPLORING HELSINKI

There's something about a harbour. See one and it becomes the pivotal part of a town or city. In Helsinki that feeling is accentuated by the grand hubbub of the daily market that takes place there. It's a colourful gathering of farmers and fishermen, traders and crafts people, and the buzzy atmosphere is enhanced by the aromas from impromptu cafés selling fresh and smoked fish grilled on planks of cedar. For the surrounding elegant neoclassical look, we can thank the German architect Carl Engel, who engraved on a clean slate nearly 200 years ago. This chunk of the city is an ideal place just to stroll round for an hour or two, enjoying the juxtaposition of fine architecture and waterfront life.

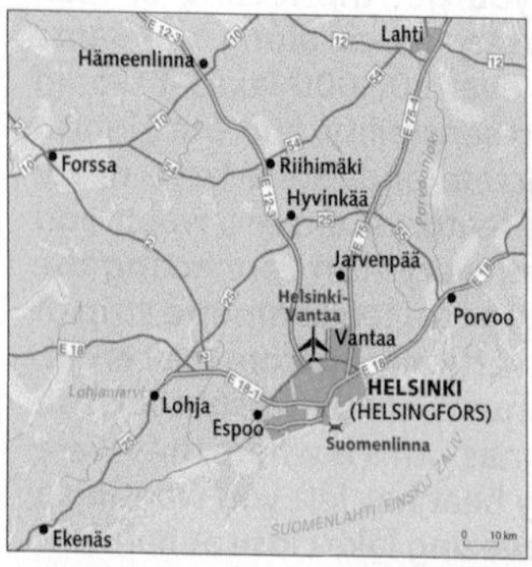

When it comes to cathedrals, you'll encounter double vision as you step off your boat onto the waterside. The vivid green dome of the **Lutheran Cathedral** has been a focal point for visitors for over 150 years, standing majestically up the hill from the harbour in **Senate Square**. The buildings that surround it create a fine symmetry; this is recognized as one of Europe's most aesthetically satisfying squares. Dominating the far side of the harbour, meanwhile, is **Uspensky Cathedral,** western Europe's largest Orthodox church, a confident testimony to Russia's past influence in Finland. It has thirteen gold cupolas, and an equally elaborate interior redolent of black marble and glinting gold. Helsinki spreads westwards along the boutique-edged avenues of **Esplanadi,** a strip of parkland that comes alive on summer evenings as everyone promenades during the long hours of light.

This is a city that takes its culture seriously. There are a host of good museums within a small area up from Senate Square and Esplanadi. The **Ateneum** (National Gallery) is a suitably grand building to house the best of Finnish art, given international enhancement by a splattering of works by Gauguin, Cézanne, Degas, Modogliani and Van Gogh. Half a mile up the road stands the eye-catching, decade old **Kiasma,** a picture itself with its curvy zinc roof and vertical aluminium elevations. This is the home of Finnish modern art, complete with theatre for experimental drama, dance and music. Carry on a little further up Mannerheimintie and you reach the **National Museum**, another show-stopping building, chock full with Finnish artefacts from prehistoric times to the present day. The sense of classy cool so permeates these places that it's no surprise to find a museum itself dedicated to style: The **DesignMuseo** (go back south past Esplanadi) pits all the famous design styles side-by-side in a kaleidoscope of good taste, with a main emphasis on Finnish masters of the art.

→ NOUVEAU RICH

If you get a slight feeling of déjà vu when your eyes alight on the DesignMuseo's art nouveau exhibits, there's a good chance you've already spent some time in Katajanokka, the art nouveau quarter of the city jutting out like a wiggly foot as you approach the harbour by boat. art nouveau took off in Helsinki as the Arts and Crafts Movement of the early twentieth century happily coincided with a flowering of inspired Finnish architects, and dozens of their landmark buildings are found in eye-catching clusters, chief of which is Katajanokka, the first neighbourhood of this type in Europe, and still the continent's best preserved. As you walk along its streets, you'll notice fine stone ornamentation, dreamy towers and fanciful details of all kinds. Two other examples of jaw-dropping art nouveau are the **Helsinki Railway Station** with its sumptuous interior and iconic lamp-holding figures to welcome you in (if somewhat menacingly), and the **Pohjola** insurance building, near Esplanadi, which mixes stone with local wood to dramatic effect. Head to the west of the city, though, for one of Finland's top visitor attractions. **Temppeliaukio**, or the Church in the Rock, is exactly that. It was hollowed out from living bedrock in 1969, and to visit is like staring at an altar in a quarry. The copper roof offsets the deadening effect of the granite walls, and the acoustics are stunning: it's a top-notch venue for concerts.

→ SOUR NOTE

The world of Finnish music is dominated by one man…**Jean Sibelius**. In Helsinki they think so much of him they not only gave him a monument, they gave him a park to go with it. It's in the west of the city and the monument certainly caused a stir when it was unveiled back in 1967. Made up of a collection of different sized metallic pipes that make their own kind of music when the wind blows, it was subject to a torrent of abuse at the time because people couldn't see the connection with Sibelius. So they added a statue of his head (some way from the pipes) and things quietened down. Judge for yourself. Whatever you may think, the park is a lovely, peaceful place to take a stroll, and it's very close to the water's edge. The best place to hear the music of Sibelius is the impressive **Finlandia Hall**, opposite the National Museum and overlooking Toolo Bay. It's a stunning building of white marble and black granite to remind you of a piano keyboard, and its acoustics do wonders for the likes of the Helsinki Philharmonic who regularly hold court there.

→ GOING UNDERGROUND

This is an excellent city for shopping. Just looking in the windows is like a lesson in artistic design. Actually, just looking in the windows may be your wisest move, especially if you're on a tight budget, as prices tend to shoot in a distinctly northerly direction. The smartest shops are around Esplanadi and Mannerheimintie, where fashion, furniture, jewellery and homeware stores jostle for attention. Go to Senate Square and its surrounds for handicrafts and art shops. If the weather's bad, you can hide from it beneath the central streets in a maze of connected underground passages replete with shops, cafés, restaurants and food markets. You could spend a day browsing down there without ever emerging into daylight!

A short ferry trip to the island of Suomenlinna is a good idea in the summer. Certainly UNESCO thinks so: it made the sea fortress on the island's headland a World Heritage Site in 1991. The fortress, built by the Swedes in the mid-eighteenth century, was used as a defence against Russia, and some of the island's 900-strong population now lives in its converted naval buildings. There are several museums and exhibition halls, balanced by delightful walks, bays and coves, making it a good location for a whole day's excursion. The calm of the island is a kind of microcosm of Helsinki: a restful place that seems to run quietly, smoothly and apparently without much effort.

HELSINKI IN...

→ ONE DAY

Harbour market place, Uspensky Cathedral, Lutheran Cathedral, Katajanokka, a slow stroll up Mannerheimintie taking in the cultural sights

→ TWO DAYS

A ferry to Suomenlinna and most of the day at the sea fortress, Church in the Rock, the lively nightlife of Fredrikinkatu area (west of city)

→ THREE DAYS

A trip through Central Park, the Sibelius monument, the design area round Esplanadi

CALENDAR HIGHLIGHTS

Helsinki has been around since 1550, and Helsinki Day, its birthday, is celebrated on 12 June. There are plenty of festivities and events around the city – Esplanadi and Senate Square are filled with music and the performing arts, while sailing boats in the harbour let you on-board (for a fee). Also in June, Juhannus (midsummer) is celebrated with bonfires and gusto. Football fans can get a summer fix at the International Youth Tournament when hundreds of young players from around the world gather to compete for the Helsinki Cup. August's Helsinki Festival includes a Night of Arts with street shows till dawn, as well as classical music, dance, theatre and visual arts. Herring lovers should make for the Market Square in October – the Baltic Herring Festival has been held here for over 200 years. Traditional Christmas markets light up the harbour in December, when there's also the dramatic Lucia Parade to the Lutheran Cathedral.

EATING OUT

Jacques Chirac may not have been very complimentary about the Finnish diet but he had clearly never visited any of the superbly stylish restaurants in Helsinki regularly serving imaginative cuisine where local – and we mean local – ingredients are very much to the fore. Produce is sourced from the country's abundant lakes, forests and seas, so that your menu will assuredly be laden with the likes of reindeer, smoked reindeer, reindeer's tongue, elk in aspic, lampreys, Arctic char, Baltic herring, snow grouse and cloudberries. Generally speaking, complicated, fussy preparations are overlooked for those that let the natural flavours shine through. In the autumn, markets are piled high with woodland mushrooms, often from Lapland, and chefs make the most of this bounty. Local alcoholic drinks include schnapps, vodka and liqueurs made from local berries, while *lakka* (made from cloudberries) and *mesimarja* (brambleberries) are definitely worth discovering – you may not find them in any other European city. You'd find coffee anywhere in Europe, but not to the same extent as here: Finns are among the world's biggest coffee drinkers. In the gastronomic restaurants, lunch is a simpler affair with limited choice. Many serve customers until 11pm, and most of the time service charges are included in restaurant bills.

→ WILD CITY

If you go for a walk in Central Park, you'll be surrounded by animal life. These include weasel, raccoon dog, muskrat, elk, arctic and brown hare. Birds are everywhere in the spring; in particular keep an eye open for Eurasian jay, dunnock, red-breasted flycatcher and garden and wood warblers.

→ OLYMPIAN HEIGHTS

Although Helsinki is a pretty low-lying city, you can reach the heights at the 240ft Olympic Stadium tower, built in 1938. The view takes in the whole of the city and the outlying Gulf of Finland.

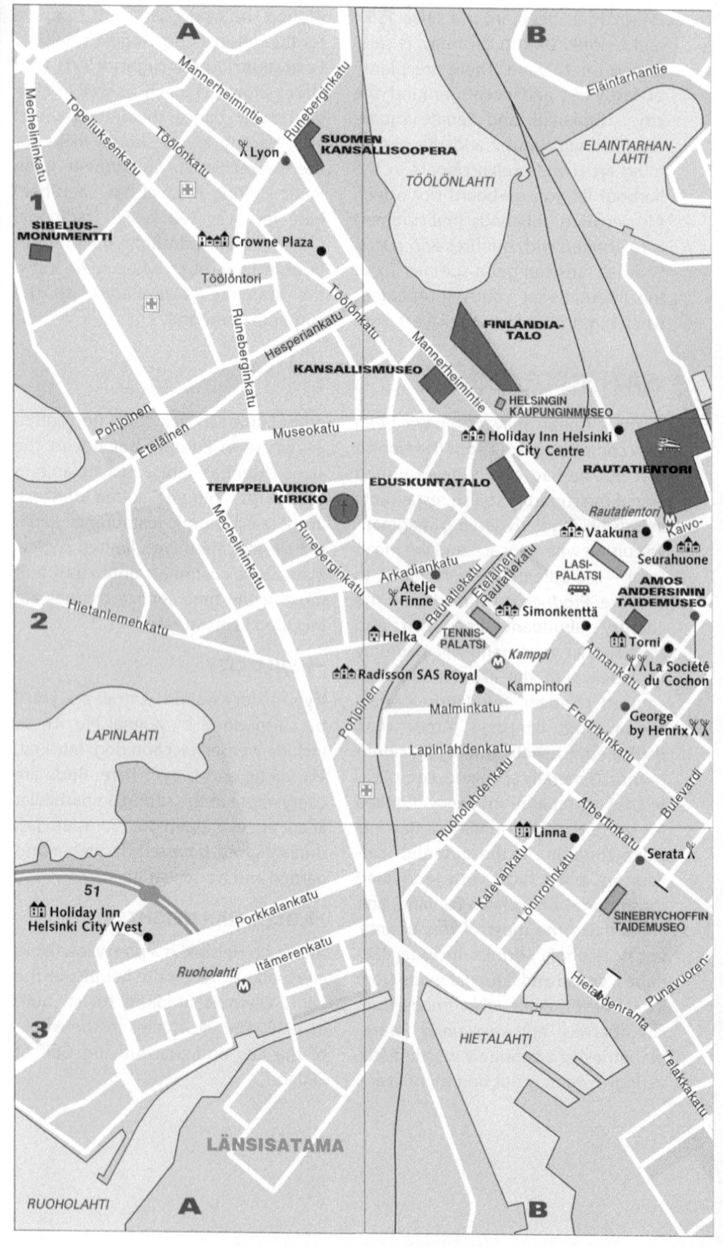
A
B
1
2
3
Mannerheimintie
Runeberginkatu
Mechelininkatu
Topeliuksenkatu
Töölönkatu
Lyon
SUOMEN KANSALLISOOPERA
Eläintarhantie
ELAINTARHAN-LAHTI
TÖÖLÖNLAHTI
SIBELIUS-MONUMENTTI
Crowne Plaza
Töölöntori
Hesperiankatu
FINLANDIA-TALO
KANSALLISMUSEO
HELSINGIN KAUPUNGINMUSEO
Pohjoinen
Eteläinen
Museokatu
Holiday Inn Helsinki City Centre
RAUTATIENTORI
TEMPPELIAUKION KIRKKO
EDUSKUNTATALO
Rautatientori
Vaakuna
Kaivo-
Seurahuone
LASI-PALATSI
AMOS ANDERSININ TAIDEMUSEO
Arkadiankatu
Rautatiekatu
Eteläinen Rautatiekatu
Atelje Finne
Simonkenttä
Hietaniemenkatu
Helka
TENNIS-PALATSI
Torni
Kamppi
Annankatu
La Société du Cochon
Radisson SAS Royal
Kampintori
Malminkatu
George by Henrix
Fredrikinkatu
LAPINLAHTI
Lapinlahdenkatu
Ruoholahdenkatu
Bulevardi
Albertinkatu
Linna
Serata
Kalevankatu
Lönnrotinkatu
51
Holiday Inn Helsinki City West
Porkkalankatu
SINEBRYCHOFFIN TAIDEMUSEO
Itämerenkatu
Ruoholahti
Hietalahdenranta
Punavuoren-
HIETALAHTI
Telakkakatu
LÄNSISATAMA
RUOHOLAHTI

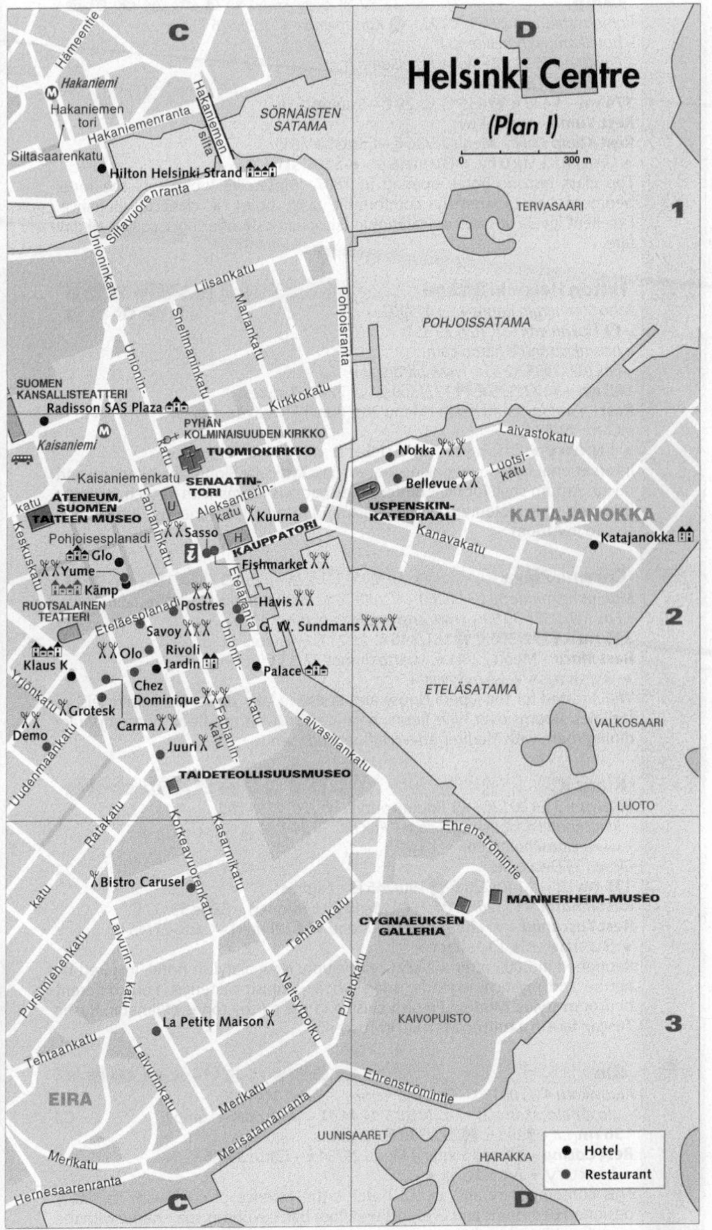
Helsinki Centre
(Plan I)
0
300 m
C
D
1
2
3
Hämeentie
Hakaniemi
Hakaniemen tori
Hakaniemenranta
Hakaniemen silta
SÖRNÄISTEN SATAMA
Siltasaarenkatu
Hilton Helsinki Strand
Siltavuorenranta
TERVASAARI
Unioninkatu
Liisankatu
Pohjoisranta
Snellmaninkatu
Mariankatu
POHJOISSATAMA
SUOMEN KANSALLISTEATTERI
Radisson SAS Plaza
Kirkkokatu
PYHÄN KOLMINAISUUDEN KIRKKO
Kaisaniemi
TUOMIOKIRKKO
Laivastokatu
Nokka
Bellevue
Luotsikatu
Kaisaniemenkatu
SENAATINTORI
ATENEUM, SUOMEN TAITEEN MUSEO
Aleksanterinkatu
Kuurna
USPENSKIN-KATEDRAALI
KATAJANOKKA
Keskuskatu
Pohjoisesplanadi
Sasso
KAUPPATORI
Kanavakatu
Katajanokka
Glo
Yume
Kämp
Fishmarket
Fabianinkatu
RUOTSALAINEN TEATTERI
Eteläesplanadi
Postres
Eteläranta
Havis
Savoy
G. W. Sundmans
Olo
Rivoli Jardin
Unioninkatu
Klaus K
Palace
Chez Dominique
ETELÄSATAMA
Yrjönkatu
Grotesk
Carma
Demo
Laivasillankatu
VALKOSAARI
Uudenmaankatu
Juuri
TAIDETEOLLISUUSMUSEO
LUOTO
Ratakatu
Korkeavuorenkatu
Kasarmikatu
Ehrenströmintie
Bistro Carusel
MANNERHEIM-MUSEO
Tehtaankatu
CYGNAEUKSEN GALLERIA
Laivurinkatu
Pursimiehenkatu
Neitsytpolku
Puistokatu
KAIVOPUISTO
La Petite Maison
Tehtaankatu
EIRA
Merikatu
Merisatamanranta
UUNISAARET
HARAKKA
Hotel
Restaurant
Hernesaarenranta

Kämp

Pohjoisesplanadi 29 ✉ 00100 – Ⓜ Kaisaniemi – ☎ (09) 576 111 – hotelkamp@hotelkamp.fi – Fax (09) 576 11 22 – www.hotelkamp.fi
closed 23-27 December **C2**
174 rm – 435 € 435 €, ☕ 29 € – 5 suites
Rest Yume – see below
Rest *Kämp Café* – Menu 25/36 € – Carte 28/68 €
♦ Grand Luxury ♦ Business ♦ Stylish ♦
Top class historic hotel, opened in 1887. Impressive lobby sets the tone; bedrooms are extremely comfortable and boast a classical elegance. Excellent levels of service. Traditional European café offering assorted all day fare.

Hilton Helsinki Strand

John Stenbergin Ranta 4 ✉ 00530 – Ⓜ Hakaniemi – ☎ (09) 39 351 – helsinkistrand@hilton.com – Fax (09) 3935 32 55 – www.hilton.com **C1**
185 rm – 122/325 € 122/360 €, ☕ 22 € – 7 suites
Rest – *(Sunday brunch only)* Menu 28 € (lunch) (weekdays only) – Carte 39/57 €
♦ Luxury ♦ Business ♦ Modern ♦
International hotel overlooking waterfront. Typically Finnish architecture and décor. Atrium style lobby. Comfortable spacious rooms with hi-tech facilities. Brasserie style restaurant with Finnish and international menus; light snacks served in Atrium.

Crowne Plaza

Mannerheimintie 50 ✉ 00260 – ☎ (09) 2521 0000 – helsinki-cph@restel.fi – Fax (09) 2521 39 99 – www.crowneplaza-helsinki.fi **A1**
345 rm – 172/306 € 161/346 €, ☕ 21 € – 4 suites
Rest *Macu* – Menu 22/41 € – Carte dinner 27/45 €
♦ Business ♦ Modern ♦
Well located for the Opera House and boasting lake views. Impressive leisure facilities. Rooms over nine floors: best are 'Club' on top floor. Contemporary dining room with Mediterranean influenced menus.

Klaus K

Bulevardi 2 ✉ 00120 – Ⓜ Rautatientori – ☎ (20) 7704 700 – klauskhotel@klauskhotel.com – Fax (20) 7704 7 30 – www.klauskhotel.com
Closed 25 December **C2**
135 rm ☕ – 140/220 € 190/245 € – 2 suites
Rest *Ilmatar* – *☎ (20) 7704 714* – Menu 50 € (dinner) – Carte 35/52 €
Rest *Toscanini* – *☎ (20) 7704 713* – Menu 44 € (dinner) – Carte 27/46 €
♦ Business ♦ Design ♦
Reopened in 2005 after a 2 year renovation. Now a stylish hotel, inspired by nature and mystical legends, using wholly Finnish materials. Four different bedroom styles. Modern Finnish cuisine in the earthy tones of Ilmatar. Rustic Tuscan fare in a trattoria setting in Toscanini.

Glo

Kluuvikatu 4 ✉ 00100 – Ⓜ Kaisaniemi – ☎ (010) 3444400 – glo@palacekamp.fi – Fax (010) 3 44 44 01 – www.palacekamp.fi **C2**
136 rm ☕ – 295 € 295/330 € – 8 suites
Rest *Cocina* – *(Closed Sunday)* Menu 29/54 € – Carte 39/46 €
♦ Luxury ♦ Modern ♦
This contemporary and stylish hotel is the essence of cool, with its slickly designed bedrooms and lively ground floor bar. Luxurious spa, shared with the next door Kämp hotel. Intense red and black décor in La Cocina. Modern Spanish cuisine.

Simonkenttä

Simonkatu 9 ✉ 00100 – Ⓜ Kamppi – ✆ (09) 68 380 – simonkentta@scandic-hotels.com – Fax (09) 683 81 11 – www.scandic-hotels.com
Closed 22-27 December

B2

357 rm ☕ – †95/279 € ††115/299 € – 3 suites
Rest *Simonkatu* – *(Closed Saturday lunch and Sunday)* Menu 20/42 € – Carte 25/45 €

♦ Business ♦ Modern ♦

Ultra modern well-located hotel with imposing glazed façade. Stylish designer décor with colourful fabrics and parquet flooring in all rooms. Some rooms with a view. Stylish restaurant offers range of popular traditional dishes.

Holiday Inn Helsinki City Centre

Elielinaukio 5 ✉ 00100 – Ⓜ Rautatientori – ✆ (09) 5425 5000 – helsinki.hihcc@restel.fi – Fax (09) 5425 52 99 – www.holidayinn.com/hihelsinkicc

B2

174 rm ☕ – †145/250 € ††160/265 €
Rest *Verde* – *(Closed Sunday and lunch Saturday and Bank Holidays) (buffet lunch)* Menu 9 € (lunch) – Carte 27/51 €

♦ Business ♦ Functional ♦

Modern city centre hotel near railway station, post office and all main shopping areas. Modern well-equipped bedrooms; good city view from 8th floor. Open style dining room serving popular menu using Finnish produce; lighter dishes available at lunchtime.

Seurahuone

Kaivokatu 12 ✉ 00100 – Ⓜ Rautatientori – ✆ (09) 69 141 – helsinki.seurahuone@restel.fi – Fax (09) 691 40 10 – www.hotelseurahuone.fi

B2

118 rm ☕ – †175/230 € ††195/290 €
Rest – *(Closed Sunday dinner)* Menu 45 € – Carte 29/56 €

♦ Luxury ♦ Classic ♦

The hotel opened on this site in 1914 and was renovated in 2006. Spacious and smart bedrooms are classically decorated and respectful of the hotel's rich traditions. Dining room offers a traditional menu in elegant surroundings.

Holiday Inn Helsinki

Messuaukio 1 (near Pasila Railway Station)
(North : 4 km by Mannerheimintie, Nordenskiöldink, Savonkatu off Ratapihantie) ✉ 00520 – ✆ (09) 150 900 – hi.reception@holidayinnhelsinki.fi – Fax (09) 150 9 01 – www.holidayinn.com
239 rm – †115/245 € ††145/275 €, ☕ 16 € – 5 suites
Rest *Terra Nova* – Carte approx. 30 €

♦ Business ♦ Classic ♦

Purpose-built hotel in same building as congress centre; popular for conferences. Take breakfast in the winter garden style atrium. Spacious well-equipped rooms with warm décor. International menu for all tastes in the large restaurant.

Radisson SAS Royal

Runeberginkatu 2 ✉ 00100 – Ⓜ Kamppi – ✆ (20) 1234 701 – reservations.finland@radissonsas.com – Fax (20) 1234 7 02 – www.radissonsas.com
Closed 22-28 December

B2

255 rm ☕ – †100/250 € ††100/270 € – 7 suites
Rest – Carte 27/53 €

♦ Business ♦ Modern ♦

Usefully located purpose-built hotel offering easy transport links. Good-sized, well-maintained bedrooms and comprehensive conference facilities. Steaks and traditional cuisine feature in the restaurant.

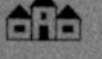

Palace

Eteläranta 10 ✉ 00130 – Ⓜ Kaisaniemi – ✆ (09) 1345 6661 – palacehotel@palacekamp.fi – Fax (09) 654 7 86 – www.palacekamphotel.fi

Closed Easter and Christmas **C2**

37 rm – 275 € 255/280 € – 2 suites

Rest *Palace Gourmet* – *✆ (09) 1345 6715 (Closed Saturday and Sunday)* Menu 58/70 €

♦ Business ♦ Classic ♦

1950s hotel by harbour, occupying upper floors of building with street level reception. Spacious, comfortable rooms with modern facilities. Some with balconies and views. 10th-floor restaurant serves traditional Finnish cuisine with hint of France.

Radisson SAS Plaza

Mikonkatu 23 ✉ 00100 – Ⓜ Kaisaniemi – ✆ (20) 1234 703 – reservations.finland@radissonsas.com – Fax (20) 1234 7 04 – www.radissonsas.com **C1-2**

290 rm – 120/200 € 240/320 € – 1 suite

Rest – *(Closed lunch Saturday, Sunday and Bank Holidays)* Menu 32 € (dinner) – Carte 28/52 €

♦ Business ♦ Functional ♦

Near the station, this sizeable modern business hotel maintains the reputation of this international group. Well-equipped rooms, in "Nordic", "Classic" or "Italian" style. Informal brasserie in a period townhouse; striking, painted windows.

Torni

Yrjönkatu 26 ✉ 00100 – Ⓜ Rautatientori – ✆ (20) 1234 604 – torni.helsinki@sokoshotels.fi – Fax (09) 4336 71 00 – www.sokoshotels.fi

Closed 20-27 December **B2**

146 rm – 180/240 € 200/260 € – 6 suites

Rest – *(Closed Sunday)* Menu 30/44 € – Carte 35/51 €

♦ Business ♦ Stylish ♦

Refurbished hotel in converted row of 1920s town houses in city centre. Rooms vary in size and are more Art Deco in style in the annexe. Choice of bars available. Inviting restaurant overlooking street offering a traditional menu.

Holiday Inn Helsinki City West

Sulhasenkuja 3 ✉ 00180 – Ⓜ Ruoholahti – ✆ (09) 4152 1000 – helsinki.hihcw@restel.fi – Fax (09) 4152 12 99 – www.hi-helsinkiwest.fi **A3**

256 rm – 118/228 € 136/246 €

Rest – *(Closed lunch Saturday and Sunday)* Carte 27/51 €

♦ Business ♦ Modern ♦

Opened in 2005 and well located for the business parks west of the city. 9th floor Executive Rooms have king size beds and good views. Complimentary use of sauna. Huge ground floor bar and restaurant with global menus.

Vaakuna

Asema-aukio 2 ✉ 00100 – Ⓜ Rautatientori – ✆ (20) 1234 610 – vaakuna.helsinki@sokoshotels.fi – Fax (09) 4337 71 00 – www.sokoshotels.fi

Closed Easter, 21-24 June and 22 December-1 January **B2**

258 rm – 75/275 € 275 € – 12 suites

Rest – Carte 29/67 €

♦ Business ♦ Classic ♦

Modern accommodation: spacious, colourful and well-appointed in this sizeable hotel, built for 1952 Olympics. Conveniently located for station. 10th-floor restaurant with views; lighter meals served in coffee shop.

Katajanokka

Vyökatu 1 ✉ 00160 – ✆ (09) 686450 – sales@bwkatajanokka.fi – Fax (09) 67 02 90 – www.bwkatajanokka.fi
Closed Christmas **D2**
106 rm – 160/245 € 202/309 €
Rest – *(buffet lunch)* Carte dinner 43 €
♦ Historic ♦ Classic ♦
Stay in a converted prison! Bedrooms boast all modern amenities, Premier rooms come with sofas and Junior suites have their own saunas. Do porridge in the candlelit basement restaurant, featuring a preserved prison cell. Relaxed atmosphere; international menu.

Rivoli Jardin without rest

Kasarmikatu 40 ✉ 00130 – Ⓜ Kaisaniemi – ✆ (09) 681 500 – rivoli.jardin@rivoli.fi – Fax (09) 656 9 88 – www.rivoli.fi **C2**
55 rm – 210 € 240 €
♦ Business ♦ Classic ♦
Well-run, traditional hotel close to city centre. Rooms are functional and comfortable, two on top floor have terrace. Winter garden style breakfast area.

Linna

Lönnrotinkatu 29 ✉ 00180 – Ⓜ Kamppi – ✆ (010) 3444 100 – linna@palacekamp.fi – Fax (010) 3444 1 01 – www.palacekamp.fi
Closed 20-24 March and 15 December-11 January **B3**
47 rm – 189/209 € 209/405 € – 1 suite
Rest – *(Closed Sunday and Bank Holidays) (dinner only)* Menu 42 €
♦ Business ♦ Modern ♦
An established local landmark, built in 1903, and a striking example of Finnish Art Nouveau. Renovated in 2005, it offers modern, well-equipped and quiet accommodation. Cosy 1st floor dining room with classic French cooking.

Pasila

Maistraatinportti 3 (North : 4 km by Mannerheimintie, Nordenskiöldink off Vetuvitie) ✉ 00240 – ✆ (20) 123 4613 – pasila.helsinki@sokoshotels.fi – Fax (09) 143 7 71 – www.sokoshotels.fi
Closed 21 December-2 January
172 rm – 95/205 € 105/225 € – 6 suites
Rest *Sevilla* – Carte 18/25 €
♦ Business ♦ Modern ♦
Large, modern business hotel in tranquil district out of town, a short tram ride from city centre. Rooms feature contemporary local décor and furnishings. Informal Spanish-influenced restaurant; popular menu with grills.

Helka

Pohjoinen Rautatiekatu 23 ✉ 00100 – Ⓜ Kamppi – ✆ (09) 613 580 – reservations@helka.fi – Fax (09) 441 0 87 – www.helka.fi
Closed 23-27 December **B2**
143 rm – 90/136 € 112/171 € – 4 suites
Rest *Helkan keittiö* – *(Buffet lunch)* Menu 33 € – Carte 30/45 €
♦ Family ♦ Functional ♦
A family-owned hotel offering affordable accommodation over five floors. The bedrooms were redecorated in 2005; if travelling alone ask for one of the larger single rooms. Clean, simple restaurant with a seasonal, contemporary Finnish menu.

Cumulus Olympia

Läntinen Brahenkatu 2 (North : 2 km by Siltasaarenkatu) ✉ 00510 – ✆ (09) 69 151 – olympia.cumulus@restel.fi – Fax (09) 691 52 19 – www.cumulus.fi
Closed 20-24 March and 21-28 December
101 rm – 105/180 € 125/205 € – **Rest** – *(dinner only)* Carte 20/46 €
♦ Business ♦ Functional ♦
Situated in a residential area near the amusement park, 10 min. by tram from city centre. Modern bedrooms with standard décor and furnishings. Nightclub and Irish Pub. International menu in the restaurant.

XXXX **G. W. Sundmans**

Eteläranta 16 (1st floor) ✉ 00130 – Ⓜ Kaisaniemi – ✆ (09) 622 6410 – myyntipalvelu@royalravintolat.com – Fax (09) 661 3 31 – www.royalravintolat.com/sundmans
Closed Easter, Christmas, Saturday lunch, Sunday and Bank Holidays **C2**
Rest – Menu 45/67 € – Carte 65/84 €
Rest *Krog (ground floor)* – Menu 47 € (dinner) – Carte 33/51 €
♦ Traditional ♦ Formal ♦
19C sea captain's Empire style mansion opposite harbour. Five classically decorated dining rooms with view. Elegantly laid tables; professional service. Classically-based cuisine with hints of modernity. Informal ground floor Krog restaurant features local seafood and traditional dishes.

XXX **Chez Dominique** (Hans Valimaki/Matti Wikberg)

Rikhardinkatu 4 ✉ 00130 – Ⓜ Rautatientori – ✆ (09) 612 7393 – info@chezdominique.fi – Fax (09) 6124 42 20 – www.chezdominique.fi
Closed 4 weeks July, Sunday, lunch Monday and Saturday and Bank Holidays **C2**
Rest – *(booking essential)* Menu 39 € (lunch) – Carte 87/107 €
Spec. Lobster poached in vanilla butter with avocado lasagna. Anjou pigeon "pastille cacao" and pigeon consommé. "Exotic fruit salad" eucalyptus and pineapple jus.
♦ Inventive ♦ Elegant ♦
Elegant, very comfortable dining room, sleekly styled in black, white and red. Highly accomplished, original cooking with delicate touches and bold flavours. Surprise menus on Saturday and Monday nights.

XXX **Savoy**

Eteläesplanadi 14 (8th floor) ✉ 00130 – Ⓜ Kaisaniemi – ✆ (09) 684 4020 – kai.kallio@royalravintolat.com – Fax (09) 628 7 15 – www.royalravintolat.com
Closed 20-24 March, 19-22 June, 23 December-6 January, Saturday and Sunday **C2**
Rest – Menu 58/86 € – Carte 72/92 €
♦ Traditional ♦ Formal ♦
Panoramic restaurant in city centre with typical Finnish design dating from 1937. Classic traditional menu of local specialities. Ask for a table in the conservatory.

XXX **Nokka**

Kanavaranta 7F ✉ 00160 – ✆ (09) 687 7330 – Fax (09) 6877 33 30 – www.royalravintolat.com
Closed 21-23 March, 20-22 June, 21 December-4 January, lunch Saturday and Sunday **D2**
Rest – *(booking essential)* Menu 45/58 € – Carte dinner 64/71 €
♦ Modern ♦ Design ♦
Converted warehouse divided into two striking rooms; glazed wine cellar; waterfront terrace. Watch the chefs prepare appealing, modern Finnish cuisine. Good service.

XX **Olo**

Kasarmikatu 44 ✉ 00130 – Ⓜ Kaisaneimi – ✆ (09) 665 565 – info@olo-restaurant.com – Fax (09) 665 5 75 – www.olo-restaurant.com
Closed Easter, 3 weeks July, Saturday lunch, Monday dinner and Sunday **C2**
Rest – Menu 38/42 € – Carte 45/60 €
♦ Contemporary ♦ Design ♦
Opened in 2006 and the new place to be seen. Comfortable, well-organised restaurant with a discreet atmosphere. Contemporary Finnish cuisine using good quality ingredients.

XX **Sasso**

Pohjoisesplanadi 17 ✉ 00170 Helsinki – Ⓜ Kaisaniemi – ☎ (09) 1345 6240 – tables@palacekamp.fi – Fax (09) 1345 62 42 – www.palacekamp.fi
Closed Sunday and Bank Holidays **C2**
Rest – Menu 58 € (dinner) – Carte 36/50 €
♦ Italian ♦ Fashionable ♦
Spacious, open-plan restaurant near market place and harbour. Stylish bar and lounge open all day. Shimmering fabrics typical of smart, contemporary interior with earthy and olive hues. Northern Italian dishes using top Finnish ingredients.

XX **Havis**

Eteläranta 16 ✉ 00130 – ☎ (09) 6869 5660 – nina.koiranen@royalravintolat.com – Fax (09) 6869 56 56 – www.royalravintolat.com/havis
Closed Easter, 23 December-1 January, Sunday October-April and lunch Saturday and Sunday **C2**
Rest – Menu 42/48 € – Carte dinner 50/71 €
♦ Seafood ♦ Formal ♦
Divided into two contrasting styles of room: one classic and ornate, the other more lively with views into the kitchen. Same menu throughout features carefully prepared seafood.

XX ✿ **Postres** (Vesa Parviainen/Samuli Wirgentius)

Eteläesplanadi 8 ✉ 00130 – Ⓜ Kaisaniemi – ☎ (09) 663 300 – info@postres.fi – Fax 663 3 01 – www.postres.fi
Closed 1-30 July, 23 December-8 January, Sunday, Monday and Saturday lunch **C2**
Rest – Menu 27/49 € – Carte dinner 53/68 €
Spec. Poached lobster with vegetable salad. Pigeon and Appenzeller with gratinated endive. Tarte Tatin and vanilla ice cream.
♦ Modern ♦ Design ♦
Opened by a keen, dedicated young team in 2006. Bright and inviting dining room divided into two. Contemporary cooking draws on French techniques and has innovative touches.

XX ✿ **Demo** (Tommi Tuominen/Teemu Aura)

Uudenmaankatu 11 ✉ 00120 Helsinki – Ⓜ Rautatientori – ☎ (09) 228 90840 – demo@restaurantdemo.fi – Fax (09) 228 9 08 41 – www.restaurantdemo.fi
Closed 2 weeks Christmas and New Year, Sunday, Monday and Bank Holidays **C2**
Rest – *(booking essential) (dinner only)* Menu 52 € – Carte 52/63 €
Spec. Slightly smoked tuna with wasabi mayonnaise. Elk shoulder with wild mushrooms, elk sausage and blackcurrant sauce. Lime soufflé and sorbet.
♦ Contemporary ♦ Trendy ♦
Locally renowned restaurant with trendy red fabric, chrome chairs and a warm candle-lit atmosphere. Modern Scandinavian and French menu; highly confident and assured cooking uses local produce.

XX **Yume** – at Kämp H.

Kluuvikatu 2 ✉ 00100 – Ⓜ Kaisaniemi – ☎ (09) 576 117 18 – sales@palacekamp.fi – Fax (09) 576 115 15 – www.palacekamp.fi
Closed Sunday, Monday and Bank Holidays **C2**
Rest – *(dinner only)* Carte 50/75 €
♦ Japanese ♦ Fashionable ♦
Both the menu and the décor change with the seasons at this smart Japanese restaurant. Located within the Kämp Hotel but with its own street entrance. Japanese cuisine with European flavours to the fore.

Carma (Markus Aremo)
Ludviginkatu 3-5 ✉ 00100 – Ⓜ Rautatientori – ☎ (09) 673236 – carma@carma.fi – www.carma.fi
Closed 21-24 March, 13 July-4 August, 23-26 December, Saturday lunch and Sunday **C2**
Rest – Menu 31/48 € – Carte dinner 59/66 €
Spec. Pumpkin soup with lobster and ginger cream. Red deer with white bean purée and juniper berry sauce. Dark chocolate mousse, ice cream and Indian sugar syrup.
◆ Modern ◆ Design ◆
Intimate restaurant with arty, serene ambience. Confident, modern Scandinavian/French cooking uses the best seasonal products. Passionate chef is celebrated master of chocolate.

La Société du Cochon
Mannerheimintie 14, (1st floor) ✉ 00100 – Ⓜ Rautatientori – ☎ (020) 7619888 – info@cochon.fi – Fax (020) 7 61 98 89 – www.cochon.fi
Closed Christmas **B2**
Rest – Menu 25 € (lunch) – Carte dinner 28/48 €
◆ Modern ◆ Brasserie ◆
Owned by one of the proprietors of Chez Dominique. Centrally located, stylish first floor brasserie with striking décor; ask for a window table. Prime seasonal, organic ingredients create flavourful dishes.

George by Henri'x
Kalevankatu 17 ✉ 00100 – Ⓜ kamppi – ☎ (010) 270 1702 – sales@henrix.fi – Fax (010) 672 7 89 – www.henrix.fi
Closed Christmas and Sunday **B2**
Rest – Menu 28/50 € – Carte dinner 42/54 €
◆ Traditional ◆ Intimate ◆
Smart 19C town house where the traditional meets the modern, with cloth-clad tables, wood panelling and leather chairs. The food reflects the décor: traditional at the core, but with some contemporary influences and imaginative Asian hints.

FishMarket
Pohjoisesplanadi 17 ✉ 00170 Helsinki – Ⓜ Kaisaniemi – ☎ (09) 1345 6220 – sales@palacekamp.fi – Fax (09) 1345 62 22 – www.palacekamp.fi
Closed Christmas, Easter, 21-22 June and Sunday **C2**
Rest – *(dinner only)* Carte 46/57 €
◆ Seafood ◆ Design ◆
Basement restaurant on the market place with appealing shellfish bar. Bright white décor complemented by attentive, friendly service. Seafood menus change seasonally, highlighted by original combinations.

Bellevue
Rahapajankatu 3 ✉ 00160 – Ⓜ Kaisaniemi – ☎ (09) 179 560 – info@restaurantbellevue.com – Fax (09) 636 9 85 – www.restaurantbellevue.com
Closed 23 December-1 January, lunch in July and Sunday **D2**
Rest – Menu 29/34 € – Carte 42/70 €
◆ Russian ◆ Cosy ◆
Opened in 1917 in a period townhouse and claims to be the oldest outside Russia. Fairly sombre traditionally styled décor and cosy, intimate atmosphere. Menu features Russian delicacies.

Grotesk
Ludviginkatu 10 ✉ 00130 – Ⓜ Rautatientori – ☎ ((10)) 4702100 – grotesk@grotesk.fi – Fax ((10)) 4 70 20 01 – www.grotesk.fi
Closed Christmas, Saturday lunch and Sunday **C2**
Rest – Menu 22 € (lunch) – Carte dinner 35/47 €
◆ Traditional ◆ Fashionable ◆
Trendy, informal restaurant in early 19C building in heart of the city, with open kitchen and stylish black and red décor. Good value heartwarming and flavoursome Finnish cooking. Buzzy atmosphere.

Lyon

A/C VISA MC AE D

Mannerheimintie 56 ✉ 00260 – ✆ (09) 408 131
– ravintola.lyon@kolumbus.fi
– Fax (09) 422 0 74 – www.ravintolalyon.fi
Restricted opening in summer and closed July, Sunday, Monday and Saturday lunch and Bank Holidays **A1**
Rest – Menu 29/45 € – Carte dinner 50/64 €
♦ French ♦ Bistro ♦
Traditional, well-established restaurant near the Opera. Menu has varied choice: seasonal, vegetarian or Helsinki, as well as the main à la carte serving French-style dishes.

La Petite Maison

VISA MC AE D

Huvilakatu 28A ✉ 00150 – Ⓜ Eiran Sai Raala – ✆ (09) 270 1704
– sales@henrix.fi – Fax (09) 6842 56 66 – www.henrix.fi
Closed July, Sunday and Monday **C3**
Rest – *(booking essential) (dinner only)* Menu 70 € – Carte 57/74 €
♦ French ♦ Cosy ♦
Cosy restaurant popular with local clientele in a quiet street known for its Art Deco architecture. Traditional décor with strong French note in the classic fare. Reasonably priced wine list.

Serata

VISA MC AE D

Bulevardi 32 ✉ 00120 – Ⓜ Kamppi Kampen – ✆ (09) 680 1365
– serata@serata.net – www.serata.net
Closed 20 December-7 January, Easter, Sunday, Monday dinner, Saturday lunch and Bank Holidays **B3**
Rest – *(booking essential)* Menu 35/40 € – Carte 35/54 €
♦ Italian ♦ Friendly ♦
Warm and relaxed corner restaurant with a convivial atmosphere. Open kitchen with some counter seating. Authentic Italian cooking with good value set menus including wine.

Juuri

A/C VISA MC AE D

Korkeavuorenkatu 27 ✉ 00130 – ✆ (09) 635 732 – ravintola@juuri.fi
– Fax (09) 635 7 32 – www.juuri.fi
Closed 6 and 25-26 December **C2**
Rest – Carte 33/41 €
♦ Finnish ♦ Bistro ♦
Close to the Design museum, a bistro with lots of wood brightened by large windows. The kitchen is keen to promote traditional Finnish home and country cooking. Starters served in tapas style.

Bistro Carusel

A/C VISA MC AE D

Korkeavuorenkatu 4B – ✆ (09) 42427650 – bistro@carusel.fi – Fax (09) 67 94 72 – www.carusel.fi
Closed Christmas-New Year, Sunday and Monday **C3**
Rest – Menu 28/52 € – Carte dinner 29/43 €
♦ Italian ♦ Neighbourhood ♦
Small neighbourhood restaurant with fresh, neat interior in earthy colours. Limited lunch; à la carte at dinner; rustic Italian cooking with a modern edge. Friendly service.

Ateljé Finne

A/C VISA MC AE D

Arkadiankatu 14 ✉ 00100 – Ⓜ Kamppi – ✆ ((09)) 493 110
– info@ateljefinne.fi
– Fax ((040)) 411 53 16 – www.ateljefinne.fi
Closed Christmas, Sunday and Monday **B2**
Rest – Menu 20/35 €
♦ Traditional ♦ Bistro ♦
Spacious bohemian restaurant serving well-priced rustic Finnish cooking. Meaning 'Finne's studio,' it's named after the famous sculptor whose workplace it was until the '60s.

Kuurna

Meritullinkatu 6 ✉ 00170 – Ⓜ Kaisaniemi – ✆ (09) 670 849 – info@kuurna.fi – www.kuurna.fi
Closed 22 June-July, 22 December-5 January, Sunday and Monday C2
Rest – *(booking essential) (dinner only)* Menu 32 €
♦ Finnish ♦ Cosy ♦
Small and intimate restaurant with vaulted ceiling seating just 20. Always busy, creating plenty of noise. Traditional Finnish home cooking with blackboard supplements.

at Helsinki-Vantaa Airport North : 19 km by A 137

Hilton Helsinki Vantaa

Lentàjànkuja 1 ✉ 01530 – ✆ (09) 73220 – helsinkivantaa.airport@hilton – Fax (09) 73 22 22 11 – www.hilton.com/helsinki
241 rm – †170/250 € ††170/250 € – 5 suites
Rest – Menu 32 € (lunch) – Carte 40/55 €
♦ Business ♦ Modern ♦
Brand new spacious and ultra-modern hotel, an easy walk to the airport terminal. Bedrooms are cool, fresh and light with contemporary Scandinavian décor; executive bedrooms come with saunas. International cuisine served in large open plan restaurant.

Vantaa

Hertaksentie 2 (near Tikkurila Railway Station) ✉ 00420 – ✆ (20) 1234 618 – hotelvantaa@sokoshotels.fi – Fax (09) 8578 55 55 – www.sokoshotels.fi
closed 23-27 December
265 rm – †125/200 € ††145/220 €
Rest *Vantaa* – Carte 20/43 €
♦ Business ♦ Functional ♦
Beside the railway station and convenient for the airport (bus number 61). Busy, corporate hotel with well-equipped rooms in a Scandinavian style. Rooms in the new wing are best.

FRANCE

PROFILE

→ **Area:**
551 500 km² (212 934 sq mi).

→ **Population:**
60 656 000 inhabitants (est. 2005), density = 110 per km².

→ **Capital:**
Paris (conurbation 9 928 000 inhabitants).

→ **Currency:**
Euro (€); rate of exchange: € 1 = US$ 1.46 (Dec 2007).

→ **Government:**
Parliamentary republic (since 1946). Member of European Union since 1957 (one of the 6 founding countries).

→ **Language:**
French.

→ **Specific public holidays:**
Victory Day 1945 (8 May), Bastille Day-National Day (14 July), Armistice Day 1918 (11 November).

→ **Local Time:**
GMT + 1 hour in winter and GMT + 2 hours in summer.

→ **Climate:**
Temperate with cool winters and warm summers (Paris: January: 3°C, July: 20°C). Mediterranean climate in the south (mild winters, hot and sunny summers, occasional strong wind called the mistral).

→ **International dialling Code:**
00 33 followed by regional code without the initial **0** and then the local number.

→ **Emergency:**
Police: ✆ **17**; Ambulance: ✆ **15**; Fire Brigade: ✆ **18**.

→ **Electricity:**
220 volts AC, 50Hz. 2-pin round-shaped continental plugs.

→ **Formalities**
Travellers from the European Union (EU), Switzerland, Iceland and the main countries of North and South America need a national identity card or passport (America: passport required) to visit France for less than three months (tourism or business purpose). For visitors from other countries a visa may be required, in addition to a passport, especially for those wishing to stay for longer than three months. We advise you to check with your embassy before travelling.

PARIS
PARIS

Population (est.2005): 2 107 000 (conurbation 9 928 000) – Altitude: 60m

R. Visage/SUNSET

It may be the city of a hundred and one clichés, but Paris never fails to come up with the goods. The French capital is one of the truly great cities of the world, a metropolis that eternally satisfies the desires of its beguiled visitors. With its harmonious layout, typified by the grand geometric boulevards radiating from the Arc de Triomphe like the spokes of a wheel, Paris is designed to enrapture.

Despite its ever-widening tentacles, most of the things worth seeing are contained within the city's ring road, the Boulevard Périphérique. The very heart of Paris is an island, the Ile de la Cité, where over two thousand years ago Celtic tribes first eked out a living. Later the Romans took control, attracted by the strategic possibilities of this settlement in the middle of the Seine. In time, a series of French kings achieved the centralisation of France, with Paris its cultural, political and economic nerve centre. Romance still pervades the streets of the twenty-first century city – a stroll along the Left Bank conjures images of Doisneau's magical monochrome photographs, while the narrow, cobbled streets of Montmartre vividly call up the colourful cool of Toulouse-Lautrec. But Paris is not resting on its laurels. New buildings and new cultural sensations are never far away: most recent has been the headline-grabbing Musée du Quai Branly. Les Grands Travaux are forever in the wings, waiting to inspire.

LIVING THE CITY

Paris wouldn't be Paris *sans* its Left and Right Banks. The **Left Bank** takes in the city south of the Seine; the **Right Bank** comprises the north and west. There are twenty **arrondissements** (quarters) set within the **Boulevard Périphérique**. The **Ile de la Cité** is the nucleus around which the city grew and the oldest quarters around this site are the 1st, 2nd, 3rd, 4th arrondisements on the Right Bank and 5th and 6th on the Left Bank. The remaining arrondisements fan out in a clockwise direction from here. Landmarks are universally known: the **Eiffel Tower** and the **Arc de Triomphe** are to the west of the centre (though on different sides of the river), the **Sacré-Coeur** is to the north, **Montparnasse Tower** to the south, and, of course, **Notre-Dame Cathedral** slap bang in the middle (of the Seine).

PRACTICAL INFORMATION

ARRIVAL-DEPARTURE

Roissy-Charles-de-Gaulle Airport is 23km northeast of Paris and by taxi will cost around €45. Air France Bus to Montparnasse or Porte Maillot runs every 15min. Orly Airport is 14km south and a taxi will be approximately €35. The Air France Bus runs to Invalides or Montparnasse. The Eurostar runs from the Gare du Nord, on the Rue de Dunkerque in the 10th arrondissement.

TRANSPORT

Paris has an excellent public transport system, and it's inexpensive too. Choose between the bus or the metro. A single ticket has a flat fare however far you travel; a carnet (book of ten tickets) works out at very good value for money.

There are three different travel cards you can also buy. Paris Visite is a one-day pass for three zones, or five-day pass for five zones; Mobilis is a one-day pass giving unlimited travel in either zones 1-2, or zones 1-8; Carte Orange is a weekly or monthly pass valid from Monday-Sunday or from the first of the month, offering an advantageous rate (you'll need a photograph for this one).

In 2007 Paris introduced the Velib. It's a self-service bicycle system – you pick up one of the twenty thousand bikes stationed at any of 750 points across the city, and leave it at another one. Subscription is a euro a day - the first half-hour of the journey is free, then after that you pay another euro if you require another half hour. Swiping a normal travel card will free up your bike – then it's just you versus the Parisian traffic…

EXPLORING PARIS

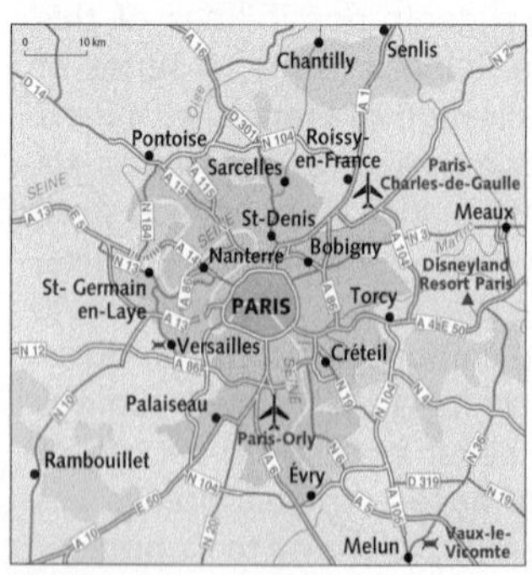

There are so many ways to enjoy the aura of Paris that even those who have never set foot in the city will recognise the familiar poetic selling points. A boat trip along the **Seine**; a café pose in **Boulevard St Germain**; the majestic glories of Notre-Dame cathedral; the utterly emblematic **Eiffel Tower**; a casual meander through the arty alleyways of **Montmartre** (enjoying the fabulous view, of course); the importance of the **Louvre's** mighty collection; getting to grips with the

Centre Pompidou (still futuristic after thirty years). However often you're reminded of them, these are images that never lose their power to seduce.

More than any other European city, Paris is defined by its river. The Seine slices its way through the centre, dividing the capital into two distinct areas. The Left Bank has, for centuries, been the home of poets, writers and artists. Inspired by the proximity of **the Sorbonne**, France's first university, radicals and intellectuals have throughout the ages flourished their quills and philosophised upon the world; many of their tracts can be found languishing in *les bouquinistes*, the Seine-side bookstalls it's impossible not to stop and browse over. Latin speaking students of the Sorbonne gave this area its name; today the **Latin Quarter** is filled with art galleries, cafés and bookshops. It's still the done thing to linger in the legendary cafés and brasseries of Boulevard St-Germain and reflect on more than the price of handbags in the smart boutiques lining the street. The classic trio – **Café de Flore, Les Deux Magots** and **Brasserie Lipp** – sit within a beguiling proximity to each other: a triangle of culinary and intellectual temptation.

→ THE SEINE CHOICE

Many of the major sights of Paris are famously strung out along the river, like an imposing architectural necklace. Two, of more recent vintage, have created quite a stir on the waterfront. If you're in Paris in the summer time, go down to the river at the eastern end of the Louvre, in the shadow of the **Pont des Arts**, and there you'll find sandy beaches, palm trees, ice-cream stalls, water sprinklers and deckchairs, not to mention fitness classes, too. This is **Paris Plage**, which, over the last five years, has become a bit of an institution. Further west, in the long shadow of the Eiffel Tower, a new museum (opened in 2006) has been pulling in visitors by the thousand. The **Musée du Quai Branly** squats low like a barge and invites you in along a sensuously swooping white ramp, while inside, mud-coloured walls form the dimly lit backdrop to powerful displays of tribal and folk art from France's colonial past. This was President Chirac's pet project, and it's shaping up to become as popular as those of his predecessors Pompidou and Mitterrand.

→ CREATING AN IMPRESSION

Mind you, it'll have to go some to catch the city's other artistic institutions. Further east along the riverfront, for example, the magical **Musée d'Orsay** continues to inspire. Everything about it is striking, from its Industrial Age railway station shell to its fabulous collections of nineteenth century art, which read like the greatest hits of Impressionist painting; realists and symbolists are there too, and substantial arrays of Van Gogh, Gauguin and Cézanne. Across the Seine, The Louvre – the museum to end all museums – is where to go for a daunting array of antiquities and French neo-classical grandeur, while the Centre Pompidou brings you bang up to date with a peerless collection of works by the likes of Picasso, Kandinsky, Matisse and Miro, right up to the latest trends.

→ EAST SIDE STORY

Taking a trip on the water doesn't have to mean taking a trip on the Seine. There's a hauntingly evocative sojourn you can take to a forgotten Paris – a liquid journey that takes you right under the **Bastille**. The **Canal Saint-Martin** winds its way up the eastern side of the city from the **Porte de l'Arsenal**, just below the Bastille, to **Parc de la Villette**, some four kilometres away. Alleys of chestnut trees cloak the peaceful, still waters of the two hundred year old canal, at one point just a stone's throw from the roaring **Place de la République**. The journey includes idyllic stretches with arching iron footbridges and boatman's pathways. It has ghoulish landmarks, too: the elegant **Maison des Morts** is where they used to pay rewards for bodies fished from the canal, and immediately below the Bastille, in a deep, dark netherworld, the boat slows to reveal a crypt, wherein lie the remains of the victims of the revolutions of 1830 and 1848. Open-topped tourist boats cover the fascinating two-and-a-half hour trip a few times a day.

→ THREE CEMETERIES

A cemetery may not be on every city's visitor hit-list, but every city isn't Paris, which has three great *cimetières*, full of history's rich and famous, and **Père-Lachaise** is the greatest of them all. Visit this massive sea of sepulchres, where the only movement appears to be the flapping of crows' wings above the deadly calm, and you'll pick out a long list of the great and the good who happen to have breathed their last in the city. Then you'll understand the wisdom of the saying: "You haven't lived until you've died in Paris". The twelfth century lovers Abelard and Heloise were the first to be reburied here, and in the last two hundred years, they've been followed by a veritable A-list Who's Who. The range is phenomenal, from Chopin to Jim Morrison, Balzac to Piaf, Rossini to Oscar Wilde and Molière to Isadora Duncan. Despite the great clamour they may have made in their lives, they now rest in a stunningly tranquil oasis of peace, the largest green space in Paris.

For contrast, what better than the life-affirming paintings of the twentieth century's most acclaimed artist. The **Picasso Museum** is hidden in a fine seventeenth century mansion in R**ue de Thorigny**, a back street in the fascinating **Marais Quarter**. It holds nearly four thousand of his works, from childhood sketches to important late works.

CALENDAR HIGHLIGHTS

Whatever your fancy, Paris can satisfy it. March is a good time for book lovers to indulge a wordy fix: the Salon du Livre Paris at the Parc des Expositions Paris-Nord Villepinte is a five day orgy *des mots* with a shelf-full of performances, while Poets' Springtime has over five thousand well versed events in streets, cafés, markets, museums, schools and stations. Later in the year, October's Reading Festival boasts hundreds of written word events. The music world takes to the City of Light with an eclectic flourish. The Open-Air Classical Music Festival on weekends in August and September brings world-class performers to Parc Floral, and in the same month Jazz à la Villette,

PARIS IN...

→ ONE DAY

Eiffel Tower and a boat trip on the Seine, Musée d'Orsay, people watching in a St-Germain brasserie

→ TWO DAYS

Musée du Quai Branly (or The Louvre), Montmartre, Picasso Museum and the Marais

→ THREE DAYS

Père-Lachaise, Canal Saint-Martin, Centre Pompidou

in Parc de la Villette, grows annually in stature as a home for innovative, experimental jazz. Dramatic Spanish rhythms cut through the springtime air in March's International Flamenco Festival at Le Grand Rex. Meantime, in north-east Paris, Seine St-Denis chills to the Banlieues Bleues, also in March. If your springtime fancy turns to art, then head to Art Paris, at Grand Palais, for a high quality small collection of paintings, sculptures and photos. You can stay up late either at La Nuit des Musées (May) when museums keep their doors open until 1am, or at Nuit Blanche (October) when it seems every public space in the city lets you in for a nocturnal cultural nose around. Catch a diverse programme of movies at springtime's Paris Film Festival, at the Cinéma Gaumont Marignan on the Champs-Élysées, or indulge your taste for wine at October's Montmartre Grape Harvest Festival (la Butte has its own vineyard). Hang around for a month and you can carouse on the Carrousel du Louvre at November's Great Wines Fair. If your taste is for beer and chips, a world away from the cultural clichés of Paris, then lose yourself amongst five million others at Europe's largest funfair, the Foire du Trône, at Pelouse de Reuilly, in the spring.

EATING OUT

Three hundred years ago, the social philosopher Montesquieu famously said, "Lunch kills half of Paris, supper the other half." Food plays such an important role in Gallic life that eating well is deemed a citizen's birthright. Stroll around any part of the capital and lavish looking shops offer perfectly presented treats: the Place de la Madeleine, for instance, has a lip-smacking range of treats. Parisians are intensely knowledgeable about their food and wine to the extent that restaurant, bistro and brasserie offerings here are of a higher quality than just about any other European city. Mind you, the French capital has had a lot on its plate in recent years with the rest of Europe seemingly playing catch up, by way of strong gastronomic performances coming from the likes of Barcelona, London and Copenhagen. As though Paris would rest on its laurels! Young chefs have taken up the cudgels and are opening their own crowd-pulling bistros and inventing their own styles; they've broken away from more formulaic regimes to achieve their own goals. They can call on the strongest backup team around: specialist produce shops line every Parisian thoroughfare, and there are not far short of a hundred city-wide markets teeming with fresh produce. Remember, when eating in Paris, to enjoy your meal at a leisurely pace – this is the city, after all, that practically shuts up shop at 12.30pm for lunch. People think nothing of spending up to three hours at the table, so if you're pressed for time, go to a brasserie or café. A service charge of fifteen per cent is normally included in the price of the meal, but locals leave an additional five per cent in smaller restaurants, and five to ten per cent in the grander establishments, which pride themselves on their service. (If you think the service has been a bit brusque or haughty, just remember that a Parisian waiter walks on average between six and twelve miles a day attending to customers' whims).

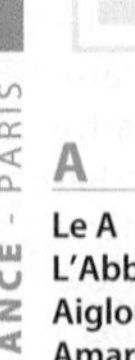

HOTELS FROM A TO Z

RESTAURANTS FROM A TO Z

A

A Beauvilliers XXX 233
A et M Restaurant N XX ☺ 238
Afaria N X ☺ 238
L'Affriolé X ☺ 212
Aida N X ✿ 212
Alain Ducasse au Plaza Athénée XXXXX ✿✿✿ 180
Al Ajami XX 188
Alcazar XX 224
Ambassade d'Auvergne XX ☺ 203
Les Ambassadeurs XXXXX ✿✿ 199
L'Ambroisie XXXX ✿✿✿ 231
L'Angle du Faubourg XX ✿ 186
Apicius XXXXX ✿✿ 181
Arpège XXX ✿✿✿ 208
Astrance XXX ✿✿✿ 209
L'Atelier de Joël Robuchon N X ✿✿ 224
Atelier Maître Albert XX 223
Au Bon Accueil X ☺ 211
Au Clair de la Lune XX 234
Au Gourmand N XX ☺ 203
Auguste XX ✿ 210
Au Petit Riche XX 202
Au Pied de Cochon XX 203
Au Trou Gascon XX ✿ 237
Aux Lyonnais X ☺ 204

B

Ballon des Ternes XX 187
Bath's X ✿ 189
Benkay XXX 237
Benoit XX ✿ 223
La Biche au Bois X 232
Le Bistrot des Soupirs "Chez les On" X 239
Bistrot du Sommelier XX 187
Bofinger XX 231
La Braisière XX ✿ 187
Le Bristol XXXXX ✿✿ 180
Buisson Ardent X ☺ 225

C

Café Constant N X ☺ 212
Café de la Paix XXX 201
Café Lenôtre - Pavillon Elysée X 188
Café Panique N XX ☺ 203
Caïus X 188
Caroubier XX ☺ 238
Carré des Feuillants XXXX ✿✿ 200
La Cave Gourmande X ☺ 239
Caves Petrissans X ☺ 189
Le Céladon XXX ✿ 200
La Cerisaie X ☺ 228
Chez Georges X 204
Chez Georges XX 188
Chez Géraud XX ☺ 237
Chez l'Ami Jean X ☺ 212
Chez les Anges XX ☺ 210
Chez Michel N X ☺ 205
Le Chiberta XXX ✿ 184
Cigale Récamier XX 223
Le "Cinq" XXXXX ✿✿ 180
Citrus Étoile XX 186
Clos des Gourmets X ☺ 211
Copenhague XXX ✿ 184
Le Cottage Marcadet XX 234
La Coupole XX 228
Cristal Room Baccarat XX 185

D

D'Chez Eux XX 210
Daru X 189
Le Dirigeable N X ☺ 239
Le Dôme XXX 228
Dominique Bouchet X ✿ 188
Drouant XXX 201

E

Les Élysées XXX ✿✿ 182
L'Enoteca X 232
L'Épi Dupin X ☺ 224
L'Épopée XX 211
L'Espadon XXXXX ✿ 199

F

Les Fables de La Fontaine X ✿ 211
Fermette Marbeuf 1900 XX 186
La Fontaine Gaillon XXX 201
Fouquet's XXX 183

G

Gallopin XX 202
La Gauloise XX 211
Gaya Rive Gauche par Pierre Gagnaire X ✿ 224
Gérard Besson XXX ✿ 201
Goumard XXXX ✿ 200
Graindorge XX ☺ 187
La Grande Cascade XXXX ✿ 237
Le Grand Pan N X ☺ 238
Le Grand Véfour XXXX ✿✿ 200
Guy Savoy XXXX ✿✿✿ 181

FRANCE - PARIS

OPEN SATURDAY AND SUNDAY

Restaurant		Page
Al Ajami	XX	188
Alcazar	XX	224
Ambassade d'Auvergne	XX ☺	203
L'Atelier de Joël Robuchon N	X ✿✿	224
Au Pied de Cochon	XX	203
Ballon des Ternes	XX	187
Benkay	XXX	237
Benoit	XX ✿	223
Bofinger	XX	231
Le Bristol	XXXXX ✿✿	180
Café de la Paix	XXX	201
Caroubier	XX ☺	238
Chez Georges	XX	188
Le "Cinq"	XXXXX ✿✿	180
La Coupole	XX	228
Drouant	XXX	201
L'Enoteca	X	232
L'Espadon	XXXXX ✿	199
Les Fables de La Fontaine	X ✿	211
Fermette Marbeuf 1900	XX	186
Fouquet's	XXX	183
Gallopin	XX	202
La Gauloise	XX	211
Goumard	XXXX ✿	200
La Grande Cascade	XXXX ✿	237
Il Vino d'Enrico Bernardo N	XX ✿	209
Le Jules Verne	XXX	209
Marius et Janette	XX	186
Market	XX	187
Mon Vieil Ami	X	225
Le Moulin de la Galette	XX	234
New Jawad	XX	210
Les Ombres	XX	210
L'Orangerie	XX	223
Pinxo	XX	203
Le Pur' Grill N	XXX ✿	201
Le Relais Plaza	XX	185
Senderens	XXX ✿✿	200
La Table de Joël Robuchon	XXX ✿✿	183
Terminus Nord	XX	203
Timgad	XX	186
La Tour d'Argent	XXXXX ✿	222
Tsé Yang	XX	185
Vaudeville	XX	203
Yugaraj	XX	223

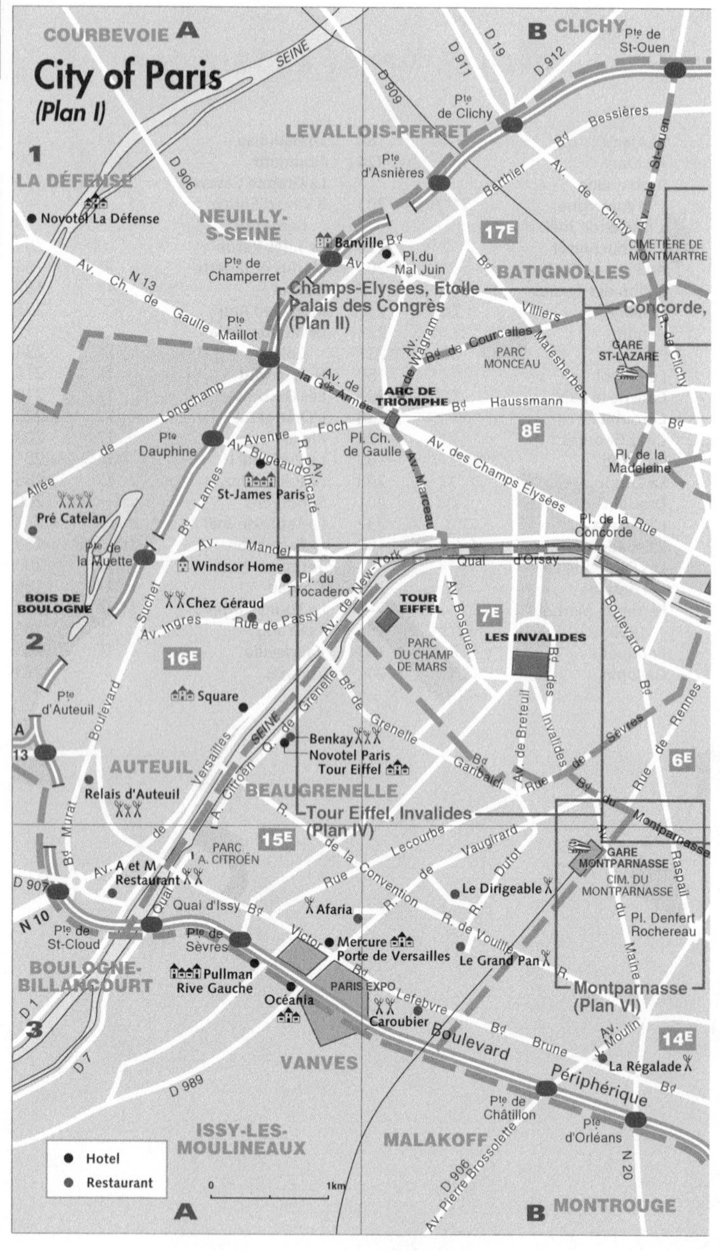
City of Paris
(Plan I)
COURBEVOIE
LA DÉFENSE
Novotel La Défense
NEUILLY-S-SEINE
LEVALLOIS-PERRET
CLICHY
Banville
Pré Catelan
St-James Paris
Windsor Home
Chez Géraud
BOIS DE BOULOGNE
Square
Benkay
Novotel Paris Tour Eiffel
Relais d'Auteuil
AUTEUIL
BEAUGRENELLE
A et M Restaurant
Afaria
Mercure Porte de Versailles
Le Dirigeable
Le Grand Pan
Pullman Rive Gauche
Océania
Caroubier
La Régalade
BOULOGNE-BILLANCOURT
VANVES
ISSY-LES-MOULINEAUX
MALAKOFF
MONTROUGE
Champs-Elysées, Etoile Palais des Congrès (Plan II)
Concorde,
Tour Eiffel, Invalides (Plan IV)
Montparnasse (Plan VI)
ARC DE TRIOMPHE
TOUR EIFFEL
LES INVALIDES
GARE ST-LAZARE
GARE MONTPARNASSE
PARIS EXPO
Boulevard Périphérique
Hotel
Restaurant

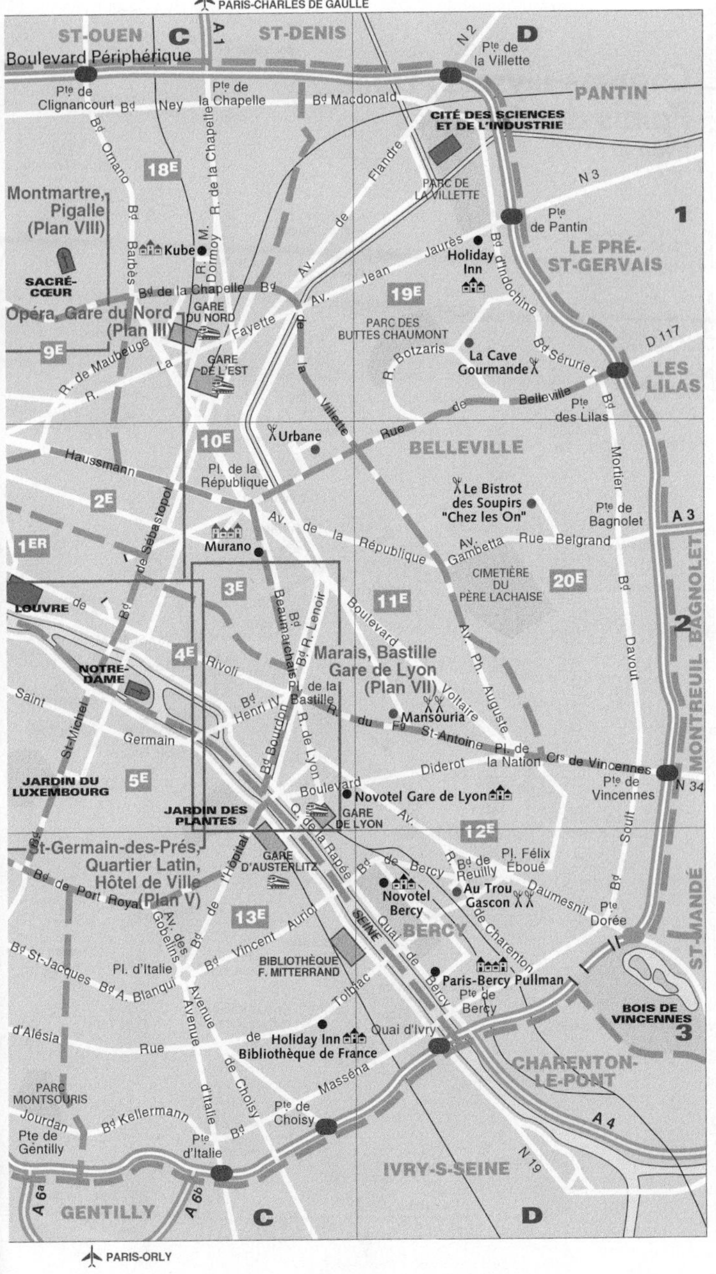
PARIS-CHARLES DE GAULLE
ST-OUEN
C
A 1
ST-DENIS
N 2
D
Pte de la Villette
Boulevard Périphérique
Pte de Clignancourt
Bd Ney
Pte de la Chapelle
Bd Macdonald
PANTIN
CITÉ DES SCIENCES ET DE L'INDUSTRIE
Bd Ornano
18E
R. de la Chapelle
Av. de Flandre
PARC DE LA VILLETTE
N 3
Montmartre, Pigalle (Plan VIII)
Bd Barbès
R. M. Dormoy
Pte de Pantin
1
Kube
Holiday Inn
LE PRÉ-ST-GERVAIS
SACRÉ-CŒUR
Av. Jean Jaurès
Bd d'Indochine
Bd de la Chapelle
19E
Opéra, Gare du Nord (Plan III)
GARE DU NORD
La Fayette
PARC DES BUTTES CHAUMONT
9E
R. de Maubeuge
R. Botzaris
La Cave Gourmande
Bd Sérurier
D 117
LES LILAS
GARE DE L'EST
Av. de la Villette
Rue de Belleville
Pte des Lilas
10E
Urbane
BELLEVILLE
Haussmann
Pl. de la République
Bd Mortier
Le Bistrot des Soupirs "Chez les On"
2E
Bd de Sébastopol
Pte de Bagnolet
A 3
1ER
Av. de la République
Murano
Av. Gambetta
Rue Belgrand
MONTREUIL BAGNOLET
CIMETIÈRE DU PÈRE LACHAISE
20E
3E
Bd Beaumarchais
Bd R. Lenoir
11E
LOUVRE
Rue de Rivoli
Boulevard Voltaire
2
4E
Marais, Bastille Gare de Lyon (Plan VII)
Av. Ph. Auguste
Bd Davout
NOTRE-DAME
Pl. de la Bastille
Bd Henri IV
Saint Germain
R. de Lyon
Mansouria
Fg St-Antoine
Pl. de la Nation
Crs de Vincennes
Bd St-Michel
Bd Bourdon
Diderot
JARDIN DU LUXEMBOURG
5E
Boulevard
Novotel Gare de Lyon
Pte de Vincennes
N 34
JARDIN DES PLANTES
GARE DE LYON
Av.
Bd Soult
12E
St-Germain-des-Prés, Quartier Latin, Hôtel de Ville (Plan V)
Bd de l'Hôpital
Q. de la Rapée
Pl. Félix Éboué
GARE D'AUSTERLITZ
Bd de Bercy
R. de Reuilly
Bd de Port Royal
Novotel Bercy
Au Trou Gascon
Daumesnil
Pte Dorée
ST-MANDÉ
Av. des Gobelins
13E
SEINE
Quai de Bercy
BERCY
de Charenton
Bd St-Jacques
Bd Vincent Auriol
BIBLIOTHÈQUE F. MITTERRAND
Pl. d'Italie
Bd A. Blanqui
Avenue d'Italie
Tolbiac
Paris-Bercy Pullman
Pte de Bercy
BOIS DE VINCENNES
3
d'Alésia
Rue de Tolbiac
Holiday Inn Bibliothèque de France
Quai d'Ivry
Avenue de Choisy
CHARENTON-LE-PONT
Masséna
PARC MONTSOURIS
Jourdan
Pte de Gentilly
Bd Kellermann
Bd
Pte de Choisy
A 4
Pte d'Italie
N 19
IVRY-S-SEINE
A 6a
A 6b
GENTILLY
C
D
PARIS-ORLY

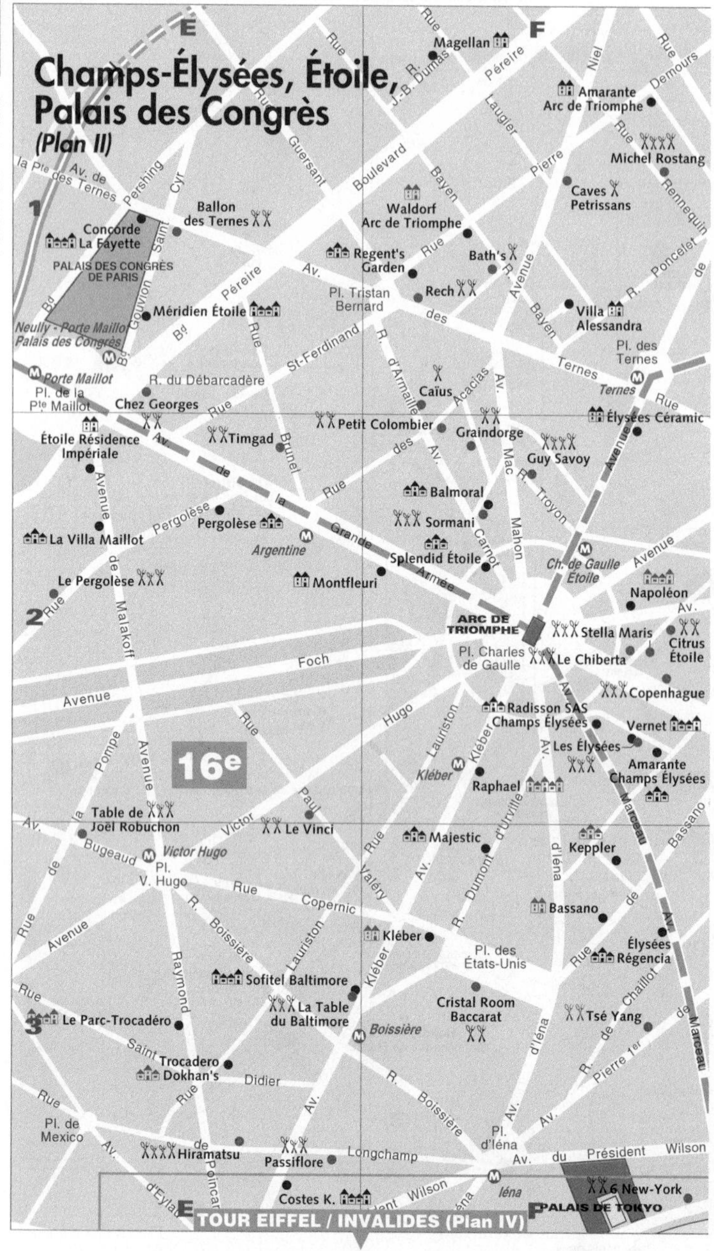
Champs-Élysées, Étoile, Palais des Congrès
(Plan II)
Magellan
Amarante Arc de Triomphe
Michel Rostang
Caves Petrissans
Ballon des Ternes
Waldorf Arc de Triomphe
Concorde La Fayette
PALAIS DES CONGRÈS DE PARIS
Regent's Garden
Bath's
Rech
Méridien Étoile
Villa Alessandra
Neuilly - Porte Maillot Palais des Congrès
Porte Maillot
Caïus
Ternes
Chez Georges
Élysées Céramic
Petit Colombier
Étoile Résidence Impériale
Timgad
Graindorge
Guy Savoy
Balmoral
Sormani
Pergolèse
La Villa Maillot
Argentine
Splendid Étoile
Ch. de Gaulle Étoile
Le Pergolèse
Montfleuri
Napoléon
ARC DE TRIOMPHE
Stella Maris
Citrus Étoile
Le Chiberta
Copenhague
Radisson SAS Champs Élysées
Vernet
Les Élysées
Amarante Champs Élysées
16e
Kléber
Raphael
Table de Joël Robuchon
Le Vinci
Majestic
Keppler
Victor Hugo
Bassano
Kléber
Élysées Régencia
Sofitel Baltimore
Cristal Room Baccarat
Tsé Yang
La Table du Baltimore
Le Parc-Trocadéro
Boissière
Trocadero Dokhan's
Hiramatsu
Passiflore
Costes K.
Iéna
6 New-York
PALAIS DE TOKYO
TOUR EIFFEL / INVALIDES (Plan IV)

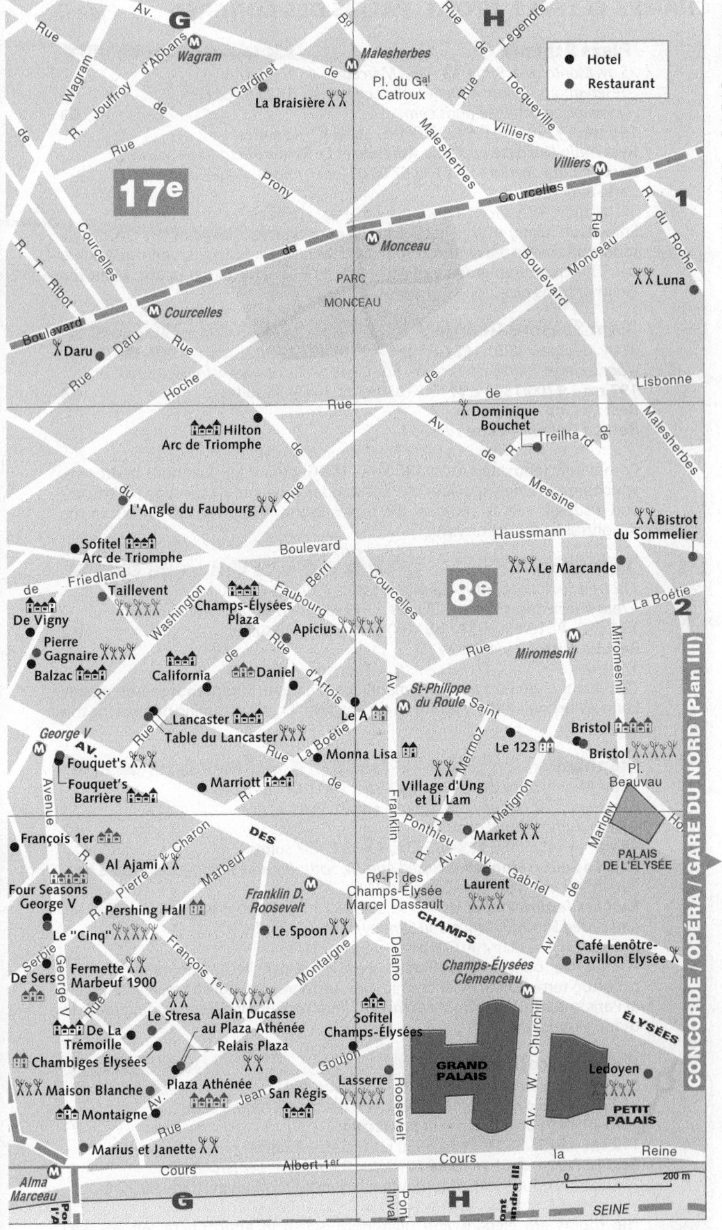
Hotel
Restaurant
17e
8e
G
H
1
2
Wagram
Malesherbes
Pl. du Gal Catroux
La Braisière
Villiers
Monceau
PARC MONCEAU
Courcelles
Luna
Daru
Lisbonne
Dominique Bouchet
Hilton Arc de Triomphe
L'Angle du Faubourg
Bistrot du Sommelier
Sofitel Arc de Triomphe
Le Marcande
Taillevent
Champs-Élysées Plaza
De Vigny
Apicius
Pierre Gagnaire
Miromesnil
Balzac
California
Daniel
St-Philippe du Roule
Lancaster
Table du Lancaster
Le A
George V
Fouquet's
Monna Lisa
Le 123
Bristol
Bristol
Pl. Beauvau
Fouquet's Barrière
Marriott
Village d'Ung et Li Lam
François 1er
Market
Al Ajami
PALAIS DE L'ÉLYSÉE
Four Seasons George V
Pershing Hall
Franklin D. Roosevelt
Rd-Pt des Champs-Élysée Marcel Dassault
Laurent
Le "Cinq"
Le Spoon
Café Lenôtre-Pavillon Elysée
De Sers
Fermette Marbeuf 1900
Champs-Élysées Clemenceau
Le Stresa
Alain Ducasse au Plaza Athénée
De La Trémoille
Relais Plaza
Sofitel Champs-Élysées
Chambiges Élysées
GRAND PALAIS
Ledoyen
Maison Blanche
Plaza Athénée
San Régis
Lasserre
PETIT PALAIS
Montaigne
Marius et Janette
Alma Marceau
SEINE
200 m

CONCORDE / OPÉRA / GARE DU NORD (Plan III)

CHAMPS-ÉLYSÉES, ÉTOILE, PALAIS DES CONGRÈS *Plan II*

Plaza Athénée

25 av. Montaigne (8th) – Ⓜ Alma Marceau – ✆ 01 53 67 66 65 – reservations@plaza-athenee-paris.com – Fax 01 53 67 66 66 – www.plaza-athenee-paris.com **G3**

146 rm – 720/740 € 820/840 €, ☕ 48 € – 45 suites

Rest *Alain Ducasse au Plaza Athénée* et ***Le Relais Plaza*** – see below

Rest *La Cour Jardin* – *✆ 01 53 67 66 02 (open mid May-mid September)* Carte 82/118 €

◆ Palace ◆ Grand Luxury ◆ Personalised ◆

Enjoy true luxury in this hotel with its comfortable, Classic or Art Deco-style rooms, afternoon teas with music in the Gobelins gallery and a stunning designer bar. The charming, greenery-filled terrace of La Cour Jardin opens when the weather turns nice.

Four Seasons George V

31 av. George-V (8th) – Ⓜ George V – ✆ 01 49 52 70 00 – par.lecinq@fourseasons.com – Fax 01 49 52 70 10 – www.fourseasons.com

197 rm – 700/1350 € 730/1350 €, ☕ 38 € – 48 suites **G3**

Rest *Le Cinq* – see below

Rest *La Galerie* – Carte 72/130 €

◆ Palace ◆ Grand Luxury ◆ Personalised ◆

Completely renovated in an 18C style, the George V has luxurious bedrooms, which are extremely spacious by Paris standards. Beautiful collections of artwork and a superb spa. In summer, the tables in this restaurant are set out in the delightful interior courtyard.

Le Bristol

112 r. Fg St-Honoré (8th) – Ⓜ Miromesnil – ✆ 01 53 43 43 00 – resa@lebristolparis.com – Fax 01 53 43 43 01 – www.lebristolparis.com

124 rm – 610/630 € 710/1160 €, ☕ 53 € – 38 suites **H2**

Rest *Le Bristol* – see below

◆ Palace ◆ Grand Luxury ◆ Personalised ◆

1925 luxury hotel set around a magnificent garden. Sumptuous rooms, mainly Louis XV or Louis XVI-style with an exceptional "boat" swimming pool on the top floor.

Raphael

17 av. Kléber (16th) ✉ 75116 – Ⓜ Kléber – ✆ 01 53 64 32 00 – reservation@raphael-hotel.com – Fax 01 53 64 32 01 – www.raphael-hotel.com **F2**

48 rm – 345/490 € 345/570 €, ☕ 38 € – 37 suites

Rest *La Salle à Manger* – *(closed August, Saturday and Sunday)* Menu 50 € bi (lunch)/60 € bi (dinner) – Carte 63/85 €

Rest *Les Jardins Plein Ciel* – *✆ 01 53 64 32 30 (open from May to September and closed Saturday lunch and Sunday)* Menu 70/90 €

◆ Grand Luxury ◆ Palace ◆ Stylish ◆

The Raphael, built in 1925, offers a superb wood-panelled gallery, refined rooms, a rooftop terrace with a panoramic view and a trendy English bar. A lovely view of Paris and a buffet formula at this 7th floor restaurant. Superb dining room in Grand Hotel style.

Le Parc-Trocadéro

55 av. R. Poincaré (16th) ✉ 75116 – Ⓜ Victor Hugo – ✆ 01 44 05 66 66 – corinne.leponner@renaissancehotels.com – Fax 01 44 05 66 00 – www.marriott.com **E3**

112 rm – 195/450 € 245/950 €, ☕ 27 € – 4 suites

Rest *Le Parc* – *✆ 01 44 05 66 10 (closed 3 August-1st September, 21 December-5 January, Saturday lunch, Sunday an Monday)* Carte 60/77 €

◆ Grand Luxury ◆ Modern ◆

The rooms are elegant and pleasingly British in atmosphere. All are well equipped (with wifi) and distributed around a garden terrace. Part of the bar décor is by Arman.

Fouquet's Barrière

46 av. George-V (8th) – Ⓜ George V – ✆ 01 40 69 60 00 – hotelfouquets@lucienbarriere.com – Fax 01 40 69 60 05 – www.fouquets-barriere.com **G2**

67 rm – 🚹690/910 € 🚹🚹690/910 €, ☕ 35 € – 40 suites

Rest *Fouquet's* – see below

Rest *Le Diane* – *(closed 19 July-18 August, 3-12 January, Sunday and Monday)* Menu 60 € (weekday lunch), 90/135 € – Carte 96/188 €

♦ Grand Luxury ♦ Modern ♦

A hushed ambience at Le Diane with its brightly-lit niches adorned with flowers. Contemporary cuisine.

Hilton Arc de Triomphe

51 r. de Courcelles (8th) – Ⓜ Courcelles – ✆ 01 58 36 67 00 – reservation.adt@hilton.com – Fax 01 58 36 67 84 **G2**

438 rm – 🚹290/680 € 🚹🚹290/730 €, ☕ 30 € – 25 suites

Rest *Safran* – *✆ 01 58 36 67 96* – Menu 49 € (dinner) – Carte 46/69 €

♦ Luxury ♦ Chain hotel ♦ Personalised ♦

This new hotel, inspired by the liners of the 1930s, has successfully created a luxurious and refined atmosphere. Elegant Art Deco rooms designed by Jacques Garcia, patio with a fountain, fitness centre etc. At Safran, contemporary cuisine influenced by the flavours and scents of Asia.

Lancaster

7 r. Berri (8th) – Ⓜ George V – ✆ 01 40 76 40 76 – reservations@hotel-lancaster.fr – Fax 01 40 76 40 00 – www.hotel-lancaster.fr **G2**

46 rm – 🚹320 € 🚹🚹490 €, ☕ 37 € – 11 suites

Rest *La Table du Lancaster* – see below

♦ Luxury ♦ Classical ♦

Boris Pastoukhoff paid for his lodging in this hotel with paintings, thus adding richly to this old townhouse's elegant decor, so beloved by Marlene Dietrich.

Sofitel Baltimore

88 bis av. Kléber (16th) ✉ 75116 – Ⓜ Boissière – ✆ 01 44 34 54 54 – h2789@accor.com – Fax 01 44 34 54 44 – www.baltimore-sofitel-paris.com **E3**

103 rm – 🚹420/820 € 🚹🚹420/820 €, ☕ 25 € – 1 suite

Rest *Table du Baltimore* – see below

♦ Luxury ♦ Modern ♦

Simple furniture, trendy fabrics, old photos of the city of Baltimore: the contemporary décor of the rooms contrasts with the architecture of this 19C building.

Vernet

25 r. Vernet (8th) – Ⓜ Charles de Gaulle-Etoile – ✆ 01 44 31 98 00 – reservations@hotelvernet.com – Fax 01 44 31 85 69 – www.hotelvernet.com **F2**

42 rm – 🚹320/340 € 🚹🚹370/450 €, ☕ 35 € – 9 suites

Rest *Les Elysées* – see below

♦ Luxury ♦ Classical ♦

A fine building dating from the 1920s, with a dressed-stone façade and wrought-iron balconies. Empire- or Louis XVI-style rooms. Fashionable bar and grill.

Napoléon

40 av. Friedland (8th) – Ⓜ Charles de Gaulle-Etoile – ✆ 01 56 68 43 21 – napoleon@hotelnapoleon.com – Fax 01 47 66 82 33 – www.hotelnapoleonparis.com **F2**

101 rm – 🚹440/630 € 🚹🚹440/690 €, ☕ 26 €

Rest – *(closed dinner, Saturday and Sunday)* Menu 45 € bi (weekday lunch), 85/120 €

♦ Luxury ♦ Retro ♦

A stone's throw from Place de l'Étoile, this hotel-museum honours the emperor's memory via autographs, figurines and paintings from the period. Directoire or Empire style bedrooms. A traditional menu served in the restrained, cosy, wainscoted restaurant.

Balzac without rest

6 r. Balzac (8th) – Ⓜ George V – ✆ 01 44 35 18 00 – reservation-balzac@jjwhotels.com – Fax 01 44 35 18 05 – www.hotelbalzac.com **G2**

69 rm – †420/470 € ††470/550 €, ☕ 38 € – 13 suites

♦ Luxury ♦ Personalised ♦

Hotel completely refurbished in luxury style, with neo-Classical décor, a vibrant colour scheme and references to the writer Balzac. Period furniture and high-tech facilities in the guestrooms.

Costes K. without rest

81 av. Kléber (16th) ✉ 75116 – Ⓜ Trocadéro – ✆ 01 44 05 75 75 – resak@hotelcostesk.com – Fax 01 44 05 74 74 – www.hotelcostesk.com **E3**

83 rm – †300 € ††350/500 €, ☕ 20 €

♦ Luxury ♦ Modern ♦

This hotel by Ricardo Bofill is ultra-modern. It invites you to enjoy the discreet calm of its vast rooms with their pure lines, laid out around a Japanese-style patio.

San Régis

12 r. J. Goujon (8th) – Ⓜ Champs-Elysées Clemenceau – ✆ 01 44 95 16 16 – message@hotel-sanregis.fr – Fax 01 45 61 05 48 – www.hotel-sanregis.fr **G3**

41 rm – †340 € ††450/725 €, ☕ 34 € – 3 suites

Rest – *(closed August and Sunday)* Menu 35 € (lunch) – Carte 46/61 €

♦ Luxury ♦ Personalised ♦

This 1857 townhouse has been remodelled with taste. A fine staircase adorned with stained glass and statues leads to delightful guestrooms furnished with a diverse range of furniture. The hotel's exquisitely appointed restaurant occupies a subdued but luxurious lounge-library.

Sofitel Arc de Triomphe

14 r. Beaujon (8th) – Ⓜ Charles de Gaulle-Etoile – ✆ 01 53 89 50 50 – h1296@accor.com – Fax 01 53 89 50 51 – www.arcdetriomphe-sofitel-paris.com **G2**

134 rm – †510/590 € ††580/620 €, ☕ 29 € – 1 suite

Rest *Le Clovis* – *✆ 01 53 89 50 53 (closed 26 July-24 August, 20-30 December, Saturday, Sunday and public holidays)* Menu 35 € (lunch) – Carte 48/90 €

♦ Luxury ♦ Chain hotel ♦ Personalised ♦

Typical late-19C Parisian building, with 18C-inspired decoration but fitted up to 21C standards. Elegant rooms. Try and book the amazing "Concept Room". Le Clovis is renowned for its contemporary décor and cuisine and attentive service.

Méridien Étoile

81 bd Gouvion St-Cyr (17th) – Ⓜ Neuilly-Porte Maillot – ✆ 01 40 68 34 34 – guest.etoile@lemeridien.com – Fax 01 40 68 31 31 – www.lemeriden.com/etoile **E1**

1025 rm – †185/504 € ††185/504 €, ☕ 25 € – 17 suites

Rest *L'Orenoc* – *✆ 01 40 68 30 40 (closed from end July to end August, 20-28 December, Saturday and Sunday)* Menu 44 € – Carte 54/73 €

♦ Business ♦ Chain hotel ♦ Modern ♦

Facilities at this huge hotel include a jazz club, bar, boutiques and an impressive conference centre. Black granite and shades of beige predominate in the contemporary-style guestrooms. The Orenoc reflects current tastes in food, and has warm, colonial-style decor. A simple menu and buffets are on offer at La Terrasse.

Concorde La Fayette

3 pl. Gén. Koenig (17th) – Ⓜ Porte Maillot – ✆ 01 40 68 50 68 – booking@concorde-hotels.com – Fax 01 40 68 50 43 – www.concorde-lafayette.com **E1**

931 rm – †165/450 € ††165/540 €, ☕ 27 € – 19 suites

Rest *La Fayette* – *✆ 01 40 68 51 19* – Menu 38/70 € bi – Carte 46/72 €

♦ Business ♦ Modern ♦

This 33-floor tower, part of the city's convention centre, offers wonderful views of Paris from most of its spacious and comfortable rooms, as well as from the panoramic bar. Buffet meals are served in the stained glass setting of La Fayette.

De Vigny

9 r. Balzac (8th) – George V – 01 42 99 80 80 – reservation@hoteldevigny.com – Fax 01 42 99 80 40 – www.hoteldevigny.com **G2**

26 rm – 305/395 € 320/440 €, 29 € – 11 suites

Rest *Baretto* – *(closed 15-24 August)* Menu 60 € bi/95 € bi – Carte 54/84 €

♦ Luxury ♦ Personalised ♦

A discreet hotel close to the Champs-Elysées with refined bedrooms with personalised touches including four-poster beds. Cosy lounge with attractive fireplace. The Baretto serves traditional cuisine in a stylish, low-key atmosphere and Art Deco setting.

Champs-Élysées Plaza without rest

35 r. de Berri (8th) – George V – 01 53 53 20 20 – info@champselyseesplaza.com – Fax 01 53 53 20 21 – www.champselyseesplaza.com **G2**

35 rm – 490/690 € 490/690 €, 24 € – 10 suites

♦ Luxury ♦ Personalised ♦

The spacious and elegant rooms of this opulent (and completely non-smoking) hotel near the Champs-Élysées all have fireplaces and Art Deco-style bathrooms.

Marriott

70 av. des Champs-Élysées (8th) – Franklin D. Roosevelt – 01 53 93 55 00 – mhrs.pardt.ays@marriotthotels.com – Fax 01 53 93 55 01 – www.marriott.com **G2**

174 rm – 365/650 € 365/650 €, 29 € – 18 suites

Rest *Sur les Champs* – *01 53 93 55 44* – Carte 39/71 €

♦ Chain hotel ♦ Business ♦ Modern ♦

Enjoy American efficiency and cocoon-like comfort in this smart hotel. Most of the bedrooms overlook the Champs-Élysées. The fanciful décor of lampposts and frescoes in this restaurant plays to a clichéd image of Paris in bygone days.

California

16 r. Berri (8th) – George V – 01 43 59 93 00 – cal@hroy.com – Fax 01 45 61 03 62 – www.hotel-california-paris.com **G2**

158 rm – 415/440 € 415/495 €, 30 € – 16 suites

Rest – *(closed August, Saturday and Sunday) (lunch only)* Menu 35/45 €

♦ Luxury ♦ Classical ♦

Several thousand paintings adorn the walls of this old luxury hotel dating from the 1920s. The collection of 200 whiskies in the piano-bar is equally impressive! The restaurant room has a stunning patio-terrace extension (fountain, mosaics, and greenery).

La Trémoille

14 r. Trémoille (8th) – Alma Marceau – 01 56 52 14 00 – reservation@hotel-tremoille.com – Fax 01 40 70 01 08 – www.hotel-tremoille.com **G3**

90 rm – 350/475 € 400/560 €, 28 € – 3 suites

Rest *Louis 2* – *(closed Saturday lunch, Sunday and public holidays)* Carte 48/72 €

♦ Luxury ♦ Modern ♦

The hotel has been successfully refurbished with contemporary decor combining the old and the ultra-modern, the latest high-tech equipment, and marble bathrooms with Portuguese tiles. An elegant dining room with a low key atmosphere; contemporary cuisine.

Keppler without rest

10 r. Keppler (16th) 75116 – George V – 01 47 20 65 05 – hotel@keppler.fr – Fax 01 47 23 02 29 – wwww.keppler.fr **F3**

34 rm – 300/350 € 420/490 €, 22 € – 5 suites

♦ Luxury ♦ Personalised ♦

This luxurious, sophisticated establishment is the work of designer Pierre-Yves Rochon. A magical blend of styles, materials and light sets the tone in the lobby and rooms.

Trocadero Dokhan's without rest

117 r. Lauriston (16th) ✉ 75116 – Ⓜ Trocadéro – ☎ 01 53 65 66 99 – reservation@dokhans.com – Fax 01 53 65 66 88 – www.dokhans-sofitel-paris.com **E3**

45 rm – ♦430/460 € ♦♦430/460 €, ☕ 27 € – 4 suites

♦ Townhouse ♦ Personalised ♦

Attractive town house (1910) with Palladian architecture and neo-Classical interior décor. 18C celadon wood panelling in the cosy lounges and intimate champagne bar.

De Sers

41 av. Pierre 1er de Serbie (8th) – Ⓜ George V – ☎ 01 53 23 75 75 – contact@hoteldesers.com – Fax 01 53 23 75 76 – www.hoteldesers.com **G3**

49 rm – ♦480/550 € ♦♦550/900 €, ☕ 29 € – 3 suites

Rest – *(closed August and Sunday)* Carte 34/180 €

♦ Luxury ♦ Modern ♦

Successfully refurbished late-19C townhouse. While the hall has kept its original character, the rooms are thoroughly modern. The food reflects current tastes and is served in a designer dining room or, in summer, on the pleasant terrace.

François 1er without rest

7 r. Magellan (8th) – Ⓜ George V – ☎ 01 47 23 44 04 – hotel@hotel-francois1er.fr – Fax 01 47 23 93 43 – www.the-paris-hotel.com **G3**

40 rm – ♦300/780 € ♦♦350/1000 €, ☕ 22 € – 2 suites

♦ Luxury ♦ Personalised ♦

Mexican marble, mouldings, curios, antique furniture and a plethora of paintings make up the luxurious décor created by French architect Pierre Yves Rochon. Substantial buffet breakfasts.

Montaigne without rest

6 av. Montaigne (8th) – Ⓜ Alma Marceau – ☎ 01 47 20 30 50 – contact@hotel-montaigne.com – Fax 01 47 20 94 12 – www.hotel-montaigne.com **G3**

29 rm – ♦200/300 € ♦♦300/450 €, ☕ 20 €

♦ Family ♦ Luxury ♦ Personalised ♦

The wrought-iron grilles, beautiful flower-decked façade and graciously cosy interior all contribute to the Hotel Montaigne's appeal. The avenue is lined by haute couture fashion designers.

La Villa Maillot without rest

143 av. Malakoff (16th) ✉ 75116 – Ⓜ Porte Maillot – ☎ 01 53 64 52 52 – resa@lavillamaillot.fr – Fax 01 45 00 60 61 – www.lavillamaillot.fr **E2**

39 rm – ♦270/350 € ♦♦300/400 €, ☕ 27 € – 3 suites

♦ Business ♦ Modern ♦

A step away from Porte Maillot. Soft colours, a high level of comfort and good soundproofing in the rooms. Glassed-in space for breakfasts, opening onto the greenery.

Daniel

8 r. Frédéric Bastiat (8th) – Ⓜ St-Philippe du Roule – ☎ 01 42 56 17 00 – danielparis@relaischateaux.com – Fax 01 42 56 17 01 – www.hoteldanielparis.com **G2**

22 rm – ♦350/490 € ♦♦410/490 €, ☕ 32 € – 4 suites

Rest – *(closed 26 July-25 August, Saturday and Sunday)* Menu 80 € – Carte 45/67 €

♦ Luxury ♦ Personalised ♦

This hotel likes travel! Furniture and objects brought back from all over the world combined with toile de Jouy create a refined and welcoming décor for Parisian globetrotters.

Sofitel Champs-Élysées

8 r. J. Goujon (8th) – Ⓜ Champs-Elysées Clemenceau – ✆ 01 40 74 64 64 – h1184-re@accor.com – Fax 01 40 74 79 66 – www.sofitel-champselysees-paris.com **G-H3**

40 rm – 🚹395/560 € 🚹🚹395/560 €, ☕ 27 € – 2 suites

Rest *Les Signatures* – *✆ 01 40 74 64 94 (closed 27 July-17 August, 25 December-4 January, Saturday, Sunday and public holidays) (lunch only)*

Menu 48 € – Carte 52/64 €

♦ Chain hotel ♦ Luxury ♦ Personalised ♦

A Second Empire building shared with the Press Club de France. The rooms have a contemporary new look and are equipped with state-of-the-art facilities. Business centre. Simple décor and a lovely terrace. A restaurant popular with journalists.

Majestic without rest

29 r. Dumont d'Urville (16th) ✉ 75116 – Ⓜ Kléber – ✆ 01 45 00 83 70 – management@majestic-hotel.com – Fax 01 45 00 29 48 – www.majestic-hotel.com

closed for refurbishment from April to September **F3**

27 rm – 🚹265 € 🚹🚹370 €, ☕ 19 € – 3 suites

♦ Traditional ♦ Classic ♦

A step away from the Champs-Elysées, this discreet building dating from the 1960s has quiet rooms, with an 'old-money' comfort, well-proportioned and impeccably well-maintained.

Splendid Étoile

1bis av. Carnot (17th) – Ⓜ Charles de Gaulle-Etoile – ✆ 01 45 72 72 00 – hotel@hsplendid.com – Fax 01 45 72 72 01 – www.hsplendid.com **F2**

50 rm – 🚹295 € 🚹🚹295 €, ☕ 23 € – 7 suites

Rest *Le Pré Carré* – 1bis av. Carnot – Menu 34 € bi (dinner) – Carte 34/69 €

♦ Traditional ♦ Classical ♦

Beautiful classical façade with wrought-iron balconies. Spacious rooms full of character, embellished with Louis XV furnishings; some look out onto the Arc de Triomphe.

Pergolèse without rest

3 r. Pergolèse (16th) ✉ 75116 – Ⓜ Argentine – ✆ 01 53 64 04 04 – hotel@pergolese.com – Fax 01 53 64 04 40 – www.hotelpergolese.com **E2**

40 rm – 🚹220/380 € 🚹🚹264/456 €, ☕ 18 €

♦ Business ♦ Design ♦

Restrained 16th arrondissement chic on the outside hides a successful designer interior combining mahogany, glass bricks, chrome and bright colours. Breakfast facing a pleasant patio.

Radisson SAS Champs-Élysées

78 av. Marceau (8th) – Ⓜ Charles de Gaulle-Etoile – ✆ 01 53 23 43 43 – reservations.paris@radissonsas.com – Fax 01 53 23 43 44 – www.champselysees.paris.radissonsas.com **F2**

46 rm – 🚹250/550 € 🚹🚹250/650 €, ☕ 26 €

Rest *La Place* – *(closed August, Christmas holidays, Saturday and Sunday)*

Carte 57/79 €

♦ Chain hotel ♦ Luxury ♦ Modern ♦

A new hotel occupying the former headquarters of Louis Vuitton. Restful, contemporary rooms, high-tech equipment (plasma TVs) and excellent soundproofing. Take a seat at the bar or on the summer terrace; concise Provençal-styled menu.

Élysées Régencia without rest

41 av. Marceau (16th) ✉ 75116 – Ⓜ George V – ✆ 01 47 20 42 65 – info@regencia.com – Fax 01 49 52 03 42 – www.regencia.com **F3**

43 rm – 🚹195/370 € 🚹🚹215/550 €, ☕ 18 €

♦ Traditional ♦ Personalised ♦

Tastefully renovated in a designer style, this hotel offers modern, stylish rooms (blue, fuchsia or aniseed), an elegant sitting room, and a bar/library (red and chocolate coloured wainscoting).

Regent's Garden without rest

6 r. P. Demours (17th) – Ⓜ Ternes – ✆ 01 45 74 07 30 – hotel.regents.garden@wanadoo.fr – Fax 01 40 55 01 42 – www.bestwestern-regents.com **F1**

40 rm – †109/319 € ††109/319 €, ☕ 16 €

♦ Traditional ♦ Personalised ♦

Attractive, elegant townhouse commissioned by Napoleon III for his doctor. Vast period rooms, some giving onto the garden, which is very pleasant in summer.

Balmoral without rest

6 r. Gén. Lanrezac (17th) – Ⓜ Charles de Gaulle-Etoile – ✆ 01 43 80 30 50 – hotel@hotelbalmoral.fr – Fax 01 43 80 51 56 – www.hotel-balmoral.com **F2**

57 rm – †128/140 € ††148/180 €, ☕ 10 €

♦ Traditional ♦ Personalised ♦

A personalised welcome and calm atmosphere characterise this old hotel (1911) a stone's throw from the Étoile. Brightly coloured bedrooms, and elegant wood panelling in the lounge.

Pershing Hall

49 r. P. Charon (8th) – Ⓜ George V – ✆ 01 58 36 58 00 – info@pershinghall.com – Fax 01 58 36 58 01 – www.pershinghall.com **G3**

26 rm – †312/420 € ††420/500 €, ☕ 26 € – 6 suites

Rest – Carte 57/91 €

♦ Luxury ♦ Modern ♦

Once the home of General Pershing, then a veterans club and finally a charming hotel designed by Andrée Putman. Chic interior, original and enchanting hanging garden. Behind the curtain of glass beads, the decor is trendy and the cuisine fashionable. Lounge evenings.

Chambiges Élysées without rest

8 r. Chambiges (8th) – Ⓜ Alma Marceau – ✆ 01 44 31 83 83 – reservation@hotelchambiges.com – Fax 01 40 70 95 51 – www.hotelchambiges.com **G3**

32 rm ☕ – †270/310 € ††270/390 € – 2 suites

♦ Luxury ♦ Personalised ♦

Wood panelling, select drapes and fabrics, period furniture; a romantic, cosy atmosphere reigns in this fully renovated hotel. Comfy rooms and a pretty interior garden.

Le A without rest

4 r. d'Artois (8th) – Ⓜ St-Philippe du Roule – ✆ 01 42 56 99 99 – hotel-le-a@wanadoo.fr – Fax 01 42 56 99 90 – www.paris-hotel-a.com **G-H2**

16 rm – †355/485 € ††355/485 €, ☕ 23 € – 10 suites

♦ Luxury ♦ Modern ♦

F. Hybert, a visual artist, and F. Méchiche, an interior designer, masterminded this trendy hotel (or museum, perhaps?) in black and white. Relaxing lounge-library and bar-lounge.

Kléber without rest

7 r. Belloy (16th) ✉ 75116 – Ⓜ Boissière – ✆ 01 47 23 80 22 – kleberhotel@wanadoo.fr – Fax 01 49 52 07 20 – www.kleberhotel.com **F3**

23 rm – †99/299 € ††99/299 €, ☕ 14 € – 1 suite

♦ Traditional ♦ Classic ♦

The sitting rooms of this 1853 hotel have Louis XV style furniture, original frescoes and old paintings. Exposed stonework and parquet floors in the rooms.

Bassano without rest

15 r. Bassano (16th) ✉ 75116 – Ⓜ George V – ✆ 01 47 23 78 23 – info@hotel-bassano.com – Fax 01 47 20 41 22 – www.hotel-bassano.com **F3**

28 rm – †175/290 € ††195/310 €, ☕ 18 € – 3 suites

♦ Family ♦ Personalised ♦

Cosy atmosphere, wrought-iron furniture, sunny fabrics (it feels like being at a friend's home in Provence, but is only a few hundred metres from the Champs-Elysées).

Montfleuri without rest

21 av. Grande Armée (16th) ✉ 75116 – Ⓜ Charles de Gaulle-Etoile – ✆ 01 45 00 33 65 – montfleuri@wanadoo – Fax 01 45 00 06 36 – www.montfleuri.fr **E-F2**

42 rm – 230/250 € 270/290 €, ☕ 13 € – 3 suites

◆ Modern ◆

Two steps from the Arc de Triomphe, this hotel has been entirely redecorated in a modern style. Peaceful, refined rooms in muted tones, elegantly furnished and adorned with fine fabrics.

Monna Lisa

97 r. La Boétie (8th) – Ⓜ St-Philippe du Roule – ✆ 01 56 43 38 38 – contact@hotelmonnalisa.com – Fax 01 45 62 39 90 **G-H2**

22 rm – 220/235 € 245/265 €, ☕ 17 €

Rest *Caffe Ristretto* – *(closed 3-24 August, 20-28 December, Saturday and Sunday)* Carte 48/66 €

◆ Luxury ◆ Minimalist ◆

This fine hotel built in 1860 is a showpiece for audacious Italian design. Larger rooms on the street side. The Caffe Ristretto offers a delicious journey through the specialities of the Italian peninsula in a wonderfully modern setting.

Le 123 without rest

123 r. du Faubourg St Honoré (8th) – Ⓜ St-Philippe du Roule – ✆ 01 53 89 01 23 – hotel.le123@astotel.com – Fax 01 45 61 09 07 – www.astotel.com **H2**

41 rm – 269/420 € 309/450 €, ☕ 24 €

◆ Luxury ◆ Personalised ◆

Contemporary decor and a mix of styles, materials and colours. The personalised rooms, which are decorated with fashion sketches, are both appealing and unusual.

Waldorf Arc de Triomphe without rest

36 r. Pierre Demours (17th) – Ⓜ Ternes – ✆ 01 47 64 67 67 – arc@hotelswaldorfparis.com – Fax 01 40 53 91 34 – www.hotelswaldorfparis.com **F1**

44 rm – 340/460 € 370/460 €, ☕ 20 €

◆ Business ◆ Design ◆

Attractively refurbished, elegant contemporary rooms. Good fitness centre, a small pool, sauna and steam bath: ideal after a hard day's work or sightseeing!

Amarante Arc de Triomphe without rest

25 r. Th.-de-Banville (17th) – Ⓜ Pereire – ✆ 01 47 63 76 69 – amarante-arcdetriomphe@jjwhotels.com – Fax 01 43 80 63 96 – www.jjwhotels.com **F1**

50 rm – 170/250 € 190/300 €, ☕ 22 €

◆ Chain hotel ◆

This hotel has Directoire-style rooms which are popular with its business clientele. Attic-type rooms on the top floor, with some rooms opening onto the patio.

Étoile Résidence Impériale without rest

155 av. de Malakoff (16th) ✉ 75116 – Ⓜ Porte Maillot – ✆ 01 45 00 23 45 – reservation@residenceimperiale.com – Fax 01 45 01 88 82 – www.residenceimperiale.com **E2**

37 rm – 170/250 € 170/250 €, ☕ 14 €

◆ Traditional ◆ Personalised ◆

Recently-renovated and well-soundproofed hotel, with theme rooms (Africa, Asia, etc.). Some have retained their exposed beams, while others (ground floor) open onto the patio.

Villa Alessandra without rest

9 pl. Boulnois (17th) – Ⓜ Ternes – ✆ 01 56 33 24 24 – alessandra@leshotelsdeparis.com – Fax 01 56 33 24 30 – www.villa-alessandra.com **F1**

49 rm – 310 € 320/385 €, ☕ 20 €

◆ Business ◆ Functional ◆

This Ternes quarter hotel is on a delightful quiet little square and is appreciated for its calm. Colours of southern France in the rooms, with wrought-iron beds and painted wood furniture.

Élysées Céramic without rest

34 av. Wagram (8th) – Ⓜ Ternes – ✆ 01 42 27 20 30 – info@elysees-ceramic.com – Fax 01 46 22 95 83 – www.elysees-ceramic.com **F2**

57 rm – 🚹175/195 € 🚹🚹210/230 €, ☕ 12 €

♦ Family ♦ Retro ♦

The Art Nouveau glazed stoneware façade (1904) is an architectural gem. The interior lives up to the same standard with furniture and decor in the same spirit.

Magellan without rest

17 r. J.-B. Dumas (17th) – Ⓜ Porte de Champerret – ✆ 01 45 72 44 51 – paris@hotelmagellan.com – Fax 01 40 68 90 36 – www.hotelmagellan.com **F1**

72 rm – 🚹135/149 € 🚹🚹150/168 €, ☕ 13 €

♦ Business ♦ Design ♦

Large, functional rooms in a beautiful building dating from 1900. The small pavilion at the far end of the garden is used as a breakfast room in summer. Art Deco-style lounge.

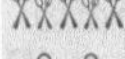

Le "Cinq" – Hôtel Four Seasons George V

31 av. George V (8th) – Ⓜ George V – ✆ 01 49 52 71 54 – par.lecinq@fourseasons.com – Fax 01 49 52 71 81 – www.fourseasons.com **G3**

Rest – Menu 75 € (lunch), 135/210 € – Carte 136/360 €

Spec. Tarialini à la fonduta et à la truffe d'Alba (beg. October-mid December). Poireau cuit à la ficelle aux saveurs d'hiver et à la truffe noire (beg. December-mid March). Poularde de Bresse et homard George V en cocotte lutée.

♦ Innovative ♦ Luxury ♦

The superb dining room, a majestic evocation of the Grand Trianon, opens onto a delightful interior garden. A refined atmosphere and masterful classic cuisine.

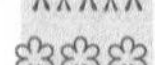

Alain Ducasse au Plaza Athénée – Hôtel Plaza Athénée

25 av. Montaigne (8th) – Ⓜ Alma Marceau – ✆ 01 53 67 65 00 – adpa@alain-ducasse.com – Fax 01 53 67 65 12 – www.alain-ducasse.com

closed 18 July-25 August, 19-30 December, Monday lunch, Tuesday lunch, Wednesday lunch, Saturday and Sunday **G3**

Rest – Menu 240/340 € – Carte 180/330 €

Spec. Caviar osciètre d'Iran, langoustines rafraîchies, nage réduite, bouillon parfumé. Volaille de Bresse, sauce albuféra aux truffes d'Alba (15 October to 31 December). Fraises des bois en coupe glacée, sablé coco.

♦ Luxury ♦

The sumptuous regency décor has been redone with a "design and organza" look; creative menus from a talented team overseen by Alain Ducasse. 1001 selected wines available!

Le Bristol – Hôtel Bristol

112 r. Fg St-Honoré (8th) – Ⓜ Miromesnil – ✆ 01 53 43 43 00 – resa@lebristolparis.com – Fax 01 53 43 43 01 – www.lebristolparis.com **H2**

Rest – Menu 95 € (lunch)/210 € – Carte 118/222 €

Spec. Macaroni farcis, truffe noire, artichaut et foie gras de canard, gratinés au parmesan. Merlan de ligne en croûte de pain aux amandes, tétragone mi-cuite, huile de péquillos. Poularde de Bresse cuite en vessie aux écrevisses, royale d'abats et morilles.

♦ Luxury ♦

With its splendid wood panelling, the winter dining room resembles a small theatre. The summer dining room overlooks the hotel's charming garden.

Ledoyen

carré Champs-Élysées (8th) – Ⓜ Champs Elysées Clemenceau – ☎ 01 53 05 10 01 – pavillon.ledoyen@ledoyen.com – Fax 01 47 42 55 01 – www.ledoyen.com
closed 2-24 August, Monday lunch, Saturday and Sunday **H3**

Rest – Menu 88 € (lunch), 198/284 € bi – Carte 149/227 €

Spec. Grosses langoustines bretonnes croustillantes, émulsion d'agrumes à l'huile d'olive. Blanc de turbot de ligne braisé, pommes rattes truffées. Noix de ris de veau en brochette de bois de citronnelle, jus d'herbes.

◆ Luxury ◆

A neo-Classical lodge built on the Champs Élysées in 1848. Magnificent Napoleon III style decor, view of the gardens designed by Hittorff and delicious surf'n'turf cuisine.

Taillevent

15 r. Lamennais (8th) – Ⓜ Charles de Gaulle-Etoile – ☎ 01 44 95 15 01 – mail@taillevent.com – Fax 01 42 25 95 18 – www.taillevent.com
closed 26 July-25 August, Saturday, Sunday and public holidays **G2**

Rest – *(number of covers limited, pre-book)* Menu 70 € (lunch), 140/190 € – Carte 116/204 €

Spec. Rémoulade de tourteau à l'aneth, sauce fleurette citronnée. Foie gras de canard au banyuls, fruits et légumes caramélisés. Trilogie gourmande.

◆ Luxury ◆

Wainscoting and works of art adorn this 19C townhouse, once home to the duke of Morny, and now a guardian of French haute cuisine. Exquisite cuisine and magnificent wine list.

Apicius (Jean-Pierre Vigato)

20 r. d'Artois (8th) – Ⓜ St-Philippe du Roule – ☎ 01 43 80 19 66 – restaurant-apicius@wanadoo.fr – Fax 01 44 40 09 57 – www.restaurant-apicius.com
closed August, Saturday, Sunday and public holidays **G2**

Rest – Menu 150 € (lunch), 160/180 € – Carte 89/166 €

Spec. Déclinaison sur le thème de la langoustine. Saint-Pierre grillé sur la peau, pâtes en risotto d'anchois. Grand dessert "tout caramel".

◆ Elegant ◆

This elegant restaurant, in a townhouse, is adorned with 19C Flemish paintings and 17C Indian sculptures. Up-to-date cuisine and superb wine list.

Lasserre

17 av. F.-D.-Roosevelt (8th) – Ⓜ Franklin D. Roosevelt – ☎ 01 43 59 53 43 – lasserre@lasserre.fr – Fax 01 45 63 72 23 – www.restaurant-lasserre.com
closed August, Saturday lunchtime, Monday lunchtime, Tuesday lunchtime, Wednesday lunchtime and Sunday **H3**

Rest – Menu 75 (lunch)/185 € – Carte 125/233 €

Spec. Macaroni fourrés aux truffes et foie gras. Turbot aux cèpes et échalotes, palourdes gratinées (September-October). Pigeon André Malraux.

◆ Luxury ◆

Considered an institution by Parisian gourmets, the neo-Classical dining room features an amazing retractable roof decorated with a fresco of dancers. Superb wine list.

Guy Savoy

18 r. Troyon (17th) – Ⓜ Charles de Gaulle-Etoile – ☎ 01 43 80 40 61 – reserv@guysavoy.com – Fax 01 46 22 43 09 – www.guysavoy.com
closed August, 24 December-2 January, Saturday lunchtime, Sunday and Monday **F2**

Rest – Menu 245/295 € – Carte 134/267 €

Spec. Soupe d'artichaut à la truffe noire, brioche feuilletée aux champignons et truffes. Bar en écaille grillées aux épices douces. Ris de veau rissolés, "petits chaussons" de pommes de terre et truffes.

◆ Innovative ◆ Trendy ◆

Glasswork, leather and Wenge, works by great names in contemporary art, African sculpture and inventive cuisine make this 'the hotel of the 21C' par excellence.

Michel Rostang

20 r. Rennequin (17th) – Ⓜ Ternes – 01 47 63 40 77 – rostang@relaischateaux.com – Fax 01 47 63 82 75 – www.michelrostang.com
closed 3-25 August, Monday lunch, Saturday lunch and Sunday **F1**

Rest – Menu 78 € (lunch), 185/285 € – Carte 125/210 €

Spec. "Menu truffe" (15 December to 15 March). Grosse sole de ligne "cuisson meunière", marinière de coquillages au curry mauricien. Canette au sang servie saignante en deux services.

♦ Classic ♦ Friendly ♦

Find wainscoting, Robj statuettes, works by Lalique, and Art Deco stained glass in this luxurious and unusual setting. Exquisite cuisine and outstanding wine list.

Pierre Gagnaire

6 r. Balzac (8th) – Ⓜ George V – 01 58 36 12 50 – p.gagnaire@wanadoo.fr – Fax 01 58 36 12 51 – www.pierre-gagnaire.com
closed 2-22 August, 22 December-4 January, Sunday lunch and Saturday **G2**

Rest – Menu 95 € (weekday lunch), 250/350 € – Carte 230/449 €

Spec. Langoustines de trois façons. Canard Pékin rôti entier. Grand dessert Pierre Gagnaire.

♦ Trendy ♦

The low key, chic, contemporary décor (light wood panelling, modern art) provides the setting for this temple of modern French cuisine. Unbridled creativity, akin to free-form jazz. Music maestro!

Hiramatsu

(dinner)

52 r. Longchamp (16th) ✉ 75116 – Ⓜ Trocadéro – 01 56 81 08 80 – paris@hiramatsu.co.jp – Fax 01 56 81 08 81 – www.hiratamatsu.co.jp
closed 2-31 August, 29 December-6 January, Saturday and Sunday **E3**

Rest – *(number of covers limited, pre-book)* Menu 48 € (lunch), 95/130 € – Carte 104/140 €

Spec. Foie gras de canard aux choux frisés, jus de truffe. Feuilleté de homard aux parfums de truffes, jus d'estragon. Gâteau au chocolat "Hiramatsu".

♦ Fashionable ♦

Hiramatsu's team has moved from the 4th to the 16th district. New décor and inventive cuisine, as skilful as ever. High class Japanese gastronomy!

Laurent

41 av. Gabriel (8th) – Ⓜ Champs Elysées Clemenceau – 01 42 25 00 39 – info@le-laurent.com – Fax 01 45 62 45 21 – www.le-laurent.com
closed 25 December-2 January, Saturday lunch, Sunday and public holidays **H3**

Rest – Menu 80/160 € – Carte 130/216 €

Spec. Araignée de mer dans ses sucs en gelée, crème de fenouil. Foie gras de canard grillé, posé sur une "cracotte". Flanchet de veau de lait braisé, blettes à la moelle et au jus.

♦ Luxury ♦

A lodge built by Hittorff has elegant, shaded terraces and cuisine that continues to uphold culinary traditions: a little corner of paradise in the Champs Élysées gardens.

Les Élysées – Hôtel Vernet

25 r. Vernet (8th) – Ⓜ Charles de Gaulle-Etoile – 01 44 31 98 98 – elysees@hotelvernet.com – Fax 01 44 31 85 69 – www.hotelvernet.com
closed 26 July-25 August, Monday lunch, Saturday and Sunday **F2**

Rest – Menu 64 € (lunch), 105/140 € – Carte 102/159 €

Spec. Langoustines bretonnes dorées au curry, galettes de pois chiches aux légumes croquants. Pithiviers de perdreau, grouse et poule faisane au miel de châtaignier (season). Vrai baba au vieux rhum agricole, sorbet ananas.

♦ Innovative ♦ Friendly ♦

Sample masterfully inventive cuisine based on classic culinary principles beneath Eiffel's splendid Belle Époque glass dome that bathes the dining room in a soft light.

La Table du Lancaster - Hôtel Lancaster

7 r. Berri (8th) – Ⓜ George V – ✆ 01 40 76 40 18 – restaurant@hotel-lancaster.fr – Fax 01 40 76 40 00 – www.hotel-lancaster.fr

VISA MC AE **G2**

Rest – *(closed Saturday lunch)* Menu 52 € (weekday lunch)/120 € – Carte 73/132 €

Spec. Cuisses de grenouilles au tamarin, chou-fleur en copeaux. Pièce de thon au ponzu, sur un riz "koshi hikari". Soufflé au citron vert et sirop au miel d'acacia.

♦ Friendly ♦

Inventive food supervised by Michel Troisgros, and a pleasant, contemporary setting (Chinese prints) opening onto the garden. A fitting restaurant for the Lancaster.

La Table de Joël Robuchon

VISA MC

16 av. Bugeaud (16th) ✉ 75116 – Ⓜ Victor Hugo – ✆ 01 56 28 16 16 – latabledejoelrobuchon@wanadoo.fr – Fax 01 56 28 16 78 **E3**

Rest – Menu 55 € bi (lunch)/150 € – Carte 55/145 €

Spec. La Langoustine en papillotes croustillantes au basilic. La caille au foie gras et caramélisée avec une pomme purée truffée. Le "chocolat sensation" crème onctueuse au chocolat araguani, glace chocolat au biscuit oréo

♦ A la mode ♦ Trendy ♦

In the elegant setting you are sure to enjoy your meal here: sample tapas style snacks and classic dishes subtly updated by Joël Robuchon.

Maison Blanche

VISA MC AE

15 av. Montaigne (8th) – Ⓜ Alma Marceau – ✆ 01 47 23 55 99 – info@maison-blanche.fr – Fax 01 47 20 09 56 – www.maison-blanche.fr closed Saturday lunch and Sunday lunch **G3**

Rest – Menu 55 € bi (lunch)/65 € bi – Carte 77/139 €

♦ Trendy ♦

On top of the Théâtre des Champs Élysées, whose loft-duplex design features a huge glass roof facing the golden dome of Les Invalides. Languedoc-inspired cuisine.

Fouquet's

VISA MC AE

99 av. Champs Élysées (8th) – Ⓜ George V – ✆ 01 40 69 60 50 – fouquets@lucienbarriere.com – Fax 01 40 69 60 35 – www.lucienbarriere.com **G2**

Rest – Menu 78 € – Carte 60/142 €

♦ Fashionable ♦

A listed dining room, updated by J. Garcia, a terrace that is popular come summer or winter and brasserie cuisine: Fouquet's has been catering to the jet set since 1889.

La Table du Baltimore - Hôtel Sofitel Baltimore

1 r. Léo Delibes (16th) ✉ 75016 – Ⓜ Boissière – ✆ 01 44 34 54 34 – h2789-fb@accor.com – Fax 01 44 34 54 44 – www.sofitel.com closed August, Saturday and Sunday

VISA MC AE **E3**

Rest – Menu 48 € bi (lunch)/50 € – Carte 54/71 €

Spec. Tourteau assaisonné à la badiane roulé dans une feuille d'algue. Selle d'agneau rôtie en croûte d'herbes, céleri rave mijoté aux sucs. Dos de cabillaud cuit au plat, confit de poireaux au curcuma et thym.

♦ A la mode ♦ Friendly ♦

Antique wood panelling, modern furnishings, warm colours and a collection of drawings all combine to create the subtle decor of this restaurant. Fine, up-to-date cuisine.

Copenhague

142 av. des Champs-Élysées (8th) – Ⓜ George V – ✆ 01 44 13 86 26 – reservation.copenhague@blanc.net – Fax 01 58 05 44 98 – www.floradanica-paris.com

closed 2-24 August, Saturday, Sunday and public holidays **F2**

Rest – *(1st floor)* Menu 50 €, 69/109 € – Carte 74/115 €

Rest *Flora Danica* – Menu 43 € – Carte 40/78 €

Spec. Foie gras poché à la bière. Cabillaud rôti et braisé au fumet de palourdes, émulsion aux coquillages. Renne légérement fumé et rôti, champignons, légumes et fruits de saison.

♦ Design ♦

This restaurant within the Maison du Danemark offers Scandinavian cuisine, elegant Danish design, a view of the Champs Elysée and a terrace facing a lovely garden. At the Flora Danica, salmon is given pride of place in the shop and on the menu.

Le Chiberta

3 r. Arsène-Houssaye (8th) – Ⓜ Charles de Gaulle-Etoile – ✆ 01 53 53 42 00 – chiberta@guysavoy.com – Fax 01 45 62 85 08 – www.lechiberta.com

closed 2-24 August, Saturday lunch and Sunday **F2**

Rest – Menu 60/100 € – Carte 73/120 €

Spec. Crème de langoustines et carottes, citronnelle-gingembre. Côte de Boeuf Hereford rôtie, sabayon ciboulette. Moelleux guanaja au pralin feuilleté.

♦ Design ♦

The Chiberta is off to a new start in the J.M. Wilmotte designed restaurant (dark colours and unusual wine bottle walls). The inventive cuisine is supervised by Guy Savoy.

Sormani

4 r. Gén. Lanrezac (17th) – Ⓜ Charles de Gaulle-Etoile – ✆ 01 43 80 13 91 – sasormani@wanadoo.fr – Fax 01 40 55 07 37

closed 1st-25 August, Saturday, Sunday and public holidays **F2**

Rest – Carte 50/114 €

♦ Italian ♦ Formal ♦

Latin charm predominates in this restaurant near the Place de l'Etoile, with its new décor (red tones and Murano-glass chandeliers), dolce vita atmosphere and Italian cuisine.

Le Pergolèse (Stéphane Gaborieau)

40 r. Pergolèse (16th) ✉ 75116 – Ⓜ Porte Maillot – ✆ 01 45 00 21 40 – le-pergolese@wanadoo.fr – Fax 01 45 00 81 31 – www.lepergolese.com

closed August, Saturday and Sunday **E2**

Rest – Menu 42 (lunch)/90 € – Carte 73/107 €

Spec. Ravioli de langoustines, duxelles de champignons, émulsion de crustacés au foie gras. Aiguillette de Saint-Pierre dorée, cannelloni farcis aux multi saveurs, émulsion de verveine. Pigeon fermier au soupçon de gingembre et cannelle.

♦ Classic ♦ Fashionable ♦

Yellow wall hangings, pale wood wainscoting and surprising sculptures reflect in the mirrors, forming an elegant décor a step away from select Avenue Foch. Impeccable classic cuisine.

Le Marcande

52 r. Miromesnil (8th) – Ⓜ Miromesnil – ✆ 01 42 65 19 14 – info@marcande.com – Fax 01 42 65 76 85 – www.marcande.com

closed 11-25 August, 24 December-5 January, Friday dinner from October to April, Saturday except dinner from May to September and Sunday **H2**

Rest – Menu 35/41 € – Carte 54/83 €

♦ Classic ♦ Intimate ♦

Discreet restaurant frequented by a business clientele. Contemporary dining room, facing a pleasant patio terrace that is often overflowing in summertime.

Passiflore (Roland Durand)

33 r. Longchamp (16th) ✉ 75016 – Ⓜ Trocadéro – ✆ 01 47 04 96 81 – passiflore@club-internet.fr – Fax 01 47 04 32 27 – www.restaurantpassiflore.com
closed 20 July-20 August, Saturday lunch and Sunday **E3**
Rest – Menu 35 € (lunch), 45/54 € (dinner) – Carte 64/100 €
Spec. Ravioles de homard en mulligatowny. Riz noir et langoustines en saté au citron vert. Quatre sorbets verts pimentés.
♦ A la mode ♦ Fashionable ♦
An unassumingly elegant décor of ethnic inspiration (yellow tones and wood panelling) and a classic, personalised cuisine combine to rejoice the taste buds of Parisian society.

Stella Maris (Tateru Yoshino)

4 r. Arsène Houssaye (8th) – Ⓜ Charles de Gaulle-Etoile – ✆ 01 42 89 16 22 – stella.maris.paris@wanadoo.fr – Fax 01 42 89 16 01 – www.stellamaris.com
closed 10-24 August, Saturday lunch, Sunday and public holidays lunch **F2**
Rest – Menu 49 € (lunch), 99/130 € – Carte 112/156 €
Spec. Terrine de chou au foie gras et truffes (winter). Lièvre à la royale (autumn). Saumon mi-cuit à l'émulsion de citron confit.
♦ A la mode ♦ Design ♦
A pleasant restaurant with a refined decor and warm welcome near the Arc de Triomphe. Classic French cuisine with a modern touch added by a skilful Japanese chef.

Cristal Room Baccarat

11 pl. des Etats-Unis (16th) ✉ 75116 – Ⓜ Boissière – ✆ 01 40 22 11 10 – cristalroom@baccarat.fr – Fax 01 40 22 11 99
closed Sunday **F3**
Rest – *(pre-book)* Menu 59 € (lunch), 92/200 € bi – Carte 90/123 €
♦ Design ♦
This mansion was used by M-L de Noailles and now belongs to Baccarat. It offers a Starck decor and modern dishes at V.I.P. prices. Beauty can be far from reasonable!

Tsé Yang

25 av. Pierre 1er de Serbie (16th) ✉ 75116 – Ⓜ Iéna – ✆ 01 47 20 70 22 – Fax 01 47 20 75 34 – www.tseyang.fr **F3**
Rest – Menu 49/59 € – Carte 35/133 €
♦ Chinese ♦
Two architect-decorators have revamped this chic embassy of traditional Chinese cuisine: dominant use of black, ceiling with gilded coffers, pretty layout, etc.

Le Relais Plaza – Hôtel Plaza Athénée

25 av. Montaigne (8th) – Ⓜ Alma Marceau – ✆ 01 53 67 64 00 – reservation@plaza-athenee-paris.com – Fax 01 53 67 66 66 – www.plaza-athenee-paris.com
closed August **G3**
Rest – Menu 50 € – Carte 76/148 €
♦ Classic ♦ Friendly ♦
The chic, intimate "local" for the nearby fashion houses. Timeless atmosphere and beautiful 1930s décor inspired by the Normandie cruise ship. Classic, refined cuisine.

Spoon

12 r. Marignan (8th) – Ⓜ Franklin D. Roosevelt – ✆ 01 40 76 34 44 – spoonfood@hotelmarignan.fr – Fax 01 40 76 34 37 – www.spoon.tm.fr
closed 2 August-1st September, 25 December-5 January, Saturday and Sunday **G3**
Rest – Menu 47 (lunch)/89 € – Carte 57/84 €
♦ Innovative ♦ Design ♦
Designer furniture, exotic wood and an open kitchen: a décor that mingles contemporary and Zen influences. Unusual, modular menu and wines from around the globe.

XX **Citrus Étoile**

6 r. Arsène-Houssaye (8th) – Ⓜ Charles de Gaulle-Étoile – ✆ 01 42 89 15 51 – info@citrusetoile.fr – Fax 01 42 89 28 67 – www.citrusetoile.fr **F2**
closed 8-19 August, 21 December-3 January, Saturday, Sunday and public holidays
Rest – Menu 39/90 € – Carte 77/91 €
♦ A la mode ♦
Chef Gilles Épié creates dishes full of interesting flavours inspired by his travels in California and Japan. Elegant, simple décor and a delicious welcome.

XX **Fermette Marbeuf 1900**

5 r. Marbeuf (8th) – Ⓜ Alma Marceau – ✆ 01 53 23 08 00 – fermettemarbeuf@blanc.net – Fax 01 53 23 08 09 – www.fermettemarbeuf.com **G3**
Rest – Menu 32 € – Carte 35/63 €
♦ Traditional ♦ Retro ♦
One must reserve a table to enjoy the Art Nouveau décor of this glass dining hall dating back to 1898 and discovered by chance in the course of renovation. Classic cuisine.

XX **Marius et Janette**

4 av. George V (8th) – Ⓜ Alma Marceau – ✆ 01 47 23 41 88 – Fax 01 47 23 07 19
closed 27 July-5 August **G3**
Rest – Menu 46 (lunch)/100 € bi – Carte 88/168 €
♦ Bistro ♦
The name of this restaurant recalls Robert Guédiguian's films and Marseille's Estaque quarter. Elegant nautical décor, a pleasant street terrace and seafood fare.

XX **Timgad**

21 r. Brunel (17th) – Ⓜ Argentine – ✆ 01 45 74 23 70 – contact@timgad.fr – Fax 01 40 68 76 46 – www.timgad.fr **E2**
Rest – Menu 45/60 € bi – Carte 38/71 €
♦ Moroccan ♦ Friendly ♦
Delve into the past splendour of the city of Timgad: the elegant Moorish decor of the rooms was carried out by Moroccan stucco-workers. Fragrant North African cuisine.

XX **Le Stresa**

7 r. Chambiges (8th) – Ⓜ Alma Marceau – ✆ 01 47 23 51 62
closed 1st-8 May, August, 21 December-3 January, Saturday and Sunday **G3**
Rest – *(pre-book)* Carte 57/105 €
♦ Italian ♦ Family ♦
Golden Triangle trattoria frequented by a very jet-set clientele. Paintings by Buffet and compressed sculptural art by César – artists also appreciate the Italian cuisine here.

XX ✿ **L'Angle du Faubourg**

195 r. Fg St-Honoré (8th) – Ⓜ Ternes – ✆ 01 40 74 20 20 – angledufaubourg@cavestaillevent.com – Fax 01 40 74 20 21 – www.angledufaubourg.com
closed 26 July-25 August, Saturday, Sunday and public holidays **G2**
Rest – Menu 35/70 € (dinner) – Carte 45/71 €
Spec. Sablé de thon aux épices. Râble de lapin rôti à la marjolaine. Cannelloni au citron, sorbet basilic.
♦ A la mode ♦ Friendly ♦
On the corner of Rue du Faubourg-St-Honoré and Rue Balzac. This modern bistrot serves skilfully updated classic cuisine to suit current tastes. Simple décor.

XX **Rech**

62 av. des Ternes (17th) – Ⓜ Ternes – ✆ 01 45 72 29 47 – Fax 01 45 72 41 60 – www.alain-ducasse.com
closed August, Sunday and Monday **F1**
Rest – Menu 34/53 € – Carte 46/74 €
♦ Traditional ♦ Retro ♦
Recently renovated, Art Deco-inspired dining rooms (mirrors, stained glass) at this venerable restaurant. Principally fine fish and seafood specialities, but the odd meat dish too.

XX

Graindorge VISA MC AE

15 r. Arc de Triomphe (17th) – M Charles de Gaulle-Etoile – ✆ 01 47 54 00 28 – le.graindorge@wanadoo.fr

closed 1st-15 August, Saturday lunch and Sunday **F2**

Rest – Menu 28 € (weekday lunch)/34 € – Carte 42/56 €

♦ Flemish cuisine ♦ Retro ♦

Here you can choose between beer and wine, generous Flemish cuisine and appealing market dishes in an attractive Art Deco setting.

XX

Bistrot du Sommelier A/C VISA MC AE

97 bd Haussmann (8th) – M St-Augustin – ✆ 01 42 65 24 85 – bistrot-du-sommelier@noos.fr – Fax 01 53 75 23 23 – www.bistrotdusommelier.com

closed 25 July-24 August, 24 December-5 January, Saturday and Sunday **H2**

Rest – Menu 39 € (lunch), 60 € bi/100 € bi – Carte 47/56 €

♦ A la mode ♦ Bistro ♦

This bistro of free-flowing Bacchanalian pleasure belongs to Philippe Faure-Brac, elected World's Best Cellarman in 1992.

XX

La Braisière (Jacques Faussat) A/C VISA MC AE

54 r. Cardinet (17th) – M Malesherbes – ✆ 01 47 63 40 37 – labraisiere@free.fr – Fax 01 47 63 04 76

closed August, 1st-8 January, Saturday and Sunday **G1**

Rest – Menu 38 € (lunch)– Carte 51/67 €

Spec. Gâteau de pommes de terre au foie gras et aux girolles. Pavé de thon rouge laqué au galanga. Gibier (October to January).

♦ South-western France ♦ Friendly ♦

Comfortable, modern restaurant in tasteful pastel colours. The menu is influenced by the cuisine of southwest France but also changes with the seasons and the chef's whims.

XX

Market A/C VISA MC AE

15 av. Matignon (8th) – M Franklin D. Roosevelt – ✆ 01 56 43 40 90 – prmarketsa@aol.com – Fax 01 43 59 10 87 – www.jean-georges.com **H3**

Rest – Menu 34 € (lunch) – Carte 49/87 €

♦ Design ♦

A trendy establishment with a prestigious location. Wood and marble décor, including African masks in niches. Mixed cuisine (French, Italian and Asian).

XX

Le Vinci A/C (dinner) VISA MC AE

23 r. P. Valéry (16th) ✉ 75116 – M Victor Hugo – ✆ 01 45 01 68 18 – levinci@wanadoo.fr – Fax 01 45 01 60 37

closed 2-24 August, Saturday and Sunday **E2-3**

Rest – Carte 39/68 €

♦ Italian ♦

Tasty Italian cuisine, pleasant colourful interior and friendly service (a highly-prized establishment a step away from the chic shopping in Avenue Victor-Hugo.

XX

6 New-York A/C VISA MC AE

6 av. New-York (16th) ✉ 75016 – M Alma Marceau – ✆ 01 40 70 03 30 – 6newyork@wanadoo.fr – Fax 01 40 70 04 77

closed August, Saturday lunch and Sunday **F3**

Rest – Menu 30 € (lunch) – Carte 48/62 €

♦ A la mode ♦ Design ♦

The sign gives you a clue to the address but does not tell you that this stylish bistro prepares dishes perfectly suited to its modern and refined setting.

XX

Ballon des Ternes VISA MC AE

103 av. Ternes (17th) – M Porte Maillot – ✆ 01 45 74 17 98 – leballondesternes@fr.oleane.com – Fax 01 45 72 18 84 **E1**

Rest – Carte 35/60 €

♦ Retro ♦

No, you have not had a "ballon" (glass of wine) too many! The table set upside down on the ceiling is part of the 1900 décor of this brasserie next to the Palais des Congrès.

FRANCE - PARIS

Village d'Ung et Li Lam

10 r. J. Mermoz (8th) – Ⓜ Franklin D. Roosevelt – ✆ 01 42 25 99 79
– Fax 01 42 25 12 06
closed Saturday lunchtime and Sunday lunchtime **H2**
Rest – Menu 19/35 € – Carte 25/40 €
♦ Exotic ♦
Ung and Li welcome you into a very original Asian setting: suspended aquariums and a flooring of glass-and-sand tiles. Chinese-Thai cuisine.

Al Ajami

58 r. François 1er (8th) – Ⓜ George V – ✆ 01 42 25 38 44 – ajami@free.fr
– Fax 01 42 25 38 39 – www.ajami.com **G3**
Rest – Menu 25 (weekdays)/46 € – Carte 36/61 €
♦ Lebanese ♦ Exotic ♦
This temple of traditional Lebanese cuisine has been run by the same family since 1920. Near East décor, family atmosphere and a faithful band of regulars.

Chez Georges

273 bd Péreire (17th) – Ⓜ Porte Maillot – ✆ 01 45 74 31 00
– chez-georges@hotmail.fr – Fax 01 45 72 18 84 **E1**
Rest – Carte 40/67 €
♦ Brasserie ♦ Bistro ♦
An institution in Paris since 1926, the ambience and décor of this brasserie are perfectly in keeping with its appetising bistro cuisine. Menu and daily suggestions.

Dominique Bouchet

11 r. Treilhard (8th) – Ⓜ Miromesnil – ✆ 01 45 61 09 46
– dominiquebouchet@yahoo.fr – Fax 01 42 89 11 14
– www.dominique-bouchet.com
closed in August, Saturday and Sunday **H2**
Rest – *(pre-book)* Menu 55/87 – Carte 55/75
Spec. Charlotte de crabe et tomate, chiffonnade de laitue, mangue fraiche et basilic (April to September). Gros macaroni de homard sur purée de champignons, noyé de sa bisque. Gigot d'agneau de sept heures, sauce parfumée au cacao torréfié, pomme purée.
♦ A la mode ♦
Tasteful contemporary décor, a friendly atmosphere and delicious, traditionally-based cuisine using market produce are the hallmarks of this small, successful and trendy bistro.

Café Lenôtre - Pavillon Elysée

10 av. Champs-Elysées (8th) – Ⓜ Champs Elysées Clemenceau
– ✆ 01 42 65 85 10 – Fax 01 42 65 76 23 – www.lenotre.fr
closed 3 weeks in August, 1 week in February, Monday dinner from November to February and Sunday dinner **H3**
Rest – Carte 44/64 €
♦ Trendy ♦
This elegant pavilion built for the 1900 World Fair has been treated to a make over. It houses a boutique, a catering school and a distinctly modern restaurant.

Caïus

6 r. d'Armaillé (17th) – Ⓜ Charles de Gaulle-Etoile – ✆ 01 42 27 19 20
– Fax 01 40 55 00 93
closed August, Saturday and Sunday **F1**
Rest – Menu 39 €
♦ Trendy ♦
Warm wood panelling, bench seating, and coffee and spice themed photos set the scene in this smart bistro devoted to personalised, tasty, market fresh cuisine.

Bath's — AC VISA MC AE

25 r. Bayen (17th) – Ⓜ Ternes – ✆ 01 45 74 74 74 – contact@baths.fr – Fax 01 45 74 71 15 – www.baths.fr
closed 2 August-1st September, 22-28 December, Saturday lunch, Monday lunch, Sunday and public holidays **E7**
Rest – Menu 25 (lunch)/42 € – Carte 50/64 €
Spec. Pétales de jambon ibérique "bellota". Encornets juste sautés, riz paëlla, sauce chorizo. Filet de bœuf de Salers aux épices douces.

◆ A la mode ◆

Sculptures of the owner and contemporary paintings pepper this restaurant's modern surroundings, where shades of orange and black dominate. Delicious market-based cuisine.

Caves Petrissans — VISA MC AE

30 bis av. Niel (17th) – Ⓜ Pereire – ✆ 01 42 27 52 03 – cavespetrissans@noos.fr – Fax 01 40 54 87 56
closed 1st-11 May, 25 July-25 August, Saturday, Sunday and public holidays
Rest – *(pre-book)* Menu 35 € – Carte 38/55 € **F1**

◆ Bistro ◆

Céline, Abel Gance and Roland Dorgelès loved to visit these cellars over a century old, which now double as a wine shop and restaurant. Tasty, bistro-style cooking.

Daru — AC (dinner) VISA MC AE

19 r. Daru (8th) – Ⓜ Courcelles – ✆ 01 42 27 23 60 – restaurant.daru@orange.fr – Fax 01 47 54 08 14 – www.daru.fr
closed August and Sunday **G1**
Rest – Carte 40/70 €

◆ Russian ◆ Formal ◆

Founded in 1918, Daru was the first Russian grocery store in Paris. Today it still offers customers a choice of zakouskis, blinis and caviar in its renowned red and black interior.

CONCORDE, OPÉRA, BOURSE, GARE DU NORD — *Plan III*

Le Meurice — rm AC rm SAT VISA MC AE

228 r. Rivoli (1st) – Ⓜ Tuileries – ✆ 01 44 58 10 10 – reservations@lemeurice.com – Fax 01 44 58 10 15 – www.lemeurice.com **J3**
137 rm – †520/620 € ††680/2100 €, ☕ 48 € – 23 suites
Rest ***le Meurice*** – see below
Rest ***Le Dali*** – ✆ *01 44 58 10 44* – Carte 65/86 €

◆ Palace ◆ Grand Luxury ◆ Historic ◆

One of the first luxury hotels, built in 1817, converted into a "palace" in 1907. Sumptuous rooms and a superb top floor suite with a breathtaking view of Paris. Philippe Starck has added a touch of modernity in the lobby area. Stunning Art Nouveau glass roof at Le Dali.

Ritz — AC SAT VISA MC AE

15 pl. Vendôme (1st) – Ⓜ Opéra – ✆ 01 43 16 30 30 – resa@ritzparis.com – Fax 01 43 16 36 68 – www.ritzparis.com **K3**
124 rm – †710/810 € ††710/810 €, ☕ 36 € – 37 suites
Rest ***L'Espadon*** – see below
Rest ***Bar Vendôme*** – ✆ *01 43 16 33 63* – Carte 75/142 €

◆ Grand Luxury ◆ Palace ◆ Stylish ◆

In 1898, César Ritz opened the 'perfect hotel' of his dreams, boasting Valentino, Proust, Hemingway and Coco Chanel among its guests. Exquisitely sophisticated. Superb pool. A chic interior and superb terrace can be found at the Bar Vendôme, which turns into a tearoom in the afternoon.

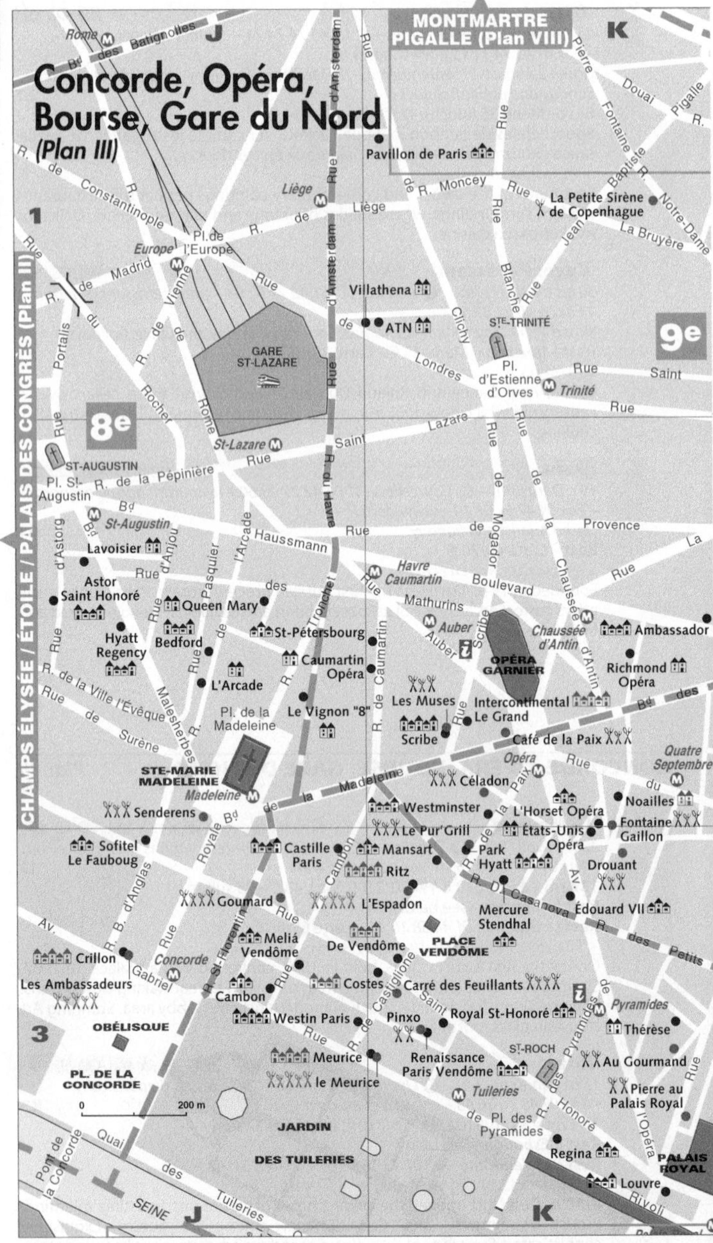
Concorde, Opéra, Bourse, Gare du Nord
(Plan III)
MONTMARTRE PIGALLE (Plan VIII)
CHAMPS ÉLYSÉE / ÉTOILE / PALAIS DES CONGRÈS (Plan II)
J
K
1
3
8e
9e
Rome
Bd des Batignolles
R. de Constantinople
Liège
R. de Liège
Pl. de l'Europe
Europe
Rue de Madrid
R. de Vienne
R. du Rocher
Rue de Rome
GARE ST-LAZARE
St-Lazare
Rue Saint Lazare
Rue d'Amsterdam
R. du Havre
Rue de Londres
Rue de Clichy
Rue Blanche
Rue Moncey
Rue de Douai
Rue Fontaine
Rue Pierre
R. Pigalle
R. Jean Baptiste
R. Notre-Dame
Rue La Bruyère
Pavillon de Paris
La Petite Sirène de Copenhague
Villathena
ATN
STE-TRINITÉ
Pl. d'Estienne d'Orves
Trinité
Rue Saint
Rue de Mogador
Rue de la Chaussée d'Antin
Rue de Provence
Boulevard Haussmann
ST-AUGUSTIN
Pl. St-Augustin
R. de la Pépinière
Bd Malesherbes
St-Augustin
Rue Portalis
Rue d'Astorg
Rue d'Anjou
Rue Pasquier
Rue de l'Arcade
R. Tronchet
Rue des Mathurins
Havre Caumartin
Rue Caumartin
Rue Auber
Auber
Rue Scribe
OPÉRA GARNIER
Chaussée d'Antin
Lavoisier
Astor Saint Honoré
Queen Mary
Hyatt Regency
Bedford
St-Pétersbourg
Caumartin Opéra
L'Arcade
Le Vignon "8"
Les Muses
Scribe
Intercontinental Le Grand
Café de la Paix
Ambassador
Richmond Opéra
R. de la Ville l'Évêque
Rue de Surène
Pl. de la Madeleine
STE-MARIE MADELEINE
Madeleine
Bd de la Madeleine
Bd des Capucines
Opéra
Rue du Quatre Septembre
Quatre Septembre
Senderens
Céladon
Westminster
L'Horset Opéra
Noailles
Fontaine Gaillon
Le Pur'Grill
États-Unis Opéra
Rue de la Paix
Park Hyatt
Drouant
Sofitel Le Faubourg
Castille Paris
Mansart
Ritz
Rue Royale
Rue Cambon
R. D. Casanova
Av. de l'Opéra
Goumard
L'Espadon
Mercure Stendhal
Édouard VII
R. des Petits
Av. Gabriel
R. B. d'Anglas
Rue St-Florentin
Melià Vendôme
De Vendôme
PLACE VENDÔME
Crillon
Les Ambassadeurs
Concorde
Cambon
Costes
Carré des Feuillants
Rue de Castiglione
Rue Saint Honoré
Royal St-Honoré
Pyramides
Thérèse
Westin Paris
Pinxo
ST-ROCH
Au Gourmand
OBÉLISQUE
PL. DE LA CONCORDE
Meurice
le Meurice
Renaissance Paris Vendôme
Tuileries
Pierre au Palais Royal
Rue de Rivoli
0
200 m
JARDIN DES TUILERIES
Pl. des Pyramides
R. des Pyramides
Regina
PALAIS ROYAL
Louvre
Pont de la Concorde
Quai des Tuileries
SEINE

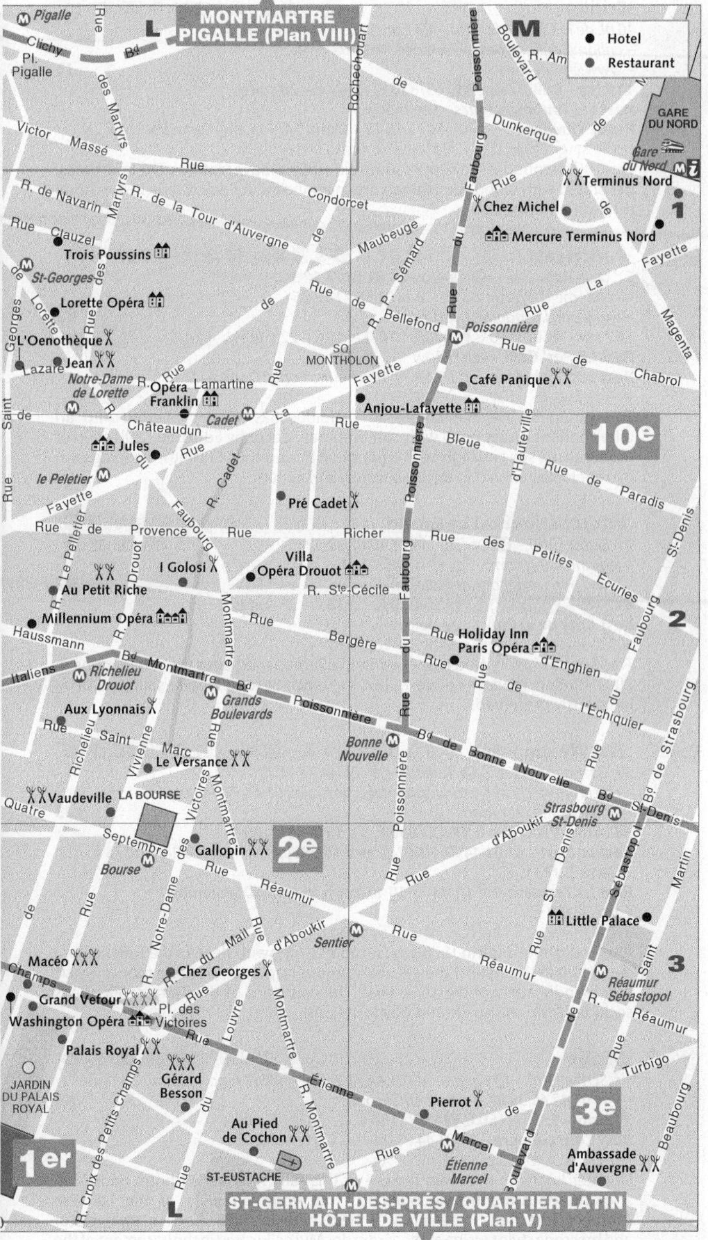
MONTMARTRE
PIGALLE (Plan VIII)
Hotel
Restaurant
GARE DU NORD
Terminus Nord
Chez Michel
Mercure Terminus Nord
Trois Poussins
Lorette Opéra
L'Oenothèque
Jean
Opéra Franklin
Café Panique
Anjou-Lafayette
Jules
Pré Cadet
I Golosi
Villa Opéra Drouot
Au Petit Riche
Millennium Opéra
Holiday Inn Paris Opéra
Aux Lyonnais
Le Versance
Vaudeville
LA BOURSE
Gallopin
Little Palace
Macéo
Chez Georges
Grand Vefour
Washington Opéra
Palais Royal
Gérard Besson
Pierrot
Au Pied de Cochon
Ambassade d'Auvergne
JARDIN DU PALAIS ROYAL
ST-EUSTACHE
10e
2e
3e
1er
ST-GERMAIN-DES-PRÉS / QUARTIER LATIN
HÔTEL DE VILLE (Plan V)

Crillon

10 pl. de la Concorde (8th) – Ⓜ Concorde – ✆ 01 44 71 15 00 – crillon@crillon.com – Fax 01 44 71 15 02 – www.crillon.com **J3**

119 rm – 695/750 € 765/830 €, 47 € – 28 suites

Rest *Les Ambassadeurs* – see below

Rest *L'Obélisque* – *✆ 01 44 71 15 15* – Menu 54/94 € bi – Carte 59/114 €

♦ Grand Luxury ♦ Palace ♦ Personalised ♦

This 18C townhouse has kept its sumptuous, decorative features. The bedrooms, decorated with wood-furnishings, are magnificent. A French style luxury hotel through-and-through.

Park Hyatt

5 r. de la Paix (2th) – Ⓜ Opéra – ✆ 01 58 71 12 34 – vendome@hyattintl.com – Fax 01 58 71 12 35 – www.paris.vendome.hyatt.com **K3**

167 rm – 600/810 € 600/810 €, 40 € – 22 suites

Rest Le Pur' Grill – see below

Rest *Les Orchidées* – *✆ 01 58 71 10 61 (lunch only)* Carte 61/123 €

♦ Grand Luxury ♦ Modern ♦

This group of five Haussmannian buildings has been converted into an ultra-modern luxury hotel with contemporary decor by Ed Tuttle. Collection of modern art, a spa and high-tech equipment throughout. Cuisine in keeping with current tastes, served to diners beneath a glass roof.

Intercontinental Le Grand

2 r. Scribe (9th) – Ⓜ Opéra – ✆ 01 40 07 32 32 – legrand@ihg.com – Fax 01 42 66 12 51 – www.paris.intercontinental.com **K2**

442 rm – 650/830 € 650/830 €, 38 € – 28 suites

Rest *Café de la Paix* – see below

♦ Grand Luxury ♦ Personalised ♦

This famous luxury hotel, opened in 1862, reopened after full renovations in 2003. It offers modern comforts, but its French Second Empire spirit has been judiciously preserved.

The Westin Paris

3 r. Castiglione (1st) – Ⓜ Tuileries – ✆ 01 44 77 11 11 – reservation.01729@starwoodhotels.com – Fax 01 44 77 14 60 – www.westin.com/paris **J3**

397 rm – 300/850 € 300/850 €, 35 € – 41 suites

Rest *Le First* – *✆ 01 44 77 10 40 (closed 14-28 July)* Menu 32 € (lunch)/75 € – Carte 32/73 €

Rest *La Terrasse* – *✆ 01 44 77 10 40 (open 1st April-30 September)* Carte 31/69 €

♦ Luxury ♦ Traditional ♦ Stylish ♦

A splendid hotel built in 1878, whose rooms (some with views of the Tuileries) are decorated in the style of the 19C. Sumptuous Napoleon III sitting rooms. Smart and friendly atmosphere at Le First. The courtyard of the Terrasse Fleurie is secluded from the hustle and bustle of Paris.

Scribe

1 r. Scribe (9th) – Ⓜ Opéra – ✆ 01 44 71 24 24 – h0663@accor.com – Fax 01 42 65 39 97 – www.sofitel.com **K2**

213 rm – 555/1150 € 555/1150 €, 28 € – 5 suites

Rest *Café Lumière* – *✆ 01 44 71 24 19* – Carte 41/67 €

♦ Luxury ♦ Cosy ♦

Discreet luxury is the main feature of this fully refurbished hotel housed in a grand Haussmann-style building. The world première of the Lumière brothers' first film screening was held here in 1895. English style décor and brasserie style cuisine at the Jardin des Muses, located in the basement of the Scribe.

Costes
239 r. St-Honoré (1st) – Ⓜ Concorde – ☎ 01 42 44 50 00 – Fax 01 42 44 50 01 – www.hotelcostes.com J-K3
82 rm – 400 € 550 €, ☕ 30 € – 3 suites
Rest – Carte 44/92 €
♦ Luxury ♦ Personalised ♦
Updated Napoleon III style in the hotel's purple and gold guestrooms. Splendid Italianate courtyard and impressive fitness centre. An extravagant luxury hotel popular with the hip crowd. The restaurant of the Hôtel Costes is a shrine to the latest lounge trend.

De Vendôme
1 pl. Vendôme (1st) – Ⓜ Opéra – ☎ 01 55 04 55 00 – reservations@hoteldevendome.com – Fax 01 49 27 97 89 – www.hoteldevendome.com K3
29 rm – 450/660 € 535/855 €, ☕ 30 € – 10 suites
Rest – Menu 40/45 € – Carte 61/83 €
♦ Grand Luxury ♦ Palace ♦ Stylish ♦
Place Vendôme provides the splendid backdrop for this fine 18C townhouse converted into a luxury hotel. Bedrooms with antique furniture, marble fittings and high tech equipment.

Astor Saint Honoré
11 r. d'Astorg (8th) – Ⓜ St-Augustin – ☎ 01 53 05 05 05 – reservation@astor.3ahotels.com – Fax 01 53 05 05 30 – www.hotel-astorsainthonore.com J2
128 rm – 290/520 € 290/520 €, ☕ 25 € – 4 suites
Rest *L'Astor* – ☎ *01 53 05 05 20 (closed August, Saturday lunch, Sunday and Monday)* Menu 48/76 € – Carte 53/71 €
♦ Luxury ♦ Personalised ♦
A successful marriage of Regency and Art Deco styles endows this cosy hotel with its unique appearance. A handful of small terraces. The light coloured elegant oval dining room is furnished in a dark wood Directoire style.

Renaissance Paris Vendôme
4 r. Mont-Thabor (1st) – Ⓜ Tuileries – ☎ 01 40 20 20 00 – francereservations@marriotthotels.com – Fax 01 40 20 20 01 – www.renaissanceparisvendome.com K3
97 rm – 330/610 € 330/610 €, ☕ 29 € – 8 suites
Rest *Pinxo* – see below
♦ Business ♦ Traditional ♦ Cosy ♦
A 19C building converted into a contemporary hotel with interesting décor from the 1930s to 1950s. Honey and chocolate tones and wood predominate in the high-tech bedrooms. Attractive Chinese bar.

Castille Paris
33 r. Cambon (1st) – Ⓜ Madeleine – ☎ 01 44 58 44 58 – reservations@castille.com – Fax 01 44 58 44 00 – www.castille.com J3
86 rm – 380/780 € 380/780 €, ☕ 28 € – 21 suites
Rest *Il Cortile* – 37 r. Cambon, ☎ *01 44 58 45 67 (closed August, 24-30 December, Saturday and Sunday)* Menu 48 (lunch)/95 € – Carte 53/80 €
♦ Luxury ♦ Traditional ♦ Personalised ♦
Delightful Venetian-inspired décor in the Opéra wing, with black and white chic in the Rivoli wing (in reverence to nearby fashion house Chanel). Il Cortile serves Italian cuisine in a Villa d'Este-style dining room. Attractive patio-terrace.

Louvre
pl. A. Malraux (1st) – Ⓜ Palais Royal Musée du Louvre – ☎ 01 44 58 38 38 – hoteldulouvre@hoteldulouvre.com – Fax 01 44 58 38 01 – www.hoteldulouvre.com K3
132 rm – 220/600 € 220/600 €, ☕ 27 € – 45 suites
Rest *Brasserie Le Louvre* – ☎ *01 42 96 27 98* – Menu 40 € (lunch) – Carte 45/73 €
♦ Luxury ♦ Traditional ♦ Historic ♦
One of the first great Parisian hotels, where the painter Pissarro stayed. Some rooms offer a unique view of the Avenue de l'Opéra and the 'Palais Garnier' (Paris Opera House). The Brasserie Le Louvre is traditional both in its 1900s décor and in its cuisine.

Westminster
13 r. de la Paix (2nd) – Ⓜ Opéra – ✆ 01 42 61 57 46
– resa.westminster@warwickhotels.com – Fax 01 42 60 30 66
– www.hotelwestminster.com **K2**
101 rm – 280/630 € 280/630 €, 28 € – 21 suites
Rest *Le Céladon* – see below
Rest *Le Petit Céladon* – *✆ 01 47 03 40 42 (closed August, Monday, Tuesday, Wednesday, Thursday and Friday)* Menu 51 € bi
◆ Luxury ◆ Cosy ◆
In was in 1846 that this elegant hotel took the name of its most loyal guest, the Duke of Westminster. Sumptuous rooms, luxurious apartments. The hall is redecorated every season. The Céladon becomes the Petit Céladon at the weekend, with a simplified menu and more relaxed service.

Hyatt Regency
24 bd Malhesherbes (8th) – Ⓜ Madeleine – ✆ 01 55 27 12 34
– madeleine@hyattintl.com – Fax 01 55 27 12 35
– www.paris.madeleine.hyatt.com **J2**
86 rm – 330/520 € 330/1005 €, 28 €
Rest *Café M* – *(closed Sunday dinner)* Menu 54 € – Carte 46/75 €
◆ Luxury ◆ Chain hotel ◆ Modern ◆
Near the Madeleine, the discreet façade hides a distinctly contemporary interior that is both restrained and warm. Spacious personalised guestrooms. The Café M is popular for its delicious modern cuisine and its tempting weekend brunches.

Millennium Opéra
12 bd Haussmann (9th) – Ⓜ Richelieu Drouot – ✆ 01 49 49 16 00
– opera@mill-cop.com – Fax 01 49 49 17 00
– www.millenniumhotels.com **L2**
157 rm – 400/450 € 500/550 €, 25 € – 6 suites
Rest *Brasserie Haussmann* – *✆ 01 49 49 16 64* – Carte 28/61 €
◆ Luxury ◆ Business ◆ Modern ◆
This 1927 hotel has lost none of its period lustre. Tastefully appointed rooms with Art Deco furniture. Modern facilities. Carefully renovated with modern décor, and typical brasserie fare at the Brasserie Haussman.

Ambassador without rest
16 bd Haussmann (9th) – Ⓜ Richelieu Drouot – ✆ 01 44 83 40 40
– ambass@concorde-hotels.com – Fax 01 44 83 40 57
– www.hotelambassader-paris.com
274 rm – 500 € 500 €, 26 € – 20 suites **K2**
Rest *16 Haussmann* – *✆ 01 48 00 06 38* – Menu 44 (lunch)/37 (dinner)/52 € – Carte 48/59 €
◆ Luxury ◆ Business ◆ Classic ◆
Painted panels, crystal chandeliers and antiques adorn this elegant hotel dating from the 1920s. The renovated rooms are decorated in simple, contemporary style; the others somewhat more traditional.

Bedford
17 r. de l'Arcade (8th) – Ⓜ Madeleine – ✆ 01 44 94 77 77
– reservation@hotel-bedford.com – Fax 01 44 94 77 97
– www.hotel-bedford.com **J2**
135 rm – 168 € 222 €, 18 € – 10 suites
Rest – *(closed 28 July-24 August, Saturday and Sunday) (lunch only)* Menu 42 € – Carte 58/74 €
◆ Luxury ◆ Personalised ◆
This hotel, built in 1860 in the elegant Madeleine district, offers guests tastefully decorated rooms of varying size. 1900s-style décor with an abundance of decorative, stucco motifs and a lovely cupola. The restaurant room is the Bedford's real jewel.

Regina

2 pl. des Pyramides (1st) – Ⓜ Tuileries – ☎ 01 42 60 31 10 – reservation@regina-hotel.com – Fax 01 40 15 95 16 – www.regina-hotel.com **K3**

120 rm – †360/430 € ††430/495 €, ☕ 31 € – 8 suites

Rest – Carte 32/53 €

♦ Traditional ♦ Business ♦ Personalised ♦

The superb Art Nouveau reception of this 1900 hotel has been preserved. The rooms, rich in antique furniture, are quieter on the patio side; some offer views of the Eiffel Tower. Dining room with a pretty "Majorelle" fireplace and a courtyard-terrace that is very popular in summer.

Cambon without rest

3 r. Cambon (1st) – Ⓜ Concorde – ☎ 01 44 58 93 93 – info@hotelcambon.com – Fax 01 42 60 30 59 – www.hotelcambon.com **J3**

40 rm – †250/280 € ††320/360 €, ☕ 18 € – 2 suites

♦ Traditional ♦ Functional ♦

Between the gardens of the Tuileries and Rue St-Honoré, pleasant rooms combining contemporary furniture, attractive engravings and old paintings. Regular clientele.

Royal St-Honoré without rest

221 r. St-Honoré (1st) – Ⓜ Tuileries – ☎ 01 42 60 32 79 – rsh@hroy.com – Fax 01 42 60 47 44 – www.hotel-royal-st-honore.com **K3**

72 rm – †330/380 € ††380/590 €, ☕ 22 €

♦ Business ♦ Traditional ♦ Classical ♦

An opulent-looking 19C building on the site of the former Hôtel de Noailles. Elegant and refined guestrooms, with Louis XVI décor in the breakfast room. Cosy bar.

Villa Opéra Drouot without rest

2 r. Geoffroy Marie (9th) – Ⓜ Grands Boulevards – ☎ 01 48 00 08 08 – drouot@leshotelsdeparis.com – Fax 01 48 00 80 60 **L2**

29 rm – †139/370 € ††149/380 €, ☕ 20 €

♦ Business ♦ Stylish ♦

A surprising and subtle blend of Baroque décor and the latest in elegant comfort in these rooms embellished with wall hangings, velvets, silks and wood panelling.

Meliá Vendôme without rest

8 r. Cambon (1st) – Ⓜ Concorde – ☎ 01 44 77 54 00 – melia.vendome@solmelia.com – Fax 01 44 77 54 01 – www.solmelia.com **J3**

83 rm – †347/407 € ††347/407 €, ☕ 27 € – 4 suites

♦ Business ♦ Traditional ♦ Functional ♦

Smart, restrained décor in tones of red and gold. Bedrooms with period furniture, elegant lounge with a Belle Époque glass roof, chic bar and attractive breakfast area.

Édouard VII

39 av. Opéra (2nd) – Ⓜ Opéra – ☎ 01 42 61 56 90 – info@edouard7hotel.com – Fax 01 42 61 47 73 – www.edouard7hotel.com **K3**

71 rm – †345/445 € ††405/595 €, ☕ 23 € – 5 suites

Rest *Angl' Opéra* – *☎ 01 42 61 86 25* – (closed 11-24 August, Saturday and Sunday) Menu 29 € (lunch) – Carte 48/58 €

♦ Luxury ♦ Modern ♦

Edward VII, Prince of Wales liked to stay here on his trips through Paris. Spacious, luxurious rooms. Dark wood panelling and stained glass decorate the bar. The warm contemporary decor of the Angl' Opéra is as pleasant as its unusual fusion food.

Mercure Terminus Nord without rest

12 bd Denain (10th) – Ⓜ Gare du Nord – ☎ 01 42 80 20 00 – h2761@accor.com – Fax 01 42 80 63 89 – www.mercure.com **M1**

236 rm – †148/288 € ††168/368 €, ☕ 16 €

♦ Chain hotel ♦ Business ♦ Cosy ♦

A sympathetic renovation has restored this 19C hotel to its former glory. Art Nouveau stained glass, "British" décor and a cosy atmosphere give it the air of an elegant Victorian mansion.

Holiday Inn Paris Opéra

38 r. Échiquier (10th) – Ⓜ Bonne Nouvelle – ☎ 01 42 46 92 75 – information@hi-parisopera.com – Fax 01 42 47 03 97 – www.holiday-inn.com/paris-opera **M2**

92 rm – 🚹159/219 € 🚹🚹259/319 €, ☕ 20 €

Rest – *(closed Saturday lunch and Sunday)* Menu 35/39 € bi – Carte approx. 40 €

◆ Chain hotel ◆ Business ◆ Retro ◆

A step away from the Grands Boulevards and their string of theatres and brasseries. This hotel offers large rooms decorated in the style of the Belle Époque. The dining room is an authentic gem from the year 1900: mosaics, glass roof, woodwork and fine Art Nouveau furniture.

Pavillon de Paris without rest

7 r. Parme (9th) – Ⓜ Liège – ☎ 01 55 31 60 00 – mail@pavillondeparis.com – Fax 01 55 31 60 01 – www.pavillondeparis.com **K1**

30 rm – 🚹215/240 € 🚹🚹270/296 €, ☕ 16 €

◆ Business ◆ Minimalist ◆

Contemporary-style hotel in a quiet street. The rooms are on the small side, but have a sober, luxurious décor and a pleasant intimate atmosphere. Japanese garden in the mini-courtyard.

Washington Opéra without rest

50 r. Richelieu (1st) – Ⓜ Palais Royal – ☎ 01 42 96 68 06 – hotel@washingtonopera.com – Fax 01 40 15 01 12 – www.washingtonopera.com **L3**

36 rm – 🚹195/245 € 🚹🚹215/275 €, ☕ 15 €

◆ Traditional ◆ Luxury ◆ Classical ◆

Former townhouse of the Marquise de Pompadour. Directoire or 'Gustavian'-style rooms. The 6th floor terrace offers beautiful views over the gardens of the Palais-Royal.

Mercure Stendhal without rest

22 r. D. Casanova (2nd) – Ⓜ Opéra – ☎ 01 44 58 52 52 – h1610@accor.com – Fax 01 44 58 52 00 – www.mercure.com **K3**

20 rm – 🚹225/330 € 🚹🚹235/340 €, ☕ 17 €

◆ Luxury ◆ Modern ◆

On the trail of the famous writer, stay in the "Red and Black" suite of this stylish residence. Smart, personalised rooms and snug lounge-bar with fireplace.

Mansart without rest

5 r. des Capucines (1st) – Ⓜ Opéra – ☎ 01 42 61 50 28 – mansart@espritfrance.com – Fax 01 49 27 97 44 – www.esprit-de-france.com **K3**

57 rm – 🚹155/335 € 🚹🚹155/335 €, ☕ 12 €

◆ Business ◆ Traditional ◆ Functional ◆

Close to Place Vendôme, this hotel pays homage to Mansart, architect to Louis XIV. Classic rooms furnished in Empire or Directoire style. A more modern lobby-lounge.

L'Horset Opéra without rest

18 r. d'Antin (2nd) – Ⓜ Opéra – ☎ 01 44 71 87 00 – reservation@hotelhorsetopera.com – Fax 01 42 66 55 54 – www.paris-hotels-charm.com **K2**

54 rm ☕ – 🚹180/255 € 🚹🚹195/285 €

◆ Luxury ◆ Cosy ◆

Colourful wall hangings, warm wood panelling and fine furnishings add style to the rooms of this traditional hotel a short distance from the Opera House. Cosy atmosphere in the lounge.

Jules without rest

49 r. La Fayette (9th) – Ⓜ Le Peletier – ☎ 01 42 85 05 44 – info@hoteljules.com – Fax 01 49 95 06 60 – www.hoteljules.com **L2**

101 rm – 🚹128/260 € 🚹🚹128/260 €, ☕ 14 €

◆ Traditional ◆ Business ◆ Cosy ◆

This hotel has embraced contemporary design without sacrificing any of its inherent elegance with the emphasis on refined décor in the refurbished bedrooms. Winter garden-style breakfast room. Wellness centre.

St-Pétersbourg without rest

33 r. Caumartin (9th) – Ⓜ Havre Caumartin – ☎ 01 42 66 60 38 – info@hotelpeters.com – Fax 01 42 66 53 54 – www.hotelsaintpetersbourg.com **J2**

100 rm – **†**151/189 € **††**193/250 €

♦ Traditional ♦ Business ♦ Classic ♦

A large, traditional, family-run hotel. Elegant entrance with chandeliers and a marble floor, numerous lounges and meeting rooms. Spacious guestrooms.

Sofitel le Faubourg

15 r. Boissy d'Anglas (8th) – Ⓜ Concorde – ☎ 01 44 94 14 14 – h1295@accor.com – Fax 01 44 94 14 28 – www.sofitelfaubourg.com **J3**

163 rm – **†**460/560 € **††**560/850 €, 30 € – 10 suites

Rest *Café Faubourg* – *(closed August, Saturday lunch and Sunday lunch)*
Carte 53/73 €

♦ Chain hotel ♦ Luxury ♦ Modern ♦

This Sofitel is housed in two buildings, one 18C, the other 19C. Rooms with high-tech facilities; a 1930s bar; plus a lounge with a glass roof. Trendy décor, relaxing interior garden and modern cuisine at the Café Faubourg.

Richmond Opéra without rest

11 r. Helder (9th) – Ⓜ Chaussée d'Antin – ☎ 01 47 70 53 20 – paris@richmond-hotel.com – Fax 01 48 00 02 10 **K2**

59 rm – **†**134/149 € **††**154/225 €, 10 €

♦ Traditional ♦ Business ♦ Classic ♦

The spacious, elegant rooms almost all give onto the courtyard. The lounge is rather grandly decorated in the Empire style.

Noailles without rest

9 r. Michodière (2nd) – Ⓜ Quatre Septembre – ☎ 01 47 42 92 90 – goldentulip.denoailles@wanadoo.fr – Fax 01 49 24 92 71 – www.hoteldenoailles.com **K2**

59 rm – **†**180/255 € **††**200/345 €, 15 € – 2 suites

♦ Traditional ♦ Modern ♦

Staunch contemporary elegance behind a pretty old façade. Minimalist décor in the rooms, most of which open onto a patio-terrace. Fashionable lounge (jazz on Thursdays).

ATN without rest

21 r. d'Athènes (9th) – Ⓜ St-Lazare – ☎ 01 48 74 00 55 – atn@atnhotel.fr – Fax 01 42 81 04 75 – www.atnhotel.fr **K1**

36 rm – **†**139/350 € **††**139/399 €, 11 €

♦ Design ♦

Situated a stone's throw from St-Lazare station, completely refurbished hotel in a trendy, contemporary style. Quality materials and attention to detail add to the appeal.

Lorette Opéra without rest

36 r. Notre-Dame de Lorette (9th) – Ⓜ St-Georges – ☎ 01 42 85 18 81 – hotel.lorette@astotel.com – Fax 01 42 81 32 19 – www.asthotel.com **L1**

84 rm – **†**136/240 € **††**136/240 €, 14 €

♦ Business ♦ Modern ♦

The décor in this completely renovated hotel is a harmonious mix of bare stone and designer style. Pleasant, contemporary rooms; breakfast is served in the cellar with its vaulted ceiling.

Villathéna without rest

23 r. d'Athènes (9th) – Ⓜ St-Lazare – ☎ 01 44 63 07 07 – reservation@villathena.com – Fax 01 44 63 07 60 – www.villathena.com

43 rm – **†**185/215 € **††**185/215 €, 17 € **K1**

♦ Modern ♦

Housed in the former Social Security offices, this brand-new hotel has a resolutely contemporary feel. Lobby decorated in red, white and black; well-appointed guestrooms with light wood furniture.

De l'Arcade without rest

9 r. Arcade (8th) – Ⓜ Madeleine – ✆ 01 53 30 60 00 – reservation@hotel-arcade.com – Fax 01 40 07 03 07 – www.hotel-arcade.com **J2**

41 rm – 🚹160/194 € 🚹🚹194/240 €, ☕ 12 €

◆ Luxury ◆ Personalised ◆

The marble and wood panels in the hall and lounges, and the soft colours and carefully-chosen furniture in the rooms, all contribute to the charm of this elegant and discreet hotel near the Madeleine.

Le Lavoisier without rest

21 r. Lavoisier (8th) – Ⓜ St-Augustin – ✆ 01 53 30 06 06 – info@hotellavoisier.com – Fax 01 53 30 23 00 – www.hotellavoisier.com **J2**

27 rm – 🚹179/270 € 🚹🚹179/270 €, ☕ 14 € – 3 suites

◆ Luxury ◆ Modern ◆

Contemporary rooms, cosy little library-cum-lounge also serving as a bar, and a vaulted breakfast room are the hallmarks of this hotel in the St-Augustin district.

Little Palace

4 r. Salomon de Caus (3nd) – Ⓜ Réaumur Sébastopol – ✆ 01 42 72 08 15 – info@littlepalacehotel.com – Fax 01 42 72 45 81 – www.littlepalacehotel.com **M3**

49 rm – 🚹155/220 € 🚹🚹175/255 €, ☕ 13 € – 4 suites

Rest – *(closed 2 August-1st September, Friday dinner, Saturday and Sunday)*
Carte 28/44 €

◆ Family ◆ Traditional ◆ Modern ◆

A charming address with décor combining Belle Époque and contemporary styles. Attractive guestrooms; those on the 5th and 6th have a balcony with views of Paris. Lovely brown, sculpted wood panelling, light tones and minimalist furniture can be found in the restaurant.

Queen Mary without rest

9 r. Greffulhe (8th) – Ⓜ Madeleine – ✆ 01 42 66 40 50 – reservations@hotelqueenmary.com – Fax 01 42 66 94 92 – www.hotelqueenmary.com **J2**

36 rm – 🚹175/230 € 🚹🚹199/254 €, ☕ 19 €

◆ Family ◆ Personalised ◆

A refined establishment with a "British" feel to it, where a welcome gift of a carafe of sherry awaits you. Attentive service, pleasant patio, charming breakfast room and hushed bedrooms.

Le Vignon "8" without rest

23 r. Vignon (8th) – Ⓜ Madeleine – ✆ 01 47 42 93 00 – reservation@hotelvignon.com – Fax 01 47 42 04 60 – www.levignon.com **J2**

28 rm – 🚹195/390 € 🚹🚹195/390 €, ☕ 20 €

◆ Chain hotel ◆ Personalised ◆

A friendly, discreet hotel just a few steps away from Place de la Madeleine. Cosy rooms – those on the top floor have just been refurbished in a distinctly contemporary style.

États-Unis Opéra without rest

16 r. d'Antin (2nd) – Ⓜ Opéra – ✆ 01 42 65 05 05 – us-opera@wanadoo.fr – Fax 01 42 65 93 70 – www.hotel-paris-opera.com **K3**

45 rm – 🚹100/215 € 🚹🚹130/330 €, ☕ 12 €

◆ Traditional ◆ Classical ◆

This hotel in a 1930s building offers modern, comfortable, recently renovated rooms. Breakfast is served in the inviting English-style bar.

Thérèse without rest

5 r. Thérèse (1st) – Ⓜ Pyramides – ✆ 01 42 96 10 01 – info@hoteltherese.com – Fax 01 42 96 15 22 – www.hoteltherese.com **K3**

43 rm – 🚹150/298 € 🚹🚹150/311 €, ☕ 13 €

◆ Traditional ◆ Business ◆ Personalised ◆

The charm of this hotel lies in its refined contemporary décor of paintings, attractive fabrics and pastel shades. Vaulted breakfast room occupying the former cellars.

Opéra Franklin without rest
19 r. Buffault (9th) – Ⓜ Cadet – ✆ 01 42 80 27 27 – info@operafranklin.com – Fax 01 48 78 13 04 – www.operafranklin.com **L1**
67 rm – 🚹139/163 € 🚹🚹152/216 €, ☕ 13 €
♦ Family ♦ Traditional ♦ Historic ♦
Located in a quiet street, this business hotel is built around a central courtyard. Large lobby with a glass roof and bar. Functional, simply decorated rooms.

Caumartin Opéra without rest
27 r. Caumartin (9th) – Ⓜ Havre Caumartin – ✆ 01 47 42 95 95 – hotel.caumartin@astotel.com – Fax 01 47 42 88 19 – www.astotel.com
40 rm – 🚹155/240 € 🚹🚹165/240 €, ☕ 14 € **J2**
♦ Chain hotel ♦ Business ♦ Modern ♦
This small hotel in the Grand Magasins district has had a complete face-lift. Contemporary-style guestrooms with immaculate white bathrooms.

Anjou Lafayette without rest
4 r. Riboutté (9th) – Ⓜ Cadet – ✆ 01 42 46 83 44 – hotel.anjou.lafayette@wanadoo.fr – Fax 01 48 00 08 97 – www.hotelanjoulafayette.com **M1**
39 rm – 🚹98/170 € 🚹🚹118/190 €, ☕ 12 €
♦ Business ♦ Modern ♦
Near the leafy Square Montholon, with its Second Empire wrought-iron gates, this hotel offers guests comfortable, soundproofed rooms decorated in warm tones.

Trois Poussins without rest
15 r. Clauzel (9th) – Ⓜ St-Georges – ✆ 01 53 32 81 81 – h3p@les3poussins.com – Fax 01 53 32 81 82 – www.les3poussins.com **L1**
40 rm – 🚹110/140 € 🚹🚹119/156 €, ☕ 10 €
♦ Traditional ♦ Business ♦ Cosy ♦
Elegant rooms offering several levels of comfort. View of Paris from the top floors. Prettily vaulted breakfast room. Small courtyard-terrace.

le Meurice – Hôtel Le Meurice
228 r. Rivoli (1st) – Ⓜ Tuileries – ✆ 01 44 58 10 55 – restaurant@lemeurice.com – Fax 01 44 58 10 76 – www.lemeurice.com
closed 26 July-24 August, 14 February-1st March, Saturday and Sunday
Rest – Menu 90 € (lunch)/220 € – Carte 164/292 € **J-K3**
Spec. Jaunes d'œuf de poule au caviar "golden osciètre". Selle d'agneau parfumée à la fleur d'oranger en cours de cuisson (June to October). Palet fondant au chocolat.
♦ Luxury ♦
The dining room in this hotel has clearly drawn its inspiration from the state apartments of Versailles. Talented, updated cuisine much appreciated by gourmets.

Les Ambassadeurs – Hôtel Crillon
10 pl. Concorde (8th) – Ⓜ Concorde – ✆ 01 44 71 16 16 – restaurants@crillon.com – Fax 01 44 71 15 02 – www.crillon.com
closed August, 1st-8 January, Sunday and Monday **J3**
Rest – Menu 75 (weekday lunch)/200 € – Carte 156/275 €
Spec. Blanc à manger d'œuf, truffe noire (January to March). Pigeonneau désossé, foie gras, jus à l'olive. "Paquet gâteau" à manger, chocolat, banane.
♦ Luxury ♦
This splendid dining room was once the ballroom of an 18C mansion. Sophisticated, inventive cuisine and a superb wine list.

L'Espadon – Hôtel Ritz
15 pl. Vendôme (1st) – Ⓜ Opéra – ✆ 01 43 16 30 80 – espadon@ritzparis.com – Fax 01 43 16 33 75 – www.ritzparis.com **K3**
Rest – Menu 75 € (lunch), 170/305 € bi – Carte 134/217 €
Spec. Belons au sabayon gratiné et mousseline d' épinards. Tronçon de turbot rôti à la fleur de sel, gnocchi au parmesan. Noix de ris de veau doré, jus perlé et pommes soufflées.
♦ Luxury ♦
The restaurant area is weighted in gold and drapery, a dazzling décor reminiscent of its famous guests. Pleasant terrace in a flower garden. A ritzy extravaganza!

XXXX ✿✿ **Le Grand Véfour**

17 r. Beaujolais (1st) – Ⓜ Palais Royal – ☎ 01 42 96 56 27 – grand.vefour@wanadoo.fr – Fax 01 42 86 80 71 – www.grand-vefour.com
closed 28 April-4 May, 28 July-25 August, 24 December-1st January, Friday dinner, Saturday and Sunday **L3**

Rest – Menu 88 (lunch)/268 € – Carte 194/235 €

Spec. Ravioles de foie gras, crème foisonnée truffée. Pigeon Prince Rainier III. Palet noisette et chocolat au lait.

◆ Innovative ◆ Romantic ◆

Many famous personalities have dined in the elegant Directoire-style "salons" of this luxurious restaurant, located in the gardens of the Palais-Royal. Innovative cuisine created by an inspired chef.

XXXX ✿✿ **Carré des Feuillants** (Alain Dutournier)

14 r. Castiglione (1st) – Ⓜ Tuileries – ☎ 01 42 86 82 82 – carrédesfeuillants@orange.fr – Fax 01 42 86 07 71 – www.carredesfeuillants.fr
closed August, Saturday and Sunday **K3**

Rest – Menu 65 (lunch)/165 € – Carte 127/159 €

Spec. Cuisses de grenouilles épicées, blé cassé, écume de roquette et cresson, girolles en tempura (summer-autumn). Tronçons de Saint-Pierre ficelés de pommes de terre et caviar (winter). "Envie de vacherin", grosses framboises, meringue légère au yuzu, crème fermière mascavo (summer).

◆ Traditional ◆ Cosy ◆

A modern restaurant on the site of the former Feuillants convent. The cuisine shows distinct Gascon influences and there is a superb choice of wines.

XXXX ✿ **Goumard**

9 r. Duphot (1st) – Ⓜ Madeleine – ☎ 01 42 60 36 07 – goumard.philippe@wanadoo.fr – Fax 01 42 60 04 54 – www.goumard.com

Rest – Menu 46 € (lunch)/60 € bi (lunch) – Carte 75/127 € **J3**

Spec. Fleur de courgette farcie de chair de tourteau, jus à l' orange sanguine (May to October). Bar de ligne rôti, poêlée d'artichaut poivrade et crevettes grises (May to October). Homard bleu rôti, cocotte de blettes et tronçons de macaroni.

◆ Formal ◆

Small intimate dining rooms whose Art Deco style is enhanced by seascapes. Don't miss the toilets, where the original décor by Majorelle can still be seen. Fine seafood menu.

XXX ✿✿ **Senderens**

9 pl. de la Madeleine (8th) – Ⓜ Madeleine – ☎ 01 42 65 22 90 – restaurant@senderens.fr – Fax 01 42 65 06 23 – www.senderens.fr
closed 3-25 August **J2**

Rest – Carte 72/91 €

Spec. Langoustines croustillantes, chou pak-choï, coriandre et livèche. Agneau de lait de Castille, péquillos et cocos. Tarte tatin aux coings, glace séchouan et orange (autumn-winter).

◆ Innovative ◆ Design ◆

Designer furnishings and Art Nouveau wood panels by Majorelle combine well in this elegant, lively brasserie. Innovative cuisine with a fine choice of accompanying wines.

XXX ✿ **Le Céladon** – Hôtel Westminster

15 r. Daunou (2nd) – Ⓜ Opéra – ☎ 01 47 03 40 42 – christophemoisand@leceladon.com – Fax 01 42 61 33 78 – www.leceladon.com
closed August, Saturday and Sunday **K2**

Rest – Menu 48 € (lunch), 72 € bi/110 € – Carte 82/111 €

Spec. Langoustines bretonnes en carpaccio. Lapin du Poitou farci de ses abats. Chocolat de Tanzanie sur sablé breton.

◆ Romantic ◆

Sophisticated décor that combines Regency-style furniture, green walls and a collection of Chinese porcelain. Cuisine suited to current tastes.

XXX ✿

Gérard Besson

5 r. Coq Héron (1st) – Ⓜ Louvre Rivoli – ✆ 01 42 33 14 74 – gerard.besson4@libertysurf.fr – Fax 01 42 33 85 71 – www.gerardbesson.com

closed 26 July-18 August, Monday lunch, Saturday lunch and Sunday **L3**

Rest – Menu 120/125 € – Carte 113/157 €

Spec. Homard bleu en fricassée "Georges Garin", macaroni à la duxelles. Gibier (season). Fenouil confit aux épices, glace vanille de Tahiti.

♦ Traditional ♦ Formal ♦

Elegant restaurant near Les Halles decorated in beige tones with still life paintings and Jouy wall hangings. Subtly reinterpreted classic cuisine.

XXX

Café de la Paix – Intercontinental Le Grand

12 bd Capucines (9th) – Ⓜ Opéra – ✆ 01 40 07 36 36 – reservation@cafedelapaix.fr – Fax 01 40 07 36 13 – www.cafedelapaix.fr **K2**

Rest – Menu 45 € (lunch)/85 € – Carte 51/118 €

♦ Brasserie ♦

Fine murals, gold wainscoting and French Second Empire-inspired furniture: this famous luxury brasserie, open from 7am to midnight, has been treated to a masterful makeover.

XXX ✿

Le Pur' Grill – Hôtel Park Hyatt

5 r. de la Paix (2nd) – Ⓜ Opéra – ✆ 01 58 71 10 60

closed August **K3**

Rest – *(dinner only)* Menu 125/300 € bi – Carte 92/225 €

Spec. Vapeur d'escargots petits gris, radis rouge et raifort. Déclinaison d'agneau allaiton, haricots coco cuisinés au chorizo."Choco Tag", chutney banane/galanga et épine vinette.

♦ Fashionable ♦

Simplicity and refinement best describe the modern dinner menu served in the chic and contemporary rotunda-shaped dining room (kitchen in full view). Attractive summer terrace.

XXX

Drouant

16 pl. Gaillon (2nd) – Ⓜ Quatre Septembre – ✆ 01 42 65 15 16 – reservations@drouant.com – Fax 01 49 24 02 15 – www.drouant.com **K3**

Rest – Menu 42 (weekday lunch)/67 € – Carte 40/87 €

♦ Traditional ♦

Small Art Deco dining rooms set around a splendid Ruhlmann staircase. The Louis XVI sitting room upstairs is where the Goncourt (literary prize) jury has met since 31 October 1914.

XXX

La Fontaine Gaillon

pl. Gaillon (2nd) – Ⓜ Quatre Septembre – ✆ 01 47 42 63 22 – Fax 01 47 42 82 84 – www.la-fontaine-gaillon.com

closed 9 August-1st September, Saturday and Sunday **K2-3**

Rest – Menu 41 € (lunch) – Carte 48/64 €

♦ Seafood ♦ Cosy ♦

Seafood dishes and wine selection supervised by the actor Gérard Depardieu in an elegant, 17C townhouse dining room. Terrace with central fountain.

XXX

Macéo

15 r. Petits-Champs (1st) – Ⓜ Bourse – ✆ 01 42 97 53 85 – info@maceorestaurant.com – Fax 01 47 03 36 93 – www.maceorestaurant.com

closed 2-17 August, Saturday lunch and Sunday **L3**

Rest – Menu 30/49 € – Carte 52/76 €

♦ Friendly ♦

A daring marriage of French Second Empire décor and modern furnishings. Updated cuisine, a vegetarian menu and international wine list. Friendly lounge-bar.

XX **Pierre au Palais Royal**

10 r. Richelieu (1st) – Ⓜ Palais Royal – ✆ 01 42 96 09 17
– pierreaupalaisroyal@wanadoo.fr – Fax 01 42 96 26 40
closed August, Saturday lunch and Sunday **K3**
Rest – Menu 39 €
◆ A la mode ◆ Neighbourhood ◆
Discreet and pleasant décor in aubergine shades with prints of the neighbouring Palais Royal. Contemporary cuisine based on seasonal market produce.

XX **Palais Royal**

110 Galerie de Valois - Jardin du Palais Royal (1st) – Ⓜ Bourse
– ✆ 01 40 20 00 27 – palaisrest@aol.com – Fax 01 40 20 00 82
– www.restaurantdupalaisroyal.com
closed 21 December-1st January and Sunday **L3**
Rest – Carte 45/76 €
◆ Traditional ◆ Retro ◆
Beneath the windows of Colette's apartment, an Art Deco-style restaurant with an idyllic terrace, opening onto the Palais-Royal garden.

XX ✿ **Jean**

8 r. St-Lazare (9th) – Ⓜ Notre-Dame-de-Lorette
– ✆ 01 48 78 62 73
– chezjean@wanadoo.fr – Fax 01 48 78 66 04
– www.restaurantjean.fr
closed 28 July-25 August, 25 February-3 March, Saturday and Sunday **L1**
Rest – Menu 46 € (lunch), 60/75 € – Carte 63/71 €
Spec. Jus tremblotant de crevettes grises, herbes parfumées. Noix de veau, yaourt à l' anchois et jus de prune à l' orchidée. Dacquoise à la fleur d'oranger, chasselas, sorbet bière blanche.
◆ Friendly ◆
A recent makeover for this restaurant serving up-to-the-minute cuisine: beige tones, stained woodwork, light fabrics, bench seating and an Oriental-style lounge upstairs.

XX **Au Petit Riche**

25 r. Le Peletier (9th) – Ⓜ Richelieu Drouot – ✆ 01 47 70 68 68
– aupetitriche@wanadoo.fr – Fax 01 48 24 10 79
– www.aupetitriche.com
closed Saturday from 14 July to 20 August and Sunday **L2**
Rest – Menu 27/36 € – Carte 30/62 €
◆ Brasserie ◆
A favourite haunt of Maurice Chevalier and Mistinguett, the gracious sitting-dining rooms, decorated in a late 19C style, are adorned with mirrors and hat stands.

XX **Gallopin**

40 r. N.-D.-des-Victoires (2nd) – Ⓜ Bourse – ✆ 01 42 36 45 38
– administration@brasseriegallopin.com – Fax 01 42 36 10 32
– www.brasseriegallopin.com **L3**
Rest – Menu 28/34 € bi – Carte 28/76 €
◆ Retro ◆
Arletty, Raimu and the plush Victorian décor have brought fame to this brasserie situated opposite the Palais Brongniart. Lovely conservatory in the rear room.

XX **La Luna**

69 r. Rocher (8th) – Ⓜ Villiers – ✆ 01 42 93 77 61 – laluna75008@yahoo.fr
– Fax 01 40 08 02 44
closed 30 July-26 August and Sunday *Plan II* **H1**
Rest – Carte 68/105 €
◆ Fish ◆ Friendly ◆
A restrained Art Deco setting and fine cuisine based on fish and seafood delivered fresh from the Atlantic. Don't miss the rum baba...

XX

Au Pied de Cochon

6 r. Coquillière (1st) – Ⓜ Châtelet-Les Halles – ✆ 01 40 13 77 00 – pieddecochon@blanc.net – Fax 01 40 13 77 09 – www.pieddecochon.com **L3**

Rest – Menu 24 € – Carte 28/75 €

♦ Brasserie ♦

This brasserie, founded in 1946 and renowned for its pigs' trotters, stays open late into the night. Original period frescoes and fruit themed chandeliers.

XX

Ambassade d'Auvergne

22 r. Grenier St-Lazare (3rd) – Ⓜ Rambuteau – ✆ 01 42 72 31 22 – info@ambassade-auvergne.com – Fax 01 42 78 85 47 – www.ambassade-auvergne.com **M3**

Rest – Menu 28 € – Carte 30/46 €

♦ Traditional ♦ Friendly ♦

True ambassadors of a province rich in flavours and traditions; Auvergne-style furniture and setting offering products, recipes and wines of the region.

XX

Café Panique

12 r. des Messageries (10th) – Ⓜ Poissonnière – ✆ 01 47 70 06 84 – www.cafepanique.com

closed August, February school holidays, Saturday and Sunday **M1**

Rest – Menu 27 € bi (lunch)/32 €

♦ A la mode ♦ Intimate ♦

Secluded, this textile workshop has been converted into a pleasant modern restaurant with the appeal of a contemporary loft: glass screens, a mezzanine, temporary exhibitions and visible kitchens.

XX

Terminus Nord

23 r. Dunkerque (10th) – Ⓜ Gare du Nord – ✆ 01 42 85 05 15 – Fax 01 40 16 13 98 – www.terminusnord.com **M1**

Rest – Menu 31 € – Carte 32/80 €

♦ Brasserie ♦

High ceilings, frescoes, posters and sculptures are reflected in the mirrors of this brasserie that successfully mixes Art Deco and Art Nouveau. Cosmopolitan clientele.

XX

Au Gourmand

17 r. Molière (1st) – Ⓜ Pyramides – ✆ 01 42 96 22 19 – Fax 01 42 96 05 72 – www.augourmand.fr

closed August, Saturday lunch, Monday lunch, Sunday and public holidays **K3**

Rest – Menu 30 € (weekday lunch)/36 €

♦ Traditional ♦ Neighbourhood ♦

Traditional cuisine with a contemporary twist (including a menu based on Joël Thiébault's famous vegetables) prepared by a self-taught chef. Knowledgeable sommelier and friendly, welcoming ambience.

XX

Pinxo – Hôtel Renaissance Paris Vendôme

9 r. d'Alger (1st) – Ⓜ Tuileries – ✆ 01 40 20 72 00 – Fax 01 40 20 72 02 – www.pinxo.fr

closed 5-25 August **K3**

Rest – Carte 38/57 €

♦ Fashionable ♦

A restaurant with minimalist furniture, black and white shades, an open kitchen and understated but stylish decoration, serving simple, tasty dishes à la Dutournier.

XX

Vaudeville

29 r. Vivienne (2nd) – Ⓜ Bourse – ✆ 01 40 20 04 62 – Fax 01 40 20 14 35 – www.vaudevilleparis.com **L2**

Rest – Menu 24 € (weekdays)/31 € – Carte 33/69 €

♦ Retro ♦

This large brasserie with its sparkling Art Deco details has become the 'canteen' of numerous journalists. It is especially lively after theatre performances.

XX **Le Versance** AC VISA MC AE

16 r. Feydeau (2nd) – Ⓜ Bourse – ✆ 01 45 08 00 08 – contact@leversance.fr – Fax 01 45 08 47 99 – www.leversance.fr

closed August, 24 December-2 January, Saturday lunch, Sunday and Monday

Rest – Menu 38 € bi – Carte 46/68 € **L2**

◆ A la mode ◆

A tasteful combination of elegant modern (white/grey tones, designer furniture) and period décor (exposed beams, stained glass). Contemporary cuisine from a globetrotting chef.

X **Chez Georges** AC VISA MC AE

1 r. du Mail (2nd) – Ⓜ Bourse – ✆ 01 42 60 07 11

closed August, 24 December-2 January, Saturday, Sunday and public holidays

Rest – Carte 42/66 € **L3**

◆ Retro ◆

This authentic Parisian bistro has conserved its original 1900s décor: bar, seats, stucco and mirrors. A neighbourhood institution.

X **Aux Lyonnais** AC VISA MC AE

32 r. St-Marc (2nd) – Ⓜ Richelieu Drouot – ✆ 01 42 96 65 04 – auxlyonnais@online.fr – Fax 01 42 97 42 95

closed 20 July-18 August, Saturday lunch, Sunday and Monday **L2**

Rest – *(pre-book)* Menu 30 € – Carte 38/55 €

◆ Bistro ◆

This bistro founded in 1890 proposes delicious, intelligently updated Lyonnais recipes. A delightfully retro setting with bar counter, bench seating, bevelled mirrors and mouldings.

X **La Petite Sirène de Copenhague** VISA MC AE

47 r. N.-D. de Lorette (9th) – Ⓜ St-Georges – ✆ 01 45 26 66 66

closed 2-25 August, 23 December-5 January, Saturday lunch, Sunday and Monday **K1**

Rest – *(pre-book)* Menu 29 € (lunch)/34 € – Carte 43/71 €

◆ Danish ◆ Friendly ◆

A tasteful dining room, colour washed walls and soft Danish lighting set the scene for recipes from Andersen's homeland. Attentive service.

X **L'Oenothèque** AC VISA MC AE

20 r. St-Lazare (9th) – Ⓜ Notre-Dame-de-Lorette – ✆ 01 48 78 08 76 – Fax 01 40 16 10 27

closed 1st-8 May, 2 weeks in August, 24 December-1st January, Saturday and Sunday **L1**

Rest – Carte 25/53 €

◆ Bistro ◆

Neighbourhood establishment combining a simple restaurant with a wine shop. Fine selection of wines to accompany the market fresh fare presented on the chalkboard.

X **I Golosi** AC VISA MC

6 r. Grange Batelière (9th) – Ⓜ Richelieu Drouot – ✆ 01 48 24 18 63 – i.golosi@wanadoo.fr – Fax 01 45 23 18 96

closed 5-20 August, Saturday dinner and Sunday **L2**

Rest – Carte 25/41 €

◆ Minimalist ◆

On the 1st floor, Italian designer décor with a minimalism made up for by the joviality of the service. Café, shop and little spot for tasting things on the ground floor. Italian cuisine.

X **Le Pré Cadet** AC VISA MC AE

10 r. Saulnier (9th) – Ⓜ Cadet – ✆ 01 48 24 99 64 – Fax 01 47 70 55 96

closed 1st-8 May, 3-21 August, 24 December-1st January, Saturday lunch and Sunday

Rest – *(number of covers limited, pre-book)* Menu 30/45 € – Carte 39/52 € **L2**

◆ Friendly ◆

This friendly, unpretentious restaurant in the vicinity of the 'Folies' is renowned for its specials, such as veal brawn - its pride and joy. Very good coffee list.

Pierrot
18 r. Étienne Marcel (2nd) – Ⓜ Etienne Marcel – ✆ 01 45 08 00 10 – Fax 01 42 77 35 92
closed 30 July-22 August and Sunday **M3**
Rest – Menu 50 € bi – Carte 34/50 €
♦ Bistro ♦
In the lively Sentier district, this bistro offers a discovery tour of the flavours and produce of the Aveyron. Summer pavement terrace.

Chez Michel
10 r. Belzunce (10th) – Ⓜ Gare du Nord – ✆ 01 44 53 06 20
closed 29 July-20 August, Monday lunch, Saturday and Sunday **M1**
Rest – Menu 30 € – Carte 45/65 €
♦ Traditional ♦ Bistro ♦
Unpretentious and popular retro-style bistro proposing delicious traditional dishes, with a slight Breton slant (the chef's origins and name!) Excellent game in season.

TOUR EIFFEL, INVALIDES *Plan IV*

Sezz without rest
6 av. Frémiet (16th) ✉ 75016 – Ⓜ Passy – ✆ 01 56 75 26 26 – mail@hotelsezz.com – Fax 01 56 75 26 16 – www.hotelsezz.com **N2**
22 rm – †280/335 € ††330/460 €, ☕ 25 € – 5 suites
♦ Luxury ♦ Design ♦
Revamped hotel in a modern style: spacious, minimalist interior (shades of grey, giant vases), hi-tech gadgets and attentive staff. Steam bath and jacuzzi.

Mercure Suffren Tour Eiffel
20 r. Jean Rey (15th) – Ⓜ Bir-Hakeim – ✆ 01 45 78 50 00 – h2175@accor.com – Fax 01 45 78 91 42 – www.mercure.com **N2**
405 rm – †150/310 € ††160/310 €, ☕ 19 €
Rest – Carte 27/43 €
♦ Business ♦ Chain hotel ♦ Functional ♦
A thorough, careful renovation has been carried out in this perfectly soundproofed hotel, whose new décor sports a 'nature and garden' theme. Some rooms offer a view of the Eiffel Tower. The dining room opens onto a pleasant terrace surrounded by trees and greenery.

Bourgogne et Montana without rest
3 r. de Bourgogne (7th) – Ⓜ Assemblée Nationale – ✆ 01 45 51 20 22 – bmontana@bourgogne-montana.com – Fax 01 45 56 11 98 – bourgogne-montana.com **Q1**
28 rm ☕ – †160/180 € ††180/340 € – 4 suites
♦ Traditional ♦ Business ♦ Classic ♦
Elegance and beauty fill every room of this discreet 18C hotel. The top floor rooms offer superb views over the "Palais-Bourbon" (French Parliament buildings).

Le Walt without rest
37 av. de La Motte Picquet (7th) – Ⓜ Ecole Militaire – ✆ 01 45 51 55 83 – lewalt@inwoodhotel.com – Fax 01 47 05 77 59 – www.lewaltparis.com **P2**
25 rm – †275/325 € ††295/345 €, ☕ 19 €
♦ Business ♦ Luxury ♦ Modern ♦
The imposing reproductions of classical masterpieces and "panther" or "zebra" bedspreads add originality to the comfortable, contemporary rooms.

Muguet without rest
11 r. Chevert (7th) – Ⓜ Ecole Militaire – ✆ 01 47 05 05 93 – muguet@wanadoo.fr – Fax 01 45 50 25 37 – www.hotelmuguet.com **P2**
43 rm – †103 € ††135/190 €, ☕ 9.50 €
♦ Business ♦ Family ♦ Functional ♦
Hotel spruced up in a classic spirit.Sitting room furnished in Louis Philippe style, well-appointed rooms (7 overlook the Eiffel Tower or the Invalides), veranda and small garden.

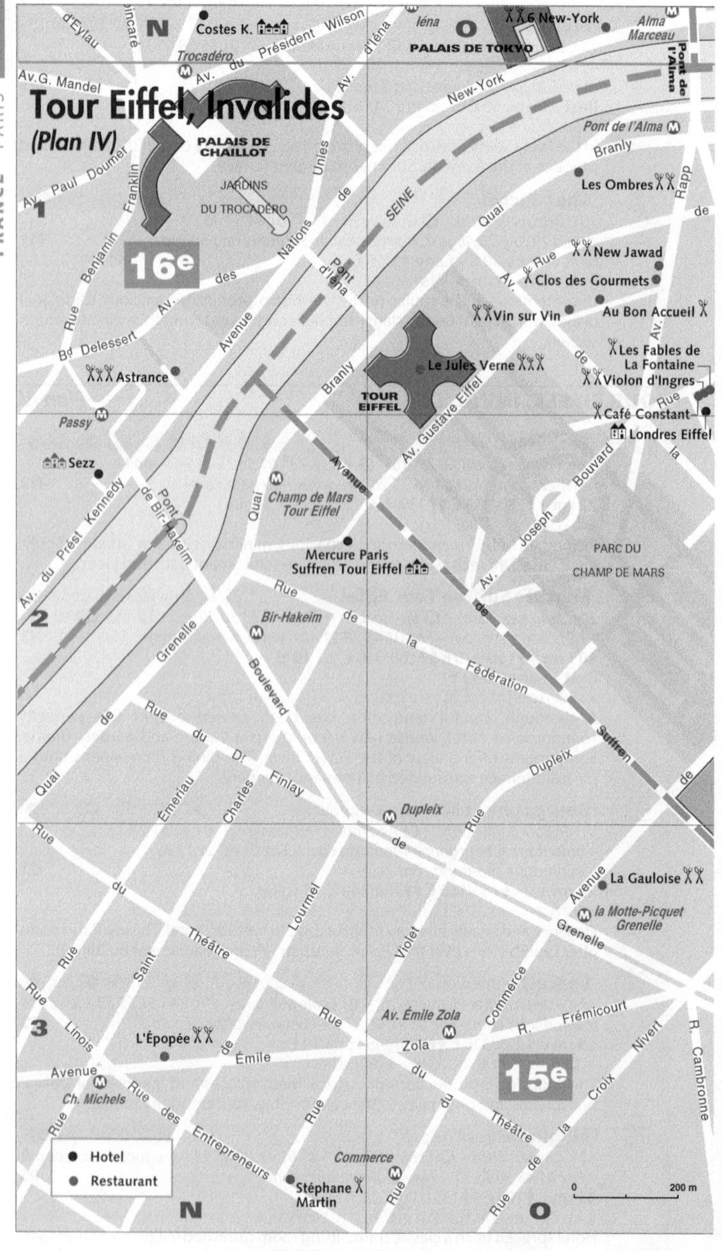
Tour Eiffel, Invalides
(Plan IV)
PALAIS DE CHAILLOT
JARDINS DU TROCADÉRO
PALAIS DE TOKYO
TOUR EIFFEL
PARC DU CHAMP DE MARS
16e
15e
SEINE
Costes K.
6 New-York
Les Ombres
New Jawad
Clos des Gourmets
Au Bon Accueil
Vin sur Vin
Les Fables de La Fontaine
Violon d'Ingres
Café Constant
Londres Eiffel
Le Jules Verne
Astrance
Sezz
Mercure Paris Suffren Tour Eiffel
La Gauloise
L'Épopée
Stéphane Martin
Trocadéro
Iéna
Alma Marceau
Pont de l'Alma
Passy
Champ de Mars Tour Eiffel
Bir-Hakeim
Dupleix
la Motte-Picquet Grenelle
Av. Émile Zola
Ch. Michels
Commerce
Hotel
Restaurant
0
200 m

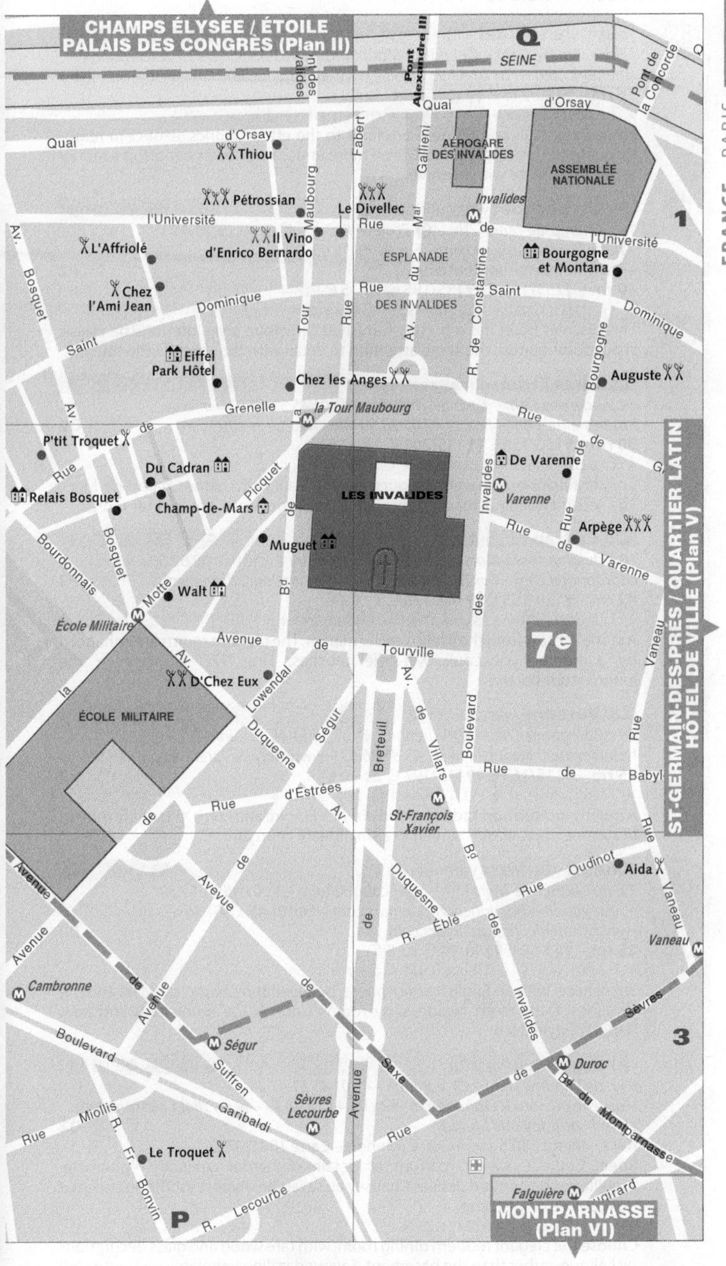
CHAMPS ÉLYSÉE / ÉTOILE
PALAIS DES CONGRÈS (Plan II)
SEINE
Quai d'Orsay
Pont Alexandre III
Pont de la Concorde
AÉROGARE DES INVALIDES
ASSEMBLÉE NATIONALE
Thiou
Pétrossian
Le Divellec
Invalides
Il Vino d'Enrico Bernardo
L'Affriolé
Chez l'Ami Jean
Bourgogne et Montana
ESPLANADE DES INVALIDES
Rue de l'Université
Rue Saint Dominique
Eiffel Park Hôtel
Chez les Anges
Auguste
la Tour Maubourg
Rue de Grenelle
P'tit Troquet
Du Cadran
De Varenne
Relais Bosquet
Champ-de-Mars
LES INVALIDES
Varenne
Arpège
Muguet
Walt
École Militaire
Avenue de Tourville
D'Chez Eux
7e
ÉCOLE MILITAIRE
Rue de Babylone
St-François Xavier
Aida
Vaneau
Cambronne
Ségur
Duroc
Sèvres Lecourbe
Le Troquet
Falguière
MONTPARNASSE (Plan VI)
ST-GERMAIN-DES-PRÉS / QUARTIER LATIN HÔTEL DE VILLE (Plan V)
1
3
P
Q

Eiffel Park Hôtel without rest
17bis r. Amélie (7th) – Ⓜ La Tour Maubourg – ✆ 01 45 55 10 01 – reservation@eiffelpark.com – Fax 01 47 05 28 68 – www.eiffelpark.com **P1**
36 rm – 🚹160/215 € 🚹🚹160/240 €, ☕ 12 €
◆ Traditional ◆ Family ◆ Personalised ◆
From the Indian and Chinese artefacts to the ethnic fabrics, exoticism reigns throughout this elegant hotel. Even more unusual, it boasts a rooftop summer terrace complete with beehives.

Relais Bosquet without rest
19 r. Champ-de-Mars (7th) – Ⓜ Ecole Militaire – ✆ 01 47 05 25 45 – hotel@relaisbosquet.com – Fax 01 45 55 08 24 – www.hotelrelaisbosquet.com **P2**
40 rm – 🚹135/180 € 🚹🚹135/195 €, ☕ 15 €
◆ Traditional ◆ Business ◆ Classic ◆
This discreet hotel has a prettily furnished Directoire style interior. The classic style rooms feature the same attention to detail with thoughtful little touches.

Londres Eiffel without rest
1 r. Augereau (7th) – Ⓜ Ecole Militaire – ✆ 01 45 51 63 02 – info@londres-eiffel.com – Fax 01 47 05 28 96 – www.londres-eiffel.com **O2**
30 rm – 🚹130/150 € 🚹🚹135/205 €, ☕ 12 €
◆ Traditional ◆ Family ◆ Cosy ◆
Cosy hotel done up in warm colours near the leafy paths of the Champ-de-Mars. The second building, reached through a small courtyard, has quieter rooms.

Du Cadran without rest
10 r. du Champ-de-Mars (7th) – Ⓜ Ecole Militaire – ✆ 01 40 62 67 00 – info@cadranhotel.com – Fax 01 40 62 67 13 – www.hotelducadran.com **P2**
42 rm – 🚹129/165 € 🚹🚹142/178 €, ☕ 13 €
◆ Traditional ◆ Business ◆ Modern ◆
A stone's throw from the lively rue Cler market. The modern rooms are enhanced by a number of Louis XVI-style touches. Fine 17C fireplace in the lounge-cum-library.

De Varenne without rest
44 r. Bourgogne (7th) – Ⓜ Varenne – ✆ 01 45 51 45 55 – info@hoteldevarenne.com – Fax 01 45 51 86 63 – www.hoteldevarenne.com
25 rm – 🚹115/167 € 🚹🚹115/197 €, ☕ 10 € **Q2**
◆ Traditional ◆ Family ◆ Functional ◆
A quietly located hotel adorned with French Empire and Louis XVI style furniture. In summer, breakfast is served in a small, leafy courtyard.

Champ-de-Mars without rest
7 r. du Champ-de-Mars (7th) – Ⓜ Ecole Militaire – ✆ 01 45 51 52 30 – reservation@hotelduchampdemars.com – Fax 01 45 51 64 36 – www.hotelduchampdemars.com **P2**
25 rm – 🚹84/90 € 🚹🚹90/94 €, ☕ 8 €
◆ Family ◆ Traditional ◆ Cosy ◆
Small hotel with an English atmosphere, between the Champ-de-Mars and the Invalides. Dark green façade, cosy rooms (soon to be renovated) and neat "Liberty" style décor.

Arpège (Alain Passard)
84 r. de Varenne (7th) – Ⓜ Varenne – ✆ 01 45 51 47 33 – arpege.passard@wanadoo.fr – Fax 01 44 18 98 39 – www.alain-passard.com
closed Saturday and Sunday **Q2**
Rest – Menu 130 (lunch)/340 € (dinner) – Carte 188/247 €
Spec. Couleur, saveur, parfum et dessin du jardin cueillette éphémère. Aiguillettes de homard des îles Chausey au savagnin. Avocat soufflé au chocolat noir, pointe de pistache.
◆ Innovative ◆ Formal ◆
Choose the elegant modern dining room, with rare wood and glass decorations by Lalique, rather than the basement. Savour dazzling vegetable garden-based cuisine by a master chef and poet of the land.

XXX

Le Jules Verne

< Paris, AC VISA MC AE

2nd floor Eiffel Tower, private lift South pillar (7th) – Ⓜ Bir-Hakeim – ✆ 01 45 55 61 44 – Fax 01 47 05 29 41 – www.lejulesverne-paris.com **O1**

Rest – Menu 75 € (lunch), 155/450 € – Carte 132/195 €

♦ Classic ♦ Elegant ♦

Although the views of Paris remain the same, the décor in this famous restaurant in the Eiffel Tower has been modernised. For a truly memorable experience, book a window table.

XXX ✿✿✿

Astrance (Pascal Barbot)

AC VISA MC AE

4 r. Beethoven (16th) ✉ 75016 – Ⓜ Passy – ✆ 01 40 50 84 40
closed 1st-9 March, August, autumn half-term holidays, Saturday, Sunday and Monday **N1**

Rest – *(number of covers limited, pre-book)* Menu 70 € (lunch), 190/290 € bi

Spec. Foie gras mariné au verjus, galette de champignons de Paris, citron confit. Selle d'agneau grillée, aubergine laquée au miso, curry noir. Croustillant chocolat blanc-gingembre, glace thé vert.

♦ Innovative ♦ Fashionable ♦

The Astrance (from the Latin Aster, a star-like flower) boasts delicious, inventive cuisine, a surprise evening menu, choice wines and an attractive modern décor.

XXX ✿

Le Divellec (Jacques Le Divellec)

AC VISA MC AE

107 r. Université (7th) – Ⓜ Invalides – ✆ 01 45 51 91 96 – ledivellec@noos.fr – Fax 01 45 51 31 75
closed 25 July-25 August, 25 December-2 January, Saturday and Sunday **P-Q1**

Rest – Menu 55 (lunch)/70 € (lunch) – Carte 105/205 €

Spec. Carpaccio de turbot et truffe, citronnelle et huile d'olive. Homard bleu à la presse avec son corail. Harmonie d'huitres chaudes et froides.

♦ Seafood ♦ Formal ♦

A chic nautical interior: frosted glass, lobster tank and blue and white colour scheme. Outstanding seafood menu direct from the Atlantic ocean.

XXX

Pétrossian

AC VISA MC AE

144 r. de l'Université (7th) – Ⓜ Invalides – ✆ 01 44 11 32 32 – Fax 01 44 11 32 35
closed August, Sunday and Monday **P1**

Rest – Menu 35 € (weekday lunch), 45/100 € – Carte 56/98 €

♦ Seafood ♦ Formal ♦

The Petrossians have treated Parisians to caviar from the Caspian sea since 1920. Above the boutique, inventive cuisine is served in a comfortable, elegant dining room.

XX ✿

Le Violon d'Ingres (Christian Constant et Stéphane Schmidt)

AC VISA MC AE

135 r. St-Dominique (7th) – Ⓜ Ecole Militaire – ✆ 01 45 55 15 05 – violondingres@wanadoo.fr – Fax 01 45 55 48 42 – www.leviolondingres.com
closed in August, Sunday and Monday **O1**

Rest – Menu 48/65 € – Carte 50/67 €

Spec. Millefeuille de langue et foie gras façon Lucullus. Cassoulet montalbanais. Soufflé vanille, sauce caramel au beurre salé.

♦ A la mode ♦ Fashionable ♦

Wood-furnishings enliven the atmosphere of this dining room which is an elegant meeting point for gourmets attracted by the very individual cuisine of the master chef.

XX ✿

Il Vino d'Enrico Bernardo

AC VISA MC AE

13 bd La Tour-Maubourg (7th) – Ⓜ Invalides – ✆ 01 44 11 72 00 – info@ilvinobyenricobernardo.com – Fax 01 44 11 72 02 – www.ilvinobyenricobernardo.com **P1**

Rest – Menu 50 € bi (lunch), 100 € bi/1000 € bi – Carte 70/120 €

Spec. Risotto aux cèpes. Agneau de sept heures. Dacquoise à la poire.

♦ Elegant ♦

Choose the wine and don't interfere with the cooking! In his chic, designer restaurant, the World's Best Sommelier of 2005 bucks the trend by selecting a meal to go with the wine.

XX

Les Ombres

Paris, AC, VISA, MC, AE

27 quai Branly (7th) – Ⓜ Alma Marceau – ✆ 01 47 53 68 00
– ombres.restaurant@elior.com – Fax 01 47 53 68 18
– www.lesombres.fr **H8**

Rest – Menu 37 (lunch)/95 € – Carte 61/98 €

♦ A la mode ♦

This restaurant enjoys fine views of the Eiffel Tower and its nocturnal illuminations from the roof-terrace of the Musée du Quai Branly. Contemporary dining.

XX ✿

Vin sur Vin

AC VISA MC

20 r. de Monttessuy (7th) – Ⓜ Pont de l'Alma – ✆ 01 47 05 14 20
closed 1st-11 May, 27 July-25 August, 22 December-6 January, Monday except dinner from mid September to end-March, Saturday lunch and Sunday

Rest – *(number of covers limited, pre-book)* Carte 68/118 € **O1**

Spec. Ravioles de jaune d'œuf aux truffes. Gros turbot sauvage. Ris de veau de lait français.

♦ Traditional ♦ Cosy ♦

Warm welcome, elegant décor, delicious traditional dishes and extensive wine list (600 vintages) – full marks for this restaurant close to the Eiffel Tower!

XX

Chez les Anges

AC VISA MC AE

54 bd de la Tour Maubourg (7th) – Ⓜ La Tour Maubourg – ✆ 01 47 05 89 86
– mail@chezlesanges.com – Fax 01 47 05 45 56 – www.chezlesanges.com
closed Saturday and Sunday **P1**

Rest – Menu 34 € – Carte 44/73 €

♦ Traditional ♦

A trendy atmosphere, minimalist contemporary décor and long counter where you can take a seat to sample the tasty cuisine, half-traditional, half-modern.

XX

New Jawad

AC VISA MC AE

12 av. Rapp (7th) – Ⓜ Ecole Militaire – ✆ 01 47 05 91 37 – Fax 01 45 50 31 27

Rest – Menu 16/40 € – Carte 21/42 € **O1**

♦ Indian-Pakistani ♦ Friendly ♦

Pakistani and Indian specialities, attentive service and a plush, cosy setting characterise this restaurant in the vicinity of the Pont de l'Alma.

XX

Thiou

AC VISA MC AE

49 quai d'Orsay (7th) – Ⓜ Invalides – ✆ 01 40 62 96 50 – Fax 01 40 62 97 30
closed August, Saturday lunch and Sunday **P1**

Rest – Carte 46/91 €

♦ Thai ♦

Thiou is the nickname of the lady chef of this restaurant, often mentioned in the press, whose regular customers include celebrities. Thai dishes served in a discreetly exotic, comfortable dining room.

XX ✿

Auguste (Gaël Orieux)

AC MC AE

54 r. Bourgogne (7th) – Ⓜ Varenne – ✆ 01 45 51 61 09 – Fax 01 45 51 27 34
– www.restaurantauguste.fr
closed 3-24 August, Saturday and Sunday **Q1**

Rest – Menu 35 € (lunch) – Carte 58/76 €

Spec. Foie gras de canard poêlé, supions et enokis. Noix de ris de veau croustillante aux cacahuètes caramelisées. Soufflé au chocolat pur Caraïbe.

♦ A la mode ♦ Design ♦

The pleasant colourful décor of this up-to-date establishment is the setting for a cuisine that is as flavourful as it is inventive. A fine tribute to Auguste Escoffier.

XX

D'Chez Eux

AC VISA MC

2 av. Lowendal (7th) – Ⓜ Ecole Militaire – ✆ 01 47 05 52 55
– contact@chezeux.com – Fax 01 45 55 60 74 – www.chezeux.com
closed 1st-18 August and Sunday **P2**

Rest – Menu 40 € (lunch) – Carte 46/77 €

♦ South-West of France ♦ Rustic ♦

For 40 years customers have been seduced by this restaurant where hearty dishes from Auvergne and southwest France are served by waiters in smocks in a "provincial inn" atmosphere.

La Gauloise

59 av. La Motte-Picquet (15th) – Ⓜ La Motte Picquet Grenelle – ✆ 01 47 34 11 64 – Fax 01 40 61 09 70 **O3**

Rest – Carte 33/52 €

♦ Brasserie ♦

This 1900 brasserie must have seen many celebrities pass through, judging from the signed photos on the walls. A pleasant, kerbside terrace.

L'Épopée

89 av. É. Zola (15th) – Ⓜ Charles Michels – ✆ 01 45 77 71 37 – Fax 01 45 77 71 37

closed 26 July-20 August, 24 December-3 January, Saturday lunch and Sunday **N3**

Rest – Menu 35 €

♦ Traditional ♦

Despite the grandeur of its name (The Epic), this is a small, convivial restaurant. Regulars keep coming back for its excellent wine list and traditional cuisine.

Au Bon Accueil

14 r. Monttessuy (7th) – Ⓜ Pont de l'Alma – ✆ 01 47 05 46 11 – Fax 01 45 56 15 80

closed 7-20 August, Saturday and Sunday **O1**

Rest – Menu 27/31 € – Carte 50/75 €

♦ Bistro ♦

Beneath the shadow of the Eiffel Tower, this modern restaurant and small adjacent room offer delicious up-to-date dishes pleasantly reflecting the changing seasons.

Les Fables de La Fontaine (Sébastien Gravé)

131 r. Saint-Dominique (7th) – Ⓜ Ecole Militaire – ✆ 01 44 18 37 55 – Fax 01 44 18 37 57

closed 23-28 December **J8**

Rest – Carte approx. 50 €

Spec. Saint-Jacques à la plancha, velouté de topinambour à la truffe noire (December to March). Merlu de Saint-Jean de Luz rôti au lard, caviar d'aubergine fumé, velouté de cèpes (September to December). Gâteau Basque.

♦ Seafood ♦

Restaurant dedicated to seafood set in a small low-key dining room (brown tones, velvet benches). Short, intelligent menu and good wine list.

Stéphane Martin

67 r. Entrepreneurs (15th) – Ⓜ Charles Michels – ✆ 01 45 79 03 31 – resto.stephanemartin@free.fr – Fax 01 45 79 44 69

closed 3 weeks in August, Christmas holidays, Easter holidays, Sunday and Monday **N3**

Rest – Menu 22 € (weekday lunch)/35 € – Carte 38/49 €

♦ A la mode ♦

This inviting restaurant with a library theme (mural of bookshelves), serves up-to-date market fresh cuisine.

Clos des Gourmets

16 av. Rapp (7th) – Ⓜ Alma Marceau – ✆ 01 45 51 75 61 – closdesgourmets@wanadoo.fr – Fax 01 47 05 74 20 – www.closdesgourmets.com

closed 10-25 August, Sunday and Monday **O1**

Rest – Menu 29 € (weekday lunch)/35 €

♦ Fashionable ♦

Many regulars love this discreet restaurant decorated in warm colours. The tempting menu varies according to the availability of market produce.

Aida (Koji Aida)

1 r. Pierre Leroux (7th) – Ⓜ Vaneau – ✆ 01 43 06 14 18 – Fax 01 43 06 14 18 – www.aidaparis.com

closed 5-25 August, February holidays and Monday **Q3**

Rest – *(dinner only) (number of covers limited, pre-book)* Menu 90/160 € – Carte 87/200 €

Spec. Huîtres sautées au beurre d'algues sur lit de cresson. Chateaubriant cuit au teppanyaki. Menu omakase.

◆ Japanese ◆ Minimalist ◆

A minimalist feel to this Japanese restaurant with softly lit counter and private dining room. Choice of teppanyaki menus and fine Burgundies chosen by the wine buff chef.

P'tit Troquet

28 r. Exposition (7th) – Ⓜ Ecole Militaire – ✆ 01 47 05 80 39 – Fax 01 47 05 80 39

closed 1st-24 August, Saturday lunch, Monday lunch and Sunday **P2**

Rest – *(number of covers limited, pre-book)* Menu 28 € (weekday lunch)/32 € – Carte approx. 40 €

◆ Retro ◆

This bistro is certainly as small as its name suggests! But it has so much going for it: a charming setting enlivened by old advertisements, friendly atmosphere and tasty market fresh cuisine.

L'Affriolé

17 r. Malar (7th) – Ⓜ Invalides – ✆ 01 44 18 31 33

closed 3 weeks in August, Sunday and Monday **P1**

Rest – Menu 29 € (lunch)/34 €

◆ Bistro ◆

This bistro's chef prepares seasonal dishes with fresh market produce, which are announced as daily specials on the blackboard or in a set menu that changes every month.

Chez l'Ami Jean

27 r. Malar (7th) – Ⓜ La Tour Maubourg – ✆ 01 47 05 86 89 – Fax 01 45 55 41 82

closed August, 23 December-2 January, Sunday and Monday **P1**

Rest – Menu 32 €

◆ South-West of France ◆ Rustic ◆

Chez l'Ami Jean offers tasty, copious dishes, with market produce, and from Southwest France (game specialities in season) in a warm, Basque Country setting.

Le Troquet

21 r. François Bonvin (15th) – Ⓜ Cambronne – ✆ 01 45 66 89 00 – Fax 01 45 66 89 83

closed 2-10 May, 1st-24 August, 24 December-1st January, Sunday and Monday **P3**

Rest – Menu 28 € (weekday lunch), 30/40 €

◆ De Terroir ◆ Neighbourhood ◆

An authentic Parisian "troquet" – single set menu shown on a slate, retro-style dining hall and cuisine redolent of the local market. For locals... and others!

Café Constant

139 r. Saint-Dominique (7th) – Ⓜ Ecole Militaire – ✆ 01 47 53 73 34 – Fax 01 45 55 48 42

closed 2 weeks in August, Sunday and Monday **O1**

Rest – Menu 31/35 €

◆ Traditional ◆ Bistro ◆

Convivial simplicity is the order of the day in this café annexe developed by Christian Constant. Tasty, good value market cuisine showing the chef's obvious hallmark.

SAINT-GERMAIN DES PRES, QUARTIER LATIN, HOTEL DE VILLE

Plan V

Lutetia

45 bd Raspail (6th) – Ⓜ Sèvres Babylone – ✆ 01 49 54 46 46 – lutetia-paris@lutetia-paris.com – Fax 01 49 54 46 00 – www.lutetia-paris.com **R2**

231 rm – 🚹250/950 € 🚹🚹250/950 €, ☕ 27 € – 11 suites

Rest *Paris* – see below

Rest *Brasserie Lutetia* – *✆ 01 49 54 46 76* – Menu 45 € – Carte 59/72 €

♦ Palace ♦ Historic ♦

Built in 1910, this luxury hotel on the Left Bank has lost none of its sparkle. It happily blends Art Deco fixtures with contemporary details (sculptures by César, Arman, etc). Refurbished rooms. Popular with well-heeled Parisians, Brasserie Lutetia is famous for its seafood menu.

Victoria Palace without rest

6 r. Blaise-Desgoffe (6th) – Ⓜ St-Placide – ✆ 01 45 49 70 00 – info@victoriapalace.com – Fax 01 45 49 23 75 – www.victoriapalace.com **R3**

62 rm – 🚹332/390 € 🚹🚹332/620 €, ☕ 18 €

♦ Luxury ♦ Historic ♦

Small luxury hotel with undeniable charm: toiles de Jouy, Louis XVI-style furniture and marble bathrooms in the rooms. Paintings, red velvet and porcelain in the lounges.

Pont Royal without rest

7 r. Montalembert (7th) – Ⓜ Rue du Bac – ✆ 01 42 84 70 00 – hpr@hotel-pont-royal.com – Fax 01 42 84 71 00 – www.hotel-pont-royal.com **R1**

65 rm – 🚹395/455 € 🚹🚹395/455 €, ☕ 27 € – 10 suites

Rest *L'Atelier de Joël Robuchon* – see below

♦ Luxury ♦ Stylish ♦

Bold colours and mahogany walls adorn the bedrooms; the romance of the salad days of St-Germain-des-Prés with all the comfort of an elegant "literary hotel"!

Duc de St-Simon without rest

14 r. St-Simon (7th) – Ⓜ Rue du Bac – ✆ 01 44 39 20 20 – duc.de.saint.simon@wanadoo.fr – Fax 01 45 48 68 25 – www.hotelducdesaintsimon.com **R1**

34 rm – 🚹225/290 € 🚹🚹225/395 €, ☕ 15 €

♦ Luxury ♦ Business ♦ Stylish ♦

Cheerful colours, wood panelling, antique furniture and objects. The atmosphere here is that of a beautiful house of olden times, with the additional appeal of a friendly welcome and peaceful surroundings.

D'Aubusson without rest

33 r. Dauphine (6th) – Ⓜ Odéon – ✆ 01 43 29 43 43 – reservations@hoteldaubusson.com – Fax 01 43 29 12 62 – www.hoteldaubusson.com **T2**

49 rm – 🚹310/470 € 🚹🚹310/470 €, ☕ 23 €

♦ Luxury ♦ Traditional ♦ Historic ♦

A 17C townhouse with character, offering elegant rooms with Versailles parquet, Aubusson tapestries and jazz evenings at the Café Laurent on weekends.

Relais Christine without rest

3 r. Christine (6th) – Ⓜ St-Michel – ✆ 01 40 51 60 80 – contact@relais-christine.com – Fax 01 40 51 60 81 – www.relais-christine.com **T2**

51 rm – 🚹370/540 € 🚹🚹415/780 €, ☕ 25 €

♦ Luxury ♦ Traditional ♦ Historic ♦

Townhouse built on the site of a medieval convent (the vaulted breakfast room is 13C). Handsome cobbled courtyard, small garden, rooms with a personal touch.

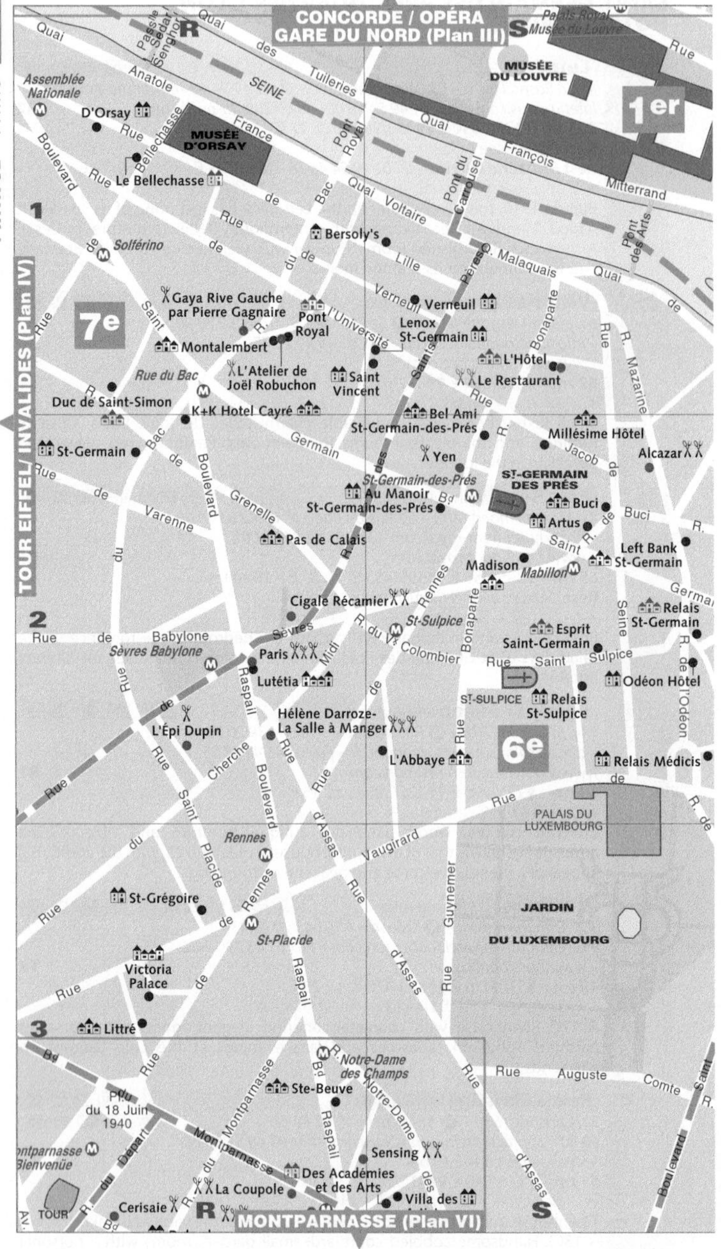
CONCORDE / OPÉRA
GARE DU NORD (Plan III)
TOUR EIFFEL/ INVALIDES (Plan IV)
MONTPARNASSE (Plan VI)
MUSÉE DU LOUVRE
MUSÉE D'ORSAY
1er
7e
6e
D'Orsay
Le Bellechasse
Bersoly's
Gaya Rive Gauche par Pierre Gagnaire
Pont Royal
Montalembert
L'Atelier de Joël Robuchon
Saint Vincent
Verneuil
Lenox St-Germain
L'Hôtel
Le Restaurant
Duc de Saint-Simon
K+K Hotel Cayré
Bel Ami St-Germain-des-Prés
Millésime Hôtel
St-Germain
Yen
Alcazar
ST-GERMAIN DES PRÉS
Au Manoir St-Germain-des-Prés
Buci
Artus
Pas de Calais
Left Bank St-Germain
Madison
Cigale Récamier
Relais St-Germain
Esprit Saint-Germain
Paris
Lutétia
Odéon Hôtel
Relais St-Sulpice
L'Épi Dupin
Hélène Darroze-La Salle à Manger
L'Abbaye
Relais Médicis
PALAIS DU LUXEMBOURG
JARDIN DU LUXEMBOURG
St-Grégoire
Victoria Palace
Littré
Ste-Beuve
Sensing
Des Académies et des Arts
La Coupole
Villa des
Cerisaie
Solférino
Rue du Bac
St-Germain-des-Prés
Mabillon
St-Sulpice
Sèvres Babylone
Rennes
St-Placide
Notre-Dame des Champs
Assemblée Nationale
Quai Anatole France
SEINE
Quai Voltaire
Quai François Mitterrand
Quai des Tuileries
Q. Malaquais
Rue de Lille
Rue de Verneuil
Rue de l'Université
Boulevard Saint-Germain
Rue du Bac
Rue de Grenelle
Rue de Varenne
Rue de Babylone
Rue de Sèvres
Boulevard Raspail
Rue de Rennes
Rue Bonaparte
Rue Jacob
Rue de Buci
Rue Mazarine
Rue de Seine
Rue Saint-Sulpice
R. du Vx Colombier
Rue du Cherche-Midi
Rue d'Assas
Rue de Vaugirard
Rue Guynemer
Rue Auguste Comte
Rue Saint-Placide
Boulevard du Montparnasse
Rue de l'Odéon
Pont Royal
Pont du Carrousel
Pont des Arts
Pl. du 18 Juin 1940
Montparnasse Bienvenüe
1
2
3
R
S

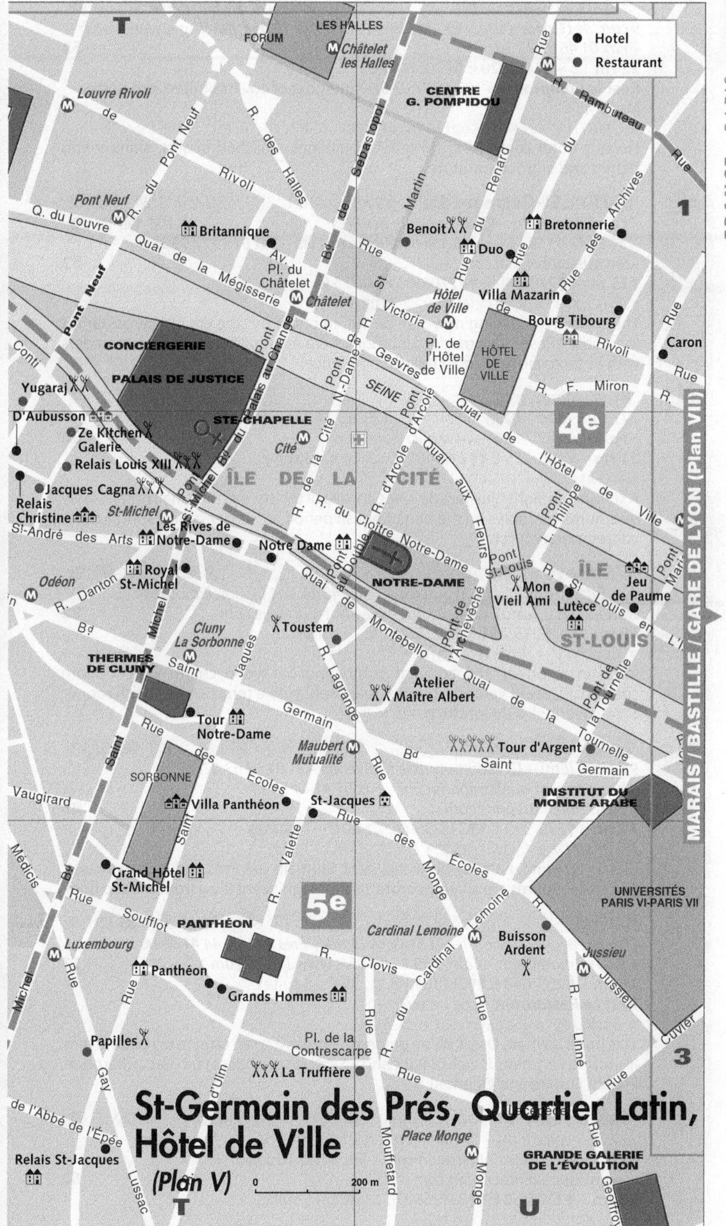
St-Germain des Prés, Quartier Latin, Hôtel de Ville
(Plan V)
Hotel
Restaurant
T
U
1
3
4e
5e
0
200 m
MARAIS / BASTILLE / GARE DE LYON (Plan VII)
LES HALLES
FORUM
Châtelet les Halles
CENTRE G. POMPIDOU
Louvre Rivoli
Pont Neuf
Q. du Louvre
Quai de la Mégisserie
Britannique
Benoit
Bretonnerie
Duo
Villa Mazarin
Bourg Tibourg
Caron
Pl. du Châtelet
Châtelet
Hôtel de Ville
Pl. de l'Hôtel de Ville
HÔTEL DE VILLE
CONCIERGERIE
PALAIS DE JUSTICE
STE-CHAPELLE
Cité
ÎLE DE LA CITÉ
SEINE
Yugaraj
D'Aubusson
Ze Kitchen Galerie
Relais Louis XIII
Jacques Cagna
Relais Christine
St-Michel
Les Rives de Notre-Dame
Notre Dame
NOTRE-DAME
Royal St-Michel
Odéon
Mon Vieil Ami
Lutèce
Jeu de Paume
ÎLE ST-LOUIS
Toustem
Cluny La Sorbonne
THERMES DE CLUNY
Atelier Maître Albert
Tour Notre-Dame
Maubert Mutualité
Tour d'Argent
INSTITUT DU MONDE ARABE
SORBONNE
Villa Panthéon
St-Jacques
UNIVERSITÉS PARIS VI-PARIS VII
Grand Hôtel St-Michel
PANTHÉON
Cardinal Lemoine
Buisson Ardent
Jussieu
Luxembourg
Panthéon
Grands Hommes
Papilles
Pl. de la Contrescarpe
La Truffière
Relais St-Jacques
Place Monge
GRANDE GALERIE DE L'ÉVOLUTION
Rue de Rivoli
Rue Rambuteau
Bd de Sébastopol
Bd St-Michel
Bd Saint Germain
Rue des Écoles
Rue Soufflot
Rue Monge
Rue Mouffetard
Rue Gay Lussac
Rue St-Jacques
Rue du Cardinal Lemoine
Quai de Montebello
Quai de la Tournelle
Quai de l'Hôtel de Ville
Quai aux Fleurs
Vaugirard
Médicis
R. Clovis
Rue Cuvier
R. Linné
Rue Jussieu
R. Lagrange
R. Valette
R. Danton
St-André des Arts
Conti
de l'Abbé de l'Épée
Rue d'Ulm
R. F. Miron
Rue du Renard
Martin
Pont au Change
Pont Notre-Dame
Pont d'Arcole
Pont au Double
Pont de l'Archevêché
Pont St-Louis
Pont L. Philippe
Pont de la Tournelle
Pont Marie
R. du Cloître Notre-Dame
R. d'Arcole
R. de la Cité
Rue des Archives
Rue des Halles
Q. de Gesvres
Victoria

Relais St-Germain

9 carr. de l'Odéon (6th) – Ⓜ Odéon – ✆ 01 43 29 12 05 – hotelrsg@wanadoo.fr – Fax 01 46 33 45 30 **S2**

22 rm ☕ – †165/220 € ††205/440 €

Rest *le Comptoir* – ✆ 01 44 27 07 97 – (number of covers limited, pre-book) – Menu 45 €

♦ Luxury ♦ Traditional ♦ Historic ♦

Elegant hotel comprising three 17C buildings. Polished beams, shimmering fabrics and antique furniture.

Bel Ami St-Germain des Prés without rest

7 r. St-Benoit (6th) – Ⓜ St-Germain des Prés – ✆ 01 42 61 53 53 – contact@hotel-bel-ami.com – Fax 01 49 27 09 33 – www.hotel-bel-ami.com **S2**

115 rm – †270/540 € ††270/600 €, ☕ 25 €

♦ Business ♦ Luxury ♦ Design ♦

This attractive building may well be 19C in origin but the era of Maupassant is long gone! Resolutely modern interior where minimalist luxury rubs shoulders with hi-tech gadgets and a relaxed ambience.

Buci without rest

22 r. Buci (6th) – Ⓜ Mabillon – ✆ 01 55 42 74 74 – hotelbuci@wanadoo.fr – Fax 01 55 42 74 44 – www.buci-hotel.com **S2**

21 rm – †185/215 € ††215/400 €, ☕ 18 € – 3 suites

♦ Luxury ♦ Personalised ♦

A stylish midnight blue façade gives an idea of the style of this small hotel. Classy bedrooms (canopies on the beds, English period furniture), others sport a more contemporary finish.

L'Abbaye without rest

10 r. Cassette (6th) – Ⓜ St-Sulpice – ✆ 01 45 44 38 11 – hotel.abbaye@wanadoo.fr – Fax 01 45 48 07 86 – www.hotel-abbaye.com **S2**

40 rm ☕ – †215/251 € ††215/251 € – 4 suites

♦ Luxury ♦ Traditional ♦ Stylish ♦

Hotel in a former 18C convent combining old-world charm with modern comfort. Pleasant veranda, duplex apartment with a terrace, and stylish rooms. Some overlook a delightful patio.

Littré without rest

9 r. Littré (6th) – Ⓜ Montparnasse Bienvenüe – ✆ 01 53 63 07 07 – hotellittre@hotellittreparis.com – Fax 01 45 44 88 13 – www.hotellittreparis.com **R3**

79 rm – †275/315 € ††315/350 €, ☕ 20 € – 11 suites

♦ Luxury ♦ Business ♦ Stylish ♦

Classic building, halfway between Saint Germain des Prés and Montparnasse. The stylish rooms are all very comfortable. Magnificent view from the top floor.

L'Hôtel

13 r. des Beaux-Arts (6th) – Ⓜ St-Germain-des-Prés – ✆ 01 44 41 99 00 – stay@l-hotel.com – Fax 01 43 25 64 81 – www.l-hotel.com **S1**

16 rm – †255/640 € ††280/640 €, ☕ 18 € – 4 suites

Rest *Le Restaurant* – see below

♦ Luxury ♦ Personalised ♦

This hotel is where Oscar Wilde passed away, leaving an unpaid bill behind him. It sports a vertiginous well of light and an extravagant décor by Garcia (Baroque, French Empire and Oriental).

Esprit Saint-Germain without rest

22 r. St-Sulpice (6th) – Ⓜ Mabillon – ✆ 01 53 10 55 55 – contact@espritsaintgermain.com – Fax 01 53 10 55 56 – www.espritsaintgermain.com **S2**

28 rm – †310/550 € ††310/550 €, ☕ 26 € – 5 suites

♦ Luxury ♦ Design ♦

Elegant and contemporary rooms pleasantly combining red, chocolate and beige colours with modern paintings and furniture; bathrooms with slate walls.

Montalembert

3 r. Montalembert (7th) – Ⓜ Rue du Bac – ✆ 01 45 49 68 68 – welcome@montalembert.com – Fax 01 45 49 69 49 – www.montalembert.com **R1**

56 rm – 380/500 € 380/500 €, 24 € – 7 suites

Rest – Carte 39/85 €

◆ Luxury ◆ Modern ◆

Dark wood, leather, glass and steel, with tobacco, plum and lilac-coloured décor. The rooms combine all the components of contemporary style. Designer dining room, terrace protected by a boxwood partition, and cuisine for appetites large and small!

Pas de Calais without rest

59 r. des Saints-Pères (6th) – Ⓜ St-Germain-des-Prés – ✆ 01 45 48 78 74 – infos@hotelpasdecalais.com – Fax 01 45 44 94 57 – www.hotelpasdecalais.com

38 rm – 145/300 € 160/300 €, 15 € **R2**

◆ Traditional ◆ Family ◆ Functional ◆

The hotel lobby is lit by a glass ceiling and has a beautiful vertical garden made up of orchids. Lovely rooms with individual touches; exposed beams on the top floor.

K+K Hotel Cayré without rest

4 bd Raspail (7th) – Ⓜ Rue du Bac – ✆ 01 45 44 38 88 – reservations@kkhotels.fr – Fax 01 45 44 98 13 – www.kkhotels.com/cayre **R1-2**

125 rm – 320/412 € 348/680 €, 25 €

◆ Luxury ◆ Business ◆ Modern ◆

The discreet Haussmann façade contrasts with the elegant designer rooms within. Fitness centre (with sauna), elegant lounge and bar serving simple bistro-style dishes.

Madison without rest

143 bd St-Germain (6th) – Ⓜ St-Germain des Prés – ✆ 01 40 51 60 00 – resa@hotel-madison.com – Fax 01 40 51 60 01 **S2**

54 rm – 150/345 € 157/385 €, 15 € – 1 suite

◆ Luxury ◆ Family ◆ Cosy ◆

This hotel was popular with Albert Camus. Some of its elegant rooms offer views of the church of St-Germain-des Prés. Attractive Louis Philippe lounge.

Villa Panthéon without rest

41 r. des Écoles (5th) – Ⓜ Maubert Mutualité – ✆ 01 53 10 95 95 – pantheon@leshotelsdeparis.com – Fax 01 53 10 95 96 – www.leshotelsdeparis.com **T2**

59 rm – 160/350 € 160/350 €, 18 €

◆ Townhouse ◆ Traditional ◆ Stylish ◆

The reception, rooms and bar (with a good selection of whiskies) have a British feel, with parquet floors, colourful hangings, exotic wood furniture and Liberty-style lights.

Jeu de Paume without rest

54 r. St-Louis-en-l'Ile (4th) – Ⓜ Pont Marie – ✆ 01 43 26 14 18 – info@jeudepaumehotel.com – Fax 01 40 46 02 76 – www.jeudepaumehotel.com closed 4-18 August **U2**

30 rm – 165/255 € 275/900 €, 18 €

◆ Traditional ◆ Personalised ◆

This 17C building at the heart of the Ile St-Louis was once a venue for real tennis. Nowadays it is a unique hotel with plenty of character and a clever use of space.

Left Bank St-Germain without rest

9 r. de l'Ancienne Comédie (6th) – Ⓜ Odéon – ✆ 01 43 54 01 70 – reservation@hotelleftbank.com – Fax 01 43 26 17 14 – www.paris-hotels-charm.com **S2**

31 rm – 140/250 € 150/370 €

◆ Traditional ◆ Family ◆ Classic ◆

Wainscoting, damask, Jouy drapes, Louis XIII style furniture and half-timbered walls set the scene. Some rooms command views of Notre Dame.

Millésime without rest

15 r. Jacob (6th) – St-Germain des Prés – 01 44 07 97 97 – reservation@millesimehotel.com – Fax 01 46 34 55 97 – www.millesimehotel.com **S2**

22 rm – 190/220 € 190/380 €, 16 €

◆ Traditional ◆ Family ◆ Cosy ◆

Colours of the south and select furniture and fabrics create a warm atmosphere in the splendid rooms at this hotel. Superb 17C staircase, patio and fine vaulted dining room.

Bourg Tibourg without rest

19 r. Bourg Tibourg (4th) – Hôtel de Ville – 01 42 78 47 39 – hotel@bourgtibourg.com – Fax 01 40 29 07 00 – www.hotelbourgtibourg.com **U1**

30 rm – 180 € 230/360 €, 16 €

◆ Luxury ◆ Family ◆ Personalised ◆

The pleasant rooms in this charming hotel are decorated in a variety of styles (neo-Gothic, Baroque or Oriental). A little gem at the heart of the Marais quarter.

Saint Vincent without rest

5 r. Pré aux Clercs (7th) – Rue du Bac – 01 42 61 01 51 – reservation@hotel-st-vincent.com – Fax 01 42 61 01 54 – www.hotel-st-vincent.com **R-S1**

22 rm – 190/210 € 220/240 €, 12 € – 2 suites

◆ Luxury ◆ Personalised ◆

A delightful luxury hotel in the heart of the Left Bank. This 18C private mansion is home to warm, spacious rooms appointed in a Napoleon III spirit.

Le Bellechasse without rest

8 r. de Bellechasse (7th) – Musée d'Orsay – 01 45 50 22 31 – info@lebellechasse.com – Fax 01 45 51 52 36 – www.lebellechasse.com **R1**

34 rm – 290/440 € 320/490 €, 25 €

◆ Luxury ◆ Personalised ◆

Top couturier Christian Lacroix designed the rooms of this hotel. He has joyfully mixed colour with antique and modern details to create an almost dreamlike but distinctly fashionable setting.

Les Rives de Notre-Dame without rest

15 quai St-Michel (5th) – St-Michel – 01 43 54 81 16 – hotel@rivesdenotredame.com – Fax 01 43 26 27 09 – www.rivesdenotredame.com **T2**

10 rm – 195/255 € 195/550 €, 14 €

◆ Traditional ◆ Family ◆ Classic ◆

Splendidly preserved 16C residence with spacious Provençal-style rooms all overlooking the Seine and Notre-Dame. Penthouse.

Royal St-Michel without rest

3 bd St-Michel (5th) – St-Michel – 01 44 07 06 06 – hotelroyalsaintmichel@wanadoo.fr – Fax 01 44 07 36 25 – www.hotelroyalsaintmichel.com **T2**

39 rm – 180/240 € 195/290 €, 18 €

◆ Family ◆ Traditional ◆ Modern ◆

On the Boulevard St Michel, opposite the fountain of the same name, this hotel enjoys an excellent location in the heart of the lively Latin Quarter. Attractive, modern rooms.

Relais Médicis without rest

23 r. Racine (6th) – Odéon – 01 43 26 00 60 – reservation@relaismedicis.com – Fax 01 40 46 83 39 – www.relaismedicis.com **S2**

16 rm – 142/172 € 172/258 €

◆ Traditional ◆ Family ◆ Stylish ◆

A hint of Provence enhances the rooms of this hotel near the Odeon theatre; those overlooking the patio are quieter. Interesting antique furniture.

Au Manoir St-Germain-des-Prés without rest

153 bd St-Germain (6th) – Ⓜ St-Germain des Prés – ✆ 01 42 22 21 65 – reservation@hotelaumanoir.com – Fax 01 45 48 22 25 – www.paris-hotels-charm.com **S2**

32 rm ☕ – 🚹150/330 € 🚹🚹150/330 €

◆ Traditional ◆ Stylish ◆

Elegant hotel, opposite the Flore and Deux Magots (famous St Germain des Prés cafés) with period furniture, murals, wood panelling and toile de Jouy prints.

St-Grégoire without rest

43 r. Abbé-Grégoire (6th) – Ⓜ St-Placide – ✆ 01 45 48 23 23 – hotel@saintgregoire.com – Fax 01 45 48 33 95 – www.hotelsaintgregoire.com **R3**

20 rm – 🚹195/250 € 🚹🚹250/300 €, ☕ 14 €

◆ Traditional ◆ Cosy ◆

Elegant and welcoming décor at this establishment. Two of the rooms have small leafy terraces. Attractive vaulted breakfast room.

Panthéon without rest

19 pl. Panthéon (5th) – Ⓜ Luxembourg – ✆ 01 43 54 32 95 – reservation@hoteldupantheon.com – Fax 01 43 26 64 65 – www.hoteldupantheon.com **T3**

36 rm – 🚹130/250 € 🚹🚹160/270 €, ☕ 12 €

◆ Traditional ◆ Cosy ◆

The cosy or Louis XVI-style rooms offer a view of the Temple de la Renommée dome. Attractive sitting room and vaulted breakfast room.

Grands Hommes without rest

17 pl. Panthéon (5th) – Ⓜ Luxembourg – ✆ 01 46 34 19 60 – reservation@hoteldesgrandshommes.com – Fax 01 43 26 67 32 – www.hoteldesgrandshommes.com **T3**

31 rm – 🚹80/310 € 🚹🚹90/430 €, ☕ 12 €

◆ Traditional ◆ Historic ◆

Facing the Panthéon, pleasant hotel decorated in Directoire style (with antique furnishings). Over half the rooms overlook the final resting place of some of France's most eminent citizens.

Villa Mazarin without rest

6 r. des Archives (4th) – Ⓜ Hôtel de Ville – ✆ 01 53 01 90 90 – paris@villamazarin.com – Fax 01 53 01 90 91 – www.villamalraux.com **U1**

29 rm – 🚹130/400 € 🚹🚹130/400 €, ☕ 12 €

◆ Business ◆ Design ◆

With its high tech equipment (wifi, flat screen TVs) and mix of modern and period furniture, this comfortable hotel near the Hôtel de Ville combines tradition and modernity.

Tour Notre-Dame without rest

20 r. Sommerard (5th) – Ⓜ Cluny la Sorbonne – ✆ 01 43 54 47 60 – tour-notre-dame@magic.fr – Fax 01 43 26 42 34 – www.la-tour-notre-dame.com **T2**

48 rm – 🚹129/176 € 🚹🚹139/190 €, ☕ 12 €

◆ Traditional ◆ Family ◆ Stylish ◆

This hotel is very well situated, almost adjoining the Cluny museum. Comfortable, recently-renovated rooms. Those at the back are quieter.

Relais St-Sulpice without rest

3 r. Garancière (6th) – Ⓜ St-Sulpice – ✆ 01 46 33 99 00 – relaisstsulpice@wanadoo.fr – Fax 01 46 33 00 10 – www.relais-saint-sulpice.com **S2**

26 rm – 🚹176/215 € 🚹🚹177/216 €, ☕ 12 €

◆ Traditional ◆ Personalised ◆

Appealing hotel not far from the Sénat and the Luxembourg gardens housing spacious, well-decorated rooms. Those at the back are very quiet.

Grand Hôtel St-Michel without rest

19 r. Cujas (5th) – Ⓜ Luxembourg – ☎ 01 46 33 33 02 – grand.hotel.st.michel@wanadoo.fr – Fax 01 40 46 96 33 – www.grand-hotel-st-michel.com **T3**

40 rm – †140/170 € ††170/220 €, ☕ 14 € – 5 suites

◆ Family ◆ Traditional ◆ Classic ◆

Hotel in a Haussmannian building offering comfortable rooms adorned with painted furniture. Napoleon III-style lounge. Breakfast served beneath a vaulted ceiling.

Notre Dame without rest

1 quai St-Michel (5th) – Ⓜ St-Michel – ☎ 01 43 54 20 43 – hotel.denotredame@libertysurf.fr – Fax 01 43 26 61 75 **T2**

26 rm – †150 € ††199 €, ☕ 7 €

◆ Traditional ◆ Family ◆ Cosy ◆

The cosy little rooms in this hotel have all been refurbished and are air-conditioned and well appointed. Most rooms have a view over Notre-Dame cathedral.

Relais St-Jacques without rest

3 r. Abbé de l'Épée (5th) – Ⓜ Luxembourg – ☎ 01 53 73 26 00 – hotel-relais@wanadoo.fr – Fax 01 43 26 17 81 – www.relais-saint-jacques.com **T3**

22 rm – †179/320 € ††179/499 €, ☕ 17 €

◆ Traditional ◆ Family ◆ Stylish ◆

Rooms of various styles (Directoire, Louis Philippe, etc.), a glass-roofed breakfast room, Louis XV lounge and 1920s bar, make this a stylish hotchpotch hotel!

Artus without rest

34 r. de Buci (6th) – Ⓜ Mabillon – ☎ 01 43 29 07 20 – info@artushotel.com – Fax 01 43 29 67 44 – www.artushotel.com **BX 10**

27 rm – †240/285 € ††250/300 €, ☕ 15 €

◆ Traditional ◆Design◆

Contemporary yet intimate, with modern bedrooms ornamented with antiques, an attractive vaulted cellar, designer bar, and paintings from nearby galleries on display.

Odéon without rest

3 r. Odéon (6th) – Ⓜ Odéon – ☎ 01 43 25 90 67 – odeon@odeonhotel.fr – Fax 01 43 25 55 98 – www.odeonhotel.fr **S2**

33 rm – †130/180 € ††180/270 €, ☕ 12 €

◆ Family ◆ Classic ◆

The façade, stone walls and exposed beams bear witness to the age of this building (17C). Personalised guestrooms, some with views of the Eiffel Tower.

Verneuil without rest

8 r. Verneuil (7th) – Ⓜ Rue du Bac – ☎ 01 42 60 82 14 – info@hotelverneuil.com – Fax 01 42 61 40 38 – www.hotelverneuil.com **S1**

26 rm – †140 € ††170/215 €, ☕ 13 €

◆ Traditional ◆ Family ◆ Classic ◆

This old building on the Left Bank is decorated in the style of a private house. Elegant rooms adorned with 18C prints. Serge Gainsbourg lived opposite.

Lenox St-Germain without rest

9 r. de l'Université (7th) – Ⓜ St-Germain des Prés – ☎ 01 42 96 10 95 – hotel@lenoxsaintgermain.com – Fax 01 42 61 52 83 – www.lenoxsaintgermain.com

32 rm – †130/175 € ††130/200 €, ☕ 14 € – 2 suites **R-S1**

◆ Traditional ◆ Business ◆ Functional ◆

A discreetly luxurious Art Deco style depicts this hotel. Rooms are a little on the small side but attractively decorated. "Egyptian" frescoes adorn the breakfast room. Pleasant bar.

D'Orsay without rest

93 r. Lille (7th) – Ⓜ Solférino – ☎ 01 47 05 85 54 – orsay@espritfrance.com – Fax 01 45 55 51 16 – www.esprit-de-france.com **R1**

41 rm – †150/210 € ††170/360 €, ☕ 13 €

◆ Traditional ◆ Business ◆ Modern ◆

The hotel occupies two handsome, late-18C buildings. Attractive classical style rooms and welcoming lounge overlooking a small leafy patio.

St-Germain without rest

88 r. du Bac (7th) – Ⓜ Rue du Bac – ✆ 01 49 54 70 00 – info@hotel-saint-germain.fr – Fax 01 45 48 26 89 – www.hotel-saint-germain.fr **R2**

29 rm – †150/220 € ††150/240 €, ☕ 12 €

♦ Traditional ♦ Family ♦ Functional ♦

Empire, Louis-Philippe, high-tech design, antique objects, contemporary paintings - the charm of variety. Comfortable library, patio pleasant in summer.

Duo without rest

11 r. Temple (4th) – Ⓜ Hôtel de Ville – ✆ 01 42 72 72 22 – contact@duoparis.com – Fax 01 42 72 03 53 – www.duoparis.com **U1**

56 rm – †130/340 € ††200/340 €, ☕ 15 € – 2 suites

♦ Modern ♦

The trendily refurbished second wing with its warm and vivid tones has given new life to this hotel full of character, run by the same family for three generations. Fitness room.

Bretonnerie without rest

22 r. Ste-Croix-de-la-Bretonnerie (4th) – Ⓜ Hôtel de Ville – ✆ 01 48 87 77 63 – hotel@bretonnerie.com – Fax 01 42 77 26 78 – www.bretonnerie.com **U1**

29 rm – †120/180 € ††120/180 €, ☕ 9.50 €

♦ Traditional ♦ Family ♦ Stylish ♦

Some of the rooms in this elegant 17C mansion in the Marais include four-poster beds and exposed beams. Vaulted ceiling in the breakfast room.

Lutèce without rest

65 r. St-Louis-en-l'Ile (4th) – Ⓜ Pont Marie – ✆ 01 43 26 23 52 – hotel.lutece@free.fr – Fax 01 43 29 60 25 – www.hoteldelutece.com **U2**

23 rm – †160 € ††195 €, ☕ 12 €

♦ Traditional ♦ Family ♦ Retro ♦

The rustic charm of this mansion on the Ile St-Louis is particularly popular with American visitors. Modernised guestrooms with a country feel, plus attractive old woodwork in the lounge.

Britannique without rest

20 av. Victoria (1st) – Ⓜ Châtelet – ✆ 01 42 33 74 59 – mailbox@hotel-britannique.fr – Fax 01 42 33 82 65 – www.hotel-britannique.fr **T1**

39 rm – †124/155 € ††172/215 €, ☕ 16 €

♦ Traditional ♦ Family ♦ Cosy ♦

Founded by an English family during the reign of Queen Victoria, this hotel has retained its elegantly British Imperial charm and refined exotic feel. Charming lounge.

Bersoly's without rest

28 r. de Lille (7th) – Ⓜ Musée d'Orsay – ✆ 01 42 60 73 79 – hotelbersolys@wanadoo.fr – Fax 01 49 27 05 55 – www.bersolyshotel.com **R-S1**

16 rm – †100/106 € ††120/150 €, ☕ 10 €

♦ Traditional ♦ Business ♦ Personalised ♦

Impressionist nights in this 17C building in which each room honours an artist whose works are displayed in the nearby Musée d'Orsay (Renoir, Gauguin, etc.).

St-Jacques without rest

35 r. des Écoles (5th) – Ⓜ Maubert Mutualité – ✆ 01 44 07 45 45 – hotelsaintjacques@wanadoo.fr – Fax 01 43 25 65 50 – www.paris-hotel-stjacques.com **T2**

38 rm – †61/92 € ††105/137 €, ☕ 9.50 €

♦ Traditional ♦ Family ♦ Stylish ♦

Modern comfort allies with old-style charm in the rooms of this hotel. Library with 18C and 19C works. Breakfast room with Roaring Twenties cabaret-style décor.

XXXXX ✿

La Tour d'Argent ← Notre-Dame, AC VISA MC AE

15 quai Tournelle (5th) – M Maubert Mutualité – ☎ 01 43 54 23 31
– resa@latourdargent.com – Fax 01 44 07 12 04 – www.latourdargent.com
closed August and Monday **U2**

Rest – Menu 70 € (lunch) – Carte 140/487 €

Spec. Quenelles de brochet "André Terrail". Noisette d'agneau des Tournelles. Gâteau au chocolat "Vasco de Gama".

♦ Traditional ♦ Luxury ♦

The 'skyline' dining room offers a magnificent view of Notre Dame Cathedral. Exceptional wine list, famous Challans duck and a celebrity clientele since the 16C. An institution!

XXX ✿

Paris – Hôtel Lutetia AC VISA MC AE

45 bd Raspail (6th) – M Sèvres Babylone – ☎ 01 49 54 46 90
– lutetia-paris@lutetia-paris.com – Fax 01 49 54 46 00 – www.lutetia-paris.com
Closed August, Saturday, Sunday and public holidays **R2**

Rest – Menu 60 € bi (lunch), 80/130 € – Carte 98/130 €

Spec. Araignée de mer au pamplemousse, jus parfumé de colombo au pollen grillé. Homard à la vanille, avocat à la tomate au citron vert. Saint-Honoré aux fruits rouges.

♦ Retro ♦

In keeping with the style of the hotel, the Sonia Rykiel Art Deco dining room is a recreation of one of the lounges from the Normandie ocean liner. Inspired traditional cuisine.

XXX ✿

Jacques Cagna AC (dinner) VISA MC AE

14 r. Grands Augustins (6th) – M St-Michel – ☎ 01 43 26 49 39
– jacquescagna@hotmail.com – Fax 01 43 54 54 48 – www.jacques-cagna.com
closed 27 July-24 August, Monday lunch, Saturday lunch and Sunday **T2**

Rest – Menu 48 (lunch)/100 € – Carte 87/153 €

Spec. Foie gras de canard poêlé aux fruits de saison caramélisés. Noix de ris de veau en croûte de sel au romarin. Gibier (season).

♦ Rustic ♦

Located in one of the oldest homes in old Paris, the comfortable dining hall is embellished by massive rafters, 16C woodwork and Flemish paintings. Refined cuisine.

XXX ✿✿

Relais Louis XIII (Manuel Martinez) AC VISA MC AE

8 r. Grands Augustins (6th) – M Odéon – ☎ 01 43 26 75 96
– contact@relaislouis13.com – Fax 01 44 07 07 80 – www.relaislouis13.com
closed August, 22 December-3 January, Sunday and Monday **T2**

Rest – Menu 50 € (lunch), 80/110 € – Carte 115/133 €

Spec. Ravioli de homard, foie gras et crème de cèpes. Caneton challandais rôti entier aux épices, cuisse confite en parmentier. Millefeuille, crème légère à la vanille bourbon.

♦ Cosy ♦

The building dates from the 16C and there are three Louis XIII-style dining rooms with balustrades, tapestries and open stonework. The cuisine is subtle and up-to-date.

XXX ✿✿

Hélène Darroze-La Salle à Manger AC VISA MC AE

4 r. d'Assas (6th) – M Sèvres Babylone – ☎ 01 42 22 00 11
– reservation@helenedarroze.com – Fax 01 42 22 25 40 **R2**

Rest – *(1st floor) (closed lunch 19 July-30 August, Monday except dinner19 July-30 August and Sunday)* Menu 72 € (lunch), 175/280 € – Carte 111/189 €

Rest *Le Salon* – *(closed 19 July-30 August, Sunday and Monday)* Menu 45 € (lunch)/88 € – Carte 64/141 €

Rest *Le Boudoir* – *(closed 19 July-30 August, Sunday and Monday)* Menu 45 € (lunch)/88 € – Carte 70/141 €

Spec. Riz carnaroli acquarello noir et crémeux, chipirons au chorizo et tomates confites, jus au persil, émulsion de parmesan. Grosses langoustines bretonnes rôties aux épices tandoori, mousseline de carottes aux agrumes. Pigeonneau fermier de Racan flambé au capucin et foie gras de canard des Landes grillé au feu de bois.

♦ South-western France ♦ Cosy ♦

Close to the Bon Marché store, the décor is modern, low key and softly lit in aubergine and oranges. Delicious cuisine and wines from southwest France. On the ground floor of the restaurant, Hélène Darroze presides over the Salon and serves tapas and small dishes with a rustic flavour of the Landes.

XXX

La Truffière

4 r. Blainville (5th) – Ⓜ Place Monge – ✆ 01 46 33 29 82
– restaurant.latruffiere@wanadoo.fr – Fax 01 46 33 64 74 – www.latruffiere.com
closed 20-26 December, Sunday and Monday **T3**
Rest – Menu 24 € (weekday lunch), 105/180 € – Carte 71/164 €

◆ Cosy ◆

A 17C house with two dining rooms. One is rustic with exposed beams and the other is vaulted. Traditional cuisine from southwest France and a fine wine list.

XX

Cigale Récamier

4 r. Récamier (7th) – Ⓜ Sèvres Babylone – ✆ 01 45 48 86 58
closed Sunday **R2**
Rest – Carte approx. 55 €

◆ Friendly ◆

A welcoming establishment with a literary clientele. Classic cuisine and sweet and savoury soufflé specialities, renewed every month. Peaceful terrace.

XX ✿

Benoit

20 r. St-Martin (4th) – Ⓜ Châtelet-Les Halles – ✆ 01 42 72 25 76
– restaurant.benoit@wanadoo.fr – Fax 01 42 72 45 68 – www.alain-ducasse.com
closed 26 July-25 August and 25 February-2 March **U1**
Rest – Menu 38 € (lunch)– Carte 55/88 €
Spec. Escargots en coquille, beurre d'ail, fines herbes. Filet de sole nantua, épinards à peine crémés. Tête de veau traditionnelle sauce ravigote.

◆ Retro ◆

Venture into this smart, lively bistro run by the same family since 1912 and sample its authentic, carefully prepared cuisine.

XX

L'Orangerie

28 r. St-Louis-en-L'Ile (4th) – Ⓜ Pont Marie – ✆ 01 46 33 93 98
– lorangerie75@orange.fr – Fax 01 43 29 25 52
closed 3-24 August, Wednesday lunch and Tuesday **U2**
Rest – Menu 35 € (weekday lunch), 75/130 € – Carte 80/102 €

◆ A la mode ◆

An experienced team runs this new restaurant on the Ile Saint-Louis. Long and narrow dining room, elegant table settings and lively, inventive cuisine.

XX

Yugaraj

14 r. Dauphine (6th) – Ⓜ Odéon – ✆ 01 43 26 44 91 – contact@yugaraj.com
– Fax 01 46 33 50 77
closed 1st-4 May, 5-27 August, 1st-4 January, Thursday lunch and Monday
Rest – Menu 31/46 € – Carte 36/60 € **T1**

◆ Exotic ◆

New look but the same refinement at this highly acclaimed Indian restaurant with its museum-like décor (wood panelling, silks and antiques). Comprehensive menu.

XX ✿

Le Restaurant – Hôtel L'Hôtel

13 r. des Beaux-Arts (6th) – Ⓜ St-Germain-des-Prés – ✆ 01 44 41 99 01 **S1**
Rest – *(closed August, 21-29 December, Sunday and Monday)* Menu 75/125 € bi – Carte 74/83 €
Spec. Le Saint Pierre. Le Cochon de Lait. Le Chocolat.

◆ Elegant ◆

Part of "L'Hôtel", the equally simply named "Le Restaurant" boasts décor by Jacques Garcia and a small inner courtyard. Refined, contemporary cuisine.

XX

Atelier Maître Albert

1 r. Maître Albert (5th) – Ⓜ Maubert Mutualité – ✆ 01 56 81 30 01
– ateliermaitrealbert@guysavoy.com – Fax 01 53 10 83 23
– www.ateliermaitrealbert.com
closed 5-25 August, Christmas holidays, Saturday lunch and Sunday lunch
Rest – Menu 24 € (weekday lunch), 40/50 € – Carte approx. 44 € **U2**

◆ Bistro ◆

Guy Savoy and his team propose carefully prepared dishes in a modern designer setting that also features a huge medieval fireplace, a spit for roasted meat and exposed beams.

Alcazar

62 r. Mazarine (6th) – Odéon – 01 53 10 19 99 – contact@alcazar.fr – Fax 01 53 10 23 23 – www.alcazar.fr **S2**

Rest – Menu 20 € bi (weekday lunch)/40 € – Carte 37/60 €

◆ Trendy ◆

The famous cabaret has been transformed into a huge, trendy designer restaurant. The cooking hobs are visible from the tables, and the cuisine is contemporary.

L'Atelier de Joël Robuchon

5 r. Montalembert (7th) – Rue du Bac – 01 42 22 56 56 – latelierdejoelrobuchon@wanadoo.fr – Fax 01 42 22 97 91

Reception from 11.30 am to 3.30 pm and from 6.30 pm to midnight.

Reservations only for certain services : please inquire **R1**

Rest – Menu 110 € – Carte 53/100 €

Spec. La langoustine en ravioli à l'étuvée de chou vert. Le ris de veau clouté de laurier frais à la feuille de romaine farcie. La Chartreuse en soufflé chaud et sa crème glacée à la pistache.

◆ Design ◆

An original concept in a chic décor designed by Rochon. No tables, just high stools in a row facing the counter where you can sample a selection of fine, modern dishes, served tapas style. Car parking service.

Yen

22 r. St-Benoît (6th) – St-Germain des Prés – 01 45 44 11 18 – restau.yen@wanadoo.fr – Fax 01 45 44 19 48

closed Sunday **S2**

Rest – Menu 55 € (dinner) – Carte 31/64 €

◆ Minimalist ◆

Two dining rooms with highly refined Japanese decor, the one on the first floor is slightly warmer in style. Pride of place on the menu for the chef's speciality: soba (buckwheat noodles).

Gaya Rive Gauche par Pierre Gagnaire

44 r. Bac (7th) – Rue du Bac – 01 45 44 73 73 – p.gagnaire@wanadoo.fr – Fax 01 45 44 73 73 – www.pierre-gagnaire.com

closed 3-24 August, 23 December-4 January, Sunday and public holidays

Rest – Carte 63/102 € **R1**

Spec. Croque-monsieur noir. Langoustines. Gâteau au chocolat.

◆ Design ◆

Popular with a well-heeled left bank clientele, seafood takes pride of place in this restaurant. Tasteful marine décor and chinaware signed by Jean Cocteau.

L'Épi Dupin

11 r. Dupin (6th) – Sèvres Babylone – 01 42 22 64 56 – lepidupin@wanadoo.fr – Fax 01 42 22 30 42

closed 1st-24 August, Monday lunch, Saturday and Sunday **R2**

Rest – *(number of covers limited, pre-book)* Menu 34 €

◆ Friendly ◆

Beams and stonework for character, closely-packed tables for conviviality and delicious cuisine to delight the palate; this pocket-handkerchief-sized restaurant has captivated people in the Bon Marché area.

Ze Kitchen Galerie (William Ledeuil)

4 r. Grands Augustins (6th) – St-Michel – 01 44 32 00 32 – zekitchen.galerie@wanadoo.fr – Fax 01 44 32 00 33 – www.zekitchengalerie.fr

closed Saturday lunchtime and Sunday **T2**

Rest – Menu 36 € – Carte 55/59 €

Spec. Légumes marinés et grillés, tomates, girolles, émulsion parmesan. Joue de veau, jus thaï, marmelade de tomate, gingembre. Chocolat gianduja, sésame, cacahuète, glace coco.

◆ Design ◆

Ze Kitchen is 'ze' hip place to be on the Left Bank. Minimalist décor, contemporary works of art, designer furniture and in vogue cuisine prepared in front of your eyes.

Toustem

(dinner) VISA

12 r. de l'Hôtel Colbert (5th) – Maubert Mutualité – 01 40 51 99 87
– toustem@helenedarroze.com
closed Monday lunch, Saturday lunch and Sunday **T2**
Rest – Menu 32 € (lunch) – Carte 45/49 €
♦ South-West of France ♦ Neighbourhood ♦
With Toustem ("always" in the Landes' dialect), Hélène Darroze launched her regional bistro (Southwest). In the setting of an ancient 13th century house, it has contemporary touches and intimate vaults.

Papilles

VISA

30 r. Gay Lussac (5th) – Luxembourg – 01 43 25 20 79
– lespapilles@hotmail.fr – Fax 01 43 25 24 35
closed Easter holidays, 1st-21 August, 1st-8 January, Sunday and Monday **T3**
Rest – Menu 31 € – Carte 36/43 €
♦ South-western France ♦
Bistro, cellar and grocer's: on one side are wine racks, on the other shelves with jars of southwest specialities and in the middle...you can enjoy market-inspired food!

Mon Vieil Ami

VISA

69 r. St-Louis-en-l'Ile (4th) – Pont Marie – 01 40 46 01 35
– mon.vieil.ami@wanadoo.fr – Fax 01 40 46 01 35 – www.mon-vieil-ami.com
closed 1st-20 August, 1st-20 January, Monday and Tuesday **U2**
Rest – Menu 41 €
♦ Traditional ♦
In this old house with a refurbished interior on Ile St Louis, sample tasty, traditional recipes infused with modern touches and Alsatian culinary influences.

Buisson Ardent

VISA

25 r. Jussieu (5th) – Jussieu – 01 43 54 93 02 – jtlopez@noos.fr
– www.lebuissonardent.fr
closed August, Saturday lunch and Sunday **U3**
Rest – Menu 31/45 €
♦ Bistro ♦
An informal atmosphere in this small, local restaurant packed at lunchtime with students from Jussieu University. Classic cuisine. Original 1923 frescoes.

MONTPARNASSE-DENFERT *Plan VI*

Méridien Montparnasse

rm rm VISA

19 r. Cdt Mouchotte (14th)
– Montparnasse Bienvenüe – 01 44 36 44 36
– meridien.montparnasse@lemeridien.com – Fax 01 44 36 49 00
– www.lemeridien.com/montparnasse **V1**
918 rm – †145/329 € ††145/329 €, 26 € – 35 suites
Rest *Montparnasse'25* – see below
Rest *Justine* – *01 44 36 44 00* – Menu 42/46 € – Carte 38/49 €
♦ Chain hotel ♦ Business ♦
The spacious rooms in this glass and concrete building have been redone in a modern spirit with Art Deco details. Beautiful view of the capital from the top floors. At Justine's, winter garden décor, green terrace and buffet menus.

Concorde Montparnasse

rm rm VISA

40 r. Cdt Mouchotte (14th) – Gaîté
– 01 56 54 84 00 – montparnasse@concorde-hotels.com – Fax 01 56 54 84 84
– www.concorde-hotels.com **V1**
354 rm – †140/350 € ††140/350 €, 20 €
Rest – Menu 34 € – Carte 35/43 €
♦ Chain hotel ♦ Business ♦
This hotel, on Place de Catalogne, was treated to a facelift recently. Calm and refined rooms, interior garden, fitness centre and bar. This restaurant, with exotic wood and coloured fabrics, offers buffets and à la carte dishes.

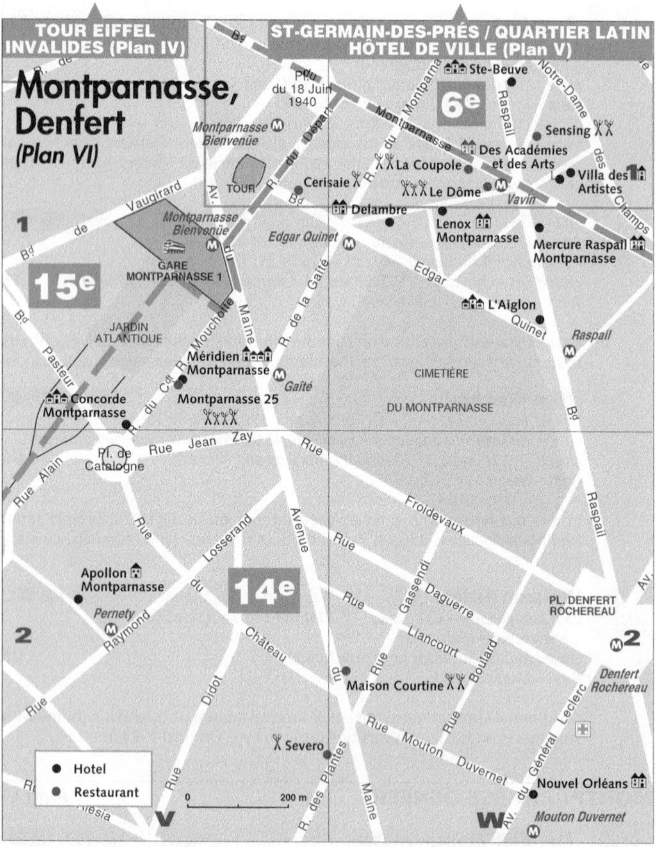

Montparnasse, Denfert (Plan VI)

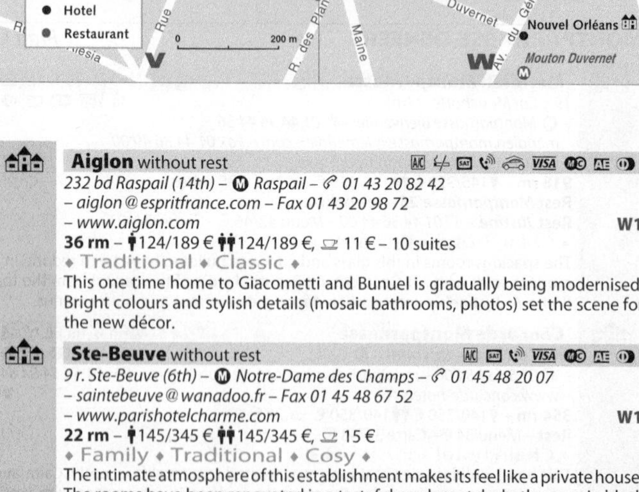

Aiglon without rest

232 bd Raspail (14th) – Ⓜ Raspail – ✆ 01 43 20 82 42
– aiglon@espritfrance.com – Fax 01 43 20 98 72
– www.aiglon.com **W1**

36 rm – ♦124/189 € ♦♦124/189 €, ☕ 11 € – 10 suites

♦ Traditional ♦ Classic ♦

This one time home to Giacometti and Bunuel is gradually being modernised. Bright colours and stylish details (mosaic bathrooms, photos) set the scene for the new décor.

Ste-Beuve without rest

9 r. Ste-Beuve (6th) – Ⓜ Notre-Dame des Champs – ✆ 01 45 48 20 07
– saintebeuve@wanadoo.fr – Fax 01 45 48 67 52
– www.parishotelcharme.com **W1**

22 rm – ♦145/345 € ♦♦145/345 €, ☕ 15 €

♦ Family ♦ Traditional ♦ Cosy ♦

The intimate atmosphere of this establishment makes its feel like a private house. The rooms have been renovated in a tasteful modern style; bathrooms in black and white.

Des Académies et des Arts without rest

15 r. de la Grande-Chaumière (6th) – Ⓜ Vavin – ✆ 01 43 26 66 44 – reservation@hoteldesacademies.com – Fax 01 40 46 86 85 – www.hoteldesacademies.com **W1**

20 rm – †220/285 € ††220/285 €, ☕ 16 €

♦ Cosy ♦

The walls of this creative and artistic hotel are adorned with white figures painted by Jérôme Mesnager and sculptures by Sophie de Watrigant. Elegant, well-appointed guestrooms.

Villa des Artistes without rest

9 r. Grande-Chaumière (6th) – Ⓜ Vavin – ✆ 01 43 26 60 86 – hotel@villa-artistes.com – Fax 01 43 54 73 70 – www.villa-artistes.com **W1**

55 rm – †158/190 € ††158/190 €, ☕ 15 €

♦ Family ♦ Traditional ♦ Stylish ♦

The name pays tribute to the artists who embellished the history of the Montparnasse district. Pleasant rooms, most overlooking the courtyard. Glass-roofed breakfast room.

Lenox Montparnasse without rest

15 r. Delambre (14th) – Ⓜ Vavin – ✆ 01 43 35 34 50 – hotel@lenoxmontparnasse.com – Fax 01 43 20 46 64 – www.hotellenox.com **W1**

52 rm – †165/310 € ††165/310 €, ☕ 16 €

♦ Traditional ♦ Cosy ♦

Establishment noted for its elegance: plush, low-key bar and sitting rooms, personalised stylish rooms, pleasant suites on the sixth floor.

Nouvel Orléans without rest

25 av. Gén. Leclerc (14th) – Ⓜ Mouton Duvernet – ✆ 01 43 27 80 20 – nouvelorleans@aol.com – Fax 01 43 35 36 57 – www.hotelnouvelorleans.com **W2**

46 rm – †90/155 € ††90/190 €, ☕ 10 €

♦ Traditional ♦ Modern ♦

The name comes from the Porte d'Orléans, 800m away. In this entirely renovated hotel, modern furniture and warm colourful materials decorate the rooms.

Delambre without rest

35 r. Delambre (14th) – Ⓜ Edgar Quinet – ✆ 01 43 20 66 31 – delambre@club-internet.fr – Fax 01 45 38 91 76 – www.hoteldelambre.com **W1**

30 rm – †85/115 € ††85/160 €, ☕ 9 €

♦ Traditional ♦ Modern ♦

André Breton stayed in this hotel located in a quiet street close to Montparnasse railway station. The décor is modern, the rooms simple but bright, and many are spacious.

Mercure Raspail Montparnasse without rest

207 bd Raspail (14th) – Ⓜ Vavin – ✆ 01 43 20 62 94 – h0351@accor.com – Fax 01 43 27 39 69 – www.mercure.com **W1**

63 rm – †150/210 € ††155/210 €, ☕ 14 €

♦ Chain hotel ♦ Business ♦ Functional ♦

Enjoy an overnight stay in this Haussmann building near the famous Montparnasse brasseries. Modern rooms with contemporary, light wood furniture, nearly all refurbished.

Apollon Montparnasse without rest

91 r. Ouest (14th) – Ⓜ Pernety – ✆ 01 43 95 62 00 – apollonm@wanadoo.fr – Fax 01 43 95 62 10 – www.apollon-montparnasse.com **V2**

33 rm – †75/89 € ††86/109 €, ☕ 8.50 €

♦ Traditional ♦ Functional ♦

Gradually renovated family hotel near the station. Tastefully decorated rooms, a smiling welcome, and a quiet location in a side street.

Montparnasse'25 – Hôtel Méridien Montparnasse

19 r. Cdt Mouchotte (14th) – Montparnasse Bienvenüe – 01 44 36 44 25 – meridien.montparnasse@lemeridien.com – Fax 01 44 36 49 03 – www.montparnasse.lemeridien.com

closed 28 April-4 May, 14 July-31 August, 22 December-6 January, Saturday, Sunday and public holidays **V1**

Rest – Menu 49 € (lunch)/110 € (dinner) – Carte 93/109 €

Spec. Saint-Jaques dorées à la plancha (season). Saint-Pierre à l'huile de truffe aux blanc de poireaux. Canard laqué aux fruits tamarin.

♦ A la mode ♦ Formal ♦

The modern setting based around black lacquer may surprise but this restaurant turns out to be comfortable and warm. Contemporary cuisine, superb cheese boards.

Le Dôme

108 bd Montparnasse (14th) – Vavin – 01 43 35 25 81 – Fax 01 42 79 01 19

closed Sunday and Monday in July-August **W1**

Rest – Carte 52/123 €

♦ Retro ♦

A temple of literary and artistic bohemian life in the Twenties has been turned into a stylish and trendy Left-Bank brasserie, with its Art Deco style intact. Fish and seafood.

Maison Courtine (Yves Charles)

157 av. du Maine (14th) – Mouton Duvernet – 01 45 43 08 04 – yves.charles@wanadoo.fr – Fax 01 45 45 91 35

closed 2 August-1st September, 23 December-2 January, Monday lunch, Saturday lunch and Sunday **W2**

Rest – Menu 39/44 €

Spec. Crémeux froid d'araignée de mer et croûtons au cumin. Petites escalopes de foie gras de canard poêlées aux raisins. Médaillon de veau de lait et lentilles blondes de la Planèze.

♦ South-western France ♦ Cosy ♦

Here one can enjoy a culinary Tour de France; the brightly-coloured interiors are modern and the furnishing is in the Louis-Philippe style. A popular establishment.

Sensing

19 r. Bréa (6th) – Vavin – 01 43 27 08 80 – sensing@orange.fr – Fax 01 43 26 99 27 – www.restaurantsensing.com

closed August, Monday lunch and Sunday **W1**

Rest – Menu 55 € (weekday lunch), 95/140 € – Carte 60/73 €

♦ Innovative ♦

A short menu with refined, contemporary dishes prepared using excellent produce and served in an uncluttered, ultra-stylish setting. Run by the famous French chef, Guy Martin.

La Coupole

102 bd Montparnasse (14th) – Vavin – 01 43 20 14 20 – jtosi@groupeflo.fr – Fax 01 43 35 46 14 – www.flobrasseries.com **W1**

Rest – Menu 31 € – Carte 32/130 €

♦ Retro ♦

The spirit of Montparnasse lives on in this immense Art Deco brasserie, first opened in 1927. The 32 pillars were decorated by artists of the period. A lively atmosphere.

La Cerisaie

70 bd E. Quinet (14th) – Edgar Quinet – 01 43 20 98 98 – Fax 01 43 20 98 98

closed 1st-11 May, 28 July-25 August, 20 December – 4 January, Saturday and Sunday **V1**

Rest – *(pre-book)* Menu 32/39 €

♦ South-western France ♦ Bistro ♦

A tiny restaurant in the heart of the Breton quarter. Every day, the owner chalks up the carefully prepared dishes of the southwest on a blackboard.

Severo

8 r. Plantes (14th) – Ⓜ Mouton Duvernet – ✆ 01 45 40 40 91
closed 27 April-4 May, 26 July-24 August, 20-28 December, Saturday and Sunday **V2**
Rest – Carte 27/54 €
◆ Bistro ◆
Products from Auvergne (meat, charcuterie) take centre stage on the daily slate menu of this friendly bistro. The wine list is enticingly eclectic.

MARAIS-BASTILLE-GARE DE LYON *Plan VII*

Pavillon de la Reine without rest

28 pl. des Vosges (3rd) – Ⓜ Bastille – ✆ 01 40 29 19 19
– contact@pavillon-de-la-reine.com – Fax 01 40 29 19 20
– www.pavillon-de-la-reine.com **Y2**
41 rm – †370/460 € ††430/460 €, ☕ 25 € – 15 suites
◆ Luxury ◆ Historic ◆
Behind one of the 36 brick houses lining the Place des Vosges stand two buildings, one of which is 17C, housing elegant rooms on the courtyard or (private) garden side.

Les Jardins du Marais

74 r. Amelot (11th) – Ⓜ St-Sébastien Froissart – ✆ 01 40 21 20 00
– resabastille@homeplazza.com – Fax 01 47 00 82 40
– www.homeplazza.com **Y1**
201 rm – †350 € ††370 €, ☕ 32 € – 64 suites
Rest – *(closed Sunday)* Carte 27/47 €
◆ Luxury ◆ Art Deco ◆
A quiet night's sleep is guaranteed in this hotel made up of several buildings overlooking a large interior garden. Designer entrance hall and bar, and comfortable Art Deco-style bedrooms.

Villa Beaumarchais without rest

5 r. Arquebusiers (3rd) – Ⓜ Chemin Vert
– ✆ 01 40 29 14 00 – beaumarchais@leshotelsdeparis.com – Fax 01 40 29 14 01
– www.leshotelsdeparis.com **X-Y1**
50 rm – †380/480 € ††380/680 €, ☕ 19 € – 4 suites
◆ Luxury ◆ Stylish ◆
Set back from the hustle and bustle of the boulevard Beaumarchais. Refined rooms graced with gold-leafed furniture; all rooms overlook a pretty winter garden.

Mercure Gare de Lyon without rest

2 pl. Louis Armand (12th) – Ⓜ Gare de Lyon
– ✆ 01 43 44 84 84 – h2217@accor.com
– Fax 01 43 47 41 94 – www.mercure.com **Y3**
315 rm – †89/250 € ††99/265 €, ☕ 15 €
◆ Chain hotel ◆ Functional ◆
The modern architecture of this hotel contrasts with the nearby belfry of the Gare de Lyon. The bedrooms are furnished in ceruse wood and have the benefit of good soundproofing. Wine bar.

Du Petit Moulin without rest

29 r. du Poitou (3rd) – Ⓜ St-Sébastien Froissart – ✆ 01 42 74 10 10
– contact@hoteldupetitmoulin.com – Fax 01 42 74 10 97
– www.hoteldupetitmoulin.com **X1**
17 rm – †190/350 € ††190/350 €, ☕ 15 €
◆ Traditional ◆ Design ◆
For this hotel in the Marais, Christian Lacroix has designed a unique and refined décor, playing on the contrasts between traditional and modern. Each room has a different design. Cosy bar.

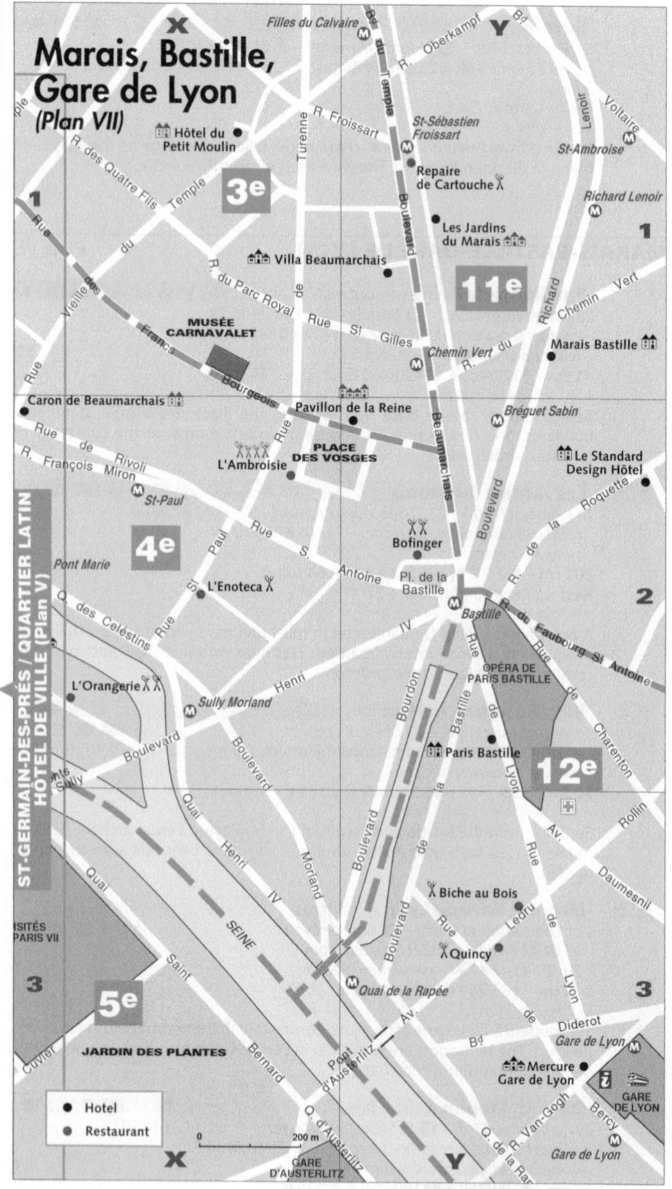
Marais, Bastille, Gare de Lyon
(Plan VII)
Hôtel du Petit Moulin
Repaire de Cartouche
Les Jardins du Marais
Villa Beaumarchais
MUSÉE CARNAVALET
Marais Bastille
Caron de Beaumarchais
Pavillon de la Reine
PLACE DES VOSGES
L'Ambroisie
Le Standard Design Hôtel
Bofinger
Pl. de la Bastille
L'Enoteca
OPÉRA DE PARIS BASTILLE
L'Orangerie
Paris Bastille
Biche au Bois
Quincy
JARDIN DES PLANTES
Mercure Gare de Lyon
GARE DE LYON
GARE D'AUSTERLITZ
SEINE
Filles du Calvaire
St-Sébastien Froissart
St-Ambroise
Richard Lenoir
Chemin Vert
Bréguet Sabin
St-Paul
Pont Marie
Bastille
Sully Morland
Quai de la Rapée
Gare de Lyon
3e
11e
4e
12e
5e
ST-GERMAIN-DES-PRÉS / QUARTIER LATIN
HÔTEL DE VILLE (Plan V)
Hotel
Restaurant
0
200 m

Caron de Beaumarchais without rest
12 r. Vieille-du-Temple (4th) – Ⓜ Hôtel de Ville – ✆ 01 42 72 34 12 – hotel@carondebeaumarchais.com – Fax 01 42 72 34 63 – www.carondebeaumarchais.com **X2**
19 rm – 125/162 € 125/162 €, 12 €
◆ Traditional ◆ Business ◆ Historic ◆
Figaro's creator lived on this historic Marais street, and the stylish decoration in this charming hotel pays a faithful tribute to him. Small, comfortable rooms.

Le Standard Design without rest
29 r. des Taillandiers (11th) – Ⓜ Bastille – ✆ 01 48 05 30 97 – reservation@standard-hotel.com – Fax 01 47 00 29 26 – www.standard-hotel.com **Y2**
34 rm – 95/140 € 130/195 €, 12 €
◆ Traditional ◆Cosy◆
A resolutely contemporary interior in black and white, with touches of colour in the bedrooms. A trendy and unique hotel embellished with numerous designer objects.

Paris Bastille without rest
67 r. Lyon (12th) – Ⓜ Bastille – ✆ 01 40 01 07 17 – infosbastille@wanadoo.fr – Fax 01 40 01 07 27 – www.hotelparisbastille.com **Y2**
37 rm – 165/240 € 175/240 €, 12 €
◆ Business ◆ Functional ◆
Up-to-date comfort, modern furnishings and carefully chosen colour schemes characterise the rooms in this hotel facing the Opéra.

Marais Bastille without rest
36 bd Richard Lenoir (11th) – Ⓜ Bréguet Sabin – ✆ 01 48 05 75 00 – maraisbastille@wanadoo.fr – Fax 01 43 57 42 85 – www.bestwestern.com/fr/maraisbastille **Y1**
36 rm – 145 € 145 €, 10 €
◆ Chain hotel ◆ Classical ◆
The hotel runs along the boulevard which has covered the Canal St-Martin since 1860. Comfortable, spacious and modern bedrooms embellished with oak and cherry wood furniture.

L'Ambroisie (Bernard Pacaud)
9 pl. des Vosges (4th) – Ⓜ St-Paul – ✆ 01 42 78 51 45
closed August, 23 February-11 March, Sunday and Monday **X2**
Rest – Carte 196/252 €
Spec. Feuillantine de langoustines aux graines de sésame. Escalopines de bar à l'émincé d'artichaut, caviar osciètre gold. Tarte fine sablée au chocolat, glace vanille.
◆ A la mode ◆ Luxury ◆
Under the arcades of the Place des Vosges, royal décor and subtle cuisine, close to perfection. The name is most appropriate: ambrosia was the food of the gods of Antiquity.

Bofinger (dinner)
5 r. Bastille (4th) – Ⓜ Bastille – ✆ 01 42 72 87 82 – ebern@groupeflo.fr – Fax 01 42 72 97 68 – www.bofingerparis.com **Y2**
Rest – Menu 32 € – Carte 32/79 €
◆ Retro ◆
The famous clients and remarkable décor have bestowed enduring renown on this brasserie created in 1864. The interior boasts a finely worked cupola, and a room on the first floor decorated by Hansi.

Quincy
28 av. Ledru-Rollin (12th) – Ⓜ Gare de Lyon – ✆ 01 46 28 46 76 – Fax 01 46 28 46 76 – www.lequincy.fr
closed 15 August-15 September, Saturday, Sunday and Monday **Y3**
Rest – Carte 44/76 €
◆ Rustic ◆
A warm atmosphere in this rustic bistrot serving hearty cusine which, like "Bobosse" the jovial owner, has plenty of character.

L'Enoteca
25 r. Charles V (4th) – Ⓜ St-Paul – ✆ 01 42 78 91 44 – enoteca@enoteca.fr – Fax 01 44 59 31 72 – www.enoteca.fr
closed 9-18 August and lunch in August **X2**
Rest – *(pre-book)* Menu 30/45 € bi – Carte 30/45 €
♦ Italian ♦ Friendly ♦
A 16C building housing a restaurant whose superb wine list of about 500 Italian wines is its main asset. Italian dishes and a very lively atmosphere.

Repaire de Cartouche
99 r. Amelot (11th) – Ⓜ St-Sébastien Froissart – ✆ 01 47 00 25 86 – Fax 01 43 38 85 91
closed 1st-8 May, August, Sunday and Monday **Y1**
Rest – Menu 26 € (weekday lunch) – Carte 35/48 €
♦ Traditional ♦ Friendly ♦
Cartouche, the impetuous yet honourable bandit, took refuge here in 1713 after deserting from the army; the restaurant murals recall his epic life. Attractive wine list.

La Biche au Bois
45 av. Ledru-Rollin (12th) – Ⓜ Gare de Lyon – ✆ 01 43 43 34 38
closed 20 July-20 August, 23 December-2 January, Monday lunch, Saturday and Sunday **Y3**
Rest – Menu 25 € – Carte approx. 30 €
♦ Classic ♦ Rustic ♦
An unpretentious decor in the noisy and smoke-filled dining room, but the service is attentive and the traditional cuisine generously served. Game in season.

MONTMARTRE, PIGALLE *Plan VIII*

Terrass'Hôtel
12 r. J. de Maistre (18th) – Ⓜ Place de Clichy – ✆ 01 46 06 72 85 – reservation@terrass-hotel.com – Fax 01 44 92 34 30 – www.terrass-hotel.com **Z1**
85 rm – †270/290 € ††320/345 €, ☕ 18 € – 15 suites
Rest *Le Diapason* – *✆ 01 44 92 34 00 (closed Sunday dinner 16 September-30 April and Saturday lunch)* Menu 29 (lunch)/35 € bi (dinner) – Carte 45/63 €
♦ Traditional ♦ Family ♦ Modern ♦
Situated at the foot of the Sacré-Coeur basilica, this hotel has stunning views of Paris from its upper-floor rooms and top-floor terrace. Elegant interior adorned with ornaments and wood panelling. Attractive Provençal-inspired dining room and rooftop terrace overlooking the capital.

Mercure Montmartre without rest
3 r. Caulaincourt (18th) – Ⓜ Place de Clichy – ✆ 01 44 69 70 70 – h0373@accor.com – Fax 01 44 69 70 71 – www.mercure.com **Z2**
305 rm – †143/192 € ††161/202 €, ☕ 14 €
♦ Chain hotel ♦ Business ♦ Functional ♦
A stone's throw from the famous Moulin Rouge, the hotel lobby is decorated on the theme of Montmartre and its painters. The rooms on the top three floors enjoy lovely views of the rooftops of Paris.

Holiday Inn Garden Court Montmartre without rest
23 r. Damrémont (18th) – Ⓜ Lamarck Caulaincourt – ✆ 01 44 92 33 40 – hiparmm@aol.com – Fax 01 44 92 09 30 – www.holiday-inn.com/parismontmart **Z1**
54 rm – †90/170 € ††110/190 €, ☕ 13 €
♦ Chain hotel ♦ Business ♦ Functional ♦
A recently built hotel with renovated, functional rooms on a typically steep Montmartre street. The breakfast room opens onto a small terrace.

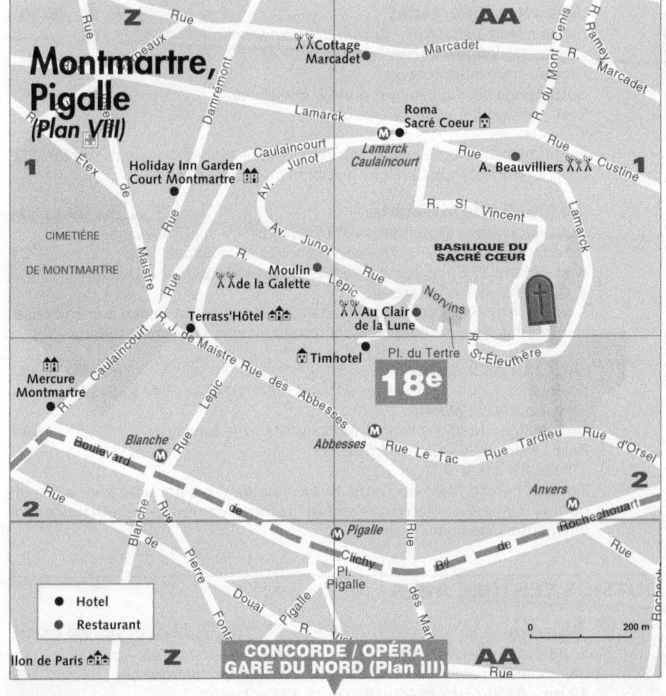

Timhotel without rest

11 r. Ravignan (18th) – Ⓜ Abbesses – ✆ 01 42 55 74 79
– montmartre.manager@timhotel.fr – Fax 01 42 55 71 01
– www.my-paris-hotel.com **AA2**

59 rm – 75/180 € 75/180 €, ☕ 8.50 €

◆ Chain hotel ◆ Functional ◆

Smart, functional hotel on one of the neighbourhood's most charming squares. The rooms on the 4th and 5th floors have been renovated and offer superb views of the capital.

Roma Sacré Cœur without rest

101 r. Caulaincourt (18th) – Ⓜ Lamarck Caulaincourt – ✆ 01 42 62 02 02
– hotel.roma@wanadoo.fr – Fax 01 42 54 34 92 – www.hotelroma.fr

57 rm – 75/115 € 85/140 €, ☕ 8 € **AA1**

◆ Traditional ◆ Family ◆ Classic ◆

This hotel has a charming location in Montmartre, with a garden to the front, typical flights of steps to the side and Sacré-Cœur above. Attractive, brightly coloured guestrooms.

A Beauvilliers

52 r. Lamarck (18th) – Ⓜ Lamarck Caulaincourt – ✆ 01 42 55 05 42
– www.abeauvilliers.com
closed 10-20 August, Sunday dinner and Monday **AA1**

Rest – Menu 35 € (lunch), 45/68 € – Carte 71/83 €

◆ A la mode ◆ Romantic ◆

There is change in the air at this Montmartre institution: delicious contemporary cuisine with a personal touch in the elegant décor. Pleasant terrace for fine weather.

Le Cottage Marcadet

151 bis r. Marcadet (18th) – Ⓜ Lamarck Caulaincourt – ✆ 01 42 57 71 22 – contact@cottagemarcadet.com – Fax 01 42 57 71 24 – www.cottagemarcadet.com
closed spring holidays, August, Sunday and Monday **AA1**
Rest – Menu 35 € – Carte 64/96 €
♦ Retro ♦
An intimate ambience awaits you in this classic dining room with comfortable Louis XVI furnishings. Carefully prepared traditional cuisine.

Le Moulin de la Galette

83 r. Lepic (18th) – Ⓜ Abbesses – ✆ 01 46 06 84 77 – moulindelagalette@yahoo.fr – Fax 01 46 06 84 78 – www.lemoulindelagalette.fr **Z1**
Rest – Menu 25 € (lunch)/42 € (dinner) – Carte 50/78 €
♦ A la mode ♦ Retro ♦
A windmill in 1622, then a popular dance hall painted by Renoir and Toulouse-Lautrec, this place is now a pleasant restaurant with a charming terrace.

Au Clair de la Lune

9 r. Poulbot (18th) – Ⓜ Abbesses – ✆ 01 42 58 97 03 – Fax 01 42 55 64 74 – www.auclairdelalune.fr
closed 18 August-15 September, Monday lunch and Sunday **AA1**
Rest – Menu 32 € – Carte 37/69 €
♦ Traditional ♦ Rustic ♦
Situated behind Place du Tertre, this restaurant takes its name from a French nursery rhyme. Classical cuisine served in a friendly atmosphere with frescoes of old Montmartre on the walls.

OUTSIDE CENTRAL AREA

Murano

13 bd du Temple (3rd) – Ⓜ Filles du Calvaire – ✆ 01 42 71 20 00 – paris@muranoresort.com – Fax 01 42 71 21 01 – www.muranoresort.com **C2**
49 rm – 🛉360/650 € 🛉🛉440/1850 €, ☕ 32 € – 2 suites
Rest – Menu 55 € bi, 85 € bi (weekday lunch)/130 € bi – Carte 41/145 €
♦ Grand Luxury ♦ Design ♦
The Murano is a trendy hotel that stands out from the crowd with its immaculate designer décor, play of colours, high-tech equipment and pop-art bar (150 types of vodka). The restaurant has a colourful contemporary style, international food and a D.J. at the decks.

St-James Paris

43 av. Bugeaud (16th) ✉ 75116 – Ⓜ Porte Dauphine – ✆ 01 44 05 81 81 – contact@saint-james-paris.com – Fax 01 44 05 81 82 – www.saint-james-paris.com **A2**
38 rm – 🛉380/630 € 🛉🛉490/630 €, ☕ 28 € – 10 suites
Rest – *(closed Saturday, Sunday and public holidays) (residents only)* Menu 50 € – Carte 67/190 €
♦ Grand Luxury ♦ Personalised ♦
Beautiful private townhouse built in 1892 by Mrs. Thiers, in the heart of a shady garden. Majestic staircase, spacious rooms and a bar-library with the atmosphere of an English club.

Paris Bercy Pullman

1 r. Libourne (12th) – Ⓜ Cour St-Emilion – ✆ 01 44 67 34 00 – h2192@accor.com – Fax 01 44 67 34 01 – www.sofitel-paris-bercy.com **D3**
386 rm – 🛉230/460 € 🛉🛉230/460 €, ☕ 26 € – 10 suites
Rest *Café Ké* – *(closed 4-25 August, 22-29 December, Saturday and Sunday)*
Menu 36 € – Carte 49/81 €
♦ Chain hotel ♦ Functional ♦
A beautiful glass façade, contemporary interior in shades of brown, beige and blue, and modern facilities. Some of the rooms enjoy views across Paris. The stylish Café Ké is a pleasant option in the Bercy village; modern cuisine.

Pullman Rive Gauche

8 r. L. Armand (15th) – Ⓜ Balard – ☎ 01 40 60 30 30 – h0572@accor.com – Fax 01 40 60 30 00 – www.pullman-hotels.com **A3**

606 rm – 320/390 € 320/390 €, 25 € – 12 suites

Rest *Brasserie* – ☎ 01 40 60 33 77 – Menu 27 € (weekday lunch) – Carte 37/69 €

◆ Business ◆ Chain hotel ◆ Functional ◆

Opposite the heliport, this hotel offers soundproofed rooms, some of which have been refurbished in an elegantly modern style. The upper floors have a lovely view over western Paris. Brasserie with a setting from the Roaring Twenties: Mosaics, cupola, benches, etc..

Square

3 r. Boulainvilliers (16th) ✉ 75016 – Ⓜ Mirabeau – ☎ 01 44 14 91 90 – reservation@hotelsquare.com – Fax 01 44 14 91 99 – ww.hotelsquare.com **A2**

20 rm – 300/480 € 300/480 €, 22 € – 2 suites

Rest *Zébra Square* – ☎ 01 44 14 91 91 – Menu 34 € bi – Carte 35/57 €

◆ Luxury ◆ Business ◆ Design ◆

A jewel of contemporary architecture across from the Maison de la Radio. Curves, colours, high-tech facilities and abstract paintings: a hymn to modern art! Trendy décor with striped theme in the restaurant, a cellar-library and contemporary cuisine on the menu.

Kube without rest

1 passage Ruelle (18th) – Ⓜ La Chapelle – ☎ 01 42 05 20 00 – paris@kubehotel.com – Fax 01 42 05 21 01 – www.kubehotel.com **C1**

41 rm – 250 € 300/750 €, 25 €

◆ Business ◆ Design ◆

The 19C façade belies this hotel's 21C high-tech designer interior. The bar – built entirely from ice (-10°C) – makes for an unusual and unforgettable experience.

Holiday Inn

216 av. J. Jaurès (19th) – Ⓜ Porte de Pantin – ☎ 01 44 84 18 18 – hilavillette@alliance-hospitality.com – Fax 01 44 84 18 20 – www.holidayinn-parisvillette.com **D1**

182 rm – 230/600 € 230/600 €, 18 €

Rest – *(closed Saturday and Sunday)* Menu 28 € (dinner) – Carte 26/51 €

◆ Business ◆ Chain hotel ◆ Functional ◆

Modern construction across from the Cité de la Musique. Spacious and soundproofed rooms, offering modern comfort. Métro station a few metres away. Simple brasserie-style restaurant and small terrace protected from the street by a curtain of plants.

Novotel Tour Eiffel

61 quai de Grenelle (15th) – Ⓜ Charles Michels – ☎ 01 40 58 20 00 – h3546@accor.com – Fax 01 40 58 24 44 – www.novotel.com **A2**

752 rm – 260/450 € 290/450 €, 20 € – 12 suites

Rest *Benkay* – see below

Rest *Tour Eiffel Café* – ☎ 01 40 58 20 75 – Menu 33/42 € bi – Carte 29/46 €

◆ Chain hotel ◆ Business ◆ Functional ◆

A hotel overlooking the Seine with comfortable modern rooms (wood, light shades), most of which have views of the river. High-tech conference centre. A pleasant, minimalist decor, modern cuisine and a delicatessen area at the Café Lenôtre.

Océania without rest

52 r. Oradour sur Glane (15th) – Ⓜ Porte de Versailles – ☎ 01 56 09 09 09 – oceania.paris@oceaniahotels.com – Fax 01 56 09 09 19 – www.oceaniahotels.com **A3**

232 rm – 160/270 € 175/285 €, 15 € – 18 suites

◆ Business ◆ Modern ◆

Modern comfort in an elegant, contemporary setting. This new hotel offers well-equipped bedrooms, a relaxation centre and an exotic terrace-garden.

Mercure Porte de Versailles without rest

69 bd Victor (15th) – Porte de Versailles – 01 44 19 03 03 – h1131@accor.com – Fax 01 48 28 22 11 – www.accorhotels.com/mercure_paris_porte_de_versailles.htm **A3**

91 rm – 115/300 € 130/315 €, 16 € – 7 suites

◆ Chain hotel ◆ Business ◆ Functional ◆

A hotel in a 1970s building opposite the Parc des Expositions, built on the site of the old Gordini car factory. Simply furnished, functional rooms.

Novotel Bercy

85 r. Bercy (12th) – Bercy – 01 43 42 30 00 – h0935@accor.com – Fax 01 43 45 30 60 **D3**

151 rm – 135/250 € 135/270 €, 15 €

Rest – Carte 24/45 €

◆ Business ◆ Functional ◆

The bright rooms in this Novotel are decorated in the chain's new "Novation" style. The nearby Parc de Bercy occupies the site of an old wine depot. Dining room/veranda and popular outdoor terrace in summertime.

Novotel Gare de Lyon

2 r. Hector Malot (12th) – Gare de Lyon – 01 44 67 60 00 – h1735@accor.com – Fax 01 44 67 60 60 – www.novotel.com **D2**

253 rm – 140/250 € 150/260 €, 16 €

Rest – Carte 20/43 €

◆ Chain hotel ◆ Functional ◆

This modern hotel overlooking a tranquil square offers comfortable, typical Novotel-style guestrooms; those on the sixth floor have a terrace. 24-hour swimming pool and well-designed children's area. Brasserie style restaurant (modern décor, benches, bay windows) and traditional fare.

Banville without rest

166 bd Berthier (17th) – Porte de Champerret – 01 42 67 70 16 – info@hotelbanville.fr – Fax 01 44 40 42 77 – www.hotelbanville.fr **B1**

38 rm – 280/400 € 280/400 €, 18 €

◆ Luxury ◆ Personalised ◆

Tastefully restored building from 1926. Charm pervades throughout from the elegant lobby and lounges to the refined rooms with personal (Provençal) touches. Live music on Tuesday evenings.

Holiday Inn Bibliothèque de France without rest

21 r. Tolbiac (13th) – Bibliothèque F. Mitterrand – 01 45 84 61 61 – hibdf@wanadoo.fr – Fax 01 45 84 43 38 – www.holiday-inn.com/paris-tolbiac **C3**

71 rm – 97/187 € 97/187 €, 14 €

◆ Chain hotel ◆ Functional ◆

In a busy street 20m from the métro station, this hotel offers comfortable, well-kept rooms with double glazing. Simple dishes available in the evening.

Windsor Home without rest

3 r. Vital (16th) 75016 – La Muette – 01 45 04 49 49 – whparis@wanadoo.fr – Fax 01 45 04 59 50 – www.windsorhomeparis.fr **A2**

8 rm – 120/160 € 130/170 €, 11 €

◆ Traditional ◆ Cosy ◆

This charming, hundred-year-old residence with a garden in front is decorated like a private house: old furniture, mouldings, light colours and contemporary touches.

XXXX ✿✿✿ **Pré Catelan**

rte Suresnes (in the Bois de Boulogne) (16th) ✉ 75016 – ✆ 01 44 14 41 14 – leprecatelan-restaurant@lenotre.fr – Fax 01 45 24 43 25 – www.lenotre.fr closed 3-25 August, 27 October-3 November, February holidays, Sunday and Monday **A2**

Rest – Menu 85 € (weekday lunch), 180/230 € – Carte 180/224 €

Spec. La Tomate (summer). La langoustine. La Pomme.

◆ Innovative ◆ Luxury ◆

Inventive cuisine provides the perfect foil to this elegant Napoleon III pavilion in the woods near the Shakespeare Theatre. Interior by Caran d'Ache.

XXXX ✿ **La Grande Cascade**

allée de Longchamp (opposite the hippodrome) (16th) ✉ 75016 – ✆ 01 45 27 33 51 – grandecascade@wanadoo.fr – Fax 01 42 88 99 06 – lagrandecascade.fr closed 20 February-10 March

Rest – Menu 75/177 € – Carte 130/200 €

Spec. Grosses langoustines snackées et huître en cromesqui, chou vert croquant et nage réduite au beurre iodé. Thon rouge croustillant poivre et sel, graines de sésame et coriandre en condiment. Pomme de ris de veau cuite lentement, olives, câpres et croûtons frits, herbes à tortue comme au Moyen Âge.

◆ A la mode ◆ Retro ◆

A Parisian paradise at the foot of the Grande Cascade (10m!) in the Bois de Boulogne. Delicately distinctive cuisine served in the 1850 pavilion or on the splendid terrace.

XXX **Benkay** - Novotel Paris Tour Eiffel

61 quai de Grenelle (4th floor) (15th) – Ⓜ Bir-Hakeim – ✆ 01 40 58 21 26 – h3546@accor.com – Fax 01 40 58 21 30 – www.novotel.com **A2**

Rest – Menu 30 € (lunch), 75/125 € – Carte 42/131 €

◆ Japanese ◆ Exotic ◆

On the top floor of a small building, the restaurant commands a fine view of the Seine. A tasteful décor of marble and wood and a sushi and teppanyaki counter.

XXX ✿ **Relais d'Auteuil** (Patrick Pignol)

31 bd. Murat (16th) ✉ 75016 – Ⓜ Michel Ange Molitor – ✆ 01 46 51 09 54 – pignol.p@wanadoo.fr – Fax 01 40 71 05 03 closed August, Christmas holidays, Monday lunchtime, Saturday lunchtime and Sunday **A2**

Rest – Menu 58 € (lunch), 119/149 € – Carte 116/171 €

Spec. Amandine de foie gras de canard des Landes et son lobe poêlé. Grosse sole de ligne dorée entière sur l'arête. Gibier (season).

◆ Classic ◆ Fashionable ◆

Modern decor and period furniture in this restaurant where the cuisine is both sophisticated and masterful. Take the time to peruse the exceptional wine list.

XX ✿ **Au Trou Gascon**

40 r. Taine (12th) – Ⓜ Daumesnil – ✆ 01 43 44 34 26 – trougascon@orange.fr – Fax 01 43 07 80 55 – www.autrougascon.fr closed August, Saturday and Sunday **D2**

Rest – Menu 36 (lunch)/50 € (dinner) – Carte 52/60 €

Spec. Chipirons cuits à la plaque (summer). Lièvre à la mode d'Aquitaine (autumn). Poire pochée au miel d'arbousier, baba punché.

◆ South-western France ◆

The decor of this old 1900 bistro combines period mouldings, designer furniture and grey hues. On the menu: Landes and Chalosse produce and southwestern wines.

XX **Chez Géraud**

31 r. Vital (16th) ✉ 75016 – Ⓜ La Muette – ✆ 01 45 20 33 00 – Fax 01 45 20 46 60 closed 1st August-1st September, 23 December-5 January, Saturday and Sunday

Rest – Menu 32 € – Carte 48/71 € **A2**

◆ Traditional ◆ Bistro ◆

The façade and the inside mural, both in Longwy earthenware tiles, are most eye-catching. Stylish bistro setting with a cuisine that highlights game in season.

Mansouria

11 r. Faidherbe (11th) – Ⓜ Faidherbe Chaligny – ✆ 01 43 71 00 16 – lollisoraya@yahoo.fr – Fax 01 40 24 21 97
closed 10-18 August, Monday lunch, Tuesday lunch and Sunday **D2**
Rest – Menu 30/46 € bi – Carte 30/49 €
♦ Moroccan ♦ Exotic ♦
Run by a former ethnologist, well-known in Paris in the field of Moroccan cuisine. The delicate, aromatic dishes are prepared by women and served in a Moorish surroundings.

Caroubier

82 bd Lefebvre (15th) – Ⓜ Porte de Vanves – ✆ 01 40 43 16 12 – Fax 01 40 43 16 12
closed 19 July-25 August and Monday **B3**
Rest – Menu 19 € (weekday lunch)/28 € – Carte 28/47 €
♦ Moroccan ♦
Modern decor enhanced with touches of the oriental. A family atmosphere and warm welcome presage generous helpings of sun-gorged Moroccan cuisine.

A et M Restaurant

136 bd Murat (16th) ✉ 75016 – Ⓜ Porte de St-Cloud – ✆ 01 45 27 39 60 – am-bistrot-16@wanadoo.fr – Fax 01 45 27 69 71
closed August, Saturday lunch and Sunday **A3**
Rest – Menu 30 € – Carte 35/48 €
♦ A la mode ♦ Fashionable ♦
Fashionable contemporary bistro close to the Seine. Tasteful colour scheme of creams and browns, designer lighting and carefully prepared up-to-date cuisine.

La Régalade

49 av. J. Moulin (14th) – Ⓜ Porte d'Orléans – ✆ 01 45 45 68 58 – la_regalade@yahoo.fr – Fax 01 45 40 96 74
closed 25 July-20 August, 1st-10 January, Monday lunch, Saturday and Sunday **B3**
Rest – *(pre-book)* Menu 32 €
♦ Bistro ♦
A welcoming smile, tasty country cuisine and a simple décor are the assets of this small bistro near the Porte de Châtillon.

Urbane

12 r. Arthur-Groussier (10th) – Ⓜ Goncourt – ✆ 01 42 40 74 75 – urbane.resto@gmail.com
closed 3 weeks in August, Saturday lunch, Sunday dinner and Monday **C2**
Rest – Menu 19 € (weekday lunch)/29 €
♦ Innovative ♦ Trendy ♦
A trendy, yet simply decorated restaurant (white walls, bistro-style furniture, imitation leather banquettes and industrial lamps). Modern dishes with an emphasis on quality ingredients.

Afaria

15 r. Desnouettes (15th) – Ⓜ Convention – ✆ 01 48 56 15 36 – Fax 01 48 56 15 36
closed 24-30 December, 3-24 August, Sunday and Monday lunch **A-B3**
Rest – Menu 27 € (lunch) – Carte 30/49 €
♦ South-western France ♦
Find tasty, well-prepared cuisine from southwest France in this bistro inspired restaurant (striped tablecloths and large mirrors). Drinks and tapas at the bar.

Le Grand Pan

20 r. Rosenwald (15th) – Ⓜ Plaisance – ✆ 01 42 50 02 50 – Fax 01 42 50 02 66
closed 1st-24 August, Christmas holidays, Saturday and Sunday **B3**
Rest – Menu 28/32 €
♦ Meat specialities ♦ Bistro ♦
Old-fashioned Parisian bistro (copper-topped bar, wood tables and blackboards) decorated in warm shades of brown. Meat specialities (game in season) and soup starter.

Le Dirigeable VISA MC AE

37 r. d' Alleray (15th) – Ⓜ Vaugirard – ✆ 01 45 32 01 54
closed 1st-24 August, 24-31 December, Sunday and Monday **B3**
Rest – Menu 22 € (lunch) – Carte 30/52 €
♦ Friendly ♦
Relaxed atmosphere, unpretentious setting and small traditional dishes at attractive prices: embark now for a cruise on the Dirigeable!

La Cave Gourmande AC VISA MC

10 r. Gén. Brunet (19th) – Ⓜ Botzaris – ✆ 01 40 40 03 30
– lacavegourmande@wanadoo.fr – Fax 01 40 40 03 30
closed 1st-24 August, February holidays, Saturday lunch and Sunday **D1**
Rest – Menu 31/36 €
♦ Bistro ♦
A friendly ambience, decorative bottle racks, wooden tables and market-inspired dishes are the main features of this pleasant bistro near the Buttes-Chaumont park.

Le Bistrot des Soupirs "Chez les On" VISA MC

49 r. Chine (20th) – Ⓜ Gambetta – ✆ 01 44 62 93 31 – Fax 01 44 62 77 83
closed 1st-10 May, 5-25 August, 25 December-1st January, Sunday and Monday
Rest – Menu 16 € (lunch), 35/50 € – Carte 28/43 € **D2**
♦ Bistro ♦
Next to the picturesque Soupirs lane, Auvergne and Lyons specialities take pride of place in this pleasant countrified inn. Resolutely jovial in spirit.

LA DÉFENSE *Plan I*

Pullman La Défense rm AC rm VISA MC AE

11 av. Arche (Défense 6 exit) ✉ 92081 – ✆ 01 47 17 50 00
– h3013@accor.com – Fax 01 47 17 56 78 – www.pullman-hotels.com
368 rm – 380 € 380 €, 25 € – 16 suites
Rest *Avant Seine* – rôtisserie – *✆ 01 47 17 50 99 (closed 5-20 August, 20-27 December, Friday dinner, Saturday, Sunday and public holidays)*
Carte approx. 51 €
♦ Chain hotel ♦ Luxury ♦ Stylish ♦
Beautiful architecture, resembling a ship's hull, a combination of glass and ochre stonework. Spacious, elegant rooms, lounges and very well-equipped auditorium (with simultaneous translation booths). The Avant Seine offers you quality designer décor and spit-roast dishes.

Renaissance rm AC rm VISA MC AE

60 Jardin de Valmy (on the circular road, exit La Défense 7) ✉ 92918
– ✆ 01 41 97 50 50 – rhi.parld.exec.sec@renaissancehotels.com – Fax 01 41 97 51 51
– www.renaissancehotels.com/parld
324 rm – 210/450 € 210/450 €, 25 € – 3 suites
Rest – *(closed Saturday lunch, Sunday lunch and public holidays lunch)* Menu 31 € – Carte 32/59 €
♦ Chain hotel ♦ Luxury ♦ Cosy ♦
At the foot of the Carrare marble Grande Arche, this contemporary hotel has well-equipped rooms, with refined decoration. Good fitness facilities. In the restaurant, all-wood features with a "retro" brasserie atmosphere and a view of the gardens of Valmy.

Hilton La Défense rm AC rm P VISA MC AE

2 pl. de la Défense ✉ 92053 – ✆ 01 46 92 10 10
– parldhirm@hilton.com – Fax 01 46 92 10 50 – www.hilton.com
139 rm – 245/550 € 245/550 €, 26 € – 6 suites
Rest *Coté Parvis* – *✆ 01 46 92 10 30* – Menu 56 € bi – Carte 31/65 €
♦ Chain hotel ♦ Business ♦ Modern ♦
Hotel situated within the CNIT complex. Some warmly decorated, designer-style rooms ideal for the business traveller. At Côté Parvis, modern cuisine and fine views.

Sofitel Centre

34 cours Michelet (via ring road, La Défense 4 exit) ✉ 92060 Puteaux – ☎ 01 47 76 44 43 – h0912@accor.com – Fax 01 47 76 72 10 – http://sofitel-paris-ladefense-centre.com

150 rm – 115/540 € 115/540 €, ☕ 27 € – 1 suite

Rest *L'Italian Lounge* – ☎ *01 47 76 72 40* – Carte 40/63 €

◆ Chain hotel ◆ Business ◆ Design ◆

The scalloped façade of this hotel stands out amid the skyscrapers of la Défense. Spacious, well-equipped rooms, which have been refurbished in a more trendy style. A contemporary setting for Mediterranean cuisine and an attractive choice of house wines. A relaxed atmosphere pervades the Italian Lounge.

Novotel La Défense

2 bd Neuilly (Défense 1 exit) – ☎ 01 41 45 23 23 – h0747@accor.com – Fax 01 41 45 23 24 – www.novotel.com **A1**

280 rm – 184/340 € 184/420 €, ☕ 16 €

Rest – buffet – Carte 21/43 €

◆ Chain hotel ◆ Business ◆ Classic ◆

Sculpture and architecture: La Défense, a veritable open-air museum, is right at the foot of this hotel. Practical rooms, some overlooking Paris. The bar has a trendy new décor. Contemporary décor in the dining room, which also has a buffet area.

PARIS AIRPORTS

Orly

Hilton Orly

(near Orly Sud airport) ✉ 94544 – ☎ 01 45 12 45 12 – rm.orly@hilton.com – Fax 01 45 12 45 00 – www.hilton.fr

351 rm – 130/215 € 130/230 €, ☕ 19 €

Rest – brasserie – Menu 35 € (weekdays) – Carte 22/56 €

◆ Chain hotel ◆Functional◆

A popular choice for corporate clients, this 1960s hotel has a designer interior, discreet yet elegant bedrooms and state of the art business facilities. Modern, entirely revamped decor and a classic menu.

Mercure

aérogare ✉ 94547 – ☎ 01 49 75 15 50 – h1246@accor.com – Fax 01 49 75 15 51 – www.mercure.com

192 rm – 79/215 € 89/225 €, ☕ 13.50 €

Rest – Menu 25 € – Carte approx. 32 €

◆ Chain hotel ◆Functional◆

Convenient for travellers between flights. Smiling staff, pleasant verdant setting and above all, well-kept, gradually refurbished rooms. Bar snacks and traditional dishes adapted to the timetables of travellers in transit.

Roissy-en-France

Z. I. Paris Nord II

Hyatt Regency

351 av. Bois de la Pie – ☎ 01 48 17 12 34 – cdg@hyattintl.com – Fax 01 48 17 17 17 – www.paris.charlesdegaulle.hyatt.com

376 rm – 550/725 € 550/725 €, ☕ 27 € – 12 suites

Rest – lunch buffet – Menu 46 € – Carte 52/72 €

◆ Chain hotel ◆ Business ◆ Modern ◆

Spectacular, contemporary architecture in a good location close to the airport. Large, stylish bedrooms equipped with ultra-modern facilities for its predominantly corporate guests. Enjoy buffet cuisine or classic à la carte choices in the Hyatt Regency's glass-ceilinged restaurant.

à l'aérogare nº 2

Sheraton

– *01 49 19 70 70 – Fax 01 49 19 70 71*
– *www.sheraton.com/parisairport*
254 rm – 199/599 € 199/999 €, 30 €
Rest *Les Étoiles* – *01 41 84 64 54 (closed 28 July-31 August, Saturday, Sunday and public holidays)* Menu 57 € – Carte 67/86 €
Rest *Les Saisons* – Menu 43/49 €
♦ Chain hotel ♦ Business ♦ Modern ♦

Leave your plane or train and take a trip on this "luxury liner" with its futuristic architecture. Décor by Andrée Putman, a view of the runways, absolute quiet and refined rooms. Les Étoiles offers modern cuisine and beautiful contemporary setting. Brasserie dishes at Les Saisons.

à Roissypole

Hilton

– *01 49 19 77 77 – cdghitwsal@hilton.com*
– *Fax 01 49 19 77 78*
385 rm – 159/759 € 159/1059 €, 24 €
Rest *Les Aviateurs* – *01 49 19 77 95* – Menu 37/47 € – Carte 31/65 €
♦ Chain hotel ♦ Business ♦ Modern ♦

Daring architecture, space and light are the main features of this hotel. Its ultra-modern facilities make it an ideal place in which to work and relax. The Aviateurs offers a small choice of brasserie dishes.

Pullman

Zone centrale Ouest – 01 49 19 29 29 – h0577@accor.com
– *Fax 01 49 19 29 00 – www.pullmanhotels.com*
342 rm – 290/345 € 320/375 €, 25 € – 8 suites
Rest *L'Escale* – Menu 31/45 € – Carte 30/72 €
♦ Chain hotel ♦ Business ♦ Modern ♦

A personal welcome, comfortable atmosphere, conference rooms, an elegant bar and well-looked-after rooms are the advantages of this hotel between two airport terminals. A restaurant with a nautical flavour and seafood. A pleasant port of call dedicated to the sea.

à Roissy-Ville

Courtyard by Marriott

allée du Verger – 01 34 38 53 53
– *alexander.krips@courtyard.com – Fax 01 34 38 53 54*
– *www.marriott.com*
300 rm – 169/259 € 169/259 €, 22 € – 4 suites
Rest – Menu 35 € – Carte 33/58 €
♦ Business ♦ Modern ♦

Behind its colonnaded white façade, this establishment has modern facilities perfectly in tune with the requirements of businessmen transiting through Paris. Themed brasserie menu served in a large and carefully decorated dining room.

Millennium

allée du Verger – 01 34 29 33 33 – sales.cdg@mill-cop.com
– *Fax 01 34 29 03 05 – www.millenniumhotels.com*
239 rm – 380 € 380/500 €, 20 €
Rest – Menu 40 € – Carte 28/46 €
♦ Business ♦ Modern ♦

Bar, Irish pub, fitness centre, attractive swimming pool, conference rooms, and spacious bedrooms with one floor specially equipped for businessmen: a hotel with good facilities. International cuisine and brasserie buffet or fast food served at the bar.

Novotel Convention et Wellness

allée des Vergers – ✆ 01 30 18 20 00 – h5418@accor.com – Fax 01 34 29 95 60 – www.novotel.com

288 rm – †99/290 € ††99/290 €, ☕ 18 € – 1 suite

Rest – Menu 24/27 € – Carte 28/44 €

♦ Chain hotel ♦ Business ♦ Modern ♦

The latest arrival in the hotel zone at Roissy offers impressive services: extensive seminar facilities, kids' corner and comprehensive wellness centre. Lenôtre brasserie dishes available twenty-four hours a day at Novotel Café and Côté Jardin.

Mercure

allée des Vergers – ✆ 01 34 29 40 00 – h1245@accor.com – Fax 01 34 29 00 18 – www.mercure.com

203 rm – †89/210 € ††99/250 €, ☕ 14 €

Rest – Carte 27/44 €

♦ Chain hotel ♦ Business ♦ Modern ♦

This hotel has a meticulous décor comprising Provençal style in the hall, old-fashioned zinc in the bar and spacious rooms in light wood. A contemporary menu that changes with the seasons served in the pleasant dining room or on the terrace overlooking the garden.

Lyons

Lyon

Population (est.2005): 468 000 (conurbation 1 449 000) Altitude: 175m

onos/PHOTONONSTOP

Lyons is a city that needs a second look. The first may be to its disadvantage: from the outlying autoroute, passers speeding by get a vision of the petrochemical industry. But strip away that industrial façade and look what lies within: the gastronomic epicentre of France; a wonderfully characterful old town with medieval and Renaissance buildings plus a World Heritage Site stamp of approval; and the peaceful flow of not one but two great rivers, the Rhône and the Saône.

Lyons has been a wealthy place since the Roman Empire, but it really came of age in the sixteenth century thanks to its silk industry; many of the city's finest buildings were erected by Italian silk merchants who flocked here at the time. What they left behind was the largest Renaissance quarter in France, with glorious architecture and an imposing cathedral. Much of this character could have been lost when demolition of the old town was threatened, but an enlightened twentieth century mayor instead made it safe, sanitary and a living embodiment of the past. Nowadays it's an energised city whose modern industries give it a twenty first century buzz – on the outside. But that feeling hasn't pervaded the three-hour lunch ethos of the older quarters: there are more restaurants per square metre of the old town than anywhere else on earth. Step inside a Lyonnais bouchon for a real encounter with the city…

LIVING THE CITY

Two great waterways, the rivers **Saône** (west) and **Rhône** (east) have their confluence in Lyons, and provide the liquid heart of the city. Modern Lyons in the shape of the shiny new Villeurbanne and La Part Dieu districts are to the east of the Rhône. The medieval sector, the old town, is west of the Saône.

Between the two rivers is a peninsula, the **Presqu'ile**, which is indeed almost an island, and appears on maps like an extended tongue. This area is renowned for its red-roofed sixteenth and seventeenth century houses. Just north of here on a hill is the old silk-weavers' district, La Croix-Rousse.

PRACTICAL INFORMATION

ARRIVAL-DEPARTURE

Lyon-Saint-Exupéry Airport is 27km east of the city centre. The Express Bus takes 45min and runs every 20min. A taxi will cost around € 45.

TRANSPORT

The transport system in the city even includes the funicular, as well as bus, tram and metro. The 'Liberty' ticket is valid for one day for travel on the network. You can also buy single tickets and a carnet of ten tickets.

The Lyons City Card is available for one, two or three days, and grants unlimited access to the transport network, plus nineteen museums (including the Roman ruins in St-Romain-en-Gal), short river trips and guided city tours. The card is available from the tourist office and major public transport offices.

Lyons boasts one of Europe's biggest 'swipe a bike' schemes: with a smart card, you help yourself to a cycle at two hundred places around town, at a flat rate for every hour in which you're pedalling.

EXPLORING LYONS

So you've worked your way into the heart of Lyons past the not-so-endearing outskirts. Standing in the Presqu'ile, you can see why France's second biggest city made its name in history. The two rivers holding you in their grip ensured this old Roman town evolved into an essential stopover for Renaissance merchants arriving from Italy and northern Europe. Lyons became the French land and river trade capital, and four annual fairs took place here, ensnaring merchants from all over the continent. But you'll need to take one of the city's twenty-eight bridges, and cross the Saône into the old town, to discover where Lyons' ancient heart really began to beat.

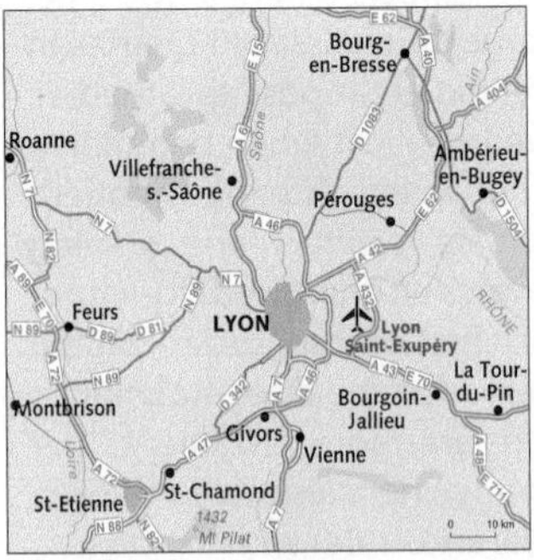

→ TRIPS ALONG THE TRABOULES

Old town is made up of three villages: **St-Georges, St-Jean**, and **St-Paul**. The characterful streets are pressed close together displaying a winning picture of medieval and Renaissance facades, interspersed with narrow alleys, paved courtyards, Italian built towers, and dozens of restaurants to settle into and absorb the atmosphere. Many diners will be enjoying the rest after taking on another element of the old town that's unique to Lyons: the traboules, or tunnelled passageways leading to courtyards open to the sky. There are more than three hundred of these shortcuts through ancient buildings, built in the 15C to make the transport of silk easier in rainy weather. Many traboules wind their way around the Croix-Rousse district as well as the old town, but you'll get lost trying to locate these fascinating medieval tunnels unless you've got a special traboule guide from the tourist office in your hand. The longest, by the way, is at number 27 in the old town's enchanting Rue du Boeuf.

→ OLD TREASURES

If you like your landmarks to be a little bit more familiar than the traboules, then you can't do much better than the old town's two massive churches. St Jean Cathedral is an imposing Gothic structure built from the 12C to the 15C, and boasts eight hundred year old stained glass above the altar and in the rose windows. Its main glory, though, is an astronomical clock built by 14C monks to calculate thousands of moveable feast days, such as Easter. Amazingly, it'll stop its workings in 2019 when its seven-hundred-year programme runs out! Up on Fourvière hill (reached by funicular) behind the Cathedral is an even more conspicuous pile: the **Notre-Dame Basilica** of Fourvière, built in the 19C. It's a monumental church with an outlandish interior that throws together marble and mosaics in an anarchic free for all, and the outside is a bit of a wedding cake, too. Best thing about your journey up here is the superb view you get of the city ranged below, showing the sweep of the rivers and the distinguishing marks of the different quartiers. Other highlights of the old town include the remains of two ruined Roman theatres, close to the basilica, and, from the other end of the cultural compass, an entertaining Marionnette Museum, whose biggest draw is the 18C Lyonnais creations Guignol and Madelon, the famous puppets who embody the spirit of the local people.

→ ALMOST PERFECT!

The Presqu'ile is dominated by its great red-sanded square Place Bellecour: it's a vast space, with good views across the Saône to the basilica. It has some interesting streets running off it: to the south the rue Auguste Comte is an antiquarian's heaven. This is the place to come if you're looking for a French Regency sideboard, Louis XVI armchair, tapestry or early edition of Voltaire. More than one hundred antiques shops are nestled around here. Meanwhile, running parallel is Rue Victor Hugo, renowned for its stylish, contemporary boutiques. North of the Place Bellecour, a leisurely stroll takes you to possibly Lyons' most beautiful square, **Place des Terreaux**, an arresting space with magnificent fountains and a mighty hôtel de ville. It also lays claim to the **Musée des Beaux-Arts**, which just happens to be rated the best art collection in France outside the Louvre. You name it: they've got it, from Tintoretto, El Greco and Rubens, to Picasso, Matisse, Canova and Rodin. The museum also includes an eye-catching collection of medieval woodcarvings, plus an eclectic range of objets d'art and antiquities.

→ A TISSUS

A more unexpected highlight of the Presqu'ile is to be found back south of Place Bellecour: the **Musée des Tissus** is considered by many - despite the competition - to be the best in Lyons. It tells the story of silk, with luxurious 17C to 19C hangings produced in Lyons, including those from a rather impressive client list that includes Marie-Antoinette, Empress Josephine, and Catherine the Great of Russia. It's not just local silks that are on display; there are also superb examples from Baghdad, as well as carpets from Iran, Turkey and India, and beautifully artistic decorative work from almost two thousand years ago. Afterwards, you'll probably be tempted to venture up to La Croix-Rousse, the old silk-weavers' district north of Place des Terreaux. Only a few looms still operate in the neighbourhood, but if you attempt the long ascent of Montée de la Grande Côte, you'll get a fair impression of what the area was like five hundred years ago. This is a quartier of many traboules and giant street murals depicting local life. At the top of **Croix-Rousse** (you can get there by metro) is a pleasant square of cafés and swaying trees, and, maybe best of all, grand city views.

→ FOOD AND WATER

Although Lyons is rightly renowned for its restaurants and bouchons, you can also grab your food on the hoof with confidence. A great bet is the bustling open-air market which runs along Quai des Célestins and St Antoine, two quays by the Saône in the heart of the Presqu'ile. Saunter along here and you can pick up any amount of French delicacies, including sausages, cakes, breads, hams, chocolates, fruits and jams. After lunch à pied, a good idea is to unwind on a river jaunt. Boats set off regularly along the Saône, travel around the southern end of the peninsula, and return by the Rhône. A night cruise is the top tip, when this beautifully illuminated city bathes its best bits in sumptuous light. If it's not too late, the ideal way to end the evening is a concert at Lyons' swanky Opera House, behind the hotel de ville. Its silver stairways are set off by a totally black interior, and its concerts range all the way from opera to jazz.

CALENDAR HIGHLIGHTS

As Lyons is famous for its gastronomy, what better than being here in October to celebrate Tasting Week? Chefs and cooks demonstrate their art, while markets and festivals bring the joys of Lyonnais' produce and recipes to one and all. The city's most time-honoured event occurs in December: it's the Festival of Lights, when a lantern lit procession, inaugurated in 1852, brings even more aura to the famously lauded illuminations of Lyons. Concerts and activities all add weight to this now four-day extravaganza. Also in December is the Vieux-Lyon Ancient Music Festival (at the Chapelle de la Trinité), which is one of the major events of its kind in

LYONS IN…

→ ONE DAY

Old town including funicular up Fourvière hill, Musée des Beaux-Arts, dining in a bouchon

→ TWO DAYS

Musée des Tissus, La Croix-Rousse, evening river trip, Opera House

→ THREE DAYS

Traboule hunting (map in hand), antique shops in rue Auguste Comte, meal in one of Lyons' famously starred restaurants

France, and features inspiring music by the likes of Mozart, Handel and Bach. On the same theme, Les Musicades (March) is an international chamber music festival which takes place in a number of venues around Lyons, while May's Nuits Sonores Panorama of Electronic Music is pretty much self-explanatory: electronic dance music through the night in various streets and squares. Les Estivales in May continues the musical thread, with a host of free events in outdoor spaces and parks; particularly noteworthy are the shows in the courtyard of the Hotel de Ville. Theatre and music dominates the Nuits de Fourvière Festival in June, when the two Roman amphitheatres on the hill provide an atmospheric setting. Day long street parties and fireworks (also on Fourvière Hill) provide the blistering backdrop to Bastille Day festivities in July. The action's fast and furious at September's Lyons Dance Biennial, with the dance traditions of twenty world cities being celebrated at twenty-three different venues, not to mention three hundred thousand parade-goers thronging the city streets. Things slow down to a more sedate air at the Red Carpet Antiques Festival (October) when a huge red carpet is thrown down on Rue Auguste Comte and all sorts of wonderful antiques are put on display for buyers and browsers.

EATING OUT

Lyons is a great place for eating. If your budget won't run to one of the smarter breed of restaurants, then pop into a local bouchon. These are the true gastronomic heart and soul of the city, atmospheric little establishments where the cuisine revolves round the sort of thing the silkworkers ate all those years ago: tripe, pigs' trotters, calf's head. Fish lovers will instead go for quenelles (fish dumplings); typical are quenelles de brochet of blended pike in a crayfish sauce. For the most atmospheric example of the bouchon, try and get to one in the tunnel-like recess inside a medieval building in the old town. Lyons also offers restaurants serving dishes from every region in France, as well as most places you can think of overseas. It's a city that loves its wine: it's said that Lyons is kept afloat on three rivers: the Saône, the Rhône, and the Beaujolais...Hours of repast in the city begin at 12.30 for lunch (and can continue for many an hour afterwards) and 7.30 in the evenings. With the reputation the city has for its restaurants, it's advisable to book ahead. The bill will include a service charge, but if you've been particularly happy with the service, then a tip of five to ten per cent is normal.

→ SPYING AS YOU'RE FRYING

On sunny summer days, the Lyonnais find their green relaxation in the Parc de la Tête d'Or, on the modern side of town east of the Rhône. Here there are ponds, botanical gardens, rose gardens and a small zoo. One curious interloper you can't miss: the spindly antennae overlooking the park that happens to be part of the international HQ of Interpol...

→ CORKING GOOD LUNCH

'Bouchon' is translated as 'cork'. The theory is that the buzzy local food hotspots acquired their name in the old days when corks from empty bottles were lined up along the bar and the waiter counted them to work out the bill. Earthy locals pour scorn on Parisians, who they believe have abandoned the concept of lunch. In Lyons, regulars at the bouchon embrace the three-hour midday meal with passion and flair.

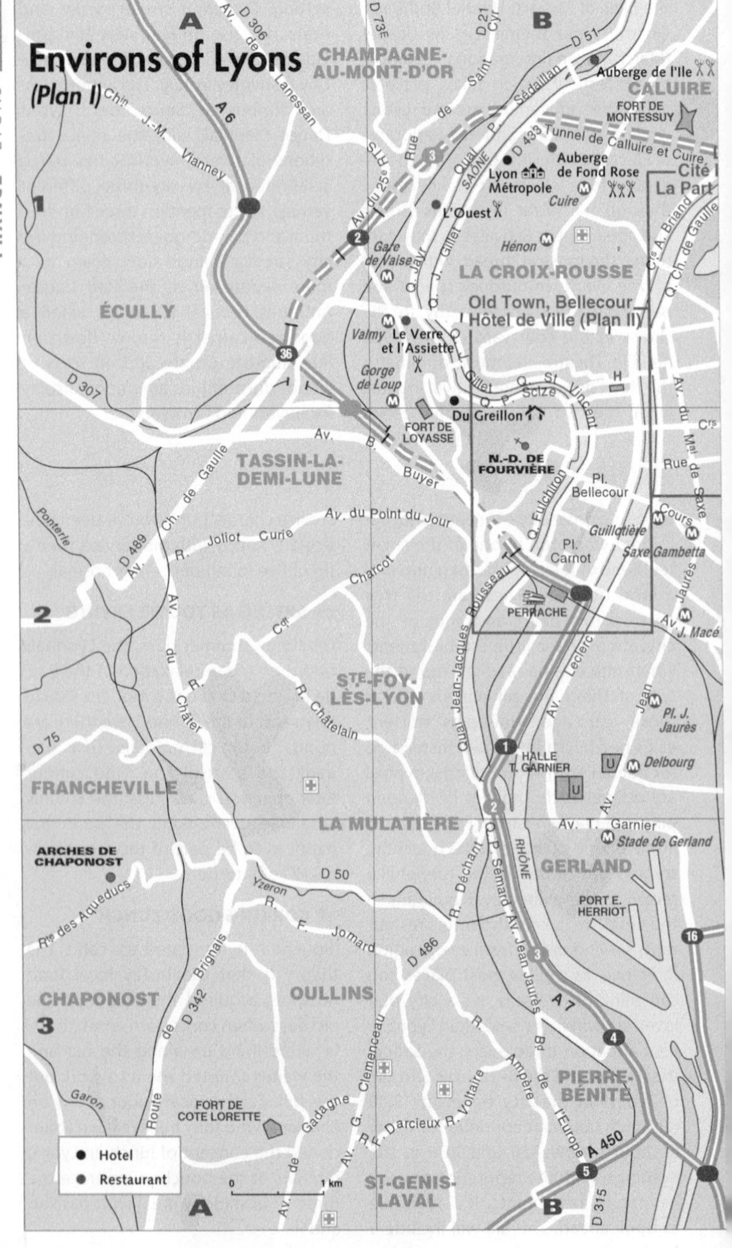
Environs of Lyons
(Plan I)
A
B
1
2
3
CHAMPAGNE-AU-MONT-D'OR
CALUIRE
FORT DE MONTESSUY
Auberge de l'Ile
Tunnel de Calluire et Cuire
Auberge de Fond Rose
Lyon Métropole
Cuire
L'Ouest
Hénon
LA CROIX-ROUSSE
Old Town, Bellecour
Hôtel de Ville (Plan II)
Gare de Vaise
ÉCULLY
Valmy
Le Verre et l'Assiette
Gorge de Loup
FORT DE LOYASSE
Du Greillon
N.-D. DE FOURVIÈRE
Pl. Bellecour
TASSIN-LA-DEMI-LUNE
Av. du Point du Jour
Guillotière
Saxe Gambetta
Pl. Carnot
PERRACHE
J. Macé
STE-FOY-LÈS-LYON
R. Châtelain
Pl. J. Jaurès
HALLE T. GARNIER
Delbourg
FRANCHEVILLE
LA MULATIÈRE
Av. T. Garnier
Stade de Gerland
ARCHES DE CHAPONOST
GERLAND
PORT E. HERRIOT
Rte des Aqueducs
D 50
Yzeron
R. F. Jomard
RHÔNE
A 7
OULLINS
CHAPONOST
FORT DE COTE LORETTE
PIERRE-BÉNITE
A 450
Hotel
Restaurant
ST-GENIS-LAVAL
D 315
D 307
D 489
D 75
D 342
D 486
A 6
D 306
D 51
Quai Jean-Jacques Rousseau
Av. Leclerc
Q. P. Sémard
Av. Jean Jaurès
Bd de l'Europe
R. Ampère
R. Voltaire
R. F. Darcieux
Av. G. Clemenceau
Av. de Gadagne
Route de Brignais
Av. du Châter
Av. Ch. de Gaulle
R. Joliot Curie
Cdt Charcot
Av. B. Buyer
Chin J.-M. Vianney
Av. de Lanessan
Av. du 25e RTS
Q. Jayr
Q. J. Gillet
Quai Saône
Q. St Vincent
Q. P. Scize
Q. Fulchiron
Cours Gambetta
Av. du Mal de Saxe
Q. Ch. de Gaulle
Crs A. Briand
Garon
R. Déchant
0
1 km

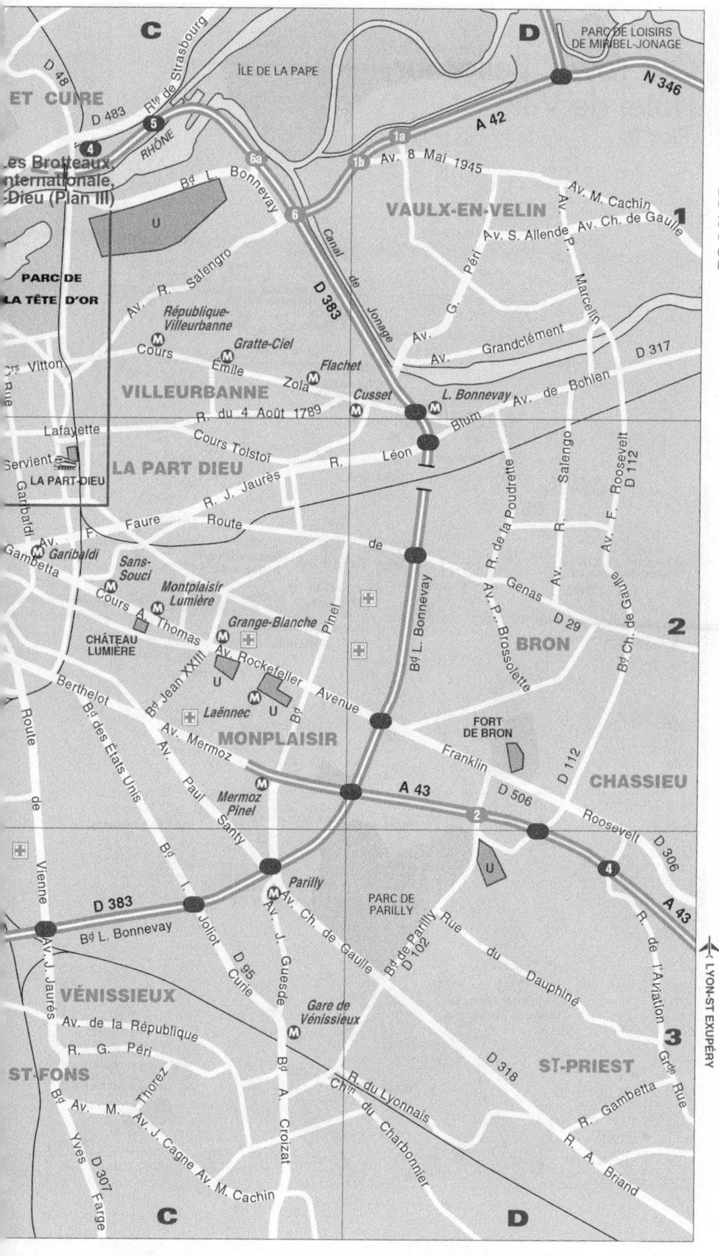
C
D
PARC DE LOISIRS DE MIRIBEL-JONAGE
ÎLE DE LA PAPE
N 346
A 42
D 48
ET CUIRE
D 483
Rte de Strasbourg
RHÔNE
Les Brotteaux, Internationale, Part-Dieu (Plan III)
Av. 8 Mai 1945
Bd L. Bonnevay
VAULX-EN-VELIN
Av. M. Cachin
Av. S. Allende
Av. Ch. de Gaulle
Av. P. Marcelin
Canal de Jonage
D 383
PARC DE LA TÊTE D'OR
Av. R. Salengro
République-Villeurbanne
Av. G. Péri
Av. Grandclément
D 317
Cours Émile Zola
Gratte-Ciel
Flachet
Crs Vitton
VILLEURBANNE
Cusset
L. Bonnevay
Av. de Bohlen
R. du 4 Août 1789
Lafayette
Cours Tolstoï
Blum
R. Léon
Servient
LA PART DIEU
R. J. Jaurès
R. de la Poudrette
Av. R. Salengo
Av. F. Roosevelt
D 112
Garibaldi
Av. F. Faure
Route de Genas
Gambetta
Sans-Souci
Montplaisir Lumière
Cours A. Thomas
Grange-Blanche
Pinel
Bd L. Bonnevay
Av. P. Brossolette
D 29
Bd Ch. de Gaulle
CHÂTEAU LUMIÈRE
BRON
Av. Rockefeller
Berthelot
Bd Jean XXIII
Laënnec
Avenue Franklin Roosevelt
Bd des États Unis
Av. Mermoz
MONPLAISIR
FORT DE BRON
Route de Vienne
Av. Paul Santy
Mermoz Pinel
A 43
D 506
D 112
CHASSIEU
D 306
Bd I. Joliot Curie
Parilly
PARC DE PARILLY
D 383
Bd L. Bonnevay
Av. Ch. de Gaulle
Bd de Parilly
D 102
Rue du Dauphiné
R. de l'Aviation
Av. J. Jaurès
D 95
Av. J. Guesde
VÉNISSIEUX
Gare de Vénissieux
Av. de la République
R. G. Péri
D 318
ST-PRIEST
ST-FONS
R. du Lyonnais
Chin du Charbonnier
Grde Rue
R. Gambetta
Bd Yves Farge
Av. M. Thorez
Bd A. Croizat
R. A. Briand
Av. J. Cagne
Av. M. Cachin
D 307
1
2
3
LYON-ST EXUPÉRY

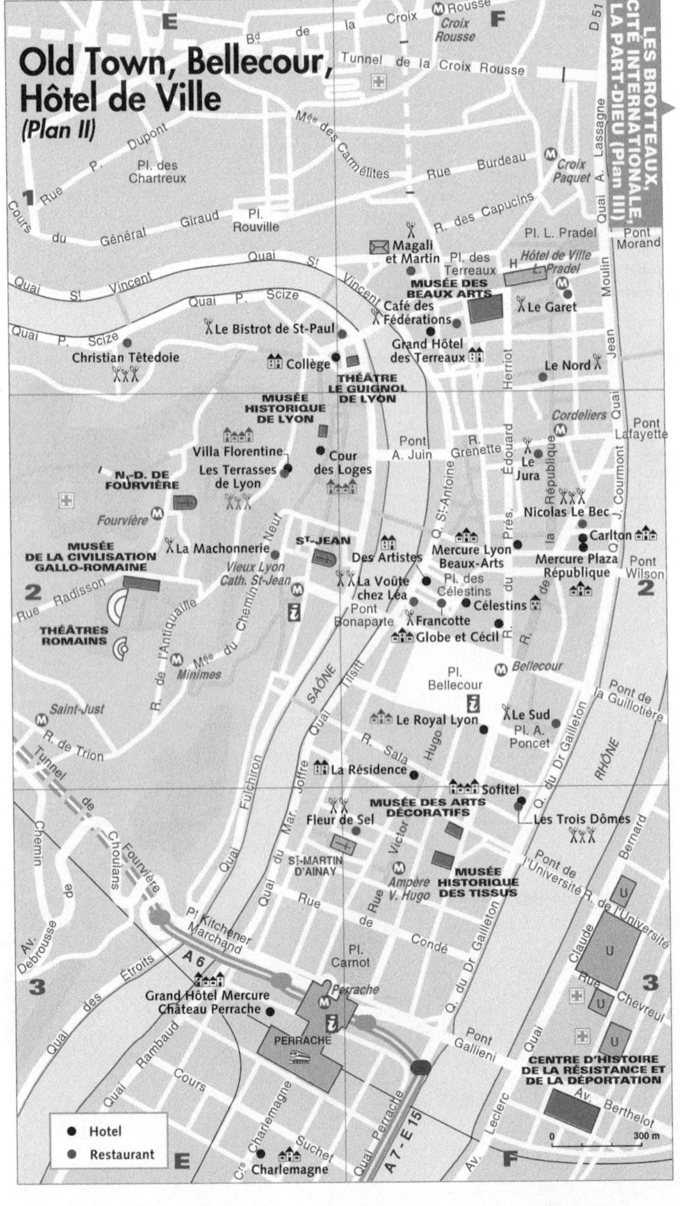
Old Town, Bellecour, Hôtel de Ville
(Plan II)
LES BROTTEAUX, CITÉ INTERNATIONALE, LA PART-DIEU (Plan III)
MUSÉE DES BEAUX ARTS
Magali et Martin
Café des Fédérations
Grand Hôtel des Terreaux
Le Garet
Le Nord
Le Bistrot de St-Paul
Christian Têtedoie
Collège
THÉÂTRE LE GUIGNOL DE LYON
MUSÉE HISTORIQUE DE LYON
Villa Florentine
Les Terrasses de Lyon
Cour des Loges
N.-D. DE FOURVIÈRE
Le Jura
Nicolas Le Bec
Carlton
Mercure Lyon Beaux-Arts
Mercure Plaza République
MUSÉE DE LA CIVILISATION GALLO-ROMAINE
La Machonnerie
ST-JEAN
Des Artistes
La Voûte chez Léa
Célestins
Francotte
Globe et Cécil
THÉÂTRES ROMAINS
Le Royal Lyon
Le Sud
La Résidence
Sofitel
Les Trois Dômes
MUSÉE DES ARTS DÉCORATIFS
Fleur de Sel
ST-MARTIN D'AINAY
MUSÉE HISTORIQUE DES TISSUS
Grand Hôtel Mercure Château Perrache
PERRACHE
CENTRE D'HISTOIRE DE LA RÉSISTANCE ET DE LA DÉPORTATION
Charlemagne
Hotel
Restaurant
300 m

TOWN CENTRE — Plan II

Sofitel VISA AE
20 quai Gailleton ✉ 69002 – Ⓜ Bellecour – ✆ 04 72 41 20 20 – h0553@accor.com – Fax 04 72 40 05 50 – www.sofitel.com **F3**
164 rm – 205/350 € 230/375 €, 26 € – 29 suites
Rest Les Trois Dômes – see below
Rest *Sofishop* – ✆ *04 72 41 20 80* – Menu 28 € (weekdays)/40 € – Carte 31/52 €
♦ Luxury ♦ Modern ♦
The cuboid exterior contrasts with the luxurious interior: contemporary rooms in good taste, modern conference facilities, smart shops and a hair-dressing salon. Brasserie atmosphere and fare at the Sofishop (oyster bar).

Le Royal Lyon without rest VISA AE
20 pl. Bellecour ✉ 69002 – Ⓜ Bellecour – ✆ 04 78 37 57 31 – h2952@accor.com – Fax 04 78 37 01 36 – www.lyonhotel-leroyal.com **F2**
77 rm – 210/450 € 290/450 €, 22 € – 3 suites
♦ Traditional ♦ Personalised ♦
After renovation, this 19C hotel run by the Paul Bocuse Institute has regained its former splendour. Magnificent rooms. The breakfast room is decorated in the manner of a kitchen.

Carlton without rest VISA AE
4 r. Jussieu ✉ 69002 – Ⓜ Cordeliers – ✆ 04 78 42 56 51 – h2950@accor.com – Fax 04 78 42 10 71 **F2**
83 rm – 89/199 € 99/209 €, 14 €
♦ Traditional ♦ Classical ♦
Purple and gold prevail in this traditional hotel, decorated in the manner of an old-fashioned luxury hotel. The period lift cage has a charm of its own. Comfortable rooms.

Globe et Cécil without rest VISA AE
21 r. Gasparin ✉ 69002 – Ⓜ Bellecour – ✆ 04 78 42 58 95 – accueil@globeetcecilhotel.com – Fax 04 72 41 99 06 – www.globeetcecilhotel.com
60 rm – 130/135 € 160/165 € **F2**
♦ Traditional ♦ Personalised ♦
One of the last silk-merchants of the town decorated the conference room of this hotel. Antique and modern furniture adorns the tastefully decorated rooms. Irresistible welcome.

Mercure Plaza République without rest
5 r. Stella ✉ 69002 – Ⓜ Cordeliers VISA AE
– ✆ 04 78 37 50 50 – h2951@accor.com – Fax 04 78 42 33 34 – www.mercure.com **F2**
78 rm – 109/169 € 119/179 €, 14 €
♦ Business ♦ Modern ♦
19C architecture, central location, modern interior, full range of comforts and conference facilities: a hotel especially popular with its business clientele.

Mercure Lyon Beaux-Arts without rest
75 r. Prés. E. Herriot ✉ 69002 – Ⓜ Cordeliers VISA AE
– ✆ 04 78 38 09 50 – h2949@accor.com – Fax 04 78 42 19 19 **F2**
75 rm – 109/179 € 119/189 €, 14 € – 4 suites
♦ Chain hotel ♦ Modern ♦
Beautiful building from 1900, most of the bedrooms are furnished in Art Deco style. Four are more unusual and are decorated by contemporary artists.

Grand Hôtel des Terreaux without rest
16 r. Lanterne ✉ 69001 – Ⓜ Hôtel de ville VISA AE
– ✆ 04 78 27 04 10 – ght@hotel-lyon.fr – Fax 04 78 27 97 75 – www.hotel-lyon.fr **F1**
53 rm – 85/105 € 115/164 €, 12 €
♦ Traditional ♦ Personalised ♦
Personalised, tastefully decorated rooms, a pretty indoor pool and attentive service ensure that guests can relax to the full in this former 19C post house.

Des Artistes without rest

8 r. G. André ✉ 69002 – Ⓜ Cordeliers – ☎ 04 78 42 04 88 – hartiste@club-internet.fr – Fax 04 78 42 93 76 – www.hoteldesartistes.fr **F2**

45 rm – †78/130 € ††90/140 €, ☕ 10 €

♦ Traditional ♦ Personalised ♦

The hotel is named after the "artistes" of the neighbouring Célestins theatre. Stylish rooms; a Cocteau style fresco adorns the breakfast room.

La Résidence without rest

18 r. V. Hugo ✉ 69002 – Ⓜ Bellecour – ☎ 04 78 42 63 28 – hotel-la-residence@wanadoo.fr – Fax 04 78 42 85 76 – www.hotel-la-residence.com **F2**

67 rm – †78 € ††78 €, ☕ 7 €

♦ Business ♦ Functional ♦

In a pedestrian street near Bellecour square, this hotel provides rooms and a lounge in a 1970s style. A few rooms are more elegant and graced with wainscoting.

Célestins without rest

4 r. Archers ✉ 69002 – Ⓜ Guillotière – ☎ 04 72 56 08 98 – info@hotelcelestins.com – Fax 04 72 56 08 65 – www.hotelcelestins.com **F2**

25 rm – †62/90 € ††68/100 €, ☕ 8 €

♦ Traditional ♦Cosy♦

Hotel occupying several floors in a residential building. Light rooms with simple furnishings; those at the front have a view over the Fourvière hillside.

Nicolas Le Bec

14 r. Grolée ✉ 69002 – Ⓜ Cordeliers – ☎ 04 78 42 15 00 – restaurant@nicolaslebec.com – Fax 04 72 40 98 97 – www.nicolaslebec.com

closed 3-24 August, 1st-11 January, Sunday, Monday and public holidays

Rest – Menu 58 € (weekday lunch), 98/148 € – Carte 75/100 € **F2**

Spec. Foie gras, anguille fumée et asperges vertes au bouillon de poule. Homard breton poché minute. Tartelette au caramel mou.

♦ Design ♦

Restaurant with a modern welcoming feel, serving food that is as refined as it is subtle. Wine list rejoicing in the nation's diversity; smoking lounge.

Les Trois Dômes – Hôtel Sofitel — < Lyon

20 quai Gailleton ✉ 69002 – Ⓜ Bellecour – ☎ 04 72 41 20 97 – reservation@les-3-domes.com – Fax 04 72 40 05 50 – www.les-trois-domes.com

closed 27 July-28 August, 24 February-4 March, Sunday and Monday **F3**

Rest – Menu 53 € (weekday lunch), 75/143 € bi – Carte 92/121 €

Spec. Quenelle de brochet soufflée, écrevisses, coques et palourdes. Saint-Jacques au thé vert et parfum de truffe (end December to mid February). Agneau de lait au pistou, poupeton d'aubergine et fèves (end January to mid May).

♦ Formal ♦

Admire the matchless panorama from the top floor of the Sofitel hotel, where you can also enjoy delicious cuisine in keeping with current tastes. Flawless wine list.

Fleur de Sel

3 r. Remparts d'Ainay ✉ 69002 – Ⓜ Ampère Victor Hugo – ☎ 04 78 37 40 37 – Fax 04 78 37 26 37 – www.fleurdesel-restaurant.fr

closed August, Sunday and Monday **F3**

Rest – Menu 19/29 € – Carte 22/43 €

♦ Cosy ♦

The light gently filters through the green and yellow curtains of this vast plush dining room. Personalised up-to-date cooking, inspired by spices from near and far.

La Voûte - Chez Léa

11 pl. A. Gourju ✉ 69002 – Ⓜ Bellecour – ☎ 04 78 42 01 33 – Fax 04 78 37 36 41

closed Sunday **F2**

Rest – Menu 19 € (weekday lunch), 28/40 € – Carte 29/48 €

♦ Friendly ♦

One of the oldest restaurants in Lyons, it continues to brilliantly uphold the region's gastronomic traditions. Welcoming ambience and décor. Game menu in autumn.

Le Nord

AC VISA MC AE

18 r. Neuve ✉ 69002 – Ⓜ Hôtel de ville – ✆ 04 72 10 69 69 – commercial@brasseries-bocuse.com – Fax 04 72 10 69 68 – www.bocuse.fr **F1**

Rest – Menu 23 (weekdays)/28 € – Carte 26/55 €

◆ Brasserie ◆

Authentic 1900s décor in the first of Bocuse's brasseries: banquettes, colourful tiled floor, wood panelling and spherical lamps. Traditional cuisine.

Le Sud

AC VISA MC AE

11 pl. Antonin Poncet ✉ 69002 – Ⓜ Bellecour – ✆ 04 72 77 80 00 – Fax 04 72 77 80 01 – www.bocuse.fr **F2**

Rest – Menu 23 (weekdays)/28 € – Carte 30/48 €

◆ Brasserie ◆

"Le Sud" is another of chef Paul Bocuse's creations, with Mediterranean cuisine and décor. Delightful summer terrace overlooking the square.

Francotte

AC VISA MC AE

8 pl. Célestins ✉ 69002 – Ⓜ Bellecour – ✆ 04 78 37 38 64 – infos@francotte.fr – Fax 04 78 38 20 35 – www.francotte.fr
closed 1st-20 August, Sunday and Monday **F2**

Rest – Menu 23/33 € – Carte 28/43 €

◆ Neighbourhood ◆

Brasserie-style cuisine in a bistro/bouchon-inspired setting adorned with photos of matriarchs and famous chefs from the region. Breakfasts served in the morning; tea room in the afternoon.

Magali et Martin

AC VISA MC

11 r. des Augustins ✉ 69001 – Ⓜ Place des Terreaux – ✆ 04 72 00 88 01
closed 4-24 August, 24 December-14 January, Saturday and Sunday **F1**

Rest – Menu 19 € (lunch), 28/50 € – Carte 27/36 €

Magali is in charge of welcoming guests and advising them on their choice of wine. Martin for his part is responsible for the tasty cuisine inspired by local market produce. A winning duet!

BOUCHONS *Regional wine tasting and local cuisine in a typical Lyonnais atmosphere*

Daniel et Denise

AC VISA MC AE

156 r. Créqui ✉ 69003 – Ⓜ Place Guichard – ✆ 04 78 60 66 53 – Fax 04 78 60 66 53 – www.daniel-et-denise.fr
Closed August, 23 December-3 January, Saturday, Sunday and public holidays

Rest – Carte 28/41 € **G3**

◆ Lyons cuisine ◆ Bistro ◆

Attractive well-worn setting and a relaxed informal atmosphere in this welcoming bistro, that serves traditionally prepared tasty Lyon specialities.

Le Garet

AC VISA MC AE

7 r. Garet ✉ 69001 – Ⓜ Hôtel de ville – ✆ 04 78 28 16 94 – legaret@wanadoo.fr – Fax 04 72 00 06 84
closed 25 July-25 August, 14-22 February, Saturday and Sunday **F1**

Rest – *(pre-book)* Menu 18 € (lunch)/23 € – Carte 20/35 €

◆ Bistro ◆

This institution in Lyon is well-known to lovers of good cooking: calf's head, tripe, quenelles and andouillettes served in a relaxed characteristic setting.

Café des Fédérations

AC VISA MC

8 r. Major Martin ✉ 69001 – Ⓜ Hôtel de ville – ✆ 04 78 28 26 00 – yr@lesfedeslyon.com – Fax 04 72 07 74 52 – www.lesfedeslyon.com
closed 22 December-2 January and Sunday **F1**

Rest – *(pre-book)* Menu 20 (lunch)/24 €

◆ Lyons cuisine ◆ Bistro ◆

Checked tablecloths, tightly packed tables, giant sausages hanging from the ceiling and a relaxed informal atmosphere: a genuine "bouchon" for sure!

Le Jura

25 r. Tupin ✉ 69002 – Ⓜ Cordeliers – ✆ 04 78 42 20 57
closed August, Monday from September to April, Saturday from May to September and Sunday **F2**
Rest – *(pre-book)* Menu 20 € – Carte 25/38 €
◆ Lyons cuisine ◆ Bistro ◆
This authentic "bouchon", in existence since 1864, has scrupulously preserved a stylish 1930s décor. Traditional tasty dishes of Lyons.

OLD TOWN *Plan II*

Villa Florentine

< Lyon,

25 montée St-Barthélémy ✉ 69005
– Ⓜ Fourvière – ✆ 04 72 56 56 56 – florentine@relaischateaux.com
– Fax 04 72 40 90 56 – www.villaflorentine.com **E2**
20 rm – 160/410 € 160/410 €, 24 € – 8 suites
Rest *Les Terrasses de Lyon* – see below
◆ Luxury ◆ Personalised ◆
On the Fourvière hill, this Renaissance-inspired abode commands a matchless view of the town. The interior sports an elegant blend of old and new.

Cour des Loges

rm

6 r. Boeuf ✉ 69005 – Ⓜ Vieux Lyon Cathédrale Saint-Jean
– ✆ 04 72 77 44 44 – contact@courdesloges.com – Fax 04 72 40 93 61
– www.courdesloges.com **E2**
58 rm – 240/290 € 240/290 €, 27 € – 4 suites
Rest *Les Loges* – *(closed July, August, Sunday and Monday) (dinner only)*
Menu 55/80 € – Carte 69/82 €
◆ Luxury ◆ Personalised ◆
An exceptional group of 14C-18C houses set around a splendid galleried courtyard have been decorated by contemporary designers and artists. Creative cuisine and décor with a personal touch.

Collège without rest

5 pl. St Paul ✉ 69005 – Ⓜ Vieux Lyon Cathédrale St-Jean
– ✆ 04 72 10 05 05 – contact@college-hotel.com – Fax 04 78 27 98 84
– www.college-hotel.com **E1**
39 rm – 105/125 € 125/140 €, 12 €
◆ Business ◆ Minimalist ◆
Take a trip down memory lane: old-fashioned school desks, a pommel horse and geography maps. The rooms are white, resolutely modern, with a balcony or terrace.

Les Terrasses de Lyon – Hôtel Villa Florentine

< Lyon,

25 montée St-Barthélémy ✉ 69005
– Ⓜ Fourvière – ✆ 04 72 56 56 56 – lesterrassesdelyon@villaflorentine.com
– Fax 04 72 40 90 56 – www.villaflorentine.com
closed Sunday and Monday **E2**
Rest – Menu 48 (weekday lunch except July-August)/104 €
– Carte 84/127 €
Spec. Homard en fine gelée, tartine de guacamole et barigoule de légumes. Darne de turbot rôti à la fève de cacao, pommes soufflées. Filet de boeuf de Salers cuit au sautoir, jus corsé au vieux vinaigre de vin.
◆ Formal ◆
Breathtaking view of Lyon from the terrace. The interior and conservatory are stylish and the modern cuisine subtly enhances excellent produce.

Christian Têtedoie

54 quai Pierre Scize ✉ 69005 – ✆ 04 78 29 40 10 – restaurant@tetedoie.com – Fax 04 72 07 05 65 – www.tetedoie.com

closed 4-24 August, 16-22 February, Saturday lunch, Monday lunch and Sunday **E1**

Rest – Menu 48 € (weekdays)/80 € – Carte 64/76 €

Spec. Fraîcheur de concombre aux agrumes, coquillages et homard (spring-summer). Pastilla de pigeonneau rôti aux agrumes et fleur d'oranger. Carpaccio de figues au vinaigre de Banyuls.

◆ Formal ◆

On the banks of the Saône, this smart cosy restaurant sports a happy mix of old and new. Contemporary cuisine and a magnificent wine list with over 700 appellations.

La Machonnerie

36 r. Tramassac ✉ 69005 – Ⓜ Ampère Victor Hugo – ✆ 04 78 42 24 62 – felix@lamachonnerie.com – Fax 04 72 40 23 32 – www.lamachonnerie.com

closed 15-30 July, 2 weeks in January, Sunday and lunch except Saturday **E2**

Rest – *(pre-book)* Menu 20/43 € bi – Carte 25/47 €

◆ Lyons cuisine ◆ Rustic ◆

The traditions of informal service, a friendly atmosphere and authentic regional cuisine are perpetuated in this typical neighbourhood "mâchon". Attractive lounge devoted to jazz.

Le Bistrot de St-Paul

2 quai de Bondy ✉ 69005 – Ⓜ Vieux Lyon Cathédrale St-Jean – ✆ 04 78 28 63 19 – jplabaste@orange.fr – Fax 04 78 28 63 19 – www.bistrotdesaintpaul.fr

closed 1st-7 May, 1st-23 August, Saturday lunch from 15 May to 15 September and Sunday **F1**

Rest – Menu 13.50 € (weekday lunch), 20/31 € – Carte 32/57 €

◆ South-western France ◆

Cassoulet, duck breast, Bordeaux and Cahors wines, etc.: the essence of south-west France in this friendly bistro on an embankment of the Saône.

PERRACHE

Plan II

Grand Hôtel Mercure Château Perrache

12 cours Verdun ✉ 69002 – Ⓜ Perrache – ✆ 04 72 77 15 00 – h1292@accor.com – Fax 04 78 37 06 56 – www.mercure.com **E3**

111 rm – 145/195 € 145/195 €, 14 € – 2 suites

Rest *Les Belles Saisons* – *(closed 25 July-25 August, weekends and holidays)* Carte 25/35 €

◆ Traditional ◆ Art Deco ◆

This hotel built in 1900 has partially conserved its Art Nouveau setting: intricate wood carving in the lobby and period furniture in some of the rooms and suites. The full effect of the Majorelle style is reflected in this superb restaurant.

Charlemagne

23 cours Charlemagne ✉ 69002 – Ⓜ Perrache – ✆ 04 72 77 70 00 – charlemagne@hotel-lyon.fr – Fax 04 78 42 94 84 – www.charlemagne-hotel.fr **E3**

116 rm – 80/155 € 85/170 €, 10 €

Rest – *(closed Saturday and Sunday)* Menu 22 € – Carte 24/31 €

◆ Business ◆ Modern ◆

Two buildings home to renovated, comfortable and tastefully appointed rooms; a business centre; winter-garden style breakfast room. Modern restaurant with a pleasant terrace in summer and unpretentious, standard fare.

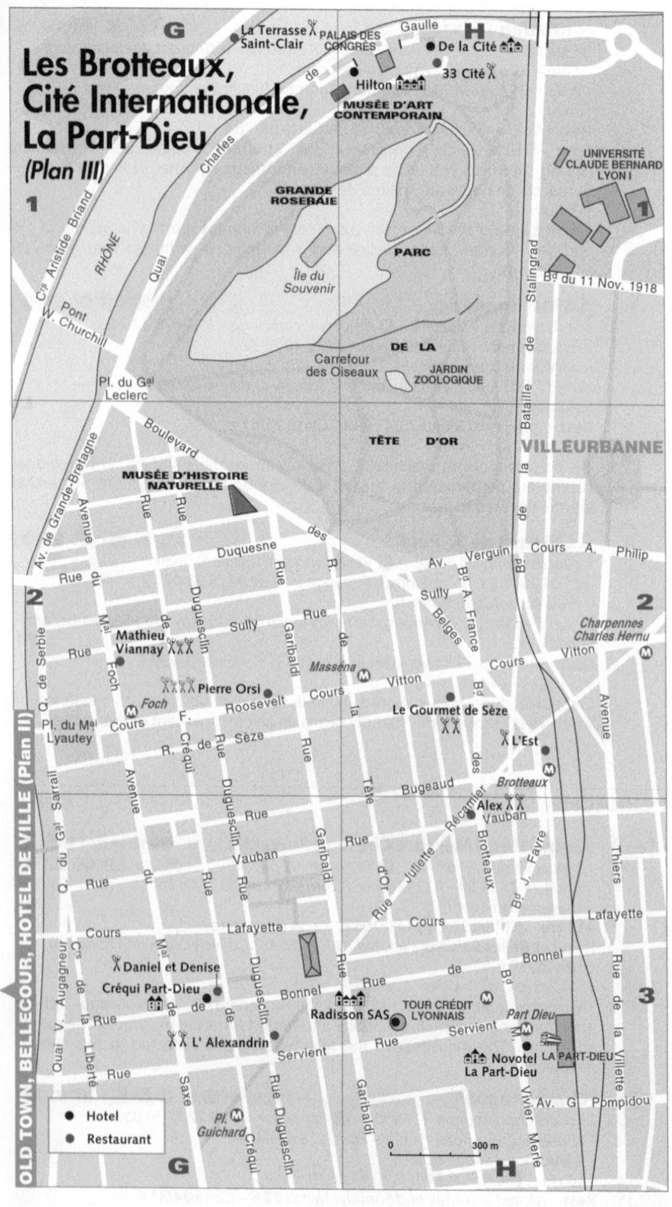
Les Brotteaux, Cité Internationale, La Part-Dieu
(Plan III)
G
H
1
2
3
La Terrasse Saint-Clair
PALAIS DES CONGRÈS
Gaulle
De la Cité
33 Cité
Hilton
MUSÉE D'ART CONTEMPORAIN
Charles
de
Quai
Cᵉˢ Aristide Briand
RHÔNE
GRANDE ROSERAIE
Île du Souvenir
PARC
DE LA
TÊTE D'OR
Carrefour des Oiseaux
JARDIN ZOOLOGIQUE
UNIVERSITÉ CLAUDE BERNARD LYON I
Bᵈ du 11 Nov. 1918
Bᵈ de la Bataille de Stalingrad
VILLEURBANNE
Pont W. Churchill
Pl. du Gᵃˡ Leclerc
Boulevard des Belges
Av. de Grande-Bretagne
MUSÉE D'HISTOIRE NATURELLE
Duquesne
Av. Verguin
Cours A. Philip
Sully
Bᵈ A. France
Charpennes Charles Hernu
Vitton
Mathieu Viannay
Pierre Orsi
Masséna
Foch
Pl. du Mᵃˡ Lyautey
Cours F. Roosevelt
R. de Sèze
Le Gourmet de Sèze
L'Est
Brotteaux
Bugeaud
Alex
Vauban
Juliette Récamier
Bᵈ J. Favre
Rue Tête d'Or
Rue Garibaldi
Rue Duguesclin
Rue Créqui
Avenue Thiers
Cours Lafayette
Daniel et Denise
Créqui Part-Dieu
Cours de la Liberté
Quai V. Augagneur
Q. du Gᵃˡ Sarrail
Q. de Serbie
Avenue du Mᵃˡ Foch
Avenue du Mᵃˡ de Saxe
Rue de Bonnel
Radisson SAS
TOUR CRÉDIT LYONNAIS
Part Dieu
Rue Servient
L' Alexandrin
Novotel La Part-Dieu
LA PART-DIEU
Rue de la Villette
Av. G. Pompidou
M. Vivier Merle
Pl. Guichard
Hotel
Restaurant
0
300 m
OLD TOWN, BELLECOUR, HOTEL DE VILLE (Plan II)

LES BROTTEAUX - CITÉ INTERNATIONALE - LA PART-DIEU

Plan III

Hilton

rm rm VISA

70 quai Ch. de Gaulle ✉ *69006 –* ✆ *04 78 17 50 50 – reservations.lyon@hilton.com – Fax 04 78 17 52 52 – www.hilton.com* **H1**

200 rm – 🛉148/365 € 🛉🛉148/530 €, ☕ 24 €

Rest *Blue Elephant* – ✆ *04 78 17 50 00 (closed 21 July-18 August, Saturday lunch and Sunday)* Menu 28 € (weekday lunch), 43/55 € – Carte 30/51 €

Rest *Brasserie* – ✆ *04 78 17 51 00* – Menu 23 € (lunch) – Carte 31/56 €

♦ Chain hotel ♦ Modern ♦

This impressive modern hotel built in brick and glass is equipped with a comprehensive business centre. Fully equipped bedrooms and apartments facing the Tête d'Or park or the Rhône. Thai specialities and decor at the Blue Elephant. Traditional food is to be found at the Brasserie.

Radisson SAS

Lyon and Rhône valley, rm VISA

129 r. Servient (32th Floor) ✉ *69003 –* Ⓜ *Part Dieu – ✆ 04 78 63 55 00 – info.lyon@radissonsas.com – Fax 04 78 63 55 20 – lyon.radissonsas.com* **H3**

245 rm – 🛉120/300 € 🛉🛉120/300 €, ☕ 20 €

Rest *L'Arc-en-Ciel* – *(closed 15 July-25 August, Saturday lunch and Sunday)* Menu 42/90 € – Carte 62/96 €

Rest *Bistrot de la Tour* – *(closed Saturday and Sunday) (lunch only)* Menu 19 € – Carte 24/43 €

♦ Business ♦ Functional ♦

At the top of the "pencil" (100m high), interior layout inspired by the houses of old Lyons: interior courtyards and superimposed galleries. Exceptional view from some rooms. The Arc-en-Ciel is on the 32nd floor of the tower. Packed at lunchtime.

De la Cité

VISA

22 quai Ch.-de-Gaulle ✉ *69006 –* ✆ *04 78 17 86 86 – hoteldelacite@concorde-hotel.com – Fax 04 78 17 86 99 – www.lyon.concorde-hotels.com* **H1**

159 rm – 🛉95/320 € 🛉🛉95/320 €, ☕ 22 € – 5 suites

Rest – Menu 23/36 € – Carte 42/67 €

♦ Chain hotel ♦ Modern ♦

This modern building designed by Renzo Piano stands between the Tête d'Or park and the Rhône. Bright rooms decorated in a contemporary vein. Traditional meals (buffet lunch). Terrace overlooking the patio of the Cité Internationale. Cocktail bar.

Novotel La Part-Dieu

rm rm VISA

47 bd Vivier-Merle ✉ *69003 –* Ⓜ *Part Dieu – ✆ 04 72 13 51 51 – h0735@accor.com – Fax 04 72 13 51 99 – www.novotel.com* **H3**

124 rm – 🛉118/153 € 🛉🛉126/161 €, ☕ 13.50 €

Rest – Menu 24 € – Carte 24/43 €

♦ Business ♦ Functional ♦

Two minutes from the railway station. The rooms are being progressively revamped in line with latest Novotel standards. Lounge-bar with an internet area. This Novotel restaurant is practical for business travellers with a train to catch or between meetings.

Créqui Part-Dieu

rm rm VISA

37 r. Bonnel ✉ *69003 –* Ⓜ *Place Guichard – ✆ 04 78 60 20 47 – inforesa@hotel-crequi.com – Fax 04 78 62 21 12 – www.bestwestern-lyonpartdieu.com closed August, Saturday and Sunday* **G3**

46 rm – 🛉71/150 € 🛉🛉71/160 €, ☕ 12 € – 3 suites

Rest – Menu 18/30 € – Carte 26/41 €

♦ Business ♦ Functional ♦

The establishment is located opposite the law courts district. The renovated rooms are decorated in warm tones; those in the new wing are particularly modern in style.

XXXX ✿ **Pierre Orsi**

3 pl. Kléber ✉ 69006 – Ⓜ Masséna – ✆ 04 78 89 57 68 – orsi@relaischateaux.com – Fax 04 72 44 93 34 – www.pierreorsi.com
closed Sunday and Monday except public holidays **G2**
Rest – Menu 60 € (weekday lunch), 85/115 € – Carte 70/155 €
Spec. Ravioles de foie gras de canard au jus de porto et truffes. Homard acadien en carapace. Pigeonneau en cocotte aux gousses d'ail confites.
◆ Formal ◆
This old house is home to elegant dining rooms and a rose garden terrace. Fine up-to-date cuisine and good wine list.

XXX ✿ **Mathieu Viannay**

47 av. Foch ✉ 69006 – Ⓜ Foch – ✆ 04 78 89 55 19 – Fax 04 78 89 08 39
closed 2-31 August, 14-22 February, Saturday and Sunday **G2**
Rest – Menu 35 € (lunch), 53/90 € – Carte 66/91 €
Spec. Pâté en croûte de volaille de Bresse et foie gras. Tombée d'ormeaux et pignons de pin aux champignons des bois (October to June). Fricassée de homard et ris de veau de lait à l'émulsion de carapace (winter and spring).
◆ Fashionable ◆
Resolutely modern dining room with parquet flooring, colourful chairs and an original candelabra created by the Lyon designer, Alain Vavro. Delicious contemporary cuisine.

XX ✿ **L'Alexandrin** (Laurent Rigal)

83 r. Moncey ✉ 69003 – Ⓜ Place Guichard – ✆ 04 72 61 15 69 – lalexandrin@lalexandrin.com – Fax 04 78 62 75 57 – www.lalexandrin.com
closed 3-25 August, 21 December-5 January, Sunday and Monday **G3**
Rest – Menu 38 € (weekday lunch), 60/115 € – Carte 62/80 €
Spec. Mousseline de brochet au crémeux d'écrevisse. Filet de bar rôti en croûte d'épices (June to August). Cocotte de légumes aux châtaignes (October to December).
◆ Cosy ◆
New management and new décor at this popular restaurant. Impressive choice of Côtes-du-Rhône, and regional dishes prepared with an original flair. Terrace.

XX ✿ **Le Gourmet de Sèze** (Bernard Mariller)

129 r. Sèze ✉ 69006 – Ⓜ Masséna – ✆ 04 78 24 23 42 – legourmetdeseze@wanadoo.fr – Fax 04 78 24 66 81 – www.le-gourmet-de-seze.com
closed 8-12 May, 18 July-19 August, 15-23 February, Sunday, Monday and public holidays **H2**
Rest – *(number of covers limited, pre-book)* Menu 38 € (lunch), 47/72 €
Spec. Croustillants de pieds de cochon. Ravioles de langoustines de Loctudy (April to September). Grand dessert.
◆ Cosy ◆
A brand new brown and white look for this non-smoking restaurant. The classic recipes are cleverly modernised and have universal appeal.

XX **Alex**

44 bd des Brotteaux ✉ 69006 – Ⓜ Brotteaux – ✆ 04 78 52 30 11 – chez.alex@club-internet.fr – Fax 04 78 52 34 16 – closed August, Sunday and Monday
Rest – Menu 20 € (weekday lunch), 44/59 € **H3**
◆ Design ◆
Restaurant whose smart, refined setting boldly allies colour, designer furniture and contemporary artworks. Menu concocted by the owner-chef from market produce.

X **L'Est**

14 pl. J. Ferry ✉ 69006 – Ⓜ Brotteaux – ✆ 04 37 24 25 26 – Fax 04 37 24 25 25 – www.bocuse.fr **H2**
Rest – Menu 23 € (weekdays)/28 € – Carte 31/57 €
◆ Bistro ◆
Trendy brasserie popular with the locals. The kitchens can be seen from the dining room, miniature trains chug round above diners' heads and world cooking is on the menu.

33 Cité

33 quai Charles de Gaulle ✉ 69006 – ✆ 04 37 45 45 45 – 33cite.restaurant@free.fr – Fax 04 37 45 45 46 **H1**

Rest – Menu 23 € (weekdays)/27 € – Carte 29/52 €

◆ Design ◆

Contemporary designer setting opposite the Salle 3000 at the Cité Internationale. View of the Parc de la Tête d'Or through the large windows. Choice of modern and classic dishes.

La Terrasse St-Clair

2 Grande Rue St-Clair ✉ 69300 Caluire-et-Cuire – ✆ 04 72 27 37 37 – Fax 04 72 27 37 38 – www.terrasse-saint-clair.com

closed 5-22 August, 23 December-15 January, Sunday and Monday **G1**

Rest – Menu 24 €

◆ Bistro ◆

There is a slight air of an open-air dance hall about the restaurant and especially the terrace shaded by plane trees. Pétanque pitch.

AROUND LYONS

Lyon Métropole

85 quai J. Gillet ✉ 69004 – ✆ 04 72 10 44 44 – metropole@lyonmetropole.com – Fax 04 72 10 44 42 – www.lyonmetropole.com **B1**

118 rm – †170/250 € ††170/250 €, ☕ 18 €

Rest ***Brasserie Lyon Plage*** – ✆ *04 72 10 44 30* – Menu 27 € – Carte 34/53 €

◆ Business ◆ Modern ◆

This 1980s hotel, reflected in the Olympic swimming pool, offers a superb spa, fitness facilities, tennis and squash courts, as well as golf practice areas. Modern rooms. Seafood takes pride of place on the menu of the Brasserie Lyon Plage.

Du Greillon without rest

12 montée du Greillon ✉ 69009 – ✆ 06 08 22 26 33 – contact@legreillon.com – Fax 04 72 29 10 97 – www.legreillon.com

closed 1st-12 August and 18-24 February **B1**

5 rm ☕ – †78/92 € ††85/100 €

◆ Traditional ◆ Personalised ◆

The former property of sculptor J. Chinard has been turned into a guesthouse. Pretty rooms, old furniture and ornaments, gorgeous garden and superb view of the Saône and Croix-Rousse.

Auberge de Fond Rose (Gérard Vignat)

23 quai G. Clemenceau ✉ 69300 Caluire-et-Cuire – ✆ 04 78 29 34 61 – contact@aubergedefondrose.com – Fax 04 72 00 28 67 – www.aubergedefondrose.com

closed 18 February-5 March, Tuesday lunch October-April, Sunday dinner and Monday except public holidays **B1**

Rest – Menu 38 € bi (weekday lunch), 51/78 € – Carte 75/80 €

Spec. Mesclun de langoustines aux céréales et citron confit. Féra du lac Léman au caviar d'aubergine. Pigeonneau cuit dans la rôtissoire, jus aux olives.

◆ Formal ◆

This handsome 1920s house features an idyllic terrace leading into the garden planted with ancient trees. Fine up-to-date menu and interesting wine list.

Auberge de l'Île (Jean-Christophe Ansanay-Alex)

(dinner)

(On Barbe Island) ✉ 69009 – ✆ 04 78 83 99 49 – info@aubergedelile.com – Fax 04 78 47 80 46 – www.aubergedelile.com

closed Sunday and Monday **B1**

Rest – Menu 60 € (weekday lunch), 90/120 €

Spec. Salade tiède exotique de homard breton. Saint-Jacques à la feuille d'or, beurre de truffe noire (winter). Crème glacée à la réglisse, cornet de pain d'épice.

◆ Friendly ◆

Situated on Ile Barbe, this charming 17C inn is known for its fine cuisine made from local, seasonal produce. The chef himself comes to your table to announce his legendary dish of the day.

L'Ouest

1 quai Commerce (North via the banks of the Saône (D 51)) ✉ 69009
– ✆ 04 37 64 64 64 – commercial@brasseries-bocuse.com – Fax 04 37 64 64 65
– www.bocuse.fr **B1**
Rest – Menu 23 (weekdays)/28 € – Carte 31/56 €
◆ Fashionable ◆
A distinctive modern building of wood, concrete and metal. Bar, giant screens, open kitchen, river facing terrace and exotic dishes. Bocuse is on a western course!

Le Verre et l'Assiette

20 Grande Rue de Vaise ✉ *69009 – ✆ 04 78 83 32 25 – leverreetlassiette@free.fr*
– www.leverreetlassiette.com
closed 26 July-19 August, 7-16 February, dinner except Thursday and Friday, Saturday, Sunday and holidays **B1**
Rest – Menu 28/39 €
◆ Classic ◆ Bistro ◆
The talented chef reinvents and personalises traditional Lyons specialities as well as a few French classics. Stone and wood prevail in the modern decor. Smiling service.

Collonges-au-Mont-d'Or

Paul Bocuse

au pont de Collonges, 12 km north along the Saône (D 433, D 51) ✉ 69660
– ✆ 04 72 42 90 90 – paul.bocuse@bocuse.fr – Fax 04 72 27 85 87
– www.bocuse.fr
Rest – Menu 125/200 € – Carte 102/183 €
Spec. Soupe aux truffes noires VGE. Loup en croûte feuilletée. Volaille de Bresse en vessie "Mère Fillioux".
◆ Formal ◆
The culinary world beats a path to the colourful, elegant inn of "Monsieur Paul". His celebrated dishes in the dining room, murals of great chefs in the courtyard.

Charbonnières-les-Bains

Le Pavillon de la Rotonde without rest

3 av. du Casino – ✆ 04 78 87 79 79
– contact@pavillon-rotonde.com – Fax 04 78 87 79 78
– www.pavillon-rotonde.com
closed 20 July-20 August
16 rm – †295 € ††325/525 €, ☕ 24 €
Rest ***La Rotonde*** – see below
◆ Luxury ◆ Design ◆
A stone's throw from the casino, a luxurious hotel with contemporary décor and discreet Art Deco touches. Spacious rooms with terrace giving onto the gardens. Heated indoor swimming pool and spa.

La Rotonde

au casino Le Lyon Vert ✉ *69890 La Tour de Salvagny – ✆ 04 78 87 00 97*
– restaurant-rotonde@g-partouche.fr – Fax 04 78 87 81 39
– www.restaurant-rotonde.com
closed 1st-12 May, 20 July-22 August, Sunday and Monday
Rest – Menu 43 € (weekday lunch), 95/150 € – Carte 98/169 €
Spec. Grosse morille "jumbo" farcie de cuisses de grenouilles et queues d'écrevisses. Canard étouffé de Challans cuit à la broche rosé. Cannelloni de chocolat amer à la glace crème brûlée.
◆ Formal ◆
A renowned gourmet restaurant on the first floor of the casino. Elegant Art Deco-style dining room opening onto the gardens and park, subtle cuisine and fine wine list.

STRASBOURG

STRASBOURG

Population (est. 2004): 273 100 (conurbation 427 300) – Altitude: 143m

J. Hampe/www.ot-strasbourg.fr

Would it be stretching things to call Strasbourg the ultimate European city? It can make an impressive claim: although in France, it sits just across the Rhine from Germany; it's home to the Court of Human Rights and the Council of Europe; its stunning Cathedral is the highest medieval building on the continent; and it's a major communications hub as it connects the Mediterranean with the Rhineland, Central Europe, the North Sea and the Baltic. Oh, and the Old Town is a UNESCO World Heritage Site.

What's more, there's a real cosmopolitan buzz here. A large student population, courtesy of the city's ancient university, helps generate a year-round feeling of liveliness. The name 'Strasbourg' translates as 'crossroads' and the city bounced back and forth between France and Germany for over three hundred years before its final acceptance as French over half a century ago. Its unique geographical position also lends the city a great gastronomic tradition, with two cuisine cultures colliding head on, and hungry visitors reaping the culinary benefits. Meantime, street signs in both French and Alsatian add to a gently teasing schizophrenia, enhanced by distinct areas of medieval French and German architecture. The final brushwork of this striking picture is the handsome waterway that completely encircles the Old Town, the ideal setting for a lingering boat journey on a summer's afternoon.

LIVING THE CITY

The **River Rhine** flows a short distance to the east of Strasbourg; the waterway that encircles the historical centre is the **River Ill** and the **Fossé des Remparts** canal. This effectively means that the heart of the city, the tourist epicentre, is an island: The Grande Ile. The **Petite France** neighbourhood is on the island's southwest tip, while the '**German district**' is northeast. The smart **European Parliament** zone is a couple of miles beyond this. Strasbourg's 'happening' district, **Krutenau**, lies near the university campus to the east of town. Right across from here, on the western fringes, is the main arrival point to the city, the central railway station.

PRACTICAL INFORMATION

ARRIVAL-DEPARTURE

Strasbourg-Entzheim International Airport is found 12km southwest of the city. The train to Central Station runs from Entzheim Station (a 5min walk from the terminal) and takes 15min. A taxi to the city centre will be about €30.

TRANSPORT

Strasbourg is covered by a bus and tram service. Tickets are valid for the whole transport network. You can buy a single ticket or carnets (multipass). There's also a Tour-Pass which gives unlimited travel for 24hr.

The city has impressive green credentials. Buses run on natural gas, trams are slick and efficient, and there are 130,000 cyclists and 270 miles of cycle paths – hiring a bike is a great way of getting about here.

If you're staying longer, invest in a Strasbourg-Pass. This is a three-day pass which offers free travel, plus free admission (and numerous discounts) to city-wide monuments and visitor attractions.

EXPLORING STRASBOURG

Set on its island between the tree-lined embrace of the River Ill, Strasbourg's old town is a classic medieval gem, but the capital of Alsace is a lot more than one-dimensional. The strikingly modern European Parliament building ensures the presence of smart shops; the large population of university students guarantees a youthful buzz; and what look like German wine taverns turn out to be cosy French bistros.

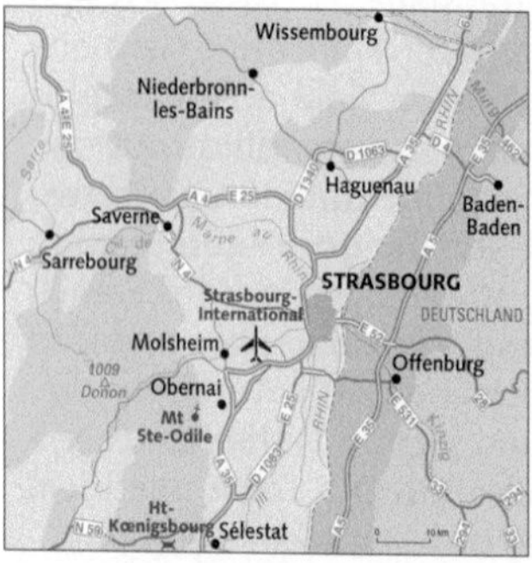

Visitors who arrive expecting a rather straight-laced city full of politicians are knocked out by its time-honed beauty and elegance. The World Heritage Site status is richly deserved: there are rows of half-timbered medieval buildings, glorious mansions and narrow pedestrianised streets dotted with leafy squares and lined with pavement cafés. The German quarter is the more northerly stretch of the old town, marked by sturdy public buildings and graceful gardens. Much of the architecture in these parts is of the grand nineteenth century neoclassical sort: witness a group of imposing structures such as the **Palace of the Rhine** and the **Strasbourg National Theatre** in the rather un-Germanic sounding Place de la Republique. Then a bit further down, on **Place Broglie**, nip inside the much-frequented **Rhine Opera** building to book tickets: performances here have earned Strasbourg a worldwide reputation for classical music.

→ TRULY IN-SPIRED

The centre of the old town is also its busiest point. Many people here are making tracks to the magnificent **Notre-Dame Cathedral**. It's not hard to find, as its unmistakable single spire towers over crouching medieval roofs lying humbly in its wake. The cathedral's stark silhouette is visible from miles round, but on closer inspection, lace-like stonework softens its lines, though it won't do much to lessen the leering stares of countless gargoyles. This is a tremendous 11C sandstone confection that changes colour with the light, from dawn pink to afternoon ochre. Inside there's an elaborate astronomical clock that brings forth a parade of apostles when it chimes at 12.30pm. Crowning glory is the kaleidoscope of the rose window: on sunny days, the stained glass is a joy to behold. Two other medieval churches in the old town are worth visiting: **St-Pierre-le-Jeune** (in Place St-Pierre-Le-Jeune) is a superb Gothic pile from 1053, and you can still see the base of the bell tower and a number of walls from the original building, though what you might appreciate most are the church's wonderful 14C frescoes. Meantime, a similar reverie can be felt at the **Church of Saint Thomas** on the Quai Saint-Thomas. It dates back to the 13C, and pride of place within goes to the organ that was played by Mozart and Albert Schweitzer.

→ PETITE PLEASURES

The southern district of the old town (which contains St Thomas) is the predominantly Gallic part of Strasbourg – Petite France. This is the prettiest area of all, like a fairytale scene peopled by 21C tourists. It's made up of 15C black-and-white half-timbered houses, once the homes of tanners and dyers, with geranium-filled balconies. All around is a jumble of cobbled streets punctuated by canals and camel-back stone bridges. Stop at the characterful **Pont des Moulins** and listen to the gushing water as it's channelled through a narrow passageway. All around here you can take in memorable views. Climb to the top of the nearby **Vauban Dam**, which crosses the Ill at its widest point, and look across to the **Ponts Couverts**, covered bridges linked by grand medieval watchtowers that in turn provide an observation point for the four Ill canals.

→ ART OF THE MATTER

Looking the other way from the dam you see the modish façade of the **Museum of Modern and Contemporary Art**. This is the crème de la crème of Strasbourg's museums, perhaps because of the striking steel-and-plate-glass structure in which it's housed as much as for the artworks themselves. Step inside and admire delightful floor-to-ceiling windows that enhance the powerful paintings on the walls…then finish your coffee in the Art Café and head on through to the actual permanent collection. This features Picasso, Braque, Ernst, Gauguin, Kandinsky and Magritte. The museum's upper gallery is a different concept altogether: an off-the-wall contemporary art ragbag that might have had even Picasso stroking his chin. If your taste in museums is a bit more conservative, check out the elegant **Rohan Palace**, in the shadow of the cathedral. Not only is this a fine eighteenth century building, it also boasts three museums, which delve into the worlds of archaeology, fine and applied arts. Across the water, on **quai Saint-Nicolas**, three adjoining sixteenth century houses make up the **Alsatian Museum**, dedicated to the history and traditions of the city and area you're visiting. If local history (or local signposts) have left you confused, this is the place to sort yourself out.

→ MEET THE KRU

Strasbourg's 'playground' is Krutenau, a bohemian quarter that used to be occupied by 'water folk' such as fishermen and boatmen. It always had an alternative air, and it's kept that bohemian feel to this day, enhanced by the big student population that descends on its bars and clubs. This funky district has an eclectic mix of hole-in-the-wall restaurants serving everything from spicy Lebanese meals to rich Thai curries. If, however, your idea of playing is a gentle cruise on a boat, then it's simplicity itself to jump on one at the landing stage behind the Rohan Palace, and relax on a one-hour trip that does the classic circular trip taking in the grandiose European Parliament building to the north and the Ponts-Couverts to the south. Then again, a stroll along the banks of the Ill gives you a first-hand chance to appreciate the tastefully landscaped river-banks that typify a superior kind of European city.

CALENDAR HIGHLIGHTS

Alsatians look forward to September in the city, not for any particularly autumnal reasons, but because this is the month when Festival Musica comes to town, and wonderfully diverse works from the modern classical music genre are performed at venues throughout Strasbourg. This lights the blue touch paper for two more influential events in the city. November's St'Art at the Strasbourg Centre de Congrès is lauded as the second-biggest contemporary art fair in France (after the FIAC in Paris) and draws art-lovers from around Europe to the 'crossroads' of the continent. That same month sees Jazz d'Or, a highly popular jazz festival over two weeks with forty concerts spread across venues in the city. The main summer event here is the Route Romane Festival (August and September), when Strasbourg's shared Franco-German cultural heritage is celebrated with a feast of medieval and traditional music. Christmas markets in the city are worth a particular mention. They're amongst the oldest and the best in Europe, and have been

STRASBOURG IN...

→ ONE DAY

Old Town, Notre-Dame Cathedral, Petite France

→ TWO DAYS

Boat trip on the Ill, Museum of Modern and Contemporary Art, meal in a winstub

→ THREE DAYS

Alsatian Museum (or Rohan Palace museums), European Parliament, Orangerie

held here since 1570. The market in Place Broglie, in the old town, is recognised as the one at the top of the tree.

EATING OUT

Strasbourg is generally considered one of the best cities in France for delicious cuisine and places in which to eat it. There's the attention to quality and detail that's the epitome of the French gourmet philosophy allied to bold and hearty Alsatian fare with its roots firmly set across the Rhine. A favourite of the region is choucroute (or sauerkraut if you're leaning towards Germany), which is a rumbustious mixture of cabbage, potatoes, pork, sausage and ham; then there's baeckoffe, a tasty Alsace stew, which translates as 'ovenbake' and blends pieces of stewing lamb, beef and pork with liberal dollops of Riesling. Talking of which, the fragrant wines of the area have a distinct character of their own: they're white, spicy and floral. The local fruit liquor, eau de vie, has a definite Alsatian kick, too – it's sweetened entirely by fruit without a hint of sugar. A good place in which to sample the local produce is a typical Strasbourg winstub. The smarter restaurants – highly prized and requiring advance reservation – are around the cathedral, in the Petite France quarter, and along the canal and river banks. As this is a eurocrat zone, expect a smart set to be at a table close to you. As in other parts of France, a fifteen per cent service charge is already added to your bill, but round it up for good service.

→ FOLLY IN THE PARK

The Orangerie is Strasbourg's most popular park, just across from the European Council offices. Not only is it full of people in serious suits – it also boasts a zoo and a bowling alley.

→ ARTY ANTHEM

Strasbourg can lay claim to three famous sons. Two of them, Gustave Dore and Jean Arp, became world renowned for their abilities with a paintbrush. The third, Frederic de Dietrich, was the mayor who commissioned the French national anthem, La Marseillaise.

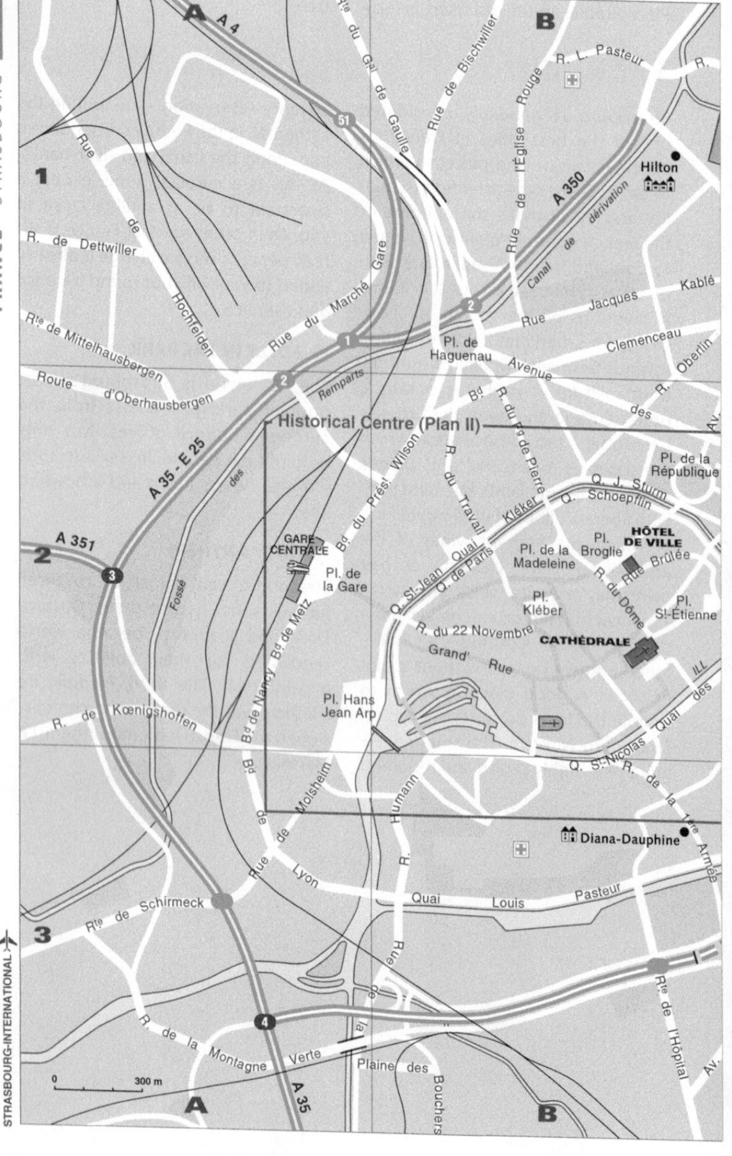
Historical Centre (Plan II)
A4
A 350
A 35 - E 25
A 351
A 35
Rte du Gal de Gaulle
Rue de Bischwiller
R. L. Pasteur
Rue de l'Église Rouge
Hilton
Canal de dérivation
Rue Jacques Kablé
Avenue Clemenceau
R. Oberlin
Pl. de Haguenau
Rue de Hochfelden
R. de Dettwiller
Rte de Mittelhausbergen
Route d'Oberhausbergen
Rue du Marché Gare
Remparts
Bd du Prés! Wilson
R. du Fg de Pierre
R. du Travail
Bd des
Pl. de la République
Q. J. Sturm
Q. Schoepflin
Quai Kléber
Q. St-Jean
Q. de Paris
Pl. de la Madeleine
Pl. Broglie
HÔTEL DE VILLE
Rue Brûlée
R. du Dôme
Pl. St-Étienne
Pl. Kléber
CATHÉDRALE
R. du 22 Novembre
Grand' Rue
GARE CENTRALE
Pl. de la Gare
Fossé des
Bd de Metz
Bd de Nancy
Pl. Hans Jean Arp
R. de Kœnigshoffen
ILL
Quai des
Q. St-Nicolas
R. de la 1ère Armée
Bd de Molsheim
R. Humann
Diana-Dauphine
Rue de Lyon
Quai Louis Pasteur
Rte de Schirmeck
Rue de la
Rte de l'Hôpital
R. de la Montagne Verte
Plaine des Bouchers
Av.
0
300 m
A
B
1
2
3
STRASBOURG-INTERNATIONAL

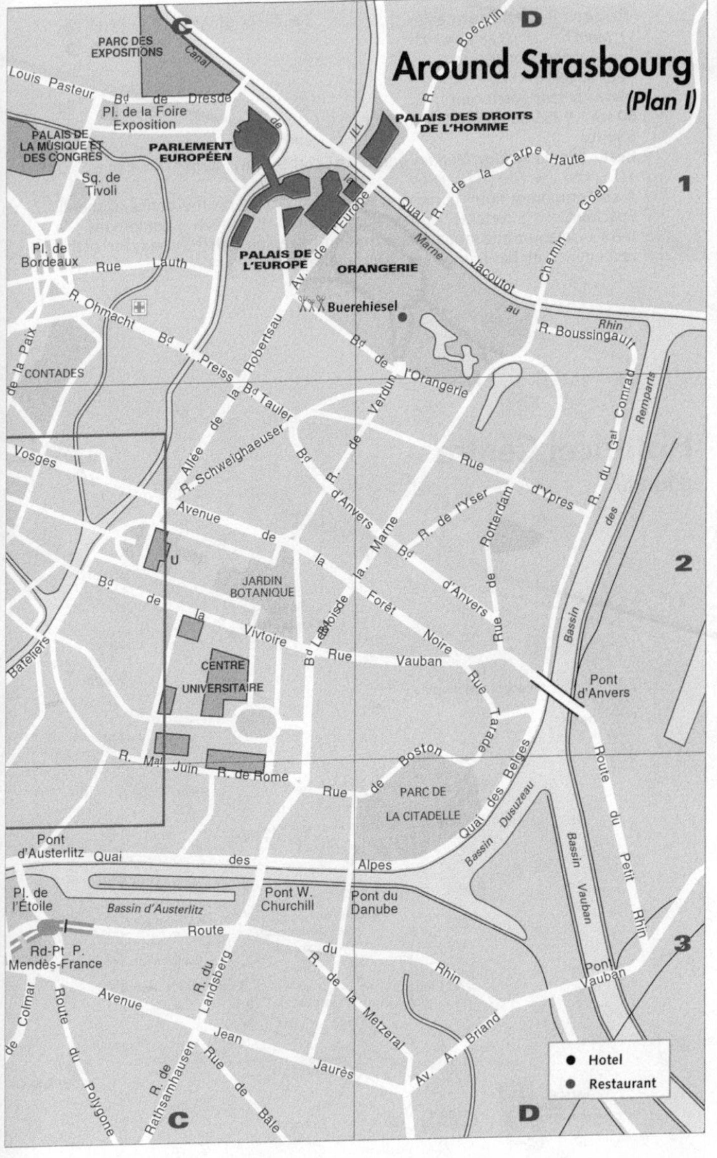
Around Strasbourg
(Plan I)
PARC DES EXPOSITIONS
PALAIS DE LA MUSIQUE ET DES CONGRES
PARLEMENT EUROPÉEN
PALAIS DES DROITS DE L'HOMME
PALAIS DE L'EUROPE
ORANGERIE
Buerehiesel
CONTADES
JARDIN BOTANIQUE
CENTRE UNIVERSITAIRE
PARC DE LA CITADELLE
Pont d'Anvers
Pont d'Austerlitz
Pl. de l'Étoile
Bassin d'Austerlitz
Pont W. Churchill
Pont du Danube
Rd-Pt P. Mendès-France
Pont Vauban
Hotel
Restaurant

Régent Petite France

5 r. Moulins – ✆ 03 88 76 43 43
– rpf@regent-hotels.com
– Fax 03 88 76 43 76
– www.regent-hotels.com

60 rm – 🚹255/380 € 🚹🚹276/401 €, ☕ 21 €
6 suites

F2

Rest – *(closed Sunday, Monday and lunch October-May)* Menu 41/71 € bi

◆ Luxury ◆ Design ◆

A contemporary hotel occupying an old ice factory on the banks of the Ill. Spacious, comfortable guestrooms with high-tech equipment, a terrace-solarium and sauna. Modern menu in keeping with the trendy feel of this restaurant with bar-lounge and views of the river.

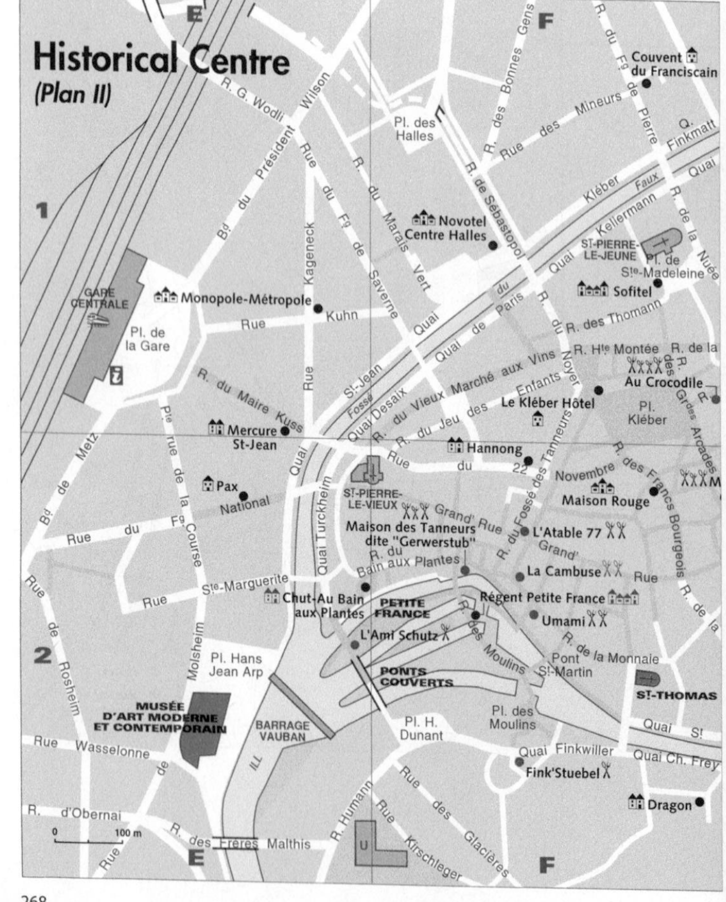

Sofitel

F1

pl. St-Pierre-le-Jeune – ✆ *03 88 15 49 00*
– h0568@accor.com – Fax 03 88 15 49 99
– www.sofitel-strasbourg.com
153 rm – 135/380 € 155/400 €, 23 €
2 suites
Rest *Sofitel* – *(closed Saturday lunch, Sunday and public holidays)*
Carte 43/61 €

♦ Chain hotel ♦ Business ♦ Modern ♦

Two types of room – classic and those designed on a European political theme on offer at this Sofitel. A full range of modern facilities, plus patio and fitness centre. Modern, Japanese-inspired design and luxury brasserie-style service at the restaurant.

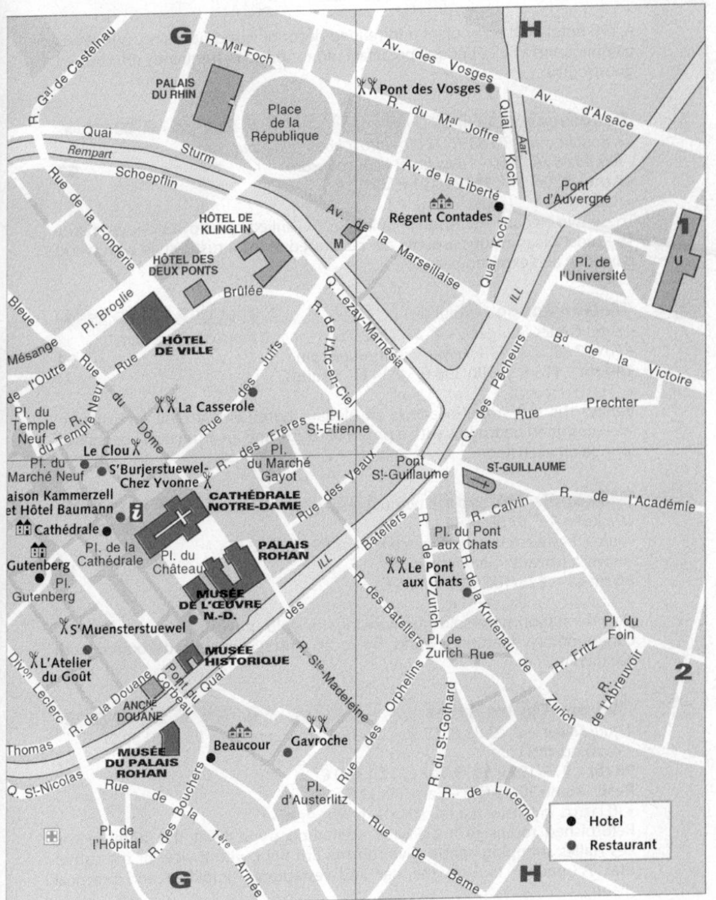

Hilton

av. Herrenschmidt – ✆ 03 88 37 10 10 – info@hilton-strasbourg.com
– Fax 03 88 36 83 27 – www.hilton.fr *Plan I* **B1**
238 rm – 🛉152/345 € 🛉🛉152/345 €, ☕ 27 € – 5 suites
Rest *La Table du Chef* – ✆ *03 88 37 41 42 (closed July-August, Saturday and Sunday) (lunch only)* Menu 35 €
Rest *Le Jardin du Tivoli* – ✆ *03 88 35 72 61* – Menu 30 € – Carte 34/46 €

◆ Chain hotel ◆ Business ◆ Modern ◆

This glass and steel hotel provides standardised comfort in its spacious guestrooms. Lobby with shops, a multimedia centre and bars. Traditional lunches and a British feel at La Table du Chef; wine bar in the evening. Buffet dining at the Jardin du Tivoli.

Régent Contades without rest

8 av. de la Liberté – ✆ 03 88 15 05 05 – rc@regent-hotels.com
– Fax 03 88 15 05 15 – www.regent-hotels.com **H1**
47 rm – 🛉190/255 € 🛉🛉210/480 €, ☕ 18.50 €

◆ Luxury ◆ Traditional ◆

A 19C hotel with an opulent and refined décor of wood panelling, numerous paintings and a Belle-Époque breakfast room. Spacious, frequently refurbished guestrooms.

Beaucour without rest

5 r. Bouchers – ✆ 03 88 76 72 00 – info@hotel-beaucour.com
– Fax 03 88 76 72 60 – www.hotel-beaucour.com **G2**
49 rm – 🛉70/101 € 🛉🛉124/191 €, ☕ 12 €

◆ Luxury ◆ Traditional ◆

These two elegant 18C Alsatian buildings are linked by a flower-decked patio. The most pleasant guestrooms are decorated in local rustic style with wood panelling and exposed beams.

Maison Rouge without rest

4 r. des Francs-Bourgeois – ✆ 03 88 32 08 60 – info@maison-rouge.com
– Fax 03 88 22 43 73 – www.maison-rouge.com **F2**
140 rm – 🛉85 € 🛉🛉100/330 €, ☕ 14 € – 2 suites

◆ Traditional ◆ Classic ◆

Behind the red stone façade is an elegant hotel with a cosy atmosphere. Well-designed bedrooms with a personal touch, and an attractively decorated lounge on each floor.

Monopole-Métropole without rest

16 r. Kuhn – ✆ 03 88 14 39 14
– info@bestwestern-monopole.com – Fax 03 88 32 82 55
– www.bestwestern-monopole.com **E1**
86 rm ☕ – 🛉75/185 € 🛉🛉85/185 €

◆ Family ◆ Rustic ◆

Near the station, hotel split into two wings (one old and rustic, the other far more contemporary, featuring works by local artists). Lounges decorated with handicrafts.

Novotel Centre Halles

4 quai Kléber – ✆ 03 88 21 50 50 – h0439@accor.com – Fax 03 88 21 50 51
– www.novotel.com **F1**
96 rm – 🛉79/197 € 🛉🛉79/207 €, ☕ 13.50 €
Rest – Menu 20/75 € bi – Carte 20/39 €

◆ Chain hotel ◆ Business ◆ Modern ◆

Refurbished rooms in a pleasant, contemporary style at this hotel in the Les Halles shopping centre. Gym on the 8th floor with a view of the cathedral. A modern look in the bar and restaurant; simplified and practical menu.

Chut - Au Bain aux Plantes rm rm VISA

4 r. Bain-aux-Plantes – ✆ 03 88 32 05 06 – contact@hote-strasbourg.fr – Fax 03 88 32 05 50 – www.hote-strasbourg.fr **E2**

8 rm – 80/90 € 90/160 €, 8 € – 1 suite

Rest – *(closed 25-31 March, 12-22 August, 3-20 January, Sunday and Monday)*
Carte 22/45 €

♦ Inn ♦ Luxury ♦ Personalised ♦

Designer or antique materials and furniture, spacious guestrooms and a relaxing, minimalist feel are the hallmarks of this stylish hotel-cum-guesthouse. The varied menu, featuring the subtle use of myriad spices, changes daily. Charming courtyard terrace.

Diana-Dauphine without rest VISA AE

30 r. de la 1ère Armée – ✆ 03 88 36 26 61 – info@hotel-diana-dauphine.com – Fax 03 88 35 50 07 – www.hotel-diana-dauphine.com
Closed 22 December-2 January *Plan I* **B3**

45 rm – 90/135 € 90/135 €, 11 €

♦ Traditional ♦ Modern ♦

Located by the tram line leading to the old town, this hotel has had a radical contemporary facelift. Modern comforts.

Hannong without rest VISA AE

15 r. du 22 Novembre – ✆ 03 88 32 16 22 – info@hotel-hannong.com – Fax 03 88 22 63 87 – www.hotel-hannong.com
closed 1st-4 January **F2**

72 rm – 82/191 € 104/191 €, 14 €

♦ Family ♦ Classic ♦

A mix of styles (classic, cosy, modern) with parquet, wood panelling, sculptures and paintings in this fine hotel built on the site of the Hannong earthenware factory (18C). Pleasant wine bar.

Du Dragon without rest VISA AE

2 r. Écarlate – ✆ 03 88 35 79 80 – hotel@dragon.fr – Fax 03 88 25 78 95 – www.dragon.fr **F2**

32 rm – 69/112 € 89/124 €, 11 €

♦ Traditional ♦ Business ♦ Modern ♦

17C building around a small quiet courtyard with a clearly contemporary feel. Shades of grey, designer furniture, rooms in a pared-down style and art exhibitions.

Mercure St-Jean without rest VISA AE

3 r. Maire Kuss – ✆ 03 88 32 80 80 – h1813@accor.com – Fax 03 88 23 05 39 **E1**

52 rm – 59/125 € 79/125 €, 13 €

♦ Chain hotel ♦ Business ♦ Design ♦

Chain hotel between the station and the "Petite France" quarter. Contemporary décor; practical guestrooms in coffee-coloured tones. Patio with mini-fountains.

Gutenberg without rest VISA AE

31 r. des Serruriers – ✆ 03 88 32 17 15 – info@hotel-gutenberg.com – Fax 03 88 75 76 67 – www.hotel-gutenberg.com **G2**

42 rm – 74/98 € 74/98 €, 9 €

♦ Traditional ♦ Classic ♦

This building dating back to 1745 is now a hotel with an eclectic mix of spacious guestrooms. The bright breakfast room is crowned by a glass roof.

Cathédrale without rest VISA AE

12-13 pl. Cathédrale – ✆ 03 88 22 12 12 – reserv@hotel-cathedrale.fr – Fax 03 88 23 28 00 – www.hotel-cathedrale.fr **G2**

47 rm – 75 € 150 €, 13 €

♦ Family ♦ Classic ♦

This century-old residence enjoys an ideal location opposite the cathedral, which is visible from the breakfast room and some of the comfortable rooms. Religious architecture-inspired décor in some rooms.

Le Kléber without rest

29 pl. Kléber – ✆ 03 88 32 09 53 – hotel-kleber-strasbourg@wanadoo.fr – Fax 03 88 32 50 41 – www.hotel-kleber.com **F1**

30 rm – 55/72 € 62/80 €, 8 €

◆ Traditional ◆ Personalised ◆

"Meringue", "Strawberry" and "Cinnamon" are just a few of the names of the rooms in this comfortable hotel. Contemporary, colourful décor with a sweet-and-savoury theme.

Couvent du Franciscain without rest

18 r. du Fg de Pierre – ✆ 03 88 32 93 93 – info@hotel-franciscain.com – Fax 03 88 75 68 46 – www.hotel-franciscain.com

closed 24 December-4 January **F1**

43 rm – 39/40 € 66/72 €, 9 €

◆ Traditional ◆ Functional ◆

A simple yet comfortable hotel at the end of a cul-de-sac. Pleasant lounge; breakfast in a "winstub-style" basement (amusing mural).

Pax rm rest rm

24 r. Fg National – ✆ 03 88 32 14 54 – info@paxhotel.com – Fax 03 88 32 01 16 – www.paxhotel.com

closed 2-11 January **E2**

106 rm – 55/60 € 73 €, 8.50 €

Rest – *(closed Sunday in January and February)* Menu 18/24 € – Carte 22/45 €

◆ Traditional ◆ Functional ◆

This hotel is on a street accessible only to tramway traffic. Simply furnished but immaculate guestrooms. On fine days, dining is outside on the pretty terrace-patio under the Virginia creeper. Regional cuisine.

Au Crocodile (Emile Jung)

10 r. Outre – ✆ 03 88 32 13 02 – info@au-crocodile.com – Fax 03 88 75 72 01 – www.au-crocodile.com

closed 15 July-5 August, 24 December-6 January, Sunday and Monday **F1**

Rest – Menu 60 € (weekday lunch), 88/130 € – Carte 75/151 €

Spec. Sandre et laitance de carpe au mille-choux. Lièvre à la royale (season). Meringue glacée à l'extrême aux fruits chauds, sorbet aux lychees.

◆ Formal ◆

Splendid wood panelling, paintings and the famous crocodile brought back from the Egyptian campaign by an Alsatian captain adorn this restaurant. Refined classical cuisine.

Buerehiesel (Eric Westermann)

dans le parc de l'Orangerie – ✆ 03 88 45 56 65 – contact@buerehiesel.fr – Fax 03 88 61 32 00 – www.buerehiesel.com

closed 1st-21 August, 31 December-21 January, Sunday and Monday *Plan I* **D1**

Rest – Menu 35 € (weekday lunch), 65/108 € – Carte 48/84 €

Spec. Pâté en croûte de veau et cochon au foie de canard. Brochet d'Alsace rôti, jus de volaille à la coriandre. Brioche à la bière, caramélisée à la bière, glace à la bière et poire rôtie.

◆ Romantic ◆

An attractive half-timbered house with a modern conservatory surrounded by trees in the Parc de l'Orangerie. Eric Westermann has replaced his father Antoine as chef.

Maison Kammerzell et Hôtel Baumann with rm

16 pl. de la Cathédrale – ✆ 03 88 32 42 14 – info@maison-kammerzell.com – Fax 03 88 23 03 92 – www.maison-kammerzell.com

closed 3 weeks in February **G2**

9 rm – 75 € 108/121 €, 10 €

Rest – Menu 30/45 € – Carte 29/57 €

◆ Retro ◆

With its stained-glass windows, paintings, wood carvings and Gothic vaulting, this 16C construction retains the feel of the Middle Ages. Sober guestrooms. An excellent brasserie menu based around traditional local cuisine. Choucroute a speciality.

XXX **Maison des Tanneurs dite "Gerwerstub"** VISA MC AE

42 r. Bain aux Plantes – ✆ 03 88 32 79 70 – maison.des.tanneurs@wanadoo.fr – Fax 03 88 22 17 26
closed 27 July-11 August, 29 December-23 January, Sunday and Monday
Rest – Menu 25 (weekday lunch)/30 € – Carte 41/62 € **F2**
♦ Rustic ♦
Ideally located by the Ill, this typical Alsatian house in La Petite France district is the place to go to if you love sauerkraut.

XX **L'Atable 77** AC VISA MC AE

77 Grand'Rue – ✆ 03 88 32 23 37 – latable77@free.fr – Fax 03 88 32 50 24 – www.latable77.com
closed 4-12 May, 13 July-4 August, 11-26 January, Sunday, Monday and lunch on public holidays **F2**
Rest – Menu 30/75 € bi
♦ Trendy ♦
A trendy restaurant with a resolutely contemporary feel throughout, from the paintings on the walls to the designer tableware and appetising creative cuisine.

XX **La Cambuse** AC VISA MC

1 r. des Dentelles – ✆ 03 88 22 10 22 – Fax 03 88 23 24 99
closed 6-21 April, 27 July-18 August, 21 December-5 January, Sunday and Monday **F2**
Rest – *(number of covers limited, pre-book)* Carte 45/53 €
♦ Fish ♦ Cosy ♦
Intimate dining room decorated in the style of a boat cabin. Fish and seafood are the specialities here, prepared in a blend of French and Asian styles (herbs, spices etc).

XX ✿ **La Casserole** (Eric Girardin) VISA MC AE

24 r. des Juifs – ✆ 03 88 36 49 68 – Fax 03 88 24 25 12
closed 21 March-1st April, 3-25 August, Christmas holidays, Saturday lunch, Sunday and Monday **G1**
Rest – *(pre-book)* Menu 38/58 €
Spec. Oeuf à la coque, meurette de betterave, jeunes pousses de red chard. Carré d'agneau rôti, endive confite, jus de viande. Mousse soufflée chaude de chocolat, crème glacée au Grand Marnier.
♦ Neighbourhood ♦
Carefully-chosen wines at reasonable prices at this restaurant, run by two sommeliers. Contemporary cuisine, in tune with the original designer décor.

XX **Umami** AC MC AE

8 r. des Dentelles – ✆ 03 88 32 80 53 – contact@restaurant-umami.com – www.restaurant-umami.com
closed 1st-12 January, Sunday and Monday **F2**
Rest – Menu 18 € (weekday lunch), 50/70 € – Carte 48/54 €
♦ Innovative ♦ Cosy ♦
The gifted chef creates resolutely modern cuisine in this contemporary and bright restaurant in the town centre, in the heart of "Little France". Worth discovering...

XX ✿ **Serge and Co** (Serge Burckel) AC VISA MC AE

14 r. Pompiers ✉ 67300 Schiltigheim – ✆ 03 88 18 96 19 – serge.burckel@wanadoo.fr – Fax 03 88 83 41 99 – www.serge-and-co.com
closed Saturday lunch, Sunday dinner and Monday
Rest – Menu 28 € (weekday lunch), 49/88 € – Carte 60/88 €
Spec. Thon rouge mariné. Grenouilles "clin d'œil aux escargots". "Cigare" au chocolat.
♦ Trendy ♦
After a long trip through Asia and America, chef Serge is back home serving appetising cuisine inspired by his travels. Contemporary décor with a slightly exotic feel.

XX **Gavroche**

4 r. Klein – ✆ 03 88 36 82 89 – restaurant.gavroche@free.fr – www.restaurant-gavroche.fr
closed 5-11 March, 30 July-19 August, 24 December-1st January, Saturday and Sunday **G2**

Rest – Menu 35 € – Carte 43/52 €

♦ Cosy ♦

Adorned with window-boxes, the red façade of the Gavroche conceals a cosy dining room (straw tones, wooden banquettes) serving delicious, market-inspired contemporary cuisine.

XX **Le Pont aux Chats**

42 r. de la Krutenau – ✆ 03 88 24 08 77 – le-pont-aux-chats.restaurant@orange.fr – Fax 03 88 24 08 77
closed 2 weeks in August, February holidays, Saturday lunch, Tuesday and Wednesday **H2**

Rest – Carte 42/63 €

♦ Trendy ♦

A charming interior featuring a successful fusion of ancient timbers and contemporary furniture, with an adorable courtyard terrace. Modern menu based around seasonal produce.

XX **Pont des Vosges**

15 quai Koch – ✆ 03 88 36 47 75 – pontdesvosges@noos.fr – Fax 03 88 25 16 85 closed Sunday **H1**

Rest – Carte 32/60 €

♦ Retro ♦

Located on the corner of a stone building, this brasserie is renowned for its copious traditional cuisine. Antique advertising posters and mirrors decorate the dining room.

X **L'Atelier du Goût**

17 r. des Tonneliers – ✆ 03 88 21 01 01 – ateliergout.morabito@free.fr – Fax 03 88 23 64 36
closed February holidays, 28 July-10 August, Saturday except dinner in December, Sunday and public holidays **G2**

Rest – Carte 35/48 €

♦ Trendy ♦

Colourful, designer décor provides the backdrop for this former winstub, transformed into a laid-back restaurant. Appetising dishes feature high-quality organic and seasonal produce.

WINSTUBS *Regional specialities and wine tasting in a typical alsatian atmosphere*

X **L'Ami Schutz**

1 Ponts Couverts – ✆ 03 88 32 76 98 – info@ami-schutz.com – Fax 03 88 32 38 40 – www.ami-schutz.com
Closed Christmas holidays **E-F2**

Rest – Menu 24/48 € bi – Carte 32/55 €

♦ Alsatian cuisine ♦ Inn ♦

Between the meanders of the Ill, typical "winstub" with wood panelling and cosy banquettes (the smaller dining room has greater charm). Terrace beneath the lime trees.

X **S'Burjerstuewel - Chez Yvonne**

10 r. Sanglier – ✆ 03 88 32 84 15 – info@chez-yvonne.net – Fax 03 88 23 00 18 – www.chez-yvonne.net
closed Christmas holidays **G2**

Rest – *(pre-book)* Carte 24/53 €

This winstub has become one of the city's institutions, witnessed by the photos and dedications of its famous guests. Regional cuisine with a modern twist.

Toulouse

TOULOUSE

Population (est. 2004): 390 350 (conurbation 761 100) – Altitude: 146m

S. Frances/HEMIS.fr

The first thing you notice about Toulouse is its pink buildings, leaving you in little doubt as to why France's fourth biggest city has the enchanting epithet 'La Ville Rose'. The rouge shade of brickwork lends the place a distinctly sunny charm, enhanced by a lovely old town infused with sixteenth century merchant houses and grand Romanesque churches.

It's here that the Toulousains throng, particularly at dusk when the town's bars and cafes are bathed in a sumptuous rosy glow. This is a confident, easy-going city whose rich architectural heritage is matched by an intellectual verve: its 115,000 students make it second only to Paris as a French university centre. You wouldn't think it to be sitting at a sunny bar with an Armagnac, but Toulouse is also at the heart of the European aerospace industry, and it's on the outskirts here that the space shuttle programme is based. Pre-eminence has come the way of this city before. From the tenth to the thirteenth centuries, the Counts of Toulouse ran a resplendent court populated by troubadours and poets whose works inspired the likes of Dante and Chaucer. Then in the sixteenth century, it flourished again through the cultivation of woad, and newly enriched merchants built the most magnificent town houses - ***hotels particuliers*** -which make up one of the best reasons to wander the streets on a sunny day.

LIVING THE CITY

Toulouse sits handsomely midway between the Mediterranean and the Atlantic. The visitor-friendly old town is bounded to the east by the Canal du Midi and to the west by the gently curving River Garonne. This charming area is even more tightly hemmed in by a ring of nineteenth-century boulevards (d'Arcole, Strasbourg, Lazare Carnot, Verdier and Jules Guesde). A sharply defined 'cross' of streets cuts the centre into four quarters (Rue d'Alsace Lorraine/Rue du Languedoc running north/south; Rue de Metz east/west). Over the river three kilometres to the northwest is Toulouse Blagnac airport, while the same distance southeast is the huge Cité de l'Espace centre.

PRACTICAL INFORMATION

ARRIVAL-DEPARTURE

Toulouse-Blagnac Airport is located 7km west of the city centre. The Express bus takes 20min while a taxi will cost about €26. High speed trains to Paris go from Gare Matabiau.

TRANSPORT

Toulouse offers a bus and metro system to get you around town. A one-trip red ticket allows you to travel anywhere on the network for an hour. There's a slightly more expensive round trip ticket, plus a Day ticket and 10-12 trip tickets.

The main railway station is situated in a picturesque setting by the Canal du Midi. It's a short five minute hop on the metro to the old town centre, but if you're not weighed down by luggage it's a pleasant twenty minute stroll over the canal on foot. On your walk into town, just before the central Place du Capitole, you'll find the main tourist office on the square Charles-de-Gaulle.

EXPLORING TOULOUSE

"Pink at dawn, red at noon and purple at dusk." How many cities can you say that about? At around the time of the colour purple, particularly in the summertime, you'll hear the sound of screeching chairs as everyone grabs a table at the bars around the capacious **Place du Capitole**, and waits for the daily free light show. As the sun sets, the long, neoclassical facade of the city hall begins to glow. At first it's a soft blush, then a warm fiery light, as the sun works on the golden balconies of its eighteenth century, rose-coloured frontage. All this, and dinner too.

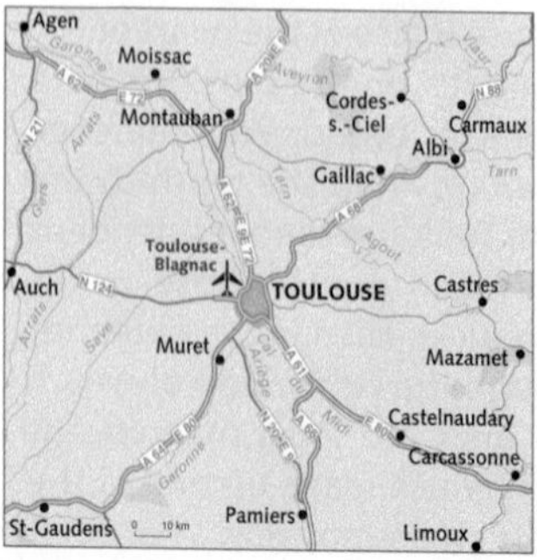

You don't have to go far to find another great treasure of old Toulouse. Just to the north of Capitole is **St-Sernin**, the largest Romanesque basilica in Europe and considered the finest in France. It was begun in 1080 as a stopping point for pilgrims on their way to Santiago de Compostela, and took another three centuries to complete. Nearly a thousand years after the first brick was laid it still has the power to knock you back in your stride. Its octagonal belfry is a masterpiece of its kind, while its cavernous, pale pink interior is full of soaring arches, and there's an array of ancient relics in the crypt. If St-Sernin is the towering landmark here, it's not the only church to impress. As the medieval streets spill out in a rich patchwork southwest of the basilica, you come across **Les Jacobins** on Rue Lakanal. A great Gothic pile built in the thirteenth century, it boasts elegant vaulting ribs like sprouting palm fronds, and lovingly maintained cloisters full of quiet, atmospheric splendour; beneath the altar lie the remains of the philosopher St Thomas Aquinas. Down Rue Gambetta from here is the baroque **Notre-Dame-de-la-Daurade**, whose dark and brooding interior is watched over by a black Madonna.

➔ PARTICULIER-LY FINE

When the visitor's eye hasn't been taken by one of the churches, there's a good chance it's seized on the delights of a ***hôtel particulier***. These are the superb Renaissance town houses and mansions which were built by the city's merchants from the wealth of the woad trade. Nearly all are built of red Toulousain brick, decorated with costly stone (brought over from the Pyrenees) in the form of ornate doorways, vaulted cloisters, statues, turrets and pillars. Most are closed, but you can peek at many by strolling casually into courtyards; particularly good is the elaborate **Hôtel de Bernuy** with its fine stone-galleried courtyard on Rue Gambetta. But the pick of les *particuliers* is **Hôtel d'Assezat**, on Rue de Metz, not least because it's open to the public. It's a superb twenty eight metre high building of brick and stone, enhanced by classic columns and a tower with octagonal lantern. Thanks to its Bemberg collection, there's a great assortment of artwork on view, including a roomful of Bonnards, and works by Monet, Canaletto, Dufy and Cranach the Elder. Eclectic is the word!

➔ SCULPTURE, SPACE – AND A SLAUGHTERHOUSE

In keeping with its venerable surroundings, Toulouse's old town offers up a museum dedicated to the distant past. **Musée des Augustins** is itself a nineteenth-century building based round the cloisters of an Augustinian priory. Inside, the wonderful collections of Romanesque and medieval sculpture bring alive the fashions of the day; these are 'fleshed out' by sixteenth to nineteenth century European paintings. For the shock of the new, you have to head over the Garonne to the left bank and a mighty brick-built former nineteenth-century slaughterhouse – **Les Abattoirs**, opened in 2000 – which dives head first into the world of modern art from the 1950s onwards. It includes the head-turning La Depouille du Minotaure by Picasso – a stage curtain from 1936 (okay, not *everything* here is post-50s). Toulouse's up-to-the-minute face, however, is found in the southeastern suburbs at **Cité de l'Espace**, the science park that leaves earth to deal with all things galactic. This is the place to come if you want to dock your virtual capsule on a space station, or find out about weightlessness, satellite communications and planetary movements. You can also walk inside a mock-up of the Mir space station (but the bus back to Place du Capitole may seem a bit mundane afterwards).

➔ KEEPING WATCH

Back on the old town's reassuring 'terra firma', fine detail appears in every nook and cranny; for somewhere apparently timeless, there's a fascination with the hours of the day, whether it's via the charming twenty-four hour clock on the face of an eighteenth-century townhouse, or in the absorbing **Musee Paul-Dupuy** (south of Capitole), which has an elegantly displayed collection of clocks and watches. All round this part of town are narrow lanes and pretty streets; the prettiest **is Rue Croix-Baragnon**, with its galleries and designer boutiques renowned for their chic interiors. Stroll about here to pick up interesting art and antiques or funky, bohemian one-offs. And when you've had your fill of street life, you'll be pleased to know that this is also the area where the city's best green spots are to be found. You can take your pick from either the enchanting formal gardens of the **Grand-Rond**, or the slightly larger and equally beguiling **Jardin des Plantes.**

→ MARKET FRESH

This is a city that makes the most of the outdoor life, and that includes its markets. The Place du Capitole is the place to be on a Wednesday, when a huge market sells food, clothes and bric-à-brac. And twice a week, they bring out the organic food, too: hang around and you'll be able to try all manner of breads, cheeses and cakes before you delve in your pocket for cash. Up at the Basilica St-Sernin on a Sunday, the antiques and bric-à-brac market is way too good to just call a flea-market – this is the place for gilded mirrors and chandeliers, so better keep some extra space in your rucksack. Market or not, the little squares dotted all over town are always humming with life, be it unicyclists or accordionists, roller-bladers or skateboarders. Or maybe just students. There are 115,000 of them here, not just adding to the weight of grey matter within the city walls, but, even more crucially if you're visiting, helping keep the prices down in the cafés and bars.

CALENDAR HIGHLIGHTS

La Ville Rose views its festivals and events through violet-tinted spectacles, even in the gloom of February, when it hosts the International Violet Meeting. Toulouse is the world capital of violets, and this celebration of the city's favourite flower includes exhibitions, markets, and various flower-based attractions. A month later, the Parc des Expositions de Toulouse is the venue for the Toulouse International Fair, when 150,000 visitors congregate for exhibitions and activities based around an international theme (in 2008 it's 'People of the Himalayas'). In June, the action moves down to the river. The Garonne Festival livens up the banksides with art happenings, music and parades, while also that month the Electronic Siestas Festival brings free afternoon concerts to the Garonne: it's innovative music to snooze-in-the-sun

TOULOUSE IN...

→ ONE DAY

Place du Capitole, St-Sernin, Les Jacobins, Hôtel d'Assezat, dusk back at Capitole

→ TWO DAYS

Musée des Augustins, Les Abattoirs (or Cité de l'Espace), the streets around rue Croix-Baragnon, a stroll along the banks of the Canal du Midi (or the Garonne)

→ THREE DAYS

Jardin des Plantes, Musée Paul-Dupuy, a boisterous market (if Sunday, at St-Sernin)

by. Toulouse is a cultural hothouse, and the Marathon des Mots, also in June, celebrates the written word, with more than three hundred writers and artists taking part in a series of readings and performances at more than forty venues. There's an eclectic air about the Toulouse d'Éte Music Festival in July and August. International names rub shoulders with local musicians in a wide range of concerts at venues across the city, and the music ranges from flamenco to jazz to piano recital. Fans of the latter will be in seventh heaven, because September sees the Piano Aux Jacobins Festival, at the Church of the Jacobins, an atmospheric occasion with recitals by some of the world's best pianists in the cloisters of the ancient church. A huge contemporary art showpiece dominates the end of September and October: Printemps de Septembre is a free exhibition covering many artistic genres that takes place all over the city with special street lighting to enhance the effect. Alongside runs the Festival Occitania (also September) with more than fifty cultural events covering film, music, poetry, theatre, painting and more besides. To top it all off, November's Toulouse Antiques Fair, at the Parc des Expositions, has been voted France's premier event in its category by the trade press, so expect three impressive displays: Prestige, Antiques and Arts and Crafts.

EATING OUT

The food of the Toulousain is not for the faint-hearted. A lot of the city's favoured dishes concentrate on the parts of animals many prefer to forget. Neck, brain, ears and liver find their way onto the menu stuffed, slow-cooked or in eye-popping combinations. At the smart restaurants, it's possible to order the likes of pigeon stuffed with langoustines or foie gras with spiced fruits. Traditionally, the mainstay of the southwest is the cassoulet, a hearty stew with basic ingredients such as pork, duck fat, beans and garlic. You need to be hungry to take it on, so you'll be pleased to know that proper evening dining in Toulouse doesn't really start till at least 8.30 or 9 in the evening when your appetite should be well and truly whetted. Get there earlier and you'll be dining alone. This is a city that lives the late life: it's only sixty miles from the Spanish border, and its dining style is cheerily overseen as 'la mode espagnole'. There's a third element to the food scene here: wander down some of the narrower streets in the evening and you'll realise how close you are to North Africa. Exotic scents waft from darkened doorways and Moroccan restaurants – lots of them – tempt you inside. Wherever you decide to eat, the bill includes a service charge, but if you're happy with the service, it's usual to leave a tip of between five and ten per cent. And remember, if you've been excited by a particular ingredient then stock up at the farmers' markets that are popular in the city: these are the places for foie gras, sausages, creamy wads of goats' cheese, and bread the size of local rugby balls.

→ TOULOUSE L'EAU-TREK

If you get the chance, come into the city by the Canal du Midi. It's lined with plane trees and fine nineteenth-century houses, and winds its calm way up from the Mediterranean. The most atmospheric way to see it is by cycling, walking or just floating along its seductive course on a slow boat.

→ BIG ON OPERA

The city hall in the Place du Capitole is so big because it also contains Toulouse's main musical venue, the Opera House. This is a refurbished eighteenth century gem, with opulent gilt mouldings and painted cartouches. It's one of France's most prestigious homes of opera, but get along to see ballet, chamber music and recitals as well.

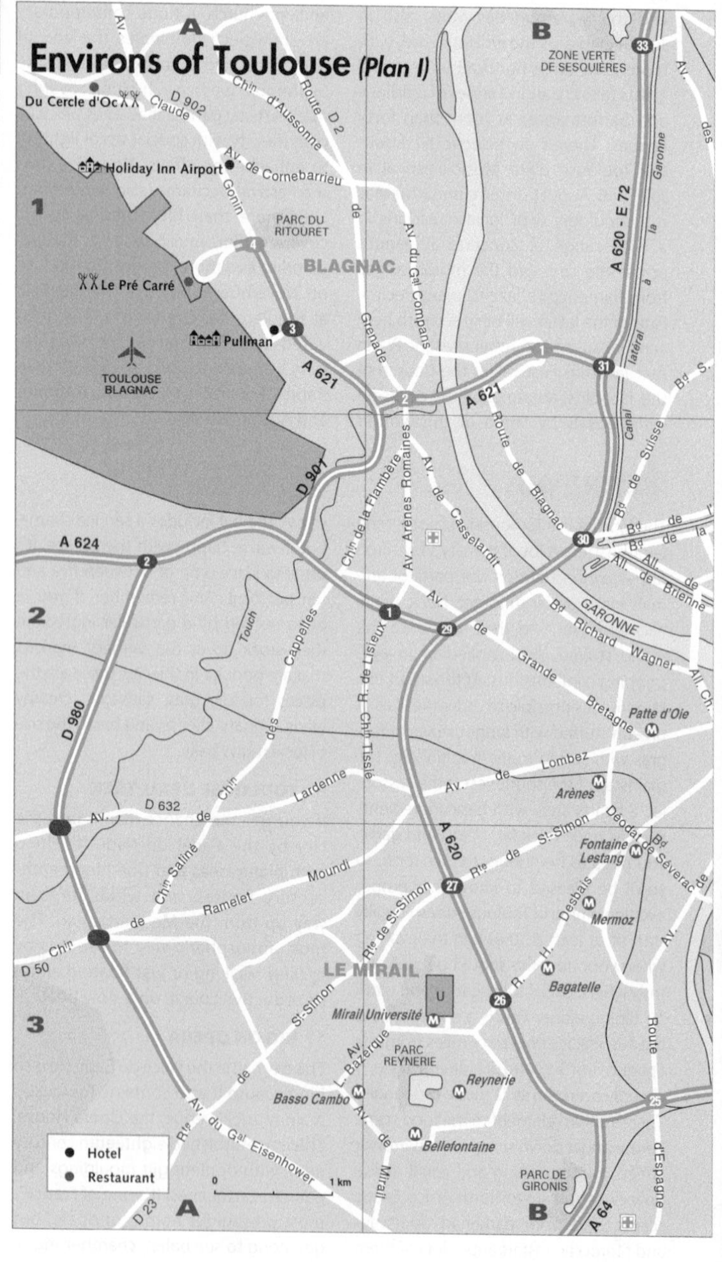
Environs of Toulouse (Plan I)
Du Cercle d'Oc
Holiday Inn Airport
Le Pré Carré
Pullman
TOULOUSE BLAGNAC
PARC DU RITOURET
BLAGNAC
ZONE VERTE DE SESQUIÈRES
A 620 - E 72
A 621
A 624
D 901
D 902
D 980
D 632
D 50
D 23
A 620
A 64
GARONNE
Patte d'Oie
Arènes
Fontaine Lestang
Mermoz
Bagatelle
LE MIRAIL
Mirail Université
PARC REYNERIE
Reynerie
Basso Cambo
Bellefontaine
PARC DE GIRONIS
Hotel
Restaurant
0
1 km

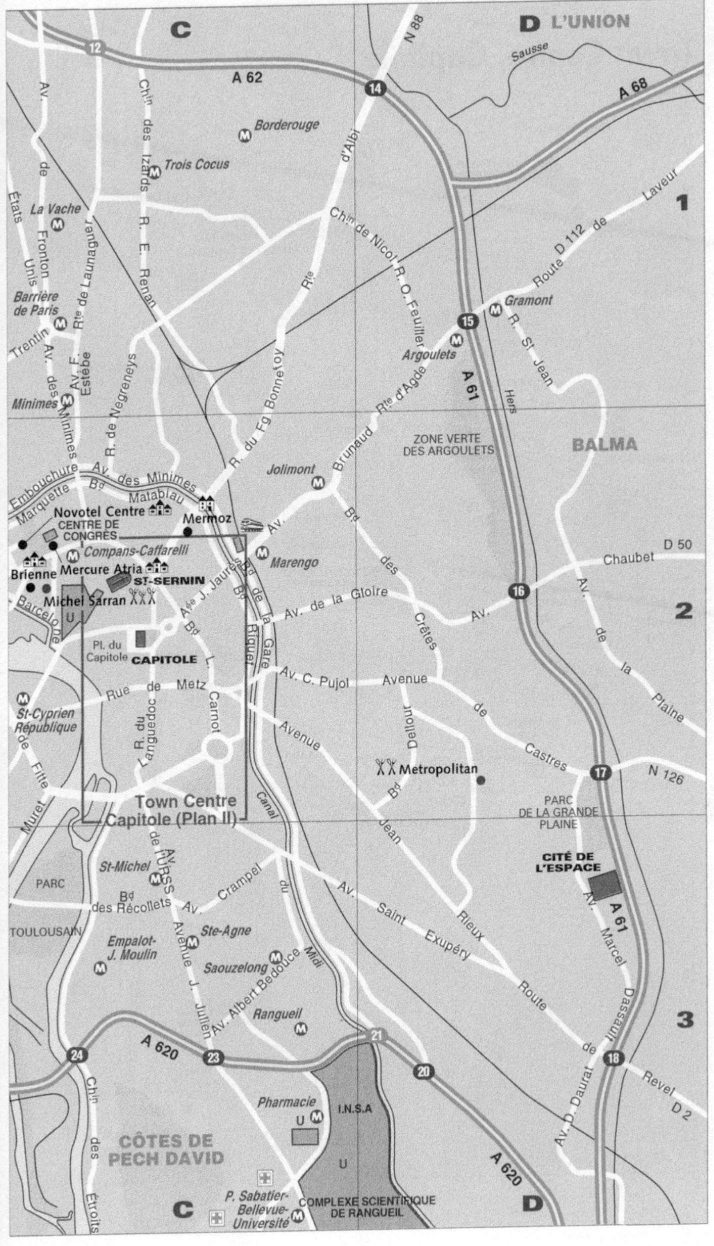
C
D
L'UNION
A 62
A 68
A 61
A 620
N 88
Borderouge
Trois Cocus
La Vache
Barrière de Paris
Minimes
Gramont
Argoulets
ZONE VERTE DES ARGOULETS
BALMA
Jolimont
Novotel Centre
CENTRE DE CONGRÈS
Mermoz
Compans-Caffarelli
Marengo
Brienne
Mercure Atria
ST-SERNIN
Michel Sarran
Pl. du Capitole
CAPITOLE
St-Cyprien République
Metropolitan
Town Centre Capitole (Plan II)
PARC DE LA GRANDE PLAINE
CITÉ DE L'ESPACE
St-Michel
PARC
TOULOUSAIN
Empalot-J. Moulin
Ste-Agne
Saouzelong
Rangueil
Pharmacie
I.N.S.A
CÔTES DE PECH DAVID
P. Sabatier-Bellevue-Université
COMPLEXE SCIENTIFIQUE DE RANGUEIL
Route D 112 de Laveur
Av. de la Gloire
Chaubet
D 50
N 126
Route de Revel
D 2
Av. de Castres
Av. de la Plaine
Av. Marcel Dassault
Av. D. Daurat
Av. Saint Exupéry
Rue de Metz
Bd des Récollets
Av. J. Julien
Av. Albert Bedouce
Canal du Midi
1
2
3

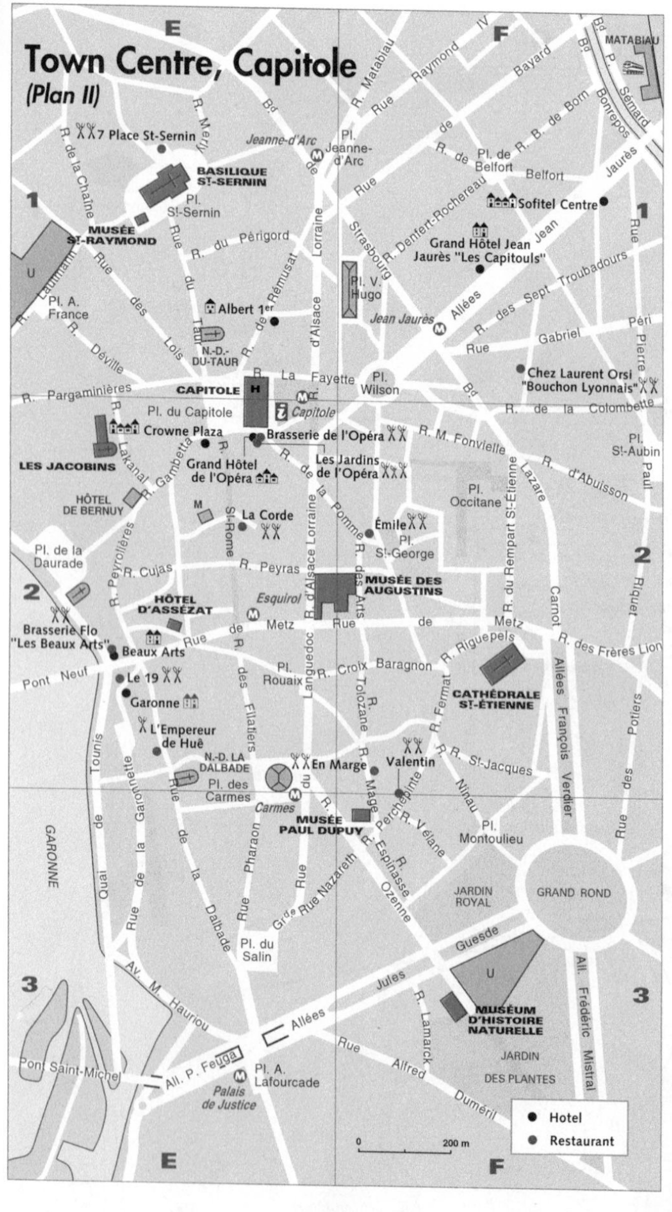
Town Centre, Capitole
(Plan II)
7 Place St-Sernin
BASILIQUE ST-SERNIN
MUSÉE ST-RAYMOND
Albert 1er
N.-D.-DU-TAUR
CAPITOLE
Pl. du Capitole
Capitole
Crowne Plaza
Brasserie de l'Opéra
Grand Hôtel de l'Opéra
Les Jardins de l'Opéra
LES JACOBINS
HÔTEL DE BERNUY
La Corde
Émile
Pl. St-George
MUSÉE DES AUGUSTINS
HÔTEL D'ASSÉZAT
Esquirol
Brasserie Flo "Les Beaux Arts"
Beaux Arts
Le 19
Garonne
L'Empereur de Huê
N.-D. LA DALBADE
Pl. des Carmes
Carmes
En Marge
Valentin
MUSÉE PAUL DUPUY
CATHÉDRALE ST-ÉTIENNE
Pl. Occitane
Sofitel Centre
Grand Hôtel Jean Jaurès "Les Capitouls"
Chez Laurent Orsi "Bouchon Lyonnais"
Jean Jaurès
Pl. Wilson
Pl. de Belfort
Pl. Jeanne-d'Arc
Pl. V. Hugo
MATABIAU
Pl. A. France
Pl. de la Daurade
Pl. Rouaix
Pl. Montoulieu
GRAND ROND
JARDIN ROYAL
MUSÉUM D'HISTOIRE NATURELLE
JARDIN DES PLANTES
Pl. du Salin
Pl. A. Lafourcade
Palais de Justice
Pont Neuf
Pont Saint-Michel
GARONNE
Hotel
Restaurant
200 m

TOWN CENTRE

Plan II

Sofitel Centre

84 allées J. Jaurès – ✆ 05 61 10 23 10 – h1091@accor.com – Fax 05 61 10 23 20 – www.sofitel-toulouse-centre.com **F1**

119 rm – 280/320 € 310/350 €, 22 € – 14 suites

Rest *S W Café* – Carte 34/59 €

♦ Luxury ♦ Chain hotel ♦ Classical ♦

The hotel occupies an imposing red-brick and glass building. Discreetly luxurious rooms, with good soundproofing. Business centre and good seminar facilities. Modern setting and recipes combining regional products and foreign spices at the SW café.

Crowne Plaza

7 pl. Capitole – ✆ 05 61 61 19 19 – hicptoulouse@alliance-hospitality.com – Fax 05 61 23 79 96 – www.crowne-plaza-toulouse.com **E2**

162 rm – 280/350 € 280/350 €, 23 € – 3 suites

Rest – *(closed August)* Menu 29/60 € bi – Carte 46/69 €

♦ Business ♦ Chain hotel ♦ Classical ♦

This luxury hotel enjoys a prestigious location on the famous Place du Capitole. Spacious, comfortable rooms, some of which overlook the town hall. Business centre. The restaurant opens onto a delightful Florentine-inspired patio.

Grand Hôtel de l'Opéra without rest

1 pl. du Capitole – ✆ 05 61 21 82 66 – hotelopera@guichard.fr – Fax 05 61 23 41 04 – www.grand-hotel-opera.com **E2**

49 rm – 185/484 € 185/484 €, 22 €

♦ Luxury ♦ Cosy ♦

This hotel in a 17C convent has an air of serenity and charm. Beautiful rooms with wood panels and velvet. Pleasant bar lounge and attractive vaulted reception hall.

de Brienne without rest

20 bd du Mar. Leclerc – ✆ 05 61 23 60 60 – brienne@hoteldebrienne.com – Fax 05 61 23 18 94 – www.hoteldebrienne.com *Plan I* **C2**

70 rm – 70/93 € 70/93 €, 10 € – 1 suite

♦ Chain hotel ♦ Classical ♦

Colourful and impeccably maintained rooms, numerous work and leisure areas (bar-library, patio): very popular with a business clientele.

Mercure Atria

8 espl. Compans Caffarelli – ✆ 05 61 11 09 09 – h1585@accor.com – Fax 05 61 23 14 12 – www.mercure.com *Plan I* **C2**

134 rm – 121/153 € 131/163 €, 14 € – 2 suites

Rest – Carte 16/27 €

♦ Chain hotel ♦ Modern ♦

Modern comfortable furnishings, decorative wood panels and warm colours in rooms that have been recently refurbished in line with the chain's new look. Vast business area. The restaurant offers a soothing view of the public park, and another, busier one of the kitchen.

Novotel Centre

5 pl. A. Jourdain – ✆ 05 61 21 74 74 – h0906@accor.com – Fax 05 61 22 81 22 – www.novotel.com *Plan I* **C2**

135 rm – 101/165 € 101/165 €, 14 € – 2 suites

Rest – Carte 22/40 €

♦ Chain hotel ♦ Modern ♦

This regional-style building adjacent to a Japanese garden and large park has spacious rooms renovated in a contemporary spirit, some with a terrace. A festival of colour in this dining room. Traditional and local cuisine.

Garonne without rest

22 descente de la Halle aux Poissons – ✆ 05 34 31 94 80 – contact@hotelgaronne.com – Fax 05 34 31 94 81 – www.hotelsdecharmetoulouse.com **E2**

14 rm – 165/185 € 165/185 €, 20 €

◆ Traditional ◆ Modern ◆

An old building in one of the Old Town's narrow streets. A fine contemporary interior: stained-oak parquet flooring, design furniture, silk draperies and the odd Japanese touch.

Des Beaux Arts without rest

1 pl. du Pont-Neuf – ✆ 05 34 45 42 42 – contact@hoteldesbeauxarts.com – Fax 05 34 45 42 43 – www.hoteldesbeauxarts.com **E2**

20 rm – 108 € 178/230 €, 16 €

◆ Business ◆ Modern ◆

Tastefully done 18C establishment with cosy refined rooms, most with a view of the Garonne. Number 42 enjoys the additional benefit of a mini-terrace.

Les Capitouls without rest

29 allées J. Jaurès – ✆ 05 34 41 31 21 – reservation@hotel-capitouls.com – Fax 05 61 63 15 17 – www.bestwestern-capitouls.com **F1**

55 rm – 130/181 € 130/181 €, 13.50 € – 2 suites

◆ Chain hotel ◆ Classical ◆

Right by the Jean Jaurès metro station, this old town house has a distinctive foyer with pink brick vaulting. The rooms have Wifi access.

Mermoz without rest

50 r. Matabiau – ✆ 05 61 63 04 04 – reservation@hotel-mermoz.com – Fax 05 61 63 15 64 – www.hotel-mermoz.com *Plan I* **C2**

52 rm – 125 € 125 €, 12 €

◆ Family ◆ Art Deco ◆

This hotel's spare décor recalls the Aeropostale's heroic pilots. Bright, candy-coloured rooms. Flower-decked glassed-in area or tree-shaded outside tables for breakfast.

Albert 1er without rest

8 r. Rivals – ✆ 05 61 21 17 91 – toulouse@hotel-albert1.com – Fax 05 61 21 09 64 – www.hotel-albert1.com **E1**

47 rm – 55/98 € 65/98 €, 10 €

◆ Family ◆ Functional ◆

A very practical base for discovering the "pink city" by foot. Ask for one of the refurbished rooms, or one at the rear for peace and quiet.

Les Jardins de l'Opéra

1 pl. Capitole – ✆ 05 61 23 07 76 – contact@lesjardinsdelopera.com – Fax 05 61 23 63 00 – www.lesjardinsdelopera.com

closed 4-25 August, 1st-7 January, Sunday and Monday **E2**

Rest – Menu 42 € bi (lunch), 70/100 € – Carte approx. 92 €

◆ Luxury ◆

The elegant dining rooms under a glass roof and separated by a fountain dedicated to Neptune. Unusually, the menu offers dishes in "trilogy": three dishes on the same plate.

Michel Sarran

21 bd A. Duportal – ✆ 05 61 12 32 32 – restaurant@michel-sarran.com – Fax 05 61 12 32 33 – www.michel-sarran.com

closed 2 August-1st September, 20-28 December, Wednesday lunch, Saturday and Sunday *Plan I* **C2**

Rest – *(pre-book)* Menu 48 € bi (lunch), 98/165 € bi – Carte 88/126 €

Spec. Soupe tiède de foie gras à l'huître belon. Turbot, jus mousseux au combawa. L'oeuf et la poule au caviar d'Aquitaine.

◆ Fashionable ◆

This delightful 19C abode, whose friendly atmosphere immediately makes one feel at home, has been decorated in a purposely minimalist style to better set off the chef's inventive cuisine.

XX ✿ **En Marge** (Frank Renimel)

8 r. Mage – ✆ 05 61 53 07 24 – contact@restaurantenmarge.com – www.restaurantenmarge.com
closed 10 August-9 September and 21 December-6 January **F2**
Rest – *(number of covers limited, pre-book)* Menu 30 € (lunch), 50 (dinner)/75 €
Spec. Crevettes pimentées en gaspacho. Noix de veau et pata negra. Soufflé rhum et caramel.

◆ Friendly ◆

A new restaurant with a homely atmosphere, friendly service and delicious, innovative cuisine. Limited number of tables in a modern décor with a hint of Baroque.

XX ✿ **Metropolitan**

2 pl. Auguste-Albert – ✆ 05 61 34 63 11 – Fax 05 61 52 88 91 – www.metropolitan-restaurant.fr *Plan I* **D2**
Rest – Menu 26 € (weekday lunch), 39/53 € – Carte 48/72 €
closed 1st-21 August, 25-30 December, Saturday lunch, Sunday and Monday **Spec.** Déclinaison autour de la tomate. Filet de canette rôti. Barre fondante au chocolat amer et praliné.

A modern restaurant which gets full marks for its delicious, contemporary cuisine, designer-style dining room (with bar), small interior terrace adorned with vines, and efficient, friendly service.

XX **Valentin**

21 r. Perchepinte – ✆ 05 61 53 11 15 – www.valentin-restaurant.fr
closed Saturday lunch, Sunday and Monday **F2**
Rest – Menu 13.50 € (lunch), 33/54 € bi – Carte 45/61 €

A glass door crowned with an arch leads to this attractive restaurant, whose young chef specialises in inventive cuisine. Elegant decor with period furniture, vaulted cellar and brick walls.

XX **7 Place St-Sernin**

7 pl. St-Sernin – ✆ 05 62 30 05 30 – restaurant@7placesaintsernin.com – Fax 05 62 30 04 06 – www.7placesaintsernin.com
Closed Saturday and Sunday **E1**
Rest – Menu 24 € bi (weekday lunch), 34/60 € bi – Carte 48/66 €

◆ Fashionable ◆

This restaurant set in a typical Toulouse house boasts flamboyant colours and is elegantly arranged and brightened with contemporary paintings. Modern dishes.

XX **La Corde**

4 r. Chalande – ✆ 05 61 29 09 43 – Fax 05 61 29 09 43 – www.lacorde.com
Rest – Menu 20 € (weekday lunch), 32/100 € – Carte 51/105 € **E2**

◆ Fashionable ◆

This impressive 15C tower, all that remains of a mansion that used to belong to prominent families of Toulouse, is home to the city's oldest restaurant (1881). Updated regional dishes.

XX **Brasserie Flo "Les Beaux Arts"**

1 quai Daurade – ✆ 05 61 21 12 12 – Fax 05 61 21 14 80 – www.brasserielesbeauxarts.com **E2**
Rest – Menu 30 € – Carte 28/68 €

◆ Retro ◆

Popular with locals, this brasserie on the banks of the Garonne was once frequented by Ingres, Matisse and Bourdelle. Retro décor and a varied menu.

XX **Le 19**

19 descente de la Halle aux Poissons – ✆ 05 34 31 94 84 – contact@restaurantle19.com – Fax 05 34 31 94 85 – www.restaurantle19.com
closed 1st-12 May, 11-17 August, 22 December-6 January, Monday lunch, Saturday lunch and Sunday **E2**
Rest – Menu 25 € bi, 40/60 € (b.i.) – Carte 47/70 €

◆ Trendy ◆

Welcoming, contemporary-style dining rooms (one with a superb 16C rib-vaulted ceiling), plus an open-view wine cellar. Hearty local cuisine.

XX **Chez Laurent Orsi "Bouchon Lyonnais"**

13 r. de l'Industrie – ✆ 05 61 62 97 43 – orsi.le-bouchon-lyonnais@wanadoo.fr – Fax 05 61 63 00 71 – www.le-bouchon-lyonnais.com

VISA

closed Saturday lunch and Sunday except public holidays **F1**

Rest – Menu 20 € (lunch)/33 € – Carte 33/58 €

◆ Brasserie ◆

A large bistro whose leather banquettes, closely-packed tables and mirrors are reminiscent of the brasseries of the 1930s. Dishes from the southwest and Lyon, as well as fish and seafood.

XX **Émile**

VISA

13 pl. St-Georges – ✆ 05 61 21 05 56 – restaurant-emile@wanadoo.fr – Fax 05 61 21 42 26 – www.restaurant-emile.com

closed 21 December-5 January, Monday except dinner May-September and Sunday **F2**

Rest – Menu 19 € (lunch), 35/50 € – Carte 37/60 €

◆ Friendly ◆

A restaurant with a popular terrace and a menu focused on local dishes and fish (cassoulet is the house speciality). Fine wine list.

XX **Brasserie de l'Opéra**

VISA

1 pl. Capitole – ✆ 05 61 21 37 03 – infojpgroupe@gmail.com – Fax 05 62 27 16 49 – www.brasserieopera.com

closed Sunday and Monday **E2**

Rest – Menu 18 € (lunch), 25/32 € – Carte 26/50 €

◆ Retro ◆

Chic 1930s style brasserie where you meet everyone in Toulouse, along with stars who leave their photo to mark a visit. Typical, seasonally influenced brasserie cuisine.

X **L'Empereur de Huê**

VISA

17 r. Couteliers – ✆ 05 61 53 55 72 – www.empereurdehue.com

closed Sunday and Monday **E2**

Rest – *(dinner only) (pre-book)* Menu 36 € – Carte 43/51 €

◆ Vietnamese ◆

If the decor of this family restaurant is contemporary, the cooking retains its Vietnamese roots.

AROUND TOULOUSE

Blagnac

Plan I

Pullman

rm VISA

2 av. Didier Daurat, dir. airport (exit n° 3) – ✆ 05 34 56 11 11 – h0565@accor.com – Fax 05 61 30 02 43 **A1**

100 rm – †175/290 € ††175/290 €, ☐ 22 €

Rest *Le Caouec* – *(closed 2-17 August, Saturday, Sunday and public holidays)* Carte 31/63 €

◆ Chain hotel ◆ Business ◆ Modern ◆

1970s hotel being treated to a complete facelift. Contemporary style public areas, with some guestrooms updated in a similar vein. Free shuttle to the airport. Tapas-type snacks served at the bar and more traditional menu in the dining room.

Holiday Inn Airport

rm rm VISA

pl. Révolution – ✆ 05 34 36 00 20 – tlsap@ichotelsgroup.com – Fax 05 34 36 00 30 – www.toulouseairport.holiday-inn.com

149 rm – †105/240 € ††105/255 €, ☐ 21 € **A1**

Rest – *(closed Saturday and Sunday)* Menu 22/35 € – Carte 22/46 €

◆ Chain hotel ◆ Business ◆ Modern ◆

Both peaceful and warm shades adorn the rooms decorated with modern furniture. A well-appointed seminar area. A shuttle links the hotel to the airport. A pleasant brasserie-style restaurant decorated with frescoes depicting olive trees.

Le Cercle d'Oc

6 pl. M. Dassault – 05 62 74 71 71 – cercledoc@wanadoo.fr – Fax 05 62 74 71 72
closed 3-24 August, 25 December-1st January, Saturday and Sunday **A1**
Rest – Menu 34 € bi (lunch), 43/55 €
♦ Fashionable ♦
This pretty 18C farm is an island of greenery in the middle of a shopping area. English club atmosphere in the elegant dining rooms, billiards room and pleasant terrace.

Le Pré Carré

aéroport Toulouse-Blagnac (2nd flour) – 05 61 16 70 40 – Fax 05 61 16 70 51
closed beg. May-end August, Saturday and Sunday **A1**
Rest – *(lunch only)* Menu 42/45 €
♦ Brasserie ♦
Pleasant airport restaurant overlooking the runways, in a brasserie setting. Design décor in red tones and wood furnishings. Modern menu.

Colomiers

L'Amphitryon (Yannick Delpech)

chemin de Gramont – 05 61 15 55 55 – contact@lamphitryon.com – Fax 05 61 15 42 30 – www.lamphitryon.com
Rest – Menu 32 € (weekday lunch), 58/105 € – Carte 87/114 €
Spec. Sardine fraîche taillée au couteau, crème de morue et caviar de hareng. Thon rouge mariné puis juste saisi. Canette du Lauragais en croûte de poivre noir, coriandre et cumin.
♦ Fashionable ♦
A welcoming, modern dining room-veranda overlooking the surrounding countryside. Brilliantly inventive cuisine takes local produce to new heights.

GERMANY
DEUTSCHLAND

PROFILE

→ **Area:**
356 733 km^2
(137 735 sq mi).

→ **Population:**
82 431 000 inhabitants (est. 2005), density = 231 per km^2.

→ **Capital:**
Berlin (conurbation 3 761 000 inhabitants).

→ **Currency:**
Euro (€); rate of exchange: € 1 = US$ 1.46 (Dec 2007).

→ **Government:**
Parliamentary federal republic, comprising 16 states (Länder) since 1990. Member of European Union since 1957 (one of the 6 founding countries).

→ **Language:**
German.

→ **Specific public holidays:**
Epiphany (6 January – in Baden-Württemberg, Bayern and Sachsen-Anhalt only); Good Friday (Friday before Easter); Corpus Christi (in Baden-Württemberg, Bayern, Hessen, Nordrhein-Westfalen, Rheinland-Pfalz, Saarland, Sachsen, Thüringen and those communities with a predominantly Roman Catholic population only); Day of German Unity (3 October); Reformation Day (31 October – in new Federal States only); 26 December.

→ **Local Time:**
GMT + 1 hour in winter and GMT + 2 hours in summer.

→ **Climate:**
Temperate continental, with cold winters and warm summers (Berlin: January: 0°C, July: 20°C).

→ **International dialling Code:**
00 49 followed by area code and then the local number. International directory enquiries ✆ **11 834**.

→ **Emergency:**
Police: ✆ **110**; Fire Brigade: ✆ **112**.

→ **Electricity:**
220 volts AC, 50HZ; 2-pin round-shaped continental plugs.

→ **Formalities**
Travellers from the European Union (EU), Switzerland, Iceland and the main countries of North and South America need a national identity card or passport (America: passport required) to visit Germany for less than three months (tourism or business purpose). For visitors from other countries a visa may be required, in addition to a passport, especially for those wishing to stay for longer than three months. We advise you to check with your embassy before travelling.

BERLIN

BERLIN

Population: 3 373 000 (conurbation 3 761 000) – Altitude: 40m

S. Guillot/MICHELIN

It's not every city parliament that has to scratch its head and decide where to put its centre, but that's the intriguing dilemma facing Berlin. Although homogeneous in many other ways, the east and the west of the city still lay claim to centres after their forty years of partition, and it may be that in time the exciting new – and central - Potsdamer Platz comes to be accepted as the city's hub. That's the thing about Germany's biggest metropolis – it's an invigorating mix of old and new, and constantly redefining itself.

After 1990, there were a tempestuous few years as Berlin sought to resolve its new identity, but it now stands proud as one of the most dynamic and forward thinking cities in the world. Alongside its idea of tomorrow, it's never lost sight of its bohemian past, and many parts of the city retain the arty sense of adventure that characterised downtown Berlin during the 1920s. Turn any corner and you might find a modernist art gallery, a tiny cinema or a cutting-edge club. Culture seeps through the very pores of life here.

LIVING THE CITY

The eastern side of the river Spree, around Nikolaiviertel, is the historic heart of the city, dating back to the 13C. Meanwhile, way over to the west of the centre lie Kurfürstendamm and Charlottenburg, smart districts which came to the fore after World War II as the heart of West Berlin. Between the two lie imposing areas which swarm with visitors: **Tiergarten** is the green lung of the city, and just to its east is the great boulevard of Unter den Linden. Continuing eastward, the self-explanatory Museum Island sits snugly and securely in the tributaries of the Spree. The most southerly of Berlin's sprawling districts is **Kreuzberg**, renowned for its bohemian, alternative character.

PRACTICAL INFORMATION

ARRIVAL-DEPARTURE

Berlin is served by three airports: Berlin-Tegel Airport lies 12km northwest of the city centre ; Berlin-Templehof is 7km to the south and Berlin-Schönefeld is 21km to the southeast. U-Bahn and S-Bahn trains operate from all three.

TRANSPORT

Invest in a Berlin-Potsdam Welcome Card. It gives you unlimited travel on the S-Bahn (trains), and discounts for selected theatres, museums, attractions and city tours. Available at public transport ticket desks, many hotels, and tourist information offices.

To get from one side of Berlin to the other, you'll need to travel by public transport. The U- and S-Bahn are quick and efficient, but the bus is another good alternative. Routes 100 and 200 are special double-decker services ideal for the visitor, as they incorporate most of the top attractions. Trams operate mainly within East Berlin. A tram ticket can be used on buses, U- and S-Bahn trains. There are various ticketing options which prevail in the city: check with tourist information offices.

Cyclists are well looked after here, so a good idea might be to hire a bike. There are many cycling routes around the city: most of the main roads have separate cycling lanes and even special traffic lights at intersections.

EXPLORING BERLIN

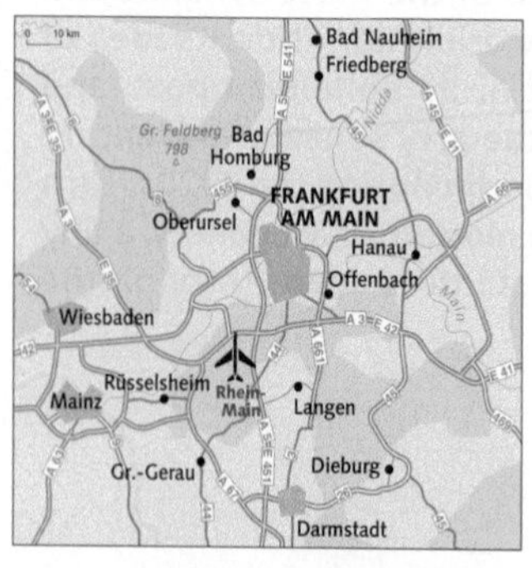

Sooner or later, the visitor to Berlin will take a stroll down Unter den Linden. To all intents and purposes, this is the city's central avenue, and you'll find none more attractive. It's an imposing boulevard, and it begins at its western end with the symbol of German reunification, The Brandenburg Gate. This magnificent neo-classical structure was completed in 1795, and has borne witness to many of the city's momentous episodes, most recently the celebrations of 1989 when the detested Wall it overlooked was triumphantly torn down. Earlier this decade the Gate was painstakingly renovated to its original Acropolis-like glory.

The wide, tree-lined Unter den Linden contains many of the city's historic landmarks, with a high concentration of 18C buildings sporting a prestigious pedigree. There's a line of fine stop-off points a little way up, the highlight being the **German History Museum**, which is housed in a magnificent former arsenal of pink baroque built just over three hundred years ago. Its fascinating exhibits range from a stern looking Martin Luther to the jacket of a concentration camp prisoner. Close to here is the neo-classical façade of the **State Opera House**, home to some of Berlin's finest performances, and the **State Library**, which boasts a tranquil inner courtyard with fountain and snug café providing a welcome break from the bustling grandeur of the boulevard.

→ ON A SPREE

Crossing **Schlossbrücke**, the eye-catching bridge over the Spree, you're on Berlin's very own island, named after what's made it famous. There are five museums here, and they're all in a grand huddle to your left. Pick of the bunch is the **Pergamon Museum**, which has one of the best collections of antiquities in the world, impressive enough to draw thousands of art lovers from across the globe. The other museums are hardly put in the shade: the **Alte Nationalgalerie** has a fine collection of German Romantics and French Impressionists; the **Altes** and **Neues Museums** highlight intriguing collections of Greek and Roman antiquities, and Egyptian art respectively; and the **Bodemuseum** has an eclectic mix of sculpture and coins. Much-needed restoration to the museums may possibly limit your access; nevertheless, give yourself an hour in each to do them justice. Most visually arresting of the island's buildings is the huge **Berliner Dom**, the city's cathedral, which has been painstakingly rebuilt since the War. Its impressive neo-Baroque exterior is modelled on St Peter's in Rome.

→ MEDIEVAL RECREATION

Just east from the island, across another bridge, lies the historic centre of Berlin, the Nikolaiviertel. By the time the city celebrated its seven hundred and fiftieth anniversary in 1987, the East German authorities of the time had rebuilt the area's pristine buildings: many of them having been lost in the War. What you see now is their attempt to recreate a medieval village. Centrepiece is the (originally) 13C **Nikolai Church**, which now includes a fascinating Berlin history exhibition. For true authenticity, make for the nearby **Knoblauchhaus**. This is the only house in Nikolaiviertel to escape War damage, and it's the oldest building still standing in Berlin. It's a beautiful mid-eighteenth century merchant's home, and its interior is now a household museum. For a radically different experience, head a little further east to the **TV Tower** – you're bound to have spotted it from practically any vantage point in the city. It's Berlin's tallest structure, like a giant toothpick that's bored its way up from the ground, and the view from its revolving café is spectacular: you'll see the whole of the city from up here, and you can enjoy a *Kaffee und Kuchen* while you're at it.

→ TOP OF THE POTS

Will **Potsdamer Platz** be recognised one day as the centrepoint of Berlin? It's ticking all the right boxes. Located just off the luxuriant Tiergarten, it was a mass of rubble not too many years ago. Now it's been developed as Germany's architectural showpiece, a shimmering zone of shiny new arcades and office buildings, where corporate domes merge with bright-as-a-button cafés and splashy fountains. This reborn area also does a nice line in irony: step out from one of its swish 21C entertainment complexes and spot the line of metal plaques thrusting from the street paving to denote where the Berlin Wall once stood. Potsdamer Platz also draws in a lot of visitors who've been to the nearby **Gemäldegalerie**, generally considered to be the best in Berlin. It contains nearly three thousand paintings covering five hundred years from the thirteenth to the eighteenth centuries, painstakingly acquired by experts whose task was to select high quality examples from all major European schools. Thus one can admire great works by Botticelli, Caravaggio, Rubens, Rembrandt, Bruegel, Vermeer and others. In keeping with the zeitgeist feel of Potsdamer Platz is the nearby **Reichstag** parliament building. Its wondrous late twentieth century glass beehive dome is visible for miles around, and adds another powerful visual statement to Berlin's modernist account. One more architectural wonder near the Gemäldegalerie is the 'circus tent' **Philharmonie** building, home to one of Europe's most renowned orchestras, the Berlin Philharmonic.

→ ALTERNATIVE CHECKPOINT

South of the centre is the 'alternative' highlight, Kreuzberg, the city's most bohemian quarter. Bizarrely enough, the 'entry point' to Kreuzberg could hardly be less bohemian (though it could possibly be termed 'alternative'): **Checkpoint Charlie** was the notorious crossing point between East and West Berlin during the Cold War. It's now marked by a single hut, but nearby is a fascinating Checkpoint Charlie museum full of weird ephemera relating to it. These days, this buzzing quarter is more renowned for its Turkish bazaars, arty boutiques, galleries and nightclubs: the latter often open in the early hours, not closing until long after the rising of the sun.

→ WEST SIDE STORY

Many tourists concentrate on the district that was East Berlin, where the origins of the city lie, but the western side also has much to commend it. Kurfürstendamm is a snazzy boulevard that runs through the heart of the area. It's not hard to realise that this was the 'free market' side of Berlin during the days of the Wall, as Ku'damm (the locals' name) runs the gamut of exclusive designer stores. The fashionable side-streets off it are also lined with boutiques and cafés tailor made to ensnare the *beau monde*. The area also boasts Europe's largest department store, **Kaufhaus des Westens** ('KaDeWe'), now over a hundred years old. The main attraction here is the gourmet's paradise, which has the largest collection of foodstuffs in the whole of Europe, including live fish and nearly two thousand five hundred different wines. Further west, Charlottenburg is possibly the most enchanting part of the city. It only became part of Berlin in 1920, and its heart is the seventeenth cen-

BERLIN IN...

→ ONE DAY

Unter Den Linden, Museum Island, Nikolaiviertel, coffee at TV Tower

→ TWO DAYS

Potsdamer Platz, Reichstag, Gemäldegalerie, concert at Philharmonie

→ THREE DAYS

KaDeWe, Kurfürstendamm, Charlottenburg Palace

tury former royal summer palace of Queen Sophie Charlotte. Its collection of richly decorated interiors is unequalled in Berlin, and the beautifully picturesque park that surrounds it is a magnet for weekending locals.

CALENDAR HIGHLIGHTS

The importance of Berlin as a cultural centre begins early in the year with the world renowned Berlin Film Festival, which attracts top international movies and stars. Throughout the summer the city holds the Museumsinsel Festival, during which special music, theatre and film productions are held for the public: Potsdamer Platz's open-air cinema is a popular venue. At the beginning of summer, in May, Kreuzberg's hip streets play host to the Karneval der Kulturen, which is three days of singing and dancing in celebration of multicultural Berlin. Bach lovers are in their element in July with Bach Tage Berlin, which features nine days' worth of the maestro's music, performed throughout the city. The same month, and on into August, World Music takes centre stage with open air concerts under the banner Heimatklange. The massive Global City celebration in August attracts up to three million visitors to Ku'damm. Now twenty years old, it hosts ten stages, featuring music of every description. A month later Musikfest Berlin offers two weeks of top classical performances in the Opera House and Philharmonie. The International Literary Festival (September) packs out Bebelplatz, as writers and poets from all over the world read to thousands. In October the focus is on a glittering metropolis when its top attractions are seductively illuminated in the Berlin Festival of Lights.

EATING OUT

Although by tradition Berlin hasn't been a gourmet stronghold, it does have a reputation for simple, hearty dishes, inspired by the long, hard winters. It's amazing how when the temperatures plummet, the city's comfort food can have an irresistible allure. Come the winter, who's for pork knuckle, Schnitzel, Bratwurst in mustard, chunky dumplings…or the real Berlin favourite Currywurst, which enjoins curry sauce and sausage. Be sure to try the local beer – Berliner Weisse mit Schuss – which is a light beer with a dash of raspberry or woodruff. Of course, that's not the whole story. Over the last fifteen years or so, Berlin has become so cosmopolitan that it can now claim a wider range of restaurants than any other German city. Many of the best restaurants are found within grand hotels and you only have to get to Savignyplatz near Ku'damm to realise how smart dining has taken off in a big way: the square is bursting with popular cafés and restaurants serving good food. There are lots too in Gendarmenmarkt. In the city as a whole there are almost unlimited options for the visitor: Asian restaurants of all kinds have sprung up in recent years. On the local front, bread and potatoes are ubiquitous – indeed Berlin has its own unique breads and rolls – but since reunification, the signature dishes have incorporated a global influence, so produce from the local forests, rivers and lakes may well have an Asian or Mediterranean twist. You can invariably eat late in Berlin: lots of places stay open until late, which can mean 2 or 3 in the morning. As dinner is the popular meal so there are plenty of inexpensive lunch menus available. Service is included in the price of your meal, but it's customary to round up the bill.

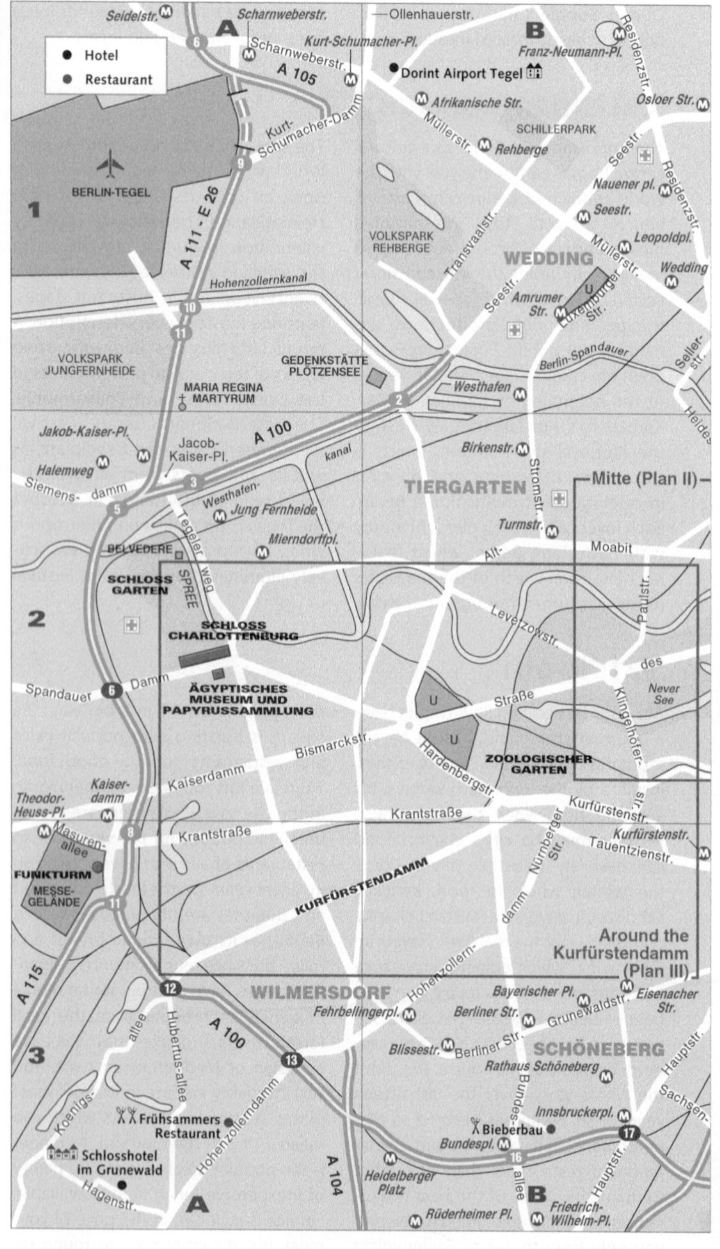

Hotel
Restaurant
A
B
1
2
3
Seidelstr.
Scharnweberstr.
Ollenhauerstr.
Kurt-Schumacher-Pl.
Franz-Neumann-Pl.
Residenzstr.
Dorint Airport Tegel
A 105
Afrikanische Str.
Osloer Str.
Kurt-Schumacher-Damm
Müllerstr.
Rehberge
SCHILLERPARK
BERLIN-TEGEL
Seestr.
Nauener pl.
Leopoldpl.
A 111 - E 26
VOLKSPARK REHBERGE
Transvaalstr.
WEDDING
Wedding
Hohenzollernkanal
Amrumer Str.
Luxemburger Str.
VOLKSPARK JUNGFERNHEIDE
GEDENKSTÄTTE PLÖTZENSEE
Berlin-Spandauer
Seller-str.
MARIA REGINA MARTYRUM
Westhafen
Jakob-Kaiser-Pl.
Jacob-Kaiser-Pl.
A 100
kanal
Birkenstr.
Halemweg
Siemens-damm
Westhafen-
Jung Fernheide
TIERGARTEN
Stromstr.
Mitte (Plan II)
Turmstr.
Mierndorffpl.
BELVEDERE
Tegeler weg
Alt-
Moabit
SCHLOSS GARTEN
SPREE
Paulstr.
Levetzowstr.
SCHLOSS CHARLOTTENBURG
des
Never See
Spandauer Damm
ÄGYPTISCHES MUSEUM UND PAPYRUSSAMMLUNG
Straße
Klingelhöfer-str.
Bismarckstr.
Hardenbergstr.
ZOOLOGISCHER GARTEN
Kaiser-damm
Kaiserdamm
Theodor-Heuss-Pl.
Krantstraße
Kurfürstenstr.
Masuren-allee
Nürnberger Str.
Tauentzienstr.
FUNKTURM
MESSE-GELÄNDE
KURFÜRSTENDAMM
Around the Kurfürstendamm (Plan III)
Hohenzollern-damm
A 115
WILMERSDORF
Bayerischer Pl.
Eisenacher Str.
Fehrbellingerpl.
Berliner Str.
Grunewaldstr.
allee
Hubertus-allee
A 100
Blissestr.
Berliner Str.
SCHÖNEBERG
Hauptstr.
Rathaus Schöneberg
Koenigs-allee
Hohenzollerndamm
Innsbruckerpl.
Sachsen-
Frühsammers Restaurant
Bieberbau
Bundespl.
Schlosshotel im Grunewald
A 104
Heidelberger Platz
Bundes-allee
Hagenstr.
Friedrich-Wilhelm-Pl.
Rüderheimer Pl.

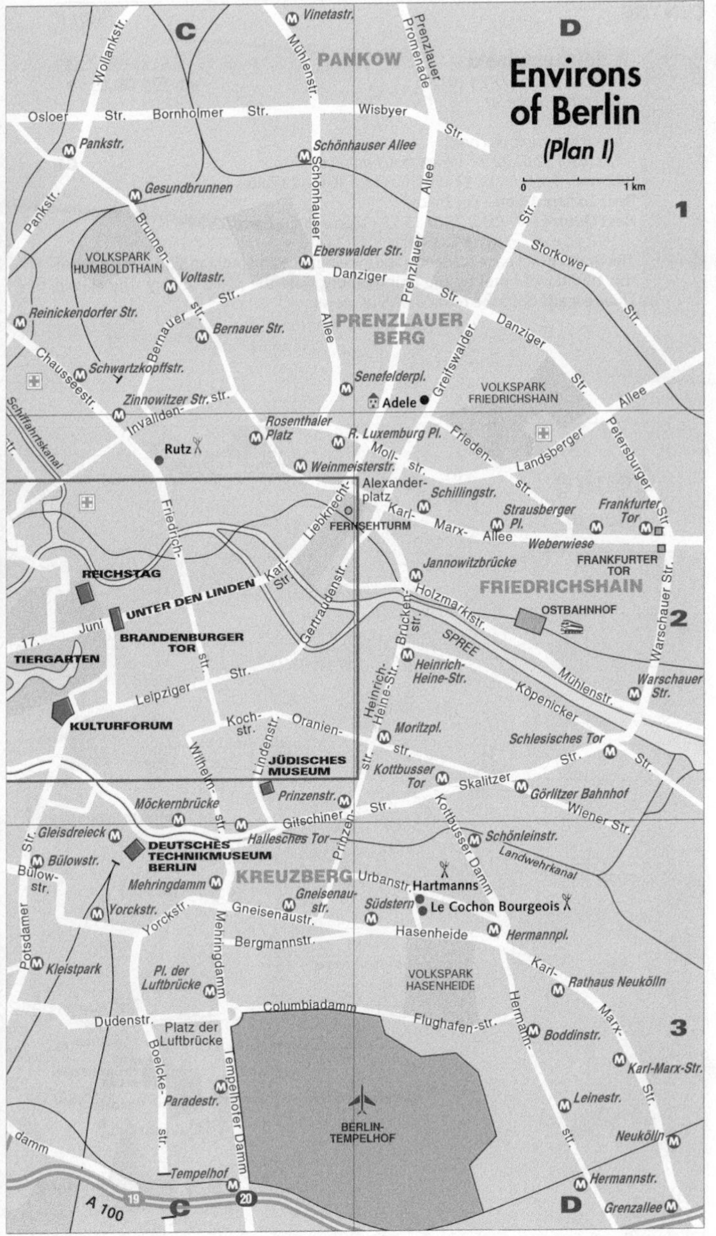
Environs of Berlin
(Plan I)
0
1 km
C
D
1
2
3
PANKOW
PRENZLAUER BERG
FRIEDRICHSHAIN
KREUZBERG
TIERGARTEN
VOLKSPARK HUMBOLDTHAIN
VOLKSPARK FRIEDRICHSHAIN
VOLKSPARK HASENHEIDE
REICHSTAG
UNTER DEN LINDEN
BRANDENBURGER TOR
KULTURFORUM
JÜDISCHES MUSEUM
DEUTSCHES TECHNIKMUSEUM BERLIN
FERNSEHTURM
OSTBAHNHOF
FRANKFURTER TOR
BERLIN-TEMPELHOF
SPREE
Adele
Rutz
Hartmanns
Le Cochon Bourgeois
Vinetastr.
Pankstr.
Gesundbrunnen
Schönhauser Allee
Eberswalder Str.
Voltastr.
Reinickendorfer Str.
Bernauer Str.
Schwartzkopffstr.
Senefelderpl.
Zinnowitzer Str.
Rosenthaler Platz
R. Luxemburg Pl.
Weinmeisterstr.
Alexanderplatz
Schillingstr.
Strausberger Pl.
Frankfurter Tor
Weberwiese
Jannowitzbrücke
Heinrich-Heine-Str.
Warschauer Str.
Moritzpl.
Schlesisches Tor
Kottbusser Tor
Görlitzer Bahnhof
Prinzenstr.
Möckernbrücke
Gleisdreieck
Hallesches Tor
Schönleinstr.
Bülowstr.
Mehringdamm
Gneisenaustr.
Südstern
Yorckstr.
Hermannpl.
Kleistpark
Pl. der Luftbrücke
Rathaus Neukölln
Boddinstr.
Karl-Marx-Str.
Paradestr.
Leinestr.
Neukölln
Tempelhof
Hermannstr.
Grenzallee
Osloer Str.
Bornholmer Str.
Wisbyer Str.
Wollankstr.
Mühlenstr.
Prenzlauer Promenade
Schönhauser Allee
Prenzlauer Allee
Pankstr.
Brunnen-str.
Danziger Str.
Storkower Str.
Bernauer Str.
Chausseestr.
Invaliden-str.
Greifswalder Str.
Frieden-str.
Landsberger Allee
Petersburger Str.
Moll-str.
Karl-Marx-Allee
Schiffahrtskanal
Friedrich-str.
Liebknecht-str.
Karl-Str.
Gertraudenstr.
Holzmarktstr.
Brücken-str.
Warschauer Str.
17. Juni
Leipziger Str.
Heinrich-Heine-Str.
Mühlenstr.
Köpenicker Str.
Koch-str.
Oranien-str.
Lindenstr.
Wilhelm-str.
Skalitzer Str.
Kottbusser Damm
Wiener Str.
Gitschiner Str.
Prinzen-str.
Landwehrkanal
Potsdamer Str.
Bülow-str.
Urbanstr.
Yorckstr.
Gneisenaustr.
Bergmannstr.
Hasenheide
Mehringdamm
Karl-Marx-Str.
Columbiadamm
Dudenstr.
Flughafen-str.
Platz der Luftbrücke
Hermann-str.
Boelcke-str.
Tempelhofer Damm
damm
A 100
19
20

CENTRE

Plan II

Adlon Kempinski

Unter den Linden 77 ✉ 10117
– Ⓜ Französische Str.
– ☎ (030) 2 26 10
– adlon@kempinski.com
– Fax (030) 22 61 22 22 – www.hotel-adlon.de **G1**

382 rm – †450/560 € ††450/560 €, ☕ 36 € – 29 suites
Rest *Lorenz Adlon* – see below
Rest *Quarré* – ☎ (030) 22 61 15 55 – Menu 75 € – Carte 52/89 €

◆ Palace ◆ Grand Luxury ◆ Classic ◆

The grand hotel par excellence: luxury, elegance and outstanding service make this traditional hotel by the Brandenburg Gate the place to stay. The classic Quarré leads onto the terrace with its views.

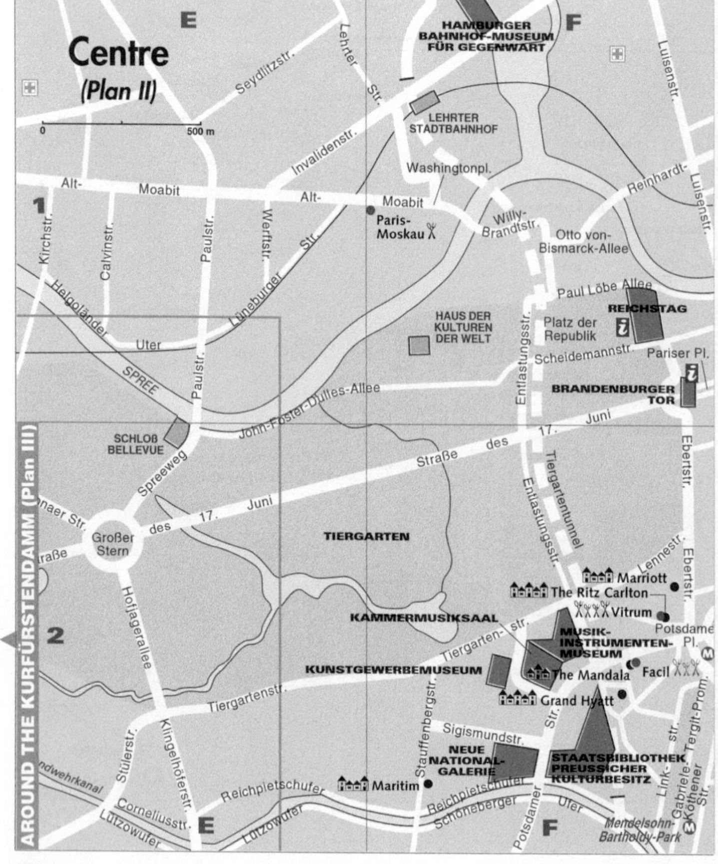

The Ritz-Carlton

Potsdamer Platz 3 ✉ *10785*
– Ⓜ *Potsdamer Platz*
– ✆ *(030) 33 77 77 – berlin@ritzcarlton.com*
– *Fax (030) 3 37 77 55 55*
– *www.ritzcarlton.com*

F2

302 rm – 🛉285/365 € 🛉🛉315/445 €, ☕ 29 € – 32 suites
Rest *Vitrum* – see below
Rest *Brasserie Desbrosses* – ✆ *(030) 3 37 77 63 41*
– Carte 31/62 €

◆ Chain hotel ◆ Grand Luxury ◆ Classic ◆

An impressive, expensively decorated lobby with free-standing marble staircase and gold leaf décor takes you to the uniformly noble, elegant rooms. Desbrosses: the original French brasserie from 1875, with a typical range of dishes.

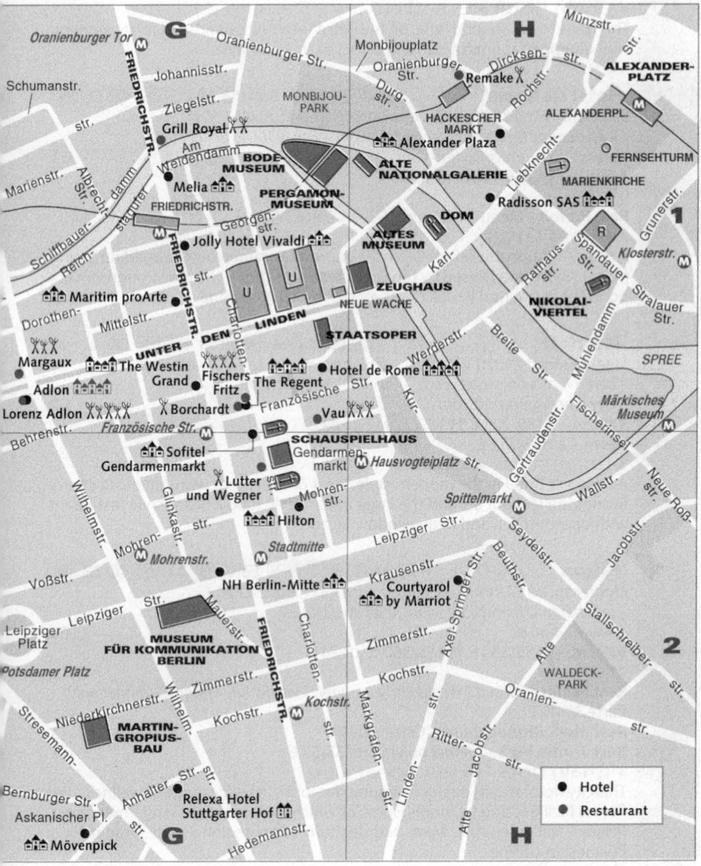

The Regent

Charlottenstr. 49 ✉ 10117 – Ⓜ Französische Str. – ✆ (030) 2 03 38 – info.berlin@rezidorregent.com – Fax (030) 20 33 61 19 – www.regenthotels.com **G1**

195 rm – †230/335 € ††260/370 €, ☕ 29 €
39 suites

Rest *Fischers Fritz* – see below

◆ Grand Luxury ◆ Classic ◆

Refined and luxurious is how to describe the atmosphere in this hotel right on the Gendarmenmarkt. The emphasis is on service and elegant ambience. Some rooms have beautiful views.

Grand Hyatt

Marlene-Dietrich-Platz 2 ✉ 10785 – Ⓜ Potsdamer Platz – ✆ (030) 25 53 12 34 – berlin@hyatt.de – Fax (030) 25 53 12 35 – www.berlin.grand.hyatt.com **F2**

342 rm – †245/540 € ††275/540 €, ☕ 27 €
12 suites

Rest *Vox* – *✆ (030) 25 53 17 72 (closed Saturday lunch and Sunday lunch)*
Menu 46/56 € – Carte 44/64 €

◆ Chain hotel ◆ Grand Luxury ◆ Design ◆

This trapezoidal-shaped hotel on the Potsdamer Platz stands out for its modern, well-equipped rooms of purist design. Vox in Asian style.

Hotel de Rome

Behrenstr. 37 ✉ 10117 – Ⓜ Französische Str. – ✆ (030) 4 60 60 90 – info.derome@roccofortecollection.com – Fax (030) 46 06 09 20 00 – www.roccofortecollection.com **G1**

146 rm – †420 € ††520 €, ☕ 26 €
9 suites

Rest *Parioli* – Menu 34 € (lunch)/75 € – Carte 54/79 €

◆ Grand Luxury ◆ Classic ◆

A luxury hotel on the Bebelplatz in the impressive framework of a building dating from 1889, formerly used by the Dresdner Bank. Today, the old strongroom is a pool. The restaurant Parioli offers ambitious Italian cuisine.

Marriott

Inge-Beisheim-Platz 1 ✉ 10785 – Ⓜ Potsdamer Platz – ✆ (030) 22 00 00 – berlin@marriotthotels.com – Fax (030) 2 20 00 10 00 – www.berlinmarriott.com **F2**

379 rm – †189/229 € ††189/229 €, ☕ 24 €

Rest – Carte 24/52 €

◆ Chain hotel ◆ Modern ◆

A business hotel in the modern style. Most of the rooms with American cherry fittings are laid out around the large atrium style lobby. Bistro style restaurant with open kitchen and large window façade.

Hilton

Mohrenstr. 30 ✉ 10117 – Ⓜ Stadtmitte – ✆ (030) 2 02 30 – info.berlin@hilton.com – Fax (030) 20 23 42 69 – www.hilton.de **G2**

591 rm – †155/360 € ††155/360 €, ☕ 24 €
14 suites

Rest *Fellini* – *(closed 2 weeks early January, 3 weeks July - August) (dinner only)*
Carte 30/40 €

Rest *Mark Brandenburg* – Carte 32/40 €

Rest *Trader Vic's* – *(dinner only)* Carte 33/52 €

◆ Chain hotel ◆ Functional ◆

This city hotel stands out for its impressive lobby, its wide range of wellness and fitness facilities and its rooms, some of which look onto the Gendarmenmarkt. Fellini – Italian cuisine. Mark Brandenburg offers regional style. Trader Vic's: Polynesian cuisine.

Radisson SAS
Karl-Liebknecht-Str. 3 ✉ 10178 – Ⓜ Alexanderplatz – ✆ (030) 23 82 80 – info.berlin@radissonsas.com – Fax (030) 2 38 28 10 – www.berlin.radissonsas.com **H1**
427 rm – 140/380 € 140/380 €, 22 €
Rest *HEat* – Carte 27/50 €
Rest *Noodle Kitchen* – *(dinner only)* Carte 28/41 €
♦ Chain hotel ♦ Business ♦ Stylish ♦
What catches your eye when you look into the purist atrium lobby of this hotel is a cylindrical aquarium 25 m high. The rooms are light and stylish. HEat: international cuisine in a modern bistro ambience. Noodle Kitchen with southeast Asian cuisine.

Maritim
Stauffenbergstr. 26 ✉ 10785 – Ⓜ Mendelssohn-Bartholdy-Park – ✆ (030) 2 06 50 – info.ber@maritim.de – Fax (030) 20 65 10 10 – www.maritim.de **F2**
505 rm – 151/289 € 170/310 €, 22 €
Rest *Grandrestaurant M* – Menu 51/72 € – Carte 31/62 €
♦ Chain hotel ♦ Luxury ♦ Modern ♦
Stands out for its elegant setting, high-quality, well-equipped rooms and excellent conference and event facilities. The Presidential Suite is 350 m²! A 1920s style restaurant.

The Westin Grand
Friedrichstr. 158 ✉ 10117 – Ⓜ Französische Str. – ✆ (030) 2 02 70 – info@westin-grand.com – Fax (030) 20 27 33 62 – www.westin.com/berlin **G1**
359 rm – 390/640 € 420/640 €, 26 € – 18 suites
Rest *Friedrichs* – Carte 27/56 €
Rest *Stammhaus* – Carte 22/30 €
Rest *Lobster House* – *(closed Monday - Tuesday)* Carte 34/65 €
♦ Chain hotel ♦ Luxury ♦ Classic ♦
'Refined' is the word for the atmosphere in this comfortable hotel in the city centre. You enter the building through a pleasant lobby with a glass roof 30 m up. Friedrichs in classic style. The Stammhaus offers Berlin specialities. Lobster House offers a seafood menu.

The Mandala
Potsdamer Str. 3 ✉ 10785 – Ⓜ Potsdamer Platz – ✆ (030) 5 90 05 00 00 – welcome@themandala.de – Fax (030) 5 90 05 05 00 – www.themandala.de
166 rm – 170/310 € 200/310 €, 23 € – 17 suites **F2**
Rest *Facil* – see below
♦ Business ♦ Stylish ♦
An impressive location on Potsdamer Platz, opposite the Sony-Center, offering spacious, modern rooms with good technical facilities.

Mövenpick
Schönebergerstr. 3 ✉ 10963 – Ⓜ Potsdamer Platz – ✆ (030) 23 00 60 – hotel.berlin@moevenpick.com – Fax (030) 23 00 61 99 – www.moevenpick-berlin.com **G2**
243 rm – 119/190 € 129/210 €, 19 €
Rest – Carte 24/36 €
♦ Chain hotel ♦ Modern ♦
Formerly a Siemens building, now listed, providing a mixture of modern design and historical touches to create an unusual interior. Restaurant with glass-covered interior courtyard.

Maritim proArte
Friedrichstr. 151 ✉ 10117 – Ⓜ Friedrichstr. – ✆ (030) 2 03 35 – info.bpa@maritim.de – Fax (030) 20 33 42 09 – www.maritim.de **G1**
403 rm – 137/278 € 154/297 €, 20 €
Rest *Atelier* – *(closed 23 July - 18 August and Sunday) (dinner only)* Menu 55 € – Carte 38/54 €
Rest *Bistro media* – Carte 20/24 €
♦ Chain hotel ♦ Business ♦ Modern ♦
An avant-garde hotel near the lime tree-lined Pracht blvd. providing well-appointed rooms with Jungen Wilden art on display. A modern designer style restaurant.

Jolly Hotel Vivaldi

Friedrichstr. 96 ✉ 10117 – Ⓜ Friedrichstr. – ✆ (030) 2 06 26 60 – vivaldi.jhb@jollyhotels.de – Fax (030) 2 06 26 69 99 – www.jollyhotels.de **G1**

262 rm – 🚹145/210 € 🚹🚹160/230 €, ☕ 19 €

Rest – Carte 36/47 €

◆ Business ◆ Stylish ◆

When entering this modern, well-run hotel you will notice the spacious hall. High-quality wooden furniture and agreeable colours make the rooms a pleasant place to stay. Light, open-plan restaurant with Italian cuisine.

Sofitel Gendarmenmarkt

Charlottenstr. 50 ✉ 10117 – Ⓜ Französische Str. – ✆ (030) 20 37 50 – h5342@accor.com – Fax (030) 20 37 51 00 – www.sofitel.com **G1-2**

92 rm – 🚹270/380 € 🚹🚹285/395 €, ☕ 25 €

Rest *Aigner* – *✆ (030) 2 03 75 18 50* – Carte 30/47 €

◆ Chain hotel ◆ Business ◆ Design ◆

The hotel is directly opposite the French cathedral at the Gendarmenmarkt and has modern, designer rooms and a recreation area on the top floor. The Aigner was built from original parts of a Viennese coffeehouse.

Courtyard by Marriott

Axel-Springer-Str. 55 ✉ 10117 – Ⓜ Spittelmarkt – ✆ (030) 8 00 92 80 – berlin.mitte@courtyard.com – Fax (030) 80 09 28 10 00 – www.courtyard.com/bermt **H2**

267 rm – 🚹139/189 € 🚹🚹139/189 €, ☕ 17 € – 4 suites

Rest – Carte 19/29 €

◆ Chain hotel ◆ Business ◆ Functional ◆

A centrally located business hotel providing homely, well-equipped rooms with functional furnishings. A Mediterranean bistro style restaurant with bar.

Alexander Plaza

Rosenstr. 1 ✉ 10178 – Ⓜ Alexanderplatz – ✆ (030) 24 00 10 – info@hotel-alexander-plaza.de – Fax (030) 24 00 17 77 – www.hotel-alexander-plaza.de **H1**

92 rm – 🚹100/180 € 🚹🚹100/180 €, ☕ 17 €

Rest – *(closed Sunday) (dinner only)* Carte 25/35 €

◆ Business ◆ Functional ◆

Between the Marienkirche and the market, this restored old building provides modern rooms and apartments with small kitchen facilities. International dishes are served in the restaurant with conservatory.

Melia

Friedrichstr. 103 ✉ 10117 – Ⓜ Friedrichstr. – ✆ (030) 20 60 79 00 – melia.berlin@solmelia.com – Fax (030) 20 60 79 04 44 – www.meliaberlin.com **G1**

364 rm ☕ – 🚹140/200 € 🚹🚹160/220 € – 3 suites

Rest – Carte 33/52 €

◆ Business ◆ Functional ◆

Its central location and modern and functional décor are features of the first Berlin hotel of the Spanish Sol-Melia Group. Executive facilities on the seventh and eighth floors. Restaurant with an international range of food and a tapas bar.

NH Berlin-Mitte

Leipziger Str. 106 ✉ 10117 – Ⓜ Stadtmitte – ✆ (030) 20 37 60 – nhberlinmitte@nh-hotels.com – Fax (030) 20 37 66 00 – www.nh-hotels.com **G2**

392 rm – 🚹99/229 € 🚹🚹99/229 €, ☕ 19 €

Rest – Carte 23/42 €

◆ Chain hotel ◆ Functional ◆

This residence with its spacious hall and rooms, which are modern, functional and comfortable, is well situated in the centre of Berlin. Leisure area on the 8th floor. The bistro-style restaurant is open to the lobby.

relexa Hotel Stuttgarter Hof

Anhalter Str. 8 ✉ 10963 – Ⓜ Kochstr. – ✆ (030) 26 48 30
– berlin@relexa-hotel.de – Fax (030) 26 48 39 00
– www.relexa-hotels.de **G2**

206 rm – 120/250 € 140/265 € – 10 suites
Rest – Carte 31/46 €

◆ Business ◆ Functional ◆

This hotel has a large reception area and provides rooms with light beech wood furniture and warm décor. Contemporary restaurant.

Adele

Greifswalder Str. 227 ✉ 10405 – Ⓜ Alexanderplatz
– ✆ (030) 44 32 43 10 – info@adele-berlin.de – Fax (030) 44 32 43 11
– www.adele-berlin.de *Plan I* **D1**

14 rm – 105/145 € 150/200 €
Rest – *(closed Saturday lunch and Sunday lunch)* Carte 21/34 €

◆ Townhouse ◆ Classic ◆

Great personal attention is lavished on guests in this small hotel near to Friedrichshain park. The rooms, furnished in a high quality, Art Deco style are captivating. This restaurant with a modern design has a bistro and lounge.

Lorenz Adlon – Hotel Adlon Kempinski

Unter den Linden 77 ✉ 10117 – Ⓜ Französische Str.
– ✆ (030) 22 61 19 60 – adlon@kempinski.com – Fax (030) 22 61 22 22
– www.hotel-adlon.de
closed 22 July - 19 August and Sunday - Monday **G1**

Rest – *(dinner only)* Menu 120/165 € – Carte 80/122 €

Spec. Tatar vom Taschenkrebs mit leichter Limonen-Ingwer-Crème-fraîche. Gebratener Spargel in der Morchelnage mit gegrillter Jakobsmuschel und Petersilienravioli. Caneton à la presse mit Pommes Maximes und Sauce Rouennaise.

◆ Classic ◆ Formal ◆

Here the guest experiences the unique luxurious atmosphere of the legendary Adlon Hotel. The fine French cuisine also includes classics prepared in a contemporary manner.

Fischers Fritz – Hotel The Regent

Charlottenstr. 49 ✉ 10117 – Ⓜ Französische Str. – ✆ (030) 2 03 36363
– fischersfritz.berlin@rezidorregent.com – Fax (030) 20 33 61 19
– www.fischersfritzberlin.com **G1**

Rest – Menu 36 € (lunch)/135 € – Carte 79/124 €

Spec. Terrine von Gänsestopfleber und geräuchertem Aal mit Pfefferkaramell. Geangelter Wolfsbarsch im Salzteig gegart mit gegrilltem Marktgemüse (2 people). Homard à la presse (by arrangement).

◆ Inventive ◆ Formal ◆

As the name suggests, fish dishes are the speciality here. Prepared in both a traditional and modern way by Christian Lohse and his kitchen team.

Vitrum – Hotel The Ritz Carlton

Potsdamer Platz 3 ✉ 10785 – Ⓜ Potsdamer Platz – ✆ (030) 3 37 77 63 40
– ccr.berlin@ritzcarlton.com – Fax (030) 3 37 77 53 41
– www.restaurant-vitrum.de
closed 2 weeks January, 4 weeks August and Sunday - Monday **F2**

Rest – *(dinner only) (booking advisable)* Menu 68 € (veg.)/108 €
– Carte 64/76 €

Spec. Kleiner Eintopf mit Rotbarbe und flüssigen Trüffel-Ravioli. Mit Gewürzen gebratener Rehrücken mit Blumenkohl-Graupengemüse und Rotweinsabayon. Dessert von Roter Bete mit Ananas und Griesflammerie.

◆ Inventive ◆ Formal ◆

With its noble classic ambience this restaurant is in keeping with the grand hotel setting. Creativity defines the cuisine.

XXX ✿ **Margaux** (Michael Hoffmann)

Unter den Linden 78 (Entrance Wilhelmstraße) ✉ 10117 – Ⓜ Französische Str. – ☎ (030) 22 65 26 11 – hoffmann@margaux-berlin.de – Fax (030) 22 65 26 12 – www.margaux-berlin.de
closed Sunday, mid July - end August, Sunday - Monday **G1**

Rest – *(dinner only)* Menu 80/140 € – Carte 74/110 €

Spec. Entenstopfleber in 3 Varianten mariniert. Hummer und Melone mit Sellerie, Sauerampfer und Ingwer. Steinbutt mit gebratenen Austern und Austernparfait.

♦ Inventive ♦ Fashionable ♦

Cuisine avant garde classique is how Michael Hoffman describes his cooking. The creative dishes are served in a modern restaurant close to the Brandenburg Gate.

XXX ✿ **FACIL** – Hotel The Mandala

Potsdamer Str. 3 (5th floor) ✉ 10785 – Ⓜ Potsdamer Platz – ☎ (030) 5 90 05 12 34 – welcome@facil.de – Fax (030) 5 90 05 05 00 – www.facil.de
closed 3 weeks January, 3 weeks July - August and Saturday - Sunday **F2**

Rest – *(booking advisable)* Menu 39 € (lunch)/110 € – Carte 72/96 €

Spec. Terrine vom Felsenoktopus mit Tomaten-Chorizomarmelade und Gewürzfenchel. Geschmorte Lammschulter mit exotischem Lammsugo und Ackersenf. Dessert von Passionsfrucht, Babybanane und Kaffee Arabica.

♦ Inventive ♦ Minimalist ♦

Located on the Potsdamer Platz, this restaurant with a modern design serves creative cuisine. An attractive feature is the opening glass roof and window frontage facing the inner courtyard.

XXX ✿ **VAU** (Kolja Kleeberg)

Jägerstr. 54 ✉ 10117 – Ⓜ Französische Str. – ☎ (030) 2 02 97 30 – restaurant@vau-berlin.de – Fax (030) 20 29 73 11 – www.vau-berlin.de
closed Sunday **G1**

Rest – Menu 42 € (lunch)/110 € – Carte 71/92 €

Spec. Soufflierter Kartoffelschmarrn mit Kaviar. Kross gebratener Loup de mer mit Paprikakutteln, Zitrone und Spitzkohl. Roastbeef vom Bison mit Pak Choi, Haselnüssen und Kakao.

♦ Inventive ♦ Fashionable ♦

The restaurant on the Gendarmenmarkt is known for its modern design and creative cuisine with classic roots. Pleasant seating on the terrace and in the inner courtyard. Bar in the basement.

XX **Grill Royal**

Friedrichstr. 105b ✉ 10117 – Ⓜ Oranienburger Tor – ☎ (030) 28 87 92 88 – office@grillroyal.com – Fax (030) 28 87 92 84 – www.grillroyal.com **G1**

Rest – *(booking advisable) (dinner only)* Carte 33/98 €

♦ International ♦ Trendy ♦

A trendy restaurant with modern, high quality décor in earth colours. Diners select the meat themselves from a glass cool store!

X ✿ **Rutz**

Chausseestr. 8 ✉ 10115 – Ⓜ Oranienburger Tor – ☎ (030) 24 62 87 60 – info@rutz-weinbar.de – Fax (030) 24 62 87 61 – www.rutz-weinbar.de
closed Sunday *Plan I* **C2**

Rest – *(dinner only)* Menu 55/65 € – Carte 47/62 €

Spec. Zweimal Thunfisch mit Crunchy Sardine. Geschmorte Stelze vom Müritz Lamm mit Parmesankeks. Gepfefferter weißer Pfirsich, Balsamico-Eis, Vanille, Olivenöl.

♦ Inventive ♦ Trendy ♦

There is a pleasant modern style in this establishment. The wine bar is on the ground floor, the restaurant on the first floor, and there is outdoor seating in the inner courtyard. Creative Mediterranean cuisine.

Remake

Große Hamburger Str. 32 ✉ 10115 – ✆ (030) 20 05 41 02 – restaurantremake@aol.com – Fax (030) 97 89 48 60 – www.restaurant-remake.de **H1**

Rest – *(dinner only)* Menu 42/65 € – Carte 44/57 €

♦ International ♦ Fashionable ♦

Light, friendly atmosphere and modern ambience and a contemporary international menu are what make this restaurant stand out.

Paris-Moskau

Alt-Moabit 141 ✉ 10557 – ✆ (030) 3 94 20 81 – restaurant@paris-moskau.de – Fax (030) 3 94 26 02 – www.paris-moskau.de

closed Saturday lunch and Sunday lunch **F1**

Rest – *(booking advisable)* Menu 60/77 € – Carte 36/45 €

♦ International ♦ Rustic ♦

This old timber-framed hotel near where the Wall used to be not far from Lehrter station, offers international cuisine (reduced lunchtime menu).

Borchardt

Französische Str. 47 ✉ 10117 – Ⓜ Französische Str. – ✆ (030) 81 88 62 62 – Fax (030) 81 88 62 49 **G1**

Rest – Carte 26/44 €

♦ International ♦ Trendy ♦

Columns with gold-plated chapters and stucco ceilings impress guests. It is no wonder at this fine address. Here you have to "see and be seen"! Courtyard terrace.

Lutter und Wegner

Charlottenstr. 56 ✉ 10117 – Ⓜ Französische Str. – ✆ (030) 2 02 95 40 – info@l-w-berlin.de – Fax (030) 20 29 54 25 – www.l-w-berlin.de **G2**

Rest – Carte 29/45 €

♦ Austrian ♦ Wine bar ♦

The writer and composer E.T.A. Hoffman once lived in this building. Three large columns painted by contemporary artists set the motto: Wine, women and song. Cosy wine bar.

Hartmanns

Fichtestr. 31 ✉ 10967 – Ⓜ Südstern – ✆ (030) 61 20 10 03 – mail@hartmanns-restaurant.de – Fax (030) 61 20 13 80 – www.hartmanns-restaurant.de

closed Sunday *Plan I* **D3**

Rest – *(booking advisable) (dinner only)* Menu 37/58 € – Carte 39/48 €

♦ International ♦ Cosy♦

This contemporary restaurant serves ambitious international food with regional influences. The works of two artists decorate the room.

Le Cochon Bourgeois

Fichtestr. 24 ✉ 10967 – Ⓜ Südstern – ✆ (030) 6 93 01 01 – Fax (030) 6 94 34 80 – www.lecochon.de

closed 2 weeks early January and Sunday - Monday *Plan I* **D3**

Rest – *(dinner only)* Menu 40/59 € – Carte 38/56 €

♦ French ♦ Cosy ♦

With a character all its own: cosy rustic décor forms the backdrop for the French cuisine served here.

AROUND THE KURFÜRSTENDAMM *Plan III*

Concorde

Augsburger Str. 41 ✉ 10789 – Ⓜ Kurfürstendamm – ✆ (030) 8 00 99 90 – info-berlin@concorde-hotels.com – Fax (030) 80 09 99 99 – www.hotelconcordeberlin.com **K2**

311 rm – †190/435 € ††210/455 €, ☕ 22 € – 44 suites

Rest *Le Faubourg* – , ✆ (030) 80 09 99 77 00 – Carte 34/57 €

♦ Business ♦ Grand Luxury ♦

A luxury hotel in an outstanding location – generous and contemporary throughout. The rooms have all the latest technology, most suites offer beautiful views. VIP lounge. The Brasserie Le Faubourg is elegant and modern.

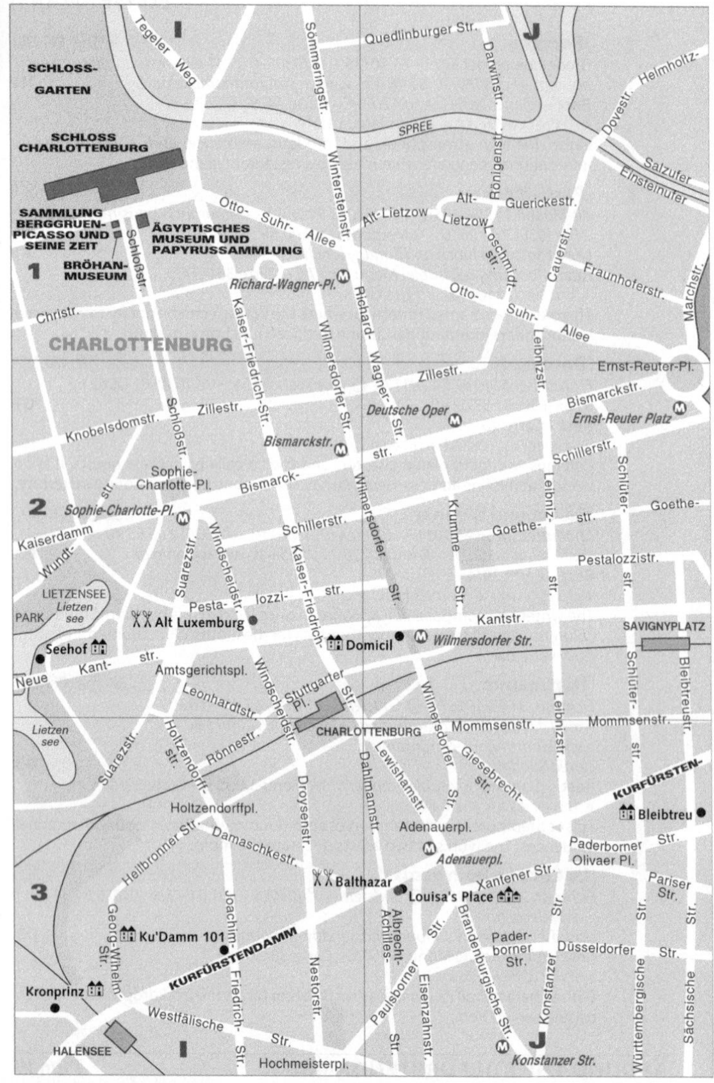

Palace

Budapester Str. 45 ✉ 10787 – Ⓜ Zoologischer Garten – ✆ (030) 2 50 20
– hotel@palace.de – Fax (030) 25 02 11 19
– www.palace.de **K2**

282 rm – †250/355 € ††250/355 €, ☕ 24 € – 19 suites

Rest *First Floor* – see below

◆ Grand Luxury ◆ Classic ◆

Guests in this private hotel enjoy modern, smart rooms with extensive technical facilities, luxurious suites and an elegant Mediterranean 800 m² spa area.

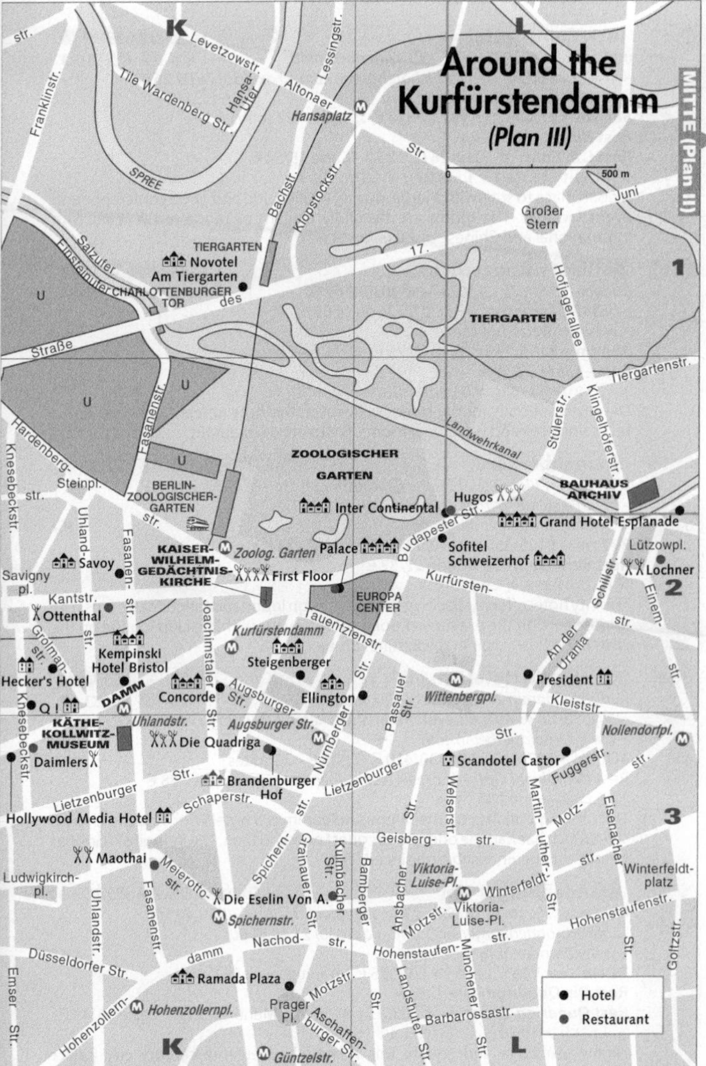

Grand Hotel Esplanade

Lützowufer 15 ✉ 10785 – ✆ (030) 25 47 80
– info@esplanade.de – Fax (030) 2 54 78 82 22 – www.esplanade.de **L2**

VISA

390 rm – 129/279 € 129/279 €, 22 € – 23 suites – **Rest** – Carte 32/48 €
Rest *Eckrestaurant* – *(closed Sunday) (dinner only)* Carte 17/38 €

♦ Grand Luxury ♦ Modern ♦

Modern design through and through marks this grand hotel on the Landwehr canal. Outside the building is the MS Esplanade yacht, a highlight for events of all kinds. The Ellipse Lounge offers international cuisine. Local specialities in the corner restaurant.

InterContinental

Budapester Str. 2 ✉ 10787 – Ⓤ Wittenbergplatz – ✆ (030) 2 60 20 – berlin@ichotelsgroup.com – Fax (030) 26 02 26 00 – www.berlin.intercontinental.com **L2**

584 rm – †130/320 € ††130/320 €, ☕ 24 € – 50 suites

Rest *Hugos* – see below

Rest *L.A. Cafe* – *✆ (030) 26 02 12 50* – Carte 35/54 €

♦ Chain hotel ♦ Luxury ♦ Classic ♦

A good place to stay, with a large, quality Vitality Club and good conference and event facilities. The rooms are tastefully elegant or modern. L.A. Cafe with international and Chinese dishes.

Sofitel Schweizerhof

Budapester Str. 25 ✉ 10787 – ✆ (030) 2 69 60 – h5347@accor.com – Fax (030) 26 96 10 00 – www.schweizerhof.com **L2**

384 rm – †135/275 € ††135/275 €, ☕ 21 € – 10 suites

Rest – Carte 31/38 €

♦ Chain hotel ♦ Business ♦ Design ♦

Designed specially for the business traveller, this hotel offers a light, generous reception area and functional rooms. Bistro-style restaurant.

Steigenberger

Los-Angeles-Platz 1 ✉ 10789 – Ⓤ Augsburger Str. – ✆ (030) 2 12 70 – berlin@steigenberger.de – Fax (030) 2 12 71 17 – www.berlin.steigenberger.de **K2**

397 rm – †125/355 € ††125/355 €, ☕ 22 € – 11 suites

Rest *Berliner Stube* – Carte 22/32 €

♦ Business ♦ Classic ♦

This city hotel offers a spacious, modern design lobby and functional rooms. The atmosphere on the executive floor is more private, with the club lounge on the sixth floor. Rustic flair in the Berliner Stube.

Kempinski Hotel Bristol

Kurfürstendamm 27 ✉ 10719 – Ⓤ Uhlandstr. – ✆ (030) 88 43 40 – reservations.bristol@kempinski.com – Fax (030) 8 83 60 75 – www.kempinski-berlin.com **K2**

301 rm – †270/350 € ††330/420 €, ☕ 25 € – 22 suites

Rest *Kempinski Grill* – *(closed 4 weeks July - August)* Carte 41/68 €

♦ Luxury ♦ Classic ♦

This striking building on the famous Ku'damm is a hotel with a classic elegant style which has had the odd famous guest now and then. The Kempinski Grill has been a true Berlin institution since 1952.

Brandenburger Hof

Eislebener Str. 14 ✉ 10789 – Ⓤ Augsburger Str. – ✆ (030) 21 40 50 – info@brandenburger-hof.com – Fax (030) 21 40 51 00 – www.brandenburger-hof.com **K3**

72 rm ☕ – †185/285 € ††270/325 € – 8 suites

Rest *Die Quadriga* – see below

Rest *Quadriga-Lounge* – *✆ (030) 21 40 56 51* – Menu 26/95 € – Carte 36/48 €

♦ Traditional ♦ Design ♦

Highly attractive and stylish, this beautiful nineteenth-century city palace combines historical elements with noble modern design. Pure elegance: the Quadriga-Lounge extending into the Bar area.

Louisa's Place

Kurfürstendamm 160 ✉ 10709 – Ⓤ Adenauerplatz – ✆ (030) 63 10 30 – info@louisas-place.de – Fax (030) 63 10 31 00 – www.louisas-place.de **J3**

47 suites – †155/595 € ††155/595 €, ☕ 20 €

Rest Balthazar – see below

♦ Business ♦ Personalised ♦

Tasteful, spacious suites with kitchens and friendly service in this exclusive hotel. Also features a stylish breakfast room and library.

Ramada Plaza VISA

Pragerstr. 12 ✉ *10779* – Ⓜ *Güntzelstr.* – ✆ *(030) 2 36 25 00*
– berlin.plaza@ramada.de – Fax (030) 2 36 25 05 50
– www.ramada-plaza-berlin.de **K3**

184 rm – 🛉139/199 € 🛉🛉139/199 €, ☕ 18 € – 60 suites

Rest – Carte 31/43 €

♦ Chain hotel ♦ Modern ♦

A business hotel providing elegant rooms and suites with American cherry wood furnishings and the latest technical facilities, with executive suites on the sixth floor. A classic style restaurant.

Ellington VISA

Nürnberger Str. 50 ✉ *10789* – Ⓜ *Wittenbergplatz* – ✆ *(030) 68 31 50*
– contact@ellington-hotel.com – Fax (030) 6 83 15 55 55
– www.ellington-hotel.com **L2**

285 rm – 🛉98/178 € 🛉🛉108/188 €, ☕ 15 €

Rest – Carte 29/45 €

♦ Business ♦ Modern ♦ Minimalist ♦

Hause Nürnberg, built in 1928-31, now houses a hotel with a modern design. The façade and many beautiful interior details preserve the historic charm. This restaurant has a straightforward, simple, elegant style with a pretty inner courtyard.

Novotel am Tiergarten VISA

Straße des 17. Juni 106 ✉ *10623* – ✆ *(030) 60 03 50 – h3649@accor.com*
– Fax (030) 60 03 56 66 – www.accorhotels.com **K1**

274 rm – 🛉99/209 € 🛉🛉114/224 €, ☕ 17 € – 11 suites

Rest – Carte 29/44 €

♦ Chain hotel ♦ Modern ♦

Located near the Tiergarten station, this business hotel provides well-equipped rooms in modern design.

Savoy rm VISA

Fasanenstr. 9 ✉ *10623* – Ⓜ *Zoologischer Garten* – ✆ *(030) 31 10 30*
– info@hotel-savoy.com – Fax (030) 31 10 33 33
– www.hotel-savoy.com **K2**

125 rm – 🛉119/248 € 🛉🛉146/277 €, ☕ 19 € – 18 suites

Rest – *(closed Sunday dinner)* Carte 31/44 €

♦ Business ♦ Modern ♦

A charming hotel, mentioned in the writings of Thomas Mann, and where celebrities still come and go. Established in 1928, it is the oldest in the town. Modern interior with red upholstered armchairs in the restaurant.

Q! VISA

Knesebeckstr. 67 ✉ *10623* – Ⓜ *Uhlandstr.* – ✆ *(030) 8 10 06 60*
– q-berlin@loock-hotels.com – Fax (030) 8 10 06 66 66
– www.loock-hotels.com **K2**

77 rm ☕ – 🛉159/217 € 🛉🛉179/235 €

Rest – *(dinner only for residents)* Carte 33/44 €

♦ Business ♦ Stylish ♦

Design wins: Minimalist design, dark tones and modern atmosphere in the technically well-equipped rooms. Stylish restaurant with Euro-Asian fare.

Seehof VISA

Lietzensee-Ufer 11 ✉ *14057* – Ⓜ *Sophie-Charlotte-Platz* – ✆ *(030) 32 00 20*
– info@hotel-seehof-berlin.de – Fax (030) 32 00 22 51
– www.hotel-seehof-berlin.de **I2**

75 rm ☕ – 🛉99/175 € 🛉🛉108/195 €

Rest – *(closed 2 to 13 January)* Carte 28/51 €

♦ Business ♦ Classic ♦

This hotel is located on the green shores of Lake Lietzen and features refined and elegant guest rooms, some furnished with period furniture. Convenient travel distance to the trade fair centre. Restaurant with classic ambience and beautiful terrace overlooking the lake.

President
An der Urania 16 ✉ 10787 – Ⓜ Wittenbergplatz – ✆ (030) 21 90 30
– info@president.bestwestern.de – Fax (030) 2 18 61 20
– www.president.bestwestern.de **L2**
177 rm – 145/230 € 175/250 €, 15 € – 3 suites
Rest – Carte 31/38 €
◆ Business ◆ Functional ◆
As well as functional economy and business rooms, this hotel also has more comfortable club rooms, with extra-large desks and comfortable leather armchairs. Wicker chairs and contemporary design in the restaurant.

Hollywood Media Hotel without rest
Kurfürstendamm 202 ✉ 10719 – Ⓜ Uhlandstr.
– ✆ (030) 88 91 00 – info@filmhotel.de – Fax (030) 88 91 02 80
– www.filmhotel.de **K3**
182 rm – 99/190 € 119/211 € – 12 suites
◆ Business ◆ Modern ◆
This residence is devoted to the world of film. The tasteful, contemporary rooms are decorated with numerous film posters and photos of stars. The hotel has its own small cinema.

Domicil
Kantstr. 111a ✉ 10627 – Ⓜ Wilmersdorfer Str. – ✆ (030) 32 90 30
– info@hotel-domicil-berlin.de – Fax (030) 32 90 32 99
– www.hotel-domicil-berlin.de **J2**
70 rm – 118/150 € 154/190 € – 3 suites
Rest – Carte 20/31 €
◆ Business ◆ Modern ◆
In this hotel high above the city you will stay in attractive rooms in Italian style, in which the highlights are contemporary art and Tuscan fabrics. Rooftop restaurant with a roof garden. Cuisine with international influences.

Hecker's Hotel
Grolmanstr. 35 ✉ 10623 – Ⓜ Uhlandstr. – ✆ (030) 8 89 00
– info@heckers-hotel.de – Fax (030) 8 89 02 60
– www.heckers-hotel.de **K2**
69 rm – 120/250 € 140/330 €, 16 €
Rest *Cassambalis* – *✆ (030) 8 85 47 47 (closed Sunday lunch)* Carte 31/42 €
◆ Business ◆ Design ◆
A hotel which values individuality and service. The rooms, some cosy and functional, some in modern designer style or tastefully fitted out as themed rooms. Mediterranean flair and offer in the Cassambalis.

Bleibtreu
Bleibtreustr. 31 ✉ 10707 – Ⓜ Uhlandstr. – ✆ (030) 88 47 40
– info@bleibtreu.com – Fax (030) 88 47 44 44
– www.bleibtreu.com **J3**
60 rm – 119/195 € 124/227 €, 15 €
Rest – Carte 22/29 €
◆ Business ◆ Design ◆
This town house from the Gründerzeit [founders' era] has been carefully restored, creating an attractive modern style hotel. The restaurant offers sandwiches, steaks and burgers.

Ku' Damm 101 without rest
Kurfürstendamm 101 ✉ 10711 – ✆ (030) 5 20 05 50
– info@kudamm101.com – Fax (030) 5 20 05 55 55
– www.kudamm101.com **I3**
170 rm – 99/205 € 101/222 €, 15 €
◆ Business ◆ Design ◆
Deliberately understated designer style. Rooms with modern colour schemes, large windows and modern facilities. The breakfast room on the seventh floor offers a view over the town.

Kronprinz without rest

Kronprinzendamm 1 ✉ 10711 – ✆ (030) 89 60 30 – reception@kronprinz-hotel.de – Fax (030) 8 93 12 15 – www.kronprinz-hotel.de **I3**

78 rm – 98/185 € 150/215 €

◆ Traditional ◆ Cosy ◆

A late 19th century building is home to light, homely rooms and a charming "Romantic room". Convention centre within walking distance. Terrace shaded by chestnut trees.

Scandotel Castor without rest

Fuggerstr. 8 ✉ 10777 – Ⓜ Nollendorfplatz – ✆ (030) 21 30 30 – scandotel@t-online.de – Fax (030) 21 30 31 60 – www.scandotel-castor.de **L3**

78 rm – 90/107 € 100/135 €, 10 €

◆ Business ◆ Functional ◆

Whether it's the Ku'damm or KaDeWe, the cinema or the pub: this contemporary hotel with its functional rooms and good technical facilities is close to them all.

First Floor – Hotel Palace

Budapester Str. 45 ✉ 10787 – Ⓜ Zoologischer Garten – ✆ (030) 25 02 10 20 – hotel@palace.de – Fax (030) 25 02 11 19 – www.firstfloor.palace.de

closed 27 July - 25 August and Sunday - Monday **K2**

Rest – Menu 42 € (lunch)/108 € – Carte 64/92 €

Spec. Carpaccio vom Pulpo mit weißem Tomatenmousse und Jakobsmuschel. Gebratener Kabeljau auf Kartoffel-Limonenpüree mit Kapern. Rücken und Schulter vom Müritz Lamm mit Couscous und Ziegenfrischkäse im Karamell.

◆ Classic ◆ Formal ◆

This classically run restaurant is famous for the filigree cuisine of Matthias Buchholz and an extensive wine list with some rarities.

Hugos – Hotel InterContinental

< Berlin,

Budapester Str. 2 (14th floor) ✉ 10787 – Ⓜ Wittenbergplatz – ✆ (030) 26 02 12 63 – mail@hugos-restaurant.de – Fax (030) 26 02 12 39 – www.hugos-restaurant.de

closed 2 weeks January, 4 weeks July - August and Sunday **L2**

Rest – *(dinner only)* Menu 85/130 € – Carte 77/89 €

Spec. Hecht mit Serrano Schinken und Wildkräutern. Spanferkel und Langustino mit arabischen Aromen. Melone, Kokoseis, Schokolade und Zitronengras.

◆ Classic ◆ Design ◆

There is a splendid view of the city from the 14th floor of the InterContinental. The ambience is elegant, the cuisine modern and creative.

Die Quadriga – Hotel Brandenburger Hof

Eislebener Str. 14 ✉ 10789 – Ⓜ Augsburger Str. – ✆ (030) 21 40 56 51 – info@brandenburger-hof.com – Fax (030) 21 40 51 00 – www.brandenburger-hof.com

closed 1 - 13 January, 20 July - 17 August and Saturday lunch, Sunday - Monday lunch **K3**

Rest – Menu 70/135 € – Carte 73/103 €

Spec. Gänseleber und Berliner Eisbein mit Verjus und Gewürzlauch. Taube mit Pinienkernen, Kapern und Rosinen. Glacierte Ananas mit Zartbitter-Schokolade, Chili und Meersalz.

◆ Classic ◆ Formal ◆

The two tastefully decorated lounges in Art Deco style create an atmosphere in which classic creative cuisine and friendly service can be enjoyed. Views onto the inner courtyard.

Alt Luxemburg

Windscheidstr. 31 ✉ 10627 – Ⓜ Wilmersdorfer Str. – ✆ (030) 3 23 87 30 – info@altluxemburg.de – Fax (030) 3 27 40 03 – www.altluxemburg.de

closed Sunday **I2**

Rest – *(dinner only) (booking advisable)* Menu 64/70 € – Carte 57/64 €

◆ Classic ◆ Family ◆

Beautiful, cheery colours define the ambience of this restaurant, under the management of the Wannemacher family since 1982. In this restaurant, tradition is maintained and classic cuisine is enjoyed.

XX **Balthazar** – Hotel Louisa's Place VISA AE

Kurfürstendamm 160 ✉ 10709 – Ⓜ Adenauerplatz – ✆ (030) 89 04 91 87 – info@balthazar-restaurant.de – Fax (030) 89 04 91 89 – www.balthazar-restaurant.de **J3**

Rest – Menu 40/44 € – Carte 31/45 €

♦ International ♦ Friendly ♦

With its contemporary purist style, this restaurant on the 'Ku'damm' offers an international cuisine – it's nice to sit outside on the terrace, too. Reduced lunchtime menu.

XX **Lochner** VISA AE

Lützowplatz 5 ✉ 10785 – Ⓜ Nollendorfplatz – ✆ (030) 23 00 52 20 – info@lochner-restaurant.de – Fax (030) 23 00 40 21 – www.lochner-restaurant.de

closed 2 weeks August and Monday **L2**

Rest – *(dinner only)* Menu 60/85 € – Carte 37/56 €

♦ International ♦ Friendly ♦

A pleasantly light, tastefully decorated restaurant offering an international menu. There is a small terrace in front of the building.

XX **Maothai** VISA AE

Meierottostr. 1 ✉ 10719 – Ⓜ Spichernstr. – ✆ (030) 8 83 28 23 – maothaiaf@aol.com – Fax (030) 88 67 56 58 – www.maothai-am-fasanenplatz.de **K3**

Rest – *(Monday - Friday dinner only)* Carte 20/48 €

♦ Asian ♦ Exotic ♦

An intimate, candle-lit atmosphere in this restaurant near the Fasanen square, serving Thai cuisine. Charming terrace dining area.

X **Bieberbau**

Durlacher Str. 15 ✉ 10715 – Ⓜ Bundesplatz – ✆ (030) 8 53 23 90 – webmaster@bieberbau-berlin.de – Fax (030) 81 00 68 65 – www.bieberbau-berlin.de

closed 3 weeks July - August and Sunday - Monday *Plan I* **B3**

Rest – *(dinner only) (booking advisable)* Menu 30/49 €

♦ International ♦ Cosy ♦

The restaurant is half-timbered, wood panelled and stucco. A friendly young staff serve set menu dishes.

X **Die Eselin von A.**

Kulmbacher Str. 15 ✉ 10777 – Ⓜ Spichernstr. – ✆ (030) 2 14 12 84 – info@die-eselin-von-a.de – Fax (030) 21 47 69 48 – www.die-eselin-von-a.de

closed 1 to 16 January, 2 weeks August **K3**

Rest – *(dinner only)* Menu 37/59 € – Carte 29/43 €

♦ International ♦ Bistro ♦

This friendly restaurant offers modern international cuisine, welcoming not just to its many regular customers.

X **Ottenthal** VISA AE

Kantstr. 153 ✉ 10623 – Ⓜ Uhlandstr. – ✆ (030) 3 13 31 62 – restaurant@ottenthal.com – Fax (030) 3 13 37 32 – www.ottenthal.com **K2**

Rest – *(dinner only) (booking advisable)* Carte 27/43 €

♦ Austrian ♦ Bistro ♦

This restaurant is named after a wine estate in Austria, serving food from that country, and featuring décor inspired by the old church.

X **Daimlers** VISA AE

Kurfürstendamm 203 ✉ 10719 – Ⓜ Uhlandstr. – ✆ (030) 39 01 16 98 – info@daimlers.de – Fax (030) 39 01 44 66 – www.daimlers.de **K3**

Rest – Menu 32/52 € – Carte 32/44 €

♦ International ♦ Bistro ♦

A car showroom gives this restaurant its unusual setting. Behind the glass façade sample international cuisine, and tapas in the afternoon, served in a pleasant bistro atmosphere.

ENVIRONS OF BERLIN

at Berlin-Grunewald *Plan I*

Schlosshotel im Grunewald

Brahmsstr. 10 ✉ 14193 – ✆ (030) 89 58 40 – info@schlosshotelberlin.com – Fax (030) 89 58 48 00 – www.schlosshotelberlin.com **A3**

54 rm – 300/450 € 300/450 €, 26 € – 12 suites

Rest *Vivaldi* – Menu 79/110 €

♦ Castle ♦ Luxury ♦ Design ♦

Stylish and tasteful, with Karl Lagerfeld's touch, this beautiful stately home combines a sumptuous historic setting and contemporary hotel comforts. The Vivaldi offers a highly elegant atmosphere.

Frühsammers Restaurant

Flinsberger Platz 8 ✉ 14193 – ✆ (030) 89 73 86 28 – info@fruesammers-restaurant.de – Fax (030) 89 73 86 28 – www.fruehsammers-restaurant.de

closed 31 March - 13 April and Sunday - Monday **A3**

Rest – *(dinner only)* Menu 30/65 € – Carte 23/31 €

♦ International ♦ Friendly ♦

In this villa belonging to the Grundewald tennis club with a terrace overlooking the courts, Peter and Sonja Frühsammer prepare good international dishes. Small club menu at lunchtime.

at Berlin-Tegel (Airport) *Plan I*

Dorint Airport Tegel

Gotthardstr. 96 ✉ 13403 – ✆ (030) 49 88 40 – info.berlin-tegel@dorint.com – Fax (030) 49 88 45 55 – www.dorint.com/berlin-tegel **B1**

303 rm – 57/166 € 57/176 €, 14 €

Rest – Carte 20/33 €

♦ Chain hotel ♦ Functional ♦

The bus for Tegel airport stops on the doorstep. There are also good connections to the extensive transport system. Rooms are furnished in functional and contemporary style. Restaurant serving international cuisine.

COLOGNE
KÖLN

Population (est 2005) 976,000 - Altitude: 53m.

goodshoot.com

Based in the very centre of Europe on the banks of the Rhine, Cologne is Germany's oldest city (its name was instigated by the Romans, a 'colony' set up to fend off Barbarians). It became a Free City, and later fell under the rule of Napoleon and then the Prussians; all of which has given the locals a cosmopolitan, laid-back and sociable outlook. To illustrate the point, they have their own beer named after them, *Kölsch*, which enjoys the same regional status as Champagne, meaning it can't be brewed anywhere else in the country.

Although it may never be described as Europe's prettiest city, it has an eye-catching old town (largely rebuilt after World War II) and some world-class museums, with subjects ranging from modern art via sport and the Olympics to chocolate. It also boasts one of the finest collections of medieval churches in Europe (lovingly restored in the last half-century), and ploughs its own furrow by celebrating Carnival like it's Rio (no-one seems to care that there's no beach and not much sunshine). Most famously, Cologne has its Cathedral, a massive structure that stood tall during the War, and remains the biggest tourist attraction in Germany. Many of the people craning their necks to take in the exterior are also marvelling at the fact that the whole great edifice took over half a millennium to build…

LIVING THE CITY

The **River Rhine** cuts a swathe right through the heart of Cologne, with four central bridges allowing you plentiful passage from east to west. The main hub of the city is on the west bank, with the **Altstadt** (old town), dominated by its **Cathedral**, practically on the river bank itself. Out to the west, the old medieval walls are now a ring road, which neatly encircles the city centre. Just northwest of the ring road is **Mediapark,** a brash modern development, while to the east of the Rhine is the massive **Trade Fair Centre**, with its 80m-high tower. To its north is Cologne's biggest and most popular park, **Rheinpark.**

PRACTICAL INFORMATION

ARRIVAL-DEPARTURE

Cologne-Bonn Airport lies 17km southeast of the city centre. A taxi will cost approximately €30 or take the S13 train.

TRANSPORT

You can get around Cologne by bus, tram or metro. Validate (stamp) each ticket whenever you board. You can buy a single trip ticket for Cologne, which is valid for anywhere in the city. This is also valid for a journey to nearby Bonn. There are also day tickets covering the same area.

If you're in the city for a while, invest in a Köln Welcome Card. This offers almost ninety offers of reduced admission, ranging from art and culture, leisure facilities, shopping and eating establishments, to free travel on the public transport network. It's available from tourist information offices and many hotels.

EXPLORING COLOGNE

A lot of people come to Cologne for its trade fairs; this is a city renowned across Germany for people in suits making a beeline for the great redbrick Kölnmesse building on the Rhine's right bank. Any visitor not heading for this imposing Trade Fair Centre is invariably headed towards the city's other mighty landmark, rearing like a huge blackened monster over on the left bank. When Cologne **Cathedral** was completed in 1880, it was the tallest building in the world, a record it held for nine years until the rise of the Eiffel Tower. The massive Dom on the Rhine took an astonishing 632 years to complete, because its high Gothic style fell out of fashion in the mid-sixteenth century and tools were downed for another three hundred years, when it became popular again.

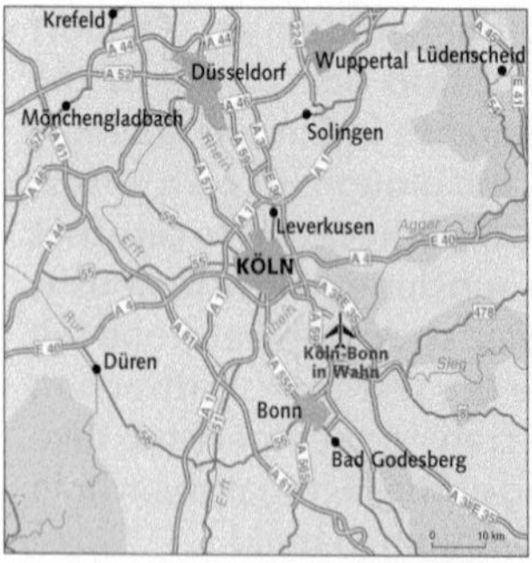

Two million visitors pass through its huge main door each year; the pluckier ones ascend the 509 steps that lead to an observation platform in one of the towers. Halfway up, many take a breather to look at the largest free-swinging bell in the world. At ground level, the massive oak stalls, now seven hundred years old, are the largest ever made in Germany; there's a beautiful fifteenth century altar painting of the patrons of Cologne, and a huge Romanesque reliquary, the Shrine of the Three Kings. After all this, the rest of the city might appear to suffer from an inferiority complex. Look closer, though, and you'll see the city's been fighting back.

➜ ALL ROADS LEAD TO ROMANESQUE

Cologne was a powerful centre for the Church in medieval times and the result is the impressive circle of **Romanesque churches** huddled together in a circle in the old town. They were all badly damaged in the War, but the loving reparations carried out since have returned most to their former glory. Amongst the most startling are **St Ursula**, with a Baroque golden chamber full of ornate, gilded carving, wild-eyed busts and hundreds of skulls wearing sequinned caps, and **St Gereon**, with its massive, ten-sided dome making it one of the most distinctive and unusual buildings in Germany. The Romanesque church most identified with the city is **Great St Martin's**, mainly because its wonderful tower and steeple dominate the **Fischmarkt**, a popular tourist spot by the river. The houses and street layout around here have been rebuilt to historic designs, making it a romantically picturesque neighbourhood in which to wander.

➜ DOM-MINIONS

Over the last few years, Cologne has rightly built itself a reputation as a cultural metropolis. Its museums are a byword for excellence, and two of them are within the shadow of the Dom. The **Romano-Germanic Museum** is essential viewing for anyone keen on 'what the Romans did for us'. Its centrepiece is a fabulous Dionysius mosaic discovered in 1941 during excavations for an air-raid shelter. The mosaic features maids in flowing blue capes being attended by muscular satyrs, and it's made from over a million pieces of ceramic. On display elsewhere is a superb array of artefacts, including beautiful oil lamps, jewellery, sandals, snake thread glassware, dice and even bridge foundations. Almost next door, perfectly placed to provide a nice contrast, is the **Museum Ludwig**, which propels you forward two thousand years with a mind-blowing collection of twentieth century art. It's in a magically light, airy building that seems just right for the biggest collection of Pop Art outside the US. Over four floors, you cross continents and all sorts of borders and boundaries to take in Russian avant-garde, German Expressionism, surrealism, and contemporary installations. Expect the ubiquitous Picasso, Dali, Magritte and Chagall, and a whole lot more besides.

➜ TASTY SELECTION

If your taste is for art from earlier, more classical, times, Cologne has that covered, too. A few minutes' walk south leads you to the **Wallraf-Richartz Museum**, a shiny edifice opened only in 2001. This should cater to most tastes, as the range of Western art from the thirteenth to the nineteenth centuries is pretty comprehensive. On the second floor is the very earliest depiction of Cologne – six hundred years old – in *The Martyrdom of St Ursula at the City of Cologne*. Go up a floor and you're face to face with a fantastic collection of works by the masters of Dutch and Flemish painting; up again and you'll find the Impressionists, plus the likes of Cezanne, Munch and Van Gogh. Nearby, on the banks of the Rhine, you'll find two more museum big hitters, rather incongruously plonked down next to each other. The **German Sport and Olympic Museum** gives you the chance to burn off energy by racing a cycle through a wind tunnel or playing football up on the roof, while at the **Chocolate Museum** you can put the pounds back on via a very tasty trip through three millennia's worth of the brown stuff.

➜ OUT OF STEP?

Underground music takes on a very literal meaning in Cologne. Go down the steps of the Ludwig Museum and immediately underneath is the **Philharmonic Hall**, home to a wide range of concerts from classical to folk and pop. In the past, the Hall has also played host to the unwelcome sound of intrusive footsteps from pedestrians in the street above, so perhaps you should avoid performances with too many quiet passages. No such considerations at the city's classy **Opera House**, in the heart of the city centre, south west of the Dom. It's situated in Germany's largest theatre complex, and holds 1300, so you've a pretty good chance of getting a seat; as well as classic and modern opera, ballet is featured heavily, too. One of the city's coolest musical venues is in the peaceful confines of the **Stadtgarten** (City Park) just beyond the ring road. **Stadtgarten** is set on the **Venloer Strasse** side of the park and has been the top jazz venue in the city for over thirty years. These days, it's widened its remit and features other strands of contemporary music. This is in general the 'cool' side of town, frequented by students and the media denizens who work in the nearby Mediapark. There are lots of fashionable restaurants and clubs, and, just to the west of the ring road, the **Belgian Quarter**, easily identified by its street names. This boasts handsome old buildings and chic apartments which make it one of the classiest places to live – and to stroll – in the city.

CALENDAR HIGHLIGHTS

As Cologne is a city of museums, it's fitting that one of its most acclaimed events is the Long Night of Cologne Museums (October). Around forty of them are open through most of the hours of darkness at a very low price. There's no real question, though, about what's the main festival in the city: Carnival. Unlike Rio or Venice, it begins on 11 November at 11.11am with a day of fancy dress and drinking in the old town and goes on until it reaches its climax about three months later with five days of hard partying, culminating in a street parade on Rose Monday (just before Lent) watched by a million spectators. As a complete contrast, the city takes on a bookish air in March when it hosts Europe's largest international literature festival, lit.cologne, featuring a whole array of renowned authors. In June, half a million pairs of

COLOGNE IN...

➜ ONE DAY

Altstadt, Dom, Romanesque churches

➜ TWO DAYS

Museum Ludwig, Wallraf-Richartz Museum (or Chocolate Museum, depending on your taste), Stadtgarten (or Opera House, again depending on your taste)

➜ THREE DAYS

Romano-Germanic Museum, Rheinpark

eyes look upwards as Cologne Lights illuminates the skies over the Rhine with the world's largest musically synchronised fireworks display; a convoy of boats adds to the spectacle. A month later, the Christopher Street Day gay pride gathering descends on an open-air stage in the old town for its off-the-wall parade; these days the event actually takes up a whole weekend. Also in July, the Summerjam (around the fields of Lake Fuhlinger) brings a Caribbean flair to Cologne in the shape of a reggae and world music jamboree. Not many cities can lay claim to concerts on their ring road, but Ringfest (August) sees a line of stages set up for two miles along the Ringstrassen (don't worry, it's closed to traffic) and two million rock fans descend on the area for a batch of free concerts.

EATING OUT

Cologne has a good variety of international restaurants, but before you consider eating, you should consider the local beer. The city is renowned throughout Germany for its Kölsch. It's the name of the local people and it's the name of their brew, a light beer with the yeast risen to the top rather than sunk to the bottom of the glass. There are twenty local breweries producing their own versions, and you can try them out in an old town brauhaus, atmospheric places with dark wood-panelled interiors and buzzy waiters always at hand to fill your empty stangen (small 0.2 litre glasses) whether you want them to or not. You haven't experienced Cologne properly till you've downed your Kölsch. That accomplished, you can make the most of the city's ethnic diversity by selecting a restaurant from an impressive global range; pick of the bunch are the fine Italian, Japanese and Turkish establishments. Seek out an Italian ice-cream parlour in the summertime, sit under a parasol and tuck into their renowned, full-on sundaes. If your preference is for something local, your best bet is not to be an animal lover. Favoured dishes include Himmer un Äad (bloodsausage and mash), Sauerbraten vom Pferd (braised horse) or Töttchen (ragout of brains and calf's head, cooked with herbs). As well as restaurants, cafés and bars stay open through the afternoon until late, maybe 11.00pm or midnight. Service charge is generally included but a tip of up to ten per cent is the norm.

ON THE RHEIN LINES

Pop over to the east bank for the city's biggest green space, Rheinpark. It's a whopping 125 acres and if you want to get from one end to the other you can climb aboard the park's very own miniature railway, or, if you fancy reaching it in dramatic fashion from the west bank, take a trip on the cable car that leaves from the zoo and crosses the river at head-spinning height.

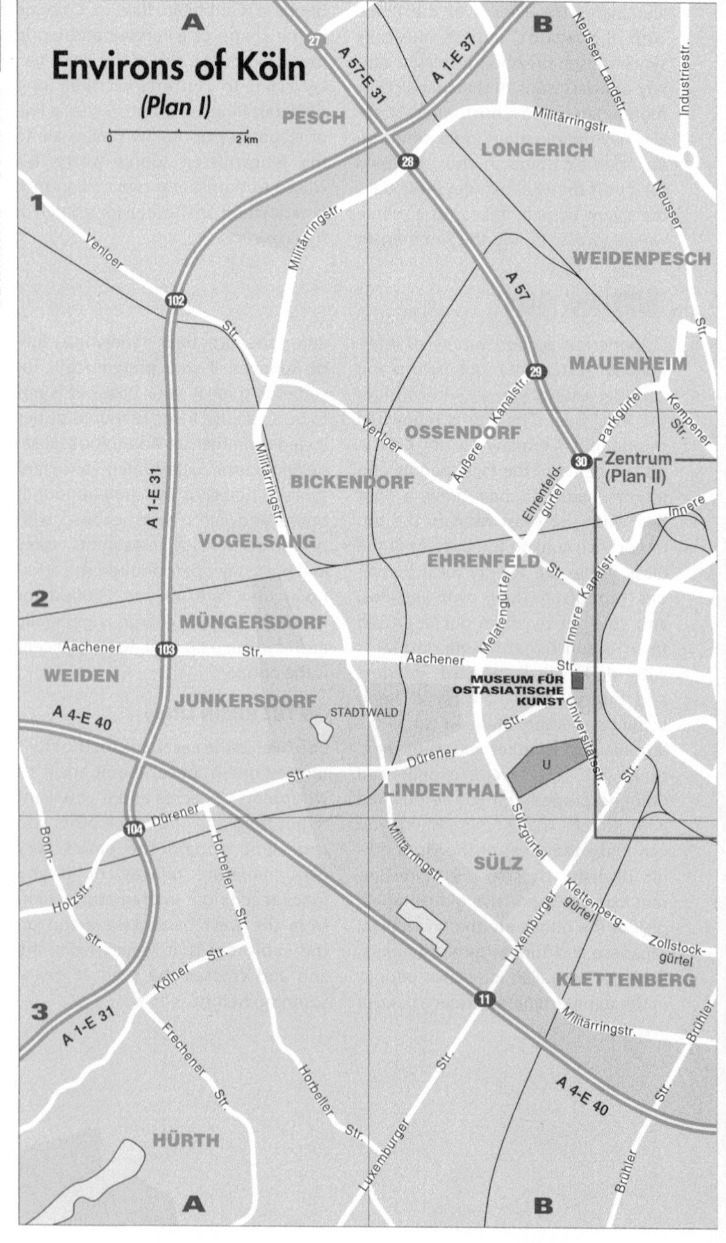
Environs of Köln
(Plan I)
0
2 km
A
B
1
2
3
PESCH
LONGERICH
WEIDENPESCH
MAUENHEIM
OSSENDORF
BICKENDORF
VOGELSANG
EHRENFELD
MÜNGERSDORF
WEIDEN
JUNKERSDORF
STADTWALD
LINDENTHAL
SÜLZ
KLETTENBERG
HÜRTH
MUSEUM FÜR OSTASIATISCHE KUNST
Zentrum (Plan II)
U
A 57-E 31
A 1-E 37
A 57
A 1-E 31
A 4-E 40
Militärringstr.
Neusser Landstr.
Industriestr.
Neusser Str.
Kempener Str.
Parkgürtel
Äußere Kanalstr.
Venloer Str.
Ehrenfeldgürtel
Innere Kanalstr.
Melarengürtel
Aachener Str.
Universitätsstr.
Dürener Str.
Sülzgürtel
Klettenberggürtel
Zollstockgürtel
Luxemburger Str.
Brühler Str.
Bonn-Holzstr.
Horbeller Str.
Kölner Str.
Frechener Str.
27
28
29
30
102
103
104
11

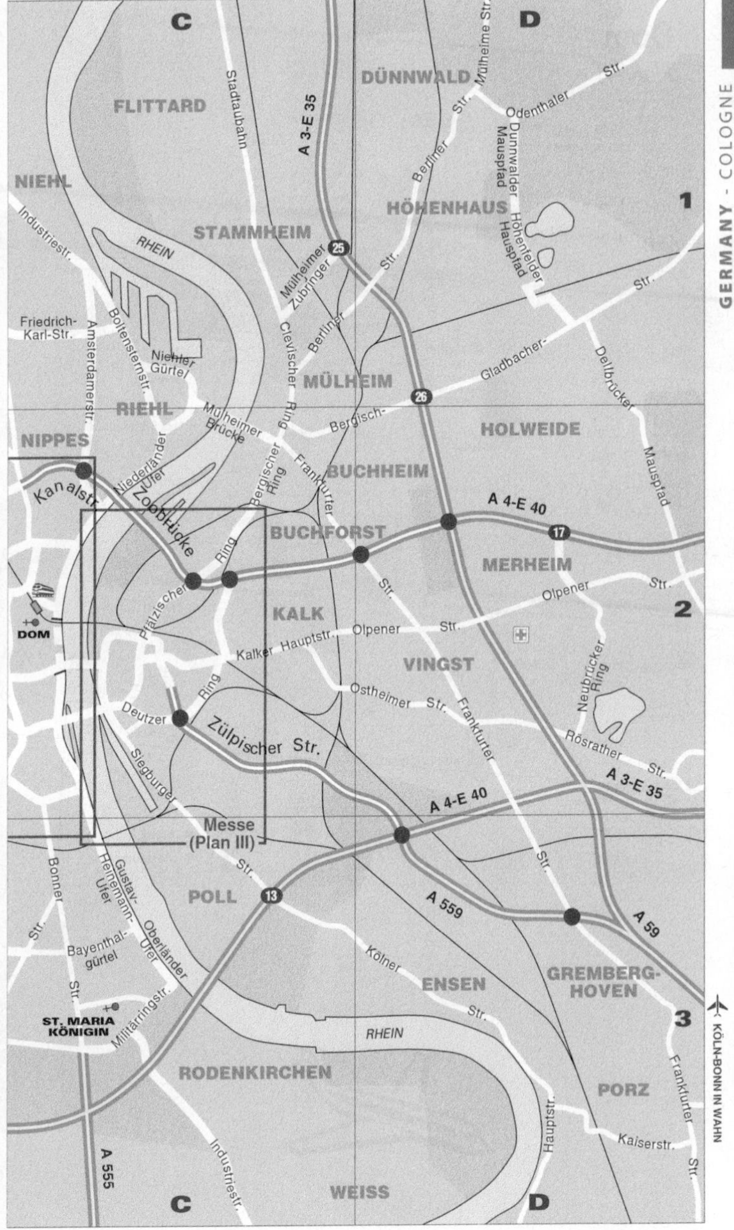
C
D
DÜNNWALD
FLITTARD
NIEHL
STAMMHEIM
HÖHENHAUS
MÜLHEIM
RIEHL
NIPPES
HOLWEIDE
BUCHHEIM
BUCHFORST
MERHEIM
KALK
VINGST
DOM
POLL
ENSEN
GREMBERG-
HOVEN
ST. MARIA
KÖNIGIN
RODENKIRCHEN
PORZ
WEISS
RHEIN
Stadtaubahn
A 3-E 35
Mülheime Str.
Odenthaler Str.
Berliner Str.
Dünnwalder Mauspfad
Höhenfelder Hauspfad
Industriestr.
Mülheimer Zubringer
Friedrich-Karl-Str.
Boltensternstr.
Amsterdamerstr.
Niehler Gürtel
Clevischer Ring
Berliner
Gladbacher-
Dellbrücker Mauspfad
Bergisch-
Mülheimer Brücke
Niederländer Ufer
Bergischer Ring
Frankfurter Str.
Kanalstr.
Zoobrücke
Ring
A 4-E 40
Pfälzischer
Olpener Str.
Kalker Hauptstr.
Ostheimer Str.
Neubrücker Ring
Deutzer
Zülpischer Str.
Siegburger Str.
Rösrather Str.
A 3-E 35
Messe
(Plan III)
Bonner Str.
Gustav-Heinemann-Ufer
Oberländer Ufer
A 559
A 59
Bayenthal-gürtel
Kölner Str.
Militäringstr.
Frankfurter Str.
Hauptstr.
Kaiserstr.
A 555
KÖLN-BONN IN WAHN
25
26
17
13
1
2
3

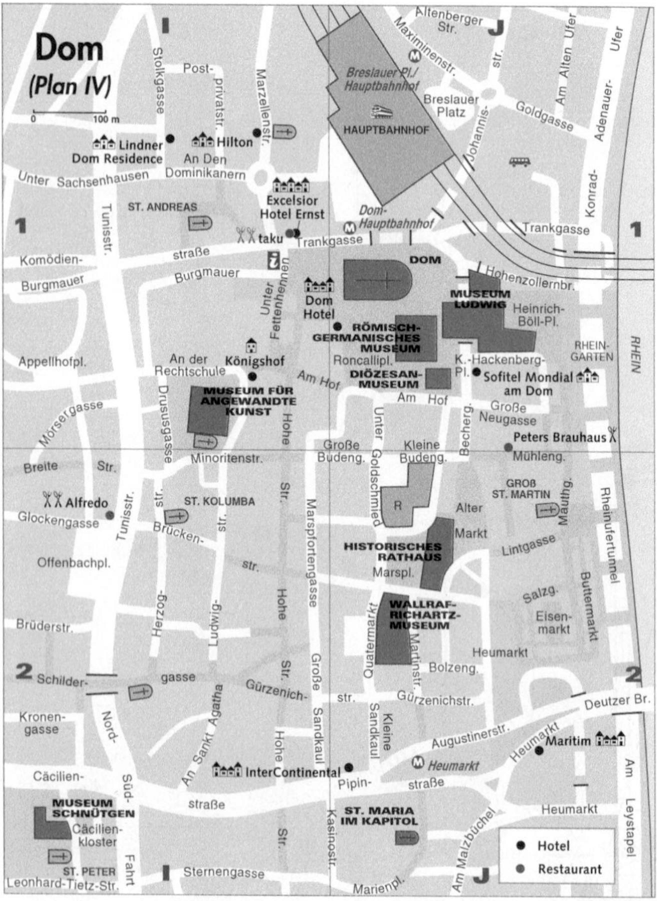

Dom
(Plan IV)

0 100 m

I
J
1
2

Lindner Dom Residence
Hilton
Excelsior Hotel Ernst
taku
Dom Hotel
Königshof
Sofitel Mondial am Dom
Peters Brauhaus
Alfredo
InterContinental
Maritim

Breslauer Pl./Hauptbahnhof
HAUPTBAHNHOF
Breslauer Platz
Dom-Hauptbahnhof
DOM
MUSEUM LUDWIG
RÖMISCH-GERMANISCHES MUSEUM
DIÖZESAN-MUSEUM
MUSEUM FÜR ANGEWANDTE KUNST
ST. ANDREAS
ST. KOLUMBA
GROß ST. MARTIN
HISTORISCHES RATHAUS
WALLRAF-RICHARTZ-MUSEUM
ST. MARIA IM KAPITOL
MUSEUM SCHNÜTGEN
ST. PETER
Heumarkt
RHEIN
RHEIN-GARTEN

Altenberger Str.
Maximinenstr.
Johannisstr.
Goldgasse
Am Alten Ufer
Konrad-Adenauer-Ufer
Trankgasse
Hohenzollernbr.
Heinrich-Böll-Pl.
K.-Hackenberg-Pl.
Stolkgasse
Post-privatstr.
Marzellenstr.
An Den Dominikanern
Unter Sachsenhausen
Tunisstr.
Komödienstraße
Burgmauer
Unter Fettenhennen
Appellhofpl.
An der Rechtschule
Am Hof
Roncallipl.
Große Neugasse
Becherg.
Mörsergasse
Drususgasse
Hohe Str.
Große Budeng.
Kleine Budeng.
Unter Goldschmied
Mühleng.
Breite Str.
Minoritenstr.
Alter Markt
Mauthg.
Rheinufertunnel
Glockengasse
Brückenstr.
Marspfortengasse
Lintgasse
Offenbachpl.
Marspl.
Salzg.
Buttermarkt
Eisenmarkt
Brüderstr.
Herzogstr.
Ludwigstr.
Quatermarkt
Martinstr.
Heumarkt
Bolzeng.
Schildergasse
Gürzenichstr.
Große Sandkaul
Sandkaul
Kleine Sandkaul
Deutzer Br.
Kronengasse
Nord-Süd-Fahrt
An Sankt Agatha
Augustinerstr.
Heumarkt
Cäcilienstraße
Pipinstraße
Kasinostr.
Cäcilienkloster
Am Malzbüchel
Am Leystapel
Leonhard-Tietz-Str.
Sternengasse
Marienpl.

● Hotel
● Restaurant

Excelsior Hotel Ernst

Domplatz/Trankgasse 1 ✉ 50667 – Ⓜ Dom-Hauptbahnhof – ✆ (0221) 27 01 – info@excelsior-hotel-ernst.de – Fax (0221) 2 70 33 33 – www.excelsior-hotel-ernst.de **I1**

142 rm – 🚹245/325 € 🚹🚹325/440 €, ☕ 25 € – 27 suites

Rest taku – see below

Rest *Hanse Stube* – *✆ (0221) 2 70 34 02* – Carte 54/86 €

◆ Grand Luxury ◆ Traditional ◆ Classic ◆

Tradition-rich grand hotel, in a central location by the cathedral, with its elegant ambience from the lobby to the rooms. Piano bar. High-grade sauna and fitness area. A stylish classical atmosphere prevails in the Hanse Stube.

InterContinental

Pipinstr. 1 ✉ 50667 – Ⓜ Heumarkt – ✆ (0221) 2 80 60 – cologne@ihg.com – Fax (0221) 28 06 11 11 – www.cologne.intercontinental.com **J2**

262 rm ☕ – 🚹160/425 € 🚹🚹190/455 € – 12 suites

Rest *Maulbeers* – *(closed Sunday - Monday) (dinner only)* Menu 42/46 € – Carte 47/54 €

◆ Business ◆ Luxury ◆ Retro ◆

Modern design with '70s-revival elements are the key theme here. This hotel stands out for its generous setting and comfortable rooms with state of the art fittings. The Maulbeers restaurant on the first floor offers international cuisine.

Dom Hotel

Domkloster 2a ✉ 50667 – Ⓜ Dom-Hauptbahnhof – ✆ (0221) 2 02 40 – sales.domhotel@lemeridien.com – Fax (0221) 2 02 44 44 – www.koeln.lemeridien.de **J1**

124 rm – 🚹360 € 🚹🚹415 €, ☕ 21 € – 5 suites

Rest – Carte 43/52 €

◆ Luxury ◆ Traditional ◆ Classic ◆

This pleasant hotel right by the cathedral has been here since 1857. A successful combination of classical elegant and modern style. The rooms are very well equipped. Restaurant with bistro ambience, complemented by a large terrace looking onto the Roncalliplatz.

Maritim

Heumarkt 20 ✉ 50667 – Ⓜ Heumarkt – ✆ (0221) 2 02 70 – info.kol@maritim.de – Fax (0221) 2 02 78 26 – www.maritim.de **J2**

454 rm – 🚹133/339 € 🚹🚹153/367 €, ☕ 19 € – 24 suites

Rest *Bellevue* – Carte 41/50 €

◆ Chain hotel ◆ Functional ◆

This hotel, by the Deutz bridge, stands out for its impressive setting. The airy glass-roofed lobby with its boulevard flair is impressive. Functional rooms. The Bellevue offers classic ambience and views of the Rhine and Old Town.

Hilton

Marzellenstr. 13 ✉ 50668 – Ⓜ Dom-Hauptbahnhof – ✆ (0221) 13 07 10 – info.cologne@hilton.com – Fax (0221) 13 07 20 – www.hilton.de/koeln **I1**

296 rm – 🚹149/449 € 🚹🚹145/499 €, ☕ 25 €

Rest – Carte 31/54 €

◆ Business ◆ Modern ◆

Modern minimalist design sets the scene in this very central business hotel which was once a post office. Linear ambience in the Konrad restaurant. Trendy: the Ice Bar.

Sofitel Mondial Am Dom

Kurt-Hackenberg-Platz 1 ✉ 50667
– Ⓤ Dom-Hauptbahnhof – ✆ (0221) 2 06 30 – h1306@accor.com
– Fax (0221) 2 06 35 27 – www.sofitel.com **J1**

207 rm – 🚹105/305 € 🚹🚹125/325 €, ☕ 22 €

Rest – Carte 32/45 €

♦ Business ♦ Modern ♦

There could hardly be a better location than next to the Dom. The hotel offers modern, functional rooms with good technology. Spacious Deluxe rooms. Contemporary restaurant with tapas bar.

Lindner Dom Residence

An den Dominikanern 4a (entrance Stolkgasse)
✉ 50668 – Ⓤ Dom-Hauptbahnhof – ✆ (0221) 1 64 40
– info.domresidence@lindner.de – Fax (0221) 1 64 44 40 – www.lindner.de
closed 22 December - 2 January **I1**

125 rm – 🚹99/279 € 🚹🚹119/299 €, ☕ 18 €

Rest *La Gazetta* – Carte 29/47 €

♦ Townhouse ♦ Functional ♦

A modern atrium building with its large expanse of glass makes this functionally equipped business hotel not far from the cathedral. The rooms on the 7th floor have a terrace! The large glass frontage of "La Gazetta" allows a view of the inner courtyard.

Königshof without rest

Richartzstr. 14 ✉ 50667 – Ⓤ Dom-Hauptbahnhof – ✆ (0221) 2 57 87 71
– hotel@hotelkoenigshof.com – Fax (0221) 2 57 87 62
– www.hotelkoenigshof.com **I1**

82 rm ☕ – 🚹90/198 € 🚹🚹110/225 €

♦ Townhouse ♦ Functional ♦

This well-run hotel is situated a stone's throw away from Cologne Cathedral and the shopping mall. It has very clean, functionally furnished rooms.

XX

taku – Excelsior Hotel Ernst

Domplatz/Trankgasse 1 ✉ 50667 – Ⓤ Dom-Hauptbahnhof
– ✆ (0221) 2 70 39 10 – info@excelsior-hotel-ernst.de – Fax (0221) 2 70 33 33
– www.taku.de **I1**

Rest – *(closed 4 weeks July - August)* Carte 50/87 €

♦ Asian ♦ Minimalist ♦

Highly attentive service offering authentically prepared Japanese, Thai, Chinese and Vietnamese dishes, in a clean, purist setting.

XX

Alfredo

Tunisstr. 3 ✉ 50667 – ✆ (0221) 2 57 73 80
– info@ristorante-alfredo.com – Fax (0221) 2 57 73 80
– www.ristoante-alfredo.com
closed 3 weeks July - August and Saturday dinner - Sunday,
Bank Holidays **I2**

Rest – *(booking advisable)* Carte 37/54 €

♦ Italian ♦ Friendly ♦

Italian tradition in Cologne: now in its second generation, delights its guests with dishes from high-class Italian cuisine, recommended by word of mouth at your table.

X

Peters Brauhaus

Mühlengasse 1 ✉ 50667 – Ⓤ Dom-Hauptbahnhof
– ✆ (0221) 2 57 39 50 – info@peters-brauhaus.de
– Fax (0221) 2 57 39 62 – www.peters-brauhaus.de
closed by Christmas **J1**

Rest – Carte 20/29 €

♦ Regional ♦ Cosy ♦

A rustic inn with a beautiful decorated façade. Worth a look around: each room has a character of its own. Serves good, solid food with fresh Kölsch beer on draught.

Marriott
Johannisstr. 76 ✉ 50668 – Ⓜ Breslauer Pl. / Hauptbahnhof – ✆ (0221) 94 22 20 – cologne.marriott@marriotthotels.com – Fax (0221) 94 22 27 77 – www.koelnmarriott.com **F1-2**
282 rm – 169 € 169 € – 11 suites
Rest *Fou* – Carte 26/41 €
◆ Business ◆ Modern ◆
A spacious lobby and "Plüsch-Bar" greet you at this comfortable business hotel near the cathedral. The rooms are comfortable and very modern. Fou: a restaurant in French brasserie style – with singing serving staff on bicycles in the evenings!

Im Wasserturm
Kaygasse 2 ✉ 50676 – Ⓜ Poststr. – ✆ (0221) 2 00 80 – info@hotel-im-wasserturm.de – Fax (0221) 2 00 88 88 – www.hotel-im-wasserturm.de **F2**
88 rm – 180/275 € 215/355 €, 22 € – 7 suites
Rest La Vision – see below
Rest *d/\blju "W"* – Menu 29 € – Carte 30/49 €
◆ Historic ◆ Business ◆ Design ◆
What is remarkable about this hotel is its unusual architecture – a former water tower (a listed building) from the 19th century with an 11-m high lobby. Designer style rooms. The d/\blju 'W' has a clear, modern, elegant style. Regional and international cuisine.

Renaissance
Magnusstr. 20 ✉ 50672 – Ⓜ Friesenplatz – ✆ (0221) 2 03 40 – info.cologne@renaissancehotels.com – Fax (0221) 2 03 47 77 – www.renaissancekoeln.de **E2**
236 rm – 125/450 € 145/500 €, 23 €
Rest *Raffael* – Carte 26/43 €
◆ Chain hotel ◆ Classic ◆
This city centre hotel is timelessly elegant, from the lobby to the comfortable rooms. The Raffael restaurant serves international cuisine.

Savoy
Turiner Str. 9 ✉ 50668 – Ⓜ Breslauer Pl. / Hauptbahnhof – ✆ (0221) 1 62 30 – info@savoy.de – Fax (0221) 1 62 32 00 – www.savoy.de **F1**
102 rm – 140 € 170 € – 6 suites
Rest – Carte 41/51 €
◆ Business ◆ Individual ◆
The tasteful use of the themes of Africa, Asia, Italy and the Orient is what gives this passionately managed hotel its individual tone. Extensive wellness area. A roof terrace completes the light, friendly restaurant.

Classic Hotel Harmonie without rest
Ursulaplatz 13 ✉ 50668 – Ⓜ Breslauer Pl. / Hauptbahnhof – ✆ (0221) 1 65 70 – harmonie@classic-hotels.com – Fax (0221) 1 65 72 00 – www.classic-hotel-harmonie.de **F1-2**
72 rm – 59/99 € 99/149 €
◆ Townhouse ◆ Cosy ◆
The atmosphere in this beautifully renovated former monastery is relaxed with an Italian flair. Modern furniture and warm Mediterranean colours set the tone.

Ascot without rest
Hohenzollernring 95 ✉ 50672 – Ⓜ Friesenplatz – ✆ (0221) 9 52 96 50 – info@ascot.bestwestern.de – Fax (0221) 9 52 96 51 00 – www.ascot.bestwestern.de closed 22 December - 2 January **E2**
44 rm – 109/225 € 136/245 €
◆ Townhouse ◆ Cosy ◆
This listed patrician house is an elegant English-style hotel. Pretty foyer with small library and lovely inner courtyard.

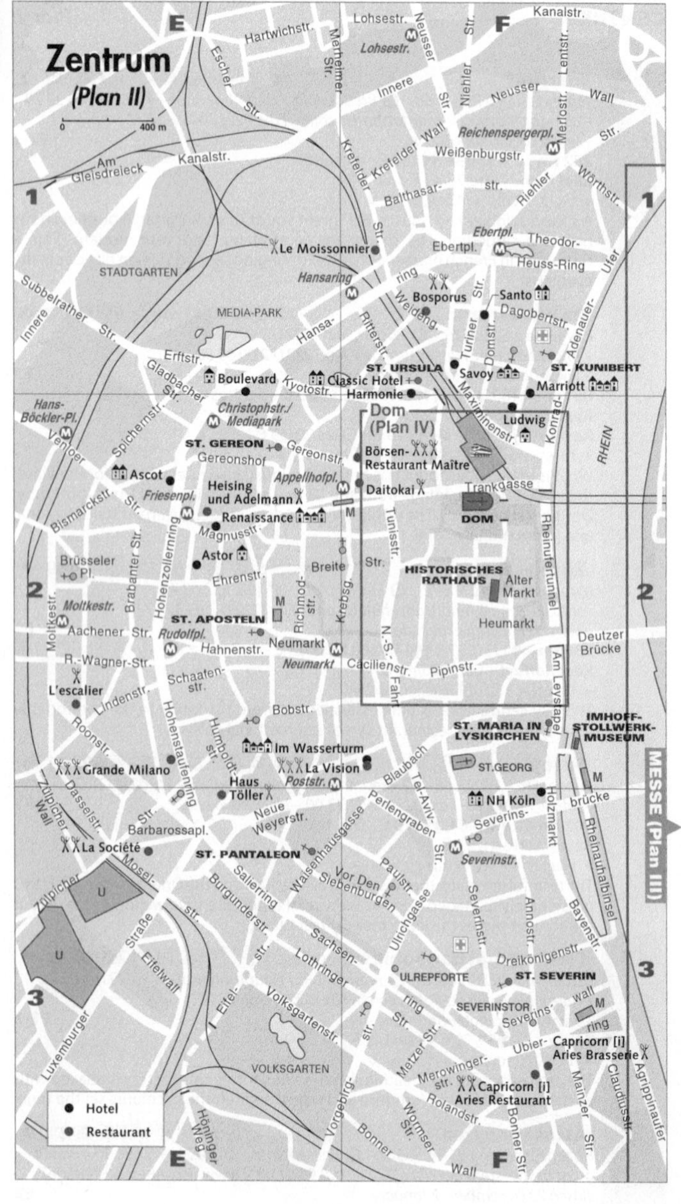
Zentrum
(Plan II)
0
400 m
E
F
1
2
3
Kanalstr.
Lohsestr.
Lohsestr.
Hartwichstr.
Merheimer Str.
Neusser Str.
Escher Str.
Innere
Niehler Str.
Neusser Wall
Lentstr.
Merlostr.
Reichenspergerpl.
Str.
Krefelder Wall
Weißenburgstr.
Am Gleisdreieck
Kanalstr.
Krefelder Str.
Balthasar- str.
Riehler Str.
Worthstr.
Le Moissonnier
Ebertpl.
Ebertpl.
Theodor-Heuss-Ring
Ufer
STADTGARTEN
Hansaring
Bosporus
Santo
Dagobertstr.
Subbelrather Str.
MEDIA-PARK
Weideng.
Turiner Str.
Domstr.
Adenauer-
Innere
Hansa-ring
Rittersstr.
Erftstr.
ST. URSULA
Savoy
ST. KUNIBERT
Gladbacher Str.
Boulevard
Classic Hotel
Kyotostr.
Harmonie
Marriott
Hans-Böckler-Pl.
Christophstr./ Mediapark
Dom (Plan IV)
Maximinenstr.
Ludwig
Konrad-
RHEIN
Venloer
Spichernstr.
ST. GEREON
Gereonshof
Gereonstr.
Börsen-Restaurant Maître
Ascot
Appellhofpl.
Bismarckstr.
Str.
Friesenpl.
Heising und Adelmann
Daitokai
Trankgasse
DOM
Renaissance
M
Magnusstr.
Rheinufertunnel
Tunisstr.
Brüsseler Pl.
Brabanter Str.
Hohenzollernring
Astor
Breite
Str.
HISTORISCHES RATHAUS
Alter Markt
Ehrenstr.
Moltkestr.
M
ST. APOSTELN
Richmodstr.
Krebsg.
Heumarkt
Moltkestr.
Aachener Str.
Rudolfpl.
Neumarkt
Deutzer Brücke
Hahnenstr.
R.-Wagner-Str.
Neumarkt
Cäcilienstr.
Pipinstr.
Am Leystapel
N.-S.-Fahrt
Schaafenstr.
L'escalier
Lindenstr.
Hohenstaufenring
Humboldt-str.
Bobstr.
IMHOFF-STOLLWERK-MUSEUM
ST. MARIA IN LYSKIRCHEN
Roonstr.
Im Wasserturm
Blaubach
ST.GEORG
Grande Milano
La Vision
M
MESSE (Plan III)
Zülpicher Wall
Haus Töller
Poststr.
Tel-Aviv-Str.
NH Köln
Holzmarkt
Dasselstr.
Str.
Neue Weyerstr.
Perlengraben
Severins-brücke
Barbarossapl.
Waisenhausgasse
La Société
ST. PANTALEON
Severinstr.
Rheinauhafen
Mosel-str.
Zülpicher
Salierring
Vor Den Siebenburgen
Paulstr.
U
Burgunderstr.
Ulrichgasse
Severinstr.
Annostr.
Bayenstr.
Straße
Sachsen-ring
U
Eifelwall
str.
Lothringer Str.
ULREPFORTE
Dreikönigenstr.
ST. SEVERIN
Eifel-str.
Volksgartenstr.
SEVERINSTOR
Severins-wall
ring
M
Capricorn [i] Aries Brasserie
Ubier-ring
Agrippinaufer
Luxemburger
Metzer Str.
Merowinger-str.
Claudiusstr.
VOLKSGARTEN
Capricorn [i] Aries Restaurant
Mainzer Str.
Hotel
Restaurant
Vorgebirgstr.
Rolandstr.
Höninger Weg
Wormser Str.
Bonner Wall
Bonner Str.

Santo without rest

Dagobertstr. 22 ✉ 50668 – Ⓜ Ebertplatz – ✆ (0221) 9 13 97 70 – info@hotelsanto.de – Fax (0221) 9 13 97 77 77 – www.hotelsanto.de **F1**

69 rm – 65/140 € 75/160 €

◆ Business ◆ Cosy ◆

An unusual hotel: fine woods, natural stone floors and a specially-designed lighting concept blend into an avant-garde living concept with every comfort.

NH Köln

Holzmarkt 47 ✉ 50676 – Ⓜ Severinstr. – ✆ (0221) 2 72 28 80 – nhkoeln@nh-hotels.com – Fax (0221) 2 72 28 81 00 – www.nh-hotels.com **F3**

204 rm – 116/286 € 133/303 €

Rest – Carte 21/32 €

◆ Chain hotel ◆ Modern ◆

Next to the Severinsbrücke and not far from the Stollwerck Chocolate Museum is this hotel with functional modern rooms featuring relaxation chairs and marble desks. The modern restaurant has a small conservatory facing the courtyard.

Astor without rest

Friesenwall 68 ✉ 50672 – Ⓜ Friesenplatz – ✆ (0221) 20 71 20 – mail@hotelastor.de – Fax (0221) 25 31 06 – www.hotelastor.de closed 21 December - 4 January **E2**

50 rm – 92/115 € 115/138 €

◆ Townhouse ◆ Functional ◆

This highly personally managed hotel consists of two houses which have been joined together. Some of the rooms are particularly comfortable and modern.

Ludwig without rest

Brandenburger Str. 24 ✉ 50668 – Ⓜ Breslauer Pl. / Hauptbahnhof – ✆ (0221) 16 05 40 – hotel@hotelludwig.com – Fax (0221) 16 05 44 44 – www.hotelludwig.de closed 21 December - 1 January **F2**

55 rm – 78/95 € 105/125 €

◆ Townhouse ◆ Functional ◆

This hotel is close to the city centre, not far from the station, and offers contemporary, functionally equipped rooms and a reception staffed around the clock.

Boulevard without rest

Hansaring 14 ✉ 50670 – Ⓜ Christophstr./Mediapark – ✆ (0221) 3 55 84 40 – hotel@hotelboulevard.de – Fax (0221) 13 83 07 – www.hotelboulevard.de closed 23 December - 2 January **E1**

27 rm – 82/175 € 110/220 €

◆ Townhouse ◆ Functional ◆

Conveniently located on the Stadtring, this hotel also attracts guests with its very well-presented, functional rooms.

La Vision – Hotel Im Wasserturm < Köln,

Kaygasse 2 (11th floor) ✉ 50676 – Ⓜ Poststr. – ✆ (0221) 2 00 80 – info@hotel-im-wasserturm.de – Fax (0221) 2 00 88 88 – www.hotel-im-wasserturm.de closed 4 weeks July - August and Sunday - Monday **F2**

Rest – Menu 64/94 € – Carte 60/83 €

Spec. Hummervariation "Favorit". Filet vom St. Pierre mit Fondue von eingeweckten Tomaten und Artischocken. Feines Mousse von Erdbeere und Waldmeister mit lauwarmem Grießknödel (season).

◆ Inventive ◆ Elegant ◆

The restaurant in a glass, round building high above the town offers creative cuisine with a classic base. Fantastic view from the roof terrace.

XXX

Börsen-Restaurant Maître

Unter Sachsenhausen 10 ✉ 50667 – Ⓜ Appellhofpl. – ✆ (0221) 13 30 21 – Fax (0221) 13 30 40 – www.boersen-restaurant.de
closed at carnival, 2 weeks Easter, 4 weeks June - July **F2**
Rest – *(closed Saturday lunch, Sunday and Bank Holidays)* Menu 52/94 € – Carte 55/77 €
Rest *Börsen-Stube* – *(closed Saturday dinner - Sunday and Bank Holidays)* Menu 24 € – Carte 28/38 €
◆ Classic ◆ Formal ◆
This light, airy restaurant with its large plate glass windows offers timeless ambience and classic food in the centre of town. A simpler alternative to the Börsen-Restaurant: the Börsen-Stube with terrace.

XXX

Grande Milano

Hohenstaufenring 29 ✉ 50674 – Ⓜ Rudolfpl. – ✆ (0221) 24 21 21 – info@grandemilano.com – Fax (0221) 24 48 46 – www.grandemilano.com
closed 1 to 14 January and Saturday lunch, Sunday, Bank Holidays **E2**
Rest – Menu 43/63 € – Carte 35/57 €
Rest *Pinot di Pinot* – Menu 13 € (lunch) – Carte 20/30 €
◆ Italian ◆ Friendly ◆
Elegant Italian restaurant with fine service. Menu features a truffle specialty. A relaxed, typically bistro-style atmosphere in the Pinot di Pinot.

XX ✿

Capricorn [i] Aries Restaurant

Alteburger Str. 34 ✉ 50678 – ✆ (0221) 32 31 82 – Fax (0221) 32 31 82 – www.capricorniaries.com
closed 31 January-6 February, 2 weeks July and Monday - Tuesday except exhibitions
Rest – *(dinner only) (booking essential)* Menu 57/99 € **F3**
Spec. Matchatee-Olivenölgelee mit geräuchertem Aal und Gänsestopfleber. Roulade von Kaisergranat mit Muschel-Beurre blanc. Reh mit Kartoffelbaumkuchen und Morcheln.
◆ Classic ◆ Individual ◆
In this small, pure white, intimate restaurant classic cuisine with a creative touch is served by the patron.

XX ✿

La Société

Kyffhäuser Str. 53 ✉ 50674 – ✆ (0221) 23 24 64 – Fax (0221) 21 04 51 – www.lasociete.info
closed 2 weeks July **E3**
Rest – *(dinner only) (booking advisable)* Menu 55/95 € – Carte 45/73 €
Spec. Langostinos und Spargel. Fünf Suppen mit Kondimenten. Gebratener Seeteufel (2 people).
◆ Inventive ◆ Individual ◆
Not much to look at from outside, this restaurant does have plenty to offer on the inside: creative cuisine, a good selection of wines, and very competent service.

XX

Bosporus

Weidengasse 36 ✉ 50668 – Ⓜ Hansaring – ✆ (0221) 12 52 65 – info@bosporus.de – Fax (0221) 9 12 38 29 – www.bosporus.de – closed Sunday lunch **F1**
Rest – Carte 23/34 €
◆ Turkish ◆ Friendly ◆
A classical interior with an Oriental touch awaits you here, and an authentic Turkish menu. Nice terrace.

X ✿

L'escalier (Jens Dannenfeld)

Brüsseler Str. 11 ✉ 50674 – Ⓜ Moltkestr. – ✆ (0221) 2 05 39 98 – info@lescalier-restaurant.de – Fax (0221) 5 69 12 80 – www.lescalier-restaurant.de
closed 31 January - 6 February, 21 to 27 March, 11 to 15 May, 29 September - 9 October and Saturday lunch, Sunday - Monday lunch
Rest – Menu 38/56 € – Carte 43/55 € **E2**
Spec. Ravioli von Kalb und Birnen mit geschmortem Treviso und Endivien. Seesaibling mit gebratenem Ingwer-Wurzelgemüse und Pastinaken. Vanillesoufflé mit Schokoladensorbet.
◆ Classic ◆ Modern ◆
The small staircase takes you down into a cosy and intimate restaurant with a bistro ambience: modern international cuisine with surprise menus.

Le Moissonnier

Krefelder Str. 25 ✉ 50670 – Ⓜ Hansaring – ✆ (0221) 72 94 79 – Fax (0221) 7 32 54 61 – www.lemoissonnier.de
closed 24 December - early January, 1 week Easter, 3 weeks July and Sunday - Monday, Bank Holidays **F1**
Rest – *(booking essential)* Menu 51/81 € – Carte 47/83 €
Spec. Entenleberpastete mit Gewürztraminer Gelee. Gebratene Jakobsmuscheln und Ravioli von Räucherhering. Suprême von der Taube.
♦ Inventive ♦ Friendly ♦
With its authentic atmosphere and pretty Art Nouveau decor, this restaurant is a bistro just like you would find in Paris. Creative French cuisine.

Capricorn [i] Aries Brasserie

Alteburgerstr. 31 ✉ 50678 – ✆ (0221) 3 97 57 10 – Fax (0221) 32 31 82 – www.capricorniaries.com
closed by carnival and Saturday lunch, Sunday **F3**
Rest – Menu 36 € (dinner) – Carte 21/40 €
♦ International ♦ Cosy ♦
A rather more laid-back version of the restaurant of the same name opposite, this friendly, contemporary brasserie with its easy, comfortable ambience offers attentive service.

Heising und Adelmann

Friesenstr. 58 ✉ 50670 – Ⓜ Friesenplatz – ✆ (0221) 1 30 94 24 – info@heising-und-adelmann.de – Fax (0221) 1 30 94 25 – www.heising-und-adelmann.de
closed Sunday and Bank Holidays **E2**
Rest – *(dinner only)* Carte 37/47 €
♦ International ♦ Trendy ♦
This lively restaurant in its pronounced bistro style with its pleasant terrace serves modern international cuisine in a relaxed atmosphere. Large bar area.

Daitokai

Kattenbug 2 ✉ 50667 – Ⓜ Appellhofpl. – ✆ (0221) 12 00 48 – Fax (0221) 13 75 03 – www.daitokai.de
closed Monday - Tuesday lunch **F2**
Rest – *(booking advisable for dinner)* Menu 24 € (lunch)/53 € – Carte 37/61 €
♦ Japanese ♦ Friendly ♦
In this typical Japanese style restaurant in the city centre, the cooks show what they can do at teppanyaki tables.

Haus Töller

Weyerstr. 96 ✉ 50676 – Ⓜ Poststr. – ✆ (0221) 2 58 93 16 – Fax (0211) 3 97 50 67 – www.haus-toeller.de
closed 24 December - 14 January and Sunday, Bank Holidays **E3**
Rest – *(dinner only) (booking advisable)* Carte 20/23 €
♦ Regional ♦ Cosy ♦
A Cologne pub like no other. Everything is still the same as when it opened back in 1889 – including a 'confessional' – creating a really cosy atmosphere.

AT THE EXHIBITION CENTRE *Plan III*

Hyatt Regency

Kennedy-Ufer 2a ✉ 50679 – Ⓜ Deutzer Freiheit – ✆ (0221) 8 28 12 34 – cologne@hyatt.de – Fax (0221) 8 28 13 70 – www.cologne.regency.hyatt.de **G2**
306 rm – †170/360 € ††195/385 €, ☕ 23 € – 18 suites
Rest *Graugans* – *(closed 2 weeks January, 2 weeks August and Sunday - Monday) (dinner only)* Menu 79/109 € – Carte 60/75 €
Rest *Glashaus* – Carte 43/60 €
♦ Chain hotel ♦ Luxury ♦ Classic ♦
Its location on the Rhine and its luxurious setting are what make this hotel stand out. The impressive airy atrium lobby leads to elegant rooms. Graugans restaurant has a Euro-Asian menu. The Glashaus offers Italian cuisine.

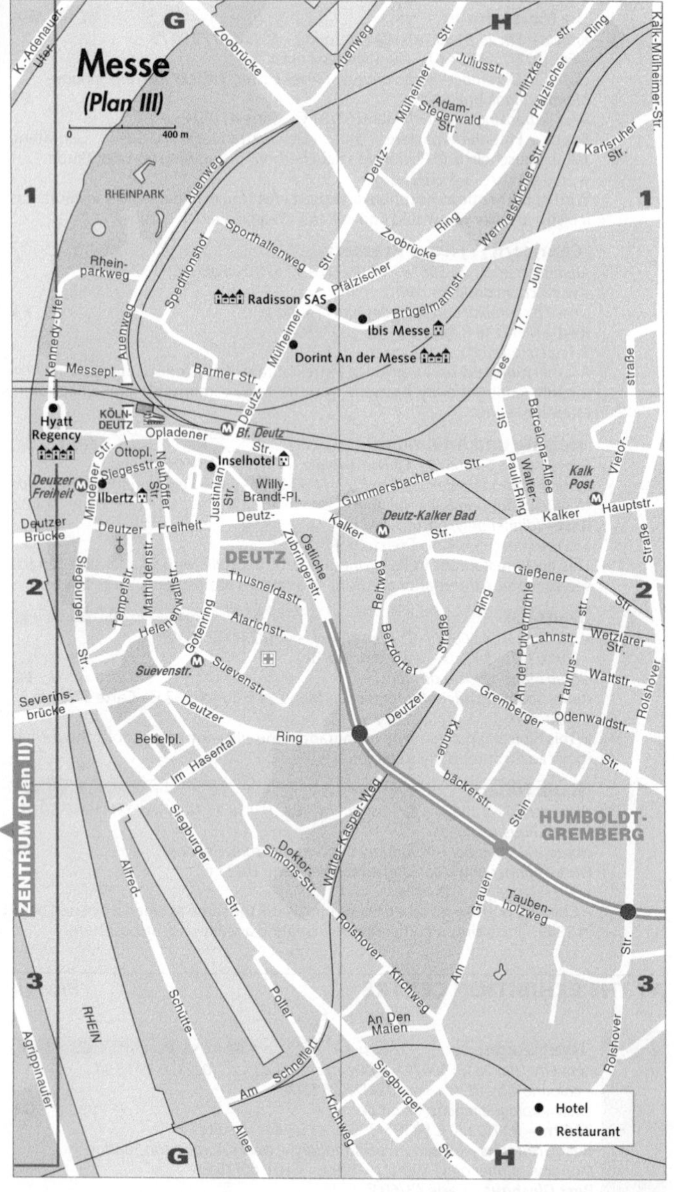
Messe
(Plan III)
0
400 m
G
H
1
2
3
RHEINPARK
Rhein-parkweg
Kennedy-Ufer
Messepl.
Auenweg
Zoobrücke
Sporthallenweg
Speditionshof
Radisson SAS
Ibis Messe
Dorint An der Messe
Pfälzischer Ring
Brügelmannstr.
Barmer Str.
Deutz-Mülheimer Str.
Wermelskirchener Str.
Des 17. Juni Str.
Karlsruher Str.
Juliusstr.
Adam-Stegerwald Str.
Ulitzka-str.
Kalk-Mülheimer-Str.
Hyatt Regency
KÖLN-DEUTZ
Opladener Str.
Bf. Deutz
Ottopl.
Siegesstr.
Inselhotel
Deutzer Freiheit
Ilbertz
Mindener Str.
Neuhöffer Str.
Justinianstr.
Willy-Brandt-Pl.
Gummersbacher Str.
Barcelona-Allee
Walter-Pauli-Ring
Kalk Post
Vietorstraße
Kalker Hauptstr.
Deutzer Brücke
Deutz-Kalker Str.
Deutz-Kalker Bad
DEUTZ
Östliche Zubringerstr.
Reitweg
Gießener Str.
Siegburger Str.
Tempelstr.
Mathildenstr.
Helenenwallstr.
Thusneldastr.
Alarichstr.
Gotenring
Suevenstr.
Betzdorfer Straße
Ring
An der Pulvermühle
Lahnstr.
Wetzlarer Str.
Taunusstr.
Wattstr.
Rolshover Straße
Severinsbrücke
Deutzer Ring
Bebelpl.
Im Hasental
Gremberger Str.
Odenwaldstr.
Kannebäckerstr.
Walter-Kasper-Weg
Stein
HUMBOLDT-GREMBERG
ZENTRUM (Plan II)
Alfred-Schütte-Allee
Doktor-Simons-Str.
Rolshover Kirchweg
Grauen
Am
Taubenholzweg
Str.
RHEIN
Poller Kirchweg
An Den Maien
Am Schnellert
Agrippinaufer
Rolshover
Hotel
Restaurant

Dorint An der Messe VISA MC AE
Deutz-Mülheimer-Str. 22 ✉ 50679 – Ⓜ Bf. Deutz
– ✆ (0221) 80 19 00 – info.koeln-messe@dorint.com – Fax (0221) 80 19 08 00
– www.dorint.com/koeln **G1**
313 rm – †128/188 € ††167/227 €, ☕ 19 € – 32 suites
Rest *L'Adresse* – *(closed 4 weeks August and Sunday - Tuesday) (dinner only)* Carte 44/68 €
Rest *Bell Arte* – *(lunch only)* Carte 26/36 €
Rest *Düx* – Carte 27/37 €
♦ Chain hotel ♦ Business ♦ Modern ♦
This elegant modern hotel is opposite the exhibition centre. Generous lobby, well-equipped rooms and a 650 m² wellness centre. The elegant L'Adresse restaurant. The Düx, a typical Cologne pub.

Radisson SAS VISA MC AE
Messe Kreisel 3 ✉ 50679 – Ⓜ Bf. Deutz – ✆ (0221) 27 72 00
– reservations.cologne@radissonsas.com – Fax (0221) 2 77 20 10
– www.radissonsas.com **G1**
393 rm – †115/190 € ††115/190 €, ☕ 19 €
Rest – Carte 33/48 €
♦ Chain hotel ♦ Business ♦ Modern ♦
This comfortable V-shaped conference hotel is impressive for its quality, state-of-the-art fittings. The light 15 m high reception area is impressive. Paparazzi serves as an a la carte restaurant, with its large pizza oven.

Inselhotel without rest VISA MC AE
Constantinstr. 96 ✉ 50679 – Ⓜ Bf. Deutz – ✆ (0221) 8 80 34 50
– mail@inselhotel-koeln.de – Fax (0221) 8 80 34 90
– www.inselhotel-koeln.de **G2**
42 rm ☕ – †89/179 € ††119/229 €
♦ Townhouse ♦ Functional ♦
The hotel is opposite Deutz station, not far from the exhibition centre site and the Köln-Arena event centre. Sensible, comfortably furnished rooms.

Ibis Messe VISA MC AE
Brügelmannstr. 1 ✉ 50679 – Ⓜ Bf. Deutz – ✆ (0221) 98 93 10
– h3744@accor.com – Fax (0221) 98 93 15 55 – www.ibishotel.com **H1**
180 rm – †59/139 € ††59/159 €, ☕ 10 €
Rest – Carte 15/22 €
♦ Chain hotel ♦ Functional ♦
Ideal for business travellers, this hotel near the conference centre provides modern, well-furnished rooms. A pub-style restaurant with much wooden décor.

Ilbertz without rest VISA MC AE
Mindener Str.6 (corner Siegesstraße) ✉ 50679 – Ⓜ Deutzer Freiheit
– ✆ (0221) 8 29 59 20 – hotel@hotel-ilbertz.de – Fax (0221) 8 29 59 21 55
– www.hotel-ilbertz.de **G2**
26 rm ☕ – †82/145 € ††105/185 €
♦ Family ♦ Functional ♦
Pleasant, spotlessly clean overnight accommodation. Guests stay in comfortable, contemporary rooms with light cherry wood furniture and technical fittings.

AT THE AIRPORT Southeast: 17 km by A59 D3:

Holiday Inn Airport P VISA MC AE
Waldstr. 255 ✉ 51147 Köln – ✆ (02203) 56 10
– reservation.hi-cologne-bonn-airport@queensgruppe.de – Fax (02203) 56 19
– www.koeln-bonn-airport-holiday-inn.de
177 rm – †165/219 € ††215/255 €, ☕ 17 €
Rest – Carte 29/46 €
♦ Chain hotel ♦ Functional ♦
Easy access to the airport, this business hotel provides functional well-equipped rooms for guests. Classic restaurant with conservatory and international cuisine.

ENVIRONS OF COLOGNE

at Köln - Porz-Langel South: 17 km by Hauptstr. D3:

XXX ✿

Zur Tant (Franz und Alexander Hütter)

Rheinbergstr. 49 ✉ 51143 – ✆ (02203) 8 18 83 – info@zurtant.de – Fax (02203) 8 73 27 – www.zurtant.de

closed 2 weeks by carnival and Thursday

Rest – Menu 65/85 € – Carte 50/68 €

Rest *Hütter's Piccolo* – *(closed Thursday)* Carte 27/38 €

Spec. Knusper-Lasagne mit Thunfisch "Mediterran". Loup de mer mit Krustentierhaube und Mango-Chutney. Lende vom steirischen Alm-Ochsen mit Mark und Bäckchenragout.

♦ Classic ♦ Friendly ♦

In this elegant restaurant classic dishes are served. There is a lovely view of the Rhine. Mediterranean décor emphasises the friendly atmosphere in the bistro-like Hütter's Piccolo restaurant.

FRANKFURT

FRANKFURT AM MAIN

Population (est.2005) 649 000 (conurbation 1 489 000) – Altitude:40m

Sime/PHOTONONSTOP

European travellers might feel there's no need to go all the way to New York when they've got Frankfurt. After all, it's earned itself the nickname 'Mainhattan' what with all those slinky, shiny skyscrapers reaching up from the banks of the river Main. This may be a city of brash towers housing big corporations (hence its other nickname 'Bankfurt') but you'll also find half-timbered medieval houses (admittedly rebuilt), and a blistering array of museums along the south bank of the river.

Located at the crossing point of Germany's north-south and east-west roads, Frankfurt is the financial powerhouse of the country, but a city that takes its cultural scene very seriously. It's said that it spends more money on the arts per year than any other European city, and from being something of a gastronomic back water, it's become a gourmet hotspot with its cuisine range becoming more eclectic by the month. The city has also joined the recent trend in turning local venues into summer beach clubs, complete with palm trees and sand. One man who wouldn't believe his eyes if he saw Frankfurt today is Germany's great poet, novelist and dramatist Johann Wolfgang von Goethe…he was born and bred here.

LIVING THE CITY

The centre of Frankfurt is **Cathedral Hill**, where the cathedral has stood for eight hundred years. It towers over **Römerberg**, the medieval square, rebuilt following the War. To the west, amongst the mighty skyscrapers of international banks and corporations, lies the main railway station and **Exhibition Centre**, while south of the **river Main**, which cuts east-west through the city, is the famous **'museum embankment'** and Frankfurt's oldest area, **Sachsenhausen**, full of bars, cafés and restaurants.

PRACTICAL INFORMATION

ARRIVAL-DEPARTURE

Frankfurt Airport is only 9km southeast from the city centre. A taxi will cost around €25. S-Bahn trains S8 and S9 leave every 15min for Frankfurt station and the journey takes just over 10min.

TRANSPORT

Frankfurt runs an efficient bus, metro and tram system. You can buy a day ticket for one person or a group (maximum five), which is valid until the last ride of the day. Tickets are available at vending machines and from bus drivers, but not on trams, the U-Bahn or S-Bahn.

Be a smart Frankfurter and invest in a Frankfurt Card. This entitles you to free public transport and discounts at a variety of museums and attractions. There are also reductions of up to thirty per cent on selected boat trips. You can buy the Card at many travel agencies, at tourist information offices and in both terminals at the airport. It's valid for 24 or 48 hours.

EXPLORING FRANKFURT

During Germany's post-war economic miracle, Frankfurt soon re-established itself as the economic hub of the country. As part of a big drive to show that there was more to the city than Deutschmarks, the authorities poured millions into invigorating its cultural life, using old plans to faithfully rebuild key parts of the war-torn old town and at the same time launch a succession of exciting opera companies, museums and theatres. The city was reborn, and is now the closest thing western Germany has to a high-rise metropolis. To view its skyline from the south bank at night is to see a twinkling fairyland of light, its resemblance to Manhattan evident to all.

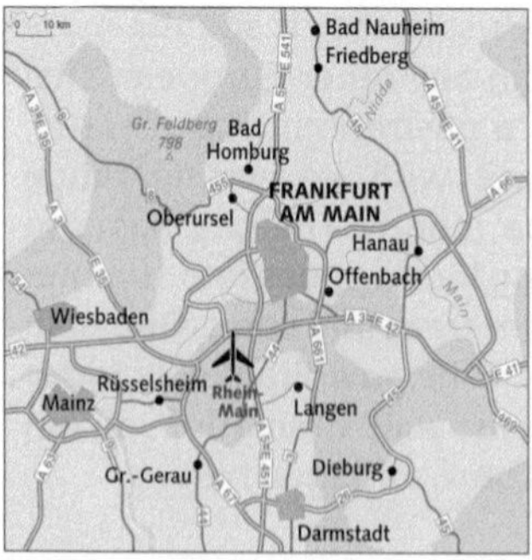

Just to the north of the curving River Main is a compact area that speaks of a far older Frankfurt, where once Holy Roman Emperors were crowned, and where market fairs rang to the cries of traders over a thousand years ago. The dominant feature of the district is the Römerberg, the old centre with its eye-catching half-timbered buildings lovingly rebuilt in 1986 with the aid of historical plans. Römerberg is a cobbled, octagonal square known locally as the 'Great Parlour', and its most striking landmark is the **town hall**, originally three 14C town houses linked by a Gothic triple-gabled frontage. It's not just pretty façades around here, there's a great gallery on the square – the **Kunsthalle Schirn**, opened little more than twenty years ago. It hosts a range of high-powered art, archaeology and cultural exhibitions, and in a short period has become one of Europe's most prestigious spaces. As a contrast, the twin-naved church of **St Nicholas**, just west of the Schirn, dates back to 1290, and twice a day reverberates to the sound of German folk songs. On the eastern side of the old town is the Kaiserdom, the city's thirteenth century cathedral, which remained standing throughout Allied bombing, and boasts stunning views from its Gothic tower: you'll have to climb 324 steps first, though.

→ BANKING ON CULTURE

Visitors don't have to travel far to find out more about the centuries long, incident-filled history of Frankfurt. Close by St Nicholas is the **History Museum**, finished in 1972, which includes a fascinating model of the medieval town, and colourful fragments of buildings that were lost in World War II. By now, you're just about at the water's edge. Cross the river and you'll be face to face with one of the best cultural neighbourhoods in Europe: the Museum Embankment. Along here, strung out like pearls, are nine exhibition buildings, enough to keep an art lover engrossed for many hours, if not days. Some of the museums are quite new (such as those looking at **German Film**, or **World Cultures**), but the **Stadel Art Institute** – perhaps the jewel in the crown – is nearly two hundred years old. The imposing neo-renaissance building boasts work by the likes of Vermeer, Rembrandt, Botticelli, Bosch and van Eyck. If Old Masters are not to your taste, then you can try your luck at other exhibitions around here, which deal with architecture, icons, sculpture, communications, applied art, or – the newest baby on the block – local artists from the Rhine-Main area. In terms of sheer novelty, head back over the Main for the **Modern Art Museum**: the collections from the 1960s onwards are innovative enough, but just gazing at the building itself is an absorbing experience – it looks like a rather tasty slice of cake.

→ MAIN PLAYERS

You can't avoid looking at buildings in this city. In the centre, the now emblematic skyscrapers tower endlessly up to the clouds; if you're of a mind, you could even call them gigantic works of art themselves. One of them, the **Commerzbank Tower**, just happens to be the tallest office building in Europe. Slightly dwarfed, but still very large indeed, is the **Main Tower**, and this is the one that's of interest to visitors. It's the only one in Frankfurt with a public viewing platform, which can be located up on the roof. It hardly needs saying that the vista from here is astounding.

The contrast between the new and the old is thrown up again back in the old town where, a short way up from the north bank of the Main, stands the **Goethe house**. The great man was born here in 1749, and it's where he lived for the next twenty-six years. It's a fascinating example of a mid-eighteenth century home of the upper middle classes, lovingly restored with an interior that includes his writing desk and an astronomical clock. Next door is the decade-old **Goethemuseum**, which includes a collection of items related to Goethe, and an absorbing library with his writings. Another cultural highlight of the area is the **Opera House**, completely rebuilt in a compelling Italian Renaissance style. What happens inside, too, is of a high order: this is Frankfurt's top venue for a wide range of concerts, which take place in either the Great Hall or the Mozart Hall – expect anything from chamber and symphony concerts to jazz, pop and comedy.

Frankfurt is home to some of the country's best shopping streets. Number one on the list is the pedestrianised **Zeil Promenade**, which is lined with department stores. There are more specialised streets dotted around: the nearby **Goethestrasse** (for exclusive designer boutiques); **Berger Strasse** (for trendy fashion); **Schillerstrasse** (for shoes). Seek out the **Kleinmarkthalle,** the city's huge indoor grocery market, for some superbly fresh German foodstuffs. A slightly more out of the way quarter to hit is Sachsenhausen, which is over the river and to the southeast of Museum Embankment. It's a leafy, laidback area, very popular for chilling out, so, after checking its quirky little specialist shops (and Saturday flea market), locals like to sip beer or coffee in one of the neighbourhood's many bars and restaurants.

Of course, if relaxing by a beach is more your thing, then even somewhere seriously landlocked like Frankfurt can come up with a solution. In the summer, many of the city's venues set up outdoor beach clubs, complete with sand and palm trees. The rooftops of some city centre buildings are fair game to double as the faux-seaside; for instance, the roof of the car park of the **Frankfurt Stock Exchange** boasts two pools and a five-hundred strong capacity, while **City Beach Frankfurt**, on the roof of the car park of (this time) a department store, goes that extra mile, with a pool and sand, open air cinema, beach volley ball, and salsa evenings.

CALENDAR HIGHLIGHTS

Practically everyone in Europe's heard of Frankfurt's main event, and with good reason. The Book Fair (in October) is a major jamboree for publishers and book lovers, and reflects the latest trends in global literature. Not by any means is every celebration in the city so cerebral. Frankfurt's Carnival in February is a riot of colour, music and festivities, and it kick-starts an impressive array of spring and summer events. The Forest Folk Festival (May) in Niederrad Forest, a stone's throw from the city, boasts a fairground, bustling market and traditional festivities. A month later, the Opernplatz Festival (in the square with the Opera House) has a stage with music, a motley collective of cabaret artists and a fine range of international gourmet treats (enough to bring local bankers down from their towers). The Rose and Light Festival (also June) transforms the city's Palm

FRANKFURT IN...

→ ONE DAY
Old Town, Römerberg, the view from Main Tower

→ TWO DAYS
Goethe House, Museum Embankment (take your pick of one or two museums), a restaurant in Sachsenhausen

→ THREE DAYS
Boat trip on the Main, window shopping in Zeil, concert at Opera House

Garden into a wonderland of lanterns and candles, which complement the music going on all around. Zeil's inner-city pavements are shaken in July by the Sound of Frankfurt, when the likes of techno, rock and pop throb round the pedestrian zones. Refuge may be sought with Frankfurt Cinema Week, where you can lose yourself watching films in unusual places (don't expect a cinema!). The river hosts two big entertainments in August: the River Main Festival, and the Museum Quay Festival. Both rejoice in Frankfurt's waterway, with music, fireworks, a regatta, the museums, and local concert halls all playing a big part. The end of summer is announced with Autumn Dippe Fair, at Festplatz am Ratsweg in September. The last big open-air fair before winter is a riot of old-fashioned fun, with carousels, rollercoasters, and fireworks to set it all off and close it down.

EATING OUT

Not so long ago, Frankfurt's gastronomic fame came courtesy of its Apfelwein (a sweet or dry variant of cider) and Handkäs mit Musik (small yellow cheese with vinegar, oil and onions). Not forgetting Grüne Sauce (a mixture of various herbs and sour cream served with boiled eggs). That's not the case now. Head along to the Fressgass (near Opernplatz) and you've got a pedestrian mile of fine eateries – food on the hoof or to graze over at good prices. Fressgass, by the way, translates as 'Eatery Alley' or 'Glutton's Lane', so you get the picture. Nearly thirty per cent of Frankfurt's citizens have come to live here from overseas, so a wealth of eating possibilities has been opened up and it's now no problem to 'eat globally' all round the city. Foreign communities have added a real touch of spice to the culinary landscape, which is full of the likes of Turkish, Italian and Chinese establishments. Nevertheless, a visit to this city wouldn't be complete without a trip to the äppelwoilokale in Sachsenhausen, the casual but lively cafés where tradition is the key, and Apfelwein served up in ceramic mugs is the drink. Any down sides to eating here? In a city full of bankers, it can prove a bit difficult locating good but inexpensive food, but if in doubt (or potential penury) - hit the Fressgass!

➜ EXPRESS DELIVERY

For a leisurely trip round Frankfurt, try the Ebbelwei Express. This colourful tram takes visitors all over the city from Römer to the zoo, across the river to Sachsenhausen and back – and you get a free bottle of cider. But it only runs at weekends and on public holidays.

➜ A RIVER RUNS

Taking to the water makes a great day out here. Only a few steps away from the Römerberg is the Main quay at the Eiserner Steg, from where you can catch boats up and down the river. You can choose between day trips up to the Rhine or shorter journeys taking in the amazing skyline of the city.

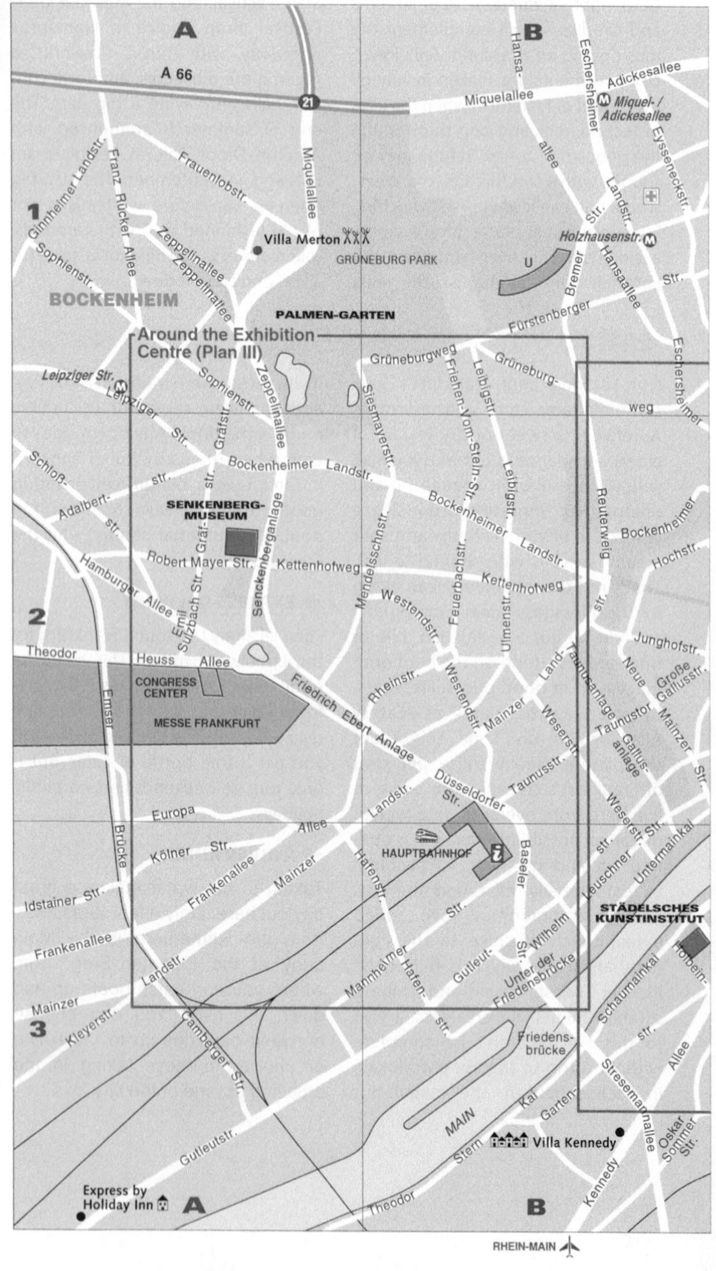
A
B
A 66
21
Miquelallee
Adickesallee
Miquel-/Adickesallee
Hansa-allee
Eschersheimer Landstr.
Eyssenecksstr.
Frauenlobstr.
Ginnheimer Landstr.
Franz Rücker Allee
Zeppelinallee
Villa Merton
GRÜNEBURG PARK
Holzhausenstr.
U
Bremer Str.
Hansaallee
Sophienstr.
BOCKENHEIM
PALMEN-GARTEN
Fürstenberger Str.
Around the Exhibition Centre (Plan III)
Grüneburgweg
Grüneburg-weg
Leipziger Str.
Siesmayerstr.
Friehen-Vom-Stein-Str.
Leibigstr.
Gräfstr.
Bockenheimer Landstr.
Schloß-str.
Adalbert-str.
SENKENBERG-MUSEUM
Senckenberganlage
Mendelsschnstr.
Reuterweg
Bockenheimer
Hochstr.
Robert Mayer Str.
Kettenhofweg
Hamburger Allee
Emil Sulzbach Str.
Westendstr.
Feuerbachstr.
Ulmenstr.
Junghofstr.
Theodor Heuss Allee
Taunusanlage
Neue Mainzer Str.
Große Gallusstr.
CONGRESS CENTER
MESSE FRANKFURT
Emser Brücke
Friedrich Ebert Anlage
Rheinstr.
Mainzer Landstr.
Wesersstr.
Taunustor
Gallus-anlage
Düsseldorfer Str.
Taunusstr.
Europa Allee
Kölner Str.
Frankenallee
Hafenstr.
HAUPTBAHNHOF
Baseler Str.
Leuschner Str.
Untermainkai
Idstainer Str.
STÄDELSCHES KUNSTINSTITUT
Wilhelm Str.
Gutleut-str.
Unter der Friedensbrücke
Mannheimer Str.
Hafen-str.
Schaumainkai
Holbein-str.
Kleyerstr.
Camberger Str.
Friedens-brücke
Stresemannallee
Allee
MAIN
Kai
Garten-str.
Gutleutstr.
Villa Kennedy
Stern
Oskar Sommer Str.
Kennedy
Express by Holiday Inn
Theodor
RHEIN-MAIN
1
2
3

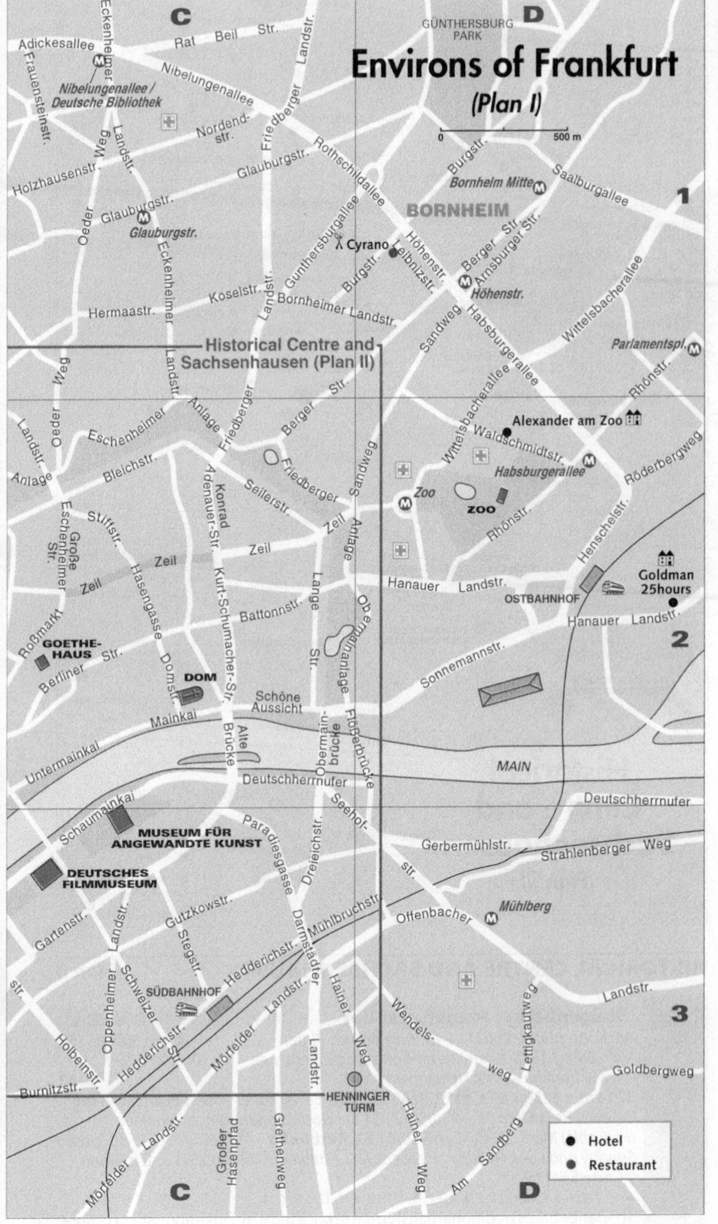
Environs of Frankfurt
(Plan I)
0
500 m
C
D
1
2
3
GÜNTHERSBURG PARK
BORNHEIM
Adickesallee
Nibelungenallee / Deutsche Bibliothek
Glauburgstr.
Bornheim Mitte
Höhenstr.
Cyrano
Historical Centre and Sachsenhausen (Plan II)
Parlamentspl.
Alexander am Zoo
Habsburgerallee
Zoo
ZOO
OSTBAHNHOF
Goldman 25hours
GOETHE-HAUS
DOM
MAIN
MUSEUM FÜR ANGEWANDTE KUNST
DEUTSCHES FILMMUSEUM
Mühlberg
SÜDBAHNHOF
HENNINGER TURM
Hotel
Restaurant

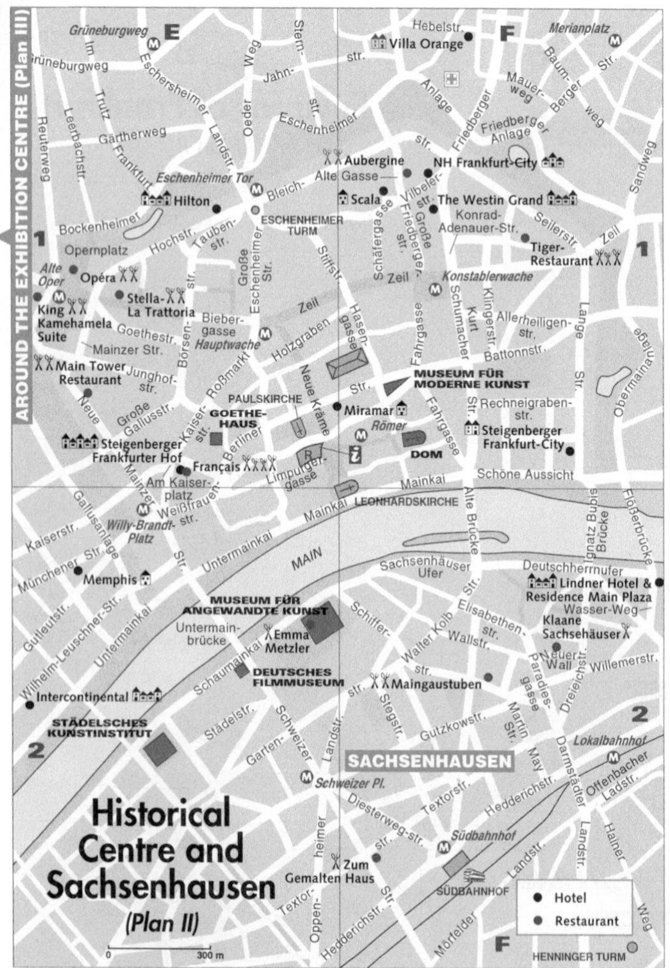

HISTORICAL CENTRE AND SACHSENHAUSEN *Plan II*

Steigenberger Frankfurter Hof

Am Kaiserplatz ✉ 60311 – Ⓜ Willy-Brandt-Platz – ☎ (069) 2 15 02 – frankfurter-hof@steigenberger.de – Fax (069) 21 59 00 – www.frankfurter-hof.steigenberger.de **E1**

321 rm – 🚹230/669 € 🚹🚹230/669 €, ☕ 28 € – 20 suites – **Rest Français** – see below – **Rest *Oscar's*** – ☎ *(069) 21 51 50 (closed Sunday lunch) (booking advisable)* Menu 30 € – Carte 39/61 € – **Rest *Iroha*** – ☎ *(069) 21 99 49 30 (closed Sunday and Bank Holidays except during exhibitions)* Menu 25/120 € (dinner) – Carte 55/73 €

♦ Grand Luxury ♦ Business ♦ Classic ♦

Steigenberger's traditional flagship dates back to 1876. This impressive, comprehensively refurbished building conveys exclusiveness. Cosmetics and massage facilities. Oscar's, with its light bistro atmosphere Far East cuisine in the Iroha.

Villa Kennedy

Kennedyallee 70 ✉ 60596 – Ⓜ Schweizer Platz – ✆ (069) 71 71 20 – info.villakennedy@roccofortehotels.com – Fax (069) 71 71 22 00 – www.roccofortehotels.com Plan I **B3**

163 rm – 460/565 € 460/565 €, ☕ 26 € – 29 suites

Rest – Carte 49/86 €

♦ Grand Luxury ♦ Classic ♦

The former Villa Speyer (1904) has now been extended to give an impressive hotel complex in the historical style, with a tasteful atmosphere and elegant spa area. Restaurant in charming inner courtyard, with Italian-influenced international cuisine.

The Westin Grand

Konrad-Adenauer Str. 7 ✉ 60313 – Ⓜ Konstablerwache – ✆ (069) 2 98 10 – grandhotel.frankfurt@arabellastarwood.com – Fax (069) 2 98 18 10 – www.starwoodhotels.com/frankfurt **F1**

371 rm – 190/700 € 230/740 €, ☕ 29 € – 17 suites

Rest *Aquaterra* – Carte 36/68 €

Rest *san san* – *✆ (069) 91 39 90 50 (closed Sunday)* Menu 16 € – Carte 25/36 €

Rest *Sushimoto* – *✆ (069) 2 98 11 87 (closed 2 weeks end July - early August, 2 weeks end December and Monday except during exhibitions) (Sunday and Bank Holidays dinner only)* Menu 40/82 € – Carte 27/56 €

♦ Chain hotel ♦ Luxury ♦ Modern ♦

Now extensively renovated, the Grand hotel downtown has a new shine: the rooms have been decorated in contemporary style, very easy to live in. Aquaterra with its Mediterranean cuisine. san san: Thai and Indo-Chinese flavours. Japanese in the Sushimoto.

Hilton

Hochstr. 4 ✉ 60313 – Ⓜ Eschenheimer Tor – ✆ (069) 1 33 80 00 – sales.frankfurt@hilton.com – Fax (069) 13 38 20 – www.hilton.de/frankfurt **E1**

342 rm – 179/499 € 179/499 €, ☕ 29 € – 3 suites

Rest – Carte 36/50 €

♦ Chain hotel ♦ Luxury ♦ Modern ♦

A generous, airy atrium takes you into this green-surrounded hotel in the centre. The "Wave, Health and Fitness Club" includes a 25 m indoor pool. Restaurant with international and American fare.

InterContinental

Wilhelm-Leuschner-Str. 43 ✉ 60329 – ✆ (069) 2 60 50 – frankfurt@ihg.com – Fax (069) 25 24 67 – www.frankfurt.intercontinental.com **E2**

770 rm – 199 € 199 €, ☕ 27 € – 28 suites

Rest *Signatures* – Carte 36/58 €

♦ Chain hotel ♦ Luxury ♦ Functional ♦

The rooms in this hotel on the river Main are divided into two wings, the River Wing and City Wing. Club floor on the 21st floor, with great views over Frankfurt. A restaurant in warm tones, with a modern conservatory.

Lindner Hotel & Residence Main Plaza ≤ Skyline,

Walther-von-Cronberg Platz 1 ✉ 60594 – Ⓜ Lokalbahnhof – ✆ (069) 66 40 10 – info.mainplaza@lindner.de – Fax (069) 6 64 01 40 04 – www.lindner.de **F2**

118 rm – 149/179 € 179/209 €, ☕ 20 € – 7 suites

Rest *New Brick* – Carte 38/51 €

♦ Business ♦ Luxury ♦

Right on the Main, behind its high-rise facade, the redbrick front hides a luxurious hotel with a modern elegant ambience. 450 m² beauty spa. The New Brick offers Californian cuisine, prepared before your eyes.

Holiday Inn City-South
Mailänder Str. 1 (by Darmstädter Landstr. C 3) ✉ 60598 – ✆ (069) 6 80 20 – info.hi-frankfurt-citysouth@queensgruppe.de – Fax (069) 6 80 23 33 – www.frankfurt-citysouth-holiday-inn.de
439 rm – 🛉129/420 € 🛉🛉145/480 €, ☕ 19 €
Rest – *(dinner only)* Carte 27/45 €
◆ Chain hotel ◆ Functional ◆
Newly furnished rooms await you in the hotel opposite the Henninger tower. The rooms on the 25th floor offer breathtaking views of the city. Elegant hotel restaurant "Le Chef" with international dishes.

NH Frankfurt-City
Vilbelerstr. 2 ✉ 60313 – Ⓜ Konstablerwache – ✆ (069) 9 28 85 90 – nhfrankfurtcity@nh-hotels.com – Fax (069) 9 28 85 91 00 – www.nh-hotels.com **F1**
256 rm – 🛉149/240 € 🛉🛉149/240 €, ☕ 22 € – 8 suites
Rest – Carte 35/53 €
◆ Chain hotel ◆ Functional ◆
Centrally located, this well run hotel is right on the pedestrian zone of town providing modern comfortable rooms with all mod cons. Restaurant on the first floor with a large buffet.

Villa Orange without rest
Hebelstr. 1 ✉ 60318 – ✆ (069) 40 58 40 – contact@villa-orange.de – Fax (069) 40 58 41 00 – www.villa-orange.de **F1**
38 rm ☕ – 🛉125/145 € 🛉🛉140/155 €
◆ Business ◆ Personalised ◆
Hotel with striking orange façade. Bedrooms are comfortably modern and some bathrooms come with free-standing bath. Passionately run by friendly owner.

Steigenberger Frankfurt-City
Lange Str. 5 ✉ 60311 – ✆ (069) 21 93 00 – frankfurt-city@steigenberger.de – Fax (069) 21 93 05 99 – www.frankfurt-city.steigenberger.de **F1**
149 rm – 🛉105/159 € 🛉🛉120/174 €, ☕ 18 €
Rest – Carte 19/35 €
◆ Business ◆ Functional ◆
This hotel, a favourite of business travellers, offers elegant, homelike guest rooms in a casual Italian style with a view of the city skyline. Restaurant with an open kitchen and international specialties.

Alexander am Zoo without rest
Waldschmidtstr. 59 ✉ 60316 – Ⓜ Habsburgerallee – ✆ (069) 94 96 00 – info@alexanderamzoo.de – Fax (069) 94 96 07 20 – www.alexanderamzoo.de *Plan I* **D2**
66 rm ☕ – 🛉130 € 🛉🛉155 € – 9 suites
◆ Business ◆ Modern ◆
A modern angular facade with equally modern, elegant rooms. Spend your leisure time during meetings and conferences on the terraces, admiring the views of the city.

Goldman 25hours
Hanauer Landstr. 127 ✉ 60314 – ✆ (069) 40 58 68 90 – frankfurt@25hours-hotels.com – Fax (069) 40 58 68 98 90 – www.25hours-hotels.com *Plan I* **D2**
49 rm – 🛉115/135 € 🛉🛉115/135 €, ☕ 14 €
Rest – *(closed Sunday)* Menu 48 € – Carte 33/51 €
◆ Business ◆ Personalised ◆ Design ◆
An unusual hotel in which modern design and interesting details of different styles come together to create a very attractive and comfortable décor and ambience. Restaurant with a maritime feel.

Memphis without rest

Münchener Str. 15 ✉ 60329 – Ⓜ Willy-Brandt-Platz – ☎ (069) 2 42 60 90 – memphis-hotel@t-online.de – Fax (069) 24 26 09 99 – www.memphis-hotel.de **E2**

42 rm ☕ – 🚹110/140 € 🚹🚹130/170 €

♦ Business ♦ Design ♦

In the centre of town, in a lively arts scene, is this charming hotel with its pleasant rooms in contemporary colours. The rooms on the inner courtyard are quiet.

Miramar without rest

Berliner Str. 31 ✉ 60311 – ☎ (069) 9 20 39 70 – info@miramar-frankfurt.de – Fax (069) 92 03 97 69 – www.miramar-frankfurt.de

closed 22 to 31 December **E-F1**

39 rm ☕ – 🚹100/130 € 🚹🚹140/150 €

♦ Business ♦ Functional ♦

Between the Zeil and the Römer, with well-tended, functional rooms and a friendly breakfast room.

Scala without rest

Schäfergasse 31 ✉ 60313 – Ⓜ Konstablerwache – ☎ (069) 1 38 11 10 – info@scala.bestwestern.de – Fax (069) 13 81 11 38 – www.scala.bestwestern.de **F1**

40 rm – 🚹95/139 € 🚹🚹118/165 €, ☕ 13 €

♦ Business ♦ Functional ♦

Its central location in the centre of the city and its modern, functionally equipped rooms are what make this hotel. The reception and drinks service is staffed 24 hours a day.

Français – Hotel Steigenberger Frankfurter Hof

Am Kaiserplatz ✉ 60311 – Ⓜ Willy-Brand-Platz – ☎ (069) 21 51 38 – frankfurter-hof@steigenberger.de – Fax (069) 21 59 19 – www.frankfurter-hof.steigenberger.de

closed 21 March - 6 April, 12 July - 10 August and Saturday - Sunday, Bank Holidays except during exhibitions **E1**

Rest – Menu 45 € (lunch)/118 € (dinner) – Carte 57/77 €

♦ French ♦ Elegant ♦

In the evenings, this elegant restaurant serves classic style dishes: at lunchtime, it offers a smaller, simpler menu under the name "Français Light".

Tiger-Restaurant

Heiligkreuzgasse 20 ✉ 60313 – Ⓜ Konstablerwache – ☎ (069) 92 00 22 25 – info@tigerpalast.de – Fax (069) 92 00 22 17 – www.tigerpalast.de

closed 2 to 5 February, 13 July - 12 August and Sunday - Monday **F1**

Rest – *(dinner only) (booking essential)* Menu 68 € (veg.)/110 € – Carte 66/81 €

Rest *Palast-Bistrot* – ☎ *(069) 92 00 22 92 (closed 2 to 5 February, 13 July-12 August and Monday) (dinner only)* Menu 66/83 € – Carte 58/78 €

Spec. Mit Guacamole gefüllter Gemüsecannelloni, Tomatenconfit und Chicoréesalat. Lammrückenfilet mit Gremolada im Foccaciamantel gebacken. Schokoladenschnitte mit eingelegten Aprikosen und Gelee von Holunderblütenessig.

♦ Classic ♦ Fashionable ♦

The variety theatre building, the Tiger Palace, is home to this modern restaurant with Mediterranean influenced classic cuisine. Good selection of French wine. The historic brick-vaulted ceiling gives the Palast-Bistrot its nice setting.

Opéra

Opernplatz 1 (level 3) ✉ 60313 – Ⓜ Alte Oper – ☎ (069) 1 34 02 15 – info@opera-restauration.de – Fax (069) 1 34 02 39 – www.opera-restauration.de **E1**

Rest – Menu 32 € – Carte 37/58 €

♦ International ♦ Formal ♦

A restaurant in the former foyer of the Alte Oper, with impressive ceiling paintings and original Art Nouveau chandeliers. Terrace with pretty views. Saturday Jause (cold dishes) and Sunday brunch.

XX **Aubergine** VISA MC AE

Alte Gasse 14 ✉ 60313 – Ⓜ Konstablerwache – ✆ (069) 9 20 07 80
– info@aubergine-frankfurt.de – Fax (069) 9 20 07 86
– www.aubergine-frankfurt.de
closed 3 weeks July - August and Saturday lunch, Sunday **F1**

Rest – *(booking advisable)* Menu 28 € (lunch)/55 € (dinner) – Carte 48/61 €

♦ International ♦ Cosy ♦

In friendly, family style, they look after their guests with an ambitious cuisine with a whiff of Italian influences, presented on Versace crockery. Many wines from Tuscany.

XX **Maingaustuben** VISA MC AE

Schifferstr. 38 ✉ 60594 – ✆ (069) 61 07 52 – maingau@t-online.de
– Fax (069) 61 99 53 72 – www.maingau.de
closed Saturday lunch, Sunday dinner - Monday **F2**

Rest – Menu 17 € (lunch)/75 € (dinner) – Carte 31/47 €

♦ International ♦ Friendly ♦

Refined décor and stylish ambience characterize this restaurant, which offers both international and classic cuisine. A smaller version of the regular menu is available at midday.

XX **Stella - La Trattoria** VISA MC AE

Große Bockenheimer Str. 52 (Gallerie Fressgass) ✉ 60313 – Ⓜ Alte Oper
– ✆ (069) 90 50 12 71 – info@stella-ffm.de – Fax (069) 90 50 16 69
– www.stella-ffm.de
closed Sunday except during exhibitions **E1**

Rest – Menu 27 € (lunch)/65 € (dinner) – Carte 45/55 €

♦ Italian ♦ Fashionable ♦

The Stella family offers Italian cuisine and good Tuscan wines in this friendly restaurant and in La Trattoria on the first floor. There are also tables outside in the glass-roofed passage.

XX **Main Tower Restaurant** ≤ Frankfurt, VISA MC AE

Neue Mainzer Str. 52 (53th floor, charge) ✉ 60311 – Ⓜ Alte Oper
– ✆ (069) 36 50 47 77 – maintower.restaurant@compass-group.de
– Fax (069) 36 50 48 71 – www.maintower-restaurant.de
closed Sunday - Monday **E1**

Rest – *(dinner only) (booking essential)* Menu 57/98 €

♦ Mediterranean ♦ Trendy ♦

The modern restaurant and bar are 187 m up, and stand out for their fantastic views over the city. Contemporary Mediterranean cuisine.

XX **King Kamehameha Suite** VISA MC AE

Taunusanlage 20 ✉ 60235 – Ⓜ Alte Oper – ✆ (069) 71 03 52 77
– suite@king-kamehameha.de – Fax (069) 71 03 59 80
– www.king-kamehameda.de **E1**

Rest – *(closed Sunday) (dinner only) (booking essential)* Menu 51/91 €
– Carte 46/73 €

Rest *Atrium* – Carte 36/64 €

♦ Inventive ♦ Trendy ♦ Modern ♦

A stylish and popular meeting place within a classical building. The trendy restaurant and bar offers creative cuisine. Atrium serves international cuisine.

X **Emma Metzler** P VISA MC AE

Schaumainkai 17 ✉ 60594 – Ⓜ Schweizer Platz – ✆ (069) 61 99 59 06
– office@emma-metzler.com – Fax (069) 61 99 59 09 – www.emma-metzler.com
closed during carnival, 29 to 31 August, 23 December - 4 January and Sunday dinner - Monday except during exhibitions **E2**

Rest – Menu 23 € (lunch)/69 € (dinner) – Carte 51/64 €

♦ Modern ♦ Trendy ♦

The bright, simple and modern restaurant in the museum of applied art offers contemporary dishes with a creative touch and views over the park

Cyrano VISA MC AE
Leibnizstr. 13 ✉ 60385 – Ⓜ Höhenstr. – ✆ (069) 43 05 59 64
– info@cyrano-restaurant.de – Fax (069) 43 05 59 65
– www.cyrano-restaurant.de
closed 24 December - 10 January *Plan I* **D1**
Rest – *(dinner only)* Menu 55/63 € – Carte 41/51 €
♦ Inventive ♦ Minimalist ♦
A small, friendly trained restaurant serving classical food with a slightly creative touch on well covered tables. Nice terrace.

Klaane Sachsehäuser
Neuer Wall 11 ✉ 60594 – ✆ (069) 61 59 83 – klaanesachse@web.de
– Fax (069) 62 21 41 – www.klaanesachsehaeuser.de
closed 22 December - 3 January and Sunday **F2**
Rest – *(open from 4pm)* Carte 12/22 €
♦ Regional ♦ Rustic ♦
The home-brewed "Stöffche" and good Frankfurt food have been served in this traditional pub since 1876. And no one ever has to sit alone!

Zum gemalten Haus VISA
Schweizer Str. 67 ✉ 60594 – Ⓜ Schweizer Platz – ✆ (069) 61 45 59
– Fax (069) 6 03 14 57 – www.zumgemaltenhaus.de
closed Monday **F2**
Rest – Carte 13/20 €
♦ Regional ♦ Rustic ♦
Huddle up, talk shop and chat in the midst of these wall murals and mementoes from bygone days. The main thing is the "Bembel" is always full!

WESTEND, EXHIBITION-CENTRE AND STATION *Plan III*

Hessischer Hof A/C SAT VISA MC AE
Friedrich-Ebert-Anlage 40 ✉ 60325 – ✆ (069) 7 54 00 – info@hessischer-hof.de
– Fax (069) 75 40 29 24 – www.hessischer-hof.de **G2**
117 rm – 233/561 € 281/561 €, 23 € – 3 suites
Rest – Menu 31 € (lunch)/60 € (dinner) – Carte 50/69 €
♦ Luxury ♦ Traditional ♦ Classic ♦
Combines classic hotel style with the latest standards in luxury, devoting itself to its guests with exemplary commitment. A display of Sèvres porcelain decorates this elegant restaurant.

Radisson SAS A/C SAT VISA MC AE
Franklinstr. 65 (by Theodor Heuss Allee A2) ✉ 60486 – ✆ (069) 7 70 15 50
– info.frankfurt@radissonsas.com – Fax (069) 77 01 55 10
– www.frankfurt.radissonsas.com
428 rm – 190/265 € 190/265 €, 26 € – 10 suites
Rest *Gaia* – Carte 27/43 €
Rest *Coast* – *(closed Sunday - Monday) (dinner only)* Carte 26/45 €
♦ Business ♦ Chain hotel ♦ Design ♦
Very modern and trendy, this is not your average hotel, with its designer rooms "At home", "Chic", "Fashion" and "Fresh". The upper floors offer inspiring views. Gaia with Mediterranean cuisine. Sample the seafood at Coast Brassiere Oyster Bar.

Marriott Frankfurt, A/C SAT VISA MC AE
Hamburger Allee 2 ✉ 60486 – ✆ (069) 7 95 50
– info.frankfurt@marriotthotels.com – Fax (069) 79 55 24 32
– www.frankfurt-marriott.com **G1**
588 rm – 159/259 € 159/259 €, 23 € – 11 suites
Rest – Menu 39 € – Carte 32/53 €
♦ Chain hotel ♦ Luxury ♦ Modern ♦
Opposite the exhibition centre, this hotel stands out for its well-equipped rooms in an elegant classical style – all looking onto the city. Restaurant with a pleasant brasserie ambience and French cuisine.

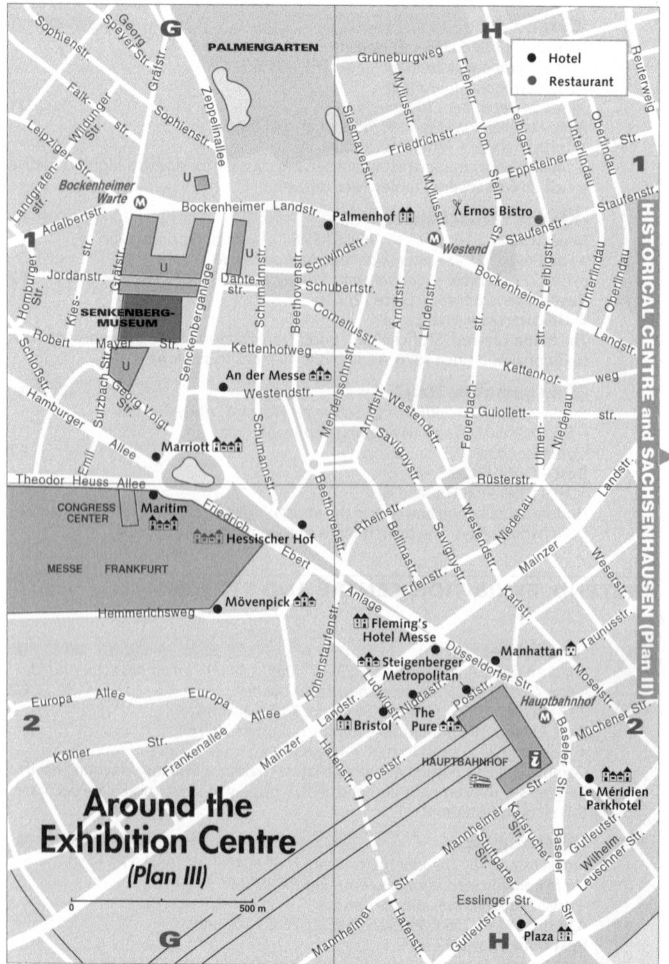

Maritim

Theodor-Heuss-Allee 3 ✉ 60486 – ✆ (069) 7 57 80 – info.fra@maritim.de – Fax (069) 75 78 10 00 – www.maritim.de **G2**

543 rm – †260/535 € ††305/580 €, ☕ 27 € – 24 suites

Rest *Classico* – *(dinner only)* Menu 38/57 € – Carte 44/55 €

Rest *SushiSho* – *(closed 4 weeks July - August, 24 to 31 December and Saturday - Sunday, except during exhibitions)* Menu 38 € (dinner)/95 € – Carte 32/73 €

♦ Chain hotel ♦ Business ♦ Modern ♦

This hotel, by the exhibition centre, offers modern, spacious rooms and a generous wellness area on the sixth floor. The elegant "Classico" offers international cuisine. SushiSho, Japanese style.

Le Méridien Parkhotel

Wiesenhüttenplatz 28 ✉ 60329 – Ⓜ Hauptbahnhof – ✆ (069) 2 69 70 – info.frankfurt@lemeridien.com – Fax (069) 2 69 78 84 – www.frankfurt.lemeridien.com **H2**

300 rm – 🚹360/440 € 🚹🚹380/440 €, ☕ 24 €

Rest – Menu 37 € – Carte 27/50 €

♦ Chain hotel ♦ Luxury ♦ Design ♦

This comfortable town hotel comprises a historical palace and a modern business like extension. The elegant Casablanca Bar in the old building is attractive. Le Parc bistro-style restaurant.

Steigenberger Metropolitan

Poststr. 6 ✉ 60329 – Ⓜ Hauptbahnhof – ✆ (069) 5 06 07 00 – metropolitan@steigenberger.de – Fax (069) 5 06 07 05 55 – www.metropolitan.steigenberger.de **H2**

131 rm – 🚹169/229 € 🚹🚹194/294 €, ☕ 21 € – 3 suites

Rest – Carte 26/56 €

♦ Chain hotel ♦ Modern ♦

This beautiful city palace by the main station dates from the 19th century, and is fitted out in a modern style which is both functional and elegant. The Brasserie M restaurant is kept in contemporary style.

The Pure without rest

Niddastr. 86 ✉ 60329 – Ⓜ Hauptbahnhof – ✆ (069) 7 10 45 70 – info@the-pure.de – Fax (069) 7 10 45 71 77 – www.the-pure.de **H2**

50 rm ☕ – 🚹160/230 € 🚹🚹190/260 €

♦ Business ♦ Design ♦

Minimalist, modern elegance. The interior of this hotel is exclusively in white. Close to the railway station. Dark furnishings create an interesting contrast.

Mövenpick Frankfurt City

Den Haager Str. 5 ✉ 60327 – ✆ (069) 7 88 07 50 – hotel.frankfurt.city@moevenpick.com – Fax (069) 7 88 07 58 88 – www.moevenpick-frankfurt-city.com **G2**

288 rm – 🚹133/189 € 🚹🚹133/189 €, ☕ 19 €

Rest – Carte 22/48 €

♦ Chain hotel ♦ Business ♦

Located directly next to the exhibition centre is this business hotel with conspicuous red-green facade. The rooms feature clean, modern and functional design. Fitness area with roof terrace. Bistro-style restaurant with international menu.

An der Messe without rest

Westendstr. 104 ✉ 60325 – ✆ (069) 74 79 79 – hotel.an.der.messe@web.de – Fax (069) 74 83 49 – www.hotel-an-der-messe.de **G1**

45 rm ☕ – 🚹130/295 € 🚹🚹155/330 €

♦ Business ♦ Personalised ♦

Individually designed rooms ranging from rustic-style to elegant, as well as a few interesting theme rooms set this hotel apart. Located near the trade fair centre.

Palmenhof without rest

Bockenheimer Landstr. 89 ✉ 60325 – Ⓜ Westend – ✆ (069) 7 53 00 60 – info@palmenhof.com – Fax (069) 75 30 06 66 – www.palmenhof.com closed 23 December - 2 January **G1**

46 rm – 🚹99/139 € 🚹🚹139/169 €, ☕ 15 €

♦ Business ♦ Classic ♦

This hotel in the financial district features individually decorated rooms, some with beautiful secretary desks and most with brass beds.

Fleming's Hotel Messe

Mainzer Landstr. 87 ✉ 60329 – Ⓜ Hauptbahnhof – ✆ (069) 8080800
– frankfurt-messe@fleming-hotels.com – Fax (069) 8 08 08 04 99
– www.flemings-hotel.com **H2**

96 rm – 109/165 € 139/195 €, ☕ 15 €
Rest – Carte 19/35 €

♦ Business ♦ Modern ♦

A business hotel in the centre of town with modern, functional rooms equipped with the latest technology. Bistro style restaurant with international cuisine.

Bristol

Ludwigstr. 15 ✉ 60327 – Ⓜ Hauptbahnhof – ✆ (069) 24 23 90
– info@bristol-hotel.de – Fax (069) 25 15 39 – www.bristol-hotel.de **H2**

145 rm ☕ – 90/120 € 140/160 €
Rest – *(dinner for residents only)*

♦ Business ♦ Modern ♦

Very close to the main railway station and inner city is this contemporary hotel with modern, functional décor. Summer lounge. Bar and reception with 24 hour service.

Plaza without rest

Esslinger Str. 8 ✉ 60329 – ✆ (069) 2 71 37 80
– info@plaza-frankfurt.bestwestern.de – Fax (069) 23 76 50
– www.plaza-frankfurt.bestwestern.de **H2**

45 rm – 92/102 € 133/143 €, ☕ 13 €

♦ Business ♦ Modern ♦

This hotel, in a quiet side street near the train station, offers functional, modern, light-toned beech furnishings and warm fabrics and colours.

Express by Holiday Inn without rest

Gutleutstr. 296 ✉ 60327 – ✆ (069) 50 69 60
– express.frankfurtmesse@whgen.com – Fax (069) 50 69 61 00
– www.hiexpress.com/lexfrankfurtmes *Plan I* **A3**

175 rm ☕ – 99/119 € 99/119 €

♦ Chain hotel ♦ Functional ♦

Ideal for business travellers, this modern well-equipped hotel is conveniently located near the exhibition centre and the local station.

Manhattan without rest

Düsseldorfer Str. 10 ✉ 60329 – ✆ (069) 2 69 59 70
– manhattan-hotel@t-online.de – Fax (069) 2 69 59 77 77
– www.manhattan-hotel.com **H2**

59 rm ☕ – 87/189 € 102/240 €

♦ Business ♦ Modern ♦

The modern design of the hotel extends from the lobby to the chic guest rooms that have a Manhattan-style ambience. Trade fairs, banks, art and culture are just a short walk away.

Villa Merton

Am Leonhardsbrunn 12 ✉ 60487 – ✆ (069) 70 30 33
– jp@kofler-company.de – Fax (069) 7 07 38 20
– www.kofler-company.de
closed 21 December - 10 January and Saturday - Sunday *Plan I* **A1**

Rest – *(booking advisable)* Menu 64/115 € – Carte 60/75 €

Spec. Marinierte Scheiben von der Jakobsmuschel mit Seeigelcorail. Schwarzes Schwein mit Pinienkern-Spinat und Sauce Charcutière. Kacinkoa-Schokolade und Passionsfrucht.

♦ Inventive ♦ Formal ♦

The villa built for the entrepreneur R Merton is situated in the diplomatic quarter. It has an elegant atmosphere and classically based creative cuisine. Simple midday menu for €30.

X

Ernos Bistro

Liebigstr. 15 ✉ 60323 – Ⓜ Westend – ✆ (069) 72 19 97 – Fax (069) 17 38 38
closed 22 December - 8 January, 21 March - 1 April, 3 weeks July and Saturday - Sunday, Bank Holidays **H1**
Rest – *(booking advisable)* Menu 36 € (lunch)/105 € – Carte 67/95 €
Spec. Hausgemachte Gänsestopfleber. Baeckeoffe vom Hummer mit Morcheln, grünem Spargel und Trüffeljus. Lammrücken und Kotelett mit Artischocken und Oliven.

♦ French ♦ Bistro ♦

There is a cosy atmosphere in this restaurant in the Westend. Classic cuisine with a personal touch and a very good selection of French wines.

ENVIRONS OF FRANKFURT

at Frankfurt-Fechenheim by Hanauer Landstr. D2

XX

Silk (Mario Lohninger)

Carl-Benz-Str. 21 ✉ 60386 – ✆ (069) 90 02 00 – reservierung@cocoonclub.net – Fax (069) 90 02 02 90 – www.cocoonclub.net
closed 2 weeks January, July and Sunday - Monday
Rest – *(dinner only)* Menu 88 €
Rest *Micro* – *(dinner only)* Menu 49 € – Carte 35/52 €
Spec. Cornetto mit Bisontatar und Senföl. 3-Stunden-Bio-Ei mit Gemüseconfetti und Trüffel. Hummer mit Avocado und geräucherter Paprika.

♦ Innovative ♦ Trendy ♦

The design of this trendy restaurant in the Cocoon Club is very unusual. The innovative cuisine, which is served to guests on their upholstered loungers, is excellent. Micro features an open kitchen serving fusion cuisine. The disco is next door.

at Frankfurt-Rödelheim by Theodor Heuss Allee A2

XX

Osteria Enoteca

Arnoldshainer Str. 2 (corner of Lorscher Straße) ✉ 60489 – ✆ (069) 7 89 22 16 – Fax (069) 7 89 22 16 – www.osteria-enoteca.de
closed 22 December - 7 January and Saturday lunch, Sunday, Bank Holidays
Rest – Menu 68/108 € – Carte 49/59 €
Spec. Lauwarmer Polposalat mit Kartoffeln und geräucherter Blutwurst. Gedämpfter Kabeljau mit Bohnencrème und Salsa Verde. Geschmorte Lammschulter mit Pilzpolenta.

♦ Italian ♦ Friendly ♦

The Italian cuisine in this pleasant, light restaurant is both full of flavour and creative. Attentive and friendly sevice.

at the Rhein-Main Airport by Kennedy Allee B3

Sheraton Frankfurt Hotel & Towers

Hugo-Eckener-Ring 15 (terminal 1)
✉ 60549 Frankfurt – ✆ (069) 6 97 70 – reservationsfrankfurt@sheraton.com – Fax (069) 69 77 22 09 – www.sheraton.com/frankfurt
1008 rm – †211/482 € ††231/518 €, ☕ 28 € – 21 suites
Rest *Flavors* – *✆ (069) 69 77 12 46* – Carte 43/72 €
Rest *Taverne* – *✆ (069) 69 77 12 59 (closed Saturday - Sunday)* Carte 39/57 €

♦ Chain hotel ♦ Business ♦ Modern ♦

Directly opposite Terminal 1 is this hotel, with its impressive lobby. Light, functional rooms and a fitness centre with sauna and massage. Modern ambience and good choice of international cuisine in Flavors. Rural charm in Taverne.

Kempinski Hotel Gravenbruch (heated)

Graf zu Ysenburg und Büdingen-Platz 1
✉ 63263 Frankfurt – ✆ (069) 38 98 80 – reservations.gravenbruch@kempinski.com – Fax (069) 38 98 89 00 – www.kempinski-frankfurt.com
285 rm – 🚹131/234 € 🚹🚹157/281 €, ☕ 24 € – 15 suites
Rest – Carte 40/69 €
Rest *L'Olivo* – *(closed Saturday - Sunday) (dinner only)* Carte 32/54 €
♦ Chain hotel ♦ Classic ♦
With the charm of a country house villa, this hotel lies in the countryside with its own lake. The rooms are classic, and the suites generous. Leisure area etc. with beauty farm. A fine restaurant with garden views. L'Olivo with Italian cuisine

Steigenberger Airport

Unterschweinstiege 16 ✉ 60549 Frankfurt
– ✆ (069) 6 97 50 – info@airporthotel.steigenberger.de – Fax (069) 69 75 25 05
– www.airporthotel.steigenberger.de
570 rm – 🚹159/335 € 🚹🚹169/335 €, ☕ 25 € – 10 suites
Rest *Unterschweinstiege* – Carte 32/61 €
Rest *Faces* – *(closed 4 weeks July - early August and Sunday - Monday) (dinner only)* Menu 49/71 € – Carte 52/71 €
♦ Chain hotel ♦ Modern ♦
The elegant reception area greets you with its light marble. Comfortable rooms and a leisure area on the top floor with pleasant views. A cosy atmosphere in the historic Unterschweinstiege restaurant. Faces: a fine bistro atmosphere.

InterCityHotel Frankfurt Airport

Cargo City Süd ✉ 60549 Frankfurt – ✆ (069) 69 70 99
– frankfurt-airport@intercityhotel.de – Fax (069) 69 70 94 44
– www.frankfurt-airport.intercityhotel.de
360 rm ☕ – 🚹124/227 € 🚹🚹134/237 €
Rest – Carte 24/33 €
♦ Chain hotel ♦ Functional ♦
Convenient Autobahn access and an airport location – with shuttle service to the terminals – as well as functional, up-to-date guest rooms highlight this hotel. Modern restaurant with international cuisine and buffet.

HAMBURG

HAMBURG

Population (est.2005): 1 750 000 (conurbation 2 290 000) – Altitude: at sea level

Sime/PHOTONONSTOP

With a maritime role stretching back centuries, Germany's second largest city has a lively and liberal ambience. Hamburg's motto is 'The Gateway to the World', and there's certainly a visceral feel here, particularly around the big, buzzy and bustling port area. Locals enjoy a long-held reputation for their tolerance and outward looking stance, cosmopolitan to the core. This tolerance extends famously to the city's nightlife, which in the St Pauli area is renowned for its racy characteristics.

But there's another side to Hamburg. Despite its northerly position, it sits easily with a Mediterranean style café culture, and boasts waterside areas that have seen a significant amount of renovation and restyling in recent years. This is a big city for culture; it's where you come for the Long Theatre Night and the Art Mile Day. And, of course, it's where the Beatles paid their dues: the Reeperbahn is a classic first stop for many visitors. Eight hundred years' worth of trading with the world has left another favourable legacy: Hamburg's cuisine scene touches on all four corners of the globe. And space to breathe is seen as very important here: the city authorities have paid much attention to green spaces, and Hamburg can proudly claim an enviable amount of parks, lakes and tree-lined canals.

LIVING THE CITY

There's no cathedral in Hamburg (at least not a standing one, as war-destroyed St Nikolai remains a ruin) so the **Town Hall** acts as the central landmark. Just north of here is the Binnenalster (inner) and Aussenalster (outer) lake. The old walls of the city, dating back over eight hundred years, are delineated by a distinct semicircle of boulevards that curve attractively in a wide arc south of the lakes. Further south from here is the port and harbour area, defined by Landungsbrücken to the west, and Speicherstadt to the east. The district to the west of the centre is **St Pauli**, famed for its clubs and bars, particularly along the notorious Reeperbahn, which pierces the district from east to west. The contrastingly smart **Altona** suburb and delightful **Blankenese** village are west of St Pauli.

PRACTICAL INFORMATION

ARRIVAL-DEPARTURE

Hamburg Airport is 15km from the city centre. A taxi costs approximately €20. Airport buses leave for Hamburg Hauptbahnhof every 15-20min and Altona Station every 30min, with a journey time for both of 20min.

TRANSPORT

Hamburg Transport Authority controls all bus routes, S-Bahn and U-Bahn underground lines, and several river and ferry services. Tickets are available for single journeys, or for one day or three day duration. Buy from vending machines or bus drivers. Information available from many underground stations and the main railway station (Hauptbahnhof).

The Hamburg Card is valid for the transport network, and offers free entrance to eleven state-run museums, discounts on other activities, and on tours on water and land. Buy it from Tourist Information offices, vending machines, hotels and travel agents.

EXPLORING HAMBURG

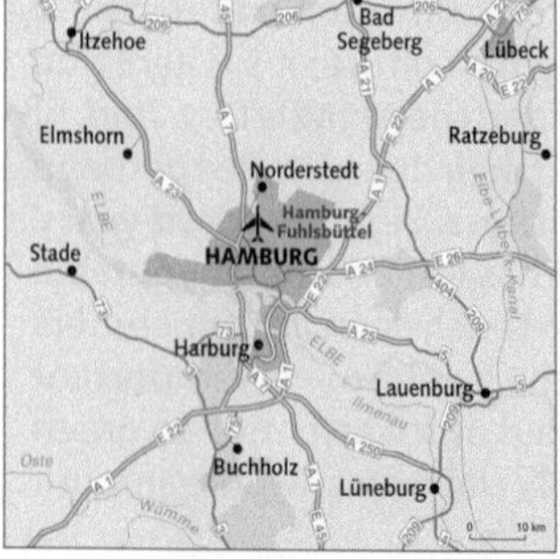

If it weren't for the **Elbe**, there would be no Hamburg, so why not get the feel of the place by heading down to the water and sniffing the salty harbour air? An endless stream of ships calls at the twenty-seven miles of quayside to transport goods to and from ports far and wide. Take a boat yourself from the Landungsbrücken pier for an invigorating harbour tour. The views of the Elbe are wonderful, and you can pick and choose how you want to travel, either by basic boat or slinky cruiser. These will carry you upriver towards the huge modern container docks or eastwards through a network of canals, leading to the fascinating **Speicherstadt**. This is a wondrous place to be, the biggest warehouse complex in the world – the 'City of Warehouses'. It's a hauntingly Hanseatic dark-red brick complex from the mid-nineteenth century, and it's no ghost building: wholesalers still keep a range of goods here. It's also alive with museums (four in total) relating to the Speicherstadt's history. Close to here, in Deichstrasse, and the near-by old Cremon road, stand charmingly romantic merchants' houses, dating back to the seventeenth and eighteenth centuries. As much of the city was rebuilt after the War, this nugget of old Hamburg offers a tantalising flavour of what the port quarter must once have been like.

→ WATER, WATER EVERYWHERE

Water dominates this city. Go up through the old town, and the liquid quality takes on a different feel altogether, as you arrive at the shimmering **Alster**. Locals proudly ask a rhetorical question: what other bustling metropolis can boast such a wondrous lake in its centre? Surrounded by cafés, promenades and invigorating lungfuls of greenery, you can actually walk around the entire 160-hectare lake without having to cross a single road. For the energetically challenged, steamboats leave from the Jungfernstieg pier, pass under two bridges connecting the outer lake from the inner, and take in a view which incorporates elaborate nineteenth century merchants' villas and delightful parks full of poplars, chestnuts and oaks. If the chance arises, hop off your boat and down a coffee at one of the tempting lakeside cafés: memorable views of the Hamburg skyline, with its dominant spires and steeples, are guaranteed. The third watery option is a cruise along inner-city canals, where weeping willows bow down gracefully and grand-looking villas offer a haughty eye as you make your stately procession between Alster and Elbe.

→ PICTURE PERFECT

Not only can Hamburgers crow about the glory of their lake, they can also lay claim to the most important art gallery in northern Germany. The **Kunsthalle** is made up of three interconnected buildings and the paintings and artworks contained within make an entrance in the fifteenth century and an exit at the present day, taking in the likes of Master Bertram of Minden, Friedrichs, Runge, Monet, Manet, Renoir, Warhol and Beuys. A refuelling point well worth a look round itself is the Café Liebermann, where you can enjoy cake and coffee in the rarefied splendour of marble-columned surroundings. If your appreciation of art isn't quite yet sated, then continue south along the boulevard arc, past the railway station, and very soon you'll reach the Arts and Crafts Museum. This is an eclectic wonderland, with exhibits ranging from the Orient, ancient Greece and Rome right through to musical instruments down the ages and handsome examples of Art Nouveau.

You have to go right across to the inner city's west side to locate the third in Hamburg's winning triumvirate of galleries and museums, and many think this is the most satisfying of the three. The **Hamburg History Museum** covers just about every aspect of the city; particularly impressive are the models of Hamburg showing the stark differences over a five hundred year period. It's interesting, too, to enter into the elegant seventeenth century merchant's home, or see just what the medieval authorities did with huge nails and the skulls of pirates who dared terrorise the port.

→ CONVERSION OF ST PAULI

Of course, lots of tourists come to Hamburg and make a beeline for the St Pauli district, just up from the western docks, and it's safe to say that visiting churches and opera houses is probably not top of their tour agenda. St Pauli is the district where the Beatles cut their teeth in the early 60s, and its pulsating nightlife is still a big draw.

The Reeperbahn has kept its reputation as the street where you wouldn't bring your great aunt: the sex shows and strip clubs are as lurid as ever, but times are a-changing. Tourists are making for the area because in recent years it's become a lively theatre and restaurant quarter in its own right. Hip young Hamburgers come here too because the bars and clubs have taken on a trendy, rather than garish, aspect. It's now a well-regulated area, and the nightlife is multi-layered, rather than notoriously one-dimensional as of old. In fact, your great aunt may demand to be taken there.

→ FOR FISH

If early starts are your thing, then St Pauli's world-famous **fishmarket**, down by the Elbe, is the ideal destination. A Sunday stalwart for three hundred years, it kicks off at five in the morning, and is often frequented by revellers unwilling to draw a line under their Saturday night. It's a cross between a rock concert and a flea-market with an impressive sideline in exotic fruit and smoked fish. There are great bargains to be had in plants and vegetables, too, and the salty-sounding vendors are an integral part of the experience. A cavernous steel and glass hall, on two floors, is given over for the morning to eating, drinking and live bands belting out a fine collection of old favourites to sing along with. For anyone still in the mood to savour the delights of St Pauli, just up the road is the Erotic Art Museum, which has nearly two thousand exhibits spanning five hundred years.

→ TOP PERFORMERS

Performance venues of another shade are high on Hamburg's cultural hit-list. In fact, they're the best of their kind in northern Germany. Just west of the inner Alster lake is the **Hamburg State Opera** and Ballet, where the best international names regularly perform. Meanwhile, The Musikhalle, which is by the Wallanlagen Gardens on aptly named Johannes-Brahms-Platz, celebrates its hundredth birthday in 2008. It's one of the most beautiful concert venues in Germany, an ornate building with three fine halls offering a wide range of orchestral and vocal performances. Hamburg can even boast two local orchestras of high renown, and the Musikhalle is their home.

CALENDAR HIGHLIGHTS

The event that really puts Hamburg on the map is the **Dom Festival**, which happens three times a year (usually March, July and August). It goes back to the fourteenth century, and translates as the Cathedral Festival. Basically, it's a huge funfair, with thrill rides, live music and beer tents – it attracts a phenomenal nine million visitors a year. The city's other major annual event

HAMBURG IN...

→ ONE DAY

Boat trip from Landungsbrücken, Speicherstadt, Kunsthalle, Fishmarket (if it's a Sunday morning!)

→ TWO DAYS

Steamboat on the Alster, Hamburg History Museum, St Pauli by night

→ THREE DAYS

Arts and Crafts Museum, canal trip between lake and harbour, concert at Musikhalle

is the harbour's birthday celebration every May – Hafengeburtstag - fun and games (and tug boats dancing) happen all along the harbour. There's a month-long market to celebrate the arrival of Spring, every March and April, in St Pauli's Heiligengeistfeld. Fiery entertainment lights up the Bürgerhaus Wilhelmsburg, when the Flamenco Festival hits town in April, while in September movie fans wallow in a glut of celluloid at the Film Festival Hamburg. May's Long Night of Hamburg Museums and November's Art Mile Day cement the city's reputation as a cultural behemoth: on both occasions arty hothouses are kept open deep into the night.

EATING OUT

Being a city immersed in water, it's no surprise to find Hamburg is pretty hot on fish. Though its fishing industry isn't the powerhouse of old, the city still boasts a giant trawler's worth of seafood places to eat. Eel dishes are mainstays of the traditional restaurant's menu, as is the herring stew with vegetables called Labskaus. Also unsurprisingly, considering it's the country's gateway to the world, this is somewhere that offers a vast range of international dishes. As good restaurants tend to open where the media gathers, and Hamburg is Germany's media capital, you're assured of a range of smart and swanky places to dine. Wherever you eat here, the portions are likely to be generous. There's no problem with finding somewhere early: cafes are often open at seven, with the belief that it's never too early for coffee and cake. Bakeries, too, believe in an early start, and the calorie content here, too, can be pretty high. Bistros and restaurants, usually open by midday, are proud of their local ingredients, so keep your eyes open for Hamburgisch on the menu. Service charges are always included in the bill, so tipping is not compulsory, although most people will round it up to the next euro, and possibly add five to ten per cent.

→ TIME FOR THE TOWN HALL

Hamburg's nineteenth-century town hall, in **Rathausplatz**, is an eye-catching place with nearly six hundred and fifty rooms. It does battle as the city's main landmark with 'Michel' – St Michael's Church – which stands proudly over the port as a centuries-old guide to sailors. Its massive clock face is the biggest in Germany, and at midday every day its three organs put on an awesome, ear-piercing show.

→ VIEW FROM A BRIDGE

Hamburg's a great place to look at the world from a bridge. You won't have trouble finding one. There are a whopping 2,247 of them around the city. Bear in mind that Venice has a measly 450, and you might begin to get the picture.

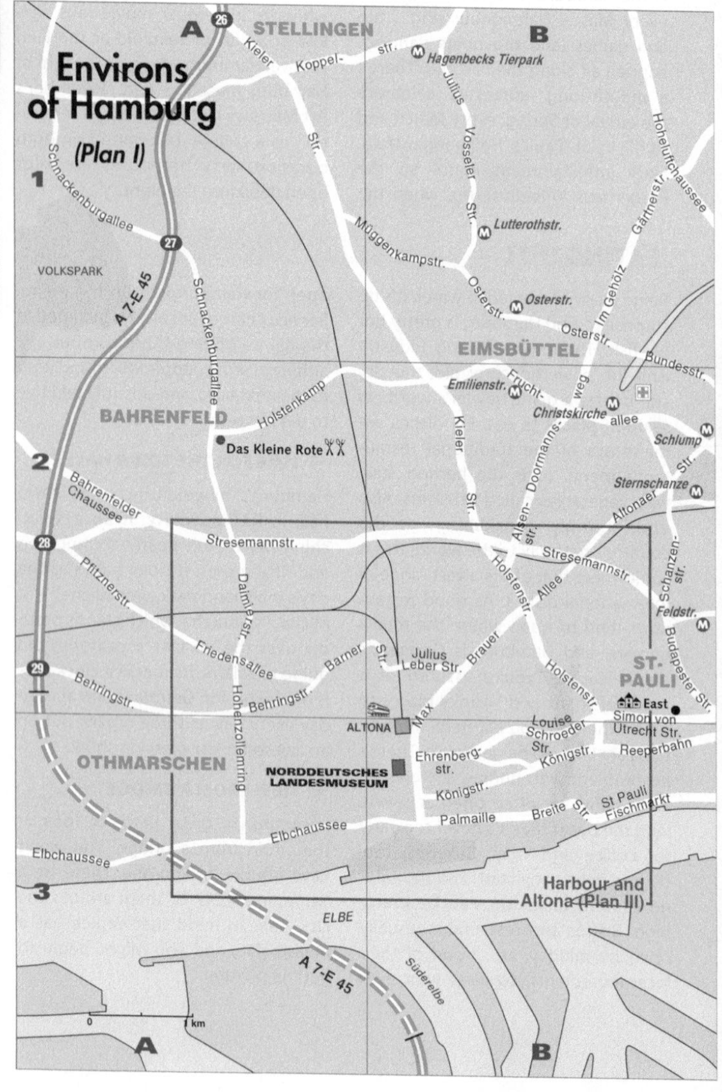
Environs of Hamburg
(Plan I)
A
B
1
2
3
STELLINGEN
EIMSBÜTTEL
BAHRENFELD
OTHMARSCHEN
ST-PAULI
VOLKSPARK
Hagenbecks Tierpark
Lutterothstr.
Osterstr.
Emilienstr.
Christskirche
Schlump
Sternschanze
Feldstr.
Das Kleine Rote
ALTONA
NORDDEUTSCHES LANDESMUSEUM
East
Harbour and Altona (Plan III)
ELBE
Süderelbe
A 7-E 45
Stresemannstr.
Elbchaussee
Palmaille
Reeperbahn
Holstenstr.
Max Brauer Allee
Königstr.
0
1 km

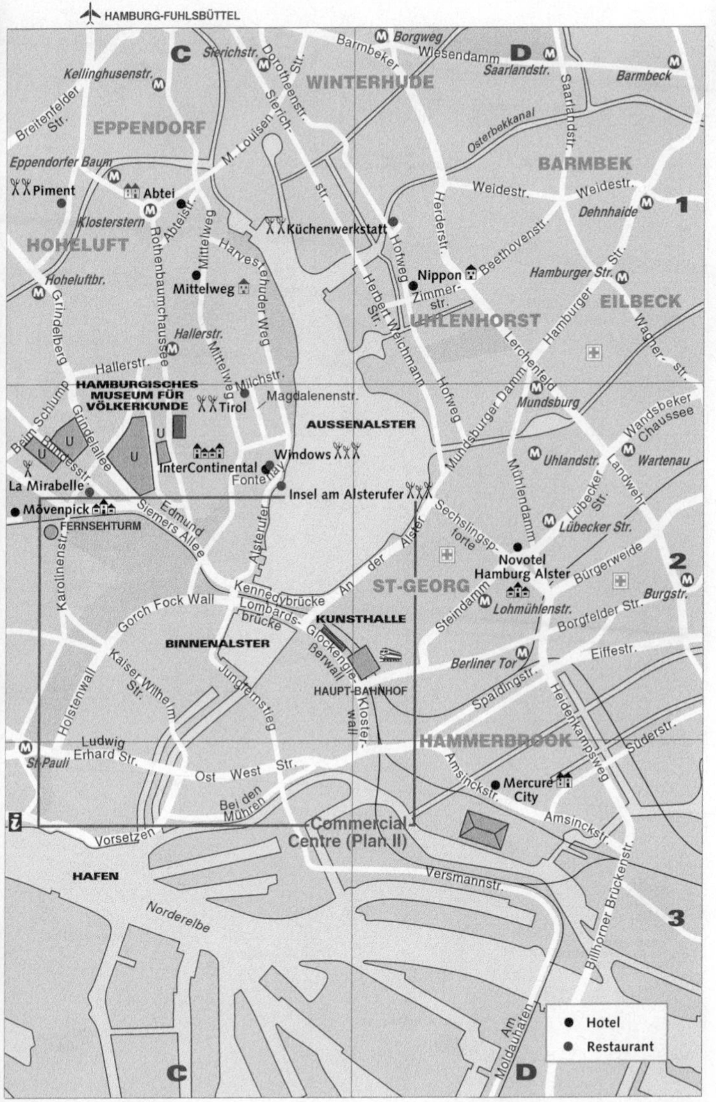
HAMBURG-FUHLSBÜTTEL
C
D
1
2
3
WINTERHUDE
EPPENDORF
BARMBEK
HOHELUFT
UHLENHORST
EILBECK
AUSSENALSTER
ST-GEORG
BINNENALSTER
HAMMERBROOK
HAFEN
HAMBURGISCHES MUSEUM FÜR VÖLKERKUNDE
KUNSTHALLE
HAUPT-BAHNHOF
FERNSEHTURM
Commercial Centre (Plan II)
Piment
Abtei
Küchenwerkstatt
Nippon
Mittelweg
Tirol
Windows
InterContinental
Insel am Alsterufer
La Mirabelle
Mövenpick
Novotel Hamburg Alster
Mercure City
Borgweg
Barmbeker
Wiesendamm
Saarlandstr.
Barmbeck
Sierichstr.
Dorotheenstr.
Kellinghusenstr.
Breitenfelder Str.
Eppendorfer Baum
Klosterstern
Hoheluftbr.
M. Louisen Str.
Sierich-str.
Osterbekkanal
Weidestr.
Dehnhaide
Herderstr.
Hofweg
Beethovenstr.
Hamburger Str.
Zimmer-str.
Herbert Weichmann Str.
Rothenbaumchaussee
Abteistr.
Mittelweg
Harvestehuder Weg
Grindelberg
Hallerstr.
Milchstr.
Magdalenenstr.
Lerchenfeld
Mundsburger Damm
Mundsburg
Wagnerstr.
Wandsbeker Chaussee
Wartenau
Uhlandstr.
Landwehr
Mühlendamm
Lübecker Str.
Beim Schlump
Grindelallee
Bundesstr.
Fontenay
Edmund Siemers Allee
Alsterufer
Sechslingspforte
An der Alster
Bürgerweide
Burgstr.
Karolinenstr.
Gorch Fock Wall
Kennedybrücke
Lombardsbrücke
Glockengießerwall
Steindamm
Lohmühlenstr.
Borgfelder Str.
Eiffestr.
Berliner Tor
Kaiser Wilhelm Str.
Jungfernstieg
Klosterwall
Spaldingstr.
Heidenkampsweg
Holstenwall
Ludwig Erhard Str.
St-Pauli
Ost West Str.
Süderstr.
Amsinckstr.
Bei den Mühren
Vorsetzen
Versmannstr.
Norderelbe
Billhorner Brückenstr.
Am Moldauhafen
Hotel
Restaurant

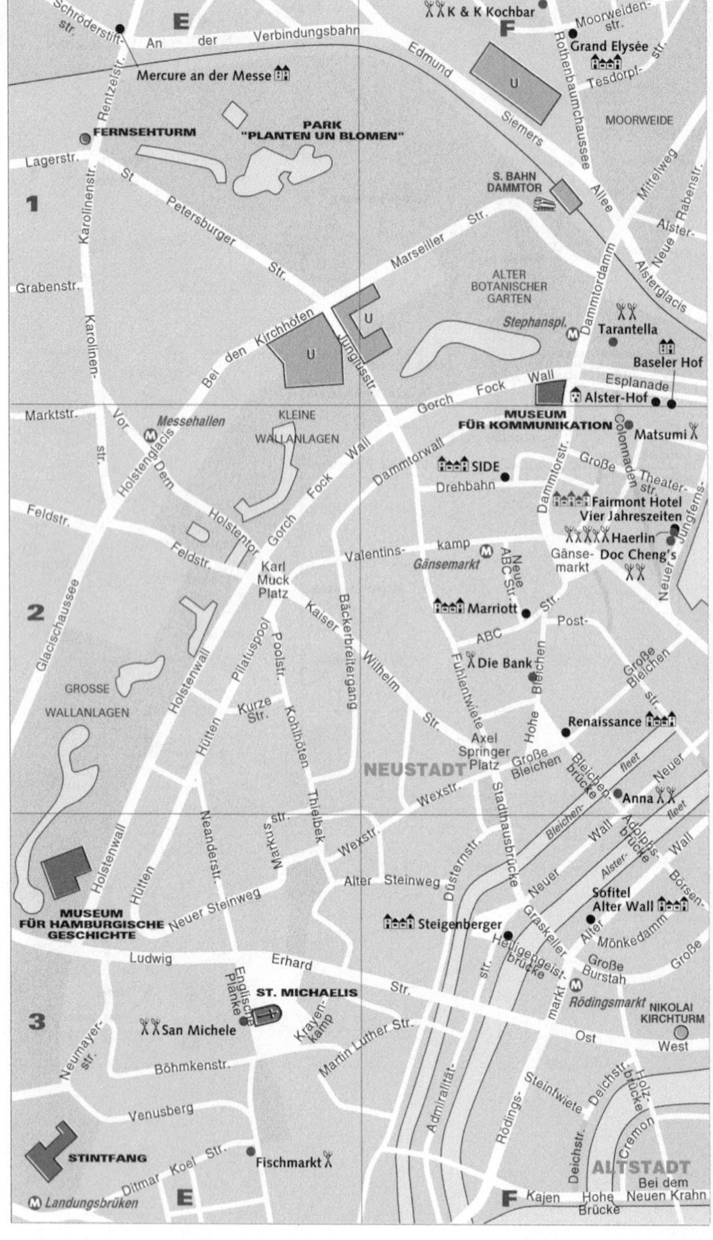
E
F
1
2
3
K & K Kochbar
Grand Elysée
Mercure an der Messe
FERNSEHTURM
PARK "PLANTEN UN BLOMEN"
MOORWEIDE
S. BAHN DAMMTOR
ALTER BOTANISCHER GARTEN
Stephanspl.
Tarantella
Baseler Hof
Alster-Hof
MUSEUM FÜR KOMMUNIKATION
Matsumi
KLEINE WALLANLAGEN
Messehallen
SIDE
Fairmont Hotel Vier Jahreszeiten
Haerlin
Doc Cheng's
Gänsemarkt
Marriott
Karl Muck Platz
Die Bank
Renaissance
GROSSE WALLANLAGEN
NEUSTADT
Axel Springer Platz
Anna
Sofitel Alter Wall
Steigenberger
MUSEUM FÜR HAMBURGISCHE GESCHICHTE
ST. MICHAELIS
San Michele
Rödingsmarkt
NIKOLAI KIRCHTURM
STINTFANG
Fischmarkt
ALTSTADT
Landungsbrüken
Schröderstift-str.
An der Verbindungsbahn
Edmund Siemers Allee
Moorweiden-str.
Rothenbaumchaussee
Tesdorpf-str.
Rentzelstr.
Lagerstr.
St. Petersburger Str.
Karolinenstr.
Grabenstr.
Karolinen-str.
Marseiller Str.
Mittelweg
Neue Rabenstr.
Alster-
Alsterglacis
Dammtordamm
Bei den Kirchhöfen
Jungiusstr.
Esplanade
Gorch Fock Wall
Marktstr.
Vor dem Holstentor
Holstenglacis
Colonnaden
Große Theater-str.
Dammtorwall
Drehbahn
Dammtorstr.
Neuer Jungfernstieg
Feldstr.
Holstentor
Valentinskamp
Neue ABC Str.
Gänsemarkt
Glacischaussee
Kaiser Wilhelm Str.
Bäckerbreitergang
Poolstr.
Pilatuspool
ABC Str.
Post-str.
Fuhlentwiete
Bleichen
Große Bleichen
Holstenwall
Kurze Str.
Kohlhöfen
Hohe Bleichen
Bleichenbrücke
Bleichenfleet
Neuer Wall
Hütten
Thielbek
Wexstr.
Neanderstr.
Markusstr.
Stadthausbrücke
Düsternstr.
Alsterfleet
Adolphsbrücke
Börsen-
Alter Steinweg
Neuer Steinweg
Graskeller
Alter Wall
Mönkedamm
Heiligengeistbrücke
Große Burstah
Ludwig Erhard Str.
Englische Planke
Krayenkamp
Martin Luther Str.
Ost West Str.
Neumayer-str.
Böhmkenstr.
Admiralitätstr.
Rödingsmarkt
Steinfwiete
Deichstr.
Holzbrücke
Cremon
Venusberg
Ditmar Koel Str.
Kajen
Hohe Brücke
Bei dem Neuen Krahn

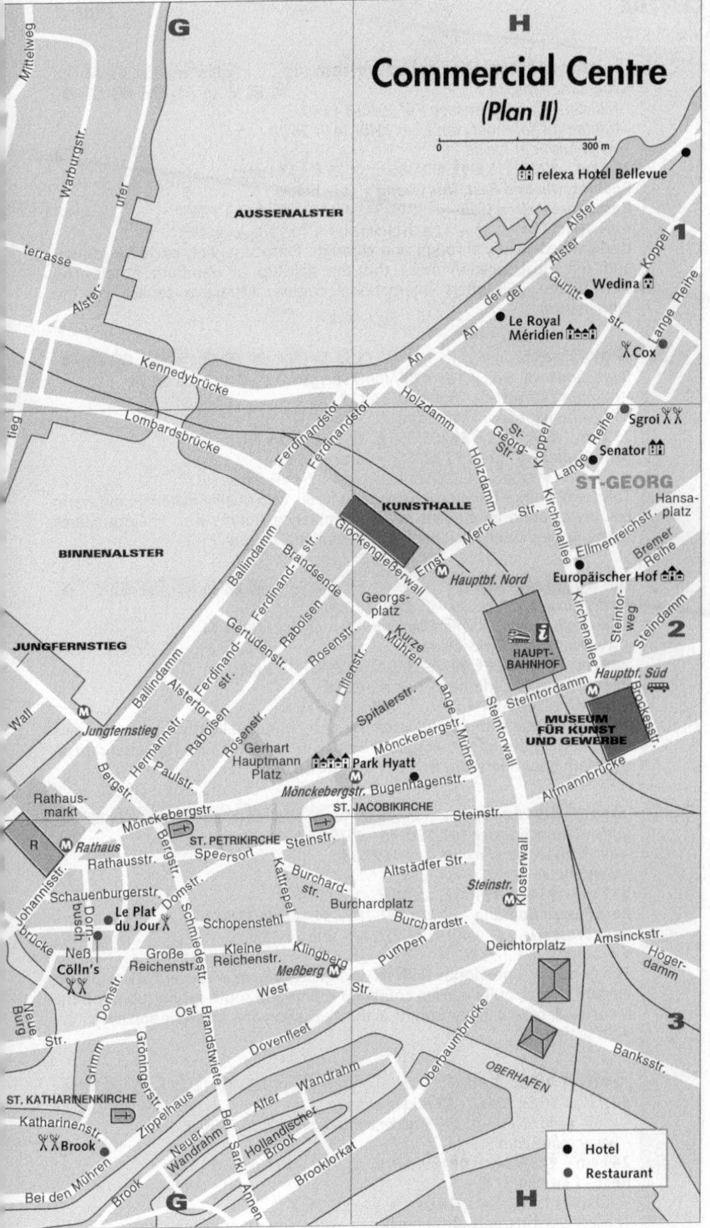
Commercial Centre
(Plan II)
0
300 m
G
H
1
2
3
AUSSENALSTER
BINNENALSTER
JUNGFERNSTIEG
KUNSTHALLE
ST-GEORG
HAUPT-BAHNHOF
MUSEUM FÜR KUNST UND GEWERBE
ST. JACOBIKIRCHE
ST. PETRIKIRCHE
ST. KATHARINENKIRCHE
OBERHAFEN
relexa Hotel Bellevue
Wedina
Le Royal Méridien
Cox
Sgroi
Senator
Europäischer Hof
Park Hyatt
Le Plat du Jour
Cölln's
Brook
Hauptbf. Nord
Hauptbf. Süd
Jungfernstieg
Mönckebergstr.
Rathaus
Steinstr.
Meßberg
Mittelweg
Warburgstr.
Alster-ufer
Alster-terrasse
Kennedybrücke
Lombardsbrücke
An der Alster
Koppel
Gurlitt-str.
Lange Reihe
Holzdamm
St.-Georg-Str.
Ferdinandstor
Ballindamm
Glockengießerwall
Ernst Merck Str.
Kirchenallee
Ellmenreichstr.
Hansa-platz
Bremer Reihe
Brandsende
Ferdinand-str.
Gertudenstr.
Raboisen
Georgs-platz
Kurze Mühren
Rosenstr.
Lilienstr.
Spitalerstr.
Lange Mühren
Steintorwall
Steintordamm
Steintor-weg
Steindamm
Brockesstr.
Hermannstr.
Alstertor
Paulstr.
Gerhart Hauptmann Platz
Bugenhagenstr.
Altmannbrücke
Wall
Bergstr.
Rathaus-markt
R
Rathausstr.
Speersort
Kattrepel
Burchard-str.
Altstädter Str.
Burchardplatz
Burchardstr.
Klosterwall
Johannisstr.
Schauenburgerstr.
Domstr.
Schmiedestr.
Dorn-busch
Schopenstehl
Neß
Große Reichenstr.
Kleine Reichenstr.
Klingberg
Pumpen
Deichtorplatz
Amsinckstr.
Höger-damm
Ost West Str.
Neue Burg
Grimm
Gröningerstr.
Brandstwiete
Dovenfleet
Oberbaumbrücke
Banksstr.
Zippelhaus
Katharinenstr.
Alter Wandrahm
Neuer Wandrahm
Holländischer Brook
Brooktorkai
Bei den Mühren
Brook
Bei St. Annen
Hotel
Restaurant

Fairmont Hotel Vier Jahreszeiten

< Binnenalster,

Neuer Jungfernstieg 9
✉ 20354 – Ⓜ Jungfernstieg – ✆ (040) 3 49 40
– hamburg@fairmont.com – Fax (040) 34 94 26 00
– www.fairmont-hvj.de **F2**

157 rm – ♦230/315 € ♦♦300/385 €, ☐ 25 € – 17 suites
Rest *Haerlin and Rest. Doc Cheng's* – see below
Rest *Jahreszeiten Grill* – *✆ (040) 34 94 33 12* – Carte 39/70 €

♦ Grand Luxury ♦ Traditional ♦ Classic ♦

Understated luxury through and through. Perfect service, exclusive design and the ideal location make this the flagship of Hamburg hotels. The Jahreszeiten grill offers international cuisine. Attractive terrace on the Binnenalster.

Park Hyatt

Bugenhagenstr. 8 ✉ 20095 – Ⓜ Mönckebergstr. – ✆ (040) 33 32 12 34
– hamburg@hyatt.de – Fax (040) 33 32 12 35
– www.hamburg.park.hyatt.com **H2**

252 rm – ♦175/325 € ♦♦205/355 €, ☐ 28 € – 21 suites
Rest *Apples* – *✆ (040) 33 321511* – Carte 36/64 €

♦ Chain hotel ♦ Grand Luxury ♦ Stylish ♦

This former office building is a luxurious hotel, with quality materials and warm colours creating an elegant modern ambience. Rooms with Philippe Starck baths. Apples' open kitchen offers international cuisine.

Le Royal Méridien

An der Alster 52 ✉ 20099 – ✆ (040) 2 10 00
– info.lrmhamburg@lemeridien.com – Fax (040) 21 00 11 11
– www.hamburg.lemeridien.com **H1**

284 rm – ♦149/329 € ♦♦169/349 €, ☐ 26 € – 19 suites
Rest – Menu 59 € (dinner) – Carte 39/65 €

♦ Chain hotel ♦ Luxury ♦ Modern ♦

A modern hotel with a clear, attractive style, from the lightly furnished rooms with specially designed therapeutic beds to the wellness area. The restaurant on the ninth floor offers fantastic views of the Aussenalster.

Grand Elysée

Rothenbaumchaussee 10 ✉ 20148 – ✆ (040) 41 41 20
– info@elysee.de – Fax (040) 41 41 27 33
– www.elysee.de **F1**

511 rm – ♦140 € ♦♦160 €, ☐ 18 € – 13 suites
Rest *Piazza Romana* – *✆ (040) 41 41 27 34* – Carte 30/51 €
Rest *Brasserie* – *✆ (040) 41 41 27 24* – Carte 24/35 €

♦ Luxury ♦ Classic ♦

The generous hotel lobby with its café greets you in boulevard style. Classic, elegant rooms, quiet garden courtyard rooms and south-facing rooms on the Moorweiden park. Italian cuisine in the Piazza Romana. Brasserie and oyster bar with seafood.

Sofitel Alter Wall

Alter Wall 40 ✉ 20457 – Ⓜ Rödingsmarkt
– ✆ (040) 36 95 00 – h5395@accor.com – Fax (040) 36 95 10 00
– www.sofitel.com **F3**

241 rm – ♦139/349 € ♦♦139/349 €, ☐ 21 € – 10 suites
Rest – Carte 34/51 €

♦ Chain hotel ♦ Luxury ♦ Design ♦

The last word in trendy designer hotels, with its own landing direct on one of the Alster canals. The rooms offer an interesting mix of materials. Restaurant with a sleek, minimalist style.

Steigenberger

Heiligengeistbrücke 4 ✉ 20459 – Ⓜ Rödingsmarkt – ☎ (040) 36 80 60 – hamburg@steigenberger.de – Fax (040) 36 80 67 77 – www.hamburg.steigenberger.de **F3**

233 rm – 🚹200/245 € 🚹🚹220/265 €, ☕ 20 € – 6 suites

Rest *Calla* – *(closed 21 December - 5 January, 17 July - 27 August and Sunday - Monday) (dinner only)* Menu 38/57 € – Carte 37/57 €

Rest *Bistro am Fleet* – Menu 27 € – Carte 26/44 €

◆ Luxury ◆ Classic ◆

An elegant building with its redbrick façade in a picturesque setting on the Alsterfleet. Guests can use conference rooms with views over the city roofs. Calla with its Euro-Asian menu, looking onto the Alster. International cuisine from the open bistro kitchen.

SIDE

Drehbahn 49 ✉ 20354 – Ⓜ Stephansplatz – ☎ (040) 30 99 90 – info@side-hamburg.de – Fax (040) 30 99 93 99 – www.side-hamburg.de **F2**

178 rm – 🚹190/315 € 🚹🚹190/315 €, ☕ 23 € – 10 suites

Rest – *(dinner only Saturday, Sunday and Bank Holidays)* Carte 30/62 €

◆ Luxury ◆ Design ◆

Part of the "Design hotels" partnership, designed to be modern and attractive accordingly. Generous rooms and suites. The Fusion restaurant is linear and minimalist.

Renaissance

Große Bleichen ✉ 20354 – Ⓜ Jungfernstieg – ☎ (040) 34 91 80 – rhi.hamrn.info@renaissancehotels.com – Fax (040) 34 91 89 19 – www.renaissance-hamburg.com **F2**

205 rm – 🚹169/279 € 🚹🚹179/289 €, ☕ 20 €

Rest – Carte 27/39 €

◆ Luxury ◆ Classic ◆

In typical renaissance style, this classic, tastefully designed hotel has functional, comfortable rooms. Sauna on the sixth floor with beautiful views. The restaurant has a bar and an open kitchen.

Marriott

ABC-Str. 52 ✉ 20354 – Ⓜ Gänsemarkt – ☎ (040) 3 50 50 – hamburg.marriott@marriotthotels.com – Fax (040) 35 05 17 77 – www.hamburgmarriott.com **F2**

277 rm – 🚹199/269 € 🚹🚹199/269 €, ☕ 24 € – 5 suites

Rest – Carte 24/48 €

◆ Chain hotel ◆ Luxury ◆ Modern ◆

Close to the Gänsemarkt is this classic hotel, with a hint of America, with its tasteful, functional rooms, a wellness area, hair salon and beauty studio. Modern designs and an abundance of light wood in Restaurant Speicher 52.

Europäischer Hof

Kirchenallee 45 ✉ 20099 – Ⓜ Hauptbahnhof Süd – ☎ (040) 24 82 48 – info@europaeischer-hof.de – Fax (040) 24 82 47 99 – www.europaeischer-hof.de **H2**

275 rm ☕ – 🚹115/190 € 🚹🚹145/230 €

Rest *Paulaner's* – Carte 19/35 €

◆ Business ◆ Classic ◆

A spacious, refined and elegant lobby welcomes you into this hotel across from the main train station. The highlight of the recreation area is a six-level waterslide down to the swimming pool. Paulaner's: rustic and relaxed.

Novotel Hamburg Alster

Lübecker Str. 3 ✉ 22087 – Ⓜ Lübecker Str. – ☎ (040) 39 19 00 – h3737@accor.com – Fax (040) 39 19 02 72 – www.novotel.com **D2**

210 rm – 🚹89/179 € 🚹🚹89/179 €, ☕ 17 €

Rest – Carte 29/47 €

◆ Chain hotel ◆ Modern ◆

A modern hotel providing well-equipped rooms in comfortable, functional style. Conference facilities available. Restaurant accessed from the hotel lobby.

Mövenpick ≤ Hamburg
Sternschanze 6 ✉ 20357 – Ⓜ Sternschanze – ☎ (040) 3 34 41 10 – hotel.hamburg@moevenpick.com – Fax (040) 33 44 11 33 33 – www.moevenpick-hamburg.com Plan I **C2**
226 rm – †150/290 € ††170/310 €, ☕ 19 €
Rest – Carte 26/48 €
♦ Chain hotel ♦ Functional ♦
The beautiful old water tower from 1907 has been extended with an annex. It houses rooms in warm tones with very good technical facilities and views over Hamburg. International cuisine is served in the restaurant with a terrace facing the park.

relexa Hotel Bellevue
An der Alster 14 ✉ 20099 – ☎ (040) 28 44 40 – hamburg@relexa-hotel.de – Fax (040) 28 44 42 22 – www.relexa-hotels.de **H1**
85 rm ☕ – †90/117 € ††117/130 €
Rest – Carte 28/42 €
♦ Business ♦ Functional ♦
Classical white hotel building. The rooms are pretty - some in the main building have nice views of the Alster, while those in the St. Georg building are smaller single rooms. Lunch restaurant on the Außenalster. Dinner in the basement with tasteful, cosy atmosphere.

Mercure an der Messe
Schröderstiftstr. 3 ✉ 20146 – ☎ (040) 45 06 90 – h5394@accor.com – Fax (040) 4 50 69 10 00 – www.mercure.com **E1**
180 rm – †93/275 € ††93/295 €, ☕ 15 €
Rest – *(closed Sunday dinner)* Carte 24/38 €
♦ Business ♦ Functional ♦
Right next to the exhibition centre, just a stone's throw from the TV tower, this business hotel offers modern design and functional equipment.

Mercure City
Amsinckstr. 53 ✉ 20097 – ☎ (040) 23 63 80 – h1163@accor.com – Fax (040) 23 42 30 – www.mercure.com Plan I **D3**
187 rm – †99/159 € ††99/159 €, ☕ 17 €
Rest – Carte 24/37 €
♦ Chain hotel ♦ Modern ♦
Modern functional rooms in this inner city hotel, ideal for business guests.

Senator without rest
Lange Reihe 18 ✉ 20099 – Ⓜ Hauptbahnhof Nord – ☎ (040) 24 12 03 – info@hotel-senator-hamburg.de – Fax (040) 2 80 37 17 – www.hotel-senator-hamburg.de **H2**
56 rm ☕ – †99/185 € ††99/185 €
♦ Business ♦ Functional ♦
Pale wood and pastel tones create a harmonious atmosphere in the rooms, some of which have a waterbed for a perfect night's sleep.

Baseler Hof
Esplanade 11 ✉ 20354 – Ⓜ Stephansplatz – ☎ (040) 35 90 60 – info@baselerhof.de – Fax (040) 35 90 69 18 – www.baselerhof.de **F1**
168 rm ☕ – †89/109 € ††129/149 €
Rest *Kleinhuis* – *☎ (040) 353399* – Carte 26/34 €
♦ Traditional ♦ Functional ♦
This hotel is located between the Außenalster and the Botanical Gardens, and is a member of the Association of Christian Hotels. A range of rooms, some with rattan furniture. The Kleinhuis is a nice bistro-style restaurant.

Wedina without rest
Gurlittstr. 23 ✉ 20099 – ☎ (040) 2 80 89 00 – info@wedina.de – Fax (040) 2 80 38 94 – www.wedina.de **H1**
59 rm ☕ – †88/155 € ††108/175 €
♦ Family ♦ Cosy ♦
The different buildings which make up this hotel are aglow with Bauhaus colours. The interior is also attractively designed featuring natural materials.

Alster-Hof without rest
Esplanade 12 ✉ 20354 – Ⓜ Stephansplatz – ✆ (040) 35 00 70 – info@alster-hof.de – Fax (040) 35 00 75 14 – www.alster-hof.de
closed 22 December - 2 January **F1**
113 rm – †80/96 € ††120/130 €
♦ Traditional ♦ Functional ♦
This centrally located hotel provides functional rooms with a refined atmosphere.

Haerlin – Fairmont Hotel Vier Jahreszeiten ≤ Binnenalster,
Neuer Jungfernstieg 9 ✉ 20354 – Ⓜ Jungfernstieg – ✆ (040) 34 94 33 10 – hamburg@fairmont.com – Fax (040) 34 94 26 08 – www.fairmont-hvj.de
closed 27 December - 7 January, 1 week Easter, 20 July - 25 August and Sunday - Monday **F2**
Rest – *(dinner only)* Menu 95/115 € – Carte 70/97 €
Spec. Lauwarmer Hummer mit Blumenkohl-Couscous. Filet vom St. Pierre mit Safran-Muschelnage und Spinatpüree. Zweierlei Carameldessert mit Himbeer-Balsamicosorbet.
♦ Classic ♦ Formal ♦
In this restaurant there is an elegant atmosphere with attentive and meticulously trained staff. The presentation and flavour of the classic dishes is excellent.

Insel am Alsterufer
Alsterufer 35 (1st floor) ✉ 20354 – ✆ (040) 4 50 18 50 – info@insel-am-alsterufer.de – Fax (040) 45 01 85 11 – www.insel-am-alsterufer.de
closed Saturday lunch and Sunday *Plan I* **C2**
Rest – Menu 20 € (lunch)/56 € – Carte 36/63 €
♦ Classic ♦ Formal ♦
This little white jewel of a villa houses an elegant restaurant with warm tones, offering its guests international cuisine. Some of the tables look out on the Aussenalster.

Cölln's
Brodschrangen 1 ✉ 20457 – Ⓜ Rathaus – ✆ (040) 36 41 53 – Fax (040) 37 22 01 **G3**
Rest – *(booking advisable)* Carte 28/70 €
♦ Classic ♦ Cosy ♦
This tastefully renovated historic establishment offers classic and regional dishes. Details such as old tiles and wood panelling feature within their comfortable rooms.

Sgroi
Lange Reihe 40 ✉ 20099 – ✆ (040) 28 00 39 30 – Fax (040) 28 00 39 31 – www.sgroi.de
closed 3 weeks July and Saturday lunch, Sunday - Monday **H1-2**
Rest – Menu 60/70 € – Carte 58/71 €
Spec. Tatar von wilden Garnelen und Couscous-Gemüse in der Zucchiniblüte. Jakobsmuscheln im Kopfsalatblatt mit Barbera-Kompott. Zicklein aus dem Ofen mit Topinambur-Törtchen.
♦ Italian ♦ Minimalist ♦
With a straightforward and modern design, this restaurant serves excellent, tasty Italian cuisine. There is also a small lounge.

Anna
Bleichenbrücke 2 ✉ 20354 – Ⓜ Rathaus – ✆ (040) 36 70 14 – Fax (040) 37 50 07 36
closed Sunday and Bank Holidays **F2**
Rest – Carte 31/41 €
♦ International ♦ Friendly ♦
Mediterranean tones set the ambience of this two-floor restaurant with its wide range of international cuisine. Pleasant terrace on the Fleet.

XX **San Michele** VISA MC AE ①

Englische Planke 8 ✉ 20459 – Ⓜ Landungsbrücken – ☎ (040) 37 11 27 – info@san-michele.de – Fax (040) 37 81 21 – www.san-michele.de
closed early to mid August and Monday **E3**
Rest – Carte 36/56 €

♦ Italian ♦ Friendly ♦

This restaurant opposite the 'Michel' is pleasantly light and Mediterranean, offering typical Italian cuisine. Small bistro on ground floor.

XX **Tarantella** VISA MC AE

Stephansplatz 10 (at Casino Esplanade) ✉ 20354 – Ⓜ Stephanspl. – ☎ (040) 65 06 77 90 – Fax (040) 65 06 77 87 – www.tarantella.cc **F1**
Rest – Carte 31/66 €

♦ International ♦ Modern ♦

This modern style restaurant with a bistro area is located in the casino building. International dishes are prepared in the open kitchen.

XX **Brook** AE

Bei den Mühren 91 ✉ 20457 – ☎ (040) 37 50 31 28 – Fax (040) 37 50 31 27 – www.restaurant-brook.de
closed Sunday **G3**
Rest – Menu 31/35 € – Carte 34/48 €

♦ International ♦ Minimalist ♦

A modern restaurant with friendly service and good international cuisine. In the evening you have views of the illuminated old warehouse district.

XX **Doc Cheng's** – Fairmont Hotel Vier Jahreszeiten AC VISA MC AE ①

Neuer Jungfernstieg 9 ✉ 20354 – Ⓜ Jungfernstieg – ☎ (040) 3 49 43 33 – hamburg@fairmont.com – Fax (040) 34 94 26 00 – www.fairmont-hvj.de
closed Saturday lunch and Sunday **F2**
Rest – *(July - August dinner only)* Carte 38/48 €

♦ Asian ♦ Exotic ♦

The Far East inspires both the stylish design and cuisine here. Euro-Asian cuisine, with reduced lunch menu.

X **Die Bank** VISA AE

Hohe Bleichen 17 ✉ 20354 – Ⓜ Gänsemarkt – ☎ (040) 2 38 00 30 – info@diebank-brasserie.de – Fax (040) 23 80 03 33 – www.diebank-brasserie.de
closed Sunday lunch and Bank Holidays **F2**
Rest – Carte 39/52 €

♦ International ♦ Brasserie ♦

A lively brasserie and bar in the imposing cashiers' hall on the first floor of what used to be a bank, offers contemporary cuisine.

X **La Mirabelle** VISA MC AE

Bundesstr. 15 ✉ 20146 – ☎ (040) 4 10 75 85 – Fax (040) 4 10 75 85 – www.la-mirabelle-hamburg.de
closed Sunday *Plan I* **C2**
Rest – *(dinner only)* Menu 33/39 € – Carte 34/48 €

♦ French ♦ Cosy ♦

In this small, friendly restaurant with its relaxed atmosphere and French flair, Pierre Moissonnier serves his guests in a friendly but passionate style.

X **Fischmarkt** VISA MC AE

Ditmar-Koel-Str. 1 ✉ 20459 – Ⓜ Landungsbrücken – ☎ (040) 36 38 09 – Fax (040) 36 21 91 – www.restaurant-fischmarkt.de
closed Saturday lunch **E3**
Rest – *(booking advisable)* Menu 30/48 € – Carte 30/46 €

♦ Fish ♦ Bistro ♦

Around 300 m from the docks is this well-cared-for restaurant with its slightly Mediterranean décor, bistro ambience and open kitchen. Mainly fish dishes.

Le Plat du Jour

Dornbusch 4 ✉ 20095 – Ⓜ Rathaus – ✆ (040) 32 14 14 – Fax (040) 32 52 63 93
closed Sunday and Bank Holidays, July - August Saturday - Sunday **G3**
Rest – *(booking advisable)* Menu 27 € – Carte 26/34 €
♦ French ♦ Bistro ♦
This pleasant French bistro has black and white photos on the walls and friendly service. For Hamburg, they serve very good value French dishes!

Cox

Lange Reihe 68 ✉ 20099 – ✆ (040) 24 94 22 – info@restaurant-cox.de – Fax (040) 28 05 09 02 – www.restaurant-cox.de
closed Saturday lunch, Sunday lunch **H1**
Rest – Carte 25/41 €
♦ International ♦ Bistro ♦
This restaurant close to the theatre serves international dishes with a Mediterranean influence in a warm, friendly bistro ambience.

Matsumi

Colonnaden 96 (1st floor) ✉ 20354 – Ⓜ Stephansplatz – ✆ (040) 34 31 25 – Fax (040) 34 42 19 – www.matsumi.de
closed 24 December - 8 January lunch Bank Holidays and Sunday **F2**
Rest – Menu 43/50 € – Carte 20/51 €
♦ Japanese ♦ Minimalist ♦
You will find this classic Japanese restaurant in the pedestrian zone. The authentic fare is served at the table, at the sushi bar or in the tatami rooms (for groups).

NORTH OF THE CENTRE

Plan I

InterContinental

< Hamburg and Alster,

Fontenay 10 ✉ 20354 – ✆ (040) 4 14 20 – hamburg@interconti.com – Fax (040) 41 42 22 99 – www.hamburg.intercontinental.com **C2**
281 rm – †185/295 € ††185/295 €, ☕ 21 € – 12 suites
Rest *Windows* – see below
Rest *Signatures* – Carte 29/43 €
♦ Chain hotel ♦ Luxury ♦ Functional ♦
In a pleasant location on the Alster, this hotel offers generous, perfectly equipped and comfortable rooms. Pleasantly bright: the conservatory restaurant. International cuisine.

Abtei

Abteistr. 14 ✉ 20149 – ✆ (040) 44 29 05 – abtei@relaischateaux.com – Fax (040) 44 98 20 – www.abtei-hotel.de
closed 24 to 26 December **C1**
11 rm ☕ – †155/200 € ††190/250 €
Rest – *(closed Sunday - Monday) (dinner only) (booking essential)* Menu 65/95 €
Spec. Erbsen-Royal gefüllt mit Gänsestopfleber, gebratener Wachtelbrust und Trüffelvinaigrette. Gebeiztes Entrecôte mit Soja und Balsamico. Mille Feuille von der Schokolade mit Bergamotte-Aroma und Orangengelee.
♦ Townhouse ♦ Personalised ♦
Surrounded by trees, this beautiful building lies in a quiet, elegant residential quarter. Extremely pleasant, private atmosphere and highly tasteful individual rooms. Intimate restaurant with a cosy refined lounge. Snooker evenings with food and instruction.

Mittelweg without rest

Mittelweg 59 ✉ 20149 – Ⓜ Klosterstern – ✆ (040) 4 14 10 10 – hotel.mittelweg@gmx.de – Fax (040) 41 41 01 20 – www.hotel-mittelweg.de **C1**
30 rm ☕ – †95/128 € ††115/168 €
♦ Townhouse ♦ Cosy ♦
Built by a Bremen merchant as his town house in 1890, this hotel stands out for its friendly, private atmosphere and old-style charm and classic, comfortable rooms.

Nippon

Hofweg 75 ✉ 22085 – ✆ (040) 2 27 11 40 – reservations@nipponhotel.de – Fax (040) 22 71 14 90 – www.nipponhotel.de
closed 23 December - 1 January **D1**
42 rm – †98/121 € ††116/150 €, ☕ 11 €
Rest – *(closed Monday) (dinner only)* Carte 26/39 €
♦ Business ♦ Minimalist ♦
Furnished in a modern, purist Japanese style with light colours and clear shapes: tatami floors, shoji walls and futons. A Japanese restaurant and sushi bar.

Windows – Hotel InterContinental

≤ Hamburg and Alster,

Fontenay 10 ✉ 20354 – ✆ (040) 41422531 – hamburg@interconti.com – Fax (040) 41 42 22 99 – www.hamburg.intercontinental.com
closed 1 - 21 January, 12 July - 22 August and Sunday - Monday **C2**
Rest – *(dinner only)* Carte 45/69 €
♦ Classic ♦ Formal ♦
As well as its French cuisine, this restaurant offers outstanding views from its two window facades and an elegant ambience.

Poletto

Eppendorfer Landstr. 145 (by Breitenfelder Str. C 1) ✉ 20251 – ✆ (040) 4 80 21 59 – Fax (040) 41 40 69 93 – www.poletto.de
closed 1 week January, 2 weeks July - August and Saturday lunch, Sunday - Monday and Bank Holidays
Rest – *(booking advisable)* Menu 35 € (lunch)/115 € – Carte 75/90 €
Spec. Spargel-Tortelloni mit mariniertem Bachsaibling und Nussbutterverjus. Steinbutt an der Gräte gegart mit violetten Artischocken und Kapernäpfeln. Weinbergpfirsich aus dem Ofen mit gebackener Amarettinipraline.
♦ Mediterranean ♦ Friendly ♦
Cornelia and Remigio Poletto attend to their guests with commitment, and serve Italian Mediterranean cuisine. The restaurant is pleasantly bright and elegant.

Piment (Wahabi Nouri)

Lehmweg 29 ✉ 20251 – ✆ (040) 42 93 77 88 – info@restaurant-piment.de – Fax (040) 42 93 77 89
closed 10 to 20 March and Sunday **C1**
Rest – *(dinner only) (booking advisable)* Menu 65/82 € – Carte 57/64 €
Spec. Gänsestopfleberterrine mit Topinambur-Carpaccio und Ingwerkrokant. Meeräsche mit Maracuja-Fenchelgemüse und Olivennage. Rücken und B'stilla vom Lamm.
♦ Inventive ♦ Friendly ♦
In this pretty Art Nouveau building Wahabi Nouri serves classic cuisine with north African elements. Reddish tones create a warm atmosphere.

Allegria

Hudtwalckerstr. 13 (by Sierichstr. C 1) ✉ 22299 – ✆ (040) 46 07 28 28 – info@allegria-restaurant.de – Fax (040) 46 07 26 07 – www.allegria-restaurant.de
closed Monday
Rest – *(weekdays dinner only)* Menu 34/70 € – Carte 34/56 €
♦ International ♦ Fashionable ♦
In the Winterhuder Fährhaus, a modern steel and glass building, offering good international cuisine with an Austrian influence. The manageress heads a friendly service team.

Küchenwerkstatt

Hans-Henny-Jahnn-Weg 1 (entrance by Hofweg) ✉ 22085 – ✆ (040) 22 92 75 88 – mail@kuechenwerkstatt-hamburg.de – Fax (040) 22 92 75 99 – www.kuechenwerkstatt-hamburg.de
closed 2 weeks early January and Sunday - Monday **D1**
Rest – Menu 22 € (lunch)/69 € (dinner) – Carte 36/49 €
♦ Inventive ♦ Trendy ♦
This former ferry building has been done out in an attractive cool modern style. Here you'll find committed service and creative cuisine. Short lunchtime menu.

XX

Tirol

Milchstr. 19 ✉ 20148 – ✆ (040) 44 60 82 – Fax (040) 44 80 93 27

closed Sunday **C2**

Rest – Carte 28/46 €

◆ Austrian ◆ Cosy ◆

For anyone who is homesick for Austria! Austrian specialties are served in the cosy, rustic atmosphere of this restaurant.

XX

K & K Kochbar

Rothenbaumchaussee 11 (at the Curio-Haus) ✉ 20148 – ✆ (040) 36 11 16 36 – kochbar@koflerkompanie.com – Fax (040) 36 11 16 11 – www.koflerkompanie.com

closed 22 December - 7 January and Saturday lunch, Sunday - Monday *Plan II* **F1**

Rest – Menu 49 € – Carte 41/51 €

◆ Innovative ◆ Trendy ◆

The restaurant is decorated with modern art work and sits within a beautiful historic Curio House of 1911 at a trendy address. The centrally positioned show kitchen is an eye catcher.

HARBOUR AND ALTONA *Plan III*

East

Simon-von-Utrecht-Str. 31 ✉ 20359 – Ⓜ St. Pauli – ✆ (040) 30 99 30 – info@east-hamburg.de – Fax (040) 30 99 32 00 – www.east-hamburg.de *Plan I* **B2**

125 rm – †155/175 € ††175/195 €, ☕ 14 € – 3 suites

Rest – Carte 32/43 €

◆ Business ◆ Design ◆

In an old foundry, this pleasant designer hotel with the latest word in rooms and bar/lounge occupies two floors. Cinema, indoor golf, putting green in the garden. Not your average restaurant, in an old factory.

XXXX ✿

Landhaus Scherrer (Heinz Wehmann)

Elbchaussee 130 ✉ 22763 – ✆ (040) 8 80 13 25 – info@landhausscherrer.de – Fax (040) 8 80 62 60 – www.landhausscherrer.de

closed Easter, Whitsun and Sunday **I1**

Rest – Menu 79/108 € – Carte 54/99 €

Rest *Bistro* – *(closed Sunday)* Carte 32/45 €

Spec. Graupengemüse mit Kalbskopf und gebratenem Hummer. Jakobsmuscheln mit warmem Selleriegelee und Bleichsellerieschaum, Olivenaroma. Gebratener Steinbutt mit Tomatenvinaigrette und Ruccola-Pesto.

◆ Classic ◆ Formal ◆

This country house built in 1827 has been an institution in Hamburg for over 30 years. Heinz Wehmann's classic cuisine is served in an elegant ambience. The wine cellar is worthy of note. Nice friendly bistro with light wood panelling.

XXX ✿

Le Canard nouveau (Ali Güngörmüs)

Elbchaussee 139 ✉ 22763 – ✆ (040) 88 12 95 31 – info@lecanard-hamburg.de – Fax (040) 88 12 95 33 – www.lecanard-hamburg.de

closed 1 to 7 January and Monday, Saturday lunch, Sunday lunch **I1**

Rest – Menu 33 € (lunch)/98 € – Carte 58/69 €

Spec. Ziegenkäse-Feigentortellini mit krossem Parmaschinken und Lorbeerjus. Paniertes Kotelett und gratinierter Rücken vom Lamm mit Gurken-Joghurtdip. Schokoladenkuchen mit Mango-Chilisorbet.

◆ International ◆ Fashionable ◆

This simple, modern restaurant overlooking the Elbe is semi-circular in shape. At lunchtimes plainer, more inexpensive variants of the menu are served.

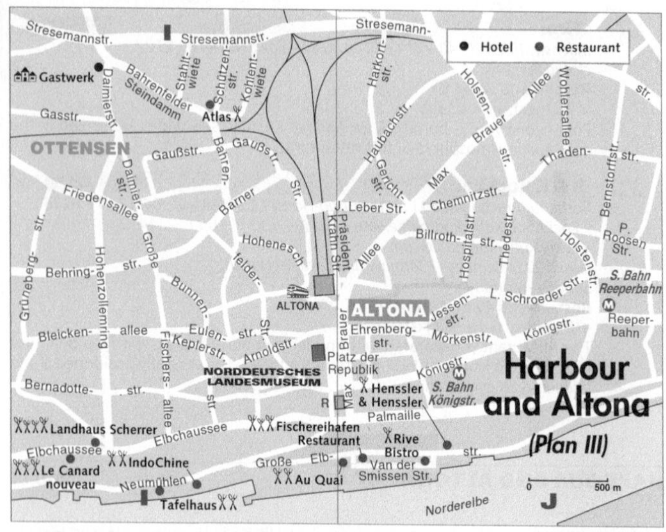

XXX Fischereihafen Restaurant

Große Elbstr. 143 ✉ 22767 – ✆ (040) 38 18 16 – info@fischereihafenrestaurant.de – Fax (040) 3 89 30 21 – www.fischereihafenrestaurant.de **J1**

Rest – *(booking advisable)* Menu 19 € (lunch)/50 € – Carte 32/72 €

◆ Fish ◆ Formal ◆

This classic restaurant is a Hamburg institution serving regional cuisine and featuring fish dishes. Terrace overlooking the Elbe.

XX Au Quai

Große Elbstr. 145 b ✉ 22767 – ✆ (040) 38 03 77 30 – info@au-quai.com – Fax (040) 38 03 77 32 – www.au-quai.com
closed Saturday lunch and Sunday **J1**

Rest – Menu 18 € (lunch) – Carte 34/58 €

◆ Fusion ◆ Trendy ◆

This popular establishment is situated close to the harbour and has a terrace facing the water. The modern interior is complemented by designer items and holographs.

XX IndoChine

Neumühlen 11 ✉ 22763 – ✆ (040) 39 80 78 80 – info@indochine.de – Fax (040) 39 80 78 82 – www.indochine.de **I1**

Rest – Menu 44/55 € – Carte 36/52 €

◆ Asian ◆ Trendy ◆

Great views, especially from the window seats, in this elegant modern restaurant on the Elbe. Cambodian, Laotian and Vietnamese cuisine. The IceBar is worth seeing.

XX ✿ Tafelhaus (Christian Rach)

Neumühlen 17 ✉ 22763 – ✆ (040) 89 27 60 – anfrage@tafelhaus.de – Fax (040) 8 99 33 24 – www.tafelhaus.de
closed Saturday lunch, Sunday - Monday **I1**

Rest – *(booking advisable)* Menu 45 € (lunch)/93 € – Carte 70/83 €

Spec. Jakobsmuscheln mit vier Aromen. Ganzer Steinbutt (2 people). Rehschulter mit Zitronenpesto und Lavendel.

◆ Inventive ◆ Fashionable ◆

This contemporary style restaurant on the Elbe features creative French cuisine. Guests can observe the busy shipping traffic from the restaurant and terrace.

Henssler Henssler

Große Elbstr. 160 ✉ 22767 – Ⓜ Königstr. – ✆ (040) 38 69 90 00 – Fax (040) 38 69 90 55 – www.hensslerhenssler.de
closed 4 weeks July and Sunday, Bank Holidays **J1**
Rest – *(booking advisable)* Carte 30/55 €
♦ Japanese ♦ Minimalist ♦

Father and son run this Far East-inspired simple modern restaurant in an old fishmonger's hall: Japanese cuisine with the Californian touch. Sushi bar.

Rive Bistro

Van-der-Smissen Str. 1 (at Cruise-Centre) ✉ 22767 – Ⓜ Königstr. – ✆ (040) 3 80 59 19 – info@rive.de – Fax (040) 3 89 47 75 – www.rive.de **J1**
Rest – *(booking advisable)* Carte 26/42 €
♦ Fish ♦ Fashionable ♦

Directly on the harbour, close to the Fischmarkt is this modern restaurant. The international menu has a strong emphasis on fish dishes. Fresh oysters at the bar.

ELBE-WESTERN DISTRICTS *Plan III*

Louis C. Jacob

Elbe River,
Elbchaussee 401 (by Elbchaussee A3) ✉ 22609 – ✆ (040) 82 25 50 – jacob@hotel-jacob.de – Fax (040) 82 25 54 44 – www.hotel-jacob.de
85 rm – †195/245 € ††255/485 €, ☕ 26 € – 8 suites
Rest *Weinwirtschaft Kleines Jacob* – see below
Rest – *(booking advisable)* Menu 63 € (lunch)/98 € – Carte 67/95 €
Spec. In Milch pochierter Steinbutt mit Pommerysenf-Nussbutter und Pellkartoffelsalat. Taube mit Sauce Rouennaise und Dattelpüree. Himbeer-Mille-Feuille mit Basilikumöl und Sauerrahmeis.
♦ Luxury ♦ Traditional ♦ Personalised ♦

This elegant hotel on the Elbe river stands out for its professional service and pleasant rooms, combining classic and modern elements successfully. French cuisine is served in the stylish restaurant and on the lovely terrace under lime trees.

Gastwerk

Beim Alten Gaswerk 3 (corner of Daimlerstraße) ✉ 22761 – ✆ (040) 89 06 20 – info@gastwerk-hotel.de – Fax (040) 8 90 62 20 – www.gastwerk-hotel.de *Plan III* **I1**
141 rm – †136/182 € ††136/182 €, ☕ 18 € – 3 suites
Rest – *(closed Saturday lunch, Sunday lunch)* Carte 36/42 €
♦ Business ♦ Stylish ♦

A successful combination of imposing industrial architecture and modern design. Pleasant rooms, lofts and suites – two of the suites have room terraces. A modern restaurant serving Italian cuisine.

Landhaus Flottbek

Baron-Voght-Str. 179 (by Stresemannstr. A 2) ✉ 22607 – ✆ (040) 8 22 74 10 – info@landhaus-flottbek.de – Fax (040) 82 27 41 51 – www.landhaus-flottbek.de
25 rm – †90/120 € ††115/150 €, ☕ 13 €
Rest – *(closed Saturday lunch, Sunday lunch)* Carte 34/43 €
♦ Family ♦ Cosy ♦

A group of 18C farmhouses with a beautiful garden. The lovely, individually furnished, country-style rooms are rustic and elegant. This restaurant offers international cuisine from good produce. Garden terrace.

XXXX ✿

Süllberg-Seven Seas (Karlheinz Hauser) with rm
Süllbergsterrasse 12 (by Elbchaussee A 3) ✉ 22587
– ✆ (040) 8 66 25 20 – info@suellberg-hamburg.de – Fax (040) 86 62 52 13
– www.suellberg-hamburg.de
11 rm – 🛉170/190 € 🛉🛉190/220 €, ☕ 17 €
Rest – *(closed 2 to 22 January and Monday - Tuesday) (weekdays dinner only)*
Menu 65/128 € – Carte 74/100 €
Rest *Bistro* – Carte 37/57 €
Spec. Thunfisch und Jakobsmuscheln mit grüner Mango und tasmanischem Pfeffer. Bar de Ligne mit Lardo di Colonata. Lammrücken und confierte Keule mit Polentanudeln.
♦ Mediterranean ♦ Formal ♦
The Süllberg ensemble high above the Elbe is a showpiece from the era of Kaiser Wilhelm. Enjoy Mediterranean cuisine and a fabulous view in a modern and elegant atmosphere. Tasteful rooms and beauty facilities await guests in the hotel area.

XX ✿

Das Kleine Rote (Gunnar Hinz)
Holstenkamp 71 ✉ 22525 – ✆ (040) 89 72 68 13 – das-kleine-rote@web.de
– Fax (040) 89 72 68 14 – www.das-kleine-rote.de
closed Saturday lunch, Sunday - Monday Plan I **A2**
Rest – *(booking advisable)* Menu 39 € (lunch)/79 € – Carte 50/80 €
Spec. Tatar vom Wolfsbarsch mit Gurken und gebackenen Austern. Butterpochierter Hummer mit grünem Spargel und Tomaten-Vanillejus. Haxe, Bries und Filet vom Kalb mit Bohnenkernen und Kartoffelkrapfen.
♦ Inventive ♦ Friendly ♦
A small red house with a pretty garden is home to this modern restaurant decorated in warm tones. Discrete lighting creates a pleasant atmosphere, particularly in the evenings.

X

Atlas
Schützenstr. 9a (entrance Phoenixhof) ✉ 22761 – ✆ (040) 8 51 78 10
– atlas@atlas.at – Fax (040) 8 51 78 11 – www.atlas.at
closed Saturday lunch Plan III **I1**
Rest – Menu 28 € (dinner) – Carte 27/39 €
♦ International ♦ Bistro ♦
This old fish smokery is now a restaurant with a modern bistro style. Short menu at lunchtimes, Sunday brunch. Nice ivy-wreathed terrace.

X

Weinwirtschaft Kleines Jacob – Hotel Louis C. Jacob
Elbchaussee 404 (by Elbchaussee A 3) ✉ 22609 – ✆ (040) 82 25 55 10
– kleines-jacob@hotel-jacob.de – Fax (040) 82 25 54 44 – www.hotel-jacob.de
closed mid July - mid August and Tuesday
Rest – *(weekdays dinner only)* Carte 24/41 €
♦ Mediterranean ♦ Cosy ♦
A very cosy wine bar atmosphere prevails in this little house opposite the Louis C. Jacob Hotel. Mediterranean-style cuisine.

AT THE AIRPORT

Courtyard by Marriott
Flughafenstr. 47 ✉ 22415 – ✆ (040) 53 10 20
– service@airporthh.com – Fax (040) 53 10 22 22 – www.courtyard.com/hamcy
159 rm – 🛉149/179 € 🛉🛉149/179 €, ☕ 17 €
Rest – Carte 27/50 €
♦ Business ♦ Functional ♦
This country house style hotel is just 500 m from the airport, and stands out for its functional but classic elegant design. Restaurant with international menu.

MUNICH
MÜNCHEN

Population: 1 205 000 (conurbation 1 656 000) – Altitude: 520m

Sime/PHOTONONSTOP

Situated in a stunning position not far north of the Alps, Munich is a cultural titan, rather unfairly overshadowed in publicity terms by its world-famous Oktoberfest bier extravaganza. Famously described as the 'village with a million inhabitants', its mix of German organisation and Italian lifestyle makes for a magical merge, with an enviable amount of Italian restaurants to seek out and enjoy.

This capital of Southern Germany boasts over forty theatres and dozens of museums, temples of culture that blend charmingly with the Bavarian love of folklore and lederhosen – the cliché actually does ring true, and locals will proudly don their traditional garb at the drop of a green hat (with jauntily set feather). Perhaps in no other world location – certainly not in Western Europe – is there such an enjoyable abundance of folk festivals and groups dedicated to playing the local music. And there's an abundance of places to see them, too: Munich is awash with Bierhallen, Bierkeller, and Biergarten. Surrounded by green fields and rolling hills (on good days, you can see across to the Alps) it's not difficult to see why Munich is currently seen as one of – if not the most – liveable city in the world.

LIVING THE CITY

The heart of Munich is the Old Town, and its epicentre the **Marienplatz** in the south and **Residenz** to the north: there are many fine historic buildings around here. Running to the east is the **River Isar**, with fine urban thoroughfares and green areas for walks. Head north for the area dissected by the **Ludwigstrasse** and **Leopoldstrasse** – **Schwabing** – which is full of students as it's the University district. To the east is the **English Garden**, a denizen of peace. West of here, the Museums district, dominated by the **Pinakothek**, is characterised by bookshops, antique stores and galleries.

PRACTICAL INFORMATION

ARRIVAL-DEPARTURE

A taxi from Airport Frank-Josef Strauss, which is 28km northeast of the city, will cost around €55. Alternatively, take the Munich S-Bahn Lines S1 or S8 to the centre, which will take 45 minutes.

TRANSPORT

On buses and trams, Munich's not the most straightforward city to travel around. It's divided into four ring-shaped price zones; zone 1 (the white zone) is the most important for visitors, as it covers the city centre. Prices rise in accordance with the amount of zones you intend to travel. If you plan to make several journeys, invest in a strip card, which costs ten euros. You can also buy a one- or three-day Tageskarte, which are good value for tourists. Available from tourist information offices, hotel receptions, travel agents and newsagents.

The underground network (U-Bahn) opened in 1971, and some stretches of the network are still not finished. It operates the same fare system as on Munich's buses and trams.

The München Welcome Card is valid for use on public transport in the city centre and for discounts of up to fifty per cent for more than thirty sights, museums, castles and palaces, city tours and bicycle hire. The card is available for one or three days.

EXPLORING MUNICH

There's really only one building you can identify as your marker for a tour of Munich, and that's the **Frauenkirche**, the largest Gothic church in Southern Germany. Its distinctive onion domes, standing high and mighty on twin towers, have been an impressive sight since the mid-fifteenth century. Around them sits snugly the old town, a tourist mecca with an intimacy and warmth enhanced by fine historic architecture and an absence of modern buildings zooming to the sky. Aesthetically, this looks great, but the reason for it is more prosaic: if the top rung of the city's fire engines can't reach, then it won't get built...

Marienplatz is the focal point for visitors. It's the central square, just a stone's throw from Frauenkirche, and Munich life emanates from this busy, bustling hub. In its immediate vicinity stand three other distinctive churches: **Peterskirche**, built in the twelfth century, is the oldest in Munich; **Michaelskirche** is famous for its magnificent barrel vaulting; and **Asamkirche** is a riot of colourful frescoes and gold leaf. Marienplatz's town hall – the **Rathaus** – took over fifty years to build at the end of the 19C, and is a testimony to Gothic splendour, with Glockenspiel marionettes performing a daily dance high up the façade. Just up the road (or, more precisely, medieval street) from here is the majestic Residenz, the grand palatial home of the Wittelsbach dynasty who ruled over Bavaria for seven hundred years, right up until the end of the First World War. It boasts the jaw-dropping **Antiquarium** – a great hall built in the 17C – and a Rococo theatre (the **Cuvillies**) just bursting with grand operatic pomp.

→ DRINK, ANYONE?

You might feel the need to balance all this civic glory with something a little more down-to-earth: a drink maybe. Well, just a hop, skip and jump away from Residenz, across the luxurious boulevard **Maximilianstrasse,** is what locals modestly call the most famous pub in the world. **Hofbräuhaus** was opened in 1830, and, perhaps unsurprisingly, it's the city's greatest tourist attraction. It can seat around 2,500 drinkers. There's a hall with long tables for a thousand on the ground floor, and a vaulted hall for thirteen hundred on the first. Side rooms make up the number. Every day, nearly eighteen thousand pints of beer are drunk, but Muncheners rather turn their noses up at it as a tourist honeypot. They have their more cherished and authentic bierhallen to keep them in liquid company.

If induced to claustrophobia at the thought of all that humanity reaching for a frothing litre of ale, then head to the **Viktualienmarkt**. It's another great landmark of the old town, and it celebrated its two hundredth birthday in 2007. Here you can get your beer and wine on the hoof, along with fruit and vegetables, meat and fish, cheese and flowers, sausages and salamis. This is Munich's oldest and most picturesque market, where you'll find fellow shoppers knocking back mugs of beer and tots of schnapps under canvas awnings.

→ PICTURE THIS

Head north and you hit the newer part of Munich, much of it built in the 19C. This part of town is famous for its stylish art galleries, and they don't come much more stylish than the Pinakothek, which boasts no less than three completely individual galleries each with its own distinctive allure. The oldest is the **Alte Pinakothek**, now considered one of the world's most important art galleries, with an outstanding collection of work from the 14C and 18C. Cross the road to the **Neue Pinakothek**, opened in 1853 and home to an impressive range of European art from the 19C. Most recent addition to this revered grouping is the **Pinakothek der Moderne**, opened only in 2002. As you might have guessed from the name, this is a temple to the world of modern art, architecture and design, housed in a spacious, three-floor structure of glass and concrete just demanding to be noticed by the passing public. Museums abound in this district; jostling for your attention in one compact and classy area are grand buildings with collections that include ancient classical antiquities, dazzling mineral formations, Greek and Roman sculpture, fossilised palm trees (and a mastodon), and artworks by Kandinsky, Klee, Beuys and Warhol. A respite from cultural overload can be taken at the **Old Botanical Gardens**, a short walk south from the museums. It has a delightful café garden, shaded by exotic trees.

IN AN ENGLISH CITY GARDEN

Mind you, when it comes to green spaces, there's nothing in the city to compare with the **English Garden**, so called because of its naturalistic landscaped style. It's one of Europe's largest city parks, and, looked at on a map, resembles a great green lung breathing life into the surrounding *strassen*. It's in a favourable position on the east side of Munich, close to the river Isar, and is a huge attraction in the summer months. You can, if you so wish, sunbathe naked here, or go for a swim in the winding streams that weave their way amongst the trees and shrubs. Many head for the 18C **Chinese Tower**, not for the view it offers (though that's good) but because it proffers a famous biergarten in its shadow. This is the university quarter: there are sixty thousand students, and the streets in the vicinity are full of life and noise. A grand boulevard runs right through, south to north. Ludwigstrasse, at the southern end, is elegantly neo-Classical in style, but as you walk northwards along Leopoldstrasse, the ambience becomes much less formal. The students come into their own, and there are pubs and swish boutiques lining the way. This is the famous Schwabing area, renowned since the late nineteenth century as a bohemian hang out, populated in its pre-World War I heyday by the likes of Thomas Mann, Kandinsky and Klee.

BEER IN BAVARIA

One of the main attractions of Munich lies in wait in a most fortuitous spot between the English Garden and the Isar. It's the **Bavarian National Museum** and it covers all aspects of life in this part of Germany from classical antiquity until the nineteenth century. It's laid out over three fascinating floors, and leaves barely a stone unturned if that stone may reveal an interesting nugget of Bavarian life. What it doesn't feature, ironically, is the one subject great hordes come exclusively to Munich for...the Oktoberfest. The largest beer orgy in the world takes up two weeks of September (and a little bit of October) and welcomes six million (yes, six million) visitors, who quaff around six million litres of golden stuff in fourteen giant tents. Sausages, ox meat and roast chickens are devoured in frightening proportions, and the songs hammered out with much gusto are invariably of the Bavarian kind. The Oktoberfest began life in 1810 to celebrate royal nuptials, so in two years' time it'll be putting on its two hundredth anniversary party. Imagine what *that's* going to be like...

CALENDAR HIGHLIGHTS

Festivals, many of them free, come thick and fast in Munich. The beer festivals (unfortunately, not free) kick off in March with Starkbierfest

MUNICH IN...

ONE DAY

The old town, Frauenkirche, English Garden, Wagner (if possible!) at the National Theatre

TWO DAYS

Schwabing, Pinakothek, Hofbräuhaus

THREE DAYS

Olympic Park, Schloss Nymphenburg, last night 'hurrah' at a traditional Bavarian inn

(The Festival of Strong Beer), carry on with the Maibockausschank at the Hofbräuhaus in May, and end with a quiet little affair in September and October…A few measures will probably be raised at the Biennale in April; this is Germany's largest contemporary music festival, heralding a host of musical events in the city. The Tollwood Festival in June, in the Olympic Park, features jazz and rock, while in July the Münchner Opernfestspiele is for opera and ballet lovers. Jazz Summer, also in July, lights up the swish Hotel Bayerischer Hof; meanwhile, rock and jazz fans are catered for in August's Theatron Music Summer in the Olympic Park's open-air theatre. The dramatic sounding Long Night of Museums is a dream for culture vultures, with over seventy museums and galleries staying open till 2am (October). Runners can get their hit also in October with the Munich Media Marathon, not a long-distance run for journos, but a twenty-six miler for one and all – over six thousand 'ordinary' runners took part in 2006.

EATING OUT

Munich is a city in which you can eat well (especially if you're not vegetarian), and in large quantities. The local specialities are meat and potatoes, with large dollops of cabbage on the side; you won't have trouble finding roast pork and dumplings or meatloaf and don't forget the local white veal sausage or weisswurst. The meat is invariably succulent, and cabbage is often adorned with the likes of juniper berries. Potatoes, meanwhile, have a tendency to evolve into soft and buttery dumplings. And sausage? Take your pick from over 1,500 recognised species. Other specialities include Schweinshaxe (knuckle of pork) or Leberkäs (meat and offal pâté). Eating out in Munich, or anywhere in Bavaria, is an experience in itself, with the distinctive background din of laughter, singing and the clinking of mugs of Bavarian Weissbier. It's famous for the Brauereigaststätten or brewery inns. When you've found your inn, be prepared for much noise, and don't be afraid to 'muck in' on a long bench, i.e. fall into conversation of a kind with fellow diners and drinkers. If that's not your idea of a good night out, then the many Italian restaurants in the city provide an excellent alternative. Most restaurants stay open until midnight or 1am. Service is included in the bill, but it's customary to leave an extra 10 per cent tip.

→ BAROQUE

Head west from the city for the baroque palace to beat all baroque palaces. The Schloss Nymphenburg – the Nymphs' Castle - was once the home of Bavaria's monarchs, and it boasts wondrous landscaping with canals, a gallery of thirty-six beautiful women, and a museum that includes 'mad' king Ludwig's coronation coach.

→ RING FIRST

If you want a night at the opera, then head to the National Theatre, right next to the Residenz. Modelled on a Greek temple, it specialises in the work of Wagner; in fact, it's where the great man actually made his name. He would have loved the latest version of the auditorium: its décor is sky blue, ivory, purple and gold.

→ PARK LIFE

Munich's most arguably famous sight is actually a few miles to the northwest of the city itself. The Olympic Park, and its iconic Olympic Tower, was built for the 1972 Games. The hills around the park aren't natural…they were made from rubble taken away from the city at the end of World War II.

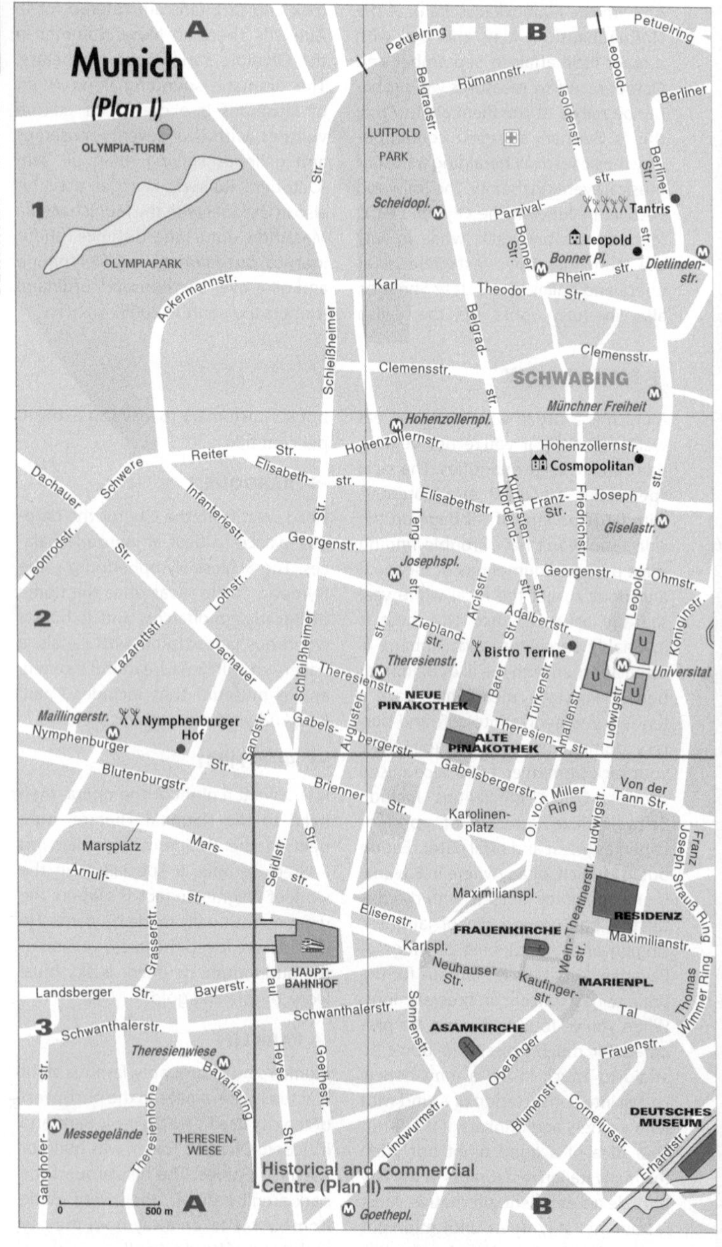
Munich
(Plan I)
A
B
1
2
3
OLYMPIA-TURM
OLYMPIAPARK
Petuelring
Rümannstr.
Belgradstr.
Isoldenstr.
Leopold-
Berliner
Berliner Str.
LUITPOLD PARK
Scheidopl.
Parzival-
str.
Tantris
Leopold
Bonner Str.
Bonner Pl.
Rhein-
Dietlinden-str.
Ackermannstr.
Karl
Theodor
Str.
Schleißheimer Str.
Belgrad-str.
Clemensstr.
SCHWABING
Münchner Freiheit
Hohenzollernpl.
Hohenzollernstr.
Cosmopolitan
Reiter
Schwere
Dachauer
Elisabeth-
str.
Elisabethstr.
Kurfürsten-Nordend-str.
Franz-Joseph Str.
Friedrichstr.
Giselastr.
Infanteriestr.
Leonrodstr.
Georgenstr.
Teng-str.
Josephspl.
Arcisstr.
Ohmstr.
Adalbertstr.
Königinstr.
Lothstr.
Ziebland-str.
Bistro Terrine
Universitat
Lazarettstr.
Theresienstr.
Barer Str.
Türkenstr.
Amalienstr.
Ludwigstr.
NEUE PINAKOTHEK
ALTE PINAKOTHEK
Augusten-str.
Maillingerstr.
Nymphenburger Hof
Nymphenburger Str.
Sandstr.
Gabels-bergerstr.
Theresien-str.
Blutenburgstr.
Brienner Str.
Gabelsbergerstr.
O. von Miller Ring
Von der Tann Str.
Karolinen-platz
Franz Joseph Strauß Ring
Marsplatz
Mars-
Arnulf-
str.
Seidlstr.
Maximilianspl.
Wein-Theatinerstr.
RESIDENZ
Elisenstr.
FRAUENKIRCHE
Maximilianstr.
Karlspl.
Neuhauser Str.
Kaufinger-str.
MARIENPL.
Grasserstr.
Paul
HAUPT-BAHNHOF
Landsberger Str.
Bayerstr.
Sonnenstr.
Tal
Thomas Wimmer Ring
Schwanthalerstr.
ASAMKIRCHE
Theresienwiese
Bavariaring
Heyse Str.
Goethestr.
Oberanger
Frauenstr.
Theresienhöhe
Messegelände
THERESIEN-WIESE
Lindwurmstr.
Blumenstr.
Corneliusstr.
DEUTSCHES MUSEUM
Erhardtstr.
Ganghofer-str.
Historical and Commercial Centre (Plan II)
0
500 m
Goethepl.

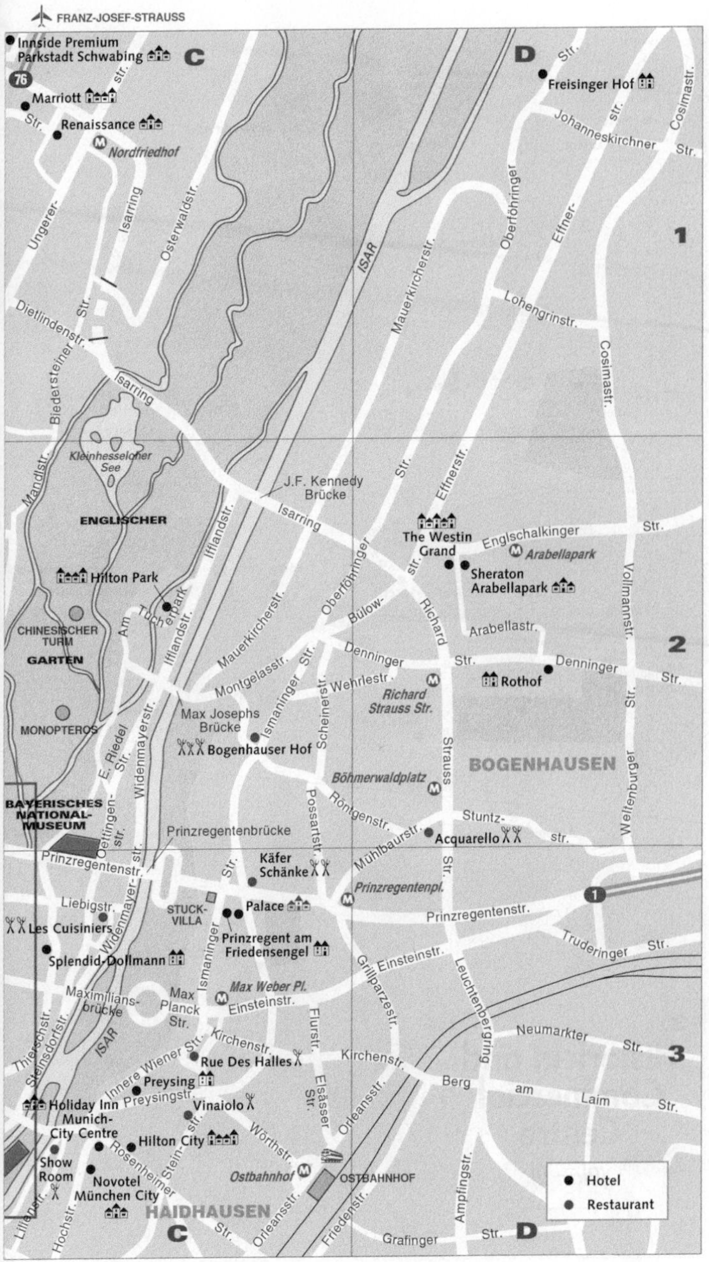
FRANZ-JOSEF-STRAUSS
Innside Premium Parkstadt Schwabing
Marriott
Renaissance
Nordfriedhof
Freisinger Hof
Johanneskirchner Str.
Cosimastr.
ISAR
Mauerkirchenstr.
Oberföhringer
Effner-
Lohengrinstr.
Ungerer-
Isarring
Osterwaldstr.
Dietlindenstr.
Biedersteiner Str.
Kleinhesselocher See
Mandlstr.
ENGLISCHER
GARTEN
J.F. Kennedy Brücke
The Westin Grand
Englschalkinger Str.
Arabellapark
Sheraton Arabellapark
Hilton Park
Tucherpark
Ifflandstr.
CHINESISCHER TURM
MONOPTEROS
Bülow-
Richard Strauss Str.
Arabellastr.
Denninger Str.
Rothof
Vollmannstr.
Montgelasstr.
Wehrlestr.
Max Josephs Brücke
Bogenhauser Hof
Ismaninger Str.
Scheinerstr.
BOGENHAUSEN
Böhmerwaldplatz
Weltenburger Str.
BAYERISCHES NATIONAL-MUSEUM
E. Riedel Str.
Widenmayerstr.
Oettingenstr.
Prinzregentenbrücke
Röntgenstr.
Possartstr.
Stuntzstr.
Acquarello
Mühlbaurstr.
Prinzregentenstr.
Käfer Schänke
Prinzregentenpl.
Liebigstr.
STUCK-VILLA
Palace
Les Cuisiniers
Prinzregent am Friedensengel
Splendid-Dollmann
Truderinger Str.
Einsteinstr.
Grillparzerstr.
Leuchtenbergring
Maximiliansbrücke
Max Planck Str.
Max Weber Pl.
Neumarkter Str.
Thierschstr.
Steinsdorfstr.
Kirchenstr.
Flurstr.
Innere Wiener Str.
Rue Des Halles
Berg am Laim Str.
Preysing
Preysingstr.
Holiday Inn Munich-City Centre
Vinaiolo
Elsässer Str.
Orleansstr.
Wörthstr.
Hilton City
Rosenheimer Str.
Show Room
Novotel München City
Stein-str.
Ostbahnhof
OSTBAHNHOF
Amptingstr.
Lilienstr.
Hochstr.
HAIDHAUSEN
Friedenstr.
Grafinger Str.
Hotel
Restaurant
C
D
1
2
3
76

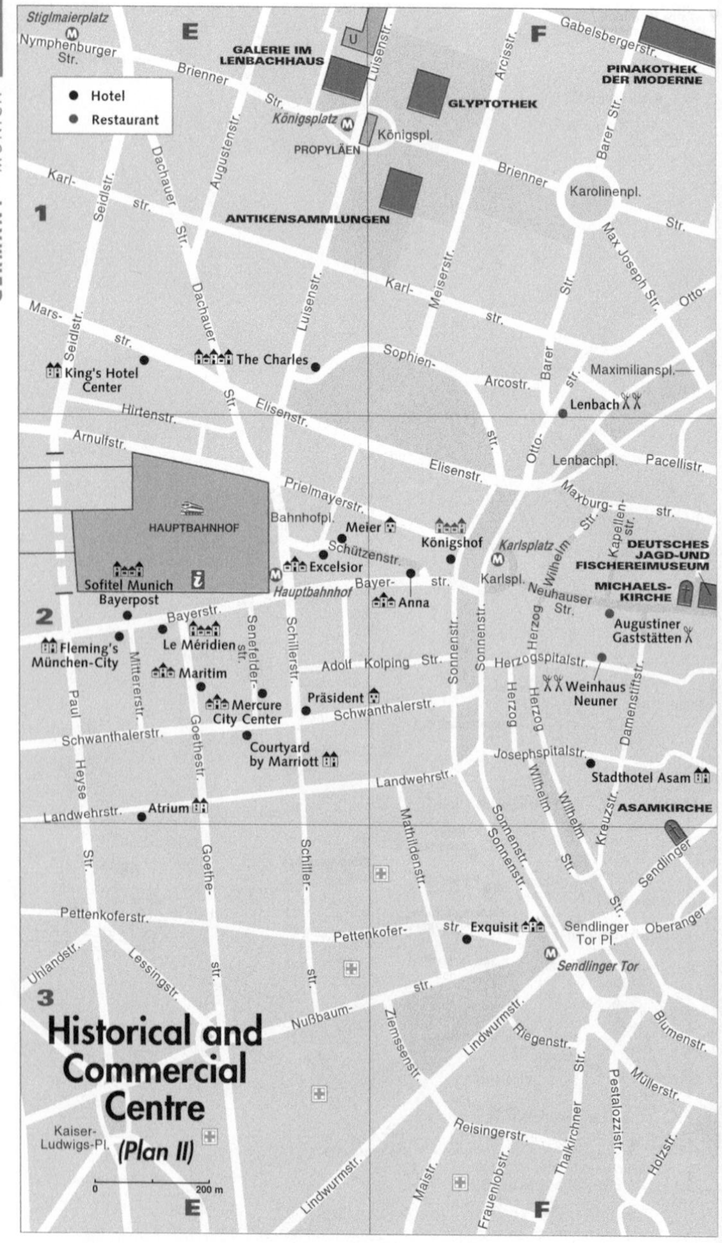
Historical and Commercial Centre (Plan II)
Hotel
Restaurant
GALERIE IM LENBACHHAUS
GLYPTOTHEK
PINAKOTHEK DER MODERNE
PROPYLÄEN
ANTIKENSAMMLUNGEN
HAUPTBAHNHOF
DEUTSCHES JAGD-UND FISCHEREIMUSEUM
MICHAELS-KIRCHE
ASAMKIRCHE
The Charles
King's Hotel Center
Lenbach
Meier
Königshof
Excelsior
Anna
Sofitel Munich Bayerpost
Le Méridien
Fleming's München-City
Maritim
Mercure City Center
Präsident
Courtyard by Marriott
Atrium
Augustiner Gaststätten
Weinhaus Neuner
Stadthotel Asam
Exquisit
Stiglmaierplatz
Königsplatz
Karlsplatz
Hauptbahnhof
Sendlinger Tor
0
200 m

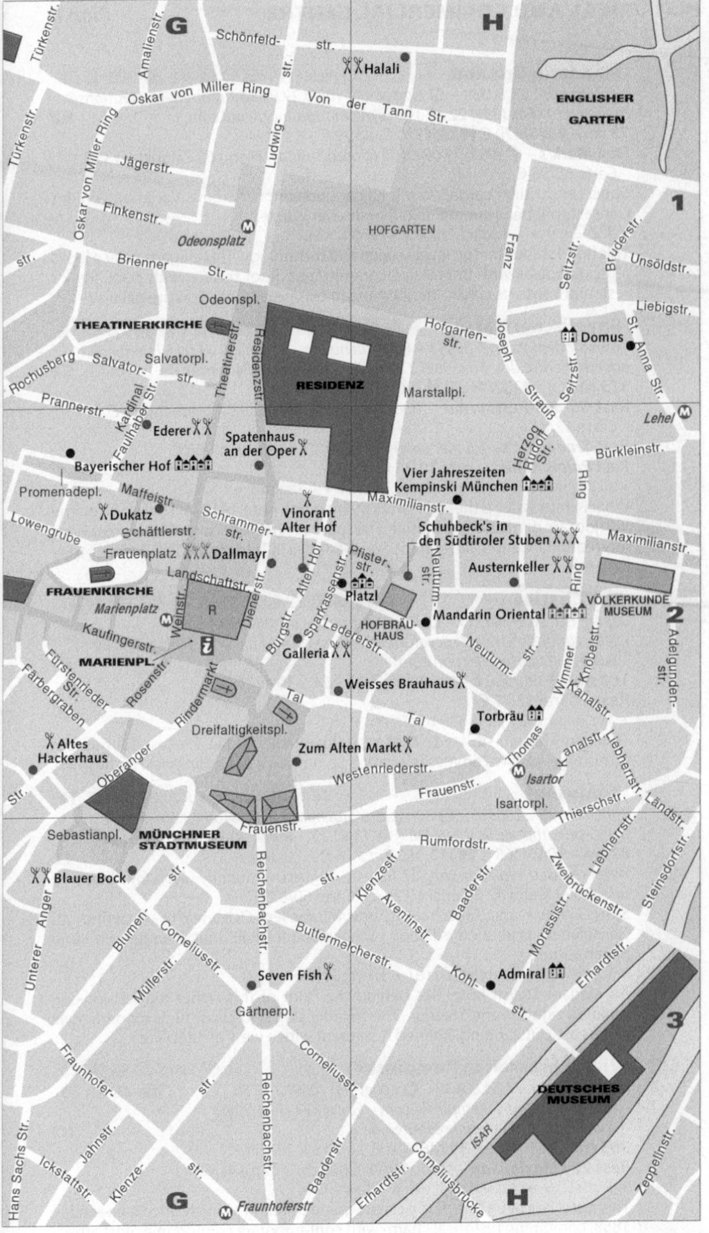
G
H
Schönfeld-str.
Halali
ENGLISHER GARTEN
Oskar von Miller Ring
Von der Tann Str.
Ludwig-str.
Türkenstr.
Amalienstr.
Jägerstr.
Finkenstr.
Oskar von Miller Ring
Odeonsplatz
HOFGARTEN
Brienner Str.
Franz Joseph Strauß Ring
Seitzstr.
Bruderstr.
Unsöldstr.
Liebigstr.
Odeonspl.
THEATINERKIRCHE
Hofgarten-str.
Domus
St. Anna Str.
Rochusberg
Salvatorpl.
Salvator-str.
Theatinerstr.
Residenzstr.
RESIDENZ
Marstallpl.
Prannerstr.
Kardinal Faulhaber Str.
Lehel
Ederer
Spatenhaus an der Oper
Herzog Rudolf Str.
Bürkleinstr.
Bayerischer Hof
Vier Jahreszeiten Kempinski München
Promenadepl.
Maffeistr.
Maximilianstr.
Dukatz
Schrammer-str.
Vinorant Alter Hof
Schuhbeck's in den Südtiroler Stuben
Lowengrube
Schäftlerstr.
Maximilianstr.
Frauenplatz
Dallmayr
Pfister-str.
Neuturm-str.
Austernkeller
Landschaftstr.
Dienerstr.
Alter Hof
Sparkassenstr.
Platzl
FRAUENKIRCHE
Marienplatz
Weinstr.
R
Mandarin Oriental
VÖLKERKUNDE MUSEUM
2
Kaufingerstr.
HOFBRÄU-HAUS
Ledererstr.
Burgstr.
Galleria
Neuturm-str.
Adelgunden-str.
MARIENPL.
Rosenstr.
Knöbelstr.
Fürstenrieder Str.
Färbergraben
Rindermarkt
Weisses Brauhaus
Kanalstr.
Wimmer
Tal
Tal
Torbräu
Dreifaltigkeitspl.
Altes Hackerhaus
Oberanger
Zum Alten Markt
Liebherrstr.
Thomas
Kanalstr.
Westenriederstr.
Isartor
Frauenstr.
Isartorpl.
Thierschstr.
Lärchstr.
Frauenstr.
Sebastianpl.
MÜNCHNER STADTMUSEUM
Rumfordstr.
Liebherrstr.
Blauer Bock
Reichenbachstr.
Klenzestr.
Baaderstr.
Zweibrückenstr.
Steinsdorfstr.
Unterer Anger
Blumen-str.
Corneliusstr.
Aventinstr.
Buttermelcherstr.
Morassistr.
Müllerstr.
Seven Fish
Kohl-str.
Admiral
Erhardtstr.
Gärtnerpl.
3
Fraunhofer-str.
Corneliusstr.
DEUTSCHES MUSEUM
Reichenbachstr.
ISAR
Hans Sachs Str.
Jahnstr.
Baaderstr.
Corneliusbrücke
Zeppelinstr.
Ickstattstr.
Klenze-str.
Erhardtstr.
Fraunhoferstr
H

HISTORICAL AND COMMERCIAL CENTRE *Plan II*

Mandarin Oriental
(heated)

Neuturmstr. 1 ✉ 80331 – Ⓜ Isartor – ☎ (089) 29 09 80 – momuc-reservations@mohg.com – Fax (089) 22 25 39 – www.mandarinoriental.com **H2**

73 rm – ♦325/470 € ♦♦395/520 €, ☕ 29 € – 8 suites

Rest *Mark's* – *☎ (089) 29 09 88 75 (closed Sunday)* Menu 65 € (lunch)/135 € – Carte 65/80 €

Spec. Langustinencarpaccio mit Kaviar und Limonencrème. Variation von der Gänsestopfleber. Hummer in orientalischer Würze.

♦ Palace ♦ Grand Luxury ♦ Modern ♦

This hotel stands for top level service and technology. This elegant palace looks after its guests with impressive commitment. Roof terrace with pool. Mark's restaurant with its classic Mediterranean cuisine is located on the gallery.

Bayerischer Hof

Promenadeplatz 2 ✉ 80333 – Ⓜ Marienplatz – ☎ (089) 2 12 00 – info@bayerischerhof.de – Fax (089) 2 12 09 06 – www.bayerischerhof.de **G2**

373 rm ☕ – ♦237/445 € ♦♦320/470 € – 16 suites

Rest *Garden-Restaurant* – *(booking advisable)* Menu 37 € (lunch)/76 € – Carte 52/81 €

Rest *Trader Vic's* – *(dinner only)* Menu 40/77 € – Carte 30/63 €

Rest *Palais Keller* – Carte 19/35 €

♦ Grand Luxury ♦ Traditional ♦ Classic ♦

What is impressive is the framework of this grand hotel of 1841. The rooms on the VIP floor are particularly exclusive. The spa area on three floors offers a great view. International Garden Restaurant. South Sea flair in Trader Vic's. Palais-Keller: truly Bavarian.

The Charles

Sophienstr. 28 ✉ 80333 – Ⓜ Hauptbahnhof – ☎ (089) 5 44 55 50 – reservations.charles@roccofortecollection.com – Fax (089) 54 45 55 20 00 – www.roccofortecollection.com **E1**

160 rm – ♦390/530 € ♦♦390/530 €, ☕ 26 € – 19 suites

Rest – Carte 42/77 €

♦ Grand Luxury ♦ Modern ♦

This luxury hotel is situated close to the old botanic garden. The tasteful, modern furnishings impart a timeless elegance. Some rooms have a fine view of the town.

Königshof

Karlsplatz 25 ✉ 80335 – Ⓜ Karlsplatz (Stachus) – ☎ (089) 55 13 60 – koenigshof@geisel-privathotels.de – Fax (089) 55 13 61 13 – www.geisel-privathotels.de

87 rm – ♦240/365 € ♦♦310/380 €, ☕ 26 € – 11 suites **F2**

Rest – *(closed 1 to 7 January, 27 July - 27 August and Sunday - Monday) (booking advisable)* Menu 42 € (lunch)/125 € – Carte 60/82 €

Spec. Gambas mit Artischocken und Mirabellen. Ochsenschwanzterrine mit Gänseleber und Petersilienöl. Schokoladenbiskuit mit Himbeeren und Sauerrahmeis.

♦ Luxury ♦ Traditional ♦ Elegant ♦

An elegant stylish hotel lies behind the front of this rather modest-looking building right on the Stachus. The friendly staff and classical or modern style rooms are outstanding. Refined restaurant with a view of Karlplatz.

Vier Jahreszeiten Kempinski

Maximilianstr. 17 ✉ 80539 – Ⓜ Lehel – ☎ (089) 2 12 50 – reservations.nvj@kempinski.com – Fax (089) 21 25 20 00 – www.kempinski-vierjahreszeiten.de **H2**

303 rm – ♦215/410 € ♦♦246/410 €, ☕ 34 € – 27 suites

Rest *Vue Maximilian* – Menu 59/98 € (lunch) – Carte 41/62 €

♦ Luxury ♦ Traditional ♦ Classic ♦

This hotel has been one of the classic grand hotels in Munich since it opened in 1858, combining historical charm with contemporary comfort in a most attractive way. Diners in the Vue Maximilian restaurant enjoy the view overlooking Maximilianstrasse.

Sofitel Munich Bayerpost

Bayerstr. 12 ✉ 80335 – Ⓜ Hauptbahnhof – ✆ (089) 59 94 80 – h5413@accor.com – Fax (089) 5 99 48 10 00 – www.sofitel.com **E2**

396 rm – †189/399 € ††189/399 €, ☕ 26 € – 14 suites

Rest – *(dinner only)* Carte 43/68 €

Rest *Suzie W.* – Carte 34/37 €

♦ Chain hotel ♦ Luxury ♦ Design ♦

This hotel with its beautiful sandstone facade is impressive with its generous framework. Tasteful avant-garde design, from the atrium lobby to the rooms. The restaurant offers an international menu. Suzie W. with its Asian-influenced cuisine.

Hilton Park

Am Tucherpark 7 ✉ 80538 – ✆ (089) 3 84 50 – info.munich@hilton.com – Fax (089) 38 45 25 88 – www.hilton.de *Plan I* **C2**

478 rm – †119/429 € ††144/429 €, ☕ 24 € – 3 suites

Rest *Tivoli & Club* – Carte 27/44 €

♦ Chain hotel ♦ Luxury ♦ Modern ♦

Besides being located on the Englischer Garten, the benefits of this hotel also include its contemporary, well-equipped rooms. Business and executive rooms also available.

Le Méridien

Bayerstr. 41 ✉ 80335 – Ⓜ Hauptbahnhof – ✆ (089) 2 42 20 – info.muenchen@lemeridien.com – Fax (089) 24 22 20 25 – www.lemeridien.com/munich

381 rm – †175/429 € ††175/429 €, ☕ 26 € – 9 suites **E2**

Rest – Carte 38/52 €

♦ Chain hotel ♦ Luxury ♦ Design ♦

Opposite the main station, this hotel offers a contemporary, understated ambience. The rooms are furnished in high-quality style. The restaurant looks onto the pleasant courtyard garden.

Excelsior

Schützenstr. 11 ✉ 80335 – Ⓜ Hauptbahnhof – ✆ (089) 55 13 70 – excelsior@geisel-privathotels.de – Fax (089) 55 13 71 21 – www.geisel-privathotels.de

114 rm – †150/285 € ††190/285 €, ☕ 18 € **E2**

Rest *Geisel's Vinothek* – *(closed Saturday lunch)* Menu 19 € (lunch)/38 € (dinner) – Carte 31/40 €

♦ Business ♦ Classic ♦

The rooms are individual and elegant in this hotel in the city centre. Guests can use the Königshof leisure area. Nice, rustic-style vinotheque offering a wide range of wines.

Maritim

Goethestr. 7 ✉ 80336 – Ⓜ Hauptbahnhof – ✆ (089) 55 23 50 – info.mun@maritim.de – Fax (089) 55 23 59 00 – www.maritim.de **E2**

339 rm – †159/307 € ††184/332 €, ☕ 20 € – 6 suites

Rest – Carte 27/47 €

♦ Business ♦ Functional ♦

Close to the Deutsches Theater, the Stachus and the Theresienwiese, with tastefully elegant rooms. The grill-room and bistro restaurants serve international cuisine.

Exquisit

Pettenkoferstr. 3 ✉ 80336 – Ⓜ Sendlinger Tor – ✆ (089) 5 51 99 00 – info@hotel-exquisit.com – Fax (089) 55 19 94 99 – www.hotel-exquisit.com **F3**

50 rm ☕ – †139/225 € ††175/275 € – 5 suites

Rest – *(closed 4 to 31 August and Saturday - Sunday) (lunch only)* Menu 13 € (buffet) – Carte 20/30 €

♦ Business ♦ Classic ♦

This hotel offers attentive service and is located near the Sendlinger Tor. It combines classical style and quality furnishings. Not far from the Sendlinger gate, this hotel provides stylish mahogany furnished rooms. Fine, comfortable suites also available.

Anna

Schützenstr. 1 ✉ 80335 – Ⓜ Karlsplatz (Stachus) – ✆ (089) 59 99 40 – anna@geisel-privathotels.de – Fax (089) 59 99 43 33 – www.geisel-privathotel.de **F2**

73 rm – 175/230 € 195/250 €

Rest – Carte 28/35 €

◆ Business ◆ Modern ◆

Modern design is what marks the atmosphere of this comfortable hotel, right on the Stachus. The rooms have state of the art technology, with panoramic views on the top floor. Bistro-style restaurant and sushi bar.

Mercure City Center

Senefelder Str. 9 ✉ 80336 – Ⓜ Hauptbahnhof – ✆ (089) 55 13 20 – h0878@accor.com – Fax (089) 59 64 44 – www.mercure.com **E2**

167 rm – 99/184 € 99/204 €, 17 €

Rest – Carte 29/43 €

◆ Chain hotel ◆ Modern ◆

Modern style and warm tones accompany the guest from the reception through to the well-equipped rooms of this hotel located close to the main railway station. Opening off the lobby, the restaurant features international fare.

Platzl

Sparkassenstr. 10 ✉ 80331 – Ⓜ Marienplatz – ✆ (089) 23 70 30 – info@platzl.de – Fax (089) 23 70 38 00 – www.platzl.de **G2**

167 rm – 125/190 € 200/236 €

Rest *Pfistermühle* – *(closed Sunday) (August dinner only)* Carte 32/47 €

Rest *Ayingers* – Carte 19/33 €

◆ Traditional ◆ Cosy ◆

Hotel in the centre of the Old Town, with rooms very successfully combining classic and modern style. Recreation area in the style of Ludwig II's Moorish Kiosk. Old Munich flair awaits you under the vaults of the Pfistermühle. Ayingers offers tavern tradition.

Stadthotel Asam without rest

Josephspitalstr. 3 ✉ 80331 – Ⓜ Sendlinger Tor – ✆ (089) 2 30 97 00 – info@hotel-asam.de – Fax (089) 23 09 70 97 – www.hotel-asam.de closed Christmas **F2**

25 rm – 125/158 € 169/189 €, 18 € – 8 suites

◆ Business ◆ Personalised ◆

A small hotel with a touch of luxury in the City Centre. The rooms are stylish and tasteful with very carefully chosen details.

Courtyard by Marriott

Schwanthalerstr. 27 ✉ 80336 – Ⓜ Hauptbahnhof – ✆ (089) 54 88 48 80 – Fax (089) 54 88 48 83 33 – www.coutyardmunichcitycenter.com **E2**

248 rm – 155 € 155 €, 19 €

Rest – Carte 23/38 €

◆ Business ◆ Modern ◆

Located in the city centre, not far from the railway station, is this hotel with contemporary rooms and studios aimed at business travellers. Good breakfast buffet.

Torbräu

Tal 41 ✉ 80331 – Ⓜ Isartor – ✆ (089) 24 23 40 – info@torbraeu.de – Fax (089) 24 23 42 35 – www.torbraeu.de closed Christmas **H2**

91 rm – 147/258 € 185/342 € – 3 suites

Rest *La Famiglia* – ✆ (089) 22 80 75 33 – Menu 41 € – Carte 35/44 €

◆ Traditional ◆ Classic ◆

Built in the 15C, this hotel must be the oldest in the city. Pleasant spacious rooms, all with air conditioning. Tuscan flair and Italian cuisine in the terracotta-tiled "La Famiglia".

Admiral without rest

Kohlstr. 9 ✉ 80469 – Ⓜ Isartor – ✆ (089) 21 63 50 – info@hotel-admiral.de – Fax (089) 29 36 74 – www.hotel-admiral.de **H3**

33 rm ☕ – 🚹170/220 € 🚹🚹200/250 €

◆ Business ◆ Functional ◆

Just a few minutes by foot from the City Centre this hotel has functional rooms, some of which are extremely quiet. In fine weather you can enjoy breakfast in the small garden.

King's Hotel Center without rest

Marsstr. 15 ✉ 80335 – ✆ (089) 51 55 30 – center@kingshotels.de – Fax (089) 51 55 33 00 – www.kingshotels.de **E1**

90 rm – 🚹99/140 € 🚹🚹140 €, ☕ 12 €

◆ Business ◆ Classic ◆

Centrally located hotel with inviting wooden lobby and comfortable rooms with four-poster beds.

Atrium without rest

Landwehrstr. 59 ✉ 80336 – Ⓜ Theresienwiese – ✆ (089) 51 41 90 – info@atrium-hotel.de – Fax (089) 53 50 66 – www.atrium-hotel.de **E2**

162 rm ☕ – 🚹84/329 € 🚹🚹114/359 €

◆ Business ◆ Functional ◆

Marble and mirrors welcome you into the lobby of this modern hotel. The rooms are furnished in natural wood with modern technical facilities. Lovely, small, leafy courtyard.

Splendid-Dollmann without rest

Thierschstr. 49 ✉ 80538 – Ⓜ Lehel – ✆ (089) 23 80 80 – splendid-muc@t-online.de – Fax (089) 23 80 83 65 – www.hotel-splendid-dollmann.de *Plan I* **C3**

36 rm – 🚹130/170 € 🚹🚹160/200 €, ☕ 13 €

◆ Traditional ◆ Personalised ◆

A 19C middle-class house with a stylish lobby, presented as a library; individually decorated rooms, some with antiques, and a pretty breakfast room with arched ceiling.

Fleming's München-City

Bayerstr. 47 ✉ 80335 – Ⓜ Hauptbahnhof – ✆ (089) 4 44 46 60 – muenchen-city@flemings-hotels.com – Fax (089) 4 44 46 69 99 – www.flemings-hotels.com **E2**

112 rm ☕ – 🚹108/175 € 🚹🚹133/210 €

Rest – Carte 19/41 €

◆ Business ◆ Modern ◆

Centrally located near the main railway station, this hotel offers functional, modern rooms. Bistro-style restaurant with bar and delicatessen.

Domus

St-Anna-Str.31 ✉ 80538 – Ⓜ Lehel – ✆ (089) 2 17 77 30 – reservation@domus-hotel.de – Fax (089) 2 28 53 59 – www.domus-hotel.de closed Christmas **H1**

45 rm ☕ – 🚹115/160 € 🚹🚹145/195 €

Rest *facile* – *✆ (089) 21 77 73 67 (closed Saturday lunch, Sunday and Bank Holidays)* Carte 26/36 €

◆ Business ◆ Functional ◆

Embedded between the Maximilianstrasse and Prinzregentenstrasse, this tastefully furnished establishment is ideal as a base from which to explore the town's art, culture and shopping. Modern atmosphere and Italian cuisine served.

Präsident without rest

Schwanthalerstr. 20 ✉ 80336 – Ⓜ Hauptbahnhof – ✆ (089) 5 49 00 60 – hotel.praesident@t-online.de – Fax (089) 54 90 06 28 – www.hotel-praesident.de **E2**

42 rm ☕ – 🚹79/209 € 🚹🚹95/299 €

◆ Business ◆ Functional ◆

The location of this fairly central hotel is ideal for theatre-goers and is diagonally opposite the Deutsche Theater. Contemporary rooms with light-coloured wooden furniture.

Meier without rest

Schützenstr. 12 ✉ 80335 – Ⓜ Hauptbahnhof – ✆ (089) 5 49 03 40 – info@hotel-meier.de – Fax (089) 5 49 03 43 40 – www.hotel-meier.de
closed 23 to 27 December **E2**
50 rm – ♦80/95 € ♦♦100/145 €
♦ Business ♦ Functional ♦
This multi-floored hotel between the main station and Stachus offers visitors uniform, functional rooms.

XXX ✿ **Schuhbeck's in den Südtiroler Stuben**

Platzl 6 ✉ 80331 – Ⓜ Isartor – ✆ (089) 2 16 69 00 – info@schuhbeck.de – Fax (089) 21 66 90 25 – www.schubeck.de
closed 2 weeks early January and Sunday - Monday lunch, Bank Holidays **H2**
Rest – Menu 73/118 €
Spec. Lauwarme Forelle mit Apfel-Ingwer und grünen Mandeln. Milchkalbsfilet in Bauernbrot mit Artischocken, Ofentomaten und Steinpilzen. Topfenpalatschinken mit eingelegten Süßkirschen und Sauerrahm-Hollerblüteneis.
♦ Regional ♦ Rustic ♦
At the heart of the gastronomic world of Alfons Schuhbeck are the Südtiroler Stuben in which regional cusine is served. Also on site is a wine bistro, chocolate and spice shop and ice cream parlour.

XXX ✿ **Dallmayr**

Dienerstr. 14 (1st floor) ✉ 80331 – Ⓜ Marienplatz – ✆ (089) 2 13 51 00 – gastro@dallmayr.de – Fax (089) 2 13 54 43 – www.dallmayr.de
closed 1 to 25 August and Sunday - Monday, Bank Holidays **G2**
Rest – *(booking advisable)* Menu 55 € (lunch)/115 € (dinner) – Carte 63/87 €
Spec. Jakobsmuscheln mit Chicorée und Nussbutterschaum. Steinbutt mit gefüllter Artischocke und Basilikum-Olivenölnage. Schokoladensoufflé mit eingelegten Blutorangen und Tahiti-Vanilleeis.
♦ Classic ♦ Elegant ♦
This well-known traditional delicatessen is located in the centre of Munich. On the first floor enjoy professional service and classic cuisine in a noble ambience.

XX **G**

Geyerstr. 52 (by Lindwurmstr. A 3 and Kapuzinerstr.) ✉ 80469 – ✆ (089) 74 74 79 99 – info@g-munich.de – Fax (089) 74 74 79 29 – www.g-munich.de
closed 23 December - 6 January, 21 to 24 March and Sunday - Monday
Rest – *(dinner only) (booking advisable)* Menu 100 € – Carte 60/79 €
♦ Inventive ♦ Fashionable ♦
A purist contemporary restaurant offering guests creative cuisine. Sit back on elegant leather-upholstered seats in the stylish lounge.

XX **Blauer Bock**

Sebastiansplatz 9 ✉ 80331 – Ⓜ Marienplatz – ✆ (089) 45 22 23 33 – mail@restaurant-blauerbock.de – Fax (089) 45 22 23 30 – www.restaurant-blauerbock.de
closed July - September Saturday dinner - Sunday and Bank Holidays **G3**
Rest – Menu 22 € (lunch)/72 € (dinner) – Carte 45/75 €
♦ International ♦ Minimalist ♦
Just a stone's throw from the Viktualienmarkt is this very modern, warm-coloured restaurant with its pleasant terrace. International French-based cuisine.

XX **Halali**

Schönfeldstr. 22 ✉ 80539 – Ⓜ Odeonsplatz – ✆ (089) 28 59 09 – halali-muenchen@t-online.de – Fax (089) 28 27 86 – www.halali-muenchen.de
closed Saturday lunch, Sunday and Bank Holidays **H1**
Rest – *(booking advisable)* Menu 22 € (lunch)/52 € – Carte 33/53 €
♦ International ♦ Cosy ♦
A historic 19th century guest house with a cosy, rustic-style restaurant, a favourite of many long-time guests.

XX

Ederer

Kardinal-Faulhaber-Str. 10 ✉ 80333 – Ⓜ Odeonsplatz – ✆ (089) 24 23 13 10 – restaurant-ederer@t-online.de – Fax (089) 24 23 13 12 – www.restaurant-ederer.de
closed 1 week Christmas and Sunday, Bank Holidays **G2**
Rest – *(booking advisable)* Menu 35 € (lunch)/65 € (dinner) – Carte 42/78 €
♦ International ♦ Fashionable ♦
A chic location for this restaurant with modern, stylish atmosphere. International cuisine. Nice inner courtyard dining.

XX

Austernkeller

Stollbergstr. 11 ✉ 80539 – Ⓜ Isartor – ✆ (089) 29 87 87 – Fax (089) 22 31 66 – www.austernkeller.de **H2**
Rest – *(dinner only) (booking advisable)* Carte 32/52 €
♦ Fish ♦ Cosy ♦
If your taste is for crustaceans and freshly-caught fruits de mer, try this listed cellar vault decorated with porcelain plates.

XX

Nymphenburger Hof

Nymphenburger Str. 24 ✉ 80335 – Ⓜ Maillingerstr. – ✆ (089) 1 23 38 30 – Fax (089) 1 23 38 52 – www.nymphenburgerhof.de
closed 24 December - 10 January and Saturday lunch, Sunday, Bank Holidays *Plan I* **A2**
Rest – *(booking advisable)* Menu 22 € (lunch) – Carte 31/54 €
♦ International ♦ Friendly ♦
This restaurant awaits you with its international range of dishes with an Austrian touch. Sitting on the terrace in front of the building is also nice.

XX

Lenbach

Ottostr. 6 ✉ 80333 – Ⓜ Karlsplatz (Stachus) – ✆ (089) 5 49 13 00 – info@lenbach.de – Fax (089) 54 91 30 75 – www.lenbach.de
closed Sunday and Bank Holidays **F1**
Rest – Carte 32/60 €
♦ Inventive ♦ Trendy ♦
The Lenbach Palais houses trend-setting gastronomy in a 2200-square metre space that was designed by Sir Terence Conran. The restaurant is a blend of modern and historic. Sushi bar.

XX

Galleria

Sparkassenstr. 11 (corner of Ledererstraße) ✉ 80331 – Ⓜ Marienplatz – ✆ (089) 29 79 95 – ristorantegalleria@yahoo.de – Fax (089) 2 91 36 53
closed Sunday except December **G2**
Rest – *(booking advisable)* Menu 25 € (lunch)/55 € – Carte 38/43 €
♦ Italian ♦ Rustic ♦
A small, cosy restaurant in the inner city with Italian cuisine. Temporary art displays in the dining area.

XX

Weinhaus Neuner

Herzogspitalstr. 8 ✉ 80331 – Ⓜ Karlsplatz (Stachus) – ✆ (089) 2 60 39 54 – info@weinhaus-neuner.de – Fax (089) 26 69 33 – www.weinhaus-neuner.de
closed Sunday and Bank Holidays **F2**
Rest – Menu 19 € (lunch)/40 € – Carte 29/45 €
♦ International ♦ Rustic ♦
As the "oldest wine bar" in Munich, this building dating back to 1852 stands out with its cross-shaped vaults and lovely wall paintings. International cuisine.

XX

Les Cuisiniers

Reitmorstr. 21 ✉ 80538 – Ⓜ Lehel – ✆ (089) 23 70 98 90 – Fax (089) 23 70 98 91 – www.lescuisiniers.de
closed Saturday lunch, Sunday - Monday lunch *Plan I* **C3**
Rest – Menu 36 € – Carte 29/37 €
♦ Mediterranean ♦ Bistro ♦
This friendly, bistro type restaurant is light with modern pictures adorning the walls. Uncomplicated Mediterranean cuisine.

Dukatz

Maffeistr. 3a (1st floor) ✉ 80333 – Ⓜ Marienplatz – ☎ (089) 7 10 40 73 73 – info@dukatz.de – Fax (089) 7 10 40 73 74 – www.dukatz.de
closed Sunday and Bank Holidays **G2**
Rest – *(booking advisable)* Carte 24/50 €
♦ French ♦ Bistro ♦
A pleasant atmosphere reigns in this bistro type restaurant in a central location on Salvadorplatz. French cuisine is served.

Show Room

Lilienstr. 6 ✉ 81669 – ☎ (089) 44 42 90 82 – info@show-room.info – Fax (089) 44 42 90 82 – www.show-room.info
closed 4 to 17 August, 24 to 30 December and Saturday, Sunday, Bank Holidays *Plan I* **C3**
Rest – *(dinner only) (booking advisable)* Menu 67/90 € – Carte 35/47 €
♦ Inventive ♦ Friendly ♦
The chef recommends his creative dishes to guests at the table in this small, modern restaurant.

Seven Fish

Gärtnerplatz 6 ✉ 80469 – Ⓜ Fraunhoferstr. – ☎ (089) 23 00 02 19 – info@seven-fish.de – Fax (089) 48 95 21 81 – www.sevenfish.de **G3**
Rest – Menu 40 € – Carte 32/50 €
♦ Fish ♦ Friendly ♦
Creative fish dishes prepared from quality produce and served by friendly staff in a modern atmosphere. A selection of Greek wines. More modest menu at lunch.

Vinorant Alter Hof

Alter Hof 3 ✉ 80331 – Ⓜ Marienplatz – ☎ (089) 24 24 37 33 – mail@alter-hof-muenchen.de – Fax (089) 24 24 37 34 – www.alter-hof-muenchen.de
closed Sunday and Bank Holidays dinner **G2**
Rest – Carte 21/35 €
♦ Regional ♦ Rustic ♦
At the former Wittelsbach residence, one of the oldest buildings in Munich, guests dine in two halls with attractive vaulted ceilings and simple modern decoration. Downstairs there is a vinotheque and bar.

Zum Alten Markt

Dreifaltigkeitsplatz 3 ✉ 80331 – Ⓜ Marienplatz – ☎ (089) 29 99 95 – lehner.gastro@zumaltenmarkt.de – Fax (089) 2 28 50 76 – www.zumaltenmarkt.de
closed Sunday and Bank Holidays **G2**
Rest – Menu 39 € – Carte 22/36 €
♦ Regional ♦ Cosy ♦
With lavish wood panelling in the style of a South Tyrolean councillor's office, part of which is authentic and over 400 years old, this establishment on the Viktualienmarkt has a very cosy atmosphere.

Spatenhaus an der Oper

Residenzstr. 12 ✉ 80333 – Ⓜ Marienplatz – ☎ (089) 2 90 70 60 – spatenhaus@kuffler.de – Fax (089) 2 91 30 54 – www.kuffler.de **G2**
Rest – Carte 23/44 €
♦ Bavarian specialities ♦ Traditional ♦
This town house, over 100 years old, houses a lovely rustic restaurant. The different rooms on the 1st floor are particularly cosy.

Weisses Brauhaus

Tal 7 ✉ 80331 – Ⓜ Isartor – ☎ (089) 2 90 13 80 – info@weisses-brauhaus.de – Fax (089) 29 01 38 15 – www.weisses-brauhaus.de **G2**
Rest – Carte 18/32 €
♦ Bavarian specialities ♦ Cosy ♦
This house in the Old Town, built around 1900, has a fine façade and cosy furnishings. The restaurant serves authentic regional specialities.

Augustiner Gaststätten

Neuhauser Str. 27 ✉ 80331 – Ⓜ Karlsplatz (Stachus) – ✆ (089) 23 18 32 57 – mail@augustiner-restaurant.com – Fax (089) 2 60 53 79 – www.augustiner-restaurant.com **F2**

Rest – Carte 16/37 €

◆ Bavarian specialities ◆ Inn ◆

Until 1885, beer was still brewed in the Augustinians' "headquarters" on the Neuhauser Strasse. An arcaded garden and a "Muschelsaal" are among the monuments of Munich's Art Nouveau period. Lovely beer garden.

Altes Hackerhaus

Sendlinger Str. 14 ✉ 80331 – Ⓜ Marienplatz – ✆ (089) 2 60 50 26 – hackerhaus@aol.com – Fax (089) 2 60 50 27 – www.hackerhaus.de **G2**

Rest – Carte 18/39 €

◆ Bavarian specialities ◆ Cosy ◆

The lovingly decorated rooms of this inn are really cosy with their rustic panelling and sturdy seating. Extremely pretty inner courtyard terrace. Good home cooking.

ENVIRONS *Plan I*

The Westin Grand

Arabellastr. 6 ✉ 81925 – Ⓜ Arabellapark – ✆ (089) 9 26 40 – grandhotel.muenchen@arabellasheraton.com – Fax (089) 92 64 86 99 – www.sheraton.com/grandmunich **D2**

629 rm – †138/478 € ††138/478 €, ☕ 27 € – 28 suites

Rest – *(closed Sunday) (lunch only)* Carte 28/39 €

Rest *Die Ente vom Lehel* – *(closed 2 weeks Easter, August, 25 December - 7 January and Sunday - Monday) (dinner only)* Menu 66/76 € – Carte 48/59 €

Rest *Paulaner's* – *(closed Saturday lunch, Sunday and Bank Holidays lunch)* Carte 22/43 €

◆ Chain hotel ◆ Grand Luxury ◆ Modern ◆

A luxurious hotel with an impressive lobby and large conference area. The top four floors convey an atmosphere of exclusivity, with the Towers rooms and their own lounge. A lively atmosphere welcomes you in the elegant Ente vom Lehel, which opens onto the foyer.

Marriott

Berliner Str. 93 ✉ 80805 – Ⓜ Nordfriedhof – ✆ (089) 36 00 20 – muenchen.marriott@marriotthotels.com – Fax (089) 36 00 22 00 – www.marriott.com/mucno **C1**

348 rm – †109/429 € ††109/429 €, ☕ 22 € – 14 suites

Rest – Carte 29/40 €

◆ Luxury ◆ Functional ◆

In this comfortable business hotel, with its generous rooms, you can look forward to a tasteful atrium-style lobby and comfortable, well-equipped rooms. Restaurant with large buffet and show kitchen.

Hilton City

Rosenheimer Str. 15 ✉ 81667 – ✆ (089) 4 80 40 – info.munich@hilton.com – Fax (089) 48 04 48 04 – www.hilton.de **C3**

480 rm – †99/219 € ††99/249 €, ☕ 24 € – 4 suites

Rest – Carte 25/44 €

◆ Chain hotel ◆ Functional ◆

This hotel is located centrally, next to the Philharmonie and Gasteig cultural centre. The contemporary functional rooms are particularly suited to business travellers. Rustic restaurant offering regional and international cuisine.

Palace

Trogerstr. 21 ✉ *81675 –* Ⓜ *Prinzregentenplatz –* ✆ *(089) 41 97 10 – palace@kuffler.de – Fax (089) 41 97 18 19 – www.muenchenpalace.de* **C3**

74 rm – †165/250 € ††205/295 €, ☕ 24 € – 3 suites

Rest – Carte 32/41 €

◆ Luxury ◆ Traditional ◆ Personalised ◆

This beautiful hotel is all about looking after the guests. The rooms are extremely comfortable, with Louis XVI style furniture. Pleasant garden and roof terrace. Timelessly elegant Palace restaurant.

Innside Premium Parkstadt Schwabing

Mies-van-der-Rohe-Str. 10 ✉ *80807 –* ✆ *(089) 35 40 80 – muenchen.schwabing@innside.de – Fax (089) 35 40 82 99 – www.innside.de* **C1**

160 rm – †173/459 € ††187/473 €, ☕ 16 €

Rest – *(closed Saturday lunch, Sunday lunch)* Carte 34/40 €

◆ Business ◆ Functional ◆

This modern building with its glass façade also features contemporary design on the inside. Rooms are well-equipped. Bistro style restaurant with interesting lighting. International cuisine served.

Renaissance

Theodor-Dombart-Str. 4 (corner of Berliner Straße) ✉ *80805 –* Ⓜ *Nordfriedhof –* ✆ *(089) 36 09 90 – rhi.mucbr.night.audit@renaissancehotels.com – Fax (089) 3 60 99 65 00 – www.marriott.com/mucbr* **C1**

261 rm – †155/179 € ††155/179 €, ☕ 21 € – 40 suites

Rest – Carte 20/39 €

◆ Chain hotel ◆ Modern ◆

Close to the English Garden. Comfortable rooms and elegant suites offer a high level of quality. Relax in the "Oasis of Rest". Modern bistro in Mediterranean colours. International cuisine with emphasis on the Mediterranean.

Novotel München City

Hochstr. 11 ✉ *81669 –* ✆ *(089) 66 10 70 – h3280@accor.com – Fax (089) 66 10 79 99 – www.novotel.com* **C3**

307 rm – †99/169 € ††122/192 €, ☕ 17 €

Rest – Carte 23/46 €

◆ Chain hotel ◆ Modern ◆

The well-equipped rooms of this business hotel are presented in pleasant tones and with smart design, some with a lovely view of the inner city. Light, contemporary restaurant.

Holiday Inn Munich - City Centre

Hochstr. 3 ✉ *81669 –* ✆ *(089) 4 80 30 – hi.muenchen@whgen.com – Fax (089) 4 48 82 77 – www.holidayinn.de* **C3**

582 rm – †169/329 € ††169/329 €, ☕ 20 €

Rest – Menu 22 € (buffet)

◆ Chain hotel ◆ Functional ◆

A modern hotel designed for conference visitors, with a comfortable setting, functional rooms and a 2100 m² conference area. A colourful, Mediterranean-style bistro with a rustic-style pub.

Sheraton Arabellapark

← Munich,

Arabellastr. 5 ✉ *81925 –* Ⓜ *Arabellapark –* ✆ *(089) 9 23 20 – bogenhausen@arabellastarwood.com – Fax (089) 92 32 44 49 – www.sheraton.com/bogenhausen* **D2**

446 rm – †175/328 € ††175/328 €, ☕ 20 € – 61 suites

Rest – Carte 32/58 €

◆ Business ◆ Modern ◆

This high rise building near the English Garden offers a comfortable ambience and fantastic view. A clean, modern, multifunctional style sets the scene here. Restaurant serving international cuisine.

Cosmopolitan without rest
Hohenzollernstr. 5 ✉ 80801 – Ⓜ Münchner Freiheit – ✆ (089) 38 38 10 – cosmo@cosmopolitan-hotel.de – Fax (089) 38 38 11 11 – www.cosmopolitan-hotel.de B2
71 rm ☕ – 🚹120/175 € 🚹🚹130/185 €
♦ Business ♦ Modern ♦
Two annexed houses in the heart of Schwabing provide modern rooms with functional furnishings and modern, technical equipment.

Prinzregent am Friedensengel without rest
Ismaninger Str. 42 ✉ 81675 – Ⓜ Prinzregentenplatz – ✆ (089) 41 60 50 – friedensengel@prinzregent.de – Fax (089) 41 60 54 66 – www.prinzregent.de
closed 23 December - 5 January C3
65 rm ☕ – 🚹139/219 € 🚹🚹164/244 €
♦ Traditional ♦ Cosy ♦
This hotel, with its comfortable Alpine-style rooms is just five minutes from the Englischer Garten. Breakfast room with fine settings and conservatory.

Freisinger Hof
Oberföhringer Str. 189 ✉ 81925 – ✆ (089) 95 23 02 – office@freisinger-hof-de – Fax (089) 9 57 85 16 – www.freisinger-hof.de D1
51 rm ☕ – 🚹115/125 € 🚹🚹145 €
Rest – Carte 27/50 €
♦ Family ♦ Cosy ♦
This old tavern from 1875 has been extended with a hotel annex. Look forward to good, homely country-style rooms. Regional dishes offered in a cosy rustic ambience. Nice garden.

Preysing without rest
Preysingstr. 1 ✉ 81667 – ✆ (089) 45 84 50 – info@hotel-preysing.de – Fax (089) 45 84 54 44 – www.hotel-preysing.de
closed 22 December - 6 January C3
62 rm ☕ – 🚹138/210 € 🚹🚹189/265 € – 5 suites
♦ Family ♦ Functional ♦
The attention to detail in these rooms furnished in modern pale wood furniture makes them comfortable and welcoming. Attractive also is the bright breakfast room with a generous buffet.

Rothof without rest
Denninger Str. 114 ✉ 81925 – Ⓜ Richard-Strauss-Str. – ✆ (089) 9 10 09 50 – reservierung@rothof-muc.de – Fax (089) 91 50 66 – www.hotel-rothof.de
closed 22 December - 6 January D2
37 rm ☕ – 🚹126/146 € 🚹🚹168/212 €
♦ Family ♦ Functional ♦
The well-run hotel offers light, spacious rooms with large windows and modern facilities - some looking onto the park.

Leopold
Leopoldstr. 119 ✉ 80804 – Ⓜ Dietlindenstr. – ✆ (089) 36 04 30 – hotel-leopold@t-online.de – Fax (089) 36 04 31 50 – www.hotel-leopold.de
closed 23 to 28 December B1
63 rm ☕ – 🚹105/159 € 🚹🚹128/195 €
Rest – Carte 20/29 €
♦ Family ♦ Classic ♦
Traditional family hotel with a wide range of rooms in various styles. Ask for a room with a view of the beautiful garden.

Tantris

Johann-Fichte-Str. 7 ✉ 80805 – Ⓜ Dietlindenstr. – ☎ (089) 3 61 95 90 – info@tantris.de – Fax (089) 36 19 59 22 – www.tantris.de
closed 1 to 13 January and Sunday - Monday, Bank Holidays **B1**
Rest – *(booking advisable)* Menu 62 € (lunch)/120 € – Carte 69/108 €
Spec. Sepioline mit lauwarmem Eigelb gefüllt. Marinierte Scheiben vom Spanferkelrücken mit Räucheraal und Dörrpflaumen. Mousse und leicht gelierte Suppe von Champagner mit Walderdbeeren und Litchisorbet.
♦ Classic ♦ Retro ♦
In an elegant setting with a 1970s style, Hans Haas offers classic cuisine with a personal touch. Competent and pleasant service.

Bogenhauser Hof

Ismaninger Str. 85 ✉ 81675 – ☎ (089) 98 55 86 – info@bogenhauser-hof.de – Fax (089) 9 81 02 21 – www.bogenhauser-hof.de
closed 24 December - 7 January, 21 to 30 March and Sunday, Bank Holidays **C2**
Rest – *(booking advisable)* Menu 74 € – Carte 43/70 €
♦ Classic ♦ Rustic ♦
This hunting lodge dating from 1825 is a classic of Munich gastronomy. Superior classical cuisine, which can also be enjoyed in the idyllic summer garden.

Acquarello (Mario Gamba)

Mühlbaurstr. 36 ✉ 81677 – Ⓜ Böhmerwaldplatz – ☎ (089) 4 70 48 48 – info@acquarello.com – Fax (089) 47 64 64 – www.acquarello.com
closed 1 to 3 January and Saturday lunch, Sunday, Bank Holidays lunch **D2**
Rest – Menu 29 € (lunch)/88 € – Carte 41/80 €
Spec. Vitello Tonnato. Feigentortelli mit Gänseleber und Cassissauce. Von Kopf bis Fuß vom Kalb.
♦ Italian ♦ Friendly ♦
Large wall paintings underline the Mediterranean ambience of this restaurant. Guests are served classic Italian cuisine by friendly staff.

Käfer Schänke

Prinzregentenstr. 73 ✉ 81675 – Ⓜ Prinzregentenplatz – ☎ (089) 4 16 82 47 – kaeferschaenke@feinkost-kaefer.de – Fax (089) 4 16 86 23 – www.feinkost-kaefer.de
closed Sunday and Bank Holidays **C3**
Rest – *(booking essential)* Carte 47/75 €
♦ Classic ♦ Cosy ♦
The restaurant is comfortable, and the small rooms have been lovingly decorated, from the "Cutlery Parlour" to the "Tobacco Parlour".

Acetaia

Nymphenburger Str. 215 (A 2) ✉ 80639 – ☎ (089) 13 92 90 77 – info@restaurant-acetaia.de – Fax (089) 13 92 90 78 – www.restaurant-acetaia.de
closed Saturday lunch
Rest – Menu 25 € (lunch)/62 € – Carte 39/50 €
♦ Italian ♦ Cosy ♦
A friendly atmosphere prevails in this restaurant, with its tasteful art nouveau décor, serving Italian and Mediterranean dishes.

Terrine

Amalienstr. 89 (Amalien-Passage) ✉ 80799 – Ⓜ Universität – ☎ (089) 28 17 80 – geniessen@terrine.de – Fax (089) 2 80 93 16 – www.terrine.de
closed 1 to 9 January and Saturday lunch, Sunday - Monday, Bank Holidays **B2**
Rest – Menu 23 € (lunch)/69 € (dinner) – Carte 52/58 €
Spec. Lauwarmer Donau Lachs mit Lauch und Kartoffelnudeln. Rinderfilet und Ochsenschwanzragout mit Rotweinzwiebeln. Passionsfruchtmousse mit Gewürzkaffee-Espuma und weißem Schokoladeneis.
♦ Seasonal cuisine ♦ Bistro ♦
In this bistro with an art nouveau touch, contemporary, seasonal dishes are served. At lunchtimes there is a cheaper à la carte menu.

Rue Des Halles
Steinstr. 18 ✉ 81667 – Ⓜ Max Weber Platz – ✆ (089) 48 56 75 – Fax (089) 44 45 10 76
C3
Rest – *(dinner only) (booking advisable)* Menu 37/52 € – Carte 27/46 €
♦ French ♦ Bistro ♦
Experience the typical French flair of this town house restaurant in the bistro style, with both classic and regional French dishes on the menu.

Vinaiolo
Steinstr. 42 ✉ 81667 – Ⓜ Ostbahnhof – ✆ (089) 48 95 03 56 – Fax (089) 48 06 80 11 – www.vinaiolo.de
closed Saturday lunch
C3
Rest – Menu 48 € – Carte 42/49 €
♦ Italian ♦ Friendly ♦
A restaurant styled as a colonial warehouse. The wines are displayed in original cabinets from the former apothecary. Italian cuisine.

AT THE EXHIBITION CENTRE

Innside Premium Neue Messe
Humboldtstr. 12 (Industrialpark-West) ✉ 85609 – ✆ (089) 94 00 50 – muenchen@innside.de – Fax (089) 94 00 52 99 – www.innside.de
closed 20 December - 3 January
134 rm – 🛉149/429 € 🛉🛉160/459 €, ☕ 16 €
Rest – *(closed Saturday lunch, Sunday lunch)* Carte 29/35 €
♦ Business ♦ Modern ♦
Modern design stays with you from the airy atrium-style lobby to the friendly rooms – the freestanding glass showers here are originals. Bistro-style restaurant with international cuisine.

Schreiberhof
Erdinger Str. 2 ✉ 85609 – ✆ (089) 90 00 60 – info@schreiberhof.de – Fax (089) 90 00 64 59 – www.schreiberhof.de
87 rm ☕ – 🛉78/177 € 🛉🛉98/188 €
Rest *Alte Gaststube* – Carte 25/39 €
♦ Family ♦ Classic ♦
An upgraded former hotel with spacious, contemporary, functional rooms. The light-filled conservatory is available for meetings. Delicious international and regional dishes are served in the cosy Alte Gaststube.

Prinzregent an der Messe
Riemer Str. 350 ✉ 81829 – ✆ (089) 94 53 90 – messe@prinzregent.de – Fax (089) 94 53 95 66 – www.prinzregent.de
closed 23 December - 4 January
91 rm ☕ – 🛉139/159 € 🛉🛉169/189 € – 4 suites
Rest – Menu 33/49 € – Carte 35/44 €
♦ Traditional ♦ Classic ♦
Near the exhibition centre, this hotel is an 18th century building with a modern extension. The tasteful, comfortable rooms and leisure area are attractive. The cosy restaurant is located in the historical part of the building.

Novotel München Messe
Willy-Brandt-Platz 1 ✉ 81829 – ✆ (089) 99 40 00 – h5563@accor.com – Fax (089) 99 40 01 00 – www.novotel.com
278 rm – 🛉85/155 € 🛉🛉95/165 €, ☕ 17 €
Rest – Menu 25 € – Carte 25/44 €
♦ Chain hotel ♦ Business ♦ Modern ♦
Located in the former airport grounds next to the conference centre, this hotel features modern décor from the spacious lobby to the rooms. Light, friendly restaurant with glass frontage.

AT THE AIRPORT

Kempinski Airport München

Terminalstraße Mitte 20 ✉ 85356 Munich
– ✆ (089) 9 78 20 – info@kempinski-airport.de – Fax (089) 97 82 26 10
– www.kempinski-airport.de
389 rm – †165/465 € ††165/465 €, ☕ 26 € – 46 suites
Rest – Menu 26 € – Carte 22/52 €
Rest *Safran* – *(closed August and Sunday - Monday) (dinner only)* Menu 43/79 € – Carte 44/63 €

♦ Business ♦ Functional ♦

Designed by leading architect Helmut Jahn, this hotel is a massive building with a glass atrium, with ever-changing lighting in the evenings. All extremely functional and generous. Enjoy Thai and Mediterranean food in the Safran restaurant.

STUTTGART

STUTTGART

Population: 589,170 – Altitude: 245m

R. Brayan/Arcaid/CORBIS

Baden-Württemberg, in Germany's south west, is one of the country's most popular tourist destinations, defined by superb castles, delectable resorts, and renowned wine-growing areas. The capital of the region, Stuttgart, sits easily within this framework. Its valley location, surrounded by steeply rising slopes, has allowed vineyards to approach the city centre from all around: the twisting branches of grapes are as much a part of the inner city picture as the sleek museums for Mercedes or Porsche.

There's an enviable amount of open space in Stuttgart. Parks, forests and orchards cover more than half of its area. It seems appropriate that the city started life as a horse stud farm in the tenth century, growing to become Germany's most prosperous metropolis by way – incongruously or not - of its association with the world's sleekest cars. This is also a city of fine squares, majestic palaces, architecturally diverse buildings and cultural vigour. Three years ago a spectacular glass cube announced itself as the city's new museum of art, while theatre, ballet and opera are housed together in the largest 'three function' building in Europe. Meanwhile, many visitors keep an eye open for Stuttgart's Beer Festival, which gives Munich's Oktoberfest a run for its money.

LIVING THE CITY

Stuttgart is enviably situated amongst picturesque hills. It's surrounded on three sides by wooded elevations, while to the east it's open to the river **Neckar.** The old town is bounded to the east by the district of **Obertürkheim**, a popular destination as it's the home of the Mercedes-Benz Museum. The city is in the heart of Germany's most scenic state (with the possible exception of Bavaria), and to its northwest lies Heidelberg, and to its west is Baden-Baden.

PRACTICAL INFORMATION

ARRIVAL-DEPARTURE

The Airport is 13km south of the city centre. S-Bahn commuter trains S2 and S3 run to Central Station in 30min, while a taxi will cost around € 20.

TRANSPORT

There's an impressively integrated public transport system in Stuttgart, which covers nearby towns as well as the city itself. Once you've bought a ticket, you can switch between buses, trams, U-Bahns, and mainline and S-Bahn trains.

There are three types of ticket you might need. If you're only in town for a short time, buy a day ticket. If you're around for longer, invest in either a city explorer Stuttcard or Stuttcard plus; these give free admission to most museums, reduced entry to theatres, and free travel on public transport for three days, including transport to the airport (the Stuttcard plus is more expensive, but offers a few more benefits).

EXPLORING STUTTGART

Stuttgart breathes well-being and good living. Even its neighbours are of the very top drawer, in the shape of nearby Heidelberg and Baden-Baden. It's a city that was always favoured by the local bigwigs, becoming first ducal, then royal, capital of Württemberg. Its beautiful position, cosseted by rolling hills, may have had something to do with this, but the local hierarchy of the past would have been bamboozled at the source of Stuttgart's current success: fast cars. Both Mercedes-Benz and Porsche have made their names in this city, and both manufacturers boast slinky museums devoted to their pride and joy.

→ SQUARE DEAL

Visitors here invariably make for **Schlossplatz,** the imposing square at the centre of the city. Its huge dimensions are breath-taking, especially when you take in the proportions of the vast **Neues Schloss**, the palace that eats up the whole of the square's east side. It was the last Baroque castle-residence to be built in Germany, and its construction lasted throughout much of the eighteenth century's latter half. The idea was to make it a second Versailles, and a pretty good job they made of it. The only part you can visit are the cellars, but it's worth it to see the **Römisches Lapidarium**, a collection of Roman stone fragments dating back to 200AD. The grandeur of the square extends still further: opposite the Neues Schloss is **Königsbau**, a fine Neo-Classical structure from the mid-nineteenth century, which has been turned to modern day use by lining it with glitzy shops.

→ STATE OF PERFECTION

You get a clue to Stuttgart's cultural import a short stroll from Schlossplatz, by arriving at the nineteenth century **Staatsgalerie**, or Old State Gallery. Reckoned to be one of the top art museums in the country, it boasts a fantastic collection of old masters and a fascinating inventory of graphics, which includes illustrated books, posters and photographs. Its stature was enhanced in 1984 when a dazzling new extension was added – the New State Gallery – which contains works from the twentieth century by the likes of Modigliani, Picasso and Beuys. This is now one of Germany's most visited museums, but its status has been challenged in the past couple of years by the new kid on the block, The **Kunstmuseum,** just off Schlossplatz. Maybe that should read the new *block* on the block, because this twenty first century upstart is in the shape of a cube made of glass, and even if you don't intend going in, you'll want to stop and look at it. It features the work of German artists, including Otto Dix and Swabian Impressionists, and its hidden tunnels of art are an unexpected delight for the first-time visitor.

→ SCHILL-OUT ZONE

You only have to cross the smart shopping street, **Königstrasse,** to indulge in a bit more of Stuttgart's cultural scene. On the beautiful **Schillerplatz**, the remains of a fourteenth century castle were given a sixteenth century makeover, and the **Altes Schloss** got its Renaissance look with atmospheric arcaded cloisters encircling a spooky inner courtyard. You might not expect to find a museum here, but this is the home of the **Württembergisches Landesmuseum**, which has an eclectic mix of Italian sculptures, Renaissance curios, and – on the top floor – the nineteenth century crown jewels.

Hang around a bit on Schillerplatz. It's the city's one example of a truly historic square, as it was here that the stud farm that gave Stuttgart its name is said to have stood. It's surrounded by historic buildings: apart from the Altes Schloss, there's the sixteenth century **Old Chancellery**, which is now a restaurant; a **gabled granary**, also from the sixteenth century, where you can find a museum of musical instruments and the elegant seventeenth century **Prinzenbau**.

→ GET YOUR MOTOR RUNNING

You often read about somewhere being a 'city of contrasts', but in Stuttgart they really mean it. To the east of the centre, away from the charms of the past, lies the roaring glory of the **Mercedes-Benz Museum**, a must for petrol-heads. Here you can see the first cars in the world, Carl Benz's three-wheeled automobile from 1886, and Gottlieb Daimler's horseless carriage. There are over seventy vehicles on display, all in mint condition, from the earliest models to today's state-of-the-art cars. One of the most impressive exhibits is the Blitzen Benz, which was driven at 228mph to set the world record at Daytona Beach nearly one hundred years ago. Of course, where there's Merc, there's **Porsche,** and Stuttgart's other legendary car manufacturer has its own museum, too, ranging from the 356 Roadster of 1948 to the latest models. In Autumn 2008 a spectacular new Porsche Museum opens in the city, and it promises to be even more comprehensive than its predecessor.

If you like to see a play, or you're a bit partial to the opera or the ballet, it's possible to combine all three at Stuttgart's **State Theatre**. It's big enough and it's bold enough to house all three within the same premises, either in the **Playhouse** or the **Opera house.** The foyer, with its busts of writers and composers, is an imposing place to gather, and there should be a special buzz about the place next year (2009) as it's the hundredth anniversary of the theatre's construction.

→ GREEN U-TURN

Stuttgart cherishes its verdant surroundings. Not only swathed in hills and vineyards, it also boasts an enviable amount of parks and green space. In fact, this has a collective name, The Green U, named after the rough shape this 'natural trail' takes. It's eight kilometres in length, starting at the Schlossplatz, and heading away via magnificent gardens (the Schlossgarten) north of Neues Schloss, before taking in the glorious Rosenstein Park, with its lake, rose garden, grand old trees, and showy Schloss Rosenstein, the former country house of the Württemberg kings. If it sounds rather idyllic from ground level, get bird's eye confirmation by heading nearly 220m up the city's famous TV Tower. Now over fifty years old, it stands on top of a wooded hill, and from either its observation platform or crows nest café you can indulge uninterrupted, jaw-dropping views of Stuttgart, the vineyards of the Neckar Valley, the Black Forest and the Alps.

CALENDAR HIGHLIGHTS

As the home to two of the world's most famous marques, it's not surprising that Stuttgart should honour the motor car. It does this in March with Retroclassics (at the Messe Stuttgart), which is a show full of vintage favourites, such as Aston Martins, Rolls Royces and Porsches, alongside a 'history of classic cars' exhibit. A month earlier, the year gets a stately opening with the Stuttgart Bach Week, at the Liederhalle, during which international artists celebrate the great man's music over a ten-day festival. The art world comes to the fore in March with Long Art Night at the Staatsgalerie: the idea is to enjoy an evening meal, then head to the museum and get into the unique experience of taking on Picasso and Munch till the midnight hour. The coming of summer is a good time to be a beer drinker in this city. The Stuttgart Spring Beer Festival (April/May), at Cannstatter Wasen, is a three-week ale celebration, with the distraction of hot-air balloon flights and fireworks. July sees three big events. Schlossplatz hosts the Viva

STUTTGART IN...

→ ONE DAY

Schlossplatz, Staatsgalerie, Mercedes-Benz Museum

→ TWO DAYS

Kunstmuseum, Altes Schloss, amble through Schlossgarten, Porsche Museum, State Theatre Stuttgart

→ THREE DAYS

Stroll in Rosenstein park, outing to Heidelberg or Baden-Baden

AfroBrasil Festival, Europe's biggest and longest-running Latino event, with samba, salsa, reggae and funk, while the Jazz Open features many international artists giving it their all for a week at the Liederhalle or on the adjacent open-air stage. Meanwhile, the Stuttgart Christopher Street Day parade is a gay pride event lasting a week, with special events running alongside stage and cabaret shows. The elegant Summer Festival (August) shimmers across three days of white pavilions, fairy lights and lanterns, with music, food and entertainment keeping thousands happy outside Neues Schloss and the Opera House. The grape and the grain hit the forefront again with the city's final two big festivals of the year. The Stuttgarter Weindorf (Aug/Sep) attracts a million wine lovers to the Marktplatz and Schlossplatz for twelve days of serious imbibing. Fifty local wineries create the famous "wine village", with over one hundred lovingly-decorated arbours. A month later, the Stuttgart Beer Festival at Cannstatter Wasen has almost two hundred years of history behind it. 'Fleshed out' with a giant Ferris wheel and numerous fairground attractions, it's the world's second biggest beer extravaganza, behind Munich's Oktoberfest.

EATING OUT

Württemberg's viniculture has a tradition of more than a thousand years and the most popular variety amongst the locals is the ruby red Trollinger. You might be surprised how it's served to you: in quarter litre glasses with handles. You won't be surprised that the 'Schwäbische Weinstuben' (local wine taverns) are rollicking good places to go. Beer is a flourishing trade too, with large Stuttgart breweries vying for your palate. That's not to say that food takes a back seat. On the contrary, this south western city isn't far from the French border, and prides itself on accomplished French inspired menus. Italian restaurants, and lots of them, jostle for position as well. There's a renowned 'local kitchen', with *Gaisburger Marsch* the pick of the dishes: it's a tasty stew made of *Spätzle* (the staple Stuttgart noodle), potatoes, beef pieces, vegetables, broth and roasted onions. *Spätzles* turn up everywhere, and are very popular *'mit Linsen* (lentils), especially when they're teamed up and served with warm sausages, or accompanying a Swabian roast, another hearty dish featuring roasted slices of beef with lots of roasted onions, served with Sauerkraut and *Maultaschen* (square dumplings with a savoury filling). There's an impressive range of international restaurants in the city, so if you want to eat good cuisine from beyond European borders, you won't have a problem. Prices include service, but it's usual to leave a tip of around ten per cent of the bill.

→ NATURAL MAGNETISM

Plant and animal lovers in Stuttgart will want to head for the Wilhelma, Europe's largest zoological/botanical gardens. Not only can you gaze at more than ten thousand animals, you can also take in the glory of rare orchids, a large magnolia grove, and all kinds of exotic plants. It can get rather crowded: nearly two million visitors turn up each year, so be prepared to have your space invaded.

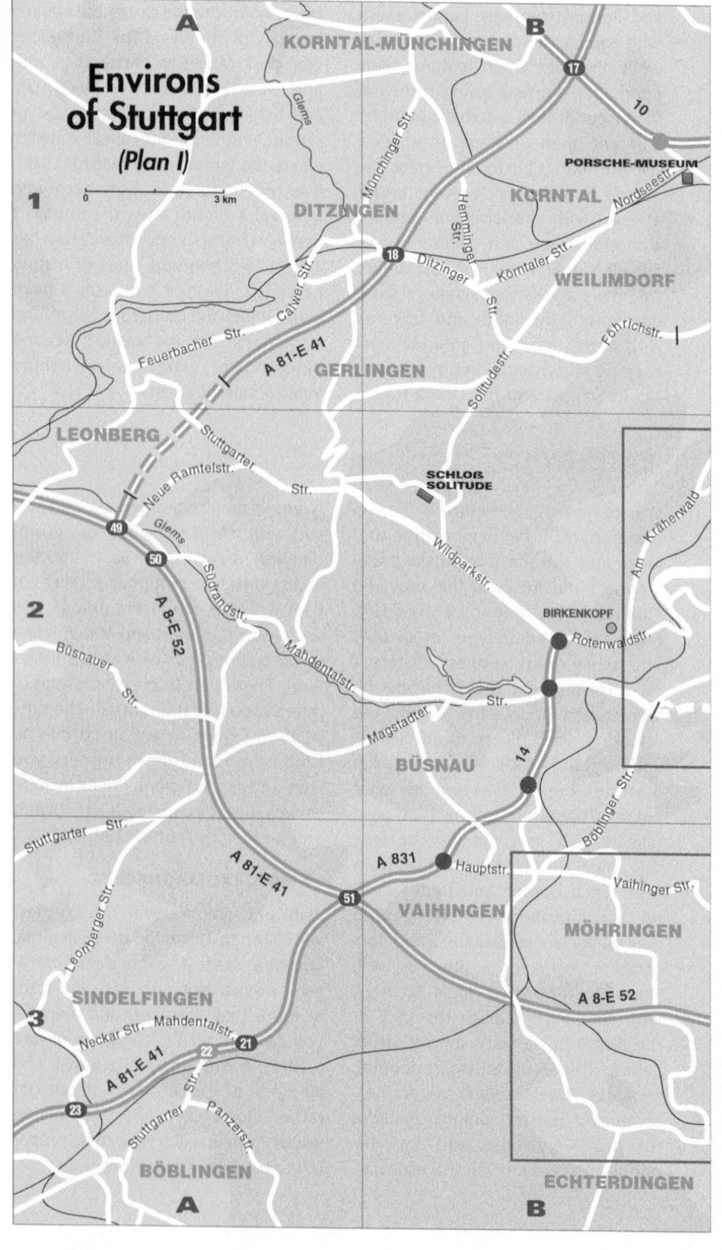
Environs of Stuttgart
(Plan I)
0
3 km
A
B
1
2
3
KORNTAL-MÜNCHINGEN
PORSCHE-MUSEUM
KORNTAL
DITZINGEN
WEILIMDORF
GERLINGEN
LEONBERG
SCHLOß SOLITUDE
BIRKENKOPF
BÜSNAU
VAIHINGEN
MÖHRINGEN
SINDELFINGEN
BÖBLINGEN
ECHTERDINGEN
Glems
Münchinger Str.
Hemminger Str.
Nordseestr.
Ditzinger Str.
Korntaler Str.
Calwer Str.
Feuerbacher Str.
Föhrichstr.
Solitudestr.
A 81-E 41
Stuttgarter Str.
Neue Ramtelstr.
Wildparkstr.
Am Kräherwald
Rotenwaldstr.
Südrandstr.
Mahdentalstr.
A 8-E 52
Büsnauer Str.
Magstadter Str.
Böblinger Str.
A 831
Hauptstr.
Vaihinger Str.
Leonberger Str.
Neckar Str.
Panzerstr.
10
14
17
18
49
50
51
21
22
23

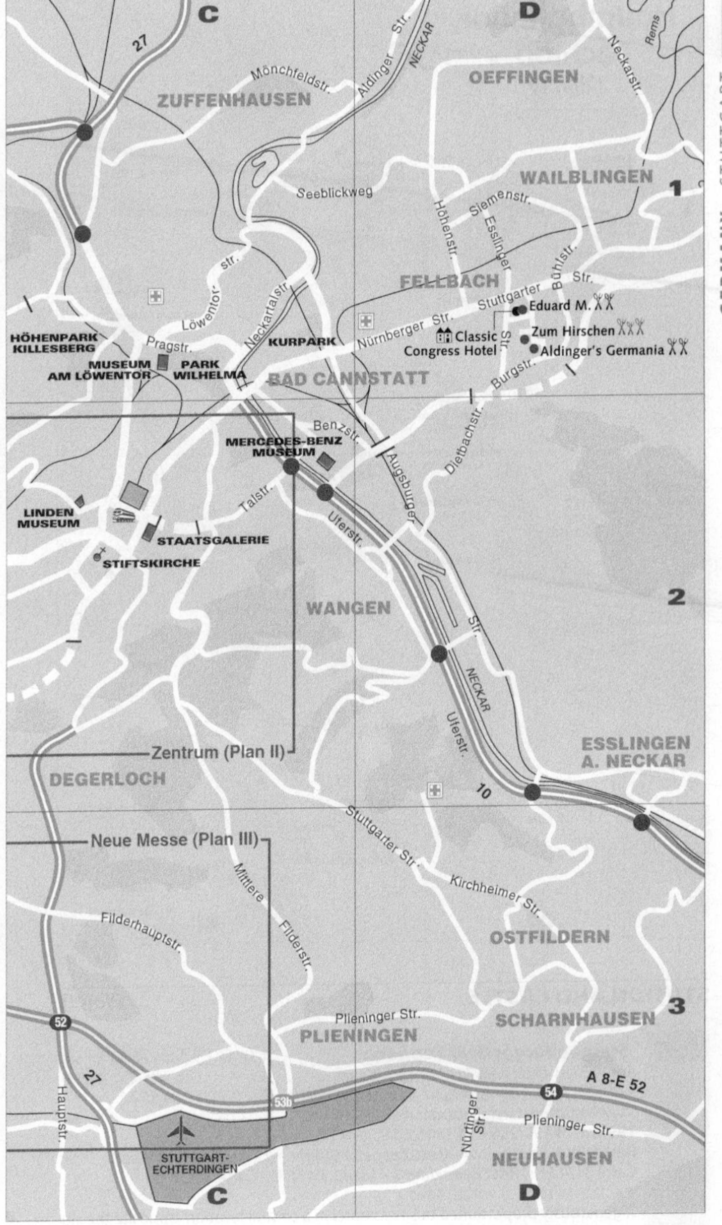
C
D
ZUFFENHAUSEN
OEFFINGEN
WAILBLINGEN
FELLBACH
BAD CANNSTATT
WANGEN
DEGERLOCH
ESSLINGEN A. NECKAR
OSTFILDERN
SCHARNHAUSEN
PLIENINGEN
NEUHAUSEN
Mönchfeldstr.
Aldinger Str.
NECKAR
Neckarstr.
Rems
Seeblickweg
Siemenstr.
Höhenstr.
Esslinger Str.
Bühlstr.
Stuttgarter Str.
Nürnberger Str.
Löwentor-str.
Neckartalstr.
Pragstr.
HÖHENPARK KILLESBERG
MUSEUM AM LÖWENTOR
PARK WILHELMA
KURPARK
Eduard M.
Classic Congress Hotel
Zum Hirschen
Aldinger's Germania
Burgstr.
Benzstr.
MERCEDES-BENZ MUSEUM
Dietbachstr.
Augsburger Str.
Talstr.
Uferstr.
LINDEN MUSEUM
STAATSGALERIE
STIFTSKIRCHE
Zentrum (Plan II)
Neue Messe (Plan III)
Stuttgarter Str.
Kirchheimer Str.
Mittlere Filderstr.
Filderhauptstr.
Plieninger Str.
A 8-E 52
Nürtinger Str.
Hauptstr.
STUTTGART-ECHTERDINGEN
27
52
53b
54
10
1
2
3

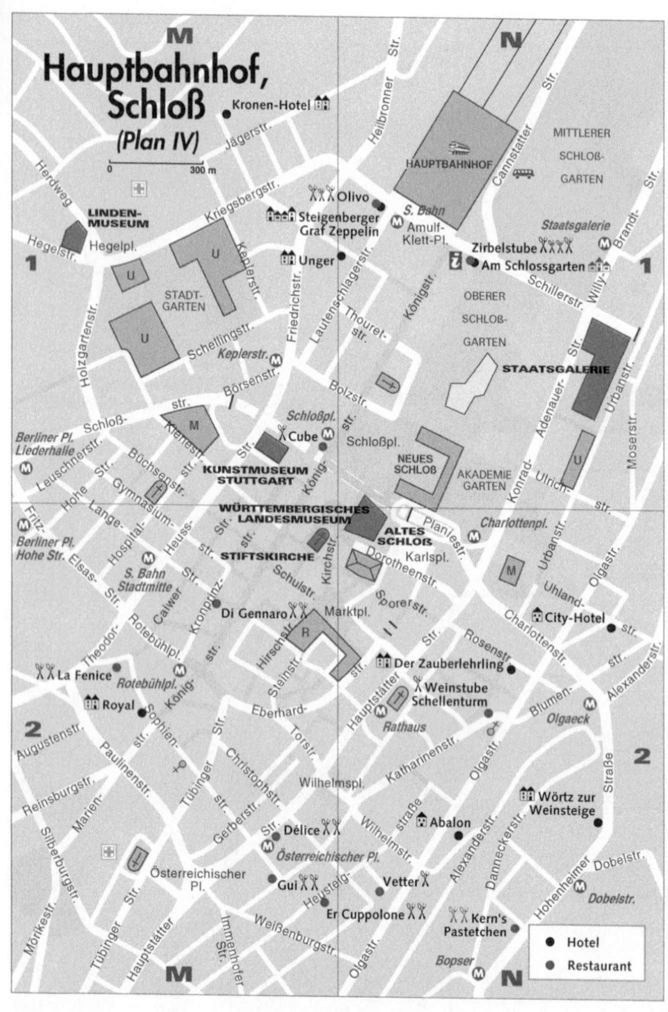

STATION AND CASTLE

Plan IV

Steigenberger Graf Zeppelin

Arnulf-Klett-Platz 7 ✉ 70173 – Ⓜ S. Bahn
– ✆ (0711) 2 04 80 – stuttgart@steigenberger.de – Fax (0711) 2 04 85 42
– www.stuttgart.steigenberger.de **N1**

189 rm – 🚹155/235 € 🚹🚹180/260 €, ☕ 21 €
Rest Olivo – see below – **Rest *Zeppelin Stüble*** – *(closed Sunday dinner)*
Carte 31/42 € – **Rest *Zeppelino's*** – Menu 39/56 € – Carte 36/56 €

♦ Chain hotel ♦ Classic ♦

A generously proportioned business hotel in a central location, opposite the station, with Classic, Elegance and Avantgarde rooms. Try the Zeppelin-Stüble with its rustic atmosphere. The cuisine at Zeppelino's is Italian. With cigar lounge and bistro.

Am Schlossgarten

Schillerstr. 23 ✉ 70173 – Ⓜ S. Bahn – ✆ (0711) 2 02 60
– info@hotelschlossgarten.com – Fax (0711) 2 02 68 88
– www.hotelschlossgarten.com **N1**

116 rm – 🚹221/248 € 🚹🚹270/297 €, ☕ 20 € – 4 suites
Rest Zirbelstube – see below
Rest *Schlossgarten-Restaurant* – *(closed Friday lunch and Saturday lunch)* Carte 40/53 €
Rest *Vinothek* – *(closed Sunday - Monday)* Menu 25 € – Carte 30/35 €

◆ Townhouse ◆ Classic ◆

This passionately managed hotel stands out for its friendliness and its pleasant, comfortable atmosphere. Some rooms look onto the castle garden. Tasteful atmosphere in the Schlossgarten restaurant. Vinothek. Mediterranean style.

Kronen-Hotel without rest

Kronenstr. 48 ✉ 70174 – Ⓜ S. Bahn – ✆ (0711) 2 25 10
– info@kronenhotel-stuttgart.de – Fax (0711) 2 25 14 04
– www.kronenhotel-stuttgart.de
closed 22 December - 2 January **M1**

80 rm ☕ – 🚹105/120 € 🚹🚹135/175 €

◆ Business ◆ Functional ◆

This hotel offers, functional rooms tailored to business people. From the breakfast room, you have a beautiful view of the greenery.

Wörtz zur Weinsteige

Hohenheimer Str. 30 ✉ 70184 – Ⓜ Dobelstr. – ✆ (0711) 2 36 70 00
– info@zur-weinsteige.de – Fax (0711) 2 36 70 07 – www.zur-weinsteige.de **N2**

33 rm ☕ – 🚹95/135 € 🚹🚹99/155 €
Rest – *(closed 1 to 14 January, 1 to 18 August and Sunday - Monday, Bank Holidays)* Menu 10 € (lunch)/29 € – Carte 30/49 €

◆ Townhouse ◆ Rustic ◆

The Scherle family really look after their guests in their hotel. The rooms in the little Schloss are particularly comfortable and elegant; or there's the stylish Louis-XVI Junior suite. Rustic décor defines the character of this restaurant.

Der Zauberlehrling

Rosenstr. 38 ✉ 70182 – Ⓜ Olgaeck – ✆ (0711) 2 37 77 70
– kontakt@zauberlehrling.de – Fax (0711) 2 37 77 75
– www.zauberlehrling.de **N2**

17 rm ☕ – 🚹135/250 € 🚹🚹195/280 € – 3 suites
Rest – *(closed Saturday lunch and Sunday lunch)* Menu 35/78 € – Carte 43/65 €

◆ Townhouse ◆ Design ◆

The rooms in this hotel are quite individual, in contemporary designer style. Each room embodies a well-known phrase or saying. Also suites/junior suites. Tasteful and modern, this cosy rustic restaurant serves international cuisine.

Royal

Sophienstr. 35 ✉ 70178 – Ⓜ Rotebühlpl. – ✆ (0711) 6 25 05 00
– royalhotel@t-online.de – Fax (0711) 62 88 09
– www.royalstuttgart.de **M2**

100 rm – 🚹102/155 € 🚹🚹129/190 €, ☕ 12 € – 5 suites
Rest – *(closed 4 to 26 August and Sunday, Bank Holidays)* Menu 50 € – Carte 22/47 €

◆ Townhouse ◆ Functional ◆

A well-run hotel in a central location, just a stone's throw from the pedestrian area. The rooms are refined and comfortable. Restaurant serving international cuisine.

Unger without rest

Kronenstr. 17 ✉ 70173 – Ⓜ S. Bahn – ✆ (0711) 2 09 90 – info@hotel-unger.de
– Fax (0711) 2 09 91 00 – www.hotel-unger.de **N1**

114 rm ☕ – 🚹119/147 € 🚹🚹165/204 €

◆ Townhouse ◆ Functional ◆

This hotel is right behind the pedestrian area, and offers functional rooms (some rooms are new and more modern).

Abalon without rest

Zimmermannstr.7 (access via Olgastraße 79) ✉ 70182 – Ⓜ Olgaeck – ✆ (0711) 2 17 10 – info@abalon.de – Fax (0711) 2 17 12 17 – www.abalon.de

42 rm – 79/86 € 99/112 € **N2**

♦ Business ♦ Functional ♦

This modern building with its pretty planted roof terrace offers relatively quiet, suitably designed rooms, despite its downtown location. Juice and water are part of the service.

City-Hotel without rest

Uhlandstr. 18 ✉ 70182 – Ⓜ Olgaeck – ✆ (0711) 21 08 10 – ch@bbv-hotels.de – Fax (0711) 2 36 97 72 – www.cityhotel-stuttgart.de **N2**

31 rm – 79/89 € 99/115 €

♦ Townhouse ♦ Functional ♦

This contemporary hotel is right in the city centre. It has a nice friendly breakfast room with a conservatory – or you can breakfast on the terrace in summer.

Zirbelstube – Hotel Am Schlossgarten

Schillerstr. 23 ✉ 70173 – Ⓜ S. Bahn – ✆ (0711) 2 02 68 28 – info@hotelschlossgarten.com – Fax (0711) 2 02 68 88 – www.hotelschlossgarten.com

closed 2 weeks January, 3 weeks August and Sunday - Monday **N1**

Rest – *(booking advisable)* Menu 56 € (lunch)/116 € – Carte 70/106 €

Spec. Marinierter Thunfisch mit Gelee von getrockneten Aprikosen und Pulpo im Tempurateig gebacken. Wachtel und Gänseleber im Steinchampignon mit Pfifferlingscrème. Prime Beef mit Artischocken-Lauch-Fondue und Pestojus.

♦ Classic ♦ Elegant ♦

Excellent service in this elegant, wood panelled restaurant where Bernhard Diers offers modern interpretations of classic dishes. Terrace with a view of the castle park.

Olivo – Hotel Steigenberger Graf Zeppelin

Arnulf-Klett-Platz 7 ✉ 70173 – Ⓜ S. Bahn – ✆ (0711) 2 04 82 77 – stuttgart@steigenberger.de – Fax (0711) 2 04 85 42 – www.stuttgart.steigenberger.de

closed 3 weeks January, 3 weeks July - August and Sunday - Monday **N1**

Rest – Menu 42 € (lunch)/119 € – Carte 47/59 €

Spec. Schwarze Bandnudeln mit Tintenfisch, Krake und Pfifferlingen. Weißweinrisotto mit grünem Spargel und Scampi. Wildschweinbraten mit Rotweinsauce und gefüllter Zwiebel.

♦ Italian ♦ Elegant ♦

A modern elegant style and a Mediterranean touch define the setting here. Various Italian provinces influence the cuisine of Thomas Heilemann.

Kern's Pastetchen

Hohenheimer Str. 64 ✉ 70184 – Ⓜ Bopser – ✆ (0711) 48 48 55 – info@kerns-pastetchen.de – Fax (0711) 48 75 65 – www.kerns-pastetchen.de

closed 14 to 29 July and Sunday **N2**

Rest – *(dinner only) (booking advisable)* Menu 50/60 € – Carte 37/58 €

♦ Classic ♦ Friendly ♦

The Kern family's pleasant restaurant successfully combines the elegant and rustic, offering Austrian- and French-influenced cuisine.

Délice (Friedrich Gutscher)

Hauptstätter Str. 61 ✉ 70178 – Ⓜ Österreichischer Pl. – ✆ (0711) 6 40 32 22 – www.restaurant-delice.de **M2**

Rest – *(closed 23 December - 6 January, 15 to 24 March and Saturday - Sunday, Bank Holidays) (dinner only) (booking essential)* Menu 90 € – Carte 52/74 €

Spec. Räucheraal mit getrüffeltem Kartoffelsalat und Passionsfruchtsaft. Seeteufel aus dem Ofen mit Steinpilzen und Aromaten auf Kartoffelpüree. Topfentarte mit Marillensauce und Eiscrème mit Trockenfrüchten.

♦ Classic ♦ Friendly ♦

In this vaulted cellar restaurant with a visible kitchen, classic dishes are served along with a good selection of wine with some rare Rieslings.

La Fenice

Rotebühlplatz 29 ✉ 70178 – Ⓜ Rotebühlpl. – ✆ (0711) 6 15 11 44 – g.vincenzo@t-online.de – Fax (0711) 6 15 11 46 – www.ristorante-la-fenice.de closed Saturday lunch, Sunday and Bank Holidays **M2**

Rest – Menu 51 € – Carte 33/58 €

◆ Italian ◆ Cosy ◆

A light, friendly restaurant with the elegant touch, where the Gorgoglione sisters offer Italian cuisine.

Di Gennaro

Kronprinzstr. 11 ✉ 70173 – Ⓜ Rotebühlpl. – ✆ (0711) 22 29 60 51 – kp@digennaro.de – Fax (0711) 22 29 60 40 – www.digennaro.de closed Sunday and Bank Holidays **M2**

Rest – Carte 41/57 €

◆ Italian ◆ Bistro ◆

A modern townhouse with its glass facade houses this lightly elegant Italian restaurant, delicatessen and vinotheque.

Er Cuppolone

Heusteigstr. 45 ✉ 70180 – Ⓜ Österreichischer Pl. – ✆ (0711) 6 07 18 80 – sante@schwaben.de – Fax (0711) 6 20 83 66 – www.santedesantis.de closed 1 to 21 August and Sunday **M2**

Rest – *(dinner only)* Menu 69/75 € – Carte 43/48 €

◆ Italian ◆ Elegant ◆

The old state parliament walls hide a cookery school, wine bar and an elegant restaurant, offering authentic Italian cuisine.

Gui

Sophienstr. 3 ✉ 70180 – Ⓜ Österreichischer Pl. – ✆ (0711) 6 45 67 77 – ruebel@gui-stuttgart.de – Fax (0711) 6 45 60 07 – www.gui-stuttgart.de closed 24 December - 7 January, 20 July - 11 August and Sunday - Monday

Rest – *(dinner only)* Menu 47/69 € **M2**

◆ International ◆ Friendly ◆

This restaurant in its small natural stone barrel vaults offers friendly service and ambitious international cuisine. Dishes come in menu form.

Cube

< Schlosspark,

Kleiner Schlossplatz 1 (at the Kunstmuseum, 4th floor) ✉ 70173 – Ⓜ Schloßpl. – ✆ (0711) 2 80 44 41 – info@cube-restaurant.de – Fax (0711) 2 80 44 42 – www.cube-restaurant.de **M1**

Rest – Menu 30 € (lunch) – Carte 42/57 €

◆ Mediterranean ◆ Fashionable ◆

A modern restaurant in the art museum. Simple design with unique view and Mediterranean/Asian cuisine. Simple menus available at midday.

Vetter

Bopserstr. 18 ✉ 70180 – Ⓜ Österreichischer Pl. – ✆ (0711) 24 19 16 – Fax (0711) 60 18 96 40 closed Christmas - New Year, mid to end August and Sunday, Bank Holidays

Rest – *(dinner only) (booking advisable)* Carte 23/42 € **N2**

◆ Regional ◆ Cosy ◆

This comfortable establishment is down a side street in the town centre. Modern interior and a selection of regional and international dishes.

Weinstube Schellenturm

Weberstr. 72 ✉ 70182 – Ⓜ Olgaeck – ✆ (0711) 2 36 48 88 – weinstube-schellenturm@t-online.de – Fax (0711) 2 26 26 99 – www.schellenturm.de closed Sunday and Bank Holidays **N2**

Rest – *(dinner only)* Carte 20/31 €

◆ Regional ◆ Cosy ◆

This 16th century fortified tower offers real local Swabian atmosphere. There is good wine, large Swabian ravioli (Maultaschen), and cheese spaetzle (noodles).

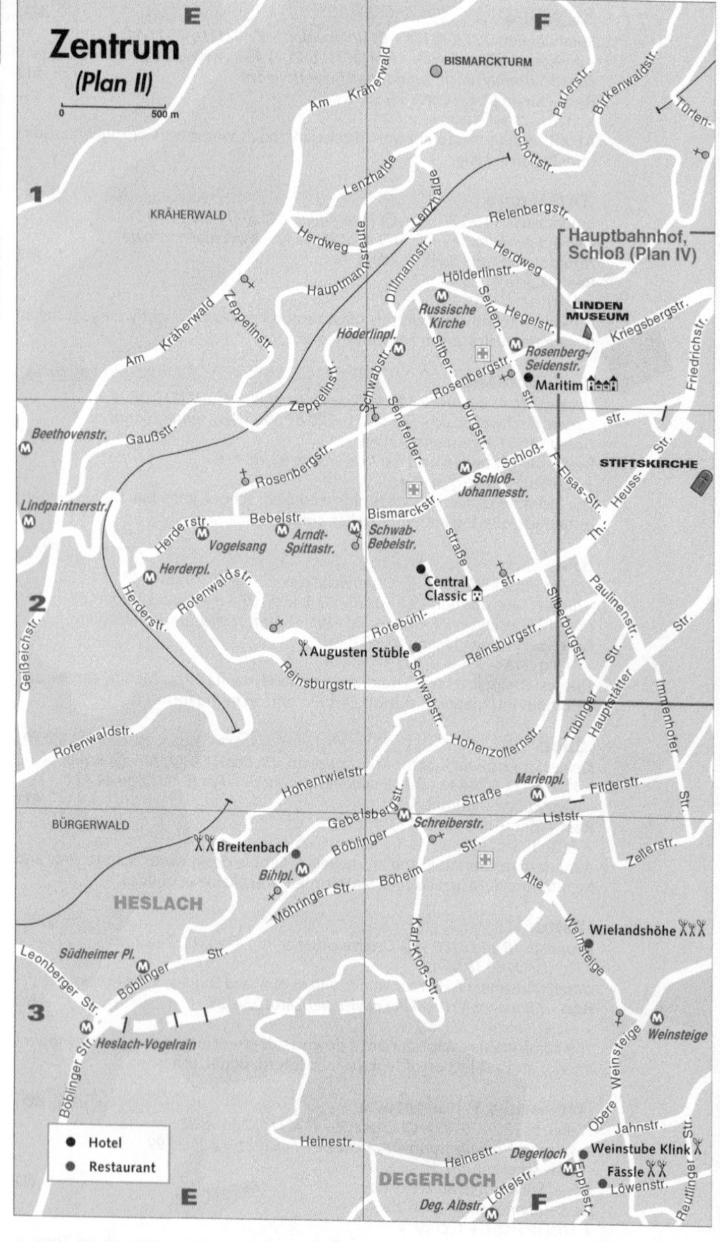
Zentrum
(Plan II)
0
500 m
E
F
1
2
3
BISMARCKTURM
KRÄHERWALD
Hauptbahnhof, Schloß (Plan IV)
LINDEN MUSEUM
Maritim
Rosenberg-/Seidenstr.
Russische Kirche
Höderlinpl.
Beethovenstr.
Lindpaintnerstr.
STIFTSKIRCHE
Schloß-Johannesstr.
Vogelsang
Arndt-Spittastr.
Schwab-Bebelstr.
Herderpl.
Central Classic
Augusten Stüble
BÜRGERWALD
Breitenbach
Bihlpl.
HESLACH
Schreiberstr.
Marienpl.
Wielandshöhe
Südheimer Pl.
Heslach-Vogelrain
Weinsteige
Weinstube Klink
Fässle
Degerloch
DEGERLOCH
Deg. Albstr.
Hotel
Restaurant

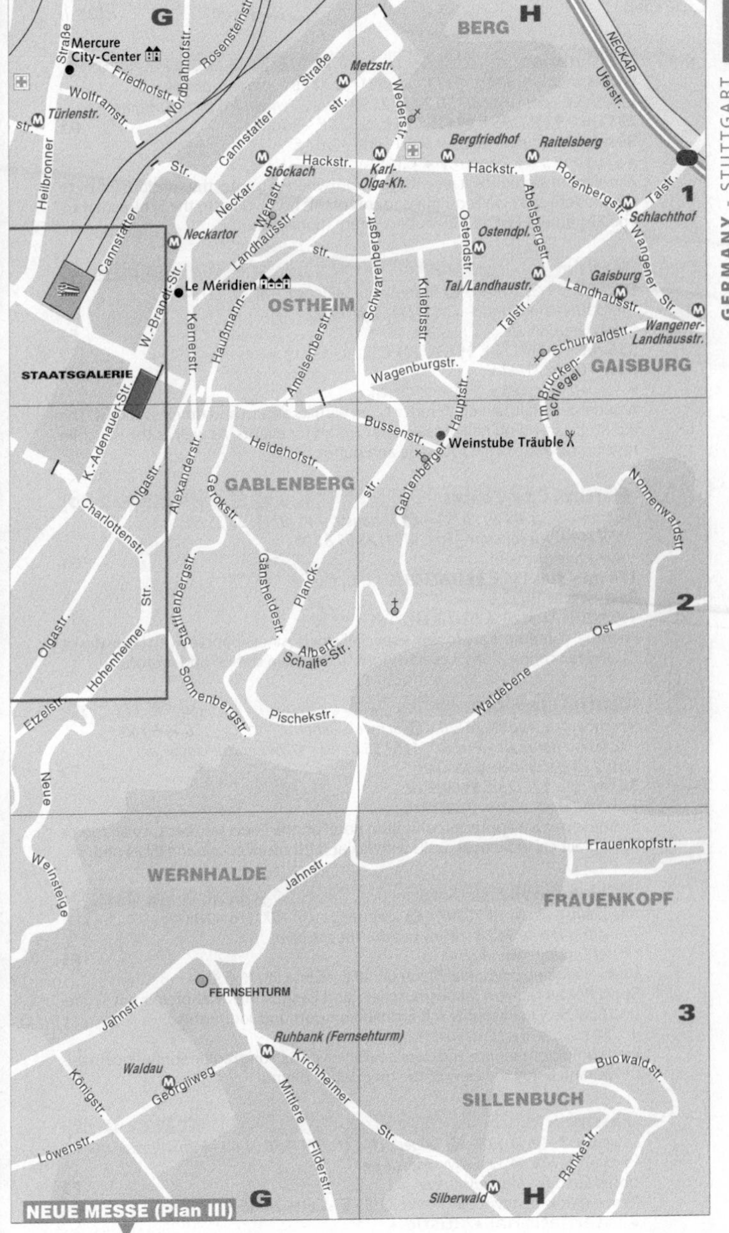
G
H
1
2
3
BERG
OSTHEIM
GAISBURG
GABLENBERG
WERNHALDE
FRAUENKOPF
SILLENBUCH
STAATSGALERIE
FERNSEHTURM
Mercure City-Center
Le Méridien
Weinstube Träuble
NECKAR
Metzstr.
Türlenstr.
Stöckach
Karl-Olga-Kh.
Bergfriedhof
Raitelsberg
Schlachthof
Neckartor
Ostendpl.
Tal./Landhausstr.
Gaisburg
Wangener-Landhausstr.
Ruhbank (Fernsehturm)
Waldau
Silberwald
Heilbronner Straße
Friedhofstr.
Wolframstr.
Nordbahnhofstr.
Rosensteinstr.
Cannstatter Straße
Hackstr.
Wederstr.
Uferstr.
Rotenbergstr.
Talstr.
Neckar-Str.
Werastr.
Landhausstr.
Schwarenbergstr.
Ostendstr.
Abelsbergstr.
Wangener Str.
Kniebisstr.
Landhausstr.
W.-Brandt-Str.
Kernerstr.
Haußmannstr.
Amelsenbergstr.
Wagenburgstr.
Schurwaldstr.
Im Bruckenschlegel
Hauptstr.
Bussenstr.
Gablenberger Hauptstr.
K.-Adenauer-Str.
Olgastr.
Alexanderstr.
Heidehofstr.
Gerokstr.
Nonnenwaldstr.
Charlottenstr.
Stafflenbergstr.
Gänsheidestr.
Planck-str.
Hohenheimer Str.
Albert-Schäffle-Str.
Ost
Waldebene
Etzelstr.
Sonnenbergstr.
Pischekstr.
Neue Weinsteige
Frauenkopfstr.
Jahnstr.
Kirchheimer Str.
Buowaldstr.
Georgiiweg
Königstr.
Mittlere Filderstr.
Rankestr.
Löwenstr.
NEUE MESSE (Plan III)

CENTRE

Plan II

Le Méridien

Willy-Brandt-Str. 30 ✉ 70173 – ☎ (0711) 2 22 10 – info.stuttgart@lemeridien.com – Fax (0711) 22 21 25 99 – www.lemeridien.com/stuttgart

281 rm – 🚹135/295 € 🚹🚹135/295 €, ☕ 22 € – 5 suites **G1**

Rest *Le Cassoulet* – *(dinner only)* Carte 40/67 €

♦ Business ♦ Luxury ♦ Classic ♦

The elegant ambience stays with you from when you enter the spacious lobby to the modern, very well equipped rooms of this hotel, close to the Schlossgarten. The Restaurant Le Cassoulet offers international cuisine.

Maritim

Seidenstr. 34 ✉ 70174 – Ⓜ Rosenberg-/Seidenstr. – ☎ (0711) 94 20 – info.stu@maritim.de – Fax (0711) 9 42 10 00 – www.maritim.de **F1**

555 rm – 🚹156/176 € 🚹🚹181/201 €, ☕ 17 € – 12 suites

Rest – Carte 27/41 €

♦ Chain hotel ♦ Functional ♦

A generously laid out conference hotel with its atrium and timeless rooms. The old Stuttgart riding hall of 1885 offers room for events. As well as the Reuchlin restaurant, there is the rotisserie and buffet.

Mercure City-Center

Heilbronner Str. 88 ✉ 70191 – Ⓜ Türlenstr. – ☎ (0711) 25 55 80 – h5424-re@accor.com – Fax (0711) 25 55 81 00 – www.mercure.com **G1**

174 rm – 🚹99/139 € 🚹🚹109/149 €, ☕ 15 €

Rest – Carte 19/32 €

♦ Chain hotel ♦ Functional ♦

Friendly, contemporary rooms, especially for business people, with large desks, PC and fax connections. Located close to the main station and motorway.

Central Classic without rest

Hasenbergstr. 49a ✉ 70176 – Ⓜ Schwab-Bebelstr. – ☎ (0711) 6 15 50 50 – cc@bbv-hotels.de – Fax (0711) 61 55 05 30 – www.central-classic.de

closed 23 December - 6 January **F2**

34 rm ☕ – 🚹73/78 € 🚹🚹89/95 €

♦ Townhouse ♦ Functional ♦

Business people appreciate this little hotel on the Feuersee, because all rooms have practical individual desks with fax and PC connections and ISDN phones.

Wielandshöhe (Vincent Klink)

< Stuttgart,

Alte Weinsteige 71 ✉ 70597 – Ⓜ Weinsteige – ☎ (0711) 6 40 88 48 – Fax (0711) 6 40 94 08 – www.wielandshoehe.com

closed Sunday - Monday **F3**

Rest – *(booking advisable)* Menu 68/98 € – Carte 58/76 €

Spec. Pot au feu von Jakobsmuscheln und Langustinos. Rehpfeffer mit Trüffel und Spätzle. Quarksoufflé mit Erdbeerkompott und Joghurteis.

♦ Classic ♦ Fashionable ♦

Find competent service and classic cuisine with a strong regional influence in this restaurant. Enjoy the view of the town while dining.

Fässle

Löwenstr. 51 ✉ 70597 – Ⓜ Degerloch – ☎ (0711) 76 01 00 – info@faessle.de – Fax (0711) 76 44 32 – www.faessle.de

closed Sunday - Monday lunch **F3**

Rest – *(booking advisable)* Menu 33/55 € – Carte 24/46 €

♦ International ♦ Rustic ♦

The cosy traditional restaurant and blue lounge make up this restaurant. Sample international and regional cuisine with attentive service.

XX ✿ **Breitenbach**

Gebelsbergstr. 97 ✉ 70199 – Ⓤ Bihlpl. – ☎ (0711) 6 40 64 67
– restaurantbreitenbach@t-online.de – Fax (0711) 6 74 42 34
– www.restaurant-breitenbach.de
closed 1 to 12 January, 13 to 17 May, 4 to 30 August and Sunday - Monday **E3**
Rest – *(dinner only) (booking advisable)* Menu 56/68 € – Carte 56/76 €
Spec. Sushi-Thunfisch in der Sesam-Szechuanpfeffer-Kruste mit Birnen-Rettich-Vinaigrette und Wasabi-Mango-Dip. Hummer-Maultaschen mit Krustentiersauce. Zander und Tafelspitz mit Flusskrebsen und Meerrettichschaum.
♦ Inventive ♦ Friendly ♦
Very friendly and competent service in this restrained elegant restaurant. Creatively influenced dishes have a classic base.

X **Augusten Stüble**

Augustenstr. 104 ✉ 70197 – Ⓤ Schwab-Bebelstr. – ☎ (0711) 62 12 48
closed Sunday and Bank Holidays **F2**
Rest – *(dinner only) (booking advisable)* Carte 18/34 €
♦ Regional ♦ Cosy ♦
The décor of this bistro-style restaurant on the edge of the centre features lots of dark wooden detail. Regional fare and a good selection of wines. Open until midnight.

X **Weinstube Klink**

Epplestr. 1e (Degerloch) ✉ 70597 – Ⓤ Degerloch – ☎ (0711) 7 65 32 05
– Fax (0711) 7 87 42 21 – www.weinstube-klink.de
closed Sunday and Bank Holidays **F3**
Rest – *(dinner only) (booking advisable)* Carte 22/39 €
♦ Regional ♦ Rustic ♦
Somewhat hidden in a courtyard, this establishment offers a small Swabian menu complemented by a specials board. Excellent wine list.

X **Weinstube Träuble**

Gablenberger Hauptstr. 66 (entrance on Bussenstraße) ✉ 70186
– ☎ (0711) 46 54 28 – Fax (0711) 4 20 79 61
closed 24 August - 7 September and Sunday, Bank Holidays **H2**
Rest – *(open from 5 pm)* Carte 17/29 €
♦ Regional ♦ Wine bar ♦
A wonderfully cosy wood-panelled dining room in this 200 year old cottage. Snack and lunch menus.

AIRPORT AND NEW TRADE FAIR CENTRE *Plan III*

Mövenpick-Hotel Messe

Flughafenstr. 50 ✉ 70629 – ☎ (0711) 7 90 70
– hotel.stuttgart.messe@moevenpick.com – Fax (0711) 79 35 85
– www.moevenpick-stuttgart-messe.com **L2**
229 rm – †131/245 € ††131/270 €, ☕ 18 €
Rest – Carte 22/33 €
♦ Conference hotel ♦ Business ♦ Functional ♦
The hotel is just 200 m from the airport terminals. Very well sound-proofed, homely rooms. S-Bahn train access nearby. Restaurant with international menu. Popular for Sunday brunch.

Millennium Hotel & Resort

Plieninger Str. 100 ✉ 70567 – Ⓤ Salzacker
– ☎ (0711) 72 10 – sales.stuttgart@mill-cop.com – Fax (0711) 7 21 29 50
– www.si-centrum.de **J1**
454 rm – †119/195 € ††119/195 €, ☕ 18 € – 22 suites
Rest – Carte 27/41 €
♦ Conference hotel ♦ Personalised ♦
This modern hotel in a high-rise by the music theatres in the SI experience centre offers its guests elegant rooms in a wide range of categories. You can choose between nineteen different restaurants, bars and cafés.

AIRPORT AND NEW TRADE FAIR CENTRE - PLAN III

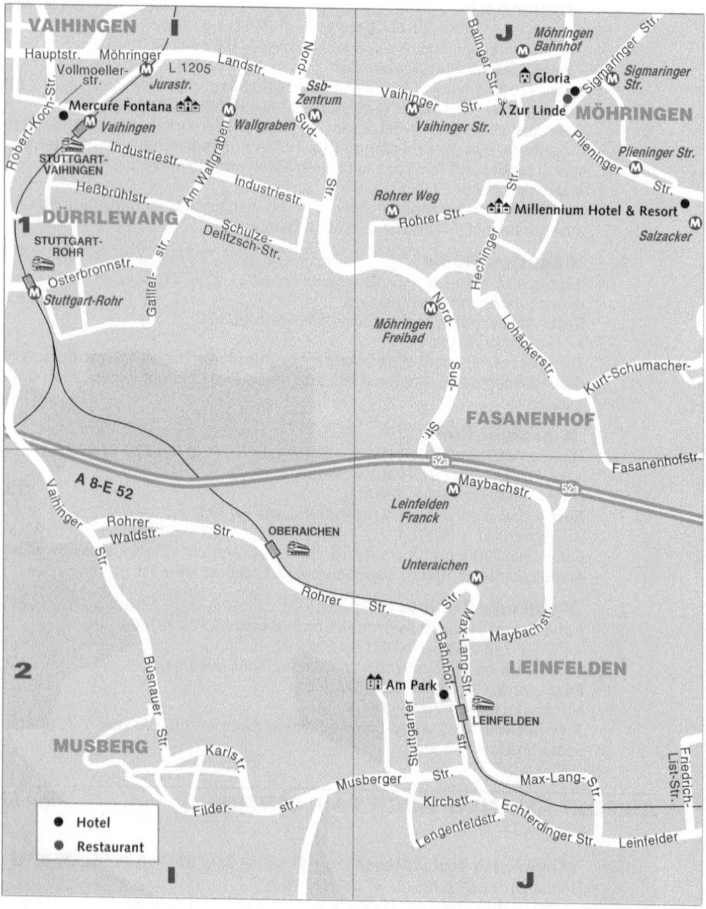

Mercure Fontana

Vollmoellerstr. 5 ✉ 70563 – Ⓜ Vaihingen
– ✆ (0711) 73 00
– h5425@accor.com
– Fax (0711) 7 30 25 25
– www.mercure.com **I1**

252 rm – 🚹119/169 € 🚹🚹139/189 €, ☕ 18 €
Rest – Carte 23/42 €

◆ Chain hotel ◆ Business ◆ Classic ◆

Eighteen floors of elegant rooms. They are tastefully furnished with desks and small living areas, and some have exquisite upholstered beds. You can choose from the elegant and the rustic sections of the restaurant.

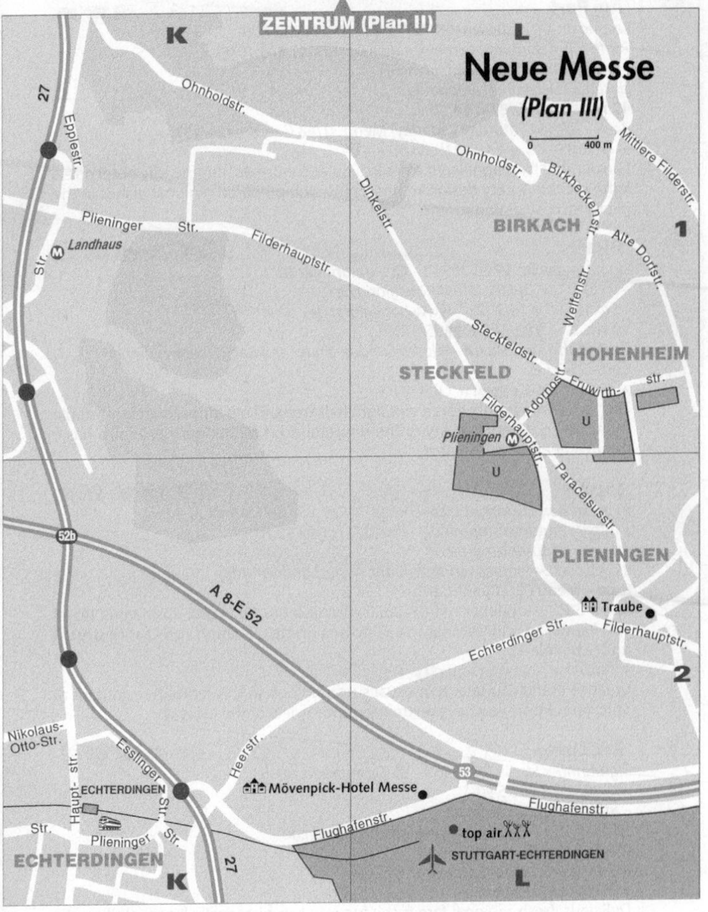

Traube

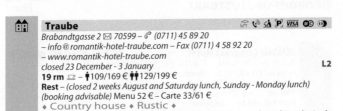

Brabandtgasse 2 ✉ 70599 – ✆ (0711) 45 89 20
– info@romantik-hotel-traube.com – Fax (0711) 4 58 92 20
– www.romantik-hotel-traube.com
closed 23 December - 3 January **L2**

19 rm ☕ – 🚹109/169 € 🚹🚹129/199 €
Rest – *(closed 2 weeks August and Saturday lunch, Sunday - Monday lunch) (booking advisable)* Menu 52 € – Carte 33/61 €

◆ Country house ◆ Rustic ◆

Behind the historical half-timbered façade, all the rooms have been lovingly renovated. Some are furnished with antiques, some in rustic style with lots of wood. Elegant, country-style restaurant bar.

Am Park

Lessingstr. 4 (Leinfelden) ✉ 70771 – ✆ (0711) 90 31 00
– info@hotelampark-leinfelden.de – Fax (0711) 9 03 10 99
– www.hotelampark-leinfelden.de
closed 22 December - 9 January **J2**
42 rm – 80/87 € 120 €
Rest – *(closed Saturday - Sunday)* Menu 31/48 € – Carte 24/45 €
♦ Business ♦ Functional ♦
Surrounded by magnificent trees in a quiet cul-de-sac, this friendly hotel offers light, contemporary design rooms. Enjoy well-prepared regional dishes in the pleasant, cosy dining rooms.

Gloria

Sigmaringer Str. 59 ✉ 70567 – Ⓤ Sigmaringer Str.
– ✆ (0711) 7 18 50 – info@hotelgloria.de
– Fax (0711) 7 18 51 21 – www.hotelgloria.de **J1**
90 rm – 85/105 € 95/125 €
Rest *Möhringer Hexle* – *(closed Sunday dinner and Bank Holidays dinner)*
Carte 25/37 €
♦ Business ♦ Functional ♦
This family-run hotel offers a nice light hall area and functional but comfortable rooms in contemporary style. The unpretentious Möhringer Hexle also has a bright, cheerful conservatory.

top air

at the airport (Terminal 1, Level 4) ✉ 70629 – ✆ (0711) 9 48 21 37
– info@restaurant-top-air.de – Fax (0711) 7 97 92 10
– www.restaurant-top-air.de
closed end December - early January, August and Saturday - Sunday **L2**
Rest – Menu 69/106 € – Carte 75/113 €
Spec. Gänsestopfleber mit Dreierlei vom grünem Apfel und Rosinenjus. Royal von Parmesan und Gambas mit Pestovinaigrette. Variation von Passionsfrucht und Schokolade.
♦ Inventive ♦ Friendly ♦
Creative French cuisine in unusual surroundings. In this modern restaurant at Stuttgart airport you have an uninterrupted view of the runway.

Zur Linde

Sigmaringer Str. 49 ✉ 70567 – Ⓤ Sigmaringer Str.
– ✆ (0711) 7 19 95 90
– info@gasthauszurlin.de
– Fax (0711) 7 19 95 92 – www.gasthauszurlin.de
closed Saturday lunch **J1**
Rest – *(booking advisable)* Carte 22/44 €
♦ Regional ♦ Inn ♦
Delicious, fresh regional fare is the focus in this historically listed, cosily rustic building with prettily decorated dining rooms. Traditional vaulted cellar for functions.

ENVIRONS OF STUTTGART *Plan I*

at Fellbach

Classic Congress Hotel

Tainer Str. 7 ✉ 70734 – ✆ (0711) 5 85 90 – info@cch-bw.de
– Fax (0711) 5 85 93 04 – www.cch-bw.de
closed 23 to 31 December **D1**
149 rm – 129/169 € 153/193 €
Rest Eduard M. – see below
♦ Business ♦ Conference hotel ♦ Functional ♦
Right by the Schwabenlandhalle is this hotel, with its functional rooms with their light furniture. Spacious hall, extensive conference rooms.

XXX ✿

Zum Hirschen (Armin Karrer) with rm

Hirschstr. 1 ✉ 70734 – ✆ (0711) 9 57 93 70 – info@zumhirschen-fellbach.de – Fax (0711) 95 79 37 10 – www.zumhirschen-fellbach.de

closed 1 to 7 January and 2 weeks August **D1**

9 rm – 75/95 € 95/135 €

Rest – *(closed Sunday - Monday) (booking advisable)* Menu 43 € (lunch)/115 € – Carte 79 €

Rest *Finca* – *(closed Sunday - Monday)* Menu 29/43 € – Carte 33/45 €

Spec. Confiertes Kaninchen mit Saubohnen und Espressosatz. Gegrillter Ingwerspargel mit Champignontapenade und Mandelschaum (April - June). Lammcarré mit Zitronensenfkruste und Olivenöljus.

♦ Classic ♦ Elegant ♦

In this pleasant, bright and modern restaurant gourmet cuisine is served in the evening. During the day a lunch menu and simpler dishes are offered. Eat Mediterranean-style in the Finca restaurant with its vaulted ceilings.

XX

Eduard M. – Classic Congress Hotel

Tainer Str. 7 ✉ 70734 – ✆ (0711) 5 85 94 11 – restaurant@eduardm.de – Fax (0711) 5 85 94 27 – www.eduardm.de

closed 23 to 31 December **D1**

Rest – Menu 52 € – Carte 27/52 €

♦ International ♦ Friendly ♦

This classic conference hotel's cultivated restaurant is refined and friendly, with its split-level layout. International cuisine.

XX

Aldinger's Germania

Schmerstr. 6 ✉ 70734 – ✆ (0711) 58 20 37 – aldingers@t-online.de – Fax (0711) 58 20 77 – www.aldingers-germania.de

closed 4 to 19 February, 3 to 27 August and Sunday - Monday **D1**

Rest – *(booking advisable)* Menu 35 € – Carte 25/44 €

♦ Regional ♦ Cosy ♦

Rural ambience with a touch of modernity. The owner is in the kitchen, preparing regional and international fare.

GREECE
ELLÁDA

PROFILE

→ **Area:**
131 944 km²
(50 944 sq mi).

→ **Population:**
10 668 000 inhabitants (est. 2005), density = 81 per km².

→ **Capital:**
Athens (conurbation 3 368 000 inhabitants).

→ **Currency:**
Euro (€); rate of exchange: € 1 = US$ 1.46 (Dec 2007).

→ **Government:**
Parliamentary republic (since 1974). Member of European Union since 1981.

→ **Language:**
Greek.

→ **Specific public holidays:**
Epiphany (6 January); Orthodox Shrove Monday (late February-March); Independence Day (25 March); Orthodox Good Friday (Friday before Easter); Orthodox Easter Monday; Day of the Holy Spirit (late May-June); Ochi Day (28 October); Boxing Day (26 December).

→ **Local Time:**
GMT + 2 hours in winter and GMT + 3 hours in summer.

→ **Climate:**
Temperate Mediterranean, with mild winters and hot, sunny summers (Athens: January: 10°C, July: 27°C).

→ **International dialling code:**
00 30 followed by local number.

→ **Emergency:**
General Police: ✆ **100**, Tourist Police: ✆ **171**, Ambulance: ✆ **166.**

→ **Electricity:**
220 volts AC, 50Hz; 2-pin round-shaped continental plugs.

→ **Formalities**
Travellers from the European Union (EU), Switzerland, Iceland and the main countries of North and South America need a national identity card or passport (America: passport required) to visit Greece for less than three months (tourism or business purpose). For visitors from other countries a visa may be required, in addition to a passport, especially for those wishing to stay for longer than three months. We advise you to check with your embassy before travelling.

ATHENS
ATHÍNA

Population: 732 000 (conurbation 3 368 000) – Altitude: 156m

Sime/PHOTONONSTOP

So what did the Greeks ever do for us? Apart from inventing democracy, the theatre and the Olympic Games, that is... and planting the seeds of philosophy and Western Civilisation, of course... Athens was central to all of these, a city that became a byword for glory and learning, a place whose golden reputation could inspire such awe in later centuries that just the mention of its name was enough to turn people misty-eyed and reverential: the poets Lamartine and Byron are just two who waxed lyrical over its splendours.

It's a truly magical place, built upon eight hills and plains, with a recorded history stretching back at least 3,000 years. Its short but highly productive golden age (roughly 470BC to 430BC) resulted in the architectural glory of The Acropolis, while the likes of Plato, Aristotle and Socrates were in the business of changing the mindset of society. In more recent times, Athens suffered at the hands of the motor car, the heat and the mountains, a notorious cocktail producing a fog that would hang over the city like a heavy hand, reaching such gruesome levels that even tourists stayed away. But since the 1980s and up to and beyond the 2004 Olympics, the city has made great efforts to regenerate itself with imaginative planning and a much-needed metro. Hip clubs and restaurants have sprung up. Quaint inner city areas have been restored. Could the glory days of Athens be returning?

LIVING THE CITY

No one could possibly argue with the fact that **The Acropolis** dominates Athens. It can be seen peeking through alleyways and turnings all over the city. Beneath it lies a teeming metropolis, part urban melting pot, part uber-buzzy neighbourhood. **Plaka**, below the Acropolis, is the old quarter, and the most visited, a mixture of great charm and cheap gift shops. North and west, **Monastiraki** and **Psirri** has become a trendy zone after decades of decay; to the east, Syntagma and Kolonaki are notably modern and smart, home to the Greek parliament and the rich and famous; you can look down on them – literally and metaphorically, if you wish – from the glorious green heights of Lykkavittos Hill. The most northerly districts of central Athens are **Omonia** and **Exarcheia**, distinguished by their rugged appearance, and steeped in history; much of the life in these parts is centred round the polytechnic and the central marketplace.

PRACTICAL INFORMATION

ARRIVAL-DEPARTURE

If you're coming to the city by sea, or intending to visit the islands, then your port of call is Piraeus, a few miles from Athens. Piraeus is now the third largest port in the Mediterranean.

Athens International Airport is 33km east of the city. A taxi can take a while so your best bet is to hop on the metro and take Line 3 to Monastiraki.

TRANSPORT

Because of that traffic, the sensible way of getting around town is by the metro. Two new lines were opened in 2001 and accessibility round Athens is now markedly better than a decade ago.

Buses and trolley-buses run an excellent service (though hampered by traffic). Carnets of 10 tickets are available from newsstands, OASA booths and kiosks and at metro or subway stations.

EXPLORING ATHENS

Where can you start exploring Athens other than at the **Acropolis**? The world's most famous hill shows evidence of settlements as far back as Neolithic times,

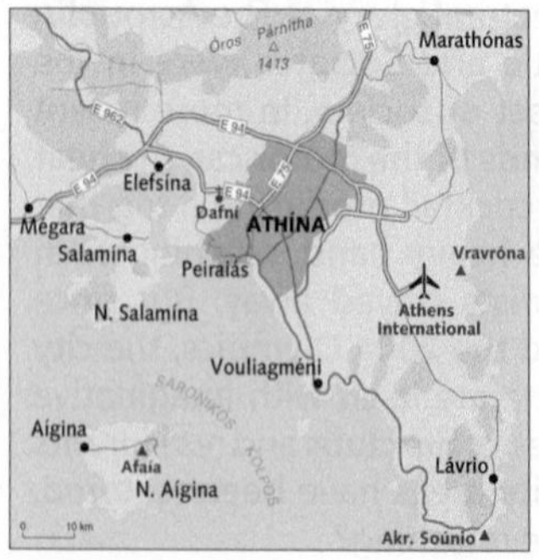

but the reign of Pericles in the fifth century BC produced buildings so stylistically perfect that they're considered, 2,500 years later, the most important monuments in the Western world and the greatest-ever influence on our architecture. These great marble masterpieces were mostly temples built to honour **Athena**, the city's patron goddess. Their scale and breathtaking proportion manage to triumph on both a majestic and a human level, a testament to the ancient architects Iktinos and Kallikrates and the unerring eye of their supervising sculptor Phidias. The **Parthenon**, much of which still stands before us today, was completed in just 10 years, an amazing achievement. When you're up at the summit of the sacred rock of Athens, take your pick of the temples around you: The Parthenon (a must), Propyleia (the grand entrance temple), the small Temple of Athena Nike, or the exceptional Ionic structure of the Erechtheion. There are two ancient theatres also on the Acropolis, including one still used for the Athens Festival (Herodes Atticus Theatre). The other is the Dionysus Theatre, the world's oldest, where plays by Sophocles and Euripedes were staged. When visiting the Acropolis, try to get there in the early morning or evening, because crowds and midday heat can sap even the most enthusiastic classicist.

If it's just too damn hot up there at the summit, you don't have to walk far to find shady relief…and buildings dating back even further than the Parthenon. The ancient **Agora** is a grassy haven at the base of the hill, the one-time marketplace founded in the sixth century BC where the likes of Socrates would make impassioned speeches to interested passers-by. Its rambling and varied remains can confuse the unwary visitor, but it doesn't take much to fall into a reverie about the lively events that once happened here (it was the centre for civic activities such as commerce, politics, arts and athletics) and it's also where you come face-to-face with the best-preserved Classical temple in Greece, the **Temple of Hephaestus**. Stroll across to the area east of this at the bottom of the Acropolis and you're in **Plaka**, the old town section that's become the gathering place for tourists and travellers, especially in the warm Athenian evenings. Its charming ambience is captured in winding alleyways haunted by a medieval air (and touts in midsummer). Seek out nuggets of sheer delight, such as the irresistible Byzantine courtyards, and the delightful hidden neighbourhood of **Anafiotika**, which clings to the foot of the Acropolis, and contains idyllic blue-and-white houses built in the 19 C by Cycladic workmen. Just up from here stands The Tower of the Winds, built in 50 BC by a Syrian astronomer, with personifications of the winds on each of its eight sides – there's no other building like it in the ancient world.

→ THE PAST AND THE PRESENTS

You can go from one end of the retail extreme to the other in central Athens; if you favour the cheaper option, then get up early on a Sunday and head for the **Monastiraki flea market**. Fabled throughout the Hellenic world, it takes place right next to the Agora, with traders and buyers filling the surrounding streets. Everything's for sale, from tat to things like antique furnishings and rare books. Just remember to haggle. At the other end of the shopping scale are the designer boutiques of **Kolonaki**, where haggling is most definitely not an option. This is the area where you can find the Parliament building, adjacent to which, along the avenue of Vassilissis Sofias, is the renowned **Museum Row**, home to four of Athens' finest. Nearest the Parliament building, The **Benaki Museum** is one of the best in Greece. It contains a fabulously all-encompassing range of prehistoric to 20 C Greek art, and its lovely rooftop garden restaurant is worth the visit in itself. Next along is the Museum of Cycladic Art, featuring elegant female figures carved 2,000 years before the Parthenon; the Byzantine Museum chronicles the rise and fall of the great Byzantine Empire from the third to the nineteenth century; and finally, the War Museum, on two huge floors, tells the history of conflict in Greece from prehistoric to modern times. Trumping all these fine collections, though, is the **National Archaeological Museum**, up in Exarcheia. Not only is this the number one museum in Greece, it's also one of the best in the world, containing a week's worth of ancient wonders to discover. Chief of these are arguably the treasures of the Mycenaean civilization, including hoards of gold and fantastical golden swords.

→ TECHNO ART

So, where does an Athenian go for the edgy, the arty and the gallery-strewn? Answer: a one-time toxin-spewing foundry in the Gaslands ('Gazi' in Greek), a former dingy neck of the woods just northwest of the Agora. This old foundry has been converted into a huge arts centre called **Technopolis**, where concerts, exhibits and arts spaces, generally of the first order, come together under one gargantuan roof with coloured lights illuminating the old chimneys. Some of the city's sleekest restaurants now nestle in the surrounding streets, while the neighbouring quarters of Thissio and Psirri have benefitted too, with grungy Greek music dives and squares dotted with bars and cafés sidling in alongside the industrial behemoths of yesteryear.

Athens is a hot and steamy place in the summer, so areas of green refuge are not just welcome but essential. South of the Acropolis is **Filopappou Hill**, the highest point in southern Athens, boasting superb views out to sea and, on its pathway up to the peak, a small cave that's said to be where Socrates was held after being sentenced to death for corrupting the youth of the city. The hill is full of shade and interesting paths. Back down to earth, you can escape the traffic in the rather wonderful National Gardens, next to the Parliament Building in Syntagma. These are full of exotic plants and winding paths, statuary and fountains. You may feel so intoxicated by this abundantly verdant oasis that you get lost (it has been known). Lykkavittos Hill, to the east of town, is accessible by foot, but most people take the funicular. It boasts stupendous views over the city from its Chapel of St George at the peak. There are a few little cafés dotted around the hill, great places to sip a drink or two as the sun goes down.

CALENDAR HIGHLIGHTS

Summer time is party time for Athenians. The Hellenic Festival runs from June to September and performances take place in a wonderful setting - the awe-inspiring Odeon of Herodes Atticus, which is backed by the floodlit Acropolis: other events featuring music, theatre and dance take place at venues around town. During the same months, The International Petra Festival at Petra Theatre gives it a good run for its money with an eclectic variety of music and theatre. The European Jazz Festival blasted off in Athens in 2001 and is now a renowned event for

ATHENS IN...

→ ONE DAY

Acropolis, Parthenon, Agora and Temple of Hephaestus, Plaka

→ TWO DAYS

Kolonaki, National Archaeological Museum, Filopappou Hill

→ THREE DAYS

Monastiraki flea-market (on Sunday), Benaki Museum, Technopolis, National Gardens, Lykkavittos Hill

international names - it takes place in June at Gazi's Technopolis. Rock fans, meanwhile, should make for Terravibe in June for Rockwave Festival, the best in Greece. It's a full-on rock celebration and includes bungee jumping and a skate park. The Dora Stratou Theatre is home to a renowned program of Greek folk dances from May to September, while The Greek Orthodox calendar highlight occurs at Easter, when a most impressive looking candlelit procession climbs Lykavittos Hill to the chapel of Agios Georgos. Talking of atmosphere: every August all Athens' monuments and archaeological sights are open to the public for free for moonlit classical performances under the title 'Nights Under The Full Moon'.

EATING OUT

In recent times, Michelin has been busy in Athens awarding stars for the smart new wave of restaurants that has hit the city. With many chefs now going abroad to train and returning home to put their nifty skills to good use, this is a fine time to eat out in the shadow of the Acropolis. If you want to get the full experience and dine with the locals (rather than the tourists), make your reservation for late evening, as Greeks rarely go out for dinner before 10pm. There's a good range of flavours in vogue, as ethnic menus have come to the fore, highlighted by Asian and Moroccan dishes. Sushi is now a big fish in Athens, too. And the trend towards a more eclectic restaurant scene now means that classic French and Italian cuisine is easily found. New modern tavernas offer good attention to detail, but this doesn't mean they're replacing the wonderfully traditional old favourites. These tavernas, along with mezedopoleia, are the backbone of Greek dining, and most visitors wouldn't think their trip was complete without eating in at least one or two. Often the waiter will just tell you what's cooking today, and you're often very welcome to go into the kitchen and make your selection. Greece is a country where it is customary to tip good service; ten per cent is the normal rate.

→ UNIFORM APPEAL

A time-honoured tourist ritual is having a gander at the changing of the guard outside the Parliament Building, on the hour every hour. Individual soldiers perform an eye-catching high kicking march, wearing mini skirts, white stockings, and red clogs with pom-poms. Selected from the ranks of Greek military conscripts, they're chosen these days not because of any war-like efficiency, but because of crowd-pleasing height and good looks.

→ MARBLES RE-FOUND

The exciting, brand new Acropolis Museum in Makrigianni, at the foot of Acropolis hill, is more than just a stunning, all-glass showpiece for its fabulous treasures. It's a sharp reminder that Greece now has a safe and adequate home for its **Marbles**, purloined by the Earl of Elgin in 1799 and sold to the British Museum where they remain to this day. After gazing at them for hours, Keats summed up the beauty of the Marbles when he famously wrote: 'Beauty is truth, truth beauty – that is all ye know on earth, and all ye need to know.'

→ A LONG WAIT FOR THE METRO

If you fancy a trip to a museum, you could do worse than nip down into the metro. During construction, many of the stations unearthed ancient remains, and these have been put on display for travellers or curious tourists; expect to find the likes of pottery and gravestones, even a skeleton still entombed. Two of the best stations are Syntagma and Akropoli. Catching a train afterwards is optional.

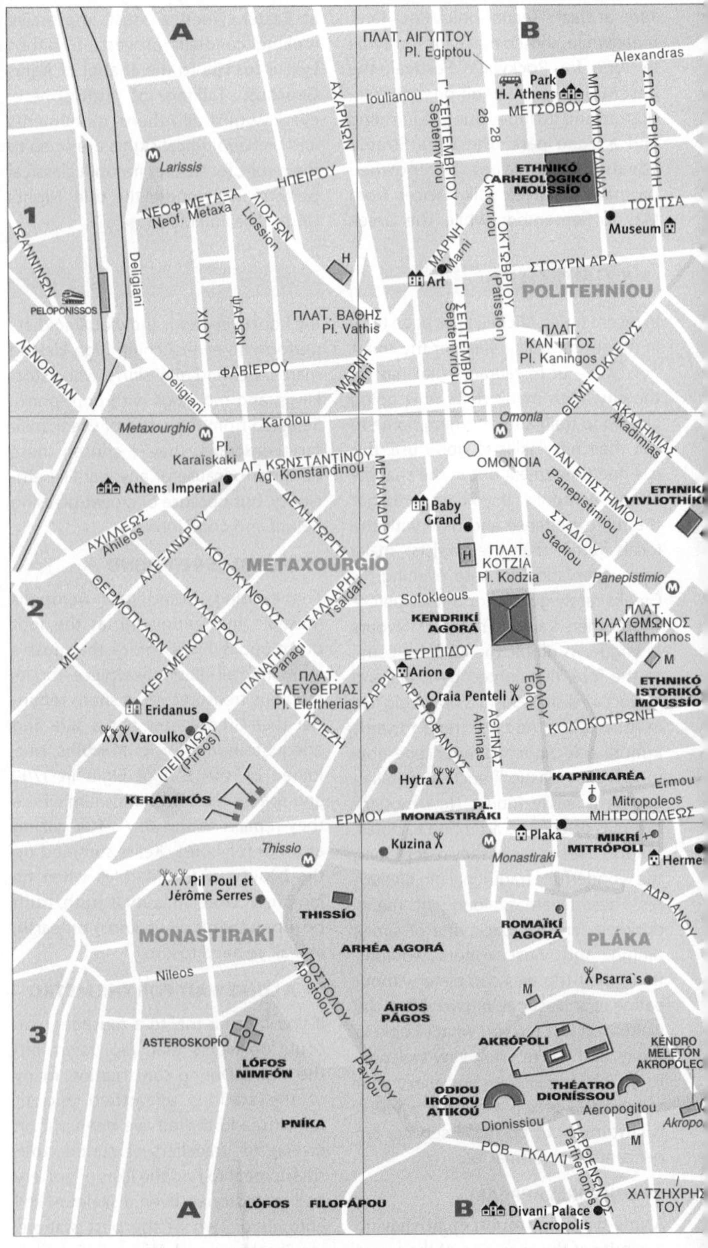
A
B
1
2
3
ΠΛΑΤ. ΑΙΓΥΠΤΟΥ
Pl. Egiptou
Alexandras
Park
H. Athens
ΜΕΤΣΟΒΟΥ
ΜΠΟΥΜΠΟΥΛΙΝΑΣ
ΣΠΥΡ. ΤΡΙΚΟΥΠΗ
Ioulianou
ΑΧΑΡΝΩΝ
Γ' ΣΕΠΤΕΜΒΡΙΟΥ
Septemvriou
28
ETHNIKÓ ARHEOLOGIKÓ MOUSSÍO
Larissis
ΗΠΕΙΡΟΥ
ΝΕΟΦ ΜΕΤΑΞΑ
Neof. Metaxa
ΛΙΟΣΙΩΝ
Liossion
ΤΟΣΙΤΣΑ
Museum
ΙΩΑΝΝΙΝΩΝ
Deligiani
ΜΑΡΝΗ
Marni
ΟΚΤΩΒΡΙΟΥ
Oktovriou
(Patission)
ΣΤΟΥΡΝ ΑΡΑ
Art
POLITEHNÍOU
PELOPONISSOS
ΧΙΟΥ
ΨΑΡΩΝ
ΠΛΑΤ. ΒΑΘΗΣ
Pl. Vathis
ΠΛΑΤ. ΚΑΝ ΙΓΓΟΣ
Pl. Kaningos
ΛΕΝΟΡΜΑΝ
ΦΑΒΙΕΡΟΥ
ΘΕΜΙΣΤΟΚΛΕΟΥΣ
Omonia
Metaxourghio
Karolou
Pl. Karaïskaki
ΑΓ. ΚΩΝΣΤΑΝΤΙΝΟΥ
Ag. Konstandinou
ΜΕΝΑΝΔΡΟΥ
ΟΜΟΝΟΙΑ
ΑΚΑΔΗΜΙΑΣ
Akadimias
ΠΑΝ ΕΠΙΣΤΗΜΙΟΥ
Panepistimiou
ETHNIKÍ VIVLIOTHÍKI
Athens Imperial
ΔΕΛΗΓΙΩΡΓΗ
Baby Grand
ΑΧΙΛΛΕΩΣ
Ahileos
ΑΛΕΞΑΝΔΡΟΥ
ΚΟΛΟΚΥΝΘΟΥΣ
METAXOURGÍO
H
ΠΛΑΤ. ΚΟΤΖΙΑ
Pl. Kodzia
ΣΤΑΔΙΟΥ
Stadiou
Panepistimio
ΘΕΡΜΟΠΥΛΩΝ
ΜΥΛΛΕΡΟΥ
ΤΣΑΛΔΑΡΗ
Tsaldari
Sofokleous
KENDRIKÍ AGORÁ
ΠΛΑΤ. ΚΛΑΥΘΜΩΝΟΣ
Pl. Klafthmonos
ΜΕΓ.
ΚΕΡΑΜΕΙΚΟΥ
ΠΑΝΑΓΗ
Panagi
ΕΥΡΙΠΙΔΟΥ
Arion
ΑΙΟΛΟΥ
Eolou
M
ETHNIKÓ ISTORIKÓ MOUSSÍO
ΠΛΑΤ. ΕΛΕΥΘΕΡΙΑΣ
Pl. Eleftherias
ΣΑΡΡΗ
ΑΡΙΣΤΟΦΑΝΟΥΣ
Oraia Penteli
Eridanus
ΑΘΗΝΑΣ
Athinas
ΚΟΛΟΚΟΤΡΩΝΗ
Varoulko
(ΠΕΙΡΑΙΩΣ)
(Pireos)
ΚΡΙΕΖΗ
KAPNIKARÉA
Ermou
Hytra
Mitropoleos
ΜΗΤΡΟΠΟΛΕΩΣ
KERAMIKÓS
PL. MONASTIRÁKI
ΕΡΜΟΥ
Plaka
MIKRÍ MITRÓPOLI
Kuzina
Thissio
Monastiraki
Herme
Pil Poul et Jérôme Serres
ΑΔΡΙΑΝΟΥ
THISSÍO
MONASTIRAKÍ
ROMAÏKÍ AGORÁ
PLÁKA
ARHÉA AGORÁ
ΑΠΟΣΤΟΛΟΥ
Apostolou
Nileos
Psarra`s
ÁRIOS PÁGOS
ASTEROSKOPÍO
AKRÓPOLI
KÉNDRO MELETÓN AKROPOLEO
LÓFOS NIMFÓN
ΠΑΥΛΟΥ
Pavlou
ODIOU IRÓDOU ATIKOÚ
THÉATRO DIONÍSSOU
Aeropogitou
Dionissiou
Akropo
PNÍKA
ΡΟΒ. ΓΚΑΛΛΙ
ΠΑΡΘΕΝΩΝΟΣ
Parthenonos
ΧΑΤΖΗΧΡΗΣ ΤΟΥ
LÓFOS FILOPÁPOU
Divani Palace Acropolis

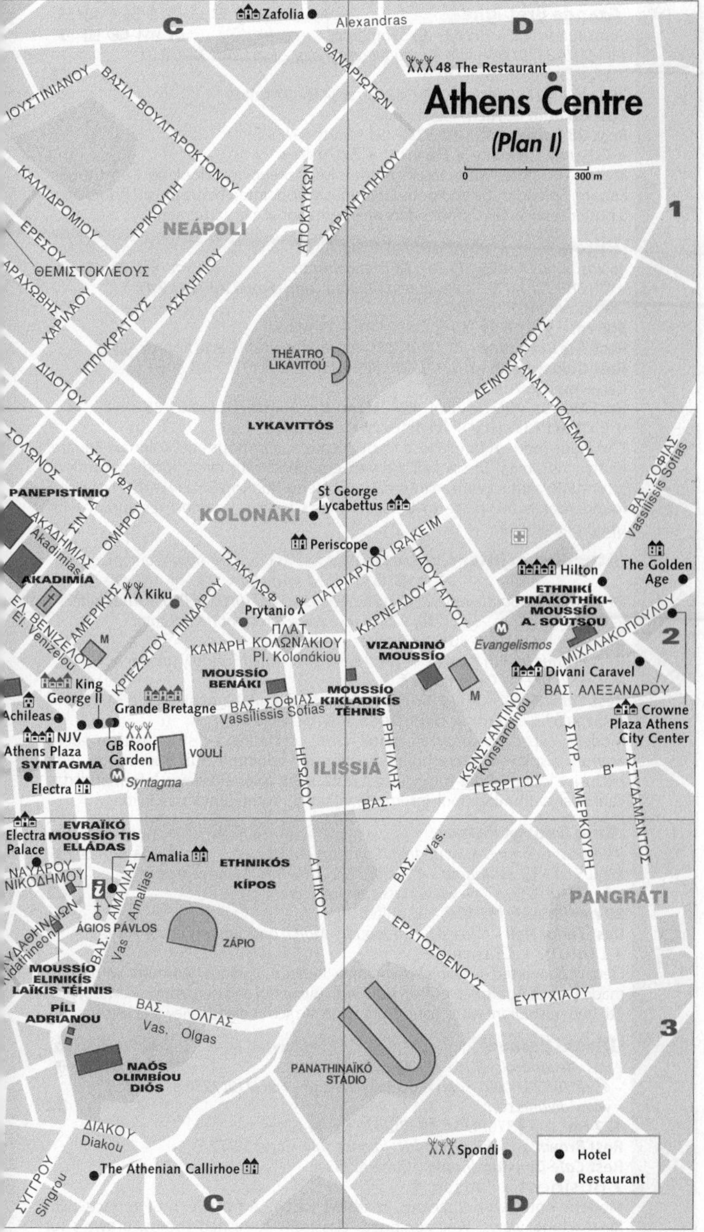
Athens Centre
(Plan I)
0
300 m
Zafolia
Alexandras
48 The Restaurant
NEÁPOLI
THÉATRO LIKAVITOÚ
LYKAVITTÓS
PANEPISTÍMIO
AKADIMÍA
KOLONÁKI
St George Lycabettus
Periscope
Kiku
Prytanio
ΠΛΑΤ. ΚΟΛΩΝΑΚΙΟΥ
Pl. Kolonákiou
VIZANDINÓ MOUSSÍO
MOUSSÍO BENÁKI
MOUSSÍO KIKLADIKÍS TÉHNIS
Hilton
The Golden Age
ETHNIKÍ PINAKOTHÍKI-MOUSSÍO A. SOÚTSOU
Evangelismos
Divani Caravel
Crowne Plaza Athens City Center
King George II
Grande Bretagne
Achileas
NJV Athens Plaza
GB Roof Garden
VOULÍ
SYNTAGMA
Syntagma
Electra
ILISSIÁ
Electra Palace
EVRAÏKÓ MOUSSÍO TIS ELLÁDAS
Amalia
ETHNIKÓS KÍPOS
ÁGIOS PÁVLOS
ZÁPIO
MOUSSÍO ELINIKÍS LAÏKIS TÉHNIS
PÍLI ADRIANOU
NAÓS OLIMBÍOU DIÓS
PANATHINAÏKÓ STÁDIO
PANGRÁTI
Spondi
The Athenian Callirhoe
Hotel
Restaurant
C
D
1
2
3

Grande Bretagne

< Athens, rm

Constitution Sq ✉ 105 63 – Ⓜ Syntagma
– ☎ (210) 3330 000 – info@grandebretagne.gr – Fax (210) 3220 8 01
– www.grandebretagne.gr **C2**

284 rm – †275/365 € ††295/385 €, ☕ 34 € – 37 suites
Rest *GB Roof Garden* – see below
Rest *GB Corner* – *☎ (210) 3330 750* – Carte 59/75 €

◆ Grand Luxury ◆ Palace ◆ Stylish ◆

Stylish 19C hotel with classic, modernised interior overlooking Constitution Square. Splendid spa and pool. Luxuriously-appointed bedrooms; 2 floors offer a butler service. GB Corner offers an international à la carte menu.

Hilton

< Athens and Acropolis, rm

46 Vas. Sofias Ave ✉ 115 28 – Ⓜ Evangelismos
– ☎ (210) 7281 000 – sales.athens@hilton.com – Fax (210) 7281 2 41
– www.athens.hilton.com **D2**

505 rm – †229 € ††359 €, ☕ 32.50 € – 19 suites
Rest *The Byzantine* – *☎ (210) 7281 400 (Buffet lunch)* Carte approx. 60 €
Rest *Galaxy Roof* – *☎ (210) 7281 402 (May-October) (dinner only)* Carte approx. 70 €
Rest *Milo's* – *☎ (210) 7244 400* – Menu 20 € (lunch) – Carte 65/85 €

◆ Grand Luxury ◆ Modern ◆

Luxurious modern hotel close to city centre, near shops and Kolonaki Square. Bedrooms similar in size; all are well-equipped with every modern comfort. Informal Byzantine with an international menu. Rooftop Galaxy with terrace and lounge/bar is the place to be seen. Milo's is large seafood restaurant with open-plan kitchen.

Athenaeum Inter-Continental

< Athens and Acropolis, rm

89-93 Singrou (Southwest : 2 ¾ km) ✉ 117 45 – ☎ (210) 9206 000 – attha.hotel@ichotelsgroup.com – Fax (210) 9206 5 06 – www.intercontinental.com

543 rm – †230 € ††230 €, – 60 suites
Rest *Première (9th floor)* – *☎ (210) 9206 981 (closed Sunday) (dinner only)* Menu 57/102 € – Carte 63/85 €
Rest *Cafezoe* – *☎ (210) 9206 655* – Menu 36 € (buffet lunch) – Carte 34/75 €

◆ Grand Luxury ◆ Business ◆ Modern ◆

Modern, top class corporate hotel, close to business district, with modern artwork displayed throughout. Luxuriously-appointed club floor rooms with exclusive lounge. Roof-top gourmet restaurant; splendid views. Informal all day café near swimming pool; international menu, some Greek specialities.

King George Palace

rm

3 Vasileos Georgiou A, Syntagma (Constitution) Sq
✉ 105 64 – Ⓜ Syntagma – ☎ (210) 3222 210 – info@kinggeorge.gr
– Fax (210) 3250 5 04 – www.classicalhotels.com **C2**

89 rm – †640 € ††640 €, – 13 suites
Rest *Tudor Hall* – *(Closed lunch January-March and Sunday)* Carte 76/92 €

◆ Luxury ◆ Classic ◆

Elegant converted mansion in Syntagma Square. Luxurious bedrooms with hand-made French furniture; rooftop suite with own pool and panoramic views. Stylish 7th floor restaurant with chandeliers, large terrace and good views. Eclectic menu.

Divani Caravel

< Athens,

2 Vas. Alexandrou ✉ 161 21 – Ⓜ Evangelismos
– ☎ (210) 7207 000 – sales@divanicaravel.gr – Fax (210) 7236 6 83
– www.divanis.com **D2**

427 rm ☕ – †370/470 € ††370/470 € – 44 suites
Rest *Brown's* – *(Closed Sunday) (dinner only)* Carte 59/72 €
Rest *Café Constantinople* – Carte 42/53 €

◆ Business ◆ Classic ◆

Modern hotel with spacious, marbled lobby. Attractive roof terrace with far-reaching views. Well-equipped, classically furnished rooms. Brown's for stylish dining and elegant cigar lounge; international cuisine with Asian influences. Café Constantinople is open all day and serves buffet lunch.

Metropolitan

385 Singrou Ave (Southwest : 7 km) ✉ 175 64 – ☎ (210) 9471 000
– metropolitan@chandris.gr – Fax (210) 9471 0 10
– www.chandris.gr
362 rm – †545 € ††545 €, ☕ 20 € – 12 suites
Rest *Trocadero* – Menu 28 € (buffet lunch Monday-Friday) – Carte 34/46 €
♦ Business ♦ Modern ♦
Striking, modern corporate hotel with easy access into and out of the city. Spacious, comfortable rooms with state-of-the-art facilities. Popular for business conventions. International or Italian fare can be taken overlooking the garden or beside the pool.

Ledra Marriott

115 Singrou (Southwest : 3 km) ✉ 117 45 – ☎ (210) 9300 000
– mhrs.athgr.exec.asst@marriott.com – Fax (210) 9559 1 53
– www.marriott.com
296 rm – †199 € ††249 €, ☕ 26 € – 18 suites
Rest *Kona Kai* – *(Closed 10 days August, Easter, 1 January, Sunday and Monday) (dinner only)* Carte 44/72 €
Rest *Zephyros* – *(buffet lunch)* Carte 32/50 €
♦ Business ♦ Modern ♦
Commercial hotel with panoramic views from rooftop terrace. Executive rooms have exclusive lounge and high-tech extras. Ornate Kona Kai for authentic Polynesian dishes and teppan-yaki. Zephyros on 1st floor for traditional and international buffet.

NJV Athens Plaza

2 Vas. Georgiou A, Syntagma Sq ✉ 105 64 – Ⓜ Syntagma
– ☎ (210) 3352 400 – sales_njv@grecotel.gr – Fax (210) 3235 8 56
– www.grecotel.gr **C2**
159 rm – †380/440 € ††440 €, ☕ 25 € – 23 suites
Rest *The Parliament* – Carte 65/104 €
♦ Business ♦ Classic ♦
Modern hotel handy for the shopping and business districts. Local stone adorns the contemporary lobby and bar. Boldly decorated, hi-tech bedrooms and luxurious suites. Modern menu of international dishes served in stylish first floor restaurant.

Athens Imperial

Karaiskaki Sq ✉ 104 37 – Ⓜ Metaxourghio – ☎ (210) 5201 600
– sales_ai@classicalhotels.gr – Fax (210) 5225 5 21
– www.classicalhotels.com **A2**
235 rm – †117 € ††148 €, ☕ 22 € – 25 suites
Rest – Carte 33/58 €
♦ Business ♦ Modern ♦
Modern hotel, its impressive atrium boasting opulent lounge and bar with suspended arboreal artwork. Lovely rooftop decked pool area with superb views to Acropolis. Mod cons match smart, stylish rooms. Views over the square from restaurant; international cuisine served.

St George Lycabettus

≤ Athens,

2 Kleomenous St ✉ 106 75 – ☎ (210) 7290 711
– sales@sglycabettus.gr – Fax (210) 7290 4 39
– www.sglycabettus.gr **C2**
148 rm ☕ – †338/442 € ††413/507 € – 6 suites
Rest *Le Grand Balcon* – *(Closed Sunday and Monday) (dinner only)* Menu 60 €
Rest *Frame* – Carte 35/45 €
♦ Business ♦ Modern ♦
Elevated position on Lycabettus Hill. Greek artwork and artefacts throughout. Roof-top pool. South-facing rooms with balconies, view of Acropolis and Athens skyline. Le Grand Balcon roof-top restaurant for international menu. All day Frame for Greek dishes.

Electra Palace

Acropolis and Plaka, rm VISA AE

18-20 Nikodimou St ✉ 105 57 – Ⓜ Syntagma – ☎ (210) 3370 000 – salesepath@electrahotels.gr – Fax (210) 3241 8 75 – www.electrahotels.gr **C3**

145 rm – †170/300 € ††180/360 € – 10 suites

Rest – *(dinner only)* Carte 44/59 €

♦ Business ♦ Classic ♦

Modern interior behind a classical façade on a quiet street in Plaka. Ultra-modern bedrooms and suites with classical décor; some with view of the Acropolis. Electra rooftop restaurant with beautiful terrace and superb view. Creative Greek cuisine.

Stratos Vassilikos

rm VISA AE

Mihalakopoulou 114 (via Mihalakopoulou, past Holiday Inn) ✉ 115 27 – Ⓜ Megaro Moussikis – ☎ (210) 7706 611 – stratos-vassilikos@airotel.gr – Fax (210) 7708 1 37 – www.airotel.gr

82 rm – †142 € ††142 € – 6 suites

Rest – Carte approx. 40 €

♦ Business ♦ Modern ♦

Elegant, modern hotel with an interesting décor, set away from the city centre. Well-furnished bedrooms, some with balconies. Spacious suites. Atrium restaurant for lunch or formal dinner; contemporary French cuisine.

Park H. Athens

Athens, rm VISA AE

10 Alexandras Ave ✉ 106 82 – Ⓜ Victoria – ☎ (210) 8894 500 – sales@athensparkhotel.gr – Fax (210) 8238 4 20 – www.athensparkhotel.gr **B1**

140 rm – †320/360 € ††380/420 € – 10 suites

Rest *Alexandra's* – Carte 22/45 €

Rest *Park Café* – Carte 18/40 €

Rest *St'Astra* – *(closed Sunday) (dinner only)* Carte 60/110 €

♦ Business ♦ Traditional ♦ Classic ♦

Modern, family-owned hotel between the archaeological museum and Pedio Areos Park. Smartly fitted rooms, suites with spa baths. Classic French and Greek cuisine in Alexandra's. All day Park Café for a light meal. Enjoy view from St'Astra by rooftop pool. Mediterranean menu and live jazz in evenings.

Zafolia

Athens, rm VISA AE

87-89 Alexandras Ave ✉ 114 74 – Ⓜ Ambelokipi – ☎ (210) 6449 002 – info@zafoliahotel.gr – Fax (210) 6442 0 42 – www.zafoliahotel.gr **C1**

185 rm – †138/180 € ††145/180 € – 7 suites

Rest – Menu 24/42 €

♦ Business ♦ Modern ♦

Privately-owned, commercial hotel on east side of city. Well-equipped rooms with modern amenities, some with private balcony. Excellent views from rooftop bar and pool. Shop-fitted mezzanine level restaurant. Greek and international menu.

Crowne Plaza Athens City Center

rm VISA AE

50 Mihalakopoulou ✉ 115 28 – Ⓜ Megaro Moussikis ☎ (210) 7278 000 – info@hiathens.com – Fax (210) 7278 6 00 – www.hiathens.com **D2**

193 rm – †440/540 € ††490/600 €, 27 €

Rest – Carte 30/57 €

♦ Chain hotel ♦ Business ♦ Modern ♦

Modern corporate hotel with extensive state-of-the-art conference facilities. All bedrooms are aimed at the commercial traveller. Restaurant offers international menu; light meals in summer in poolside roof garden commanding far-reaching city views. Hotel being refurbished in 2008.

Holiday Suites without rest

VISA AE

4 Arnis St (by Mihalakopoulou) ✉ 115 28 – Ⓜ Megaro Moussikis – ☎ (210) 7278 500 – info@holiday-suites.com – Fax (210) 7278 6 00 – www.holiday-suites.com

16 rm – †540 € ††570 € – 18 suites, 19 €

♦ Business ♦ Modern ♦

Converted apartments in quiet residential area. Spacious rooms each with kitchenette, sofa and work area, superbly equipped with CD/DVD/fax. Breakfast here or at the Crowne Plaza Athens City Center.

Divani Palace Acropolis ⊠ ▭ ⇸rm ▭ ♨ VISA ◉ AE ◑

19-25 Parthenonos ✉ 117 42 – Ⓜ Akropolis – ✆ (210) 9280 100 – divanis@divaniacropolis.gr – Fax (210) 9214 9 93 – www.divaniacropolis.gr **B3**

242 rm – †260/310 € ††260/310 €, ☕ 20 € – 8 suites

Rest *Aspassia* – Menu 30 € – Carte 36/68 €

Rest *Roof Garden* – *(Closed Tuesday) (dinner only)* Carte 60/90 €

♦ Traditional ♦ Classic ♦

Near the Parthenon yet fairly quiet with parts of Themistocles' wall in the basement. Particularly comfortable suites. All day Aspassia for international and Greek meals. Roof Garden for summer barbecue buffet with live music.

The Athenian Callirhoe without rest

32 Kallirois Ave and Petmeza ✉ 117 43 – Ⓜ Singrou-Fix – ✆ (210) 9215 353 – hotel@tac.gr – Fax (210) 9215 3 42 – www.tac.gr **C3**

84 rm ☕ – †130/160 € ††150/180 €

♦ Business ♦ Stylish ♦

A bright, contemporary boutique hotel with subtle art deco styling. City views from the rooftop terrace and balconies of the smartly fitted executive rooms.

Eridanus without rest

78 Pireaus Ave, Keramikos ✉ 104 35 – Ⓜ Thissio – ✆ (210) 5205 360 – eridanus@eridanus.gr – Fax (210) 5200 5 50 – www.eridanus.gr **A2**

38 rm ☕ – †160/220 € ††160/400 €

♦ Business ♦ Stylish ♦

Contemporary design hotel on a busy main road. Luxurious bedrooms with high-tech equipment and hydro massage showers; some with views of the Acropolis.

Baby Grand

65 Athens St ✉ 105 52 – Ⓜ Omonia – ✆ (210) 3250 900 – athenagrand@grecotel.gr – Fax (210) 3743 6 43 – www.grecotel.gr **B2**

70 rm – †116 € ††148 €, ☕ 20 € – 6 suites

Rest *Baby Grand* – Menu 27 € – Carte 24/31 €

♦ Business ♦ Modern ♦

Eclectically-furnished city centre hotel featuring Mini Cooper reception desks. Relax in colourful lounge with squashy sofas. Individually designed rooms are well equipped. Ground floor restaurant serves international and Greek dishes.

Alexandros

8 Timoleontos Vassou St (via Vas. Sofias off Soutsou D.) ✉ 115 21 – Ⓜ Megaro Moussikis – ✆ (210) 6430 464 – alexandros@airotel.gr – Fax (210) 6441 0 84 – www.airotel.gr

92 rm ☕ – †128 € ††128 € – 3 suites

Rest *Don Giovanni* – Carte 20/32 €

♦ Business ♦ Modern ♦

A relaxed, commercial hotel off a busy avenue in residential area. Simple accommodation is offered in comfortably appointed bedrooms. Don Giovanni is an elegant little restaurant offering mostly Greek cuisine, with some Italian dishes too.

Electra

5 Ermou ✉ 105 63 – Ⓜ Syntagma – ✆ (210) 3378 000 – saleselath@electrahotels.gr – Fax (210) 3220 3 10 – www.electrahotels.gr **C2**

106 rm ☕ – †130/312 € ††150/312 € – 3 suites

Rest – Carte 18/30 €

♦ Business ♦ Modern ♦

Popular tourist hotel within the lively pedestrianised shopping area. Soundproofed, refurbished bedrooms are thoughtfully equipped and well maintained, some have spa baths. International dishes in mezzanine restaurant.

Art

27 Marni St ✉ 104 32 – Ⓜ Omonia – ☎ (210) 5240 501 – info@arthotelathens.gr – Fax (210) 5243 3 84 – www.arthotelathens.gr **B1**

30 rm – 79/129 € 79/160 €

Rest – Carte 40/60 €

◆ Family ◆ Personalised ◆

The name's the clue: artwork in all areas of this family-owned 21C boutique hotel behind a classic 1930s façade on busy central street. Simply furnished bedrooms; some with balcony. Classically-styled restaurant; short international menu.

Periscope without rest

22 Haritos St, Kolonaki ✉ 106 75 – Ⓜ Evangelismos – ☎ (210) 7297 200 – info@periscope.gr – Fax (210) 7297 2 06 – www.periscope.gr **D2**

21 rm – 160/200 € 200/500 €

◆ Business ◆ Modern ◆

Minimalism in quiet area; trendy bar has plasma screens and reconditioned Mini Cooper seats! Uniquely-styled rooms boast balconies; executive rooms are quietest and have enlarged Athenian images on ceiling.

Amalia

10 Amalia Ave ✉ 105 57 – Ⓜ Syntagma – ☎ ((210)) 3237 300 – reserve@amaliaathens.gr – Fax ((210)) 3237 3 09 – www.amaliahotels.com

97 rm – 150/210 € 165/225 € – 1 suite **C3**

Rest – Carte 34/50 €

◆ Chain hotel ◆ Modern ◆

Well located just in front of the National Gardens. Spacious, modern bedrooms, refurbished in 2007; those in front have balconies overlooking the gardens. First floor restaurant serves Mediterranean and Greek cuisine.

The Golden Age

57 Michaelakopoulou ✉ 115 28 – Ⓜ Megaro Moussikis – ☎ ((210)) 7213 965 – goldenage@ath.forthnet.gr – Fax ((210)) 7240 8 61 – www.goldenage.gr **D2**

122 rm – 126 € 126/210 €

Rest – Carte 25/39 €

◆ Business ◆ Functional ◆

This refurbished hotel boasts a new steely high-tech façade and good-sized bedrooms with up-to-date facilities; those at the front have balconies, while those at the back are quieter. International cuisine.

Hermes without rest

19 Apollonos St ✉ 105 57 – Ⓜ Syntagma – ☎ (210) 3235 514 – hermes@tourhotel.gr – Fax (210) 3211 8 00 – www.hermeshotel.gr **B3**

45 rm – 90/120 € 95/145 €

◆ Family ◆ Modern ◆

Small modern hotel near the shops in Plaka. Stylish lobby and breakfast room. Tidy bedrooms have all mod cons; those at the front have balconies.

Arion without rest

18 Aglou Dimitriou St ✉ 105 54 – Ⓜ Monastiraki – ☎ (210) 3240 415 – arion@tourhotel.gr – Fax (210) 3222 4 19 – www.arionhotel.gr **B2**

51 rm – 70/110 € 80/135 €

◆ Family ◆ Modern ◆

A sensibly priced tourist hotel in a lively part of city. Roof-top terrace with superb views. Compact, impressive rooms - ask for one that overlooks Acropolis.

Plaka without rest

< Athens,

7 Kapnikareas and Mitropoleos St ✉ 105 56 – Ⓜ Monastiraki – ☎ (210) 3222 096 – plaka@tourhotel.gr – Fax (210) 3211 8 00 – www.plakahotel.gr **B3**

67 rm – 90/145 € 95/145 €

◆ Traditional ◆ Family ◆

Privately owned hotel among shops and tavernas, with a rooftop bar overlooking the old town. Spotless, sensibly priced modern rooms; ask for one with a view of the Acropolis.

Museum without rest
16 Bouboulinas St ✉ 106 82 – Ⓜ Victoria – ☎ (210) 3805 611
– museum@hotelsofathens.com – Fax (210) 3800 5 07
– www.hotelsofathens.com **B1**
93 rm – †65/150 € ††70/230 €
◆ Family ◆ Functional ◆
Overlooking the National Archaeological Museum and offering comfy facilities. Extension rooms are spacious, stylish and modern. Others are classically-furnished, with balcony views.

Achilleas without rest
21 Lekka St ✉ 105 54 – Ⓜ Syntagma – ☎ ((210)) 2335 605
– marilena@tourhotel.gr – Fax ((210)) 3241 0 92 – www.achilleashotel.gr **C2**
34 rm – †70/110 € ††80/135 €
◆ Family ◆ Functional ◆
In small street known for its silversmiths, near Constitution Square. Spacious bedrooms, ideal for families. Clean compact bathrooms. Mezzanine for self-service breakfast.

Spondi
5 Pyronos, off Varnava Sq, Pangrati ✉ 116 36 – ☎ (210) 7564 021
– spond@relaischateaux.com – Fax (210) 7567 0 21 – www.spondi.gr
Closed 1 week August and Easter **D3**
Rest – *(dinner only)* Menu 65/115 € – Carte 84/102 €
Spec. Iced soup, sea bass and avruga caviar with walnut crust, ouzo and lime foam. Sea bream with orange, seasonal vegetables and olive foam. Geometry of pure arabica with lemon thyme, praline broth.
◆ French ◆ Formal ◆
Attractive converted villa creating an intimate atmosphere in its elegant rooms and external courtyard and terraces. Outstanding modern French cooking; well crafted, balanced and precise.

Pil Poul et Jérôme Serres ← Acropolis,
51 Apostolou Pavlou, Thissio ✉ 118 51 – Ⓜ Thissio
– ☎ (210) 342 36 65 – info@pilpoul.gr – Fax (210) 341 30 46 – www.pilpoul.gr
Closed Easter, 13-19 August, 25-26 December,
1-2 January and Sunday **A3**
Rest – *(dinner only)* Carte 78/96 €
Spec. Coquilles St. Jacques, carotte, cumin avec coulis de rose. Dos de canard petillant. Macaron frappé.
◆ French ◆ Elegant ◆
Opened in 2006 on the first floor of a restored former hat maker's mansion in a lively part of the city. Superb Acropolis views from the rooftop terrace. Classic French cuisine in a modern idiom.

GB Roof Garden – Grande Bretagne H. ← Athens and Acropolis,
Constitution Sq ✉ 105 63 – Ⓜ Syntagma
– ☎ (210) 3330 000 – info@grandebretagne.gr – Fax (210) 3228 0 34 **C2**
Rest – *(May-October (dinner only)* Menu 55/65 € – Carte 52/70 €
◆ Mediterranean ◆ Formal ◆
The full length windows make the most of the spectacular views. Plush and very comfortable roof-top dining room with lively bar. Elegantly dressed tables and formal service.

Varoulko (Lazarou Lefteris)
80 Pireaus Ave, Keramikos ✉ 104 35 – Ⓜ Thissio – ☎ (210) 5228 400
– info@varoulko.gr – Fax (210) 5228 8 00 – www.varoulko.gr
Closed Sunday **A2**
Rest – *(booking essential) (dinner only)* Menu 55 € – Carte 52/62 €
Spec. Moussaka of crayfish ragoût and olive oil béchamel. John Dory with vegetable broth and curry. Gianduja mousse with chocolate sorbet.
◆ Seafood ◆ Fashionable ◆
Modern, stylish restaurant in converted house with roof terrace and view of the Acropolis. Daily-changing menu of freshest and finest local seafood. Accomplished cooking.

XXX

48 The Restaurant

48 Armatolon and Klefton ✉ 114 71 – Ⓜ Ambelokipi – ☎ (210) 6411 082 – 48_ilta@otenet.gr – Fax 6462 1 82 – www.48therestaurant.com

Closed 1 July-1 September and Sunday **D1**

Rest – *(dinner only)* Menu 70 € – Carte 59/82 €

♦ Inventive ♦ Design ♦

Trendy, atmospheric restaurant where minimalism holds sway, underpinned by modern art on the walls. Dishes, accordingly, are an evolving, modish reworking of Greek classics.

XX

Hytra

Navarhou Apostoli 7, Psirri ✉ *105 54* – Ⓜ *Monastiraki* – ☎ *(210) 3316 767 – Fax (210) 3316 7 67*

Closed 25 October-10 April and Sunday **B2**

Rest – *(dinner only)* Carte approx. 49 €

♦ Inventive ♦ Trendy ♦

Refurbished, vibrant modern restaurant in trendy Psirri. Modish Greek menus, innovative in places; reworking of Greek classics. Friendly, knowledgeable service.

XX

Kiku

12 Dimokritou St, Kolonaki ✉ *106 73* – Ⓜ *Syntagma* – ☎ *(210) 3647 033 – athenskiku@yahoo.gr – Fax (210) 3626 2 39 – www.kiku.gr*

Closed August, Easter, Christmas, New Year and Sunday **C2**

Rest – Menu 35/64 € – Carte 57/64 €

♦ Japanese ♦ Minimalist ♦

Authentic Japanese restaurant hidden away in a quiet side street. Clean, crisp, minimalist interior and large sushi counter with mood changing lighting.

XX

Luna Rossa

213 Sokratous, Kallithea (Southwest : 4 km) ✉ *176 74* – ☎ *(210) 9423 777 – info@lunarossa.gr – Fax (210) 9328 1 46 – www.lunarossa.gr*

Closed mid July-mid September, Easter, 25 December and Sunday

Rest – *(lunch by arrangement)* Menu 60/80 € – Carte 63/95 €

♦ Italian ♦ Family ♦

Delightful and intimate converted house which still feels like a family home. Divided into four dining rooms and small terrace. Authentic Italian cooking with Roman base. Comprehensive and impressive wine list.

X

Psarra's

16 Erehtheos and Erotokritou St, Plaka ✉ *105 56* – Ⓜ *Monastiraki – ☎ (210) 3218 733 – Fax (210) 3218 7 34* **B3**

Rest – Menu 15/40 € – Carte 19/31 €

♦ Traditional ♦ Rustic ♦

Just below the Acropolis; has been a taverna since 1898. Refurbished rustic style within two yellow-washed houses with terrace. Fresh ingredients enhance classic taverna menus.

X

Prytanio

7 Milioni St, Kolonaki ✉ *106 73* – ☎ *(210) 3643 353 – info@prytaneion.gr – Fax (210) 8082 5 77 – www.prytaneion.gr* **C2**

Rest – Carte 22/69 €

♦ Mediterranean ♦ Bistro ♦

Watch the fashionable shoppers go by from a table on the terrace or choose the more intimate interior or the garden. Pleasant service and modern Mediterranean-influenced menu.

X

Oraia Penteli

Iroon Sq, Psirri ✉ *105 54* – Ⓜ *Monastiraki* – ☎ *(210) 3218 627 – Fax (210) 3218 6 27* **B2**

Rest – Carte 12/31 €

♦ Traditional ♦ Rustic ♦

Historic building converted into rustic café-restaurant with terrace on lively square in the centre of the Psirri district. Traditional Greek cooking; menu changes daily.

Kuzina

9 Adrianou St ✉ 105 55 – Ⓜ Thissio – ✆ (210) 3240 133 – Fax (210) 3240 1 35 – www.kuzina.gr
Closed 25 and 31 December and Easter **B3**
Rest – Carte 32/59 €
♦ Modern ♦ Bistro ♦
Modern taverna-style restaurant in the Thissio area, with large front terrace, open kitchen and lively atmosphere. Contemporary cooking makes good use of local produce.

ENVIRONS OF ATHENS

at Kifissia Northeast : 15 km by Vas. Sofias

Pentelikon

66 Diligianni St, Kefalari (off Harilaou Trikoupi, follow signs to Politia) ✉ 145 62 – Ⓜ Kifissia – ✆ (210) 6230 650 – pentelik@otenet.gr – Fax (210) 8019 2 23 – www.pentelikon.gr
101 rm – †325/380 € ††325/380 €, ☕ 28 € – 11 suites
Rest ***Vardis*** – see below
Rest ***La Terrasse*** – Carte 52/74 €
♦ Grand Luxury ♦ Traditional ♦ Classic ♦
Imposing mansion in affluent residential suburb. Opulence and antiques throughout. Most charming and tranquil rooms overlook the gardens. Traditional service. La Terrasse offers a full range of dishes with piano music nightly.

Theoxenia Palace

2 Filadelfeos St ✉ 145 62 – Ⓜ Kifissia – ✆ (210) 6233 622 – reservations@theoxeniapalace.com – Fax (210) 6231 6 75 – www.theoxeniapalace.com
69 rm ☕ – †310/345 € ††370/490 € – 2 suites
Rest – *(dinner only)* Carte 38/50 €
♦ Business ♦ Classic ♦
Renovated 1920s hotel with imposing façade. Spacious well-equipped rooms. Good leisure and large conference/banqueting facilities. Shogun for Asian cuisine, with sushi bar.

Theoxenia House without rest

42 Charilaou Trikoupi St and 9 Pentelis St ✉ 145 62 – Ⓜ Kifissia – ✆ (210) 6233 622 – reservations@theoxeniapalace.com – Fax (210) 6231 6 75 – www.theoxeniapalace.com
11 rm ☕ – †355 € ††380 € – 1 suite
♦ Business ♦ Classic ♦
Stylish house in pleasant suburb converted to provide very large, well-equipped rooms, each with lounge area and cooking facilities, plus full use of Theoxenia Palace hotel.

The Kefalari Suites without rest

1 Pentelis and Kolokotroni St, Kefalari ✉ 145 62 – Ⓜ Kifissia – ✆ (210) 6233 333 – info@kefalarisuites.gr – Fax (210) 6233 3 30 – www.kefalarisuites.gr
12 rm ☕ – †210 € ††210 € – 1 suite
♦ Townhouse ♦ Stylish ♦
Early 20C villa set in a smart, quiet suburb; stylish, airy, thoughtfully appointed rooms, each on a subtle, imaginative theme, including one with Arabian arch, palm tree and terrace.

Semiramis

48 Charilaou Trikoupi St, Kefalari ✉ 145 62 – Ⓜ Kifissia – ✆ (210) 6284 400 – info@semiramisathens.com – Fax (210) 6284 4 99 – www.semiramisathens.com
50 rm ☕ – †200/230 € ††200/230 € – 1 suite
Rest – Carte 30/53 €
♦ Business ♦ Design ♦
Striking 1930s conversion accentuated by lime green balconies, boldly hued public areas and organic shaped pool. Rooms with no numbers on the doors and stunning interiors. Spacious restaurant serving Italian cuisine, with view of pool and terrace and music from DJ.

Twenty One

21 Kolokotroni and Mykonou St, Kefalari ✉ *145 62 – Ⓜ Kifissia – ✆ (210) 6233 521 – info@twentyone.gr – Fax (210) 6233 8 21 – www.twentyone.gr*
21 rm – 🛉190/200 € 🛉🛉200/260 €, ☐ 15 €
Rest – Carte 23/37 €
◆ Business ◆ Modern ◆
Converted slate grey 19C former watermill in pleasant suburb. Flowing minimalistic interior. Standard rooms are well designed, some with balconies; five trendy loft suites. Informal dining room and expansive terrace; Italian menus.

Vardis – at Pentelikon H.

66 Diligianni St, Kefalari (off Harilaou Trikoupi, follow signs to Politia) ✉ *145 62 – Ⓜ Kifissia – ✆ (210) 6230 660 – vardis@hotelpentelikon.gr – Fax (210) 8019 2 23 – www.hotelpentelikon.gr*
Closed Sunday
Rest – *(booking essential) (dinner only)* Carte 70/84 €
Spec. Scallops with a Jerusalem artichoke velouté and truffle. Duck breast with orange, "soufflé" potatoes. Chocolate "Grand Cru".
◆ French ◆ Formal ◆
Elegant, ornately decorated restaurant with extensive terrace. Fine table settings. Formal and polished service of carefully-crafted, contemporary French cuisine. Passionate sommelier.

at Ekali Northeast : 20 km by Vas. Sofias

Life Gallery

103 Thisseos Ave ✉ *145 78 – ✆ (210) 6260 400 – info-lifegallery@bluegr.com – Fax (210) 6229 3 53 – www.bluegr.com*
30 rm ☐ – 🛉690 € 🛉🛉725/1040 €
Rest – *(Closed Sunday and Monday dinner)* Carte 50/78 €
◆ Luxury ◆ Design ◆
Strikingly smart 'glass cube' with discreet yet eye-catchingly contemporary décor at every turn: don't miss the modern library. Sleek, stylish bedrooms all boast balconies. Bright, spacious restaurant with capacious outdoor terrace. Mediterranean-influenced menus.

at Athens International Airport East : 35 km by Vas. Sofias

Sofitel Athens Airport

✉ *190 19 – Ⓜ Airport – ✆ (210) 3544 000 – h3167@accor.com – Fax (210) 3544 4 44 – www.sofitel.com*
332 rm – 🛉300 € 🛉🛉360 €, ☐ € – 13 suites
Rest *Karavi* – *(dinner only except Saturday and Sunday brunch)* Carte dinner 72/114 €
Rest *Mesoghaia* – *✆ (210) 3544 920* – Menu 37 € – Carte 37/79 €
◆ Business ◆ Modern ◆
First hotel at the new airport. Modern and very well equipped, from comfy library bar to exclusive leisure club. Spacious, soundproofed rooms and impressive bathrooms. French menus on the 9th floor in Karavi. Informal brightly decorated Mediterranean-themed Mesoghaia.

at Vouliagmeni South : 18 km by Singrou

The Westin Athens ≤ Bay,

40 Apollonos St ✉ *166 71 – ✆ (210) 8902 000 – reservation@astir.gr – Fax (210) 8962 5 82 – www.westin.com*
153 rm ☐ – 🛉395 € 🛉🛉425 € – 9 suites
Rest *Sao* – Menu 50 €
Rest *Kymata* – *(lunch only)(buffet only)* Carte 39/55 €
◆ Luxury ◆ Palace ◆ Modern ◆
Recently transformed vast 75 acre resort complex on its own peninsula. Supremely comfortable hotel with private beaches and extensive facilities. Delightful bedrooms are spacious with sea views. Fusion cooking in Sao with its own terrace. Buffet menu in Kymata.

Arion Resort & Spa
40 Apollonos St ✉ 166 71
– ✆ (210) 8902 000 – reservation@astir.gr – Fax (210) 8962 5 82
– www.luxurycollection.com
107 rm – 395 € 425 € – 16 suites
Rest *Alia* – Carte 30/50 €
Rest *Grill Room* – Menu 70 € – Carte 60/90 €
♦ Luxury ♦ Modern ♦
Next door to the Westin on private peninsula and sharing many of the wide-ranging facilities. Bedrooms are large, contemporary in style and most have balconies.
Relaxed sophistication and a Mediterranean menu at Alia.
International cuisine and local seafood in the Grill Room.

Divani Apollon Palace & Spa Saronic Gulf,
10 Ag. Nikolaou and Iliou St (Kavouri) off Athinas ✉ 166 71
– ✆ (210) 8911 100
– divanis@divaniapollon.gr – Fax (210) 9658 0 10
– www.divanis.com
286 rm – 420/560 € 460/600 €, 26 €
Rest *Mythos* – *(Closed Sunday) (dinner only)* Carte 59/71 €
Rest *Anemos* – Carte 51/61 €
♦ Luxury ♦ Classic ♦
Modern hotel in fashionable resort. Poolside lounge. Spa and thalassotherapy centre. Every bedroom boasts balcony overlooking the Saronic Gulf. Small private beach.
Dine in Mythos on the beach with local dishes. Anemos is modern with global fare.

Apollon Suites without rest
11 Nikolaou St ✉ 166 71 – ✆ ((210)) 8911 100 – suites@divaniapollen.gr
– Fax ((210)) 9658 0 10 – www.divanis.gr
56 rm
♦ Luxury ♦ Modern ♦
New annex for the Divani Apollon Palace, whose facilities it shares, with the added benefit of a slightly quieter atmosphere. Well-equipped, luxury suites with modern style.

The Margi
11 Litous St, off Athinas by Apollonos ✉ 166 71
– ✆ (210) 8929 000
– sales@themargi.gr – Fax (210) 8929 1 43
– www.themargi.gr
88 rm – 210 € 210/280 € – 7 suites
Rest – Carte 30/70 €
♦ Business ♦ Stylish ♦
A stylish hotel that combines contemporary elegance with a colonial feel. Breakfast can be taken on the poolside terrace. Bedrooms have antique pieces and smart marble bathrooms. Bistro restaurant serving Mediterranean menu.

at Pireas Southwest: 8 km by Singrou

Delfino
60 A.Komoundourou St ✉ 185 32 – ✆ ((210)) 4120 388
– mail@delfino.gr
– Fax ((210)) 4128 5 00
– www.delfino.gr
Rest – Carte 33/41 €
♦ Italian ♦ Family ♦
Popular, family-owned seafood restaurant with maritime décor and decked terrace overlooking the yachts in the harbour. Italian à la carte menu of fresh, flavourful seafood dishes.

at Kalamaki Southwest : 14 km by Singrou

XXX **Akrotiri**

Vas. Georgiou B5, Agios Kosmas, Helliniko ✉ *167 77*
– ✆ (210) 9859 147
– akrotiri@enternet.gr
– Fax (210) 9859 1 49
– www.akrotirilounge.gr
Friday and Saturday only November-April
Rest – *(dinner only)* Menu 80 € – Carte 59/90 €
♦ French ♦ Fashionable ♦
A trendy seaside restaurant combining simplicity and luxury. Candlelit dinners on the pool terrace; DJ music. Menu of good quality international cuisine with French influence.

HUNGARY
MAGYARORSZÁG

PROFILE

→ **Area:**
93 032 km^2
(35 920 sq mi).

→ **Population:**
10 007 000 inhabitants (est. 2005), density = 108 per km^2.

→ **Capital:**
Budapest (conurbation 2 232 000 inhabitants).

→ **Currency:**
Forint (Ft or HUF); rate of exchange: HUF 100 = € 0.39 = US$ 0.51 (Nov 2008).

→ **Government:**
Parliamentary republic (since 1989). Member of European Union since 2004.

→ **Language:**
Hungarian; many Hungarians also speak English and German.

→ **Specific public holidays:**
1848 Revolution Day (15 March); National Day-St. Stephen Day (20 August); Republic Day-1956 Uprising Remembrance Day (23 October); All Saints' Day (1 November); Boxing Day (25-26 December).

→ **Local time:**
GMT + 1 hour in winter and GMT + 2 hours in summer.

→ **Climate:**
Temperate continental with cold winters and warm summers (Budapest: January: -1°C, July: 22°C).

→ **International dialling Code:**
00 36 followed by area code (1 for Budapest) and local number. International enquiries: ✆ **199**.

→ **Emergency:**
Central emergency line: ✆ **112**; Ambulance: ✆ **104**, Fire Brigade: ✆ **105**, Police: ✆ **107**, Roadside breakdown service: ✆ **188**.

→ **Electricity:**
220 volts, 50 Hz; 2-pin round-shaped continental plugs.

→ **Formalities**
Travellers from the European Union (EU), Switzerland, Iceland and the main countries of North and South America need a national identity card or passport (America: passport required) to visit Hungary for less than three months (tourism or business purpose). For visitors from other countries a visa may be required, in addition to a passport, especially for those wishing to stay for longer than three months. We advise you to check with your embassy before travelling.

BUDAPEST

BUDAPEST

BUDAPEST

Population: 1 702 000 (conurbation 2 232 000) – Altitude: 102m

J. Warbuton-Lee/PHOTONONSTOP

No one knows quite where the Hungarian language came from. It's not quite Slavic, not quite Turkic, and its closest relatives appear to be in Finland and Siberia. In much the same way, Hungary's capital is a bit of an enigma. A lot of what you see is not as old as it appears. Classical and Gothic buildings are mostly Neoclassical and neo-Gothic, and the fabled Baroque of the city is of a more recent vintage than in other European capitals. That's because Budapest's frequent invaders and conquerors, from all compass points of the map, left little but rubble behind them when they left; the grand look of today took shape for the most part no earlier than the mid 19C.

It's still a beautiful place to look at, with hilly Buda keeping watch via eight great bridges over sprawling Pest on the other side of the lilting, bending Danube. These were formerly two separate towns, united in 1873 to form a capital city. It reached its heyday around that time, a magnificent city that was the hub of the Austro-Hungarian Empire. Defeats in two world wars and fifty years behind the Iron Curtain put paid to the glory, but battered Budapest is used to rising from the ashes, and now it's Europe's most earthily beautiful capital, particularly when winter mists rise from the river to shroud it in a thick white cloak. The spas are good, too.

LIVING THE CITY

It's not easy to get lost in Budapest. Despite its size, it's split asunder by the great **Danube**, whose ubiquitous liquid pathway helps you keep your bearings. **Buda**, on the west bank, is very hilly and provides constant views of the river. Its southern quarter, Gellert and Taban, is smartly residential, while northern Buda is dominated by visitor hotspot The Royal Palace. This stares across to the imposing Parliament Building in **Pest**, around which large squares and wide avenues offer reminders of the Austro-Hungarian Empire. South of here is the commercial hub of Belvaros, or inner city, full of shops, cafes and summer tourists. The northeast quarter of the city, furthest from the river, is Varosliget, which translates as City Park, and it's the place the locals come to play and lounge around in the sun; this is also an area renowned for its grand buildings and monuments. In the middle of the Danube, as the city reaches its northern boundary, stands the green oasis of Margaret Island.

PRACTICAL INFORMATION

ARRIVAL-DEPARTURE

Ferihegy Budapest National Airport is 24km southeast of the city. A taxi will take about 45min and cost around 4000 HUF ; there are Shuttle Mini-buses doing the rounds of the hotels or, from Terminal 1, a train will take you to the Western train station for 300 HUF.

TRANSPORT

Budapest has an extensive public transport system: its metro, with three lines, is second oldest in the world after the London Underground. Above ground, you can take your pick of buses, trolley buses or trams. Tickets must be bought in advance and validated in the ticket stampers at the start of the journey. Buy your tickets at metro stations, ticket machines, newsagents or tobacconists.

If you're in town for more than a day, then the Budapest Card is a sound investment. It includes unlimited travel on public transport, free or reduced price admission to many museums and sights, cultural and folklore programmes, as well as discounts in some shops, restaurants and thermal baths. The Card is valid for two or three days, and can be bought at the airport, main metro stations, tourist offices and some hotels.

If you're going shopping on the weekend, make sure you do it on Saturday morning. Most high street shops are shut on Saturday afternoons, and there is almost no Sunday opening, apart from the shopping malls.

EXPLORING BUDAPEST

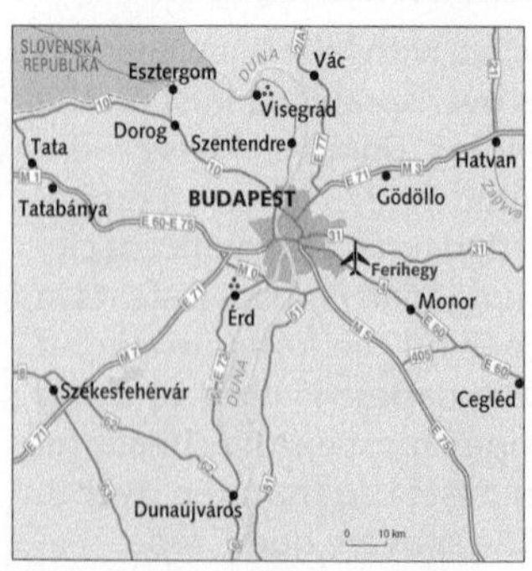

Budapest offers a thick slice of East European charm that hasn't been ruined by monotonously grey communist architecture. It's grander in scale than Vienna and Prague, the other two members of the 'Habsburg triumvirate', and you can't help but get the feeling that its art nouveau delights are modelled on nineteenth century Paris (which indeed they are, at least in Pest). Ask two locals to tell you the city's defining tourist location – its unmissable sight - and one will probably say "The Royal Palace", the other "The Parliament Building". The **Royal Palace** can certainly stake a strong claim. There's been a dominant castle or palace overlooking Buda since 1255. The latest incarnation was built in the eighteenth century after the Habsburg Empire claimed it from the Ottomans in a bloody siege. They developed not one palace but an amalgamation of buildings, spreading out along the hill. These took a big hit during World War II, and what we see today has been healthily patched up over the past sixty years: the dome, for instance, was entirely rebuilt. The **Hungarian National Gallery** was inaugurated at the Palace just over fifty years ago, in 1957, and nowhere in the city is there more treasure than here; it displays art from medieval times to the present day in six permanent exhibitions which lavish upon the visitor the very best of Hungarian creativity. Fans of the Secession (the nineteenth century arts movement devoted to bright colours and fantastical designs) will be in their element. There are actually more than 10,000 exhibits spread over much of the Royal Palace, making it one of the greatest collections in the world.

➜ PARLIAMENTARY PRIVILEGE

So how does the **Parliament building** compare with all that? It's certainly nowhere near as old, as it was only completed in 1902 after two decades of construction. A symbol of Hungarian self-confidence at the beginning of the twentieth century, it certainly looks the part. It's one of Europe's finest neo-Gothic buildings and when you gaze at it from across the water its dazzling symmetry imbues it with a real sense of magnificence. Inside, its two biggest 'vote catchers' are its sweeping Grand Staircase and its Domed Hall, which houses the Crown Jewels. To see them, you'll have to join a guided tour, but as our imaginary second local would tell you, that's something well worth doing.

➜ GET YOUR THERMALS ON

If you're in Budapest in the summer, you'll very likely be hot; this is a place that swelters. The good news is you won't have any trouble finding somewhere to cool down. The city is renowned for its therapeutic **thermal baths**, and when the weather's hot it can seem like the whole of Budapest is immersed. The Ottomans loved the natural springs and built some wonderful domed baths with steam rooms, hot and cold pools and peaceful chambers in which to relax. Enough original Turkish baths remain to give you (something like) the full Oriental experience. It was when spa bathing became a craze across central Europe in the nineteenth and early twentieth century that Budapest's two most famous bathing complexes opened, and they remain top visitor attractions: the Gellert Baths, in Buda, are part of the Secessionist Gellert Hotel and the stunning neoclassical main pool is surrounded by high galleries and marble columns, and studded with colourful mosaics. Meanwhile, to say Central Park's Szechenyi baths are big is like saying that Paris does some nice food and Athens has one or two interesting relics. Szechenyi is vast, the biggest in Europe, its neo-Baroque façade more like a Grand Central rail station than a bathing complex. There are splendid Belle Epoque foyers, an all-weather mixed swimming area, which includes Hungary's deepest thermal baths, single sex steam baths, and chessplayers who congregate around stone chessboards in one of the expansive open-air pools.

➜ PEST CONTROL

You'll know you're in the heart of Pest when you get to **Vaci Utca**. A teeming street in two parts (one for eating and drinking, one for hitting the shops) this is the city's buzziest thoroughfare, running parallel to the Danube. At the top end is Gerbeaud Cukraszda, the smartest and most famous coffee house in Budapest, at the bottom end the bustling Central Market Hall, where the locals go for their fruit and veg from local allotments on one side, and more exotic global fare on the other. Vaci Utca is the true hub of the city, lined with many types of store, though perhaps lacking the 'designer' glamour of more fashion-conscious cities.

Staying in Pest, go for a wonderful cultural hit at two of its most stunning buildings. The **State Opera House**, inland from the Parliament building, is a neo-Renaissance masterpiece, its interior so full of opulent splendour, you'll feel you're back at the height of the Austro-Hungarian Empire. Best of all, though: take in a concert there. Further south, beyond Vaci Utca, is the outstanding **Museum of Applied Arts**, its appearance a fitting tribute to the Secessionist movement and its stunning green domes worth the trip alone. Inside, dazzling Oriental artefacts complement the graceful white architecture. The creative genius behind the building was Odon Lechner, who, in the late nineteenth century, was to Budapest what Gaudi was to Barcelona. Lechner's designs adorn many structures in the city.

→ THE GREAT ESCAPE

If you need a break from the crowds, there's one very visible, and another not so visible, refuge. **Margaret Island** (the visible one) is a tranquil oasis plonked down in the middle of the Danube. Locals sprawl around during high summer, but there's enough room for anyone to find a cool spot and relax under a tree. In the winter, with the wind gushing through the swirling branches and not a soul to be seen, it takes on a distinctly romantic feel. 2008 is its one hundredth anniversary as a public park. And as for the hidden escape? Well, you won't discover it anywhere above ground. North of the Royal Palace, walk up Uri Utca (Lords' Street) till you get to number nine, which is the entrance to the bizarre but wonderful Buda Castle Labyrinth, an underground maze of tunnels and chambers formed by hot springs half a million years ago. In the seventeenth century, a part of these catacombs was used to store wine, and there's a room today where fruity red wine gushes from a fountain – but you'll have to find it! (Your best bet is to join a guided tour). Incidentally, Úri Utca itself is something to see with its Gothic and Baroque façades lining the way, but spare a thought that much of this fine street was rebuilt in the 1950s after that great shadow over Budapest – war – had once more taken its heavy toll.

BUDAPEST IN...

→ ONE DAY

Royal Palace, the Parliament Building, a trip on the Danube

→ TWO DAYS

Gellert Baths, a stroll down Váci Utca, a concert at the State Opera House

→ THREE DAYS

Museum of Applied Arts, Margaret Island, coffee and cake at Gerbeaud Cukrazda

CALENDAR HIGHLIGHTS

Music is high on the list of Hungarian passions: this is the country that gave us Liszt and Bartok. Winter is the time for high calibre concerts at great prices in venues like the Opera House, Franz Liszt Music Academy, and the National Concert Hall. The Spring Festival, in March, is the city's largest cultural jamboree, with a heady mixture of ballet, opera and chamber music fusing with the likes of jazz and folk dance. An entire Danube island is taken over by rock fans in August for the huge Sziget Festival, which goes on for a week and features roots music as well as ubiquitous four/four rhythms. World music takes centre stage at July's WoMuFe, where musicians from Central, Eastern Europe and beyond join forces for a fine old mash-up. The Autumn Festival, in October, is a kind of counterbalance to the Spring Festival: this one acts as a showcase for cutting edge theatre, dance and media arts, as well as music and film.

EATING OUT

The city is most famous for its coffee houses so before you dive into a restaurant tuck into a cream cake with a double espresso in, say, the Ruszwurm on Castle Hill, the city's oldest, and possibly cosiest, café. In tourist areas, it's not difficult to locate goulash on your menu, and you never have to travel far to find beans, dumplings and cabbage in profusion. Having said that, Budapest's culinary scene has moved on apace since the fall of communism, and Hungarian chefs have become inventive with their use of local seasonal produce. Pest is where you'll find most choice but even in Buda there are plenty of worthy restaurants in among the tourist traps. Lots of locals like to eat sausage on the run and if you fancy the idea, buy a pocket knife. Sunday brunch is popular in Budapest, especially at the best hotels. If you're in a restaurant, it might well include a service charge. Don't feel obliged to pay it, as tipping is entirely at your own discretion but you may find that the persistence of the little folk groups that pop up in many of the restaurants hard to resist.

→ WAITING FOR THE DAY

There are two outstanding places of worship in the city. The **Matyas Church**, towering over Buda, dates from 1255, but its most recent addition, the multi-coloured tiled roof, was built as recently as 1970. The magnificent **St Stephen's Basilica,** in the heart of Pest and seen from all over the city, was only completed in 1905, fifty-five years after it was begun. The great length of time in construction led to the local equivalent of 'pigs might fly' – 'when the basilica is finished'.

→ CHAIN REACTION

Budapest's most magnificent bridge is **The Chain Bridge**, linking the towns since 1848. It was designed by an Englishman, built by a Scotsman, and loved by the world: its huge towers are superbly lit at night, making it one of the city's most photographed sights.

→ TERROR TRIP

Fancy a trip to the House of Terror? You might not when you get there. Based in **Andrassy Street**, it's the former HQ of the fascist, then communist, secret police who ran the city for much of the twentieth century. Now a museum, it's dedicated to those who perished under both dictatorships. This is the place where confessions were extracted and victims sentenced to death. A sobering experience.

HUNGARY - BUDAPEST

Four Seasons Gresham Palace
Roosevelt tér 5-6 ✉ 1051 – Ⓜ Vörösmarty tér
– ✆ (01) 268 6000 – budapest.reservations@fourseasons.com – Fax 268 50 00
– www.fourseasons.com/budapest **E2**
165 rm – †77165/120175 HUF ††127765/223905 HUF, ☕ 8230 HUF – 14 suites
Rest *Páva* – *(Closed Sunday) (dinner only)* Carte 13500/18100 HUF
Rest *Gresham Kávéház* – *✆ (01) 268 5110* – Carte 6200/11900 HUF
♦ Grand Luxury ♦ Palace ♦ Art Deco ♦
Art Nouveau palace on the Danube converted into an elegant, modern hotel with excellent service; stunning atrium. Riverside Páva restaurant and terrace offers a menu of seasonal Italian-influenced dishes with modish twist. Kávéház is a coffee house renowned for traditional dishes - and its cakes.

Corinthia Grand H. Royal
Erzsébet krt 43-49 ✉ 1073 – Ⓜ Oktogon
– ✆ (01) 479 4000 – royal@corinthia.hu – Fax 479 43 33
– www.corinthia.hu Plan I **B2**
383 rm – †87500 HUF ††87500 HUF, ☕ 5500 HUF – 31 suites
Rest *Brasserie Royale* – Carte 7500/12800 HUF
Rest *Rickshaw* – *(Closed Monday) (dinner only)* Menu 5500 HUF – Carte 6600/10700 HUF
♦ Grand Luxury ♦ Business ♦ Modern ♦
Early 20C grand hotel with impressive atrium. Well-appointed bedrooms - particularly Executive - with modern décor in warm colours. Stylish new spa. Brasserie Royale for pleasant atrium dining, with family brunch on Sundays. Wok dishes and sushi bar in Rickshaw.

New York Palace
Erzébet Krt 9-11 ✉ 1073 – Ⓜ Blaha Tér – ✆ (01) 886 6111 – info@newyorkboscolo.com – Fax 886 61 99 – www.boscolohotels.com Plan 1 **B 2**
103 rm – †43010/63250 HUF ††60720/73370 HUF, ☕ 6325 HUF – 4 suites
Rest *Deep Water* – *✆ (01) 886 6166 (dinner only)* Menu 17710 HUF – Carte 15180/17457 HUF
Rest *New York Cafe* – Menu 11385/15180 HUF – Carte 12144/14168 HUF
♦ Grand Luxury ♦ Business ♦ Classic ♦
This stunning 1894 former insurance company building opened as a hotel in 2006. Sympathetic renovation has created impressive levels of comfort. Deep Water, with wood panelling and formal settings, for Hungarian and Italian dishes. The New York Cafe is rightly celebrated for its striking baroque style and long history.

Kempinski H. Corvinus
Erzsébet tér 7-8 ✉ 1051 – Ⓜ Deàk tér
– ✆ (01) 429 3777 – hotel.corvinus@kempinski.com – Fax 429 47 77
– www.kempinski-budapest.com **E2**
335 rm – †47817/75647 HUF ††47817/75647 HUF, ☕ 7590 HUF – 31 suites
Rest *Ristorante Giardino* – *(dinner only)* Carte 12650/27830 HUF
Rest *Bistro Jardin* – Carte 7350/14000 HUF
♦ Grand Luxury ♦ Business ♦ Modern ♦
Modern hotel in the heart of the city. Spa boasts panoply of up-to-date treatments. Rooms provide top class comforts and facilities. Italian Ristorante Giardino. Bistro Jardin buffet restaurant.

Sofitel Budapest
Roosevelt tér 2 ✉ 1051 – Ⓜ Vörösmarty tér – ✆ (01) 266 1234
– h3229-re@accor.com – Fax 235 91 01 – www.sofitel-budapest.com **E2**
328 rm – †32637 HUF ††55407 HUF, ☕ 6325 HUF – 22 suites
Rest *Paris Budapest Café* – Menu 5000 HUF – Carte 5100/11750 HUF
♦ Business ♦ Chain hotel ♦ Modern ♦
Modern hotel near Chain Bridge. 'Bibliotheque' and coffee lounge; plane suspended in mid-air. Comfortable, well-equipped rooms. Contemporary restaurant with open kitchen offers modern fusion cooking with Thai influences.

Le Meridien

Erzsébet tér 9-10 ✉ 1051 – Ⓜ Deák tér
– ✆ (01) 429 5500
– sales@le-meridien.hu
– Fax 429 55 55
– www.budapest.lemeridien.com **E2**

203 rm – 🚹100947 HUF 🚹🚹100947 HUF, ☕ 7084 HUF
15 suites
Rest *Le Bourbon* – Carte 9361/12903 HUF

♦ Business ♦ Traditional ♦ Modern ♦

Top class hotel, ideally located for both business and leisure. Classically furnished, very comfortable bedrooms and particularly smart bathrooms. Atrium styled restaurant with Art Deco glass dome and impressive French-influenced desserts.

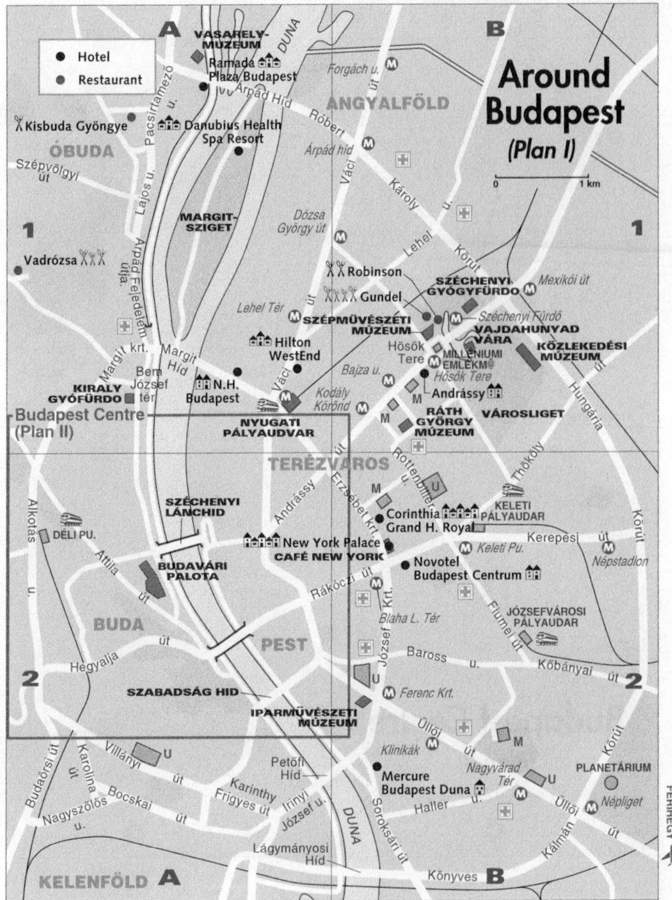

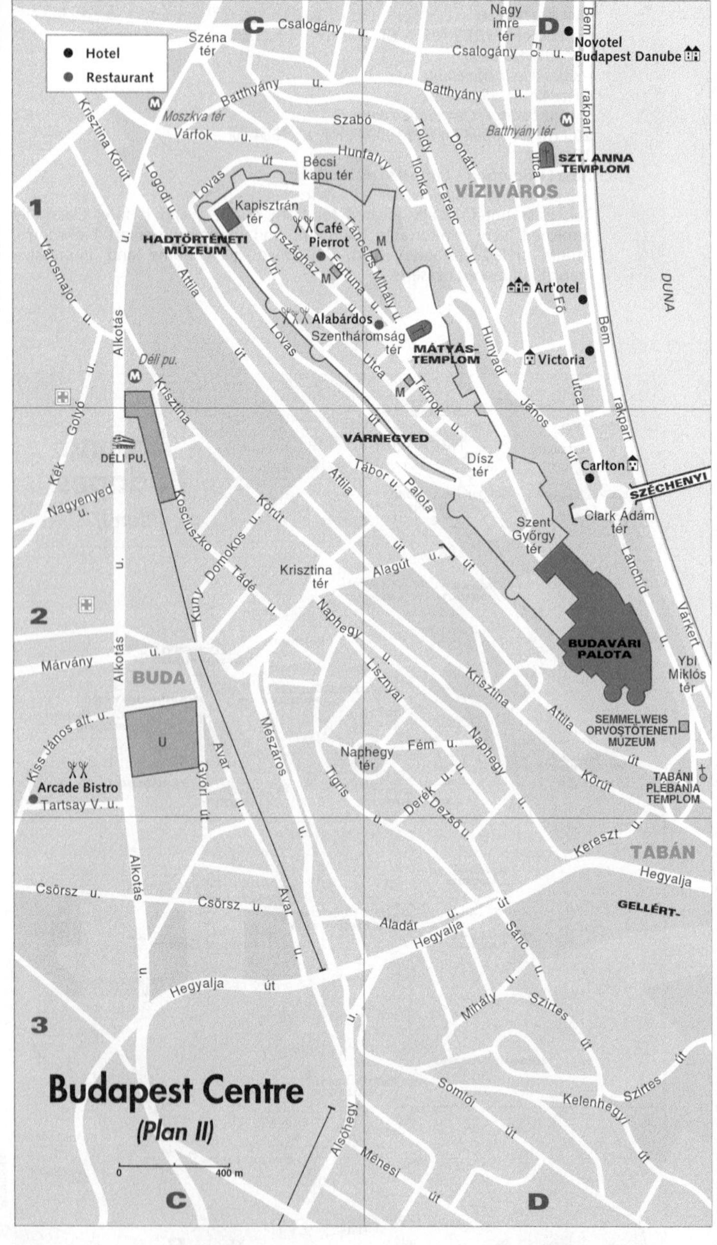
Budapest Centre
(Plan II)
Hotel
Restaurant
Novotel Budapest Danube
SZT. ANNA TEMPLOM
VÍZIVÁROS
HADTÖRTÉNETI MÚZEUM
Café Pierrot
Alabárdos
Art'otel
MÁTYÁS-TEMPLOM
Victoria
VÁRNEGYED
DÉLI PU.
Carlton
SZÉCHENYI
Clark Ádám tér
BUDAVÁRI PALOTA
SEMMELWEIS ORVOSTÖTENETI MÚZEUM
TABÁNI PLÉBÁNIA TEMPLOM
BUDA
TABÁN
GELLÉRT-
Arcade Bistro
DUNA
0
400 m

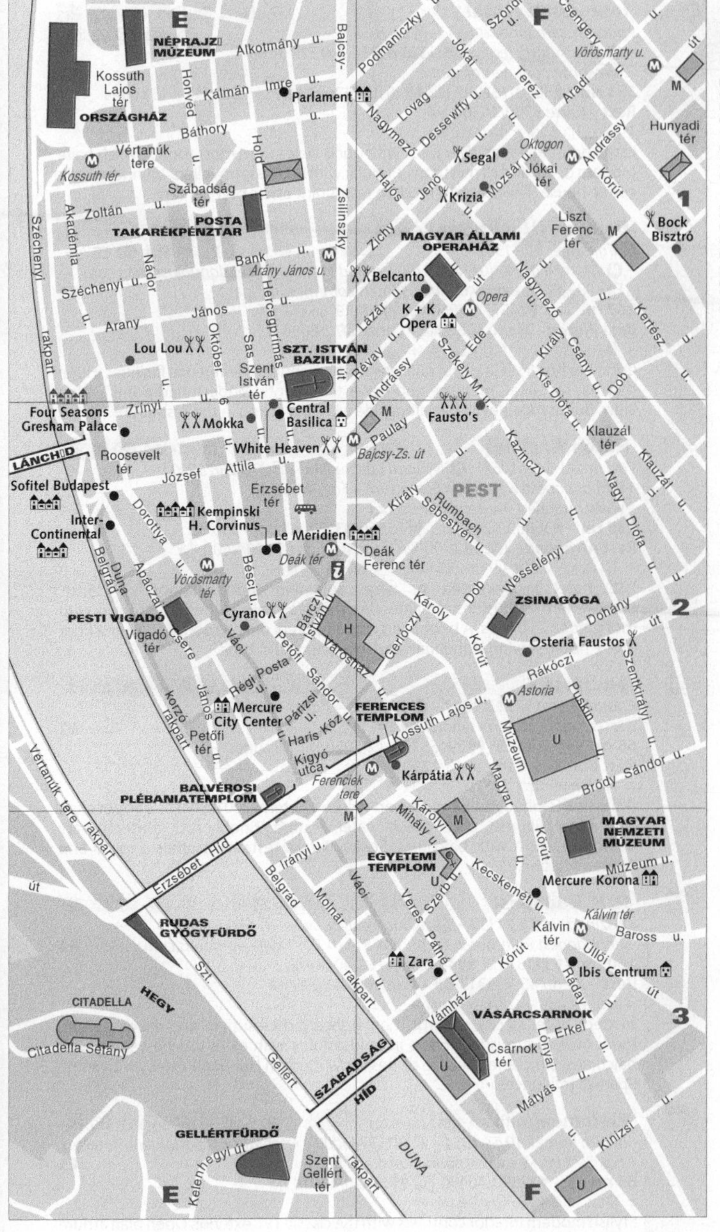
E
F
1
2
3
NÉPRAJZI MÚZEUM
Alkotmány u.
Kossuth Lajos tér
ORSZÁGHÁZ
Honvéd u.
Kálmán Imre u.
Parlament
Podmaniczky u.
Szondi u.
Csengery u.
Vörösmarty u.
Jókai u.
Teréz
Aradi u.
Hunyadi tér
Lovag u.
Nagymező u.
Dessewffy u.
Báthory u.
Vértanúk tere
Kossuth tér
Hold u.
Segal
Oktogon
Andrássy
Jókai tér
Mozsár u.
Körút
Hajós u.
Jenő u.
Krizia
Szabadság tér
POSTA TAKARÉKPÉNZTÁR
Zoltán u.
Akadémia u.
Széchenyi rakpart
Zsilinszky
Bajcsy-
Zichy u.
MAGYAR ÁLLAMI OPERAHÁZ
Liszt Ferenc tér
Bock Bisztró
Bank u.
Arany János u.
Nádor u.
Széchenyi u.
Hercegprímás u.
Belcanto
K + K Opera
Opera
Lázár u.
Nagymező u.
Kertész u.
Arany János u.
Október 6 u.
Sas u.
Lou Lou
SZT. ISTVÁN BAZILIKA
Szent István tér
Révay u.
Andrássy út
Székely M. u.
Ede
Király u.
Csányi u.
Dob u.
Kis Diófa u.
Four Seasons Gresham Palace
Zrínyi u.
Mokka
Central Basilica
Paulay
Fausto's
Klauzál tér
LÁNCHÍD
Roosevelt tér
White Heaven
Bajcsy-Zs. út
Kazinczy u.
Klauzál u.
József Attila u.
Sofitel Budapest
Erzsébet tér
PEST
Király u.
Rumbach Sebestyén u.
Nagy Diófa u.
Inter-Continental
Kempinski H. Corvinus
Le Meridien
Deák Ferenc tér
Deák tér
Dorottya u.
Duna Belgrád
Apáczai
Vörösmarty tér
Bécsi u.
Wesselényi u.
Károly
Dob u.
PESTI VIGADÓ
Vigadó tér
Csere
Cyrano
Bárczy István u.
Városház u.
Gerlóczy u.
ZSINAGÓGA
Dohány
Osteria Faustos
Váci u.
Petőfi Sándor u.
Körút
Rákóczi út
Régi Posta u.
Mercure City Center
Párizsi u.
FERENCES TEMPLOM
Astoria
Puskin u.
Szentkirályi u.
Korzó rakpart
János u.
Petőfi tér
Haris Köz
Kossuth Lajos u.
Múzeum
Kígyó utca
Kárpátia
Magyar
Bródy Sándor u.
Vértanúk tere
BALVÉROSI PLÉBANIATEMPLOM
Ferenciek tere
Károlyi Mihály u.
MAGYAR NEMZETI MÚZEUM
rakpart
Erzsébet Híd
Irányi u.
EGYETEMI TEMPLOM
Körút
Múzeum u.
út
Belgrád
Váci
Kecskeméti u.
Mercure Korona
Molnár
Veres Pálné u.
Szerb u.
RUDAS GYÓGYFÜRDŐ
Kálvin tér
Baross u.
Üllői út
Zara
Ibis Centrum
Ráday u.
Szt.
rakpart
CITADELLA
HEGY
VÁSÁRCSARNOK
Vámház
Erkel u.
Lónyai u.
Citadella Sétány
Gellért
Csarnok tér
SZABADSÁG HÍD
Mátyás u.
GELLÉRTFÜRDŐ
Kinizsi u.
Kelenhegyi út
Szent Gellért tér
rakpart
DUNA
H
M
U

Inter-Continental

Apáczai Csere János útca 12-14 ✉ 1052 – Ⓜ Vörösmarty tér – ☎ (01) 327 6333 – Fax 327 64 66 – www.intercontinental.com **E2**

383 rm – †30107/62997 HUF ††30107/62997 HUF, ☕ 7084 HUF – 15 suites

Rest – Carte 5700/10300 HUF

♦ Business ♦ Modern ♦

Large hotel tower on river bank with good views from most rooms which have modern décor and all mod cons. Popular with business travellers. Viennese-style coffee house. The pleasant modern restaurant offers popular fare.

Danubius Health Spa Resort (heated)

Margitsziget ✉ 1138 – Ⓜ Árpád híd – ☎ (01) 889 4700 – resind@margitsziget.danubiusgroup.com – Fax 889 49 88 – www.danubiushotels.com/margitsziget Plan I **A1**

267 rm ☕ – †27577/37950 HUF ††31119/66792 HUF

Rest *Platan* – Menu 5060 HUF – Carte 6072/8096 HUF

♦ Business ♦ Modern ♦

Concrete hotel set in island gardens on the Danube. Conference facilities. Huge thermal spa: heat, massage and water treatments. Modern bedrooms with a view. Buffet meals available alongside à la carte menu in the restaurant.

Hilton WestEnd

Váci útca 1-3 ✉ 1062 – Ⓜ Nyugati pályaudvar – ☎ (01) 288 5500 – info.budapest-westend@hilton.com – Fax 288 55 88 – www.budapest-westend.hilton.com Plan I **A1**

230 rm – †30360/57937 HUF ††55660/83237 HUF, ☕ 7590 HUF

Rest *Arrabona* – Menu 1790 HUF (lunch) – Carte 7400/9600 HUF

♦ Business ♦ Chain hotel ♦ Modern ♦

21C hotel incorporated in large adjoining indoor shopping centre. Comprehensive business facilities. Very comfortable modern bedrooms with roof garden as bonus. A bright and contemporary dining room on the first floor of the hotel, serving Hungarian and international cuisine.

Andrássy

Andrássy útca 111 ✉ 1063 – Ⓜ Bajza u. – ☎ (01) 462 2100 – reservation@andrassyhotel.com – Fax 322 94 45 Plan I **B1**

65 rm – †53130 HUF ††59455 HUF, ☕ 5060 HUF – 5 suites

Rest *Baraka* – Carte 5313/12903 HUF

♦ Business ♦ Stylish ♦

A classical Bauhaus building converted into a hotel in 2001. Stylish lobby of glass and metal filigree, plus stylish water feature. Bright and contemporary bedrooms, most with balconies. Stylish Baraka restaurant offers original and modern cuisine.

N. H. Budapest

Vigszinház u. 3 ✉ 1137 – Ⓜ Nyugati pályaudvar – ☎ (01) 814 0000 – nhbudapest@nh-hotels.com – Fax 814 01 00 – www.nh-hotels.com Plan I **A1**

160 rm – †32131 HUF ††48323 HUF, ☕ 4048 HUF

Rest – Menu 4554/5313 HUF – Carte 6072/8096 HUF

♦ Business ♦ Modern ♦

Modern hotel in city suburbs. Conference facilities; gym and sauna. Bright, modern, well-furnished rooms in bold colours with extra touches; some with balconies. Simple restaurant; dishes show modern Hungarian style, with some Spanish influences.

Parlament without rest

Kálmán Imre U. 19 ✉ 1054 – ☎ (01) 3746000 – reservation@parlament-hotel.hu – Fax 3 73 08 43 – www.parlament-hotel.hu **E1**

65 rm ☕ – †32890/40480 HUF ††35420/43010 HUF

♦ Business ♦ Design ♦

Stylish modern interior contrasts with the classic 19C exterior. Open plan atrium with display of famous Hungarians. Identical bedrooms have a clean and crisp design.

Novotel Budapest Centrum
Rákóczi útca 43-45 ✉ 1088 – Ⓜ Blaha tér
– ✆ (01) 477 5300 – h3560@accor.com – Fax 477 53 53
– www.novotel-bud-centrum.hu *Plan I* **B2**
227 rm – 41770 HUF 32910/41770 HUF
Rest *Palace Garden Brasserie* – ✆ *(01) 477 5400* – Menu 5315/7090 HUF
◆ Business ◆ Chain hotel ◆ Functional ◆
Early 20C Art Deco hotel with extensions, in the business district. Conference facilities; basement leisure club. Spacious, well-fitted and modern bedrooms. The ornate, classic Palace restaurant serves an international menu.

K + K Opera
Révay útca 24 ✉ 1065 – Ⓜ Opera – ✆ (01) 269 0222
– kk.hotel.opera@kkhotels.hu – Fax 269 02 30 – www.kkhotels.com **F1**
203 rm – 50600 HUF 63250 HUF – 2 suites
Rest – Carte 5313/8855 HUF
◆ Business ◆ Modern ◆
Well run hotel in quiet street of business district near opera. Stylish modern interior design. Good size rooms smartly furnished and well equipped. Informal dining in bar with bright modern décor and pale wood furniture; bistro-style menu.

Mercure Korona
Kecskeméti útca 14 ✉ 1053 – Ⓜ Kálvin tér – ✆ (01) 486 8800
– h1765@accor.com – Fax 318 38 67 – www.mercure.com **F3**
412 rm – 32890/63250 HUF 32890/63250 HUF, 253 HUF – 8 suites
Rest – Menu 5819 HUF (dinner) – Carte 5819/8096 HUF
◆ Business ◆ Chain hotel ◆ Modern ◆
Well-equipped modern business hotel close to Hungarian National Museum. Contemporary rooms with all mod cons. Coffee bar and modish lounge. Buzzy restaurant above lobby; informal, modern with original lighting and contemporary local menus. Hungarian wine by the glass.

Zara
Só U. 6 ✉ 1056 – ✆ (01) 5770700 – info@zarahotels.com – Fax 5 77 07 10
– www.zarahotels.com **F 3**
74 rm – 24035/49335 HUF 26565/55660 HUF
Rest – Carte 2580/5060 HUF
◆ Townhouse ◆ Modern ◆
Adjacent to the river and the main shopping street, this purpose-built hotel opened in 2006. Mirrored glass façade; compact but comfortable bedrooms with modern fabrics. Atrium bar and a simple dining room with an easy menu.

Mercure City Center
Váci utca 20 ✉ 1052 – Ⓜ Ferenciek tere – ✆ 485 3100 – h6565@accor.com
– Fax 485 31 11 – www.mercure.com **E2**
223 rm – 46500 HUF – 4 suites
Rest *Gambrinus* – *(dinner only)* Carte approx. 6000 HUF
Rest *Taverna Brasserie* – Carte approx. 2500 HUF
◆ Traditional ◆ Business ◆ Functional ◆
Business and tourist hotel on main pedestrianised shopping street. Extensive facilities offer something for everyone. Comfortable, refurbished rooms; suites have own sauna. Classical style at Gambrinus. Convivial ambience at traditional brasserie.

Central Basilica without rest
Hercegprímás u. 8 ✉ 1051 – Ⓜ Bajcsy-Zs. út – ✆ 328 5010
– info@hotelcentral-basilica.hu – Fax 328 50 19
– www.central-basilica.hu **E2**
37 rm – 21505/27577 24035/30107
◆ Traditional ◆ Functional ◆
Brand new hotel located downtown, close to the basilica. Functional bedrooms have wood furniture, double glazed windows and well-equipped bathrooms. Buffet breakfast.

Ibis Centrum without rest

Raday útca 6 ✉ 1092 – Ⓜ Kálvin tér – ☎ (01) 456 4100 – h2078@accor.com – Fax 456 41 16 – www.ibis-centrum.com **F3**

126 rm – ♦19745 HUF ♦♦16455/19745 HUF

◆ Business ◆ Chain hotel ◆ Functional ◆

Modern hotel well located for city and national museum. Good functional accommodation with all necessary facilities. Lounge, small bar, bright breakfast room and roof garden.

Mercure Budapest Duna without rest

Soroksári útca 12 ✉ 1095 – ☎ (01) 455 8300 – h2025@accor.com – Fax 455 83 85 – www.mercure.com *Plan I* **B2**

130 rm – ♦22500 HUF ♦♦27500 HUF, 3000 HUF

◆ Business ◆ Chain hotel ◆ Functional ◆

Modern hotel catering well for business people and tourists, close to river and city. Fair-sized bedrooms offer simple but modern comforts and reasonable level of mod cons.

XXXX **Gundel**

Állatkerti útca 2 ✉ 1146 – Ⓜ Hösök tere – ☎ (01) 468 4040 – info@gundel.hu – Fax 363 19 17 – www.gundel.hu

Closed 24 December *Plan I* **B1**

Rest – *(booking essential)* Menu 3500/11890 HUF – Carte 8770/12200 HUF

Rest *1894* – *(dinner only)* Menu 6500/9000 HUF – Carte 4000/8350 HUF

◆ Traditional Hungarian ◆ Elegant ◆

Hungary's best known restaurant, an elegant classic. Spacious main room with walnut panelling and ornate ceiling. Traditional cuisine. Summer terrace and live music at dinner. More relaxed atmosphere in 1894; a cellar specialising in wine and grilled dishes.

XXX **Fausto's**

Székely Mihaly U.2 ✉ 1061 – Ⓜ Opera – ☎ (01) 8776210 – www.fausto.hu

Closed 1 May, 6 August, 1 September, 23 October, 1 November, 25 December and Sunday **F1/2**

Rest – Menu 4500 HUF (lunch) – Carte 7400/12400 HUF

◆ Italian ◆ Design ◆

Relocated here in 2006. Discreet façade; sophisticated, comfortable interior divided into two. Husband and wife team deliver accomplished, well-presented Italian cooking.

XX **Lou Lou**

Vigyázó Ferenc Útca 4 ✉ 1051 – ☎ (01) 3124505 – loulou@loulourestaurant.com – Fax 4 72 05 95 – www.loulourestaurant.com

Closed Saturday lunch, Sunday and Bank Holidays **E 1**

Rest – Menu 8000 HUF (lunch) – Carte 10100/13100 HUF

◆ Innovative ◆ Fashionable ◆

Relaunched with considerable style and panache, with chocolate coloured walls and vaulted ceiling. Original and cutting-edge cuisine with vivid flavours. The place to be seen.

XX **White Heaven**

Szent István tér 4-5 ✉ 1051 – ☎ 963 1963 – info@thewhiteheaven.hu – www.thewhiteheaven.hu **D1-2**

Rest – Carte 6000/11000

◆ Asian influences ◆ Trendy ◆

Vibrant restaurant opposite the basilica, with young, trendy clientele. Eat sushi in stylishly angular white bar. International dishes on more comfortable mezzanine level.

XX **Robinson**

Városligeti tó ✉ 1146 – Ⓜ Széchenyi Fürdö – ✆ (01) 422 0222 – robinson@axelero.hu – Fax 422 00 72 – www.restaurantguide.hu/robinson
closed 24-26 December *Plan I* **B1**
Rest – Carte 4500/7000 HUF
◆ Traditional ◆ Friendly ◆
Pavilion on tiny island in park; plenty of ducks to watch in lake with fountains. Spacious conservatory with terrace. Extensive menu of traditional and modern fare. Guitar music at dinner.

XX **Cyrano**

Kristóf tér 7-8 ✉ 1052 – Ⓜ Vörösmarty tér – ✆ (01) 266 4747 – cyrano@citynet.hu – Fax 266 68 18
Closed 24 December and dinner 31 December **E2**
Rest – Carte 5819/9614 HUF
◆ Contemporary ◆ Trendy ◆
Popular informal restaurant just off main shopping street with unusual dramatic modern designer-style décor. Serves selection of good modern European and Hungarian food.

XX **Mokka**

Sas u. 4 ✉ 1051 – Ⓜ Bajcsy-Zs. út – ✆ (01) 328 0081 – mokkar@mokkarestaurant.hu – Fax 328 00 82 – www.mokkarestaurant.hu
Closed Christmas and New Year **E2**
Rest – *(booking essential)* Carte 8040/12660 HUF
◆ Fusion ◆ Trendy ◆
Trendy, warm and buzzy destination close to the Basilica; booking essential. Décor changing in 2008. Eclectic menus offer a mix of Hungarian, Italian and Asian dishes.

XX **Kárpátia**

Ferenciek tere 7-8 ✉ 1053 – Ⓜ Ferenciek tere – ✆ (01) 317 3596 – restaurant@karpatia.hu – Fax 318 05 91 – www.karpatia.hu
Closed 24 December **F2**
Rest – Carte 6600/12400 HUF
◆ Traditional Hungarian ◆ Rustic ◆
One of the city's oldest restaurants with characterful vaulted renaissance-style interior, beautifully painted walls and works of art. Extensive menu of traditional cuisine.

XX **Belcanto**

Dalszínház útca 8 ✉ 1062 – Ⓜ Opera – ✆ (01) 269 2786 – restaurant@belcanto.hu – Fax 311 95 47 – www.belcanto.hu
Closed 25 December **F1**
Rest – *(booking essential)* Menu 5566/7590 HUF – Carte 10626/14674 HUF
◆ Traditional Hungarian ◆ Musical ◆
Next to the opera and famous for classical and operatic evening recitals, including impromptu performances by waiters! Atmosphere is lively and enjoyable. Hungarian food.

X **Segal**

O utca 43-49 ✉ 1066 – Ⓜ Oktogon – ✆ (01) 3280774 **F2**
Rest – *(booking essential)* Menu 2800 HUF (lunch) – Carte 5300/9900 HUF
◆ Asian influences ◆ Fashionable ◆
Modern restaurant with simple décor and original style; quieter tables on mezzanine floor. Eclectic dishes show French and Asian influences; generous portions; moderate prices.

X **Bock Bisztró**

Erzsébet Krt 43-49 ✉ 1073 – Ⓜ Oktogon – ✆ (01) 321 0340 – bockbisztro@axelero.hu – Fax 321 03 40 **F1**
Rest – Carte 4850/9400 HUF
◆ Traditional ◆ Bistro ◆
Stylish décor with Art Deco lighting, though the feel is informal bistro. Classic local recipes with a 21C lift; tapas and cheese/ham plates available too.

Osteria Fausto's

AC VISA MC AE

Dohàny U.5 ✉ 1072 – Ⓜ Astoria – ✆ (01) 2696806 – faustos@fausto.hu – Fax 2 69 68 06 – www.fausto.hu

Closed 1 May, 23 October, 1 November, 25 December and Sunday **F 2**

Rest – Menu 3000 HUF – Carte 4600/8000 HUF

♦ Italian ♦ Bistro ♦

Informal Italian restaurant and wine bar serving simple, rustic Italian food supplemented by blackboard specials, and Hungarian and Italian wines. Expect a friendly welcome.

Krizia

AC VISA MC AE

Mozsár útca 12 ✉ 1066 – Ⓜ Oktogon – ✆ (01) 331 8711 – ristorante.krizia@axelero.hu – Fax 331 87 11 – www.ristorantekrizia.hu

Closed 2 weeks summer, 2 weeks January, 24-26 December, 2 days Easter and Sunday **F1**

Rest – Menu 2600 HUF – Carte 4580/7150 HUF

♦ Italian ♦ Cosy ♦

Dining room in vaulted cellar with a pleasant intimate atmosphere and friendly service. Carefully-prepared Italian cooking, supplemented by regularly changing specials.

BUDA

Plan II

Ramada Plaza Budapest

VISA MC AE

Arpád Fejedelem útca 94 ✉ 1036 – Ⓜ Árpád híd – ✆ (01) 436 4100 – info@aqu.hu – Fax 436 41 22 – www.corinthian.hu

Plan I **A1**

302 rm – †35420/55660 HUF ††40480/60720 HUF, ☕ 4554 HUF – 8 suites

Rest *Apicius* – Carte 6450/10600 HUF

♦ Business ♦ Modern ♦

Modern hotel on west bank, north of centre with own comprehensive thermal spa and therapy centre. Executive level rooms are best; worth the short trip from the city. Apicius restaurant with smart modern décor in warm tones and a pleasant atmosphere.

Art'otel

rm VISA MC AE

Bem Rakpart 16-19 ✉ 1011 – Ⓜ Batthyány tér – ✆ (01) 487 9487 – budapest@artotel.hu – Fax 487 94 88 – www.artotels.com **D1**

156 rm – †22517 HUF ††75647 HUF, ☕ 3036 HUF – 9 suites

Rest *Chelsea* – Carte 4200/7500 HUF

♦ Business ♦ Design ♦

Half new building, half converted baroque houses. Stylish and original interior in cool shades and clean lines. Features over 700 pieces of original art by Donald Sultan. Bright dining room with vaulted ceiling topped with glass and modern artwork.

Novotel Budapest Danube

VISA MC AE

Bem Rakpart 33-34 ✉ 1027 – Ⓜ Batthyány tér – ✆ 458 4900 – h6151@accor.com – Fax 458 49 09 – www.novotel.com **D1**

175 rm – †35100/44200 ††35100/44200 , ☕ 4400

Rest – Menu 2500 (lunch) – Carte 4200/7800

♦ Chain hotel ♦ Business ♦ Modern ♦

Well located, modern hotel boasting basement gym and sauna, meeting rooms for the business traveller and well equipped bedrooms, with a choice of 'Novation' or 'Executive.' Enjoy panoramic views of the river and the Parliament building from Café Danube, which serves international cuisine.

Uhu Villa

Keselyü I/a (Northwest : 8 km by Szilágyi Erzsébet fasor) ✉ *1025 – ☎ (01) 275 1002 – uhuvilla@uhuvilla.hu – Fax 398 05 71 – www.uhuvilla.hu*

13 rm – †29095/44275 HUF ††34155/44275 HUF, ☕ 2277 HUF – 1 suite

Rest – *(Closed Sunday) (dinner only)* Carte 6000/10100 HUF

♦ Traditional ♦ Cosy ♦

Friendly, discreet, personally-styled early 20C villa with gardens in peaceful Buda Hills. Smart, contemporary bedrooms with neat décor, some with balconies. Restaurant with terrace and view serving Italian dishes; Hungarian and Italian wine list.

Carlton without rest

Apor Péter útca 3 ✉ *1011 – Ⓜ Batthyány tér – ☎ (01) 224 0999 – carltonhotel@t-online.hu – Fax 224 09 90 – www.carltonhotel.hu* **D2**

95 rm ☕ – †18975/24035 HUF ††27505/27830 HUF

♦ Traditional ♦ Classic ♦

Usefully-located hotel on Buda side of river, offering straightforward accommodation for the cost-conscious traveller. Rooms are functional and comfortable. Small bar.

Victoria without rest

< Danube and Pest,

Bem Rakpart 11 ✉ *1011 – Ⓜ Batthyány tér – ☎ (01) 457 8080 – victoria@victoria.hu – Fax 457 80 88 – www.victoria.hu* **D1**

27 rm ☕ – †23023/31119 HUF ††24288/31119 HUF

♦ Traditional ♦ Functional ♦

Family-run hotel, popular with tourists, in a row of town houses below the castle. Spacious rooms, equipped with good range of facilities, offer fine views. Refreshing sauna.

Alabárdos

Országház útca 2 ✉ *1014 – Ⓜ Moszkva tér – ☎ (01) 356 0851 – alabardos@t-online.hu – Fax 214 38 14 – www.alabardos.hu*

Closed Sunday **D1**

Rest – *(booking essential) (dinner only and Saturday lunch)* Menu 10000 HUF – Carte 9300/11000 HUF

♦ Traditional ♦ Formal ♦

Well-run restaurant in vaulted Gothic interior of characterful 17C building with covered courtyard in castle square. Extensive menu of good traditional Hungarian classics.

Vadrózsa

Pentelei Molnár útca 15 (via Rómer Flóris útca) ✉ *1025 – ☎ (01) 326 5817 – vadrozsa@hungary.net – Fax 326 58 09 – www.vadrozsa.hu*

Closed 24-26 December *Plan I* **A1**

Rest – Menu 5000 HUF (lunch) – Carte 6980/9620 HUF

♦ Traditional Hungarian ♦ Formal ♦

Pleasant villa just out of town. Spacious wood panelled dining room with piano. Display of raw ingredients presented with the menu. Attractive summer terrace. Detailed service.

Café Pierrot

Fortuna u. 14 ✉ *1014 – Ⓜ Moszkva tér – ☎ (01) 375 6971 – info@pierrot.hu – Fax 375 69 71 – www.pierrot.hu*

closed 24 December **C1**

Rest – Menu 3500 HUF – Carte 4370/8970 HUF

♦ Modern ♦ Friendly ♦

Trees in pots, twinkling fairy lights, Pierrot clown theming with original artwork by local artists. Hungarian base underpins dishes skilfully concocted with Gallic finesse. Live jazz piano.

XX **Arcade Bistro**

Kiss Janos Alt u. 38 ✉ 1126 – Ⓜ Déli pu. – ✆ (01) 225 1969 – arcade@freestart.hu – Fax 225 19 68 – www.arcadebistro.hu

Closed Sunday and Bank Holidays **C2-3**

Rest – *(booking essential)* Carte 5566/9361 HUF

◆ Traditional ◆ Bistro ◆

Small and friendly local restaurant in drab residential area, with central column water feature and colourful modern art décor. Traditional Hungarian cooking.

X **Kisbuda Gyöngye**

Kenyeres útca 34 ✉ 1034 – Ⓜ Árpád híd – ✆ (01) 368 9246 – gyongye@remiz.hu – Fax 368 92 27 – www.remiz.hu

Closed 24 December and Sunday Plan I **A1**

Rest – *(booking essential) (music at dinner)* Carte 5540/9340 HUF

◆ Traditional Hungarian ◆ Rustic ◆

Neighbourhood restaurant in a residential street. Rustic wood panelling created by old wardrobes. Attentive service. Good choice menu; international and authentic food. Live piano.

X **Náncsi Néni**

Ördögárok útca 80, Hüvösvölgy (Northwest : 10 km by Szilágyi Erzsébetfasor) ✉ 1029 – ✆ (01) 397 2742 – info@nancsineni.hu – Fax 397 27 42 – www.nancsineni.hu

Closed 24 December and dinner 31 December

Rest – Carte 3960/6560 HUF

◆ Traditional Hungarian ◆ Minimalist ◆

Interior similar to a Swiss chalet with gingham tablecloths, convivial atmosphere and large terrace. Well-priced home-style Hungarian cooking. Worth the drive from the city.

Republic of IRELAND
ÉIRE

PROFILE

→ **Area:**
70 284 km^2 (27 137 sq mi).

→ **Population:**
4 016 000 inhabitants (est. 2005), density = 57 per km^2.

→ **Capital:**
Dublin (population 1 004 614).

→ **Currency:**
Euro (€); rate of exchange: € 1 = US$ 1.46 (Dec 2007).

→ **Government:**
Parliamentary republic (since 1921). Member of European Union since 1973.

→ **Languages:**
Irish and English.

→ **Specific public holidays:**
St. Patrick's Day (17 March) Good Friday (Friday before Easter); May Bank Holiday (first Monday in May); June Bank Holiday (first Monday in June); August Bank Holiday (first Monday in August); October Bank Holiday (last Monday in Octo-ber); St. Stephen's Day (26 December).

→ **Local Time:**
GMT in winter and GMT + 1 hour in summer.

→ **Climate:**
Temperate maritime, with cool winters and mild summers, fairly high rainfall (Dublin : January: 5°C, July: 15°C).

→ **International dialling Code:**
00 353 followed by area code and then the local number.

→ **Emergency:**
✆ **999** for all emergency services – Fire Brigade, Police, Ambulance, Mountain, Cave, Coastguard and Sea rescue.

→ **Electricity:**
230 volts AC, 50Hz; 3 pin flat or 2-pin round-shaped wall sockets are standard.

→ **Formalities**
Travellers from the European Union

(EU), Switzerland, Iceland and the main countries of North and South America need a national identity card or passport (except for British nationals travelling from the UK; America: passport required) to visit Ireland for less than three months (tourism or business purpose). For visitors from other countries a visa may be required, in addition to a passport, especially for those wishing to stay for longer than three months. We advise you to check with your embassy before travelling.

74

DUBLIN

BAILE ÁTHA CLIATH

Population: 495 101 (conurbation 1 004 614) – Altitude: sea level

R. Kord PHOTONONSTOP

For somewhere touted as the finest Georgian city in the British Isles, Dublin enjoys a very young image. As the 'Celtic Tiger' roared to prominence in the 1990s, Ireland's old capital took on a youthful expression, and for the first time revelled in the epithets 'chic' and 'trendy'. Nowadays it's not just the bastion of Guinness drinkers and those here for the 'craic', but a twenty-first century city with smart restaurants, grand new hotels, modern architecture, impressive galleries and ethnic diversity (and yes, the Guinness still tastes perfect).

Dublin hasn't known a period of such economic prosperity and growth for 250 years, when its handsome squares and façades took shape, designed by the finest architects of the time. In the intervening years, it's gone through uprising, civil war and independence from Britain, and the last decade or so has seen the Irish economy grow ever stronger so that now the city holds a strong fascination for foreign visitors – people are going to Dublin rather than leaving it, as was traditionally the case. Mind you, the locals don't always take too kindly to their guests: invading hordes of stag and hen parties crossing the Irish Sea for intense liquid refreshment, mostly in the Temple Bar area alongside the Liffey, put a strain on even a Dubliner's amiability. At least it leaves all those other fascinating parts of the city ripe for the rest of us to explore.

LIVING THE CITY

Dublin can be pretty well divided into three parts. The area southeast of the river is the classiest, defined by the glorious **Trinity College, St Stephen's Green**, and **Grafton Street's** smart shops. Just west of here is the second area, dominated by **Dublin Castle** and **Christ Church Cathedral** – ancient buildings abound, but it doesn't quite match the sleek aura of the city's Georgian quarter. Cross the **Liffey** to reach the third area. This northern section was the last part of Dublin to be developed during the eighteenth century. Although it lacks the glamour and affluence of its southern neighbours, it does boast the city's grandest avenue, **O'Connell Street,** as well as its most celebrated theatres, a fact that counts in a city which has been home to four Nobel Prize winning writers.

PRACTICAL INFORMATION

ARRIVAL-DEPARTURE

Dublin Airport is just over 7 miles north of the city and a taxi will cost around €20. There is no rail link to the airport but a number of coaches and buses, including Airlink and Aircoach, will take you to the city centre in approximately 30mins.

TRANSPORT

The bus network covers the whole city from the Central Bus Station in Store Street. The price of a single ticket varies depending on the number of stages you've travelled, but it's a cheap and efficient service.

The exciting LUAS (meaning 'speed') light rail network rushes you to areas of the city and suburbs previously only connected to the centre by bus. LUAS was introduced in 2004; like the buses, you pay more as you travel further by zones.

If you want to get out to the coast, then jump on a Dublin Area Rapid Transport (DART) train. They operate at regular intervals, are awesomely efficient, and leave central Dublin from Connolly, Tara Street and Pearse stations. They're as quick as they sound. Buy tickets at any station.

Get along to a Tourist Information Office for the Dublin Pass, which gains you access to just about anywhere in the city. Well, to over thirty attractions, anyway. Passes range from one to six days.

EXPLORING DUBLIN

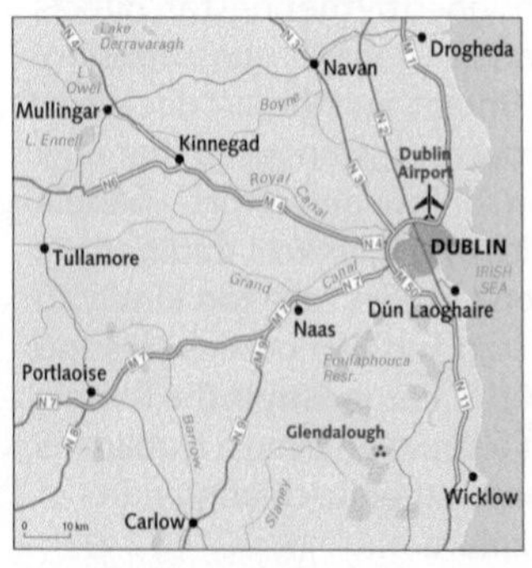

Despite its twenty-first century gloss, Dublin still enjoys a meandering pace of life with an emphasis on the slow and relaxed. Locals will advise you to take your time over a visit; this is not the biggest metropolis on the planet, so why hurry to get around it? With almost a thousand pubs inside the city limits (never mind the new bars and cafés which have sprung up) there's certainly no problem in interrupting your sightseeing schedule. Most of the tourist hotspots are in the area to the south of the Liffey, but there's a lot of fun to be had in turning into inconspicuous alleyways and seeing what shadowy hidden gem might be giving you the nod.

➜ BROUGHT TO BOOK

If you did happen to be in a rush, you could walk from the top of O'Connell Street over the river to the smart southern suburb of **Ballsbridge** in an hour. But then what would be the point of coming to Dublin? The best place to linger is the area around Trinity College, leading down Grafton Street. This section of the city was pretty much undeveloped until the college was founded in 1592, but it was another hundred years before St Stephen's Green, just to the south, was created. As we say, around here no-one's in a particular hurry. It's not difficult to see why people flock to the college. The alma mater of Samuel Beckett, Oliver Goldsmith and Edmund Burke, it's populated with attractive squares, an Old Library with a spectacular Long Room, and a dominant thirty metre high Campanile. Its main attraction, though, is in the Treasury, where the magnificent **Book of Kells** is housed. Dated from around AD 800, it's one of the oldest books in the world, a lavishly illustrated manuscript produced by monks on the remote Scottish island of Iona. It features superbly decorated opening letters of each chapter and dyes supposedly imported from the Middle East.

By way of a complete contrast to the intense intellectualism of Trinity College, step outside and there you'll find the fancy shops lining Grafton Street, the city's most fashionable thoroughfare. Its most exclusive store, Brown Thomas, is also one of its oldest, and locals look upon it as a Londoner might look upon Harvey Nichols. Grafton Street certainly pulls in the crowds, and for those heading south, there's the reward of a verdant sanctuary: St Stephen's Green. Landscaped with flowerbeds, trees, a lake and a fountain, it likes to remind you exactly where you are by displaying numerous memorials to eminent Dubliners: Joyce, Yeats and Wolfe Tone are all here.

➜ MAKING MERRION

This is where Georgian architecture really makes its impact felt; head north along **Merrion Street Upper** and you'll find **Merrion Square,** twelve swanky acres of mid-eighteenth century splendour, bordered on three sides by attractive town-houses featuring wrought-iron balconies and brightly painted doors. The area's sophisticated appeal is enhanced by a rash of museums and galleries, chief of these being the **National Museum** on Kildare Street, which announces itself with an eye-catching domed rotunda and beautiful jewellery from the Bronze Age. In the **National Gallery** on Clare Street, the major schools of European art are represented alongside Irish painting. One of the benefactors here was George Bernard Shaw (his own birthplace, a twenty minute walk south from here, is itself now a museum). Truly worth a visit when you're in the Georgian quarter is the **National Library**, fascinating because it contains first editions of every major Irish writer, and you don't have to think too hard to come up with an awesome list. But museum lovers need not yet feel sated, as also in the area are the **Heraldic Museum** and the **Natural History Museum**, or 'the Dead Zoo' as it's known to the locals.

➜ TEMPLE WORSHIP

You don't really feel you're strolling into a radically different area when you venture south-west of the Liffey: after all, it's just a hop, skip and jump across from Trinity College and Grafton Street. But this is an even older part of town, with **Temple Bar** boasting a wealth of attractive cobbled streets. The area is alive during the daytime as well, particularly around Temple Bar Square, which buzzes with little gallery shops, designer boutiques and a thriving book market at weekends. With its now legendary number of bars, pubs and restaurants jostling for your attention, you might feel the only way to find sanctuary is in a big church or even a castle. Wouldn't you know it, there are two on the doorstep. Christ Church Cathedral, in Christchurch Place, was established nearly a thousand years ago, making it Ireland's oldest. Its history continues right up to 2000, when the vast and fascinating twelfth century crypt was restored. Just across the way is Dublin Castle, first built in the thirteenth century, but with the **Record Tower** the only survivor from that time; luxurious state apartments and a throne presented by William of Orange can be found here, but the star turn is the **Chester Beatty Library**, in the Castle's Clock Tower Building. This outstanding collection of ancient works of art from around the world includes hundreds of illuminated manuscripts with exquisite calligraphy, and almost 300 copies of the Koran spread over a thousand years (considered to be the best example of illuminated Islamic texts in the world). There are striking Buddhist paintings, clay tablets and detailed miniatures. Not surprisingly, it was named European Museum of the Year in 2002. Oh, and the rooftop garden's a great place to eat your lunch if it's a sunny day.

→ NOT WRITTEN OFF

North of the Liffey has for many years been considered a bit of an Achilles Heel, an area 'down on its uppers' and in need of a facelift, an urban botox. That said, there are good reasons to cross the river in a northwards direction, not least a stroll along Dublin's grandest thoroughfare, O'Connell Street. This imposing avenue's mid-eighteenth century glory days may be long gone, but meandering along its central mall you can still get a feel for its heyday as you sample its mix of monuments, fine department stores and historic public buildings. At either end of O'Connell Street stand Dublin's two most famous theatres: **The Abbey** to the south is Ireland's national theatre where Irish playwrights are proudly to the fore; while **The Gate** in Parnell Square to the north has a great reputation for contemporary drama. Slipping very conveniently into this creative mix is the absorbing **Dublin Writers' Museum**, also in Parnell Square, which pays tribute to the city's long history as a literary giant, and includes letters, photos and other memorabilia. Fans of Joyce can then pop along a few streets east to the **James Joyce Cultural Centre**, housed neatly in a Georgian townhouse.

DUBLIN IN...

→ ONE DAY

Trinity College, Grafton Street, St Stephen's Green, Merrion Square, a drink and a meal in Temple Bar

→ TWO DAYS

Christ Church Cathedral, Dublin Castle, Chester Beatty Library, the quayside, a play at one of Dublin's theatres

→ THREE DAYS

A further amble round the alleyways of Temple Bar, O'Connell Street, Parnell Square, Dublin Writers' Museum, a DART train to the coast

CALENDAR HIGHLIGHTS

Some people think Dubliners celebrate a special event every day of the year – the moment the first pint of Guinness goes down. Well, that apart, there are many events and calendar highlights of an official kind in the city. St Patrick's Day in March is, surprise surprise, taken rather seriously here. It's a national holiday given over to music and carnival-style merriment. Around the same time, Celtic Flame lets rip, a citywide festival of traditional and modern music. Don't get this mixed up with the Temple Bar Fleadh, another mid-March mash-up, which resounds to traditional rhythms all around the Temple Bar area. On a more refined scale, April hosts the Colours Boat Race along the Liffey between Trinity College and University College teams, while a little later in the month Feis Ceoil is one of Europe's most well-established and prestigious classical music festivals. Temple Bar again plays host to Diversions right through the summer, an umbrella title for loads of free concerts and open-air theatre shows. The sixteenth of June is a sacred day for fans of Joyce's Ulysses, because it's Bloomsday, when walks, pub talks and lectures take place all over the city. Dublin's premier social event, the Horse Show, trots along in August and gives people a chance to dress in funny hats. Drama's back centre-stage in September with the Fringe Theatre Festival, and then in October with the Dublin Theatre Festival, where new plays are put under the spotlight. A different kind of traditional music sees Opera Ireland make its mark for a week in November at the Gaiety Theatre.

EATING OUT

It's still possible to indulge in Irish stew, but nowadays in Dublin you can also dine out on everything from Thai to tacos and Malaysian to Middle-Eastern. The last decade has seen a boom in global cuisine, often in the Temple Bar area. The city makes the most of its bay proximity, and seafood and fish are used abundantly ; in particular, smoked salmon and oysters. The latter is a staple diet of Dubliners, who love nothing better than to wash them down with Guinness. Portions here are generous, especially in pubs: a plate of roast meat and vegetables is invariably good value for money. For decades vegetables were seen as a bit of a curse in Ireland: a mere decoration, over-boiled to death. Now they're treated with the respect they deserve, and local chefs insist on the best seasonal produce, cooked for just the right amount of time to savour all the taste and goodness. There's never been a better time to be a vegetarian in Dublin, as every type of veg from asparagus to spinach and seaweed is used liberally in dishes. Meat is particularly tasty in Ireland, due to healthy livestock and a wet climate: Irish beef is world famous for its fulsome flavour. Dinner here is usually served till about 10pm, though many ethnic and city-centre restaurants stay open later. If you make your main meal at lunchtime, you'll pay considerably less than in the evening: the menus are often similar, but the bill in the middle of the day will probably be about half the price. Good restaurants nowadays include a fifteen per cent service charge, so there's no need to add a tip.

The Shelbourne

27 St Stephen's Green ✉ D2 – ✆ (01) 663 4500 – info@renaissancehotels.com – Fax (01) 661 60 06 – www.theshelbourne.ie **E3**

246 rm – 🚹260/340 € 🚹🚹260/340 €, ☕ 31 € – 19 suites

Rest *The Saddle Room* – see below

♦ Grand Luxury ♦ Classic ♦

A delightful refit of a grand old hotel, with elegant meeting rooms and sumptuous bedrooms offering a host of extras. The historic Horseshoe Bar and Lord Mayor's Room remain.

The Merrion

Upper Merrion St ✉ D2 – ✆ (01) 603 0600 – info@merrionhotel.com – Fax (01) 603 07 00 – www.merrionhotel.com **F3**

133 rm – 🚹475 € 🚹🚹595 €, ☕ 29 € – 10 suites

Rest The Cellar and **The Cellar Bar** – see below

♦ Grand Luxury ♦ Classic ♦

Classic hotel in series of elegantly restored Georgian town houses; many of the individually designed grand rooms overlook pleasant gardens. Irish art in opulent lounges.

The Westin

College Green, Westmoreland St ✉ D2 – ✆ (01) 645 1000 – reservations.dublin@westin.com – Fax (01) 645 12 34 – www.westin.com/dublin **E2**

150 rm – 🚹189/489 € 🚹🚹189/489 €, ☕ 27 € – 13 suites

Rest *The Exchange* – *(Closed Saturday lunch and Monday)* Menu 26 € (lunch) – Carte dinner 41/59 €

Rest *The Mint* – Carte approx. 27 €

♦ Luxury ♦ Modern ♦

Immaculately kept and consummately run hotel in a useful central location. Smart, uniform interiors and an ornate period banking hall. Excellent bedrooms with marvellous beds. Elegant, Art Deco 1920s-style dining in The Exchange. More informal fare at The Mint.

The Westbury

Grafton St ✉ D2 – ✆ (01) 679 1122 – westbury@jurysdoyle.com – Fax (01) 679 70 78 – www.jurysdoyle.com **E2**

197 rm – 🚹435 € 🚹🚹435 €, ☕ 28 € – 8 suites

Rest *Russell Room* – Menu 32/62 € – Carte 53/68 €

Rest *The Sandbank* – *✆ (01) 646 3353 (Closed Sunday and Bank Holidays)* Menu 30/50 € – Carte 40/53 €

♦ Luxury ♦ Modern ♦

Imposing marble foyer and stairs lead to lounge famous for afternoon teas. Stylish Mandarin bar. Luxurious bedrooms offer every conceivable facility. Russell Room has distinctive, formal feel. Informal, bistro-style Sandbank.

Conrad Dublin

Earlsfort Terrace ✉ D2 – ✆ (01) 602 8900 – dublininfo@conradhotels.com – Fax (01) 676 54 24 – www.conraddublin.com **E3**

191 rm – 🚹185/380 € 🚹🚹200/380 €, ☕ 24 €

Rest *Alex* – Menu 40 € (dinner) – Carte 38/68 €

♦ Luxury ♦ Modern ♦

Smart, business oriented international hotel opposite the National Concert Hall. Popular, pub-style bar. Spacious rooms with bright, modern décor and comprehensive facilities. Modern, bright and airy restaurant offers seafoodh specialities.

Dylan

rm A/C SAT VISA MC AE

Eastmoreland Place ✉ *D2 – ☎ (01) 660 3000 – justask@dylan.ie*
– Fax (01) 660 30 05 – www.dylan.ie
Closed Christmas — *Plan III* **H1**

44 rm – ♦395 € ♦♦395 €, ☕ 30 €
Rest *Still* – Menu 38 € (lunch) – Carte dinner 60/84 €

♦ Luxury ♦ Modern ♦

Modern boutique hotel with vibrant use of colour. Supremely comfortable, individually decorated bedrooms boast an opulent feel and a host of unexpected extras. Modern Irish cooking served in elegant, white-furnished dining room.

The Clarence

SAT P VISA MC AE

6-8 Wellington Quay ✉ *D2 – ☎ (01) 407 0800*
– reservations@theclarence.ie – Fax (01) 407 08 20
– www.theclarence.ie
Closed 24-26 December **D2**

43 rm – ♦370 € ♦♦370 €, ☕ 28 € – 5 suites
Rest *The Tea Room* – see below

♦ Luxury ♦ Design ♦

Discreet, stylish former warehouse overlooking river and boasting 21C interior design. Small panelled library. Modern, distinctive rooms: quietest face courtyard on fourth floor.

The Fitzwilliam

A/C SAT VISA MC AE

St Stephen's Green ✉ *D2 – ☎ (01) 478 7000*
– enq@fitzwilliamhotel.com – Fax (01) 478 78 78
– www.fitzwilliamhotel.com **E3**

136 rm – ♦380 € ♦♦380 €, ☕ 19 € – 3 suites
Rest *Thornton's* – see below
Rest *Citron* – Carte 25/50 €

♦ Business ♦ Modern ♦

Rewardingly overlooks the Green and boasts a bright contemporary interior. Spacious, finely appointed rooms offer understated elegance. Largest hotel roof garden in Europe. Very trendy, informal brasserie.

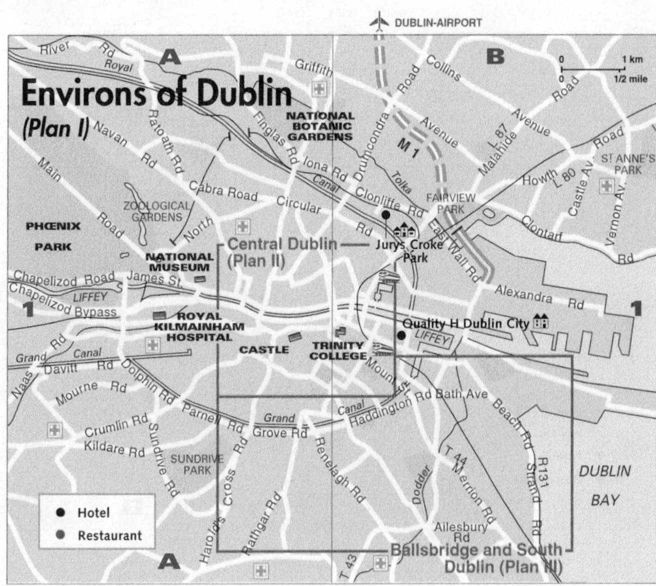

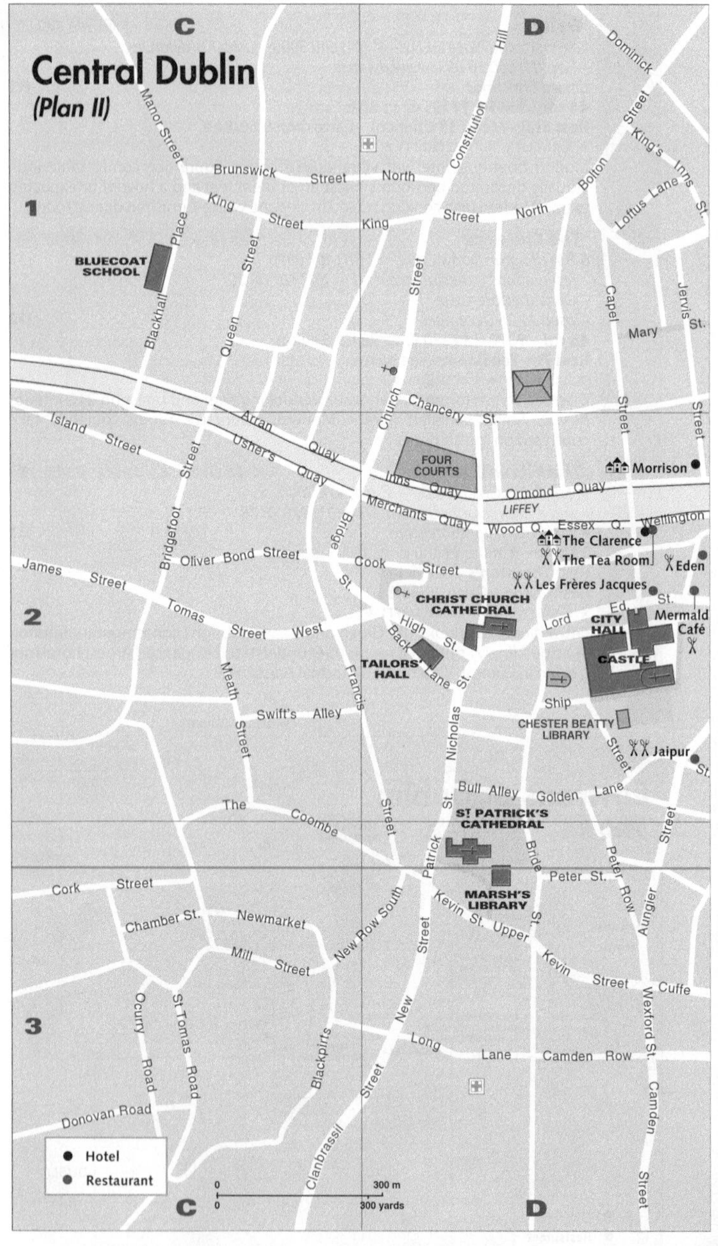
Central Dublin
(Plan II)
C
D
1
2
3
BLUECOAT SCHOOL
FOUR COURTS
CHRIST CHURCH CATHEDRAL
TAILORS' HALL
CITY HALL
CASTLE
CHESTER BEATTY LIBRARY
ST PATRICK'S CATHEDRAL
MARSH'S LIBRARY
LIFFEY
Morrison
The Clarence
The Tea Room
Eden
Les Frères Jacques
Mermald Café
Jaipur
Manor Street
Brunswick Street North
King Street North
Blackhall Place
Queen Street
Constitution Hill
Church Street
Dominick Street
Bolton Street
King's Inns St.
Loftus Lane
Capel Street
Jervis St.
Mary St.
Chancery St.
Arran Quay
Usher's Quay
Inns Quay
Ormond Quay
Merchants Quay
Wood Q.
Essex Q.
Wellington
Island Street
Bridgefoot Street
Oliver Bond Street
Bridge St.
Cook Street
James Street
Tomas Street West
High St.
Back Lane
Lord Ed. St.
Meath Street
Francis Street
Nicholas St.
Swift's Alley
Ship Street
Bull Alley
Golden Lane
The Coombe
Patrick St.
Bride St.
Peter St.
Peter Row
Aungier Street
Cork Street
Chamber St.
Newmarket
Mill Street
New Row South
Kevin St. Upper
Kevin Street
Cuffe
New Street
Wexford St.
Ocurry Road
St Tomas Road
Blackpirts
Long Lane
Camden Row
Camden Street
Clanbrassil Street
Donovan Road
Hotel
Restaurant
0 300 m
0 300 yards

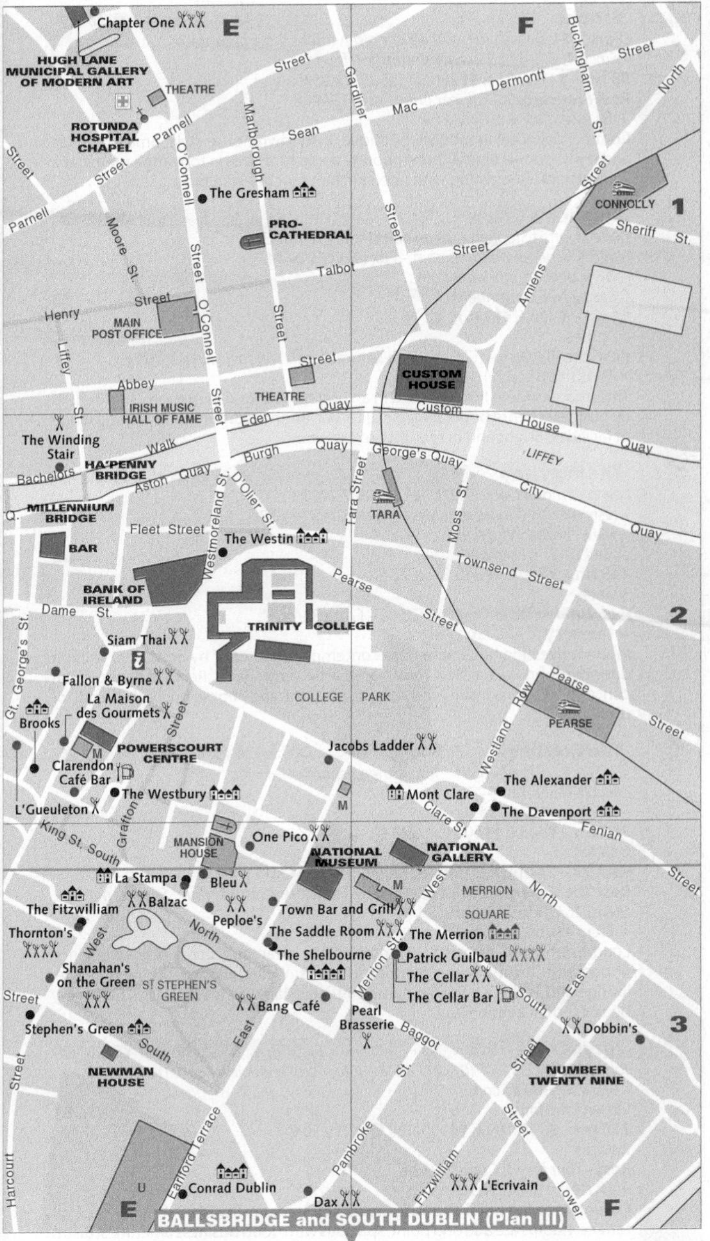
E
F
1
2
3
Chapter One
HUGH LANE MUNICIPAL GALLERY OF MODERN ART
THEATRE
ROTUNDA HOSPITAL CHAPEL
The Gresham
PRO-CATHEDRAL
CONNOLLY
MAIN POST OFFICE
THEATRE
CUSTOM HOUSE
IRISH MUSIC HALL OF FAME
The Winding Stair
HA'PENNY BRIDGE
MILLENNIUM BRIDGE
LIFFEY
TARA
BAR
The Westin
BANK OF IRELAND
TRINITY COLLEGE
COLLEGE PARK
Siam Thai
Fallon & Byrne
La Maison des Gourmets
Brooks
POWERSCOURT CENTRE
Clarendon Café Bar
The Westbury
L'Gueuleton
Jacobs Ladder
PEARSE
The Alexander
Mont Clare
The Davenport
MANSION HOUSE
One Pico
NATIONAL MUSEUM
NATIONAL GALLERY
La Stampa
Bleu
MERRION SQUARE
The Fitzwilliam
Balzac
Peploe's
Town Bar and Grill
Thornton's
The Saddle Room
The Merrion
The Shelbourne
Patrick Guilbaud
The Cellar
The Cellar Bar
Shanahan's on the Green
ST STEPHEN'S GREEN
Bang Café
Pearl Brasserie
Dobbin's
Stephen's Green
NEWMAN HOUSE
NUMBER TWENTY NINE
Conrad Dublin
Dax
L'Ecrivain
BALLSBRIDGE and SOUTH DUBLIN (Plan III)
Parnell Street
Sean Mac Dermontt Street
Buckingham St.
North Street
Marlborough Street
Gardiner Street
O'Connell Street
Moore St.
Talbot Street
Amiens Street
Sheriff St.
Henry Street
Liffey St.
Abbey Street
Eden Quay
Custom House Quay
Bachelors Walk
Aston Quay
Burgh Quay
George's Quay
City Quay
Westmoreland St.
D'Olier St.
Tara Street
Moss St.
Fleet Street
Townsend Street
Pearse Street
Dame St.
Gt. George's St.
Westland Row
Clare St.
Fenian Street
King St. South
Grafton Street
Merrion St.
Merrion Square North
Merrion Square West
Merrion Square South
Merrion Square East
St Stephen's Green North
St Stephen's Green West
St Stephen's Green South
St Stephen's Green East
Baggot St.
Earlsfort Terrace
Pembroke St.
Fitzwilliam Street
Lower
Harcourt Street
U

Brooks

Drury St ✉ D2 – ☎ (01) 670 4000 – reservations@brookshotel.ie – Fax (01) 670 44 55 – www.sinnotthotels.com **E2**

98 rm – 170/185 € 200/215 €, 17.95 €

Rest *Francesca's* – *(dinner only)* Carte 19/44 €

♦ Business ♦ Stylish ♦

Commercial hotel in modish, boutique, Irish town house style. Smart lounges and stylish rooms exude contemporary panache. Extras in top range rooms, at a supplement. Fine dining with open kitchen for chef-watching.

Stephen's Green

Cuffe St, off St Stephen's Green ✉ *D2 – ☎ (01) 607 3600 – info@ocallaghanhotels.com – Fax (01) 478 14 44 – www.ocallaghanhotels.com*

Closed 23-28 December **E3**

64 rm – 325 € 325 €, 16 €

11 suites

Rest *The Pie Dish* – *(Closed lunch Saturday and Sunday)* Carte 35/60 €

♦ Business ♦ Modern ♦

This smart modern hotel housed in an originally Georgian property frequented by business clients; popular Magic Glass bar. Bright bedrooms offer a good range of facilities. Bright and breezy bistro restaurant.

The Morrison

Lower Ormond Quay ✉ *D1 – ☎ (01) 887 2400 – reservations@morrisonhotel.ie – Fax (01) 874 40 39 – www.morrisonhotel.ie*

closed 24-27 December **D2**

135 rm – 340 € 340 €, 22 €

3 suites

Rest *Halo* – Lower Ormond Quay, – Carte 33/46 €

♦ Luxury ♦ Design ♦

Modern riverside hotel with ultra-contemporary interior by acclaimed fashion designer John Rocha. New rooms are particularly stylish. Relaxed dining room concentrates on Irish produce in modish and home-cooked blend of dishes.

The Gresham

✉ *D1 – ☎ (01) 874 6881 – info@thegresham.com – Fax (01) 878 71 75 – www.gresham-hotels.com* **E1**

283 rm – 600 € 600 €, 23 €

6 suites

Rest *23* – 23 Upper O'Connell St *(dinner only)* Carte 34/40 €

Rest *The Gallery* – 23 Upper O'Connell St *(closed Saturday and Sunday lunch)* Menu 26 € (lunch) – Carte 34/40 €

♦ Business ♦ Modern ♦

Long-established restored 19C property in a famous street offers elegance tinged with luxury. Some penthouse suites. Well-equipped business centre, lounge and Toddy's bar. 23 is named after available wines by glass. The Gallery boasts formal ambience.

Jurys Croke Park

Jones's Rd ✉ *D3 – ☎ (01) 871 4444 – info@crokepark.ie – Fax (01) 871 44 00 – www.jurysdoyle.com*

Closed Christmas *Plan I* **B1**

230 rm – 149/189 € 149/189 €, 19.50 €

2 suites

Rest – *(bar lunch)* Carte 24/32 €

♦ Business ♦ Modern ♦

Corporate styled hotel opposite Croke Park Stadium. Stylish 'Side Line' bar with terrace. Rooms are a strong point: spacious with good business amenities. Bistro boasts the Canal terrace and modern/Mediterranean influenced menus.

O'Callaghan Alexander

Fienian St, Merrion Sq ✉ D2 – ☎ (01) 607 3700 – info@ocallaghanhotels.com – Fax (01) 661 56 63 – www.ocallaghanhotels.com

Closed 23-28 December **F2**

98 rm – 450 € 450 €, 16 € – 4 suites

Rest *Caravaggio's* – *(bar lunch Saturday and Sunday)* Carte 38/45 €

◆ Business ◆ Modern ◆

This bright corporate hotel, well placed for museums and Trinity College, has a stylish contemporary interior. Spacious comfortable rooms and suites with good facilities. Stylish contemporary restaurant with wide-ranging menus.

O'Callaghan Davenport

Lower Merrion St, off Merrion Sq ✉ D2 – ☎ (01) 607 3500 – info@ocallaghanhotels.com – Fax (01) 661 56 63 – www.ocallaghanhotels.com **F2**

113 rm – 450 € 450 €, 16 € – 2 suites

Rest *Lanyon* – Carte 40/47 €

◆ Business ◆ Modern ◆

Sumptuous Victorian gospel hall façade heralds elegant hotel popular with business clientele. Tastefully furnished, well-fitted rooms. Presidents bar honours past leaders. Dining room with fine choice menu.

La Stampa

35-36 Dawson St ✉ D2 – ☎ (01) 677 4444 – hotel@lastampa.ie – Fax (01) 677 44 11 – www.lastampa.ie **E3**

27 rm – 170/220 € 170/220 €, 15 € – 1 suite

Rest Balzac – see below

Rest *Tiger Becs* – *(dinner only)* Carte approx. 40 €

◆ Business ◆ Personalised ◆

Silks and oriental furnishings give an Eastern feel to this substantial Georgian house. Elegant bar, beautiful spa and individually appointed, well-equipped bedrooms. Basement restaurant Tiger Becs serves an authentic Thai menu.

O'Callaghan Mont Clare

Lower Merrion St, off Merrion Sq ✉ D2 – ☎ (01) 607 3800 – info@ocallaghanhotels.com – Fax (01) 661 56 63 – www.ocallaghanhotels.com

Closed 23-28 December **F2**

74 rm – 330 € 330 €, 14 €

Rest *Goldsmiths* – *(closed lunch Saturday and Sunday)* Carte 30/40 €

◆ Business ◆ Modern ◆

Classic property with elegant panelled reception and tasteful comfortable rooms at heart of Georgian Dublin. Corporate suites available. Traditional pub style Gallery bar.

Quality H. Dublin City

Sir John Rogerson's Quay, Cardiff Lane ✉ D2 – ☎ (01) 643 9500 – info.dublin@qualityhotels.ie – Fax (01) 643 95 10 – www.qualitydublin.com *Plan I* **B1**

213 rm – 259 € 259 €, 13.50 €

Rest – *(bar lunch)* Menu 35 € – Carte 30/46 €

◆ Business ◆ Modern ◆

Based in 'new generation' quayside area. Sleek Vertigo bar named after U2 song. Impressive health club with large pool. Spacious, modern rooms, 48 boasting balconies. Irish and European mix of dishes in open plan restaurant.

Kilronan House without rest

70 Adelaide Rd ✉ D2 – ☎ (01) 475 5266 – info@kilronanhouse.com – Fax (01) 478 28 41 – www.kilronanhouse.com

Closed Christmas *Plan III* **G1**

12 rm – 55/120 € 160 €

◆ Traditional ◆ Classic ◆

In the heart of Georgian Dublin, a good value, well-kept town house run by knowledgeable, friendly couple. Individually styled rooms; sustaining breakfasts.

XXXX ✿✿

Patrick Guilbaud (Guillaume Lebrun) A/C ⊕ VISA MC AE

21 Upper Merrion St ✉ D2 – ✆ (01) 676 4192
– restaurantpatrickguilbaud@eircom.net – Fax (01) 661 00 52
– www.restaurantpatrickguilbaud.ie
Closed 25-26 December, 17 March, Good Friday, Sunday and Monday **F3**

Rest – Menu 47 € (lunch) – Carte 88/131 €

Spec. Lobster ravioli in coconut scented cream. Veal sweetbread in liquorice with parsnip sauce. Assiette of chocolate.

♦ Contemporary ♦ Formal ♦

Run by consummate professional offering accomplished and acclaimed Irish-influenced dishes in redesigned Georgian town house. Glass-roofed terrace planned for 2008.

XXXX ✿

Thornton's – at The Fitzwilliam H. A/C VISA MC AE

128 St Stephen's Green ✉ D2 – ✆ (01) 478 7008 – thorntonsrestaurant@eircom.net – Fax (01) 478 70 09 – www.thorntonsrestaurant.com
Closed 2 weeks Christmas, Sunday, Monday and lunch Tuesday and Wednesday

Rest – Menu 45/95 € (lunch) – Carte 92/102 € **E3**

Spec. Sautéed prawns and bisque, truffle sabayon. Magret of Mallard duck with girolles and Madeira sauce. Blood orange soufflé with sorbet.

♦ Modern ♦ Formal ♦

Sample canapés in spacious lounge; dine at linen-clad tables in restaurant, hung with the chef's striking photos. Luxury ingredients are prepared with balance and knowledge.

XXXX

Shanahan's on the Green A/C VISA MC AE

119 St Stephen's Green ✉ D2 – ✆ (01) 407 0939 – sales@shanahans.ie
– Fax (01) 407 09 40 – www.shanahans.ie
Closed 2 weeks Christmas and Good Friday **E3**

Rest – *(dinner only and Friday lunch) (booking essential)* Carte 76/122 €

♦ Beef Specialities ♦ Formal ♦

Sumptuous Georgian town house; upper floor window tables survey the Green. Supreme comfort enhances your enjoyment of strong seafood dishes and choice cuts of Irish beef.

XXX ✿

L'Ecrivain (Derry Clarke) A/C ⊕ VISA MC AE

109A Lower Baggot St ✉ D2 – ✆ (01) 661 1919 – enquiries@lecrivain.com
– Fax (01) 661 06 17 – www.lecrivain.com
Closed 10 days Christmas, Easter, Saturday lunch,
Sunday and Bank Holidays **F3**

Rest – *(booking essential)* Menu 45/80 € – Carte dinner 80/100 €

Spec. Seared tuna, pear sauce and fritter, Oscietra caviar. Suckling pig, pithivier, celeriac, apple fondant, sage and bacon foam. Chocolate fondant, mint ice cream, triple chocolate mousse.

♦ Contemporary ♦ Formal ♦

Well-established restaurant serving well prepared, modern Irish menus with emphasis on fish and game. Attentive service from well-versed team. Delightful private dining room.

XXX ✿

Chapter One (Ross Lewis) A/C ⊕ VISA MC

The Dublin Writers Museum, 18-19 Parnell Sq ✉ D1 – ✆ (01) 873 2266
– info@chapteronerestaurant.com – Fax (01) 873 23 30
– www.chapteronerestaurant.com
Closed first 2 weeks August, 24 December-8 January, Sunday, Monday and Saturday Lunch **E1**

Rest – Menu 35 € (lunch) – Carte dinner 55/75 €

Spec. Boudin of pig's trotter, lentil, apple and horseradish compote. Veal, macaroni, girolles, spinach, red wine, basil and caper sauce. Orange and Campari jelly, chocolate mousse, vanilla ice cream.

♦ Modern ♦ Formal ♦

Stylish restaurant in basement of historic building; rustic walls filled with contemporary art. Seasonal, classically-based cooking demonstrates skill and understanding.

XXX **The Saddle Room** – at The Shelbourne H.

27 St Stephen's Green ✉ D2 – ☎ (01) 663 4500 – info@renaissancehotels.com – Fax (01) 651 60 66 – www.theshelbourne.ie **E3**

Rest – Menu 50 € – Carte 50/68 €

◆ Grills ◆ Formal ◆

Smart restaurant in heart of hotel with delightful seafood bar. Grill/seafood menu offers quality Irish produce including superior 21 day hung steaks. Two private dining rooms.

XX **Balzac** – at La Stampa H.

35-36 Dawson St ✉ D2 – ☎ 677 4444 – hotel@lastampa.ie – Fax 677 44 11 closed Saturday and Sunday lunch **E3**

Rest – Menu 22 € – Carte 40/50 €

◆ French ◆ Fashionable ◆

Elegant yet spacious restaurant with high ceiling, blond wood bar, mirrors, banquette seating and a real bistro feel. Tasty, classical French cooking from an appealing menu.

XX **Locks**

Number 1, Windsor Terrace ✉ D8 – ☎ (01) 454 3391 – www.locksrestaurant.ie closed 1 week Easter, 1 week Christmas-New Year, Saturday lunch, Sunday and Bank Holidays *Plan III* **G1**

Rest – Menu 29/49 € – Carte 59/75 €

◆ French ◆ Fashionable ◆

Quirky modern restaurant by the canal boasting stylish inner with wooden floor, comfy leather seating and dining split over 2 floors. French menu includes some regional dishes.

XX **The Tea Room** – at The Clarence H.

6-8 Wellington Quay ✉ D2 – ☎ (01) 407 0813 – tearoom@theclarence.ie – Fax (01) 407 08 26
Closed 24-26 December and Saturday lunch **D2**

Rest – *(booking essential)* Menu 31 € – Carte 49/81 €

◆ Modern ◆ Fashionable ◆

Spacious elegant ground floor room with soaring coved ceiling and stylish contemporary décor offers interesting modern Irish dishes with hint of continental influence.

XX **Dax**

23 Pembroke Street Upper ✉ D2 – ☎ (01) 676 1494 – olivier@dax.ie – www.dax.ie Closed Christmas and New Year, Sunday and Monday **E3**

Rest – *(booking essential)* Menu 27 € – Carte 46/56 €

◆ French ◆ Rustic ◆

Hidden away in basement of Georgian terrace, with rustic inner, immaculately laid tables, wine cellar and bar serving tapas. Knowledgable staff serve French influenced menus.

XX **Fallon & Byrne**

First Floor, 11-17 Exchequer St ✉ D2 – ☎ (01) 472 1000 – Fax (01) 472 10 16 – www.fallonandbyrne.com
Closed 25-26 December and Good Friday **E2**

Rest – Carte 27/55 €

◆ French ◆ Bistro ◆

Food emporium boasting vast basement wine cellar, ground floor full of fresh quality produce, and first floor French style bistro with banquettes, mirrors and tasty bistro food.

XX **The Cellar** – at The Merrion H.

Upper Merrion St ✉ D2 – ☎ (01) 603 0630 – Fax (01) 603 07 00
Closed Saturday lunch **F3**

Rest – Menu 25 € (lunch) – Carte dinner 31/58 €

◆ Mediterranean ◆ Formal ◆

Smart open-plan basement restaurant with informal ambience offering well-prepared formal style fare crossing Irish with Mediterranean influences. Good value lunch menu.

XX **One Pico**

5-6 Molesworth Pl ✉ D2 – ✆ (01) 676 0300 – eamonnoreilly@ireland.com – Fax (01) 676 04 11 – www.onepico.com
Closed 25 December-3 January, Sunday and Bank Holidays **E3**
Rest – Menu 30/45 € – Carte dinner 53/102 €
♦ Modern ♦ Fashionable ♦
Wide-ranging cuisine, classic and traditional by turns, always with an original, eclectic edge. Décor and service share a pleasant formality, crisp, modern and stylish.

XX **Rhodes D7**

The Capel Buildings, Mary's Abbey ✉ D7 – ✆ (01) 804 4444 – info@rhodesd7.com – Fax (01) 804 44 45 – www.rhodesd7.com
Closed 25-26 December, dinner Sunday and Monday *Plan III* **J1**
Rest – Carte 35/48 €
♦ Modern ♦ Brasserie ♦
Cavernous restaurant: take your pick from four dining areas. Bright, warm décor incorporating bold, colourful paintings accompanies classic Rhodes menus given an Irish twist.

XX **Les Frères Jacques**

74 Dame St ✉ D2 – ✆ (01) 679 4555 – info@lesfreresjacques.com – Fax (01) 679 47 25 – www.lesfreresjacques.com
Closed 24 December-3 January, Saturday lunch, Sunday and Bank Holidays
Rest – Menu 23/36 € – Carte 50/90 € **D2**
♦ French ♦ Bistro ♦
Smart and well established, offering well prepared, classic French cuisine with fresh fish and seafood a speciality, served by efficient French staff. Warm, modern décor.

XX **Peploe's**

16 St Stephen's Green ✉ D2 – ✆ (01) 676 3144 – reception@peploes.com – Fax (01) 676 31 54 – www.peploes.com
Closed 24-29 December and Good Friday **E3**
Rest – Carte 43/56 €
♦ Mediterranean ♦ Fashionable ♦
Fashionable restaurant - a former bank vault - by the Green. Irish wall mural, Italian leather chairs, suede banquettes. Original dishes with pronounced Mediterranean accents.

XX **Town Bar and Grill**

21 Kildare St ✉ D2 – ✆ (01) 662 4724 – reservations@townbarandgrill.com – Fax (01) 662 38 57 – www.townbarandgrill.com
Closed 25-26 December, 1 January and Good Friday **E3**
Rest – Menu 28 € (lunch) – Carte dinner 39/60 €
♦ Italian Influences ♦ Rustic ♦
Located in wine merchant's old cellars: brick pillars divide a large space; fresh flowers and candles add a personal touch. Italian flair in bold cooking with innovative edge.

XX **Dobbin's**

15 Stephen's Lane, (off Stephen's Place) off Lower Mount St ✉ D2 – ✆ (01) 661 9536 – dobbinsbistro@g.mail.com – Fax (01) 661 33 31 – www.dobbins.ie
Closed 1 week Christmas-New Year, Good Friday, Saturday lunch, Sunday dinner and Bank Holidays **F3**
Rest – *(booking essential)* Menu 21/35 € – Carte 47/61 €
♦ Traditional ♦ Retro ♦
In the unlikely setting of a former Nissen hut, and now with contemporary styling, this popular restaurant, something of a local landmark, offers good food to suit all tastes.

XX

Jacobs Ladder

VISA MC AE D

4-5 Nassau St ✉ D2 – ✆ (01) 670 3865 – dining@jacobsladder.ie – Fax (01) 670 38 68 – www.jacobsladder.ie

closed 2 weeks Christmas, 1 week August, Good Friday, 17 March, Sunday and Monday **E2**

Rest – *(booking essential)* Menu 44 € (dinner) – Carte 31/62 €

◆ Modern ◆ Fashionable ◆

Up a narrow staircase, this popular small first floor restaurant with unfussy modern décor and a good view offers modern Irish fare and very personable service.

XX

Siam Thai

A/C VISA MC AE

14-15 Andrew St ✉ D2 – ✆ (01) 677 3363 – siam@eircom.net – Fax (01) 670 76 44 – www.siamthai.ie

Closed 25-26 December and lunch Saturday and Sunday **E2**

Rest – Menu 15/35 € – Carte 29/44 €

◆ Thai ◆ Exotic ◆

Invariably popular, centrally located restaurant with a warm, homely feel, embodied by woven Thai prints. Daily specials enhance Thai menus full of choice and originality.

XX

Jaipur

VISA MC AE D

41 South Great George's St ✉ D2 – ✆ (01) 677 0999 – dublin@jaipur.ie – Fax (01) 677 09 79 – www.jaipur.ie **D2**

Rest – *(dinner only and lunch in December)* Menu 50 € – Carte 35/45 €

◆ Indian ◆ Minimalist ◆

Vivid modernity in the city centre; run by knowledgeable team. Immaculately laid, linen-clad tables. Interesting, freshly prepared Indian dishes using unique variations.

XX ☺

Bang Café

A/C VISA MC D

11 Merrion Row ✉ D2 – ✆ (01) 676 0898 – bangcafe@eircom.net – Fax (01) 676 08 99 – www.bangrestaurant.com

Closed 2 weeks late December-early January and Sunday **E3**

Rest – *(booking essential)* Menu 40/50 € – Carte 31/48 €

◆ Innovative ◆ Fashionable ◆

Stylish feel, closely set tables and an open kitchen lend a lively, contemporary air to this established three-tier favourite. Menus balance the classical and the creative.

X ☺

The Winding Stair

VISA MC

40 Lower Ormond Quay ✉ D1 – ✆ (01) 872 7320 – www.winding-stair.com

Closed 25-26 December and 1 January **E2**

Rest – *(booking essential)* Carte 30/48 €

◆ Modern ◆ Rustic ◆

Delightfully rustic restaurant on banks of River Liffey, unusually set above a bookshop. Open dining room with wooden tables; frequently-changing menu has strong organic base.

X

Pearl Brasserie

A/C VISA MC AE

20 Merrion St Upper ✉ D2 – ✆ (01) 661 3572 – info@pearl-brasserie.com – Fax (01) 661 36 29 – www.pearl-brasserie.com

Closed 25 December, Saturday lunch and Sunday **F3**

Rest – Carte 29/49 €

◆ French ◆ Brasserie ◆

A metal staircase leads down to this intimate, newly refurbished, vaulted brasserie where Franco-Irish dishes are served at smart, linen-laid tables. Amiable, helpful service.

Eden

Meeting House Sq, Temple Bar ✉ D2 – ☎ (01) 670 5372 – eden@edenrestaurant.ie – Fax (01) 670 33 30 – www.edenrestaurant.ie
Closed 25 December-2 January and Bank Holidays **D2**
Rest – Menu 26/44 € (lunch) – Carte 36/48 €
♦ Modern ♦ Minimalist ♦
Modern minimalist restaurant with open plan kitchen serves good robust food. Terrace overlooks theatre square, at the heart of a busy arty district. The place for pre-theatre.

Mermaid Café

69-70 Dame St ✉ D2 – ☎ (01) 670 8236 – info@mermaid.ie – Fax (01) 670 82 05 – www.mermaid.ie **D2**
Rest – *(Sunday brunch) (booking essential)* Menu 27 € (lunch) – Carte 40/51 €
♦ Modern ♦ Fashionable ♦
This informal restaurant with unfussy décor and bustling atmosphere offers an interesting and well cooked selection of robust modern dishes. Efficient service.

L'Gueleton

1 Fade St ✉ D2 – ☎ (01) 675 3708
closed 25 December-1 January, Sunday and Bank Holidays **E2**
Rest – *(bookings not accepted)* Carte 27/42 €
♦ French ♦ Bistro ♦
Busy, highly renowned recent arrival. Rustic style: mish-mash of roughed-up chairs and tables with candles or Parisian lamps. Authentic French country dishes full of flavour.

Bleu

Joshua House, Dawson St ✉ D2 – ☎ (01) 676 7015 – Fax (01) 676 70 27 – www.bleu.ie
Closed 25-26 December **E3**
Rest – Menu 22/30 € – Carte dinner 25/42 €
♦ Modedrn ♦ Fashionable ♦
Distinctive modern interior serves as chic background to this friendly all-day restaurant. Appealing and varied menu, well executed and very tasty. Good wine selection.

La Maison des Gourmets

15 Castlemarket ✉ D2 – ☎ (01) 672 7258 – Fax (01) 672 72 38
Closed 25 December-2 January and Bank Holidays **E2**
Rest – *(lunch only) (bookings not accepted)* Carte 18/24 €
♦ French ♦ Cosy ♦
Neat, refurbished eatery on first floor above an excellent French bakery. Extremely good value Gallic meals with simplicity the key. Get there early or be prepared to wait!

The Cellar Bar – at The Merrion H.

Upper Merrion St ✉ D2 – ☎ (01) 603 0600 – info@merrionhotel.com – Fax (01) 603 07 00 – www.merrionhotel.com
Closed 25 December and Sunday **F3**
Rest – *(carvery lunch)* Carte 35/50 €
♦ Traditional ♦ Pub ♦
Characterful stone and brick bar-restaurant in the original vaulted cellars with large wood bar. Popular with Dublin's social set. Offers wholesome Irish pub lunch fare.

Clarendon Café Bar

32 Clarendon Street ✉ D2 – ☎ (01) 679 2909 – Fax (01) 670 69 00 – www.clarendon.ie
Closed 25-26 December, 1 January, dinner Friday-Sunday and Good Friday
Rest – *(Sunday brunch) (bookings not accepted)* Carte 15/42 € **E2**
♦ Modern ♦ Trendy ♦
Sleek, contemporary metal and glass dining pub on three levels. Chocolate leather box seats and scatter cushions. Modern menus all the way from casual to serious in style.

Four Seasons

Simmonscourt Rd ✉ D4 – ✆ (01) 665 4000 – sales.dublin@fourseasons.com – Fax (01) 665 40 99 – www.fourseasons.com/dublin **J2**

157 rm – ††445/490 €, ☕ 29 € – 40 suites

Rest *Seasons* – Menu 35 € (lunch) – Carte dinner 62/84 €

Rest *The Cafe* – Carte 38/75 €

♦ Grand Luxury ♦ Modern ♦

Every inch the epitome of international style - supremely comfortable rooms with every facility; richly furnished lounge; a warm mix of antiques, oils and soft piano études. Dining in Seasons guarantees luxury ingredients. Good choice menu in The Café.

Herbert Park

✉ D4 – ✆ (01) 667 2200 – reservations@herbertparkhotel.ie – Fax (01) 667 25 95 – www.herbertparkhotel.ie **J2**

151 rm – †250 € ††385 €, ☕ 21.50 € – 2 suites

Rest *The Pavilion* – Menu 26 € – Carte 36/72 €

♦ Business ♦ Modern ♦

Stylish contemporary hotel. Open, modern lobby and lounges. Excellent, well-designed rooms with tasteful décor: fifth floor Executive rooms boast several upgraded extras. French-windowed restaurant with alfresco potential; oyster/lobster specialities.

Merrion Hall without rest

54-56 Merrion Rd ✉ D4 – ✆ (01) 283 7916 – merrionhall@aol.ie – Fax (01) 283 78 77 – www.halpinsprivatehotels.com **J2**

34 rm ☕ – †99/119 € ††139/169 € – 2 suites

♦ Business ♦ Minimalist ♦

Manor house hotel has comfy sitting rooms with Georgian feel and some original features plus rear breakfast room with conservatory. Minimalist bedrooms boast quality feel.

The Schoolhouse

2-8 Northumberland Rd ✉ D4 – ✆ (01) 667 5014 – reservations@schoolhousehotel.com – Fax (01) 667 50 15 – www.schoolhousehotel.com Closed 24-26 December **H1**

31 rm ☕ – †169/500 € ††199/500 €

Rest *Canteen* – *(brunch Saturday and Sunday)* Menu 24 € (lunch) – Carte 29/49 €

♦ Business ♦ Historic ♦

Spacious converted 19C schoolhouse, close to canal, boasts modernity and charm. Inkwell bar exudes a convivial atmosphere. Rooms contain locally crafted furniture. Old classroom now a large restaurant with beamed ceilings.

Ariel House without rest

50-54 Lansdowne Rd ✉ D4 – ✆ (01) 668 5512 – reservations@ariel-house.net – Fax (01) 668 58 45 – www.ariel-house.net – Closed 21-28 December **J1**

37 rm ☕ – †72/110 € ††130/250 €

♦ Business ♦ Classic ♦

Restored, listed Victorian mansion in smart suburb houses personally run, traditional small hotel. Rooms feature period décor and some antiques; comfy four poster rooms.

Bewley's

Merrion Rd ✉ D4 – ✆ (01) 668 1111 – ballsbridge@bewleyshotels.com – Fax (01) 668 19 99 – www.bewleyshotels.com – closed 24-26 December **J2**

304 rm – †109/119 € ††109/119 €, ☕ 11 €

Rest *O'Connells* – *(carvery lunch)* Menu 28 € – Carte 27/37 €

♦ Business ♦ Functional ♦

Huge hotel offers stylish modern accommodation behind sumptuous Victorian façade of former Masonic school. Location, facilities and value for money make this a good choice. Informal modern O'Connells restaurant, cleverly constructed with terrace in stairwell.

Aberdeen Lodge

53-55 Park Ave ✉ D4 – ✆ (01) 283 8155
– aberdeen@iol.ie
– Fax (01) 283 78 77
– www.halpinsprivatehotels.com **J2**
17 rm – 99/119 € 139/300 €
Rest – *(residents only, light meals)* Carte 25/34 €
♦ Townhouse ♦ Classic ♦
Neat red brick house in smart residential suburb. Comfortable rooms with Edwardian style décor in neutral tones, wood furniture and modern facilities. Some garden views. Comfortable, traditionally decorated dining room.

Pembroke Townhouse without rest

90 Pembroke Rd ✉ D4 – ✆ (01) 660 0277
– info@pembroketownhouse.ie
– Fax (01) 660 02 91
– www.pembroketownhouse.ie
closed 22 December-3 January **H1**
48 rm – 90/165 € 130/230 €
♦ Townhouse ♦ Classic ♦
Period-inspired décor adds to the appeal of a sensitively modernised Georgian terrace town house in the smart suburbs. Neat, simple accommodation.

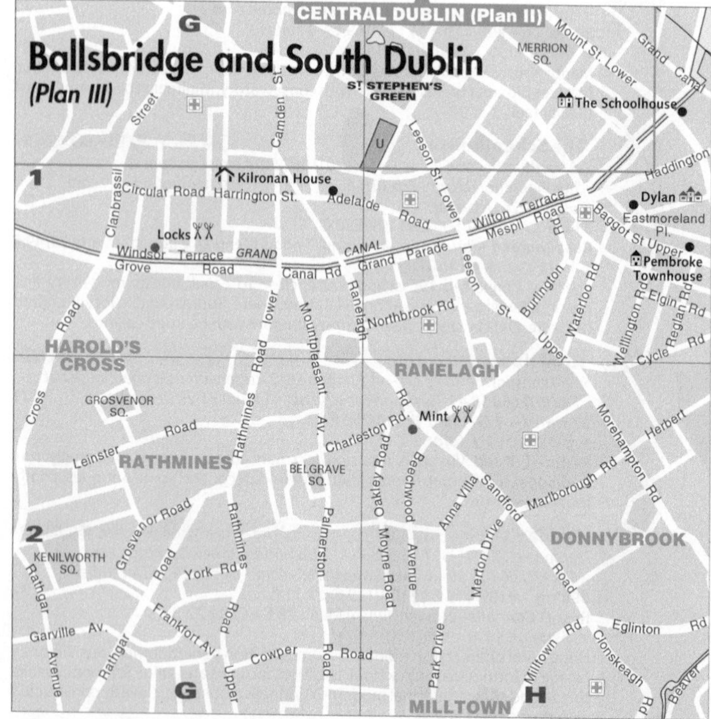

Glenogra House without rest

64 Merrion Rd ✉ D4
– ✆ (01) 668 3661
– info@glenogra.com
– Fax (01) 668 36 98
– www.glenogra.com
Closed 22 December-10 January J2
13 rm ☕ – 🚹85/105 € 🚹🚹119/159 €

◆ Family ◆ Cosy ◆

Neat and tidy bay-windowed house in smart suburb. Personally-run to good standard with bedrooms attractively decorated in keeping with a period property. Modern facilities.

Siam Thai

Sweepstake Centre ✉ D4
– ✆ (01) 660 1722
– siam@eircom.net
– Fax (01) 660 15 37 – www.siamthai.ie
Closed 25-26 December, lunch Saturday and Sunday and Good Friday
Rest – Menu 15/35 € – Carte 29/44 € J2

◆ Thai ◆ Friendly ◆

Unerringly busy restaurant that combines comfort with liveliness. Efficient staff serve authentic Thai cuisine, prepared with skill and understanding. Good value lunches.

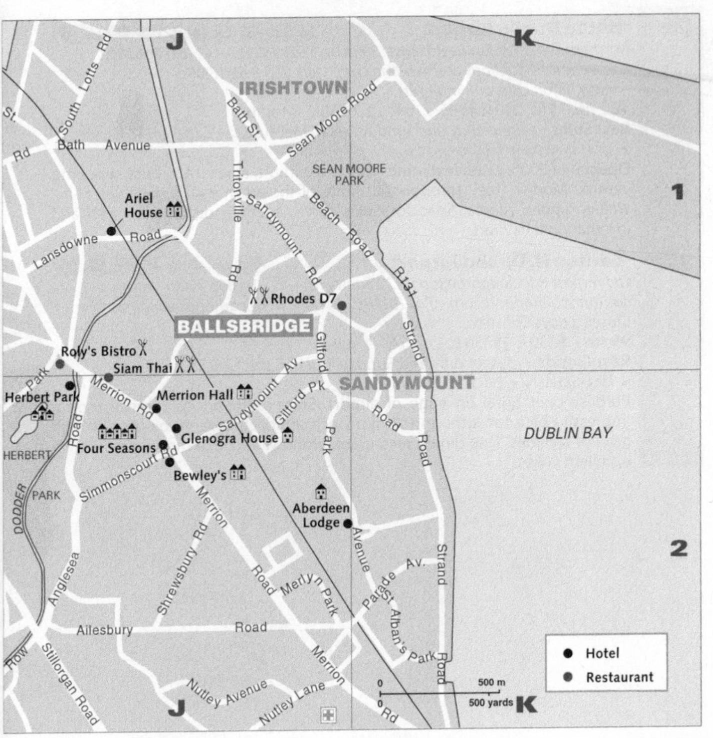

Roly's Bistro

7 Ballsbridge Terrace ✉ *D4 – ☎ (01) 668 2611 – ireland@rolysbistro.ie – Fax (01) 660 33 42 – www.rolysbistro.ie* **J1**

Rest – *(booking essential)* Menu 21/42 € – Carte 39/51 €

♦ Traditional ♦ Bistro ♦

A Dublin institution: this roadside bistro is very busy and well run with a buzzy, fun atmosphere. Its two floors offer traditional Irish dishes and a very good value lunch.

at Ranelagh

Mint (Dylan McGrath)

47 Ranelagh Rd ✉ *D6 – ☎ (01) 497 8655* **H2**
– info@mintrestaurant.ie – Fax (01) 497 90 35
– www.mintrestaurant.ie

Closed 23 December-6 January, 6-17 April, Sunday, Monday and Saturday lunch

Rest – Menu 30/75 € – Carte 37/75 €

Spec. Road lobster, minced veal, truffle macaroni, hen's egg. Roast turbot, broccoli purée, braised snails, Spanish ham and red wine. Ginger ice cream, ginger savarin and lime parfait.

♦ Inventive ♦ Intimate ♦

Intimate, pastel-hued restaurant in up and coming area of the city. Ambitious, confident kitchen serving uncompromisingly rich and elaborate dishes with French influences.

at DUBLIN AIRPORT

Hilton Dublin Airport

Northern Cross, Malahide Rd (East : 3 km by A 32) ✉ *D17 – ☎ (01) 8661800 – reservations.dublinairport@hilton.com – Fax (01) 8 66 18 66 – www.hilton.com/dublinairport*

162 rm – †86/240 € ††86/270 €, ☕ 19.50 € – 4 suites

Rest *Solas* – *(dinner only and Sunday lunch)* Menu 38 € – Carte 36/48 €

♦ Business ♦ Modern ♦

Opened in 2005, just five minutes from the airport, adjacent to busy shopping centre. Modish feel throughout. State-of-the-art meeting facilities. Airy, well-equipped rooms. Spacious Solas serves modern dishes with Irish and international flavours.

Carlton H. Dublin Airport

Old Airport Rd, Cloughran (on R 132 Santry rd) – ☎ (01) 866 7500 – info@carltondublinairport.com – Fax (01) 862 31 14 – www.carltondublinairport.com

Closed 3 days Christmas

99 rm – †330 € ††330 €, ☕ 16 € – 1 suite

Rest Clouds – (dinner only and Sunday lunch) Carte €35/53

♦ Business ♦ Modern ♦

Purpose-built hotel on edge of airport. State-of-the-art conference rooms. Impressive bedrooms, though many a touch compact, in warm colours with high level of facilities. Fine dining restaurant: worldwide cooking accompanied by excellent views.

ITALY

ITALIA

PROFILE

→ **Area:**
301 262 km^2 (116 317 sq mi).

→ **Population:**
59 131 287 inhabitants (est. 2007), density = 196 per km^2.

→ **Capital:**
Rome (conurbation 2 867 000 inhabitants).

→ **Currency:**
Euro (€); rate of exchange: € 1 = 1.46 US$ (Dec 2007).

→ **Government:**
Parliamentary republic with two chambers (since 1946). Member of European Union since 1957 (one of the 6 founding countries).

→ **Language:**
Italian.

→ **Specific public holidays:**
Epiphany (6 January); Liberation Day (25 April); Anniversary of the Republic (2 June); Immaculate Conception (8 December); St. Stephen's Day (26 December). Each town also celebrates the feast day of its patron saint (Rome: 29 June St. Peter, Milan: 7 December St. Ambrose, etc details from the local tourist offices).

→ **Local Time:**
GMT + 1 hour in winter and GMT + 2 hours in summer.

→ **Climate:**
Temperate Mediterranean, with mild winters and hot, sunny summers (Rome: January: 8°C, July: 25°C).

→ **International dialling Code:**
00 39 followed by area or city code and then the local number.

→ **Emergency:**
Police: ✆ **112**; Fire Brigade: ✆ **115**; Health services: ✆ **118**.

→ **Electricity:**
220 volts AC, 50Hz; 2-pin round-shaped continental plugs.

→ **Formalities**
Travellers from the European Union (EU), Switzerland, Iceland and the main countries of North and South America need a national identity card or passport (America: passport required) to visit Italy for less than three months (tourism or business purpose). For visitors from other countries a visa may be required, in addition to a passport, especially for those wishing to stay for longer than three months. We advise you to check with your embassy before travelling.

ROME
ROMA

Population (est. 2007): 2 705 000 (conurbation 4 013 000) – Altitude: about 100m above sea level

R. Mattès/HEMIS.fr

Rome wasn't built in a day, and it's pretty hard to do it justice in less than three. The Italian capital is so richly layered in Imperial, Renaissance, Baroque and modern architecture that it takes on the appearance of a sprawling stew, its ingredients stirred together into a spicy and multi-ingredient feast. Its broad piazzas, hooting traffic and cobbled thoroughfares all lend their part to the heady fare: a theatrical stage cradled within seven famous hills.

Being Eternal, Rome never ceases to feel like a lively, living city, while at the same time a scintillating monument to Renaissance power and an epic centre of antiquity. Nowhere else offers such a wealth of classical remains, strung together alongside palaces and churches, and bathed in the soft, golden light for which it is famous. Even when taking time off from exploring the famous sights, you can hardly fail to come across ochre-coloured façades hiding a little square with a bustling market, or stairways that lead you down to a gushing fountain. You're always aware of the steady drip of history here: over 2,700 years of it. When Augustus became the first Emperor of Rome, he could hardly have imagined the impact his city's language, laws and calendar would have upon the world.

LIVING THE CITY

The **River Tiber** snakes its way north to south through the heart of Rome. On its west bank lies the characterful and 'independent' neighbourhood of **Trastevere**, while north of here is Vatican City. Over the river the **Piazza di Spagna** area to the north has Rome's smartest shopping streets, while the southern boundary is marked by the **Aventine** and **Celian** hills, the latter overlooking the **Colosseum**. **Esquiline**'s teeming quarter is just to the east of the city's heart; that honour goes to the **Capitol,** which gave its name to the concept of a 'capital' city. Rome is surrounded by the **Lazio** countryside, beautiful in the spring and autumn months.

PRACTICAL INFORMATION

ARRIVAL-DEPARTURE

Leonardo da Vinci Airport at Fiumicino is 32km southwest of Rome; a taxi will be around €40. The Fiumicino Leonardo Express train to Stazione Termini runs every 30min and takes 32min. Every 30min the Cotral bus travels to the Anagnina Station of Metro Line A.

TRANSPORT

Rome is served by a metro, bus and tram system. Tickets are available from metro stations, bus terminals, ticket machines, tobacconists, newsagents, cafés and tourist information centres. Choose your ticket type: a single ticket, which must be time stamped on board, or travelcards for one, three or seven days.

By the very nature of its hills and piazzas, Rome is best seen on foot, so make sure you have a good pair of walking shoes. A pair of binoculars is useful to have slung round your neck, too, as lots of sights are on ceilings or the top of columns.

Remember not to overdo the dressing down if you're visiting the religious sights around the city. You won't be allowed in if you think walking into a Roman church is akin to stepping onto an Italian beach – so avoid the likes of sleeveless tops, shorts and mini skirts.

EXPLORING ROME

To get to the very heart of Rome, you need to climb stairs. But these stairs are by Michelangelo, and once you've reached the top of the **Cordonata**, you arrive at the great man's **Piazza dei Campidoglio**, a spectacular setting for Rome's city hall, whose bell tower offers incomparable views far and wide. You are now at the Capitol, which, for Romans, has been the centre of their world and the seat of municipal government for centuries. Around the piazza are two of the city's best museums, the **Capitoline Museums**, home to a fantastic collection of Classical statues and artworks by the likes of Tintoretto, Titian and Rubens. The grandeur of these two

late Middle Age temples to culture sets the tone for an even more awe-inspiring art show: the one featuring the old city's remarkable buildings themselves.

➜ FORUM...HERE TO ETERNITY

Just south of the Capitol is quite simply one of the world's great sights. It doesn't matter from which angle you come at it, there's little to compare with the drama afforded by the **Forum**'s weary old bones backed up by the brooding presence of the Colosseum. What remains of the Forum gives only a hint of its former imperial pomp, but even this relative handful of columns, temples and basilicas, scattered in a great drunken maze around you, offers a moving impression of what was once the centre of Rome's political and commercial life. Imagine it...over two thousand years ago, on this spot, Julius Caesar was building his very own temple to vanity, setting the template for future emperors from Augustus onwards. Even in its ruined state, the Colosseum, arching up in the background, is a sight to take the breath away. Rome's greatest amphitheatre was built in AD80 for over fifty thousand spectators to gawp at gladiatorial contests, but was plundered in Renaissance times for its stone. Nevertheless, it still remains an awesome presence; venture inside to the top row seats for head-spinning views.

➜ PLEASURE DOME

If you turn north from the Capitol, rather than south, you'll find not only the best-preserved ancient temple in Rome, but also one of the finest buildings in European architectural history – **The Pantheon**. This beautifully proportioned 'Temple of all the Gods' boasts a portico with granite columns, but these offer no clue as to the beauty and elegance of the building's main highlight, its vast dome. Go inside and marvel at it. The hole at the top provides the only light, and is a constant talking point for architects, who never cease to wonder just why the unreinforced dome has never come crashing to the ground!

➜ THREE COINS

A little way northeast of here is another of Rome's star turns: The **Trevi Fountain**, on the Quirinal Hill. It was only built in 1762, which makes it almost modern by the city's standards, and its theatrical figures of Neptune and two tritons take up most of the tiny **Piazza di Trevi**. The fountain resembles a stage set, and was suitably employed as the shimmering, splashy backdrop to Anita Ekberg's cavortings during Fellini's ground-breaking movie *La Dolce Vita* in 1960. Nowadays, visitors chuck coins in the Trevi, just like the secretaries in another famous 'Rome' movie, *Three Coins In the Fountain*. In the back streets around here are lots of hidden churches – neat, mysterious and charming - while further down Quirinal Hill, fine palaces built for the ancient and powerful families of the city are a splendid sight.

➜ SPANISH STROLL

Carry on northwards and you reach one of Rome's smartest areas, around Piazza di Spagna. This neighbourhood offers superb Renaissance and Baroque art in its churches, as well as one of the city's most prized ancient monuments (the **Ara Pacis**) repackaged in a 21C glass hangar. There's also fine art in the **Villa Medici**, and wonderful views of the city from the **Pincio Gardens**. But most people come up here to loll around awhile on the **Spanish Steps**. Built in 1726, the steps curve around terraces, richly flowered at Easter, to create one of the city's most famously distinctive landmarks. At their base, rather incongruously, is the **Keats-Shelley Memorial House**, a small museum dedicated to the two poets who are both buried in Rome. Latin sophistication is very much restored when you cross the Piazza di Spagna to take in the shadowy chic of **Via Condotti**. This is the home of Rome's smartest shops where early evening strollers come to gaze at the windows of the coolest designer names in the city. Another favourite is the nearby **Via del Babuino**, along which hushed art galleries and fascinating antique shops combine to create a smart feel.

Along the curving Tiber a little way south west is Rome's most handsome, most theatrical piazza – **Piazza Navona**. It's shaped like a huge oval lozenge because it was once a great athletics stadium, originally built in AD86. Today the entertainment comes from its three grandiose fountains, and the little human dramas being enacted in the pedestrian areas day and night. The eye-catching Baroque churches here provide a spectacle of their own. Close by is the fascinating **Via del Governo Vecchio**, full of 15C and 16C Renaissance houses interspersed with charming antique shops.

The east bank, just across from Trastevere, boasts a down-to-earth shrine of its own in the bustling market place of **Campo de' Fiori**, which has been in existence since medieval times when it was surrounded by inns for pilgrims; these days the lively ambience lives on and the teeming stalls of fruit and vegetables are used to supply many of the nearby restaurants. Of course, in this city you're never far from a majestic building or two to set alight the flame of inspiration. Close by is the grandiose baroque church of **Sant' Andrea della Valle**, renowned for its beautiful dome. Praying in here one day, with the cries of the market stall vendors in the distance, Puccini came up with the idea for the first act of *Tosca*.

→ THE TRASTEVERE

To get the feel for a different Rome, one that gives the impression of proletarian life in bygone times, cross the Tiber by any of the five bridges in the area, and soak up the atmosphere of **Trastevere**. It's one of the most picturesque old neighbourhoods of the city, with a distinctly laidback feel in contrast to the frenetic world over the river. The narrow cobbled alleyways here have a charm all their own and are a great place to escape to for a quiet lunch or early evening drink. The only threat to Trastevere's earthy character is the steady growth of fashionable bars, clubs and boutiques which have arrived in recent years, but in high summer the proximity of its densely packed buildings offers a welcomingly cool experience when the rest of Rome feels like a spit roast.

CALENDAR HIGHLIGHTS

You could say that Rome is an event in itself, but the city still likes to down tools for a bit of a celebration. February, for example, sees the historical thoroughfares of the city come alive for the annual Carnival. When

ROME IN...

→ ONE DAY

Capitol, Forum, Colosseum, Pantheon, Trevi Fountain, Spanish Steps

→ TWO DAYS

Via Condotti, Piazza Navona and churches in surrounding area, Capitoline museums

→ THREE DAYS

A day on the west bank of the Tiber at Trastevere and Vatican City

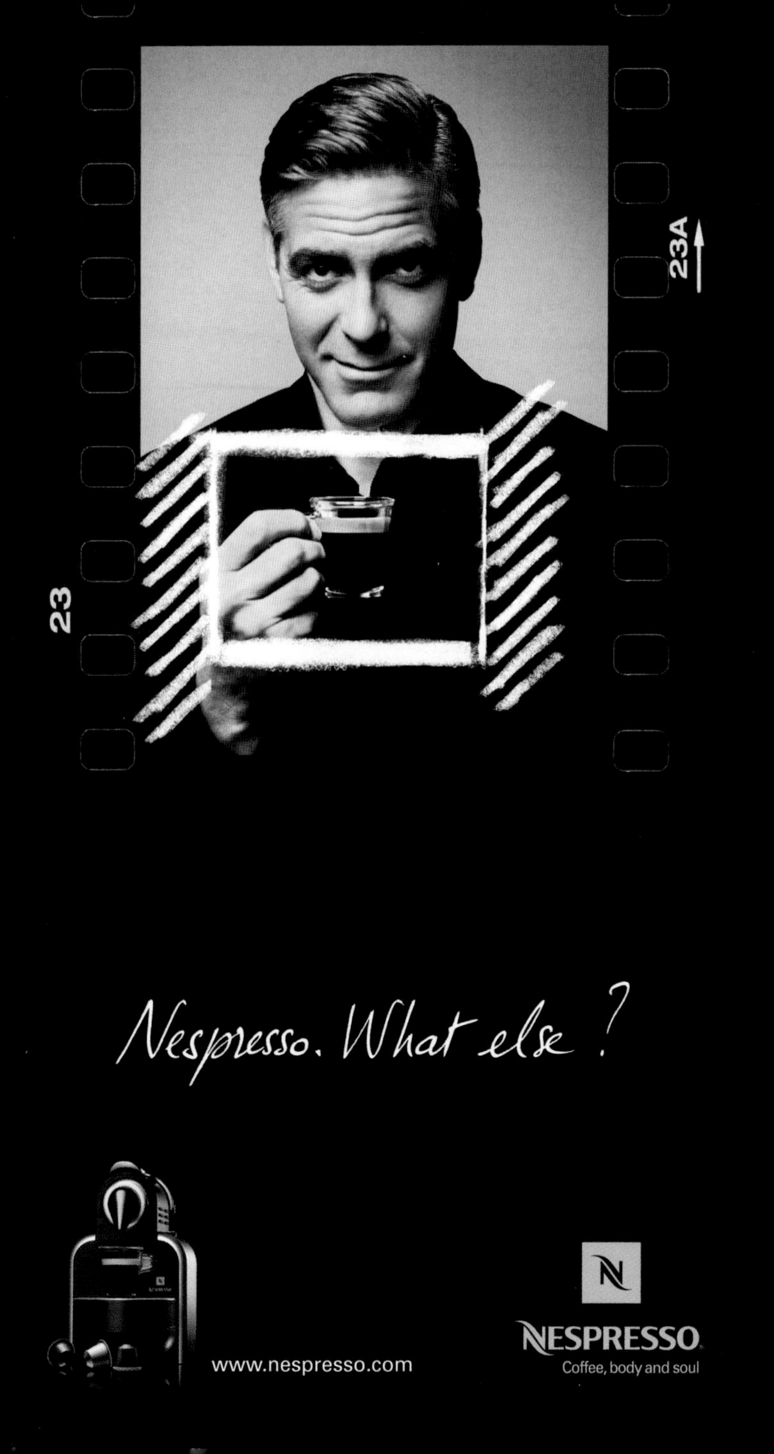

the azaleas appear in March, three thousand vases of them are arranged dramatically on the Spanish Steps for the Spring Festival. That same month, film fans celebrate the first of Rome's two big festivals with the Independent Film Festival, featuring more than sixty innovative movies from around the globe at a variety of cinemas. Also at that time, the city boasts its Cultural Heritage Week, with museums and monuments opening up to the public without charge. April is a big month here: Rome celebrates its birthday on the twenty-first (it was 'born' in 753BC) and the Campidoglio is the centre of activity with illuminated hillside palazzi and monster fireworks. There's also the Parklife festival at Fiera di Roma, which celebrates environmental culture with exhibits, films and installations promoting protected areas and natural parks in Italy. The Roman Summer is renowned for its oppressive heat, but the festival bearing that name (June-September) is hot in another way: the city's piazzas, palaces, parks and courtyards host a wide array of pop and jazz concerts (the outdoor film screenings late into the night may be a cooler choice). Tiberina Island is lit up like a film set for Cinema Isle (June-August) with retrospectives and blockbusters high on its agenda, while July's Festa de Noantri has two weeks' worth of art and street performances in honour of Trastevere's earthy proletarian beginnings. Also in July get cool on both banks of the Tiber at the Tevere Expo, when stalls full of arts and crafts, food and wine tempt you to buy. Two other summer highlights for music lovers: Secret Passages (July-August) boasts classical concerts and theatre performances at various locations in the city, while New Operafestival (July-September) at Basilica di San Clemente, just behind the Colosseum, is an operatic feast, featuring the likes of Mozart, Verdi and Donizetti. Autumn's Roma Europa Festival is a big one, with music, dance and theatre at stunning locations across Rome. Museums, galleries and theatres stay open till the early hours during White Night (September), while film from every angle is highlighted at the Rome Film Festival, at important movie venues, in October.

EATING OUT

Despite being Italy's capital, Rome largely favours a local, traditional cuisine to be found in typically unpretentious trattorie or osterie. Although not far from the sea, the city doesn't go in much for fish, and food is often connected to the rural, pastoral life with products coming from the surrounding Lazio hills, which also produce good wines. Pasta, of course, is not to be missed – mainly spaghetti, bucatini or rigatoni – combined with sauces such as amatriciana (prepared with tomatoes and unsmoked bacon), carbonara (eggs and unsmoked bacon) or arrabbiata (chilli). Lamb is favoured among meats for the main course; so too, the 'quinto quarto', which is another example of Roman cuisine's links to popular traditions based on rural tastes. The quinto quarto is a long-established way of indicating those parts of the beef (tail, tripe, liver, spleen, lungs, heart, kidney) left over after the best bits had gone to the richest families. Trastevere and the historical centre are full of restaurants featuring quinto quarto. For international, or more classic, cuisine combined with a more refined setting, head for the elegant hotels: very few other areas of Italy have such an increasing number of good quality restaurants within a hotel setting. Locals like to dine later in Rome than, say, Milan, with 1pm, or 8pm the very earliest you'd dream of appearing for lunch or dinner. In the famous tourist hotspots, of course, owners are only too pleased to open that bit earlier.

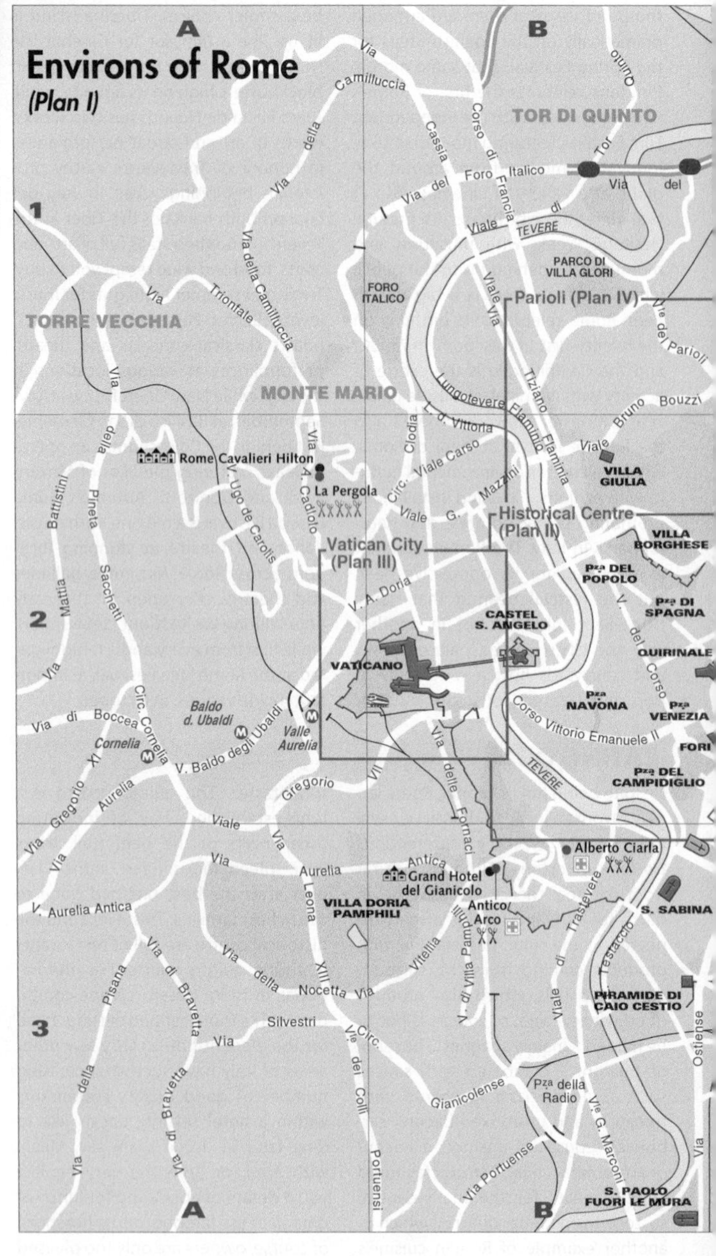
Environs of Rome
(Plan I)
A
B
1
2
3
TOR DI QUINTO
TORRE VECCHIA
MONTE MARIO
FORO ITALICO
PARCO DI VILLA GLORI
Parioli (Plan IV)
Historical Centre (Plan II)
Vatican City (Plan III)
VILLA GIULIA
VILLA BORGHESE
Pza DEL POPOLO
Pza DI SPAGNA
CASTEL S. ANGELO
QUIRINALE
VATICANO
Pza NAVONA
Pza VENEZIA
FORI
Pza DEL CAMPIDIGLIO
Rome Cavalieri Hilton
La Pergola
Baldo d. Ubaldi
Cornelia
Valle Aurelia
Alberto Ciarla
Grand Hotel del Gianicolo
Antico Arco
VILLA DORIA PAMPHILI
S. SABINA
PIRAMIDE DI CAIO CESTIO
Pza della Radio
S. PAOLO FUORI LE MURA
Via Camilluccia
Via della
Via della Camilluccia
Via Trionfale
Via Cassia
Corso di Francia
Via del Foro Italico
Viale di Tor di Quinto
Via del
Viale
TEVERE
Viale Via
Vle dei Parioli
Lungotevere Flaminio
L. d. Vittoria
Tiziano
Flaminia
Viale Bruno Bouzzi
Viale
Circ. Clodia
Viale Carso
Viale G. Mazzini
Via A. Cadlolo
V. Ugo de Carolis
Via della Pineta Sacchetti
Battistini
Mattia
V. A. Doria
V. del Corso
Corso Vittorio Emanuele II
Via di Boccea
Circ. Cornelia
V. Baldo degli Ubaldi
Via Gregorio XI
Aurelia
Viale Gregorio VII
Via delle Fornaci
Via Aurelia Antica
V. Aurelia Antica
Via Leona XIII
Via della Nocetta
Via Vitellia
V. di Villa Pamphili
Viale di Trastevere
Testaccio
Via di Bravetta
Via Pisana
Via Silvestri
Vle dei Colli Portuensi
Circ. Gianicolense
Vle G. Marconi
Via Portuense
Ostiense
Via

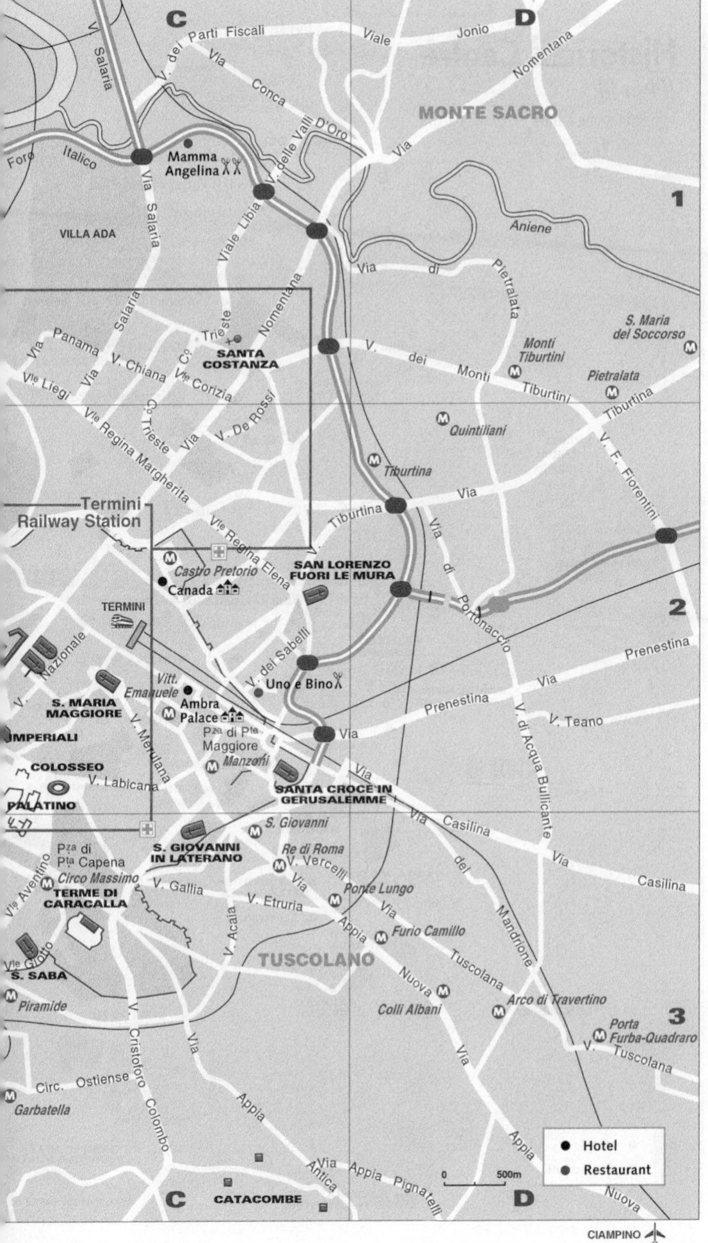
C
D
MONTE SACRO
Mamma Angelina
VILLA ADA
SANTA COSTANZA
Termini Railway Station
Castro Pretorio
Canada
SAN LORENZO FUORI LE MURA
TERMINI
Uno e Bino
Ambra Palace
S. MARIA MAGGIORE
IMPERIALI
COLOSSEO
PALATINO
SANTA CROCE IN GERUSALEMME
S. Giovanni
S. GIOVANNI IN LATERANO
Re di Roma
Circo Massimo
TERME DI CARACALLA
Ponte Lungo
Furio Camillo
TUSCOLANO
S. SABA
Piramide
Colli Albani
Arco di Travertino
Porta Furba-Quadraro
Garbatella
CATACOMBE
Tiburtina
Quintiliani
Monti Tiburtini
Pietralata
S. Maria del Soccorso
Manzoni
Aniene
1
2
3
Hotel
Restaurant
0 500m
CIAMPINO

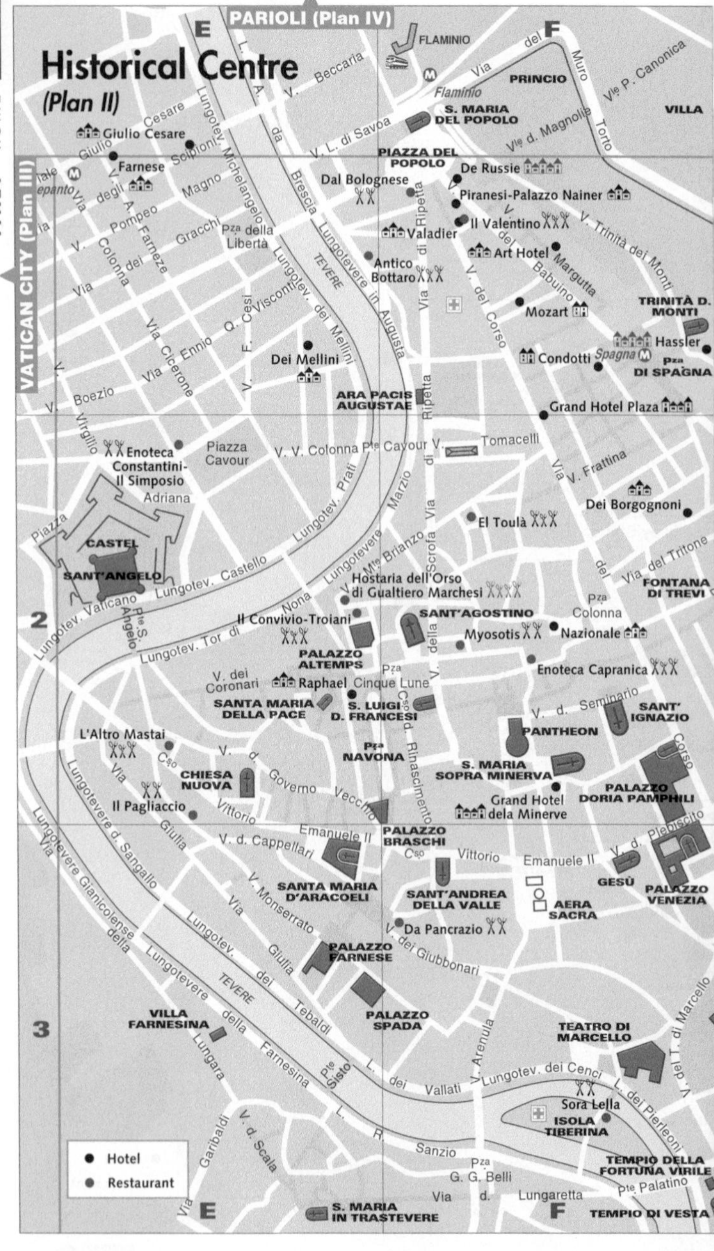

Historical Centre
(Plan II)
PARIOLI (Plan IV)
VATICAN CITY (Plan III)
E
F
2
3
FLAMINIO
Flaminio
PRINCIO
VILLA
S. MARIA DEL POPOLO
PIAZZA DEL POPOLO
Giulio Cesare
Farnese
De Russie
Dal Bolognese
Piranesi-Palazzo Nainer
Il Valentino
Valadier
Art Hotel
Antico Bottaro
Mozart
TRINITÀ D. MONTI
Hassler
Condotti
Spagna
Pza DI SPAGNA
Dei Mellini
ARA PACIS AUGUSTAE
Grand Hotel Plaza
Enoteca Constantini-Il Simposio
Piazza Cavour
Tomacelli
Dei Borgognoni
El Toulà
CASTEL SANT'ANGELO
Hostaria dell'Orso di Gualtiero Marchesi
FONTANA DI TREVI
Il Convivio-Troiani
SANT'AGOSTINO
Pza Colonna
Myosotis
Nazionale
PALAZZO ALTEMPS
Enoteca Capranica
Raphael
Pza Cinque Lune
SANTA MARIA DELLA PACE
S. LUIGI D. FRANCESI
SANT' IGNAZIO
PANTHEON
L'Altro Mastai
Pza NAVONA
S. MARIA SOPRA MINERVA
CHIESA NUOVA
PALAZZO DORIA PAMPHILI
Il Pagliaccio
Grand Hotel dela Minerve
PALAZZO BRASCHI
SANTA MARIA D'ARACOELI
SANT'ANDREA DELLA VALLE
GESÙ
PALAZZO VENEZIA
AERA SACRA
Da Pancrazio
PALAZZO FARNESE
PALAZZO SPADA
VILLA FARNESINA
TEATRO DI MARCELLO
Sora Lella
ISOLA TIBERINA
TEMPIO DELLA FORTUNA VIRILE
Pza G. G. Belli
Pte Palatino
S. MARIA IN TRASTEVERE
TEMPIO DI VESTA
TEVERE
Hotel
Restaurant

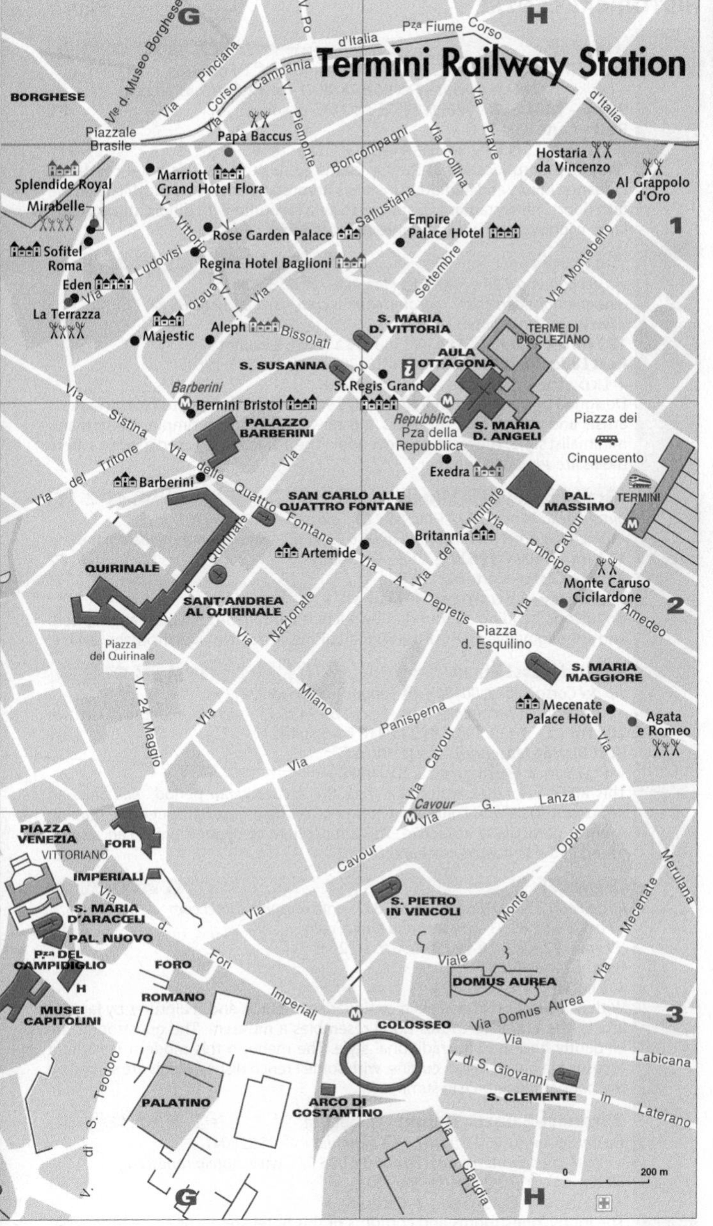
Termini Railway Station
G
H
1
2
3
BORGHESE
Piazzale Brasile
Papà Baccus
Splendide Royal
Mirabelle
Marriott Grand Hotel Flora
Rose Garden Palace
Sofitel Roma
Regina Hotel Baglioni
Eden
La Terrazza
Majestic
Aleph
Empire Palace Hotel
Hostaria da Vincenzo
Al Grappolo d'Oro
S. MARIA D. VITTORIA
TERME DI DIOCLEZIANO
AULA OTTAGONA
S. SUSANNA
St.Regis Grand
Barberini
Bernini Bristol
PALAZZO BARBERINI
Repubblica
Pza della Repubblica
S. MARIA D. ANGELI
Piazza dei Cinquecento
TERMINI
Exedra
PAL. MASSIMO
Barberini
SAN CARLO ALLE QUATTRO FONTANE
Britannia
Artemide
QUIRINALE
SANT'ANDREA AL QUIRINALE
Piazza del Quirinale
Monte Caruso Cicilardone
Piazza d. Esquilino
S. MARIA MAGGIORE
Mecenate Palace Hotel
Agata e Romeo
PIAZZA VENEZIA
VITTORIANO
FORI IMPERIALI
S. MARIA D'ARACŒLI
PAL. NUOVO
Pza DEL CAMPIDOGLIO
MUSEI CAPITOLINI
FORO ROMANO
S. PIETRO IN VINCOLI
DOMUS AUREA
COLOSSEO
ARCO DI COSTANTINO
PALATINO
S. CLEMENTE
V. Po
Pza Fiume
Corso d'Italia
Via Pinciana
Vle d. Museo Borghese
Via Campania
Corso d'Italia
V. Piemonte
Boncompagni
Via Collina
Via Piave
Sallustiana
Via Vittorio Veneto
Via Ludovisi
Via Bissolati
Settembre
Via Montebello
Via Sistina
Via del Tritone
Via delle Quattro Fontane
Via Quirinale
Via Nazionale
Via A. Depretis
Via del Viminale
Via Cavour
Via Principe Amedeo
V. 24 Maggio
Via Milano
Via Panisperna
Via Cavour
Via G. Lanza
Via d. Fori Imperiali
Viale Monte Oppio
Via Merulana
Via Mecenate
Via Domus Aurea
Via Labicana
V. di S. Giovanni in Laterano
Via Claudia
V. di S. Teodoro
0
200 m

HISTORICAL CENTRE

Plan II

Hassler

piazza Trinità dei Monti 6 ✉ 00187 – Ⓜ Spagna – ☎ 06 699340 – booking@hotelhassler.it – Fax 06 6 78 99 91 – www.hotelhassler.com

95 rm – 🛉484/517 € 🛉🛉605/935 €, ☕ 37 € – 8 suites **F1**

Rest – Carte 85/146 €

♦ Grand Luxury ♦ Business ♦ Classic ♦

With its superb location at the top of the Spanish Steps, this hotel combines elegance, luxury and tradition. Unusual interpretation of the classical style on the fifth floor. This restaurant continues to be a favourite with diners, thanks to its large windows and unforgettable views of Rome.

De Russie

via del Babuino 9 ✉ 00187 – Ⓜ Flaminio – ☎ 06 328881 – reservations.derussie@roccofortehotels.com – Fax 06 32 88 88 88 – www.roccofortehotels.com **F1**

122 rm – 🛉293/450 € 🛉🛉436/1380 €, ☕ 33 € – 26 suites

Rest *Le Jardin du Russie* – ☎ *06 32888870* – Carte 143/196 €

♦ Luxury ♦ Business ♦ Classic ♦

Designed by Valadier during the early 19C, this hotel has hosted many famous artists and writers over the years. It is now furnished in a simple, modern and minimalist style. The restaurant overlooks the attractive terraced garden, where meals are served in summer.

Grand Hotel de la Minerve

piazza della Minerva 69 ✉ 00186 – Ⓜ Colosseo – ☎ 06 695201 – minerva@hotel-invest.com – Fax 06 6 79 41 65 – www.grandhoteldelaminerve.it

134 rm – 🛉400 € 🛉🛉620 €, ☕ 31 € – 3 suites **F2**

Rest *La Cesta* – Carte 62/110 €

♦ Luxury ♦ Business ♦ Stylish ♦

An historic building surrounded by ancient monuments. Elegant atmosphere and an imaginative menu of traditional cuisine. Attractive views from the terrace.

Grand Hotel Plaza

via del Corso 126 ✉ 00186 – Ⓜ Spagna – ☎ 06 69921111 – plaza@grandhotelplaza.com – Fax 06 69 94 15 75 – www.grandhotelplaza.com

200 rm ☕ – 🛉230/290 € 🛉🛉275/410 € – 5 suites **F1**

Rest *Bistrot-Mascagni* – Carte 40/66 €

♦ Palace ♦ Business ♦ Stylish ♦

This attractive hotel, restored during the Art Nouveau period, was once an important social and cultural meeting-place. The ornate Baroque-style reading room is particularly attractive. The atmosphere of bygone times can also be found in the evocative restaurant

Raphaël

largo Febo 2 ✉ 00186 – ☎ 06 682831 – info@raphaelhotel.com – Fax 06 6 87 89 93 – www.raphaelhotel.com **E2**

55 rm – 🛉230/550 € 🛉🛉250/600 €, ☕ 26 €

Rest – Carte 49/83 €

♦ Luxury ♦ Classic ♦

With its collection of porcelain, antiquarian artefacts and sculptures by famous artists, the entrance to this hotel resembles a museum. The guestrooms are elegantly furnished in traditional style. The menu in this modern restaurant focuses mainly on Italian cuisine, with some French dishes. Meals are served on the panoramic terrace in summer.

Piranesi-Palazzo Nainer without rest

via del Babuino 196 ✉ 00187 – Ⓜ Flaminio – ☎ 06 328041 – info@hotelpiranesi.com – Fax 06 3 61 05 97 – www.hotelpiranesi.com

32 rm ☕ – 🛉170/240 € 🛉🛉198/320 € **F1**

♦ Palace ♦ Business ♦ Classic ♦

The lobby, guestrooms and corridors of this hotel are decorated with marble, elegant furnishings and an unusual exhibition of old fabrics. The hotel also boasts a roof garden and sun terrace.

Valadier

via della Fontanella 15 ✉ 00187 – Ⓜ Flaminio – ☏ 06 3611998 – info@hotelvaladier.com – Fax 06 3 20 15 58 – www.hotelvaladier.com **F1**

64 rm – †180/400 € ††220/500 € – 6 suites

Rest Il Valentino – see below

♦ Traditional ♦ Modern ♦

Elegant hotel close to Piazza del Popolo with a dark and stylish interior décor. The guestrooms have period touches such as tapestries and coffered ceilings. Panoramic roof-garden.

Art Hotel

via Margutta 56 ✉ 00187 – Ⓜ Spagna – ☏ 06 328711 – info@hotelart.it – Fax 06 36 00 39 95 – www.hotelart.it **F1**

46 rm – †250/398 € ††385/590 € – 2 suites

Rest – *(residents only)* Carte 51/66 €

♦ Luxury ♦ Art Deco ♦

Situated along a road lined with antique shops, this hotel has a contemporary décor, which uses light, colour and shape to create contrasts between old and new. Lights on the floor lead to the rooms. A simple menu is served in the original dining room.

Dei Borgognoni without rest

via del Bufalo 126 ✉ 00187 – Ⓜ Spagna – ☏ 06 69941505 – info@hotelborgognoni.it – Fax 06 69 94 15 01 – www.hotelborgognoni.it **F2**

51 rm – †195/250 € ††230/330 €

♦ Traditional ♦ Business ♦ Modern ♦

Occupying a 19C palazzo, this smart hotel has an elegant atmosphere, spacious, modern public rooms and comfortable, traditional-style bedrooms. Attractive winter garden.

Nazionale

piazza Montecitorio 131 ✉ 00186 – Ⓜ Barberini – ☏ 06 695001 – hotel@nazionaleroma.it – Fax 06 6 78 66 77 – www.nazionaleroma.it

95 rm – †280/340 € ††340/530 €, 12 € – 1 suite **F2**

Rest *31 Al Vicario* – *☏ 06 69925530 (closed August and Sunday)* Carte 30/58 €

♦ Traditional ♦ Business ♦ Classic ♦

Situated on Piazza di Montecitorio, this hotel occupies an 18C building which was once a private residence. Elegant, classical interior décor. Guests will enjoy traditional Italian cuisine in this elegant, comfortable restaurant.

Barberini without rest

via Rasella 3 ✉ 00187 – Ⓜ Barberini – ☏ 06 4814993 – info@hotelbarberini.com – Fax 06 4 81 52 11 – www.hotelbarberini.com **G2**

35 rm – †184/244 € ††238/328 €, 30 €

♦ Traditional ♦ Classic ♦

Near the Palazzo of the same name, this elegant hotel is decorated with fine marble, stylish fabrics and wood fittings. The roof-garden is perfect for a breakfast with a view or an atmospheric evening aperitif.

Grand Hotel del Gianicolo without rest

viale Mura Gianicolensi 107 ✉ 00152 – Ⓜ Cipro Musei Vaticani – ☏ 06 58333405 – info@grandhotelgianicolo.it – Fax 06 58 17 94 34 – www.grandhotelgianicolo.it *Plan I* **B3**

48 rm – †160/320 € ††200/360 €

♦ Traditional ♦ Classic ♦

Located in an elegant villa with a well-maintained garden and swimming pool, this hotel has comfortable, spacious rooms and refined public spaces.

Mozart without rest

via dei Greci 23/b ✉ 00187 – Ⓜ Spagna – ☏ 06 36001915 – info@hotelmozart.com – Fax 06 36 00 17 35 – www.hotelmozart.com **F1**

66 rm – †130/185 € ††186/265 €

♦ Traditional ♦ Classic ♦

Housed in a 19C palazzo, this restored hotel has simple rooms with elegant furnishings. More modern rooms are available in a nearby annex. Pleasant roof garden.

Condotti without rest

via Mario dè Fiori 37 ✉ 00187 – Ⓜ Spagna – ✆ 06 6794661 – info@hotelcondotti.com – Fax 06 6 79 04 57 **F1**

26 rm – 🚹139/209 € 🚹🚹179/289 €

◆ Traditional ◆ Classic ◆

The lobby of this hotel is decorated in marble and adorned with elegant chandeliers. Small guestrooms furnished in traditional style; some are in a separate building nearby. Quiet breakfast room in the basement.

Hostaria dell'Orso di Gualtiero Marchesi

via dei Soldati 25/c ✉ 00186 – Ⓜ Spagna – ✆ 06 68301192 – info@hdo.it – Fax 06 68 21 70 63 – www.hdo.it

closed 10-25 August and Sunday **E-F2**

Rest – *(booking advisable) (dinner only)* Menu 75/145 € – Carte 70/110 €

◆ Modern ◆ Fashionable ◆

Housed in an historic building, this restaurant has intimate, romantic dining rooms decorated in a simple, elegant style. The elegant cuisine is based around the highest quality ingredients.

L'Altro Mastai (Fabio Baldassare)

via Giraud 53 ang. via dei Banchi Nuovi ✉ 00186 – Ⓜ Spagna – ✆ 06 68301296 – restaurant@laltromastai.it – Fax 06 6 86 13 03 – www.laltromastai.it

closed August, 1 week in January, Sunday and Monday **E2**

Rest – *(dinner only)* Menu 100 € – Carte 74/100 €

Spec. Ostriche in gelatina di sedano con mele candite e scaglie di gorgonzola. Ravioli di testina di maiale con salsa al mascarpone di bufala e caviale. Piccione cotto nella cenere di quercia al mosto di vino rosso.

◆ Mediterranean ◆ Fashionable ◆

This restaurant, opened towards the end of 2003, will come as a pleasant surprise to many and is destined to leave its mark on Rome's culinary history. The décor is discreet and the service courteous and efficient. Fine wine cellar.

Il Convivio-Troiani

vicolo dei Soldati 31 ✉ 00186 – Ⓜ Spagna – ✆ 06 6869432 – info@ilconviviotroiani.com – Fax 06 6 86 94 32 – www.ilconviviotroiani.com

closed 13 to 17 August and Sunday **E2**

Rest – *(dinner only)* Menu 98 € – Carte 90/117 €

◆ Inventive ◆ Fashionable ◆

Hidden in the alleyways of the historical centre, this restaurant serves modern innovative cuisine, with an emphasis on meat and fish dishes. Simple, elegant décor in the three dining rooms.

El Toulà

via della Lupa 29/b ✉ 00186 – Ⓜ Spagna – ✆ 06 6873498 – toula2@libero.it – Fax 06 6 87 11 15 – www.toula.it

closed August, 24 to 26 December, Saturday lunch, Sunday and Monday **F2**

Rest – Menu 40/70 € – Carte 62/84 €

◆ Modern ◆ Formal ◆

This quiet, elegant restaurant comprises a series of small dining rooms furnished with comfortable chairs and separated by arches. The restaurant specialises in Italian and Venetian cuisine.

Antico Bottaro

Passeggiata di Ripetta 15 ✉ 00186 – Ⓜ Flaminio – ✆ 06 3236763 – anticobottaro@anticobottaro.it – Fax 06 3 23 67 63 – www.anticobottaro.it

closed 4 to 31 August and Wednesday **E-F1**

Rest – *(dinner only)* Carte 63/78 €

◆ Classic ◆ Fashionable ◆

This smart private residence is adorned with fine stucco and elegant fabrics. The restaurant here serves innovative cuisine with a French flavour, using the best ingredients.

XXX

Enoteca Capranica

piazza Capranica 99/100 ✉ 00186 – Ⓜ Spagna – ✆ 06 69940992 – Fax 06 69 94 09 89 – www.enotecacapranica.it
closed Saturday lunch and Sunday **F2**
Rest – *(dinner only in August)* Menu 65/75 € – Carte 52/82 €
♦ Mediterranean ♦ Fashionable ♦
This wine bar near Montecitorio has been transformed into an elegant restaurant serving Mediterranean cuisine. Colourful vaulted ceiling and a small exhibition of wine bottles on display.

XXX

Il Valentino – Hotel Valadier

via della Fontanella 14 ✉ 00187 – Ⓜ Flaminio – ✆ 06 3610880 – Fax 06 3 20 15 58 – www.ilvalentino.com **F1**
Rest – Carte 50/75 €
♦ Mediterranean ♦ Cosy ♦
Light wood panelling and warm colours decorate this elegant restaurant, which serves traditional Italian dishes, often with an innovative twist. Meals may be enjoyed on the roof garden in summer.

XXX

Alberto Ciarla

piazza San Cosimato 40 ✉ 00153 – ✆ 06 5816068 – alberto@albertociarla.com – Fax 06 58 33 01 62 – www.albertociarla.com
closed 1 week in August, 1 week in January and Sunday *Plan I* **B3**
Rest – *(dinner only)* Carte 52/76 €
♦ Fish ♦ Friendly ♦
A friendly, convivial atmosphere in this distinctive restaurant which has retained a 1970s ambience. Specialities include fish (fresh fish is on display near the door) and traditional Roman cuisine.

XX ✿

Il Pagliaccio (Anthony Genovese)

via dei Banchi Vecchi 129 ✉ 00186 – ✆ 06 68809595 – info@ristoranteilpagliaccio.it – Fax 06 68 21 75 04 – www.ristoranteilpagliaccio.it
closed 6 to 25 August, 9 to 17 January, Sunday, Monday and Tuesday lunch
Rest – Menu 65/85 € – Carte 62/85 € **E2**
Spec. Zuppa di piselli al te verde, uovo scottato, baccalà croccante. Ravioli di mare al vapore, brodo di crostacei. Triangolo di cioccolato caldo, carpaccio di mango, sorbetto di mango e pepe nero.
♦ Inventive ♦ Formal ♦
The young, enthusiastic team at this restaurant offers a varied menu, including Mediterranean, Eastern and traditional French dishes.

XX

Dal Bolognese

piazza del Popolo 1/2 ✉ 00187 – Ⓜ Flaminio – ✆ 06 3611426 – dalbolognese@virgilio.it – Fax 06 3 22 27 99
closed August, Christmas, New Year and Monday **F1**
Rest – Menu 60 € (+ 13 %)
♦ Classic ♦ Formal ♦
One of Rome's historic, traditional restaurants, Dal Bolognese serves specialities from the Emilia-Romagna region. Terrace overlooking the Piazza del Popolo for outdoor dining in summer.

XX

Da Pancrazio

piazza del Biscione 92 ✉ 00186 – Ⓜ Flaminio – ✆ 06 6861246 – dapancrazio@tin.it – Fax 06 97 84 02 35 – www.dapancrazio.com
closed 5 to 25 August, Christmas and Wednesday **F3**
Rest – Menu 30/35 € – Carte 33/48 €
♦ Classic ♦ Formal ♦
Da Pancrazio offers two different styles and two thousand years of history: one of its dining rooms is decorated in the style of a typical 19C tavern; the other is built over a section of the ruins of Pompey's Theatre.

XX **Sora Lella**

via di Ponte Quattro Capi 16 (Tiber Island) ✉ 00186 – Ⓜ Circo Massimo – ✆ 06 6861601 – soralella@soralella.com – Fax 06 6 86 16 01 – www.soralella.com
closed 15 to 20 August and Sunday **F3**
Rest – Menu 26/80 € – Carte 47/78 €
♦ Roman ♦ Family ♦
Son and grandchildren of the famous late ""Sora Lella"", perpetuate in a dignified way the tradition both in the warmth of the welcome and in the typical Roman elements of the offer.

XX **Myosotis**

piazza delle Coppelle 49 ✉ 00186 – Ⓜ Spagna – ✆ 06 6865554 – g.marsili@libero.it – Fax 06 6 86 55 54 – www.myosotis.it
closed 10 to 24 August, 2 to 9 January and Sunday **F2**
Rest – Menu 25/35 € – Carte 28/64 €
♦ Classic ♦ Formal ♦
Situated in a delightful pedestrianised square, this well-established family-run restaurant specialises in traditional Italian cuisine. Pleasant, bright dining room.

XX **Antico Arco**

piazzale Aurelio 7 ✉ 00152 – ✆ 06 5815274 – info@anticoarco.it – Fax 06 5 81 52 74 – www.anticoarco.it
closed 11 to 17 August and Sunday *Plan I* **B3**
Rest – *(dinner only)* Carte 52/67 €
♦ Inventive ♦
Situated in a fashionable and popular location, this restaurant has been refurbished in minimalist style. The wine-bar is near the entrance and the restaurant occupies two floors. Attentive service.

TERMINI RAILWAY STATION *Plan II*

St. Regis Grand

via Vittorio Emanuele Orlando 3 ✉ 00185 – Ⓜ Repubblica – ✆ 06 47091 – stregisgrandrome@stregis.com – Fax 06 47 09 28 31 – www.stregis.com/grandrome **H1**
153 rm – ††800/1030 €, ☕ 49 € – 8 suites
Rest *Vivendo* – *✆ 06 47092736 (closed Saturday lunch and Sunday)*
Menu 85/130 € bi – Carte 50/88 €
♦ Chain hotel ♦ Luxury ♦ Historic ♦
Frescoes, valuable furnishings and Empire-style antiques in the luxurious bedrooms and the magnificent lounges of a hotel restored to its original antique splendours (1894). The restaurant has a modern, eclectic décor.

Eden

via Ludovisi 49 ✉ 00187 – Ⓜ Barberini – ✆ 06 478121 – 1872.resevations@lemeridien.com – Fax 06 4 82 15 84 – www.lemeridien.com/eden **G1**
108 rm – †528/880 € ††880/1320 €, ☕ 54 € – 13 suites
Rest La Terrazza – see below
♦ Palace ♦ Luxury ♦ Stylish ♦
This large, top-end hotel has a formal atmosphere but the service is warm and friendly. Some of the rooms on the upper floors have what is perhaps the best view of Rome.

Exedra

piazza della Repubblica 47 ✉ 00185 – Ⓜ Repubblica – ✆ 06 48938020 – reservation@exedra.boscolo.com – Fax 06 48 93 80 00 – www.boscolo.com
238 rm – ††600 €, ☕ 30 € – 5 suites **H2**
Rest *Tazio* – ✆ 06 48938061 – Carte 76/104 €
♦ Luxury ♦ Chain hotel ♦ Classic ♦
This luxury hotel boasts spacious public lounges, comfortable guestrooms and state-of-the-art technology. The décor is tasteful and elegant, featuring a profusion of marble and inlaid wood. The Tazio restaurant serves a simple menu at lunchtime and more elaborate dishes in the evening.

Sofitel Roma

via Lombardia 47 ✉ 00187 – Ⓜ Barberini – ☎ 06 478021 – prenotazioni.sofitelroma@accor-hotels.it – Fax 06 4 82 10 19 – www.sofitel.com G1

113 rm – ♦400 € ♦♦540 €

Rest – Carte 50/67 €

♦ Luxury ♦ Business ♦ Historic ♦

The neo-Classical style of the Imperial Roman period dominates in this hotel, with statues and sculptures dotted around the historic palazzo. Choose between the terrace bar with its views of Rome, and the cosy, British atmosphere in the bar. An elegant restaurant with vaulted ceilings, housed in the former stables of the palazzo.

Majestic without rest

via Vittorio Veneto 50 ✉ 00187 – Ⓜ Barberini – ☎ 06 421441 – info@hotelmajestic.com – Fax 06 4 88 09 84 – www.hotelmajestic.com G1

98 rm – ♦465/510 € ♦♦570/675 €, ☕ 40 €

♦ Luxury ♦ Traditional ♦ Classic ♦

Although space is limited in the hotel lobby, this is compensated for by the elegant lounge areas adorned with late-19C frescoes on the first floor. Splendid lift and charming guestrooms.

Regina Hotel Baglioni

via Vittorio Veneto 72 ✉ 00187 – Ⓜ Barberini – ☎ 06 421111 – regina.roma@baglionihotels.com – Fax 06 42 01 21 30 – www.baglionihotels.com G1

112 rm – ♦253/330 € ♦♦451/517 €, ☕ 24 € – 8 suites

Rest – Carte 60/102 €

♦ Luxury ♦ Traditional ♦ Art Deco ♦

This building restructured in Art Nouveau style is home to an historic hotel with Art Deco interiors and excellent facilities. The attractive guestrooms are striking for their marble décor. Restaurant with warm, refined atmosphere; international cuisine.

Splendide Royal

via di Porta Pinciana 14 ✉ 00187 – Ⓜ Barberini – ☎ 06 421689 – reservations@splendideroyal.com – Fax 06 42 16 88 00 – www.splendideroyal.com G1

69 rm ☕ – ♦270/480 € ♦♦310/800 €

Rest Mirabelle – see below

♦ Luxury ♦ Traditional ♦ Stylish ♦

Gilded stucco, damask fabrics and sumptuous antique furnishings contribute to the Roman Baroque style of this hotel, which is in sharp contrast to the contemporary trend for minimalist design.

Aleph

via San Basilio 15 ✉ 00187 – Ⓜ Barberini – ☎ 06 422901 – reception@aleph.boscolo.com – Fax 06 42 29 00 00 – www.boscolohotels.com G1

96 rm – ♦250/350 € ♦♦350/450 €, ☕ 22 €

Rest *Maremoto* – Carte 120/195 €

♦ Luxury ♦ Design ♦

One of a group of "designer hotels". The lobby design and color scheme are incomparable, the room designs innovative. This prestigious hotel also has a fitness center. A modern restaurant with minimalist décor.

Bernini Bristol

piazza Barberini 23 ✉ 00187 – Ⓜ Barberini – ☎ 06 488931 – reservationsbb@sinahotels.it – Fax 06 4 82 42 66 – www.berninibristol.com G2

127 rm – ♦290/415 € ♦♦460/525 €, ☕ 28 € – 10 suites

Rest *L'Olimpo* – *☎ 06 488933288* – Carte 86/122 €

♦ Traditional ♦ Business ♦ Classic ♦

This stylish hotel has rooms with classic or contemporary furnishings. The rooms with a view on the upper floors are the best choice. Roof-garden restaurant, with outdoor dining in the summer and a marvellous view of the Eternal City.

Marriott Grand Hotel Flora

rest rm

via Vittorio Veneto 191 ✉ 00187 – Ⓜ Spagna – ✆ 06 489929 – info@grandhotelflora.net – Fax 06 4 82 03 59 – www.hotelfloraroma.com **G1**

156 rm – †322/478 € ††478 €, ☕ 30 € – 8 suites

Rest – Carte 42/82 €

♦ Luxury ♦ Business ♦ Classic ♦

After its total renovation, the hotel, at the end of Via Veneto, looks like a harmonious and functional building of simple and functional classical elegance, finished in a modern style. Warm parquet flooring and wood furnishings grace the elegant dining room of this restaurant. Neapolitan cuisine.

Empire Palace Hotel

rm VISA AE

via Aureliana 39 ✉ 00187 – Ⓜ Repubblica – ✆ 06 421281 – gold@empirepalacehotel.com – Fax 06 42 12 84 00 – www.empirepalacehotel.com

105 rm ☕ – †382/510 € ††405/586 € – 5 suites **H1**

Rest *Aureliano* – *(closed Sunday)* Carte 46/70 €

♦ Palace ♦ Business ♦ Design ♦

Sophisticated combination of elements of the 19C building and contemporary design, with a collection of modern art in the public areas; simple, classic bedrooms. The dining room features cherry wood décor and pink and blue table lamps.

Rose Garden Palace

rm VISA AE

via Boncompagni 19 ✉ 00187 – Ⓜ Barberini – ✆ 06 421741 – info@rosegardenpalace.com – Fax 06 4 81 56 08 **G1**

65 rm ☕ – †247 € ††440 €

Rest – *(closed Sunday) (residents only)* Carte 32/59 €

♦ Business ♦ Design ♦

A modern, minimalist design in muted colours is the inspiration behind the furnishing of this hotel housed in an early-20C palazzo.

Mecenate Palace Hotel without rest

VISA AE

via Carlo Alberto 3 ✉ 00185 – Ⓜ Vittorio Emanuele – ✆ 06 44702024 – info@mecenatepalace.com – Fax 06 4 46 13 54 – www.mecenatepalace.com

72 rm ☕ – †120/330 € ††200/390 € **H2**

♦ Business ♦ Classic ♦

The warm and elegant period-style interiors are in perfect keeping with the spirit of the 19C building which houses this new hotel. Fine views of Santa Maria Maggiore from the upper floors.

Artemide without rest

VISA AE

via Nazionale 22 ✉ 00184 – Ⓜ Repubblica – ✆ 06 489911 – info@hotelartemide.it – Fax 06 48 99 17 00 – www.hotelartemide.it

85 rm ☕ – †110/270 € ††150/370 € **G-H2**

♦ Traditional ♦ Business ♦ Classic ♦

In a precious restored Art Nouveau building, a classically elegant hotel which satsifies all the requirements of modern hospitality; very well organised conference areas.

Canada without rest

VISA AE

via Vicenza 58 ✉ 00185 – Ⓜ Castro Pretorio – ✆ 06 4457770 – info@hotelcanadaroma.com – Fax 06 4 45 07 49 – www.hotelcanadaroma.com

73 rm ☕ – †100/190 € ††132/225 € *Plan I* **C2**

♦ Business ♦ Classic ♦

In period style building near the Termini railway station, a simple but elegant hotel, with period style furnishings; luxurious rooms: some with four poster beds available on request.

Ambra Palace without rest

VISA AE

via Principe Amedeo 257 ✉ 00185 – Ⓜ Vittorio Emanuele – ✆ 06 492330 – info@ambrapalacehotel.com – Fax 06 49 23 31 00 – www.ambrapalace.com

78 rm ☕ – †109/230 € ††129/430 € *Plan I* **C2**

♦ Business ♦ Classic ♦

The building is mid-19C, the hotel is set up prevalently to meet the needs of the business visitor.

Britannia without rest

via Napoli 64 ✉ 00184 – Ⓜ Repubblica – ✆ 06 4883153 – info@hotelbritannia.it – Fax 06 48 98 63 16 – www.hotelbritannia.it **H2**

33 rm ☕ – 🛉130/200 € 🛉🛉160/280 €

◆ Traditional ◆ Business ◆ Personalised ◆

This small hotel has reasonable facilities, comfortable guestrooms and an English-style bar. Marble décor, neo-Classical reproductions and attention to detail.

La Terrazza – Hotel Eden

via Ludovisi 49 ✉ 00187 – Ⓜ Barberini – ✆ 06 47812752 – daniele.colombo@lemeridien.com – Fax 06 4 81 44 73 – www.hotel-eden.it **G1**

Rest – Carte 96/128 €

◆ Contemporary ◆ Fashionable ◆

A lift takes guests to the top floor of this building, where the dining room enjoys stunning views of the historic centre of the city. Panoramic windows allow guests to enjoy the views to the full. A unique setting for a memorable evening.

Mirabelle – Hotel Splendide Royal

via di Porta Pinciana 14 ✉ 00187 – Ⓜ Barberini – ✆ 06 42168838 – mirabelle@splendideroyal.com – Fax 06 42 16 88 70 – www.splendideroyal.com

Closed 7 to 20 January **G1**

Rest – Carte 82/120 €

Spec. Terrina di fegato grasso tartufato con gelatina al Sauternes. Tortelli di ricotta e taleggio cremolati alla purea di tartufo bianco. Settimo cielo: cioccolato con cuore di nocciola e pepite d'oro.

◆ Mediterranean ◆ Fashionable ◆

With one of the most spectacular roof gardens in Rome and views of the Vatican Gardens, this restaurant serves an interesting blend of regional and international cuisine.

Agata e Romeo (Agata Parisella)

via Carlo Alberto 45 ✉ 00185 – Ⓜ Vittorio Emanuele – ✆ 06 4466115 – ristorante@agataeromeo.it – Fax 06 4 46 58 42 – www.agataeromeo.it

closed 6 to 28 August, 1 to 27 January, Saturday and Sunday **H2**

Rest – Menu 110/160 € – Carte 90/125 €

Spec. Cappesante avvolte in pancetta croccante e salsa di porri. Cannelloncini farciti con prosciutto e salsa di cipollotto. Baccalà islandese cucinato in quattro modi.

◆ Roman ◆ Formal ◆

Despite its location in a district which is becoming more and more multicultural, this restaurant continues to specialise in inventive Roman and Italian cuisine.

Al Grappolo d'Oro

via Palestro 4/10 ✉ 00185 – Ⓜ Repubblica – ✆ 06 4941441 – info@algrappolodoro.it – Fax 06 4 45 23 50 – www.algrappolodoro.it

closed August, Saturday lunch and Sunday **H1**

Rest – Carte 32/48 €

◆ Fish ◆ Formal ◆

Not far from the Terme di Diocleziano, a classic restaurant, where recent work has improved and refined the building, and where there is a large menu of traditional dishes on offer.

Monte Caruso Cicilardone

via Farini 12 ✉ 00185 – Ⓜ Termini – ✆ 06 483549 – cicilardone@tiscali.it – www.montecaruso.com

closed August, Sunday and Monday lunch **H2**

Rest – Menu 35/50 € – Carte 30/36 €

◆ Roman ◆ Family ◆

The flavours of the South in a warm and welcoming family-run establishment, with a menu based on Lucanian specialities, achieved in a simple and genuine manner.

Papà Baccus
via Toscana 32/36 ✉ 00187 – Ⓜ Barberini – ✆ 06 42742808
– papabaccus@papabaccus.com – Fax 06 42 01 00 05
– www.papabaccus.com
closed 15 days in August, Saturday lunch and Sunday **G1**
Rest – Carte 46/66 €
◆ Regional ◆ Formal ◆
This typical restaurant in the Via Veneto district is understandably popular given its delicious seafood cuisine and Tuscan specialities, which include Chianina beef and Cinta Senese pork.

Hostaria da Vincenzo
via Castelfidardo 6 ✉ 00185 – Ⓜ Termini – ✆ 06 484596 – Fax 06 4 87 00 92
closed August and Sunday **H1**
Rest – Carte 22/41 €
◆ Fish ◆ Friendly ◆
With its traditional, friendly atmosphere and typical regional and Italian dishes, this restaurant has a loyal following and is particularly popular with business clientele.

Uno e Bino
via degli Equi 58 ✉ 00185 – Ⓜ Termini – ✆ 06 4460702
closed August and Monday *Plan I* **C2**
Rest – *(dinner only)* Carte 39/63 €
◆ Inventive ◆ Bistro ◆
The fact that it is good value for money is the trump card of this quiet and attractive restaurant. The bistro-style décor creates a cordial and informal atmosphere.

ST-PETER'S BASILICA *Plan II*

Rome Cavalieri Hilton < town, rm
via Cadlolo 101 ✉ 00136
– ✆ 06 35091 – sales.rome@hilton.com – Fax 06 35 09 22 41
– www.cavalieri-hilton.it *Plan I* **A2**
370 rm – 🚹835 € 🚹🚹860 €, ☕ 38 € – 25 suites
Rest La Pergola – see below
Rest *Il Giardino dell'Uliveto* – Carte 78/117 €
◆ Luxury ◆ Business ◆ Classic ◆
This imposing building overlooks the entire city of Rome. The hotel has excellent facilities, including extensive gardens, an outdoor swimming pool, plus a fine art collection. Restaurant with an informal atmosphere by the edge of the swimming pool for dining with live music.

Giulio Cesare without rest
via degli Scipioni 287 ✉ 00192 – Ⓜ Lepanto – ✆ 06 3210751 – giulioce@uni.net
– Fax 06 3 21 17 36 – www.hotelgiuliocesare.com **E1**
78 rm ☕ – 🚹160/265 € 🚹🚹230/350 €
◆ Luxury ◆ Stylish ◆
The elegant, aristocratic feel of the early 20C is still much in evidence in this fine Patrician villa. The welcoming interior is adorned with period carpets, a fireplace in the lobby and tasteful furniture in different styles in the hotel's public areas.

Farnese without rest
via Alessandro Farnese 30 ✉ 00192 – Ⓜ Lepanto – ✆ 06 3212553
– info@hotelfarnese.com – Fax 06 3 21 51 29
– www.hotelfarnese.com **E1**
23 rm ☕ – 🚹170/250 € 🚹🚹200/350 €
◆ Luxury ◆ Business ◆ Stylish ◆
Decorated in period style, this hotel has elegant rooms and an attractive lobby housing a 17C polychrome marble altar frontal. Fine views of St Peter's from the terrace.

Dei Mellini without rest

via Muzio Clementi 81 ✉ 00193 – Ⓜ Lepanto – ✆ 06 324771 – info@hotelmellini.com – Fax 06 32 47 78 01 – www.hotelmellini.com **E1**

67 rm – ♦255/275 € ♦♦275/385 € – 11 suites

♦ Luxury ♦ Classic ♦

This hotel is on the right bank of the Tiber; the environment is soberly elegant, comfort is of the highest level and the rooms are large, modern and well equipped. There is a solarium-terrace.

Dei Consoli without rest

via Varrone 2/d ✉ 00193 – Ⓜ Ottaviano-San Pietro – ✆ 06 68892972 – info@hoteldeiconsoli.com – Fax 06 68 21 22 74 – www.hoteldeiconsoli.com *Plan III* **K1**

28 rm – ♦150/220 € ♦♦320 €

♦ Traditional ♦ Stylish ♦

Housed in an old palazzo, this hotel caters for a discerning clientele, with its rich décor, careful attention to detail and elegant rooms furnished in Empire style.

Hotel Alimandi Vaticano without rest

viale Vaticano 99 ✉ 00165 – Ⓜ Ottaviano-San Pietro – ✆ 06 39745562 – hotelali@hotelalimandie.191.it – Fax 06 39 73 01 32 – www.alimandi.it *Plan III* **J1**

25 rm – ♦140/170 € ♦♦170/200 €

♦ Family ♦ Classic ♦

This pleasant hotel enjoys an excellent location directly opposite the Vatican Museums. The marble and wood décor in the well-appointed guestrooms adds to their elegant atmosphere.

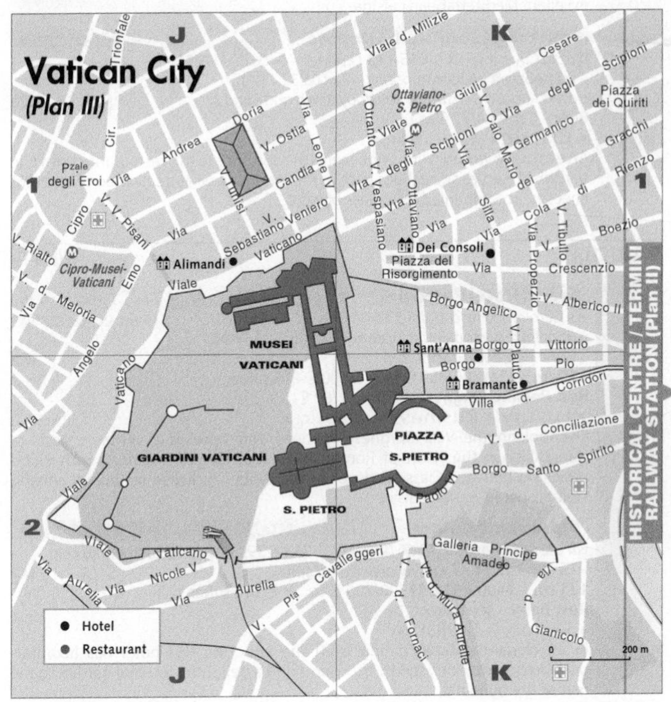

Sant'Anna without rest

borgo Pio 133 ✉ 00193 – Ⓜ Ottaviano-San Pietro – ✆ 06 68801602 – santanna@travel.it – Fax 06 68 30 87 17 – www.hotelsantanna.com

20 rm – †100/160 € ††150/230 € *Plan III* **K1-2**

♦ Traditional ♦ Personalised ♦

An original coffered ceiling and pleasant interior courtyard add a decorative touch to this small, welcoming hotel occupying a 16C building a short distance from St Peter's.

Bramante without rest

vicolo delle Palline 24 ✉ 00193 – Ⓜ Ottaviano-San Pietro – ✆ 06 68806426 – hotelbramante@libero.it – Fax 06 68 13 33 39 – www.hotelbramante.com *Plan III* **K2**

16 rm – †100/160 € ††150/220 €

♦ Traditional ♦ Family ♦ Classic ♦

This small, comfortable hotel situated a stone's throw from St Peter's is ideal for visitors wishing to stay in the heart of the Vatican district.

La Pergola (Heinz Beck) – Hotel Rome Cavalieri Hilton town,

via Cadlolo 101 ✉ 00136 – ✆ 06 35092152 – lapergola.rome@hilton.com – Fax 06 35 09 21 65 – www.cavalieri-hilton.it

closed 10 to 25 August, 1 to 28 January, Sunday and Monday *Plan I* **A2**

Rest – *(booking essential) (dinner only)* Menu 170/195 € – Carte 118/173 €

Spec. Carpaccio di capesante su amaranto al mais nero con olio allo zenzero. Maccheroncini integrali al ferretto con gamberi rossi coulis di melanzana affumicata e croccante di pane. Guanciale di manzo brasato con tartufo nero e purea di mele.

♦ Inventive ♦ Formal ♦

Enjoy an unforgettable view of Rome and its surrounding hills from the roof-garden of this restaurant. Quiet, elegant atmosphere, impeccable service, and excellent Mediterranean cuisine.

Enoteca Costantini-Il Simposio

piazza Cavour 16 ✉ 00193 – Ⓜ Lepanto – ✆ 06 32111131 – ilsimposio@pierocostantini.it – Fax 06 32 11 11 31

closed August, Christmas, Saturday lunch and Sunday **E2**

Rest – Carte 44/72 €

♦ Classic ♦ Wine bar ♦

An evocative wrought-iron vine marks the entrance to this restaurant-cum-wine bar, which serves specialities such as foie gras, as well as a selection of different cheeses, accompanied by a glass of wine.

PARIOLI *Plan IV*

Grand Hotel Parco dei Principi (heated) rm

via Gerolamo Frescobaldi 5 ✉ 00198 – ✆ 06 854421 – principi@parcodeiprincipi.com – Fax 06 8 84 51 04 – www.parcodeiprincipi.com **M2**

180 rm – †400/450 € ††540/600 € – 15 suites

Rest ***Pauline Borghese*** – Carte 62/82 €

♦ Luxury ♦ Business ♦ Classic ♦

Overlooking the Villa Borghese gardens, this hotel is a veritable oasis of tranquillity in the heart of Rome. Warm and elegant interiors, with wood panelling and neo-Classical décor in the lobby. Exclusive restaurant serving well-prepared, varied cuisine.

Aldrovandi Palace

via Ulisse Aldrovandi 15 ✉ 00197 – ✆ 06 3223993 – hotel@aldrovandi.com – Fax 06 3 22 14 35 – www.aldrovandi.com **M2**

121 rm – †400/450 € ††500/700 €, 33 € – 16 suites

Rest Baby – see below

♦ Luxury ♦ Stylish ♦

In an elegant palazzo dating from the late 19C, this hotel has luxurious period-style interiors, stylish bedrooms and a delightful internal garden to the rear of the building.

Lord Byron

via De Notaris 5 ✉ 00197 – Ⓜ Flaminio – ✆ 06 3220404 – info@lordbyronhotel.com – Fax 06 3 22 04 05 – www.lordbyronhotel.com **L-M1**

26 rm – 325/413 € 363/550 € – 6 suites

Rest *Sapori del Lord Byron* – *(closed Sunday)* Carte 51/73 €

♦ Luxury ♦ Stylish ♦

Elegant Art Deco furnishings, luxurious guestrooms and modern facilities make this hotel near the Villa Borghese gardens an excellent base. Impeccable service. This stylish restaurant adorned with mirrors, marble and fine paintings has its own entrance. Ideal for quiet, intimate dinners.

The Duke Hotel

via Archimede 69 ✉ 00197 – ✆ 06 367221 – theduke@thedukehotel.com – Fax 06 36 00 41 04 – www.thedukehotel.com **L1**

78 rm – 290/360 € 390/443 €

Rest – Carte 58/91 €

♦ Luxury ♦ Business ♦ Stylish ♦

Situated in a quiet residential area, this hotel has the discreet, muted atmosphere of an elegant English club. Decorated in typical period style, but with all the latest modern comforts. Afternoon tea is served in front of the fireplace. Italian and international dishes are reinterpreted with a creative flair at this restaurant.

Mercure Roma Corso Trieste without rest

via Gradisca 29 ✉ 00198 – Ⓜ Bologna – ✆ 06 852021 – mercure.romatrieste@accor-hotels.it – Fax 06 8 41 24 44 – www.mercure.com **O1**

97 rm – 165/180 € 185/200 €

♦ Chain hotel ♦ Business ♦ Modern ♦

A modern, comfortable hotel with a hint of Art Deco in a predominantly residential district. The tastefully furnished rooms vary in size. Gym, terrace and solarium on the top floor.

Fenix

viale Gorizia 5 ✉ 00198 – Ⓜ Bologna – ✆ 06 8540741 – info@fenixhotel.it – Fax 06 8 54 36 32 – www.fenixhotel.it **O1**

73 rm – 110/160 € 150/200 €

Rest – *(closed August, Saturday dinner and Sunday)* Carte 25/45 €

♦ Traditional ♦ Business ♦ Classic ♦

Situated near the Villa Torlonia gardens, this hotel has an modern, elegant atmosphere and is tastefully furnished with original, colourful décor. Pleasant internal garden. Soft, elegant colours dominate the dining room of the restaurant.

Mercure Roma Piazza Bologna without rest

via Reggio Calabria 54 ✉ 00161 – Ⓜ Bologna – ✆ 06 440741 – prenotazione.mercureromabologna@accor-hotels.it – Fax 06 44 24 54 61 – www.accorhotels.com **O2**

113 rm – 180/195 € 215/245 €

♦ Business ♦ Modern ♦

Situated in a residential district proposing some of Rome's best Art Deco and rationalist buildings, the lobby is modern and fluorescent while rooms are ideal for business travellers.

Villa Morgagni without rest

via G.B. Morgagni 25 ✉ 00161 – Ⓜ Policlinico – ✆ 06 44202190 – info@villamorgagni.it – Fax 06 44 20 21 90 – www.villamorgagni.it **O2**

34 rm – 70/200 € 130/250 €

♦ Luxury ♦ Classic ♦

Privacy and silence are the assets of this hotel together with its refined liberty atmosphere. Rooms are well equipped while breakfast is served on a panoramic roof garden.

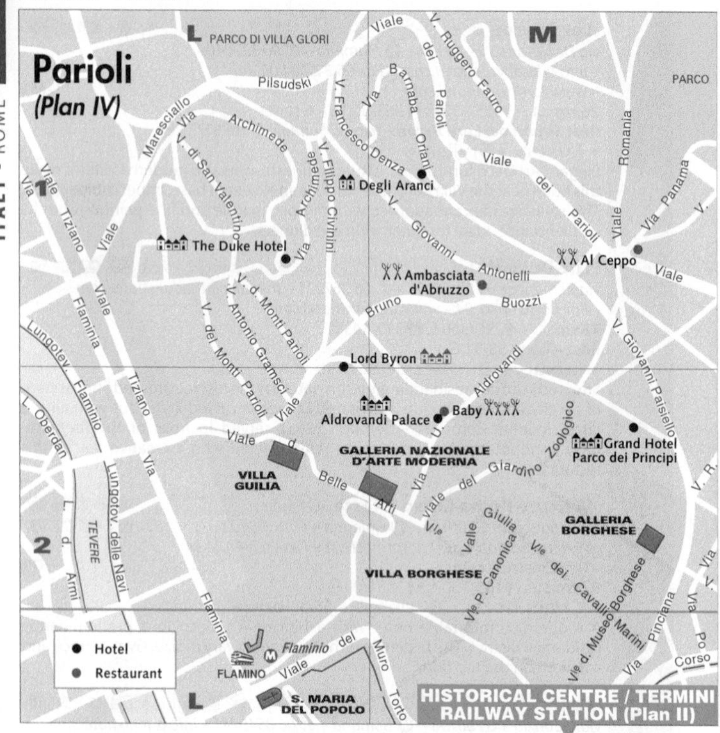

Degli Aranci

via Oriani 11 ✉ 00197 – Ⓜ Flaminio – ☎ 06 8070202 – info@hoteldegliaranci.com – Fax 06 8 07 07 04 **M1**

58 rm ☕ – 🚹210 € 🚹🚹280 € – 2 suites

Rest – Carte 35/55 €

♦ Traditional ♦ Modern ♦

This elegant hotel occupies a fine early 20C building. Situated in a quiet residential street, the hotel has a peaceful ambience and is decorated in gentle pastel colours. Polite, attentive service. The restaurant has an English feel, with windows overlooking the garden.

Baby (Alfonso Iaccarino) – Hotel Aldrovandi Palace

via Ulisse Aldrovandi 15 ✉ 00197 – ☎ 06 3216126 – baby@aldrovandi.com – Fax 06 3 22 14 35 – www.aldrovandi.com

closed Monday **M2**

Rest – Menu 110 € – Carte 75/95 €

Spec. Naif di astice e mozzarella di bufala con pesche bianche e bollicine. Ravioli di caciotta fresca e maggiorana con pomodorini vesuviani e basilico. Cernia ai sentori di vaniglia con zabaione ai capperi e crocchette di zucca.

♦ Inventive ♦ Fashionable ♦

The result of a partnership with a well-known chef from Sant'Agata, this restaurant specialises in dishes from the Campania region. Belonging to the elegant Aldovrandi Palace hotel, the restaurant is decorated in a bright minimalist style.

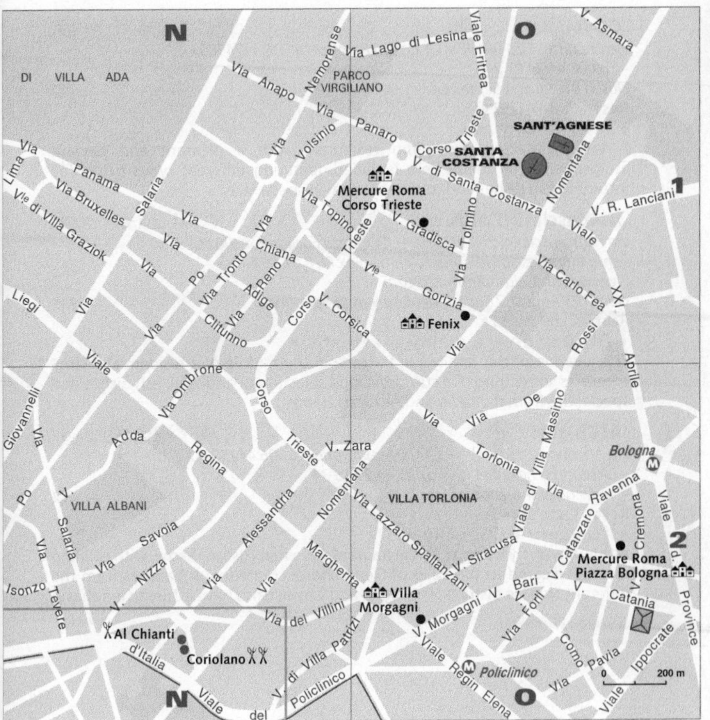

Al Ceppo

via Panama 2 ✉ 00198
– ✆ 06 8551379
– info@ristorantealceppo.it
– Fax 06 85 30 13 70
– www.ristorantealceppo.it
closed 8 to 24 August and Monday **M1**

Rest – Carte 48/63 €

◆ Classic ◆ Rustic ◆

Innovative Mediterranean cuisine served in an elegantly rustic setting. Main courses include meat and fish grilled in the dining room.

Mamma Angelina

viale Arrigo Boito 65 ✉ 00199
– ✆ 06 8608928
– mammangelina@libero.it
– Fax 06 8 61 03 55
closed August and Wednesday Plan I **C1**

Rest – Carte 20/33 €

◆ Fish ◆ Friendly ◆

Traditional Italian cuisine is the hallmark of this friendly restaurant. Specialities include an excellent buffet of antipasti, fish and seafood dishes and typical Roman delicacies.

XX **Coriolano**

via Ancona 14 ✉ 00198 – Ⓜ Castro Petorio – ✆ 06 44249863 – Fax 06 44 24 97 24
closed 8 August-1 September **N2**
Rest – Carte 41/57 €
♦ Fish ♦ Formal ♦
A well-maintained, family-run restaurant with a pleasant and elegant atmosphere. The menu here is varied, featuring different types of cuisine including fish dishes and traditional Roman specialities.

XX **Ambasciata d'Abruzzo**

via Pietro Tacchini 26 ✉ 00197 – Ⓜ Piazza Euclide – ✆ 06 8078256 – info@ambasciatadiabruzzo.com – Fax 06 8 07 49 64 – www.ambasciatadiabruzzo.com
closed 23 August-7 September and 9 to 23 January **M1**
Rest – Carte 25/35 €
♦ Abruzzian specialities ♦ Rustic ♦
The location of this family-run trattoria in the middle of a residential district comes as something of a surprise. Good selection of antipasti, fish dishes and specialities from the Lazio and Abruzzi regions.

X **Al Chianti**

via Ancona 17 ✉ 00198 – Ⓜ Castro Pretorio – ✆ 06 44250242 – alchianti@nexianet.it – Fax 06 44 29 15 34 – www.alchiantiristorante.it **N2**
Rest – Carte 29/48 €
♦ Tuscany ♦ Friendly ♦
Although run by Romans, this restaurant has a real Tuscan theme, with a dining room dedicated to the Palio of Siena and decorated with banners from the different Sienese districts. The menu and winelist also have a Tuscan emphasis.

MILAN

MILANO

Population (est. 2007): 1 303 000 (conurbation 3 884 000) – Altitude: 122m

Ph. Renault/HEMIS.fr

If it's the romantic charm of places like Venice, Florence or Rome you're looking for, then best avoid Milan. If you're hankering for a permanent panorama of Renaissance chapels, palazzi, shimmering canals and bastions of fine art, then you're in the wrong place. What Milan does is relentless fashion, churned out with oodles of attitude and style. Italy's second largest city is constantly reinventing itself, and when Milan does a makeover, it invariably does it with flair and panache.

That's not to say that Italy's capital of fast money and fast fashion doesn't have an eye for its past. The centrepiece of the whole city is the magnificent gleaming white Duomo, which took five hundred years to complete, while up *la via* a little way, La Scala is quite simply the world's most famous opera house. But this city is known primarily for its sleek and modern towers, many housing the very latest threads from the very latest fashion gurus. There are cutting-edge art galleries here, rubbing shoulders with space-age spas and bars, some of them opened by exclusive high-street designers. You know you've arrived in Milan not so much when you stare at a Renaissance piece of art as when you take an *aperitivo* at cocktail hour in a snazzy bar.

LIVING THE CITY

When you see the great bulk of the **Duomo**, you know you're in the centre of landlocked Milan. Just north lies **Brera,** with its much prized old-world charm, and **Quadrilatero d'Oro**, with no little new-world glitz. The popular **Giardini Pubblici** are a little way further north east from here. South of the centre is the **Navigli** quarter, home to rejuvenated Middle Age canals, while to the west are the green lungs of the **Parco Sempione.** The artily trendy neighbourhood of **Lambrate** is way up to the north east of Milan.

PRACTICAL INFORMATION

ARRIVAL-DEPARTURE

Malpensa Airport is 48km northwest of the city and Linate Airport 7km east. A train connects Malpensa with Stazione Cadorna every 30min which takes 40min, while a taxi will cost around €70. From Linate take the Airport bus no. 73 to Piazza San Babila metro station (every 10min, time 25min).

TRANSPORT

The best way to get about Milan is by bus, tram or metro. Tickets are valid for one metro ride, or seventy five minutes of travel on buses or trams. You can also purchase books of ten tickets, or unlimited one-day or two-day passes. Buy them at metro stations, kiosks, bars or tobacconists.

The metro provides a fast and efficient service, with frequent trains running on three different coloured lines. If you don't fancy waiting around for public transport, then walking is also advised: although Milan may seem too big to conquer on foot, most of its attractions are based in the small and compact centre.

EXPLORING MILAN

Milan's fashion designers pride themselves on peering into the future and dreaming up the garments of tomorrow. But high up in the city centre you get the chance to project your own vision even further than them. Just climb to the roof of the mighty Duomo and take in the spectacular views, which, on a clear day, will let you gaze on the Alps sixty miles away. Come back down to comprehend the wonders of a building which took half a millennium to complete. This immense Gothic cathedral, begun in 1387, reflects the whims of fashion over the centuries and is a surreal amalgam of architectural styles. The spires are capped by thousands of sculptures in an awesome embrace of High Gothic. Much of the building is marble, but the interior highlight, La Madonnina, is pure gold. It doesn't take very long to realise that this is the shade of choice for much of Milan: you'll see it in the glitter of handbags and the flash of credit cards. Cross the piazza and the sight of gold will be much in evidence at the **Galleria Vittorio Emanuele II**. Built in 1878, this fabulous salotto (drawing room)

lays claim to being the first shopping arcade in Europe. For much more than a century, stylish Milanese have browsed in this elegant neoclassical structure with its landmark glass roof.

→ FADING GLORY

Head west for the city's most lauded artistic experience (but make sure you've booked first). Invariably most visitors will find their way to see Leonardo da Vinci's **The Last Supper**. It's not in a cathedral or church, but is painted on the wall of a convent dining hall at the **Santa Maria delle Grazie**, half a mile west of the Duomo. The effect of the years (over six hundred of them) and damp Milan winters has resulted in the masterpiece literally fading in front of the onlookers' eyes. But you can still read the apostles' reactions in their movements and positions; you can still admire the brilliant colours used in the original. Your appetite for high culture whetted, head a short distance north east to the city's very own castle stronghold, **Castello Sforzesco**. Built in the fourteenth century to protect Milan's assets, over the centuries its use was adapted to showcase what the city does best: creativity. Now it's the home to no less than ten museums, and some are well worth a visit. Particularly impressive is the **Museo d'Arte Antica**, which includes a fresco believed to be by Leonardo -Sala delle Asse - and Michelangelo's extraordinary, unfinished final work, Rondanini Pieta, which he toiled over for years until his death in 1564. There's also the **Photographic Archive**, full of fascinating pictures of Italian life dating back to 1840, and the **Achille Bertarelli Prints Collection**, which seems to show that before Milan was obsessed with fashion it was rather partial to postcards, maps and all kinds of printed ephemera.

→ PARK ART

Step out of Castello Sforzesco, and you're in one of the city's top green spaces - the Parco Sempione. It's a rambling quadrangle of grassy hillocks and leafy avenues named after philosophers and writers. Because this is Milan, there's also a temple to design here, **The Triennale,** where the way the temporary exhibitions are presented is often as impressive as the subject matter. More evidence that they like to mix relaxation and up-to-the-minute art can be found in the city's other main park, Giardini Publicci, northeast of the centre, where a double dose of culture lies in wait amongst the rose bushes and pebble paths. The **Galleria d'Arte Moderna** is chock full of Futurists and twentieth century Realists; next door the **Padiglione d'Arte Contemporanea** puts on the gutsiest and most daring exhibitions in town. Afterwards step back outside and enjoy an ice cream in the park.

The city's best art collection is in the Brera quarter, the one neighbourhood of Milan that breathes old-style Italian charm, with its low stucco buildings and cobblestone streets. This is the ideal setting for **Pinacoteca Brera**, which celebrates its two hundredth birthday in 2009. It contains over seven hundred years' worth of Italian art, including Raphael's Marriage of the Virgin, Piero della Francesca's Brera Altarpiece and Veronese's Last Supper (a very different take to Leonardo's!). Throw in the likes of Caravaggio, Canaletto, Titian, Tintoretto, Botticelli and Mantegna, and you may well convince yourself that, despite its best efforts, Milan does appreciate things other than shopping and fashion.

→ FOOLS' GOLD?

Mind you, if that really is the reason you're here, then you'll certainly have no trouble striking gold – quite literally, in the quarter north east of the Duomo, which the locals call Quadrilatero d'Oro, or 'Golden Quad'. This is the part of town where plastic is the only currency, and if you're here on a tight budget, then a visit will be for anecdotal or research purposes only. The 'Quad' lies along and between four lengthy streets, and has earned its gold status because of the outlandishly expensive boutiques all around here. The big design names are gathered in clusters; many are so exclusive they don't bother with price tags. The good news for those financially challenged is that it isn't really necessary to shop here: the primary pastime is to perfect your strutting.

For a complete contrast, go to the south of the city centre where, in Navigli, you'll find canals from the Middle Ages. This is a rather shabby but fascinating district; artists and designers are taking over the old warehouses, particularly in **Zona Tortona**, where you can pick up well-priced trinkets from the refashioned artisans' studios. A leisurely stroll along the main drag of Ripa di Porta Ticinese brings you into contact with antiques shops during the day and trendy bars by night.

→ DIVA

To 'do' Milan properly, there's only one way to finish the evening, and that's to take in a performance at **La Scala**. The legendary venue was completely refurbished in 2004, but the history lives on: in the eighteenth and nineteenth centuries it was normal practice for the audience to chat, gamble and walk in and out during shows, while up to the middle of the last century even Italy's top divas would shy away from performing here because of the cat calls and whistles that could come their way courtesy of the nation's harshest critics located in the upper tiers. Nowadays, the diva is safe: aficionados reserve their thoughts until the bar at intermission.

CALENDAR HIGHLIGHTS

Some locals would say that the Milan calendar means nothing until early December, when the opera season at La Scala gets underway. But if you can't grab a seat for a performance for love or money, you can instead get all at sea at the Milan Aquarium's The Sea In Milan (also in December), a series of aquatic activities with marine related exhibitions and art-based events. The Fiera Milano plays host to MiArt in March, an international modern art fair that gives you the chance to check out four fascinatingly different sections: Preview, Modern, Contemporary, and Art&Co. April is the time to head down to the canals for the Naviglio Grande Flower Market, when two hundred 'flower pros' from all over Italy set up a beautiful carnival of flowers and fragrance along the wharf complex. Something completely different in June: the Gods of Metal Festival at Idropark Fila, when heavy metal music reigns for two days. In the same month, the rhythms are of a very different nature at the Festival Latino Americando, in

MILAN IN…

→ ONE DAY

Duomo, The Last Supper (remember to book first), Brera, Navigli

→ TWO DAYS

Pinacoteca Brera, Castello Sforzesco, Parco Sempione, a night at La Scala

→ THREE DAYS

Giardini Publicci and its museums, trendy Lambrate district

the grounds of Datchforum: a South American village is set up to host not only top musicians from that continent, but also literature, art and films. June's a busy month in Milan: there's the Festa del Naviglio, with music, food and special events around the canals, and also Notte Bianca (on the third Saturday of the month) when a variety of concerts and performances go on right through the night. During September Music, they continue right through a whole month, and feature the work of famous composers, as well as the world's regional music. Panoramica (also in September) is a top film festival featuring a selection of the best movies from the Venice and Locarno Festivals: get along to the Anteo or Multisala Plinius cinemas for the reel deal. More than twenty thousand visitors jog along to the Fiera Milano in October for a fitness fiesta at the Wellness World Exhibition, while the ambience is more on the decadent side the same month for the Celtic New Year celebrations, when the Castello Sforzesco is turned into a medieval north European site for traditional music and revelry.

EATING OUT

For a taste of Italy's regional cuisines, Milan is a great place to be. The city is often the goal of those leaving their home regions in the south or centre of the country; many open trattoria or restaurants with the result that Milan offers a wide range of provincial menus. Excellent fish restaurants, inspired by recipes from the south, are a big draw despite the fact that the city is a long way from the sea. Going beyond the local borders, that emphasis on really good food continues and the quality (if not always the number) of ethnically diverse places to eat is better in Milan than just about anywhere else in Italy, including Rome. Japanese restaurants are all the rage now and they're having a growing influence on menus here: raw fish is very popular. You'd expect avant-garde eating destinations to be the thing in this city of fashion and style, and you'd be right: there are some top-notch cutting-edge restaurants, thanks to Milan's famous tendency to reshape and experiment as it goes. For those who want to try out the local gastronomic traditions, *risotto allo zafferano* is not to be missed, nor either the *cotoletta alla Milanese* (veal cutlet), or the *casoeula* (a winter special made with pork and cabbage). Then, of course, there's the ubiquitous *panettone*, to be enjoyed at Christmas. Milanesi tend to eat earlier than diners in Rome, starting the evening meal at roughly eight o'clock. If you want to stay up that much later lingering with the beautiful people, your best bet is the bohemian Navigli quarter, with its unique atmosphere created by old fashioned houses and laidback canal side eateries. The bill will always include service charge.

→ HAVING A BALL AT THE GALLERIA

A couple of things you should know about the oh-so-stylish Galleria Vittorio Emanuele II. Architect Giuseppe Mengoni spent fourteen years working on this, his pet project, but died falling from the roof the day before it opened in 1878. Bring yourself good luck by rubbing your feet on the genitals of the bull in the central mosaic. Decades of grinding stilettos meant the bull required a recent touch up.

If you can't get enough of this century's art scene, then head out of town (fifteen minutes on the metro) to the suburb of Lambrate. The provocative and highly singular gallerias beckon you inside for audacious artworks and flights of fancy with a technological twist. What would Leonardo have made of it all?

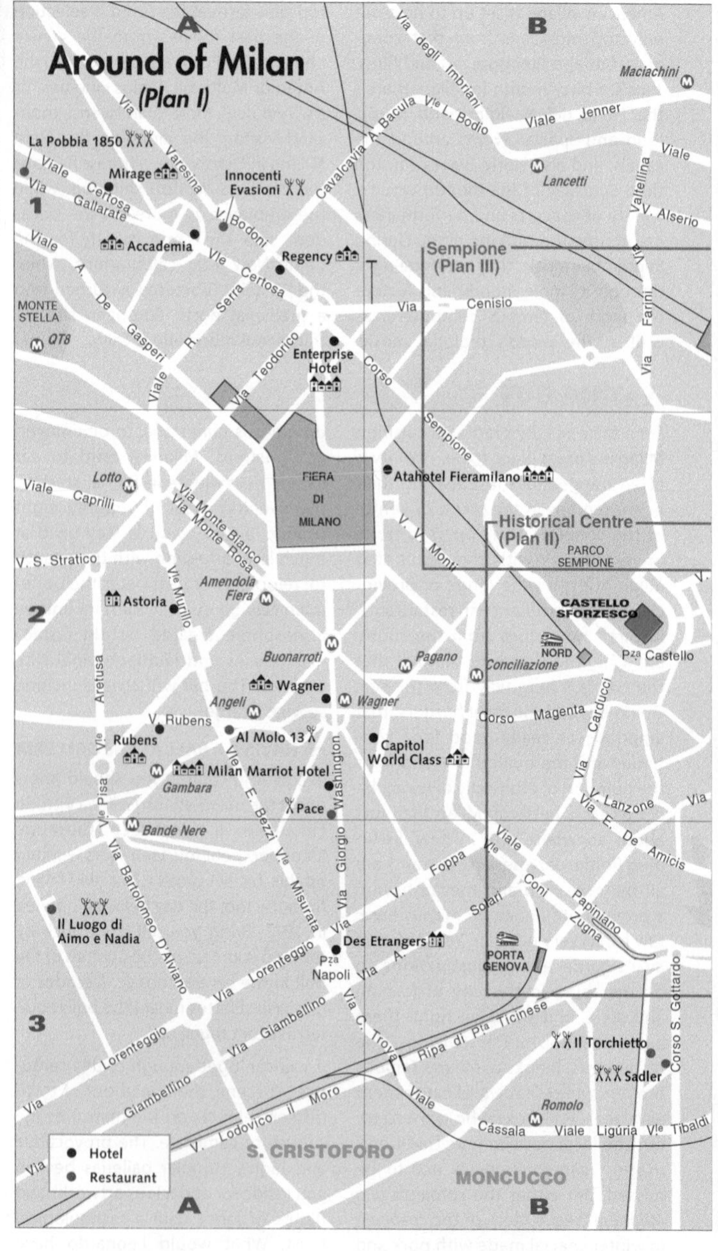
Around of Milan
(Plan I)
A
B
1
2
3
La Pobbia 1850
Mirage
Innocenti Evasioni
Accademia
Regency
Enterprise Hotel
Atahotel Fieramilano
FIERA DI MILANO
Sempione (Plan III)
Historical Centre (Plan II)
PARCO SEMPIONE
CASTELLO SFORZESCO
P^za Castello
NORD
Maciachini
Lancetti
MONTE STELLA
QT8
Lotto
Amendola Fiera
Buonarroti
Pagano
Conciliazione
Astoria
Wagner
Angeli
Rubens
Al Molo 13
Capitol World Class
Milan Marriot Hotel
Gambara
Pace
Bande Nere
Il Luogo di Aimo e Nadia
Des Etrangers
P^za Napoli
PORTA GENOVA
Il Torchietto
Sadler
Romolo
S. CRISTOFORO
MONCUCCO
Hotel
Restaurant

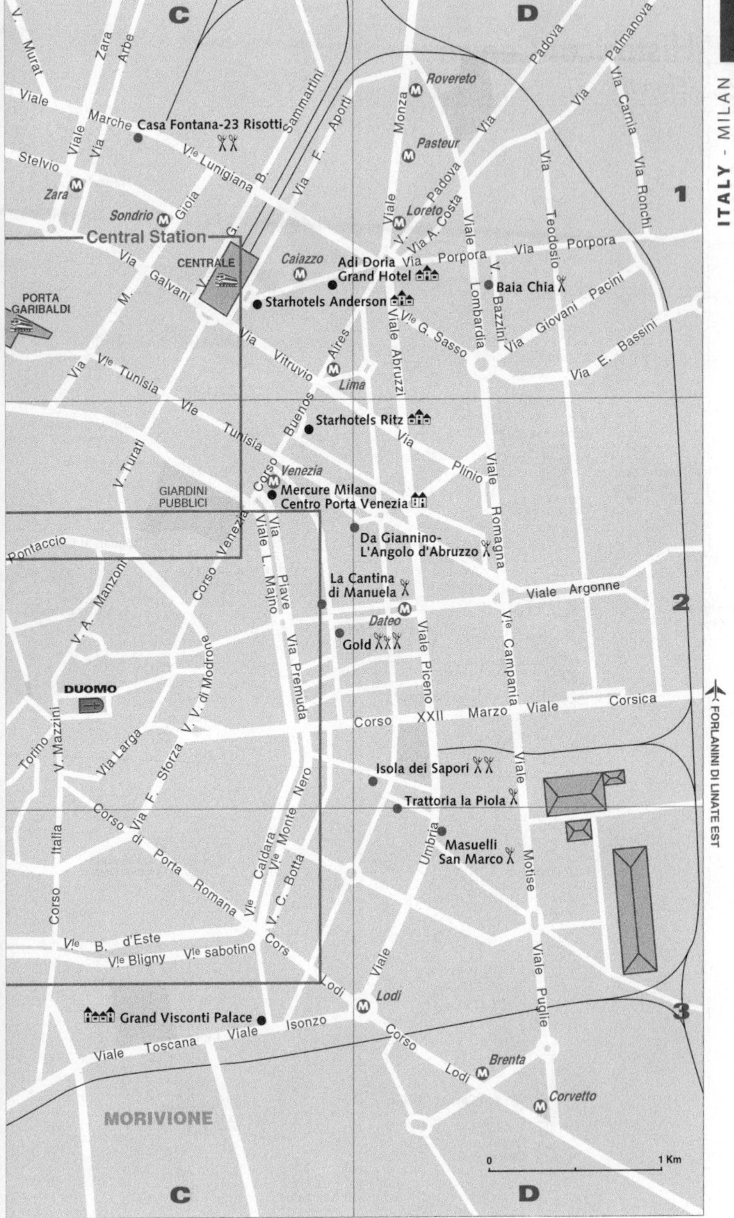

C
D
1
2
3
Central Station
CENTRALE
PORTA GARIBALDI
Casa Fontana-23 Risotti
Adi Doria Grand Hotel
Starhotels Anderson
Baia Chia
Starhotels Ritz
Mercure Milano Centro Porta Venezia
Da Giannino-L'Angolo d'Abruzzo
La Cantina di Manuela
Gold
Isola dei Sapori
Trattoria la Piola
Masuelli San Marco
Grand Visconti Palace
GIARDINI PUBBLICI
DUOMO
MORIVIONE
Rovereto
Pasteur
Loreto
Caiazzo
Lima
Venezia
Dateo
Zara
Sondrio
Lodi
Brenta
Corvetto
FORLANINI DI LINATE EST
0
1 Km

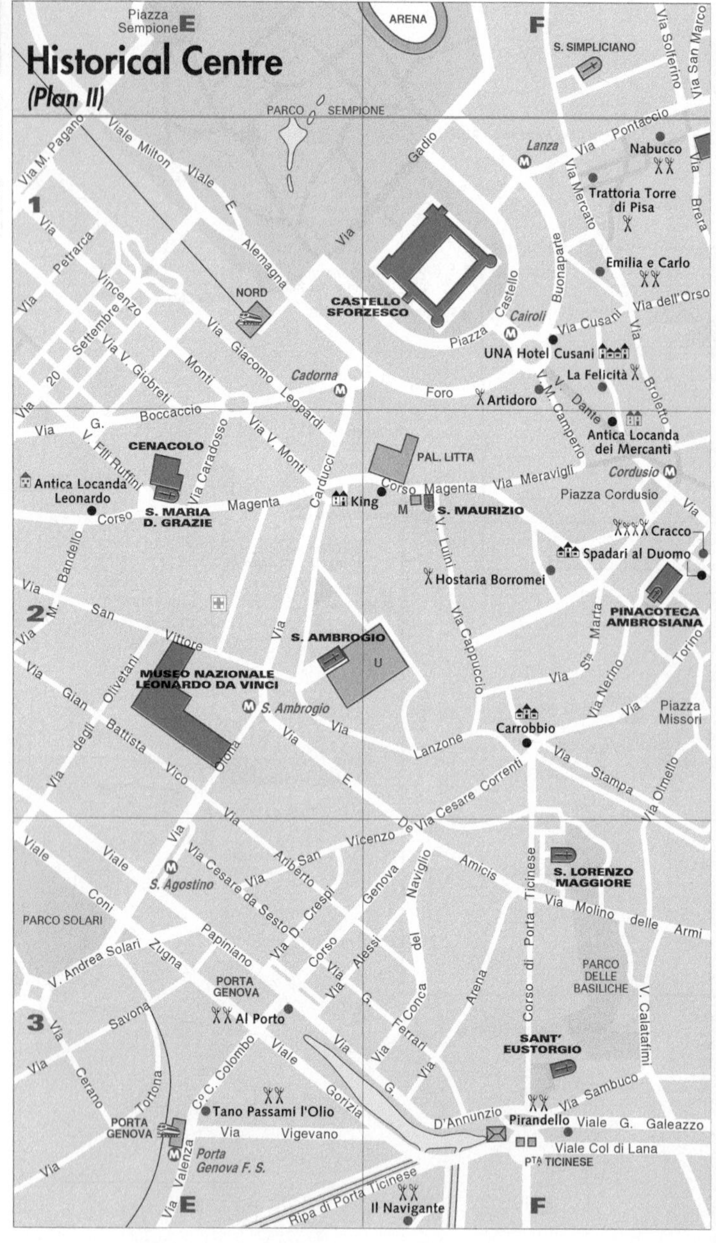
Historical Centre
(Plan II)
ARENA
PARCO SEMPIONE
Piazza Sempione
S. SIMPLICIANO
Via Solferino
Via San Marco
Via Pontaccio
Lanza
Nabucco
Trattoria Torre di Pisa
Emilia e Carlo
Via Mercato
Via Brera
Via dell'Orso
Via Cusani
Cairoli
Piazza Castello
Buonaparte
CASTELLO SFORZESCO
NORD
Via Gadio
Viale Milton
Viale E. Alemagna
Via M. Pagano
Via Petrarca
Via Vincenzo
20 Settembre
Via V. Giobreti
Monti
Via Giacomo Leopardi
Cadorna
Foro
Artidoro
UNA Hotel Cusani
La Felicità
V. M. Camperio
V. Dante
Via Broletto
Antica Locanda dei Mercanti
Cordusio
Piazza Cordusio
Via Meravigli
PAL. LITTA
Corso Magenta
S. MAURIZIO
King
Carducci
Via V. Monti
Boccaccio
Via G. Boccaccio
V. F.lli Ruffini
CENACOLO
S. MARIA D. GRAZIE
Via Caradosso
Antica Locanda Leonardo
Corso Magenta
Via Bandello
Cracco
Spadari al Duomo
Hostaria Borromei
V. Luini
Via Cappuccio
PINACOTECA AMBROSIANA
Via Torino
Via Sta Marta
Via M. San Vittore
MUSEO NAZIONALE LEONARDO DA VINCI
S. AMBROGIO
S. Ambrogio
Via Lanzone
Carrobbio
Via Nerino
Piazza Missori
Via Stampa
Via Olmetto
Via Gian Battista Vico
Via degli Olivetani
Olona
Via E. De Amicis
Via Cesare Correnti
Via San Vicenzo
Via Aribert
S. Agostino
Via Cesare da Sesto
S. LORENZO MAGGIORE
Corso di Porta Ticinese
Via Molino delle Armi
Viale Coni Zugna
PARCO SOLARI
V. Andrea Solari
Papiniano
Via D. Crespi
Corso Genova
Naviglio
Via Alessi
Via G. Conca del Naviglio
Via Ferrari
Arena
PARCO DELLE BASILICHE
V. Calatafimi
PORTA GENOVA
Al Porto
Savona
Via Cerano
Tortona
Co C. Colombo
Viale Gorizia
Tano Passami l'Olio
SANT' EUSTORGIO
Via Sambuco
Pirandello
D'Annunzio
Viale G. Galeazzo
Viale Col di Lana
PTA TICINESE
Via Vigevano
Porta Genova F. S.
Via Valenza
Ripa di Porta Ticinese
Il Navigante
E
F
1
2
3

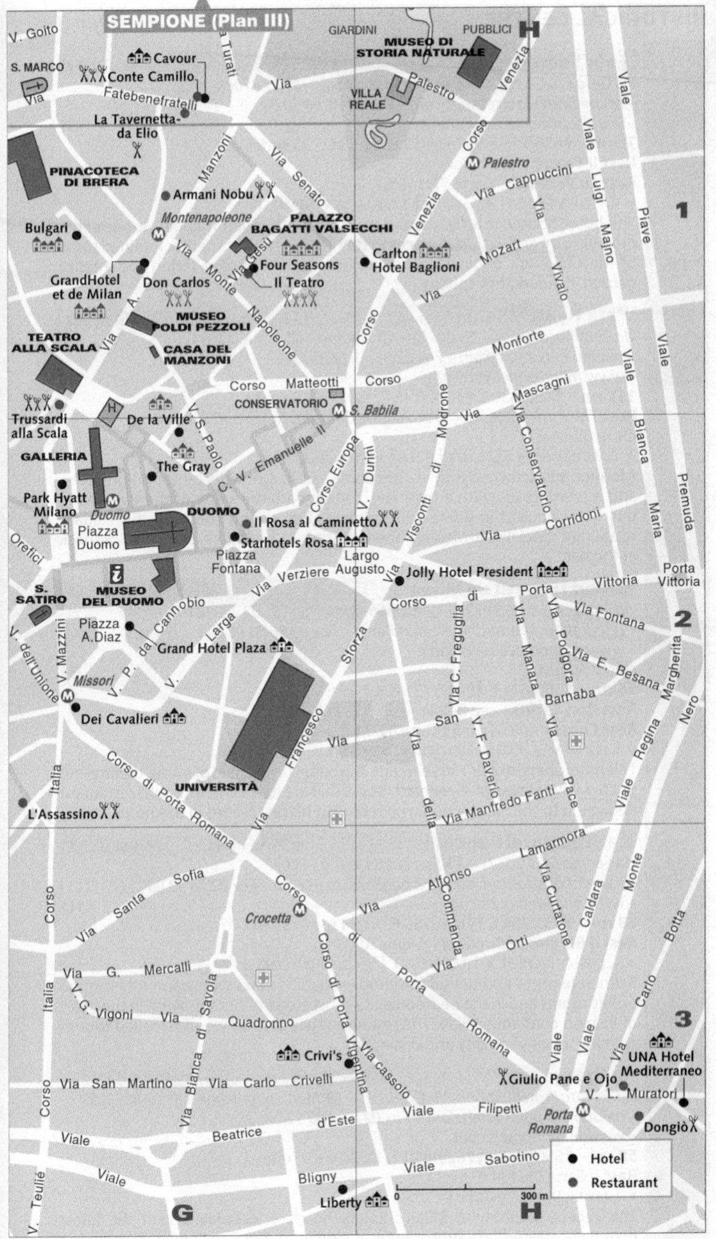
SEMPIONE (Plan III)
GIARDINI
PUBBLICI
MUSEO DI STORIA NATURALE
VILLA REALE
PINACOTECA DI BRERA
PALAZZO BAGATTI VALSECCHI
MUSEO POLDI PEZZOLI
CASA DEL MANZONI
TEATRO ALLA SCALA
CONSERVATORIO
GALLERIA
DUOMO
MUSEO DEL DUOMO
S. SATIRO
UNIVERSITÀ
Cavour
Conte Camillo
La Tavernetta-da Elio
Armani Nobu
Bulgari
GrandHotel et de Milan
Don Carlos
Four Seasons
Il Teatro
Carlton Hotel Baglioni
Trussardi alla Scala
De la Ville
The Gray
Park Hyatt Milano
Il Rosa al Caminetto
Starhotels Rosa
Jolly Hotel President
Grand Hotel Plaza
Dei Cavalieri
L'Assassino
Crivi's
Giulio Pane e Ojo
UNA Hotel Mediterraneo
Dongiò
Liberty
Palestro
Montenapoleone
S. Babila
Duomo
Missori
Crocetta
Porta Romana
Piazza Duomo
Piazza Fontana
Largo Augusto
Piazza A.Diaz
Porta Vittoria
Corso Venezia
Corso Matteotti
Corso Monforte
Corso Europa
Corso di Porta Romana
Corso di Porta Vigentina
Corso Italia
Via Manzoni
Via Senato
Via Monte Napoleone
Via Palestro
Viale Piave
Viale Bianca Maria
Viale Premuda
Viale Regina Margherita
Viale Monte Nero
Via Francesco Sforza
Via Larga
Via Orefici
Via Mazzini
Via Santa Sofia
Viale Beatrice d'Este
Viale Filipetti
Viale Sabotino
Viale Bligny
V. Teulié
1
2
3
G
H
0
300 m
Hotel
Restaurant

HISTORICAL CENTRE *Plan II*

Four Seasons

via Gesù 6/8 ✉ 20121 – Ⓜ Montenapoleone – ☏ 02 77088
– res.milano@fourseasons.com – Fax 02 77 08 50 00
– www.fourseasons.com/milan **G1**
78 rm – 616/715 € 742/852 €, 33 € – 25 suites
Rest Il Teatro – see below
Rest *La Veranda* – Carte 77/116 €
♦ Chain hotel ♦ Grand Luxury ♦ Stylish ♦
This hotel, housed in a 15C monastery in Milan's "Golden Triangle", is one of the most elegant and exclusive places to stay in the city. The hotel has retained some of the building's original decorative features. Restaurant facing the interior garden. Refined atmosphere.

Park Hyatt Milano

via Tommaso Grossi 1 ✉ 20121 – Ⓜ Duomo – ☏ 02 88211234
– milano@hyattintl.com – Fax 02 88 21 12 35
– www.milan.park.hyatt.com **G2**
117 rm – 480/630 € 530/740 €, 29 € – 9 suites
Rest *The Park* – *(closed 4 to 26 August, Saturday lunch and Sunday)*
Carte 63/94 €
♦ Business ♦ Chain hotel ♦ Modern ♦
A lounge area crowned with a large cupola, public rooms decorated in light tones and a relaxing spa with a gym and Turkish bath are some of the features of this hotel housed in a late-19C building. Two dining rooms in the elegant restaurant specialise in Mediterranean cuisine. At lunchtime, enjoy a quick snack at the bar.

Grand Hotel et de Milan

via Manzoni 29 ✉ 20121 – Ⓜ Montenapoleone – ☏ 02 723141
– reservations@grandhoteletdemilan.it – Fax 02 86 46 08 61
– www.grandhoteletdemilan.it
closed August **G1**
95 rm – 560/674 € 617/731 €, 35 € – 7 suites
Rest Don Carlos – see below
Rest *Caruso* – *(lunch only)* Carte 42/71 €
♦ Luxury ♦ Traditional ♦ Stylish ♦
This hotel opened over 150 years ago. Big names in the field of music, theatre and politics have stayed in its elegant rooms that are full of charm. Bright restaurant dedicated to the great tenor, who recorded his first record in this hotel.

Carlton Hotel Baglioni

via Senato 5 ✉ 20121 – Ⓜ San Babila – ☏ 02 77077
– reservations.carlton.milano@baglionihotels.com – Fax 02 78 33 00
– www.baglionihotels.com **H1**
83 rm – 550/700 € 600/750 €, 34 € – 9 suites
Rest *Il Baretto al Baglioni* – Menu 70/90 €
♦ Chain hotel ♦ Luxury ♦ Personalised ♦
Refined features and period furniture, valuable fabrics with warm tones in the public rooms and in the bedrooms of a most elegant "bomboniera" in the heart of fashion conscious Milan. The restaurant has several, wood-panelled rooms, creating an air of quality and distinction.

Bulgari

via privata Fratelli Gabba 7/b ✉ 20121 – Ⓜ Montenapoleone – ☏ 02 8058051
– milano@bulgarihotels.com – Fax 02 8 05 80 52 22
– www.bulgarihotels.com **G1**
58 rm – 550/790 € 620/810 €, 30 € – 9 suites
Rest – Carte 55/114 €
♦ Luxury ♦ Stylish ♦
This recent addition to Milan's luxury hotels is decorated with the finest materials, creating an atmosphere of simple, discreet elegance. A charming garden comes as a pleasant surprise. This is an exclusive restaurant surrounded by greenery.

Starhotels Rosa

via Pattari 5 ✉ 20122 – Ⓜ Duomo – ✆ 02 8831 – rosa.mi@starhotels.it – Fax 02 8 05 79 64 – www.starhotels.com **G2**

240 rm – ††160/700 €, ☕ 19 € – 3 suites

Rest Il Rosa al Caminetto – see below

♦ Business ♦ Classic ♦

Just a short walk from the Duomo, this establishment offers a discreet elegance. It has a spacious ground floor lounge with marble and stucco décor, well-designed rooms, a conference centre, and health centre.

Grand Visconti Palace

viale Isonzo 14 ✉ 20135 – Ⓜ Lodi TIBB – ✆ 02 540341 – info@grandviscontipalace.com – Fax 02 54 06 95 23 – www.grandviscontipalace.com *Plan I* **C3**

166 rm ☕ – †330/460 € ††400/530 € – 6 suites

Rest ***Al Quinto Piano*** – Carte 44/67 €

♦ Business ♦ Personalised ♦

This elegant hotel is housed in the extensive buildings of an old industrial mill. Facilities include conference rooms, a delightful garden and a first-class fitness centre. As its name suggests, this restaurant is situated on the fifth floor. Creative, imaginative cuisine.

Jolly Hotel President

largo Augusto 10 ✉ 20122 – Ⓜ San Babila – ✆ 02 77461 – milano_president@jollyhotels.com – Fax 02 78 34 49 – www.jollyhotels.com **H2**

244 rm ☕ – †130/430 € ††150/480 € – 12 suites

Rest ***Il Verziere*** – Carte 40/57 €

♦ Business ♦ Classic ♦

An international standard hotel for business travellers or tourists. It has attractive, spacious lounge areas as well as facilities for fashion shows, business lunches and conferences. The restaurant serves specialities from Lombardy, as well as Mediterranean-style dishes.

UNA Hotel Cusani

via Cusani 13 ✉ 20121 – Ⓜ Cairoli – ✆ 02 85601 – una.cusani@unahotels.it – Fax 02 8 69 36 01 – www.unahotels.it **F1**

87 rm ☕ – ††153/569 € – 5 suites

Rest – Carte 42/54 €

♦ Business ♦ Modern ♦

Located in the heart of the historic town centre, this hotel is in an ideal location for business and sightseeing. It has simple and modern, very large attractive rooms. Choose from classic Italian or international dishes at this cosy restaurant.

De la Ville

via Hoepli 6 ✉ 20121 – Ⓜ Duomo – ✆ 02 8791311 – reservationsdlv@sinahotels.it – Fax 02 86 66 09 – www.delavillemilano.com **G2**

109 rm ☕ – †380 € ††396 €

Rest ***L'Opera*** – ✆ 02 8051231 – Carte 39/60 €

♦ Luxury ♦ Cosy ♦

Located near the Duomo, this chic hotel with warm surroundings is decorated with marble and colourful silk. It has a relaxing swimming pool on the top floor covered with a transparent dome. Ideal for after theatre dinner, this restaurant serves Mediterranean cuisine reinterpreted with a creative flair.

The Gray

via San Raffaele 6 ✉ 20121 – Ⓜ Duomo – ✆ 02 7208951 – info.thegray@sinahotels.it – Fax 02 86 65 26 – www.hotelgray.com **G2**

21 rm – †391 € ††572 €, ☕ 31 €

Rest – *(residents only)* Carte 50/66 €

♦ Luxury ♦ Stylish ♦

Near the Galleria, this elegant hotel's modern design has rooms with stylish touches. There is also a fitness centre. This cosy restaurant with a creative décor offers a gourmet menu.

Spadari al Duomo without rest
via Spadari 11 ✉ 20123 – Ⓜ Duomo – ✆ 02 72002371
– reservation@spadarihotel.com – Fax 02 86 11 84
– www.spadarihotel.com
closed Christmas **F2**
40 rm – 168/328 €
◆ Business ◆ Functional ◆
With its extensive collection of contemporary art, this small hotel combines comfort with a penchant for new and exciting forms of artistic expression.

Cavour
via Fatebenefratelli 21 ✉ 20121 – Ⓜ Turati – ✆ 02 620001
– booking@hotelcavour.it – Fax 02 6 59 22 63
– www.hotelcavour.it
Closed August **G1**
113 rm – 233 € 267 €
Rest Conte Camillo – see below
◆ Business ◆ Functional ◆
This traditional, family-run hotel, situated near the city's main cultural sights, cafés and restaurants, offers its guests well-furnished, sound-proofed rooms and excellent service.

Dei Cavalieri without rest
piazza Missori 1 ✉ 20123 – Ⓜ Missori – ✆ 02 88571
– info@hoteldeicavalieri.com – Fax 02 8 85 72 41
– www.hoteldeicavalieri.com **G2**
177 rm – 309 € 720 €
◆ Traditional ◆ Functional ◆
You are sure to find a relaxing atmosphere in this hotel that has stylish, comfortably furnished rooms with contemporary décor and facilities for conferences, business lunches and banquets.

Grand Hotel Plaza without rest
piazza Diaz 3 ✉ 20123 – Ⓜ Duomo – ✆ 02 8555
– info@grandhotelplazamilano.it – Fax 02 86 72 40
– www.grandhotelplazamilano.it
closed 23 December-2 January **G2**
136 rm – 160/315 € 160/370 €
◆ Business ◆ Traditional ◆ Classic ◆
A traditional hotel in the heart of the city, with large, tastefully furnished rooms, a lobby with a bar and piano, and a new fully-equipped gym.

Carrobbio without rest
via Medici 3 ✉ 20123 – Ⓜ Duomo – ✆ 02 89010740
– info@hotelcarrobbiomilano.com – Fax 02 8 05 33 34
– www.hotelcarrobbiomilano.com
closed August and 22 December-2 January **F2**
56 rm – 185 € 436 €
◆ Business ◆ Classic ◆
This recently renovated hotel is in a quiet area and near the historic town centre. It has a small and relaxing winter garden.

Liberty without rest
viale Bligny 56 ✉ 20136 – ✆ 02 58318562
– reserve@hotelliberty-milano.com – Fax 02 58 31 90 61
– www.hotelliberty-milano.com
closed 26 July-17 August **G3**
58 rm – 95/250 € 105/360 €
◆ Traditional ◆ Personalised ◆
Near to the Bocconi University, an elegant hotel, with public areas inspired by the style from which they take their name and some antique furniture; many bedrooms with hydromassage unit.

Crivi's without rest
corso Porta Vigentina 46 ✉ 20122 – Ⓜ Crocetta – ✆ 02 582891 – crivis@tin.it – Fax 02 58 31 81 82 – www.crivis.com
closed August and Christmas G3
86 rm – †125/180 € ††140/280 €
♦ Business ♦ Functional ♦
In a convenient location near the metro, this comfortable hotel has pleasant public areas and traditionally furnished, reasonably comfortable and spacious guestrooms.

UNA Hotel Mediterraneo
via Muratori 14 ✉ 20135 – Ⓜ Porta Romana – ✆ 02 550071 – una.mediterraneo@unahotels.it – Fax 02 5 50 07 22 17 – www.unahotels.it H3
93 rm – ††107/443 €
Rest – *(residents only)* Carte 32/47 €
♦ Business ♦ Functional ♦
This business hotel, situated near the metro in the Porta Romana district, is modern in style, with functional, comfortable and sound-proofed guestrooms.

King without rest
corso Magenta 19 ✉ 20123 – Ⓜ Cadorna F.N.M. – ✆ 02 874432 – info@hotelkingmilano.com – Fax 02 89 01 07 98 – www.mokinba.it F2
48 rm – †80/231 € ††100/315 €
♦ Business ♦ Functional ♦
Housed in a six-storey building not far from the Duomo, this hotel has been renovated with opulent and elegant furnishings. The guestrooms, although not that spacious, are very comfortable.

Antica Locanda dei Mercanti without rest
via San Tomaso 8 ✉ 20121 – Ⓜ Cordusio – ✆ 02 8054080 – locanda@locanda.it – Fax 02 8 05 40 90 – www.locanda.it F2
14 rm – †155/205 € ††180/280 €, 10 €
♦ Townhouse ♦ Personalised ♦
A small, cosy hotel, simple and elegant in style, and furnished with antique furniture. Many of the light and spacious guestrooms have a small terrace.

Mercure Milano Centro Porta Venezia without rest
piazza Oberdan 12 ✉ 20129 – Ⓜ Venezia – ✆ 02 29403907 – booking@hotelmercuremilanocentro.it – Fax 02 29 52 61 71 – www.mercure.com C2
30 rm – †110/299 € ††130/349 €
♦ Chain hotel ♦ Stylish ♦
The hotel is a few steps away from the cultural heart of the city. Set in a 19C house, it has Art Nouveau furnishings and elegant, comfortable rooms.

Cracco
via Victor Hugo 4 ✉ 20123 – Ⓜ Duomo – ✆ 02 876774 – info@ristorantecracco.it – Fax 02 86 10 40 – www.peck.it
closed 3 weeks in August, 22 December-10 January, Saturday lunch (also Saturday dinner from June to August), Sunday and Monday lunch F2
Rest – Carte 98/132 €
Spec. Musetto di maiale fondente con pomodori verdi e scampi. Risotto al pepe di Sechuan, zenzero e acciuga. Rognone di vitello con ricci di mare e spugnole bianche.
♦ Inventive ♦ Fashionable ♦
Decorated in a simple, modern style, this restaurant serves excellent contemporary cuisine with a focus on innovative and inventive dishes.

XXXX

Il Teatro – Hotel Four Seasons

via Gesù 6/8 ✉ 20121 – Ⓜ Montenapoleone – ☎ 02 77081435 – milano@fourseasons.com – Fax 02 77 08 50 00 – www.fourseasons.com/milan
closed August, Christmas, 1 to 7 January and Sunday **G1**
Rest – *(dinner only)* Carte 85/118 €
◆ Modern ◆ Formal ◆
The restaurant, contained in the splendid premises of the Four Seasons hotel, is characterised by exclusiveness and class. The cuisine highlights interpretive creativity.

XXX

Don Carlos – Grand Hotel et de Milan

via Manzoni 29 ✉ 20121 – Ⓜ Montenapoleone – ☎ 02 72314640 – info@ristorantedoncarlos.it – Fax 02 86 46 08 61 – www.ristorantedoncarlos.it
closed August and Sunday **G1**
Rest – *(dinner only)* Carte 62/84 €
◆ Lombard-piedmontese ◆ Cosy ◆
A charming restaurant with a quiet atmosphere and elegant décor, including wood panelling, red appliqué and pictures and photos dating from the time of Verdi. Fine seasonal and regional cuisine with a creative touch.

XXX

Conte Camillo – Hotel Cavour

via Fatebenefratelli 21 ✉ 20121 – Ⓜ Turati – ☎ 02 6570516 – booking@hotelcavour.it – Fax 02 6 59 22 63 – www.hotelcavour.it
closed August and Saturday-Sunday lunch **G1**
Rest – Carte 36/53 €
◆ Classic ◆ Formal ◆
This discreetly stylish restaurant in the centre of Milan offers traditional dishes with a modern touch.

XXX ✿✿

Sadler

via Ascanio Sforza 77 ✉ 20136 – Ⓜ Romolo – ☎ 02 58104451 – sadler@sadler.it – Fax 02 58 11 23 43 – www.sadler.it
closed 8 August-2 September, 1 to 12 January and Sunday *Plan I* **B3**
Rest – *(dinner only)* Carte 71/114 €
Spec. Salamino di foie gras d'oca con uvetta e noci (autumn-winter). Risotto con carciofi croccanti e calamaretti spillo, pesto leggero (winter-spring). Padellata di crostacei con passatina di broccoletti, patate croccanti.
◆ Inventive ◆ Trendy ◆
The new premises of the renowned Sadler restaurant has large windows opening on to the street, offering views of the kitchen. Inventive contemporary cuisine with real attention to detail.

XXX ✿

Trussardi alla Scala

piazza della Scala 5 ✉ 20121 – Ⓜ Duomo – ☎ 02 80688201 – ristorante@trussardiallascala.com – Fax 02 80 68 82 87 – www.marinoallascala.com
closed 9 to 31 August, 22 December-6 January, Saturday lunch and Sunday **G1**
Rest – Menu 95 € – Carte 74/98 €
Spec. Noci di capesante alla plancia con polvere di zenzero e crema di arachidi. Riso mantecato alla milanese con animelle di vitello dorate. Brodo d'anatra con petto arrosto e tortino di pane con cosce brasate.
◆ Modern ◆ Trendy ◆
Housed in a beautiful palazzo in the square of the same name, this restaurant serves the best of Italian cuisine. The dining room is modern and spacious, with pleasant views from some of the tables.

XX

Il Rosa al Caminetto – Starhotels Rosa

via Beccaria 4 ✉ 20122 – Ⓜ Duomo – ☎ 02 89095235 – info@ilrosa.it – Fax 02 89 01 68 93 – www.ilrosa.it **G2**
Rest – Carte 40/60 €
◆ Classic ◆ Friendly ◆
This restaurant under new management features fast and attentive service with a menu of regional and Italian dishes. A lavish buffet lunch is also served.

XX **Armani/Nobu** A/C VISA MC AE DC

via Pisoni 1 ✉ 20121 – Ⓜ Montenapoleone – ☎ 02 62312645 – armani.nobu@giorgioarmani.it – Fax 02 62 31 26 74 – www.armaninobu.com
closed August, 25 December-7 January and Sunday lunch **G1**
Rest – Carte 45/73 €
♦ Japanese ♦ Fashionable ♦
An exotic union between fashion and gastronomy: Japanese "fusion" cuisine with South American influences in a simple, refined atmosphere inspired by Japanese design.

XX **Nabucco** A/C VISA MC AE DC

via Fiori Chiari 10 ✉ 20121 – Ⓜ Cairoli – ☎ 02 860663 – info@nabucco.it – Fax 02 8 69 25 76 – www.nabucco.it **F1**
Rest – Carte 38/46 €
♦ Classic ♦ Friendly ♦
Located in a typical alleyway in the Brera district with interesting inspired cuisine, both fish and meat dishes; evening meals by candlelight.

XX **L'Assassino** A/C VISA MC

via Amedei 8, angolo via Cornaggia ✉ 20123 – Ⓜ Missori – ☎ 02 8056144 – lambgori@tin.it – Fax 02 86 46 73 74 – www.ristorantelassassino.it
closed July, 23 December-2 January, Friday lunch and Saturday **G2**
Rest – Carte 31/62 €
♦ Mediterranean ♦ Friendly ♦
This typical restaurant in the heart of the city is always busy, and is particularly popular with a business clientele. Traditional Italian menu featuring seafood and home-made pasta.

XX **Emilia e Carlo** A/C VISA MC AE DC

via Sacchi 8 ✉ 20121 – Ⓜ Lanza – ☎ 02 875948 – emiliaecarlosas@virgilio.it – Fax 02 86 21 00 – www.emiliaecarlo.it
closed Easter, August, Christmas, Saturday lunch and Sunday **F1**
Rest – Carte 47/59 €
♦ Classic ♦ Cosy ♦
Set in an early 19th-century palazzo, this traditional-looking trattoria serves creative contemporary cuisine, and has a fine choice of wines.

XX **Al Porto** A/C VISA MC AE DC

piazzale Generale Cantore ✉ 20123 – Ⓜ Porta Genova FS – ☎ 02 89407425 – alportodimilano@acena.it – Fax 02 8 32 14 81
closed August, 24 December-3 January, Sunday and Monday lunch **E3**
Rest – Carte 45/60 €
♦ Fish ♦ Retro ♦
There is a definite maritime flavour to this restaurant, which occupies the old 19C Porta Genova toll house. Always busy, Al Porto specialises exclusively in fresh fish dishes, including raw fish.

XX **Tano Passami l'Olio** ♿ A/C VISA MC AE DC

via Villoresi 16 ✉ 20143 – Ⓜ Porta Genova FS – ☎ 02 8394139 – info@tanopassamilolio.it – Fax 02 83 24 01 04 – www.tanopassamilolio.it
closed August, 24 December-6 January and Sunday **E3**
Rest – *(dinner only)* Carte 67/89 €
♦ Inventive ♦ Cosy ♦
The key features here are the soft lighting, romantic atmosphere and creative fish and meat dishes, flavoured with a choice of extra-virgin olive oils on display in the dining room. Smoking lounge with a sofa.

XX **Il Torchietto** A/C VISA MC AE

via Ascanio Sforza 47 ✉ 20136 – Ⓜ Porta Genova FS – ☎ 02 8372910 – info@il.torchietto.com – Fax 02 8 37 20 00 – www.il-torchietto.com
closed August, 26 December-3 January, Saturday lunch and Monday *Plan I* **B3**
Rest – Carte 33/47 €
♦ Mantuan ♦ Friendly ♦
Specialising in regional cuisine using seasonal ingredients, with a particular emphasis on dishes from Mantua, this large, traditional trattoria is situated on the Naviglio Pavese canal.

XX

Il Navigante

via Magolfa 14 ✉ 20143 – Ⓜ Porta Genova FS – ☎ 02 89406320 – info@navigante.it – Fax 02 89 42 08 97 – www.navigante.it
closed August, Sunday and Monday **F3**
Rest – *(dinner only)* Carte 30/63 €
♦ Fish ♦ Friendly ♦
On a road at the back of the waterway, live music every evening in an establishment managed by an ex-ship's cook, with an unusual aquarium on the floor; seafood cuisine.

XX

Isola dei Sapori

via Anfossi 10 ✉ 20135 – Ⓜ Porta Romana – ☎ 02 54100708 – Fax 02 54 10 07 08
closed August, 23 December-3 January, Sunday and Monday lunch Plan I **D2**
Rest – Carte 28/45 €
♦ Classic ♦ Friendly ♦
Three young Sardinians have introduced a nautical note in the modern décor of this restaurant; the cuisine features fish specialties, prime quality ingredients and generous portions.

XX

Pirandello

viale Gian Galeazzo 6 ✉ 20136 – ☎ 02 89402901 – Fax 02 89 40 29 01
closed 7 to 30 August, Christmas, Saturday lunch and Sunday **F3**
Rest – Carte 42/60 €
♦ Sicilian ♦ Friendly ♦
This restaurant has a decidedly Sicilian atmosphere, management and cuisine. Sample the tasty fish dishes and traditional Sicilian cuisine in both dining rooms.

X

La Felicità

via Rovello 3 ✉ 20121 – Ⓜ Cordusio – ☎ 02 865235 – fanglei@cebichina.cn – Fax 02 86 52 35 **F1**
Rest – Carte 17/25 €
♦ Chinese ♦ Family ♦
This simple, well-run Chinese restaurant also serves Vietnamese, Thai and Korean cuisine. Elegant furnishings which are broadly Oriental in style.

X

Artidoro

via Camperio 15 ✉ 20123 – Ⓜ Cairoli – ☎ 02 8057386 – info@artidoro.it – Fax 02 85 91 04 10 – www.artidoro.it
closed 6 to 19 August and Christmas **F1**
Rest – Carte 32/52 €
♦ Regional ♦ Friendly ♦
In the heart of Milan, this tavern with a contemporary décor and young, experienced management, offers Emilian cuisine and musical evenings.

X

La Tavernetta-da Elio

via Fatebenefratelli 30 ✉ 20121 – Ⓜ Montenapoleone – ☎ 02 653441 – ristorante@tavernetta.it – Fax 02 99 98 67 42 – www.tavernetta.it
closed August, 24 December-2 January, Saturday lunch, Sunday and Bank Holidays **G1**
Rest – Carte 33/45 €
♦ Classic ♦ Family ♦
Experience consolidated for over 40 years, a simple, lively and welcoming restaurant, frequented by regulars; classic dishes with Tuscan specialities.

X

Hostaria Borromei

via Borromei 4 ✉ 20123 – Ⓜ Cordusio – ☎ 02 86453760 – Fax 02 86 45 21 78
closed 8 to 31 August, 24 December-7 January, Saturday lunch and Sunday **F2**
Rest – Carte 35/48 €
♦ Mantuan ♦ Family ♦
Housed in an 18C palazzo in the heart of the historic centre, this small restaurant serves traditional, regional cuisine, with the accent on dishes from Mantua. Outdoor dining in the courtyard in summer.

Trattoria Torre di Pisa

via Fiori Chiari 21/5 ✉ 20121 – Ⓜ Lanza – ✆ 02 874877 – Fax 02 80 44 83 – www.trattoriatorredipisa.it
closed 3 weeks August and Saturday lunch **F1**
Rest – Carte 33/59 €
◆ Tuscany ◆ Family ◆
A family-type Tuscan restaurant located at the heart of the characteristic quarter of Brera. Enjoy the cuisine of Dante's homeland at particularly attractive prices.

Masuelli San Marco

viale Umbria 80 ✉ 20135 – Ⓜ Lodi TIBB – ✆ 02 55184138 – prenotazioni@masuellitrattoria.it – Fax 02 54 12 45 12 – www.masuelli-trattoria.com
closed 3 weeks in August, 25 December-6 January, Sunday and Monday lunch *Plan I* **D3**
Rest – Carte 33/47 €
◆ Lombard specialities ◆ Friendly ◆
A rustic atmosphere with a luxurious feel in a typical trattoria, with the same management since 1921; cuisine strongly linked to traditional Lombardy and Piedmont recipes.

Giulio Pane e Ojo

via Muratori 10 ✉ 20135 – Ⓜ Porta Romana – ✆ 02 5456189 – info@giuliopaneojo.com – Fax 02 36 50 46 03 – www.giuliopaneojo.com
closed 15 August, 24 to 26 December and Sunday (except December) **H3**
Rest – Menu 10 € bi – Carte 25/30 €
◆ Roman ◆ Friendly ◆
This rustic, informal osteria, with its young managers, is very popular with locals. The emphasis here is on typically Roman cuisine, with simpler, less expensive options at lunchtime. Visitors are advised to book in advance for dinner.

Dongiò

via Corio 3 ✉ 20135 – Ⓜ Porta Romana – ✆ 02 5511372 – tosame@dongio.com – Fax 02 5 51 03 71
closed Easter, August, 2 weeks at Christmas, Saturday lunch and Sunday **H3**
Rest – Carte 22/33 €
◆ Calabrian specialities ◆ Family ◆
This typical, family-run trattoria has a simple décor and friendly atmosphere. Specialities on the menu include fresh pasta, meat and dishes from Calabria.

Trattoria la Piola

via Perugino 18 ✉ 20135 – ✆ 02 55195945 – info@lapiola.it – Fax 02 55 19 59 45 – www.lapiola.it
closed Easter, August, 24 December-2 January, Saturday lunch and Sunday *Plan I* **D2**
Rest – Carte 33/57 €
◆ Fish ◆ Rustic ◆
At this well-run trattoria, the variety of enticing fish menus is the key to their continued success.

CENTRAL STATION *Plan III*

Principe di Savoia

piazza della Repubblica 17 ✉ 20124 – Ⓜ Repubblica – ✆ 02 62301 – principe@hotelprincipedisavoia.com – Fax 02 6 59 58 38 – www.hotelprincipedisavoia.com **M2**
337 rm – †420/830 € ††480/1010 €, ☕ 45 € – 64 suites
Rest Acanto – see below
◆ Palace ◆ Grand Luxury ◆ Stylish ◆
Period furniture, luxury, and sophistication predominate in this19th-century building with an international appeal. There are also sports facilities and a health centre.

The Westin Palace

piazza della Repubblica 20 ✉ 20124 – Ⓜ Repubblica – ✆ 02 63361 – palacemilan@westin.com – Fax 02 65 44 85 – www.westin.com **M2**

228 rm – †300/790 € ††330/920 €, ☕ 35 €

Rest *Casanova* – Carte 72/89 €

◆ Grand Luxury ◆ Stylish ◆

This luxury hotel in a modern tower has rooms with designer furnishings and spacious lounge areas. This plush renovated restaurant has a private room and serves international cuisine.

Le Meridien Gallia

piazza Duca d'Aosta 9 ✉ 20124 – Ⓜ Centrale FS – ✆ 02 67851 – reservations@excelsiorgallia.it – Fax 02 6 71 32 39 – www.starwoodhotels.com **M1**

237 rm – †240/505 € ††295/600 €, ☕ 34 € – 13 suites

Rest – Carte 70/100 €

◆ Palace ◆ Classic ◆

Spacious public areas furnished in warm tones, elegant guestrooms, a beauty centre and gym are some of the features of this luxury hotel, which has long been a favourite with politicians and celebrities. An elegant and professionally run restaurant specialising in cuisine from the Lombardy region and the Mediterranean.

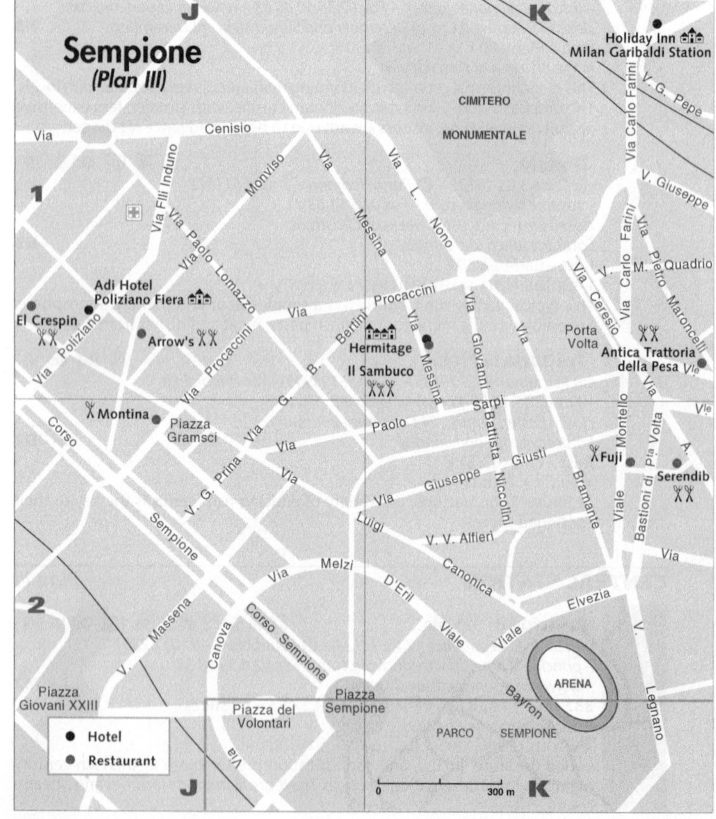

Jolly Hotel Touring

via Tarchetti 2 ✉ 20121 – Ⓜ Repubblica – ☎ 02 63351
– milano_touring@jollyhotels.com – Fax 02 6 59 22 09
– www.jollyhotels.com

M2

282 rm – 199/379 € 239/469 €
Rest – Carte 40/53 €

♦ Chain hotel ♦ Functional ♦

This hotel caters mostly to business travellers and has recently refurbished the lounge areas. Friendly reception and excellent service. Very near the centre of town. Typical regional dishes are served in these cosy, stylish surroundings.

Atahotel Executive without rest

viale Luigi Sturzo 45 ✉ 20154 – Ⓜ Porta Garibaldi FS – ☎ 02 62941
– prenotazioni.executive@atahotels.it – Fax 02 29 01 02 38
– www.hotel-executive.com

L1

414 rm – 278/378 € 338/458 € – 6 suites

♦ Chain hotel ♦ Classic ♦

Situated opposite the Garibaldi railway station, this large hotel with its well-equipped conference centre is ideal for business clients and meetings. The guestrooms are attractive and comfortable.

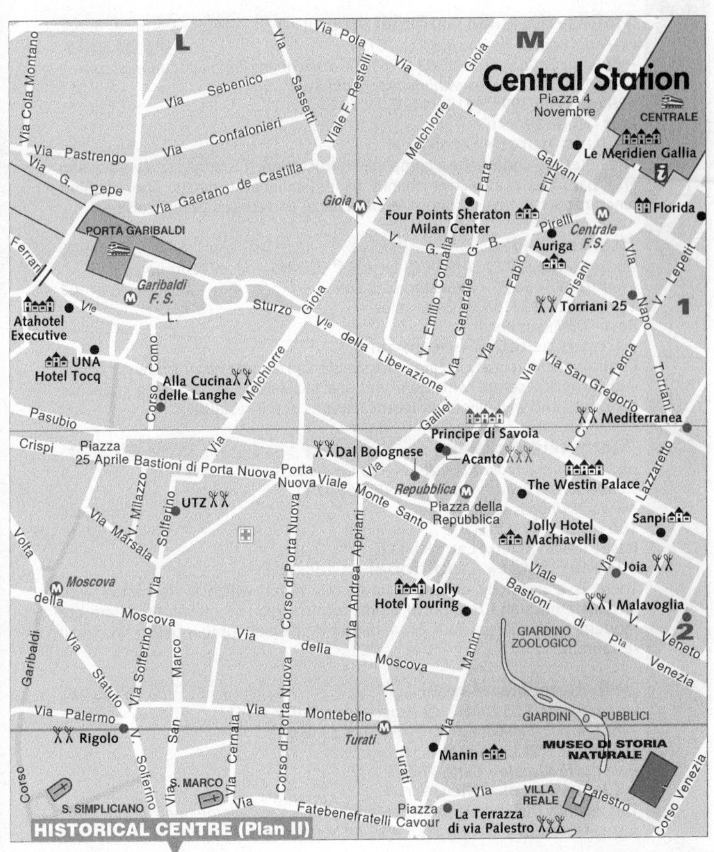

Four Points Sheraton Milan Center
via Cardano 1 ✉ 20124 – Ⓜ Gioia – ✆ 02 667461
– info@fourpointsmilano.it – Fax 02 6 70 30 24
– www.fourpointsmilano.it **M1**
254 rm – 🛉370 € 🛉🛉420 €, ☕ 25 €
Rest – Carte 37/63 €
♦ Chain hotel ♦ Modern ♦
Housed in a modern building in the centre of Milan, this hotel offers relaxing public areas furnished in a simple, elegant style, as well as pleasant and comfortable guestrooms. A bright dining room with tasteful décor.

UNA Hotel Tocq
via A. de Tocqueville 7/D ✉ 20154 – Ⓜ Porta Garibaldi FS – ✆ 02 62071
– una.tocq@unahotels.it – Fax 02 6 57 07 80 – www.unahotels.it **L1**
109 rm ☕ – 🛉🛉115/568 € – 13 suites
Rest – Carte 38/49 €
♦ Chain hotel ♦ Business ♦ Design ♦
Modern design is the key feature of this hotel, with its subtle, minimalist furnishings. Fully equipped with all the facilities expected of a contemporary hotel. Main dining room of the restaurant with summer colours and natural Danish oak parquet flooring.

Holiday Inn Milan Garibaldi Station
via Farini angolo via Ugo Bassi ✉ 20154
– Ⓜ Porta Garibaldi FS – ✆ 02 6076801 – reservations@himilangaribaldi.com
– Fax 02 6 88 07 64 – www.himilangaribaldi.com **K1**
129 rm – 🛉99/399 € 🛉🛉139/449 €, ☕ 18 €
Rest – Carte 39/59 €
♦ Chain hotel ♦ Design ♦
The hotel has undergone a complete restructuring. It is bright and welcoming and particularly attractive thanks to its minimalist décor. The pleasant lunch-room has a glass cupola. Modern décor and contemporary cuisine.

Starhotels Ritz
via Spallanzani 40 ✉ 20129 – Ⓜ Lima – ✆ 02 2055 – ritz.mi@starhotels.it
– Fax 02 29 51 86 79 – www.starhotels.com *Plan I* **C2**
187 rm ☕ – 🛉🛉115/550 € – 6 suites
Rest – *(résidents only)*
♦ Chain hotel ♦ Functional ♦
Centrally located in a quiet area, this simple and elegant hotel is now equipped with a health centre with gym and spa facilities. A large dining room for banquets, and wall paintings are the features of this restaurant.

Starhotels Anderson
piazza Luigi di Savoia 20 ✉ 20124 – Ⓜ Centrale FS – ✆ 02 6690141
– anderson.mi@starhotels.it – Fax 02 6 69 03 31
– www.starhotels.com *Plan I* **C1**
106 rm ☕ – 🛉🛉109/600 €
Rest – *(résidents only)* Carte 33/43 €
♦ Chain hotel ♦ Traditional ♦ Classic ♦
There is a distinctly exclusive air to this hotel, which is decorated with elegant fabrics and traditional ethnic furnishings. The guestrooms here are modern, light and spacious. Have dinner in the elegant lounges in this small restaurant.

Jolly Hotel Machiavelli
via Lazzaretto 5 ✉ 20124 – Ⓜ Repubblica – ✆ 02 631141
– machiavelli@jollyhotels.com – Fax 02 6 59 98 00 **M2**
103 rm ☕ – 🛉🛉330/540 €
Rest ***Caffè Niccolò*** – Carte 37/52 €
♦ Chain hotel ♦ Modern ♦
This recently built hotel has simple, bright rooms and a large open lounge area. A small restaurant serving à la carte and buffet meals.

Adi Doria Grand Hotel — AC rm VISA AE

viale Andrea Doria 22 ✉ 20124 – Ⓜ Caiazzo – ✆ 02 67411411
– info.doriagrandhotel@adihotels.com – Fax 02 6 69 66 69
– www.adihotels.com — *Plan I* **C1**

124 rm – 165/285 € 225/375 € – 2 suites

Rest – *(closed 28 July-26 August and 24 December-6 January)* Carte 37/64 €

♦ Business ♦ Personalised ♦

A classical building with an elegant lobby furnished in early-20C style and large, comfortable guestrooms. Cultural and musical events are occasionally held in the spacious public areas. This small, bright restaurant serves fine regional cuisine in elegant surroundings.

Manin — AC rm VISA AE

via Manin 7 ✉ 20121 – Ⓜ Palestro – ✆ 02 6596511 – info@hotelmanin.it
– Fax 02 6 55 21 60 – www.hotelmanin.it
closed 9 to 31 August — **M2**

118 rm – 120/240 € 140/324 €

Rest *Il Bettolino* – *(closed Saturday)* Carte 41/53 €

♦ Business ♦ Classic ♦

A hotel in the busy cultural heart of the city, with large, simply furnished guestrooms. Charming decoration above the beds. Traditional cuisine served in a quiet, cosy atmosphere.

Sanpi without rest — AC VISA AE

via Lazzaro Palazzi 18 ✉ 20124 – Ⓜ Venezia – ✆ 02 29513341
– info@hotelsanpimilano.it – Fax 02 29 40 24 51 – www.hotelsanpimilano.it
closed 24 December-2 January — **M2**

79 rm – 100/370 € 110/470 €

♦ Business ♦ Classic ♦

Comprising three buildings in the heart of the city, this quiet hotel has well-lit public areas and guestrooms decorated in pastel shades. There is a small garden in the internal courtyard.

Auriga without rest — AC VISA AE

via Giovanni Battista Pirelli 7 ✉ 20124 – Ⓜ Centrale FS – ✆ 02 66985851
– auriga@auriga-milano.com – Fax 02 66 98 06 98
– www.auriga-milano.com
closed 3 to 26 August and 21 December-7 January — **M1**

52 rm – 105/230 € 160/300 €

♦ Business ♦ Personalised ♦

The mix of styles, unusual façade and bright colours of this hotel combine to create a striking exterior. Comfortable facilities and efficient service for tourists and business travellers alike.

Florida without rest — AC VISA AE

via Lepetit 33 ✉ 20124 – Ⓜ Centrale FS – ✆ 02 6705921
– info@hotelfloridamilan.com – Fax 02 6 69 28 67
– www.hotelfloridamilan.com — **M1**

55 rm – 80/135 € 120/210 €

♦ Family ♦ Classic ♦

This modern hotel offers simple but spacious rooms furnished in a clean, geometrical style. A small office inside the hotel is available for business meetings.

Acanto – Hotel Principe di Savoia — AC VISA AE

piazza della Repubblica 17 ✉ 20124 – Ⓜ Repubblica – ✆ 02 62302026
– acanto@hotelprincipedisavoia.com – Fax 02 62 30 40 93 — **M2**

Rest – Carte 81/111 €

♦ Classic ♦ Formal ♦

This recently renovated restaurant occupies a modern, elegant building with large windows overlooking a garden. Classic, contemporary cuisine.

XXX **Gold**

via Poerio 2/A ✉ 20129 – Ⓜ Venezia – ✆ 02 7577771 – Fax 02 75 77 77 20 – www.dolcegabbanagold.it

closed Easter, 4 to 27 August and 22 December-3 January Plan I **C2**

Rest – *(dinner only)* Carte 60/80 €

Rest *Bistrot Gold* – – Carte 42/54 €

♦ Modern ♦ Fashionable ♦

This modern, contemporary-style restaurant furnished with large round tables is the creation of two leading names in the fashion world. Smoking room. Informal and yet elegant, the bistro serves food throughout the day.

XXX **La Terrazza di Via Palestro**

via Palestro 2 ✉ 20121 – Ⓜ Turati – ✆ 02 76002186 – terrazzapalestro@esperiaristorazione.it – Fax 02 76 00 33 28 – www.esperiaristorazione.it

closed August, 22 December-6 January, Saturday and Sunday **M2**

Rest – Carte 63/103 €

♦ Classic ♦ Formal ♦

This fourth-floor restaurant with covered terrace overlooks the public gardens. The mainly fish menu is innovative.

XX **Dal Bolognese**

piazza della Repubblica 13 ✉ 20124 – Ⓜ Repubblica – ✆ 02 626948 – dalbolognese@virgilio.it – Fax 02 62 69 48

closed August, Christmas, New Year's day, Saturday lunch and Sunday **M2**

Rest – Carte 49/74 €

♦ Classic ♦ Friendly ♦

Find muted colors and a lively atmosphere in this deluxe bistrot-style bar. Classic cuisine is served, and outside dining is available in the summer.

XX **Mediterranea**

piazza Cincinnato 4 ✉ 20124 – Ⓜ Venezia – ✆ 02 29522076 – ristmediterranea@fastwebnet.it – Fax 02 20 11 56 – www.ristorantemediterranea.it

closed 5 to 25 August, 30 December-10 January, Sunday and Monday lunch **M1-2**

Rest – Carte 40/63 €

♦ Fish ♦ Formal ♦

This friendly restaurant with walls decorated with picturesque views of Italy, serves fish dishes and has a good selection of wines.

XX **Joia** (Pietro Leemann)

via Panfilo Castaldi 18 ✉ 20124 – Ⓜ Repubblica – ✆ 02 29522124 – joia@joia.it – Fax 02 2 04 92 44 – www.joia.it

closed 4 to 25 August, Saturday lunch and Sunday **M2**

Rest – Menu 60/100 € – Carte 62/84 €

Spec. Appunti di viaggio (spuma di parmigiano, balsamico stravecchio e altri contrasti). Volontà (pasta leggermente arrostita con tre salse in contrasto). Sotto una coltre colorata (composizione di funghi, verdure e altri gusti).

♦ Inventive ♦ Minimalist ♦

One of the most unusual and distinctive restaurants in Milan, the Joia serves mainly vegetarian food, with some fish dishes. Creative, innovative cuisine.

XX **Torriani 25**

via Napo Torriani 25 ✉ 20124 – Ⓜ Centrale FS – ✆ 02 67078183 – acena@torriani25.it – Fax 02 67 47 95 48 – www.torriani25.it

closed 9 to 26 August, 25 December-1 January, Saturday lunch and Sunday **M1**

Rest – Carte 35/49 €

♦ Fish ♦ Design ♦

This modern restaurant is decorated in warm colours, with plenty of natural light. Choose from a wide selection of fish - the house speciality - on display on the buffet in the dining room.

XX

I Malavoglia

via Lecco 4 ✉ 20124 – Ⓜ Venezia – ✆ 02 29531387 – www.ristorante-imalavoglia.com

closed Easter, 1 May, August, 24 December-7 January and Sunday **M2**

Rest – *(dinner only)* Carte 44/64 €

♦ Sicilian ♦ Family ♦

This classic restaurant has been run by the same team for over thirty years. They serve typical Sicilian dishes in Lombardy's capital.

XX

Rigolo

largo Treves ang. via Solferino 11 ✉ 20121 – Ⓜ Moscova – ✆ 02 804589 – ristorante.rigolo@tiscalinet.it – Fax 02 86 46 32 20 – www.rigolo.it

closed August and Monday **L2**

Rest – Carte 30/41 €

♦ Classic ♦ Retro ♦

Managed by the same family for over 40 years, this traditional restaurant situated in a fashionable part of the city centre is popular with locals. Meat and fish dishes are served in the elegant dining rooms.

XX

Alla Cucina delle Langhe

corso Como 6 ✉ 20154 – Ⓜ Porta Garibaldi FS – ✆ 02 6554279 – Fax 02 29 00 68 59

closed August, Saturday in July and Sunday **L1**

Rest – Carte 35/50 €

♦ Piedmontese specialities ♦ Friendly ♦

The typical atmosphere of this beautiful trattoria is in keeping with the traditional Lombard and Piedmontese specialities served here. Comprehensive salad buffet.

XX

UTZ

via Solferino 48 ✉ 20121 – Ⓜ Moscova – ✆ 02 6551180 – parla@utz-foodemotion.net – Fax 02 31 52 22 – www.utz-foodemotion.net

closed 2 weeks in August, 2 weeks at Christmas, Saturday lunch and Monday **L2**

Rest – Carte 33/45 €

♦ Inventive ♦ Friendly ♦

The young, dynamic management at this restaurant offers an eclectic cuisine. The colourful décor recalls Iberian folklore. It also serves pizzas and Sunday brunch.

XX

Antica Trattoria della Pesa

viale Pasubio 10 ✉ 20154 – Ⓜ Porta Garibaldi FS – ✆ 02 6555741 – Fax 02 29 01 51 57

closed August and Sunday **K1**

Rest – Carte 43/62 €

♦ Lombard specialities ♦ Rustic ♦

A delightfully old-time atmosphere obtains in this Milanese trattoria that has entered into Italian history; the cuisine is consistently faithful to the Lombardian tradition. One of the rooms is dedicated to Ho Chi Minh.

XX

Casa Fontana-23 Risotti

piazza Carbonari 5 ✉ 20125 – Ⓜ Sondrio – ✆ 02 6704710 – trattoria@23risotti.it – Fax 02 66 80 04 65 – www.23risotti.it

closed 25 to 29 March, 24 June-14 July, 1 to 9 January, Monday, Saturday lunch and Saturday dinner-Sunday in July-August *Plan I* **C1**

Rest – Carte 35/49 €

♦ Lombard specialities ♦ Cosy ♦

Despite its location in the suburbs and the obligatory 25-minute wait for your food, this small, friendly restaurant is well worth a visit for its excellent risottos.

XX **Serendib**

via Pontida 2 ✉ 20121 – Ⓜ Moscova – ☏ 02 6592139 – surange@email.it – Fax 02 6 59 21 39 – www.serendib.it
closed 10 to 20 August **K2**
Rest – *(dinner only)* Carte 20/25 €
♦ Indian ♦ Friendly ♦
Loyal to the original both in the decoration and in the Indian and "cingalese" cuisine, is a pleasant establishment which bears the old name of Sri Lanka ("to make people happy").

X **La Cantina di Manuela**

via Poerio 3 ✉ 20129 – Ⓜ Venezia – ☏ 02 76318892 – info@lacantinadimanuela.it – Fax 02 76 31 29 71 – www.lacantinadimanuela.it
closed Sunday *Plan I* **C2**
Rest – Carte 30/38 €
♦ Classic ♦ Wine bar ♦
This restaurant has an especially interesting wine list that accompanies its excellent cooking. A few tables are put on the path outside during summer.

X **Da Giannino-L'Angolo d'Abruzzo**

via Pilo 20 ✉ 20129 – Ⓜ Venezia – ☏ 02 29406526 – Fax 02 29 40 65 26
closed August and Monday *Plan I* **D2**
Rest – Carte 17/30 €
♦ Abruzzian specialities ♦ Friendly ♦
Visitors can expect a warm welcome in this simple, cheerful and popular restaurant. Generous portions of typical Abruzzi cuisine.

X **Baia Chia**

via Bazzini 37 ✉ 20131 – Ⓜ Piola – ☏ 02 2361131 – fabrizio.papetti@fastwebnet.it – Fax 02 2 36 11 31
closed Easter, 3 weeks in August, 24 December-2 January, Sunday and Monday lunch *Plan I* **D1**
Rest – Carte 24/35 €
♦ Sardinian specialities ♦ Family ♦
This is a pleasant establishment with a family atmosphere that is divided into several dining areas. Sample delicious fish dishes, savoury specialities and Sardinian wines.

X **Fuji**

viale Montello 9 ✉ 20154 – Ⓜ Moscova – ☏ 02 29008349 – Fax 02 29 00 35 92
closed Easter, 1 to 23 August, 24 December-2 January and Sunday **K2**
Rest – *(dinner only)* Carte 35/48 €
♦ Japanese ♦ Minimalist ♦
Jointly managed by its Italian and Japanese owners for the past 10 years, this simple Japanese restaurant has hit on a winning formula. The restaurant also has a sushi bar next door.

FIERA-SEMPIONE *Plan I*

Hermitage

via Messina 10 ✉ 20154 – Ⓜ Porta Garibaldi FS – ☏ 02 318170 – hermitage.res@monrifhotels.it – Fax 02 33 10 73 99 – www.monrifhotels.it
closed August *Plan III* **K1**
131 rm – †200/320 € ††280/490 € – 10 suites
Rest Il Sambuco – see below
♦ Business ♦ Stylish ♦
Style and comfort are the trademarks of this hotel which combines the atmosphere of elegant period-style interiors with modern facilities; popular with models and other celebrities.

Milan Marriott Hotel
via Washington 66 ✉ 20146 – Ⓜ Wagner – ✆ 02 4852020 – milan@marriothotels.com – Fax 02 4 81 89 25 – www.marriott.com **A2**
322 rm – ††192/390 €, ☕ 24 €
Rest *La Brasserie de Milan* – ✆ 02 48522834 – Carte 49/77 €
◆ Chain hotel ◆ Modern ◆
Original contrast between the modern building and the imposing classic interiors of a hotel clearly geared towards Conference and Trade Fair business clientele; functional period style bedrooms. Restaurant dining room with the kitchen in full view; classical style.

Enterprise Hotel
corso Sempione 91 ✉ 20154 – ✆ 02 318181 – info@enterprisehotel.com – Fax 02 31 81 88 11 – www.enterprisehotel.com **A1**
123 rm ☕ – †123/590 € ††133/630 €
Rest *Sophia's* – ✆ 02 31818855 – Carte 54/106 €
◆ Business ◆ Design ◆
Attention to detail and design is evident in every aspect of this elegant modern hotel, from the marble and granite exterior to its bespoke furnishings and pleasing geometrical lines. A pleasant and original restaurant for lunch and dinner. Outdoor dining in summer.

Atahotel Fieramilano
viale Boezio 20 ✉ 20145 – ✆ 02 336221 – booking.fieramilano@atahotels.it – Fax 02 31 41 19 – www.atahotels.it
closed August **B2**
238 rm ☕ – †99/250 € ††119/330 € – 2 suites
Rest *Ambrosiano* – Carte 30/49 €
◆ Chain hotel ◆ Modern ◆
This tastefully furnished hotel opposite the Fiera Milano offers modern and comfortable rooms. In summer, breakfast is served in a gazebo in the garden. Quiet, elegant dining room.

Capitol World Class
via Cimarosa 6 ✉ 20144 – Ⓜ Pagano – ✆ 02 438591 – info@capitolmilano.com – Fax 02 4 69 47 24 – www.capitolmilano.com **B2**
66 rm ☕ – †160/280 € ††225/428 €
Rest – *(closed 10 to 20 August and 23 December-3 January)* Carte 41/65 €
◆ Business ◆ Personalised ◆
An elegant, modern hotel with warm, traditional touches both in its public areas and the fully equipped guestrooms, many of which overlook a peaceful internal courtyard. Have dinner on the terrace or in the elegant dining room.

Regency without rest
via Arimondi 12 ✉ 20155 – ✆ 02 39216021 – regency@regency-milano.com – Fax 02 39 21 77 34 – www.regency-milano.com
closed 1 to 25 August and 20 December-7 January **A1**
71 rm ☕ – †100/210 € ††150/300 € – 2 suites
◆ Traditional ◆ Personalised ◆
This charming mansion dating from the late 19C is built around a delightful courtyard. Stylish interior furnishings, including an elegant living room with a real open fire.

Adi Poliziano Fiera without rest
via Poliziano 11 ✉ 20154 – ✆ 02 3191911 – info.hotelpolizianofiera@adihotels.com – Fax 02 3 19 19 31 – www.adihotels.com
closed 27 July-26 August and 25 December-7 January *Plan III* **J1**
100 rm ☕ – †166/310 € ††186/360 € – 2 suites
◆ Business ◆ Modern ◆
Friendly, attentive service and spacious guestrooms furnished in light green and sand-coloured tones compensate for the rather small public areas in this modern hotel.

Wagner without rest — AC VISA MC AE D

via Buonarroti 13 – Ⓜ Wagner – ☎ 02 463151
– wagner@roma-wagner.com – Fax 02 48 02 09 48
– www.roma-wagner.com
closed 12 to 19 August **A2**
48 rm ☕ – 🚹119/398 € 🚹🚹149/498 € – 1 suite
♦ Business ♦ Personalised ♦
This hotel, next to the eponymous metro station, has attractive rooms with marble and modern furnishings.

Rubens — Fō AC ⊬rm SÀ P VISA MC AE D

via Rubens 21 ✉ 20148 – Ⓜ Gambara – ☎ 02 40302
– rubens@antareshotels.com – Fax 02 48 19 31 14 – www.antareshotels.com
closed 1 to 24 August **A2**
87 rm ☕ – 🚹90/270 € 🚹🚹99/350 €
Rest – Carte 31/42 €
♦ Business ♦ Personalised ♦
The spacious, comfortable guestrooms in this elegant hotel are adorned with frescoes by contemporary artists and furnished in stylish purple and cobalt-blue tones.

Accademia — AC ⊬rm SÀ VISA MC AE D

viale Certosa 68 ✉ 20155 – ☎ 02 39211122 – accademia@antareshotels.com
– Fax 02 33 10 38 78 – www.antareshotels.com
closed 4 to 17 August **A1**
67 rm ☕ – 🚹270 € 🚹🚹350 €
Rest – *(residents only)* Carte 30/50 €
♦ Business ♦ Personalised ♦
A modern feel, new rooms with designer-style furnishings, and relaxing public areas are some of the features of this attractive, recently refurbished hotel.

Mirage — ♿rm AC ⊬rm SÀ 🚗 VISA MC AE D

viale Certosa 104/106 ✉ 20156 – ☎ 02 39210471 – mirage@gruppomirage.it
– Fax 02 39 21 05 89 – www.gruppomirage.it
closed 1 to 24 August and 24 December-4 January **A1**
86 rm ☕ – 🚹102/206 € 🚹🚹142/269 €
Rest – *(closed Friday and Saturday) (dinner only) (residents only)*
Carte 34/44 €
♦ Business ♦ Functional ♦
Not far from the Trade Fair complex, this hotel offers simply furnished public areas and guestrooms renovated in classical style; the bathrooms are decorated with large tiles or mosaics.

Astoria without rest — AC ⊬ SÀ VISA MC AE D

viale Murillo 9 ✉ 20149 – Ⓜ Lotto – ☎ 02 40090095
– info@astoriahotelmilano.com – Fax 02 40 07 46 42
– www.astoriahotelmilano.com **A2**
68 rm ☕ – 🚹80/250 € 🚹🚹90/380 € – 1 suite
♦ Business ♦ Functional ♦
This hotel that caters mostly to business travellers is located along a ring road. The rooms are modern and soundproof.

Des Etrangers without rest — ♿ AC ⊬ SÀ 🚗 VISA MC AE D

via Sirte 9 ✉ 20146 – ☎ 02 48955325 – info@hde.it – Fax 02 48 95 53 59
– www.hoteldesetrangers.it
closed 8 to 24 August **A3**
94 rm ☕ – 🚹70/180 € 🚹🚹80/220 €
♦ Family ♦ Classic ♦
This well-maintained hotel in a quiet street offers its guests functional and comfortable public areas and guestrooms, as well as convenient underground parking.

Antica Locanda Leonardo without rest

corso Magenta 78 ✉ 20123 – Ⓜ Conciliazione – ✆ 02 48014197 – info@anticalocandaleonardo.com – Fax 02 48 01 90 12 – www.anticalocandaleonardo.com

closed 5 to 25 August and 31 December-6 January — *Plan II* **E2**

16 rm – 🛉95/105 € 🛉🛉150/230 €

♦ Inn ♦ Cosy ♦

The luxury atmosphere combines with the family-style welcome in a hotel which overlooks a small inner courtyard, in an ideal location near the place where Leonardo da Vinci's painting of the "Last Supper" is housed.

Il Luogo di Aimo e Nadia (Aimo Moroni)

via Montecuccoli 6 ✉ 20147 – Ⓜ Primaticcio – ✆ 02 416886 – info@aimoenadia.com – Fax 02 48 30 20 05 – www.aimoenadia.com

closed 24 to 29 March, 2 to 26 August, 1 to 9 January, Saturday lunch and Sunday — **A3**

Rest – Carte 85/136 €

Spec. Lo scampone: marinato con granita di mela e verbena, croccante al cipollotto e miele, crudo con cous cous ai porcini (summer-autumn). Petti di piccione al tè invecchiato, coscette in brodo di fagiano alla verbena con raviolo di fichi. Tria di cioccolati: bavarese con mousse di Arriba, mojito di Trinitario ghiacciato, ricotta candita e cedro in Ghana affumicato.

♦ Contemporary ♦ Formal ♦

A leading light of the city's culinary scene, this restaurant, with an impressive display of modern works of art, has cuisine memorable for its creativity.

La Pobbia 1850

via Gallarate 92 ✉ 20151 – ✆ 02 38006641 – lapobbia@lapobbia.com – Fax 02 38 00 07 24 – www.lapobbia.com

closed August and Sunday — **A1**

Rest – Carte 50/68 €

♦ Lombard specialities ♦ Formal ♦

This 19C tavern is now an elegant restaurant with an interior garden. It serves traditional Lombard and international cuisine. There is also an area set aside for smokers.

Il Sambuco – Hotel Hermitage

via Messina 10 ✉ 20154 – Ⓜ Porta Garibaldi FS – ✆ 02 33610333 – info@ilsambuco.it – Fax 02 33 61 18 50 – www.ilsambuco.it

closed Easter, 1 to 20 August, 25 December-3 January, Saturday lunch and Sunday — *Plan III* **K1**

Rest – Carte 72/87 €

♦ Fish ♦ Trendy ♦

Like the hotel of which it is a part, this restaurant is characterised by elegant décor and attentive service. The cuisine is renowned for its seafood specialities and, on Mondays, for its dishes of boiled meat.

Arrow's

via Mantegna 17/19 ✉ 20154 – ✆ 02 341533 – Fax 02 33 10 64 96

closed August, Sunday and Monday lunch — *Plan III* **J1**

Rest – Carte 37/64 €

♦ Fish ♦ Formal ♦

Packed, even at midday, the atmosphere becomes cosier in the evening but the seafood cuisine, prepared according to tradition, remains the same.

El Crespin

via Castelvetro 18 ✉ 20154 – ✆ 02 33103004 – elcrespin@hotmail.it – Fax 02 33 10 30 04 – www.pagine.gialle.it/elcrespin

closed August, 26 December-7 January, Saturday and Sunday — *Plan III* **J1**

Rest – *(dinner only)* Carte 34/43 €

♦ Classic ♦ Friendly ♦

The entrance of this restaurant is decorated with period photos, while the dining room is tastefully furnished in a simple, modern style. Both meat and fish dishes feature on the menu.

Innocenti Evasioni

via privata della Bindellina ✉ 20155 – ✆ 02 33001882
– ristorante@innocentievasioni.com – Fax 02 33 00 18 82
– www.innocentievasioni.com
closed August, 3 to 9 January and Sunday **A1**
Rest – *(dinner only)* Carte 43/54 €
♦ Innovative ♦ Cosy ♦
This pleasant establishment, with large windows facing the garden, offers classic cuisine reinterpreted with imagination. Enjoyable outdoor summer dining.

Trattoria Montina

via Procaccini 54 ✉ 20154 – Ⓜ Porta Garibaldi FS – ✆ 02 3490498
closed August 25 December-5 January, Sunday and Monday lunch *Plan III* **J2**
Rest – Carte 28/40 €
♦ Classic ♦ Friendly ♦
Nice bistro atmosphere, tables close together, defused lighting in the evening in an establishment managed by twin brothers; seasonal national and Milanese dishes.

Pace

via Washington 74 ✉ 20146 – Ⓜ Wagner – ✆ 02 43983058 – Fax 02 46 85 67
closed Easter, 1 to 24 August, 24 December-5 January,
Saturday lunch and Wednesday **A2-3**
Rest – Carte 25/35 €
♦ Classic ♦ Rustic ♦
This very popular family-run trattoria has been providing cordial hospitality for over 30 years. The surroundings are simple and the menu traditional.

Al Molo 13

via Rubens 13 ✉ 20148 – Ⓜ De Angelis – ✆ 02 4042743 – info@molo13.it
– Fax 02 40 07 26 16 – www.molo13.it
closed August, 31 December-9 January, Sunday and Monday lunch **A2**
Rest – Carte 39/77 €
♦ Fish ♦ Rustic ♦
The two colourful dining rooms of this restaurant are adorned with paintings and ceramics which give a Sardinian flavour to the décor. Specialities include seafood dishes and typical Sardinian cuisine. Generous portions.

LUXEMBOURG
LËTZEBUERG

PROFILE

→ **Area:**
2 586 km² (998 sq mi).

→ **Population:**
468 600 inhabitants (est. 2005) nearly 62% nationals, 38% resident foreigners (mostly Belgian, French, German, Italian and Portuguese). Density = 181 per km².

→ **Capital:**
Luxembourg (conurbation 125 000 inhabitants).

→ **Currency:**
Euro (€); rate of exchange: € 1 = US$ 1.46 (Dec 2007).

→ **Government:**
Constitutional parliamentary monarchy (since 1868). Member of European Union since 1957 (one of the 6 founding countries).

→ **Languages:**
The official language is Lëtzebuergesch, a variant of German, similar to the Frankish dialect of the Moselle valley; High German is used for general purposes and is the first language for teaching; French is the literary and administrative language.

→ **Specific public holidays:**
Carnival (Late February-March); National Day (23 June); Luxembourg City Kermesse (early September, applies to the Luxembourg City only); St. Stephen's Day (26 December).

→ **Local Time:**
GMT + 1 hour in winter and GMT + 2 hours in summer.

→ **Climate:**
Temperate continental with cold winters and mild summers (Luxembourg: January: 1°C, July: 17°C).

→ **International dialling Code:**
00 352 followed by the local number of 5 or 6 or (exceptionally) 8 figures. Online telephone directory: www.editus.lu

→ **Emergency numbers:**
Police : ✆ **113** ; Medical Assistance : ✆ **112**.

→ **Electricity:**
220 volts AC, 50Hz; 2-pin round-shaped continental plugs.

→ **Formalities**
Travellers from the European Union (EU), Switzerland, Iceland and the main countries of North and South America need a national identity card or passport (America: passport required) to visit the Grand Duchy of Luxembourg for less than three months (tourism or business purpose). For visitors from other countries a visa may be required, in addition to a passport, especially for those wishing to stay for longer than three months. We advise you to check with your embassy before travelling.

LUXEMBOURG
LËTZEBUERG

Population (est 2004): 77 400 (conurbation 125 000) – Altitude: 300m

N. Rung/Author's Image/PHOTONONSTOP

Luxembourg may be small but it's perfectly formed. And perfectly situated. It stands high above two rivers on a sandstone bluff, looking composedly back on a thousand year history that's been anything but composed. Its commanding position over sheer gorges may be a boon to modern day visitors, but down the centuries that very setting of enviable altitude has rendered it the subject of conquest on many occasions.

Its eye-catching geography makes it a city of distinctive districts, linked by spectacular bridges spanning lush green valleys. The city squares boast elegant façades painted in pastel colours, ideally suited as the backdrop to café culture on a warm afternoon. UNESCO liked what they saw, and in 1994 conferred World Heritage Status on the old town. It may not be instantly apparent, but Luxembourg is also a hub of activity for the European Union, with new buildings and offices mushrooming in recent years – thankfully, some way from the old centre. Most visitors head in the opposite direction for wonderful walks in the valleys and across the fine bridges, finding this the best way to appreciate the capital's uniquely charming aura.

LIVING THE CITY

The absolute heart of the city is the **old town**, unmistakable at the top of its surrounding valleys, its most prominent landmark the **cathedral** spires. Winding its way deep below to the south west is the river **Pétrusse,** which has its confluence with the river **Alzette** in the south east. Directly to the south of the old town is the rather sleazy **railway station** quarter, while down at river level to the east is the altogether more attractive **Grund** district, which has northerly neighbours **Clausen** and **Pfaffenthal**. Up in the north east, connected by the grand sounding **Pont Grand-Duchesse Charlotte**, is the EU institution quarter of **Kirchberg Plateau**.

PRACTICAL INFORMATION

ARRIVAL-DEPARTURE

Luxembourg-Findel Airport is 6km from the city centre ; a taxi should cost about €25. Alternatively, take city bus Number 16 which runs every 20min and takes 25min.

TRANSPORT

There's a good bus service in Luxembourg City, but no metro or tram. Buses run from 5am to 10pm each day, and there's an additional late night service on Fridays and Saturdays only. The most convenient bus stations for visitors are at the exit of Gare Centrale and on Place Hamilius in the old town. The fare system (valid for trains too) is simple enough: for trips of 10km or less you buy a 'short' ticket; for an unlimited day ticket (valid till 8am the next day) you buy a Billet Reseau.

You can also opt for the Luxembourg Card. This is valid for one, two or three days and, apart from giving you unlimited use of public transport, also offers free admission to lots of attractions, not just in the city but in other parts of the country too. Available from tourist offices, it's valid throughout the summer. In winter, the Stater Museeskaart offers three days of free admission to important sights in Luxembourg City.

EXPLORING LUXEMBOURG CITY

It's not every city that can boast 'Europe's Most Beautiful Balcony' in its blurb. But Luxembourg can. Along the stunning pedestrian promenade called **Chemin de la Corniche** there are scintillating views over the sheer-sided gorges that give this elegantly compact city a natural aesthetic advantage over so many others. Luxembourg City has taken a battering over the centuries. It's been taken by the Burgundians, Spanish, French, Austrians and Prussians; the stately old defensive walls that remain around the edges of the centre add an extra layer of historic charm to the place.

➜ TAKING UP D'ARMES

The old town, nestled above the gorges, is a true delight. Its narrow streets are home to arty residents, while quirky shops, traditional cafés and fine restaurants enhance the general feel of a city contented in its skin. At the centre is the slightly formal Place Guillaume II, where you'll find the town hall. Most people, though, make a beeline for the **Place d'Armes**, the 'Parlour of the City', lined with sunny pavement terraces in the summer. The feeling of informality is enhanced when you stroll a little way east and come across the **Ducal Grand Palace**. No pomp or circumstance here, despite the fact that Louis XIV and Napoleon called in. Nowadays, with the royals having left some time ago, the Moorish-style palace, built by the Spanish in 1570, is used for functions on the inside, and as a tourist spot for photos on the outside. You're not bothered by traffic or blaring horns, and there's just a single guard on duty. All very peaceful. If you *are* searching out more life, the area right behind the Ducal Palace has several restaurants.

→ HISTORY LESSON

There's a great museum here too, just round the corner from the palace. It's the **National Museum of History and Art**, and its show-stopping white contours come as quite a surprise after the Ducal Grand Palace. It's a state-of-the-art affair, with a glass atrium and exhibits housed over several levels. They range from the 13C to the present day and highlights include a superb Roman mosaic, absorbing works by Luxembourg's Expressionist artist Joseph Kutter, paintings by Cézanne, Picasso and Magritte, and a watercolour of the city by Turner. South from here, you can indulge a comprehensive primer on the life and times of this underestimated city at the impressive **Luxembourg City History Museum**, which, over six floors, does pretty much what it says on the label.

Luxembourg City has raised itself above the museum parapet and shone a light into the 21C with its brand new **Museum of Modern Art,** opened in 2006. Located in the Kirchberg district, it's a stunning white concrete-and-glass palace and home to an eclectic mix of work, including photography, painting, multimedia, fashion, design and graphic arts. Close by, another new building has seen the light of day: the **Luxembourg Philharmonic Hall** is now *the* place to catch a concert in the city. It's not just home to the Philharmonic Orchestra, but also caters to a wide range of styles including jazz and world music. There are three separate concert halls, and you can squeeze in any number from 120 to 1,500.

→ ON THE CASE

From the modern to the extremely ancient – at the end of the wonderful Chemin de la Corniche you arrive at the cliff on which the very first castle was built in 963. It's called **The Bock**, and though its mighty fort and fortifications are now no more than ruins, that's not the case with the **Casemates**. This is a labyrinth of 17C-18C underground defences carved out beneath the Bock by the Spaniards. These rock thoroughfares have known a number of uses down the years. They've seen action as slaughterhouses and bakeries and housed garrisons of soldiers. Many of the locals used them as bomb shelters during the two world wars. Further west, there are more casemates at Pétrusse, but these are slightly less accessible than those at Bock.

→ A GRUND LIFE

Another little world exists below the Bock, and it's called the Grund, or the lower town. It's an attractive area, where the cluster of cafés, bars and restaurants sits easily alongside the meandering Alzette. Its characterful charm is enhanced by clumps of ruins offset by groups of terrace houses, once home to artisans who needed the river waters to assist them in their crafts. There's an easy way to get down here: just take the elevator from the **Plateau du St Esprit**, a hilltop bluff that itself offers stunning views over the valleys and the Grund. Although it pretty much exists in its very own green heaven, Luxembourg has fashioned itself a lovely **park,** and very moreish it is too. It's down in the valley on the same level as the Grund, but west of it in the vicinity of the Pétrusse. Get down to it from the Old Bridge, or Viaduc and, if you're here in the spring, take in the stunning display of magnolias.

CALENDAR HIGHLIGHTS

For a small place, Luxembourg packs a big festive punch. From the end of November until early January, the Winter Lights Festival uses Christmas as the excuse to let rip with street art, theatre, concerts and fireworks. Spring is celebrated with the Printemps Festival, which lasts from March until June. At concert venues throughout the city, internationally acclaimed world music and jazz musicians hold centre stage. The spotlight moves to the city's great outdoors in May with the running of the Luxembourg Marathon. This is a marathon with a difference, held in the evening and to the accompaniment of revellers soaking up the atmosphere at mini festivals in the narrow streets of the old town. Locals keep the evening of 22 June clear in their diaries: this is the eve before National Day, when fireworks are set off from the bridge over the Pétrusse Valley, and there's much partying with music and dancing on Place d'Armes and Place Guillaume II. One of Europe's biggest funfairs has evolved over the centuries from an ancient shepherd's market – it's called Schueberfouer, and it lasts two weeks from the end of August, when seemingly most of the city comes along to watch the lavish fireworks that finish it all off.

EATING OUT

The taste buds of Luxembourg have been very much influenced by French classical cuisine and the results are there for all to savour, particularly around and about the old town, an area that in the summer becomes one smart open-air terrace. The centre of town is in fact an eclectic place to eat. It runs the gauntlet from fast-style pizzeria (there are lots of Italians in the

LUXEMBOURG CITY IN…

→ ONE DAY

Place d'Armes, Ducal Grand Palace, National Museum of History and Art, Chemin de la Corniche

→ TWO DAYS

Leisurely coffee back on Place d'Armes, Luxembourg City History Museum, Bock Casemates, afternoon and evening in the Grund, including a meal in one of its restaurants

→ THREE DAYS

Kirchberg Plateau, Museum of Modern Art, concert at Luxembourg Philharmonic Hall

city), taverns, cafés and brasseries up to expense account restaurants favoured by bankers and businessmen. On winter evenings, though, this part of town can be a bit quiet. A good bet for atmosphere, certainly in the darker months, is the Grund, which offers a variety of restaurants with a wide range of prices. It's certainly the area that boasts the most popular cafés and pubs. A few trendy places have sprouted over recent times near the Casemates, and these too are proving to be pretty hot with the younger crowd. On the menus here look out for the local speciality *Judd mat Gaardebounen*, which is a very hearty smoked neck of pork with broad beans. The Grand Duchy produces its own white and sparkling wines on the borders of the Moselle. These didn't have much of a reputation at first, but over the last decade a number of young winemakers have produced some interesting wines. You'll rarely find these abroad, as they're bought locally by business people and smart restaurants. At the end of your meal, a service charges is included in your bill, but if you want to tip, ten per cent is a reasonable amount.

NOTRE DAMNED

The city's Notre Dame Cathedral is unmissable, what with its black spires reaching up above the rooftops. And inside it has Luxembourg's most revered icon, The Lady Comforter of the Afflicted. But you won't see the city's greatest church in many 'must-see' lists. That's because the rest of the interior is full of renovations and mismatching styles, creating a none to inspiring mishmash. You're better off heading by on your way to the grand views of the Viaduc.

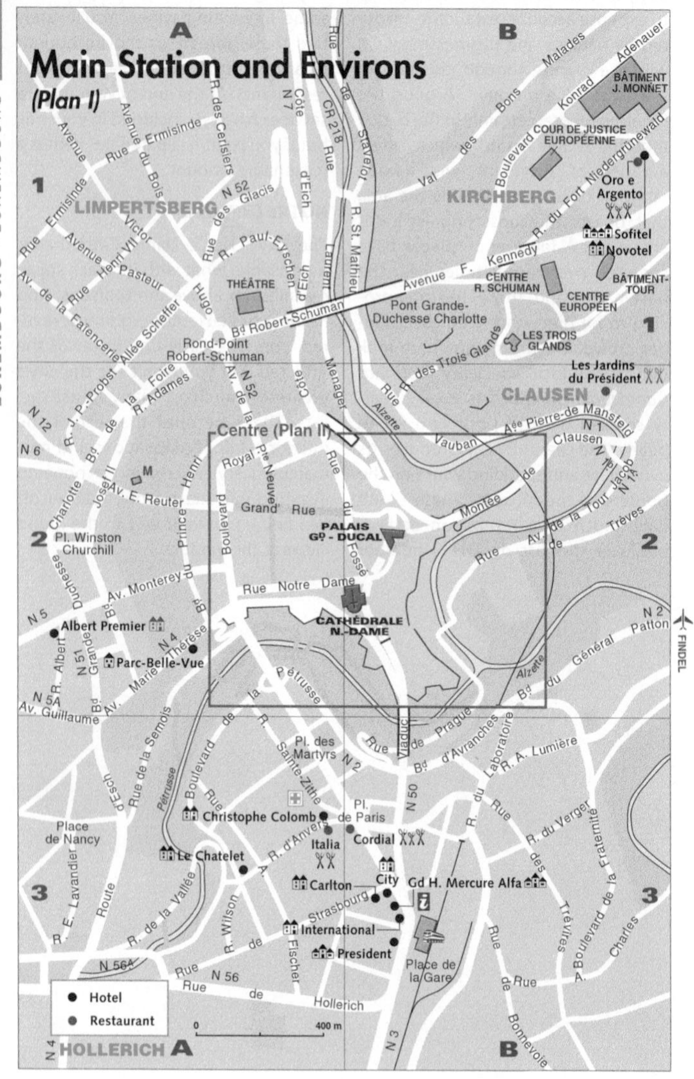
Main Station and Environs
(Plan I)
A
B
1
2
3
LIMPERTSBERG
KIRCHBERG
CLAUSEN
HOLLERICH
THÉÂTRE
Rond-Point Robert-Schuman
Bd Robert-Schuman
Pont Grande-Duchesse Charlotte
Avenue F. Kennedy
BÂTIMENT J. MONNET
COUR DE JUSTICE EUROPÉENNE
Oro e Argento
Sofitel
Novotel
BÂTIMENT-TOUR
CENTRE R. SCHUMAN
CENTRE EUROPÉEN
LES TROIS GLANDS
Les Jardins du Président
Centre (Plan II)
PALAIS Gd - DUCAL
CATHÉDRALE N.-DAME
Grand' Rue
Rue Notre Dame
Pl. Winston Churchill
Albert Premier
Parc-Belle-Vue
Christophe Colomb
Italia
Cordial
Le Chatelet
Carlton
City
Gd H. Mercure Alfa
International
President
Pl. des Martyrs
Pl. de Paris
Place de Nancy
Place de la Gare
Viaduct
FINDEL
Hotel
Restaurant
0
400 m

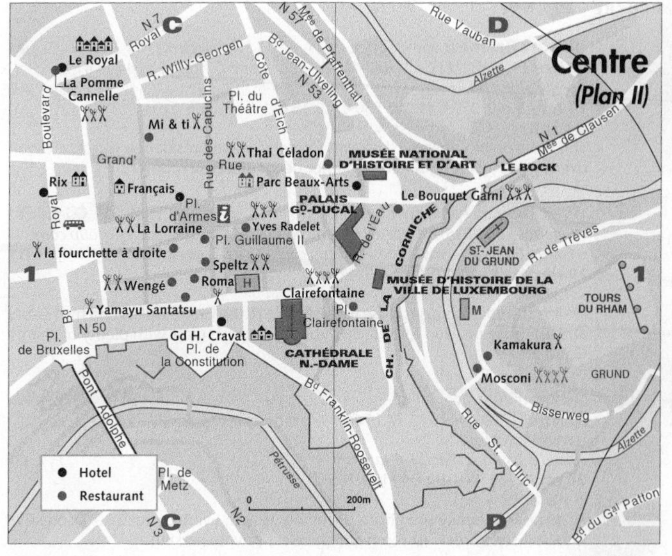

CENTRE — Plan II

Le Royal

bd Royal 12 ✉ 2449 – ✆ 241 61 61 – reservations@leroyalluxembourg.com – Fax 22 59 48 – www.leroyalluxembourg.com **C1**

190 rm – 🚹370/500 € 🚹🚹370/500 €, ☕ 26 € – 20 suites

Rest *La Pomme Cannelle* – see below

Rest *Le Jardin* – *(closed 24 December dinner)* Menu 29 €, 36/39 € – Carte 40/57 €

◆ Grand Luxury ◆ Business ◆ Classic ◆

A modern building at the heart of Luxembourg's "Wall Street" with large, modern and superbly-equipped bedrooms. Top-notch, personalised service around the clock. Mediterranean atmosphere and cuisine in the Le Jardin restaurant. Buffet lunch served on Sundays.

Grand Hôtel Cravat

bd Roosevelt 29 ✉ 2450 – ✆ 22 19 75 – contact@hotelcravat.lu – Fax 22 67 11 – www.hotelcravat.lu **C1**

60 rm ☕ – 🚹215/375 € 🚹🚹345/357 € – 1 suite

Rest *Le Normandy* – 1st floor – Menu 47 € – Carte 47/62 €

Rest *La Taverne* – Menu 13/39 €

◆ Traditional ◆ Business ◆ Classic ◆

This hotel occupies an old building on a panoramic square (affording views over the Pétrusse Valley). Its comfortable, irregularly shaped rooms are classically furnished. Gourmet restaurant at the Normandy (on the first floor). Regional cuisine served at the Taverne on the ground floor.

Parc Belair

av.du X Septembre 111 (by N5) ✉ 2551 – ✆ 442 32 31 – reception.belair@goeres-group.com – Fax 456 14 12 20 – www.goeres-group.com

52 rm ☕ – 🚹260/870 € 🚹🚹282/870 € – 1 suite

Rest – *(closed lunch Saturday, Sunday and Bank Holidays)* Carte 26/45 €

◆ Traditional ◆ Business ◆ Functional ◆

This luxury hotel on the edge of a park is appreciated by guests for its modern, comfortable rooms, including junior suites and rooms with themed décor. Pleasant lounge bar and lovely views.

Albert Premier without rest
r. Albert 1er 2a ✉ 1117 – ✆ 442 44 21 – info@albert1er.lu – Fax 44 74 41 – www.albert1er.lu *Plan I* **A2**
14 rm – 140/250 € 140/250 €, ☕ 18 €
◆ Luxury ◆ Business ◆ Stylish ◆
This hotel on the city's outskirts was formerly a grand residence. Guests are won over by its plush, English-style interior décor and cosy rooms.

Parc Beaux-Arts without rest
r. Sigefroi 1 ✉ 2536 – ✆ 268 67 61 – reception.beauxarts@goeres-group.com – Fax 26 86 76 36 – www.goeres-group.com **D1**
10 rm ☕ – 340/405 € 362/427 €
◆ Luxury ◆ Modern ◆
Well-restored old houses close to the Palace of the Grand Dukes and the history and art museum. Neo-retro-style public areas and suites with plenty of charm. Good breakfast.

Rix without rest
bd Royal 20 ✉ 2449 – ✆ 47 16 66 – info@hotelrix.lu – Fax 22 75 35 – www.hotelrix.lu
closed 8-24 August and 1-6 January **C1**
20 rm ☕ – 120/180 € 180/195 €
◆ Family ◆ Business ◆ Functional ◆
A pleasant family-run hotel offering sober, varied rooms. Impressive Classical-style breakfast room and priceless private parking.

Parc-Belle-Vue
av. Marie-Thérèse 5 ✉ 2132 – ✆ 456 14 11 – reception.bellevue@goeres-group.com – Fax 456 14 12 22 – www.goeres-group.com *Plan I* **A2**
58 rm ☕ – 135/165 € 152/182 €
Rest – *(closed lunch Saturday, Sunday and Bank Holidays) (buffets)* Carte 23/42 €
◆ Business ◆ Functional ◆
This hotel certainly lives up to its name with its park and fine views. The rooms in the new extension are the most comfortable but here the views are lacking. The restaurant and tavern serve buffet meals. Panoramic summer terrace.

Français
pl. d'Armes 14 ✉ 1136 – ✆ 47 45 34 – info@hotelfrancais.lu – Fax 46 42 74 – www.hotelfrancais.lu **C1**
25 rm ☕ – 97/110 € 120/140 €
Rest – *(open until 11 p.m.)* Menu 13 €, 21/46 € – Carte 29/58 €
◆ Family ◆ Business ◆ Functional ◆
Run by the same family since 1970, this hotel overlooks the liveliest square in the city. Works of art are dotted about the public areas and the rooms are impeccably kept. Tavern-style restaurant serving classic-traditional cuisine.

Clairefontaine (Arnaud Magnier)
pl.de Clairefontaine 9 ✉ 1341 – ✆ 46 22 11 – clairefo@pt.lu – Fax 47 08 21 – www.restaurantclairefontaine.lu
closed 1 week Easter, last 2 weeks August-first week September, 25-31 December, first week January, Saturday and Sunday **D1**
Rest – Menu 51 €, 75/95 € – Carte 67/100 €
Spec. Carpaccio et tartare de Saint-Jacques au céleri et truffe (October-March). Poularde de Bresse cuite en vessie, farce au foie gras et sauce Albufera. Soufflé léger au Grand Marnier.
◆ Innovative ◆ Formal ◆
In the old town, fronting a charming square close to the cathedral, this renowned restaurant is known for its ever-evolving cuisine, complementary, well-balanced cellar and quality service.

XXXX ✿✿ **Mosconi** (Ilario Mosconi)

r. Münster 13 ✉ 2160 – ✆ 54 69 94 – mosconi@pt.lu – Fax 54 00 43 – www.mosconi.lu
closed 1 week Easter, 12 August-4 September, Christmas- NewYear, Saturday lunch, Sunday and Monday **D1**
Rest – Menu 39 €, 55/110 € – Carte 66/94 €
Spec. Pâté de foie de poulet à la crème de truffes blanches, polenta, sauce au vin rouge. Risotto aux truffes blanches (October-December). Entrecôte de veau légèrement panée, poireau et patate douce.

♦ Italian ♦ Cosy ♦

A smart house on the banks of the River Alzette serving fine Italian cuisine. A romantic setting where the emphasis is on discreet luxury. Attractive terrace by the water's edge and fine wine list.

XXX ✿ **Le Bouquet Garni** (Thierry Duhr)

r. Eau 32 ✉ 1449 – ✆ 26 20 06 20 – bouquetgarni@pt.lu – Fax 26 20 09 11 – www.lebouquetgarni.lu
closed late August-early September, late December-early January, Sunday and Monday **D1**
Rest – Menu 35/85 € – Carte 62/88 €
Spec. Homard rôti au beurre salé. Pied de cochon farci de morilles et ris de veau (winter). Forêt noire aux griottines revisitée.

♦ Traditional ♦ Rustic ♦

An elegant, rustic-style restaurant housed in an 18C building in a street running alongside the Palace of the Grand Dukes.

XXX **La Pomme Cannelle** – Hotel Le Royal

bd Royal 12 ✉ 2449 – ✆ 241 61 67 36 – restauration@leroyalluxembourg.com – Fax 22 29 85 – www.leroyalluxembourg.com
closed mid July-mid August, 1 week January, Saturday and Sunday **C1**
Rest – Menu 39 €, 49/68 € – Carte 63/99 €

♦ Contemporary ♦ Fashionable ♦

Highly original cuisine in which high-quality ingredients, wines and spices from the New World take pride of place. The chic, yet welcoming interior calls to mind exotic locations.

XXX **Yves Radelet**

r. Curé 20 (relocation planned: av. du X Septembre 44 in Belair) ✉ 1368 – ✆ 22 26 18 – info@yvesradelet.lu – Fax 46 24 40 – www.yvesradelet.lu
closed 25 August-6 September, Sunday and Monday **C1**
Rest – Menu 26 €, 45/90 € bi – Carte 58/72 €

♦ Contemporary ♦ Cosy ♦

You will be handed an appetising menu of classic dishes with a modern twist at this restaurant whose owner, who is also the chef, produces the cheeses, charcuterie and cured foods himself.

XX **Speltz**

r. Chimay 8 (angle r. Louvigny) ✉ 1333 – ✆ 47 49 50 – info@restaurant-speltz.lu – Fax 47 46 77 – www.restaurant-speltz.lu – closed 23-31 March, 3-18 August, 24 December-1 January, Sunday and Monday **C1**
Rest – Menu 57/79 € – Carte 64/78 €

♦ Contemporary ♦ Cosy ♦

A brasserie with a summer terrace out front on a pedestrianised street and a "gastro" dining room to the rear where the focus is on contemporary cuisine. Well-informed sommelier. Tea-room in the afternoon.

XX **La Lorraine**

pl. d'Armes 7 (1st floor) ✉ 1136 – ✆ 47 14 36 – lorraine@pt.lu – Fax 47 09 64 – www.lorraine.lu – closed Sunday **C1**
Rest – Menu 42/73 € – Carte 41/69 €
Rest *Bistrot de La Lorraine* – ground floor – Carte 39/60 €

♦ Seafood ♦ Retro ♦

Two main types of cuisine are served in this fine edifice on the place d'Armes: local cuisine, with oysters (in season) on the bistro-style ground floor, and contemporary fare in an attractive Art Deco room on the first floor.

XX **Thai Céladon**
r. Nord 1 ✉ 2229 – ✆ 47 49 34 – Fax 26 38 38 27 – www.thai.lu
closed Saturday lunch and Sunday **C1**
Rest – Menu 18 €, 46/52 € – Carte 37/44 €
◆ Thai ◆ Exotic ◆
This central restaurant with two floors serves Thai cuisine and vegetarian dishes in a simple, contemporary ambience. It takes its name from a glaze used by Oriental potters.

X **Wengé**
r. Louvigny 15 ✉ 1946 – ✆ 26 20 10 58 – wenge@vo.lu – Fax 26 20 12 59 – www.wenge.lu
closed 24-31 March, 18-30 August, 1-7 January and Sunday **C1**
Rest – *(lunch only except Wednesday and Friday)* Menu 39/91 € bi – Carte 43/82 €
◆ Contemporary ◆ Fashionable ◆
Occupying the back of a pâtisserie-cum-delicatessen, this minimalist-style restaurant has a mezzanine and is adorned with Wenge panelling. Contemporary cuisine accompanied by fine wines.

X **Mi & ti**
av. de la Porte-Neuve 8 ✉ 2227 – ✆ 26 26 22 50 – mieti@pt.lu – Fax 26 26 22 51
closed 1 week Easter, last 3 weeks August, 24 and 31 December, 1-3 January, Saturday and Sunday **C1**
Rest – Menu 20 €, 40/71 € – Carte 39/49 €
◆ Italian ◆ Fashionable ◆
A new Italian restaurant with a trendy ambience on the first floor of a modern building. Good-quality products shipped directly from the homeland, with a simplified menu in La Bottega downstairs.

X **Roma**
r. Louvigny 5 ✉ 1946 – ✆ 22 36 92 – Fax 22 04 96
closed Sunday dinner and Monday **C1**
Rest – Carte 41/57 €
◆ Italian ◆ Friendly ◆
One of the oldest "ristoranti" in Luxembourg. Relaxed atmosphere and décor to match the era. Two types of menu: classic and contemporary. Good choice of Italian wines.

X **La Fourchette à droite**
av. Monterey 5 ✉ 2163 – ✆ 22 13 60 – Fax 22 24 95
closed Sunday lunch **C1**
Rest – Menu 19 €, 35/81 € – Carte 46/63 €
◆ Traditional ◆ Bistro ◆
Modern bistro set amid a variety of restaurants in a pedestrian area attracting a range of clients, including locals, tourists and workers. A second room upstairs.

X **Yamayu Santatsu**
r. Notre-Dame 26 ✉ 2240 – ✆ 46 12 49 – Fax 46 05 71
closed first 3 weeks August, Christmas-first week January, Sunday and Monday
Rest – Menu 14/28 € – Carte 18/47 € **C1**
◆ Japanese ◆ Minimalist ◆
Japanese restaurant in a minimalist setting about 200m/220yd from the cathedral. Typical and varied choice, including one fixed menu. You can see the sushi being made behind the counter in the restaurant.

X **Kamakura**
r. Münster 4 ✉ 2160 – ✆ 47 06 04 – kamakura@pt.lu – Fax 46 73 30 – www.kamakura.lu
closed 2 weeks Easter, last 2 weeks August, Bank Holidays lunch, Saturday lunch and Sunday **D1**
Rest – Menu 12 €, 29/52 € bi – Carte 34/50 €
◆ Japanese ◆ Exotic ◆
The Kamakura makes few concessions to the West with its minimalist ambience and design. Good sushi-bar and fixed menus which remain loyal to Japanese customs. A firm favourite.

MAIN STATION *Plan I*

President

pl. de la Gare 32 ✉ 1024 – ✆ 486 16 11 – info@president.lu – Fax 48 61 80 – www.president.lu **B3**

41 rm ☕ – 🚹160/190 € 🚹🚹190/250 €
1 suite

Rest *Les Jardins du President* at Environs of Luxembourg – see below

♦ Traditional ♦ Business ♦ Classic ♦

This chic hotel near the station offers guests tastefully furnished and comfortable guestrooms. Personalised service, neo-Classical lobby and an intimate ambience. A new brasserie opened here in 2006.

Mercure Grand Hotel Alfa

pl. de la Gare 16 ✉ 1616 – ✆ 490 01 11 – h2058@accor.com – Fax 49 00 09 – www.mercure.com **B3**

140 rm – 🚹180/230 € 🚹🚹180/230 €, ☕ 18 €
1 suite

Rest – Menu 21 € – Carte 32/56 €

♦ Chain hotel ♦ Business ♦ Modern ♦

This completely refurbished chain hotel is a useful address for rail travellers. Behind its imposing façade, typical of the 1930s, are pleasant rooms where a good night's sleep is guaranteed. The atmosphere of a Parisian-style brasserie reigns in the vast Art Deco restaurant.

International

pl. de la Gare 20 ✉ 1616 – ✆ 48 59 11 – info@hotelinter.lu – Fax 49 32 27 – www.hotelinter.lu **B3**

69 rm ☕ – 🚹90/250 € 🚹🚹110/300 € – 1 suite

Rest *Am Inter* – *(closed 21 December-5 January, Saturday and Sunday)*
Menu 20/50 € – Carte 30/62 €

♦ Family ♦ Business ♦ Classic ♦

Located opposite the railway station, this hotel is gradually being overhauled. Well-maintained rooms, the best being the new junior suites at the front. The restaurant occupies the corner of the building and the large bay windows allow light to flood in. Classic menu with substantial choice.

Carlton without rest

r. Strasbourg 9 ✉ 2561 – ✆ 29 96 60 – carlton@pt.lu – Fax 29 96 64 – www.carlton.lu **B3**

50 rm ☕ – 🚹88/95 € 🚹🚹100/110 €

♦ Chain hotel ♦ Classic ♦

This fine Art Deco building dating back to 1930 is home to a hotel with comfortable guestrooms, public areas reminiscent of the Roaring Twenties, and an attractive retro-style lounge. Attentive service throughout.

Le Châtelet without rest

bd de la Pétrusse 2 ✉ 2320 – ✆ 40 21 01 – contact@chatelet.lu – Fax 40 36 66 – www.chatelet.lu **A3**

40 rm ☕ – 🚹95/114 € 🚹🚹108/132 €

♦ Family ♦ Business ♦ Classic ♦

Overlooking the Pétrusse Valley, this hotel is an amalgam of several houses, one of which is crowned by an imposing turret. White-leaded furniture and Oriental carpets in the largest rooms.

City without rest

r. Strasbourg 1 ✉ 2561 – ✆ 29 11 22 – mail@cityhotel.lu – Fax 29 11 33 – www.cityhotel.lu **B3**

35 rm ☕ – 🚹90/135 € 🚹🚹124/185 €

♦ Family ♦ Business ♦ Classic ♦

This corner building dating from the inter-war period has fairly spacious rooms decorated in a style reminiscent of the 1980s, each with an individual feel. Lounge-bar offering a daily lunch special and snacks all day long.

Christophe Colomb without rest

r. Anvers 10 ✉ 1130 – ✆ 408 41 41 – mail@christophe-colomb.lu – Fax 40 84 08 – www.christophe-colomb.lu **A3**

24 rm – 75/165 € 85/175 €

◆ Family ◆ Business ◆ Modern ◆

Just 500m/550yd from the station, this pleasant small hotel is ideal for those arriving in the city by train. Standard, reasonably spacious rooms with modern furnishings.

Cordial

pl. de Paris 1 (1st floor) ✉ 2314 – ✆ 48 85 38 – info@lecordial.lu – Fax 40 77 76 – www.lecordial.lu

closed 24-30 March, 12-18 May, 4-24 August and Saturday **B3**

Rest – *(lunch only)* Menu 25/90 € bi – Carte 40/71 €

◆ French traditional ◆ Formal ◆

A large, comfortable restaurant with a conventional layout and elegant ambience. Classic culinary options including a combination of menus and daily specials.

Italia with rm

rest

r. Anvers 15 ✉ 1130 – ✆ 486 62 61 – italia@euro.lu – Fax 48 08 07 **A3**

20 rm – 70/80 € 80/90 €

Rest – Carte 35/55 €

◆ Italian ◆ Family ◆

A restaurant with classic set-up and a menu strong on Italian specialities and grilled meats. Terrace hidden at the rear. The best rooms are at the front.

ENVIRONS OF LUXEMBOURG *Plan I*

NH

rte de Trèves 1 (Airport) ✉ 2633 – ✆ 34 05 71 – nhluxembourg@nh-hotels.com – Fax 34 02 17 – www.nh-hotels.com

147 rm – 89/350 € 89/350 €, 22 € – 1 suite

Rest – *(closed dinner Sunday and Bank Holidays) (open until 11 p.m.)* Menu 23 € – Carte 30/52 €

◆ Chain hotel ◆ Business ◆ Modern ◆

A full range of creature comforts, sophisticated luxury, triple glazing, views of the airport and impeccable service are the hallmarks of this recently renovated 1970s-built hotel. Bright, simple brasserie with an international menu and a summer terrace.

Hilton

r. Jean Engling 12 ✉ 1466 Dommeldange – ✆ 4 37 81 – hilton.luxembourg@hilton.com – Fax 43 60 95 – www.hilton.com

298 rm – 90/250 € 90/250 € – 39 suites

Rest – *(buffets)* Menu 26 € – Carte 34/55 €

◆ Chain hotel ◆ Business ◆ Classic ◆

This luxury hotel situated on a wooded hillside in a valley has comfortable rooms, friendly service and a large conference centre. Modern bistro décor in the restaurant.

Sofitel Europe

rm

r. Fort Niedergrünewald 6 (European Centre) ✉ 2015 Kirchberg – ✆ 43 77 61 – h1314@accor.com – Fax 42 50 91 – www.sofitel.com **B1**

100 rm – 325/350 € 325/350 €, 22 € – 4 suites

Rest Oro e Argento – see below

Rest *Le Stübli* – *(closed July-2 September and Saturday lunch) (open until 11 p.m.)* Menu 25 € – Carte approx. 35 €

◆ Chain hotel ◆ Business ◆ Classic ◆

This bold, oval-shaped hotel with a central atrium is located at the heart of the European institutions district. Comfortable, spacious rooms with service to match. Regional cuisine served in a welcoming setting, where waiting staff are dressed in traditional attire.

Novotel
r. Fort Niedergrünewald 6 (European Centre) ✉ 2226 Kirchberg – ✆ 429 84 81 – h1930@accor.com – Fax 43 86 58 – www.novotel.com **B1**
260 rm – †190/210 € ††190/210 €, ☕ 15 €
Rest – *(open until midnight)* Carte 26/52 €
♦ Chain hotel ♦ Business ♦ Functional ♦
The Novotel is run by the same group as its neighbour, the Sofitel, and offers business customers a full range of seminar facilities as well as recently refurbished rooms. Brasserie-style restaurant with an international menu in line with the Novotel standard.

Ponte Vecchio without rest
r. Neudorf 271 ✉ 2221 Neudorf – ✆ 424 72 01 – vecchio@pt.lu – Fax 424 72 08 88 – www.vecchio.lu
46 rm ☕ – †83/93 € ††99/119 €
♦ Traditional ♦ Business ♦ Functional ♦
This old brewery has been skilfully redeveloped into a series of impressive bedrooms (with and without kitchenettes) - including nine split-level - and public areas adorned with romantic Italianate frescoes.

Ibis
rte de Trèves (Airport) ✉ 2632 – ✆ 43 88 01 – h0974@accor.com – Fax 43 88 02 – www.accorhotels.com
167 rm – †65/93 € ††65/93 €, ☕ 12 €
Rest – Menu 25 € – Carte approx. 25 €
♦ Chain hotel ♦ Business ♦ Functional ♦
A chain hotel with attractive lounge and dining areas plus a cheaper annexe for the budget-conscious. Although quite small, the bedrooms offer the level of comfort you would expect from the Ibis name. A glass rotunda provides the backdrop for the restaurant.

Oro e Argento – Hotel Sofitel Europe
r. Fort Niedergrünewald 6 (European Centre) ✉ 2015 Kirchberg – ✆ 43 77 61 – h1314@accor.com – Fax 42 50 91 – www.sofitel.com
closed Saturday **B1**
Rest – Carte 45/68 €
♦ Italian ♦ Cosy ♦
Fine Italian restaurant in a luxury hotel. Contemporary cooking, sumptuous, Venetian-inspired décor, intimate ambience and faultless service.

Hostellerie du Grünewald with rm
rte d'Echternach 10 ✉ 1453 Dommeldange – ✆ 43 18 82 – hostgrun@pt.lu – Fax 42 06 46 – www.hotel-romantik.com
24 rm – †80/130 € ††90/175 €
Rest – *(closed 4-20 August, 1-17 January, Saturday lunch, Sunday and Monday lunch)* Menu 53/92 € – Carte approx. 65 €
♦ French traditional ♦ Family ♦
A delightful, traditional-style hostelry with a hushed, romantic atmosphere. We recommend that you reserve a table in the central dining room. Well-presented classic cuisine. Attentive service.

Les Jardins du President – Hotel President with rm
pl. Ste-Cunégonde 2 ✉ 1367 Clausen – ✆ 260 90 71 – jardins@president.lu – Fax 26 09 07 73 – www.jardinspresident.lu
closed 23 December-6 January **B2**
7 rm ☕ – †250 € ††250/350 €
Rest – *(closed Saturday lunch and Sunday)* Menu 33 €, 45/69 € – Carte 54/70 €
♦ Contemporary ♦ Fashionable ♦
An elegant restaurant set amid an oasis of greenery producing dishes with a modern touch. Well-informed sommelier. The terrace overlooks a garden and waterfall. Individually designed bedrooms.

XX **Le Grimpereau**

r. Cents 140 (Airport) ✉ 1319 – ✆ 43 67 87 – bridard@pt.lu – Fax 42 60 26 – www.legrimpereau.lu
closed 1 week Easter, first 3 weeks August, 31 December-1 January, Saturday lunch, Sunday dinner and Monday
Rest – Menu 30/40 € – Carte 65/84 €
♦ Contemporary ♦ Rustic ♦
A villa reminiscent of a chalet is the setting for this simple and spacious neo-rustic restaurant with exposed beams and stone fireplace. Contemporary cuisine.

NETHERLANDS
NEDERLAND

PROFILE

→ **Area:**
41 863 km^2 (16 163 sq mi).

→ **Population:**
16 407 000 inhabitants (est. 2005), density = 392 per km^2.

→ **Capital:**
Amsterdam (conurbation1 193 000 inhabitants); The Hague is the seat of government and Parliament.

→ **Currency:**
Euro (€); rate of exchange: € 1 = US$1.46 (Dec 2007).

→ **Government:**
Constitutional parliamentary monarchy (since 1815). Member of European Union since 1957 (one of the 6 founding countries).

→ **Language:**
Dutch; many Dutch people also speak English.

→ **Specific public holidays:**
Good Friday (Friday before Easter); Queen's Day (30 April, 2006: 29 April); Liberation Day (5 May); Boxing Day (26 December).

→ **Local Time:**
GMT + 1hour in winter and GMT + 2 hours in summer.

→ **Climate:**
Temperate maritime with cool winters and mild summers (Amsterdam: January: 2°C, July: 17°C), rainfall evenly distributed throughout the year.

→ **International dialling Code:**
00 31 followed by area code without the initial **0** and then the local number. International Directory enquiries: ✆ **06 0418**.

→ **Emergency:**
Fire Brigade: ✆ **112**; Police, Ambulance, Roadside assistance: ✆ **0900 8418**.

→ **Electricity:**
220 volts AC, 50Hz; 2-pin round-shaped continental plugs.

Formalities
Travellers from the European Union (EU), Switzerland, Iceland and the main countries of North and South America need a national identity card or passport (America: passport required) to visit the Netherlands for less than three months (tourism or business purpose). For visitors from other countries a visa may be required, in addition to a passport, especially for those wishing to stay for longer than three months. We advise you to check with your embassy before travelling.

AMSTERDAM

AMSTERDAM

Population: 750 000 (conurbation 1 193 000) – Altitude: sea level

R. Mazin/PHOTONONSTOP

Once visited, never forgotten. That's Amsterdam's great claim to fame. Its endearing horseshoe shape - defined by 17C canals cut to drain land for a growing population – allied to finely detailed gabled houses, has produced a compact city centre of aesthetically splendid symmetry and matchless consistency. Exploring the city on foot or bike is the real joy here; visitors rarely need to jump on a tram or bus.

Amsterdam, 'the world's biggest small city', displays a host of distinctive characteristics ranging from the red light district to the brown cafés, from the wonderful art galleries to the tree-lined waterways. There's the feel of a northern Venice, but without the hallowed and revered atmosphere. It exists on a human scale, small enough to walk from one end to the other. Those who might moan that it's just *too* small should stroll along to the former derelict docklands on the east side and contemplate the shiny new apartments giving the waterfront a sleek twenty-first century feel. Most people who come here, though, are just happy to cosy up to old Amsterdam's sleepy, relaxed vibe. No European city does snug bars better: this is the place to go for cats kipping on beat-up chairs and candles flickering on wax-encrusted tables…

LIVING THE CITY

Arrive at the **Central station**, at the top end of Amsterdam's centre, and you really do have the city laid out in front of you. How many other famous European destinations can you say that about? You're in the **New Side**, although 'new' in this case refers to the medieval period. Just to your east is the **Old Side,** which began to develop in the 12C as a thriving village of fisher-folk on the River **Amstel**. Keeping these two ancient areas in a vice-like grip and fanning out beneath them in a kind of watery spider's web is the **Grachtengordel**, the superb semicircle of three canals lined by elegant gabled houses and connected by pretty bridges: the Western Canal ring includes the lively, bohemian **Jordaan** district. Just beyond the Grachtengordel lies the museum quarter, a tourist must-see, as it features two of the world's most prestigious museums. There's the lovely **Vondelpark** here, too. The most easterly quarter of the city is Plantage, or 'Plantation', a name mirroring its historically green qualities. This area was once parkland, and seventeenth century Amsterdammers would come here to spend leisure time. Nowadays it's elegant and tree lined, but seems strangely undiscovered by many visitors.

PRACTICAL INFORMATION

ARRIVAL-DEPARTURE

Schipol International Airport is 18km southwest of the city and trains run regularly to Amsterdam Central Station, a journey that takes about 20 minutes. A taxi costs around €38 and there are also Airport Shuttles available.

TRANSPORT

To get around Amsterdam – take a hike. Of all Europe's main cities, this is the one most geared to walking, what with its narrow streets and canals.

Avoid any thoughts of driving a car here. Word of warning: trams can be pretty silent and can move pretty fast, so look both ways when crossing tram routes. If you venture inadvertently onto a cycle path (there are many), you'll soon hear the frantic ringing of bicycle bells.

The Amsterdam Card entitles the holder to free public transport, free admission to major museums, a canal cruise and discounts in some restaurants. It's valid for 24hr, 48hr, or 72hr, and available from the Tourist Information Office opposite the central station.

Trams and buses run mostly from the central station; the metro has four short lines, mostly used by commuters. Modern white and blue trams are the most popular form of public transport; they operate from 6am on weekdays, finish just after midnight and tickets are available from the Tourist Information office or vending machines. Bus routes mainly complement the tram network.

EXPLORING AMSTERDAM

It's safe to say you won't experience the like of Amsterdam anywhere else in Europe. The city appears so well planned that it's possible to look at it on a map and sense in your head that you've got the measure of it. Most visitors arrive at the Central Railway station and get their bearings from here. Just down the road they will find two veritable old churches steeped in medieval history, a red light district famous throughout the world and a museum devoted to the history of marijuana. Such is the city they've arrived in. Central to all the action is **Dam Square** – simply 'The Dam' to locals – built on the very spot where the city's roots lie. Now somewhat faded, it nevertheless boasts the glorious Nieuwe Kerk and the Classical seventeenth century Koninklijk Palace, once the city's town hall. The Dam's size makes it a great place for markets and all shade of al fresco events. As a complete contrast to the area's seedier elements, and not far west of the Red Light district, is the beguiling Begijnhof, an enchanting sanctuary of gabled houses (including Amsterdam's oldest) overlooking a tranquil green. Its hushed atmosphere allows for no large tour groups.

→ CANAL PLUS

Amsterdam's first canal, the **Singel**, is the tight boundary for the Old and New sides, and it is just beyond here that the Grachtengordel's concentric arrangement of canals begins. They're called Herengracht, Keizersgracht and Prinsengracht, and were cut in two stages through the seventeenth century. There's no better way of getting a feel for Amsterdam's charms than taking a slow boat along one of them, taking in the timeless appeal of the narrow houses and the steady progress of bike riders on the little waterside streets, making the most of this, the flattest country on the planet. A jaunt along the canals is best in the spring or summer, when the city blooms into a café society. Chairs and tables spill outdoors to welcome the sun, and taking in the tree-lined banks here is one of Europe's greatest pleasures. A super vantage point is from the bridge at the crossing of the Herengracht with Reguliersgracht (another pretty canal in the eastern canal ring, dug after those in the Grachtengordel): this is called the 'golden curve' and gives a view of fifteen bridges all at one time.

→ THE COLOUR BROWN

If any part of the city can claim the title of the 'real' Amsterdam, that accolade belongs to the **Jordaan**. This delightful maze of canals and backstreets on the western canal ring is a short stroll from the main visitor hotspots, yet it doesn't quite draw the same crowds. Losing yourself here is all part of the fun, idling amongst the seventeenth century workers' houses and quirky shops. This is where to stop and enjoy Amsterdam's best brown cafés, so called not just because their interiors are characterised by dark wooden panelling, but also because they've turned that rather inviting nutty colour with age and cigarette smoke. They're cosy and convivial, and often form the social hub of the neighbourhood.

At the heart of the Jordaan are two of the city's most famous sights, standing within a stone's throw of each other. The **Westerkerk** is the tallest church in Amsterdam, its spire rewarding climbers with stunning views. Rembrandt, who lived close by, is buried here, though his grave has never been found. Just along Prinsengracht is a humble abode that attracts nine hundred thousand visitors a year – **Anne Frank House**. For two years during

World War II, this was where the now-famous young diarist lived with her family in a little upstairs apartment hidden behind a revolving bookcase. You can visit her room, empty except for pin-ups of wartime film stars. It's advisable, for obvious reasons, to get here either early or late in the day.

→ SEMINAL MUSEUMS

If the weather's inclement, you can easily spend a day in the museums and galleries of this city. In fact, whatever the elements are doing, be sure to head just beyond the limits of the Grachtengordel and pay homage to the district around **Museumplein**. Here you will find the **Rijksmuseum** and the **Van Gogh Museum**, two of Europe's cultural landmarks. The Rijksmuseum has been undergoing extensive renovation which began five years ago, and the reopening, due in 2008, is bound to be a stunning occasion. This neo-Gothic titan is a powerhouse of art, possessing nearly seven million works, with only a fraction on display at any one time. Over two hundred years, it's built an unrivalled collection of Dutch art; try not to miss the paintings of the 17C, the Golden Age, adorned by the likes of Rembrandt, Vermeer and Hals. There are also tremendously impressive sections on Asiatic art and sculpture/applied art. It can be quite overpowering to take in this museum in a single day; best do some planning beforehand. The Van Gogh museum, on the other hand, is on a more human scale, and includes two hundred of the great man's paintings and five hundred of his drawings. There are hundreds of letters to his brother Theo, too. As if all this wasn't enough, practically opposite the homage to Van Gogh is the Stedelijk Museum, the national Museum of Modern Art, now seventy years old. Inside are works by the likes of Chagall, Cézanne and Picasso, plus, naturally enough, a fascinating insight into the Dutch De Stijl movement, iconic in the world of twentieth century abstract art.

HIPPY TRAIL

There's only one place to head after a gallery trawl, and that's the nearby **Vondelpark**. This former hippie haven boasts about eight million visitors a year. They come for the landscaped delights, the meandering footpaths, rose gardens and waterways, the parakeets which home in on the pavilion every morning, and the sheep, goats and cows which graze lazily in the pastures. They come for the free summer musical concerts and plays which the park is famous for, and they come too for its film museum, where classic movies are shown each day, either in the lovingly restored interior or, in the summer, out on the terrace during summer. These are free to watch as well.

In recent decades Amsterdam has been famous for its enjoyment of plant life (mainly the sort you inhale in a brown

AMSTERDAM IN…

→ ONE DAY

A trip on a canal boat; evening atmosphere of a brown café ; a stroll around the red light district

→ TWO DAYS

Begijnhof. Rijksmuseum, Vondelpark,

→ THREE DAYS

The Jordaan, Van Gogh museum, Plantage and Entrepotdok

café), but the city has been cultivating medicinal herbs for about three hundred and twenty five years in the **Botanical Gardens** in the Plantage district to the east of town. These are amongst the oldest in the world, and include a three-climate greenhouse with tropical, sub-tropical and desert sections. There's an Orangery, too, with museum and terrace, which is a great place to take afternoon tea, while art shows with a botanical theme are a common sight. Plantage as a whole boasts attractively wide, tree-lined streets, and offers a vivid new take on the past: at Entrepotdok, the grand old warehouses have been redeveloped, and this dockland quarter buzzes with colour, café tables and shiny houseboats. Twenty-first century Amsterdam's evolution on water continues apace.

CALENDAR HIGHLIGHTS

Summertime is a cultural big-hit in Amsterdam. The highlight comes in the middle of August with Uitmarkt, a weekend of theatrical and musical shows on Leidseplein and Museumplein, which launches a season of dance, opera, music and drama in the city. This is also the month of the Grachtenfestival, which sees classical concerts along all sections of the Grachtengordel. September's third weekend is the time to be in Jordaan to check out its annual festival, when musical shows and fairs light up Westerkerk and its surrounding quarter. Earlier in the summer, during three weeks of June, look out for the Holland Festival, a three-week long jamboree, featuring theatrical drama in Amsterdamse Bos, southwest of the city, and a host of other plays, concerts and ballets around town: Vondelpark puts on some renowned shows al fresco. This is also the month for the Amsterdam Roots Festival, a celebration of global music and dance, and Open Garden Days, when picturesque private gardens are free for public perusal. Modern art is up for inspection in May at the Kunst RAI, a huge exhibition held in Amsterdam RAI, just southeast of the city. Every July, classical music fans make for the Concertgebouw for summer concerts, which continue throughout August. Brave Amsterdammers leave the comfort of cosy brown cafés on the first Saturday of November for Museumnacht, when many museums stay open during the night, with musical events and guided tours to keep eyelids from drooping.

EATING OUT

Amsterdam is a vibrant and multicultural city and, as such, offers a wide proliferation of restaurants offering a varied choice of cuisines where you can eat well without paying too much. Head for an eetcafe, and you'll get satisfying three-course menus at a reasonable price. The Dutch consider the evening to be the time to eat your main meal, so some restaurants shut at lunchtime. Aside from the eetcafe, you can top up your middle-of-day fuel levels at a bruin (brown) café, or one specialising in coffee and cake. If you wish to try local specialities, number one on the hit list could be rijsttafel or rice table, as the Dutch have imported much from their former colonies of Indonesia. Fresh raw herring from local waters is another nutritious local favourite, as are apple pies and pancakes of the sweet persuasion. Restaurants are never too big but are certainly atmospheric and busy so it's worth making reservations.

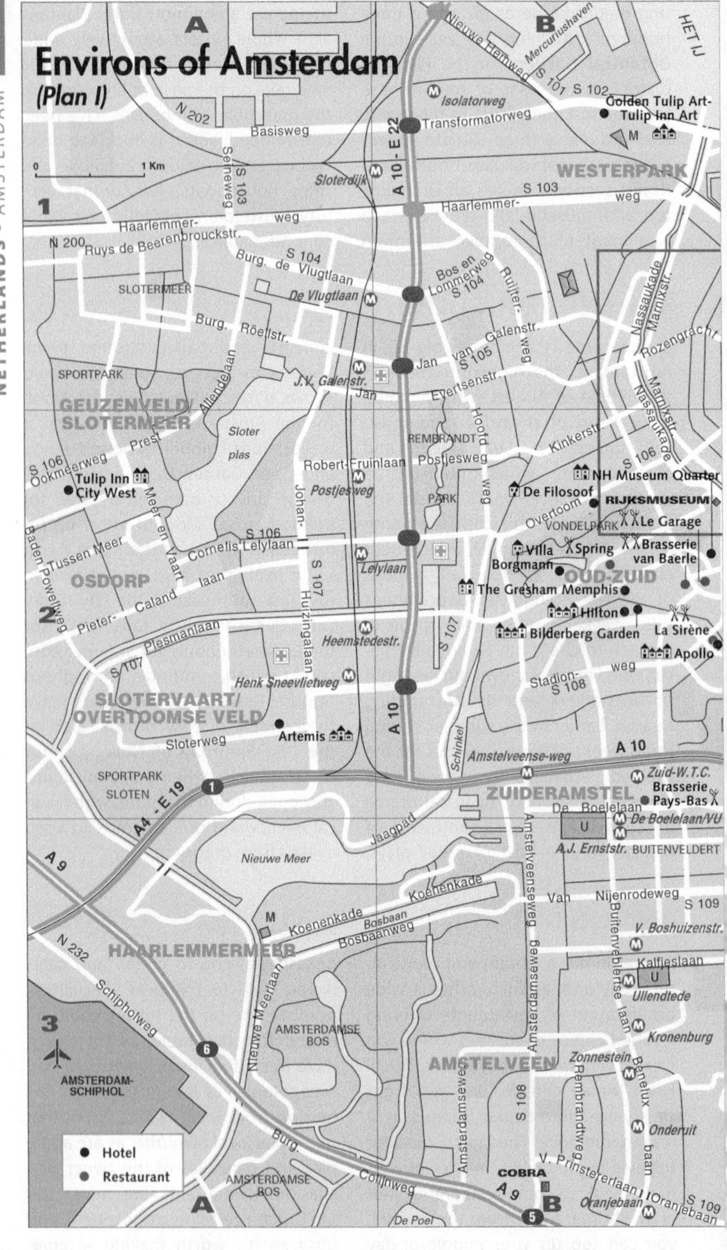
Environs of Amsterdam
(Plan I)
A
B
1
2
3
Hotel
Restaurant
WESTERPARK
GEUZENVELD/ SLOTERMEER
OSDORP
SLOTERVAART/ OVERTOOMSE VELD
OUD-ZUID
ZUIDERAMSTEL
HAARLEMMERMEER
AMSTELVEEN
Golden Tulip Art-Tulip Inn Art
Tulip Inn City West
NH Museum Quarter
De Filosoof
RIJKSMUSEUM
Le Garage
Villa Borgmann
Spring
Brasserie van Baerle
The Gresham Memphis
Hilton
Bilderberg Garden
La Sirène
Apollo
Artemis
Brasserie Pays-Bas
AMSTERDAM-SCHIPHOL
AMSTERDAMSE BOS
COBRA
Nieuwe Meer
Sloter plas

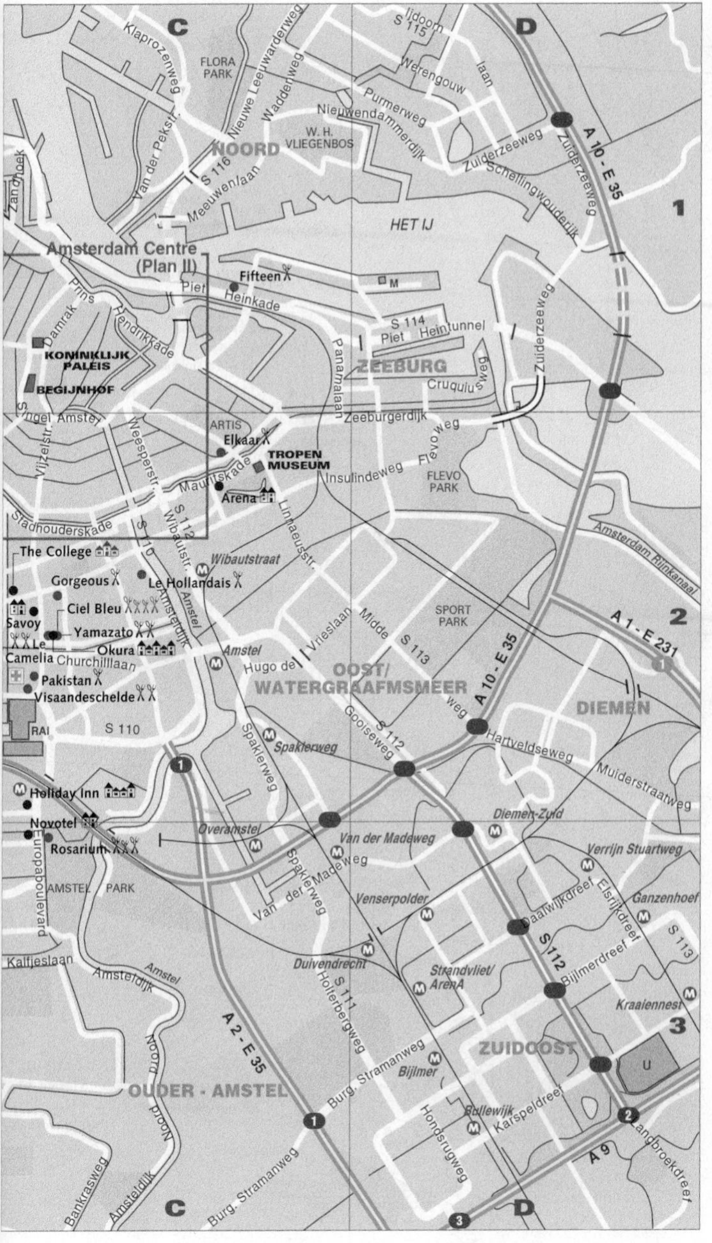
C
D
1
2
3
NOORD
HET IJ
ZEEBURG
OOST/ WATERGRAAFSMMEER
DIEMEN
ZUIDOOST
OUDER - AMSTEL
FLORA PARK
W. H. VLIEGENBOS
FLEVO PARK
SPORT PARK
AMSTEL PARK
Amsterdam Centre (Plan II)
KONINKLIJK PALEIS
BEGIJNHOF
TROPEN MUSEUM
ARTIS
Fifteen
Elkaar
Arena
The College
Gorgeous
Le Hollandais
Ciel Bleu
Savoy
Yamazato
Okura
Le Camelia
Pakistan
Visaandeschelde
RAI
Holiday Inn
Novotel
Rosarium
A 10 - E 35
A 1 - E 231
A 2 - E 35
A 9
Wibautstraat
Spaklerweg
Overamstel
Van der Madeweg
Venserpolder
Duivendrecht
Strandvliet/ ArenA
Bijlmer
Bullewijk
Diemen-Zuid
Verrijn Stuartweg
Ganzenhoef
Kraaiennest
Amsterdam Rijnkanaal
Klaprozenweg
Nieuwe Leeuwarderweg
Waddenweg
Purmerweg
Nieuwendammerdijk
Werengouw
Zuiderzeeweg
Schellingwouderdijk
Meeuwenlaan
Van der Pekstr.
Zamenhoek
Piet Heinkade
Piet Heintunnel
Prins Hendrikkade
Damrak
Panamalaan
Cruquiusweg
Zeeburgerdijk
Flevoweg
Insulindeweg
Mauritskade
Singel
Amstel
Vijzelstr.
Weesperstr.
Wibautstr.
Stadhouderskade
Linnaeusstr.
Hugo de Vrieslaan
Middelweg
Amsteldijk
Churchilllaan
Gooiseweg
Hartveldseweg
Muiderstraatweg
Europaboulevard
Kalfjeslaan
Holterbergweg
Daalwijkdreef
Elsrijkdreef
Bijlmerdreef
Burg. Stramanweg
Hondsrugweg
Karspeldreef
Langbroekdreef
Bankrasweg
Noord
S 110
S 111
S 112
S 113
S 114
S 115
S 116
M
U

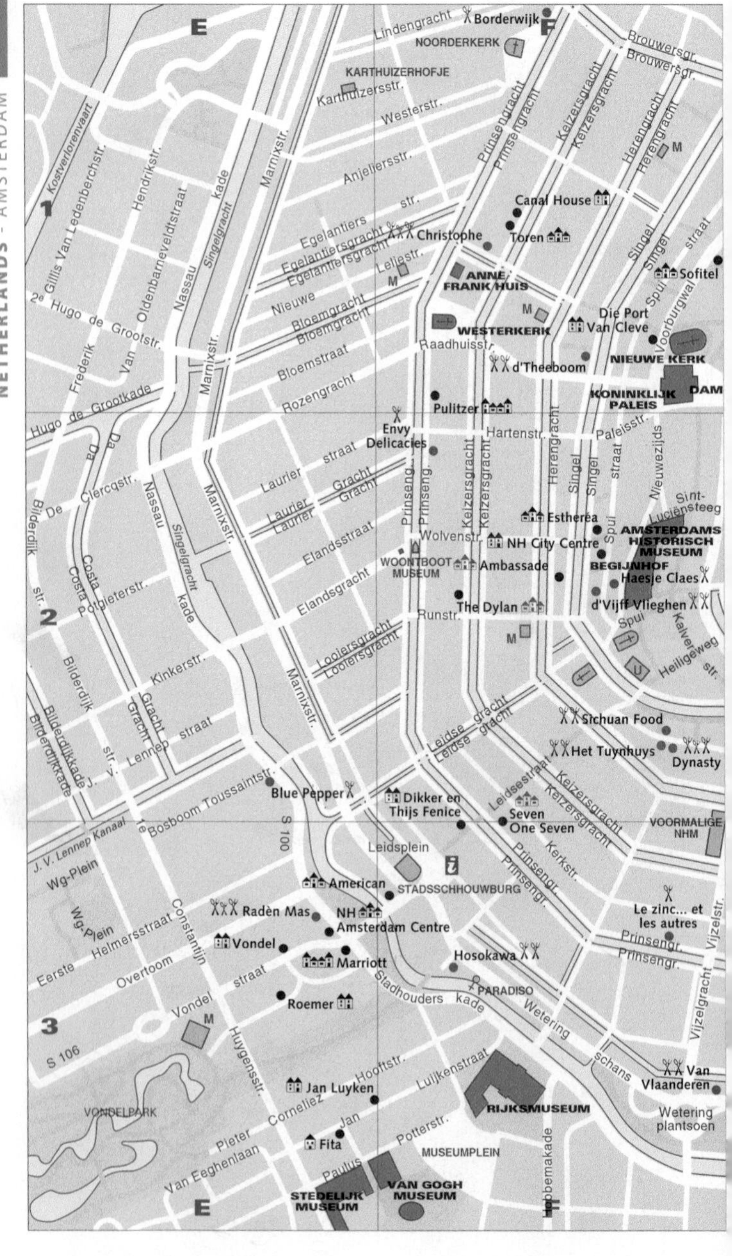
E
F
1
2
3
Lindengracht
Borderwijk
NOORDERKERK
Brouwersgr.
Brouwersgr.
KARTHUIZERHOFJE
Karthuizersstr.
Westerstr.
Anjeliersstr.
Kostverlorenvaart
Gillis Van Ledenberchstr.
Hendrikstr.
Van Oldenbarneveldtstraat
Nassau
Singelgracht
kade
Marnixstr.
Prinsengracht
Prinsengracht
Keizersgracht
Keizersgracht
Herengracht
Herengracht
M
Canal House
Toren
Egelantiers
str.
Egelantiersgracht
Egelantiersgracht
Christophe
Leliestr.
M
ANNE FRANK HUIS
Singel
Singel
straat
Sofitel
Spui
Voorburgwal
2e Hugo de Grootstr.
Frederik
Van
Nieuwe
Bloemgracht
Bloemgracht
M
WESTERKERK
Die Port Van Cleve
NIEUWE KERK
Raadhuisstr.
d'Theeboom
Bloemstraat
Rozengracht
Marnixstr.
Hugo de Grootkade
Pulitzer
KONINKLIJK PALEIS
DAM
Envy Delicacies
Hartenstr.
Paleisstr.
Nieuwezijds
Da Costa
De Clercqstr.
Laurier
straat
Laurier
Laurier
Gracht
Gracht
Prinseng.
Prinseng.
Keizersgracht
Keizersgracht
Herengracht
Singel
Singel
straat
Sint-Luciënsteeg
Bilderdijk
str.
Nassau
Singelgracht
kade
Marnixstr.
Estheréa
AMSTERDAMS HISTORISCH MUSEUM
Wolvenstr.
NH City Centre
Spui
Elandsstraat
WOONTBOOT MUSEUM
Ambassade
BEGIJNHOF
Haesje Claes
Costa
Costa
Potgieterstr.
Elandsgracht
The Dylan
d'Vijff Vlieghen
Runstr.
Spui
Kalver
str.
M
Heiligeweg
Kinkerstr.
Looiersgracht
Looiersgracht
Bilderdijk
Bilderdijkkade
Bilderdijkkade
Gracht
Gracht
J. v. Lennep
straat
str.
Marnixstr.
Leidse
Leidse
gracht
gracht
Sichuan Food
Het Tuynhuys
Dynasty
Bosboom Toussaintstr.
Blue Pepper
Dikker en Thijs Fenice
Leidsestraat
Seven One Seven
Keizersgracht
Keizersgracht
VOORMALIGE NHM
1e
J. V. Lennep Kanaal
S 100
Leidsplein
Kerkstr.
Prinsengr.
Prinsengr.
Wg-Plein
Wg-Plein
American
STADSSCHOUWBURG
Constantijn
Radèn Mas
NH Amsterdam Centre
Le zinc... et les autres
Vijzelstr.
Helmersstraat
Eerste
Vondel
Marriott
Prinsengr.
Prinsengr.
Overtoom
straat
Hosokawa
Stadhouders
kade
PARADISO
Vijzelgracht
Vondel
Roemer
Wetering
M
S 106
Huygensstr.
schans
Van Vlaanderen
Hooftstr.
Luijkenstraat
Jan Luyken
VONDELPARK
Cornelisz
RIJKSMUSEUM
Wetering plantsoen
Pieter
Jan
Fita
Potterstr.
MUSEUMPLEIN
Van Eeghenlaan
Paulus
Hobbemakade
STEDELIJK MUSEUM
VAN GOGH MUSEUM

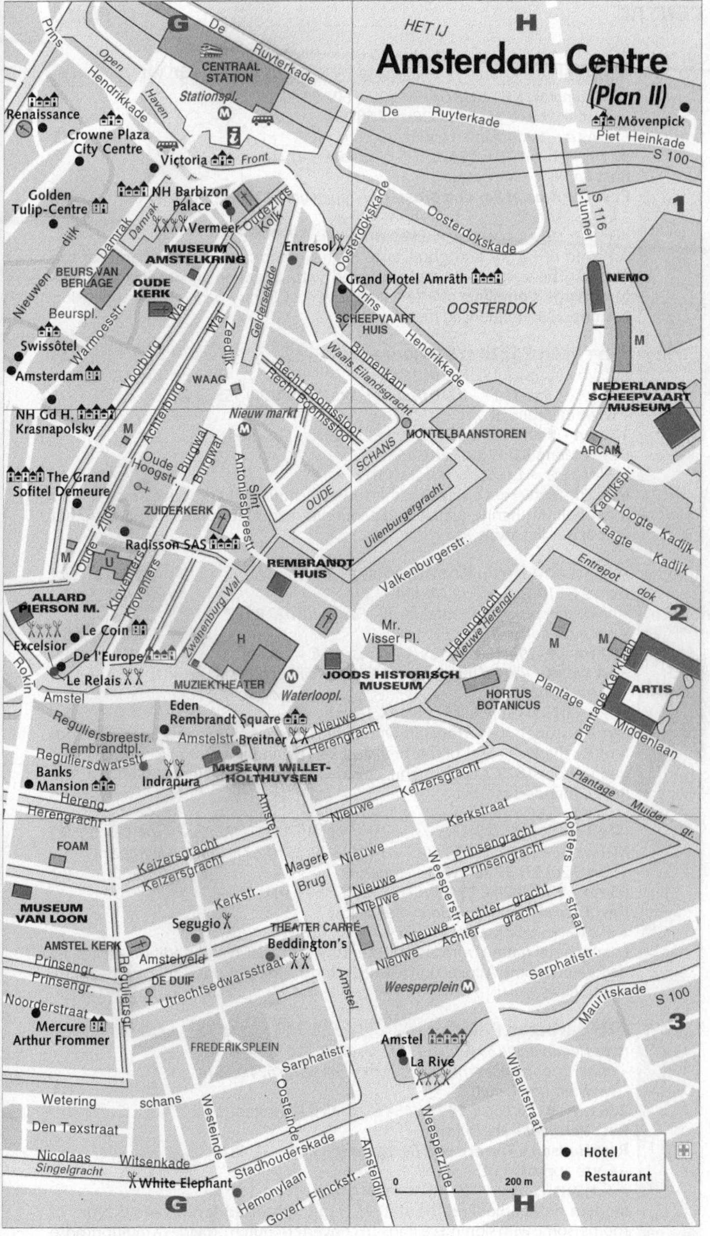
Amsterdam Centre
(Plan II)
HET IJ
G
H
1
2
3
De Ruyterkade
CENTRAAL STATION
Stationspl.
Prins Hendrikkade
Open Haven
Renaissance
Crowne Plaza City Centre
Victoria
Front
Golden Tulip-Centre
NH Barbizon Palace
Vermeer
Damrak
Oudezijds Kolk
Entresol
Oosterdokskade
MUSEUM AMSTELKRING
BEURS VAN BERLAGE
Nieuwendijk
OUDE KERK
Beurspl.
Warmoesstr.
Swissôtel
Amsterdam
Voorburgwal
Wal
Zeedijk
Geldersekade
WAAG
Nieuw markt
NH Gd H. Krasnapolsky
Achterburgwal
Oude Hoogstr.
Oude Burgwal
The Grand Sofitel Demeure
ZUIDERKERK
Sint Antoniesbreestr.
Radisson SAS
Oude Zijds
Kloveniers
ALLARD PIERSON M.
Le Coin
Excelsior
De l'Europe
Le Relais
Rokin
Amstel
Zwanenburg Wal
MUZIEKTHEATER
Waterloopl.
REMBRANDT HUIS
JOODS HISTORISCH MUSEUM
Grand Hotel Amrâth
SCHEEPVAART HUIS
Binnenkant
Waals Eilandsgracht
Recht Boomssloot
OUDE SCHANS
MONTELBAANSTOREN
Uilenburgergracht
Valkenburgerstr.
Mr. Visser Pl.
Herengracht
Nieuwe Herengr.
OOSTERDOK
De Ruyterkade
Mövenpick
Piet Heinkade
S 100
S 116
IJ-tunnel
NEMO
NEDERLANDS SCHEEPVAART MUSEUM
ARCAM
Kadijkspl.
Hoogte Kadijk
Laagte Kadijk
Entrepot dok
ARTIS
Plantage Kerklaan
Plantage Middenlaan
HORTUS BOTANICUS
Plantage Muider gr.
Eden Rembrandt Square
Reguliersbreestr.
Amstelstr.
Breitner
Nieuwe Herengracht
Rembrandtpl.
Reguliersdwarsstr.
Indrapura
MUSEUM WILLET-HOLTHUYSEN
Banks Mansion
Hereng.
Herengracht
FOAM
Keizersgracht
Nieuwe Keizersgracht
Kerkstraat
Magere Brug
Nieuwe Prinsengracht
MUSEUM VAN LOON
Kerkstr.
Segugio
THEATER CARRÉ
Beddington's
Nieuwe Achter gracht
Weesperstr.
Roeterstraat
AMSTEL KERK
Amstelveld
Prinsengr.
Reguliersgr.
DE DUIF
Utrechtsedwarsstraat
Weesperplein
Sarphatistr.
Mauritskade
Noorderstraat
Mercure Arthur Frommer
FREDERIKSPLEIN
Amstel
La Rive
Wibautstraat
Wetering schans
Westeinde
Oosteinde
Weesperzijde
Den Texstraat
Nicolaas Witsenkade
Singelgracht
White Elephant
Stadhouderskade
Hemonylaan
Govert Flinckstr.
Amsteldijk
0
200 m
Hotel
Restaurant

CENTRE *Plan II*

Amstel

Prof. Tulpplein 1 ✉ 1018 GX – ☏ (0 20) 622 60 60 – amstel@ihg.com – Fax (0 20) 622 58 08 – www.amsterdam.intercontinental.com **H3**

62 rm – 625/675 € 625/675 €, 27 € – 17 suites

Rest *La Rive* – see below

Rest *The Amstel Bar and Brasserie* – *(open until 11 p.m.)* Menu 40 € – Carte 54/99 €

♦ Palace ♦ Luxury ♦ Classic ♦

A haven of luxury and good taste in this grand hotel on the banks of the Amstel. The vast rooms are decorated with attention to detail and stylish furnishings. Complete, efficient service. A cosy library-bar, with an appetising cosmopolitan-influenced menu.

The Grand Sofitel Demeure

O.Z. Voorburgwal 197 ✉ 1012 EX – ☏ (0 20) 555 31 11 – h2783@accor.com – Fax (0 20) 555 32 22 – www.thegrand.nl **G2**

170 rm – 490/690 € 490/690 €, 28 € – 12 suites

Rest – Menu 33/39 € – Carte 45/60 €

♦ Palace ♦ Luxury ♦ Historic ♦

Maria de Medici once stayed in this superb historic building, once Amsterdam's town hall. Authentic Art Nouveau lounges, exquisite rooms and a beautiful indoor garden await you.

NH Grand Hotel Krasnapolsky

Dam 9 ✉ 1012 JS – ☏ (0 20) 554 91 11 – nhkrasnapolsky@nh-hotels.com – Fax (0 20) 622 86 07 – www.nh-hotels.com **G1**

467 rm – 129/459 € 129/459 €, 28 € – 1 suite

Rest *Reflet* – *(closed mid July-mid August) (dinner only)* Menu 48 € – Carte 43/68 €

♦ Traditional ♦ Luxury ♦ Classic ♦

Large, historic hotel on the Dam with various categories of rooms, apartments for rent by the week and buffet breakfast served under a magnificent glass roof dating from 1879. Classic menu, chic décor and well-heeled ambience at the Reflet, founded in 1883.

De l'Europe

Nieuwe Doelenstraat 2 ✉ 1012 CP – ☏ (0 20) 531 17 77 – hotel@leurope.nl – Fax (0 20) 531 17 78 – www.leurope.nl **G2**

95 rm – 345/424 € 420/510 €, 25 € – 5 suites

Rest *Excelsior* and ***Le Relais*** – see below

♦ Palace ♦ Luxury ♦ Classic ♦

Luxury hotel dating from late 19th century with charm and tradition. Tastefully decorated rooms. A collection of Dutch landscape paintings displayed. Beautiful water views.

NH Barbizon Palace

Prins Hendrikkade 59 ✉ 1012 AD – ☏ (0 20) 556 45 64 – nhbarbizonpalace@nh-hotels.com – Fax (0 20) 624 33 53 – www.nh-hotels.com **G1**

266 rm – 129/454 € 129/454 €, 25 € – 3 suites

Rest *Vermeer* – see below

Rest *Hudson's Terrace and Restaurant* – Menu 42/48 € – Carte approx. 45 €

♦ Chain hotel ♦ Business ♦ Modern ♦

Modern hotel adjoining the station. Huge, light-filled foyer, various types of rooms (some with sloping ceilings). A converted church provides a multipurpose room for groups. Vaguely nautical atmosphere, international menu and interior terrace at Hudson's.

Radisson SAS

Rusland 17 ⊠ 1012 CK – ✆ (0 20) 623 12 31 – reservations.amsterdam@radissonsas.com – Fax (0 20) 520 82 00 – www.amsterdam.radissonsas.com **G2**

240 rm – †149/369 € ††149/369 €, ☕ 24 € – 2 suites

Rest *Brasserie De Palmboom* – Menu 40 € – Carte 35/49 €

◆ Chain hotel ◆ Business ◆ Stylish ◆

A modern chain hotel with an atrium incorporating an 18th century presbytery. Walkway under the road leads to the annexe opposite. Several styles of bedroom available. International menu offered in two Scandinavian-inspired dining rooms.

Marriott

Stadhouderskade 12 ⊠ 1054 ES – ✆ (0 20) 607 55 55 – amsterdam.guest@marriott.com – Fax (0 20) 607 55 11 – www.amsterdammarriott.com **E3**

387 rm – †199/354 € ††199/354 €, ☕ 26 € – 5 suites

Rest – *(closed Sunday and Monday) (dinner only until 11 p.m.)* Carte 39/67 €

◆ Chain hotel ◆ Business ◆ Cosy ◆

A high-class, American-style hotel on a major thoroughfare. The rooms are vast and well-equipped. A good seminar infrastructure and business centre. International menu served in the restaurant; grilled meats, salads and pizza in the brasserie.

Pulitzer

Prinsengracht 323 ⊠ 1016 GZ – ✆ (0 20) 523 52 35 – pulitzers.amsterdam@luxurycollection.com – Fax (0 20) 627 67 53 – www.pulitzer.com **F1**

227 rm – †230/450 € ††255/475 €, ☕ 27 € – 3 suites

Rest *Pulitzers* – Menu 26 € – Carte 44/70 €

◆ Chain hotel ◆ Luxury ◆ Historic ◆

25 admirably-restored 17th and 18th centuries houses, around a well-tended garden. Public areas filled with works of art; refined, individualized bedrooms. Modern restaurant with novel décor (amusing reference to the painter, Frans Hals). Intimate bar.

Renaissance

Kattengat 1 ⊠ 1012 SZ – ✆ (0 20) 621 22 23 – Fax (0 20) 627 52 45 – www.renaissancehotels.com/amsrd **G1**

375 rm – †160/425 € ††189/425 €, ☕ 25 € – 6 suites

Rest – Carte approx. 35 €

◆ Traditional ◆ Business ◆ Classic ◆

Rooms, suites and junior suites with modern comfort and numerous services on offer. Excellent conference facilities beneath the dome of an old Lutheran church dating from 1671. Bar with an international menu; simplified dining in the "brown café".

Grand Hotel Amrâth

Prins Hendrikkade 108 ⊠ 1011 AK – ✆ (0 20) 552 00 00 – Fax (0 20) 552 09 00 **G1**

153 rm – †270/500 € ††270/500 €, ☕ 25 € – 10 suites

Rest – Menu 30/45 € – Carte 42/85 €

◆ Chain hotel ◆ Business ◆ Stylish ◆

The hotel opened in 2007, in the monumental Shipping House (1916), characteristic of the Amsterdam School. Stunning Art Deco interior. Contemporary cuisine served in a large, delightfully old-fashioned dining room.

Crowne Plaza City Centre

N.Z. Voorburgwal 5 ⊠ 1012 RC – ✆ (0 20) 620 05 00 – amsnl.gsc@ihg.com – Fax (0 20) 620 11 73 – www.amsterdam-citycentre.crowneplaza.com **G1**

268 rm – †135/498 € ††135/495 €, ☕ 22 € – 2 suites

Rest *Dorrius* – *(closed Sunday) (dinner only until 11 p.m.)* Menu 32/45 € – Carte 38/50 €

◆ Chain hotel ◆ Business ◆ Classic ◆

Chain hotel near the station. Functional bedrooms. Town roofscape view from the top-floor "lounge club". A restaurant featuring reconstructed 19th century décor. Classic menu accompanied by local dishes.

American

Leidsekade 97 ✉ 1017 PN – ☎ (0 20) 556 30 00 – info@amsterdamamerican.com – Fax (0 20) 556 30 01 – www.amsterdamamerican.com **F3**

174 rm – 120/300 € 120/300 €, ☕ 21 € – 1 suite

Rest *Café Americain* – Menu 30/40 € – Carte 38/57 €

♦ Palace ♦ Business ♦ Art Deco ♦

Near a lively square, this hotel with its imposing historic façade is a local institution. Bedrooms are gradually being updated. Bar popular with artists and people watchers. Elegant vaulted Art Deco café. International menu; high tea served in the afternoon.

The Dylan

Keizersgracht 384 ✉ 1016 GB – ☎ (0 20) 530 20 10 – info@dylanamsterdam.com – Fax (0 20) 530 20 30 – www.dylanamsterdam.com **F2**

38 rm – 285/330 € 455/960 €, ☕ 25 € – 3 suites

Rest – *(closed 24 March, 30 April, 1 and 12 May, 24, 25, 26 and 31 December, 1 January, Saturday lunch and Sunday)* Menu 43 €, 70/145 € bi – Carte 60/81 €

♦ Grand Luxury ♦ Design ♦

"Order and beauty; luxury, peace and delight." Discover the secret harmony of the exceptional interior design of this unique hotel. Exquisite rooms by Anouska Hempel. Modern cuisine served in a trendy décor and courtyard-terrace with modern furnishings.

Ambassade without rest

Herengracht 341 ✉ 1016 AZ – ☎ (0 20) 555 02 22 – info@ambassade-hotel.nl – Fax (0 20) 555 02 77 – www.ambassade-hotel.nl **F2**

51 rm – 185 € 185/225 €, ☕ 16 € – 8 suites

♦ Family ♦ Luxury ♦ Stylish ♦

Beautiful and stylishly personalised rooms and suites spread over ten 17th century houses next to the canal. Modern art and interesting library. Float and massage centre.

Sofitel

N.Z. Voorburgwal 67 ✉ 1012 RE – ☎ (0 20) 627 59 00 – h1159-gm@accor.com – Fax (0 20) 623 89 32 – www.sofitel.com **F1**

148 rm – 275 € 275/695 €, ☕ 22 €

Rest – Carte approx. 45 €

♦ Chain hotel ♦ Traditional ♦ Classic ♦

Chain hotel near a main road, made up of three 17th to 19th century houses. Various types of bedrooms, including about ten modern junior suites. Orient-Express atmosphere and brasserie-style cuisine in the restaurant.

Seven One Seven without rest

Prinsengracht 717 ✉ 1017 JW – ☎ (0 20) 427 07 17 – info@717hotel.nl – Fax (0 20) 423 07 17 – www.717hotel.nl **F2-3**

8 rm ☕ – 390 € 470/670 €

♦ Grand Luxury ♦ Traditional ♦ Classic ♦

Small, attractive 18th century house converted into an intimate and select place to stay. The guestrooms are veritable gems. Romantic lounges; leafy courtyard where breakfast is served in summer.

Victoria

Damrak 1 ✉ 1012 LG – ☎ (0 20) 623 42 55 – vhares@pphe.com – Fax (0 20) 625 29 97 – www.parkplaza.com **G1**

296 rm – 315/375 € 330/395 €, ☕ 20 € – 10 suites

Rest – *(open until 11 p.m.)* Menu 29 € – Carte approx. 35 €

♦ Traditional ♦ Chain hotel ♦ Classic ♦

Neo-classical 19C luxury hotel and extension dating from the 1980s near the station. Domed lobby with modern stained glass. Refurbished rooms. Tavern-restaurant with traditional menu.

Eden Rembrandt Square

Amstelstraat 17 ✉ 1017 DA – ☎ (0 20) 890 47 47
– info@edenrembrandtsquare.com – Fax (0 20) 890 47 40
– www.edenrembrandtsquare.com **G2**

165 rm – †99/295 € ††99/335 €, ☕ 18 € – 1 suite

Rest *Flo* – *(closed Saturday lunch and Sunday lunch) (open until 11 p.m.)*
Menu 29 € – Carte 35/70 €

◆ Chain hotel ◆ Functional ◆

Old hotel building with modernised interior, set on a lively square. High-tech bedrooms with contemporary minimalist décor. Classic-traditional cooking served in the atmosphere of a Parisian-style brasserie.

Banks Mansion without rest

Herengracht 519 ✉ 1017 BV – ☎ (0 20) 420 00 55 – desk@banksmansion.nl
– Fax (0 20) 420 09 93 – www.banksmansion.nl **G2**

51 rm – †159/299 € ††189/610 €

◆ Chain hotel ◆ Business ◆ Modern ◆

Building dating from 1923 whose interior combines the styles of Dutch architect Hendrik Petrus Berlage and American architect Frank Lloyd Wright. Modern rooms with retro touches. Attractive, intimate lounge.

Mövenpick

Piet Heinkade 11 ✉ 1019 BR – ☎ (0 20) 519 12 00
– hotel.amsterdam@moevenpick.com – Fax (0 20) 519 12 49
– www.moevenpick-amsterdam.com **H1**

407 rm – †169/345 € ††169/345 €, ☕ 21 € – 1 suite

Rest – Menu 25/39 € – Carte 37/45 €

◆ Chain hotel ◆ Business ◆ Modern ◆

Modern chain hotel inaugurated in 2006 in a modern district. The rooms have panoramic views. Concert hall, jazz club and congress centre next door. Restaurant serving Asian cuisine: Chinese, Thai and Indonesian.

Estheréa without rest

Singel 305 ✉ 1012 WJ – ☎ (0 20) 624 51 46 – info@estherea.nl
– Fax (0 20) 623 90 01 – www.estherea.nl **F2**

71 rm – †179/246 € ††191/314 €, ☕ 14 €

◆ Family ◆ Traditional ◆ Personalised ◆

The same family have run this hotel since 1942. Set in a row of old merchants' houses with refined, neoclassical communal areas, personalised rooms and characterful breakfast room.

Swissôtel

Damrak 96 ✉ 1012 LP – ☎ (0 20) 522 30 00 – harold.kluit@swissotel.com
– www.swissotel-amsterdam.com **G1**

104 rm – †99/380 € ††99/450 €, ☕ 18 € – 5 suites

Rest – Carte 18/44 €

◆ Chain hotel ◆ Business ◆ Functional ◆

Renovated chain hotel in a centrally-located traditional-looking building. Modern public areas, functional bedrooms and good reception. Contemporary brasserie-restaurant. International menu.

Toren without rest

Keizersgracht 164 ✉ 1015 CZ – ☎ (0 20) 622 60 33 – info@hoteltoren.nl
– Fax (0 20) 626 97 05 – www.thetoren.nl **F1**

39 rm – †110/240 € ††140/390 €, ☕ 12 € – 1 suite

◆ Traditional ◆ Classic ◆

Anne Frank's House is just 200 m away from this charming hotel with spruce rooms in a classic style. Elegant breakfast room in front of an attractive bar.

NH Amsterdam Centre

Stadhouderskade 7 ✉ 1054 ES – ✆ (0 20) 685 13 51
– nhamsterdamcentre@nh-hotels.com – Fax (0 20) 685 16 11
– www.nh-hotels.com **E3**

228 rm – 159/420 € 159/420 €, 25 € – 2 suites

Rest ***Bice*** – *(closed 16 July-5 August and Sunday) (dinner only)* Carte 34/56 €

◆ Chain hotel ◆ Business ◆ Modern ◆

Renovated chain hotel built to host athletes attending the Amsterdam Olympic Games in 1928. Designer public areas. Large modern bedrooms. Italian menu, contemporary setting and view over the Leidseplein at the Bice restaurant.

Amsterdam

Damrak 93 ✉ 1012 LP – ✆ (0 20) 555 06 66 – info@hotelamsterdam.nl
– Fax (0 20) 620 47 16 – www.hotelamsterdam.nl **G1**

79 rm – 100/250 € 100/360 €, 12 €

Rest ***De Roode Leeuw*** – Menu 33 € – Carte 36/78 €

◆ Traditional ◆ Classic ◆

This traditional Amsterdam hotel is on a very central section of the busy Damstraat. Very comfortable rooms. Public car parks nearby. A brasserie offering traditional Dutch dishes in a modernised setting with red decor.

Die Port van Cleve

rest

N.Z. Voorburgwal 178 ✉ 1012 SJ – ✆ (0 20) 718 90 13
– info@dieportvancleve.com – Fax (0 20) 421 03 10
– www.dieportvancleve.com **F1**

120 rm – 295 € 305 €, 18 € – 1 suite

Rest – Menu 30/36 € – Carte 34/49 €

◆ Traditional ◆ Functional ◆

The first Dutch brewers started work in the 19th century behind the flamboyant façade of this building (1864). Tidy rooms. Dutch gin bar decorated with Delft china and panelling. Restaurant-grill with a tally of the number of steaks served since 1870.

Dikker en Thijs Fenice without rest

Prinsengracht 444 ✉ 1017 KE – ✆ (0 20) 620 12 12 – info@dtfh.nl
– Fax (0 20) 625 89 86 – www.dtfh.nl **F3**

42 rm – 125/245 € 150/345 €

◆ Traditional ◆ Business ◆ Classic ◆

A building dating from 1921 on the corner of a shopping street, opposite the Princes Canal, where an assistant of Escoffier once owned a food shop. Large guestrooms, studio and penthouse.

Canal House without rest

Keizersgracht 148 ✉ 1015 CX – ✆ (0 20) 622 51 82 – info@canalhouse.nl
– Fax (0 20) 624 13 17 – www.canalhouse.nl **F1**

26 rm – 154/209 € 154/209 €

◆ Traditional ◆ Classic ◆

A 17th century building that has retained all its character. The personalised guestrooms look out over the canal or garden. Period decoration and furniture of varying styles.

Golden Tulip-Centre without rest

Nieuwezijdskolk 19 ✉ 1012 PV – ✆ (0 20) 530 18 18
– infoamsterdam@goldentuliphotelinntel.com – Fax (0 20) 422 19 19
– www.goldentuliphotelinntel.com **G1**

239 rm – 99/375 € 99/375 €, 20 €

◆ Chain hotel ◆ Modern ◆

A modern glass-fronted establishment in the heart of the busy Nieuwe Zijde, the shopping area next to the station. Well sound-proofed rooms. Breakfast area entirely surrounded by glass.

NH City Centre without rest

Spuistraat 288 ✉ 1012 VX – ✆ (0 20) 420 45 45 – nhcitycentre@nh.hotels.com – Fax (0 20) 420 43 00 – www.nh-hotels.com **F2**

209 rm – 🚹119/219 € 🚹🚹129/329 €, ☕ 17 €

◆ Chain hotel ◆ Business ◆ Functional ◆

Slotted between the Singel canal and the Béguine convent, this hotel has neutral, contemporary-style bedrooms typical of the NH chain. Spacious and comfortable lounge.

Mercure Arthur Frommer without rest

Noorderstraat 46 ✉ 1017 TV – ✆ (0 20) 622 03 28 – h1032@accor.com – Fax (0 20) 620 32 08 – www.accorhotels.com **G3**

90 rm – 🚹90/155 € 🚹🚹110/175 €, ☕ 15 €

◆ Chain hotel ◆ Traditional ◆ Classic ◆

A group of houses (including a former wool factory) in a quiet residential street, close to the Rijksmuseum. Public areas and bedrooms with Dutch decorative touches.

Le Coin without rest

Nieuwe Doelenstraat 5 ✉ 1012 CP – ✆ (0 20) 524 68 00 – hotel@lecoin.nl – Fax (0 20) 524 68 01 – www.lecoin.nl **G2**

42 rm – 🚹115 € 🚹🚹131/148 €, ☕ 11 €

◆ Traditional ◆ Functional ◆

Seven houses next to the University of Amsterdam make up this hotel. Rooms of various shapes and sizes, but all decorated in a contemporary style and equipped with a kitchenette.

Roemer without rest

Roemer Visscherstraat 10 ✉ 1054 EX – ✆ (0 20) 589 08 00 – info@hotelroemer.com – Fax (0 20) 589 08 01 – www.vondelhotels.com **E3**

23 rm ☕ – 🚹199/479 € 🚹🚹229/649 €

◆ Business ◆ Design ◆

This small designer-decorated hotel is located in an early 20C house not far from the Vondelpark. Well-equipped pleasant rooms. Town garden.

Vondel without rest

Vondelstraat 26 ✉ 1054 GD – ✆ (0 20) 612 01 20 – info@hotelvondel.com – Fax (0 20) 685 43 21 – www.hotelvondel.com **E3**

78 rm – 🚹99/499 € 🚹🚹99/499 €, ☕ 19 €

◆ Luxury ◆ Business ◆ Design ◆

Hotel occupying several late-19th century houses. Trendy communal areas in Italian designer style, works of modern art, contemporary bedrooms and ornamental garden.

Jan Luyken without rest

Jan Luykenstraat 58 ✉ 1071 CS – ✆ (0 20) 573 07 30 – jan-luyken@bilderberg.nl – Fax (0 20) 676 38 41 – www.janluyken.nl **E3**

62 rm – 🚹129/209 € 🚹🚹169/319 €, ☕ 19 €

◆ Chain hotel ◆ Traditional ◆ Cosy ◆

Three 1900s houses make up this hotel with contemporary interior décor. Modern bedrooms, designer bar with a few period touches and small courtyard terrace.

Fita without rest

Jan Luykenstraat 37 ✉ 1071 CL – ✆ (0 20) 679 09 76 – info@fita.nl – Fax (0 20) 664 39 69 – www.hotelfita.com

closed 15-31 December and 1-15 January **E3**

15 rm ☕ – 🚹100/145 € 🚹🚹130/160 €

◆ Family ◆ Classic ◆

This typical family-run hotel has functional rooms in three different sizes with the added advantage of being near Amsterdam's most prestigious museums. Friendly welcome.

XXXX ✿ **La Rive** – Hotel Amstel

Prof. Tulpplein 1 ✉ 1018 GX – ☎ (0 20) 520 32 64 – evert.groot@ihg.com – Fax (0 20) 520 32 66 – www.restaurantlarive.com
closed 28 July-18 August, 1-10 January, Saturday lunch, Sunday and Monday **H3**
Rest – Menu 48 €, 85/194 € bi – Carte 85/118 €
Spec. Terrine van ham, ganzenlever en sukadevlees, ossestaartgelei met sichuanpeper. Cannelloni van pepers en wortelen met kreeft en tijmbouillon. Gegrilde duif met rode paprika, maïssaus en gekonfijte boutjes.
♦ Contemporary ♦ Formal ♦
A fine atmosphere with refined décor, a prestigious wine collection and high level of comfort characterize this gastronomic restaurant on the Amstel. Views of the river from the dining area at the front.

XXXX **Excelsior** – Hotel de l'Europe

Nieuwe Doelenstraat 2 ✉ 1012 CP – ☎ (0 20) 531 17 05 – restaurant@leurope.nl – Fax (0 20) 531 17 78 – www.restaurantexcelsior.nl
closed 1-12 January, Saturday lunch and Sunday lunch **G2**
Rest – Menu 49 €, 69/96 € – Carte 55/118 €
♦ Contemporary ♦ Formal ♦
Elegant restaurant serving modern cuisine in a one-hundred-year-old luxury hotel. Enjoy views of the Munttoren and busy boats on the Amstel from the attractive terrace. Knowledgeable sommelier.

XXXX **Vermeer** – Hotel NH Barbizon Palace

Prins Hendrikkade 59 ✉ 1012 AD – ☎ (0 20) 556 48 85 – vermeer@nh-hotels.com – Fax (0 20) 624 33 53 – www.restaurantvermeer.nl
closed 30 July-4 August, 1-7 January, Saturday lunch and Sunday **G1**
Rest – Menu 40 €, 65/140 € bi – Carte approx. 80 €
♦ Innovative ♦ Minimalist ♦
Large somewhat formal restaurant within a luxury hotel. Classical repertoire in keeping with the luxury décor.

XXX **Christophe**

Leliegracht 46 ✉ 1015 DH – ☎ (0 20) 625 08 07 – info@restaurantchristophe.nl – Fax (0 20) 638 91 32 – www.restaurantchristophe.nl
closed Sunday and Monday **F1**
Rest – *(dinner only)* Menu 45/65 € – Carte 59/89 €
♦ French traditional ♦ Trendy ♦
This low-key, refined restaurant in a traditional building on the banks of the canal Lys serves good classic to modern cuisine.

XXX **Dynasty**

Reguliersdwarsstraat 30 ✉ 1017 BM – ☎ (0 20) 626 84 00 – dynasty@hetnet.nl – Fax (0 20) 622 30 38 – www.fer.nl
closed 27 December-30 January and Tuesday **F2**
Rest – *(dinner only)* Menu 38/60 € – Carte 34/65 €
♦ Chinese ♦ Exotic ♦
Stroll through the lively street before having a meal in this pleasant long-standing oriental restaurant. Walls decorated with photos of fruit taken by Hageman, a local food photographer.

XXX **Radèn Mas**

Stadhouderskade 6 ✉ 1054 ES – ☎ (0 20) 685 40 41 – Fax (0 20) 685 39 81
closed 31 December **E3**
Rest – *(dinner only until 11 p.m.)* Menu 30/46 € – Carte 33/68 €
♦ Indonesian ♦ Exotic ♦
This fine Indonesian restaurant has worthily preserved the culinary heritage of the former Dutch colony. Several "rijsttafel" (rice table) set menus. Classic-exotic setting.

XX **d'Vijff Vlieghen**

Spuistraat 294 (by Vlieghendesteeg 1) ✉ 1012 VX – ☎ (0 20) 530 40 60 – vijffvlieghen@nh-hotels.com – Fax (0 20) 623 64 04 – www.vijffvlieghen.nl
closed 23 December-1 January **F2**
Rest – *(dinner only)* Menu 34/54 € – Carte 45/67 €
◆ Dutch regional cuisine ◆ Rustic ◆
Modern cuisine prepared using typically Dutch produce and served in a restaurant taking up five 17th century townhouses. Maze of fully-renovated rustic dining rooms.

XX **Breitner**

Amstel 212 ✉ 1017 AH – ☎ (0 20) 627 78 79 – info@restaurant-breitner.nl – Fax (0 20) 330 29 98 – www.restaurant-breitner.nl
closed 28 July-10 August, 25 December-5 January and Sunday **G2**
Rest – *(dinner only)* Menu 35/58 € – Carte 48/72 €
◆ Contemporary ◆ Cosy ◆
Creative and elaborate meals served in a modern setting, with views over the Amstel and drawbridges. Designer lighting and contemporary art in the dining room.

XX **Het Tuynhuys**

Reguliersdwarsstraat 28 ✉ 1017 BM – ☎ (0 20) 627 66 03 – info@tuynhuys.nl – Fax (0 20) 423 59 97 – www.tuynhuys.nl
closed 28 December-3 January, Saturday lunch and Sunday lunch **F2**
Rest – Menu 30 €, 33/63 € – Carte 43/57 €
◆ Contemporary ◆ Fashionable ◆
Mediterranean-inspired menu, attractive modern décor (white walls, wrought iron chairs, azulejo tiles) and courtyard-garden with a fine view of the baroque façade.

XX **Indrapura**

Rembrandtplein 42 ✉ 1017 CV – ☎ (0 20) 623 73 29 – info@indrapura.nl – Fax (0 20) 624 90 78 – www.indrapura.nl
closed 31 December **G2**
Rest – *(dinner only)* Carte approx. 60 €
◆ Indonesian ◆ Exotic ◆
On a busy, crowded square. A good choice of Indonesian dishes, including the famous "rijsttafel" (rice table). A mixed clientele, exotic atmosphere and weekend pianist.

XX **Van Vlaanderen**

Weteringschans 175 ✉ 1017 XD – ☎ (0 20) 622 82 92
closed last 2 weeks July-first 2 weeks August, last week December, Sunday, Monday
Rest – *(dinner only) (booking essential)* Menu 43/50 € – Carte 53/65 € **F3**
◆ Contemporary ◆ Fashionable ◆
This trendy restaurant stands out due to its bow windowed-frontage. Cordial reception, polished, neutral dining rooms on two levels, and modern cuisine. Reservations advised.

XX **Hosokawa**

Max Euweplein 22 ✉ 1017 MB – ☎ (0 20) 638 80 86 – info@hosokawa.nl – Fax (0 20) 638 22 19 – www.hosokawa.nl – closed Sunday lunch **F3**
Rest – Menu 21 €, 40/78 € – Carte 30/89 €
◆ Japanese ◆ Minimalist ◆
A sober, modern Japanese restaurant with cooking tables, worth a detour to watch the entertaining show of food rotating past your eyes! At lunchtimes, only sushi is available.

XX **d' Theeboom**

Singel 210 ✉ 1016 AB – ☎ (0 20) 623 84 20 – info@theeboom.com – Fax (0 20) 421 25 12 – www.theeboom.com
closed 23 December-5 January and Sunday **F1**
Rest – *(dinner only)* Menu 35/40 € – Carte approx. 45 €
◆ Contemporary ◆ Retro ◆
Former cheese warehouse from 1712 where updated traditional meals are served in a pleasant setting with yellow walls, panelling, modern china and huge chandeliers.

XX **Beddington's**

Utrechtsedwarsstraat 141 ✉ 1017 WE – ✆ (0 20) 620 73 93 – Fax (0 20) 620 01 90
closed 13 July-4 August, 25 December, 1 January, Sunday and Monday
Rest – *(dinner only)* Menu 45/52 € **G3**
♦ Contemporary ♦ Fashionable ♦
A British chef runs the open kitchen of this modern restaurant serving contemporary cuisine in her adopted home of Amsterdam. Black and white décor.

XX **Sichuan Food**

Reguliersdwarsstraat 35 ✉ 1017 BK – ✆ (0 20) 626 93 27 – Fax (0 20) 627 72 81
closed 31 December **F2**
Rest – *(dinner only)* Menu 31/43 € – Carte 35/55 €
♦ Chinese ♦ Exotic ♦
Small oriental restaurant with good local reputation situated in a lively area. Typical local Chinese restaurant décor. Peking Duck prepared and served in the dining room.

XX **Le Relais** – Hotel de l'Europe

Nieuwe Doelenstraat 2 ✉ 1012 CP – ✆ (0 20) 531 17 04 – concierge@leurope.nl – Fax (0 20) 531 17 78 – www.leurope.nl **G2**
Rest – *(open until 11 p.m.)* Menu 25/30 € – Carte 29/48 €
♦ Brasserie ♦ Wine bar ♦
Despite the grand hotel location, stylish welcome and waiters in tails, this restaurant is far from stuffy! Blackboard lunchtime specials, set menus and local specialities.

X **Bordewijk**

Noordermarkt 7 ✉ 1015 MV – ✆ (0 20) 624 38 99 – www.restaurantbordewijk.nl
closed mid July-mid August, 24 December-2 January and Monday **F1**
Rest – *(dinner only)* Menu 39/59 € – Carte approx. 60 €
♦ Contemporary ♦ Minimalist ♦
Popular restaurant due to its modern menu with inventive touches and minimalist décor: bare floorboards, Formica tables and designer chairs. Noisy atmosphere when busy.

X **Entresol**

Geldersekade 29 ✉ 1011 EJ – ✆ (0 20) 623 79 12 – entresol@chello.nl – www.entresol.nl
closed 3 weeks July, 26 December-1 January, Sunday and Monday **G1**
Rest – *(dinner only)* Menu 34/46 € – Carte 39/54 €
♦ Contemporary ♦ Cosy ♦
Small modern restaurant in a narrow 17th century house. Intimate dining rooms on two levels, the one on the first floor features a Delft china fireplace.

X **Envy Delicacies**

Prinsengracht 381 ✉ 1016 HL – ✆ (0 20) 344 64 07 – info@envy.nl – Fax (0 20) 344 64 05 – www.envy.nl
closed Monday lunch and Tuesday **F2**
Rest – *(open until 11 p.m.)* Carte approx. 30 €
♦ Contemporary ♦ Brasserie ♦
Contemporary-style brasserie where guests eat on both sides of a long wenge wood bar lit by modern globe-shaped lights or at one of the neighbouring tables. Open kitchen.

X **Segugio**

Utrechtsestraat 96 ✉ 1017 VS – ✆ (0 20) 330 15 03 – adriano@segugio.nl – Fax (0 20) 330 15 16 – www.segugio.nl
closed 24 December-1 January and Sunday **G3**
Rest – *(dinner only until 11 p.m.)* Menu 55 € – Carte 46/68 €
♦ Italian ♦ Design ♦
This "ristorante" takes its name from a breed of gun dog, also used to search for truffles. Serves a good selection of regional wines.

Blue Pepper

Nassaukade 366h ✉ 1054 AB – ✆ (0 20) 489 70 39 – info@restaurantbluepepper.com – www.restaurantbluepepper.com **E2**

Rest – *(dinner only)* Menu 48/68 € bi – Carte approx. 50 €

◆ Indonesian ◆ Fashionable ◆

Soft lighting and a décor of blue monochrome and delicate floral touches make up the relaxing setting of the Blue Pepper. With fine Javanese meals served in attractive dishes.

Le zinc... et les autres

Prinsengracht 999 ✉ 1017 KM – ✆ (0 20) 622 90 44 – info@lezinc.nl – Fax (0 20) 639 02 70 – www.lezinc.nl

closed 30 April, 27 December-1 January and Sunday **F3**

Rest – *(dinner only until 11 p.m.)* Menu 33/82 € bi – Carte 41/55 €

◆ Contemporary ◆ Rustic ◆

Former warehouse from the 17th century located off the tourist trail opposite the Prinsengracht. Superb zinc bar with rustic dining room above. Modern classic cuisine.

Haesje Claes

Spuistraat 275 ✉ 1012 VR – ✆ (0 20) 624 99 98 – info@haesjeclaes.nl – Fax (0 20) 627 48 17 – www.haesjeclaes.nl

closed 30 April and 25, 26 and 31 December **F2**

Rest – Menu 20/29 € – Carte 26/43 €

◆ Dutch regional cuisine ◆ Rustic ◆

A popular restaurant reflecting the town's atmosphere. Simple and copious Dutch cuisine served in a cheerful setting. Historical museum nearby.

Fifteen

Jollemanhof 9 ✉ 1019 GW – ✆ 0 900 343 83 36 – info@fifteen.nl – Fax (0 20) 509 50 19 – www.fifteen.nl

closed 31 December-1 January *Plan I* **C1**

Rest – *(open until 11 p.m.)* Menu 31/46 € – Carte 35/50 €

◆ Contemporary ◆ Fashionable ◆

Jamie Oliver is behind the concept of this popular restaurant with a mission to give disadvantaged youngsters opportunities. Recipes made famous by "The Naked Chef".

SOUTH and WEST QUARTERS *Plan I*

Okura

Ferdinand Bolstraat 333 ✉ 1072 LH – ✆ (0 20) 678 71 11 – sales@okura.nl – Fax (0 20) 671 23 44 – www.okura.nl **C2**

286 rm – †260/395 € ††260/395 €, ☕ 30 € – 15 suites

Rest *Ciel Bleu* and ***Yamazato*** and ***Le Camelia*** – see below

Rest *Sazanka* – *(dinner only)* Menu 58/83 € – Carte 43/107 €

◆ Grand Luxury ◆ Business ◆ Modern ◆

Luxury Japanese-style hotel set in a modern tower block with 23 floors. Various types of rooms and suites, superb wellness centre and a full range of services offered. Large conference centre. Spectacular Japanese cuisine around cooking tables at the Sazanka.

Hilton

Apollolaan 138 ✉ 1077 BG – ✆ (0 20) 710 60 00 – info.amsterdam@hilton.com – Fax (0 20) 710 60 80 – www.amsterdam.hilton.com **B2**

267 rm – †205/430 € ††205/430 €, ☕ 25 € – 4 suites

Rest *Roberto's* – Carte 51/62 €

◆ Chain hotel ◆ Business ◆ Modern ◆

This modern and spacious hotel belonging to a chain has a terrace and garden with a water feature. Rooms and suites with superb views, one on a 1969 theme of 'John Lennon and Yoko Ono'. Italian menu served in a contemporary setting at Roberto's restaurant.

Apollo

Apollolaan 2 ✉ 1077 BA – ✆ (0 20) 673 59 22 – info@gtaa.nl – Fax (0 20) 570 57 44 – www.goldentulipapolloamsterdam.com **B2**

217 rm – ♦100/325 € ♦♦100/325 €, ☕ 22 € – 2 suites

Rest *La Sirène* – see below

♦ Chain hotel ♦ Business ♦ Stylish ♦

An international chain hotel located at the intersection of five canals. Guestrooms designed with the business traveller in mind. Waterside bar, terrace and landing stage.

Bilderberg Garden

Dijsselhofplantsoen 7 ✉ 1077 BJ – ✆ (0 20) 570 56 00 – gardens@bilderberg.nl – Fax (0 20) 570 56 54 – www.bilderberg.nl **B2**

122 rm – ♦169/350 € ♦♦169/350 €, ☕ 21 € – 2 suites

Rest *De Kersentuin* – *(closed Saturday lunch and Sunday)* Menu 25 €, 40/48 € – Carte approx. 55 €

♦ Luxury ♦ Business ♦ Stylish ♦

Chain hotel catering mainly to corporate customers in the business district. Fully renovated interior and bedrooms. Meals in line with current tastes, modern brasserie décor, pavement terrace.

Holiday Inn

De Boelelaan 2 ✉ 1083 HJ – ✆ (0 20) 646 23 00 – Fax (0 20) 517 25 34 – www.holidayinn.com/amsterdam **C2**

264 rm – ♦90/295 € ♦♦90/335 €, ☕ 21 €

Rest – *(open until 11 p.m.)* Menu 28 €, 30/38 € – Carte approx. 40 €

♦ Chain hotel ♦ Business ♦ Functional ♦

Chain hotel close to the RAI. Enjoy the discreet luxury and spaciousness of the communal areas and the comfortable guestrooms. Lounge-bar and restaurant in a modern setting evocative of New England. International and American cuisine.

Golden Tulip Art-Tulip Inn Art

Spaarndammerdijk 302 (Westerpark) ✉ 1013 ZX – ✆ (0 20) 410 96 70 – art@westcordhotels.nl – Fax (0 20) 681 08 02 – www.westcordhotels.nl **B1**

187 rm – ♦79/225 € ♦♦79/225 €, ☕ 15 € – 3 suites

Rest – Menu 20 €, 33/40 € – Carte 36/49 €

♦ Chain hotel ♦ Business ♦ Stylish ♦

Near a slip road off the ring, a modern hotel with very contemporary guest-rooms, available in two sizes. Exhibition of modern paintings in the public areas. Modern meals served in a trendy atmosphere; simpler set menu in the "eetcafé".

The College – Hotel school

Roelof Hartstraat 1 ✉ 1071 VE – ✆ (0 20) 571 15 11 – info@thecollegehotel.com – Fax (0 20) 571 15 13 – www.steinhotels.com/college **C2**

39 rm – ♦230 € ♦♦260/395 €, ☕ 19 € – 1 suite

Rest – *(closed Sunday dinner)* Menu 28 €, 32/55 €

♦ Grand Luxury ♦ Design ♦

This hotel is located in a former 19C "college", redecorated with refinement. Chic and fashionable lounge bar and rooms in the same style. Modern restaurant installed in a former gym. Serves modern cuisine.

Tulip Inn City West

Reimerswaalstraat 5 ✉ 1069 AE – ✆ (0 20) 410 80 00 – info@tulipinnamsterdamwest.nl – Fax (0 20) 410 80 30 – www.tulipinnamsterdamwest.nl **A2**

166 rm – ♦60/190 € ♦♦60/210 €, ☕ 8 €

Rest – Menu 20 €, 33/40 € – Carte 36/49 €

♦ Chain hotel ♦ Business ♦ Classic ♦

In a quiet area, this chain hotel boasts large rooms and public areas. With nearby parking available. Traditional-classic menu presented on a blackboard in the restaurant.

Savoy without rest
Ferdinand Bolstraat 194 ✉ 1072 LW – ☎ (0 20) 644 74 45 – info@savoyhotel.nl – www.savoyhotel.nl **C2**
43 rm ☕ – †125/165 € ††185/259 €
◆ Traditional ◆ Modern ◆
The architectural style of this brick building dating from 1933 was inspired by the Amsterdam School. Functional comfort and sufficiently-large guestrooms. Bright public areas.

Novotel rm
Europaboulevard 10 ✉ 1083 AD – ☎ (0 20) 541 11 23 – h0515@accor.com – Fax (0 20) 646 28 23 – www.novotel.com **C3**
611 rm – †395 € ††395/499 €, ☕ 21 €
Rest – *(open until midnight)* Menu 20 €, 24/40 € – Carte 22/51 €
◆ Chain hotel ◆ Business ◆ Functional ◆
Imposing hotel block, with one of the largest guest capacities in Benelux. Fully-renovated interior. Bright, modern and functional bedrooms. Functional tavern-restaurant serving traditional classic cuisine.

The Gresham Memphis without rest
De Lairessestraat 87 ✉ 1071 NX – ☎ (0 20) 673 31 41 – info@gresham-memphishotel.com – Fax (0 20) 673 73 12 – www.memphishotel.nl **B2**
74 rm – †145/295 € ††165/395 €, ☕ 20 €
◆ Chain hotel ◆ Business ◆ Classic ◆
The tram line to the city centre runs in front of this ivy-covered hotel. Modern and intimate lounge bar with hushed atmosphere. Fresh bedrooms and pleasant breakfast area.

NH Museum Quarter
Hobbemakade 50 ✉ 1071 XL – ☎ (0 20) 573 82 00 – nhmuseumquarter@nh-hotels.com – Fax (0 20) 573 82 99 – www.nh-hotels.com **B2**
163 rm – †129/279 € ††129/279 €, ☕ 17 €
Rest – Carte approx. 30 €
◆ Chain hotel ◆ Business ◆ Functional ◆
This chain hotel provides modern, standard guestrooms, the better ones located at the rear. Bright breakfast room facing the courtyard. Lounge-bar and modern dining room. Limited international menu.

Arena rest
's-Gravesandestraat 51 ✉ 1092 AA – ☎ (0 20) 850 24 11 – rheere@hotelarena.nl – Fax (0 20) 850 24 65 – www.hotelarena.nl **C2**
127 rm – †89/180 € ††109/275 €, ☕ 14 €
Rest – Menu 27 €, 28/43 € – Carte 32/46 €
◆ Business ◆ Minimalist ◆
Formerly an orphanage (1890), now an ultra-trendy hotel. Fantastic old staircase, designer bar and guestrooms of various styles and levels of comfort. Weekend nightclub (separate access). Designer setting and modern cuisine in the restaurant.

De Filosoof without rest
Anna van den Vondelstraat 6 ✉ 1054 GZ – ☎ (0 20) 683 30 13 – reservations@hotelfilosoof.nl – Fax (0 20) 685 37 50 – www.hotelfilosoof.nl **B2**
38 rm ☕ – †75/130 € ††100/125 €
◆ Family ◆ Personalised ◆
The originality of this hotel in a one-way street alongside the Vondelpark is in the décor of its rooms, based on cultural or philosophical themes. Garden.

Villa Borgmann without rest
Koningslaan 48 ✉ 1075 AE – ☎ (0 20) 673 52 52 – info@hotel-borgmann.nl – Fax (0 20) 676 25 80 – www.hotel-borgmann.nl **B2**
15 rm ☕ – †85/105 € ††120/189 €
◆ Family ◆ Functional ◆
A Russian couple play host in this large red-brick 1900s villa near the Vondelpark. Uncluttered rooms, simple breakfasts, quiet neighbourhood and easy car parking (paying).

XXXX

Ciel Bleu - Hotel Okura ≤ city, AC P VISA MC AE

Ferdinand Bolstraat 333 (23rd floor) ✉ 1072 LH – ☎ (0 20) 678 83 40 – restaurants@okura.nl – Fax (0 20) 678 77 88 – www.okura.nl

closed 3 weeks for building workers holidays and 1 week after Christmas

Rest – *(dinner only)* Menu 68/167 € bi – Carte 79/103 € **C2**

Spec. Tarbot op boerenbrood gebakken met Pata Negra, geglaceerde schorseneren en dressing van sherry. Gegrilde kalfshaas met gerookte kalfszwezerik, ravioli van kalfswang en jus van mosterdzaad. Warm taartje van chocolade met gemarineerd roodfruit en roomijs van zwarte kersen.

♦ Contemporary ♦ Formal ♦

At the top of a luxury hotel, this fully refurbished restaurant sports a cosy, modern look. Stylish service, creative cuisine, fine wine list. Admire the sunset from the lounge.

XXX

Rosarium P VISA MC AE

Amstelpark 1 ✉ 1083 HZ – ☎ (0 20) 644 40 85 – info@rosarium.net – Fax (0 20) 646 60 04 – www.rosarium.net

closed last week July-first week August, Saturday and Sunday **C3**

Rest – Menu 30 €, 40/45 € bi – Carte approx. 40 €

♦ Contemporary ♦ Fashionable ♦

Modern restaurant on the edge of the Amstelpark, located in a modern circular building with two wings. Spacious and bright designer setting, wine bar and verdant terrace.

XX

Yamazato - Hotel Okura AC P VISA MC AE

Ferdinand Bolstraat 333 ✉ 1072 LH – ☎ (0 20) 678 83 51 – restaurants@okura.nl – Fax (0 20) 678 77 88 – www.okura.nl **C2**

Rest – Menu 48 €, 65/140 € – Carte 38/97 €

Spec. Onigara-yaki van kreeft. Tsukuri van tonijn. Tempura van garnalen.

♦ Japanese ♦ Minimalist ♦

A "zen" atmosphere and setting in this Japanese restaurant, where you can savour the whole range of traditional dishes. Friendly, kimono-clad waitresses; simplified menu at lunchtime.

XX

Visaandeschelde AC (dinner) VISA MC AE

Scheldeplein 4 ✉ 1078 GR – ☎ (0 20) 675 15 83 – info@visaandeschelde.nl – Fax (0 20) 471 46 53 – www.visaandeschelde.nl

closed 30 April, 24-26 and 31 December-1 January, Saturday lunch and Sunday lunch **C2**

Rest – *(open until 11 p.m.)* Menu 32 €, 37/54 € – Carte 41/91 €

♦ Seafood ♦ Fashionable ♦

Opposite the RAI congress centre, this restaurant is popular with Amsterdammers for its dishes full of the flavours of the sea, contemporary brasserie décor and lively atmosphere.

XX

La Sirène - Hotel Apollo AC P VISA MC AE

Apollolaan 2 ✉ 1077 BA – ☎ (0 20) 570 57 24 – info@gtaa.nl – Fax (0 20) 570 57 44 – www.goldentulipapolloamsterdam.com **B2**

Rest – Menu 30 € – Carte approx. 40 €

♦ Seafood ♦ Formal ♦

Cuisine which comes in with the tide, served either in the large, bright dining room with views over the point where five canals meet or on the panoramic waterside terrace.

XX

Le Camelia - Hotel Okura AC P VISA MC AE

Ferdinand Bolstraat 333 ✉ 1072 LH – ☎ (0 20) 678 74 50 – restaurants@okura.nl – Fax (0 20) 678 77 88 – www.okura.nl **C2**

Rest – *(open until 11 p.m.)* Menu 33 € – Carte 36/41 €

♦ Contemporary ♦ Brasserie ♦

Parisian-inspired brasserie on the ground floor of a prestigious Japanese hotel. Modern menu and interior décor with light Art Deco touches.

XX **Le Garage** (dinner) VISA MC AE

Ruysdaelstraat 54 ✉ 1071 XE – ☎ (0 20) 679 71 76 – info@restaurantlegarage.nl – Fax (0 20) 662 22 49 – www.restaurantlegarage.nl
closed Easter, Whitsun, Ascension Day, 24-26 and 31 December-2 January, Saturday lunch and Sunday lunch **B2**

Rest – *(booking essential)* Menu 30 €, 35/45 € – Carte 41/70 €

♦ Brasserie ♦ Trendy ♦

An artistic and cosmopolitan atmosphere in this modern brasserie in an unusual setting where as well as coming for the food, guests come to see and be seen.

XX **Brasserie van Baerle** VISA MC AE

Van Baerlestraat 158 ✉ 1071 BG – ☎ (0 20) 679 15 32 – info@brasserievanbaerle.nl – Fax (0 20) 671 71 96 – www.brasserievanbaerle.nl
closed 25 December-January **B2**

Rest – *(open until 11 p.m.)* Menu 33/44 € – Carte 45/67 €

♦ Contemporary ♦ Retro ♦

This retro brasserie attracts regular customers, mainly from the local area because of its attractive menu, tasty steak tartare and well-matched wines. Courtyard terrace.

X **Le Hollandais** VISA MC AE

Amsteldijk 41 ✉ 1074 HV – ☎ (0 20) 679 12 48 – info@lehollandais.nl – www.lehollandais.nl
closed 3 weeks August, Sunday and Monday **C2**

Rest – *(dinner only)* Menu 32/70 € bi – Carte 43/55 €

♦ French traditional ♦ Trendy ♦

Endearing little local eatery serving classic French cuisine in a pared-down setting. Bistro dining room with covered tables and 1970s-style chairs.

X **Gorgeous** VISA MC AE

2de v.d. Helststraat 16 ✉ 1072 PD – ☎ (0 20) 379 14 00 – info@gorgeousrestaurant.nl – www.gorgeousrestaurant.nl
closed 24 December-2 January and Monday **C2**

Rest – *(dinner only)* Menu 34/60 € – Carte 41/57 €

♦ Contemporary ♦ Bistro ♦

Located in a working class district, not far from the Sarphati Park, this bistro can be spotted by its ornate tiled façade. Modernised interior. Menu read aloud.

X **Pakistan** VISA MC AE

Scheldestraat 100 ✉ 1078 GP – ☎ (0 20) 675 39 76 – Fax (0 20) 675 39 76 **C2**

Rest – *(dinner only until 11 p.m.)* Menu 25/45 € – Carte 27/45 €

♦ Indian ♦ Family ♦

An authentic Pakistani restaurant with exotic, generous menus, located not far from the RAI congress centre. Beef dishes instead of pork.

X **White Elephant** VISA MC AE

Van Woustraat 3 ✉ 1074 AA – ☎ (0 20) 679 55 56 – info@whiteelephant.nl – Fax (0 20) 679 55 58 – www.whiteelephant.nl
closed Monday *Plan II* **G3**

Rest – *(dinner only until 11 p.m.)* Menu 37/59 € – Carte 37/54 €

♦ Thai ♦ Exotic ♦

Thai restaurant with matching décor: panelling, orchids, bar in a traditional "hut", exotic terrace and friendly waiters in traditional costume. Authentic cuisine.

X **Spring** VISA MC AE

Willemsparkweg 177 ✉ 1071 GZ – ☎ (0 20) 675 44 21 – info@restaurantspring.nl – Fax (0 20) 676 94 14 – www.restaurantspring.nl
closed 30 April, 25-26 and 31 December-1 January, Saturday lunch and Sunday **B2**

Rest – Menu 30 €, 37/75 € bi – Carte 45/69 €

♦ Contemporary ♦ Minimalist ♦

Contemporary dining room with minimalist tubular décor, divided in two by a long leather bench. Mediterranean inspired cuisine. Set lunchtime menu; à la carte in the evening.

Brasserie Pays-Bas

Gustav Mahlerplein 14 ✉ 1082 MA – ☎ (0 20) 642 06 73 – info@brasseriepaysbas.nl – Fax (0 20) 642 22 27 – www.brasseriepaysbas.nl

closed lunch Saturday and Sunday **B2**

Rest – Menu 30 €, 40/55 € – Carte 39/58 €

◆ French traditional ◆ Design ◆

Recently-opened designer restaurant in a business district, where the corporate clientele from local offices flock at lunchtime. French classics and à la carte brasserie dishes.

Elkaar

Alexanderplein 6 ✉ 1018 CG – ☎ (0 20) 330 75 59 – info@etenbijelkaar.nl – www.etenbijelkaar.nl

closed 30 April, 25 and 31 December-1 January and Saturday lunch **C2**

Rest – Menu 25 €, 35/50 € – Carte 39/48 €

◆ Contemporary ◆ Bistro ◆

Warm contemporary bistro set in a smart house situated between the zoo and the Tropenmuseum. Softly-lit dining room; pavement-terrace open on fine days.

AT SCHIPHOL AIRPORT *Plan I*

Sheraton Airport

Schiphol bd 101 ✉ 1118 BG Schiphol – ☎ (0 20) 316 43 00 – sales.amsterdam@sheraton.com – Fax (0 20) 316 43 99 – www.sheraton.com/amsterdamair

400 rm – †167/409 € ††192/434 €, ☕ 27 € – 6 suites

Rest ***Voyager*** – Menu 40/58 € – Carte 40/72 €

◆ Chain hotel ◆ Business ◆ Modern ◆

Modern hotel complex near the airport, designed for a globe-trotting business clientèle. Guestrooms offer every comfort. Fine atrium. Full service. Modern brasserie with a star-decorated ceiling. International menu and buffets.

Hilton Schiphol

Schiphol Bd 701 ✉ 1118 ZK Schiphol – ☎ (0 20) 710 40 00 – hilton.schiphol@hilton.com – Fax (0 20) 710 40 80 – www.hilton.com

278 rm – †135/345 € ††150/360 €, ☕ 25 € – 2 suites

Rest ***East West*** – *(closed mid July-August, Saturday and Sunday) (dinner only)* Carte 52/69 €

◆ Chain hotel ◆ Business ◆ Functional ◆

A chain hotel, located near the airport and popular with business clientele. Modern, well-equipped guestrooms and meeting rooms. Meals combining Asian and Western flavours at the East West restaurant (Japanese cooking table during the week).

Radisson SAS Airport

Boeing Avenue 2 (South : 4 km by N 201 at Rijk) ✉ 1119 PB Schiphol – ☎ (0 20) 655 31 31 – reservations.amsterdam.airport@radissonsas.com – Fax (0 20) 655 31 00 – www.radissonsas.com

277 rm – †105/239 € ††105/239 €, ☕ 19 € – 2 suites

Rest – Menu 26 € – Carte 30/48 €

◆ Chain hotel ◆ Business ◆ Modern ◆

This hotel is ideal for business trips. It is spacious, close to the airport and motorway, with a convivial bar, meeting rooms and modern guestrooms which want for nothing. The restaurant menu offers international cuisine, dominated by Mediterranean dishes.

Courtyard by Marriott-Amsterdam Airport

Kruisweg 1401 ✉ 2131 MD Hoofddorp – ☎ (0 23) 556 90 00 – courtyard@claus.nl – Fax (0 23) 556 90 09 – www.marriott.nl

148 rm – †99/245 € ††99/245 €, ☕ 18 €

Rest – Carte 23/37 €

◆ Chain hotel ◆ Business ◆ Modern ◆

A modern-style business hotel next to a wooded area and lake. Spacious and contemporary guestrooms with king-size beds. Designer fireside lounge. Brasserie in a modern setting serving intercontinental cuisine and pizzas.

Schiphol A 4

Rijksweg A 4 nr 3 (South : 4 km, direction Amsterdam, Den Ruygen Hoek)
✉ 2132 MA Hoofddorp – ✆ (0 252) 67 53 35 – info@schiphol.valk.nl
– Fax (0 252) 62 92 45 – www.hotelschiphol.valk.nl
433 rm – †89/179 € ††100/225 €, ☕ 15 € – 2 suites
Rest – *(open until 11 p.m.)* Menu 20/23 € – Carte 22/51 €
♦ Chain hotel ♦ Business ♦ Functional ♦
Various categories of bedroom as well as huge conference facilities in this vast establishment typical of the Van der Valk hotel chain. Updated classic interior décor. Large restaurant with international menu.

Artemis

John M. Keynesplein 2 (exit ① Sloten) ✉ 1066 EP – ✆ (0 20) 718 90 00
– info@artemisamsterdam.com – Fax (0 20) 718 90 01
– www.artemisamsterdam.com **A2**
256 rm – †285 € ††285/555 €, ☕ 18 €
Rest – *(open until 11 p.m.)* Menu 25/43 € – Carte 34/45 €
♦ Luxury ♦ Design ♦
This modern building of original design in the business district features Dutch designer-style décor. There is an art gallery for exploring the subject in more detail. A large restaurant with ultra-modern décor and a big waterside terrace. Contemporary menu.

De Herbergh with rm

Sloterweg 259 ✉ 1171 CP Badhoevedorp – ✆ (0 20) 659 26 00
– info@herbergh.nl – Fax (0 20) 659 83 90 – www.herbergh.nl
24 rm – †70/111 € ††75/121 €, ☕ 12 €
Rest – Menu 28/38 € – Carte 29/38 €
♦ Contemporary ♦ Cosy ♦
Hundred-year-old auberge with cosy dining room and hidden, tree-lined terrace. The best rooms are upstairs. Small executive seminars are catered for.

Marktzicht

Marktplein 31 ✉ 2132 DA Hoofddorp – ✆ (0 23) 561 24 11
– info@restaurant-marktzicht.nl – Fax (0 23) 563 72 91
– www.restaurant-marktzicht.nl
closed 25-26 December and Sunday
Rest – Menu 33 € – Carte 42/60 €
♦ Contemporary ♦ Rustic ♦
An old 19th century inn on the Markt, built when the polder on which the airport stands was erected. Nostalgic atmosphere, modern menu and terrace to the front.

PAVILJOEN GOLFSLAG RESTAURANT

THE HAGUE

DEN HAAG – 'S GRAVENHAGE'

Population (est. 2005): 468 500 – Altitude: 3m

Iconotec/PHOTONONSTOP

The Hague appears to be a city of anomalies. Although the seat of Dutch government, it's not the capital of the Netherlands (which is Amsterdam); although a city of Europe wide importance, it's just as famous for its kiss-me-quick resort of Scheveningen; and although populated for hundreds of years by the well-to-do, its canal-side houses share little of Amsterdam's flamboyance.

The Hague earned its nickname 'the biggest village in Europe' because of its relatively small population sprawled about a large area: that 'village' is marked by an aristocratic charm, which is why it's rightly obtained another title – Holland's most elegant town. There are signs, though, that The Hague is doffing its neatly tailored cap to the 21C. Parts of the centre now shoot skywards courtesy of shiny government high-rises, while at ground level a rash of reasonably priced and buzzy restaurants and bars has brightened the streets. An outward-thinking city council has helped loosen the staid image with a lively programme of concerts and events, and there's an enticing range of museums clustered in the centre. A village, however large, wouldn't be a village without its sections of green and pleasant land, and The Hague doesn't disappoint with a kaleidoscope of leafy lanes and large parks.

LIVING THE CITY

Arrive at **Den Haag Centraal Station**, and you're only a five-minute walk from the centre of town (to your west). This is a compact quarter dominated by the **Binnenhof** parliament buildings. To the northeast of the centre are numerous green spaces and parks, while to the east and southeast lie the suburbs **Leidschendam, Voorburg** and **Rijswijk**. A couple of miles northwest of the centre is the **North Sea** and the popular beach resort of **Scheveningen**.

PRACTICAL INFORMATION

ARRIVAL-DEPARTURE

Rotterdam Airport is 16km southeast of The Hague which translates as a €45 taxi ride. Alternatively, there are shuttle and train services to Central Station which take 45 and 30min respectively.

TRANSPORT

A bus and tram system will whisk you around The Hague. Single tickets can be purchased from the bus driver but saver tickets must be bought in advance from the tourist information office, post offices, tobacconists, newsagents and hotels.

You can buy good value stripcards for your journeys. These are in two varieties; as a 15-stripcard or 45-stripcard and are valid throughout the country on buses, trams and metro. A one-day pass is also available for travel in The Hague, with price dependent on the amount of zones to be covered.

Once in The Hague, the only rail travel within the city is the line linking the two stations, Den Haag Centraal Station and Den Haag Hollands Spoor, which is a kilometre to the south of the centre, and is connected to it by frequent trams.

EXPLORING THE HAGUE

Although it gives the impression of being charmingly laid back and provincial, The Hague is a truly international city. It's home to over eighty embassies, as well as the International Court of Justice, and, of course, the Dutch Parliament. The Queen lives here too, albeit quite modestly. Not as modestly as the Crown Prince, though. His palace door opens on to the street. The air of gentle manners and 1950s calm is all-pervasive, as though the bureaucrats and bankers know that in a few minutes they can be sitting in a deckchair on the sandy beach.

→ LOUNGING ALONG THE LANGE

For all the new generation of eateries in the city, a stroll along **Lange Voorhout,** slap bang in the centre, even on a Saturday evening, can still be a serenely still experience. From here The Hague spreads through several square miles of art galleries and bistros. In the summer, the sun casts long shadows over leafy avenues and you can hear birds singing in the lime trees. A suitably bucolic spot to head for is the **Court Pond**, a dreamy lake which reflects the low-slung brick buildings of the Binnenhof – the Dutch Parliament. This is an impressive complex whose focal point is the thirteenth-century **Knights Hall**, a striking oak-roofed building in which the state opening of parliament takes place.

The tone is set for a visit to the adjacent **Mauritshuis**, not only The Hague's most important gallery, but one of the top art spaces in the world. What makes it so special is its size, or rather its lack of it. This is a compact and intimate gallery over just two floors, with around a hundred paintings on show. But what paintings! The core of the collection consists of masterpieces from the Dutch Golden Age, including works by Vermeer (yes, 'Girl With A Pearl Earring' is here), Rembrandt (the museum holds no less than twelve of his paintings), Hals and Potter. There are also stunning Flemish works from the sixteenth and seventeenth centuries by the likes of Rubens and van Dyck. Look out too for Holbein the Younger and some stark Flemish lowlife from the seventeenth century painter Brouwer, a man who knew his subject well, as he spent most of his short life in either a tavern or a prison.

→ PURE TORTURE

The feeling of cool sophistication continues as you regain Lange Voorhout. This is the main street in the city, a wide cobblestoned thoroughfare that becomes a leafy square. It boasts neoclassical mansions whose grand façades lead into foreign embassies and consulates. There's a museum on the square devoted to the vibrant works of the Dutch artist **M.C.Escher**, while two minutes' walk away yet more beautiful paintings are on offer at the **Museum Bredius**. These are packed tight like a splendid species in confinement, their setting enhanced by a sumptuous interior. The pick of the bunch are two works by Rembrandt. Just a short stroll west of the Museum Bredius, things take a darker turn as you arrive at a venue proud of its branding irons, execution swords and axes, elbow and thumb screws, racks and pillory boards, but the **Prison Gate** museum, which occupies the old town prison, and has a special section devoted to instruments of torture and interrogation. The tourist office people are quick to remind you that times have changed and the International Court of Justice really is based a few blocks from here.

→ LOOK AT THE VIEW!

If you head north past the **Noordeinde Palace**, home of the royals, you arrive, quite literally, at the Netherlands' biggest panorama. **Panorama Mesdag** was painted over the space of four months in 1880 by Hendrik Mesdag of the Hague School. It's a vast, cylindrical painting of Scheveningen, measuring 120m in circumference and standing 14m tall: it covers an amazing square mile of canvas (Mesdag did get assistance with his task!). From the viewing platform, the vista is endless in all directions: to the fishing village and its lighthouse, over the beach and the North Sea with its flat-bottomed fishing boats, to the fashionable seaside resort where bathing carriages are being rolled into the sea, over the dune landscape and on to The Hague. You can look three hundred and sixty degrees around you, and, to add to the illusion, the canvas itself blends into a 'virtual terrain' of seemingly abandoned objects on the floor. Real tufts of grass poke through the artificial beach that holds scraps of driftwood and a rusty anchor. Nearby, a weathered wooden chair lies next to a solitary clog. It all seems so real, you wonder why you can't sniff the seaweed or hear the swoosh of the waves.

→ A TRUE GEM

Heading inexorably towards the seaside, visitors are waylaid by another artistic gem – **The Gemeentemuseum**, the largest and most diverse of the city's exhibition spaces. Over seventy years old, it displays a rotated selection from a vast permanent collection. Nip down to the basement and you'll find eclectic sections on fashion and old musical instruments; upstairs the modern art section reflects changes from the early nineteenth century onwards. Many visitors are drawn to the impressive section on the De Stijl movement, which flourished between the two world wars, while others come because the museum boasts the world's largest collection of paintings by Holland's most famous twentieth century artist, Piet Mondrian. In his honour, an entire section is devoted to his early works. Trumping these, though, is his last (unfinished) painting 'Victory Boogie Woogie', a visual feast for the eye that's considered by many to be his best.

→ RATHER FRED THAN DEAD

Back in the centre of town, The Hague has some rather interesting shopping streets. First and foremost, hit the Fred, or, to be more precise, get along to **De Frederik Hendriklaan**, one of the city's most beautiful retail thoroughfares. It's lined with high-end boutiques and galleries, with a particular penchant for home furnishings and good food. There are charming streetside cafes here too. In **Hofweg,** right next to the Binnenhof, is **The Passage**, a restored covered arcade – the only one in the city – with a good selection of small boutiques and special interest shops. Meanwhile, Noordeinde is the place to go for elegant and imposing modern art galleries and boutiques, while the best antiques dealers can be found on **Denneweg**. The ideal way to round off your day is to take in a concert at the **Lucent Dans Theater**, a spankingly modern building near the Binnenhof, home to the National Dance Theatre. Their choreographed productions are of world renown and immense colour, a shimmering contrast to the coolly sedate charms of their home 'big village'.

CALENDAR HIGHLIGHTS

The Hague knows how to loosen its stays and flaunt itself when it comes to annual festivals. For instance, in April the Queen's Night Festival sees the city lighten up with five outdoor stages for a mammoth free music show…in honour of Beatrix. The focus turns seawards in May with the North Sea Regatta, which has sailing competitions between Scheveningen and Harwich in the UK. The sand stays in your eyes between April and June at the International Sand Sculpture Festival, as teams from around the

THE HAGUE IN…

→ ONE DAY

Binnenhof, Mauritshuis, Panorama Mesdag

→ TWO DAYS

Gemeentemuseum, 'The Fred', a stroll around Noordeinde, a show at Lucent Dans Theater

→ THREE DAYS

A day out at Scheveningen by the sea, Madurodam

world come up with magical creations made out of Scheveningen's shifting stuff. June's Music In My Head takes place at the Hague's Paard Van Troje over a couple of cutting-edge days: established rock acts line up alongside up-and-coming names. The city really throws off its ambassadorial trappings with July's De Parade, a travelling festival which alights in Westbroekpark with ten days of fairground rides, music, theatre, film, dance and opera. Tasty world cuisine's on offer too. Back at Scheveningen in August, the Van der Valk pier lights up twice every evening for the three nights of the International Fireworks Festival, while a month later the Todaysart Festival puts on a whole range of performing arts shows at twenty indoor and outdoor venues across the Hague. Fans of that event should also make a beeline for the Theater aan het Spui in November for the Crossing Border Festival which is, quite simply, Europe's biggest literature, music and visual arts all-in-one celebration, with over eighty acts taking part.

EATING OUT

Locals like to think that their 'biggest village in Europe' is the result of a lot made from a little. They call it the Hague Bluff. But what's that got to do with food? Well, the Hague Bluff is also a local pudding, made with eggs and sugar, representing the idea that something grand can be made from humble ingredients (in its finished state the Hague Bluff becomes a gooseberry fool). There's nothing bluff, though, about the city's restaurant scene. It's first rate in every respect, and although some are targeted full-on at the embassy army, many more are very affordable, with main courses set between fifteen and twenty euros. With the cuisine of more than twenty nationalities on offer, the choice is broad and pleasingly sophisticated: the number of exotic restaurants reflects the many cultures found here. Asian influences are everywhere, but in particular, the Indonesian connection is clear. There's a host of first-rate restaurants in the area just beyond Lange Voorhout around Denneweg and Frederikstraat. If you can't find what you want there, then head to Molenstraat, near the Noordeinde Palace, for another exciting cluster.

→ PEACE BE WITH YOU

The Peace Palace, to the north of the city, was the result of a donation by American millionaire Andrew Carnegie at the turn of the twentieth century. In turn, nations donated stained glass, marble, tapestries, urns, and a Swiss clock in the bell tower. Despite the onset of World War I, the Peace Palace's reputation went from strength to strength...today, this is where you'll find the International Court of Justice.

→ SCULPTURE BY THE SEA

If you decide to go to Scheveningen, you won't be alone. The resort is Holland's most popular seaside location and is visited by nine million a year. Its most fascinating attraction is the Museum Beelden-aan-Zee, which features modern sculptures in an old pavilion. Many leading sculptors are represented, including Fritz Koenig and Man Ray.

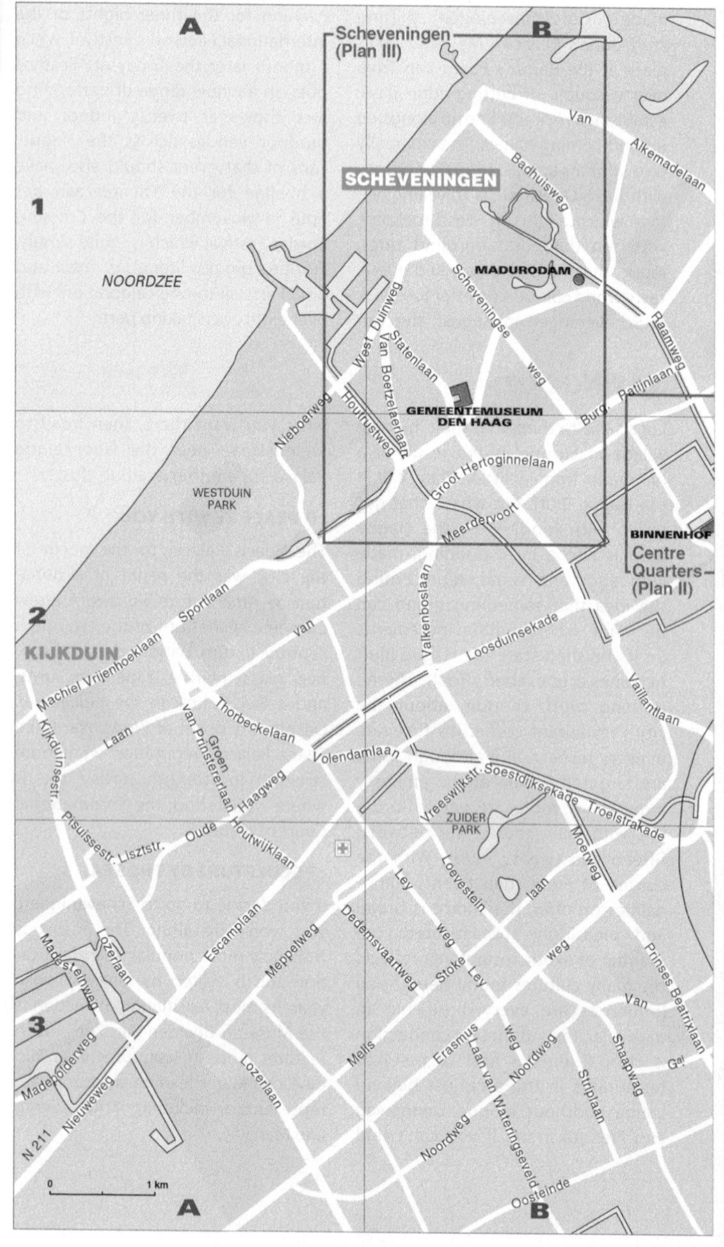
A
B
1
2
3
Scheveningen (Plan III)
SCHEVENINGEN
NOORDZEE
MADURODAM
GEMEENTEMUSEUM DEN HAAG
WESTDUIN PARK
KIJKDUIN
BINNENHOF
Centre Quarters (Plan II)
ZUIDER PARK
Van Alkemadelaan
Badhuisweg
Scheveningse weg
Raamweg
West Duinweg
Van Boetzelaerlaan
Statenlaan
Nieboerweg
Houtrustweg
Burg. Patijnlaan
Groot Hertoginnelaan
Meerdervoort
Sportlaan
Machiel Vrijenhoeklaan
Laan van
Valkenboslaan
Loosduinsekade
Vaillantlaan
Thorbeckelaan
Groen Van Prinstererlaan
Volendamlaan
Kijkduinsestr.
Haagweg
Vreeswijkstr.
Soestdijksekade
Troelstrakade
Pisuissestr.
Lisztstr.
Oude Houtwijklaan
Ley
Loevestein laan
Moerweg
Madesteinweg
Lozerlaan
Escamplaan
Meppelweg
Dedemsvaartweg
Stoke
weg
Prinses Beatrixlaan
Van
Gal
Madepolderweg
Mells
Erasmus weg
Laan van Wateringseveld
Noordweg
Striplaan
Shaapweg
Nieuweweg
N 211
0
1 km
Oosteinde

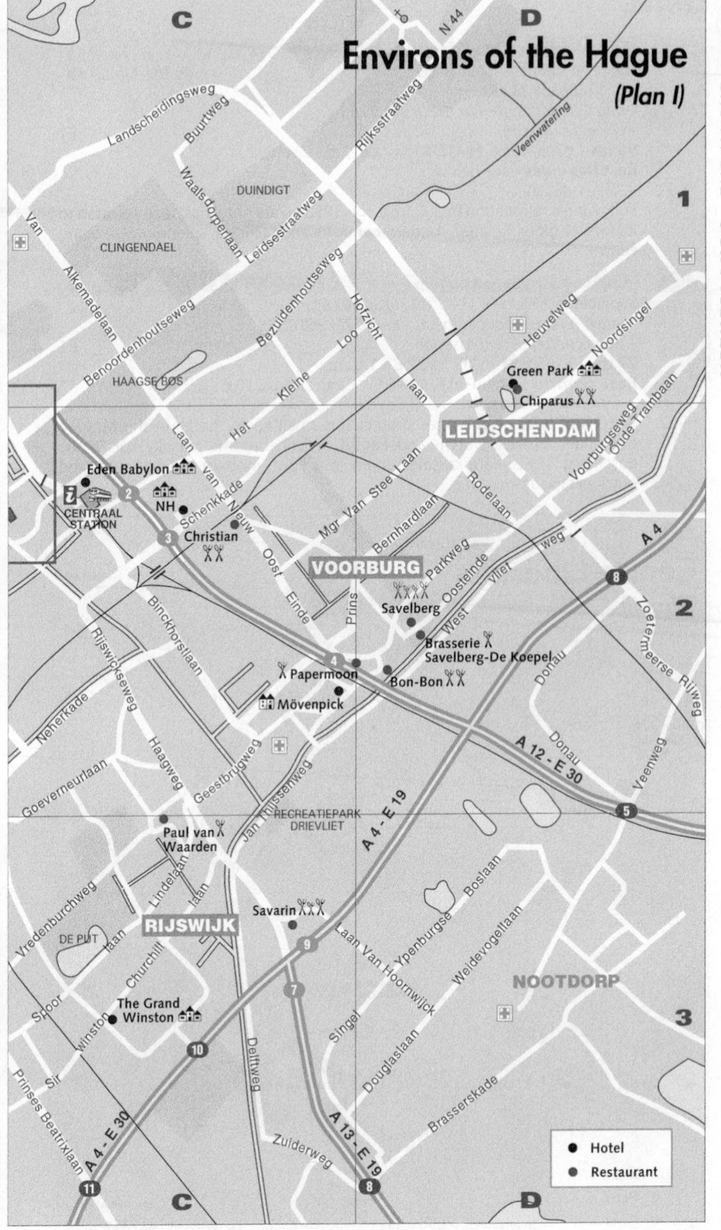

Environs of the Hague
(Plan I)
Hotel
Restaurant
LEIDSCHENDAM
VOORBURG
RIJSWIJK
NOOTDORP
DUINDIGT
CLINGENDAEL
HAAGSE BOS
RECREATIEPARK DRIEVLIET
DE PUT
CENTRAAL STATION
Green Park
Chiparus
Eden Babylon
NH
Christian
Savelberg
Brasserie Savelberg-De Koepel
Papermoon
Bon-Bon
Mövenpick
Paul van Waarden
Savarin
The Grand Winston
A 12 - E 30
A 4 - E 19
A 4 - E 30
A 13 - E 19
A 4
N 44

CENTRE

Plan II

Le Méridien Hotel des Indes

Lange Voorhout 54 ✉ 2514 EG – ✆ (0 70) 361 23 45 – info@desindes.nl – Fax (0 70) 361 23 50 – www.desindes.nl

F1

90 rm – 🚹365/465 € 🚹🚹415/515 €, ☕ 25 € – 2 suites
Rest *Des Indes* – see below

♦ Grand luxury ♦ Design ♦

Following a renovation by J. Garcia, this 1858 luxury hotel has been restored to its former glory. Refined, modern comforts and facilities; splendid well-being centre.

Carlton Ambassador

Sophialaan 2 ✉ 2514 JP – ✆ (0 70) 363 03 63 – info@ambassador.carlton.nl – Fax (0 70) 360 05 35 – www.carlton.nl/ambassador

E1

77 rm – 🚹145 € 🚹🚹160 €, ☕ 22 € – 1 suite
Rest *Henricus* – Menu 30 €, 40/48 € – Carte approx. 50 €

♦ Palace ♦ Classic ♦

Dozens of ancient oak trees protect this small luxury hotel, in the Mesdag diplomatic district. Dutch- and English-style bedrooms. Whisky bar in the basement. Up-to-date cuisine served in a light, modern dining room, and outdoors in summertime.

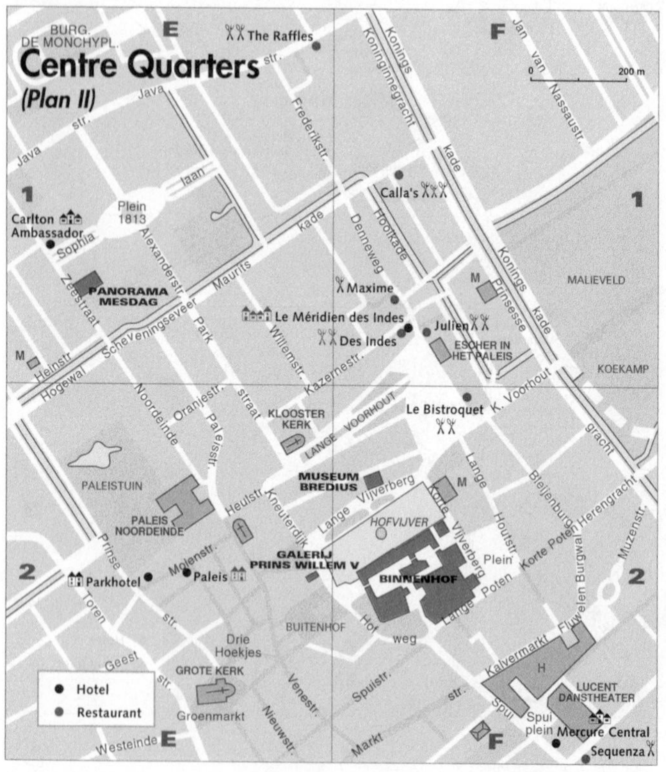

Eden Babylon

Koningin Julianaplein 35 ✉ 2595 AA – ✆ (0 70) 381 49 01 – info@edenhotelgroup.com – Fax (0 70) 382 59 27 – www.edenhotelgroup.com Plan I **C2**

142 rm – 149/260 € 169/320 €, 22 € – 1 suite

Rest – *(closed Saturday lunch and Sunday lunch)* Menu 37/82 € bi – Carte approx. 55 €

◆ Chain hotel ◆ Business ◆ Design ◆

Next-door to the station, the interior of this modern hotel was redesigned by Miguel Cancio Martins (responsible for the Paris Buddha Bar). Designer-style rooms. Trendy lounge-bar and designer-style dining room, whose large bay windows overlook the park.

Bel Air

Johan de Wittlaan 30 ✉ 2517 JR – ✆ (0 70) 352 53 54 – info@goldentulipbelairhotel.nl – Fax (0 70) 352 53 53 – www.goldentulipbelairhotel.nl Plan III **H3**

326 rm – 110/275 € 110/275 €, 18 €

Rest – Carte 31/55 €

◆ Chain hotel ◆ Classic ◆

Immense hotel whose spacious comfortable rooms overlook the park or the museum. Spacious public area, conference and fitness facilities and long-stay studios. Immense contemporary-inspired restaurant in a brasserie style.

Crowne Plaza Promenade

Van Stolkweg 1 ✉ 2585 JL – ✆ (0 70) 352 51 61 – info@crowneplazadenhaag.nl – Fax (0 70) 354 10 46 – www.crowneplazadenhaag.nl Plan III **H2**

92 rm – 275 € 295 €, 23 € – 2 suites

Rest ***Brasserie Promenade*** – Menu 30 €, 35/40 € – Carte 35/57 €

◆ Chain hotel ◆ Functional ◆

Chain hotel overlooking a vast park that is home to the Madurodam (Miniature Holland). Standard rooms and junior suites. Fine collection of modern artwork. Relaxed brasserie offering simple meals.

Mercure Central

Spui 180 ✉ 2511 BW – ✆ (0 70) 363 67 00 – h1317@accor.com – Fax (0 70) 363 93 98 – www.mercure.nl **F2**

156 rm – 79/205 € 79/210 €, 19 € – 3 suites

Rest – Menu 29 € – Carte 34/47 €

◆ Chain hotel ◆ Business ◆ Design ◆

Centrally located chain hotel, recently renovated in a contemporary spirit. Practical, well-soundproofed rooms. Business clientele. Bar decorated along the lines of Pullman carriage serving a small selection of dishes.

NH

Prinses Margrietplantsoen 100 ✉ 2595 BR – ✆ (0 70) 381 23 45 – nhdenhaag@nh-hotels.com – Fax (0 70) 381 23 33 – www.nh-hotels.com Plan I **C2**

193 rm – 75/295 € 75/295 €, 17 € – 12 suites

Rest – *(closed lunch Saturday and Sunday) (open until 11 p.m.)* Menu 30 € – Carte 35/49 €

◆ Chain hotel ◆ Business ◆ Modern ◆

Three modern tower blocks, inaugurated in 2005 in the heart of the local Manhattan, offer various categories of contemporary rooms. Glass-roofed atrium shopping centre. Trendy lounge restaurant, and culinary concept to match, appreciated for its versatility.

Parkhotel

Molenstraat 53 ✉ 2513 BJ – ✆ (0 70) 362 43 71 – info@parkhoteldenhaag.nl – Fax (0 70) 361 45 25 – www.parkhoteldenhaag.nl **E2**

120 rm – 89/145 € 99/275 €, 15 €

Rest – *(dinner only residents)*

◆ Traditional ◆ Classic ◆

Contemporary dining room, dotted with "neo-retro" influences in a hotel founded in 1912, overlooking a park. Cosy lounge, period staircase, modernised rooms and garden.

Novotel World Forum

Johan de Wittlaan 42 ✉ 2517 JR – ✆ (0 70) 416 91 11 – h5389@accor.com – Fax (0 70) 416 91 00 – www.novotel.com Plan III **H2**

214 rm – 170/260 € 185/275 € – 2 suites

Rest – Menu 16 € – Carte 37/48 €

♦ Chain hotel ♦ Functional ♦

Strategically situated "on" the congress hall. Modern hotel, with spacious and spick-and-span bedrooms, as well as a huge conference infrastructure and interesting views. Brasserie for guests and congress delegates who prefer to remain in the hotel.

Paleis without rest

Molenstraat 26 ✉ 2513 BL – ✆ (0 70) 362 46 21 – info@paleishotel.nl – Fax (0 70) 361 45 33 – www.paleishotel.nl **E2**

20 rm – 189/295 € 199/325 €, 16 €

♦ Luxury ♦ Classic ♦

Plush boutique hotel noted for its personalised welcome. Louis XVI-style rooms adorned with rich fabrics by French designer Pierre Frey. Sumptuous breakfast room.

Calla's (Marcel van der Kleijn)

Laan van Roos en Doorn 51a ✉ 2514 BC – ✆ (0 70) 345 58 66 – info@restaurantcallas.nl – Fax (0 70) 345 57 10 – www.restaurantcallas.nl

closed 27 July-18 August, 23 December-7 January, Saturday lunch, Sunday and Monday **F1**

Rest – Menu 48 €, 75/148 € bi – Carte 85/108 €

Spec. Tartelette van Jacobsmosselen, parmezaanse kaas en seizoenstruffel (October-April). Gebraden kooieend met blauwe vijg en koriander (September-October). In rhum gegaarde banaan met amandelcake en kokossorbet.

♦ Contemporary ♦ Minimalist ♦

A former warehouse turned into a smart contemporary-style restaurant. Lounge, chef's table and a view of the kitchen below. Main room is upstairs.

Des Indes – Le Méridien Hotel des Indes

Lange Voorhout 54 ✉ 2514 EG – ✆ (0 70) 361 23 45 – info@desindes.nl – Fax (0 70) 361 23 50 – www.desindes.nl **F1**

Rest – Menu 35 €, 45/93 € bi – Carte 36/71 €

♦ Contemporary ♦ Formal ♦

Following a renovation by J. Garcia, this 1858 luxury hotel has been restored to its former glory. Refined, modern comforts and facilities; splendid well-being centre.

Le Bistroquet

Lange Voorhout 98 ✉ 2514 EJ – ✆ (0 70) 360 11 70 – info@bistroquet.nl – Fax (0 70) 360 55 30 – www.bistroquet.nl

closed 24 December-1 January, Saturday lunch and Sunday **F2**

Rest – Menu 33 €, 39/67 € bi – Carte 53/68 €

♦ Contemporary ♦ Cosy ♦

This plush bistro is popular with the diplomatic-parliamentary crowd. Up-to-date cuisine served in a warm, intimate atmosphere or outdoors in the shade of the square's trees.

Julien

Vos in Tuinstraat 2a ✉ 2514 BX – ✆ (0 70) 365 86 02 – info@julien.nl – Fax (0 70) 365 31 47 – www.julien.nl

closed Sunday **F1**

Rest – Menu 38/90 € – Carte 49/72 €

♦ Traditional ♦ Retro ♦

This restaurant will delight Art Nouveau enthusiasts. Muted dining rooms, mezzanine and understated bar. Swan theme décor. Popular with politicians and Dutch royalty.

Rousseau

Van Boetzelaerlaan 134 ✉ 2581 AX – ✆ (0 70) 355 47 43
– info@restaurantrousseau.com
– www.restaurantrousseau.com
closed 3-25 August, 21 December-5 January, 23 February-3 March, Saturday lunch, Sunday and Monday *Plan III* **G3**
Rest – Menu 28 €, 33/94 € bi – Carte 49/66 €
♦ Traditional ♦ Friendly ♦
Well-thought out, traditional, seasonal menu served in front of a naïve fresco in the style of Douanier Rousseau, (the chef-owner shares his surname), or in the courtyard with pergola.

Christian

Laan van Nieuw Oost Indië 1f ✉ 2593 BH – ✆ (0 70) 383 88 56
– info@restaurantchristian.nl – Fax (0 70) 385 59 32
– www.restaurantchristian.nl
closed 2 weeks August, 1-9 January, Tuesday, Wednesday and Saturday lunch *Plan I* **C2**
Rest – Menu 35 €, 43/75 € – Carte approx. 55 €
♦ Contemporary ♦ Friendly ♦
Excellent cuisine served in this modern restaurant enhanced by a tasteful grey and orange colour scheme. Chef's table for 8 to 10 guests to the rear; courtyard terrace.

The Raffles

Javastraat 63 ✉ 2585 AG – ✆ (0 70) 345 85 87
– info@restaurantraffles.com – Fax (0 70) 356 00 84
– www.restaurantraffles.com
closed late July-early August, 1 week February, Sunday and Monday **E1**
Rest – *(dinner only)* Menu 38/47 € – Carte 36/55 €
♦ Indonesian ♦ Friendly ♦
Located on the fittingly-named Javastraat, restaurant serving authentic, flavoursome Indonesian cooking, served in a suitably exotic setting, enhanced with Colonial touches.

Maxime

Denneweg 10b ✉ 2514 CG – ✆ (0 70) 360 92 24 – info@restaurantmaxime.nl
– www.restaurantmaxime.nl
closed 28 July-17 August and Sunday lunch **F1**
Rest – *(booking essential)* Menu 26/30 €
♦ Contemporary ♦ Bistro ♦
Small hip bistro offering two set four-course menus - "links" and "rechts". Cosy designer décor. Book for the first (6-8pm) or second (8-10pm) sitting.

Shirasagi

Stadhouderslaan 76 R ✉ 2517 JA – ✆ (0 70) 346 47 00 – shirasagi@planet.nl
– Fax (0 70) 346 26 01 – www.shirasagi.nl
closed 31 December-2 January and Sunday *Plan III* **G3**
Rest – Menu 20 €, 40/60 € – Carte 29/60 €
♦ Japanese ♦ Minimalist ♦
Japanese restaurant out of the town centre in an attractive old house. Minimalist décor, teppanyaki (evenings), sushi bar, open kitchens and inviting rear terrace.

Sequenza

Spui 224 ✉ 2511 BX – ✆ (0 70) 345 28 53
closed 1 week May, 3 weeks September, Sunday and Monday **F2**
Rest – *(dinner only until 11 p.m.)* Menu 38 €
♦ Contemporary ♦ Friendly ♦
Mediterranean-inspired cusine, daily changing menu depending on the season. Wooden floorboards and rustic chairs indoors, ivy-covered walled terrace outdoors.

Steigenberger Kurhaus

Gevers Deynootplein 30 ✉ 2586 CK – ☎ (0 70) 416 26 36 – info@kurhaus.nl – Fax (0 70) 416 26 46 – www.kurhaus.nl **G1**

235 rm – 275/350 € 300/375 €, ☕ 23 € – 10 suites

Rest *Kandinsky* – see below

Rest *Kurzaal* – Menu 20 €, 25/33 €

♦ Palace ♦ Luxury ♦ Classic ♦

This beachside luxury hotel frequently hosts upmarket seminars. Extensive facilities, full spa service and sophisticated rooms equipped with modern comforts. Modern menu served under the dome of a splendid period concert hall.

Carlton Beach

Gevers Deynootweg 201 ✉ 2586 HZ – ☎ (0 70) 354 14 14 – info@beach.carlton.nl – Fax (0 70) 352 00 20 – www.carlton.nl/beach **H1**

179 rm – 145/300 € 165/300 €, ☕ 21 € – 4 suites

Rest – Carte 35/60 €

♦ Business ♦ Modern ♦

1980s building standing at the end of the dyke offering rooms that overlook the beach, dunes or street. Generous buffet and fine sea-view at breakfast time. Two restaurants: pirate-inspired grill room and modern brasserie-style dining room.

Europa

Zwolsestraat 2 ✉ 2587 VJ – ☎ (0 70) 416 95 95 – europa@bilderberg.nl – www.bilderberg.nl **H1**

173 rm – 115/215 € 140/235 €, ☕ 19 € – 1 suite

Rest – *(dinner only)* Menu 30/58 € bi – Carte 42/57 €

♦ Chain hotel ♦ Functional ♦

This modern hotel, 300m from the jetty, overlooks a busy street. Ask for one of the quieter rooms at the back to avoid the noise. The restaurant features an up-to-date menu, smart brasserie style and city terrace.

Badhotel

Gevers Deynootweg 15 ✉ 2586 BB – ☎ (0 70) 351 22 21 – info@badhotelscheveningen.nl – Fax (0 70) 355 58 70 – www.badhotelscheveningen.nl **G1**

90 rm – 108/160 € 123/160 €, ☕ 15 €

Rest – *(dinner only residents)*

♦ Traditional ♦ Classic ♦

On the main street (tramway), this building offers tastefully decorated rooms in a nautical style. Those to the rear and on the top floors are larger and quieter. Spruced up restaurant; classic, traditional dishes.

Ibis

Gevers Deynootweg 63 ✉ 2586 BJ – ☎ (0 70) 354 33 00 – h1153@accor.com – Fax (0 70) 352 39 16 – www.ibishotel.com **G1**

88 rm – 78/110 € 78/110 €, ☕ 12 €

Rest – *(closed Saturday and Sunday) (dinner only)* Carte 21/34 €

♦ Chain hotel ♦ Business ♦ Functional ♦

Centrally located and close to all the resort's main amenities, this chain hotel stands on a main street parallel with the dyke (Strandweg). Two sizes of rooms. Restaurant in the lobby; simple menu with pasta and pizzas.

Kandinsky – Hotel Steigenberger Kurhaus — sea and beach,

Gevers Deynootplein 30 ✉ 2586 CK – ☎ (0 70) 416 27 13 – info@kurhaus.nl – Fax (0 70) 416 26 71 – www.kurhaus.nl

closed 1-6 January, Saturday lunch and Sunday **G1**

Rest – *(dinner only 21 July-2 September)* Menu 38 €, 55/92 € bi – Carte 55/98 €

♦ Contemporary ♦ Formal ♦

Elegant, modern restaurant in the resort's flagship hotel. Comfortable dining area, tasty inventive cuisine, pleasant seaside view and terrace overlooking the dyke.

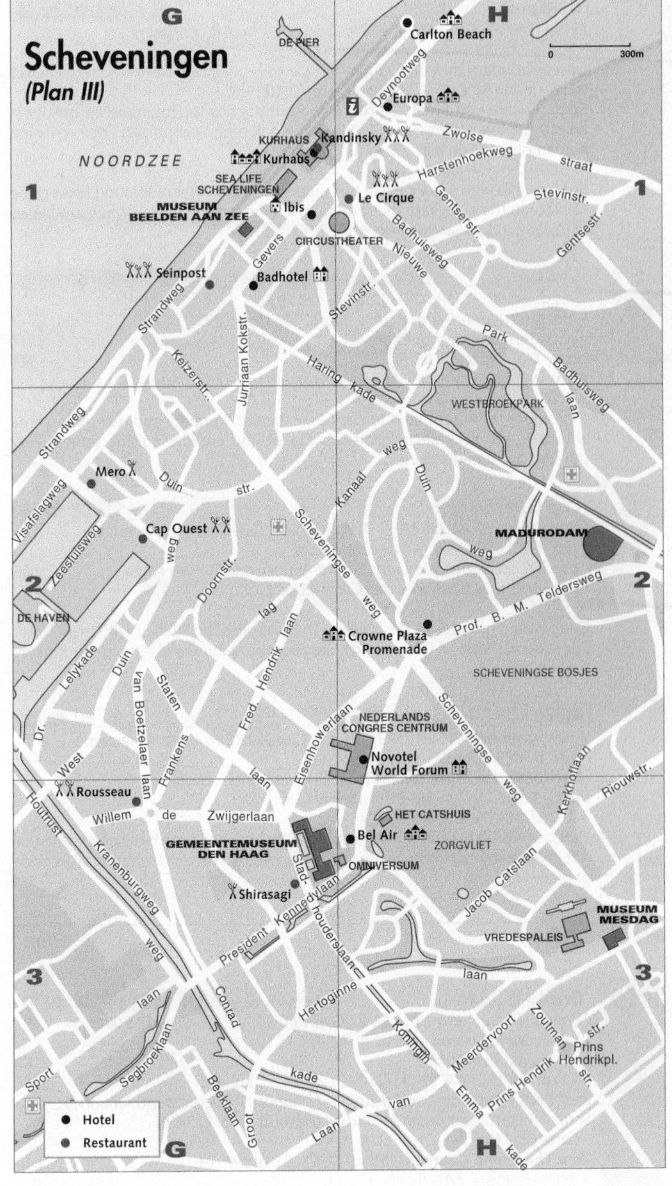
Scheveningen
(Plan III)
NOORDZEE
DE PIER
Carlton Beach
Europa
Kandinsky
KURHAUS
Kurhaus
SEA LIFE SCHEVENINGEN
MUSEUM BEELDEN AAN ZEE
Ibis
Le Cirque
CIRCUSTHEATER
Seinpost
Badhotel
WESTBROEKPARK
MADURODAM
Mero
Cap Ouest
DE HAVEN
Crowne Plaza Promenade
SCHEVENINGSE BOSJES
NEDERLANDS CONGRES CENTRUM
Novotel World Forum
Rousseau
HET CATSHUIS
Bel Air
ZORGVLIET
GEMEENTEMUSEUM DEN HAAG
OMNIVERSUM
Shirasagi
MUSEUM MESDAG
VREDESPALEIS
Prins Hendrikpl.
Hotel
Restaurant

Seinpost

Zeekant 60 ✉ 2586 AD – ✆ (0 70) 355 52 50 – mail@seinpost.nl – Fax (0 70) 355 50 93 – www.seinpost.nl
closed Saturday lunch and Sunday **G1**
Rest – Menu 50 €, 65/138 € bi – Carte 70/102 €
Spec. Tartare van kreeft en rund, yoghurtmayonaise, arganolie en gelei van kreeft. Plateau met schaal- en schelpdieren. Mango en rice crispies, kardamomgelei en kerrie-yoghurtijs (summer).
◆ Seafood ◆ Design ◆
Book a table with a sea view in this modern rotunda where seafood takes pride of place in the elaborate modern cuisine. Fine wine list. The owner supervises with care.

Le Cirque

Circusplein 50 ✉ 2586 CZ – ✆ (0 70) 416 76 76 – info@restaurantlecirque.com – Fax (0 70) 416 75 37 – www.restaurantlecirque.com
closed Monday and Tuesday **H1**
Rest – *(dinner only except Sunday)* Menu 50/165 € bi – Carte 42/71 €
◆ Innovative ◆ Design ◆
A designer restaurant next to the Circustheater. Veranda and rear dining area with red and black décor contrasts. Classic and creative cuisine served. Very popular pre-theatre menu.

Cap Ouest

Schokkerweg 37 ✉ 2583 BH – ✆ (0 70) 306 09 35 – info@capouest.nl – Fax (0 70) 350 84 54 – www.capouest.nl
closed 30 December-5 January, Saturday lunch and Sunday lunch **G2**
Rest – Menu 28 €, 43/85 € bi – Carte 43/65 €
◆ Seafood ◆ Family ◆
Establishment opposite the harbour that supplies the kitchen with fresh North Sea produce. View of the kitchens, spacious mezzanine and terrace overlooking the docks.

Mero

Vissershavenweg 61e ✉ 2583 DL – ✆ (0 70) 352 36 00 – info@merovis.nl – Fax (0 70) 306 34 37 – www.merovis.nl
closed Saturday lunch, Sunday lunch, Monday and Tuesday **G2**
Rest – Menu 29 €, 35/48 € – Carte 48/71 €
◆ Seafood ◆ Brasserie ◆
Harbour-side fish restaurant in keeping with the times, both by its post-industrial loft-style, as by its cuisine, where the daily catch of fish and seafood takes pride of place.

ENVIRONS *Plan I*

Grand Winston

Generaal Eisenhowerplein 1 ✉ 2288 AE Rijswijk – ✆ (0 70) 414 15 00 – info@grandwinston.nl – Fax (0 70) 414 15 10 – www.grandwinston.nl **C3**
245 rm – 🚹95/214 € 🚹🚹115/250 €, ☕ 19 € – 7 suites
Rest *Leds* – 2nd floor *(closed 20 July-17 August, 21 December-8 January, Saturday lunch, Sunday and Monday)* Menu 35 €, 43/112 € bi – Carte 63/113 €
Rest *The Grand Canteen* – Menu 30 € – Carte 29/51 €
◆ Business ◆ Modern ◆
A designer hotel next to the Rijswijk station with Winston Churchill watching over the lobby! Rooms in two modern blocks. Futuristic décor, modern menu and attractive selection of wines. Flamboyantly modern canteen; international menu.

Green Park

Weigelia 22 ✉ 2262 AB Leidschendam – ✆ (0 70) 320 92 80 – info@greenpark.nl – Fax (0 70) 327 49 07 – www.greenpark.nl **D1**

92 rm – 103/193 € 120/210 €, 19 € – 4 suites

Rest *Chiparus* – see below

◆ Chain hotel ◆ Business ◆ Classic ◆

Lakeside hotel built on piles not far from an immense shopping centre. The lobby is under the glass roof of an atrium and the best rooms enjoy a lake-view balcony.

Mövenpick

Stationsplein 8 ✉ 2275 AZ Voorburg – ✆ (0 70) 337 37 37 – hotel.voorburg@moevenpick.com – Fax (0 70) 337 37 00 – www.moevenpick-voorburg.com **C2**

125 rm – 65/151 € 65/171 €, 16 €

Rest – *(open until 11 p.m.)* Menu 23/25 € – Carte 21/48 €

◆ Chain hotel ◆ Functional ◆

Modern chain hotel, whose semi-circular façade overlooks the station. Functional rooms, the best ones at the rear. Designer-style bar. Modern brasserie with an Italian-Asian focus: pasta and wok-cooked dishes. Front terrace.

Savelberg with rm

Oosteinde 14 ✉ 2271 EH Voorburg – ✆ (0 70) 387 20 81 – info@restauranthotelsavelberg.nl – Fax (0 70) 387 77 15 – www.restauranthotelsavelberg.nl closed 27 December-7 January **D2**

14 rm – 150/190 € 150/350 €, 16 €

Rest – *(closed Saturday lunch, Sunday and Monday)* Menu 55 €, 72/145 € bi – Carte 80/108 €

Spec. Salade van kreeft met artisjok en groene boontjes, eendenlever met zwarte truffel. Gebakken langoustinestaartjes met gemarineerde navelsinaasappel en kletskop van zwarte peper met aceto balsamico. Gebraden duif met ravioli van ui, groene linzen en jus van duif.

◆ Traditional ◆ Formal ◆

This luxurious 18C abode is a real treat for the eyes! Good quality seasonal produce, extensive wine cellar, well-informed wine waiter and splendid terrace facing the park. Elegant rooms and suites with balcony, personalised in a plush classical register.

Savarin

Laan van Hoornwijck 29 ✉ 2289 DG Rijswijk – ✆ (0 70) 307 20 50 – info@savarin.nl – Fax (0 70) 307 20 55 – www.savarin.nl closed 27 December-1 January, Saturday lunch and Sunday lunch **C3**

Rest – Menu 33 €, 38/81 € bi – Carte approx. 50 €

◆ Contemporary ◆ Formal ◆

Former farm dating from 1916 where inventive cuisine is served in a designer inspired rustic-contemporary dining room. Modern conference room with whitewashed beams. Terrace.

Chiparus – Hotel Green Park

Weigelia 22 ✉ 2262 AB Leidschendam – ✆ (0 70) 320 92 80 – info@greenpark.nl – Fax (0 70) 327 49 07 – www.greenpark.nl – closed Sunday **D1**

Rest – Menu 33/46 € – Carte 40/51 €

◆ Contemporary ◆ Formal ◆

This restaurant, named after a 20th century Romanian sculptor, offers a dining room with a water view. Modern Mediterranean cuisine. Lakeside terrace.

Bon-Bon

Kerkstraat 52 ✉ 2271 CT Voorburg – ✆ (0 70) 386 29 00 – info@bon-bon.nl – Fax (0 70) 386 55 92 – www.bon-bon.nl closed 29 July-19 August, 1-14 January, Saturday lunch, Sunday and Monday

Rest – Menu 30 €, 32/50 € bi – Carte 37/64 € **D2**

◆ Contemporary ◆ Friendly ◆

Two 17th century houses host this warm, modern brasserie-type restaurant, with its red benches, light-grey walls, closely-placed tables and set of mirrors. Enclosed terrace.

Paul van Waarden

Tollensstraat 10 ✉ 2282 BM Rijswijk – ☎ (0 70) 414 08 12 – info@paulvanwaarden.nl – Fax (0 70) 414 03 91 – www.paulvanwaarden.nl
closed 2 weeks August, 28 December-11 January, Saturday lunch, Sunday and Monday **C3**
Rest – Menu 33/75 € bi – Carte 51/70 €
Spec. Vier bereidingen van vier verschillende soorten lever. Krokant gebakken kabeljauw, erwtensoep met gerookte paling (21 September-21 March). Tarte tatin van rabarber met gemberroomijs.
♦ Contemporary ♦ Brasserie ♦
Paul van Waarden hosts you in one of the series of rooms which make up the restaurant, designed in the style of a modern brasserie. Modern cuisine. Walled terrace.

Brasserie Savelberg-De Koepel

Oosteinde 1 ✉ 2271 EA Voorburg – ☎ (0 70) 369 35 72 – Fax (0 70) 369 32 14 – www.brasseriedekoepel.nl
closed 29 December-2 January **D2**
Rest – *(dinner only except Sunday) (open until 11 p.m.)* Menu 30/52 € bi – Carte approx. 40 €
♦ French traditional ♦ Brasserie ♦
Upmarket brasserie in an immense rotunda, topped by a cupola and adorned by modern frescoes. Lush summer terrace. Reasonably priced, tasty dishes.

Papermoon

Herenstraat 175 ✉ 2271 CE Voorburg – ☎ (0 70) 387 31 61 – info@papermoon.nl
closed 31 December-1 January and Monday **C2-3**
Rest – *(dinner only)* Menu 30/68 € bi – Carte approx. 45 €
♦ Contemporary ♦ Friendly ♦
An appealing modern menu with several set menus at this friendly restaurant where the dining room has a refined atmosphere.

ROTTERDAM

ROTTERDAM

Population (est 2005): 601 000 (conurbation 3 340 000) – Altitude: sea level

Simeone/PHOTONONSTOP

Rotterdam trades on its earthy appeal, on a rough-and-ready grittiness tied in with its status as the largest seaport in the world, handling 350 million tonnes of goods a year, with over half of all goods that are heading into Europe passing through it. Flattened during the Second World War, Rotterdam was rebuilt on a grand scale, jettisoning the idea of streets full of terraced houses in favour of a modern cityscape of concrete and glass.

The city is located on the Nieuwe Maas, but is centred round a maze of other rivers - most importantly the Rhine and the Maas - and is only a few dozen kilometres inland from the North Sea. It spills over both banks of its river, and is linked by tunnels, bridges and the metro; the most stunning connection across the water is the modern Erasmusbridge, whose sleek design has come to embody the Rotterdam of the new millennium. It's mirrored on the southern banks by the development of the previously run-down Kop Van Zuid area into a zone of new build and sleek promise.

LIVING THE CITY

Rotterdam is a sprawling city that's eaten up both banks of the **Nieuwe Maas River**. Its northern extremity is bounded by the **Zestienhoven airport,** while to the south, over the water, shimmers the modernist, once industrialised, area of **Kop Van Zuid**. Central Rotterdam's main rail station, **Centraal**, is to the north of the river; immediately to its east is a complex array of modern high-rises with the focus on the pedestrianized **Lijnbaan**. The culture zone of **Museumpark** is close to the water, and it's bounded on either side by two old harbours, **Delfshaven** and **Oude Haven**. The latter is in the compact and interesting district of **Blaak**, another of the city's modernist shrines.

PRACTICAL INFORMATION

ARRIVAL-DEPARTURE

The Airport is 6km northwest of the city, with a taxi costing about €23. Shuttle buses no.33 and 43 run every 10min and take 20min to Central Railway Station.

TRANSPORT

Metro, bus, tram and train combine to delve into every little corner of the city. There are a variety of stripcards to ease your way around: from two-strip right up to forty-five strip tickets. That could entail a lot of fiddling about and franking. A better bet could be to invest in a one-day, two-day, or three-day card, which give you unlimited travel on any form of transport.

Another good idea is to buy a Rotterdam Card, which provides unlimited use of the transport network as well as free admission to most attractions. It's available for either 24 or 72 hours.

You can hire bicycles from the Centraal station cycle shop. These work out at good value, and can be hired for either a day or a week.

EXPLORING ROTTERDAM

Whatever else anyone may say about Rotterdam, no-one denies that it has edge. Pacy, big and brash, it barged its way into the European zeitgeist earlier this decade when it was European City of Culture. It lived – and still lives – easily with that term. Constructed anew after 1945, the bustling port city on the Nieuwe Maas introduced to Europe the concept of modern building, for good or bad. Walk down the Lijnbaan, and you're face to face with the continent's first pedestrianized shopping precinct. It's now fifty-five years old, and on no-one's list for an architecture award – but it's a fascinating prototype, all the same; back in 1953, this was very much the shape of things to come.

A different kind of modernity confronts you just a half mile to the east. The district of Blaak was a working-class stronghold until it was destroyed in World War II. The phoenix that arose took everyone by surprise. For starters, a space-age metro station rose from the ashes, alongside apartments that are shaped like cubes, up-ended on one corner and perched on tall stalks. They're called **Cube Houses**, and were built to the bemusement of locals a quarter of a century ago. One of them, the **Kijk-Kubus**, is open to visitors, but beware if you're unbalanced at the thought of an 'upside-down' house. The city's trademark melding of functional and eccentric is further enhanced just a bit to the southwest with the fabulous sounding **Boompjestorens**, three dice-shaped apartment blocks in a seventeenth century double row of lime trees turned into a modish boulevard.

➔ BUILDING SIGHTS

The more you wander the city, the more you realise that Blaak isn't the sole preserve of architectural innovation. Whatever your take on it all, there's no getting away from the fact that there are few places in the world that have such an eclectic range of buildings to keep you entertained (or bewildered). Try these for size: the **Euromast Space Tower** (which, at 185m, really is a size), a spire with super-fast automatic lifts which zoom you up for awesome views of the city; the **Groothandelsgebouw** (which translates as large business building) and is, well, a large business building with a stunning post-war design; the **Witte Huis**, a twelve-storey high-rise dating from 1897, making it Europe's first skyscraper; **Willemswerf**, the sparkling global HQ of shipping giant Nedlloyd; **Huis Sonnenfeld**, a modernist house from the 1930s that sets off the adjacent **Architectuur Instituut** a treat; the soaring **KPN Telekom Building**, built by Renzo Piano in 2000, and looking in its precarious way as if it's about to topple over; and the city's two iconic bridges, the **Willemsbrug**, and **Erasmusbrug,** whose graceful, angular lines of silver tubing have earned it the nickname 'The Swan'.

➔ HAVENS OF PEACE

If you're looking for a more picturesque aspect of Rotterdam – something that might give a clue to its long lost past – then bits of the Nieuwe Maas harbourside area can nudge you in the right direction. A couple of kilometres southwest of Centraal Station is Delfshaven, an antique harbour that managed to stay pretty much intact as the bombs fell. It has history: the Pilgrim Fathers set sail from here in 1620 en route to the New World, and its quiet waterways lend it a feel of decorous charm. Way off to the east at the other end of the central waterfront is Oude Haven, the city's oldest harbour dating from 1325, and sympathetically redeveloped after the War. A tiny inlet, it adds another dimension to the 'cube house'/Witte Huis area - it's lined with peaceful cafes and houses whose origins stretch back seven hundred years. The antique boats and barges that mill around just add to the feeling of a different city at a different time.

➔ DAM CULTURED

There's no problem locating the area where culture is the name of the game – the authorities found a wide, open area not far up from the waterfront and called it Museumpark. Chief amongst its glories is Rotterdam's number one attraction, The **Museum Boijmans Van Beuningen,** which covers a mighty span of art history and holds a continuing cycle of temporary exhibitions. The permanent collection ranges across all major schools of Dutch and continental art from old masters (Bosch, Breugel, Rembrandt) through the Impressionists (Van Gogh, Degas, Gaugin, Monet), to the modernists (Dali, Duchamp, Magritte). As a perfect foil, the nearby **Kunsthal** is a great place to look at premier league exhibitions of contemporary art, design and photography, while there's the **Natuurmuseum** next door, a pure joy for lovers of taxidermy. Outside, the nature's pretty good, too, as Museumpark gives you the chance for a good stroll, with a fountain, a lake and enough benches for you to sit and ruminate on the meaning of the giant rabbit sculptures that dot the lawn.

Finding out more about the history of Rotterdam itself is the preserve of two museums east of Museumpark near the old **Leuvehaven** harbour. The **Maritiem Museum** is a salty dog of a gallery, full of the sights and sounds of the city as seaport, and with an absorbing look at what it was like to be a seafarer in the seventeenth and eighteenth centuries. Up the road, past Churchillplein metro station, the **Museum het Schielandshuis** is housed in one of the city's few preserved seventeenth century mansions, and it paints a broader brush over Rotterdam's history, with original footage of World War II bombing, and, on a lighter note, social history in photographs.

The story of modern Rotterdam is embodied in the tale of the neighbourhood to the south of the river – Kop Van Zuid. Historically, a predominantly working class area with docks, a shipyard and a terminal for ocean-going liners, its stock plummeted in the 1960s and 70s when most of the heavy waterfront industry packed up and moved way out west to **Europoort** by the North Sea. Kop Van Zuid, poorly connected to the north bank, was abandoned. Then, in 1986, development started to turn the area around, and by 2010 it's expected that fifteen thousand residents will be living in the hard-edged modern urban apartments that have helped earn the south bank its new reputation as a high quality zone with eye-catching architecture and smart cafés and bars. The icing on the cake for this, the city's most heralded up-and-coming quarter, came with the arrival of the **Luxor Theatre**, a stunning modern building that's brought a real touch of culture – through concerts, musicals and dance – to the 'other side' of the Nieuwe Maas.

CALENDAR HIGHLIGHTS

Holland's most prestigious jazz event, The North Sea Jazz Festival, has moved its base from The Hague to Rotterdam's Ahoy centre in Kop Van Zuid, a sure sign of the city's emergence on the cultural map. It attracts many of the world's top musicians and, held in mid-July, it's just part of a vibrant summer in the city. May's Dunya Festival presents a wealth of arts and culture from across the globe, with several stages around Euromast and Parklaan hosting music, storytelling and performance. The streets

ROTTERDAM IN…

→ ONE DAY

Blaak area, including Kijk-Kubus and Boompjestorens, Oude Haven, Museum Boijmans Van Beuningen

→ TWO DAYS

A fuller investigation of Museumpark, Delfshaven, the view from Euromast, a cruise along the Nieuwe Maas

→ THREE DAYS

Kop Van Zuid, including a meal at one of its restaurants, a show at the Luxor Theatre

come alive with colour at two spectacular events, one in July and one in August. The first – the Summer Carnival – matches the spirit of more exotic climes, a great street parade enlivened by ethnic groups from the likes of Cape Verde, the Antilles and Surinam. Then along comes Dance Parade, during which around forty decorated trucks wind their way through the centre, to the sound of pulsing drums, eventually arriving at Schiehaven's Lloydpier. As a complete contrast, the Municipal Theatre hosts the Poetry International Festival in June – the largest gathering of global poets in Europe; there are Dutch and English translations of their work. The action moves back outside again for September's World Port Festival, when, over three days, the secrets of the city's huge harbour are revealed: there are ship tours, rescue and aviation demos, boat cruises and bus trips. In the same month, The Kunsthal hosts Chocolad' Amour (can there *be* a more enticing name?), which does pretty much what it says on the label, with tasting sessions – surprise, surprise – a huge draw. Sticking to the food theme, the Kunsthal is also home base and kitchen for KunsthalCOOKING, a three-day food jamboree with tastings, again in September. January is the month for movie buffs with the twelve-day International Film Festival, renowned for its innovative aspect, while in March you can stay up late for Museum Night, when more than forty galleries and museums have extended opening hours – a great time for a guided tour.

EATING OUT

Rotterdam is a hot place for dining, in the literal and metaphorical sense. There are lots of places to tuck into the flavours of Holland's colonial past, in particular the spicy delicacies of Indonesia and Surinam. The long east/west stretch of Oude and Nieuwe Binnenweg is not only central and handy for many of the sights, it's also chock-full of good cafes, café-bars and restaurants. The recently smartened up canal district of Oudehaven has also introduced to the city a good selection of places to eat while taking in the relaxed vibe. Along the waterfront, various warehouses have been transformed into mega-restaurants, particularly around the Noordereiland isle in the middle of the river, while in Kop Van Zuid the Wilhelminapier quay is spot-on for a brand new area with good restaurants and tasty views to go with it. Many establishments in the city are closed at lunchtime, except business restaurants and those that set a high gastronomic standard and like to show it off in the middle of the day as well as in the evening. The bill includes service charge, and tipping is optional: round up the total if you're pleased with the service.

→ LIQUID REFRESHMENT

A satisfying – and speedy – way to get a duck's eye view of the intriguing architecture here is to take a water taxi. Introduced to the harbour just a few years ago, they whisk you along at nearly 30mph past the cranes, warehouses and giant cargo ships. They skim towards the harbour mouth, then spin round and bring you back, so that what you missed on the way out, you can catch on the return.

→ BINNEN THERE, BOUGHT IT

You may think you've *seen* a few oddities in Rotterdam, but the place to buy them is the massive Binnenrotte market, open three days of the week. It's not inconceivable to think you can get anything here, from antique dolls and Turkish bread to 1930s bikes and secondhand fishing rods.

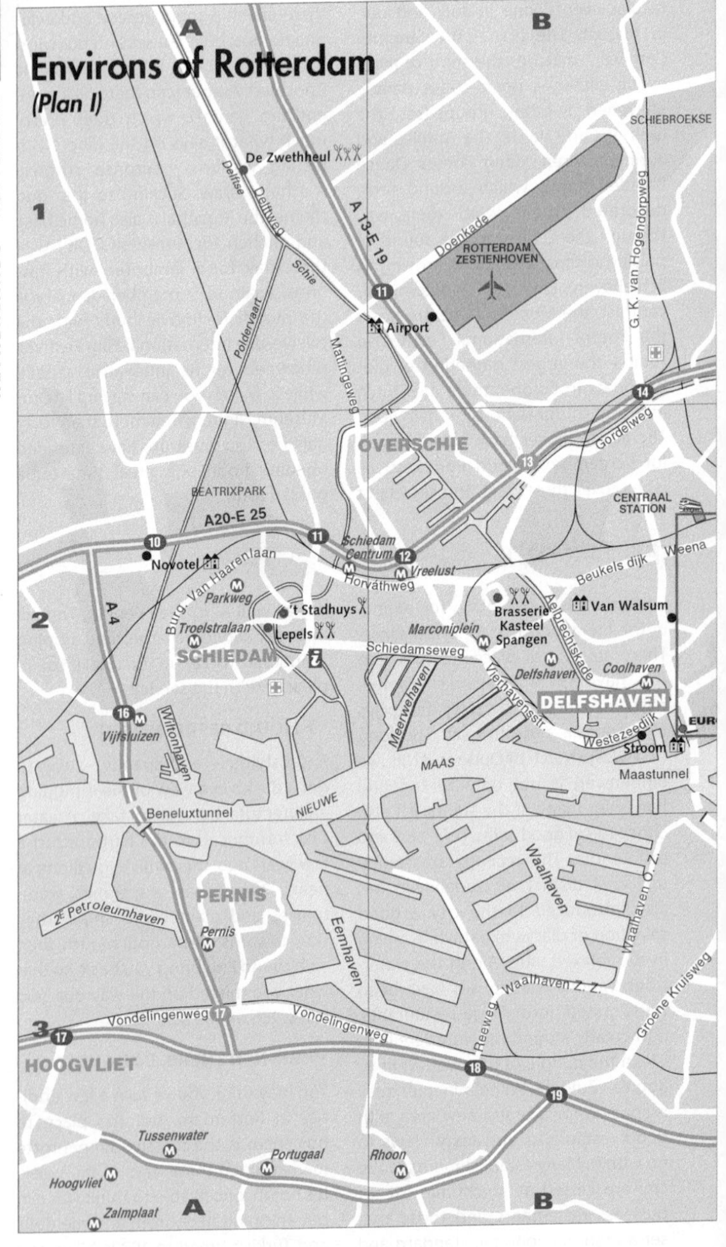
Environs of Rotterdam
(Plan I)
A
B
1
2
3
SCHIEBROEKSE
De Zwethheul
Delftse
Delftweg
Schie
A 13-E 19
Doenkade
ROTTERDAM ZESTIENHOVEN
G. K. van Hogendorpweg
Airport
Poldervaart
Matlingeweg
OVERSCHIE
Gordelweg
BEATRIXPARK
A20-E 25
CENTRAAL STATION
Schiedam Centrum
Vreelust
Weena
Novotel
Burg. Van Haarenlaan
Horvâthweg
Beukels dijk
Parkweg
't Stadhuys
Brasserie Kasteel Spangen
Van Walsum
A 4
Troelstralaan
Lepels
Marconiplein
Aelbrechtskade
SCHIEDAM
Schiedamseweg
Delfshaven
Coolhaven
Meerwehaven
Vierhavensstr.
DELFSHAVEN
Vijfsluizen
Wiltonhaven
Westezeedijk
Stroom
MAAS
Maastunnel
NIEUWE
Beneluxtunnel
Waalhaven
Waalhaven O. Z.
PERNIS
2e Petroleumhaven
Pernis
Eemhaven
Groene Kruisweg
Waalhaven Z. Z.
Vondelingenweg
Reeweg
HOOGVLIET
Tussenwater
Portugaal
Rhoon
Hoogvliet
Zalmplaat

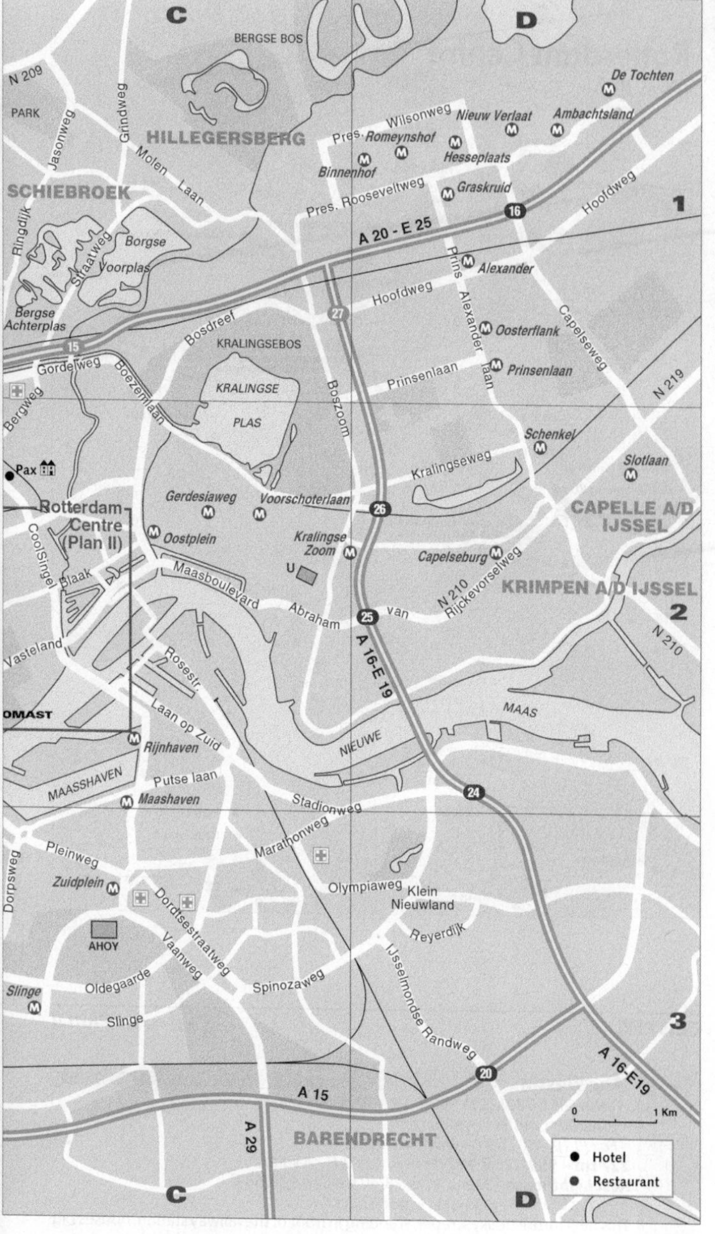
C
D
BERGSE BOS
HILLEGERSBERG
SCHIEBROEK
N 209
PARK
Jasonweg
Grindweg
Molen Laan
Ringdijk
Straatweg
Borgse Voorplas
Bergse Achterplas
Pres. Wilsonweg
Pres. Rooseveltweg
Romeynshof
Binnenhof
Nieuw Verlaat
Hesseplaats
Ambachtsland
De Tochten
Graskruid
A 20 - E 25
16
Hoofdweg
1
Prins Alexander laan
Alexander
Oosterflank
Prinsenlaan
Capelseweg
N 219
27
Bosdreef
KRALINGSEBOS
KRALINGSE PLAS
15
Gordelweg
Boezemlaan
Bergweg
Boszoom
Schenkel
Kralingseweg
Slotlaan
Pax
Rotterdam Centre (Plan II)
Gerdesiaweg
Voorschoterlaan
26
CAPELLE A/D IJSSEL
Coolsingel
Oostplein
Kralingse Zoom
Capelseburg
Blaak
U
Maasboulevard
N 210
Rijckevorselweg
KRIMPEN A/D IJSSEL
Abraham van
25
2
Vasteland
A 16-E 19
N 210
Rosestr.
MAAS
OMAST
Laan op Zuid
NIEUWE
Rijnhaven
MAASSHAVEN
Putse laan
Maashaven
24
Stadionweg
Marathonweg
Pleinweg
Dorpsweg
Zuidplein
Olympiaweg
Klein Nieuwland
Dordtsestraatweg
Reyerdijk
AHOY
Vaanweg
IJsselmondse Randweg
Oldegaarde
Spinozaweg
Slinge
Slinge
3
A 16-E19
20
A 15
A 29
0
1 Km
BARENDRECHT
Hotel
Restaurant

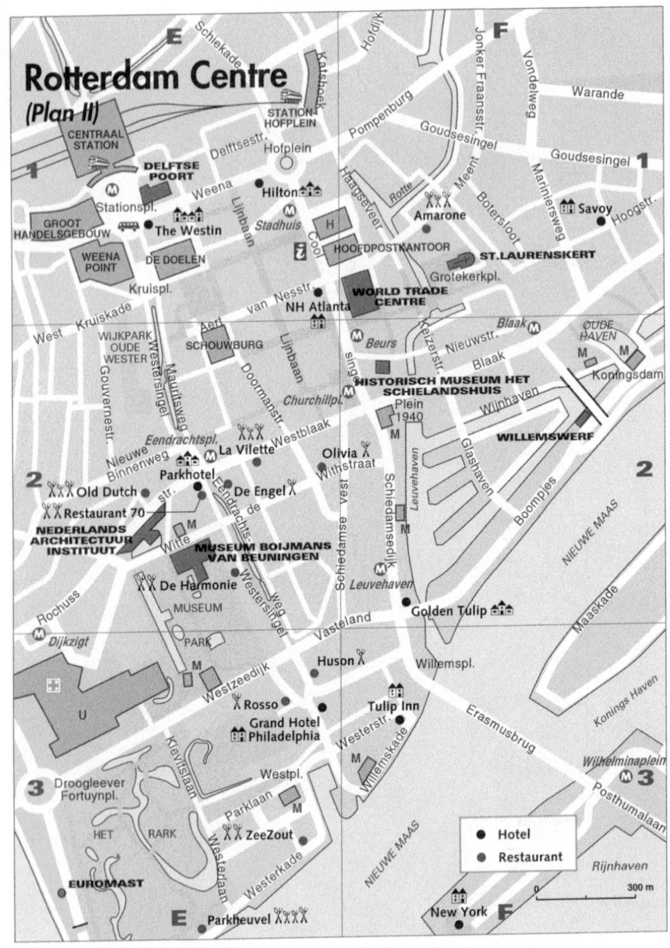

CENTRE

Plan II

The Westin

Weena 686 ✉ 3012 CN – ✆ (0 10) 430 20 00
– rotterdam.westin@westin.com
– Fax (0 10) 430 20 01 – www.westin.nl **E1**

227 rm – 🚹99/426 € 🚹🚹99/445 €, ☕ 27 € – 4 suites
Rest *Lighthouse* – Menu 25 €, 28/40 € – Carte 36/53 €

♦ Luxury ♦ Business ♦ Modern ♦

This new futuristic skyscraper, standing in front of the railway station, houses big bedrooms, with full modern comfort. Conference rooms and business centre. Up-to-date cuisine to be enjoyed in a resolutely modern décor.

Parkhotel

Westersingel 70 ✉ 3015 LB – ✆ (0 10) 436 36 11 – parkhotel@bilderberg.nl – Fax (0 10) 436 42 12 – www.parkhotelrotterdam.nl **E2**

187 rm – 🛉165/223 € 🛉🛉195/223 €, ☕ 21 € – 2 suites

Rest *Restaurant 70* – see below

♦ Traditional ♦ Business ♦ Classic ♦

Hotel established in 1922 and modernised over the years, which explains the mixed architecture. Renovated interior. Several types of guestroom. Modern meals served in a dining room decorated in blue, white and beige tones or on the pretty garden terrace.

Hilton

Weena 10 ✉ 3012 CM – ✆ (0 10) 710 80 00 – info-rotterdam@hilton.com – Fax (0 10) 710 80 00 – www.rotterdam.hilton.com **E1**

246 rm – 🛉90/250 € 🛉🛉90/250 €, ☕ 23 € – 8 suites

Rest – *(open until 11 p.m.)* Carte 35/50 €

♦ Chain hotel ♦ Business ♦ Classic ♦

Close to the WTC, the hotel was designed by the architect of the Euromast tower. Immense lobby, varying categories of rooms, business centre and fine conference facilities. Lounge-restaurant offering a modern menu and choice of wines by the glass.

Golden Tulip

Leuvehaven 80 ✉ 3011 EA – ✆ (0 10) 413 41 39 – inforotterdam@goldentuliphotelinntel.com – Fax (0 10) 413 32 22 – www.goldentuliprotterdamcentre.com **F2**

263 rm – 🛉230 € 🛉🛉230/350 €, ☕ 20 €

Rest – Carte 31/46 €

♦ Chain hotel ♦ Business ♦ Modern ♦

Chain hotel, lining a harbour museum dock, just one stride away from the majestic Erasmus Bridge (Erasmusbrug). Top-floor pool and panoramic bar.

NH Atlanta

Aert van Nesstraat 4 ✉ 3012 CA – ✆ (0 10) 206 78 00 – nhatlantarotterdam@nh-hotels.com – Fax (0 10) 413 53 20 – www.nh-hotels.com **E1**

213 rm – 🛉75/295 € 🛉🛉75/295 €, ☕ 17 € – 2 suites

Rest – *(closed Saturday and Sunday) (dinner only until 11 p.m.)* Menu 28 € – Carte 38/51 €

♦ Chain hotel ♦ Classic ♦

Next-door to the WTC, this hotel is comprised of three buildings, the oldest of which dates from the 1930s. Suites, junior suites, studios and new modern rooms. Art deco public areas. Up-to-date cuisine and bar ambience.

Savoy without rest

Hoogstraat 81 ✉ 3011 PJ – ✆ (0 10) 413 92 80 – info.savoy@edenhotelgroup.com – Fax (0 10) 404 57 12 – www.edenhotelgroup.com **F1**

94 rm – 🛉175/215 € 🛉🛉175/215 €, ☕ 17 €

♦ Traditional ♦ Business ♦ Classic ♦

A 7-storey building, just a stone's throw from Blom's famous "cube houses". Modern rooms adorned with Burberry-style fabrics, fitness facilities and a nautical-style bar.

Stroom

rest

Lloydstraat 1 ✉ 3024 EA – ✆ (0 10) 221 40 60 – info@stroomrotterdam.nl – Fax (0 10) 221 40 61 – www.stroomrotterdam.nl *Plan I* **B2**

18 rm – 🛉145/345 € 🛉🛉145/345 €, ☕ 18 €

Rest – Carte 31/43 €

♦ Business ♦ Minimalist ♦

In a newly-developed district near the docks, former power station now an ultra-trendy hotel. Remains of its industrial past displayed in the lobby. Bright minimalist-style designer rooms. Lounge-bar setting for this restaurant with modern, international menu.

New York

Koninginnenhoofd 1 (Wilhelminapier) ✉ 3072 AD – ✆ (0 10) 439 05 00 – info@hotelnewyork.nl – Fax (0 10) 484 27 01 – www.hotelnewyork.nl **F3**

72 rm – 105/230 € 105/230 €, 13 €

Rest – Menu 28 € – Carte 18/52 €

◆ Traditional ◆ Retro ◆

The former HQ of the Holland-America shipping line is now a hotel with character. Rooms overlooking the port, town or river. Vintage New York-style barbershop. Spacious historic café in a "post-industrial" style. Modern menu printed on placemats.

Pax without rest

Schiekade 658 ✉ 3032 AK – ✆ (0 10) 466 33 44 – pax@bestwestern.nl – Fax (0 10) 467 52 78 – www.paxhotel.nl *Plan I* **C2**

124 rm – 68/165 € 77/185 €

◆ Traditional ◆ Functional ◆

On a busy main street, the hotel is made up of three old houses and a modern wing at the rear, where rooms are just as comfortable, but quieter.

Tulip Inn without rest

Willemsplein 1 ✉ 3016 DN – ✆ (0 10) 413 47 90 – reservations@tulipinnrotterdam.nl – Fax (0 10) 412 78 90 – www.tulipinnrotterdam.nl **F3**

92 rm – 80/230 € 80/240 €, 14 €

◆ Business ◆ Functional ◆

Ideally located at the foot of Erasmusbrug Bridge, opposite the landing stage of the tourist boats. Spacious rooms with panoramic views at the front; simpler to the rear.

Grand Hotel Philadelphia

Van Vollenhovenstraat 48 ✉ 3016 BJ – ✆ (0 10) 240 04 25 – grandhotel@philadelphia.nl – Fax (0 10) 270 97 35 – www.grandhotelphiladelphia.nl **E3**

20 rm – 95/134 € 95/134 €, 10 €

Rest – *(closed Saturday and Sunday) (light lunch only)*

◆ Inn ◆ Modern ◆

The maritime past of this period house (1900) can still be seen in some of the interior decoration. Three types of modern rooms; opt for one at the rear. Snacks and simple lunchtime menu served in the bistro whose décor mixes old with new.

Van Walsum

Mathenesserlaan 199 ✉ 3014 HC – ✆ (0 10) 436 32 75 – info@hotelvanwalsum.nl – Fax (0 10) 436 44 10 – www.hotelvanwalsum.nl *Plan I* **B2**

closed 24 December-2 January

29 rm – 80/95 € 95/130 €

Rest – *(residents only)*

◆ Family ◆ Classic ◆

This 1895 abode has been run by the same family since 1955. The rooms, of varying appeal, are gradually being renovated. Dining room-veranda opening onto a terrace-garden.

Parkheuvel (Erik van Loo)

Heuvellaan 21 ✉ 3016 GL – ✆ (0 10) 436 07 66 – info@parkheuvel.nl – Fax (0 10) 436 71 40 – www.parkheuvel.nl

closed 21 July-10 August, 27 December-7 January, Saturday lunch and Sunday **E3**

Rest – Menu 48 €, 65/143 € bi – Carte 67/110 €

Spec. Zuiglam met knoflookbeignets en basilicumjus (spring-summer). Ravioli van kip met langoustines. Met witte chocolademousse gevulde frambozen, balsamico azijn en basilicumsiroop (summer).

◆ Contemporary ◆ Formal ◆

On the banks of the Maas and a park, a modern, semi-circular pavilion with harbour views from the bay windows and terrace. Reinterpreted Art Deco interior. Elaborate menu.

XXX

Old Dutch

Rochussenstraat 20 ✉ 3015 EK – ✆ (0 10) 436 03 44 – info@olddutch.net – Fax (0 10) 436 78 26 – www.olddutch.net

closed Saturday and Sunday **E2**

Rest – Menu 35 €, 50/95 € bi – Carte 52/74 €

♦ Traditional ♦ Formal ♦

Founded in 1932, the restaurant serves traditional fare in a conventional classical décor: stained glass, beams, period furniture, wood panelling and carving. Meat carved on the spot.

XXX ✿

La Vilette

Westblaak 160 ✉ 3012 KM – ✆ (0 10) 414 86 92 – lavilette@cistron.nl – Fax (0 10) 414 33 91 – www.lavilette.nl

closed 21 July-10 August, 23 December-6 January, Saturday lunch and Sunday

Rest – Menu 34 €, 45/118 € bi – Carte 63/80 € **E2**

Spec. Terrine van eendenlever met diverse bereidingen van appel. Langoustines met limoenrisotto en kreeftenvinaigrette. Zeetong 'à la Grenobloise' (April-November).

♦ Contemporary ♦ Formal ♦

Comfortable restaurant in a busy office district. Discreet welcome and service, smart, intimate setting, appetising modern menu that lives up to its promises.

XXX ✿

Amarone (Gert Blom)

Meent 72a ✉ 3011 JN – ✆ (0 10) 414 84 87 – info@restaurantamarone.nl – Fax (0 10) 413 36 73 – www.restaurantamarone.nl

closed 21 July-11 August, 1-7 January, Saturday lunch and Sunday **F1**

Rest – Menu 30/45 € – Carte 46/58 €

Spec. Pata Negra ham met gebakken makreel en polenta. Gebakken zeebrasem met lasagne van kingkrab. Gepocheerde appel met zoethout en kaneel.

♦ Contemporary ♦ Formal ♦

Close to the WTC, a tasty updated menu and fashionable setting: large mirrors reflecting the open kitchen, striped chairs, grey benches and a fine glass-fronted wine cellar.

XX

Brasserie Kasteel Spangen

Spartastraat 7 (Sparta stadion) ✉ 3027 ER – ✆ (0 10) 238 03 00 – brasserie@kasteelspangen.nl – Fax (0 10) 238 03 09 – www.kasteelspangen.nl

closed 1-6 January, 30 April, 1-20 July, 26-31 December, Saturday lunch, Sunday lunch and Monday *Plan I* **B2**

Rest – Menu 25 €, 33/65 € – Carte 38/82 €

♦ Contemporary ♦ Brasserie ♦

Modern brasserie underneath the Sparta stadium stands, overlooking a castle where banquets are held. Up-to-the-minute menu and fine choice of well-recommended wines.

XX

De Harmonie

Westersingel 95 ✉ 3015 LC – ✆ (0 10) 436 36 10 – deharmonie@deharmonie.demon.nl – Fax (0 10) 436 36 08 – www.restaurantdeharmonie.nl

closed 26 December-2 January, Saturday lunch and Sunday **E2**

Rest – Menu 38 €, 40/78 € bi – Carte 51/74 €

♦ Contemporary ♦ Fashionable ♦

A modern restaurant opposite the Museumpark in a chic avenue of fine houses. A modern, refined dining area opening onto the charming garden terrace.

XX

Restaurant 70 – Parkhotel

Westersingel 70 ✉ 3015 LB – ✆ (0 10) 436 36 11 – restaurant70@bilderberg.nl – Fax (0 10) 436 42 12 – www.restaurant70.nl

closed Sunday **E2**

Rest – *(dinner only)* Menu 34 €

♦ Contemporary ♦ Formal ♦

Tasteful modern restaurant within the Parkhotel. Comfy beige armchairs, blue benches and light wooden floors. Inner garden with terrace in summertime.

XX **Zeezout**
Westerkade 11b ✉ 3016 CL – ☏ (0 10) 436 50 49 – zeezout1@hetnet.nl – Fax (0 10) 225 18 47 – www.engelgroep.com
closed Saturday lunch, Sunday and Monday **E3**
Rest – *(booking essential)* Menu 32 €, 42/88 € bi – Carte approx. 45 €
♦ Seafood ♦ Formal ♦
The chic and trendy atmosphere, fish and seafood menu and waterside terrace are this modern brasserie's assets, whose name – "Sea Salt" – gives the game away.

X **Huson**
Scheepstimmermanslaan 14 ✉ 3016 CL – ☏ (0 10) 413 03 71 – lunch@huson.info – www.huson.info
closed Saturday lunch, Sunday and Monday **E3**
Rest – *(booking essential)* Menu 30/52 € – Carte 35/51 €
♦ Contemporary ♦ Brasserie ♦
Trendy atmosphere in a modern dining room in aubergine and peppermint tones. Nice leather benches. Serving a small menu of a variety of dishes from noon till 9.30pm.

X **De Engel**
Eendrachtsweg 19 ✉ 3012 LB – ☏ (0 10) 413 82 56 – restaurant@engel.nl – Fax (0 10) 412 51 96 – www.engelgroep.com
closed 25-26 and 31 December-1 January, Saturday lunch and Sunday **E2**
Rest – Menu 37 €, 43/93 € bi – Carte 49/65 €
♦ Contemporary ♦ Trendy ♦
Opulent house set in a lively neighbourhood. World cuisine, relaxed atmosphere, decorative mixture of old and new and collection of photographs illustrating the culinary arts.

X **Oliva**
Witte de Withstraat 15a ✉ 3012 BK – ☏ (0 10) 412 14 13 – info@restaurantoliva.nl – Fax (0 10) 412 70 69 – www.restaurantoliva.nl **E2**
Rest – *(dinner only)* Menu 32/62 € – Carte approx. 40 €
♦ Italian ♦ Bistro ♦
Lively Italian restaurant and a lively loft-inspired ambience. Open kitchen, simple menu and daily specials chalked on a board.

X **Rosso**
Van Vollenhovenstraat 15 (access by Westerlijk Handelsterrein) ✉ 3016 BE – ☏ (0 10) 225 07 05 – hans-veerman@hetnet.nl – Fax (0 10) 436 95 04 – www.rosso.nl
closed last week July and Sunday **E3**
Rest – *(dinner only until 11 p.m.)* Menu 35/65 € bi – Carte 37/56 €
♦ Contemporary ♦ Fashionable ♦
Bar-restaurant in a renovated 19th century warehouse, with dining area in vibrant red tones. Chic clientele and ambience. Très à la mode!

AT THE AIRPORT

Plan I

Airport
Vliegveldweg 59 ✉ 3043 NT – ☏ (0 10) 462 55 66 – info@airporthotel.nl – Fax (0 10) 462 22 66 – www.airporthotel.nl **B1**
96 rm – †89/199 € ††89/199 €, ☕ 18 € – 2 suites
Rest – Menu 32 € – Carte 30/48 €
♦ Business ♦ Classic ♦
Comfortable hotel located opposite the airport (shuttle). Soundproofed rooms; bar popular with business clientele. No air traffic between 11pm and 7am. Up-to-date menu. Waterside terrace.

Novotel

Hargalaan 2 (near A 20) ✉ 3118 JA Schiedam – ✆ (0 10) 471 33 22 – h0517@accor.com – Fax (0 10) 470 06 56 – www.novotel.com **A2**

136 rm – 🚹99/160 € 🚹🚹99/160 €, ☕ 16 €

Rest – Menu 13 €, 28/33 € – Carte 28/49 €

♦ Chain hotel ♦ Modern ♦

This renovated hotel within easy reach of the motorway is popular with business customers. Latest Novotel style in the rooms. Garden terrace and swimming pool. A modern-style brasserie with an international focus.

De Zwethheul

Rotterdamseweg 480 (at Zweth, canalside) ✉ 2636 KB Schipluiden – ✆ (0 10) 470 41 66 – info@zwethheul.nl – Fax (0 10) 470 65 22 – www.zwethheul.nl

closed 22 December-5 January, Saturday lunch, Sunday lunch and Monday **A1**

Rest – Menu 48 €, 70/152 € bi – Carte 78/115 €

Spec. 'Rosbief' van tonijn met zwarte peper, chaud-froid van krab (winter-summer). Kip gepocheerd met gesmolten ganzenlever, ragout van morieljes en truffel (spring). Reefilet met gedroogde sinaasappel en noten, jus van peperkoekkruiden (game season).

♦ Contemporary ♦ Formal ♦

This remodelled former inn (1865) serves fine meals to be enjoyed while observing the boats come and go, either from the dining room or the shaded, waterside terrace.

Lepels

Korte Haven 5 ✉ 3111 BH Schiedam – ✆ (0 10) 246 73 58 – info@marcsmeets.nl – Fax (0 10) 246 73 59 – www.marcsmeets.nl

closed 28 December-12 January, Monday and Saturday lunch **A2**

Rest – Menu 30 €, 45/85 € bi – Carte 48/63 €

♦ Contemporary ♦ Brasserie ♦

Trendy restaurant located between the covered market and the windmill, near a bascule bridge. Central open kitchen, black and white designer décor, soft lighting and lounge music.

't Stadhuys

Grote Markt 1a ✉ 3111 NG Schiedam – ✆ (0 10) 426 55 33 – info@restauranthetstadhuys.nl – www.restauranthetstadhuys.nl

closed late December **A2**

Rest – Menu 29 €, 32/75 € bi – Carte 43/55 €

♦ Traditional ♦ Brasserie ♦

Restaurant located in Schiedam's former town hall: a splendid baroque building with voluted gables and a pinnacle on the roof. Summer terrace on the Grote Markt.

NORWAY
NORGE

PROFILE

→ **Area:**
323 878 km²
(125 049 sq mi).

→ **Population:**
4 640 000 inhabitants (est. 2006), density = 14 per km².

→ **Capital:**
Oslo (conurbation 731 600 inhabitants).

→ **Currency:**
Krone (kr or NOK) divided into 100 øre; rate of exchange: NOK 1 = € 0.18 = US$ 0.12 (Dec 2007).

→ **Government:**
Constitutional parliamentary monarchy with single-chamber Parliament (since 1945).

→ **Languages:**
Norwegian has two written variants: Bokmål (influenced by Danish) spoken by 80% of the population and Nynorsk (New Norwegian). Sami is the language of the Sami people in the far north. English is widely spoken.

→ **Specific public holidays:**
Maundy Thursday and Good Friday (Thursday and Friday before Easter); Constitution Day (17 May); Boxing Day (26 December).

→ **Local Time:**
GMT + 1 hour in winter and GMT + 2 hours in summer.

→ **Climate:**
Temperate northern maritime, with cold winters and mild summers (Oslo: January: -4°C, July: 16°C). Colder interior, fairly high precipitation in the coastal regions.

→ **International dialling Code:**
00 47 followed by full local number.

→ **Emergency:**
Police: ✆ **112**; Ambulance service: ✆ **113**; Fire Brigade: ✆ **110**.

→ **Electricity:**
220 volts AC, 50Hz; 2-pin round-shaped continental plugs.

→ **Formalities**
Travellers from the European Union (EU), Switzerland, Iceland and the main countries of North and South America need a national identity card or passport (America: passport required) to visit Norway for less than three months (tourism or business purpose). For visitors from other countries a visa may be required, in addition to a passport, especially for those wishing to stay for longer than three months. We advise you to check with your embassy before travelling.

OSLO

OSLO

Population: 538 411 (conurbation 731 600) – Altitude: 96m

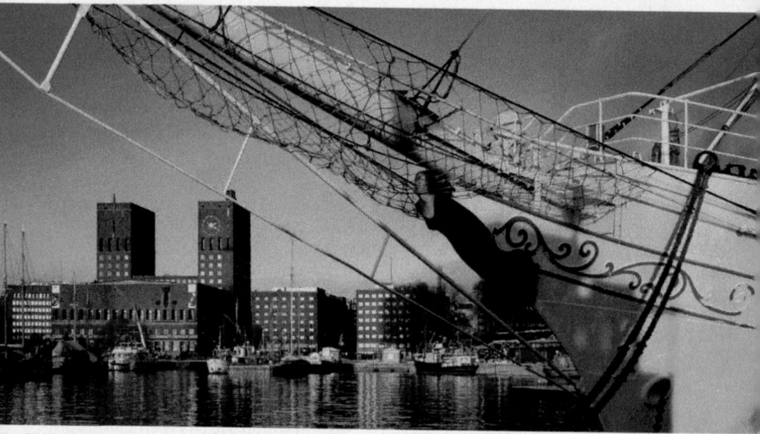

Sime/PHOTONONSTOP

Oslo has a lot going for it and one particularly striking downside. Let's get that out of the way first: it's currently the world's most expensive city, above even Tokyo, London and Paris. So don't expect the cheapest trip you've ever made. But it also rates as the city with the world's best standard of living, and its position, at the head of Oslofjord and surrounded by steep forested hills, is hard to match for drama and beauty. It's mellow and elegant, and though it can make as much of an impression on your wallet as on your memory, it's a charmingly compact place to stroll round, particularly in the summer, when the daylight hours practically abolish the night.

Oslo is rather underrated in that it lacks the urban cool of other Scandinavian cities like Copenhagen or Stockholm, but it boasts its fair share of trendy clubs and a raft of Michelin starred restaurants. Oh, and a real raft, too: Thor Hyerdahl's famous balsawood Kon-Tiki, which is one of the star turns in a city that loves its museums. You won't feel claustrophobic here; there's an uncluttered feel enhanced by parks and wide streets and, in the winter, there are times when you feel you have the whole place to yourself!

LIVING THE CITY

It's almost impossible for Oslo to live up to its lovely setting, but somehow it manages it. Drift into the city by boat down the Oslofjord and land at the smart harbour of **Aker Brygge**. To the west lies the charming **Bygdøy** peninsula, home, naturally enough, to museums permeated with the smell of the sea. North-west of your arrival point is **Frogner**, with its famous sculpture park, the place where locals hang out on long summer days. The centre of town, the commercial hub, is Karl Johans Gate, bounded at one end by the Royal Palace and at the other by the Cathedral, while further east lie two trendy multi-cultural areas, Grunerlokka and Grønland, which have taken on a vibrant edge over the last decade. This area is also home to the Edvard Munch Museum.

PRACTICAL INFORMATION

ARRIVAL-DEPARTURE

A taxi from Oslo International Airport, Gardermoen, which is 47km north of the city, will cost around NOK600. The train station is located beneath the terminal and the high speed Flytoget train takes 19 minutes to Oslo's central station. Alternatively, take the Express Bus to Galleri bus terminal – it leaves every 20min and takes 45min.

TRANSPORT

Serious sightseeing is enhanced with the Oslo Pass, which covers the transport system and entry to all those museums. It's valid for one to three days. Get it from the Information Centre next to Oslo Central Station.

Oslo is proud of its green credentials, and you'll have to pay a toll if you arrive by car. The integrated transport system within the city is efficient, comprising bus, tram or metro. You can obtain single or day tickets. For a small deposit, you can tap into the green-friendly Citybike scheme in Oslo. Go to a tourist information office, get your electronic 'Tourist Card', and hire one of the many free bicycles parked at different points around the city.

EXPLORING OSLO

Step ashore from your ferry at Akker Brygge - the swishly redeveloped harbour area of Oslo - in the summer months and it seems that the population of Norway is your escort. Locals cherish this time of year, when the sun never apparently sets, and they spend long hours in the streets and parks of the city. This is when restaurants, bars and museums stay open that much longer, and concert halls and theatres move their productions outdoors; in mid-summer bonfires are lit and the clink of glasses rustles the still air in celebration of life al fresco.

Akker Brygge itself is a bustling waterfront area and a fine place to make the acquaintance of Oslo. It used to be a full-on shipyard, but has been re-born as a trendy glass-and-chrome shopping and entertainment quarter, more Fisherman's Wharf of San Francisco than Docklands of London. It's a lovely place to settle down with a glass of wine and look at the fishing boats, and there are some snazzy eating places, but be warned that lots of them weigh in with a hefty bill. Best bet is to stroll the waterfront down to one of the most striking buildings of the city, the **Akershus Fortress**, an imposing building that has acted as Oslo's guardian since the thirteenth century. In those seven hundred plus years, Akershus has been under siege nine times, but has never fallen except during World War II.

→ OPEN GATE

Back up behind the harbour a coterie of colourful streets leads to the grand boulevard of Oslo: **Karl Johans Gate.** Aside from the shops, this is where many of Norway's most important buildings are based, including **Slottet** (the Royal Palace) and **Stortinget** (the Parliament building). Culture lovers need only pop round the corner to get a fix of Ibsen at the National Theatre, where his plays are a staple, and for good measure enjoy one of the country's finest art collections, which is included in the price of a ticket. It won't take long before you stumble on a museum. In this part of the capital alone, near the Royal Palace, are the Historical Museum, documenting Norwegian history, and the Stenersen Museum, named after the art collector who donated his entire collection to the city of Oslo. Wandering around further, you'll find museums dedicated to...well, you name it. Think architecture and zoology, and just about everything in between. Some of them have become especially well renowned. Modern art lovers, for instance, like to sniff out a couple in the streets behind Akershus, and with good reason. The Astrup Fearnley Museum of Modern Art is relatively new on the block (opened in 1993), housing recent works by Norwegian and critically acclaimed international artists in a strikingly modern building whose main entrance is two massive steel doors. Nearby is the National Museum for Art, Architecture and Design, full of disturbing works by post-war Norwegians in a rather eye-catching art nouveau building.

→ SCREAM OF THE CROP

Edvard Munch is a national institution in Norway. Though his fellow countrymen aren't particularly maudlin by nature, Munch revelled in despair, depression, disease and death. Or at least his paintings did. In the 1880s and 90s, when he was at his creative height, many people were outraged at his take on the national psyche, but now his work is lauded the length and breadth of the land, and features in two Oslo museums – The National Gallery, which contains a number of his most famous works, and the Munch Museum, out in Grunerlokka, an exhibition which is constantly changing, due to the huge amount of paintings, prints, drawings, plates and letters he produced. There are versions of The Scream in both galleries (dependent on the adroitness of thieves, of course...)

→ MARITIME MUSEUMS

A short ferry trip across the Oslofjord takes you to the **Bygdøy** peninsula, a favoured summer retreat with its meadows, groves, beaches and watery views (you can take a bus here, too, but it's not quite as spectacular). Bygdøy is home to some of the best attractions in the city (and yes, when we say attractions, we really mean – you've guessed it – museums). Being right alongside the fjord, these rightly take on a maritime quality. The **Kon-Tiki** Museum gives an evocatively vivid account of the exploits of the famed explorer Thor Heyerdahl, who sailed his balsawood raft across the South Pacific in 1947. It's there, looking remarkably flimsy, as is Ra II, in which he sailed the Atlantic in 1970. Next door, in the Fram Museum, proudly sits the Fram, 'the world's strongest ship' which sailed the North Pole and Antarctica a century ago: board her and see the preserved objects from those remarkable trips.

Hit land again and breathe in the fragrant pine before reaching the final piece of this triumvirate, the Viking Ship Museum, a church-like building containing three ancient oak ships (ancient here meaning the ninth century) whose sweeping lines are simple but elegant; their ornate prows having been preserved in the clay of chieftains' graves. However, it's not all homage to derring-do in Bygdøy. Up the road from the Viking ships stands Europe's largest open-air museum, the **Norwegian Folk Museum** – more than 150 buildings from across Norway which you can wander around to your heart's content. Exhibits range from a twelfth century stave church to a petrol station from the 1920s.

→ PARK AND GLIDE

Despite the user-friendly appeal of its other attractions, the two most popular places to visit in Oslo are a park and a ski jump. The park, in the Frogner quarter, is **Vigeland Park**, named after the sculptor Gustav Vigeland, and the thousands who flock here throughout the year add to the permanent numbers already present, resolutely naked and constructed from granite or weathered bronze. Inevitably, there's a museum on hand, with nearly 3000 sculptures and 10,000 drawings, all by Vigeland. Meanwhile, the ski jump is a metro ride away at Holmenkollen. If you visit in winter you might be lucky and catch a competition, but if you're here in the summer, go to the top of the jump and get the best view of Oslo imaginable. Yes, there's a ski museum too, located at the foot of the jump.

It *is* possible to stroll a part of Oslo without an exhibit in sight, unless you count the blond-highlighted cool cats of Grunerlokka and Grønland as exhibits. This is the east end part of the city which has evolved from worn-out working-class area to creative boho quarter and boasts a quirky range of cafés and restaurants frequented by local artists and photographers. It's by the Aker River, and the many small shops and delis are a febrile hunting ground, enhanced by many immigrant nationalities creating a buzzy, eclectic atmosphere.

OSLO IN...

→ ONE DAY

Aker Brygge, Karl Johans Gate, a central museum, a meal in Grunerlokka

→ TWO DAYS

Akershus, Astrup Fearnley Museum, ferry trip to Bygdøy, museum and picnic there

→ THREE DAYS

Vigeland Park, Holmenkollen Ski Jump, a stroll round Grunerlokka, Munch Museum, supper in Akker Brygge

CALENDAR HIGHLIGHTS

Oslo's cultural highlights are obviously dependent on the time of year. If you're a ski fancier, then go in the winter months for competitions at Holmenkollen. At Christmas, the Folk Museum on Bygdøy and the seventeenth century former foundry at Baerums Verk with its workers' houses converted into small shops are magical places to be. February and March are the months for the Winter Night Festival, a classical music extravaganza, and the Oslo International Church Music Festival, held at the cathedral and other churches within the city. Summer is welcomed with St Hallvard's Day in May, when a host of concerts and theatre productions pronounce curtain-up; a month later, the Norwegian Wood rock festival is a three-day jamboree with mostly Norwegian bands. Bonfires are lit on Midsummer Night, and in July/August the Folk Museum has daily folk dancing and helpings of traditional food. Mid-August is given over to an International Jazz Festival, while the Oslo World Music Festival blasts out from various city venues in November. The Nobel Peace Prize, awarded in December, is celebrated with parades and festivities across town.

EATING OUT

Oslo has a very vibrant dining scene, albeit one that is somewhat expensive, particularly if you drink wine. The cooking is generally quite refined and classical, although some innovative menus are beginning to appear. France has always exerted the greatest influence on the cuisine but now younger chefs are looking also to Italy and Spain for inspiration and, these days, there is generally a broader choice of food styles. What is in no doubt is the quality of the produce used, whether that's the ever-popular game or the superlative shellfish which comes from very cold water, giving it a clean and fresh flavour. Classic Norwegian dishes often include fruit, such as lingonberries with venison. Lunch is not a particularly major affair ; most prefer just a snack or sandwich at midday while making dinner the main event of the day. You'll find most diners are seated by 7pm and are offered a 6,7,or 8 course menu which they can reduce at their will, with a paired wine menu alongside. Service is another great strength of the restaurants ; staff are generally very polite, speak English and are fully versed in the menu.

It doesn't have to be expensive, though. Look out for konditoris (bakeries) where you can pick up sandwiches and pastries, while kafeterias serve substantial meals, traditional and simple, at reasonable prices.

→ TAKE THE TRAIN TO THE TRAIL

One of the reasons there aren't many people about in Oslo in the winter is that they're making use of the cross-country ski trails that encircle the city. There are 1,250 miles of them and they're floodlit at night. A local train ride gets you to them.

→ A FRIEND OF THE PEOPLE

Henrik Ibsen would walk every day from Oslo's Grand Café to the apartment in Arbiens Gate where he spent the last years of his life. He was so punctual with this sortie that the people of the city would set their watches by him.

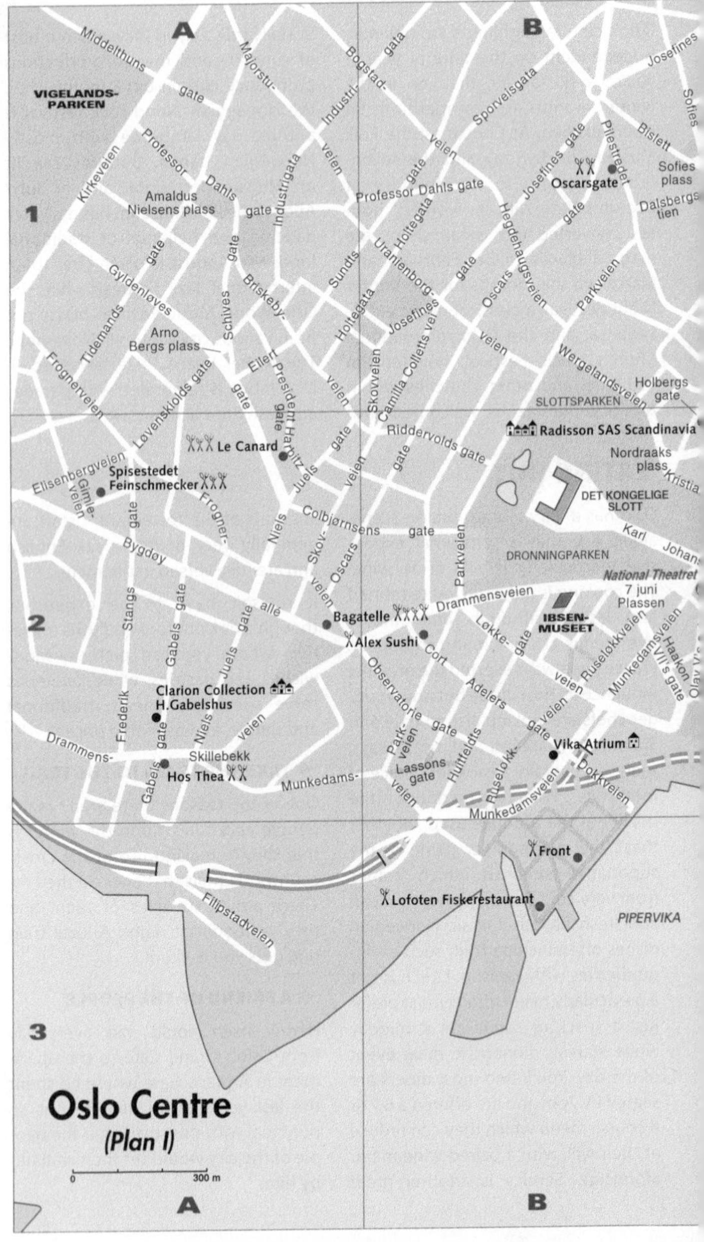
A
B
1
2
3
VIGELANDS-PARKEN
Middelthuns gate
Majorstu-veien
Bogstad-veien
Industri-gata
Sporveisgata
Josefines gate
Pilestredet
Bislett
Sofies plass
Dalsbergs-tien
Oscarsgate
Professor Dahls gate
Amaldus Nielsens plass
Kirkeveien
Industrigata
Holtegata
Uranienborg-veien
Heggehaugsveien
Parkveien
Oscars gate
Gyldenløves gate
Tidemands gate
Schives gate
Briskeby-veien
Sundts gate
Josefines gate
Camilla Colletts vei
Arno Bergs plass
Frognerveien
Løvenskiolds gate
Eilert Sundts gate
President Harbitz gate
Skovveien
Wergelandsveien
Holbergs gate
SLOTTSPARKEN
Radisson SAS Scandinavia
Riddervolds gate
Le Canard
Elisenbergveien
Gimle-veien
Spisestedet Feinschmecker
Frogner-veien
Juels gate
Nordraaks plass
Kristia
DET KONGELIGE SLOTT
Colbjørnsens gate
Karl Johans
DRONNINGPARKEN
Bygdøy allé
Stangs gate
Gabels gate
Niels Juels gate
National Theatret
7 juni Plassen
Drammensveien
Bagatelle
Alex Sushi
Cort Adelers gate
IBSEN-MUSEET
Løkke-veien
Ruseløkkveien
Munkedamsveien
Haakon VII's gate
Olav V's
Observatorie gate
Clarion Collection H.Gabelshus
Frederik Stangs gate
Drammens-veien
Skillebekk
Hos Thea
Munkedams-veien
Park-veien
Lassons gate
Huitfeldts gate
Vika Atrium
Dokkveien
Front
Lofoten Fiskerestaurant
PIPERVIKA
Filipstadveien
Oslo Centre
(Plan I)
0
300 m

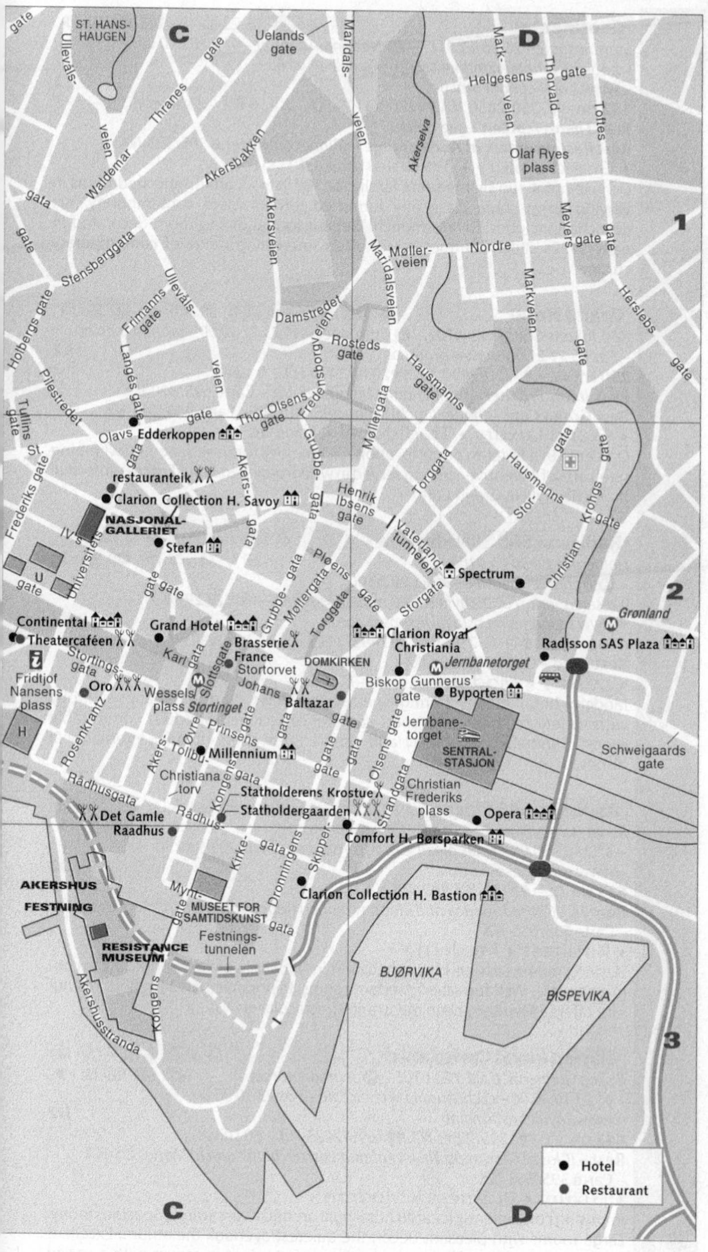
ST. HANS-HAUGEN
C
D
Uelands gate
Maridals-veien
Helgesens gate
Thorvald Meyers gate
Tofte gate
Olaf Ryes plass
Akerselva
Thranes gate
Waldemar Thranes gate
Akersbakken
Akersveien
Stensberggata
Ullevålsveien
Møller-veien
Nordre gate
Markveien
Herslebs gate
Frimanns gate
Langes gate
Damstredet
Fredensborgveien
Rosteds gate
Hausmanns gate
Holbergs gate
Pilestredet
Tullins gate
Thor Olsens gate
Møllergata
Olavs gate
Edderkoppen
restauranteik
Clarion Collection H. Savoy
NASJONAL-GALLERIET
Stefan
Grubbe-gata
Henrik Ibsens gate
Vaterland-tunnelen
Torggata
Stor-gata
Christian Krohgs gate
Frederiks gate
Universitetsgata
Pløens gate
Spectrum
Storgata
Grønland
Continental
Grand Hotel
Theatercaféen
Karl Johans gate
Brasserie France
Clarion Royal Christiania
Radisson SAS Plaza
Stortingsgata
Stortorvet
DOMKIRKEN
Jernbanetorget
Fridtjof Nansens plass
Oro
Wessels plass
Stortinget
Baltazar
Biskop Gunnerus' gate
Byporten
Rosenkrantz gate
Øvre Slottsgate
Prinsens gate
Jernbane-torget
SENTRAL-STASJON
Schweigaards gate
Akers-gata
Tollbugata
Millennium
Christiania torv
Kongens gate
Rådhusgata
Statholderens Krostue
Statholdergaarden
Christian Frederiks plass
Strandgata
Det Gamle Raadhus
Opera
Comfort H. Børsparken
Kirkegata
Dronningens gate
Skipper-gata
AKERSHUS FESTNING
Myntgate
MUSEET FOR SAMTIDSKUNST
Clarion Collection H. Bastion
RESISTANCE MUSEUM
Festnings-tunnelen
BJØRVIKA
BISPEVIKA
Akershusstranda
1
2
3
Hotel
Restaurant

NORWAY - OSLO

Continental

C2

Stortingsgaten 24-26 ✉ 0117 – Ⓜ *National Theatret* – ☏ 22 82 40 00 – *booking@hotel-continental.no* – *Fax 22 42 40 65* – *www.hotel-continental.no*

152 rm – †2250/2850 NOK ††2700/3120 NOK, ☕ 150 NOK – 3 suites

Rest *Theatercaféen* – see below

Rest *Restauranteik at Annen Etage* – *(dinner only)* Menu 395/525 NOK

♦ Grand Luxury ♦ Traditional ♦ Classic ♦

De luxe hotel, run by the same family for 100 years. Comfortable bedrooms in varying sizes; some classically furnished, others more contemporary. Art collection includes Edvard Munch. Elegant formal dining room decorated in early 1920s style. Gourmet menu offers interesting range of contemporary cuisine.

Grand Hotel

C2

Karl Johans Gate 31 ✉ *0101* – Ⓜ *Stortinget* – ☏ *23 21 20 00* – *grand@rica.no* – *Fax 23 21 21 00* – *www.grand.no*

290 rm ☕ – †1780/2490 NOK ††2030/2490 NOK – 9 suites

Rest *Julius Fritzner* – *(dinner only)* Menu 595 NOK – Carte 625/820 NOK

Rest *Grand Café* – *(buffet lunch)* Menu 395/445 NOK – Carte 445/540 NOK

♦ Grand Luxury ♦ Traditional ♦ Classic ♦

Opulent 1874 hotel, in prime location. De luxe well furnished rooms. Swimming pool on roof. Inventive cooking served in wood-panelled Julius Fritzner. Informal brasserie-style in Grand Café.

Radisson SAS Scandinavia

≤ Oslo and Fjord,

B2

Holbergsgate 30 ✉ *0166* – Ⓜ *National Theatret* – ☏ *23 29 30 00* – *reservations.scandinavia.oslo@radissonsas.com* – *Fax 23 29 30 01* – *www.scandinavia.oslo.radissonsas.com*

476 rm ☕ – †1195/2195 NOK ††1495/2495 NOK – 12 suites

Rest *Enzo* – Carte 373/561 NOK

♦ Luxury ♦ Modern ♦

Modern hotel block offering spectacular views. Vast international lobby with variety of shops and good conference facilities. Spacious comfortable rooms. Panoramic bar. Small and simple Enzo offers popular international dishes.

Radisson SAS Plaza

≤ Oslo and Fjord,

D2

Sonja Henies Plass 3 ✉ *0134* – Ⓜ *Jernbanetorget* – ☏ *22 05 80 00* – *sales.plaza@radissonsas.com* – *Fax 22 05 80 30* – *www.radissonsas.com*

673 rm ☕ – †2195 NOK ††2495 NOK

Rest *34* – *(Closed Sunday and Monday dinner) (tapas buffet lunch)* Menu 495 NOK – Carte 535/655 NOK

♦ Business ♦ Modern ♦

Business-oriented hotel block, the tallest in Norway, with footbridge link to congress centre. Well furnished modern rooms. Panoramic bar. 34th floor restaurant offers a Mediterranean menu and spectacular views.

Clarion Royal Christiania

D2

Biskop Gunnerus' Gate 3 ✉ *0106* – Ⓜ *Jernbanetorget* – ☏ *23 10 80 00* – *cl.christiania@choice.no* – *Fax 23 10 80 80* – *www.royalchristiana.no*

443 rm ☕ – †1295/2295 NOK ††1695/2495 NOK – 60 suites

Rest – *(Closed Christmas, New Year and Easter) (buffet lunch)* Menu 395 NOK – Carte 395/665 NOK

♦ Luxury ♦ Business ♦ Modern ♦

Imposing conveniently located hotel built around a vast atrium. Spacious lobby. Large rooms with pleasant décor; the quietest overlook the atrium. Excellent conference facilities. Pleasantly decorated restaurant in atrium with a varied international menu.

Opera
Christian Frederiks plass 5 ✉ 0103 – Ⓜ Jernbanetorget – ✆ 24 10 30 00 – opera@thonhotels.no – Fax 24 10 30 10 – www.thonhotels.no/opera
Closed 1 week Christmas D2
432 rm – 1195/1695 NOK 1995 NOK – 2 suites
Rest – *(buffet lunch)* Carte 505/655 NOK
♦ Business ♦ Modern ♦
Located next to the railway station and in front of the new opera house, with an imposing hall and functional yet contemporary furnishings; the best bedrooms overlook the sea. Restaurant with huge windows affording panoramic views. Elaborate traditional cooking.

Clarion Collection H. Bastion without rest
Skippergaten 7 ✉ 0152 – ✆ 22 47 77 00 – cc.bastion@choice.no – Fax 22 33 11 80 – www.hotelbastion.no
Closed 19-25 March and 20-31 December C3
93 rm – 2195 NOK 1595/2395 NOK – 5 suites
♦ Business ♦ Modern ♦
Comfortable, modern hotel handily placed for motorway. Welcoming rooms with good facilities; the best in the new wing. Furniture and paintings reminiscent of English style.

Edderkoppen
St Olavs Plass 1 ✉ 0165 – Ⓜ National Theatret – ✆ 23 15 56 00 – edderkoppen@scandic-hotels.com – Fax 23 15 56 11 – www.scandic-hotels.com
Closed 23 December-2 January C2
235 rm – 1850 NOK 1150/2050 NOK – 6 suites
Rest – *(Closed Sunday) (buffet lunch)* Menu 165/395 NOK – Carte 295/355 NOK
♦ Business ♦ Modern ♦
550 photographs of Norway's famous actors adorn the walls of this renovated building, incorporating a theatre. Modern, functional, well-equipped bedrooms. Modern restaurant offering dishes with Mediterranean and international flavours.

Clarion Collection H. Gabelshus without rest
Gabelsgate 16 ✉ 0272 – ✆ 23 27 65 00 – cc.gabelshus@choice.no – Fax 23 27 65 60 – www.choicehotels.no
Closed Easter and 22 December-2 January A2
113 rm – 2000 NOK 2000 NOK – 1 suite
♦ Traditional ♦ Classic ♦
Attractive early 20C vine-clad hotel with extension in quiet district. Modern public rooms. Large well-fitted bedrooms; some on front with balconies, quieter at the rear.

Millennium
Tollbugaten 25 ✉ 0157 – ✆ 21 02 28 00 – millennium@firsthotels.no – Fax 21 02 28 30 – www.firsthotels.com C2
102 rm – 1095/1950 NOK 1550/2000 NOK – 10 suites
Rest – *(Closed Sunday and Bank Holidays) (dinner only)* Carte approx. 550 NOK
♦ Business ♦ Functional ♦
Functional modern hotel near harbour and restaurants. Internet access. Spacious well-equipped rooms; top floor with balconies; quietest on inside although overlooked. Simple restaurant on different levels serving global cuisine, from pizza to tapas.

Stefan
Rosenkrantzgate 1 ✉ 0159 – ✆ 23 31 55 00 – stefan@thonhotels.no – Fax 23 31 55 55 – www.thonhotels.no/stefan
Closed 15-24 March and 21 December-2 January C2
150 rm – 1295/1795 NOK 1595/1795 NOK
Rest – *(Closed Sunday)* Carte approx. 230 NOK
♦ Business ♦ Functional ♦
Modern hotel on convenient corner site. Rooms are well equipped with functional furniture and good facilities; top floor recently refurbished. Families and groups catered for. Comfortable ground floor restaurant with fireplace.

Clarion Collection H. Savoy

Universitetsgata 11 ✉ 0164 – Ⓜ National Theatret – ☎ 23 35 42 00 – cc.savoy@choice.no – Fax 23 35 42 01 – www.choice.no
Closed 13-26 March and 20 December-2 January **C2**
93 rm – 1995/2495 NOK 2495 NOK
Rest *restauranteik* – see below
♦ Business ♦ Classic ♦
Classic early 20C hotel in the city centre behind the museum. Spacious well-kept bedrooms with good facilities. Free dinner buffet in elegant attic room.

Byporten without rest

Jernbanetorget 6 ✉ 0154 – Ⓜ Jernbanetorget – ☎ 23 15 55 00 – byporten@scandic-hotels.com – Fax 23 15 55 11 – www.scandic-hotels.com/byporten **D2**
235 rm – 1890/2190 NOK 2190/2390 NOK – 4 suites
♦ Business ♦ Modern ♦
Modern hotel in vast office/commercial centre block by station. Functional soundproofed rooms with environmentally friendly decor. Breakfast in nearby public restaurant.

Comfort H. Børsparken without rest

Tollbugaten 4 ✉ 0152 – Ⓜ Jernbanetorget – ☎ 22 47 17 17 – co.borsparken@choice.no – Fax 22 47 17 18 – www.choicehotels.no **C-D2**
198 rm – 1890 NOK 2110 NOK
♦ Business ♦ Functional ♦
Modern functional chain hotel on corner site in city centre. Pleasant lobby opening onto tree-lined square. Compact practical rooms, well equipped for business clientele.

Vika Atrium without rest

Munkedamsveien 45 ✉ 0121 – Ⓜ National Theatret – ☎ 22 83 33 00 – vika.atrium@thonhotels.no – Fax 22 83 09 57 – www.thonhotels.no/vikaatrium **B2**
79 rm – 1395/1595 NOK 1695/1895 NOK
♦ Business ♦ Functional ♦
Located in large office block built around an atrium. Comfortable lobby lounge. Well-serviced rooms with functional modern fittings. Good conference facilities.

Spectrum without rest

Brugata 7 ✉ 0133 – Ⓜ Grønland – ☎ 23 36 27 00 – spectrum@thonhotels.no – Fax 23 36 27 50 – www.thonhotel.no/spectrum
Closed 20 December-2 January **D2**
151 rm – 615 NOK 895 NOK
♦ Business ♦ Functional ♦
Conveniently located, basic hotel not far from station, in area full of grocery stores. Some bedrooms are fairly functional; others have more interesting décor and furniture.

Bagatelle (Eyvind Hellstrøm)

Bygdøy Allé 3 ✉ 0257 – Ⓜ National Theatret – ☎ 22 12 14 40 – bagatelle@bagatelle.no – Fax 22 43 64 20 – www.bagatelle.no
Closed Easter, 4 weeks July-August, Christmas and Sunday **A2**
Rest – *(booking essential) (dinner only)* Menu 800 NOK – Carte 800/1100 NOK
Spec. Tempura of Norwegian red King crab. Turbot "Royal", aromatic butter. Passion fruit soufflé.
♦ Contemporary ♦ Design ♦
Long-standing, elegant restaurant with well-spaced tables, colourful contemporary décor and numerous paintings on walls. Choose between classic and creative menus. Wine cellar may be viewed by diners.

XXX ✿

Le Canard

President Harbitz Gate 4 ✉ 0259 – ✆ 22 54 34 00 – lecanard@lecanard.no – Fax 22 54 34 10 – www.lecanard.no
Closed Easter, Christmas-New Year, 18-20 February, 8 July-1 August, Sunday and Bank Holidays **A2**
Rest – *(dinner only)* Menu 695/1150 NOK
Spec. King crab with avocado purée and sea urchin sauce. Duckling with golden raisins and hazelnuts, aigre-doux sauce. Manjari chocolate dessert, sour cream sorbet.

♦ Inventive ♦ Formal ♦

1900 villa in residential district, fully refurbished in 2006. Stylish and modern interior with original wall fresco. Skilled and refined cooking. Knowledgeable service.

XXX ✿

Statholdergaarden (Bent Stiansen)

Rådhusgate 11, (entrance by Kirkegate) ✉ 0151 – Ⓜ Stortinget – ✆ 22 41 88 00 – post@statholdergaarden.no – Fax 22 41 22 24 – www.statholdergaarden.no
Closed 16-24 March, 1, 11-14 and 17 May, 13 July-5 August, 21 December-7 January and Sunday **C2**
Rest Statholderens Krostue – see below
Rest – *(booking essential) (dinner only)* Menu 825/995 NOK – Carte 750/920 NOK
Spec. Scallops with halibut, cauliflower cream and tarragon sauce. Fillet of lamb with sweet potato mousseline and rosemary sauce. Pear and chocolate tart with hazelnut ice cream.

♦ Contemporary ♦ Formal ♦

Fine 17C house; elegant dining room with original décor beneath beautiful stucco ceilings. High quality cuisine draws on French classics, with hints of the Mediterranean.

XXX ✿

Spisestedet Feinschmecker

Balchensgate 5 ✉ 0265 – ✆ 22 12 93 80 – kontakt@feinschmecker.no – Fax 22 12 93 88 – www.feinschmecker.no
Closed Easter, 3 weeks in summer and Sunday **A2**
Rest – *(dinner only)* Menu 675 NOK – Carte 640/825 NOK
Spec. Sautéed scallops with cauliflower purée and truffle vinaigrette. Herb roast rack of lamb with seasonal vegetables. Gratin of raspberries.

♦ Contemporary ♦ Formal ♦

The chef personally welcomes his customers to this cosy, traditional restaurant, located in a smart neighbourhood. Inventive cuisine draws inspiration from all over Europe.

XXX

Oro

Tordenskioldsgate 6A ✉ 0160 – Ⓜ Stortinget – ✆ 23 01 02 40 – kontakt@ororestaurant.no – Fax 23 01 02 48 – www.ororestaurant.no
Closed Christmas and New Year **C2**
Rest – *(booking essential) (dinner only)* Menu 575 NOK
Rest *Del i Oro* – Menu 200/300 NOK – Carte 100/150 NOK

♦ International ♦ Trendy ♦

Elegant, modern designer décor in muted tones with an informal atmosphere. Open-plan kitchen offers inventive cuisine with French influences. Booking a must. Del i Oro, the adjoining tapas bar with a large counter displaying cold and some warm dishes.

XX

Det Gamle Raadhus

Nedre Slottsgate 1 ✉ 0157 – Ⓜ Stortinget – ✆ 22 42 01 07 – gamle.raadhus@gamle-raadhus.no – Fax 22 42 04 90 – www.gamle-raadhus.no
Closed 1 week Easter, 3 weeks July, 1 week Christmas and Sunday **C3**
Rest – *(dinner only)* Menu 425 NOK – Carte 413/649 NOK

♦ Traditional ♦ Rustic ♦

Well-run restaurant operating for over a century located in Oslo's original City Hall, dating from 1641. Elegant rustic interior décor and English-style atmosphere in bar.

XX

restauranteik – Clarion Collection H. Savoy

Universitetsgata 11 ✉ 0164 – Ⓜ Stortinget – ✆ 22 36 07 10 – eikefjord@restauranteik.no – Fax 22 36 07 11 – www.restauranteik.no

Closed 13-26 March, 20 December-2 January, Sunday and Monday **C2**

Rest – *(set menu only)(dinner only)* Menu 355 NOK

◆ Contemporary ◆ Fashionable ◆

Restaurant in striking minimalist style; open-plan kitchen with chef's table. Good value set menu of 3 or 5 courses of interesting dishes.

XX

Baltazar

Dronningensgt 27 ✉ 0154 – Ⓜ Jernbanetorget – ✆ 23 35 70 60 – baltazar@baltazar.no – Fax 23 35 70 61 – www.baltazar.no

Closed, 1 month in Summer, Easter, 1 and 17 May, July, Christmas and Sunday **C2**

Rest – *(dinner only)* Menu 545/755 NOK

Rest *Enoteca* – Carte 280/350 NOK

◆ Italian ◆ Friendly ◆

Behind cathedral, under arcades of 1852 brick market. Serious Italian wine list; small à la carte or concise chef's menu: home-made pasta, fine Italian produce and local fish. The rustic décor of the wine bar is just right for an informal lunch.

XX

Haga (Terje Ness)

Griniveien 315 (Baerum, Northwest: 11 km) – ✆ 67157515 – max@hagarestaurant.no – Fax 67 15 75 16 – www.hagarestaurant.no

Closed Christmas, Easter, Sunday and Monday

Rest – *(booking essential) (dinner only)* Menu 495

Spec. Poached turbot with caviar and fennel. Roast pigeon with foie gras. Chocolate crème with peanuts and sherbet.

◆ Inventive ◆ Minimalist ◆

Modern building set on golf course, with glass walls offering views over the surrounding countryside. Precise, classic French-inspired cuisine with hints of Spain and Italy.

XX

Oscarsgate (Björn Svensson)

Pilestredet 63 ✉ 0350 – ✆ 22465906 – Fax 22 46 59 07 – www.resaturantoscargate.no

Closed 1-21 July, 22 December-6 January, Sunday, Monday and Bank Holidays **B1**

Rest – *(booking essential) (dinner only)* Menu 595 – Carte 775/1065

Spec. Salmon and bluefin tuna, soya sauce and lime sorbet. Norwegian pigeon and foie gras with potato confit. Dark chocolate with cherries, strawberries and liquorice.

◆ Inventive ◆ Elegant ◆

Tiny restaurant with narrow tables; its dimensions reflected in the miniature dishes that are served over 8 courses, combining Norwegian, French and Italian influences. Precise, original cooking.

XX

Theatercaféen – at Continental H.

Stortingsgaten 24-26 ✉ 0117 – Ⓜ National Theatret – ✆ 22 82 40 50 – theatercafeen@hotel-continental.no – Fax 22 41 20 94 – www.hotel-continental.no **C2**

Rest – *(light lunch)* Menu 570 NOK (dinner) – Carte 455/725 NOK

◆ Traditional ◆ Brasserie ◆

An institution in the city and the place to see and be seen. Elaborate lunchtime sandwiches make way for afternoon/evening brasserie specials.

XX

Hos Thea

Gabelsgate 11 ✉ 0272 – ✆ 22 44 68 74 – post@hosthea.no – www.hosthea.no

Closed 24-26 December, 20-23 March, 7-30 July **A2**

Rest – *(dinner only)* Menu 395 NOK – Carte 345/535 NOK

◆ Italian influences ◆ Family ◆

Discreet black façade in residential area conceals this typical little restaurant fitted out with simple, Scandinavian-style décor. Appealing menu boasts Italian influences.

Brasserie France

Øvre Slottsgate 16 ✉ 0157 – Ⓜ Stortinget – ✆ 23 10 01 65 – bord@brasseriefrance.no – Fax 23 10 01 61 – www.brasseriefrance.no
Closed Easter, 23 December-3 January and Sunday **C2**
Rest – *(dinner only and Saturday light lunch)* Menu 345 NOK – Carte 345/485 NOK
♦ French ♦ Brasserie ♦
Set over 3 floors plus a dining cellar, with French brasserie-style on ground floor. Wall benches, bistro chairs and open kitchen. Interesting dishes from all areas of France.

Statholderens Krostue – at Statholdergaarden

Rådhusgate 11, 1st floor ✉ 0151 – Ⓜ Stortinget – ✆ 22 41 88 00 – post@statholdergaarden.no – Fax 22 41 22 24 – www.statholdergaarden.no
Closed 16-24 March, 1, 11-14, and 17 May, 6 July-6 August, 21 December-7 January, Sunday and Monday **C2**
Rest – Menu 500 NOK – Carte 520/550 NOK
♦ International ♦ Rustic ♦
Three vaulted basement rooms with bistro-style décor and warm candle-lit ambience. Changing themed menus for dinner and à la carte for light lunch; friendly service.

Lofoten Fiskerestaurant

Stranden 75 ✉ 0250 – ✆ 22 83 08 08 – lofoten@fiskerestaurant.no – Fax 22 83 68 66 – www.lofoten-fiskerestaurant.no
Closed 22 December-3 January **B3**
Rest – Menu 330/440 NOK – Carte 413/485 NOK
♦ Seafood ♦ Brasserie ♦
Attractive, modern fjord-side restaurant at Aker Brygge. Owner-chef offers a tempting array of seafood and shellfish. Ask for a table on the terrace so you can enjoy the view.

Alex Sushi

Cort Adelers Gate 2 ✉ 0254 – Ⓜ National Theatret – ✆ 22 43 99 99 – alex@alexsushi.no – Fax 22 43 99 98 – www.alexsushi.no
Closed Christmas, New Year and Easter **B2**
Rest – *(dinner only)* Menu 375/595 NOK – Carte 400/675 NOK
♦ Japanese ♦ Design ♦
Swish Japanese restaurant features central oval sushi bar shaped like small boat with metallic roof. Dining room enlivened by modern art. Appealing tempura and miso dishes.

Front

Stranden 7 ✉ 0250 – ✆ 22 83 64 00 – post@restaurant-front.no – Fax 22 83 64 01 – www.restaurant-front.no **B3**
Rest – *(light lunch)* Menu 425 NOK – Carte 445/589 NOK
♦ Traditional ♦ Minimalist ♦
A very popular newcomer on Aker Brygge quay, this contemporary brasserie/restaurant is flooded with light from big windows and has a smart front terrace. Tasty local dishes.

ENVIRONS OF OSLO

at Lillestrøm Northeast : 18 km by E 6

Arena

Nesgata 1 ✉ 2004 – ✆ 66 93 60 00 – arena@thonhotels.no – Fax 66 93 63 00 – www.thonhotels.no/arena
Closed 21 December-4 January
262 rm – †1345/1645 NOK ††1545/1895 NOK – 16 suites
Rest *Madame Thrane* – *(dinner only)* Menu 395 NOK – Carte 395/595 NOK
Rest *Amfi* – *(buffet lunch)* Menu 285/515 NOK
♦ Business ♦ Functional ♦
Large modern hotel in trade fair centre with direct train access to airport and city centre. Contemporary rooms with every possible facility, though the singles are fairly compact. Madame Thrane for interesting contemporary dishes. Buffet-style service at the informal Amfi.

at Holmenkollen Northwest : 10 km by Bogstadveien, Sørkedalsveien and Holmenkollveien

Holmenkollen Park

< Oslo and Fjord, rm

Kongeveien 26 ✉ 0787 – Ⓜ Holmenkollen
– ✆ 22 92 20 00 – holmenkollen.park.hotel.rica@rica.no – Fax 22 14 61 92
– www.holmenkollenparkhotel.no
Closed 22 December-3 January
222 rm – †1160/1680 NOK ††1410/1930 NOK – 11 suites
Rest *De Fem Stuer* – *(buffet lunch)* Menu 445 NOK – Carte 495/695 NOK
Rest *Galleriet* – *(Closed Saturday lunch and Sunday) (buffet lunch)* Menu 295 NOK – Carte 275/590 NOK
♦ Traditional ♦ Personalised ♦
Smart hotel near Olympic ski jump; superb views. Part built (1894) in old Norwegian "dragon style" decorated wood. Chalet-style rooms, some with balconies or views or saunas. Norwegian cuisine with global influences in De Fem Stuer. Informal Galleriet for a more popular menu.

at Oslo Airport Northeast : 45 km by E 6 at Gardermoen

Radisson SAS Airport

✉ *2061 – ✆ 63 93 30 00*
– sales.airport.oslo@radissonsas.com – Fax 63 93 30 30
– www.gardermoen.radissonsas.com
500 rm – †1450/2295 NOK ††2895 NOK
Rest – Carte approx. 450 NOK
♦ Business ♦ Modern ♦
Ultra-contemporary business hotel on a semi-circular plan overlooking runway but well soundproofed. Rooms are a good size, well equipped and have varied décor. Modern restaurant offering a variety of international dishes to appeal to all comers.

Clarion Oslo Airport

rm

(West : 6 km) ✉ *2060 – ✆ 63 94 94 94*
– cl.oslo.airport@choice.no – Fax 63 94 94 95 – www.choicehotels.no
357 rm – †1095/1995 NOK ††1295/2195 NOK – 2 suites
Rest – *buffet lunch* Carte approx. 463 NOK
♦ Business ♦ Functional ♦
Modern hotel with Norwegian design of wood and red tiles, a few minutes from airport by bus shuttle. Newly renovated rooms; elegant furnishings. Well equipped for conferences. Vast restaurant offers a standard range of international dishes to cater for all tastes.

POLAND
POLSKA

PROFILE

→ **Area:**
312 677 km^2 (120 725 sq mi).

→ **Population:**
38 635 000 inhabitants (est. 2005), density = 124 per km^2.

→ **Capital:**
Warsaw (conurbation 2 135 000 inhabitants).

→ **Currency:**
Złoty (zl or PLN); rate of exchange: PLN 1 = € 0.26 = US$ 0.40 (Dec 2007).

→ **Government:**
Parliamentary republic (since 1990). Member of European Union since 2004.

→ **Language:**
Polish.

→ **Specific public holidays:**
National 3rd of May Holiday, Corpus Christi (9th Thursday after Easter), Independence Day (11 November).

→ **Local Time:**
GMT + 1 hour in winter and GMT + 2 hours in summer.

→ **Climate:**
Temperate continental with cold winters and warm summers (Warsaw: January: -2°C; July: 20°C).

→ **International dialling Code:**
00 48 followed by the area code and then the local number. Directory enquiries: ✆ **118 912**.

→ **Emergency:**
Ambulance: ✆ **999**; Fire Brigade: ✆ **998**; Police: ✆ **997**; Police from mobile: ✆ **112**.

→ **Electricity:**
230V AC, 50Hz; 2 pin round-shaped continental plugs.

→ **Formalities**
Travellers from the European Union (EU), Switzerland, Iceland and the main countries of North and South America need a national identity card or passport (America: passport required) to visit Poland for less than three months (tourism or business purpose). For visitors from other countries a visa may be required, in addition to a passport, especially for those wishing to stay for longer than three months. We advise you to check with your embassy before travelling.

Centrum
kierunek
Kabaty

WARSAW
WARSZAWA

Population: 1 593 000 (conurbation 2 135 000) - Altitude: 106m.

Office National Polonais du Tourisme

When UNESCO added Warsaw to its World Heritage list a few years ago, it was a fitting seal of approval for an inspired refit and rebuild: eighty per cent of the city had been destroyed during World War II, with over half the city's population either killed or displaced. Using plans of the old city, architects painstakingly rebuilt the shattered Polish capital throughout the 1950s until it became an admirable mirror image of its former self. Strolling around the renovated Old Town, it's hard to believe that most of it is barely fifty years old.

The city still has its grey communist era apartment blocks, and these pall desperately when up against the old-style buildings with their pastel prettiness and aristocratic swagger, their architecture spanning a whole range of movements from Gothic to Baroque, Rococo to Secession. It's a vibrant place to be, and the locals are well known for their exuberance and warmth: chat briefly to a Varsovian at bar or bus stop and you'll soon be given a phone number and an invitation to meet up and share a vodka. Throw in the charming river views, superb parkland, and hearty cuisine now on offer, and you have a city confidently reclaiming its glories of old.

LIVING THE CITY

Warsaw sidles up along the left bank of the River Vistula; its opposite side, the district of **Praga**, is mostly marshy banks fronting a district of tower blocks. The main area for visitors is the **Old Town**, nestling against the river, which was established at the end of the thirteenth century around what is now the Royal Castle. A century later the **New Town**, to the north, began to take shape. To the south of Old Town runs 'The Royal Route', so named because from the late middle ages wealthy citizens built summer residences with lush gardens along these rural thoroughfares. Continue southwards and you're in Lazienki Park with its palaces and pavilions. To the west lie the more commercial areas of Marshal Street and Solidarity Avenue, once the commercial heart of the city. The northwest of Warsaw was traditionally the Jewish district, destroyed during World War II, and today redeveloped with housing estates and the sobering Monument to the Ghetto Heroes.

PRACTICAL INFORMATION

ARRIVAL-DEPARTURE

Warsaw Frederic Chopin Airport in Okecie is 10km from the city. Bus 179 or 188 will take you to the centre in 20 mins. Ensure you take a taxi from the rank outside arrivals.

TRANSPORT

Warsaw's metro is under development, and the best way to get about town is bus or tram (beyond the centre) or on foot for the central attractions.

Buy a pack of ten tickets for travelling on Warsaw's public transport system. Most single tickets are bought from RUCH kiosks, but as these are often closed in evenings and at weekends, it's best to get them in a pack. A flat rate fare for all single journeys applies. One-day and family tickets are also available.

It's well worth buying a Warsaw Tourist Card. Available from tourist information offices, it entitles you to free travel on public transport, free admission to 21 museums, and discounts in some shops, restaurants and leisure centres.

EXPLORING WARSAW

Warsaw is one of the youngest capital cities of Europe. It only assumed the mantle in 1596, after the royal castle in Cracow was destroyed by fire. It's been destroyed twice since then: by the Swedes in 1655 and the Germans in 1944. Visitors today are taken aback at how superbly the centre was rebuilt, using old documents and plans. The Old Town (Stare Miasto) is a masterclass of **Baroque** style in a smart geometric grid of little streets, swarming with delighted onlookers in summer.

➜ ROYAL FAMILIAR

The heartbeat of this quarter is **The Royal Castle**, the rebuild of which wasn't actually completed until 1988. It's now a museum and a focal point for formal ceremonies; it had once been the official residence of the Polish monarchs. Its interior is lavish, with many original furnishings and *objets d'art*: the Poles managed to hide many treasured statues and paintings from the Nazis. Check out the ballroom, Marble Room and Canaletto Room, each an opulent treat. Just north of Castle Square stands **Old Town Market Square**, which for centuries was the city's most important public meeting place. Here, everything from fairs to executions was carried out. The square's town hall was demolished nearly two hundred years ago, and its distinctive four sides are each named after parliamentarians of the eighteenth century; the houses grandly surrounding you were designed in the seventeenth. The Dekert side of the square is really worth discovering: all the houses are interconnected and form the Warsaw History Museum, which includes paintings, illustrations, archaeological finds, sculpture and photographs – a chronological odyssey through the city's troubled history. The cultural thrust of the square doesn't end here. On the Barss side stand two burghers' houses, a popular location for swarms of Varsovians, for this is the home of the Literature Museum, and in particular, first editions and original manuscripts of Poland's best-loved Romantic poet Adam Mickiewicz.

➜ NATIONAL TREASURE

Warsaw's real cultural gem is **The National Museum**: travel due south from Old Town Market Square for a mile to find it. Founded in 1862 with just 36 paintings, the museum now holds a mesmerising 780,000 exhibits. But you shouldn't suffer too much cultural overload: many are only on show at special exhibitions. Nevertheless, you might well feel like a park break when you stumble from the National's hallowed portals. You're in luck. A few minutes' walk and you're in **Lazienki Park,** Warsaw's green jewel, a luscious, peacock-strewn wonderland of old palaces and an orangerie with an eighteenth century court theatre. There's a second theatre here, too, on an island with a moat separating the auditorium from the stage. And a neoclassical Temple based on ancient Greek design. Not forgetting the Chopin Monument, sculpted one hundred years ago (1908) depicting the great man sitting under a willow tree in search of inspiration. In summer, the park is packed with visitors to the lakeside Palace on the Water, one of the finest examples of neoclassical architecture in Poland. There's another glorious park with palaces further south in Wilanow: again this is a lovely place to visit, with a stunning Baroque Park hiding behind the palace and, fascinatingly, a poster museum in a former stable: it includes posters by Picasso, Warhol and Mucha.

➜ GRAND TOUR

Warsaw has earned a reputation as a centre of cultural tourism thanks to numerous theatrical and musical venues. Top of the list is the grand sounding, grand looking...**Grand Theatre**, just south of Solidarity Avenue. Badly damaged during World War II, it was enlarged during reconstruction and its modern interiors have brought it bang up to date. This is where to go if you want to see top-class opera or ballet. Before going in, incidentally, you could stroll over to the nearby **Saxon Gardens**, Warsaw's first public park and another leafy oasis. Modelled on Versailles, it boasts statues, fountains, mature trees and, more sombrely, the Tomb of the Unknown Soldier, a constant reminder of the city's anguished 20C history. Mozart lovers, meanwhile, often make a beeline for the Philharmonic Hall, near prestigious Marshal Street, where his music is a well-established attraction. And the Royal Castle is a great place to go for Renaissance and Baroque music (but remember it's only on a Sunday!)

Going shopping in Warsaw, as you might imagine, is a rather different experience than it was in 1989. From famine to feast might be putting it a bit strongly, but you get the picture. An expanding number of department stores and shopping arcades have arrived in the centre of the city with the Marshal Street area being the hub. For many locals, though, markets are what this city is really all about. Muffled up against the wind and snow, doing business with a street trader is part and parcel of Warsaw life. And for market lovers there's only one place to go – the **'Russian Market'**, across the river, in the Praga district. Quite simply, it's Europe's largest open-air market, a daily hotch-potch on a massive scale, the home of thousands of traders from Russia (hence the name) to the sub-Sahara, hawking everything from mobiles to counterfeit clothes, hunting knives to rifles. It encircles a vast disused stadium, and as you get off the number 12 tram, there are stalls as far as the eye can see. A bizarre bazaar, the like of which you won't have encountered before.

→ MOVING MEMORIALS

In the northwest of the city there are a lot of memorials: they tell the sombre story, in small part, of the many thousands of Jews who lived here before 1939, and who were murdered during World War II. One of the most affecting is the Monument to the Ghetto Heroes in **Zamenhofa**. It was erected in 1948, when the city was still in ruins, and powerfully commemorates the Ghetto Uprising of 1943, with men, women and children surrounded by the burning ghetto. Other monuments in the area include the **Umschlagplatz** Monument, to denote an old railway siding where Jews were sent to concentration camps, and the Monument to 300 Victims, a small 'funeral pyre' at the location where the remains of 300 Jews and Poles were unearthed during building works. Both the last two monuments were completed just twenty years ago.

CALENDAR HIGHLIGHTS

Warsaw's a hot spot for events, particularly in spring and autumn when the weather's at neither extreme. On Easter Monday, the first public holiday of the year, don't be surprised if you get doused, or at least sprinkled, with water by a total stranger. Amid much jollity, this has become something

WARSAW IN…

→ ONE DAY
Royal Castle, Warsaw History Museum, National Museum, Lazienki Park

→ TWO DAYS
Russian Market, Monument to the Ghetto Heroes, Saxon Gardens, top-class concert at Grand Theatre or Philharmonic Hall

→ THREE DAYS
The Royal Route, Marshal Street, Solidarity Avenue, Wilanow

of an institution for Varsovians. Also around this time is the Drowning of Marzanna, symbolizing the death of winter, when children throw a raggy doll into the Vistula (don't worry, they don't pick on visitors). In May, the cultural season really gets under way: there's an International Book Fair at the Palace of Culture and Science, while the Festival of Latin American Culture lasts a week and displays art from all over that continent. Also in June is the International Street Arts Festival, which literally brings art to the streets, plus the tunnels, bus and tram stops, and subway stations of Warsaw. Music plays a special place in Varsovians' lives – Chopin, their favourite son, is celebrated in concerts on Sunday afternoons in June in Lazienki Park, while the Chopin International Piano Competition, held every five years in October, is one of the most important in the world, and only music by Chopin is performed. Another summer favourite, meanwhile, is the Mozart Festival, where all of his operas are performed. Or you can mosey on over to the Royal Castle courtyard in July and August, where you'll join forty thousand others for the Musical Gardens festival, featuring films depicting opera, ballet and art. As the leaves turn to rich autumnal tones, Warsaw hosts a plethora of fine festivals, including Warsaw Autumn (September) featuring top composers from around the world, the Film Festival (October) which blends new and classic movies in cinemas around the city, and, also that month, the Jazz Jamboree, one of Europe's most prestigious, celebrating its fiftieth year in 2008.

EATING OUT

There's an old Polish proverb that says: "Eat, drink and loosen your belt." It rather lost its edge during the communist era, but in the near twenty years since democracy returned, the quality and quantity of Warsaw's restaurants has moved unerringly northwards. New venues seem to open weekly, and long gone are the days when a waiter would tell the hapless diner that none of the items on the menu were actually available. A visitor arriving for the first time since 1989 would be astonished at the proliferation of eateries, everything from veggie to Vietnamese, with fast food joints on most corners, as well as stalls selling falafel and noodles. A large Italian business community has encouraged a boom in the amount of good Italian restaurants. Asian food is also well represented, with Japanese restaurants particularly plentiful. What about Polish food? The centuries-old traditional cuisine of Warsaw was influenced by neighbouring countries, such as Russia, Ukraine and Germany, while Jewish dishes were also added to the mix. Time-honoured classics, such as the ubiquitous pierogi (turnovers with various fillings) and assorted pork dishes, have been updated with flair by Poland's finest chefs. Accompanied, of course, by Polish vodka, which covers a bewildering range of styles and brands, but tastes like no other vodka on earth: it has a distinct character, and should be served chilled. A good number of restaurants and cafés in central Warsaw provide stylised settings, such as a burgher's house, vaulted cellar, or Secessionist sophistication. Wherever you eat, check that VAT has been included with prices (it's not always) and add ten per cent for a tip, which is customary.

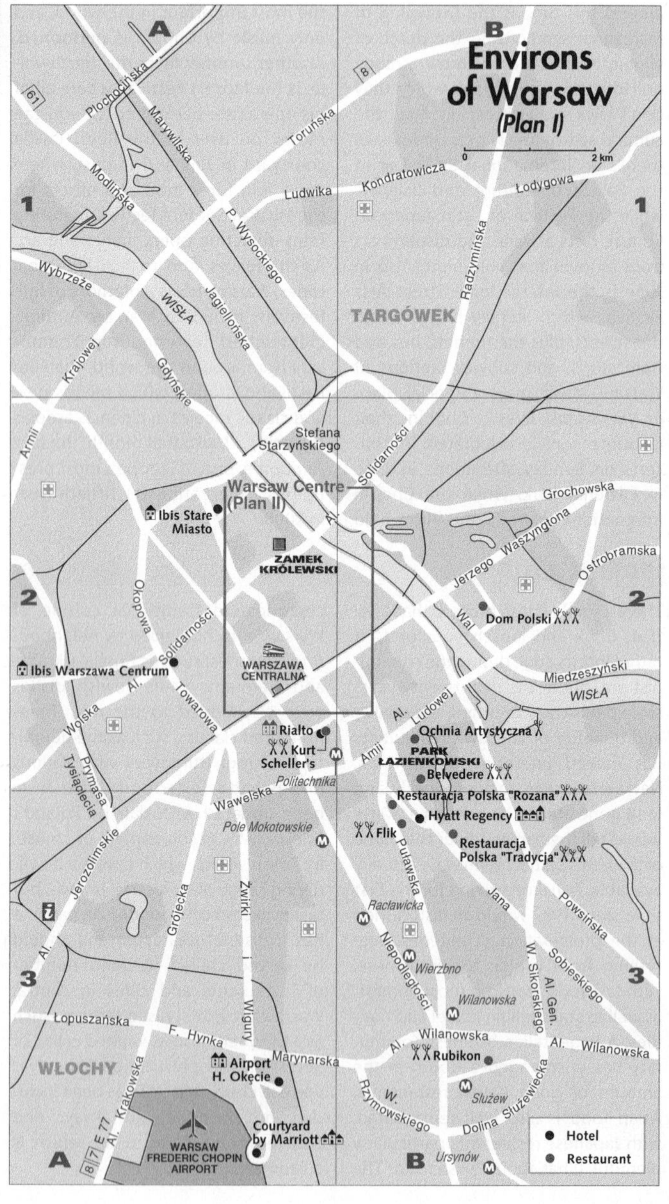
Environs of Warsaw
(Plan I)
0
2 km
A
B
1
2
3
Płochocińska
Marywilska
Toruńska
Modlińska
Ludwika
Kondratowicza
Łodygowa
P. Wysockiego
Radzymińska
Wybrzeże
WISŁA
Jagiellońska
TARGÓWEK
Krajowej
Gdyńskie
Armii
Stefana
Starzyńskiego
Solidarności
Warsaw Centre
(Plan II)
Grochowska
Ibis Stare
Miasto
ZAMEK
KRÓLEWSKI
Jerzego
Waszyngtona
Ostrobramska
Okopowa
Wał
Dom Polski
Al.
Solidarności
WARSZAWA
CENTRALNA
Ibis Warszawa Centrum
Miedzeszyński
WISŁA
Towarowa
Wolska
Al.
Ludowej
Rialto
Kurt
Scheller's
Qchnia Artystyczna
PARK
ŁAZIENKOWSKI
Armii
Belvedere
Politechnika
Prymasa
Tysiąclecia
Restauracja Polska "Rozana"
Wawelska
Hyatt Regency
Pole Mokotowskie
Flik
Restauracja
Polska "Tradycja"
Jerozolimskie
Puławska
Jana
Powsińska
Grójecka
Żwirki
Racławicka
Niepodległości
Al.
Wierzbno
W. Sikorskiego
Sobieskiego
Wilanowska
Al. Gen.
Wigury
Łopuszańska
F. Hynka
Al. Wilanowska
Al. Wilanowska
Rubikon
Marynarska
WŁOCHY
Airport
H. Okęcie
Krakowska
W.
Rzymowskiego
Służew
Służewiecka
Dolina
Courtyard
by Marriott
E 77
Al.
WARSAW
FREDERIC CHOPIN
AIRPORT
Ursynów
Hotel
Restaurant

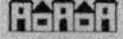

Le Royal Meridien Bristol ⁄rm
Krakowskie Przedmieście 42-44 ✉ 00 325 VISA AE
– Ⓜ Świętokrzyska – ✆ (022) 551 10 00 – bristol@lemeridien.com
– Fax (022) 625 25 77 – www.lemeridien.com/warsaw **D1**
173 rm – 1098 PLN 1098 PLN, 100 PLN – 31 suites
Rest *Marconi* – Menu 69 PLN (lunch) – Carte 137/186 PLN
Rest *Malinowa* – *✆ (022) 55 11 832 (Closed Sunday and Monday) (booking essential) (dinner only)* Carte 151/222 PLN

♦ Grand Luxury ♦ Classic ♦

Imposing late 19C façade, partly decorated in Art Nouveau style fronts classic hotel, a byword for luxury and meeting place for Warsaw high society. Spacious elegant rooms. Formal dining room with Art Nouveau décor and chandeliers adding opulence. Elaborate gourmet menu offers international cuisine with a strong French influence. Fairly informal restaurant with terrace offers a varied menu of Mediterranean fare.

Intercontinental < City, ⁄rm
Ul. Emilii Plater 49 ✉ 00 125 – Ⓜ Centrum VISA AE
– ✆ (022) 328 88 88 – wrs_reservation@interconti.com – Fax (022) 328 88 89
– www.warsaw.intercontinental.com **C2**
306 rm – 542/686 PLN 614/758 PLN, 35 PLN – 21 suites
Rest *Frida* – *(Closed Saturday and Sunday lunch)* Menu 75 PLN (lunch) – Carte 126/154 PLN
Rest *Downtown* – *(lunch only)* Carte 112/154 PLN
Rest *Hemisphere* – *(Closed Saturday-Sunday) (dinner only)* Carte 112/151 PLN

♦ Grand Luxury ♦ Business ♦ Modern ♦

Architecturally striking high-rise hotel. Richly furnished, contemporary bedrooms. Stunning 44th floor wellness centre. Frida for Mexican dishes from open-plan kitchen. Cosmopolitan New York-style in Downtown. Hemisphere with Hemingway theme and live music.

Hyatt Regency ⁄rm P
Belwederska Ave 23 ✉ 00 761 – ✆ (022) 558 12 34 VISA AE
– info@hyattwarsaw.pl – Fax (022) 558 12 35
– www.warsaw.regency.hyatt.com *Plan I* **B3**
231 rm – 740 PLN 490/780 PLN, PLN – 19 suites
Rest *Venti Tre* – *✆ (022) 558 1094* – Carte 137/187 PLN
Rest *Q Club* – *(Closed Saturday, Sunday and Bank Holidays) (dinner only)* Carte 114/156 PLN

♦ Luxury ♦ Business ♦ Modern ♦

Striking glass-fronted and ultramodern corporate hotel beside Lazienki Park. Spacious bedrooms with every facility and comfort. Contemporary Italian fare in relaxed Venti Tre. Open kitchen with wood fired specialities. Q Club for contemporary Asian menu.

The Westin ⁄rm VISA AE
Al. Jana Pawła II 21 ✉ 00 854 – Ⓜ Świętokrzyska – ✆ (022) 450 80 00
– warsaw@westin.com – Fax (022) 450 81 11 – www.westin.com/warsaw
346 rm – 454 PLN 756 PLN – 15 suites **C2**
Rest *Fusion* – Carte 138/293 PLN

♦ Luxury ♦ Business ♦ Modern ♦

Impressive modern façade, splendid glass atrium with glass lifts and spacious public areas. 'Heavenly beds' and modern facilities in comfortable bedrooms. Contemporary Fusion offers culinary delights as East meets West.

Sheraton ⁄rm VISA AE
Ul. B. Prusa 2 ✉ 00493 – Ⓜ Centrum – ✆ (022) 450 61 00 – warsaw@sheraton.com – Fax (022) 450 62 00 – www.sheraton.com/warsaw **D2**
331 rm – 454 PLN 756 PLN, 86 PLN – 19 suites
Rest *The Oriental* – *(Closed Saturday lunch and Sunday dinner)* Carte 120/190 PLN
Rest *Olive* – *(buffet lunch)* Carte 104/174 PLN

♦ Luxury ♦ Business ♦ Modern ♦

Business hotel in well-located, imposing building. Comfortable, spacious rooms; extra amenities in business class. Authentic Asian fare in ornately decorated Oriental. Mediterranean dishes in Olive.

Marriott

Al. Jerozolimskie 65-79 ✉ 00 697 – Ⓜ Centrum – ☎ (022) 630 63 06
– warsaw-reservation@marriotthotels.com – Fax (022) 830 03 11
– www.marriott.com/wawpl **C2**

483 rm – †464 PLN ††752 PLN, ☕ 72 PLN – 35 suites

Rest *Parmizzano's* – Carte 142/270 PLN

Rest *Lila Weneda* – Menu 86 PLN – Carte 69/134 PLN

♦ Business ♦ Modern ♦

Modern high-rise business hotel opposite station. Well-equipped up-to-date bedrooms with city views; good facilities for business travellers. Formal Parmizzano's offers Italian fare. Classic Polish cooking in Lila Weneda.

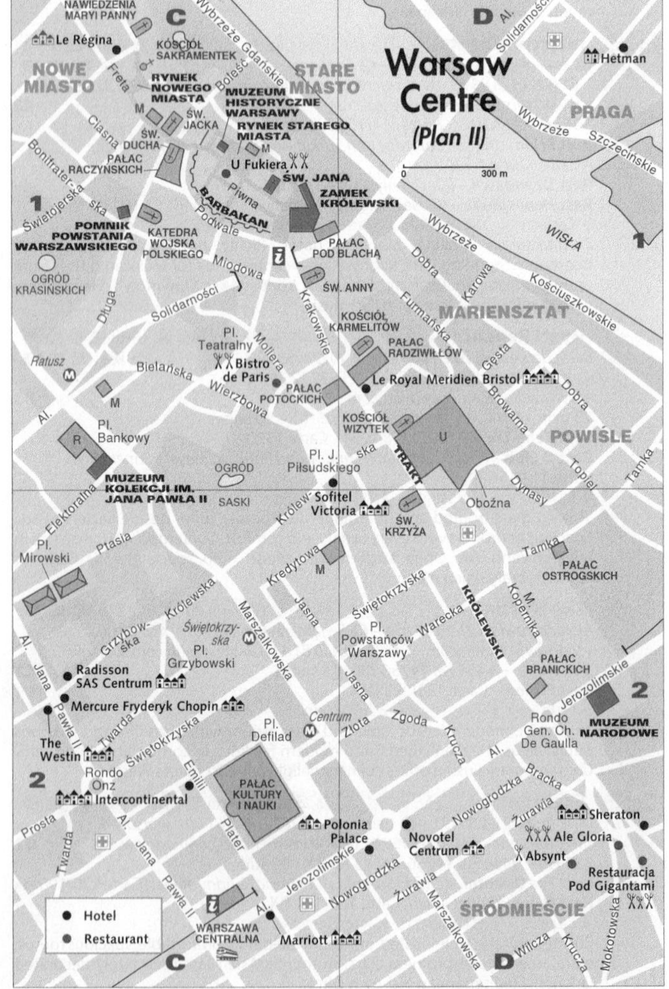

Sofitel Victoria

Ul. Krølewska 11 ✉ 00 065 – Ⓜ Świętokrzyska – ✆ (022) 657 80 11 – sof.victoria@orbis.pl – Fax (022) 657 80 57 – www.sofitel.com **C1-2**

329 rm – †720 PLN ††720 PLN – 12 suites

Rest *Canaletto* – Carte 122/169 PLN

◆ Business ◆ Classic ◆

Large hotel overlooking Pilsudski Square and Saxon Gardens. Rooms are well equipped and comfortable with muted classic décor. Good business facilities available. Formal restaurant with Italian influence.

Radisson SAS Centrum

Grzybowska 24 ✉ 00 132 – Ⓜ Świętokrzyska – ✆ (022) 321 88 88 – reservation.warsaw@radissonsas.com – Fax (022) 321 88 98 – www.radissonsas.com **C2**

292 rm – †299 PLN ††432 PLN, 72 PLN – 19 suites

Rest *Latino Brasserie at Ferdy's* – *(buffet lunch)* Carte 80/150 PLN

◆ Business ◆ Modern ◆

Popular corporate hotel in business district with state of the art meeting facilities. Modern bedrooms in maritime, Scandinavian or Italian style. Informal bar-restaurant with Latin American influences.

Le Régina

U. Kościelna 12 ✉ 00 218 – Ⓜ Ratusz – ✆ (022) 531 60 00 – info@leregina.com – Fax (022) 531 60 01 – www.leregina.com **C1**

59 rm – †1188 PLN ††1188 PLN, 72 PLN – 2 suites

Rest *La Rotisserie* – Menu 120/182 PLN – Carte 168/256 PLN

◆ Luxury ◆ Design ◆

Boutique hotel close to the Old Town; neo-18C exterior but stylish, contemporary interior. Pleasant courtyard. Individually decorated, spacious high-tech bedrooms. Small, intimate restaurant offering original modern cuisine.

Polonia Palace

Al. Jerozolimskie 45 ✉ 00 692 – Ⓜ Centrum – ✆ (022) 318 2888 – centralreservation@syrena.com.pl – Fax (022) 318 28 89 – www.poloniapalace.com **D2**

197 rm – †432 PLN ††432 PLN – 9 suites

Rest *Ludwikowska* – Carte 105/170 PLN

◆ Business ◆ Classic ◆

Architecturally striking hotel and celebrated landmark, dating from 1913. Sympathetically remodelled throughout, with bedrooms sleek and contemporary in style. Great detail in the ornate, gilded fine dining room with a menu of Polish and Mediterranean influences.

Mercure Fryderyk Chopin

Al. Jana Pawła II 22 ✉ 00 133 – Ⓜ Świętokrzyska – ✆ (022) 528 03 00 – h1597@accor.com – Fax (022) 528 03 03 – www.mercure.com **C2**

242 rm – †473 PLN ††875 PLN, 53 PLN – 7 suites

Rest *Stanislas Brasserie* – ✆ (022) 528 03 60 – Menu 60 PLN (lunch) – Carte 78/139 PLN

◆ Business ◆ Functional ◆

Located in business district, catering for business clientele. Practically appointed rooms. Comfortable brasserie-style restaurant for international dishes. Pleasant place for coffee.

Novotel Centrum

Ul. Marszalkowska 94/98 ✉ 00 510 – Ⓜ Centrum – ✆ (022) 621 02 71 – rez.nov.warszawa@orbis.pl – Fax (022) 625 04 76 **D2**

730 rm – †306 PLN ††547 PLN – 10 suites

Rest *Essencia* – Carte 85/117 PLN

◆ Business ◆ Functional ◆

1970s-style high-rise hotel in central location on main shopping street. Contemporary style, well-serviced bedrooms, all with city views. International cuisine and vibrant bar and lounge.

Rialto

Ul. Wilcza 73 ✉ 00 670 – Ⓜ Politechnika – ✆ (022) 584 87 00 – reservation@hotelrialto.com.pl – Fax (022) 584 87 01 – www.hotelrialto.com.pl *Plan I* **A2**

33 rm – 🚹800/865 PLN 🚹🚹915 PLN, ☕ 98 PLN – 11 suites

Rest *Kurt Scheller's* – see below

♦ Business ♦ Art Deco ♦

Boutique hotel with superb Art Deco features in converted 1906 building in discreet location. Individually decorated bedrooms with the latest in comfort and facilities.

Hetman

Klopotowskiego 36 ✉ 03 717 – ✆ (022) 511 98 00 – rez@hotelhetman.pl – Fax (022) 618 51 39 – www.hotelhetman.pl **D1**

68 rm ☕ – 🚹345 PLN 🚹🚹395/410 PLN

Rest – Carte 65/76 PLN

♦ Business ♦ Functional ♦

Modern hotel in a 19C converted apartment block, a short walk over the river from the Old Town and city centre. Large, uniform and immaculate bedrooms. International cuisine in restaurant.

Ibis Stare Miasto

Ul. Muranowska 2 ✉ 00 209 – ✆ (022) 310 10 00 – h3714@accor.com – Fax (022) 310 10 10 – www.ibishotel.com *Plan I* **A2**

333 rm – 🚹289 PLN 🚹🚹289 PLN, ☕ 28 PLN

Rest *L'Estaminet* – Menu 51 PLN – Carte 65/134 PLN

♦ Chain hotel ♦ Functional ♦

Modern hotel close to the Old Town with 24-hour bar and business centre. Larger rooms on 6th floor with balconies. Bistro-style restaurant providing simple traditional European dishes. Flexible breakfast times.

Ibis Warszawa Centrum

Al. Solidarności 165 ✉ 00 876 – ✆ (022) 520 30 00 – h2894@accor.com – Fax (022) 520 30 30 – www.ibishotel.com *Plan I* **A2**

189 rm – 🚹279 PLN 🚹🚹279/329 PLN, ☕ 28 PLN

Rest *L'Estaminet* – Menu 51 PLN

♦ Chain hotel ♦ Functional ♦

Located at intersection of two main roads by Warsaw Trade Tower. Good size rooms are light and airy, well soundproofed with modern functional fittings. Bistro-style restaurant providing simple traditional European dishes.

Restauracja Polska "Tradycja"

Belwederska Ave 18A ✉ 00 762 – ✆ (022) 840 09 01 – Fax (022) 840 09 50 – www.restauracjatradycja.pl *Plan I* **B3**

Rest – *(booking essential)* Carte 65/137 PLN

♦ Traditional ♦ Family ♦

Several homely dining rooms offer traditional Polish atmosphere; live piano, candles and lace tablecloths. Professional service. Well-prepared traditional Polish cooking.

Restauracja Pod Gigantami

Al. Ujazdowskie 24 ✉ 00 478 – Ⓜ Centrum – ✆ (022) 629 23 12 – podgigantami@zapart.pl – Fax (022) 621 30 59 – www.podgigantami.pl

Rest – Menu 45 PLN (lunch) – Carte 99/171 PLN **D2**

♦ International ♦ Formal ♦

This early 20C house plays host to an elegant and charming restaurant, favoured by diplomats from nearby embassies. Attentive formal service and a carefully prepared European menu.

Restauracja Polska "Rozana"

Chocimska 7 ✉ 00 791 – Ⓜ Pole Mokotowskie – ✆ (022) 848 12 25 – Fax (022) 848 15 90 – www.restauracjapolska.com.pl *Plan I* **B3**

Rest – *(booking essential)* Carte 65/137 PLN

♦ Traditional ♦ Friendly ♦

Typical of the Restauracja Polska style: traditional homely ambience; professional service; classic Polish cuisine. Home-made dessert trolley and nightly pianist.

XXX **Ale Gloria**

Pl. Trzech Krzyzy 3 ✉ 00 535 – Ⓜ Centrum – ☎ (022) 584 70 80 – alegloria@alegloria.pl – Fax (022) 584 70 81 – www.alegloria.pl **D2**

Rest – Carte 93/200 PLN

♦ Modern ♦ Design ♦

Prepare yourself for some subterranean enchantment. This fashionable restaurant, in what was once stables, has a magical, original feel. The menu is equally bold and individual.

XXX **Dom Polski**

Ul. Francuska 11 ✉ 03 906 – ☎ (022) 616 24 32 – restauracjadompolski@wp.pl – Fax (022) 616 24 88 – www.restauracjadompolski.pl *Plan I* **B2**

Rest – Carte 70/100 PLN

♦ Traditional ♦ Friendly ♦

Elegant house in city suburb with pleasant terrace-garden. Comfortable dining rooms on two floors with welcoming ambience. Interesting well-presented traditional cuisine.

XXX **Belvedere**

Ul. Agrykoli 1 (entry from Parkowa St) ✉ 00 460 – ☎ (022) 841 22 50 – restauracja@belvedere.com.pl – Fax (022) 841 71 35 – www.belvedere.com.pl Closed 24 December-6 January *Plan I* **B2**

Rest – *(booking essential)* Carte 98/214 PLN

♦ International ♦ Formal ♦

Elegant restaurant occupying late 19C orangery in Lazienki park. Dining room filled with statuesque plants. French-influenced international and Polish cuisine.

XX **Bistro de Paris**

Pl. Piłsudskiego 9 ✉ 00 073 – Ⓜ Ratusz – ☎ (022) 826 01 07 – michelmoran@02.pl – Fax (022) 827 08 08 – www.restaurantbistrodeparis.com Closed Sunday and Bank Holidays **C1**

Rest – Menu 62 PLN (lunch) – Carte 75/140 PLN

♦ French ♦ Family ♦

Expect French cooking with some eclectic touches but underscored by a traditional base. The smart façade is matched by the comfortable interior; service is taken seriously.

XX **Kurt Scheller's** – at Rialto H.

Ul. Wilcza 73 ✉ 00 670 – Ⓜ Politechnika – ☎ (022) 584 87 00 – restaurant@hotelrialto.com.pl – Fax (022) 584 87 01 *Plan I* **A2**

Rest – Carte 112/169 PLN

♦ Modern ♦ Fashionable ♦

Superb Art Deco style with reproduction 1930s furniture and posters. Modern slant on traditional Polish cooking by Kurt Scheller, renowned chef and teacher.

XX **Rubikon**

Ul. Wróbla 3/5 ✉ 02 736 – Ⓜ Służew – ☎ (022) 847 66 55 – info@rubikon.waw.pl – www.rubikon.waw.pl Closed 24-25 December and 23 March *Plan I* **B3**

Rest – *(brunch at weekends)* Menu 100 PLN (dinner) – Carte 98/134 PLN

♦ Italian ♦ Neighbourhood ♦

In a restored villa south of the city. Divided into various rooms over two floors, the style is modern with some Art Deco. Prime sourced produce, flavoursome cooking.

XX **U Fukiera**

Rynek Starego Miasta 27 ✉ 00 272 – Ⓜ Ratusz – ☎ (022) 831 10 13 – fukier@tlen.pl – Fax (022) 831 58 08 – www.ufukiera.pl **C1**

Rest – Carte 90/325 PLN

♦ Traditional ♦ Rustic ♦

On historic central city square, well-known restaurant with character; 17C vaulted cellar and pleasant rear courtyard. Traditional Polish cuisine.

XX **Flik**

Ul. Puławska 43 ✉ 02 508 – Ⓜ Pole Mokotowskie – ✆ (022) 849 44 34 – restauracja@flik.com.pl – Fax (022) 849 44 06 – www.flik.com.pl *Plan I* **B3**

Rest – Menu 59/70 PLN – Carte 70/138 PLN

◆ Traditional ◆ Neighbourhood ◆

Welcoming neighbourhood restaurant with Polish art collection, overlooking park. Friendly service, well-prepared traditional fare. Famed for lunch buffet and business clientele.

X **Qchnia Artystyczna**

Al. Ujazdowskie 6 (Ujazdowski Castle) ✉ 00 461 – Ⓜ Politechnika – ✆ (022) 625 76 27 – qchnia@qchnia.pl – Fax (022) 625 76 27 – www.qchnia.pl

Closed Easter and Christmas *Plan I* **B2**

Rest – Carte 52/97 PLN

◆ Modern ◆ Fashionable ◆

Translates as "artistic kitchen"; expect bold flavours using seasonal ingredients, from bizarrely laid out menu. Original and fresh decor; well regarded by fashionable locals.

X **Absynt**

Ul. Wspólna 35 ✉ 00 519 – Ⓜ Centrum – ✆ (022) 621 18 81 – absynt@siesta.com.pl – Fax (022) 622 11 01 – www.kregliccy.com.pl

Closed 25 December **D2**

Rest – Carte 80/133 PLN

◆ French ◆ Bistro ◆

Informal restaurant with a strong 'French' accent; more intimate basement. Good value, seasonally changing, classic French repertoire with a hint of modernity.

at Warsaw Frederick Chopin Airport Southwest : 10 km by Zwirki i Wigury *Plan I*

Courtyard by Marriott

Ul. Zwirki i Wigury 1 ✉ 00 906 – ✆ (022) 650 01 00 – wcy@courtyard.com – Fax (022) 650 01 01 – www.courtyard.com/wawcy **A3**

219 rm – †731 PLN ††731 PLN, ☕ 56 PLN – 7 suites

Rest *Brasserie* – *(buffet lunch)* Carte 100/170 PLN

◆ Business ◆ Modern ◆

Modern hotel opposite the airport entrance. Bar and cyber café with Internet access; conference facilities. Well-equipped modern bedrooms with effective soundproofing. Mezzanine brasserie offering an eclectic range of international dishes.

Airport H. Okęcie

Ul. 17 Stycznia 24 ✉ 02 146 – ✆ (022) 456 80 00 – reservation@airporthotel.pl – Fax (022) 456 80 29 – www.airporthotel.pl **A3**

165 rm – †445/600 PLN ††562/600 PLN, ☕ 45 PLN – 7 suites

Rest *Mirage* – *(buffet lunch)* Carte 58/143 PLN

◆ Business ◆ Classic ◆

Classic corporate hotel 800 metres from the airport. Large meeting rooms and bedrooms have the international traveller and conference delegate in mind. Sky Bar for drinks. Lively and popular 'Mirage' with open-plan kitchen and buffet.

CRACOW
KRAKÓW

Population: 760 000 (conurbation 1 500000) - Altitude: 219m

R. Mauritius/PHOTONONSTOP

Cracow has often been referred to as the 'new Prague', which is both good and bad news for the locals. They don't want the stag-party brigade who've recently been latching on to Poland's third biggest city as the place to go for cheap vodka. But they do want visitors who'll appreciate the superb cultural atmosphere and artistic treasures which abound here. Not for nothing was Cracow included in the very first UNESCO World Heritage List.

Unlike much of Poland, this beautiful old city - the country's capital from the eleventh to the seventeenth centuries - was spared Second World War destruction because the German Governor had his HQ here. So Cracow is still able to boast a hugely imposing market square that was the biggest in medieval Europe, and a hill that's crowned with not just a castle, but a cathedral too. And not far away there's even a glorious chapel made of salt one hundred metres underground! It's a city famous for its links with Judaism and its visitor-friendly Royal Route, but also for its cultural inheritance. During the Renaissance, Cracow became a centre of new ideas that drew the most outstanding writers, thinkers and musicians of the day. It has literally thousands of architectural monuments and millions of artefacts collected and displayed in its museums and churches. But it's very much a modern city, too, with an eye on the twenty first century.

LIVING THE CITY

The heart and soul of Cracow is its **old quarter**, which received its charter in 1257. This area is dominated by the imposing **Market Square**, and almost completely encircled by the restful green embrace of the **Planty** gardens. A short way to the south, briefly interrupted by the curving streets of **Okol** neighbourhood, is **Wawel Hill**, the second major tourist destination of the city. Further south from here is the characterful Jewish quarter of **Kazimierz.** The smartly residential areas of **Piasek** and **Nowy Swiat** are to the west of the old quarter.

PRACTICAL INFORMATION

ARRIVAL-DEPARTURE

John Paul II International Airport-Balice is 13km west of the city centre. A taxi will cost around 65PLN and take 20min. There's a free shuttle to the train station which is located 200m from the terminal building; trains to the centre take 15min. Bus 192 goes to the central Bus station.

TRANSPORT

The historic centre of the city is a largely pedestrian precinct, so getting about on foot here is a traffic-free pleasure. The streets in the old quarter are laid out in a grid pattern, which makes orientation even easier.

The public transport system in Cracow is made up of an extensive network of buses and trams (there's no metro here). You can use your tickets on both bus or tram, and there are four different types available: timed (valid for one hour from the moment of punching), daily (from punching till midnight), weekly and family. Buy your tickets from MPK outlets or newspaper kiosks.

EXPLORING CRACOW

The sound of music has rasped out from Cracow's Market Square for centuries without a break. On the hour, every hour, for six hundred years a bugler has climbed one of the towers of **St Mary's Church**, and sounded a two-and-a-half minute bugle call across the square, day and night. It's just one of the quirks that gives this city its special appeal. The church itself, a Gothic basilica, is the proud owner of two towers, one taller than the other, making it the slightly uneven and easily distinguishable main landmark of Cracow. Inside, St Mary's is pretty impressive too, boasting Baroque and Renaissance finery (in the shape of the pulpit and the tombs), but most people who come here make for the **High Altar**, because this is the scene of daily theatre. At 11.45am, on the dot, a nun arrives and, in front of an expectant gallery, peels away the outer panels of Veit Stoss's 15C 39-ft. high, 36-ft long wood-carved polyptych. The inner cabinet is dazzling, a whole array of exquisite carvings tracing the death of Mary and her Assumption in a blaze of golden sunbeams. Catch it if you can: the whole 'show' only lasts ten minutes each day.

➜ CLOTHED IN HISTORY

Another notable – and ancient – building on the Market Square is the **Cloth Hall**, which dates back to the days of the original charter. Naturally enough, it once dealt in the trade of cloth, but now plays host to a colourful parade of souvenir stalls. More interestingly, inside its much remodelled walls is the impressive **Gallery of 19th Century Polish Painting.** Outside, in the huge arena of the square, there are churches, palaces, town houses, eye-catching modern sculptures, a sprinkling of designer clothes stores, and a whole al fresco jumble (at least in summer) of café tables and chairs. Near the Cloth Hall is one of the city's most beautiful palaces, **Christopher Palace**, which boasts a spectacular arcaded courtyard to dazzle the eye. You actually get double the value here, because it's also home to the **Museum of Cracow**, a fascinating treasure trove of goodies dug up from the city's rich history.

➜ WAWEL

Jostling Market Square in the fame stakes is Wawel Hill. It's attached to the old quarter by the umbilical cord that is **Gródzska Street**, a lovely old cobbled thoroughfare with varying styles of architecture that are a delight to stroll past. Medieval kings made Wawel the seat of their political power, and a royal residence was built here, overlooking the city below. It went through much chopping and changing before evolving into the castle you see today, sprawling nonchalantly across the hill, its mishmash of styles representing Poland's turbulent history. Various captors have given it a style makeover down the centuries: in Renaissance times it was one of the most thrilling royal residences in Central Europe. Just to add more lustre, the 14C kings added a cathedral to the castle complex, and this is the final resting place of Poland's national heroes and royalty, making it the number one symbol of the country's statehood. There are beautifully carved tombs here, as well as important works of art, and the largest bell in Poland, weighing in at a mighty eleven tons.

➜ KAZIMIERZ

The neighbourhood of Kazimierz is the most southerly quarter of Cracow. It feels like a different place, which isn't surprising because, until 1791, it was an independent town in its own right. It's a characterful area of narrow streets lined with low buildings, and has been a major centre of Jewish culture for over five hundred years. It's the ideal place to discover more about the story of the Jews in Poland and contains seven synagogues and a number of Jewish cemeteries. But it's also a magnet for Cracow's young, as many of the old buildings here have been reborn as cafés and bars. Steven Spielberg's epic drama *Schindler's List* was filmed around Kazimierz and the actors were regulars in the eating establishments around here, appreciating the blasts of live klezmer that periodically ring out from many of the neighbourhood's restaurants. Klezmer is Jewish folk music, and you'd have to have feet of clay for its infectious rhythms not to get you up and dancing.

➜ SALT OF THE EARTH

The winters can get mighty cold in Cracow, and if you want to dive into a museum for cover, you'll find there are dozens hiding in all sorts of alleyways and corners. The main building of the **National Museum** takes some beating. A modern construction finished less than twenty years ago, it's west in Nowy Swiat. Suitably enough, it's full of 20C and contemporary Polish art; the Modernist section is a real stand out.

Meanwhile, back in the old quarter, the **Czartoryski Museum** is for lovers of Western art. There are works by the likes of Leonardo Da Vinci and Rembrandt on display in three houses which exude a warm and homely feel. As a complete contrast, head out on a bus to the **Wieliczka salt mine** for a truly one-off experience. The mine has been operating for over nine hundred years, and has two hundred miles of underground corridors. Down the years miners have carved out hundreds of statues, and the most awe-inspiring is the **Chapel of St Kinga**. It took three miners sixty seven years to eke out this masterpiece, which lies over a hundred metres underground, and is fifty four metres long and twelve metres high. Everything in the chapel is made from rock salt, from the statue of Christ on the cross to the chandeliers, and it all makes for a spectacular experience. Should you get hungry down there, you can go for a meal at the deepest underground restaurant in the world.

→ DIG THE PLANTY

Very much back on terra firma, don't forget a stroll around the Planty, the 'green belt' that embraces the old quarter. It replaced the medieval walls of the city early in the nineteenth century, and its gardens were landscaped to make the most of the superb vistas on offer. The Planty has always been a popular venue for strolling and socialising, and for the last twenty years it's been getting lots of tender loving care, courtesy of period fencing and street lamps that give it the look it once knew two hundred years ago.

→ OVERWHELMING VISIT

An hour's journey from Cracow is Auschwitz, now a UNESCO World Heritage site. The grounds and buildings are open to visitors as a museum and poignant memorial; many of the inhabitants of Kazimierz were sent here by the Nazis. Remember that Auschwitz can be an emotionally draining experience.

CALENDAR HIGHLIGHTS

Cracow can get so cold in the winter that it pretty much shuts down on the festival front (though it looks beautiful under a blanket of snow). Things pick up in the spring with the arrival of the first crocuses and the first visitors drawing up chairs at al fresco tables in the old quarter. Two events in June highlight the city's love of myths: The Lajkonik Festival recalls an age-old victory for the citizens of Cracow over Tartar invaders. A procession of musicians and merrymakers takes three hours to pass from the 12C Convent of St.Norbet to Market Square. Meanwhile, Wianki is based on a pagan festival, as wreaths of flowers are floated down

CRACOW IN...

→ ONE DAY

St Mary's Church, Cloth Hall, Wawel, main building of National Museum

→ TWO DAYS

Kazimierz, Czartoryski Museum, stroll round Planty

→ THREE DAYS

Trip either to Auschwitz or Wieliczka salt mine

the Vistula river, lit by huge bonfires as midsummer is celebrated to the sound of music and fireworks. The Kazimierz neighbourhood comes under the spotlight for the Cracow Jewish Culture Festival (June/July) when the quarter's lively streets, with their synagogues, cafés and pubs, celebrate Yiddish traditions with a whole range of concerts and recitals. The infectious sound of klezmer is a highlight. A month later, many of the beautiful buildings of the old quarter double as venues for Music in Old Cracow, a seventeen-day event featuring classical music from Baroque to Romantic to Modern. The sounds here will be familiar to most ears, but for those looking for something a bit different, October's intriguingly named International Festival of Forgotten Music is a treat. It features archaic songs from the Baltic region performed by country folk groups, and a good time is a cast-iron guarantee.

EATING OUT

Cracow has long had a reputation as a good place to go and eat. Even during the Communist era it kept its end up, with busy cafés serving good food unknown at the time in the rest of Poland. In the 1990s, hundreds of new restaurants opened their doors, often in pretty locations with medieval or Renaissance interiors. Other restaurateurs chose to go into ancient cellars, restored and furnished to give just the right intimate feel. As for the food itself, many Poles go misty-eyed at the thought of Bigos (Hunter's stew) on a cold winter's day. It's a game, sausage and cabbage stew that comes with sauerkraut, onion, potatoes, herbs and spices. It's reputed to get better with reheating on successive days, and lots of Cracow restaurants claim to serve the tastiest version. Pierogi is another local favourite: crescent-shaped dumplings which you can eat either in savoury or sweet style. Barszcz is a lemon and garlic flavoured beetroot soup that's invariably good value, while in Kazimierz, specialities include Jewish dumpling, filled with onion, cheese and potatoes, and Berdytchov soup, which imaginatively mixes honey and cinnamon with beef. Global grub is also on the menu here. Look around and you won't be short-changed on restaurants specialising in French, Greek, Vietnamese, Middle Eastern, Indian, Italian and Mexican food. You can eat quite late in Cracow: most restaurants don't close until around midnight, and there's no pressure on customers to rush their final drinks and leave. A tip of about ten per cent is the norm.

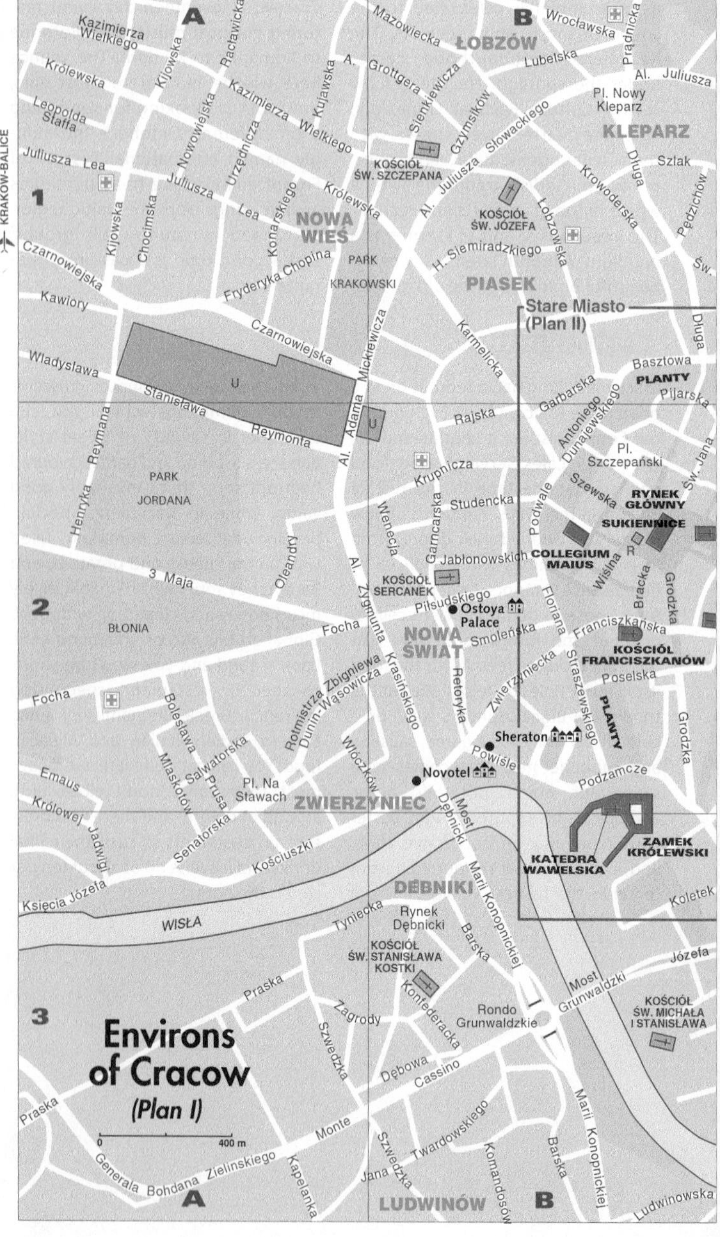

Environs of Cracow
(Plan I)

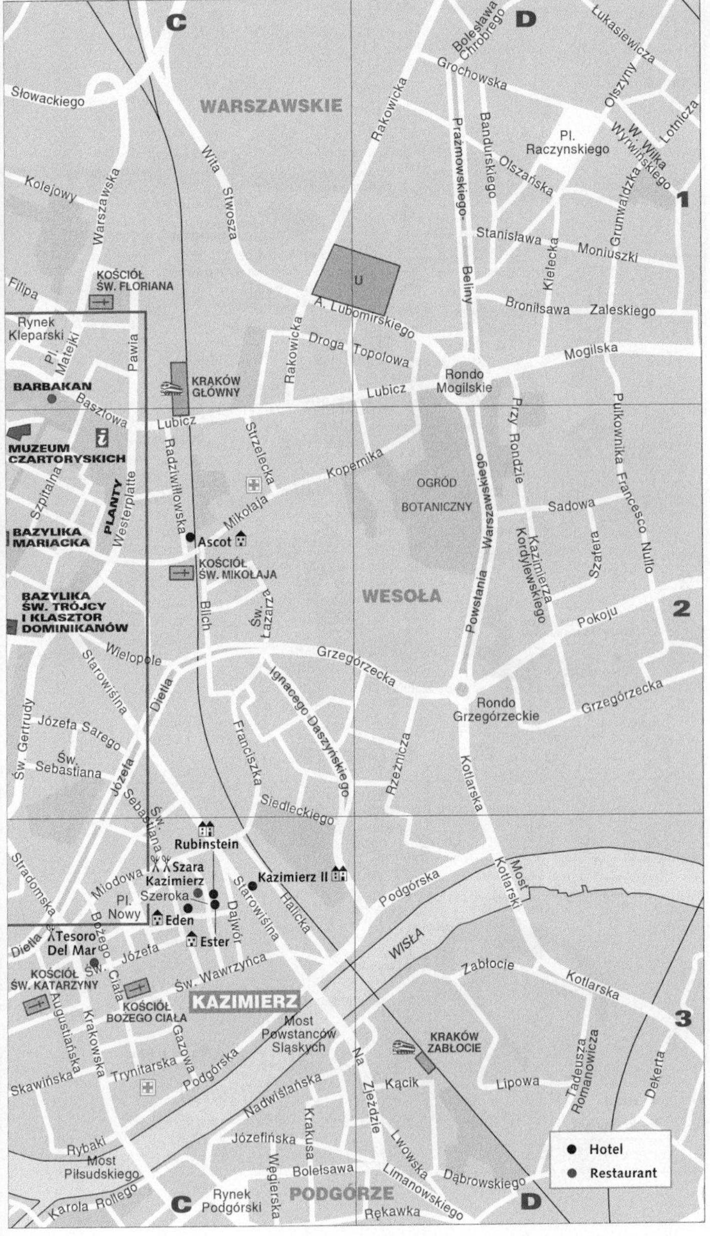
C
D
1
2
3
WARSZAWSKIE
WESOŁA
KAZIMIERZ
PODGÓRZE
OGRÓD
BOTANICZNY
WISŁA
KOŚCIÓŁ
ŚW. FLORIANA
KRAKÓW
GŁÓWNY
BARBAKAN
MUZEUM
CZARTORYSKICH
PLANTY
BAZYLIKA
MARIACKA
BAZYLIKA
ŚW. TRÓJCY
I KLASZTOR
DOMINIKANÓW
KOŚCIÓŁ
ŚW. MIKOŁAJA
Ascot
Rubinstein
Szara
Kazimierz
Kazimierz II
Eden
Ester
Tesoro
Del Mar
KOŚCIÓŁ
ŚW. KATARZYNY
KOŚCIÓŁ
BOŻEGO CIAŁA
KRAKÓW
ZABŁOCIE
Rynek
Kleparski
Pl.
Raczynskiego
Rondo
Mogilskie
Rondo
Grzegórzeckie
Pl.
Nowy
Most
Powstanców
Sląskych
Most
Piłsudskiego
Rynek
Podgórski
Most
Kotlarski
Hotel
Restaurant
Słowackiego
Kolejowy
Filipa
Warszawska
Wita
Stwosza
Rakowicka
A. Lubomirskiego
Droga
Topolowa
Lubicz
Basztowa
Pawia
Pl.
Matejki
Radziwiłłowska
Strzelecka
Kopernika
Mikołaja
Westerplatte
Szpitalna
Blich
Św.
Łazarza
Wielopole
Starowiślna
Dietla
Grzegórzecka
Ignacego Daszyńskiego
Franciszka
Siedleckiego
Rzeźnicza
Kotlarska
Józefa Sarego
Św. Gertrudy
Św.
Sebastiana
Józefa
Sebastiana
Św.
Stradomska
Miodowa
Szeroka
Dajwór
Halicka
Podgórska
Bożego
Ciała
Św. Wawrzyńca
Augustiańska
Krakowska
Gazowa
Trynitarska
Skawińska
Rybaki
Karola Rollego
Nadwiślańska
Józefińska
Krakusa
Węgierska
Bolesława
Na Zjeździe
Kącik
Lwowska
Limanowskiego
Dąbrowskiego
Rękawka
Zabłocie
Lipowa
Tadeusza
Romanowicza
Dekerta
Bolesława
Chrobrego
Grochowska
Łukasiewicza
Olszyny
W. Wilka
Wyrwińskiego
Lotnicza
Prażmowskiego-
Beliny
Bandurskiego
Olszańska
Stanisława
Moniuszki
Kielecka
Grunwaldzka
Bronisława
Zaleskiego
Mogilska
Przy Rondzie
Pułkownika Francesco Nullo
Warszawskiego
Powstania
Sadowa
Szafera
Kazimierza
Kordylewskiego
Pokoju
U

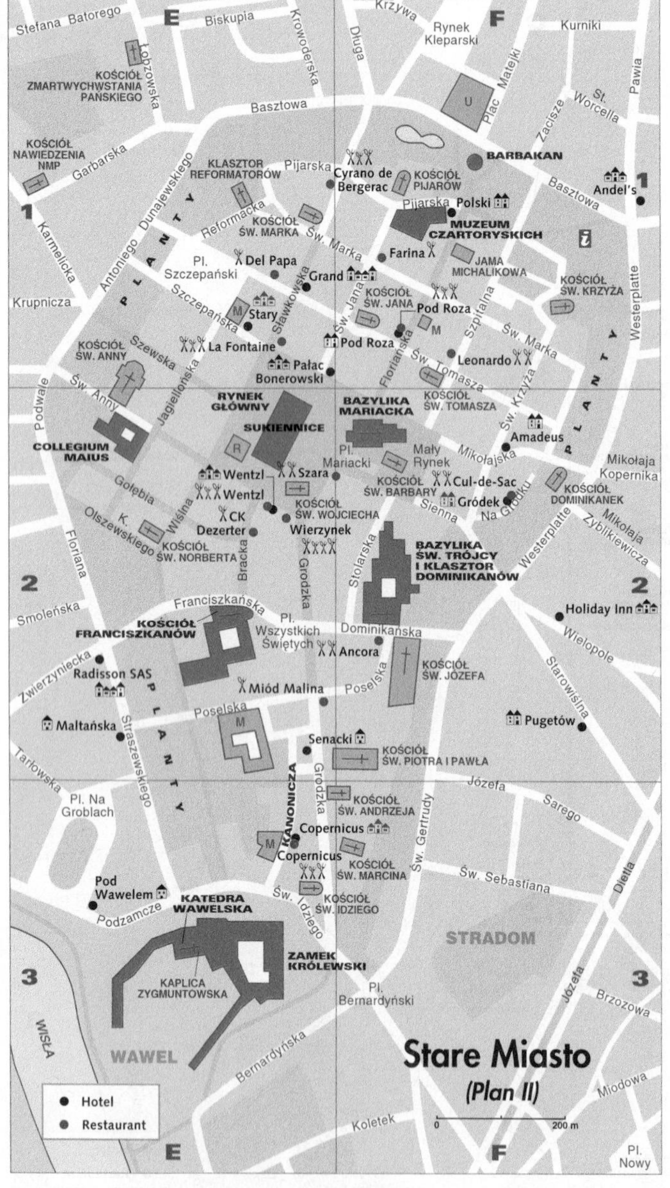
Stare Miasto
(Plan II)
Hotel
Restaurant
RYNEK GŁÓWNY
SUKIENNICE
BAZYLIKA MARIACKA
BARBAKAN
MUZEUM CZARTORYSKICH
COLLEGIUM MAIUS
KOŚCIÓŁ FRANCISZKANÓW
BAZYLIKA ŚW. TRÓJCY I KLASZTOR DOMINIKANÓW
KATEDRA WAWELSKA
ZAMEK KRÓLEWSKI
KAPLICA ZYGMUNTOWSKA
WAWEL
STRADOM
PLANTY
Wisła
Basztowa
Floriańska
Grodzka
Kanonicza
Cyrano de Bergerac
Polski
Andel's
Farina
Del Papa
Grand
Stary
Pod Roza
La Fontaine
Pałac Bonerowski
Leonardo
Amadeus
Wentzl
Szara
Cul-de-Sac
Gródek
CK Dezerter
Wierzynek
Holiday Inn
Ancora
Radisson SAS
Miód Malina
Maltańska
Pugetów
Senacki
Copernicus
Pod Wawelem
0
200 m

Sheraton

Ul. Powiśle 7 ✉ 31 101 – ✆ (12) 6621000 – krakow@sheraton.com – Fax (12) 6 62 11 00 – www.sheraton.com/krakow *Plan I* **B2**

229 rm – 828/864 PLN 886/954 PLN – 3 suites

Rest *The Olive* – Carte 77/109 PLN

♦ Business ♦ Modern ♦

Purpose-built hotel near the castle, with views of the Wisla river. Well-equipped bedrooms come with all mod cons. Qube bar serves over 200 different vodkas. Mediterranean/international menu served at The Olive; relaxed open plan restaurant situated in huge glass-roofed atrium.

Radisson SAS

Ul. Straszewskiego 17 ✉ 31 101 – ✆ (12) 618 88 88 – reservations.krakow@radissonsas.com – Fax (12) 6 18 88 89 – www.radissonsas.com **E2**

189 rm – 458/710 PLN 556/710 PLN, 65 PLN – 7 suites

Rest – Carte 103/130 PLN

♦ Business ♦ Modern ♦

Well run chain hotel, five minutes from the main square. Large open plan lobby and stylish bar. Generously proportioned, comfortable and warmly decorated bedrooms with a high level of facilities. International and Polish cuisine served in bright restaurant; regular buffets and themed evenings.

Grand

Ul. Slawkowska 5/7 ✉ 31 014 – ✆ (12) 4240800 – hotel@grand.pl – Fax (12) 4 21 72 55 – www.grand.pl **E1**

53 rm – 792/864 PLN 886/1044 PLN – 9 suites

Rest *Mirror Hall* – *(dinner only)* Carte 69/106 PLN

♦ Traditional ♦ Historic ♦

Historic hotel, formerly the palace of the Duke Czartoryski, now restored to its former glory, with gold leaf, high ceilings and stained glass windows. Sumptuous, spacious suites. Formal dining under chandeliers in the Mirror Hall.

Copernicus

Ul. Kanonicza 16 ✉ 31 002 – ✆ (12) 4243400 – copernicus@hotel.com.pl – Fax (12) 4 24 34 05 – www.hotel.com.pl **E3**

29 rm – 750/800 PLN 850/980 PLN – 4 suites

Rest *Copernicus* – see below

♦ Historic ♦ Stylish ♦

Set on one of the oldest streets in the city, restoration of this intimate, atmospheric hotel revealed 15C ceiling inscriptions and ornaments. Handmade furniture, velvet bedspreads, silk drapes. Attentive service.

Wentzl

Rynek Glówny,

Rynek Glówny 19 ✉ 31 008 – ✆ (12) 4302664 – hotel@wentzl.pl – Fax (12) 4 30 26 65 – www.wentzl.pl

Closed 25 December **E2**

18 rm – 155/169 PLN 165/189 PLN

Rest *Wentzl* – see below

♦ Townhouse ♦ Historic ♦

15C house overlooking splendour of main square. Charming, antique-furnished bedrooms bedecked with art offer high level of facilities; those on top floor are contemporary in the style, others more traditional.

Stary

Ul. Szczepańska 5 ✉ 31 011 – ✆ (12) 3840808 – stary@hotel.co.pl – Fax (12) 3 84 08 09 – www.hotel.com.pl **E1**

50 rm – 680/800 PLN 765/900 PLN – 3 suites

Rest *Trzy Rybki* – Carte 123/159 PLN

♦ Townhouse ♦ Stylish ♦

Stylish hotel, its oldest part dating from 15C, with original frescos on the walls. Atmospheric, antique-furnished rooms with marble bathrooms. Good levels of service. European menu with strong Italian influences served in Trzy Rybki.

Pałac Bonerowski

Ul. Św. Jana 1 ✉ 31 013 – ✆ (12) 374 13 00 – rezerwacja@palacbonerowski.pl – Fax (12) 3 74 13 05 – www.palacbonerowski.pl **E1**

9 rm – 860 PLN 1000/2150 PLN – 6 suites

Rest *Pod Winogronomi* – Carte 69/119 PLN

♦ Palace ♦ Personalised ♦

Characterful hotel overlooking the main square, whose historic features include medieval portals and restored 17C polychrome and ceilings. Suite 201 is probably the biggest in the city. Italian cuisine served in restaurant, with fresh fish a feature.

Andel's

Ul. Pawia 3 ✉ 31 154 – ✆ (12) 6600100 – info@andelscracow.com – Fax (12) 6 60 00 01 – www.andelscracow.com **F1**

157 rm – 612/778 PLN 705/828 PLN – 2 suites

Rest – Carte 62/97 PLN

♦ Business ♦ Modern ♦

Opened in 2007, this hotel opposite main station boasts bright, open plan public areas with original design features. Stylishly lit rooms feature flat screen TVs and DVD players. Cool lobby bar. Light, spacious restaurant opens out onto terrace and plaza and serves international and Polish cuisine.

Novotel

Ul. Tadeusza Kościuszki 5 ✉ 30 105 – ✆ (12) 2992900 – H3372@accor.com – Fax (12) 2 99 29 99 – www.novotel.com *Plan I* **B2**

192 rm – 570/630 PLN 570/630 PLN – 6 suites

Rest – Carte 96/133 PLN

♦ Chain hotel ♦ Functional ♦

Geared towards corporate customers, with simple, bright rooms over six floors, some with terrific views of Wawel castle. Large gym and pool. Children under 16 are free. Light and airy restaurant serving an international menu.

Holiday Inn

Ul.Wielopole 4 ✉ 31 072 – ✆ (12) 6190000 – smm@hik.krakow.pl – Fax (12) 6 19 00 05 – www.holidayinn.com **F2**

152 rm – 493/752 PLN 658/842 PLN – 2 suites

Rest – Carte 85/146 PLN

♦ Chain hotel ♦ Functional ♦

The converted Parenskich Palace, a short walk from the city centre, now flanked with modern extensions. Well-sized bedrooms offer modern comforts. Lobby bar and café. Basement restaurant offers Mediterranean cuisine and buffet breakfast.

Gródek

Ul. Na Gródku 4 ✉ 31 028 – ✆ (12) 4319030 – grodek@donimirski.com – Fax (12) 4 31 90 40 – www.donimirski.com **F2**

21 rm – 590/740 PLN 630/780 PLN – 2 suites

Rest *Cul-de-Sac* – see below

♦ Townhouse ♦ Personalised ♦

Charming boutique hotel with bright, comfortable feel, cosy wood-panelled bar and pleasant roof terrace. Individually decorated, immaculately kept bedrooms. Pleasing service.

Pod Róża

Ul. Floriańska 14 ✉ 31 021 – ✆ (12) 4243300 – pod-roza@hotel.com.pl – Fax (12) 4 24 33 51 – www.hotel.com.pl **F1**

53 rm – 550 PLN 650 PLN – 4 suites

Rest *Pod Różą* – see below

♦ Traditional ♦ Classic ♦

16C building - reputedly the oldest hotel in the city - whose past guests include such luminaries as Balzac and Liszt. Traditional rooms with antique furnishings. Atmospheric conference facilities in cellars.

Amadeus

Ul. Mikolajska 20 ✉ 31 027 – ✆ (12) 4296070 – amadeus@janpol.com.pl – Fax (12) 2 49 60 62 – www.hotel-amadeus.pl **F2**

20 rm – 486/522 PLN 522/612 PLN – 2 suites

Rest – Carte 93/136 PLN

♦ Traditional ♦ Classic ♦

Charming 16C house with subtle baroque character, a short stroll from main square. Characterful bedrooms boast cosy, warm feel. Intimate dining in former cellars; the vaulted ceilings brightened with paintings and frescoes. Mostly European menu; many Polish dishes.

Ostoya Palace

Ul. Pilsudskiego 24 ✉ 31 109 – ✆ (12) 4309000 – reservation@ostoyapalace.pl – Fax (12) 4 30 90 01 – www.ostoyapalace.pl *Plan I* **B2**

24 rm – 540/648 PLN 608/691 PLN

Rest – Carte 52/105 PLN

♦ Historic ♦ Stylish ♦

Discreet, comfortable and characterful hotel whose bedrooms reflect its 19C origins, with high ceilings and original stove heaters. Popular pub in basement. Restaurant features original 15C ceiling and serves international menu.

Polski without rest

Ul.Pijarska 17 ✉ 31 015 – ✆ (12) 422 11 44 – hotel.polski@podorlem.com.pl – Fax (12) 4 29 18 10 – www.podorlem.com.pl **F1**

54 rm – 295/370 PLN 355/525 PLN – 3 suites

♦ Family ♦ Classic ♦

Friendly hotel located next door to the Czartoryski Museum, which houses da Vinci's 'Lady with an Ermine.' Comfy rooms range from singles to triples. Friendly service; pleasant atmosphere.

Pugetów without rest

Ul. Starowiślna 15a ✉ 31 038 – ✆ (12) 4324950 – pugetow@donimirski.com – Fax (12) 3 78 93 25 – www.donimirski.com **F2**

5 rm – 350/480 PLN 480/520 PLN – 2 suites

♦ Traditional ♦ Historic ♦

Cosy 19C house set alongside the Pugetów Palace, away from main street, with the intimate feel of a private residence. Spacious rooms include 2 huge antique-furnished suites.

Maltański without rest

Ul. Straszewskiego 14 ✉ 31 101 – ✆ (12) 4310010 – maltanski@donimirski.com – Fax (12) 3 78 93 12 – www.donimirski.com **E2**

16 rm – 510/540 PLN 540/590 PLN

♦ Traditional ♦ Personalised ♦

Charming little hotel - a former stable block - set back from the road. Ground floor rooms are best, with doors onto small terraces, but all rooms are equally comfortable.

Senacki

Ul. Grodzska 51 ✉ 31 001 – ✆ (12) 4211161 – recepcja@senacki.krakow.pl – Fax (12) 4 22 79 34 – www.senacki.krakow.pl **E2**

20 rm – 288/432 PLN 398/504 PLN

Rest – Carte 73/91 PLN

♦ Townhouse ♦ Functional ♦

Well located, simple hotel close to the castle and opposite the 17C Church of Saint Peter and Paul. Atmospheric bar and café in converted cellars. Neat bedrooms over 3 floors. Concise menu of Polish and Italian dishes served in restaurant.

Pod Wawelem

PL. Na Groblach 22 ✉ 31 101 – ✆ (12) 4262626
– rezerwacja@hotelpodwawelem.pl – Fax (12) 4 22 33 99
– www.hotelpodwawelem.pl **E3**
47 rm – 300/500 PLN 380/600 PLN – 1 suite
Rest – Carte 48/69 PLN
◆ Family ◆ Functional ◆
Small, sensibly-priced hotel in the shadow of the Royal Castle and close to the river; purpose built, but sympathetically so. Terrific rooftop café in summer. Functional bedrooms. Bright and airy café-style restaurant serving international and Polish dishes.

Ascot without rest

Ul. Radziwillowska 3 ✉ 31 026 – ✆ (12) 384 06 06 – recepcja@hotelascot.pl
– Fax (12) 3 84 06 07 – www.hotelascot.pl *Plan I* **C2**
49 rm – 265/320 PLN 304 PLN
◆ Family ◆ Functional ◆
Purpose-built hotel, a 5 minute walk from the centre, opened in 2007. Small lobby with corner bar. Functional downstairs breakfast room. Clean, compact, fairly priced bedrooms.

Wierzynek

Rynek Glówny 15 ✉ 31 008 – ✆ (12) 4249600
– rezerwacja@wierzynek.pl – Fax (12) 4 24 96 01
– www.wierzynek.pl **E2**
Rest – Menu 165 PLN – Carte 131/195 PLN
◆ Polish ◆ Elegant ◆
Ornately decorated restaurant occupying commanding position in main square; past guests include George Bush and Steven Spielberg. Polish specialities carefully prepared using top quality ingredients. Well-organised, formal service.

Wentzl – at Wentzl H.

Rynek Glówny 19 ✉ 31 008 – ✆ (12) 4295712
– restauracja@wentzl.pl@wentzl.pl – Fax (12) 4 31 57 70
– www.wentzl.pl
Closed 25 December **E2**
Rest – Carte 87/129 PLN
◆ International ◆ Formal ◆
Hotel restaurant exuding palpable sense of history; impressive Renaissance interiors include original wood ceilings and 15C triptych. Menu adds an international note to Polish dishes.

Cyrano de Bergerac

Ul. Slawekowska 26 ✉ 31 014 – ✆ (12) 4117288
– rest@cyranodebergerac.pl – Fax (12) 4 12 15 72
– www.cyranodebergerac.pl
Closed Sunday and Bank Holidays **E1**
Rest – *(booking essential)* Carte 92/153 PLN
◆ French ◆ Romantic ◆
Characterful French cellar restaurant; antique furniture, tapestries and candlelit tables create wonderfully romantic atmosphere. Ground floor art deco piano bar. Robust classical French cooking.

Copernicus – at Copernicus H.

Ul. Kanonicza 16 ✉ 31 002 – ✆ (12) 4243421 – copernicus@hotel.com.pl
– Fax (12) 4 24 34 05 – www.hotel.com.pl **E3**
Rest – *(booking essential)* Carte 83/167 PLN
◆ Polish ◆ Formal ◆
Charming restaurant specialising in seasonal Polish cooking, artfully presented and full of flavour. A table on the gallery allows one to fully appreciate the ornate Renaissance ceiling.

XXX **La Fontaine** AC VISA MC

Ul. Slawkowska 1 ✉ 31 014 – ✆ (12) 4318930 – lafontaine@lafontaine.com.pl – Fax (12) 4 31 09 55 – www.lafontaine.com.pl
Closed 24-25 December **E1**
Rest – Carte 91/140 PLN
◆ French ◆ Formal ◆
Cellar restaurant - purportedly dating from 13C - set in 4 rooms, with well-spaced tables and a romantic feel. Classic, rich French cooking is served in very generous portions.

XXX **Pod Róża** – at Pod Róża H. AC VISA MC AE

Ul. Floriańska 14 ✉ 31 021 – ✆ (12) 4243300 – pod-roza@hotel.com.pl – Fax (12) 4 24 33 51 – www.hotel.com.pl **F1**
Rest – Carte 103/129 PLN
◆ International ◆ Friendly ◆
Capacious restaurant; its large glass roof supported by a row of columns, giving the room a proud feel. Appealing European cooking with a heavy Italian accent. Formal service.

XX **Cul-de-Sac** – at Gródek H. VISA MC AE

Ul. Na Gródku 4 ✉ 31 028 – ✆ (12) 4319030 – Fax (12) 4 31 90 40 – www.donimirski.com **F2**
Rest – Carte 59/115 PLN
◆ International ◆ Design ◆
Bright restaurant in basement of Gródek hotel, decorated with objects found during the building's renovation. International menu; its base rooted in Italy. Imaginative, ambitious cooking.

XX **Ancora** AC VISA MC AE

Ul. Dominikánska 3 ✉ 31 043 – ✆ (12) 3573355 – restauracja@ancora-restaurant.com – www.ancora-restaurant.com
Closed 24-25 December **F2**
Rest – Carte 42/85 PLN
◆ International ◆ Fashionable ◆
Large, contemporary corner restaurant with open kitchen and photos of the chef in action; equally cavernous converted cellars downstairs. Cooking is rooted in Poland with modern, international sensibilities.

XX **Leonardo** AC VISA MC AE

Ul. Szpitalna 20-22 ✉ 31 024 – ✆ (12) 4296850 – rezerwacja@leonardo.com.pl – Fax (12) 4 32 22 56 – www.leonardo.com.pl
Closed 24-25 December **F1**
Rest – Carte 72/149 PLN
◆ Italian ◆ Neighbourhood ◆
Leonardo room decorated with da Vinci's etchings and musings; cosy Wine room takes the grapevine as its motif; produce hangs from ceiling in Spice room. Italian menu features plenty of fresh fish. Friendly service.

XX **Szara** AC VISA MC AE

Rynek Glówny 6 ✉ 31 042 – ✆ (12) 4216669 – restauracja@szara.pl – www.szara.pl **E/F2**
Rest – Carte 97/117 PLN
◆ Polish ◆ Friendly ◆
Two rooms with original Gothic vaulted ceilings, situated on main square. Elaborately presented, flavourful European cuisine, with Polish and Swedish dishes to the fore. Friendly service.

X **Farina** AC VISA MC AE

Ul. Św. Marka 16 ✉ 31 017 – ✆ (12) 4221680 – Fax (12) 4 21 37 30 – www.farina.krakow.pl
Closed 24-25 December **F1**
Rest – Carte 64/117 PLN
◆ Seafood ◆ Rustic ◆
Attractive candlelit corner restaurant divided into 2 rooms with wood floors and a bright rustic style. Menu specialises in seafood with a hint of Italy. Warm, friendly service.

Miód Malina
Ul. Grodzka 40 ✉ 31 044 – ✆ (12) 4300411 – restauracja@miodmalina.pl – www.miodmalina.pl
Closed 25 December **E2**
Rest – *(booking essential)* Carte 52/94 PLN
♦ Italian ♦ Neighbourhood ♦
Busy restaurant with pleasant atmosphere serving a mix of Polish and Italian dishes, some cooked in wood fired oven. Larger, no-smoking room with vaulted ceiling is best place to sit.

Del Papa
Ul. Św. Tomasza 6 ✉ 31 014 – ✆ (12) 4218343 – delpapa@vp.pl – www.delpapa.pl **E1**
Rest – Carte 58/109 PLN
♦ Italian ♦ Rustic ♦
Characterful and popular with locals. Café style front room; distressed brick walls in middle; bright room with glass roof at back. Friendly staff. Simple Italian food with homemade pasta a speciality.

C. K. Dezerter
Ul. Bracka 6 ✉ 31 005 – ✆ (12) 4227931 – ckdezerter.bracka6@wp.pl – Fax (12) 4 22 42 51 – www.ck-dezerter.pl
Closed 25 December **E2**
Rest – Carte 40/60 PLN
♦ Polish ♦ Neighbourhood ♦
Decorated in a homely farmhouse style, with a warm, friendly atmopshere. Menu offers specialities from Austria-Hungary and the Galicia region of Poland, and includes a full page of pork dishes.

at KAZIMIERZ *Plan I*

Rubinstein
Ul. Szeroka 12 ✉ 31 053 – ✆ (12) 3840000 – recepcja@hotelrubinstein.com – Fax (12) 3 84 00 01 – www.hotelrubinstein.com **C3**
26 rm – †560/645 PLN ††645/730 PLN – 1 suite
Rest – Carte 77/107 PLN
♦ Historic ♦ Modern ♦
Well run, characterful hotel in in the Jewish quarter, converted from 15C tenement buildings and named after Helena, of cosmetics fame, who grew up in this street. Comfortable rooms reflect the age of the house. Glass-roofed restaurant, serving Jewish and Polish specialities.

Kazimierz II without rest
Ul. Starowiślna 60 ✉ 31 035 – ✆ (12) 426 80 70 – rezerwacja@hk.com.pl – Fax (12) 4 26 80 71 – www.hk.com.pl **C3**
23 rm – †180/230 PLN ††230/286 PLN
♦ Family ♦ Functional ♦
Purpose-built hotel on busy street, opened in 2006. Decently-sized blue and yellow bedrooms boast a fresh feel; those at the front are the largest. Bright breakfast room.

Ester
Ul. Szeroka 20 ✉ 31 053 – ✆ (12) 4291188 – biuro@hotel.ester.krakow.pl – Fax (12) 4 29 12 33 – www.hotel-ester.krakow.pl **C3**
32 rm – †396/536 PLN ††452/630 PLN
Rest – Carte 60/96 PLN
♦ Townhouse ♦ Personalised ♦
Friendly hotel in the heart of the Jewish quarter. Clean, functional, decently-sized bedrooms include five triple rooms. Café-style restaurant with outside summer terrace. Menu focuses on Jewish and Polish cuisine, with a few international dishes. Live music at weekends.

Eden without rest

Ul. Ciemna 15 ✉ 31 053 – ✆ (12) 430 65 65 – eden@hoteleden.pl – Fax (12) 4 30 67 67 – www.hoteleden.pl **C3**

27 rm ☕ – 🚹190/260 PLN 🚹🚹280/350 PLN

♦ Traditional ♦ Personalised ♦

Friendly hotel whose idiosyncratic bedrooms reflect its 15 and 16C history. Characterful cellar pub and pleasant breakfast room with hot and cold buffet. Hotel has own Mikveh.

Szara Kazimierz

Ul. Szeroka 39 ✉ 31 053 – ✆ (12) 429 12 19 – kazimierz@szara.pl **C3**

Rest – Carte 63/91 PLN

♦ Polish ♦ Brasserie ♦

Relaxed, brasserie style restaurant; sister to Szara in the old town, with wood burning stoves, pillars and a secluded back terrace. European cooking with a nod towards Italy. Courteous service.

Tesoro del Mar

Ul. Józefa 6 ✉ 31 056 – ✆ (12) 430 60 13 – info@tesorodelmar.pl – www.tesorodelmar.pl **C3**

Rest – Carte 72/124 PLN

♦ Seafood ♦ Neighbourhood ♦

Trendy new restaurant opened in late 2007, with cellar-like appearance; sit in the warmer, more inviting back room. Artful seafood menu with Mediterranean influences.

PORTUGAL
PORTUGAL

PROFILE

→ **Area:**
88 944 km^2
(34 341 sq mi).

→ **Population:**
10 642 836
(est. 2007), density
= 116 per km^2.

→ **Capital:**
Lisbon (conurbation
2 900 000
inhabitants).

→ **Currency:**
Euro (€); rate
of exchange: € 1
= US$1.46 (Dec 2007).

→ **Government:**
Parliamentary
republic (since 1976).
Member of European
Union since 1986.

→ **Language:**
Portuguese.

→ **Specific public holidays:**
Shrove Tuesday
(February);
Good Friday (Friday
before Easter);
Freedom Day
(25 April), Corpus
Christi (May or
June); Portugal Day
(10 June); Republic
Day (5 October);
Restoration of
Independence
Day (1 December);
Immaculate
Conception
(8 December).

→ **Local Time:**
GMT in winter and
GMT + 1 hour in
summer.

→ **Climate:**
Temperate
Mediterranean with
warm winters and
hot summers (Lisbon:
January 15°C, July
26°C).

→ **International dialling code:**
00 351 followed by
a nine-digit number.
International
directory enquiries :
✆ **098**.

→ **Emergency:**
Dial ✆ **112**.

→ **Electricity:**
230-240 volts AC,
50 Hz; 2-pin round-
shaped continental
plugs.

→ **Formalities**
Travellers from the

European Union
(EU), Switzerland,
Iceland and the main
countries of North
and South America
need a national
identity card or
passport (America:
passport required)
to visit Portugal
for less than three
months (tourism or
business purpose).
For visitors from
other countries
a visa may be
required, in addition
to a passport,
especially for those
wishing to stay for
longer than three
months. We advise
you to check with
your embassy before
travelling.

IASA

LISBON

LISBOA

Population (est. 2007): 662782 (conurbation 2 900 000) – Altitude: at sea level

Simeone/PHOTONONSTOP

Lisbon wears a time-worn look of fading grandeur sitting as it does beneath huge open skies and within an amphitheatre of seven hills. Sited on the north bank of the River Tagus as it feeds into the Atlantic, it boasts an atmosphere that few cities can match; an enchanting walk around the streets of the Bairro Alto, Alfama, the Baixa or Graça has an old-time ambience all its own, matched only by a jaunt on the trams and funiculars that run up and down the steep hills.

At first sight Lisbon is all flaky palaces, meandering alleyways and castellated horizon quarried from medieval stone. But there's a 21C element to the city, kick-started with Expo 98 and carried on with the Euro 2004 football tournament. Slinky new developments line the riverside to east and west, linking the old and the new in a kind of glorious jumble spilling down the slopes to the water's edge. It's the views of that water from various vantage points all over Lisbon that continually draw the visitor: the vistas of the 'Straw Sea', so named because of the golden reflections of the sun on the Tagus, are an inspiration whatever time of year. So too are the sounds of fado, the city's alluring folk music. Fado conjures up a melancholic yearning, and can be heard in taverns and dives all over town. They are the songs of fate, and they add another layer of intrigue to Lisbon's absorbing patchwork.

LIVING THE CITY

Lisbon is strung out along the north bank of the curving **River Tagus**. The compact heart of the city is the **Baixa**, the flat eighteenth century grid of streets flanked by seven hills. Just to the west of the Baixa is the elegant commercial district of **Chiado** and the funky hilltop **Bairro Alto** , while immediately to the east is **Alfama**, a tightly packed former Moorish quarter with kasbah-like qualities. North of here is the working-class neighbourhood of **Graça**. Way out west lies the spacious riverside suburb of **Belém**, while up the river to the east can be found the ultra modern **Parque das Nações.**

PRACTICAL INFORMATION

ARRIVAL-DEPARTURE

The airport is just 7km from the city centre and a taxi will cost about €14. Alternatively, take the Aerobus which runs every 20min.

TRANSPORT

Lisbon's an easy city to get around. Four metro lines cover much of the central part of the city, with three different ticket types: single ticket, one-day ticket, or ten tickets.

There's also a good network of trams, buses and funiculars, with six main bus routes and three funiculars. Buses and trams operate every 11-15 minutes; tram routes 15 and 28 serve the main sights. Tickets for buses and trams can be bought as a single fare, a one-day or a three-day ticket. For bus, trams and funiculars: 4-day and 7-day passes are available.

The Lisboa Card is valid for unlimited travel on public transport (except trams 15 and 28) and for free or reduced admission to most museums and cultural sites. Valid for 24, 48 or 72hr.

EXPLORING LISBON

Lisbon takes the best elements of other big cities and blends them together: the winding alleyways of Venice, the wide boulevards of Paris, the trams of Amsterdam, the cobbled streets of Brussels. And it doesn't end there: the **Ponte 25 de Abril**, slung out across the Tagus, looks just like San Francisco's Golden Gate, while the 80ft-high **statue of Christ**, on the river's far bank, is a spitting image of the original overlooking Rio. Despite all this, Lisbon is very much its own city with a distinct melancholy charm. Just wander up and down the slopes of its central core and you'll get the vibe.

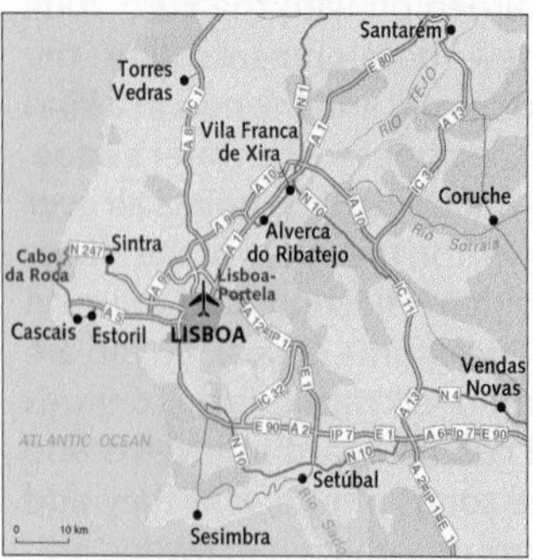

→ SO MOORISH

The Alfama district is the oldest bit of Lisbon still standing. It survived the 1755 earthquake which knocked out the rest of the city, but by then its Moorish population had moved further west. They left behind a myriad of tightly packed alleyways and steep streets lined with compact houses which exist to this day; the medieval layout has a humble allure, its alleys so narrow that the balconies on opposite sides of the street almost meet in greeting. There are local grocery stores hidden in corners, and cosy, cellar-like tavernas announcing themselves like a conspiratorial secret. Above Alfama is the city's most distinctive landmark: the **Castelo São Jorge**. The castle was built by the Moors on the site of a Roman fort, but was left in ruins for centuries until it was reconstructed in the Twentieth. Hang around the ramparts for gorgeous views of the Tagus estuary and the city lining its northern bank. Then head further north to the neighbourhood of Graça for more super views - mostly a panorama of rooftops - enjoyed best of all in the early evening at a café table beneath the swaying pines.

➜ CENTRAL PLANNING

Looked down upon from the castle, bustling Baixa was totally destroyed in the earthquake, but, under the guidance of the Marquês de Pombal, this sea-level centre of town was reborn with neo-classical buildings and a symmetrically laid out grid of elegant, broad boulevards – it was one of Europe's first examples of town planning. This is the heart of the city, where the smart shops are. They're book-ended by two imposing squares, the buzzing **Praça do Comércio** down by the river, and the **Rossio** further north. A favourite way of coming into Lisbon is by ferry from the southern bank, alighting at the Praça do Comércio, and admiring the impressive triumphal arch which towers over the north side of the square. From here, you stroll into **Rua Augusta**, Lisbon's main tourist thoroughfare, lined with open-air cafés and smart boutiques. Handsomely adorned with mosaic pavements, it's lively, bustling and pedestrianized, and it's flanked on either side by **'Goldsmiths' Street'** and **'Silversmiths' Street'**, just to give you an idea of the kind of retail going on in this compact part of town. By day, it seems all of Lisbon is here, but as soon as darkness descends, Baixa becomes a ghost town.

Not so the adjacent quarter of Bairro Alto, high up the hill to the west of Baixa. It's a raffish, bohemian warren of streets that by day is peaceful enough, with hippie shops and sedate viewpoints. When the sun goes down, though, the shutters go up, hundreds of local restaurants open their doors, and the clubs and bars pulsate to the sounds of African and samba rhythms. This is a nightlife zone that doesn't let up till the dawn. When the day does come, shopping around Bairro Alto can be a very personalised and social occasion, where bars sell clothes, hairdressers flip open a beer bottle (for the customer, that is) and the cosy neighbourhood store boasts a DJ. The nearby district of Chiado exudes a different feel again: it's an area of elegant shops and old-style cafés, typified by the century-old **Café A Brasileira** with its carved and panelled wood interior set off by gleaming, gilded mirrors.

➜ SEA THE PAST

Jump on a tram, head out west for half an hour, and you're in Belém, the riverside neighbourhood of Lisbon most in thrall to its seafaring past. When Vasco da Gama and Ferdinand Magellan were at the height of their medieval adventures, the city was celebrating their fame by building exuberant late-Gothic churches and monuments in Belem, from where they'd set sail. The real showstopper here is the **Jerónimos monastery**, an exotic structure with a richly carved cloister and portal. Vasco da Gama is buried here in a tomb of seafaring symbols; lying next to him is Portugal's most famous poet, Luis de Camões. Outside, Belém is a suburb of pocket-sized parks and gardens, a snazzy promenade with cafés and, when the sun's shining, a distinctly seaside vibe.

➔ PARQUE AND TIDE

You have to take a trip about eight kilometres east of the centre to find the glittering twenty first century face of Lisbon. You'll find it at Parque das Nações. Just fifteen years ago, this area was a wasteland, but it was developed for Expo 98, and is now a riot of modern attractions. Chief amongst these is the Portugal Pavilion, which boasts a stunning concrete canopy floating over its forecourt. There's also a science museum and an Oceanarium vying for your attention, but what might *really* grab it lies further along the riverside promenade: the **Vasco da Gama bridge** stretches for 10 miles across the wide river, making it the longest bridge in Europe.

➔ ACROSS THE RANGE

Not many art collections can claim to span 4,000 years of exhibits, but Lisbon boasts one, and it's not to be missed. The **Calouste Gulbenkian Museum**, north of the city centre, is a private collection that happens to be one of the finest in Europe. It ranges from ancient Egyptian statuettes to works by Turner, Rembrandt and Manet. There's also a stunning display of Oriental and Islamic pieces, as colourful as anything else on display here. The other hot museum of art to head for is down near the river at the western end of Bairro Alto. It's the **Museu Nacional de Arte Antiga**, which translates as the National Museum of Ancient Art. It houses a phenomenal range of Portuguese national art ranging from the twelfth to the nineteenth centuries, and it's the largest collection of paintings in the country, complemented by many works from other parts of Europe and the Orient. One look round here, taking in Portugal's historic links with so many other countries around the globe, gives another hint as to why Lisbon has bolted on all those parts of other world cities to create its magical whole.

CALENDAR HIGHLIGHTS

Despite their reputation as being more reserved than their Spanish neighbours, the Portuguese do love a party, particularly if there's a saint involved. Which means that Festas dos Santos Populares, (or Feast Days of the Popular Saints), in June, is Lisbon's biggest party. The city streets are decorated with paper lanterns, streamers and coloured lights, and balconies and railings are festooned, creating a magical sight. Another big celebration that month is Portugal's National Day, which marks the anniversary of the death of the country's greatest poet, Luis de Camões: when the city hosts various cultural events. On the theme of writing, June's Lisbon Book Fair, in Parque Eduardo VII, has been a great event since the 1930s, and you can browse old tomes, new books and comics at your leisure

LISBON IN...

➔ ONE DAY
Alfama, Castelo São Jorge, Bairro Alto

➔ TWO DAYS
Baixa, Calouste Gulbenkian Museum, Parque das Nações

➔ THREE DAYS
Museu Nacional de Arte Antiga, Belém

as you stroll amongst the trees. Also that month, the Alkantara Festival is a seventeen-day jamboree which includes theatre, dance and performance art, but which may be even more notable for its fascinating walk through Alfama, or its all-night marathon! The Parque do Tejo in Parque das Nações blasts to life in July when top names in rock give it their all at the Super Bock Super Rock Festival. Later that month, a slightly more refined air accompanies the Almada International Theatre Festival, during which various city venues host plays and exhibitions from across the globe. November's Arte Lisboa is an important event in the city's art world, with contemporary works filling sixty-six galleries at the FIL. In the spring, the Belém Cultural Centre hosts two important events: the Spring Festival (March), which puts on various shows, concerts and exhibitions, and then, in April, the CCB Music Festival: at this one, seven different stages are home to baroque orchestras, choirs and soloists in an intense three-day event. On the same theme, and running right through the winter and spring (November-May), Great Orchestras of the World, at the Coliseu dos Recreios, is presented by the influential Calouste Gulbenkian Foundation, and features various internationally renowned conductors and soloists.

EATING OUT

The cuisine of the Lisbon region can be characterised by its simplicity. *Lisboetas* love their local agricultural produce, prepared naturally, without the addition of a large number of extra ingredients. The city has an age-old maritime tradition and is open to the sea, so it's home to a range of dishes based on fish and seafood. There are a number of fishing ports nearby which supply it with ocean-fresh produce. Gastronomically, Lisbon doesn't disappoint, with all the country's regional cuisine represented: it might not be strikingly original, but there's a clear commitment to values such as simplicity and honesty. Having said that, the locals love *bacalhau* (cod), and it's said that there's a different way to prepare it each day for a year, while a Lisbon academy has identified over a thousand cod recipes. Eating in either a humble *tasca* (tavern with a few tables), *casa de pasto* (large dining room) or *restaurante*, there are some specialities to keep an eye open for. *Bacalhau* may come oven baked, slow cooked or cooked in milk, and served wrapped in cabbage, with tocino belly pork, a topping of mayonnaise or in a myriad other ways. *Amêijoas à bulhão pato* (clams cooked with garlic and coriander), *cozido à Portuguesa* (traditional stew with beef, chicken and sausage cooked with vegetables and rice), *feijao à Portuguesa* (bean casserole with tocino belly pork), or *arroz de lamprea* (lamprey eel with rice) are all mainstays of the Lisbon menu. Enjoy them with a *vinho verde*, the wine of the region. A service charge will be included on your bill, but it's customary to leave a tip of about ten per cent.

→ A BAKER'S SECRET

Belém has always been famous for its tarts; in this case, they're warm, creamy, and dripping with custard. They're made at the legendary Antiga Confeitaria de Belém, and the secret recipe used in their production is known only to three bakers. Ten thousand *pastéis de Belém* are sold on an average weekday, and eaten, time permitting, in the café's rooms, which are famous far and wide for their colourful tiles depicting the area four hundred years ago.

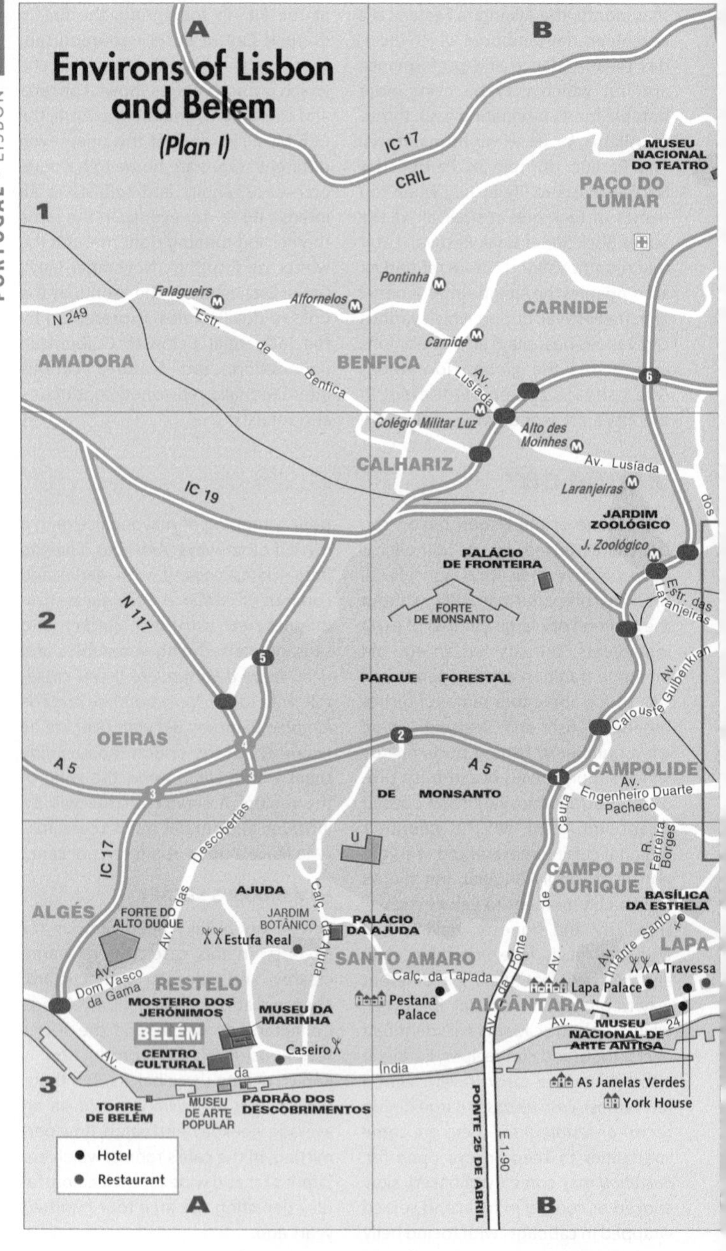
Environs of Lisbon and Belem
(Plan I)
A
B
1
2
3
IC 17
CRIL
MUSEU NACIONAL DO TEATRO
PAÇO DO LUMIAR
Pontinha
Falagueirs
Alfornelos
N 249
Estr. de Benfica
CARNIDE
Carnide
AMADORA
BENFICA
Av. Lusíada
Colégio Militar Luz
Alto des Moinhes
CALHARIZ
Av. Lusíada
Laranjeiras
IC 19
JARDIM ZOOLÓGICO
J. Zoológico
PALÁCIO DE FRONTEIRA
FORTE DE MONSANTO
Estr. das Laranjeiras
N 117
PARQUE FORESTAL
Av. Calouste Gulbenkian
OEIRAS
A 5
A 5
CAMPOLIDE
DE MONSANTO
Av. Engenheiro Duarte Pacheco
Ceuta
Descobertas
R. Ferreira Borges
IC 17
CAMPO DE OURIQUE
AJUDA
Av. das
BASÍLICA DA ESTRELA
ALGÉS
FORTE DO ALTO DUQUE
JARDIM BOTÂNICO
PALÁCIO DA AJUDA
Estufa Real
Calç. da Ajuda
SANTO AMARO
Av. da Ponte
Av. Infante Santo
LAPA
A Travessa
Av. Dom Vasco da Gama
RESTELO
Calç. da Tapada
Lapa Palace
MOSTEIRO DOS JERÓNIMOS
Pestana Palace
MUSEU DA MARINHA
ALCÂNTARA
BELÉM
Av. 24
MUSEU NACIONAL DE ARTE ANTIGA
Caseiro
CENTRO CULTURAL
Av. da Índia
As Janelas Verdes
York House
TORRE DE BELÉM
MUSEU DE ARTE POPULAR
PADRÃO DOS DESCOBRIMENTOS
PONTE 25 DE ABRIL
E 1-90
Hotel
Restaurant

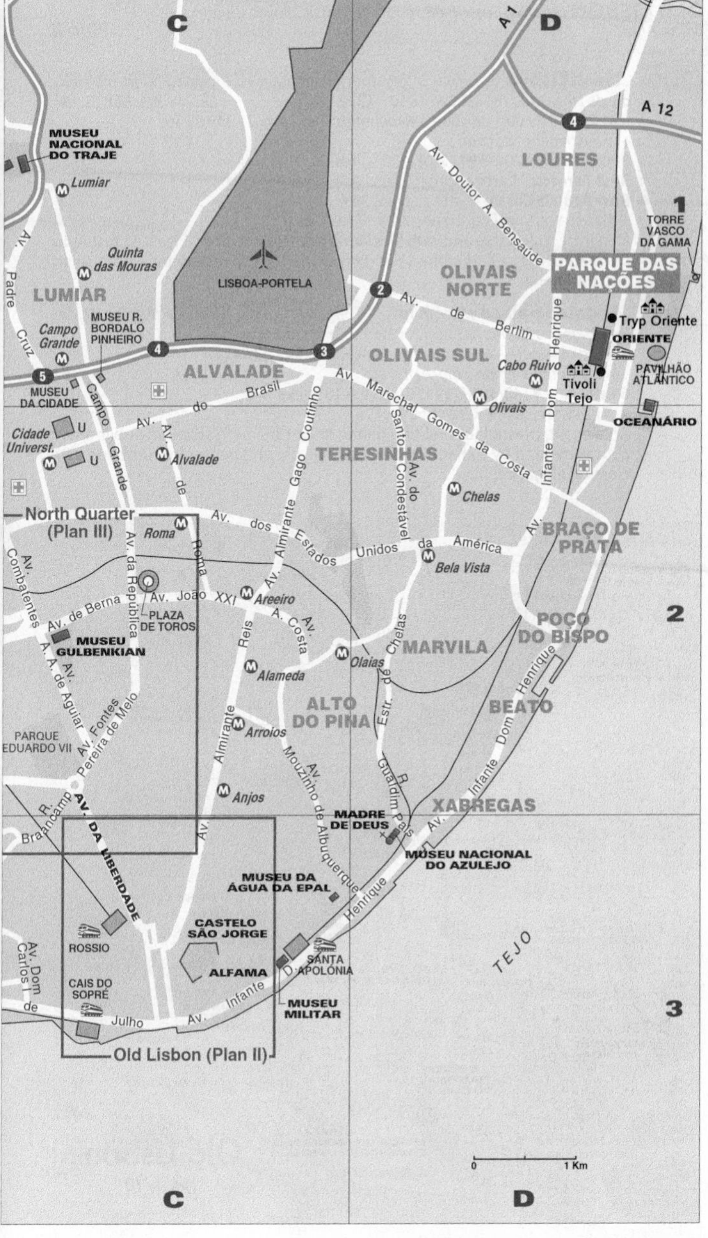
C
D
A 1
A 12
MUSEU NACIONAL DO TRAJE
Lumiar
LOURES
LUMIAR
Quinta das Mouras
LISBOA-PORTELA
OLIVAIS NORTE
PARQUE DAS NAÇÕES
TORRE VASCO DA GAMA
Tryp Oriente
ORIENTE
MUSEU R. BORDALO PINHEIRO
Campo Grande
ALVALADE
OLIVAIS SUL
Cabo Ruivo
Tivoli Tejo
PAVILHÃO ATLÂNTICO
MUSEU DA CIDADE
OCEANÁRIO
Olivais
Cidade Universt.
Alvalade
TERESINHAS
Chelas
North Quarter (Plan III)
Roma
BRAÇO DE PRATA
Bela Vista
Areeiro
PLAZA DE TOROS
MUSEU GULBENKIAN
POÇO DO BISPO
MARVILA
Olaias
Alameda
ALTO DO PINA
BEATO
PARQUE EDUARDO VII
Arroios
Anjos
XABREGAS
MADRE DE DEUS
MUSEU NACIONAL DO AZULEJO
MUSEU DA ÁGUA DA EPAL
CASTELO SÃO JORGE
ROSSIO
ALFAMA
SANTA APOLÓNIA
TEJO
CAIS DO SOPRÉ
MUSEU MILITAR
Old Lisbon (Plan II)
1
2
3
0
1 Km

OLD LISBON *(Alfama, Castelo de São Jorge, Rossio, Baixa, Chiado, Bairro Alto)*

Plan II

Tivoli Lisboa
< city from the terrace, (heated) rm

av. da Liberdade 185 ✉ 1269-050 – Ⓜ Avenida – ✆ 21 319 89 00 – htlisboa@tivolihotels.com – Fax 21 319 89 50 – www.tivolihotels.com **E1**

300 rm – 400 € 420 € – 29 suites

Rest *Terraço* – Carte approx. 60 €

Rest *Beatriz Costa* – Carte approx. 36 €

♦ Business ♦ Traditional ♦ Classic ♦

Elegant, comfortable and with fine views from the top floor. Pleasant, tastefully decorated and well-equipped bedrooms. The Terraço restaurant is both smart and traditional.

Avenida Palace without rest

Rua 1° de Dezembro 123 ✉ 1200-359 – Ⓜ Restauradores – ✆ 21 321 81 00 – reservas@hotel-avenida-palace.pt – Fax 21 342 28 84 – www.hotel-avenida-palace.pt **E1**

64 rm – 140/180 € 170/385 € – 18 suites

♦ Traditional ♦ Classic ♦

An elegant, prestigious building dating from 1892, with splendid public areas, complemented by a charming English-style bar and bedrooms furnished with classical elegance.

NORTH QUARTER (Plan III)

● Hotel
● Restaurant

Veneza
Britania
Tivoli Lisboa
Tivoli Jardim
NH Liberdade
Varanda da União
Sofitel Lisboa
Lisboa Plaza
Ad Lib
Heritage Av Liberdade
Solar dos Presuntos
Avenida Palace
Gambrinus
Olissippo Castelo
Lisboa Tejo
Metropole
Casa do Leão
Solar do Castelo
A Severa
Tavares
Solar dos Mouros
Bairro Alto H.
Lisboa Regency Chiado
Clube de Fado

Old Lisbon (Plan II)

Bairro Alto H

Praça Luis de Camões 2 ✉ 1200-243 – Ⓜ Baixa-Chiado – ☏ 21 340 82 88 – info@bairroaltohotel.com – Fax 21 340 82 99 – www.bairroaltohotel.com

51 rm – 🛉200/300 € 🛉🛉230/590 € – 4 suites **E2**

Rest – Menu 35 €

♦ Luxury ♦ Modern ♦

Beautiful restored building in the monumental zone. Boasts modern décor, with minimalist touches, and a roof terrace with views. The restaurant combines its pleasant layout with large windows overlooking the square.

Sofitel Lisboa

Av. da Liberdade 127 ✉ 1269-038 – Ⓜ Avenida – ☏ 21 322 83 00 – h1319@accor.com – Fax 21 322 83 60 – www.sofitel-lisboa.com **E1**

167 rm – 🛉265/315 € 🛉🛉335/365 €, 18 € – 4 suites

Rest Ad Lib – see below

♦ Business ♦ Design ♦

A friendly welcome, comfortable and with a contemporary classic feel. Enjoy a pleasant stay in agreeable surroundings.

Lisboa Plaza

Travessa do Salitre 7 ✉ 1269-066 – Ⓜ Avenida – ☏ 21 321 82 18 – plaza.hotels@heritage.pt – Fax 21 347 16 30 – www.heritage.pt **E1**

94 rm – 🛉152/220 € 🛉🛉162/243 €, 14 € – 12 suites

Rest – Menu 35 €

♦ Business ♦ Traditional ♦ Classic ♦

Near the famous Avenida da Liberdade. Very traditional with distinguished and tasteful atmosphere and classic décor. A large buffet is available in the dining room.

Lisboa Regency Chiado without rest

Rua Nova do Almada 114 ✉ 1200-290 – Ⓜ Baixa-Chiado – ☏ 21 325 61 00 – reservations.chiado@madeiraregency.pt – Fax 21 325 61 61 – www.regency-hotels-resorts.com **E2**

40 rm – 🛉158/398 € 🛉🛉178/398 €

♦ Business ♦ Personalised ♦

Pleasantly situated in a building in the old part of the city. Friendly, professional service with bedrooms decorated in oriental style.

Heritage Av Liberdade without rest

Av. da Liberdade 28 ✉ 1250-145 – Ⓜ Avenida – ☏ 21 340 40 40 – avliberdade@heritage.pt – Fax 21 340 40 44 – www.heritage.pt **E1**

42 rm – 🛉210/298 € 🛉🛉224/315 €, 14 €

♦ Business ♦ Chain hotel ♦ Modern ♦

Boasts a classical exterior and a multi-purpose common area, which is also used as the breakfast room, Offers well equipped, modern rooms.

NH Liberdade

Av. da Liberdade 180-B ✉ 1250-146 – Ⓜ Avenida – ☏ 21 351 40 60 – nhliberdade@nh-hotels.com – Fax 21 314 36 74 – www.nh-hotels.com

58 rm – 🛉112/255 € 🛉🛉125/275 € – 25 suites **E1**

Rest – *(closed Saturday, Sunday and Bank Holidays)* Carte 26/38 €

♦ Business ♦ Chain hotel ♦ Modern ♦

Situated in Lisbon's most important business district. A comfortable and functional hotel with all the quality and characteristic style of this hotel chain.

Tivoli Jardim

(heated)

Rua Julio Cesar Machado 7 ✉ 1250-135 – Ⓜ Avenida – ☏ 21 359 10 00 – htjardim@tivolihotels.com – Fax 21 359 12 45 – www.tivolihotels.com **E1**

119 rm – 🛉310 € 🛉🛉320 €

Rest – Menu 28 €

♦ Business ♦ Functional ♦

Modern efficiency for the business traveller. A large foyer, conference rooms and pleasantly decorated bedrooms. The brightly-lit dining room offers traditional dishes.

Britania without rest
Rua Rodrigues Sampaio 17 ✉ 1150-278 – Ⓜ Avenida – ✆ 21 315 50 16 – britania.hotel@heritage.pt – Fax 21 315 50 21 – www.heritage.pt **E1**
33 rm – 🚹165/226 € 🚹🚹175/251 €, ☕ 14 €
◆ Business ◆ Traditional ◆ Art Deco ◆
The lounge area consists of a bar which boasts a beautiful wooden floor and paintings of Portugal's former colonies. Spacious Art Deco-style rooms.

Veneza without rest
Av. da Liberdade 189 ✉ 1250-141 – Ⓜ Avenida – ✆ 21 352 26 18 – veneza@3khoteis.com.pt – Fax 21 352 66 78 – www.viphotels.com **E1**
37 rm – 🚹🚹89/98 €, ☕ 8 €
◆ Traditional ◆ Business ◆ Cosy ◆
In a small former palace with a lovely façade. A perfect balance of old grandeur and modern day functionality.

Olissippo Castelo without rest
Rua Costa do Castelo 126 ✉ 1100-179 – Ⓜ Rossio – ✆ 21 882 01 90 – info.oc@olissippohotels.com – Fax 21 882 01 94 – www.olissippohotels.com **F2**
24 rm ☕ – 🚹130/170 € 🚹🚹150/190 €
◆ Traditional ◆ Classic ◆
Next to the Castle of St George, with one of the hotel's walls built against the castle's fortifications. High-standard guestrooms, 12 of which have their own landscaped terrace and boast magnificent views.

Solar do Castelo without rest
Rua das Cozinhas 2 ✉ 1100-181 – ✆ 21 880 60 50 – solar.castelo@heritage.pt – Fax 21 887 09 07 – www.heritage.pt **F2**
14 rm – 🚹216/310 € 🚹🚹231/340 €, ☕ 14 €
◆ Family ◆ Cosy ◆
A small 18C palace in an area with lots of historic monuments. A comfortable and completely renovated interior. Modern bedrooms with attractive design details.

Metropole without rest
Praça Dom Pedro IV-30 (Rossio) ✉ 1100-200 – Ⓜ Rossio – ✆ 21 321 90 30 – metropole@almeidahotels.com – Fax 21 346 91 66 – www.almeidahotels.com **E2**
36 rm ☕ – 🚹130/175 € 🚹🚹145/190 €
◆ Traditional ◆ Classic ◆
An early-20C building in the heart of old Lisbon. Classic bedrooms offering high levels of comfort, some with a balcony overlooking Rossio Square.

Solar dos Mouros without rest
Rua do Milagre de Santo António 6 ✉ 1100-351 – Ⓜ Baixa-Chiado – ✆ 21 885 49 40 – reservation@solardosmouros.pt – Fax 21 885 49 45 – www.solardosmouros.com **F2**
11 rm – 🚹106/196 € 🚹🚹136/226 €, ☕ 14.50 €
◆ Family ◆ Personalised ◆
A typical house which has been modernised and furnished with personal touches, including four paintings by the owner himself. Colourful bedrooms, some with excellent views.

Lisboa Tejo without rest
Rua dos Condes de Monsanto 2 ✉ 1100-159 – Ⓜ Rossio – ✆ 21 886 61 82 – hotellisboatejo.reservas@evidenciagrupo.com – Fax 21 886 51 63 – www.evidenciahoteis.com **F2**
51 rm ☕ – 🚹80/105 € 🚹🚹85/120 € – 7 suites
◆ Business ◆ Traditional ◆ Personalised ◆
Moderate prices and pleasant, well-appointed bedrooms in the Baixa Pombalina district. A modern, refurbished and central hotel with a traditional atmosphere and elegant décor.

XXX **Tavares**

Rua da Misericórdia 37 ✉ 1200-270 – Ⓜ Baixa-Chiado – ☎ 21 342 11 12 – reservas@tavaresrico.pt – Fax 21 347 81 25 – www.tavaresrico.pt
closed Saturday lunch, Sunday and Monday lunch **E2**
Rest – Carte 76/85 €
◆ Inventive ◆ Formal ◆
Founded in 1784, Lisbon's oldest restaurant has retained all its aristocratic elegance and ambience. A sumptuous décor of gilded work, mirrors and chandeliers.

XXX **Gambrinus**

Rua das Portas de Santo Antão 25 ✉ 1150-264 – Ⓜ Restauradores – ☎ 21 342 14 66 – rest.gambrinus@mail.telepac.pt – Fax 21 346 50 32 **E1**
Rest – Carte 45/70 €
◆ Traditional ◆ Formal ◆
In the historic centre of the city near the Rossio district. A restaurant with a well-established reputation backed up by fine cuisine and an excellent wine list.

XXX **Casa do Leão**

Castelo de São Jorge ✉ 1100-129 – Ⓜ Rossio – ☎ 21 887 59 62 – guest@pousadas.pt – Fax 21 887 63 29 – www.pousadas.pt **F2**
Rest – Carte approx. 40 €
◆ Traditional ◆ Formal ◆
Situated in the walls of the castle of São Jorge. An elegant restaurant in traditional Portuguese-style with an exclusive ambience.

XX **Solar dos Presuntos**

Rua das Portas de Santo Antão 150 ✉ 1150-269 – Ⓜ Avenida – ☎ 21 342 42 53 – restaurante@solardospresuntos.com – Fax 21 346 84 68 – www.solardospresuntos.com
closed August, Sunday and Bank Holidays **E1**
Rest – Carte 27/44 €
◆ Minho cuisine ◆ Family ◆
A locally-run, comfortable restaurant with a wide selection of well-prepared traditional dishes and some specialities from Minho.

XX **Ad Lib** – Hotel Sofitel Lisboa

Av. da Liberdade 127 ✉ 1269-038 – Ⓜ Avenida – ☎ 21 322 83 50 – ad-lib@accor.com – Fax 21 322 83 60 – www.sofitel-lisboa.com
closed Saturday lunch and Sunday lunch **E1**
Rest – Carte 35/43 €
◆ Contemporary ◆ Bistro ◆
A friendly welcome, comfortable and with a contemporary classic feel. Enjoy a pleasant stay in agreeable surroundings.

FADO RESTAURANTS *You can hear the typical Portuguese fado songs while dining in these restaurants.* *Plan II*

XX **Clube de Fado**

São João da Praça 94 ✉ 1100-521 – Ⓜ Restauradores – ☎ 21 885 27 04 – info@clube-de-fado.com – Fax 21 888 26 94 – www.clube-de-fado.com
Rest – *(dinner only)* Carte 43/57 € **F2**
◆ Traditional ◆ Musical ◆
A restaurant with a well cared-for appearance, a pleasant ambience and a bar with a friendly atmosphere. Simple décor.

XX **A Severa**

Rua Das Gáveas 51 ✉ 1200-206 – Ⓜ Baixa-Chiado – ☎ 21 342 83 14 – Fax 21 346 40 06 – www.asevera.com
closed Thursday **E2**
Rest – Carte approx. 51 €
◆ Traditional ◆ Musical ◆
A traditional fado restaurant run by a large family who base their success on good cuisine. Comfortable and with classic Portuguese décor.

NORTH QUARTER (Av. da Liberdade, Parque Eduardo VII, Museu Gulbenkian) Plan III

Four Seasons H. Ritz Lisbon

Rua Rodrigo da Fonseca 88 ✉ 1099-039 – Ⓜ Marquês de Pombal – ✆ 21 381 14 00 – fsh.lisbon@fourseasons.com – Fax 21 383 17 83 – www.fourseasons.com G3

262 rm – †320 € ††345 €, ☕ 27 € – 20 suites

Rest *Varanda* – Carte approx. 62 €

◆ Luxury ◆ Business ◆ Classic ◆

Luxury is the keynote in these exquisite bedrooms, more than matched by the superb public rooms. The exclusive restaurant in classic style serves sophisticated, immaculately presented cuisine.

Le Meridien Park Atlantic Lisboa

Rua Castilho 149 ✉ 1099-034 – Ⓜ Marquês de Pombal – ✆ 21 381 87 00 – reservas.lisboa@lemeridien.pt – Fax 21 389 05 05 – www.lemeridien.com G3

314 rm ☕ – †125/150 € ††140/170 € – 17 suites

Rest *L'Appart* – Carte 45/56 €

◆ Business ◆ Chain hotel ◆ Modern ◆

A full range of facilities and professional service in the comfort of modern bedrooms and suites. Bathrooms fitted with marble and high quality furnishings. A pleasantly decorated restaurant offering à la carte, buffet or dish of the day.

Real Palacio

Rua Tomás Ribeiro 115 ✉ 1050-228 – Ⓜ São Sebastião – ✆ 21 319 95 00 – realpalacio@hoteisreal.com – Fax 21 319 95 01 – www.hoteisreal.com G2

143 rm ☕ – †250 € ††275 € – 4 suites

Rest *Guarda Real* – Carte 26/40 €

◆ Business ◆ Classic ◆

The Real Palacio is a mix of the modern and traditional with its stylish marble and elegant woodwork. Panelled meeting rooms and fully-equipped bedrooms. Options in the restaurant include the à la carte menu and an extensive buffet.

Holiday Inn Lisbon Continental

Rua Laura Alves 9 ✉ 1069-169 – Ⓜ Campo Pequeno – ✆ 21 004 60 00 – hic@grupo-continental.com – Fax 21 797 36 69 – www.holiday-inn.com H1

210 rm – †95/180 € ††105/205 €, ☕ 12 € – 10 suites

Rest – Menu 18 €

◆ Business ◆ Chain hotel ◆ Functional ◆

A hotel with a modern exterior that is very popular for business meetings. Pleasant, well-appointed bedrooms and adequate public areas. The dining room is not up to the standards of the rest of the hotel.

Real Parque

Av. Luís Bívar 67 ✉ 1069-146 – Ⓜ Picoas – ✆ 21 319 90 00 – realparque@hoteisreal.com – Fax 21 357 07 50 – www.hoteisreal.com G2

147 rm ☕ – †170 € ††190 € – 6 suites

Rest *Cozinha do Real* – Carte 21/33 €

◆ Business ◆ Classic ◆

Ideal for meetings, business and leisure travel. Elegant furnishings, quality and good taste everywhere. A modern exterior, classic contemporary décor and a charming lounge area. Good food served in a pleasant dining room.

Aviz

Rua Duque de Palmela 32 ✉ 1250-098 – Ⓜ Marquês de Pombal – ✆ 21 040 20 00 – geral@hotelaviz.com – Fax 21 040 21 98 – www.hotelaviz.com G3

56 rm ☕ – †120/160 € ††140/320 € – 14 suites

Rest – Carte 30/50 €

◆ Traditional ◆ Classic ◆

The name pays homage to a famous luxury hotel which no longer exists. Elegant foyer, and well-appointed bedrooms with marble bathrooms. Traditional-style restaurant decorated with objects from the former Aviz.

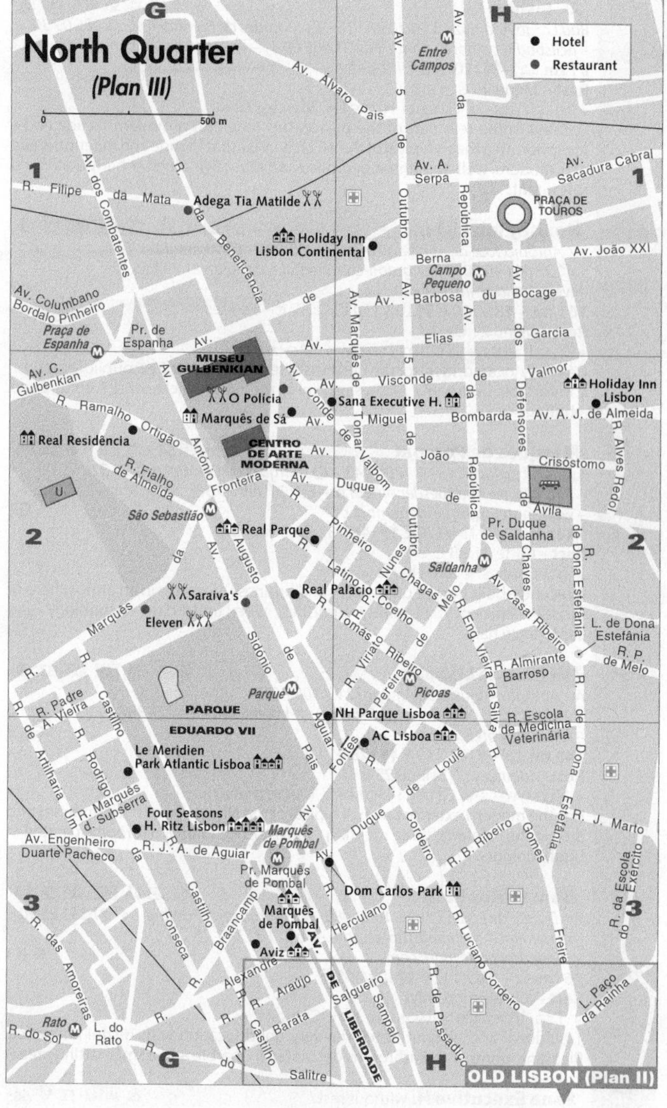
North Quarter
(Plan III)
0
500 m
Hotel
Restaurant
Adega Tia Matilde
Holiday Inn Lisbon Continental
MUSEU GULBENKIAN
O Polícia
Sana Executive H.
Marquês de Sá
Real Residência
CENTRO DE ARTE MODERNA
Holiday Inn Lisbon
PRAÇA DE TOUROS
Real Parque
Real Palacio
Saraiva's
Eleven
PARQUE EDUARDO VII
NH Parque Lisboa
AC Lisboa
Le Meridien Park Atlantic Lisboa
Four Seasons H. Ritz Lisbon
Dom Carlos Park
Marquês de Pombal
Aviz
OLD LISBON (Plan II)

AC Lisboa

Rua Largo Andaluz 13 ✉ 1050-121 – Ⓜ Marquês de Pombal – ✆ 21 005 09 30 – aclisboa@ac-hotels.com – Fax 21 005 09 31 – www.ac-hotels.com **H3**

81 rm – 120/178 € – 2 suites

Rest – Menu 25 €

♦ Business ♦ Chain hotel ♦ Modern ♦

Located in the rear part of the palace, this hotel has a modern façade and a reception area that is typical of the AC chain. Pleasant lounge and meeting areas, plus modern, well-appointed bedrooms. An attractive, albeit soberly decorated restaurant.

Holiday Inn Lisbon

Av. António José de Almeida 28-A ✉ 1000-044 – Ⓜ Alameda – ✆ 21 004 40 00 – hil@grupo-continental.com – Fax 21 793 66 72 – www.holiday-inn.com **H2**

161 rm – 85/110 € 100/150 €, 12 € – 8 suites

Rest – Menu 21 €

♦ Business ♦ Chain hotel ♦ Modern ♦

Centrally located; ideal for the business or leisure traveller. Few public rooms but comfortable bedrooms. A pleasant dining room with wickerwork furniture and a buffet.

Marquês de Pombal

Av. da Liberdade 243 ✉ 1250-143 – Ⓜ Marquês de Pombal – ✆ 21 319 79 00 – info@hotel-marquesdepombal.pt – Fax 21 319 79 90 – www.hotel-marquesdepombal.pt **G3**

120 rm – 134/170 € 146/182 € – 3 suites

Rest – Carte 21/33 €

♦ Business ♦ Modern ♦

A recently-built hotel. Conferences and business meetings in an atmosphere of modern efficiency. Elegantly furnished with up-to-date technology and conference hall.

NH Parque Lisboa

Av. António Augusto de Aguiar 12 ✉ 1050-016 – ✆ 21 351 50 00 – nhparquelisboa@nh-hotels.com – Fax 21 357 99 99 – www.nh-hotels.com **G2-3**

148 rm – 103/149 € 128/174 €

Rest – *(dinner only)* Menu 25 €

♦ Business ♦ Chain hotel ♦ Functional ♦

Has the modern exterior and hall typical of the NH chain, with a lounge seating area in the cafeteria, three meeting rooms and functional bedrooms painted in bright colours.

Dom Carlos Park

Av. Duque de Loulé 121 ✉ 1050-089 – Ⓜ Marquês de Pombal – ✆ 21 351 25 90 – comercial@domcarloshoteis.com – Fax 21 352 07 28 – www.domcarlospark.com **G-H3**

76 rm – 85/147 € 109/191 €

Rest – *(Coffee shop only)*

♦ Traditional ♦ Business ♦ Classic ♦

Traditional and elegant hotel in a very good location with restful ambience. Pleasant rooms with bathrooms decorated in marble and a small sitting area.

Sana Executive H. without rest

Av. Conde Valbom 56 ✉ 1050-069 – Ⓜ São Sebastião – ✆ 21 795 11 57 – sanaexecutive@sanahotels.com – Fax 21 795 11 66 – www.sanahotels.com **G-H2**

72 rm – 66/170 € 76/180 €

♦ Business ♦ Modern ♦

Good location and ideal for the business traveller. Practical and functional. A modern foyer-reception, comfortable, well-equipped rooms and bathrooms with marble fittings.

Marquês de Sá

Av. Miguel Bombarda 130 ✉ 1050-167 – Ⓜ São Sebastião – ✆ 21 791 10 14 – reservas.oms@olissippohotels.com – Fax 21 793 69 83 – www.olissippohotels.com **G2**

163 rm – †110/150 € ††130/170 € – 1 suite

Rest – Carte approx. 30 €

♦ Business ♦ Functional ♦

Beside the Gulbenkian Foundation. Business and pleasure in a pleasant atmosphere of quality. Friendly service and well-appointed rooms. Well-lit dining room with décor in blue tones and a large foyer.

Real Residência

Rua Ramalho Ortigão 41 ✉ 1070-228 – Ⓜ São Sebastião – ✆ 21 382 29 00 – realresidencia@hoteisreal.com – Fax 21 382 29 30 – www.hoteisreal.com **G2**

24 suites – †160 € ††180 €

Rest – Carte 22/29 €

♦ Traditional ♦ Classic ♦

Quality, comfort and elegance. Large, well-equipped apartments: bathrooms fitted with marble, traditional décor of good quality furnishings and fittings. The smallish dining room is pleasant and combines modern elements with attractive rustic details.

Eleven

park, city and river Tejo,

Rua Marquês de Fronteira ✉ 1070 – Ⓜ São Sebastião – ✆ 21 386 22 11 – 11@restauranteleven.com – Fax 21 386 22 14 – www.restauranteleven.com closed Sunday **G2**

Rest – Menu 69 € – Carte 59/74 €

Spec. Crocante de camarão sobre risotto de coco e molho de caril de Madrás, ervalimão. Costeleta de porco preto com crosta de pimentão e gratinado de batata com queijo amanteigado (January-May). Souflé de maracujá com gelado de banana (December-June).

♦ Inventive ♦ Design ♦

This establishment has already gained wide acceptance in a short time. Excellent, modern facilities, a private lobby bar and a dining room with magnificent views. Enticing creative cooking.

Saraiva's

Rua Engenheiro Canto Resende 3 ✉ 1050-104 – Ⓜ São Sebastião – ✆ 21 354 06 09 – Fax 21 353 19 87 closed Friday dinner, Saturday and Bank Holidays **G2**

Rest – Carte 20/32 €

♦ Traditional ♦ Design ♦

Carpeted floors and elegant modern-style furnishings. Very professional service, a well-heeled clientele and a lively ambience.

Adega Tia Matilde

Rua da Beneficência 77 ✉ 1600-017 – Ⓜ Praça de Espanha – ✆ 21 797 21 72 – adegatiamatilde@netcabo.pt – Fax 21 797 21 72 closed Saturday dinner and Sunday **G1**

Rest – Carte 25/33 €

♦ Traditional ♦ Family ♦

A popular establishment, friendly and professional. Portuguese specialities. Classic-modern style with plants and fresh flowers on the tables.

Varanda da União

Rua Castilho 14 C-7º ✉ 1250-069 – Ⓜ Marquês de Pombal – ✆ 21 314 10 45 – Fax 21 314 10 46 – www.varandadauniao.restaunet.pt closed Saturday lunch, Sunday and Bank Holidays lunch *Plan II* **E1**

Rest – Carte 34/43 €

♦ Traditional ♦ Formal ♦

A fine panorama of Lisbon rooftops from the 7th floor of a residential building. A large number of waiting staff and success based on the quality of the cuisine.

O Polícia

Rua Marquês Sá da Bandeira 112 ✉ 1050-150 – Ⓜ São Sebastião – ✆ 21 796 35 05 – Fax 21 796 97 91
closed Saturday dinner, Sunday and Bank Holidays **G2**
Rest – Carte 22/37 €
♦ Traditional ♦ Brasserie ♦
Renowned for fish. Well-decorated establishment with large dining room, friendly service and a busy atmosphere. Reservation recommended.

PARQUE DAS NAÇÕES *Plan I*

Tivoli Tejo

Av. D. João II (Parque das Nações) ✉ 1990-083 – Ⓜ Oriente – ✆ 21 891 51 00 – httejo@tivolihotels.com – Fax 21 891 53 45 – www.tivolitejo.com **D1**
262 rm – 80/210 € 90/210 € – 17 suites
Rest *VIII Colina* – Carte 31/50 €
♦ Chain hotel ♦ Business ♦ Classic ♦
An attractive building next to the Oriente railway station, with contemporary bedrooms and compact bathrooms. Although on the small side, the hotel's public areas are comfortable and well-appointed. The VIII Colina restaurant enjoys wonderful panoramic views of the city.

Tryp Oriente

Av. D. João II (Parque das Nações) ✉ 1990-083 – Ⓜ Oriente – ✆ 21 893 00 00 – tryp.oriente@solmeliaportugal.com – Fax 21 893 00 99 – www.solmelia.com **D1**
205 rm – 79/113 € 89/145 € – 1 suite
Rest – Menu 18 €
♦ Chain hotel ♦ Business ♦ Functional ♦
Located on the Expo site, this functional hotel has a pleasant foyer-bar and lounge, plus spacious guestrooms with views from those on the upper floors. The bright, independently accessed restaurant offers diners a concise menu.

AT WEST *Plan I*

Lapa Palace

Rua do Pau de Bandeira 4 ✉ 1249-021 – Ⓜ Rato – ✆ 21 394 94 94 – info@lapa-palace.com – Fax 21 395 06 65 – www.lapa-palace.com **B3**
92 rm – 340/445 € – 9 suites
Rest *Hotel Cipriani* – Carte 48/58 €
♦ Grand Luxury ♦ Classic ♦
Lavish, traditional elegance on a hill with the Tagus as a backdrop. A 19C palace with intimate corners and evocative gardens with a small waterfall tumbling through the trees. The restaurant is renowned for its refined cuisine focusing on Portuguese and Italian specialities.

Pestana Palace

Rua Jau 54 ✉ 1300-314 – ✆ 21 361 56 00 – sales.cph@pestana.com – Fax 21 361 56 01 – www.pestana.com **B3**
173 rm – 370 € 390 € – 17 suites
Rest *Valle Flor* – Carte 54/70 €
♦ Luxury ♦ Classic ♦
An attractive restored 19C palace decorated in keeping with its period of construction, including sumptuous lounges and meticulously appointed bedrooms. The elegant exterior is a veritable botanical paradise. A magnificent restaurant, both for its cuisine and the beauty of its luxurious dining rooms.

As Janelas Verdes without rest

Rua das Janelas Verdes 47 ✉ 1200-690 – ✆ 21 396 81 43 – jverdes@heritage.pt – Fax 21 396 81 44 – www.heritage.pt **B3**

29 rm – 🚹181/275 € 🚹🚹194/299 €, ☕ 14 €

◆ Traditional ◆ Cosy ◆

Partly occupying a seigneurial 18C mansion, with a delightful lounge-library and good views. The overall sensation here is warm, romantic and charmingly traditional.

York House

Rua das Janelas Verdes 32 ✉ 1200-691 – Ⓜ Cais do Sodré – ✆ 21 396 24 35 – reservations@yorkhouselisboa.com – Fax 21 397 27 93 – www.yorkhouselisboa.com **B3**

32 rm – 🚹135/225 € 🚹🚹155/270 €, ☕ 15 €

Rest – Carte 30/43 €

◆ Traditional ◆ Cosy ◆

Housed in a 17C convent, but with an interior that has been completely modernised, with furniture that combines the traditional and the contemporary. Traditionally decorated restaurant, including a striking panel of old azulejos.

A Travessa

Travessa do Convento das Bernardas 12 ✉ 1200-638 – ✆ 21 390 20 34 – info@atravessa.com – Fax 21 394 08 39 – www.atravessa.com closed Sunday **B3**

Rest – Carte 31/43 €

◆ French ◆ Cosy ◆

Part of a 17C convent, in which the dining room, located in what was once the refectory, is crowned by a delightful vaulted ceiling. The terrace, occupying the cloisters, adds further charm to the setting.

BELÉM

Plan I

Estufa Real

Jardim Botânico da Ajuda-Calçada do Gãlvao ✉ 1400 – ✆ 21 361 94 00 – geral@estufareal.mail.pt – Fax 21 361 90 18 – www.estufareal.com closed Saturday **A3**

Rest – *(lunch only)* Carte approx. 36 €

◆ Traditional ◆ Fashionable ◆

A relaxing location in the Jardim Botânico da Ajuda. A lovely glassed-in conservatory with attractive modern design details.

Caseiro

Rua de Belém 35 ✉ 1300-354 – ✆ 21 363 88 03 – Fax 21 364 23 39 closed August and Sunday **A3**

Rest – Carte 23/31 €

◆ Traditional ◆ Rustic ◆

Traditional establishment serving delicious, simply prepared dishes which have made this restaurant well known in the locality.

SPAIN
ESPAÑA

PROFILE

→ **Area:**
504 782 km²
(194 897 sq mi).

→ **Population:**
45 116 894 inhabitants (est. 2007), density = 88.6 per km².

→ **Capital:**
Madrid (conurbation 6 112 078 inhabitants).

→ **Currency:**
Euro (€); rate of exchange: € 1 = US$ 1.46 (Dec 2007).

→ **Government:**
Constitutional parliamentary monarchy (since 1978). Member of European Union since 1986.

→ **Languages:**
Spanish (Castilian) but also Catalan in Catalonia, Gallego in Galicia, Euskera in the Basque Country, Valencian in the Valencian Region and Mallorquin in the Balearic Isles.

→ **Specific public holidays:**
Epiphany (6 January); San Jose (19 March); Maundy Thursday (the day before Good Friday); Good Friday (Friday before Easter); National Day (12 October); Constitution Day (6 December); Immaculate Conception (8 December). Some public holidays may be replaced by the autonomous communities with another date.

→ **Local Time:**
GMT + 1 hour in winter and GMT + 2 hours in summer.

→ **Climate:**
Temperate Mediterranean with mild winters (colder in interior) and sunny, hot summers (Madrid: January: 6°C, July: 25°C).

→ **International dialling Code:**
00 34 followed by full 9-digit number. Directory enquiries: ✆ **11822**. International directory enquiries: ✆ **11825**. On-line telephone directory: www.blancas.paginasamarillas.es

→ **Emergency:**
Dial ✆ **112**; National Police: ✆ **091**.

Barcelona
MADRID
Valencia

→ **Electricity:**
220 or 225 volts AC (previously 110 V), 50 Hz; 2-pin round-shaped continental plugs.

→ **Formalities**
Travellers from the European Union (EU), Switzerland, Iceland and the main countries of North and South America need a national identity card or passport (America: passport required) to visit Spain for less than three months (tourism or business purpose). For visitors from other countries a visa may be required, in addition to a passport, especially for those wishing to stay for longer than three months. We advise you to check with your embassy before travelling.

PLAZA
MAYOR

MADRID

MADRID

Population (est. 2007): 3 186187 (conurbation 6 112078) – Altitude: 646m

Y. Travert/PHOTONONSTOP

Madrid is a city on the rise. The nightlife in Spain's proud capital is now second to none and the superb museums of art which make up the city's 'golden triangle' have all undergone thrilling reinvention in recent years.

The next big plan for Madrid is to have a square kilometre park near the river Manzanares, which runs just west of the city. In a big bid to give ***madrileños*** more clean air, the new park will be free of cars, and will boast bike lanes intermingled with eight thousand trees – and there'll be an artificial beach, too. The renaissance of Madrid has seen it develop as a big player on the world cultural stage, attracting more international music, theatre and dance than it would have dreamed of a decade ago. The new Royal Spanish Ballet will be based here, a testament to its rising cachet in the arts. This is a city that might think it has some catching up to do: it was only made the capital in 1561 on the whim of ruler, Felipe II. But its position was crucial: slap bang in the middle of the Iberian Peninsula. Ruled by Habsburgs and Bourbons, it soon made a mark in Europe.

The contemporary big wigs of Madrid are out to have the same effect with a 21C twist.

LIVING THE CITY

The central heart of Madrid is compact, defined by the teeming Habsburg hubs of **Puerta del Sol** and **Plaza Mayor**, and the mighty **Palacio Real**. East of here are the grand squares, fountains and fine museums of the Bourbon district with its easterly boundary, the **Retiro** park. West of the historical centre are the capacious green acres of **Casa de Campo**, while the affluent, regimented grid streets of **Salamanca** are to the east. Modern Madrid is just to the north, embodied in the grand north-south boulevard **Paseo de la Castellana**.

PRACTICAL INFORMATION

ARRIVAL-DEPARTURE

Madrid-Barajas Airport is approximately 13km east of the city. A taxi should cost around €25. Metro Line 8 runs every 4-7min, with a journey time of 50min. Chamartin Station is the railway station for services to the north of Spain and France ; Atocha Station for those to the south.

TRANSPORT

Madrid is covered by a bus and metro public transport system. You can buy single journey tickets, but a better bet for longer visits is a ten-trip Metrobus ticket, valid on both bus and metro networks, and better value than tickets bought individually. Get them from underground stations, bus ticket offices, newsstands and tobacconists.

Consider also the Tourist Travel Card, which is valid from one to seven days for unlimited travel on all public transport in Zone A or Zone T in the Madrid region. As well as usual outlets, it's also on sale at the city's two long-distance train stations, Chamartín and Atocha.

It's well worth forking out for a Madrid Card. You can get them for one, two, or three-day periods from a wide range of outlets. They entitle you to travel on all forms of public transport, and grant admission to more than forty museums. They're also valid for discounts in some nightclubs, shops and restaurants.

EXPLORING MADRID

All roads in Spain lead to the Puerta del Sol. This is not as fanciful as it

sounds: the square - where it seems every tourist in Madrid has congregated for orientation guidelines - also bears a symbol on the ground marking Kilometre Zero, considered the centre of Spain's road network. This was once the eastern entrance to Madrid, with a castle and gatehouse. You'd never guess it now. With its iconic 'Tio Pepe' sherry sign leering overhead, the cafés and shops here are a non-stop buzz of activity as visitors plan their itineraries in the surrounding knot of narrow streets. The crescent shaped Puerta del Sol has its charms, but the area's finest square is a little way to the west.

Plaza Mayor is a beautifully arcaded rectangle which has been the focal point over the centuries of everything from bullfights to the trials of the Inquisition. It's still the ceremonial heart of the city, so one day you can expect a fiesta, the next a political rally. Despite all this, it can be surprisingly peaceful here during weekdays, and makes the perfect setting for a coffee or a meal at one of the many cafés whose tables spill out from the arcades. It boasts a distinctly Castilian character, and its theatrical face is best shown above the arcades of the Casa de la Panadería, which is decorated with eye-catching allegorical paintings. Just two hundred metres further west is the third of the old quarter's great squares, **Plaza de la Villa**, an atmospheric space surrounded by many historic buildings, such as the early fifteenth-century **Torre de los Lujanes**, which mixes Gothic embellishments with arches in a dramatic horse-shoe style.

→ REAL HEAD-TURNER

Head even further west, up a steep slope towards the river, and you come to Madrid's ultimate showpiece building: the **Palacio Real**. This is the biggest official royal residence in the world with a bewildering three thousand rooms. It took two 18C Bourbon monarchs twenty eight years to build themselves this cosy little number. You come to it across the huge semi-circular **Plaza de Oriente**, a theatrical concoction in itself. Inside, the show continues, with highlights left, right and centre. These include the superb Throne Room with its sculptures by Velázquez, the main staircase sculpted from Toledo marble, the lavishly decorated Garparini Rooms (all silk, stucco and chinoiserie), the magnificent State Dining Room, and the Royal Armoury, which includes the armour of El Cid and his horse.

Don't get the impression Madrid is all plaza and palaccio. You can come up for air at a number of imposing green spaces. Close to the Palaccio Real is the gracefully sloping **Campo del Moro**, while the western boundary of the city is the massive Casa de Campo, almost seven square miles of tennis courts, swimming pools, funfair, pines and scrubland. Madrid's favourite park, though, is on the eastern side of town. Retiro Park was once a three hundred acre royal palace garden. When it opened to the public in 1869 *madrileños* came in their thousands, and it's still the city's number one destination for chilling out. There's a large boating lake in the middle, and two elegant glasshouses useful for delving around as they house interesting free art exhibitions.

If you're at the Retiro, you're in the city's Bourbon quarter, named after the dynasty which developed it in the eighteenth century. Strolling around the park, there's every chance you've been to, or are heading towards, one of the three fabulous museums in the area: art lovers in this neck of the woods aren't just spoilt for choice, they can positively wallow in it. Top spot goes to the **Prado**, one of the world's great museums and the capital's top cultural attraction. It contains the world's richest assembly of Spanish painting, covering the 12 to 19C, with a magnificent range of works by Velázquez, Goya and El Greco. There's also a wealth of Italian Renaissance masterpieces and Flemish works. Ground floor highlights include Hieronymus Bosch's *The Garden of Earthly Delights*, and *The Annunciation* by Fra Angelico.

→ SEVEN CENTURIES OF ART

Cross the street and you're at another superb artistic offering. The **Museo Thyssen-Bornemisza** was bequeathed to Spain as recently as 1993, and is one of the most important private collections in the world. Installed in an 18C palace, its three floors cover seven centuries of Western art, from Van Eyck, Holbein, Titian, Durer and Rubens (top floor) to the Dutch Golden Age, German Expressionism and French Impressionism (first floor), and ending up with Picasso, Hopper and Freud at ground level. If you have the energy, saunter down the Paseo del Prado for less than half a mile and you'll reach the third of the triumvirate, the **Centro de Arte Reina Sofía**, the city's museum of modern art. Most people come here primarily to take in Picasso's haunting *Guernica*, but when they arrive they're knocked out by the whole place. It's an 18C former hospital, and its exhibition space is vast. The focus is on Spanish work (the 20C was a monumental century for Spanish art), and there are rooms devoted to Miró, Dalí and the surrealist film-maker Luis Buñuel.

→ GRAN TOUR

It's useful to have eyes not only in the back of your head but on top of it too when you're passing along the **Gran Vía**. This is Madrid's bustling main thoroughfare, whose construction started exactly one hundred years ago (1908) and was completed twenty years later. Sure, you have to watch out for the traffic streaming along it, but don't miss the fine 20C buildings towering above you, either. They represent a vivid panorama of modern architecture, from neo-classical to art deco. Gran Vía even has a structure straight out of a Jimmy Cagney movie: the 1920s **Telefónica** building is a slightly squashed version of a Manhattan skyscraper. A different style of street, and a different style of window gazing, can be found further east in the Salamanca district. Here you'll come across wide, sophisticated boulevards on a grid system where the shops and boutiques are of the smartly expensive variety.

Madrid is a hip and happening place wherever you turn at whatever time of day, and tourists from, say, northern Europe may have to adjust their body clocks to the city's late hour culture. However, even in this city, there are two areas just north of Gran Vía that are instantly recognisable for their extra cool vibe. **Chueca** and **Malasaña** have an arty, bohemian feel, defined by hip bars and sassy little shops. Chueca is the gay/lesbian quarter of the city; Malasaña's grungy ambience is, if anything, heightened by its charming cobbled streets, fountains and trees. Whichever quarter you hit on, you won't forget the nightlife in a hurry.

CALENDAR HIGHLIGHTS

The highlight of the year comes in May: the Fiesta de San Isidro, the feast of the region's patron saint. For a week either side of the fifteenth, the city pulsates with fiestas, music and dance; focal points are the Plaza Mayor and Jardines de las Vistillas. Just before this, on 2 May, Dos de Mayo

MADRID IN...

→ ONE DAY

Puerta del Sol, Plaza Mayor, Palacio Real, Prado

→ TWO DAYS

Museo Thyssen-Bornemisza, Retiro, Gran Vía, tapas at a traditional taberna

→ THREE DAYS

Chueca, Malasaña, Centro de Arte Reina Sofía

festivities in Malasaña commemorate a rebellion against French occupying forces: there could be quite a party in 2008 as it's the two hundredth anniversary. A more sedate air surrounds the Madrid Book Fair in Retiro Park at the end of the month. The summer's main festival is Los Veranos de la Villa, a series of concerts featuring international musicians in various city venues: for two months, Madrid is ablaze with opera, tango, flamenco, jazz, Spanish musicals, exhibitions and films. September sees Festival de Otoño, when drama, ballet and opera descend upon they city's concert venues. One of the most colourful sights of the Madrid winter is the Twelfth Night procession (5 January) which goes from Retiro to Plaza Mayor and is full of floats and accompanying animals. Art lovers don their coats and scarves and head for ARCO in February: this is the city's internationally renowned contemporary art fair, held in Parque Ferial Juan Carlos I. And then there's Carnaval, with fancy dress parties and a parade from Plaza de Colón to Plaza de Cibeles. Día de Cervantes (23 April) celebrates the great author's death with a book fair in Alcalá de Henares.

EATING OUT

Madrileños know how to pace themselves. Breakfast is around 10am, lunch 2pm or 3pm, 5pm is the beginning of the afternoon and dinner won't be until 10pm or 11pm. A late night? Until dawn the next day or later. Madrid is the European capital which has best managed to absorb the regional cuisine of the country, largely due to massive internal migration to the city. Spain has the highest bar-restaurant per inhabitant ratio in Europe, and Madrid clocks in with one bar-restaurant per 171 inhabitants. Strange as it may seem given its geography, the quality and range of fish available in Madrid is exceptional: it's the second largest central fish market in the world, after Tokyo. Two reasons: it's established a land port in the nearby town of Coslada, and ocean fresh seafood is transported to the capital on a daily basis from the Galician coast. If you want to tuck into local specialities, you'll find them everywhere around the city. But what to try? *Callos a la madrileña* is Madrid-style tripe, dating back to 1559, while *sopas de Ajo* (garlic soup) is a favourite on cold winter days. Another popular soup (also a main course) is *cocido madrileño*, hearty and aromatic and comprised of chick peas, meat, tocino belly pork, potatoes and vegetables, slowly cooked in a rich broth. Two top fish dishes are *besugo a la madrileña* (baked sea bream with white wine, parsley and potatoes), and *bacalao a la madrileña* (Madrid-style cod, with potatoes, onions, tomatoes, garlic and olive oil). Or, of course, there's always the ubiquitous *tortilla de patata* (potato omelette) found in any bar, taberna or cafetería. To experience the real Madrid dining ambience, get to a traditional taberna in the heart of the old neighbourhood: there are about one hundred remaining in the area, distinguished by large clock, carved wooden bar with zinc counter and wine flasks, marble table tops and ceramic tiles. At the end of a meal, the bill will include service, but tips in cash are commonplace: around five per cent of the total.

→ THE OLDEST

A taberna to make for when in the old town is Botín. The roast suckling pig on offer is renowned throughout Spain, and Ernest Hemingway was known to tuck in here. The establishment's real claim to fame, though, is its appearance in the Guinness Book of Records: it dates back to 1725, making it the oldest restaurant in the world.

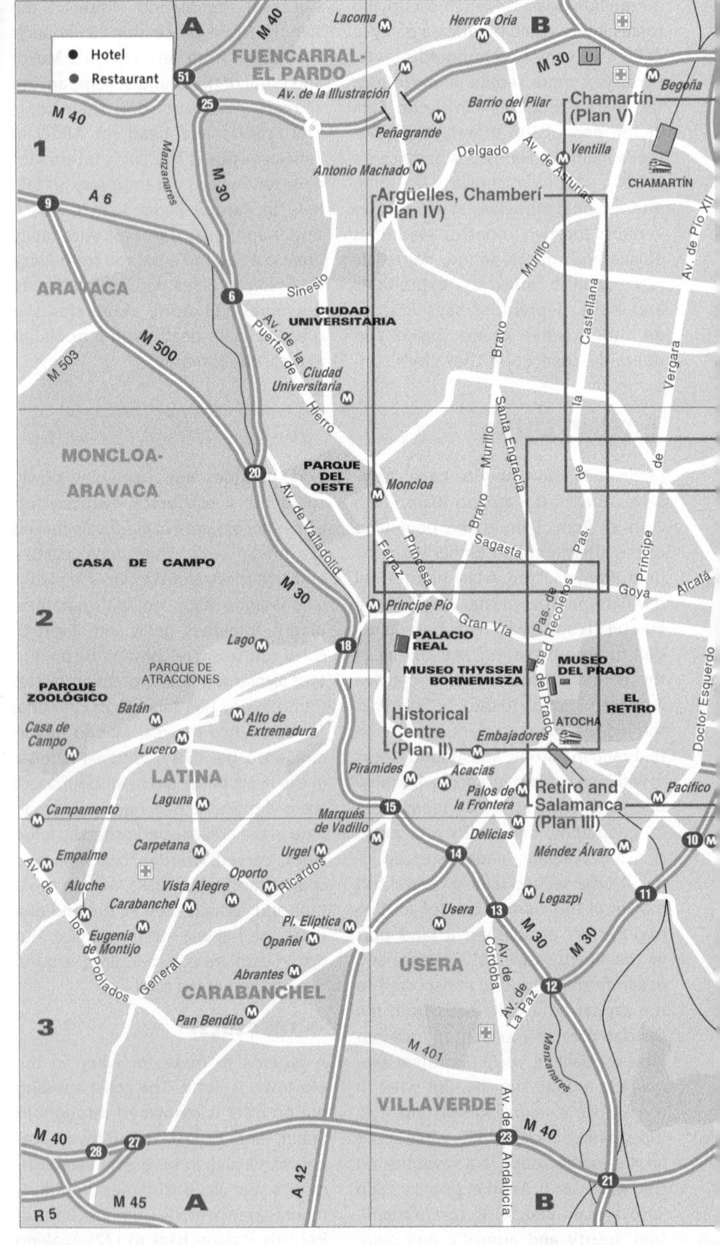
Hotel
Restaurant
A
B
1
2
3
FUENCARRAL-EL PARDO
ARAVACA
MONCLOA-ARAVACA
CASA DE CAMPO
CIUDAD UNIVERSITARIA
PARQUE DEL OESTE
PALACIO REAL
MUSEO THYSSEN BORNEMISZA
MUSEO DEL PRADO
EL RETIRO
ATOCHA
CHAMARTÍN
PARQUE DE ATRACCIONES
PARQUE ZOOLÓGICO
LATINA
CARABANCHEL
USERA
VILLAVERDE
Chamartín (Plan V)
Argüelles, Chamberí (Plan IV)
Historical Centre (Plan II)
Retiro and Salamanca (Plan III)
Lacoma
Herrera Oria
Begoña
Barrio del Pilar
Peñagrande
Antonio Machado
Ventilla
Moncloa
Príncipe Pío
Lago
Batán
Casa de Campo
Lucero
Alto de Extremadura
Laguna
Campamento
Pirámides
Acacias
Embajadores
Palos de la Frontera
Pacífico
Marqués de Vadillo
Delicias
Méndez Álvaro
Carpetana
Empalme
Urgel
Oporto
Aluche
Vista Alegre
Carabanchel
Legazpi
Usera
Eugenia de Montijo
Pl. Elíptica
Opañel
Abrantes
Pan Bendito
Ciudad Universitaria
Av. de la Illustración
Delgado
Av. de Asturias
Sinesio
Av. de la Puerta de Hierro
Av. de Valladolid
Murillo
Bravo Murillo
Santa Engracia
Castellana
Pas. de la Castellana
Av. de Pío XII
Vergara
Príncipe de Vergara
Sagasta
Ferraz
Princesa
Gran Vía
Goya
Alcalá
Pas. de Recoletos
Pas. del Prado
Doctor Esquerdo
Ricardos
General Ricardos
Av. de los Poblados
Av. de Córdoba
Av. de La Paz
Av. de Andalucía
Manzanares
M 40
M 30
M 500
M 503
M 401
M 45
A 6
A 42
R 5
U

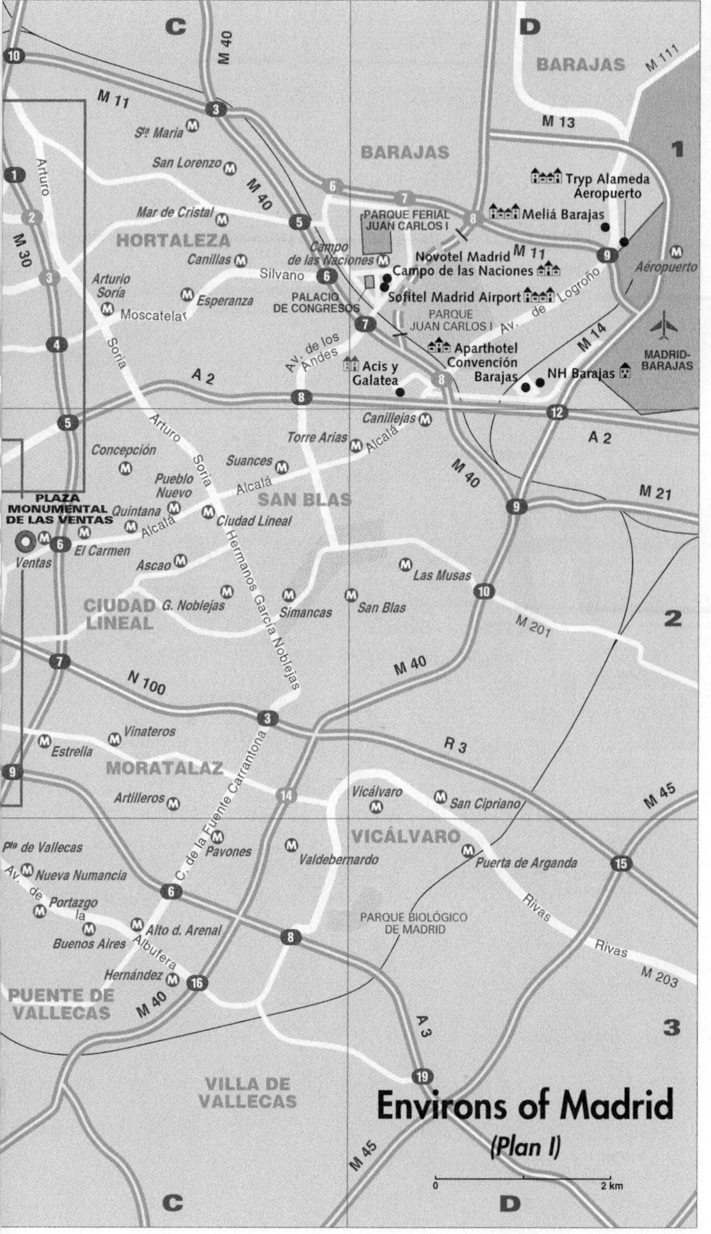

Environs of Madrid
(Plan I)
BARAJAS
HORTALEZA
SAN BLAS
CIUDAD LINEAL
MORATALAZ
VICÁLVARO
PUENTE DE VALLECAS
VILLA DE VALLECAS
Tryp Alameda Aeropuerto
Meliá Barajas
Novotel Madrid Campo de las Naciones
Sofitel Madrid Airport
Aparthotel Convención Barajas
NH Barajas
Acis y Galatea
PARQUE FERIAL JUAN CARLOS I
PALACIO DE CONGRESOS
PARQUE JUAN CARLOS I
MADRID-BARAJAS
PLAZA MONUMENTAL DE LAS VENTAS
PARQUE BIOLÓGICO DE MADRID
Aéropuerto
Sta María
San Lorenzo
Mar de Cristal
Canillas
Campo de las Naciones
Arturio Soría
Esperanza
Moscatelar
Silvano
Av. de los Andes
Av. de Logroño
Canillejas
Torre Arias
Alcalá
Suances
Concepción
Pueblo Nuevo
Quintana
Ciudad Lineal
Ventas
El Carmen
Ascao
G. Noblejas
Simancas
San Blas
Las Musas
Hermanos García Noblejas
Arturo Soria
Vinateros
Estrella
Artilleros
C. de la Fuente Carrantona
Vicálvaro
San Cipriano
Pavones
Valdebernardo
Puerta de Arganda
Pte de Vallecas
Nueva Numancia
Portazgo
Av. de la Albufera
Buenos Aires
Alto d. Arenal
Hernández
Rivas
M 11
M 40
M 30
M 13
M 111
M 14
A 2
M 21
M 201
N 100
R 3
M 45
M 203
A 3
0
2 km
C
D
1
2
3

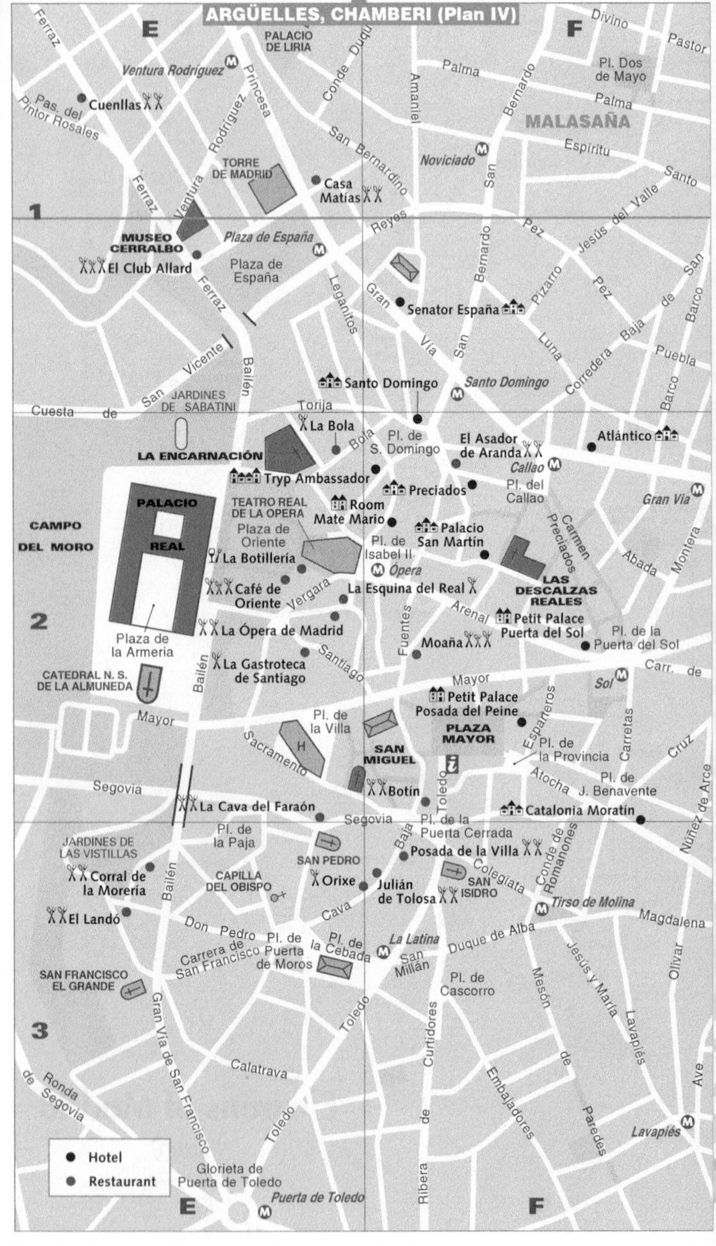
ARGÜELLES, CHAMBERI (Plan IV)
PALACIO DE LIRIA
Ventura Rodríguez
Cuenllas
TORRE DE MADRID
Casa Matías
MUSEO CERRALBO
El Club Allard
Plaza de España
Senator España
MALASAÑA
Noviciado
Santo Domingo
JARDINES DE SABATINI
LA ENCARNACIÓN
La Bola
Pl. de S. Domingo
El Asador de Aranda
Atlántico
Callao
Tryp Ambassador
Preciados
Pl. del Callao
Gran Vía
PALACIO REAL
TEATRO REAL DE LA OPERA
Room Mate Mario
Plaza de Oriente
CAMPO DEL MORO
Palacio San Martín
Pl. de Isabel II
Ópera
La Botillería
Café de Oriente
La Esquina del Real
LAS DESCALZAS REALES
Petit Palace Puerta del Sol
La Ópera de Madrid
Moaña
Pl. de la Puerta del Sol
Plaza de la Armeria
La Gastroteca de Santiago
CATEDRAL N. S. DE LA ALMUNEDA
Sol
Petit Palace Posada del Peine
Pl. de la Villa
PLAZA MAYOR
SAN MIGUEL
Pl. de la Provincia
Pl. de J. Benavente
Botín
La Cava del Faraón
Catalonia Moratín
Pl. de la Paja
Pl. de la Puerta Cerrada
JARDINES DE LAS VISTILLAS
SAN PEDRO
Posada de la Villa
Corral de la Morería
CAPILLA DEL OBISPO
Orixe
Julián de Tolosa
SAN ISIDRO
Tirso de Molina
El Landó
Pl. de Puerta de Moros
Pl. de la Cebada
La Latina
Pl. de Cascorro
SAN FRANCISCO EL GRANDE
Lavapiés
Glorieta de Puerta de Toledo
Puerta de Toledo
Hotel
Restaurant

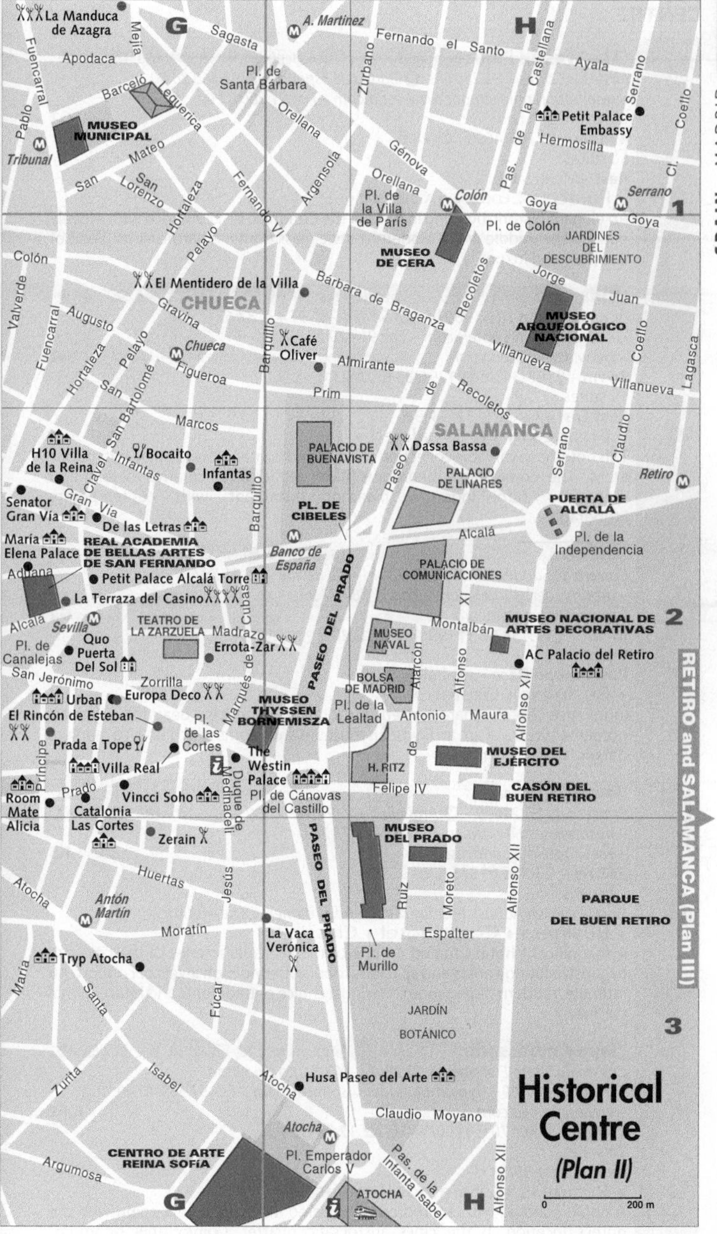
Historical Centre (Plan II)
RETIRO and SALAMANCA (Plan III)
La Manduca de Azagra
MUSEO MUNICIPAL
El Mentidero de la Villa
CHUECA
Café Oliver
H10 Villa de la Reina
Bocaito
Infantas
Senator Gran Vía
De las Letras
María Elena Palace
REAL ACADEMIA DE BELLAS ARTES DE SAN FERNANDO
Petit Palace Alcalá Torre
La Terraza del Casino
TEATRO DE LA ZARZUELA
Errota-Zar
Quo Puerta Del Sol
Urban
Europa Deco
El Rincón de Esteban
Prada a Tope
Villa Real
Room Mate Alicia
Catalonia Las Cortes
Vincci Soho
Zerain
The Westin Palace
MUSEO THYSSEN BORNEMISZA
Tryp Atocha
La Vaca Verónica
Husa Paseo del Arte
CENTRO DE ARTE REINA SOFíA
ATOCHA
MUSEO DE CERA
MUSEO ARQUEOLÓGICO NACIONAL
JARDINES DEL DESCUBRIMIENTO
Petit Palace Embassy
SALAMANCA
Dassa Bassa
PALACIO DE BUENAVISTA
PL. DE CIBELES
PALACIO DE LINARES
PUERTA DE ALCALÁ
PALACIO DE COMUNICACIONES
MUSEO NACIONAL DE ARTES DECORATIVAS
AC Palacio del Retiro
MUSEO NAVAL
BOLSA DE MADRID
H. RITZ
MUSEO DEL EJÉRCITO
CASÓN DEL BUEN RETIRO
MUSEO DEL PRADO
PARQUE DEL BUEN RETIRO
JARDÍN BOTÁNICO
PASEO DEL PRADO
Paseo de Recoletos
Pas. de la Castellana
Pl. de Colón
Pl. de la Independencia
Pl. de Cánovas del Castillo
Pl. de Murillo
Pl. Emperador Carlos V
Pl. de Santa Bárbara
Pl. de la Villa de París
Pl. de Canalejas
Pl. de las Cortes
Pl. de la Lealtad
Tribunal
A. Martínez
Colón
Serrano
Chueca
Retiro
Banco de España
Sevilla
Antón Martín
Atocha
Fuencarral
Sagasta
Fernando el Santo
Génova
Goya
Gran Vía
Alcalá
Huertas
Atocha
Moratín
Claudio Moyano
Alfonso XII
Argumosa
200 m
G
H
1
2
3

The Westin Palace

pl. de las Cortes 7 ✉ 28014 – Ⓜ Banco de España – ✆ 91 360 80 00 – reservation.palacemadrid@westin.com – Fax 91 360 81 00 – www.westin.com **G2**

418 rm – ††209/469 €, ☕ 28 €
50 suites
Rest – Menu 54 €
♦ Palace ♦ Luxury ♦ Classic ♦

An elegant historic building in front of the Congreso de Diputados with a lovely patio in the middle and a Modernist-style glass dome. A harmonious blend of tradition and luxury.

Villa Real

Smokers rest.

pl. de las Cortes 10 ✉ 28014 – Ⓜ Sevilla – ✆ 91 420 37 67 – villareal@derbyhotels.com – Fax 91 420 25 47 – www.derbyhotels.com **G2**

96 rm – †168/343 € ††179/383 €, ☕ 21 €
19 suites
Rest *East 47* – Carte 32/58 €
♦ Business ♦ Personalised ♦

This hotel has a valuable collection of Greek and Roman art on display in its public areas. The comfortable bedrooms have attractive decorative details and mahogany furnishings. A pleasant restaurant with contemporary lithographs.

Urban

Carrera de San Jerónimo 34 ✉ 28014 – Ⓜ Sevilla – ✆ 91 787 77 70 – urban@derbyhotels.com – Fax 91 787 77 99 – www.derbyhotels.com **G2**

87 rm – †199/387 € ††199/430 €, ☕ 20 €
9 suites
Rest *Europa Deco* – see below
♦ Business ♦ Design ♦

Innovative hotel, characterized by quality materials, beautiful lighting, numerous works of art, an Egyptian museum and rooms which boast a range of details.

Husa Princesa

Smokers rest.

Princesa 40 ✉ 28008 – Ⓜ Argüelles – ✆ 91 542 21 00 – husaprincesa@husa.es – Fax 91 542 73 28 – www.hotelhusaprincesa.com *Plan IV* **K3**

263 rm – †300 € ††375 €, ☕ 25 €
12 suites
Rest – *(closed August, Sunday and Monday dinner)* Carte 46/60 €
♦ Business ♦ Chain hotel ♦ Classic ♦

A magnificent hotel situated on one of the principal arteries of the city with expansive lounge areas and spacious rooms offering high levels of comfort. An intimate, modern dining room offering a choice of traditional and international cuisine.

Tryp Ambassador

Smokers rest.

Cuesta de Santo Domingo 5 ✉ 28013 – Ⓜ Santo Domingo – ✆ 91 541 67 00 – tryp.ambassador@solmelia.com – Fax 91 559 10 40 – www.solmelia.com **E-F2**

159 rm – †80/170 € ††90/240 €, ☕ 17.50 €
24 suites
Rest – Carte 35/51 €
♦ Business ♦ Chain hotel ♦ Classic ♦

A noble building with an impressive covered inner patio in keeping with the hotel's location in the city's aristocratic quarter. Comfortable bedrooms embellished with elegant, high-quality furnishings. The glass-roofed restaurant has the feel of a winter garden.

De las Letras

Gran Vía 11 ✉ 28013 – Ⓜ Sevilla – ✆ 91 523 79 80 – info@hoteldelasletras.com – Fax 91 523 79 81 – www.hoteldelasletras.com **G2**

103 rm – ♦♦198/264 €, ☕ 15 €

Rest – Carte 35/45 €

♦ Business ♦ Design ♦

The restored exterior is in distinct contrast to the colourful and contemporary interior. New York-style design features in the guestrooms, with their discreet lighting and poems on the walls. A modern, original restaurant where diners can create their own dishes.

Vincci Soho

No smokers rest.

Prado 18 ✉ 28014 – Ⓜ Antón Martín – ✆ 91 141 41 00 – reservas.soho@vinccihoteles.com – Fax 91 141 41 01 – www.vinccihoteles.com **G2**

167 rm – ♦♦81/390 €, ☕ 15 € – 2 suites

Rest – Carte approx. 40 €

♦ Business ♦ Personalised ♦

The completely renovated interior is a surprising fusion of avant-garde and minimalist décor in a distinctly relaxed and low-key ambience. Well-appointed and comfortable bedrooms. Attractive and bright restaurant and café.

María Elena Palace

Aduana 19 ✉ 28013 – Ⓜ Sol – ✆ 91 360 49 30 – mariaelenapalace@chh.es – Fax 91 360 47 89 – www.chh.es **G2**

87 rm ☕ – ♦100/225 € ♦♦115/350 €

Rest – Menu 23 €

♦ Business ♦ Traditional ♦ Classic ♦

This hotel boasts a spacious main lounge and a magnificent covered patio crowned by a glass roof. Classically styled, carpeted guestrooms with quality furnishings and marble bathrooms.

Catalonia Las Cortes

No smokers rest.

Prado 6 ✉ 28014 – Ⓜ Antón Martín – ✆ 91 389 60 51 – lascortes@hoteles-catalonia.es – Fax 91 389 60 52 – www.hoteles-catalonia.com **G2**

65 rm – ♦99/227 € ♦♦99/265 €, ☕ 15 €

Rest – *(dinner only)* Menu 23 €

♦ Traditional ♦ Classic ♦

This 18C palace once belonged to the Duke of Noblejas. Bright interior which combines the traditional and contemporary. Well-appointed guestrooms.

Senator España

No smokers rest.

Gran Vía 70 ✉ 28013 – Ⓜ Plaza de España – ✆ 91 522 82 65 – senator.espana@playasenator.com – Fax 91 522 82 64 – www.playasenator.com **F1**

171 rm – ♦70/242 € ♦♦80/294 €, ☕ 17 €

Rest – Menu 17 €

♦ Business ♦ Chain hotel ♦ Functional ♦

Excellent leisure facilities, including a beauty centre and hydromassage pools. The hotel's bedrooms are fully sound-proofed and well-appointed. The restaurant offers diners the combination of a salad buffet and a reasonably creative menu.

H10 Villa de la Reina

Gran Vía 22 ✉ 28013 – Ⓜ Gran Via – ✆ 91 523 91 01 – h10.villa.delareina@h10.es – Fax 91 521 75 22 – www.h10hotels.com **G2**

73 rm ☕ – ♦100/325 € ♦♦120/500 € – 1 suite

Rest – *(dinner only)* Carte approx. 28 €

♦ Business ♦ Chain hotel ♦ Stylish ♦

An attractive building from the early part of the last century, with an entrance-reception area adorned with attractive marble and wood. The charm of yesteryear has been retained in the hotel, which offers guests high levels of comfort in every room.

Infantas Smokers rest.

Infantas 29 ✉ 28004 – Ⓜ Chueca – ✆ 91 521 28 28 – hotelinfantas@lussohoteles.com – Fax 91 521 66 88 – www.lussohoteles.com **G2**

40 rm – 70/250 €, 13 €

Rest *Ex Libris* – Carte 28/42 €

♦ Business ♦ Modern ♦

Housed in a old building which has been completely remodelled into a hotel with a decor that is resolutely modern in style. Fully equipped bedrooms and bathrooms. A minimalist feel in the restaurant, with its creative menu.

Palacio San Martín No smokers rest.

pl. San Martín 5 ✉ 28013 – Ⓜ Callao – ✆ 91 701 50 00 – sanmartin@intur.com – Fax 91 701 50 10 – www.intur.com **F2**

93 rm – 115/180 € 115/223 €, 16 € – 1 suite

Rest – *(closed August, Sunday and Bank Holidays)* Menu 35 €

♦ Business ♦ Stylish ♦

A historic building which in the 1950s was the United States Embassy. A patio with a glass roof serves as a lounge area. Traditional-style bedrooms, plus a panoramic restaurant on the top floor.

Husa Paseo del Arte

Atocha 123 ✉ 28012 – Ⓜ Atocha – ✆ 91 298 48 00 – paseodelarte@husa.es – Fax 91 298 48 50 – www.husa.es **G3**

260 rm – 80/250 €, 18 €

Rest – Menu 23 €

♦ Business ♦ Modern ♦

As its name would imply, this hotel is ideally located to visit Madrid's most famous museums. Bright and spacious public areas, along with functional bedrooms with good-quality furnishings. The restaurant occupies the inner patio with its glass roof and small garden.

Room Mate Alicia

Prado 2 ✉ 28014 – Ⓜ Sevilla – ✆ 91 389 60 95 – alicia@room-matehoteles.com – Fax 91 369 47 95 – www.room-matehoteles.com **G2**

34 rm – 90/170 €

Rest – *(coffee shop only)*

♦ Business ♦ Modern ♦

A well-restored old building and façade with a contrasting modern interior. Spacious, well-appointed guestrooms embellished with designer furniture.

Senator Gran Vía No smokers rest.

Gran Vía 21 ✉ 28013 – Ⓜ Gran Vía – ✆ 91 531 41 51 – senator.granvia@playasenator.com – Fax 91 524 07 99 – www.playasenator.com **G2**

136 rm – 82/230 € 92/280 €, 13 €

Rest – Carte 30/45 €

♦ Business ♦ Chain hotel ♦ Functional ♦

Behind the Senator's distinctive classical façade is an interior with the latest in modern comforts, including avant-garde bedrooms. Dining options include a simply-styled restaurant offering à la carte and buffet dining and a spacious cafeteria.

Santo Domingo No smokers rest.

(under refurbishment), pl. de Santo Domingo 13 ✉ 28013 – Ⓜ Santo Domingo – ✆ 91 547 98 00 – reserva@hotelsantodomingo.com – Fax 91 547 59 95 – www.hotelsantodomingo.com **F2**

120 rm – 116/160 € 147/199 €, 12.40 €

Rest – Menu 33 €

♦ Business ♦ Traditional ♦ Personalised ♦

Numerous works of art decorate the walls of this hotel. Comfortable rooms with modern bathrooms, some with hydro-massage baths.

Preciados
Preciados 37 ✉ 28013 – Ⓜ Callao – ☎ 91 454 44 00 – preciadoshotel@preciadoshotel.com – Fax 91 454 44 01 – www.preciadoshotel.com **F2**
68 rm – 🚹95/160 € 🚹🚹105/220 €, ☕ 15 € – 5 suites
Rest – Carte 31/40 €
♦ Business ♦ Modern ♦
The severe 19C classicism of this hotel's architecture is in complete contrast to its modern and well-appointed facilities. A small but pleasant lounge.

Tryp Atocha without rest
Atocha 83 ✉ 28012 – Ⓜ Antón Martín – ☎ 91 330 05 00 – tryp.atocha@solmelia.com – Fax 91 420 15 60 – www.solmelia.com **G3**
150 rm – 🚹110/170 € 🚹🚹130/190 €, ☕ 19 €
♦ Business ♦ Chain hotel ♦ Functional ♦
This small palace dating from 1913 offers guests modern, functional facilities. The spacious lounge areas include the glass-adorned "salón de actos" and a superb staircase.

Catalonia Moratín without rest
Atocha 23 ✉ 28012 – Ⓜ Sol – ☎ 91 369 71 71 – moratin@hoteles-catalonia.es – Fax 91 360 12 31 – www.hoteles-catalonia.es **F2-3**
59 rm – 🚹70/165 € 🚹🚹90/198 €, ☕ 15 € – 4 suites
♦ Business ♦ Chain hotel ♦ Functional ♦
An 18C building combining original features, such as the staircase, and other more practical designs. Inner patio with a glass roof, plus modern bedrooms.

Atlántico without rest
Gran Vía 38 ✉ 28013 – Ⓜ Callao – ☎ 91 522 64 80 – informacion@hotelatlantico.es – Fax 91 531 02 10 – www.hotelatlantico.es **F2**
116 rm – 🚹100/150 € 🚹🚹120/200 €, ☕ 11 €
♦ Business ♦ Family ♦ Classic ♦
The comfort in this centrally located mansion has increased following a recent expansion. Harmonious décor in the bedrooms with matching wallpaper and curtains.

Husa Moncloa
Serrano Jover 1 ✉ 28015 – Ⓜ Argüelles – ☎ 91 542 45 85 – husamoncloa@husa.es – Fax 91 542 71 69 – www.hotelhusamoncloa.com *Plan IV* **K3**
116 rm – 🚹199 € 🚹🚹220 €, ☕ 18.50 € – 12 suites
Rest – *(in Hotel Husa Princesa)*
♦ Business ♦ Chain hotel ♦ Classic ♦
This hotel functions as an annexe to the Hotel Husa Princesa, which provides most of its guest services apart from breakfast. Large, well-equipped bedrooms.

Petit Palace Alcalá Torre without rest
Virgen de los Peligros 2 ✉ 28013 – Ⓜ Sevilla – ☎ 91 532 19 01 – alcala@hthoteles.com – Fax 91 522 91 30 – www.hthoteles.com **G2**
66 rm – 🚹🚹95/320 €, ☕ 14 €
♦ Chain hotel ♦ Minimalist ♦
An historic building with an unusual layout. Modern, functional furnishings associated with this hotel chain, plus hydromassage showers and fine views of the tower from guest bedrooms.

Petit Palace Puerta del Sol without rest
Arenal 4 ✉ 28013 – Ⓜ Sol – ☎ 91 521 05 42 – sol@hthoteles.com – Fax 91 521 05 61 – www.hthoteles.com **F2**
64 rm – 🚹🚹70/290 €, ☕ 10 €
♦ Chain hotel ♦ Functional ♦
A modern hotel with a spacious reception, lounge area and free Internet access zone. Functional bedrooms with hydromassage showers.

Quo Puerta Del Sol without rest

Sevilla 4 ✉ 28014 – Ⓜ Sevilla – ✆ 91 532 90 49 – puertadelsol@hotelesquo.com – Fax 91 531 28 34 – www.hotelesquo.com **G2**

61 rm – 122/240 € 122/300 €, 16 € – 1 suite

♦ Business ♦ Design ♦

The hotel's excellent facilities and refined minimalist décor more than compensate for the lack of public areas and bedrooms that are on the small side.

Petit Palace Posada del Peine without rest

Postas 17 ✉ 28012 – Ⓜ Sol – ✆ 91 523 81 51 – pos@hthoteles.com – Fax 91 523 29 93 – www.hthoteles.com **F2**

69 rm – 85/320 €, 14 €

♦ Chain hotel ♦ Functional ♦

A truly historic address, dating back to the year 1610. Completely renovated, the hotel offers guests comfortable surroundings with attractive decorative touches and the latest technology.

Room Mate Mario without rest

Campomanes 4 ✉ 28013 – ✆ 91 548 85 48 – mario@room-matehoteles.com – Fax 91 559 12 88 – www.room-matehoteles.com **F2**

54 rm – 80/160 € 90/170 €

♦ Chain hotel ♦ Modern ♦

This small hotel is characterised by its decorative, avant-garde design which combines an eclectic mix of colours, styles and furniture. Well-appointed bedrooms.

La Terraza del Casino (Paco Roncero)

Alcalá 15-3° ✉ 28014 – Ⓜ Sevilla – ✆ 91 521 87 00 – laterraza@casinodemadrid.es – Fax 91 523 44 36 – www.casinodemadrid.es

closed August, Saturday lunch, Sunday and Bank Holidays **G2**

Rest – Menu 110 € – Carte 75/95 €

Spec. Queso de aceite de oliva virgen extra variedad arbequina al parmesano. San Pedro con texturas de limón. Hígado de pato con garbanzos esféricos y su consomé.

♦ Inventive ♦ Formal ♦

In the 19C Madrid Casino building. The lounges have a classy feel and the very attractive terrace is a delightful setting in which to eat.

El Club Allard (Diego Guerrero) Smokers rest.

Ferraz 2 ✉ 28008 – Ⓜ Plaza España – ✆ 91 559 09 39 – mpellicer@elcluballard.com – Fax 91 559 12 29

closed August, Saturday lunch, Sunday and Monday dinner **E1**

Rest – Menu 65 € – Carte 42/58 €

Spec. Las huevas con pan y panceta sobre crema ligera de patata. Cochinillo confitado con canela, manzana y comino. Tatin con cremoso de zanahoria y helado de queso.

♦ Inventive ♦ Formal ♦

Occupying the ground floor of a early-20C modernist building, with a traditionally styled dining room with a high ceiling. Creative, innovative cuisine based around fresh market produce.

Café de Oriente

pl. de Oriente 2 ✉ 28013 – Ⓜ Ópera – ✆ 91 547 15 64 – cafeoriente@grupolezama.com – Fax 91 547 77 07 – www.grupolezama.es **E2**

Rest – Carte 46/59 €

♦ International ♦ Formal ♦

In front of the Palacio Real with a luxury café and an attractive wine cellar-style dining room. International menu with a modern twist.

La Manduca de Azagra

Sagasta 14 ✉ 28004 – Ⓜ Alonso Martínez – ✆ 91 591 01 12 – Fax 91 591 01 13

closed August, Sunday and Bank Holidays **G1**

Rest – Carte 37/46 €

♦ Navarrese specialities ♦ Minimalist ♦

A privileged central location for this spacious restaurant with a minimalist feel in both its design and lighting. The cuisine here is based on quality products.

XXX **Moaña**

Hileras 4 ✉ 28013 – Ⓜ Ópera – ☏ 91 548 29 14 – Fax 91 541 65 98
closed Sunday dinner **F2**
Rest – Carte 43/70 €
♦ Galician specialities ♦ Formal ♦
A hotel with an elegant and comfortable feel in the heart of the old quarter. Bar, a number of private rooms and a live fish and seafood tank.

XX **El Mentidero de la Villa** No smokers rest.

Santo Tomé 6 ✉ 28004 – Ⓜ Chueca – ☏ 91 308 12 85 – info@mentiderodelavilla.com – Fax 91 651 34 88 – www.elmentiderodelavilla.es
closed August, Saturday lunch, Sunday and Bank Holidays **G1**
Rest – Carte 40/55 €
♦ International ♦ Cosy ♦
A welcoming, intimate restaurant with a well-conceived layout and original décor. Exquisite culinary preparation of daring international cuisine.

XX **Errota-Zar**

Jovellanos 3-1° ✉ 28014 – Ⓜ Sevilla – ☏ 91 531 97 90 – errota@errota-zar.com – Fax 91 531 25 64 – www.errota-zar.com
closed Holy Week, 26 July-28 August, Sunday and Bank Holidays **G2**
Rest – Carte 45/51 €
♦ Basque ♦ Family ♦
In front of the Zarzuela theatre. The sober but elegant dining room serves Basque cuisine accompanied by an extensive wine and cigar list. One private room is also available.

XX **Casa Matías**

San Leonardo 12 ✉ 28015 – Ⓜ Plaza de España – ☏ 91 541 76 83 – Fax 91 541 93 70 – www.casamatias.es
closed Sunday dinner **E1**
Rest – Carte 40/49 €
♦ Grills ♦ Rustic ♦
This Basque-style cider house, adorned with large casks of its trademark brew for customers to taste, has two spacious rustic-modern rooms, one with an open grill.

XX **Julián de Tolosa** Smokers rest.

Cava Baja 18 ✉ 28005 – Ⓜ La Latina – ☏ 91 365 82 10 – Fax 91 366 33 08
closed Sunday dinner **F3**
Rest – Carte approx. 46 €
♦ Grills ♦ Rustic ♦
A pleasant restaurant in neo-rustic style offering the best T-bone steaks in the city. The limited menu is more than compensated for by the quality of the food.

XX **Posada de la Villa**

Cava Baja 9 ✉ 28005 – Ⓜ La Latina – ☏ 91 366 18 60 – povisa@posadadelavilla.com – Fax 91 366 70 90 – www.posadadelavilla.com
closed August and Sunday dinner except May **F3**
Rest – Carte 25/42 €
♦ Spanish ♦ Rustic ♦
An old inn with a friendly ambience and Castilian décor. Regional menu and traditional roasts cooked in a wood-fired oven. Madrid-style chickpea stew a speciality.

XX **Europa Decó** – Hotel Urban

Carrera de San Jerónimo 34 ✉ 28014 – Ⓜ Sevilla – ☏ 91 787 77 80 – europadeco@derbyhotels.com – Fax 91 787 77 70 – www.derbyhotels.com
closed August, Saturday lunch, Sunday and Bank Holidays **G2**
Rest – Carte 59/70 €
♦ Inventive ♦ Trendy ♦
The name on everyone's lips, with its innovative design and excellent restaurant, serving Mediterranean and international fusion cuisine, produced using both fresh local produce and more exotic ingredients.

XX **El Asador de Aranda** AC VISA MC AE ①

Preciados 44 ✉ 28013 – Ⓜ Callao – ☎ 91 547 21 56 – Fax 91 556 62 02 – www.asadordearanda.com

closed 21 July-10 August and Monday dinner **F2**

Rest – Carte approx. 40 €

♦ Roast lamb ♦ Rustic ♦

An attractive Castilian restaurant with beautiful wood ceilings. Traditional dishes and roast meats cooked in a wood fired oven a speciality.

XX **La Ópera de Madrid** No smokers rest. AC VISA MC AE ①

Amnistía 5 ✉ 28013 – Ⓜ Ópera – ☎ 91 559 50 92 – Fax 91 559 50 92 – www.laoperarestaurante.com

closed August and Sunday **E2**

Rest – Carte 30/40 €

♦ International ♦ Cosy ♦

A good place to start an evening out or to discuss a play seen in the nearby theatre while enjoying something delicious. Elegant décor and a well-balanced menu.

XX **El Landó** Smokers rest. AC ⇔ VISA MC AE ①

pl. Gabriel Miró 8 ✉ 28005 – Ⓜ La Latina – ☎ 91 366 76 81 – ellando@telefonica.net – Fax 91 366 25 56

closed Holy Week, August and Sunday **E3**

Rest – Carte 46/60 €

♦ Spanish ♦ Formal ♦

Near to the Basílica de San Francisco el Grande, this restaurant has a bar, dining room in the basement and private room, all classically furnished with a profusion of wood.

XX **Cuenllas** AC ⇔ VISA MC AE ①

Ferraz 5 ✉ 28008 – Ⓜ Ventura Rodríguez – ☎ 91 542 56 21 – f.cuenllas@cuenllas.com – Fax 91 559 79 01 – www.cuenllas.com

closed 1 to 7 January, Holy Week and 15 days in August **E1**

Rest – Carte approx. 48 €

♦ Inventive ♦ Formal ♦

Restaurant along modern lines, split over two floors, with two reduced-capacity dining rooms, various private rooms and a wine-bar at the entrance. Creative cuisine and an excellent wine cellar.

XX **Corral de la Morería** No smokers rest. AC VISA MC AE ①

Morería 17 ✉ 28005 – Ⓜ Ópera – ☎ 91 365 84 46 – info@corraldelamoreria.com – Fax 91 364 12 19 – www.corraldelamoreria.com **E3**

Rest – Flamenco show – *(dinner only)* Carte 52/70 €

♦ Spanish ♦ Musical ♦

A restaurant with a top-class Flamenco show and tables set tightly together around the stage. Various gastronomic menus, plus à la carte dining.

XX **Botín** No smokers rest. AC VISA MC AE ①

Cuchilleros 17 ✉ 28005 – Ⓜ Sol – ☎ 91 366 42 17 – Fax 91 366 84 94 – www.botin.es **F2**

Rest – Carte 30/46 €

♦ Spanish ♦ Rustic ♦

Founded in 1725 and said to be the oldest restaurant in the world. The old-style décor, traditional wine-cellar and wood-fired oven all convey a strong feeling of the past.

XX **El Rincón de Esteban** AC VISA MC AE ①

Santa Catalina 3 ✉ 28014 – Ⓜ Sevilla – ☎ 91 429 92 89 – Fax 91 365 87 70 – www.elrincondeesteban.com

closed August and Sunday **G2**

Rest – Carte 45/63 €

♦ Spanish ♦ Family ♦

Frequented by politicians because of its proximity to the Palacio de Congresos. Intimate and elegant and offering traditional-style dishes.

La Cava del Faraón

Segovia 8 ✉ 28005 – Ⓜ Tirso de Molina – ✆ 91 542 52 54 – f@defuny.com – Fax 91 457 45 30 – www.buenpaladar.com
closed Monday **E2**
Rest – *(dinner only)* Carte 30/44 €
♦ Egyptian ♦ Exotic ♦
A typical Egyptian setting with a tea-room, domed ceilings and a dining room where you can sample the cuisine of the country and enjoy a belly-dancing performance.

La Esquina del Real

Smokers rest.

Amnistía 4 ✉ 28013 – Ⓜ Ópera – ✆ 91 559 43 09 – Fax 91 559 43 09 – www.laesquinadelreal.com
closed 15 August-15 September, Saturday lunch, Sunday and Bank Holidays **E-F2**
Rest – Carte 41/54 €
♦ International ♦ Friendly ♦
An intimate and pleasant rustic-style restaurant with stone and brick walls. Friendly service and French dishes.

Orixe

Cava Baja 17 ✉ 28005 – Ⓜ La Latina – ✆ 91 354 04 11 – info@orixerestaurante.com – Fax 91 458 39 01 – www.orixerestaurante.com
closed Monday except Summer and Sunday dinner **E3**
Rest – Carte approx. 41 €
♦ Galician specialities ♦ Friendly ♦
An excellent setting in which to enjoy the abundant delights of traditional Galician cuisine. Bar at the entrance, as well as various dining rooms with a décor and atmosphere that are distinctly contemporary.

Zerain

Quevedo 3 ✉ 28014 – Ⓜ Antón Martín – ✆ 91 429 79 09 – Fax 91 429 17 20
closed Holy Week, August and Sunday **G3**
Rest – Carte 30/40 €
♦ Basque ♦ Rustic ♦
A Basque cider house with huge barrels. Friendly atmosphere and attractive décor with pictures of the Basque country. Traditional cider house menu at reasonable prices.

Café Oliver

Almirante 12 ✉ 28004 – Ⓜ Colón – ✆ 91 521 73 79 – info@cafeoliver.com – www.cafeoliver.com **G1**
Rest – Carte 32/45 €
♦ International ♦ Bistro ♦
A roomy yet intimate restaurant with stone walls and individual table lighting. The focus here is on traditional, international and Arab cuisine.

La Gastroteca de Santiago

Smokers rest.

pl. Santiago 1 ✉ 28013 – Ⓜ Ópera – ✆ 91 548 07 07 – lagastrotecadesantiago@yahoo.es
closed 11 to 17 August **E2**
Rest – Carte 26/52 €
♦ Inventive ♦ Cosy ♦
Behind its two large French windows you will find a limited, but inviting restaurant with friendly management and a modern atmosphere. Partly visible kitchen and modern menu.

La Bola

No smokers rest.

Bola 5 ✉ 28013 – Ⓜ Santo Domingo – ✆ 91 547 69 30 – labola1870@hotmail.com – Fax 91 541 71 64 – www.labola.es
closed Sunday dinner **E2**
Rest – Carte approx. 33 €
♦ Spanish ♦ Friendly ♦
A long-established Madrid tavern with the flavour of old Madrid. Traditional stewed dishes a speciality. Try the meat and chickpea stew.

La Vaca Verónica Smokers rest.

Moratín 38 ✉ 28014 – Ⓜ Antón Martín – ✆ 91 429 78 27
– www.lavacaveronica.es
closed Saturday lunch **G3**
Rest – Carte 26/34 €
◆ International ◆ Friendly ◆
This delightfully intimate and friendly restaurant is decorated in original style with colourful paintings, mirrored ceilings and candles on every table.

La Botillería del Café de Oriente

pl. de Oriente 4 ✉ 28013 – Ⓜ Ópera – ✆ 91 548 46 20 – cafeoriente@grupolezama.com – Fax 91 547 77 07 – www.grupolezama.es **E2**
Tapa 3.90 € **Ración** approx. 12.50 €
◆ Spanish ◆ Tapas bar ◆
In an area that is very lively at night. Traditional Viennese café-style décor and a wide variety of canapés accompanied by good wines served by the glass.

Prada a Tope Smokers rest.

Principe 11 ✉ 28012 – Ⓜ Sevilla – ✆ 91 429 59 21 – Fax 91 429 59 21
closed 15 days in August, Sunday dinner and Monday **G2**
Tapa 6 € **Ración** approx. 12 €
◆ Spanish ◆ Tapas bar ◆
A traditional establishment with a bar and rustic-style tables. Wood décor, photos on the walls and the opportunity to buy various products.

Bocaito Smokers rest.

Libertad 6 ✉ 28004 – Ⓜ Chueca – ✆ 91 532 12 19 – bocaito@bocaito.com
– Fax 91 522 56 29 – www.bocaito.com
closed August, Saturday lunch and Sunday **G2**
Tapa 3 € **Ración** approx. 10 €
◆ Spanish ◆ Tapas bar ◆
A taurine atmosphere and décor. Ideal for sampling tapas either at the splendid bar or at a table. Deep-fried and egg-based tapas are specialities.

Taberna de San Bernardo Smokers rest.

San Bernardo 85 ✉ 28015 – Ⓜ San Bernardo – ✆ 91 445 41 70 *Plan IV* **K3**
Tapa 1.80 € **Ración** approx. 6.50 €
◆ Spanish ◆ Tapas bar ◆
An informal, rustic tavern with three separate sections. Popular house specialities include two vegetarian dishes - papas con huevo and fritura de verduras.

RETIRO and SALAMANCA *Plan III*

Ritz No smokers rest.

pl. de la Lealtad 5 ✉ 28014 – Ⓜ Banco de España – ✆ 91 701 67 67
– reservations@ritz.es – Fax 91 701 67 76 – www.ritzmadrid.com **I2**
137 rm – 205/630 €, ☕ 31 € – 30 suites
Rest – Carte approx. 110 €
◆ Grand Luxury ◆ Traditional ◆ Classic ◆
An internationally prestigious hotel occupying a former palace dating from the early 20C, with long-standing associations with the diplomatic world. Extraordinarily beautiful public areas and sumptuously decorated guestrooms. The Ritz's restaurant has an elegant dining room and pleasant summer terrace.

Gran Meliá Fénix

Hermosilla 2 ✉ 28001 – Ⓜ Serrano – ✆ 91 431 67 00 – gran.melia.fenix@solmelia.com – Fax 91 576 06 61 – www.granmeliafenix.com **I2**
199 rm – 175/375 €, ☕ 25 € – 16 suites
Rest – Menu 25 €
◆ Luxury ◆ Chain hotel ◆ Classic ◆
An elegant, refined hotel with spacious public areas, such as the striking cupola-crowned lobby, and impressive, traditional bedrooms with top-notch furnishings. Somewhat limited restaurant facilities.

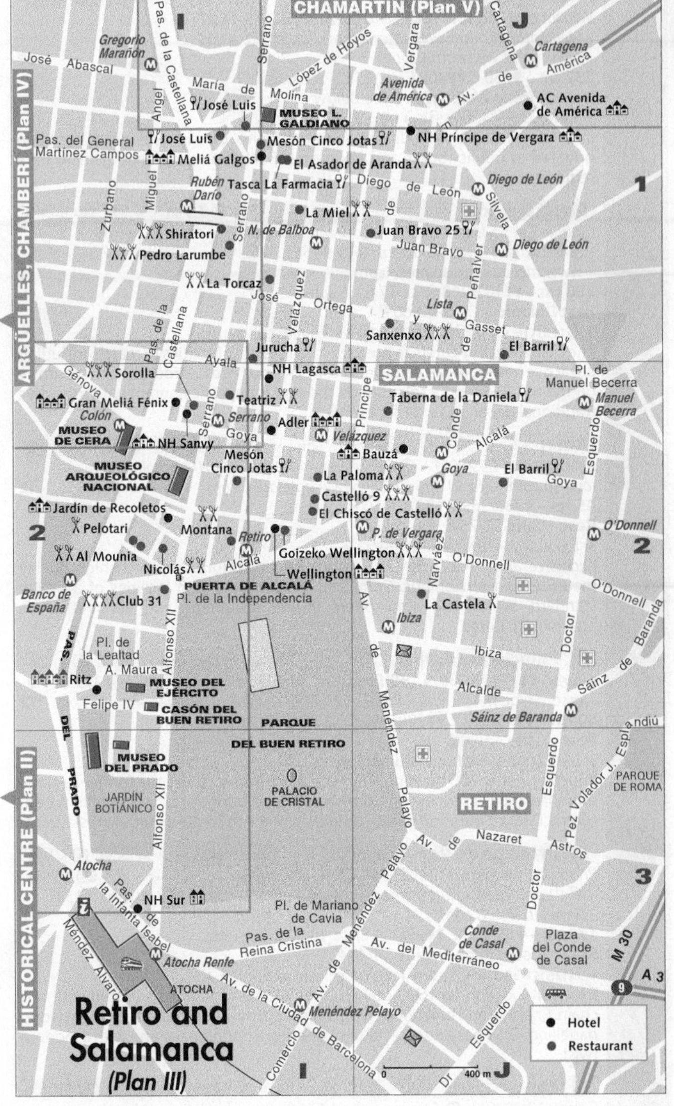

CHAMARTÍN (Plan V)
ARGÜELLES, CHAMBERÍ (Plan IV)
HISTORICAL CENTRE (Plan II)
SALAMANCA
RETIRO
MUSEO L. GALDIANO
MUSEO DE CERA
MUSEO ARQUEOLÓGICO NACIONAL
PUERTA DE ALCALÁ
MUSEO DEL EJÉRCITO
CASÓN DEL BUEN RETIRO
PARQUE DEL BUEN RETIRO
PALACIO DE CRISTAL
MUSEO DEL PRADO
JARDÍN BOTÁNICO
ATOCHA
PARQUE DE ROMA
José Luis
Mesón Cinco Jotas
NH Príncipe de Vergara
AC Avenida de América
Meliá Galgos
El Asador de Aranda
Tasca La Farmacia
La Miel
Shiratori
Juan Bravo 25
Pedro Larumbe
La Torcaz
Sanxenxo
El Barril
Jurucha
NH Lagasca
Sorolla
Taberna de la Daniela
Gran Meliá Fénix
Teatriz
Adler
NH Sanvy
Bauzá
La Paloma
Castelló 9
El Chiscó de Castelló
Jardín de Recoletos
Montana
Pelotari
Goizeko Wellington
Al Mounia
Nicolás
Wellington
Club 31
La Castela
Ritz
NH Sur
Hotel
Restaurant
0
400 m
Retiro and Salamanca (Plan III)

Wellington

Velázquez 8 ✉ 28001 – Ⓜ Velázquez – ☎ 91 575 44 00
– wellington@hotel-wellington.com – Fax 91 576 41 64
– www.hotel-wellington.com **I2**
237 rm – †250 € ††400 €, ☕ 25 € – 25 suites
Rest *Goizeko Wellington* – see below
◆ Luxury ◆ Classic ◆
In an elegant area of Madrid close to the Retiro. Classic style which has been updated in public rooms and bedrooms. Bullfighting aficionados meet here regularly.

Meliá Galgos

Claudio Coello 139 ✉ 28006 – Ⓜ Gregorio Marañón – ☎ 91 562 66 00
– melia.galgos@solmelia.com – Fax 91 561 76 62
– www.meliagalgos.solmelia.com **I1**
350 rm – ††107/260 €, ☕ 17 € – 6 suites
Rest *Diábolo* – Carte 40/60 €
◆ Business ◆ Chain hotel ◆ Functional ◆
The Galgos mainly caters to business clientele with facilities to match, including attractive lounge areas, comfortable, well-appointed bedrooms, a fitness centre on the top floor and a solarium on the roof terrace. Restaurant with attractive traditional décor and excellent service.

Adler

Smokers rest.
Velázquez 33 ✉ 28001 – Ⓜ Velázquez – ☎ 91 426 32 20 – hoteladler@iova-sa.com – Fax 91 426 32 21 – www.hoteladler.com **I2**
45 rm – †230/365 € ††275/450 €, ☕ 25 €
Rest – Carte 58/75 €
◆ Luxury ◆ Personalised ◆
Exclusive and select with an elegant interior refurbished with high-quality materials and furnishings. Comfortable bedrooms with facilities of a similar standard. Welcoming atmosphere in the restaurant, with its meticulous attention to detail.

AC Palacio del Retiro

No smokers rest.
Alfonso XII - 14 ✉ 28014 – Ⓜ Retiro – ☎ 91 523 74 60
– pretiro@ac-hotels.com – Fax 91 523 74 61 – www.ac-hotels.com *Plan II* **H2**
50 rm – †220/287 € ††220/346 €, ☕ 28 € – 1 suite
Rest – Carte 42/50 €
◆ Luxury ◆ Personalised ◆
Imposing, early 20C building. The reception area occupies the former carriage entrance and is complemented by an elegant lounge area and excellent bedrooms. Dark colours and design details combine to create a modern restaurant.

NH Príncipe de Vergara

No smokers rest.
Príncipe de Vergara 92 ✉ 28006 – Ⓜ Av. de América
– ☎ 91 563 26 95 – nhprincipedevergara@nh-hotels.com – Fax 91 563 72 53
– www.nh-hotels.com **J1**
170 rm – †85/180 € ††95/205 €, ☕ 18.50 € – 3 suites
Rest – *(closed August)* Carte 34/44 €
◆ Business ◆ Chain hotel ◆ Functional ◆
Excellent location for this hotel with the usual standards associated with this chain. Practical and functional, with bright bedrooms decorated with light wood panelling. Cosy basement restaurant offering a traditional menu with a modern twist.

NH Sanvy

Goya 3 ✉ 28001 – Ⓜ Serrano – ☎ 91 576 08 00 – nhsanvy@nh-hotels.com
– Fax 91 575 24 43 – www.nh-hotels.com **I2**
139 rm – †100/195 € ††110/230 €, ☕ 19 € – 10 suites
Rest *Sorolla* – see below
◆ Business ◆ Chain hotel ◆ Functional ◆
A functional hotel with a good level of comfort throughout. Impeccable contemporary décor, plus a large terrace on the fourth floor, with a swimming pool and solarium.

Bauzá
Goya 79 ✉ 28001 – Ⓜ Goya – ✆ 91 435 75 45 – info@hotelbauza.com – Fax 91 431 09 43 – www.hotelbauza.com **J2**
169 rm – 🚹90/187 € 🚹🚹145/260 €, ☕ 15 € – 8 suites
Rest – Carte 30/43 €
♦ Business ♦ Design ♦
An upbeat design, including a cosy lounge-library with a fireplace, and bedrooms with every creature comfort, some with a terrace. Bright, modern restaurant with décor in varying shades of white and an innovative menu.

Petit Palace Embassy No smokers rest.
Serrano 46 ✉ 28001 – Ⓜ Serrano – ✆ 91 431 30 60 – emb@hthoteles.com – Fax 91 431 30 62 – www.hthoteles.com **H1**
75 rm – 🚹135/375 € 🚹🚹145/375 €, ☕ 16 €
Rest – *(closed August, Saturday, Sunday and Bank Holidays)* Carte approx. 55 €
♦ Chain hotel ♦ Design ♦
The bold combination of a charming 19C building and a designer interior works well here to create an ambience that is warm and welcoming. Fully equipped bedrooms, each with a computer. Contemporary restaurant with a predominance of grey and metallic tones.

AC Avenida de América
Cartagena 83 ✉ 28028 – Ⓜ Av. de América – ✆ 91 724 42 40 – acamerica@ac-hotels.com – Fax 91 724 42 41 – www.ac-hotels.com **J1**
145 rm – 🚹🚹75/162 €, ☕ 15 €
Rest – *(coffee shop) (dinner only)*
♦ Business ♦ Chain hotel ♦ Functional ♦
Ideal for business executives and with good communications. Modern and functional with a coffee shop that is also a bar depending on the time of day.

Jardín de Recoletos
Gil de Santivañes 4 ✉ 28001 – Ⓜ Serrano – ✆ 91 781 16 40 – rc@vphoteles.com – Fax 91 781 16 41 – www.vphoteles.com **I2**
43 rm ☕ – 🚹135/204 € 🚹🚹143/212 €
Rest – Menu 24 €
♦ Business ♦ Classic ♦
Attractive façade with balustraded balconies. Elegant lobby-reception area with a glazed ceiling, spacious, study-like bedrooms and a pleasant patio-terrace. Small dining room decorated with landscape-inspired murals.

NH Lagasca No smokers rest.
Lagasca 64 ✉ 28001 – Ⓜ Serrano – ✆ 91 575 46 06 – nhlagasca@nh-hotels.com – Fax 91 575 16 94 – www.nh-hotels.com **I2**
100 rm – 🚹🚹215 €, ☕ 18 €
Rest – *(closed August, Saturday, Sunday and Bank Holidays)* Menu 15 €
♦ Business ♦ Chain hotel ♦ Functional ♦
Good and comfortable rooms in a functional hotel where great thought is given to the needs and comfort of guests. Professional management.

NH Sur without rest
paseo Infanta Isabel 9 ✉ 28014 – Ⓜ Atocha – ✆ 91 539 94 00 – nhsur@nh-hotels.com – Fax 91 467 09 96 **I3**
68 rm – 🚹69/172 € 🚹🚹69/190 €, ☕ 13.50 €
♦ Business ♦ Chain hotel ♦ Functional ♦
Decor in keeping with the contemporary ethos of the NH chain. Public areas limited to a breakfast room with TV. Comfortable rooms, although the single rooms are on the small side.

XXXX **Club 31** Smokers rest.
Alcalá 58 ✉ 28014 – Ⓜ Retiro – ✆ 91 531 00 92 – club31@club31.net – Fax 91 531 00 92 – www.club31.net
closed August **I2**
Rest – Carte approx. 65 €
♦ International ♦ Formal ♦
This highly respected and well-established restaurant offers a mix of traditional and modern décor, and a menu featuring a range of international cuisine. Impressive cellar.

XXX **Sanxenxo** A/C ⇔ VISA MC AE ①

José Ortega y Gasset 40 ✉ 28006 – Ⓜ Núñez de Balboa – ✆ 91 577 82 72 – combarro@combarro.com – Fax 91 435 95 12 – www.sanxenxo.com.es
closed Holy Week, August and Sunday dinner J1

Rest – Carte approx. 70 €

◆ Galician specialities ◆ Formal ◆

Superb setting with dining rooms laid out on two floors with a decorative emphasis on granite and wood. Traditional Galician cuisine focusing on high-quality fish and seafood.

XXX **Pedro Larumbe** A/C VISA MC AE ①

Serrano 61 (2nd floor) ✉ 28006 – Ⓜ Rubén Darío – ✆ 91 575 11 12 – info@larumbe.com – Fax 91 576 60 19 – www.larumbe.com
closed Holy Week, 15 days in August, Saturday lunch, Sunday and Bank Holidays I1

Rest – Carte 47/60 €

◆ International ◆ Retro ◆

On the top floor of a small palace, with three majestic dining rooms with personalised décor and exquisitely tasteful detail. International cuisine with a creative touch.

XXX **Goizeko Wellington** – Hotel Wellington A/C VISA MC AE ①

Villanueva 34 ✉ 28001 – Ⓜ Velázquez – ✆ 91 577 01 38 – goizeko@goizekowellington.com – Fax 91 557 60 26 – www.goizekogaztelupe.com
closed Sunday I2

Rest – Carte 65/95 € ✿

◆ Spanish ◆ Minimalist ◆

A combination of classic and modern décor and an elegant setting form the backdrop to this restaurant where the menu is a fusion of traditional and international cuisine with a creative flourish. Extensive cellar.

XXX **Sorolla** – Hotel NH Sanvy A/C P VISA MC AE ①

Hermosilla 4 ✉ 28001 – Ⓜ Serrano – ✆ 91 576 08 00 – Fax 91 575 24 43
closed August, Sunday and Bank Holidays I2

Rest – Carte 33/50 €

◆ Spanish ◆ Formal ◆

Impressive, classically furnished dining room, as well as four private rooms. Traditional cuisine complemented by grilled dishes and a fine selection of coffees and herbal teas.

XXX **Shiratori** A/C P VISA MC AE ①

paseo de la Castellana 36 ✉ 28046 – Ⓜ Rubén Darío – ✆ 91 577 37 34 – jarmas@r-shiratori.com – Fax 91 577 44 55
closed Holy Week, 21 days in August, Sunday and Bank Holidays I1

Rest – Carte 49/71 €

◆ Japanese ◆ Exotic ◆

A spacious restaurant serving a selective range of Japanese specialities in a relaxed atmosphere typical of the country. A choice of menus, with dishes created in front of diners.

XXX **Castelló 9** A/C ⇔ VISA MC AE ①

Castelló 9 ✉ 28001 – Ⓜ Príncipe de Vergara – ✆ 91 435 00 67 – castello9@castello9.es – Fax 91 435 91 34 – www.castello9.es
closed Holy Week, August, Sunday and Bank Holidays I2

Rest – Carte 36/53 €

◆ International ◆ Formal ◆

Classic elegance in the Salamanca district. Intimate dining rooms offering an international à la carte choice plus a tasting menu featuring a variety of shared dishes.

XX **La Paloma** Smokers rest. AC VISA MC AE

Jorge Juan 39 ✉ 28001 – Ⓜ Príncipe de Vergara – ✆ 91 576 86 92 – Fax 91 575 51 41
closed Holy Week, August, Sunday and Bank Holidays **I2**
Rest – Carte 54/64 €
♦ International ♦ Trendy ♦
A highly professional feel and superb service are the hallmarks of this restaurant attracting an elegant clientele. A dining room on two floors, where the cuisine is based around international and traditional dishes.

XX **La Torcaz** Smokers rest. AC VISA MC AE

Lagasca 81 ✉ 28006 – Ⓜ Núñez de Balboa – ✆ 91 575 41 30 – info@latorcaz.com – Fax 91 431 83 88 – www.latorcaz.com
closed Holy Week, August, Sunday and Bank Holidays **I1**
Rest – Carte 40/55 €
♦ International ♦ Formal ♦
A cosy restaurant with an attractive wine display case. Fusion of modern and traditional furnishings, excellent service and an impressive wine list.

XX **Dassa Bassa** AC VISA MC AE

Villalar 7 ✉ 28001 – Ⓜ Retiro – ✆ 91 576 73 97 – dassabassa@dassabassa.com – www.dassabassa.com
closed Holy Week, 21 days in August, Sunday, Monday and Bank Holidays *Plan II* **H2**
Rest – Carte approx. 56 €
♦ Inventive ♦ Design ♦
Occupying what was once a charcoal factory, the Dassa Barra has a large entrance and four modern dining rooms decorated with designer features. Creative cuisine with an accent on distinctive flavours.

XX **La Miel** Smokers rest. AC VISA MC AE

Maldonado 14 ✉ 28006 – Ⓜ Núñez de Balboa – ✆ 91 435 50 45 – manuelcoto@restaurantelamiel.com – www.restaurantelamiel.com
closed August and Sunday **I1**
Rest – Carte 36/49 €
♦ International ♦ Family ♦
A traditional, comfortable restaurant run by the proprietors. Attentive service, a good menu of international dishes and an impressive wine cellar.

XX **Montana** Smokers rest. AC VISA MC AE

Lagasca 5 ✉ 28001 – Ⓜ Retiro – ✆ 91 435 99 01 – restaurantemontana@hotmail.com – Fax 91 297 47 40 – www.restaurantemontana.es
closed 11 to 24 August and Sunday **I2**
Rest – Carte 31/45 €
♦ Spanish ♦ Minimalist ♦
This small restaurant is run by a young team with great enthusiasm. A modern feel, attentive service, and traditional cuisine enlivened with creative panache.

XX **Al Mounia** AC VISA MC AE

Recoletos 5 ✉ 28001 – Ⓜ Banco de España – ✆ 91 435 08 28 – almounia@terra.es – Fax 91 575 01 73
closed Holy Week, August, Sunday and Monday **I2**
Rest – Carte 22/34 €
♦ North African ♦ Exotic ♦
An exotic restaurant near the National Archaeological Museum. Moroccan décor featuring sculpted wood, moulded plasterwork, attractive rugs and typical low tables. Traditional dishes from North Africa.

XX **Teatriz** No smokers rest. AC VISA MC AE

Hermosilla 15 ✉ 28001 – Ⓜ Serrano – ✆ 91 577 53 79 – Fax 91 431 69 10 – www.grupovips.com **I2**
Rest – Carte approx. 52 €
♦ International ♦ Design ♦
In the stalls of the former Teatro Beatriz. A tapas bar near the entrance and a dining area and a bar on the stage, all with attractive Modernist décor.

XX

Nicolás Smokers rest.

Villalar 4 ✉ 28001 – Ⓜ Retiro – ✆ 91 431 77 37 – resnicolas@hotmail.com – Fax 91 577 86 65

closed Holy Week, August, Sunday and Monday **I2**

Rest – Carte 27/42 €

♦ Spanish ♦ Minimalist ♦

Modern décor provides the backdrop for this restaurant with a minimalist air. The traditional menu is a little limited, although compensated by the good choice of home cooking. Select wine list.

XX

El Chiscón de Castelló Smokers rest.

Castelló 3 ✉ 28001 – Ⓜ Príncipe de Vergara – ✆ 91 575 56 62 – Fax 91 575 56 62 – www.elchiscon.com

closed August, Sunday, Monday dinner and Bank Holidays **I2**

Rest – Carte 35/48 €

♦ Spanish ♦ Friendly ♦

Hidden behind the typical façade is a warmly decorated interior that gives it the feel of a private house, particularly on the first floor. Well-priced traditional cuisine.

XX

El Asador de Aranda No smokers rest.

Diego de León 9 ✉ 28006 – Ⓜ Núñez de Balboa – ✆ 91 563 02 46 – Fax 91 556 62 02 – www.asadordearanda.com

closed August and Sunday dinner **I1**

Rest – Carte approx. 37 €

♦ Roast lamb ♦ Rustic ♦

Classic Castilian décor and a wood-fired oven for roasting meat. The main dining room with stained-glass windows is on the 1st floor.

X

Pelotari

Recoletos 3 ✉ 28001 – Ⓜ Colón – ✆ 91 578 24 97 – informacion@asador-pelotari.com – Fax 91 431 60 04 – www.asador-pelotari.com

closed 11 to 17 August and Sunday **I2**

Rest – Carte approx. 45 €

♦ Basque ♦ Rustic ♦

A typical Basque rotisserie run by two owners, one in the kitchen, the other front of house. Four dining rooms (two convertible into private dining areas), where the traditional décor is typical of this region in the north of the country.

X

La Castela Smokers rest.

Doctor Castelo 22 ✉ 28009 – Ⓜ Ibiza – ✆ 91 574 00 15 – info@lacastela.com – www.lacastela.com

closed Holy Week, August and Sunday **J2**

Rest – Carte approx. 39 €

♦ Spanish ♦ Formal ♦

La Castela perpetuates the tradition of historic Madrid taverns, with its tapas bar at the entrance. Simple but attractive traditional dining room with a similarly conservative menu.

Juan Bravo 25 Smokers rest.

Juan Bravo 25 ✉ 28006 – Ⓜ Núñez de Balboa – ✆ 91 411 60 25 – jmb@juanbravo25.com – Fax 91 411 82 31 – www.juanbravo25.com

closed Holy Week, 15 days in August and Sunday **J1**

Tapa 3.20 € **Ración** approx. 13.50 €

♦ Spanish ♦ Tapas bar ♦

On the mezzanine with a central bar heaped with tapas and pinchos in typical Basque style. The adjoining dining room offers a more traditional menu.

José Luis Smokers rest.

General Oráa 5 ✉ 28006 – Ⓜ Rubén Darío – ✆ 91 561 64 13 – joseluis@joseluis.es **I1**

Tapa 2.20 € **Ración** approx. 16 €

♦ Spanish ♦ Tapas bar ♦

A well-known establishment with a wide range of canapés, Basque-style tapas and servings of different dishes in elegant surroundings with traditional décor.

Mesón Cinco Jotas

Puigcerdá ✉ 28001 – Ⓜ Serrano – ✆ 91 575 41 25 – m5jjorgejuan@osborne.es – Fax 91 575 56 35 – www.mesoncincojotas.com **I2**

Tapa 4 € **Ración** approx. 10 €

◆ Spanish ◆ Tapas bar ◆

Renowned for the high quality of its Iberian products, including tapas and raciones, this typical eatery has a splendid terrace and three cosy dining rooms arranged on three floors.

Tasca La Farmacia

Diego de León 9 ✉ 28006 – Ⓜ Núñez de Balboa – ✆ 91 564 86 52 – Fax 91 556 62 02 – www.asadordearanda.com
closed 20 July-10 August and Sunday **I1**

Tapa 3 € **Ración** approx. 10 €

◆ Codfish specialities ◆ Tapas bar ◆

A traditional establishment with a beautiful tiled bar. Don't miss the opportunity to try the tapas or larger servings of salt-cod dishes.

Mesón Cinco Jotas

Serrano 118 ✉ 28006 – Ⓜ Núñez de Balboa – ✆ 91 563 27 10 – m5jserrano@osborne.es – Fax 91 561 32 84 – www.mesoncincojotas.com **I1**

Tapa 4 € **Ración** approx. 10 €

◆ Spanish ◆ Tapas bar ◆

Contemporary in feel, with a good selection of tapas, toasts and raciones, with the emphasis on Iberian pork products. Pleasant dining room.

El Barril

Goya 86 ✉ 28009 – Ⓜ Goya – ✆ 91 578 39 98 – www.elbarrildegoya.com
closed Sunday dinner **J2**

Ración approx. 17 €

◆ Seafood ◆ Tapas bar ◆

A seafood restaurant with an impressive bar displaying an extensive selection of high-quality products. Good menu choices in the dining room to the rear.

José Luis

Smokers rest.

Serrano 89 ✉ 28006 – Ⓜ Gregorio Marañón – ✆ 91 563 09 58 – joseluis@joseluis.es – Fax 91 563 31 02 **I1**

Tapa 2.20 € **Ración** approx. 16 €

◆ Spanish ◆ Tapas bar ◆

Two restaurants in one with two entrances, two bars and two dining rooms. Pleasant summer terrace. Basque tapas and raciones, plus a small menu.

Taberna de la Daniela

Smokers rest.

General Pardiñas 21 ✉ 28001 – Ⓜ Goya – ✆ 91 575 23 29 – Fax 91 435 24 22 **J2**

Tapa 3.50 € **Ración** approx. 18 €

◆ Spanish ◆ Tapas bar ◆

A typical tavern in the Salamanca district, with an azulejo-adorned façade and several dining rooms in which to enjoy a range of tapas and raciones. An address famous for its cocido madrileño, the city's typical stew.

El Barril

Don Ramón de la Cruz 91 ✉ 28006 – Ⓜ Manuel Becerra – ✆ 91 401 33 05 – www.elbarrilalcantara.com **J1**

Tapa 6 € **Ración** approx. 23 €

◆ Seafood ◆ Tapas bar ◆

A seafood restaurant renowned for its high-quality cuisine and excellent service. Eat in the bar-cervecería or in one of the two dining rooms.

Jurucha

Smokers rest.

Ayala 19 ✉ 28001 – Ⓜ Serrano – ✆ 91 575 00 98 – jurucha@telefonica.net
closed August, Sunday and Bank Holidays **I1**

Tapa 1.60 € **Ración** approx. 3.50 €

◆ Spanish ◆ Tapas bar ◆

A must on any tapas tour of Madrid. Delicious Basque-style tapas and pinchos, including omelettes and croquettes.

ARGÜELLES — *Plan IV*

Sofitel Madrid Plaza de España without rest

Tutor 1 ✉ 28008 – Ⓜ Ventura Rodríguez – ✆ 91 541 98 80 – h1320@accor.com – Fax 91 542 57 36 – www.sofitel.com

96 rm – 🚹99/300 € 🚹🚹116/320 €, ☕ 24.50 € – 1 suite **K3**

◆ Business ◆ Chain hotel ◆ Cosy ◆

Well refurbished with high-quality furnishings in the bedrooms and marble fittings in the bathrooms. A perfect balance of elegance and comfort.

El Molino de los Porches

paseo Pintor Rosales 1 ✉ 28008 – Ⓜ Plaza de España – ✆ 91 548 13 36 – Fax 91 547 97 61 – www.asadorelmolino.com

closed Sunday dinner **K3**

Rest – Carte 30/42 €

◆ Grills ◆ Rustic ◆

A hotel located in the Parque del Oeste with several lounges and a pleasant glazed-in terrace. The meat produced from the wood-fired oven and charcoal grill is delicious.

CHAMBERÍ — *Plan IV*

AC Santo Mauro No smokers rest.

Zurbano 36 ✉ 28010 – Ⓜ Alonso Martínez – ✆ 91 319 69 00 – santo-mauro@ac-hotels.com – Fax 91 308 54 77 **L3**

43 rm – 🚹🚹279/355 €, ☕ 28 € – 8 suites

Rest *Santo Mauro* – *(closed August)* Carte approx. 73 €

◆ Palace ◆ Grand Luxury ◆ Classic ◆

A hotel in a beautiful French-style palace with garden situated in a classy district of Madrid. Elegant with touches of luxury in the rooms. The restaurant is in a beautiful library-room which lends distinction to the food.

Intercontinental Madrid

paseo de la Castellana 49 ✉ 28046 – Ⓜ Gregorio Marañón – ✆ 91 700 73 00 – madrid@ichotelsgroup.com – Fax 91 319 58 53 – www.madrid.intercontinental.com **L3**

279 rm – 🚹🚹199/279 €, ☕ 28 € – 28 suites

Rest – Menu 45 €

◆ Luxury ◆ Classic ◆

Superb facilities, including an elegant domed lobby with a profusion of marble, a pleasant interior patio-terrace, and bedrooms with the Intercontinental's usual high levels of comfort. A refined menu of international cuisine is the order of the day in the restaurant adjoining the lobby-bar.

Miguel Ángel

Miguel Ángel 31 ✉ 28010 – Ⓜ Gregorio Marañón – ✆ 91 442 00 22 – comercial.hma@oh-es.com – Fax 91 442 53 20 – www.miguelangelhotel.com

243 rm – 🚹145/350 € 🚹🚹160/350 €, ☕ 25 € – 20 suites **L3**

Rest *Arco* – Carte 40/52 €

◆ Luxury ◆ Classic ◆

A prestigious and up-to-date hotel located in the Castellana district of Madrid. Well-appointed rooms and large public areas with classically elegant décor. Superb restaurant with a terrace for the summer months.

Hesperia Madrid

paseo de la Castellana 57 ✉ 28046 – Ⓜ Gregorio Marañón – ✆ 91 210 88 00 – hotel@hesperia-madrid.com – Fax 91 210 88 99 – www.hesperia-madrid.com

139 rm – 🚹179/357 € 🚹🚹179/410 €, ☕ 27 € – 32 suites **L2**

Rest *Santceloni* – see below

Rest – Menu 32 €

◆ Business ◆ Modern ◆

The Hespería Madrid enjoys an excellent location in the city's business district. A small lobby, compensated by the wide choice of meeting rooms. Classically elegant bedrooms, plus a restaurant in the interior patio which doubles as the breakfast room.

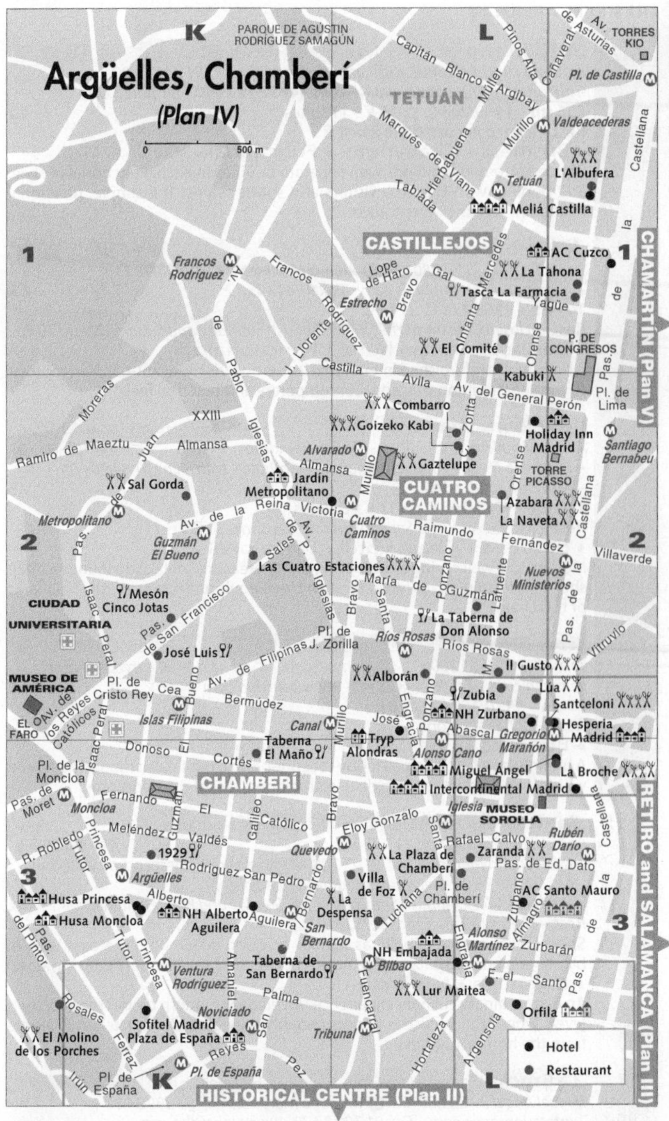

Orfila

Orfila 6 ✉ *28010 – Ⓜ Alonso Martínez – ✆ 91 702 77 70 – inforeservas@hotelorfila.com – Fax 91 702 77 72 – www.hotelorfila.com* **L3**

28 rm – 310 € 380 €, 25 € – 4 suites – **Rest** – *(closed August)* Menu 70 €

◆ Palace ◆ Luxury ◆ Classic ◆

A hotel in a late 19C palace situated in an exclusive residential zone. A grand atmosphere and rooms with traditional and elegant furnishings. A welcoming dining room and interior garden where you can enjoy the à la carte menu.

NH Zurbano
No smokers rest. VISA AE

Zurbano 79-81 ✉ *28003* – Ⓜ *Gregorio Marañón* – ☎ *91 441 45 00* – *nhzurbano@nh-hotels.com* – *Fax 91 441 32 24* – *www.nh-hotels.com* **L2**

255 rm – ††89/203 €, ☕ 16 € – 11 suites

Rest – *(closed August)* Carte 34/41 €

◆ Business ◆ Chain hotel ◆ Functional ◆

Divided into two buildings with separate facilities in each. Functional in style, and popular with business visitors and sports teams. The simple, functional restaurant has its own entrance.

NH Embajada
VISA AE

Santa Engracia 5 ✉ *28010* – Ⓜ *Alonso Martínez* – ☎ *91 594 02 13* – *nhembajada@nh-hotels.com* – *Fax 91 447 33 12* **L3**

101 rm – ††63/178 €, ☕ 14 €

Rest – *(closed Christmas, Holy Week, August, Saturday and Sunday)* Menu 30 €

◆ Business ◆ Chain hotel ◆ Functional ◆

A hotel with a refurbished interior that leans towards the avant-garde in contrast to the very traditional façade. Contemporary and practical feel.

NH Alberto Aguilera
Smokers rest. VISA AE

Alberto Aguilera 18 ✉ *28015* – Ⓜ *San Bernardo* – ☎ *91 446 09 00* – *nhalbertoaguilera@nh-hotels.com* – *Fax 91 446 09 04* – *www.nh-hotels.com* **K3**

148 rm – ††85/168 €, ☕ 15 € – 5 suites

Rest – *(closed August-2 September)* Carte approx. 30 €

◆ Business ◆ Chain hotel ◆ Functional ◆

Modern and welcoming although the public areas are limited to a lounge-coffee shop and the dining room. Comfort and well-equipped rooms are the hallmarks of this chain.

Tryp Alondras
VISA AE

José Abascal 8 ✉ *28003* – Ⓜ *Alonso Cano* – ☎ *91 447 40 00* – *tryp.alondras@solmelia.com* – *Fax 91 593 88 00* – *www.solmelia.com* **L2**

72 rm – ††70/160 €, ☕ 10 €

Rest – *(coffee shop only)*

◆ Business ◆ Chain hotel ◆ Classic ◆

A friendly hotel with a small lobby-reception and a minimalist modern cafeteria which is in contrast to the old-style, traditional feel of the bedrooms.

Santceloni (Óscar Velasco) – Hotel Hesperia Madrid
VISA AE

paseo de la Castellana 57 ✉ *28046* – Ⓜ *Gregorio Marañón* – ☎ *91 210 88 40* – *santceloni@hesperia-madrid.com* – *Fax 91 210 88 92* – *www.restaurantesantceloni.com*

closed Holy Week, August, Saturday lunch, Sunday and Bank Holidays **L2**

Rest – Menu 129 € – Carte 90/120 €

Spec. Caviar con las cebolletas cocidas en caldo de jamón. Jarrete de ternera blanca con puré de patatas. Crema de chocolate con avellana al Pedro Ximénez.

◆ Inventive ◆ Minimalist ◆

An extraordinary culinary experience. An elegant modern dining room on two levels where the service is understandably impeccable. The kitchen is visible from the hotel's lounges.

La Broche (Sergi Arola)
No smokers rest. VISA AE

Miguel Ángel 29 ✉ *28010* – Ⓜ *Gregorio Marañón* – ☎ *91 399 34 37* – *info@labroche.com* – *Fax 91 399 37 78* – *www.labroche.com*

closed Holy Week, August, Saturday and Sunday **L3**

Rest – Menu 95 € – Carte 69/88 €

Spec. Sardinas asadas en sobrasada, judías de Kenia y trompetas de los muertos. Lomo de lubina asada en citronelle y sandwich de patatas y tirabeques (spring). Chuletón de buey ahumado al romero, morillas aliñadas, puré de manzana y mostaza antigua (spring).

◆ Inventive ◆ Minimalist ◆

A spacious restaurant with bare white walls which allow all attention to be focused on the very innovative cuisine.

XXXX

Las Cuatro Estaciones

A/C VISA MC AE

General Ibáñez de Íbero 5 ✉ 28003 – Ⓜ Guzmán El Bueno – ☎ 91 553 63 05 – Fax 91 535 05 23
closed August, Saturday lunch and Sunday **K2**
Rest – Carte 50/71 €
♦ International ♦ Formal ♦
This original restaurant recalls the decorative trends of the 1980s. The carpeted dining room is laid out on several levels. Private bar and well-balanced cellar.

XXX

Il Gusto

A/C VISA MC AE

Espronceda 27 ✉ 28003 – Ⓜ Canal – ☎ 91 535 39 02 – Fax 91 535 08 61 – www.restauranteilgusto.com **L2**
Rest – Carte 35/47 €
♦ Italian ♦ Design ♦
Discover the delicious nuances of Italian cuisine in this modern restaurant with an entrance hall and elegant dining room, where the décor is a combination of wood and marble.

XXX

Lur Maitea

A/C VISA MC AE

Fernando el Santo 4 ✉ 28010 – Ⓜ Alonso Martínez – ☎ 91 308 03 50 – alex@restaurantelurmaitea.com – Fax 91 391 38 21 – www.restaurantelurmaitea.com
closed Holy Week, August and Sunday **L3**
Rest – Carte 52/72 €
♦ Basque ♦ Formal ♦
Lur Maitea has become one of Madrid's most respected addresses. Elegant dining room with a parquet floor and décor influenced by varying shades of blue. Contemporary Basque cuisine.

XX

Alborán

A/C VISA MC AE

Ponzano 39-41 ✉ 28003 – Ⓜ Alonso Cano – ☎ 91 399 21 50 – alboran@alboran-rest.com – Fax 91 399 21 50 – www.alboran-rest.com
closed Sunday dinner **L2**
Rest – Carte 43/58 €
♦ Spanish ♦ Rustic ♦
A coffee shop with tapas near the entrance and two dining areas with high-quality furnishings. Décor of a maritime theme with wooden floors and walls.

XX ✿

Zaranda (Fernando P. Arellano)

Smokers rest. A/C VISA MC AE

paseo de Eduardo Dato 5 ✉ 28010 – Ⓜ Iglesia – ☎ 91 446 45 48 – zaranda@zaranda.es – www.zaranda.es
closed August, Saturday lunch, Sunday and Monday dinner **L3**
Rest – Menu 50 € – Carte 42/70 €
Spec. Cochinillo en choucroute oriental (autumn-winter). Abalon escalopado y su salpicón al cilantro sobre sopa fría de judías verdes (spring). Cremoso de queso de cabra con sorbete de fresa al Rioja y albahaca.
♦ Inventive ♦ Friendly ♦
A well-run restaurant whose owners work both front-of-house and in the kitchen. Two modern-style dining rooms offering creative à la carte dishes and two tasting menus.

XX

La Plaza de Chamberí

A/C VISA MC AE

pl. de Chamberí 10 ✉ 28010 – Ⓜ Iglesia – ☎ 91 446 06 97 – Fax 91 594 21 20 – www.restaurantelaplazadechamberi.com
closed Sunday **L3**
Rest – Carte 35/41 €
♦ Spanish ♦ Formal ♦
A well-established, colourful local restaurant, with an old-style dining room laid out on two levels. The menu here is dominated by traditional recipes.

XX **Lúa** Smokers rest. AC VISA MC AE ①
Zurbano 85 ✉ 28003 – Ⓜ Gregorio Marañón – ☎ 91 395 28 53
closed Holy Week, 15 days in August and Sunday **L2**
Rest – *(set menu only)* Menu 45 €
◆ Inventive ◆ Cosy ◆
This small restaurant has a relaxed, youthful ambience with one dining room split into three areas. Cuisine here is based around a daily, tasting-type menu with a modern, creative edge.

X **Villa de Foz** Smokers rest. AC VISA MC AE ①
Gonzalo de Córdoba 10 ✉ 28010 – Ⓜ Bilbao – ☎ 91 446 89 93
– www.villadefoz.es
closed Holy Week, August and Sunday **L3**
Rest – Carte approx. 38 €
◆ Galician specialities ◆ Trendy ◆
Good traditional Galician cuisine in a modern dining room. The menu is limited but the food is of very high quality.

Mesón Cinco Jotas AC VISA MC AE ①
paseo de San Francisco de Sales 27 ✉ 28003 – Ⓜ Guzmán El Bueno
– ☎ 91 544 01 89 – m5jsfsales@osborne.es – Fax 91 549 06 51
– www.mesoncincojotas.com **K2**
Tapa 3.50 € **Ración** approx. 16 €
◆ Spanish ◆ Tapas bar ◆
In the style of this chain with two areas where you can have a single dish or eat à la carte. Also a variety of tapas, fine hams and pork products.

Zubia Smokers rest. AC VISA MC AE ①
Espronceda 28 ✉ 28003 – Ⓜ Ríos Rosas – ☎ 91 441 04 32
– info@restaurantezubia.com – Fax 91 441 10 43 – www.restaurantezubia.com
closed Holy Week, 15 to 30 August, Saturday lunch and Sunday **L2**
Tapa 2 € **Ración** approx. 10 €
◆ Spanish ◆ Tapas bar ◆
Enjoy a good choice of tapas and raciones standing at the Zubia's bar, seated at the small number of adjoining tables or in the small interior dining room.

José Luis Smokers rest. AC VISA MC AE ①
paseo de San Francisco de Sales 14 ✉ 28003 – Ⓜ Islas Filipinas – ☎ 91 441 20 43
– joseluis@joseluis.es **K2**
Tapa 2.20 € **Ración** approx. 16 €
◆ Spanish ◆ Tapas bar ◆
One of the more simple establishments in this well-known chain. A variety of Basque-style tapas and larger portions of dishes. Also a terrace.

La Taberna de Don Alonso Smokers rest. AC VISA MC AE ①
Alonso Cano 64 ✉ 28003 – Ⓜ Ríos Rosas – ☎ 91 533 52 49
closed Holy Week, 20 July-20 August, Sunday dinner and Monday **L2**
Tapa 2.10 € **Ración** approx. 12 €
◆ Spanish ◆ Tapas bar ◆
A tavern with a selection of Basque-style tapas and a blackboard listing tapas prepared to order and larger servings of dishes available. Wine by the glass.

Taberna El Maño Smokers rest. VISA MC
Vallehermoso 59 ✉ 28015 – Ⓜ Canal – ☎ 91 448 40 35
closed August-3 September and Monday **K3**
Taurine atmosphere – **Tapa** 5 € **Ración** approx. 15 €
◆ Spanish ◆ Tapas bar ◆
An old-fashioned, typical eatery with a bullfighting-inspired décor. A wide choice of pinchos, tapas and raciones created from high-quality ingredients.

1929 Smokers rest. AC VISA MC
Rodríguez San Pedro 66 ✉ 28015 – Ⓜ Argüelles – ☎ 91 549 91 16
closed 15 to 30 August and Sunday **K3**
Tapa 3 € **Ración** approx. 8 €
◆ Spanish ◆ Tapas bar ◆
Run by its owner, this rustic eatery includes a well-stocked bar, several barrels that serve as tables, and two dining rooms.

CASTILLEJOS and CUATRO CAMINOS *Plan IV*

Meliá Castilla
VISA AE

Capitán Haya 43 ✉ 28020 – Ⓜ Cuzco – ✆ 91 567 50 00
– melia.castilla@solmelia.com – Fax 91 567 50 51
– www.meliacastilla.solmelia.com **L1**
904 rm – 146/350 €, ☕ 23 € – 12 suites
Rest *L'Albufera* – see below
♦ Business ♦ Chain hotel ♦ Modern ♦
The main selling-points of this hotel are its extensive public areas, large auditorium, numerous function rooms for banquets and conferences, and elegant, clasically designed bedrooms.

AC Cuzco
No smokers rest. VISA AE

paseo de la Castellana 133 ✉ 28046 – Ⓜ Cuzco – ✆ 91 556 06 00
– reservas.accuzco@ac-hotels.com – Fax 91 556 03 72
– www.ac-hotels.com **L1**
315 rm – 107/235 €, ☕ 19 € – 4 suites
Rest – Carte approx. 45 €
♦ Business ♦ Functional ♦
Completely renovated with the typical comfort, design and modern feel that you come to associate with the AC hotel chain. Adequately appointed guestrooms.

Holiday Inn Madrid
VISA AE

pl. Carlos Trías Beltrán 4 (entrance by Orense 22-24) ✉ 28020
– Ⓜ Santiago Bernabeu – ✆ 91 456 80 00
– tojsp.reservations@ichotelsgroup.com – Fax 91 456 80 01
– www.holidayinnmadrid.net **L2**
280 rm – 130/250 € 150/270 €, ☕ 23 € – 33 suites
Rest *Big Blue* – Carte approx. 45 €
♦ Business ♦ Chain hotel ♦ Functional ♦
Well-located next to the Azca business district with its numerous offices and leisure facilities. Modern rooms and an extensive range of guest services. Cheerful, modernist décor in the Big Blue restaurant.

Jardín Metropolitano
VISA AE

av. Reina Victoria 12 ✉ 28003 – Ⓜ Cuatro Caminos – ✆ 91 183 18 10
– metropolitano@vphoteles.com – Fax 91 183 18 11
– www.vphoteles.com **K-L2**
96 rm ☕ – 91/162 € 104/203 € – 6 suites
Rest – Menu 23 €
♦ Business ♦ Classic ♦
This hotel occupies a building laid out around a central patio crowned by a skylight. Contemporary in feel with spacious, well-appointed and classically designed rooms.

L'Albufera – Hotel Meliá Castilla
VISA AE

Capitán Haya 45 ✉ 28020 – Ⓜ Cuzco – ✆ 91 567 51 97
– Fax 91 567 50 51 **L1**
Rest – Carte 37/51 €
♦ Rice specialities ♦ Formal ♦
A restaurant with three attractive dining rooms and another in a conservatory in a central patio with numerous plants.

Azabara
VISA AE

Hernani 75 ✉ 28020 – Ⓜ Nuevos Ministerios – ✆ 91 417 59 79
– gonzalezyugarte@gyu.e.telefonica.net – Fax 91 417 57 14
– www.lanuevafontana.com
closed August and Sunday **L2**
Rest – Carte approx. 70 €
♦ Spanish ♦ Retro ♦
Elegant and impeccably styled, with classic, 1920s décor with an emphasis on black, and individual lighting at each table.

XXX

Combarro

Reina Mercedes 12 ✉ 28020 – Ⓜ Nuevos Ministerios – ✆ 91 554 77 84 – combarro@combarro.com – Fax 91 534 25 01 – www.combarro.com
closed Holy Week, August and Sunday dinner **L2**
Rest – Carte approx. 70 €
◆ Galician specialities ◆ Formal ◆
Galician cooking based on quality products which are on view in the live fish and seafood display tanks. Public bar, dining room on the first floor and various rooms in the basement, all decorated and furnished with classical elegance.

XXX

Goizeko Kabi

Smokers rest.
Comandante Zorita 37 ✉ 28020 – Ⓜ Alvarado – ✆ 91 533 01 85 – Fax 91 533 02 14 – www.goizeko-gaztelupe.com
closed Sunday **L2**
Rest – Carte 52/63 €
◆ Basque ◆ Formal ◆
A Basque restaurant with prestige in the city. Elegant and comfortable although the tables are a little close together.

XX

La Tahona

Capitán Haya 21 (side) ✉ 28020 – Ⓜ Cuzco – ✆ 91 555 04 41 – Fax 91 556 62 02 – www.asadordearanda.com
closed August and Sunday dinner **L1**
Rest – Carte approx. 40 €
◆ Roast lamb ◆ Rustic ◆
The entrance bar, with its wood oven and wood-inspired craftwork, leads to various rooms with a medieval Castillian ambience. Traditionally roasted dishes, plus a good house red.

XX

La Naveta

Smokers rest.
Hernani 75 ✉ 28020 – Ⓜ Nuevos Ministerios – ✆ 91 417 59 79 – gonzalezyugarte@gyu.e.telefonica.net – Fax 91 417 57 14 – www.lanuevafontana.com
closed Sunday **L2**
Rest – Carte 50/90 €
◆ Traditional ◆ Trendy ◆
Elegant and spacious tapas bar, along with an enclosed and air-conditioned terrace-style dining room with designer chairs and tables on different levels.

XX

Gaztelupe

Comandante Zorita 32 ✉ 28020 – Ⓜ Alvarado – ✆ 91 534 90 28 – Fax 91 554 65 66 – www.goizeko-gaztelupe.com
closed Sunday dinner **L2**
Rest – Carte 48/54 €
◆ Basque ◆ Friendly ◆
A bar at the entrance, refurbished dining areas with décor in regional style, and two private rooms in the basement. An extensive menu of traditional Basque dishes.

XX

El Comité

Smokers rest.
pl. de San Amaro 8 ✉ 28020 – Ⓜ Santiago Bernabeu – ✆ 91 571 87 11 – Fax 91 435 43 27
closed Saturday lunch and Sunday **L1**
Rest – Carte approx. 50 €
◆ French ◆ Bistro ◆
Restaurant in a welcoming bistro-style with café-type furniture and lots of old photos on the walls. French cuisine.

XX

Sal Gorda

Smokers rest.
Beatríz de Bobadilla 9 ✉ 28040 – Ⓜ Guzmán El Bueno – ✆ 91 553 95 06
closed August and Sunday **K2**
Rest – Carte approx. 33 €
◆ Spanish ◆ Formal ◆
A warm, inviting and professionally run restaurant with a regular and loyal clientele. Traditional décor with a slightly outdated feel.

Kabuki

av. Presidente Carmona 2 ✉ 28020 – Ⓜ Santiago Bernabeu – ✆ 91 417 64 15 – Fax 91 556 02 32
closed Holy Week, 4 to 24 August, Saturday lunch, Sunday and Bank Holidays
Rest – Carte approx. 61 € **L1-2**
♦ Japanese ♦ Minimalist ♦
An intimate Japanese restaurant with tasteful, minimalist décor. A modern terrace, in addition to a bar/kitchen serving popular dishes such as sushi.

Tasca La Farmacia

No smokers rest.

Capitán Haya 19 ✉ 28020 – Ⓜ Cuzco – ✆ 91 555 81 46 – Fax 91 556 62 02 – www.asadordearanda.com
closed 17 August-8 September and Sunday **L1**
Tapa 3 € **Ración** approx. 10 €
♦ Codfish specialities ♦ Tapas bar ♦
This charming restaurant is adorned with azulejos, stone arches, exposed brickwork, wrought-iron latticework and attractive glass in the ceiling of the dining room. Famous for its cod dishes.

CHAMARTÍN *Plan V*

Puerta América

av. de América 41 ✉ 28002 – Ⓜ Cartagena – ✆ 91 744 54 00 – hotel.puertamerica@hoteles-silken.com – Fax 91 744 54 01 – www.hotelpuertamerica.com **N3**
330 rm – ††169/360 €, ☕ 25 € – 12 suites
Rest *Lágrimas Negras* – *(closed 4 to 24 August, Saturday lunch and Sunday)* Carte 61/86 €
♦ Business ♦ Design ♦
A colourful hotel with a distinct designer feel, with each floor highlighting the creativity of a famous artist. Original décor in the guestrooms. The modern restaurant has a certain New York ambience, with a bar area and high ceilings.

NH Eurobuilding

Padre Damián 23 ✉ 28036 – Ⓜ Cuzco – ✆ 91 353 73 00 – nheurobuilding@nh-hotels.com – Fax 91 345 45 76 – www.nh-hotels.com **M2**
455 rm – ††100/230 €, ☕ 20 € – 4 suites
Rest *Magerit* – *(closed August)* Carte approx. 45 €
♦ Business ♦ Chain hotel ♦ Functional ♦
In keeping with the NH chain's philosophy, the rooms here are well-appointed, modern and spacious. Numerous meeting rooms and a spa complex. High-quality restaurant with a warm, traditional atmopshere.

AC Aitana

No smokers rest.

paseo de la Castellana 152 ✉ 28046 – Ⓜ Cuzco – ✆ 91 458 49 70 – aitana@ac-hotels.com – Fax 91 458 49 71 – www.ac-hotels.com **M2**
109 rm – ††107/235 €, ☕ 19 € – 2 suites
Rest – *(closed August)* Carte approx. 35 €
♦ Business ♦ Chain hotel ♦ Functional ♦
The interior design and furniture here have an avant-garde feel, with a predominance of wood. Contemporary bedrooms with parquet flooring. The restaurant is used for breakfast, lunch and dinner.

NH La Habana

No smokers rest.

paseo de la Habana 73 ✉ 28036 – Ⓜ Colombia – ✆ 91 443 07 20 – nhhabana@nh-hotels.com – Fax 91 457 75 79 – www.nh-hotels.com
155 rm – †170 € ††205 €, ☕ 16 € – 1 suite **M2**
Rest – Menu 35 €
♦ Business ♦ Chain hotel ♦ Functional ♦
A modern hotel geared mainly to business visitors. Comfortable guestrooms, albeit on the small side, with modern furnishings and wooden flooring.

Confortel Suites Madrid

No smokers rest.

López de Hoyos 143 ✉ 28002 – Ⓜ Alfonso XIII – ✆ 91 744 50 00 – info@confortelsuitesmadrid.com – Fax 91 415 30 73 – www.confortelhoteles.com **N3**

120 rm – 85/300 €, 16 €

Rest – *(closed August, Saturday and Sunday)* Menu 17 €

♦ Business ♦ Chain hotel ♦ Modern ♦

A large, business-orientated hotel with reasonably spacious guestrooms, almost all with their own lounge, which are gradually being refurbished in a more contemporary style.

Don Pío

av. Pío XII-25 ✉ 28016 – Ⓜ Pio XII – ✆ 91 353 07 80 – hoteldonpio@hoteldonpio.com – Fax 91 353 07 81 – www.hoteldonpio.com **N2**

41 rm – 68/138 € 78/170 €, 13 €

Rest – *(coffee shop only)*

♦ Business ♦ Traditional ♦ Cosy ♦

An attractive patio foyer with a classic-modern skylight which runs through the building. The bedrooms are quite large and have facilities such as hydro-massage.

Castilla Plaza

paseo de la Castellana 220 ✉ 28046 – Ⓜ Plaza Castilla – ✆ 91 567 43 00 – castilla-plaza@abbahoteles.com – Fax 91 315 54 06 – www.abbahoteles.com **M1**

228 rm – 90/275 € 140/350 €, 16 €

Rest – Carte 32/41 €

♦ Business ♦ Modern ♦

An impressive, glass-fronted building which, along with the Kio Torres, forms part of the architectural complex known as the Puerta de Europa. Comfortable, modern and with a wealth of detail. The menu in the attractively laid-out restaurant focuses on traditional cuisine.

Aristos

av. Pío XII-34 ✉ 28016 – Ⓜ Pio XII – ✆ 91 345 04 50 – hotelaristos@elchaflan.com – Fax 91 345 10 23 – www.hotelaristos.com **N1**

22 rm – 110 € 150 €, 9 € – 1 suite

Rest *El Chaflán* – see below

♦ Traditional ♦ Functional ♦

An attractive red-brick façade, functional facilities and well-appointed rooms with white wooden flooring and contemporary furnishings.

Zalacain (Juan Antonio Medina)

Álvarez de Baena 4 ✉ 28006 – Ⓜ Gregorio Marañón – ✆ 91 561 48 40 – Fax 91 561 47 32 – www.restaurantezalacain.com closed Holy Week, August, Saturday lunch, Sunday and Bank Holidays **M3**

Rest – Menu 94 € – Carte 57/79 €

Spec. Carpaccio de hígado de oca con aceitunas verdes y salsa de romero. Bogavante guisado con salsa de anchoas y cogollo de Tudela breseado. Medallón de solomillo con salsa de fresones y manzana caramelizada.

♦ International ♦ Formal ♦

A warm and intimate setting with a keen sense of aesthetic detail. An elegant atmosphere in which to enjoy a mix of traditional and international cuisine.

Príncipe de Viana

Manuel de Falla 5 ✉ 28036 – Ⓜ Santiago Bernabeu – ✆ 91 457 15 49 – restaurante@principeviana.com – Fax 91 457 52 83 closed Holy Week, August, Saturday lunch and Sunday **M2**

Rest – Carte 60/68 €

♦ Basque ♦ Formal ♦

Well-known restaurant serving Basque-Navarrese inspired cooking. Traditional dining areas and excellent service.

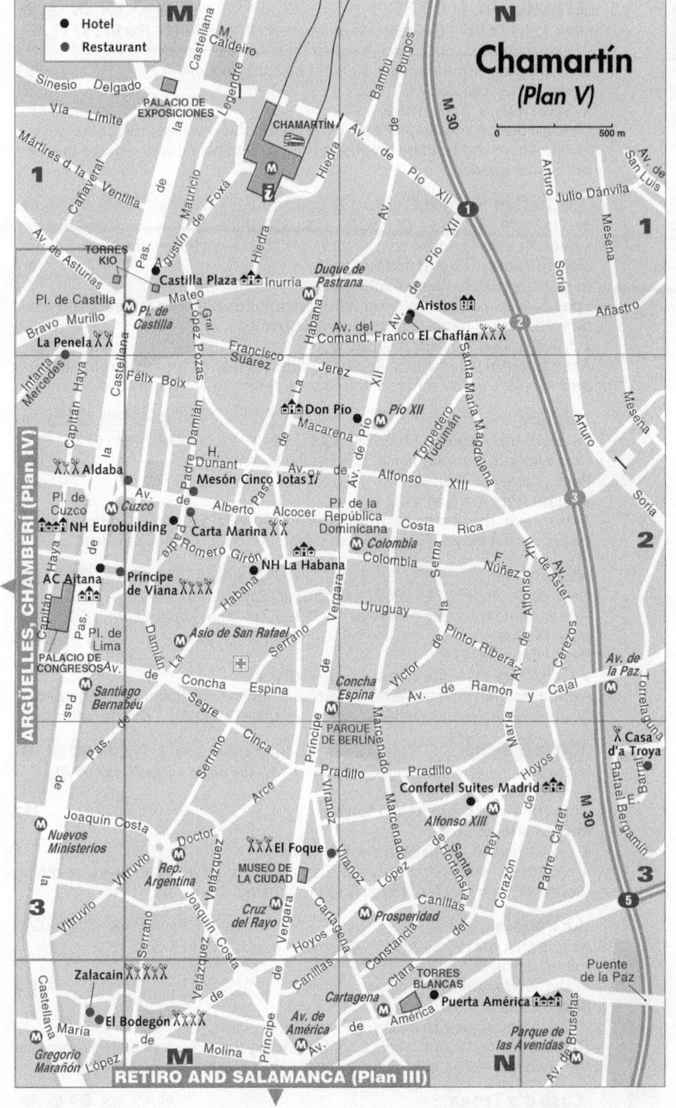
Chamartín
(Plan V)
Hotel
Restaurant
500 m
PALACIO DE EXPOSICIONES
CHAMARTÍN
TORRES KIO
Castilla Plaza
Aristos
El Chaflán
La Penela
Don Pío
Aldaba
Mesón Cinco Jotas
NH Eurobuilding
Carta Marina
NH La Habana
AC Aitana
Príncipe de Viana
PALACIO DE CONGRESOS
Confortel Suites Madrid
Casa d'a Troya
El Foque
MUSEO DE LA CIUDAD
Zalacain
El Bodegón
TORRES BLANCAS
Puerta América
ARGÜELLES, CHAMBERÍ (Plan IV)
RETIRO AND SALAMANCA (Plan III)
Pl. de Castilla
Duque de Pastrana
Pío XII
Cuzco
Colombia
Asio de San Rafael
Santiago Bernabéu
Concha Espina
PARQUE DE BERLÍN
Alfonso XIII
Nuevos Ministerios
Rep. Argentina
Cruz del Rayo
Prosperidad
Cartagena
Av. de América
Gregorio Marañón
Parque de las Avenidas
Puente de la Paz
M 30

XXXX

El Bodegón

Pinar 15 ✉ 28006 – Ⓜ Gregorio Marañón – ☎ 91 562 88 44 – Fax 91 562 97 25 – www.grupovips.com

closed August, Saturday lunch, Sunday and Bank Holidays **M3**

Rest – Carte approx. 62 €

♦ Spanish ♦ Formal ♦

Classical design and elegance are to the fore in this restaurant set out on several levels, where the culinary emphasis is on traditional cuisine. Private bar for a pre-dinner aperitif.

XXX ✿

El Chaflán (Juan Pablo Felipe) – Hotel Aristos

av. Pío XII-34 ✉ 28016 – Ⓜ Pio XII – ☎ 91 350 61 93 – restaurante@elchaflan.com – Fax 91 345 10 23 – www.elchaflan.com

closed 10 days in August and Sunday **N1**

Rest – Menu 75 € – Carte 62/90 €

Spec. Salpicón de mariscos a la soja. Atún rojo con pil-pil de tomate y cous cous de verduritas. Naranja suzette (autumn-spring).

♦ Inventive ♦ Minimalist ♦

A restaurant in minimalist style which prides itself on its service. An olive tree has pride of place in the centre of the room. Interesting and innovative cuisine.

XXX

Aldaba

av. de Alberto Alcocer 5 ✉ 28036 – Ⓜ Cuzco – ☎ 91 359 73 86 – Fax 91 345 21 93

closed August, Saturday lunch, Sunday and Bank Holidays **M2**

Rest – Carte 59/79 €

♦ Spanish ♦ Friendly ♦

A bar near the entrance from which follows a pleasant dining room in classic-modern style. There are also private rooms. Excellent wine list.

XXX

El Foque

Smokers rest.

Suero de Quiñones 22 ✉ 28002 – Ⓜ Cruz del Rayo – ☎ 91 519 25 72 – restaurante@elfoque.com – Fax 91 519 25 73 – www.elfoque.com

closed Sunday **M3**

Rest – Carte 38/45 €

♦ Codfish specialities ♦ Friendly ♦

A good location next to the National Music Auditorium. Refined dining room on two levels with maritime décor including a mast and sails. Cod specialities.

XX

Carta Marina

No smokers rest.

Padre Damián 40 ✉ 28036 – Ⓜ Cuzco – ☎ 91 458 68 26 – Fax 91 457 08 21 – www.carta-marina.com

closed Holy Week, August and Sunday **M2**

Rest – Carte 38/56 €

♦ Galician specialities ♦ Formal ♦

A restaurant with wood décor and an attractive private bar. Pleasant dining rooms with terrace. Traditional Galician cooking.

XX

La Penela

Infanta Mercedes 98 ✉ 28020 – Ⓜ Valdeacederas – ☎ 91 579 91 78 – www.lapenela.com

closed Sunday dinner **M1-2**

Rest – Carte 31/46 €

♦ Galician specialities ♦ Formal ♦

This Galician restaurant offers a bar for waiting and a modern dining room split over two floors. The products are very fresh, brought in daily from Galicia.

X

Casa d'a Troya

Emiliano Barral 14 ✉ 28043 – Ⓜ Avenida de la Paz – ☎ 91 416 44 55 – Fax 91 416 42 80

closed 24 December-2 January, Holy Week, 15 July-August, dinner Monday to Thursday, Sunday and Bank Holidays **N3**

Rest – Carte 40/60 €

♦ Galician specialities ♦ Family ♦

A family-run restaurant comprising a bar at the entrance and two comfortable dining rooms. Galician food prepared in a traditionally simple way.

Mesón Cinco Jotas

Padre Damián 42 ✉ 28036 – Ⓜ Cuzco – ✆ 91 350 31 73
– m5jpdamian@osborne.es – Fax 91 345 79 51
– www.mesoncincojotas.com **M2**

Tapa 4 € **Ración** approx. 10 €

◆ Spanish ◆ Tapas bar ◆

This establishment belongs to a chain specialising in ham and other pork products. Two attractive eating areas plus a limited choice of set menus.

PARQUE FERIAL *Plan I*

Sofitel Madrid Campo de las Naciones

av. de la Capital de España Madrid 10 ✉ 28042
– Ⓜ Campo de las Naciones – ✆ 91 721 00 70 – h1606@accor.com
– Fax 91 721 05 15 – www.sofitel.com **D1**

176 rm – ††100/348 €, ☕ 25 € – 3 suites

Rest ***Mare Nostrum*** – *(closed August, Saturday and Sunday)* Carte 56/75 €

◆ Business ◆ Chain hotel ◆ Classic ◆

Close to Madrid's exhibition site. Impressive entrance area and attractive dining room in the style of an Andalucian patio. Well-appointed, comfortable guestrooms. Distinguished ambience in the Mare Nostrum restaurant, with its interesting menu.

Novotel Madrid Campo de las Naciones

No smokers rest.

Amsterdam 3 ✉ 28042
– Ⓜ Campo de las Naciones – ✆ 91 721 18 18 – h1636@accor.com
– Fax 91 721 11 22 – www.novotel.com **D1**

240 rm – ††74/250 €, ☕ 17 € – 6 suites

Rest ***Claravía*** – Carte 32/46 €

◆ Business ◆ Chain hotel ◆ Functional ◆

A contemporary chain hotel near the city's exhibition area. Reasonably spacious public areas, and bedrooms with functional facilities and furnishings. Bright dining room with a terrace for the summer months.

Acis y Galatea

Galatea 6 ✉ 28042 – Ⓜ Canillejas – ✆ 91 743 49 01
– res.acisgalatea@hotelesglobales.com – Fax 91 741 76 97
– www.acisygalatea.com **D1**

20 rm – †75/165 € ††85/170 €, ☕ 11 €

Rest – *(coffee shop only)*

◆ Family ◆ Modern ◆

Full of charm, and noteworthy for its friendly family management and contrasting modern decoration in bright and dark colours. Well-equipped rooms.

AT BARAJAS AIRPORT *Plan I*

Meliá Barajas

av. de Logroño 305 (A2 and detour to Barajas city: 15km) ✉ 28042 – Ⓜ Barajas
– ✆ 91 747 77 00 – reservas.tryp.barajas@solmelia.com – Fax 91 747 87 17
– www.meliabarajas.solmelia.com **D1**

220 rm – ††95/210 €, ☕ 18 € – 9 suites

Rest – Menu 20 €

◆ Business ◆ Chain hotel ◆ Classic ◆

Comfortable and traditional with extremely well-equipped rooms and refurbished bathrooms. A number of conference/meeting rooms around the swimming pool and garden. One dining room serves à la carte cuisine, the other food prepared on a charcoal grill.

Tryp Alameda Aeropuerto

av. de Logroño 100 (A2 and detour to Barajas city: 15km) ✉ *28042* – Ⓜ *Barajas* – ✆ *91 747 48 00 – tryp.alameda.aeropuerto@solmelia.com – Fax 91 747 89 28 – www.trypalamedaaeropuerto.solmelia.com* **D1**

145 rm – 70/200 €, ☕ 16 € – 3 suites

Rest – Menu 15 €

◆ Business ◆ Chain hotel ◆ Modern ◆

Bright and comfortable guest rooms furnished in modern style with cherry tones and well-equipped bathrooms. The hotel's lounges and meeting areas are in the process of being refurbished.

Aparthotel Convención Barajas without rest

Noray 10 (A2 detour to Barajas city and industrial zone: 10km) ✉ *28042* – Ⓜ *El Capricho* – ✆ *91 371 74 10 – aparthotel@hotel-convencion.com – Fax 91 371 79 01 – www.hotel-convencion.com* **D1**

95 suites – 70/148 € 70/185 €, ☕ 12 €

◆ Business ◆ Functional ◆

Two towers with few areas in common although they have spacious apartment-type bedrooms with a small sitting room and kitchen.

NH Barajas without rest

Catamarán 1 (A2 detour to Barajas city and industrial zone: 10km) ✉ *28042* – Ⓜ *El Capricho* – ✆ *91 742 02 00 – exbarajas@nh-hoteles.es – Fax 91 741 11 00 – www.nh-hotels.com* **D1**

173 rm – 67/140 €, ☕ 9.50 €

◆ Business ◆ Chain hotel ◆ Functional ◆

This budget hotel, part of the NH chain, offers reasonable comfort and value for money, although its lounges and public areas are somewhat on the small side.

BARCELONA

BARCELONA

Population (est 2007): 1 605602 (conurbation 5 327872) – Altitude: sea level

B. Brillion/MICHELIN

It can't be overestimated how important Catalonia is to the locals of Barcelona. Pride in their autonomous region of Spain runs deep in the blood. Barcelona loves to mix the traditional with the avant-garde, and this exuberant opening of arms has seen it grow over the years into a pulsating city for visitors. Its rash of theatres, museums and concert halls is unmatched by most other European cities, and many artists and architects have chosen to live here. Testament to the creative zest of Barcelona lies in the fact that Picasso, Miró and Dalí, along with Gaudí and Subirachs, chose to make it their home.

The nineteenth century was a golden period in the city's artistic development, with the growth of the great Catalan Modernism movement. It was knocked back on its heels after the Spanish Civil War and the rise to power of the dictator Franco, who destroyed the hopes for an independent Catalonia. After his death, democracy came to Spain and in the last 30 years Barcelona has relished its position as capital of a restored autonomous region. Whether it's via fun-loving locals, record numbers of tourists thronging its streets, or the beloved Barça football team that reached the pinnacle of success with victory in the 2006 European Champions League, this is a city that lives by the headlines it creates.

LIVING THE CITY

If you're up on **Montjuïc**, you get a great overview of the city below. Barcelona's atmospheric old town is near the harbour and reaches into the teeming streets of the **Gothic Quarter**, while the newer area is north of this, the elegant avenues in grid formation that make up Eixample. The coastal quarter of **Barça** has been transformed in recent times with the development of Barceloneta and its trendy informality. For many, though, the epicentre of this bubbling city is **The Ramblas**, scything through the centre of town.

PRACTICAL INFORMATION

ARRIVAL-DEPARTURE

Barcelona airport is located 13km southwest of the city. A taxi will cost around €25. Alternatively take the train (marked C beside Terminal A) every 30min or Aerobýs which runs approximately every 10min.

TRANSPORT

Barcelona Card – one to five days of unlimited travel, starting at 17 euros, on metro and buses; discounts on airport bus and cable cars; reduced entry to museums and attractions; discounts in several restaurants, bars and shops. It's sold at airport, tourist offices and various participating venues.

Articket – 20 euros: gives free entry to seven museums and galleries over three months and is available from tourist offices.

Look out for two tourist buses – orange Barcelona Tours and white Bus Turistic; both offer comprehensive tours of the city.

Walking tours include Modernisme, Picasso, Gothic and Gourmet – the latter includes stops in best cafés, food shops and markets.

EXPLORING BARCELONA

Has the vibrant and visceral Catalonian capital grown too popular for its own good? Some might say so but it's not hard to make the opposite case: Barcelona has always been a city that wears its heart on its sleeve, eager to show the world a love of eccentricity and affection for life after dark. No wonder the modernist master **Gaudí** flourished here: his ideals of creativity and vivacity fitted perfectly with those of the locals.

Following the 'grey years' of Franco, Barcelona really took off. It was awarded the 1992 Olympics, and the city fathers granted free reign to acclaimed architects and designers for a face-lifting blitz. From a virtual 'green-free' city, 19 new parks were created and nearly 30,000 new trees took root. Neglected squares were transformed with paved surfaces, shimmering mosaics and innovative sculptures, not to mention new seats from which to appreciate them. And the run-down seafront was spruced up, so that swathes of shiny new beach and bustling marina were created from wasteland. It's now possible to walk along five kilometres of waterfront or laze on a beach, though you might wish to avert your gaze from the senors of a certain vintage who have taken this late opportunity in life to stand naked at the water's edge.

→ RAMBLING ON

Polls indicate that Barcelona is the European city best loved by visitors. Its beating heart, The **Ramblas**, runs straight up from the port, inexorably sucking in the world's tourists. Plane trees fan the way, and you can buy all manner of bird-life and flowers, or watch locals chatting at the newsstands. Along its three-quarter mile stretch, the Ramblas boasts numerous places to linger, from the exhibitions of the Centre d'Art Santa Mónica and waxwork likenesses at the Museu de Cera at one end, to the splendid 19C **Palau Moja** and famous Canaletes drinking fountain at the other. In between it's possible to get a feel for Gaudí's curves at the Palau Güell with its magnificently ornate chimneys, indulge in a treasure trove of musical paraphernalia at Casa Beethoven, or submerge into a feast of colourful fruit, fish and veg at the mighty Boquería market with its sturdy cast iron exterior and stained glass decorations.

You can retreat from the clamour of the Ramblas onto two of the city's most charming squares: **Plaça del Pi**, where buskers make the most of wonderful acoustics, or **Plaça Reial**, a harmonious spot with palm trees, fountains, classical buildings and lanterns designed by Gaudí.

In a city of churches, two stand out. The **Catedral de Santa Eulalia**, an imposing medieval giant that actually wasn't finished until 1913, is the star attraction of the Gothic quarter adjacent to the Ramblas. Its longevity of construction is being mirrored further across the city, where Gaudí's **Sagrada Familia**, Barcelona's most famously photographed landmark, remains unfinished, over 80 years after its creator was run down and killed by a trolley bus. Its circular towers, stretching conically to the heavens, look down eerily on a hollow interior, the project's completion date vaguely set for some time in the future. Gaudí spent the last 16 years of his life working on La Sagrada Familia. His name is entrenched in the city's recent history, his monuments to Modernism consigning design rulebooks to the scrap heap. No visitor should miss his work. La Pedrera ('The Stone Quarry' to natives) is an imposing apartment house with a fantastical, rippling façade and roof, while Casa Batlló's wonderfully sinister face depicts Sant Jordi and the Dragon: the cross on the top of the building is the knight's lance, the roof is the back of the beast, and the skeletal balconies are the skulls and bones of its wretched victims.

UNESCO has been busy in Barça. **Casa Batlló** is now one of its sites, as is the 100 year-old Palau de la Música Catalana, a richly ornate concert hall in the modernist style. Quirkiness pops up in all corners of the city with a wealth of offbeat museums dedicated to the likes of sewers, funeral carriages and shoes. The one most people head for, though, is the **Museu Picasso**, housed in five beautiful palaces, and containing over 3,600 of the great man's works, mostly from his early years and Blue Period. Picasso would have approved of the La Ribera district in which the museum is found: it's a bohemian, cutting edge area, and teems with boutiques, trendy cafés and snazzy restaurants.

→ HEAD FOR THE HILL

For a different view of the city, then **Montjuïc** is the place to head for. The 700ft. hill, home of most events at the

'92 Olympics, provides Barça's lungs. You can reach the summit in style by cable car, and take in the views via new gardens and walkways. Don't miss out on a swim in the Olympic pool while you're there. Then soak up the glories of the world-renowned **Museu Nacional d'Art de Catalunya**, in the massive Palau Nacional. This contains a unique collection of Romanesque frescoes peeled carefully from the walls of churches in remote Pyrenean valleys.

Barcelona has changed much since George Orwell stayed in the city in the mid-thirties during the time of the Civil War. He wrote in Homage to Catalonia: "The working-class was in the saddle. Practically every building of any size had been seized by the workers." You could argue that artists and architects have now seized those very buildings. A former bullring in the city (bullfighting no longer exists now in Barcelona) is being transformed into an avant-garde shopping centre by Lord Rogers: an old infatuation being replaced by a very modern one.

CALENDAR HIGHLIGHTS

Think Barcelona and you think celebration. Unsurprisingly, the city enjoys a rich musical calendar. Maldades, in May, is a fiery flamenco festival which has strong similarities with the popular Rumba Catalana, while in the same month, the Barcelona Guitar Festival highlights international talent and emerging performers in locations around the city. From October through to July, the Gran Teatre del Liceu presents a wide-ranging programme of classical performances in luxurious surroundings. Also in October, the International Jazz Festival is one of Europe's longest-running and most well respected events, and the range of styles on offer is all-encompassing. Away from the music hall, you can get out and about on two wheels in the much-hyped Bicycle Week every June, and keep the midnight fires burning during the dramatic Fiesta de la Merce in September, when a spectacular late night train of dragons, eagles and devils haunt the streets to a sizzling backdrop of fireworks. There's another great knees-up in June in celebration of Saint John's Day when concerts, dances and bonfires come together in a dazzling explosion. For those in a quieter frame of mind, the Barcelona Book Market, every September, is a fine place to find a second hand book and appreciate charming Passeig de Grácia in Eixample.

VIENNA IN...

→ ONE DAY

Catedral de Santa Eulalia, the Ramblas, La Pedrera, Museu Picasso, Sagrada Familia, chocolate shop

→ TWO DAYS

Montjuïc, Parc Güell, Nou Camp stadium, Barceloneta waterfront, Tibidabo (hill with 19C amusement park)

→ THREE DAYS

Barri Gotic and Palau de la Musica Catalana, Via Laietana (street with elegant façades and buzzy cafés), a trip to the resort of Sitges along the coast

EATING OUT

Barcelona has long had a good gastronomic tradition, not least because geographically it's been more influenced by France and Italy than other Spanish regions. But these days the sensual enjoyment of food has become something of a mainstream religion here. Not surprising, when you remember that Ferran Adriá's shrine-like El Bulli restaurant is along the Catalan coast, his reputation leading to an explosion of creative kitchens in the area. But if you want to stick with more traditional fare, the city has hundreds of tapas bars, and these are very refreshing knocked back with a draught beer. The city's location brings together produce from the land and the sea, with a firm emphasis on seasonality and quality produce. This explains why there are 39 markets in the city, all in great locations. Specialities to look out for include Pantumaca: slices of toasted bread with tomato and olive oil; Escalibada which is made with roasted vegetables; Esqueixada, a typically Catalan salad and Crema Catalana, a light custard. One little known facet of Barcelona life is its exquisite chocolate and sweet shops. Two stand out: Fargas, in the Barri Gothic, is the city's most famous chocolate shop, its 19C air giving it the status of a shrine, while Cacao Sampaka is the most elegant chocolate store you could ever wish to find and its creative concoctions, made with authentic cocoa, would make even Willie Wonka drool.

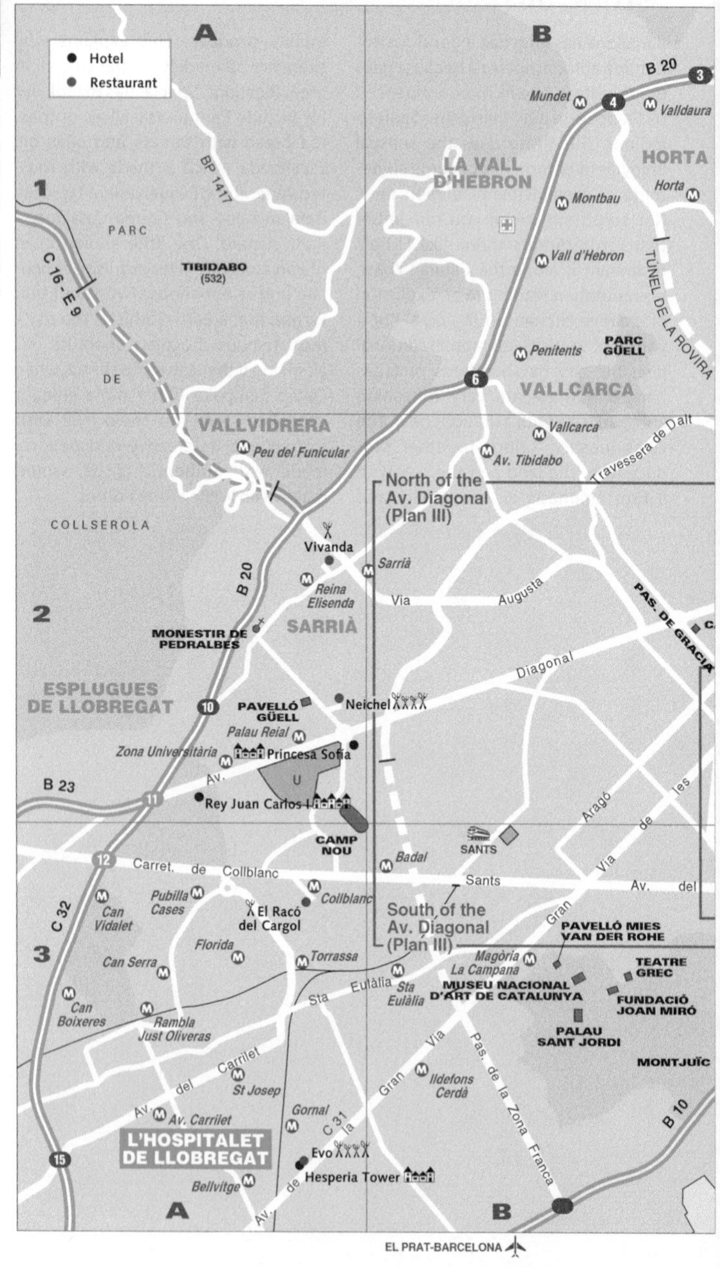
A
B
Hotel
Restaurant
B 20
Mundet
Valldaura
HORTA
Horta
LA VALL D'HEBRON
Montbau
Vall d'Hebron
TÚNEL DE LA ROVIRA
BP 1417
PARC
TIBIDABO (532)
C 16 - E 9
DE
Penitents
PARC GÜELL
VALLCARCA
VALLVIDRERA
Peu del Funicular
Vallcarca
Av. Tibidabo
Travessera de Dalt
North of the Av. Diagonal (Plan III)
COLLSEROLA
Vivanda
Sarrià
B 20
Reina Elisenda
Via Augusta
PAS. DE GRACIA
MONESTIR DE PEDRALBES
SARRIÀ
Diagonal
ESPLUGUES DE LLOBREGAT
PAVELLÓ GÜELL
Neichel
Palau Reial
Zona Universitària
Princesa Sofia
Av.
B 23
Rey Juan Carlos I
CAMP NOU
SANTS
Aragó
Badal
Carret. de Collblanc
Sants
Av. del
Gran Via de les
Pubilla Cases
El Racó del Cargol
Collblanc
Can Vidalet
C 32
South of the Av. Diagonal (Plan III)
PAVELLÓ MIES VAN DER ROHE
Florida
Torrassa
Magòria La Campana
TEATRE GREC
Can Serra
Sta Eulàlia
MUSEU NACIONAL D'ART DE CATALUNYA
FUNDACIÓ JOAN MIRÓ
Can Boixeres
Rambla Just Oliveras
PALAU SANT JORDI
MONTJUÏC
Av. del Carrilet
St Josep
Gran Via
Ildefons Cerdà
Pas. de la Zona Franca
Av. Carrilet
Gornal
C 31
B 10
L'HOSPITALET DE LLOBREGAT
Evo
Hesperia Tower
Bellvitge
Av. de la
EL PRAT-BARCELONA

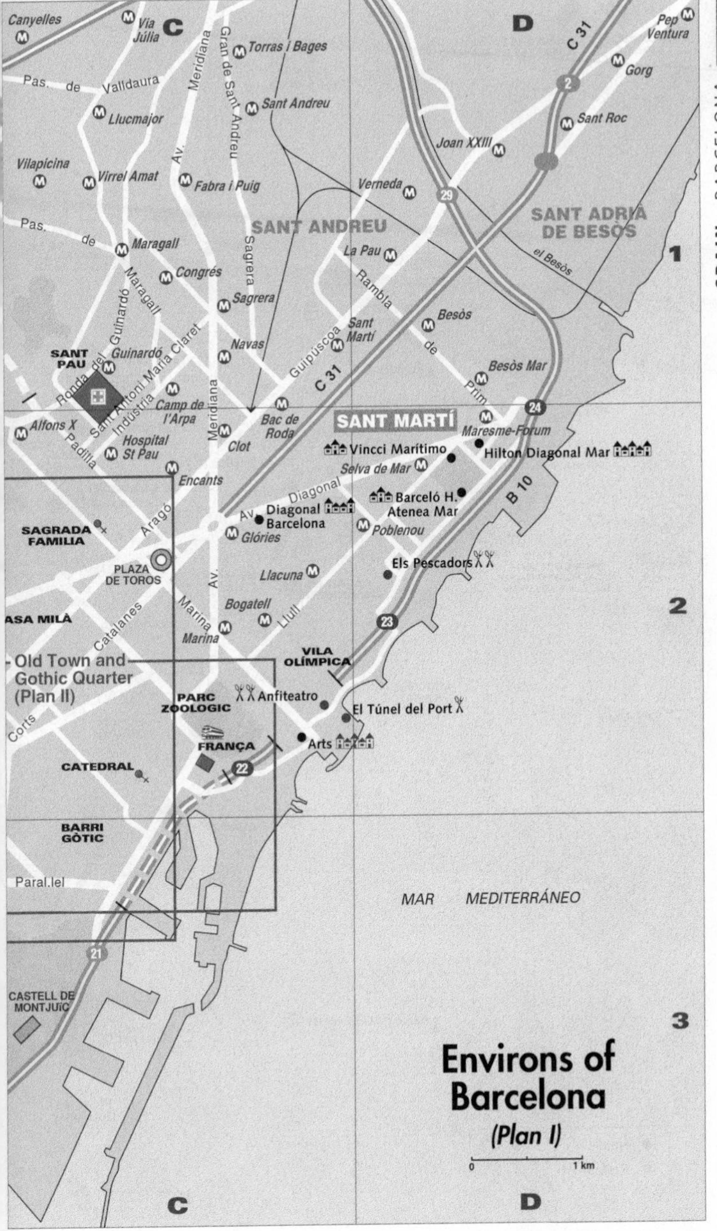

Environs of Barcelona

(Plan I)

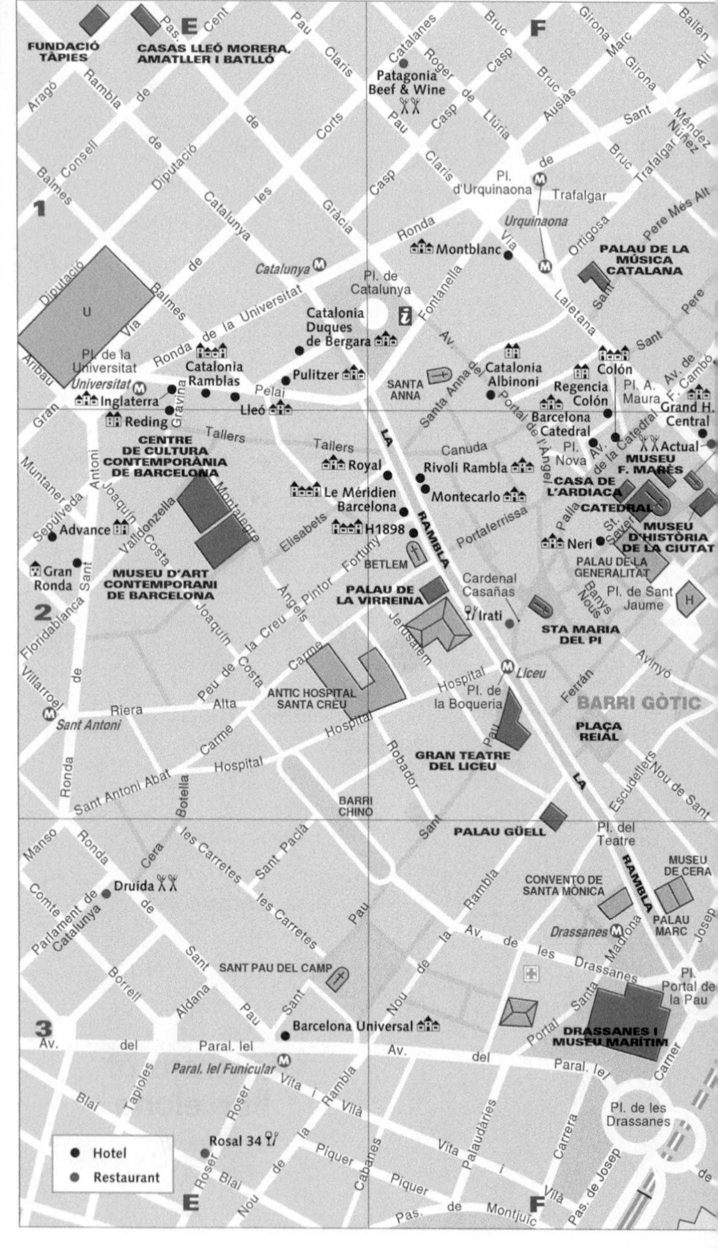
E
F
1
2
3
FUNDACIÓ TÀPIES
CASAS LLEÓ MORERA, AMATLLER I BATLLÓ
Patagonia Beef & Wine
Montblanc
PALAU DE LA MÚSICA CATALANA
Catalunya
Pl. de Catalunya
Catalonia Duques de Bergara
Pl. de la Universitat
Universitat
Catalonia Ramblas
Pulitzer
Inglaterra
Lleó
Reding
SANTA ANNA
Catalonia Albinoni
Colón
Regencia Colón
Pl. A. Maura
Grand H. Central
Barcelona Catedral
Pl. Nova
Actual
MUSEU F. MARÈS
CENTRE DE CULTURA CONTEMPORÀNIA DE BARCELONA
Royal
Rivoli Rambla
Le Méridien Barcelona
Montecarlo
CASA DE L'ARDIACA
CATEDRAL
Advance
H1898
Neri
MUSEU D'HISTÒRIA DE LA CIUTAT
PALAU DE LA GENERALITAT
Gran Ronda
MUSEU D'ART CONTEMPORANI DE BARCELONA
BETLEM
Pl. de Sant Jaume
PALAU DE LA VIRREINA
Irati
STA MARIA DEL PI
Liceu
ANTIC HOSPITAL SANTA CREU
Pl. de la Boqueria
BARRI GÒTIC
Sant Antoni
PLAÇA REIAL
GRAN TEATRE DEL LICEU
BARRI CHINO
PALAU GÜELL
Pl. del Teatre
MUSEU DE CERA
Druída
CONVENTO DE SANTA MÒNICA
Drassanes
PALAU MARC
SANT PAU DEL CAMP
Pl. Portal de la Pau
Barcelona Universal
DRASSANES I MUSEU MARÍTIM
Paral. lel Funicular
Pl. de les Drassanes
Rosal 34
LA RAMBLA
Hotel
Restaurant

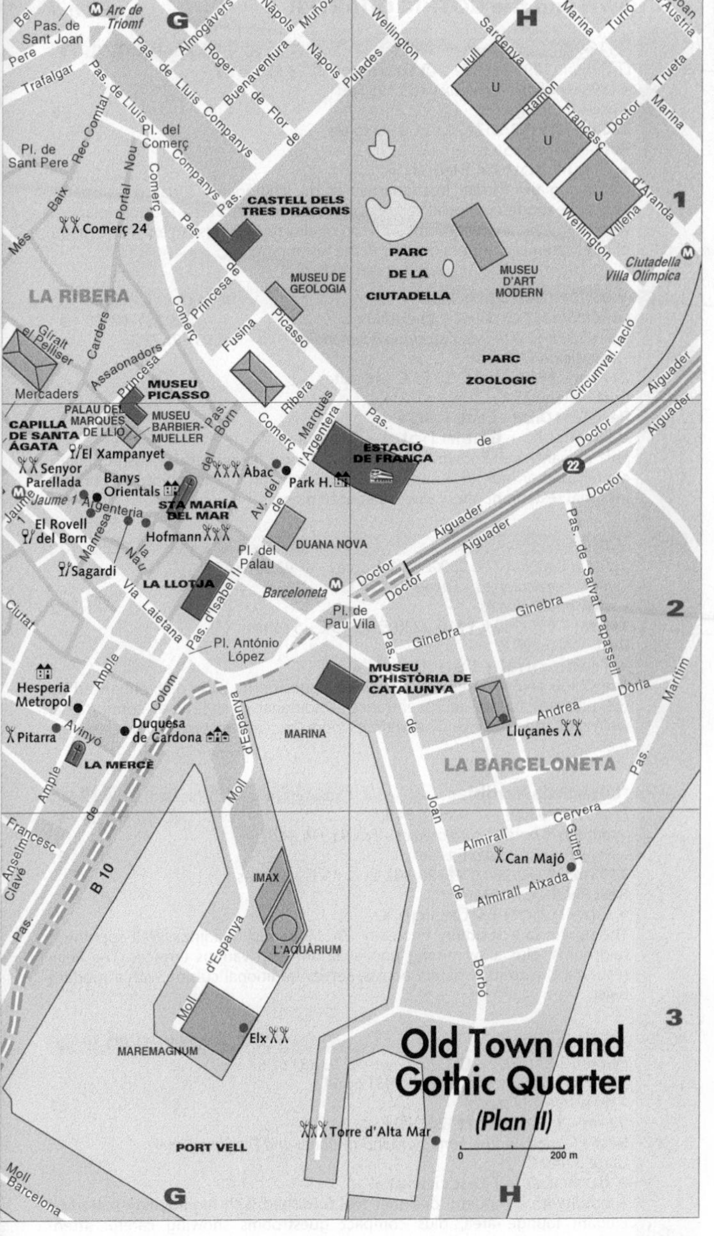

Old Town and Gothic Quarter
(Plan II)

H1898
No smokers rest.

La Rambla 109 ✉ 08002 – Ⓜ Catalunya – ✆ 93 552 95 52 – 1898@nnhotels.es – Fax 93 552 95 50 – www.nnhotels.es **F2**

166 rm – 192/267 €, ☕ 21 € – 3 suites

Rest – Carte 43/56 €

♦ Chain hotel ♦ Stylish ♦

Occupying the former headquarters of the Philippines Tobacco Company, hence the modern-colonial style. Facilities include a spa area, rooftop solarium with city views, and bedrooms with top-quality furnishings. An extensive menu of international cuisine is on offer in the restaurant.

Le Méridien Barcelona
No smokers rest.

La Rambla 111 ✉ 08002 – Ⓜ Catalunya – ✆ 93 318 62 00 – info.barcelona@lemeridien.com – Fax 93 301 77 76 – www.lemeridien.com **F2**

217 rm – 175/400 €, ☕ 25 € – 16 suites

Rest – Menu 25 €

Rest *Cent Onze* – Carte 30/45 €

♦ Business ♦ Chain hotel ♦ Classic ♦

This elegant, well-known hotel combines local flavour and a cosmopolitan contemporary look in a superb location right on the Ramblas. The bright, informal restaurant offers a well-balanced menu.

Colón
No smokers rest.

av. de la Catedral 7 ✉ 08002 – Ⓜ Jaume I – ✆ 93 301 14 04 – info@hotelcolon.es – Fax 93 317 29 15 – www.hotelcolon.es **F2**

140 rm – 90/160 € 100/230 €, ☕ 15 € – 5 suites

Rest – Menu 20 €

♦ Traditional ♦ Functional ♦

The Colón enjoys an enviable position opposite the cathedral, enhanced by the pleasant terrace at its entrance. Traditional in style with comfortable, well-appointed rooms. The dining room has a welcoming and intimate feel.

Catalonia Ramblas
Smokers rest. (heated)

Pelai 28 ✉ 08001 – ✆ 93 316 84 00 – ramblas@hoteles-catalonia.es – Fax 93 316 84 01 – www.hoteles-catalonia.com **E1**

219 rm – 160/264 € 190/302 €, ☕ 15 € – 2 suites

Rest *Pelai* – Carte 34/46 €

♦ Chain hotel ♦ Design ♦

The superb façade unifies two early-20C Modernist buildings. Well-appointed bedrooms, plus a swimming pool-solarium with various terraces. The Pelai restaurant, with its separate access, serves traditional cuisine with a modern twist.

Pulitzer

Bergara 8 ✉ 08002 – Ⓜ Catalunya – ✆ 93 481 67 67 – info@hotelpulitzer.es – Fax 93 481 64 64 – www.hotelpulitzer.es **E1**

92 rm – 120/300 € 120/330 €, ☕ 15 €

Rest – *(closed August, Sunday, Monday dinner and Tuesday dinner)* Carte 31/40 €

♦ Business ♦ Functional ♦

A hotel with a modern, designer feel furnished with high-quality materials. Elegant lounge area, plus compact guestrooms showing careful attention to detail. Informal, contemporary restaurant, which looks out onto a terrace.

Montecarlo without rest

La Rambla 124 ✉ 08002 – Ⓜ Liceu – ✆ 93 412 04 04 – hotel@montecarlobcn.com – Fax 93 318 73 23 – www.montecarlobcn.com **F2**

50 rm – 🛉144 € 🛉🛉220/386 €, ☕ 11 € – 1 suite

◆ Traditional ◆ Design ◆

This magnificent hotel, housed in a 19C palace, harmoniously combines the classicism of the past with exquisitely furnished and spacious guestrooms.

Neri

Sant Sever 5 ✉ 08002 – Ⓜ Liceu – ✆ 93 304 06 55 – info@hotelneri.com – Fax 93 304 03 37 – www.hotelneri.com **F2**

21 rm – 🛉🛉310/341 €, ☕ 25 € – 1 suite

Rest – Menu 27 €

◆ Business ◆ Design ◆

A large 18C mansion with a unique and bold avant-garde look just a few yards from the cathedral. Small library-lounge, superb bedrooms and an intimate restaurant dominated by two stone arches in which the cuisine is equally innovative.

Grand H. Central

Via Laietana 30 ✉ 08003 – Ⓜ Jaume I – ✆ 93 295 79 00 – info@grandhotelcentral.com – Fax 93 268 12 15 – www.grandhotelcentral.com **F2**

141 rm – 🛉🛉155/275 €, ☕ 19 € – 6 suites

Rest Actual – see below

◆ Business ◆ Design ◆

A new generation of hotel where the buzzwords are design and functionality and whose guestrooms are furnished with fine attention to detail. Terrace-solarium with a swimming pool and panoramic views.

Duquesa de Cardona No smokers rest.

passeig de Colom 12 ✉ 08002 – Ⓜ Drassanes – ✆ 93 268 90 90 – info@hduquesadecardona.com – Fax 93 268 29 31 – www.hduquesadecardona.com **G2**

40 rm – 🛉155/250 € 🛉🛉155/265 €, ☕ 14 €

Rest – *(closed Monday) (lunch only)* Menu 15 €

◆ Luxury ◆ Cosy ◆

By incorporating many of its original features, this 19C seigniorial mansion has retained much of its former charm. Excellent bedrooms and an attractive terrace-solarium on the roof.

Rivoli Rambla

La Rambla 128 ✉ 08002 – Ⓜ Catalunya – ✆ 93 481 76 76 – reservas@rivolihotels.com – Fax 93 317 50 53 – www.rivolihotels.com **F2**

119 rm – 🛉180/232 € 🛉🛉215/270 €, ☕ 19 € – 6 suites

Rest – Menu 18 €

◆ Business ◆ Design ◆

This historic building has a delightful façade and a contemporary, classic interior embellished with Art Deco touches. Comfortable bedrooms, plus a pleasant internal terrace. The restaurant menu offers a range of international dishes.

Royal No smokers rest.

La Rambla 117 ✉ 08002 – Ⓜ Catalunya – ✆ 93 301 94 00 – hotelroyal@hroyal.com – Fax 93 317 31 79 – www.hroyal.com **F2**

119 rm – 🛉100/250 € 🛉🛉120/305 €, ☕ 9 €

Rest ***La Poma*** – Carte 35/50 €

◆ Business ◆ Classic ◆

Located in the liveliest part of the city, this hotel's traditional feel is gradually being modernised and updated. The spacious restaurant, specialising in grilled meats, has a separate entrance.

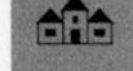

Barcelona Catedral

Dels Capellans 4 ✉ 08002 – Ⓜ Catalunya – ✆ 93 304 22 55
– hotel@barcelonacatedral.com – Fax 93 304 23 66
– www.barcelonacatedral.com **F2**

80 rm – 130/315 €, 16 €
Rest – *(closed Saturday and Sunday) (lunch only)* Menu 20.50 €
♦ Business ♦ Modern ♦
A modern hotel with a wealth of designer features and tasteful décor. Fully-equipped guestrooms and a superb terrace on an inner patio. Informal atmosphere in the restaurant, which adjoins the bar.

Catalonia Duques de Bergara

Bergara 11 ✉ 08002 – Ⓜ Catalunya – ✆ 93 301 51 51
– duques@hoteles-catalonia.es – Fax 93 317 34 42
– www.hoteles-catalonia.com **E1**

146 rm – 150/228 € 180/260 €, 15 € – 2 suites
Rest – Menu 16 €
♦ Business ♦ Chain hotel ♦ Functional ♦
Partly occupying an attractive late-19C Modernist building, with an interior that combines a sense of the past with contemporary comfort. The hotel restaurant offers a wide range of fine international cuisine.

Montblanc No smokers rest.

Via Laietana 61 ✉ 08003 – Ⓜ Urquinaona – ✆ 93 343 55 55
– montblanc@hcchotels.es – Fax 93 343 55 58 – www.hcchotels.es **F1**

157 rm – 115/180 € 132/220 €, 16 €
Rest – Menu 21 €
♦ Traditional ♦ Functional ♦
Spacious lounges, an elegant piano bar, and comfortable, functional bedrooms. Small indoor swimming pool, terrace and solarium. The circular dining room offers a limited choice of international dishes.

Barcelona Universal No smokers rest.

av. del Paral.lel 80 ✉ 08001 – Ⓜ Paral.lel
– ✆ 93 567 74 47 – bcnuniversal@nnhotels.com – Fax 93 567 74 40
– www.nnhotels.com **E3**

164 rm – 107/428 €, 15 € – 3 suites
Rest – *(dinner only)* Menu 22 €
♦ Business ♦ Functional ♦
Built in modern style, this hotel offers guests spacious, well-appointed bedrooms. Lounge area with a bar, plus a panoramic swimming pool and solarium on the roof. The simply furnished restaurant offers buffet dining accompanied by grilled meats.

Inglaterra No smokers rest.

Pelai 14 ✉ 08001 – Ⓜ Universitat – ✆ 93 505 11 00
– recepcion@hotel-inglaterra.com – Fax 93 505 11 09
– www.hotel-inglaterra.com **E1**

60 rm – 99/195 € 99/250 €, 12 €
Rest – Menu 18 €
♦ Traditional ♦ Functional ♦
A modern, welcoming hotel with an attractive, classical façade. Multi-purpose function areas, plus bedrooms with large wooden or leather headboards. Pleasant terrace-solarium. Simply furnished contemporary restaurant decorated in varying tones of red.

Lleó

Pelai 22 ✉ 08001 – Ⓜ Universitat – ✆ 93 318 13 12 – reservas@hotel-lleo.es
– Fax 93 412 26 57 – www.hotel-lleo.es **E1**

89 rm – 120/130 € 145/170 €, 11 €
Rest – *(coffee shop only)*
♦ Family ♦ Personalised ♦
A well-run family hotel with an elegant façade, functional facilities, a large lounge area, and bedrooms offering adequate levels of comfort.

Catalonia Albinoni without rest

av. Portal de l'Ángel 17 ✉ 08002 – Ⓜ Catalunya – ☎ 93 318 41 41 – albinoni@hoteles-catalonia.es – Fax 93 301 26 31 – www.hoteles-catalonia.com **F1**

74 rm – †128/174 € ††158/186 €, ☕ 15 €

♦ Business ♦ Chain hotel ♦ Functional ♦

In the former Rocamora Palace and near the Gothic Quarter. The foyer area has original decorative details and bedrooms in the style of the period.

Park H. without rest

av. Marquès de l'Argentera 11 ✉ 08003 – Ⓜ Barceloneta – ☎ 93 319 60 00 – parkhotel@parkhotelbarcelona.com – Fax 93 319 45 19 – www.parkhotelbarcelona.com **G2**

91 rm ☕ – †85/170 € ††105/210 €

♦ Traditional ♦ Modern ♦

An impeccably maintained hotel with modernised, well-appointed and welcoming rooms. Pleasant entrance-cum-reception area with adjoining bar.

Reding

Gravina 5-7 ✉ 08001 – Ⓜ Universitat – ☎ 93 412 10 97 – reding@oh-es.com – Fax 93 268 34 82 – www.hotelreding.com **E1-2**

44 rm – †123/258 € ††268 €, ☕ 13 €

Rest – *(closed Sunday and Bank Holidays)* Menu 11 €

♦ Traditional ♦ Functional ♦

Located close to Plaça de Catalunya. Relatively small lounge, adequate public areas, though the bedrooms are comfortable and well-appointed. The hotel's simply styled dining room offers a menu featuring traditional and Catalan dishes.

Banys Orientals

L'Argenteria 37 ✉ 08003 – Ⓜ Jaume I – ☎ 93 268 84 60 – reservas@hotelbanysorientals.com – Fax 93 268 84 61 – www.hotelbanysorientals.com **G2**

56 rm – †82 € ††98 €, ☕ 10 €

Rest *Senyor Parellada* – see below

♦ Business ♦ Design ♦

Comfortable minimalist rooms with design features galore, wooden floors and four-poster-style beds. No lounge area.

Regencia Colón without rest

Sagristans 13 ✉ 08002 – Ⓜ Jaume I – ☎ 93 318 98 58 – info@hotelregenciacolon.com – Fax 93 317 28 22 – www.hotelregenciacolon.com **F1-2**

50 rm – †60/130 € ††60/160 €, ☕ 10 €

♦ Traditional ♦ Functional ♦

A great base from which to explore one of the city's most distinctive districts. Functional bedrooms with modern bathrooms and wood flooring.

Hesperia Metropol without rest

Ample 31 ✉ 08002 – Ⓜ Drassanes – ☎ 93 310 51 00 – hotel@hesperia-metropol.com – Fax 93 319 12 76 – www.hesperia-metropol.com **G2**

68 rm – †60/175 € ††60/250 €, ☕ 11 €

♦ Business ♦ Chain hotel ♦ Functional ♦

Situated in the Old Town with comfortable and well-decorated rooms. Friendly atmosphere and pleasant staff.

Advance without rest

Sepúlveda 180 ✉ 08011 – ☎ 93 289 28 92 – hoteladvance@hotenco.com – Fax 93 289 30 24 – www.hotenco.com **E2**

36 rm – †80/250 € ††100/270 €, ☕ 14 €

♦ Chain hotel ♦ Modern ♦

Occupying a renovated old building, this hotel offers guests modern facilities and well-appointed, albeit somewhat small bedrooms, most of which have a built-in shower in the bathroom.

Gran Ronda without rest

Ronda de Sant Antoni 49 ✉ 08011 – ✆ 93 327 18 00 – recepcion.granronda@apsishotels.com – Fax 93 327 18 08 **E2**

65 rm – ††89/200 €, ☕ 11 €

♦ Traditional ♦ Functional ♦

Simple yet well-designed, this hotel uses an inner patio with elevators as a waiting area. Functional, well-appointed and spacious guestrooms.

Àbac (Xavier Pellicer)

(possible transfer to av. del Tibidabo 1), Rec 79-89 ✉ 08003 – Ⓜ Barceloneta – ✆ 93 319 66 00 – info@restaurantabac.com – Fax 93 319 45 19 – www.restaurantabac.com

closed August, Sunday and Monday lunch **G2**

Rest – Menu 84 € – Carte 66/95 €

Spec. Ensaladilla de primavera. Guisantes con tripa de bacalao y colmenillas (February-June). Pollo de payés al cardamomo.

♦ Inventive ♦ Minimalist ♦

Modern restaurant with minimalist design details. Excellent service and creative Mediterranean cuisine. Popular with a young clientele.

Hofmann (Mey Hoffman)

(transfer to street La Granada del Penedès 14-16), L'Argenteria 74-78 (1°) ✉ 08003 – ✆ 93 218 71 65 – restaurante@hofmann-bcn.com – www.hofmann-bcn.com

closed Christmas, Holy Week, August, Saturday and Sunday **G2**

Rest – Carte 56/81 €

Spec. Cigalas envueltas con láminas de shitake sobre parmentier y crema de ceps. Bacalao cocido a baja temperatura con sanfaina. Carré de cordero asado con berenjena rellena de queso.

♦ Inventive ♦ Design ♦

Housed in an old building which doubles as a catering school, the Hofmann is known for its classical design and innovative, imaginatively presented cuisine.

Torre d'Alta Mar No smokers rest. ← city, sea and port,

passeig Joan de Borbó 88 ✉ 08039 – Ⓜ Barceloneta – ✆ 93 221 00 07 – reserves@torredealtamar.com – Fax 93 221 00 90 – www.torredealtamar.com

closed Christmas, 7 days in August, Sunday and Monday lunch **H3**

Rest – Carte 61/76 €

♦ Traditional ♦ Trendy ♦

A unique location on top of a 75m-high metal tower. Circular dining room with modern décor and spectacular views through the surrounding windows.

Actual – Hotel Grand H. Central No smokers rest.

Pare Gallifa 3 ✉ 08003 – Ⓜ Jaume I – ✆ 93 295 79 05 – actual@grandhotelcentral.com – Fax 93 268 12 15 – www.grandhotelcentral.com **F2**

Rest – Carte approx. 35 €

♦ Inventive ♦ Design ♦

Restaurant with bags of personality, a designer setting and polite young staff. Set-price menu of inventive cuisine.

Lluçanès (Ángel Pascual) No smokers rest.

pl. de la Font ✉ 08003 – ✆ 93 224 25 25 – cuina@restaurantllucanes.com – www.restaurantllucanes.com

closed 15 to 31 March, Sunday dinner and Monday **H2**

Rest – Menu 95 € – Carte 58/63 €

Spec. Bloody Mary, guacamole de alubias y bivalbos. Galantina de pato, rebozuelos y cremoso de ajo blanco. Tocinillo de cielo, trufa de verano, helado de trufa y toffee de caramelo amargo.

♦ Inventive ♦ Family ♦

Faithful to its roots, this restaurant in the working-class district of La Barceloneta has an attractively urban feel and a kitchen visible to diners. Innovative cuisine.

XX **Druída** Smokers rest. A/C VISA MC AE
Parlament 54 ✉ 08015 – Ⓜ Sant Antoni – ✆ 93 441 10 45
– druida@restaurantedruida.com – Fax 93 324 84 67
– www.restaurantedruida.com
closed 7 to 31 August, Sunday dinner and Monday **E3**
Rest – Carte 45/65 €
♦ Inventive ♦ Formal ♦
A welcoming restaurant decorated with Louis XV-style furnishings and armchairs, providing an interesting contrast with the designer crockery. Creative menu, and a kitchen visible to customers.

XX **Comerç 24** (Carles Abellán) No smokers rest. A/C VISA MC AE
Comerç 24 ✉ 08003 – Ⓜ Arc de Triomf – ✆ 93 319 21 02
– info@comerc24.com – Fax 93 319 10 74
– www.carlesabellan.com
closed Christmas, 7 days in August, Sunday and Monday **G1**
Rest – Menu 72 € – Carte 43/60 €
Spec. Raviolis de sepia y colmenillas. Arroz de pato y foie. Tapas dulces.
♦ Inventive ♦ Design ♦
A modern restaurant with avant-garde décor where the emphasis is on creative cuisine. Tapas-influenced tasting menus, plus a small menu of "pinchos" and "raciones".

XX **Patagonia Beef & Wine** A/C VISA MC AE
Gran Via de les Corts Catalanes 660 ✉ 08010 – Ⓜ Passeig de Gràcia
– ✆ 93 304 37 35 – info.bcn@patagoniabw.com – Fax 93 304 37 34
– www.patagoniabw.com
closed Sunday **F1**
Rest – Carte 28/50 €
♦ Argentine ♦ Minimalist ♦
The attractive setting and minimalist decoration are the hallmarks of this restuarant with a reasonably extensive menu, with a focus on Argentinian red meat dishes.

XX **Senyor Parellada** – Hotel Banys Orientals A/C VISA MC AE
L'Argenteria 37 ✉ 08003 – Ⓜ Jaume I – ✆ 93 310 50 94
– diana@senyorparellada.com – Fax 93 268 31 57 **G2**
Rest – Carte approx. 28 €
♦ Catalan cuisine ♦ Cosy ♦
An updated classical-style restaurant with several dining rooms and an imposing bar. Worth noting is the mini-courtyard, protected by a glass roof. Regional cooking at reasonable prices.

XX **Elx** No smokers rest. A/C VISA MC AE
Moll d'Espanya-Maremagnum (Local 9) ✉ 08039 – Ⓜ Drassanes
– ✆ 93 225 81 17 – elx@restaurantelx.com – Fax 93 225 81 20
– www.restauratelx.com **G3**
Rest – Carte 28/41 €
♦ Rice specialities ♦ Formal ♦
A restaurant with pleasant views of the marina. Modern dining room and pleasant terrace. Popular for its fish, seafood and good choice of rice-based dishes.

X **Pitarra** A/C VISA MC AE
Avinyó 56 ✉ 08002 – Ⓜ Liceu – ✆ 93 301 16 47 – info@restaurantpitarra.cat
– Fax 93 301 85 62 – www.restaurantpitarra.cat
closed August, Sunday and dinner Bank Holidays **G2**
Rest – Carte 25/45 €
♦ Catalan cuisine ♦ Cosy ♦
A pleasant and welcoming interior adorned with old clocks and mementoes of the poet Pitarra. The comprehensive, moderately priced menu is strong on traditional cuisine.

Can Majó

Almirall Aixada 23 ✉ 08003 – Ⓜ Barceloneta – ✆ 93 221 54 55 – majocan@terra.es – Fax 93 221 54 55
closed Sunday dinner and Monday **H3**
Rest – Carte 33/53 €
◆ Seafood ◆ Family ◆
This popular, family-run restaurant is renowned for its impressive fish and seafood menu. Attractive seafood counter plus a panoramic terrace.

El Rovell del Born

Smokers rest. A/C VISA MC

L'Argenteria 6 ✉ 08003 – Ⓜ Jaume I – ✆ 93 269 04 58 – info@elrovelldelborn.com – www.elrovelldelborn.com
closed Monday except Bank Holidays **G2**
Tapa 2 € **Ración** approx. 5 €
◆ Spanish ◆ Tapas bar ◆
A tavern-style tapas bar with modern décor and a bar heaped with excellent tapas. A number of high tables for customers, who can also enjoy a range of traditional à la carte dishes with a contemporary twist.

Sagardi

L'Argenteria 62 ✉ 08003 – Ⓜ Jaume I – ✆ 93 319 99 93 – reservas@sagardi.com – Fax 93 268 48 86 – www.sagardi.com **G2**
Tapa 1.50 € **Ración** approx. 14 €
◆ Basque ◆ Tapas bar ◆
A Basque cider house situated near the historic church of Santa María del Mar. A very wide range of Basque-style tapas and dining room with cider barrels and charcoal grill.

Irati

Cardenal Casanyes 17 ✉ 08002 – Ⓜ Liceu – ✆ 93 302 30 84 – irati@sagardi.com – Fax 93 412 73 76 – www.sagardi.com **F2**
Tapa 2 € **Ración** approx. 14 €
◆ Basque ◆ Tapas bar ◆
A traditional-style Basque eatery close to the Liceo theatre. Traditional "carvery"-style dining room serving a range of inventive Basque dishes, plus a bar well-stocked with tapas.

El Xampanyet

No smokers rest. VISA MC

Montcada 22 ✉ 08003 – Ⓜ Jaume I – ✆ 93 319 70 03 – xampanyet@telefonica.net
closed Holy Week and August **G2**
Tapa 3.50 € **Ración** approx. 5 €
◆ Spanish ◆ Tapas bar ◆
This well-established family-run tavern is attractively adorned with typical azulejo panelling. A varied selection of tapas with the emphasis on fish and meat.

Rosal 34

Smokers rest. A/C VISA MC AE

Roser 34 ✉ 08004 – Ⓜ Paral.lel – ✆ 93 324 90 46 – info@rosal34.com – Fax 93 324 90 46 – www.rosal34.com
closed 15 to 31 January, 15 to 31 August, Sunday dinner and Monday (October-May), Sunday and Monday lunch for rest of the year **E3**
Ración approx. 15 €
◆ Spanish ◆ Rustic ◆
This former family bodega combines the rustic nature of exposed stone with a décor that is modern in style. Extensive menu of inventive tapas.

Rey Juan Carlos I
No smokers rest. (heated)

av. Diagonal 661 ✉ 08028
– Ⓜ Zona Universitaria – ✆ 93 364 40 40 – hotel@hrjuancarlos.com
– Fax 93 364 42 64 – www.hrjuancarlos.com — Plan I **A2**

375 rm – 160/315 € 160/420 €, 23.50 € – 37 suites
Rest – Menu 38 €

♦ Luxury ♦ Business ♦ Modern ♦

A hotel with impressive modern facilities surrounded by an area of parkland with a small lake and swimming pool. An exclusive atmosphere pervades this hotel, which is tastefully decorated throughout. Various dining options including buffet and à la carte. The Garden restaurant has a pleasant terrace.

Palace

(possible closure for works in 2008), Gran Via de les Corts Catalanes 668
✉ 08010 – Ⓜ Passeig de Gràcia – ✆ 93 510 11 30
– palace@hotelpalacebarcelona.com – Fax 93 318 01 48
– www.hotelpalacebarcelona.com — **L2**

114 rm – 204/394 € 204/421 €, 27 € – 6 suites
Rest *Caelis* – see below

♦ Grand Luxury ♦ Classic ♦

This emblematic hotel, both in terms of its luxury and its tradition, occupies an elegant building dating back to 1919. Delightful cupola-crowned lounge and splendid guestrooms.

Majestic
No smokers rest.

passeig de Gràcia 68 ✉ 08007 – Ⓜ Passeig de Gràcia
– ✆ 93 488 17 17 – recepcion@hotelmajestic.es – Fax 93 448 18 80
– www.hotelmajestic.es
271 rm – 199/450 €, 21 € – 32 suites — **K2**
Rest *Drolma* – see below
Rest – Menu 36 €

♦ Traditional ♦ Classic ♦

This classic address on the Paseo de Gràcia has benefited from a recent renovation. Perfect service and well-appointed guestrooms despite their compact size. Functional dining room offering à la carte and buffet choices.

Condes de Barcelona

passeig de Gràcia 73-75 ✉ 08008 – Ⓜ Diagonal – ✆ 93 445 00 00
– reservas@condesdebarcelona.com – Fax 93 445 32 32
– www.condesdebarcelona.com — **K2**

228 rm – 135/315 €, 17 € – 7 suites
Rest Lasarte – see below
Rest *Loidi* – *(set menu only)* Menu 32 €

♦ Traditional ♦ Modern ♦

A hotel occupying two of the city's most emblematic buildings, the Casa Batlló and the Casa Durella. Comfortable guestrooms with many period features. Attractive terrace-solarium. The Loidi restaurant offers guests a fixed-price menu.

NH Constanza
No smokers rest. (heated)

Deu i Mata 69-99 ✉ 08029 – Ⓜ Les Corts
– ✆ 93 281 15 00 – nhconstanza@nh-hotels.com – Fax 93 410 03 35
– www.nh-hotels.com — **I2**

300 rm – 126/260 €, 19 € – 8 suites
Rest *Nhube* – Carte 30/40 €

♦ Business ♦ Design ♦

Designed by Rafael Moneo to make the most of natural light and straight lines, this hotel boasts a large lobby, modular meeting rooms and luxurious yet functional guestrooms. The restaurant, decorated in varying tones of white, offers a menu centred around traditional cuisine.

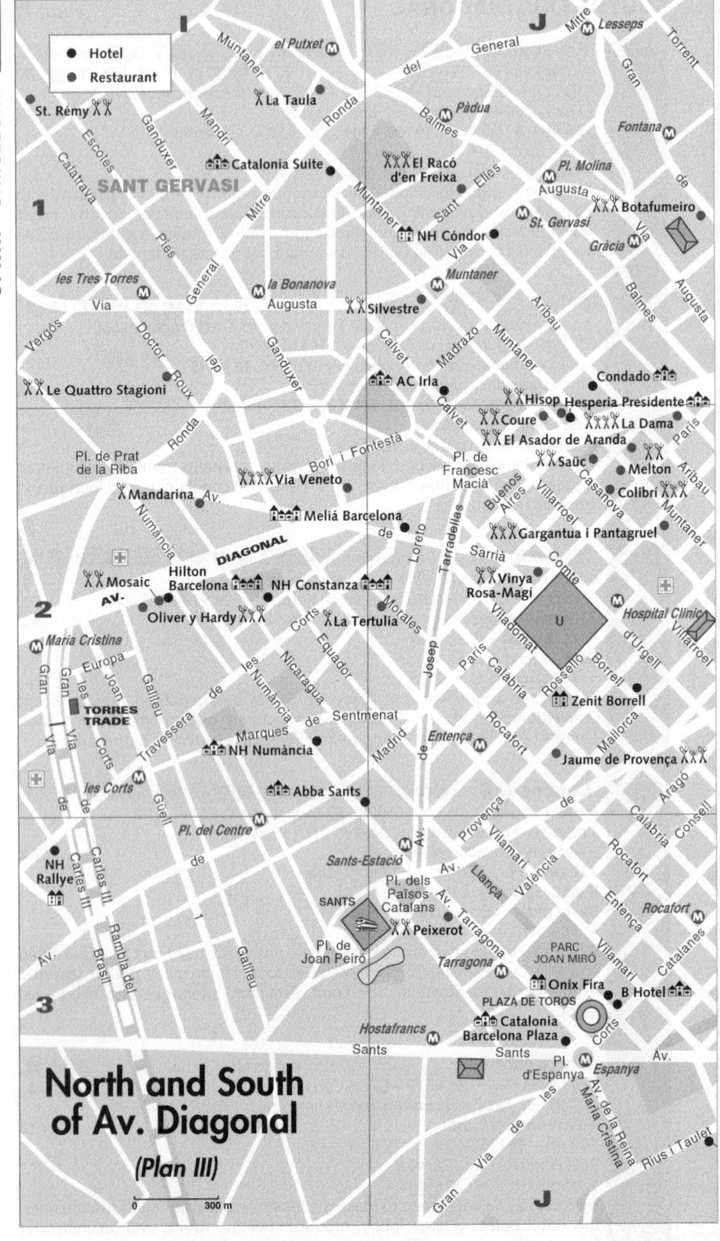

North and South of Av. Diagonal
(Plan III)
Hotel
Restaurant
SANT GERVASI
St. Rémy
La Taula
Catalonia Suite
El Racó d'en Freixa
Botafumeiro
NH Cóndor
Silvestre
Le Quattro Stagioni
AC Irla
Condado
Hisop
Hesperia Presidente
Coure
La Dama
El Asador de Aranda
Saüc
Melton
Colibrí
Via Veneto
Mandarina
Meliá Barcelona
Gargantua i Pantagruel
Mosaic
Hilton Barcelona
NH Constanza
Vinya Rosa-Magí
Oliver y Hardy
La Tertulia
Zenit Borrell
NH Numància
Jaume de Provença
Abba Sants
NH Rallye
Peixerot
Onix Fira
B Hotel
Catalonia Barcelona Plaza
TORRES TRADE
PARC JOAN MIRÓ
PLAZA DE TOROS
SANTS
el Putxet
Lesseps
Pàdua
Fontana
Pl. Molina
St. Gervasi
Gràcia
Muntaner
les Tres Torres
la Bonanova
Maria Cristina
Hospital Clínic
les Corts
Entença
Pl. del Centre
Sants-Estació
Rocafort
Tarragona
Hostafrancs
Espanya
Pl. de Prat de la Riba
Pl. de Francesc Macià
Pl. dels Països Catalans
Pl. de Joan Peiró
Pl. d'Espanya
Av. Diagonal
0 300 m

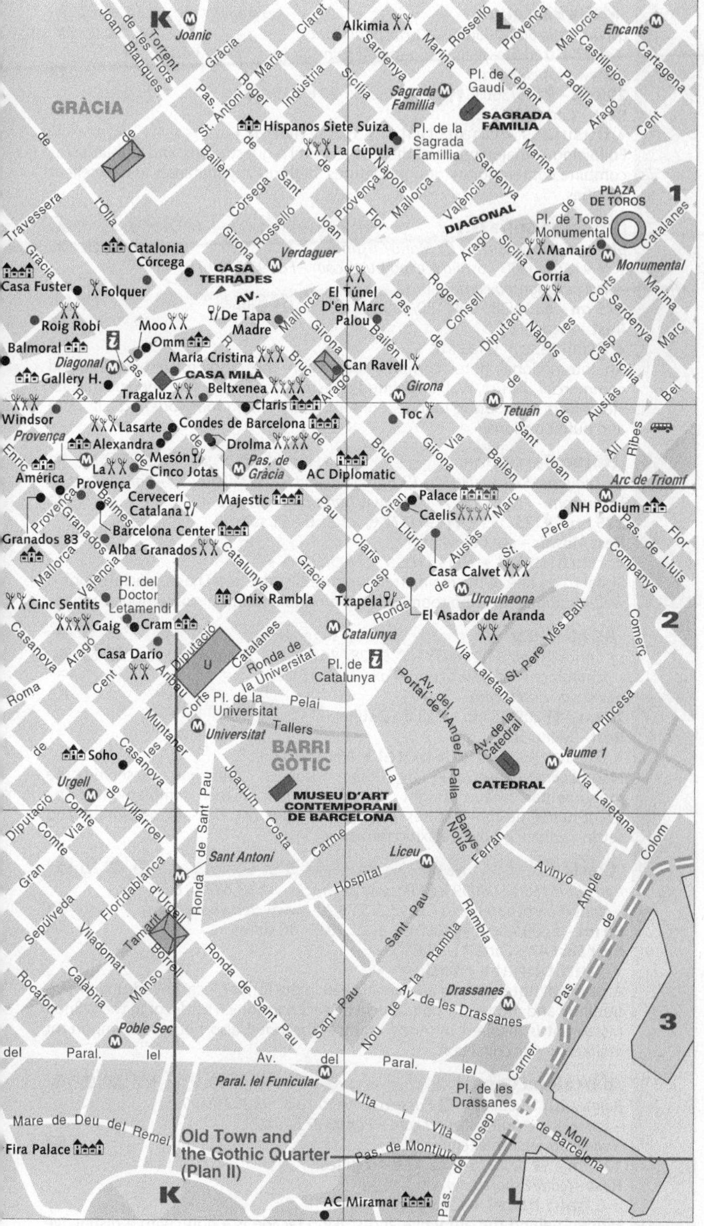
K
L
Joanic
GRÀCIA
Alkimia
Sagrada Familia
Pl. de Gaudí
SAGRADA FAMILIA
Encants
Hispanos Siete Suiza
La Cúpula
Pl. de la Sagrada Famillia
DIAGONAL
PLAZA DE TOROS
Pl. de Toros Monumental
Manairó
Monumental
Gorría
1
Catalonia Córcega
CASA TERRADES
Verdaguer
El Túnel D'en Marc Palou
Casa Fuster
Folquer
Roig Robí
De Tapa Madre
Moo
Omm
Balmoral
Diagonal
María Cristina
Can Ravell
CASA MILÀ
Gallery H.
Beltxenea
Tragaluz
Girona
Claris
Windsor
Lasarte
Condes de Barcelona
Toc
Tetuán
Provença
Alexandra
Drolma
La
Mesón
Cinco Jotas
Pas. de Gràcia
AC Diplomatic
América
Arc de Triomf
Cerveceri Catalana
Majestic
Palace
Caelis
NH Podium
Barcelona Center
Granados 83
Alba Granados
Casa Calvet
Pl. del Doctor Letamendi
Onix Rambla
Txapela
Urquinaona
Cinc Sentits
El Asador de Aranda
Gaig
Cram
2
Catalunya
Casa Darío
Pl. de Catalunya
Pl. de la Universitat
Universitat
BARRI GÒTIC
Soho
CATEDRAL
Jaume 1
Urgell
MUSEU D'ART CONTEMPORANI DE BARCELONA
Sant Antoni
Liceu
Drassanes
3
Poble Sec
Paral. lel Funicular
Pl. de les Drassanes
Fira Palace
Old Town and the Gothic Quarter (Plan II)
AC Miramar
K
L

Meliá Barcelona No smokers rest.

av. de Sarrià 50 ✉ 08029 – Ⓜ Hospital Clinic
– ☎ 93 410 60 60 – melia.barcelona@solmelia.com – Fax 93 410 77 44
– www.solmelia.com **J2**

299 rm – 125/360 € 145/360 €, 20 € – 15 suites

Rest – Carte 40/65 €

◆ Business ◆ Chain hotel ◆ Functional ◆

Following a major refurbishment, the hotel's guestrooms and public areas combine contemporary design features, high-quality materials and excellent facilities.

Princesa Sofía G. H. No smokers rest.

pl. Pius XII-4 ✉ 08028 – Ⓜ Maria Cristina
– ☎ 93 508 10 00 – psofia@expogrupo.com – Fax 93 508 10 01
– www.expogrupo.com Plan I **A2**

475 rm – 120/380 € 130/390 €, 20 € – 25 suites

Rest – Menu 22 €

◆ Business ◆ Classic ◆

An international hotel complex located in the city's main business and commercial district. Well-appointed guestrooms, a large spa, and spectacular views from the rooftop lounge. Contemporary dining room offering à la carte and buffet options.

Hilton Barcelona

av. Diagonal 589 ✉ 08014 – Ⓜ Maria Cristina – ☎ 93 495 77 77 – barcelona@hilton.com – Fax 93 495 77 00 – www.barcelona.hilton.com **I2**

275 rm – 175/355 € 197/377 €, 21 € – 11 suites

Rest ***Mosaic*** – see below

◆ Traditional ◆ Business ◆ Modern ◆

Situated on one of the main arteries of the city, the hotel has a spacious lobby, well-equipped meeting rooms and comfortable rooms in contemporary style.

AC Miramar sea and mountain,

pl. Carlos Ibáñez 3 ✉ 08038 – ☎ 93 281 16 00
– acmiramar@ac-hotels.com – Fax 93 281 16 01
– www.ac-hotels.com **K3**

73 rm – 209/353 €, 28 € – 2 suites

Rest – Menu 50 €

◆ Business ◆ Chain hotel ◆ Modern ◆

Magnificently renovated by Oscar Tusquets, who has conserved the monumental façade. Bright and airy public areas, complemented by avant-garde design features and fine furnishings. Pleasant restaurant and setting enhanced by a relaxing terrace.

Claris No smokers rest.

Pau Claris 150 ✉ 08009 – Ⓜ Passeig de Gràcia – ☎ 93 487 62 62
– claris@derbyhotels.es – Fax 93 215 79 70 – www.derbyhotels.com **K2**

80 rm – 209/406 € 209/452 €, 20 € – 40 suites

Rest ***East 47*** – Carte 41/57 €

◆ Traditional ◆ Modern ◆

An elegant hotel with an aristocratic feel in the former Palacio Vedruna, where tradition and modernity combine in perfect harmony. The décor in the refined restaurant is inspired by Andy Warhol. The hotel also houses an important archaeological collection.

Barcelona Center

Balmes 103 ✉ 08008 – Ⓜ Passeig de Gràcia – ☎ 93 273 00 00
– barcelona@hotelescenter.com – Fax 93 273 00 02
– www.hotelescenter.com **K2**

129 rm – 100/275 €, 17 € – 3 suites

Rest – *(coffee shop only)*

◆ Chain hotel ◆ Cosy ◆

Hidden behind the attractive and striking façade is a hotel with a distinctive lounge area, modern, fully-equipped guestrooms, and an enormous rooftop terrace-solarium.

Fira Palace
No smokers rest. VISA

av. Rius i Taulet 1 ✉ 08004 – Ⓜ Espanya – ☎ 93 426 22 23 – reservations@fira-palace.com – Fax 93 425 50 47 – www.fira-palace.com **J-K3**

258 rm – †299 € ††314 €, ☕ 15 € – 18 suites

Rest *El Mall* – Carte 32/40 €

♦ Business ♦ Classic ♦

Classically furnished, superbly maintained hotel with an emphasis on high-quality materials. Well-appointed and spacious guestrooms and public areas. Exposed brickwork in the rustic-style restaurant.

AC Diplomatic
No smokers rest. VISA

Pau Claris 122 ✉ 08009 – Ⓜ Passeig de Gràcia – ☎ 93 272 38 10 – diplomatic@ac-hotels.com – Fax 93 272 38 11 – www.ac-hotels.com **K2**

209 rm – ††130/294 €, ☕ 21 € – 2 suites

Rest – Carte 32/55 €

♦ Business ♦ Chain hotel ♦ Functional ♦

Recently refurbished to conform to the chain's tasteful look, this hotel combines design features, high levels of comfort and good facilities. Contemporary-style guestrooms and a large choice of meeting rooms.

Catalonia Barcelona Plaza
(heated) VISA

pl. d'Espanya 6 ✉ 08014 – Ⓜ Espanya – ☎ 93 426 26 00 – plaza@hoteles-catalonia.es – Fax 93 426 04 00 – www.hoteles-catalonia.com **J3**

338 rm – †80/228 € ††80/260 €, ☕ 15 € – 9 suites

Rest *Gourmet Plaza* – Carte 31/49 €

♦ Business ♦ Chain hotel ♦ Functional ♦

Located opposite Barcelona's main exhibition centre. Good facilities for a mainly business clientele, including excellent meeting rooms and functional furnishings. Swimming pool with a retractable roof on the top floor. Soberly decorated, functional restaurant.

Omm
VISA

Rosselló 265 ✉ 08008 – Ⓜ Diagonal – ☎ 93 445 40 00 – reservas@hotelomm.es – Fax 93 445 40 04 – www.hotelomm.es **K1**

87 rm – ††210/400 €, ☕ 22 € – 4 suites

Rest *Moo* – see below

♦ Business ♦ Design ♦

Hiding behind the original façade is a boutique hotel with a spacious lounge area laid out in three parts. Well-appointed guestrooms, plus an attractive spa.

Cram
VISA

Aribau 54 ✉ 08011 – Ⓜ Universitat – ☎ 93 216 77 00 – info@hotelcram.com – Fax 93 216 77 07 – www.hotelcram.com **K2**

67 rm – ††130/615 €, ☕ 21 €

Rest *Gaig* – see below

♦ Business ♦ Design ♦

Bedrooms on the small side are more than compensated for by the use of innovative technology and cutting-edge work by leading interior designers.

Granados 83
No smokers rest. VISA

Enric Granados 83 ✉ 08008 – Ⓜ Provença – ☎ 93 492 96 70 – granados83@derbyhotels.com – Fax 93 492 96 90 – www.derbyhotels.com **K2**

77 rm – †160/349 € ††160/389 €, ☕ 16 €

Rest – Menu 30 €

♦ Chain hotel ♦ Design ♦

An outstanding hotel featuring an avant-garde fusion of glass, steel and brick. Superbly appointed bedrooms adorned with 10C Asiatic works of art. The restaurant is embellished by a pleasant terrace.

NH Numància

Numància 74 ✉ 08029 – Ⓜ Sants-Estació – ✆ 93 322 44 51 – nhnumancia@nh-hotels.com – Fax 93 410 76 42 – www.nh-hotels.com **I2**

208 rm – †67/146 € ††83/220 €, ☕ 14 €

Rest – Menu 30 €

◆ Business ◆ Chain hotel ◆ Functional ◆

Close to Sants train station. Attractive public areas with designer features, plus spacious, comfortable bedrooms with modern décor and furnishings. Pleasant restaurant with a good reputation.

Abba Sants No smokers rest.

Numància 32 ✉ 08029 – Ⓜ Sants-Estació – ✆ 93 600 31 00 – abba-sants@abbahoteles.com – Fax 93 600 31 01 – www.abbahoteles.com **I2**

140 rm – †83/260 € ††93/280 €, ☕ 16 €

Rest *Amalur* – *(closed August)* Carte 34/41 €

◆ Business ◆ Chain hotel ◆ Modern ◆

Popular with a business clientele with its high standard throughout, modern design and well-maintained facilities. Functional guestrooms and multi-purpose lounges. Excellent à la carte choices, plus a popular daily menu.

Alexandra

Mallorca 251 ✉ 08008 – Ⓜ Passeig de Gràcia – ✆ 93 467 71 66 – informacion@hotel-alexandra.com – Fax 93 488 02 58 – www.hotel-alexandra.com

106 rm – †120/300 € ††150/350 €, ☕ 18 € – 3 suites **K2**

Rest – Carte 26/37 €

◆ Business ◆ Functional ◆

A modern, welcoming hotel with spacious, well-equipped rooms, contemporary furnishings, wood floors and fully equipped bathrooms. Simple décor in the menu-based restaurant.

B Hotel without rest

Gran Via de les Corts Catalanes 389 ✉ 08015 – Ⓜ Espanya – ✆ 93 552 95 00 – b-hotel@nnhotels.es – Fax 93 552 95 01 – www.nnhotels.es **J3**

84 rm – †130/255 € ††145/310 €, ☕ 13 €

◆ Chain hotel ◆ Modern ◆

Well-located and pleasantly modern in style. Bright lounge area, modern bedrooms and a delightful terrace-solarium on the roof with a swimming pool and superb views.

Soho without rest

Gran Via de les Corts Catalanes 543-545 ✉ 08011 – Ⓜ Urgell – ✆ 93 552 96 10 – soho@nnhotels.com – Fax 93 552 96 11 – www.hotelsohobarcelona.com

51 rm – †107/257 € ††117/315 €, ☕ 12 € **K2**

◆ Business ◆ Design ◆

An interesting combination of boutique style, designer detail, and the decorative use of light and space, allied with modern comforts and technology.

América without rest

Provença 195 ✉ 08008 – Ⓜ Provença – ✆ 93 487 62 92 – america@hotel-america-barcelona.com – Fax 93 487 25 18 – www.hotelamericabarcelona.com **K2**

60 rm – †100/196 € ††100/230 €, ☕ 15 €

◆ Traditional ◆ Cosy ◆

A bright, contemporary hotel with an attractive combination of red and white tones. Functional and comfortable guestrooms, plus an interior patio.

Gallery H. No smokers rest.

Rosselló 249 ✉ 08008 – Ⓜ Diagonal – ✆ 93 415 99 11 – galleryhotel@galleryhoteles.com – Fax 93 415 91 84 – www.galleryhotel.com **K1**

110 rm – †115/270 € ††120/300 €, ☕ 18 € – 5 suites

Rest – Menu 24 €

◆ Business ◆ Modern ◆

Renovated in modern style, this hotel boasts several meeting rooms, comfortable bedrooms designed with an eye for clean contemporary lines, and bathrooms with lots of attention to detail. The restaurant is enhanced by large windows and a welcoming terrace on an interior patio.

NH Podium No smokers rest.

Bailén 4 ✉ 08010 – Ⓜ Arc de Triomf – ✆ 93 265 02 02 – nhpodium@nh-hotels.com – Fax 93 265 05 06 – www.nh-hotels.com **L2**

140 rm – 104/182 € 116/255 €, 17.50 € – 5 suites

Rest *Corella* – Carte 37/48 €

◆ Business ◆ Chain hotel ◆ Functional ◆

The modern interior of this hotel in the Modernist section of the Ensanche district is hidden behind a façade that is resolutely traditional. Welcoming guestrooms, plus a fitness room with sauna and swimming pool on the roof. Intimate restaurant with pleasant décor and contemporary paintings.

Zenit Borrell

Comte Borrell 208 ✉ 08029 – Ⓜ Hospital Clinic – ✆ 93 452 55 66 – borrell@zenithoteles.com – Fax 93 452 55 60 – www.zenithoteles.com **J2**

73 rm – 65/350 €, 12 € – 1 suite

Rest – Carte 24/33 €

◆ Traditional ◆ Modern ◆

The emphasis here is on impeccable taste, with bedrooms that have contemporary furnishings, wood floors and marble bathrooms. Spacious reception area. Simply decorated restaurant with a pleasant interior terrace for the summer months.

NH Rallye No smokers rest.

Travessera de les Corts 150 ✉ 08028 – Ⓜ Les Corts – ✆ 93 339 90 50 – nhrallye@nh-hotels.com – Fax 93 411 07 90 – www.nh-hotels.com **I3**

105 rm – 95/185 € 100/220 €, 14 € – 1 suite

Rest – *(closed August)* Carte 33/44 €

◆ Business ◆ Chain hotel ◆ Functional ◆

A modern, functional property with the characteristic style of this hotel chain. Comfortable, well-equipped rooms, plus an attractive swimming pool and adjoining fitness room on the roof. Simply furnished, contemporary-style restaurant offering à la carte and buffet choices.

Onix Fira without rest

Llançà 30 ✉ 08015 – Ⓜ Espanya – ✆ 93 426 00 87 – reservas.hotelsonix@icyesa.es – Fax 93 426 19 81 – www.hotelsonix.com **J3**

80 rm – 88/110 € 99/138 €, 9 €

◆ Business ◆ Functional ◆

A good option if you need to be close to the "Fira de Barcelona". Simple yet comfortable furnishings, functional guestrooms, plus a spacious café.

Onix Rambla without rest

Rambla de Catalunya 24 ✉ 08007 – Ⓜ Catalunya – ✆ 93 342 79 80 – reservas.hotelsonix@icyesa.es – Fax 93 342 51 52 – www.hotelsonix.com **K2**

40 rm – 80/192 € 90/203 €, 10 €

◆ Business ◆ Functional ◆

A hotel with a modern, simple design and restrained décor based around wood, varying tones of white, and concrete. Functional guestrooms with wood flooring.

Caelis – Hotel Palace

(possible closure for works in 2008), Gran Via de les Corts Catalanes 668 ✉ 08010 – Ⓜ Passeig de Gràcia – ✆ 93 510 12 05 – restaurante@caelis.com – Fax 93 317 49 37 – www.caelis.com

closed 7 to 14 January, 7 days in April, 21 days in August, Saturday lunch, Sunday and Monday **L2**

Rest – Menu 92 € – Carte 90/100 €

Spec. El yogur. Los macarrones. El hielo.

◆ Inventive ◆ Design ◆

An amazing décor with a classical entrance contrasting with a modern designed dining room. Excellent setting for the inventive cuisine.

XXXX ✿ **Drolma** – Hotel Majestic Smokers rest. AC ⇔ P VISA MC AE ①

Passeig de Gràcia 68 ✉ 08007 – M Passeig de Gràcia – ✆ 93 496 77 10 – drolma@hotelmajestic.es – Fax 93 445 38 93 – www.drolmarestaurant.com closed Sunday **K2**

Rest – Menu 135 € – Carte 105/132 €

Spec. Lasaña de champiñones y trufa negra (15 December-15 March). Gambas con hinojo y calabacín. Cabrito embarrado a la cuchara.

♦ International ♦ Formal ♦

Traditional-style, predominantly wood, décor creating an elegant and refined atmosphere. Professional staff.

XXXX ✿ **Gaig** – Hotel Cram AC ⇔ P VISA MC AE ①

Aragó 214 ✉ 08011 – M Universitat – ✆ 93 429 10 17 – info@restaurantgaig.com – Fax 93 429 70 02 – www.restaurantgaig.com closed Holy Week, August, Sunday and Monday lunch **K2**

Rest – Menu 85 € – Carte 65/95 €

Spec. Ensalada de perdiz con vinagreta de cava. Gambas a la sal con arroz jugoso de pescados de roca y calamar. San Pedro con emulsión de setas de temporada.

♦ Inventive ♦ Design ♦

A refined setting with professional service of the highest order. Creative cuisine which takes its inspiration from the Mediterranean and Catalonia.

XXXX **La Dama** AC VISA MC AE ①

av. Diagonal 423 ✉ 08036 – M Diagonal – ✆ 93 202 06 86 – reservas@ladama-restaurant.com – Fax 93 200 72 99 – www.ladama-restaurant.com closed 3 weeks in August **J2**

Rest – Carte 54/71 €

♦ International ♦ Retro ♦

An elegant restaurant with Modernist decorative details both inside and on the façade. Professional staff.

XXXX **Beltxenea** AC VISA MC AE ①

Mallorca 275 entlo ✉ 08008 – M Diagonal – ✆ 93 215 30 24 – info@beltxenea.com – Fax 93 487 00 81 closed Christmas, Holy Week, August, Saturday lunch and Sunday **K1**

Rest – Carte 41/55 €

♦ Basque ♦ Formal ♦

An elegant restaurant in a historic building with a sense of the past. Refined traditional ambience, with two rooms overlooking a small garden.

XXX ✿ **Lasarte** – Hotel Condes de Barcelona Smokers rest. AC VISA MC AE ①

Mallorca 259 ✉ 08008 – M Diagonal – ✆ 93 445 32 42 – info@restaurantlasarte.com – Fax 93 445 32 32 – www.restaurantlasarte.com closed 4 August-7 September, Saturday, Sunday and Bank Holidays **K2**

Rest – Menu 90 € – Carte 70/85 €

Spec. Milhojas caramelizado de manzana verde, foie-gras y anguila ahumada. Pulpitos salteados, terciopelo de topinambur, tubérculos glaseados y jugo cuajado de hierbas. Agua de dátiles con helado de haba tonka, bizcocho y trufa a la esencia de naranjo.

♦ Inventive ♦ Formal ♦

A restaurant supervised by the famous chef Martin Barasategui from Lasarte in the Basque country. Two comfortable dining rooms in a modern style offering a creative menu with some traditional Basque dishes.

XXX **Casa Calvet** No smokers rest. AC ⇔ VISA MC AE ①

Casp 48 ✉ 08010 – M Urquinaona – ✆ 93 412 40 12 – restaurant@casacalvet.es – Fax 93 412 43 36 – www.casacalvet.es closed Holy Week, 15 days in August, Sunday and Bank Holidays **L2**

Rest – Carte 53/70 €

♦ Inventive ♦ Formal ♦

A restaurant in an attractive Modernist building designed by Gaudí. Traditional à la carte dishes with a modern twist, and an emphasis on excellent presentation and top-quality products.

XXX **Windsor** AC VISA MC AE

Còrsega 286 ✉ 08008 – Ⓜ Diagonal – ✆ 93 415 84 83 – info@restaurantwindsor.com – Fax 93 238 66 08 – www.restaurantwindsor.com
closed 1 to 7 January, Holy Week, August, Saturday lunch and Sunday
Rest – Carte 38/57 € **K2**
◆ Catalan cuisine ◆ Formal ◆
An elegant, traditional restaurant with one main glass-fronted dining room overlooking the garden and various private rooms. Extensive menu based on contemporary Catalan dishes, plus an impressive wine cellar.

XXX **Colibrí** No smokers rest. AC P VISA MC AE

Casanova 212 ✉ 08036 – ✆ 93 443 23 06 – info@restaurantcolibri.com – Fax 93 442 61 27 – www.restaurantcolibri.com
closed Holy Week, 21 days in August, Sunday dinner and Monday in July, Sunday and Monday for rest of the year **J2**
Rest – Carte approx. 65 €
◆ Inventive ◆ Formal ◆
A reasonably spacious restaurant known for its comfortable surroundings and good service. Bright and airy dining room where guests can enjoy inventive cuisine based around fresh market produce.

XXX **Gargantua i Pantagruel** AC VISA MC AE

Còrsega 200 ✉ 08036 – Ⓜ Hospital Clinic – ✆ 93 453 20 20 – gip@gargantuaipantagruel.com – Fax 93 419 29 22 – www.gargantuaipantagruel.com
closed August and Sunday dinner **J2**
Rest – Carte 37/60 €
◆ Catalan cuisine ◆ Trendy ◆
A spacious restaurant with a contemporary brown and grey colour scheme. Kitchen in full view of diners, who come here to enjoy traditional Catalan cuisine.

XXX **María Cristina** AC VISA MC AE

Provença 271 ✉ 08008 – Ⓜ Passeig de Gràcia – ✆ 93 215 32 37 – margaret_marga@hotmail.com – Fax 93 215 83 23
closed 10 to 20 August, Saturday lunch and Sunday **K1**
Rest – Carte 38/50 €
◆ Catalan cuisine ◆ Formal ◆
The attractive opaque glass frontage leads to a small foyer and several dining rooms with a mixed classic-modern ambience. Traditional cuisine based on high-quality products.

XXX **Oliver y Hardy** AC VISA MC AE

av. Diagonal 593 ✉ 08014 – Ⓜ Maria Cristina – ✆ 93 419 31 81 – oliveryhardy@husa.es – Fax 93 419 18 99 – www.husarestauracion.com
closed Saturday lunch and Sunday **I2**
Rest – Carte 38/50 €
◆ International ◆ Formal ◆
A renowned dinner venue divided between a nightclub and restaurant. Refined dining room with a terrace used for private functions.

XXX **Jaume de Provença** AC VISA MC AE

Provença 88 ✉ 08029 – Ⓜ Entença – ✆ 93 430 00 29 – restaurant@jaumeprovenza.com – Fax 93 439 29 50 – www.jaumeprovenza.com
closed August, Sunday dinner and Monday **J2**
Rest – Carte 44/66 €
◆ International ◆ Formal ◆
A traditional-style restaurant run by the owner. Bar for a pre-dinner aperitif, various wine cellars, plus an impressive wood-panelled dining room.

XX **Melton** Smokers rest. AC VISA MC AE

Muntaner 189 ✉ 08036 – ✆ 93 363 27 76 – meltonrestaurante@hotmail.com – Fax 93 363 27 76 – www.restaurante-melton.com **J2**
Rest – *(closed 21 days in August, Sunday dinner and Monday)* Carte approx. 45 €
◆ Italian ◆ Trendy ◆
Great attention to detail (lighting, service, décor) are the keys to the success of this small, contemporary restaurant serving imaginative Italian cuisine.

XX

Cinc Sentits No smokers rest.

Aribau 58 ✉ 08011 – Ⓜ Universitat – ☎ 93 323 94 90 – info@cincsentits.com – Fax 93 323 94 91 – www.cincsentits.com

closed Sunday and Monday **K2**

Rest – Carte 43/57 €

♦ Inventive ♦ Minimalist ♦

Attractive, minimalist décor provides the backdrop for inventive cuisine based on top-quality Catalan products.

XX ✿

Moo – Hotel Omm No smokers rest.

Rosselló 265 ✉ 08008 – Ⓜ Diagonal – ☎ 93 445 40 00 – restaurante.moo@hotelomm.es – Fax 93 445 40 04 – www.hotelomm.es

closed 21 days in August and Sunday **K1**

Rest – Menu 75 € – Carte 62/77 €

Spec. Canelón de liebre y trufa (autumn-winter). Perdiz salvaje con trigo tierno y jugo de col (autumn-winter). Maridaje entre plato y vino.

♦ Inventive ♦ Design ♦

Cosmopolitan ambience and a bright, contemporary dining room with designer detailing. Creative cuisine and original wine list.

XX ✿

Saüc (Xavier Franco) Smokers rest.

passatge Lluís Pellicer 12 ✉ 08036 – Ⓜ Hospital Clinic – ☎ 93 321 01 89 – sauc@saucrestaurant.com – www.saucrestaurant.com

closed 1 to 7 January, 21 days in August, Sunday, Monday and Bank Holidays **J2**

Rest – Menu 74 € – Carte 55/67 €

Spec. Trinxat de patata y perona con mollejas de ternera glaseadas. Papada crujiente, calamares y alcachofas, jugo de asado. Cochinillo confitado y asado, patatas y chalotas salteadas.

♦ Inventive ♦ Family ♦

The couple who run this restaurant, functional in style but with the occasional avant-garde touch, offer a personal slant on regional cuisine based on high-quality products.

XX

Tragaluz

passeig de la Concepció 5 ✉ 08006 – ☎ 93 487 06 21 – compras.tragaluz@grupotragaluz.com – Fax 93 487 70 83 – www.grupotragaluz.com **K1-2**

Rest – Carte approx. 45 €

♦ Inventive ♦ Formal ♦

A restaurant occuying three floors from street level upwards, with a distinctive retractable gabled glass roof. Moderately priced creative cuisine.

XX

La Provença

Provença 242 ✉ 08008 – Ⓜ Diagonal – ☎ 93 323 23 67 – restofi@laprovenza.com – Fax 93 451 23 89 – www.laprovenza.com **K2**

Rest – Carte 26/34 €

♦ Catalan cuisine ♦ Trendy ♦

A restaurant combining the traditional and modern with numerous private rooms making it a popular choice for business clients. Extensive menu with a good selection of daily suggestions.

XX

El Túnel D'en Marc Palou Smokers rest.

Bailén 91 ✉ 08009 – Ⓜ Girona – ☎ 93 265 86 58 – info@eltuneldenmarc.com – Fax 93 246 01 14 – www.eltuneldenmarc.com

closed August, Sunday and Monday dinner **L1**

Rest – Carte 34/42 €

♦ Inventive ♦ Trendy ♦

In a glass-fronted corner building with three small and contemporary dining rooms on various levels. A refined setting for cuisine that is interestingly inventive.

XX **Peixerot** P VISA MC AE

av. Tarragona 177 ✉ 08014 – Ⓜ Sants Estació – ✆ 93 424 69 69 – central@peixerot.net – Fax 93 426 10 63

closed 13 to 26 August and Sunday dinner **J3**

Rest – Carte 41/59 €

♦ Seafood ♦ Formal ♦

A restaurant with a traditional ambience spread across various floors. Good service, plus an extensive menu that varies daily according to the catch at the city's fish market.

XX **Alba Granados** AC VISA MC AE D

Enric Granados 34 ✉ 08036 – Ⓜ Passeig de Gràcia – ✆ 93 454 61 16 – info@albagranados.com – Fax 93 454 83 74 – www.albagranados.com

closed 12 to 26 August and Sunday dinner **K2**

Rest – Carte 26/41 €

♦ Spanish ♦ Rustic ♦

Surprising in its decoration, which refers entirely to the world of wine. With dining rooms on two floors and a traditional menu offering a good selection of grilled meats.

XX **Vinya Rosa-Magí** AC VISA MC AE D

av. de Sarrià 17 ✉ 08029 – Ⓜ Hospital Clinic – ✆ 93 430 00 03 – info@vinyarosamagi.com – Fax 93 430 00 41 – www.vinyarosamagi.com

closed Saturday lunch and Sunday **J2**

Rest – Carte 33/47 €

♦ International ♦ Friendly ♦

A small restaurant with attractive décor, an intimate and welcoming atmosphere, and a menu featuring classic dishes and daily specials.

XX **El Asador de Aranda** AC VISA MC AE D

Londres 94 ✉ 08036 – ✆ 93 414 67 90 – barcelona@asadordearanda.com – Fax 93 414 67 90 – www.asadoraranda.com

closed Sunday dinner **L2**

Rest – Carte 32/38 €

♦ Roast lamb ♦ Rustic ♦

In a street off the Avenida Diagonal. A spacious restaurant with traditional Castilian-style décor, bar and a wood-fired oven for roasting suckling pig and lamb.

XX **Gorría** AC VISA MC AE D

Diputació 421 ✉ 08013 – Ⓜ Sagrada Familia – ✆ 93 245 11 64 – info@restaurantegorria.com – Fax 93 232 78 57 – www.restaurantegorria.com

closed Holy Week, August, Sunday, Monday dinner and Bank Holidays dinner

Rest – Carte 35/52 € **L1**

♦ Basque ♦ Rustic ♦

A long-standing Basque restaurant with attractive rustic-style décor. Excellent wine list.

XX **Mosaic** – Hotel Hilton Barcelona No smokers rest. AC

av. Diagonal 589 ✉ 08014 – Ⓜ María Cristina – ✆ 93 495 77 60 – Fax 93 495 77 00 – www.barcelona.hilton.com P VISA MC AE D **I2**

Rest – Carte 37/47 €

♦ International ♦ Formal ♦

Contemporary-style interior with high ceilings, straight lines and dark wood. International and Mediterranean cuisine.

XX **El Asador de Aranda** AC VISA MC AE D

Pau Clarís 70 ✉ 08010 – Ⓜ Urquinaona – ✆ 93 342 55 77 – barcelona@asadordearanda.com – Fax 93 342 55 78 – www.asadoraranda.com

closed Sunday dinner **J2**

Rest – Carte 32/38 €

♦ Roast lamb ♦ Rustic ♦

The standard features of this chain are evident here with a bar at the entrance, a roasting oven in open view and two inviting dining rooms with elegant Castilian décor.

XX

Casa Darío

AC VISA MC AE D

Consell de Cent 256 ✉ 08011 – M Universitat – ✆ 93 453 31 35 – casadario@casadario.com – Fax 93 451 33 95 – www.casadario.com

closed August and Sunday **K2**

Rest – Carte 38/60 €

◆ Seafood ◆ Formal ◆

A long-standing, popular restaurant known for its high-quality cuisine. Private bar, three dining rooms and three private rooms. Galician and seafood specialities.

XX

Manairó

AC VISA MC AE D

Diputació 424 ✉ 08013 – M Monumental – ✆ 93 231 00 57 – info@manairo.com – Fax 93 265 23 81 – www.manairo.com

closed 6 to 27 August, Sunday and Monday **L1**

Rest – Carte 44/56 €

◆ Inventive ◆ Cosy ◆

A popular local restaurant with a small dining room decorated with works of art by various artists. Traditional cuisine with a creative and innovative twist.

X

Toc

AC VISA MC AE D

Girona 59 ✉ 08009 – M Girona – ✆ 93 488 11 48 – toc@tocbcn.com – www.tocbcn.com

closed 10 to 31 August, Saturday lunch and Sunday **L2**

Rest – Carte 38/53 €

◆ Catalan ◆ Trendy ◆

This restaurant extends over two floors and boasts modern decoration that has taken the 70s as its aesthetic model. Modernised Catalan cuisine.

X

La Tertulia

Smokers rest. AC VISA MC AE

Morales 15 ✉ 08029 – ✆ 93 419 58 97 – tertulia@arrosseriaxativa.com – Fax 93 363 21 58 – www.arrosseriaxativa.com

closed Sunday dinner **J2**

Rest – Carte 25/35 €

◆ Traditional ◆ Rustic ◆

A fairly cosy, rustic setting with large windows and a pleasant terrace. Traditional cuisine that is attentive to both price and product quality.

X

Can Ravell

AC P VISA MC AE D

Aragó 313 ✉ 08009 – M Girona – ✆ 93 457 51 14 – direccio@ravell.com – Fax 93 459 39 56 – www.ravell.com

closed Holy Week, 21 days in August and Sunday **K1**

Rest – *(lunch only except Thursday and Friday)* Carte 44/66 €

◆ Traditional ◆ Family ◆

Very curious establishment reached via an old grocery store. On the 2nd floor, there is one dining room and two private rooms. Catalan cuisine and a good selection of wines.

Mesón Cinco Jotas

VISA MC AE

Rambla de Catalunya 91-93 ✉ 08008 – M Diagonal – ✆ 93 487 89 42 – m5jrambla@osborne.es – Fax 93 487 91 21 – www.mesoncincojotas.com **K2**

Tapa 3.50 € **Ración** approx. 12 €

◆ Spanish ◆ Tapas bar ◆

A spacious bar with traditional wood décor and tables at the entrance where you savour a fine selection of cured hams, plus a dining room to the rear. Extensive tapas menu.

Cervecería Catalana

Mallorca 236 ✉ 08008 – Ⓜ Diagonal – ☎ 93 216 03 68 – jahumada@62online.com – Fax 93 488 17 97 **K2**

Tapa 5 € **Ración** approx. 10 €

♦ Spanish ♦ Brasserie ♦

A popular local bar with shelves decorated with bottles and an impressive selection of tapas created from the finest ingredients.

De Tapa Madre

Mallorca 301 ✉ 08037 – Ⓜ Verdaguer – ☎ 93 459 31 34 – detapamadre@hotmail.com – Fax 93 457 28 61 – www.detapamadre.com **K1**

Tapa 3.50 € **Ración** approx. 10.40 €

♦ Spanish ♦ Rustic ♦

Rustic tapas bar with a small terrace, a dining room and a private room on the upper floor. Its snacks and light bites are made from quality produce.

Txapela

No smokers rest.

passeig de Gràcia 8-10 ✉ 08007 – Ⓜ Passeig de Gràcia – ☎ 93 412 02 89 – txapela@angrup.com – Fax 93 412 24 78 – www.angrup.com **K2**

Tapa 1.55 €

♦ Basque ♦ Tapas bar ♦

A Basque-style bar and restaurant situated on the Paseo de Gràcia. Spacious eating area plus a pleasant terrace. Huge choice of tapas created in a kitchen in full view of diners.

SANT MARTÍ *Plan I*

Arts

No smokers rest.

Marina 19 ✉ 08005 – Ⓜ Ciutadella-Vila Olímpica – ☎ 93 221 10 00 – rc.barcelonareservations@ritzcarlton.com – Fax 93 221 10 70 – www.hotelartsbarcelona.com **C2**

397 rm – †273/404 € ††393/509 €, ☕ 30 € – 87 suites

Rest *Arola* – *(closed Monday and Tuesday)* Carte 40/60 €

Rest *Enoteca* – *(closed Sunday)* Carte 72/90 €

♦ Grand Luxury ♦ Design ♦

A superb hotel occupying one of the glass-fronted towers overlooking the Olympic port. Unbeatable views from the guestrooms which combine luxurious furnishings and ultra-modern design. The Arts has several restaurants, most notably the Arola, which is renowned for its creative cuisine.

Hilton Diagonal Mar

No smokers rest.

passeig del Taulat 262-264 ✉ 08019 – Ⓜ El Maresme/Forum – ☎ 93 507 07 07 – diagonalmarbarcelona@hilton.com – Fax 93 507 07 00 – www.hilton.com **D2**

411 rm – †215/398 € ††237/420 €, ☕ 22 € – 22 suites

Rest – Menu 40 €

♦ Business ♦ Modern ♦

Located near the Fórum and orientated towards organising conferences. Its rooms have a clean design, with modern furniture of excellent quality. The restaurant, housed on the 1st floor, has views over the grand entrance hall and outside.

Diagonal Barcelona

No smokers rest.

av. Diagonal 205 ✉ 08018 – Ⓜ Glòries – ☎ 93 489 53 00 – reservas.diagonal@hoteles-silken.com – Fax 93 489 53 09 – www.hoteldiagonalbarcelona.com **C2**

228 rm – †100/320 € ††115/350 €, ☕ 17 € – 12 suites

Rest – *(closed August and Sunday)* Carte 37/51 €

♦ Business ♦ Design ♦

The pure design of this hotel is the creative work of several well-known artists. Ultra-modern bedrooms with open-plan bathrooms, plus a sun terrace on the roof. Simply furnished, contemporary restaurant.

Barceló Atenea Mar No smokers rest.

passeig Garcia Faria 47 ✉ 08019 – Ⓜ Selva de Mar – ✆ 93 531 60 40 – ateneamar@bchoteles.com – Fax 93 531 60 90 – www.bchoteles.com **D2**

191 rm – 🚹95/180 € 🚹🚹105/195 €, ☕ 14 €

Rest *El Comedor* – Carte approx. 37 €

♦ Business ♦ Chain hotel ♦ Functional ♦

On an avenue facing the sea, this hotel offers a number of multi-purpose meeting rooms, a fitness area and functional bedrooms, most of which enjoy views of the Mediterranean. Restaurant with a separate entrance and a menu based on creative cuisine.

Vincci Marítimo No smokers rest.

Llull 340 ✉ 08019 – Ⓜ Selva de Mar – ✆ 93 356 26 00 – maritimo@vinccihoteles.com – Fax 93 356 06 69 – www.vinccihoteles.com **D2**

144 rm – 🚹🚹81/350 €, ☕ 18 €

Rest – Menu 20 €

♦ Business ♦ Chain hotel ♦ Design ♦

A bright and airy lobby, modular meeting rooms, and comfortable guestrooms with quirky design features and wood floors. Pleasant restaurant with access to the terrace.

Anfiteatro

av. Litoral (Parc del Port Olímpic) ✉ 08005 – Ⓜ Ciutadella-Vila Olímpica – ✆ 659 69 53 45 – anfiteatrobcn@telefonica.net – Fax 93 457 14 19

closed 7 to 31 January, 4 to 24 August, Sunday dinner and Monday **C2**

Rest – *(set menu only)* Menu 45 €

♦ Inventive ♦ Trendy ♦

A contemporary-style restaurant along a main artery of the city, near a small lake. Plenty of natural light and gastronomic fare centred around a tasting menu.

Els Pescadors

pl. Prim 1 ✉ 08005 – Ⓜ Poblenou – ✆ 93 225 20 18 – contacte@elspescadors.com – Fax 93 224 00 04 – www.elspescadors.com

closed Holy Week **D2**

Rest – Carte 38/61 €

♦ Rice specialities ♦ Formal ♦

This restaurant has one dining room in the style of an early 20C café-bar and two with more modern décor. A varied menu of fish and seafood, including cod and rice dishes.

El Túnel del Port

Moll de Gregal 12 (Port Olímpic) ✉ 08005 – Ⓜ Ciutadella-Vila Olímpica – ✆ 93 221 03 21 – eltunel@eltuneldelport.com – Fax 93 221 35 86 – www.eltuneldelport.com

closed Sunday dinner and Monday **C2**

Rest – Carte 34/52 €

♦ Catalan cuisine ♦ Formal ♦

A traditional restaurant with a large seating capacity. Two dining rooms on different levels, one of which is surrounded by glass and enjoys panoramic views.

NORTH of AV. DIAGONAL *Plan III*

Casa Fuster

passeig de Gràcia 132 ✉ 08008 – Ⓜ Diagonal – ✆ 93 255 30 00 – casafuster@hotelescenter.com – Fax 93 255 30 02 – www.hotelcasafuster.com **K1**

66 rm – 🚹🚹275/700 €, ☕ 25 € – 39 suites

Rest *Galaxó* – Carte approx. 65 €

♦ Luxury ♦ Modern ♦

Magnificent hotel housed in a beautiful Modernist building dating back to 1908. It has an attractive café-lounge and the bedrooms are equipped to the highest level with well-appointed bathrooms. You can enjoy sophisticated, innovative cooking in the hotel's elegant restaurant.

Hesperia Presidente No smokers rest.
av. Diagonal 570 ✉ 08021 – Ⓜ Hospital Clinic – ✆ 93 200 21 11 – hotel@hesperia-presidente.com – Fax 93 209 51 06 – www.hesperia-presidente.com **J2**
139 rm – 120/350 €, ☕ 16 € – 12 suites
Rest – Menu 25 €
♦ Business ♦ Chain hotel ♦ Functional ♦
This hotel, whose main public areas overlook the Diagonal, has been completely restored with an emphasis on bright colours. Elegant and comfortable guestrooms, plus a restaurant with a menu based around Calatan and Mediterranean dishes.

Hispanos Siete Suiza
Sicilia 255 ✉ 08025 – Ⓜ Sagrada Familia – ✆ 93 208 20 51 – comercial@hispanos7suiza.com – Fax 93 208 20 52 – www.h7s.es **L1**
19 rm ☕ – 130/190 €
Rest ***La Cúpula*** – see below
♦ Traditional ♦ Classic ♦
Comfortable establishment with a classical feel, boasting apartments with two bedrooms, two bathrooms, lounge, fully-fitted kitchen, and in most cases a balcony.

Balmoral
Via Augusta 5 ✉ 08006 – Ⓜ Diagonal – ✆ 93 217 87 00 – info@hotelbalmoral.com – Fax 93 415 14 21 – www.hotelbalmoral.com **K1**
106 rm – 60/250 €, ☕ 12.50 €
Rest – *(coffee shop only)*
♦ Traditional ♦ Classic ♦
A comfortable, traditional-style hotel offering professional service. Bright, well-appointed bedrooms and a choice of panelled-off function rooms.

AC Irla without rest
Calvet 40-42 ✉ 08021 – Ⓜ Muntaner – ✆ 93 241 62 10 – acirla@ac-hotels.com – Fax 93 241 62 11 – www.ac-hotels.com **J1**
36 rm – 84/230 €, ☕ 13 €
♦ Business ♦ Chain hotel ♦ Functional ♦
Quality materials, design features and a sense of the functional add to the overall charm of this welcoming hotel. Spacious bathrooms with showers rather than baths.

Condado without rest
Aribau 201 ✉ 08021 – Ⓜ Diagonal – ✆ 93 200 23 11 – administracion@condadohotel.com – Fax 93 200 25 86 – www.condadohotel.com **J1**
75 rm – 90/200 € 90/225 €, ☕ 12 € – 1 suite
♦ Traditional ♦ Classic ♦
A complete makeover has given this hotel a style that is both contemporary and traditional, combining quality materials and bright colours. Light, spacious guestrooms with wooden floors.

Catalonia Suite No smokers rest.
Muntaner 505 ✉ 08022 – Ⓜ El Putxet – ✆ 93 212 80 12 – suite@hoteles-catalonia.es – Fax 93 211 23 17 – www.hoteles-catalonia.com **I1**
117 rm – 110/174 € 140/186 €, ☕ 15 €
Rest – *(set menu only)* Menu 18 €
♦ Business ♦ Chain hotel ♦ Functional ♦
Located in a residential and business district, this hotel offers guests functional, contemporary bedrooms with spacious bathrooms, most of which are fitted with a separate shower and hydro-massage bathtub.

Catalonia Córcega

Còrsega 368 ✉ 08037 – Ⓜ Verdaguer – ✆ 93 208 19 19 – corcega@hoteles-catalonia.es – Fax 93 208 08 57 – www.hoteles-catalonia.com

77 rm – 🛉124/174 € 🛉🛉154/186 €, ☕ 15 € – 2 suites **K1**

Rest – Menu 18 €

◆ Business ◆ Chain hotel ◆ Functional ◆

A modern hotel with well-maintained rooms, a mix of contemporary and traditional furniture, wood floors and reasonable facilities. Compact lounge area. Fixed menu in the restaurant, with a small à la carte choice.

NH Cóndor

No smokers rest.

Via Augusta 127 ✉ 08006 – Ⓜ Muntaner – ✆ 93 209 45 11 – nhcondor@nh-hotels.com – Fax 93 202 27 13 – www.nh-hotels.com **J1**

66 rm – 🛉85/211 € 🛉🛉85/270 €, ☕ 14 € – 12 suites

Rest – *(closed August, Saturday and Sunday)* Menu 20 €

◆ Business ◆ Chain hotel ◆ Functional ◆

A functional and comfortable hotel with all the characteristic style of this hotel chain. Somewhat compact public areas, although the guest rooms are well-maintained and decorated with modern furnishings.

Neichel

Beltran i Rózpide 1 ✉ 08034 – Ⓜ Maria Cristina – ✆ 93 203 84 08 – neichel@relaischateaux.com – Fax 93 205 63 69 – www.neichel.es

closed 1 to 7 January, 1 to 24 August, Sunday, Monday and Bank Holidays

Rest – Menu 90 € – Carte 65/80 € *Plan I* **A2**

Spec. Arroz integral de Pals caldoso, espardenyes, gambitas y erizos de mar. Rodaballo al jamón serrano, migas, patata tenedor con olivas. Papillote transparente de frutas tropicales, ron, tonka y sorbete de mandarina.

◆ Inventive ◆ Design ◆

Creative and innovative cuisine to satisfy even the most demanding palate. An elegant and pleasant restaurant with a garden.

Via Veneto

Ganduxer 10 ✉ 08021 – Ⓜ Hospital Clinic – ✆ 93 200 72 44 – pmonje@adam.es – Fax 93 201 60 95 – www.viavenetorestaurant.com

closed 1 to 20 August, Saturday lunch and Sunday **I2**

Rest – Menu 85 € – Carte 60/90 €

Spec. Huevos de Calaf a baja temperatura con trío de patatas y trufa negra. Pichón de Bresse asado en dos cocciones con risotto de queso Llavina. Torrija con naranja, crema de almendras y helado de turrón.

◆ International ◆ Retro ◆

A restaurant with elegant Belle Époque décor and impeccable service with an interesting menu. A highly professional staff.

El Racó d'en Freixa (Ramón Freixa)

Smokers rest.

Sant Elies 22 ✉ 08006 – Ⓜ Plaça Molina – ✆ 93 209 75 59 – info@elracodenfreixa.com – Fax 93 209 79 18 – www.elracodenfreixa.com

closed Holy Week, 21 days in August, Sunday and Monday **J1**

Rest – Menu 72 € – Carte 68/92 €

Spec. Hamburguesa de pato azulón, pan de cereales, mostaza helada y queso Idiazábal. Cerdo ibérico, tres tipos, tres cocciones con berenjena. Chocolate 2008.

◆ Inventive ◆ Family ◆

Contemporary in style with pure, minimalist lines and designer touches to mirror the excellent service and interestingly creative and high-quality cuisine.

Botafumeiro

Gran de Gràcia 81 ✉ 08012 – Ⓜ Fontana – ✆ 93 218 42 30 – info@botafumeiro.es – Fax 93 217 13 05 – www.botafumeiro.es **J1**

Rest – Carte approx. 70 €

◆ Seafood ◆ Formal ◆

A well-known restaurant in the Gràcia district of the city, with an attractive bar at the entrance and a main dining room on several levels with a profusion of wood and maritime-inspired décor.

XXX

La Cúpula – Hotel Hispanos Siete Suiza

Sicilia 255 ✉ 08025 – Ⓜ Sagrada Familia – ✆ 93 208 20 61
– info@lacupularestaurant.com – Fax 93 208 20 52
– www.lacupularestaurant.com
closed August, Saturday lunch and Sunday L1

Rest – Carte 32/54 €

♦ Traditional ♦ Formal ♦

Displays a wonderful collection of Hispano-Suiza cars from the beginning of the twentieth century, has two dining rooms on two floors, both exquisitely laid out in a classical style with nice furniture.

XX

Roig Robí

Sèneca 20 ✉ 08006 – Ⓜ Diagonal – ✆ 93 218 92 22 – roigrobi@roigrobi.com
– Fax 93 415 78 42 – www.roigrobi.com
closed August, Saturday lunch and Sunday K1

Rest – Carte 53/73 €

♦ Catalan cuisine ♦ Family ♦

A modern restaurant in a splendid setting with a pleasant garden-terrace. A very varied and original menu.

XX

Alkimia (Jordi Vilà) No smokers rest.

Indústria 79 ✉ 08025 – Ⓜ Sagrada Familia – ✆ 93 207 61 15
– alkimia@telefonica.net
closed Holy Week, 15 days in August, Saturday and Sunday K1

Rest – Menu 68 € – Carte 50/70 €

Spec. Coca de anchoas con escalibada, mantequilla de trufa y yogur. Espardenyes con arroz Empordà y espárragos verdes. Paletilla de lechazo con fondue de queso y pan de tomillo.

♦ Inventive ♦ Minimalist ♦

Dining room with soothing, minimalist décor, attentive service and individual lighting. Modern menu featuring creative dishes and more traditional Catalan cuisine.

XX

Coure

passatge de Marimon 20 ✉ 08021 – Ⓜ Hospital Clinic – ✆ 93 200 75 32
– restaurantcoure@hotmail.com
closed Holy Week, 11 to 31 August, Sunday and Monday J2

Rest – Carte 45/52 €

♦ Inventive ♦ Formal ♦

Modern-looking restaurant with bright colours and minimalist-inspired decoration. Its owner-chef creates an interesting signature menu.

XX

Hisop Smokers rest.

passatge de Marimon 9 ✉ 08021 – Ⓜ Hospital Clinic – ✆ 93 241 32 33
– hisop@hisop.com – www.hisop.com
closed 4 to 24 August, Saturday lunch, Sunday and Bank Holidays J2

Rest – Carte 42/63 €

♦ Inventive ♦ Minimalist ♦

Hisop enjoys an excellent local reputation based upon its highly creative cuisine and good service. A minimalist look with floral decoration on the walls.

XX

St. Rémy

Iradier 12 ✉ 08017 – ✆ 93 418 75 04 – Fax 93 434 04 34
– www.stremyrestaurant.com
closed Sunday dinner I1

Rest – Carte 27/35 €

♦ Catalan cuisine ♦ Formal ♦

A restaurant housed in a small palace-style building, with attractively illuminated and spacious dining rooms and contemporary-style furniture. The menu here remains faithful to Catalan cuisine.

Le Quattro Stagioni

Dr. Roux 37 ✉ 08017 – Ⓜ Les Tres Torres – ☏ 93 205 22 79
– restaurante@4stagioni.com – Fax 93 205 78 65
– www.4stagioni.com
closed Holy Week, Sunday and Monday lunch (July-August), Sunday dinner and Monday for rest of the year **I1**

Rest – Carte 27/36 €

♦ Italian ♦ Cosy ♦

A distinct Mediterranean ambience pervades this restaurant on two floors. Glass-fronted terrace and a pleasant outdoor terrace. Large selection of Italian wines.

Silvestre

Santaló 101 ✉ 08021 – Ⓜ Muntaner – ☏ 93 241 40 31 – Fax 93 241 40 31
– www.restaurantesilvestre.com
closed Holy Week, 21 days in August, Saturday lunch, Sunday and Bank Holidays **J1**

Rest – Carte 27/35 €

♦ Catalan cuisine ♦ Cosy ♦

The couple who own this restaurant have created a popular eatery with several sections which add intimacy to this classic setting. Good value for money and seasonal produce.

Mandarina

Caravel.la "La Niña" ✉ 08017 – Ⓜ María Cristina – ☏ 93 205 60 04
– info@mandarinarestaurant.com – Fax 93 280 19 72
– www.mandarinarestaurant.com
closed 1 to 8 January, 5 to 26 August, Sunday and Monday **I2**

Rest – Carte 24/35 €

♦ Inventive ♦ Formal ♦

Offers a fresh and young atmosphere, leaving the client with the feeling of having eaten healthily and lightly. Split over two floors, with the kitchen partially in view and a pleasant terrace.

La Taula

No smokers rest.

Sant Màrius 8-12 ✉ 08022 – Ⓜ El Putxet – ☏ 93 417 28 48 – Fax 93 434 01 27
– www.lataula.com
closed August, Saturday lunch, Sunday and Bank Holidays **I1**

Rest – Carte 21/35 €

♦ International ♦ Cosy ♦

Small, cosy and with good attention to detail. A busy, lively atmosphere pervades this restaurant where the cuisine is centred around two types of menu and a list of chef's recommendations.

Vivanda

Major de Sarrià 134 ✉ 08017 – ☏ 93 203 19 18 – asisted@asisted.com
– Fax 93 212 48 85
closed Sunday, Monday lunch and Bank Holidays *Plan I* **A2**

Rest – Carte 28/35 €

♦ Inventive ♦ Formal ♦

In the Sarrià district residential area. Modern style dining room, with wicker furniture and suitable table service. Interesting menu at reasonable prices.

Folquer

Smokers rest.

Torrent de l'Olla 3 ✉ 08012 – Ⓜ Diagonal – ☏ 93 217 43 95
closed Holy Week, August, Saturday lunch and Sunday **K1**

Rest – *(only lunch) (only set meal)* Carte 27/34 €

♦ Inventive ♦ Bistro ♦

Typical bistro decoration, with 1920s-style cafeteria chairs and tables. Modern menu, but at lunch time it only offers three set menus.

Hesperia Tower

Gran Via 144 ✉ 08907 – Ⓜ Bellvitge – ☎ 93 413 50 00
– hotel@hesperia-tower.com – Fax 93 413 50 10 **A3**
258 rm – 155/340 €, 22 € – 22 suites
Rest *Evo* – see below
Rest *Bouquet* – Carte approx. 60 €

♦ Business ♦ Chain hotel ♦ Modern ♦

Innovative design and the latest technology best describe this hotel complex with spacious public areas, conference centre and fully-equipped guestrooms. The focus in the modern second-floor restaurant is on creative cuisine.

Evo – Hotel Hesperia Tower

Smokers rest.
city and mountain and sea,

Gran Via 144 ✉ 08907 – Ⓜ Bellvitge – ☎ 93 413 50 30
– evo@hesperia-tower.com – Fax 93 413 50 17 – www.evorestaurante.com
closed August, Saturday lunch, Sunday, Monday lunch and Bank Holidays
Rest – Menu 135 € **A3**

Spec. Carabineros en cocción unilateral con emulsión de citronelle. Salmonete albardado con tapenade y azafrán. Bizcocho viennois con pera, caramelo y helado de vainilla.

♦ Inventive ♦ Design ♦

A highly original restaurant with a panoramic dining room built beneath a glass cupola. Inventive cuisine based around traditional dishes and high-quality produce.

El Racó del Cargol

Smokers rest.

Dr. Martí Julià 54 ✉ 08903 – Ⓜ Collblanc – ☎ 93 449 77 18
– restaurantecargol@hotmail.com – Fax 93 449 08 16 – www.rocxi.es
closed 4 to 24 August, Sunday and Monday dinner **A3**
Rest – Carte 22/38 €

♦ Traditional ♦ Formal ♦

Surprisingly well organised, it offers traditional cuisine at reasonable prices. Classical dining room and two smaller, more modern rooms on the upper floor.

AT EL PRAT AIRPORT

Tryp Barcelona Aeropuerto

No smokers rest.

pl. del Pla de L'Estany 1-2 ✉ 08820 – ☎ 93 378 10 00
– tryp.barcelona.aeropuerto@solmelia.com – Fax 93 378 10 01
– www.tripbarcelonaaeropuerto.solmelia.com
205 rm – 80/230 €, 14 €
Rest – Menu 19 €

♦ Business ♦ Chain hotel ♦ Functional ♦

Functional establishment located in a business park close to the airport. The interesting lobby layout means that it opens directly onto all the corridors leading to the hotel's comfortable, practical bedrooms.

VALENCIA
VALÈNCIA

Population (est. 2007): 807 396 (Conurbation 1 500 000) - Altitude: 13m

Turismo Valencia/www.turisvalencia.es

Spain's third largest city remained to all intents and purposes a tourist no-go destination for too many years, hidden beneath its sunny shell. Not any more. In 2007 the prestigious America's Cup set sail from its shores in the shadow of the most eye-catching leisure complex in Europe, a stunning twenty-first century addition to the city's skyline. Valencia has announced itself in a big way.

Why it was ever relegated in the visitor stakes is a mystery to all Valencians. Friendly and unpretentious, they're only too willing to tell you of the city's undeniable character and charm, its unspoilt beaches, museums, amazing nightlife and rip-roaring fiestas. And they have a point. The buildings of the city's beautiful old town are testament to its rich history: medieval churches, Renaissance halls of trade and baroque mansions are layered on top of an earlier Roman city. This is the home of paella, and a thriving café scene gives you ample opportunity to tuck into it. The sun shines most of the time here, but if you want shelter there are more than thirty museums on hand offering a cool escape.

LIVING THE CITY

Valencia sits in an enviable position on the Mediterranean coast; the city's port and its long golden beach are to the east. A mile or so inland is the heart of the city, its old town, a labyrinth of ancient cobbled streets. It's bounded to the north by the Turia River Park, created when the actual river was diverted after floods a half a century ago, and to the south by a semicircle of wide boulevards, which follow the line of the ancient city walls. The renowned nightlife district of Carmen is the northwest area of the old town.

PRACTICAL INFORMATION

ARRIVAL-DEPARTURE

Valencia-Manises Airport is 8km west of the city and a taxi to the centre will cost about €15. Alternatively take the Metro train (lines 3 and 5) or the Airport bus which runs every 20min and takes around 15min.

TRANSPORT

Valencia has an integrated transport system, with metro, buses and trams. Single tickets for the modern metro, which has four lines, are cheap and can be purchased from station machines or ticket offices. You can buy a one-day pass for the metro, trams and buses or, alternatively, a 10-trip pass for about twice the price.

Another useful investment is the Valencia Tourist Card, available from tourism offices, hotels, tobacconists and kiosks. It offers free travel on all forms of public transport, as well as discounts in museums, shops, restaurants and various leisure activities. The cards last for one, two, or three days.

EXPLORING VALENCIA

This is a city whose centre resembles a Gothic-Renaissance theme park. Valencia can trace two thousand years of history, and at times you might well believe there's a mazy little street or alleyway for each of those years. Certainly newcomers will get lost in the compact centre, but that's part of the charm of the place. Anyway, you'll always come to a hefty landmark before too long. The reason for all the cobbled warrens and hidden plazas, the grand mixture of architectural styles is simple: over time Valencia has seen many invaders come and go, from the Romans to the Visigoths, from the Aragonese to the Moors. Each has left behind a mark of its presence.

The city's focal point is the **Plaza de la Virgen**. This is at the hub of the old town, a square constructed of marble with central fountain and array of buzzy street cafés. What mark it out as special are the two mighty churches that dominate it. The **Cathedral** is the most important religious building in the city, a beguiling mishmash of Moorish, gothic and Baroque styles built between 1262 and 1426. Alabaster windows bathe the interior in a warm Mediterranean light, suitably mellow to appreciate two paintings by Goya in a private chapel instigated by the renowned Borgia family. Climb the octagonal bell tower, 165ft above the ground, for some spectacular vertiginous views across the old rooftops. Once you've stepped out from the Cathedral, you can step straight into the neighbouring **Basćlica** and admire its seventeenth century baroque geography and gaze up at the dome for a beautiful fresco restored to its original glory. But don't look for candles to light: none are allowed in order to save the fresco from the effects of blackening.

→ SILKY SMOOTH

A hop, skip and jump to the south west – so close you're unlikely even to get lost – stands the jewel in Valencia's gothic crown: **La Lonja**. This fabulous one-time Silk Exchange was constructed in the 15C in the days when Valencia was the Spanish capital of prosperity. These days it's a UNESCO World Heritage Site. The façade is impressive enough, but it's the interior that catches your breath with its elegant columns of white stone carved to resemble twisted bolts of silk. There are high vaulted ceilings, wrought-iron chandeliers, a hall with splendid carved figures and impish gargoyles, and a prison tower where disreputable silk merchants would be sent. There's also a hidden garden with orange trees where you can sit and contemplate all you've seen. La Lonja is still in use today – for stamp fairs…

→ MARKET SHARES

Stamp lover or not, you'll come out of the Silk Exchange and face one of Valencia's most popular landmarks, the art nouveau **Central Market**, which has been a colourful centrepiece of local life for eighty years. It's a vast vaulted scrum of activity, one of the largest markets in Europe. The stalls, laden with gleaming tomatoes, hams, peppers and, above all, fish and shellfish, are an experience in themselves, set off by the wonderfully worn tiled and domed surroundings. If you counted the stalls here, you'd eventually reach an astronomical 959, so make sure you don't arrange to meet someone by the one that sells vegetables. They say that Valencians don't do things by halves, which is why there's a second great market to be found in the city: the **Mercado Colón**. This is a beautifully restored place with an ornate façade to the east of town. What it lacks in the fruit and veg stakes, it makes up for in cool cafés and boutiques which now populate most of the interior.

→ FUTURISTIC CITY

Culturally, the city has been propelled into the major league in the last decade. What's taken it there is the exciting **City of Arts and Sciences** complex, which draws over four million visitors each year. Valencian authorities had the inspired notion to build it in the confines of the Turia River Park, the fabulous nine-mile green space created when the river was diverted after flooding in 1957. This futuristic 'city' is made up of four stunning buildings made of white concrete and glass; these are home to a science museum, an opera house, an aquarium and an Imax cinema with a planetarium and laserium. Whether you're planning to go in any of them, or come face-to-face with them on a stroll through the parkland, there's no way you can ignore these weirdly compelling, other-worldly domes and pods.

For the more conventionally-minded, there are two great art galleries in Valencia. Both are on the northern edge of the old town, one just to the south of the river park, the other just to its north. The first, the Valencian Institute of Modern Art (IVAM), is only nineteen years old (as of 2008) but surprisingly it's Spain's oldest contemporary art museum. It boasts a brilliant display of sculpture by local artist Julio González, whose expressive iron masks and figures make him a true icon of modern sculpture. His work is backed up by a strong collection of international pop art and photography. Cross the Turia river bed and you'll soon arrive at the city's Museum of Fine Arts, one of the most important in Spain and generally regarded as a 'must see' by visitors. It's an easily identifiable place, with its blue-tiled dome jutting above the park; inside, it's a treasure trove of great works. There's much religious art from the 13C to 15C, mixed in with Bosch's breath-taking Triptych of the Passion. You'll also find works by most of Spain's greats such as Goya, El Greco and Velázquez, as well as plenty of modern art depicting the life of Valencia.

➜ CLASSIC CARMEN

This part of town – between the hip and happening Calle Caballeros and the Turia River Park – is also the main area to hit for nightlife and bars. It's the district known as **Carmen**, and fittingly boasts its very own operatic style. Even for a late-night country like Spain, Valencia has a revered position in the good-time stakes, and Carmen is where it happens. At the weekends the smart clubs and bars are overflowing with locals and tourists alike: there's not much point in arriving before 11pm, while it's a sure-fire bet that the sunshine will be accompanying you on your way back to your hotel. If you're more interested in a quiet stroll than the bright lights, then a good walk in the old town is to the **Serranos Tower** on Plaza Fueros by the side of the park. It's a heavily fortified survivor from the city's medieval walls, and as it doesn't close till 8.30 in the evening, climb up to its battlements as the sun goes down. From here, take in the sparkling views as you look across the lights of the old town and down the length of the Turia River Park, where the spookily illuminated City of Arts and Sciences looks like a multi-pronged night-travelling space voyager.

CALENDAR HIGHLIGHTS

Valencia is a religious city, and nowhere is this more evident than in its festivals, which fill the streets throughout the year. These are not sombre affairs, and fireworks play a significant – and noisy – role on practically every occasion. It all gets underway on 5 January when the Three Wise Men are

VALENCIA IN...

➜ ONE DAY

Plaza de la Virgen, La Lonja, central market, City of Arts and Sciences, a trip to the beach

➜ TWO DAYS

IVAM (or Museum of Fine Arts), another visit to City of Arts and Sciences, Carmen district nightlife

➜ THREE DAYS

Long, slow stroll along the Turia River Park, followed by equally long, relaxing meal of paella at café on Plaza de la Virgen or along the beach promenade lifted onto the City Hall balcony. Later that month the city's patron saint, St Vincent, is honoured in a procession from outside the cathedral. Easter sees Sailors' Holy Week and more rip-roaring processions, while kite-flying at the Turia River Park marks Easter Sunday and Monday. On the second Sunday of May all sorts of festivities coincide with the feast day of Our Lady of the Forsaken. Two months after Easter comes the feast of Corpus Christi (celebrated here for over 650 years), which sees a giant procession take to the streets led fittingly by eye-catching giant figures. As we say, a city of religion...Two festivals with a more secular tone are the Bienal de Valencia, an art-themed event from September to November (every second year, the next is in 2009) and the city's greatest extravaganza, Las Fallas. This is quite simply one of the greatest and craziest festivals in Europe; it always runs from 12-19 March and incorporates eardrum-shattering fireworks, brilliant parades, full-on parties and the ritual burning (on the last day) of satirical figures made from papier-mâché, some as tall as 25m. All this to celebrate the arrival of spring. And to add to its bizarre element, one of the giant figures is saved every year from conflagration, and stored in a special museum – the Guild of Fallas Artists Museum – way to the north of the city.

EATING OUT

Valencia is the city of paella. It was invented here, and this is the place to try it in infinite varieties. For a gargantuan helping, head off to the Las Arenas beach promenade, which is lined with a whole legion of seafood restaurants, anxious to send great platefuls your way. On a hot day (which is most days) the traditional liquid accompaniment is *agua de Valencia*, a potentially lethal combination of orange juice, Cava and vodka. Alternatively, if you're in town for Las Fallas, join a nomadic Fallas community group and eat it on the pavement amidst the firecrackers and parties. Generally speaking, food in Valencia is of the no-nonsense variety. Most restaurants remain very Spanish in character, and if you're not eating paella, then you'll probably be enjoying tapas, with an emphasis on the excellent local cured hams and cheeses. Slightly more 'off the wall' is the local delicacy of *all i pebre*, a mouth-watering meal of stewed eels from the local wetlands served in a garlic and red pepper sauce. The drink to cool down with is *horchata*. It's tigernut milk (a mixture of nuts, cinnamon, sugar and water) and is best enjoyed with a doughy cake. Meal times can throw the unwary visitor. Lunch is often not served until two in the afternoon, and dinner, in general, is never taken before nine at night. Adjust your eating habits accordingly. One thing that will be easy to get used to: service charge is always included in your bill, though if you wish to tip then five to ten per cent is ample.

→ ON THE TILES

One of the best buildings in the city is home to the Ceramics Museum. It's the 15C Palacio del Marqués de Dos Aguas, just south of Plaza de la Virgen, and it's a baroque beauty (it was revamped in 1740). The over-the-top alabaster front door surround is something to behold, as is the sumptuous interior. Oh yes, and it has a superlative range of tiles, too.

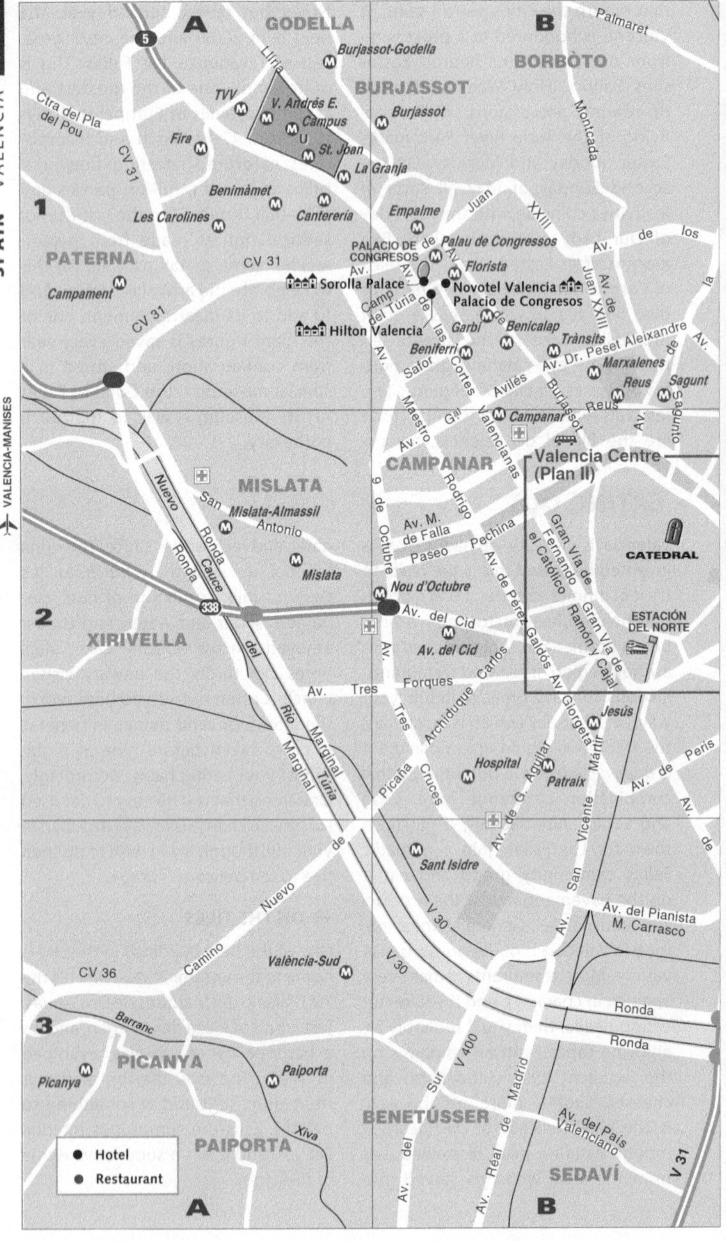
A
B
1
2
3
GODELLA
BURJASSOT
BORBÒTO
PATERNA
MISLATA
CAMPANAR
XIRIVELLA
PICANYA
PAIPORTA
BENETÚSSER
SEDAVÍ
Palmaret
Burjassot-Godella
Llíria
Burjassot
TVV
V. Andrés E.
Campus
U
St. Joan
La Granja
Fira
Ctra del Pla del Pou
CV 31
Benimàmet
Cantereria
Les Carolines
Campament
Empalme
Moncada
Juan XXIII
PALACIO DE CONGRESOS
Palau de Congressos
Florista
Sorolla Palace
Novotel Valencia Palacio de Congresos
Hilton Valencia
Camp del Túria
Garbí
Benicalap
Beniferri
Trànsits
Av. Dr. Peset Aleixandre
Marxalenes
Reus
Sagunt
Av. de los
Av. de Juan XXIII
Av. Burjassot
Av. Saguntо
Av. Maestro Rodrigo
Av. Gral. Avilés
Av. de las Cortes Valencianas
Campanar
Valencia Centre (Plan II)
CATEDRAL
ESTACIÓN DEL NORTE
Gran Vía de Fernando el Católico
Gran Vía de Ramón y Cajal
VALENCIA-MANISES
Nuevo Cauce del Río
Ronda
San Antonio
Mislata-Almassil
Mislata
Av. M. de Falla
Paseo Pechina
Av. 9 de Octubre
Nou d'Octubre
Av. del Cid
338
Av. Tres Forques
Av. Tres Cruces
Archiduque Carlos
Av. de Pérez Galdós
Av. Giorgeta
Jesús
Hospital
Patraix
Av. de G. Aguilar
Av. San Vicente Mártir
Av. de Peris
Marginal del Túria
Picaña
Camino Nuevo de
Sant Isidre
V 30
Av. del Pianista M. Carrasco
València-Sud
CV 36
Barranc
Ronda
Paiporta
Picanya
Xiva
V 400
Av. del Sur
Av. Real de Madrid
Av. del País Valenciano
V 31
Hotel
Restaurant

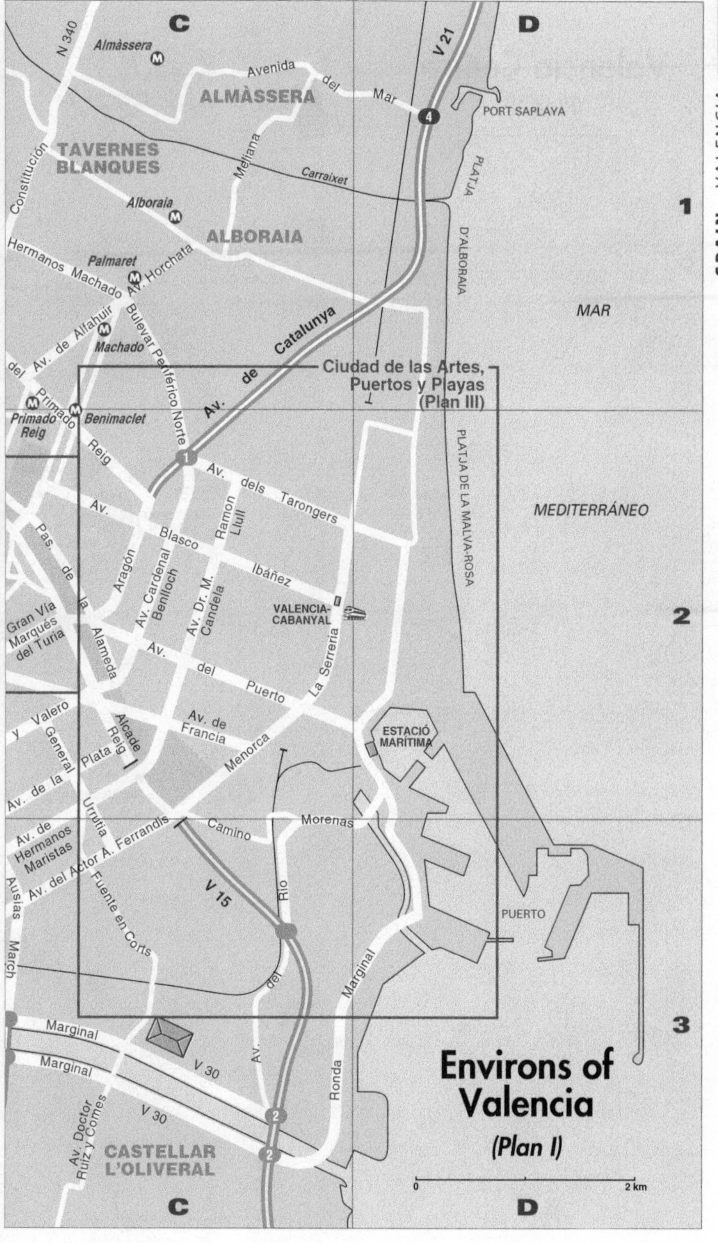

Environs of Valencia

(Plan I)

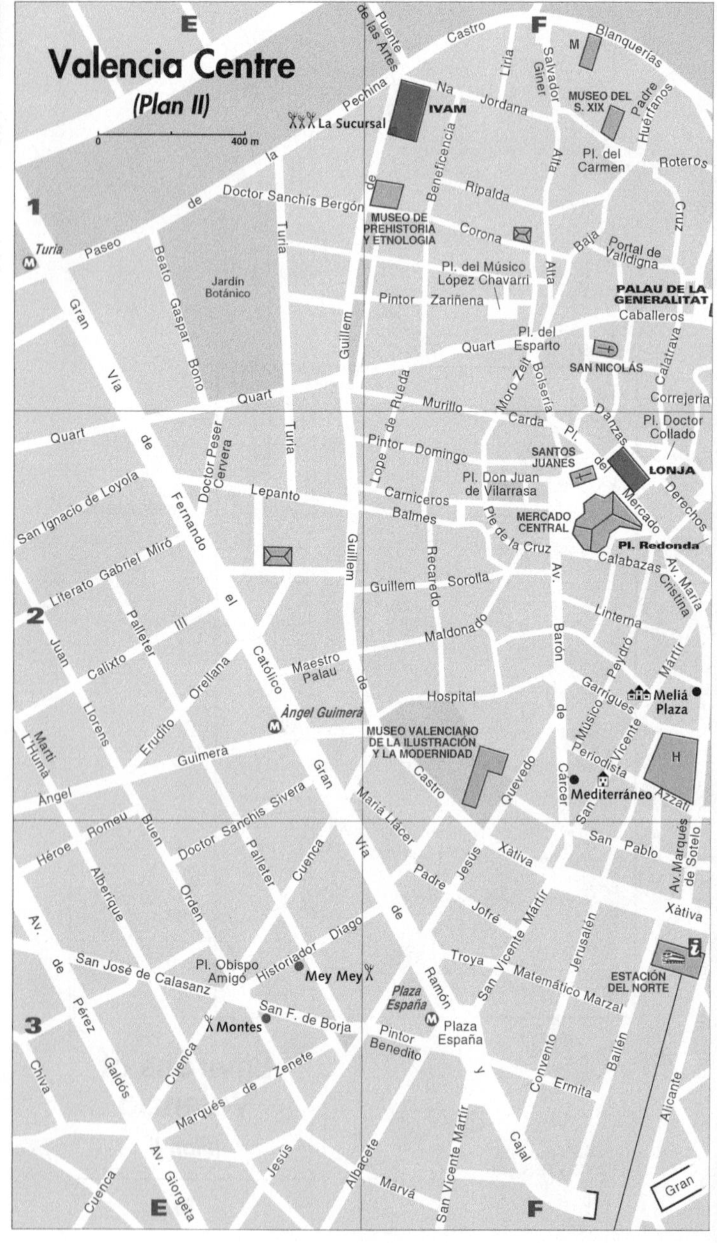
Valencia Centre
(Plan II)
0
400 m
E
F
1
2
3
Turia
Jardín Botánico
La Sucursal
IVAM
MUSEO DE PREHISTORIA Y ETNOLOGIA
MUSEO DEL S. XIX
Pl. del Carmen
Pl. del Músico López Chavarri
PALAU DE LA GENERALITAT
Pl. del Esparto
SAN NICOLÁS
Pl. Doctor Collado
SANTOS JUANES
LONJA
Pl. Don Juan de Vilarrasa
MERCADO CENTRAL
Pl. Redonda
Meliá Plaza
Àngel Guimerà
MUSEO VALENCIANO DE LA ILUSTRACIÓN Y LA MODERNIDAD
Mediterráneo
ESTACIÓN DEL NORTE
Pl. Obispo Amigó
Mey Mey
Montes
Plaza España
Castro
Blanquerías
Puente de las Artes
Pechina
Na Jordana
Liria
Salvador Giner
Padre Huérfanos
Roteros
Doctor Sanchis Bergón
Paseo de la
Beneficencia
Ripalda
Corona
Baja
Portal de Valldigna
Cruz
Alta
Pintor Zariñena
Caballeros
Calatrava
Quart
Beato Gaspar Bono
Gran Vía de Fernando el Católico
Guillem
Murillo
Carda
Correjeria
Danzas
Pl. del Mercado
Derechos
Moro Zeit
Bolsería
Pintor Domingo
Lope de Rueda
Doctor Peser Cervera
Turia
San Ignacio de Loyola
Lepanto
Carniceros
Balmes
Pie de la Cruz
Calabazas
Av. María Cristina
Literato Gabriel Miró
Guillem Sorolla
Recaredo
Av. Barón de Cárcer
Linterna
Palleter
Calixto III
Juan Llorens
Maldonado
Maestro Palau
Orellana
Peydró
Mártir
Hospital
Garrigues
Músico
Vicente
Marti L'Humà
Erudito
Guimera
Ángel
Castro
Quevedo
Periodista Azzati
Gran Vía
María Llácer
San
Héroe Romeu
Buen Orden
Doctor Sanchis Sivera
Palleter
Cuenca
San Pablo
Av. Marqués de Sotelo
Xàtiva
Alberique
Padre Jofré
Jesús
San Vicente Mártir
Av. de Pérez Galdós
Diago
Historiador
Troya
Matemático Marzal
Jerusalén
San José de Calasanz
Ramón y Cajal
San F. de Borja
Pintor Benedito
Convento
Bailén
Ermita
Chiva
Cuenca
Marqués de Zenete
Alicante
Jesús
Albacete
Marvá
San Vicente Mártir
Av. Giorgeta
Gran

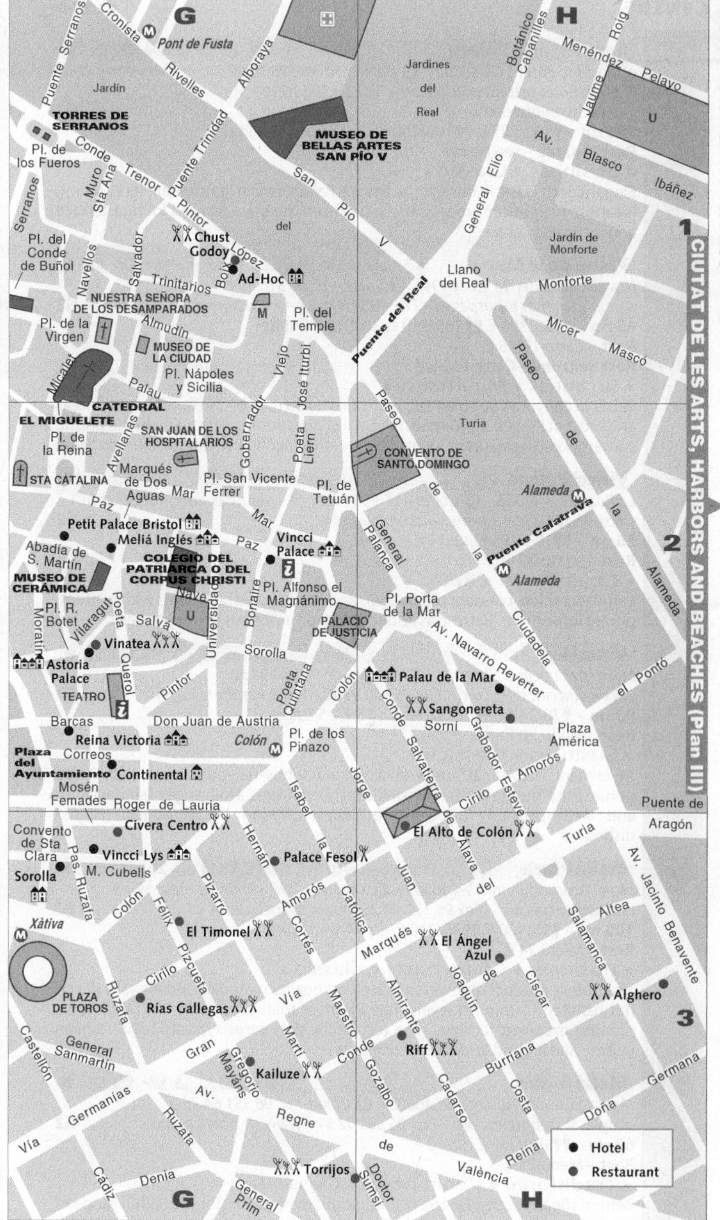
CIUTAT DE LES ARTS, HARBORS AND BEACHES (Plan III)
TORRES DE SERRANOS
MUSEO DE BELLAS ARTES SAN PÍO V
Jardines del Real
NUESTRA SEÑORA DE LOS DESAMPARADOS
MUSEO DE LA CIUDAD
CATEDRAL
EL MIGUELETE
SAN JUAN DE LOS HOSPITALARIOS
STA CATALINA
CONVENTO DE SANTO DOMINGO
COLEGIO DEL PATRIARCA O DEL CORPUS CHRISTI
MUSEO DE CERÁMICA
PALACIO DE JUSTICIA
TEATRO
Plaza del Ayuntamiento
PLAZA DE TOROS
Chust Godoy
Ad-Hoc
Petit Palace Bristol
Meliá Inglés
Vincci Palace
Vinatea
Astoria Palace
Palau de la Mar
Sangonereta
Reina Victoria
Continental
Civera Centro
Vincci Lys
Sorolla
Palace Fesol
El Alto de Colón
El Timonel
El Ángel Azul
Alghero
Rías Gallegas
Riff
Kailuze
Torrijos
Pont de Fusta
Alameda
Colón
Xàtiva
Puente del Real
Puente Calatrava
Puente de Aragón
Hotel
Restaurant

Ayre Astoria Palace

pl. Rodrigo Botet 5 ✉ 46002 – Ⓜ Colón – ☎ 96 398 10 00 – info@hotel-astoria-palace.com – Fax 96 398 10 10 – www.ayrehoteles.com **G2**

196 rm – 🚹100/225 € 🚹🚹100/260 €, ☕ 13.50 € – 8 suites

Rest Vinatea – see below

♦ Business ♦ Classic ♦

Elegant and classic in design, the Astoria Palace's main features are its stunning location, magnificent rooms, the views from the glass-fronted lounge-terrace and its fitness centre.

Palau de la Mar Smokers rest.

Navarro Reverter 14 ✉ 46004 – Ⓜ Colón – ☎ 96 316 28 84 – palaudelamar@hospes.es – Fax 96 316 28 85 – www.hospes.es **H2**

65 rm – 🚹165/300 € 🚹🚹165/350 €, ☕ 18 € – 2 suites

Rest – Carte 29/45 €

Rest *Senzone* – Carte 43/58 €

♦ Business ♦ Minimalist ♦

Partly occupying two small 19C mansions taken over by the hotel's public areas and most of its well-appointed, minimalist guestrooms. The menu in the bright, contemporary restaurant focuses on creative Mediterranean cuisine. Spa area.

Vincci Palace No smokers rest.

La Paz 42 ✉ 46003 – Ⓜ Colón – ☎ 96 206 23 77 – palace@vinccihoteles.com – Fax 96 206 23 64 – www.vinccihoteles.com **G2**

76 rm – 🚹🚹104/295 €, ☕ 14 €

Rest – Menu 26 €

♦ Chain hotel ♦ Retro ♦

Large reception, pleasant public areas and comfortable bedrooms with contemporary furnishings. Retro-classic décor with an emphasis on grey tones.

Vincci Lys No smokers rest.

Martínez Cubells 5 ✉ 46002 – Ⓜ Xàtiva – ☎ 96 350 95 50 – lys@vinccihoteles.com – Fax 96 350 95 52 – www.vincihoteles.com **G3**

95 rm – 🚹78/240 € 🚹🚹78/320 €, ☕ 15 € – 5 suites

Rest – Menu 20 €

♦ Business ♦ Classic ♦

An elegant, traditional hotel with a spacious lobby-reception area which is also home to the lounge and bar. Magnificent guestrooms, a full range of spa facilities, and an impeccably designed restaurant offering Mediterranean-inspired dishes.

Meliá Plaza Smokers rest.

pl. del Ayuntamiento 4 ✉ 46002 – Ⓜ Xàtiva – ☎ 96 352 06 12 – reservas@plazavalencia.com – Fax 96 352 04 26 – www.solmelia.com **F2**

100 rm – 🚹95/180 € 🚹🚹95/210 €, ☕ 14 € – 1 suite

Rest – Menu 24 €

♦ Business ♦ Chain hotel ♦ Classic ♦

The hotel's gradual renovation, based on quality materials and elegant décor, has resulted in comfort levels that are more than acceptable with bedrooms offering excellent facilities. The restaurant showcases typical Mediterranean cuisine and a good selection of rice dishes.

Meliá Inglés

Marqués de Dos Aguas 6 ✉ 46002 – Ⓜ Colón – ☎ 96 351 64 26 – ingles@sh-hoteles.com – Fax 96 394 02 51 – www.sh-hoteles.com **G2**

63 rm – 🚹🚹100/250 €, ☕ 10 €

Rest – Menu 23 €

♦ Traditional ♦ Chain hotel ♦ Classic ♦

Behind the attractive façade of this old building is a hotel with a full range of modern comforts and the latest technology. Superb guestrooms decorated with the utmost taste. The restaurant, divided into two rooms, serves international cuisine, plus a comprehensive menu of rice dishes.

Reina Victoria No smokers rest.
Barcas 4 ✉ 46002 – Ⓜ Xàtiva – ☎ 96 352 04 87 – hreinavictoriavalencia@husa.es – Fax 96 352 27 21 – www.husa.es
95 rm – †70/155 € ††70/205 €, ☕ 12 € – 1 suite **G2**
Rest – *(closed August)* Menu 25 €
◆ Traditional ◆ Chain hotel ◆ Classic ◆
A fine façade and an unbeatable location a stone's throw from the city's main museums. Elegant facilities, including an attractive lounge area and bedrooms which have been sympathetically modernised. The restaurant on the first floor adjoins the English-style bar.

Ad-Hoc Smokers rest.
Boix 4 ✉ 46003 – ☎ 96 391 91 40 – adhoc@adhochoteles.com – Fax 96 391 36 67 – www.adhochoteles.com **G1**
28 rm – †76/161 € ††89/207 €, ☕ 10 €
Rest – *(closed Sunday)* Carte 23/36 €
◆ Traditional ◆ Rustic ◆
An attractive hotel in a 19C building with compact public areas, and guestrooms embellished with a neo-rustic décor of exposed brickwork, wooden beams and clay tiles. Pleasant and relaxing restaurant.

Petit Palace Bristol without rest
Abadía de San Martín 3 ✉ 46002 – Ⓜ Colón – ☎ 96 394 51 00 – bristol@hthoteles.com – Fax 96 394 38 50 – www.hthoteles.com **G2**
43 rm – †75/300 € ††80/300 €, ☕ 13 €
◆ Traditional ◆ Modern ◆
In a building that has preserved its original 19C façade. Multi-purpose foyer, and contemporary-style bedrooms, all with hydro-massage columns in the bathrooms.

Sorolla without rest
Convento Santa Clara 5 ✉ 46002 – Ⓜ Xàtiva – ☎ 96 352 33 92 – reservas@hotelsorolla.com – Fax 96 352 14 65 – www.hotelsorolla.com **G3**
58 rm ☕ – †85/160 € ††85/220 €
◆ Traditional ◆ Functional ◆
With its glass-fronted façade and attractively renovated reception, the Sorolla's overall feel is pleasantly contemporary. Comfortable, functional bedrooms with parquet flooring.

Mediterráneo without rest
Barón de Cárcer 45 ✉ 46001 – Ⓜ Xàtiva – ☎ 96 351 01 42 – riasmediter@terra.es – Fax 96 351 01 42 – www.hotel-mediterraneo.es **F2**
34 rm – †68/100 € ††96/150 €, ☕ 7 €
◆ Family ◆ Functional ◆
A centrally located hotel with a welcoming and elegant foyer-reception area adorned with wood and marble. Classically furnished bedrooms. Breakfast room on the first floor.

Continental without rest
Correos 8 ✉ 46002 – Ⓜ Colón – ☎ 96 353 52 82 – continental@contitel.es – Fax 96 353 11 13 – www.contitel.es **G2**
46 rm ☕ – †48/65 € ††62/110 €
◆ Traditional ◆ Functional ◆
A contemporary, functionally furnished hotel with a central location. Small public areas, compensated by well-appointed, comfortable guestrooms, half of which overlook an inner patio.

Rías Gallegas Smokers rest.
Cirilo Amorós 4 ✉ 46004 – Ⓜ Xàtiva – ☎ 96 352 51 11 – riasgallegas@riasgallegas.es – Fax 96 351 99 10 – www.riasgallegas.es
closed Holy Week, August, Sunday and Monday dinner **G3**
Rest – Carte approx. 64 €
◆ Galician specialities ◆ Formal ◆
Specialising in traditional Galician cuisine, the menu here understandably focuses on fish and seafood. Exclusive dining room on two levels, professional service and delightful table settings.

Torrijos (Josep Quintana)
Dr. Sumsi 4 ✉ 46005 – Ⓜ Colón – ☎ 96 373 29 49 – info@restaurantetorrijos.com – Fax 96 373 29 49 – www.restaurantetorrijos.com
closed 7 to 17 January, 25 March-4 April, 15 to 31 August, 1 to 15 September and Sunday dinner **G-H3**
Rest – Menu 75 € – Carte 58/70 €
Spec. Chipirón de anzuelo con raviolis de verduras y setas. Ventresca de atún con berenjena ahumada, yogur picante y su escabeche. Albaricoque estofado con crujiente de almendras y helado de cardamomo (May-August).
♦ Inventive ♦ Formal ♦
An elegant, modern ambience, excellent service and an attractive, innovative menu. Attractive, glass-fronted wine cellar and two private rooms, one with views of the kitchen.

La Sucursal
Guillém de Castro 118 ✉ 46003 – Ⓜ Túria – ☎ 96 374 66 65 – info@restaurantelasucursal.com – Fax 96 392 41 54 – www.restaurantelasucursal.com
closed 15 to 31 August, Saturday lunch and Sunday **F1**
Rest – Menu 68 € – Carte 49/55 €
Spec. Salmonetes de roca con puré de remolacha y frambuesa. Rodaballo salvaje con emulsión de suquet. Paletilla de cordero lechal con cabello de ángel.
♦ Inventive ♦ Minimalist ♦
Part of the Instituto Valenciano de Arte Moderno, with a cafeteria open to the public on the ground floor and a minimalist room on the first. A fusion of innovative and traditional cuisine.

Vinatea – Hotel Ayre Astoria Palace — Smokers rest.
Vilaragut 4 ✉ 46002 – Ⓜ Colón – ☎ 96 398 10 00 – info@hotel-astoria-palace.com – Fax 96 398 10 10 – www.ayrehoteles.com **G2**
Rest – Carte approx. 51 €
♦ International ♦ Formal ♦
Excellent levels of comfort, with a separate entrance, offering interesting gastronomic choice. Refined classical décor with elegant furniture.

Riff — Smokers rest.
Conde de Altea 18 ✉ 46005 – Ⓜ Colón – ☎ 96 333 53 53 – restaurante@restaurante-riff.com – Fax 96 335 31 78 – www.restaurante-riff.com
closed August, Sunday and Monday **H3**
Rest – Carte 46/57 €
♦ Inventive ♦ Minimalist ♦
Hot on the heels of the latest trends in the restaurant world with its creative cuisine and minimalist design. The restaurant also has its own delicatessen next door.

Kailuze — Smokers rest.
Gregorio Mayáns 5 ✉ 46005 – Ⓜ Xàtiva – ☎ 96 335 45 39 – kailuze@menjariviure.com – Fax 96 335 48 93 – www.kailuze.com
closed Holy Week, August, Saturday lunch and Sunday **G3**
Rest – Carte 43/57 €
♦ Basque ♦ Formal ♦
Warm décor, excellent service and reliable Basque-Navarran cuisine are the hallmarks of this restaurant with a reception area and cosy dining room.

El Ángel Azul — Smokers rest.
Conde de Altea 33 ✉ 46005 – Ⓜ Colón – ☎ 96 374 56 56 – www.angelazul.com
closed 12 August-13 September, Sunday and Monday **H3**
Rest – Carte 42/49 €
♦ Inventive ♦ Formal ♦
A centrally located restaurant with an elegant main dining room and two rooms for private functions. Creative à la carte choices, in addition to several tasting menus.

XX **Civera Centro**

Mosén Femades 10 ✉ 46002 – Ⓜ Colón – ✆ 96 352 97 64 – civeracentro@marisqueriascivera.com – Fax 96 346 50 50 – www.marisqueriascivera.com
closed Holy Week, 15 to 31 July and 4 to 10 August **G3**
Rest – Carte 38/55 €
♦ Seafood ♦ Formal ♦
A restaurant renowned for the high quality of its ingredients. Tapas bar, maritime-influenced décor in the dining room and various private rooms. The seafood platter is a house speciality.

XX **Chust Godoy** Smokers rest.

Boix 6 ✉ 46003 – Ⓜ Colón – ✆ 96 391 38 15 – chustgodoy@chustgodoy.com – Fax 96 392 22 39 – www.chustgodoy.com
closed Holy Week, August, Saturday lunch and Sunday **G1**
Rest – Carte 44/55 €
♦ Traditional ♦ Family ♦
Professionally run by the owner-chef and his wife, the Chust Godoy has one neo-rustic dining room and one cellar-type private area. Menu based on seasonal market products, with a good choice of savoury rice dishes.

XX **Sangonereta** Smokers rest.

Sorni 31 ✉ 46004 – Ⓜ Colón – ✆ 96 373 81 70 – rtesangonereta@hotmail.com – Fax 96 373 81 70 – www.sangonereta.com
closed Holy Week, 15 to 31 August, Saturday lunch and Sunday **H2**
Rest – Carte 34/50 €
♦ Inventive ♦ Formal ♦
A classic restaurant whose name pays homage to a character in the novel and TV series "Cañas y Barro". Creative cuisine, including a tasting menu.

XX **El Alto de Colón**

Jorge Juan 19 ✉ 46004 – Ⓜ Colón – ✆ 96 353 09 00
closed Holy Week, August, Saturday lunch and Sunday **H3**
Rest – Carte 41/55 €
♦ Traditional ♦ Formal ♦
Remarkable establishment located in one of the towers of the Colón market, with a modern style. Boasts attractive tiled ceilings and modern Mediterranean cuisine.

XX **El Timonel**

Félix Pizcueta 13 ✉ 46004 – Ⓜ Xàtiva – ✆ 96 352 63 00 – restaurante@eltimonel.com – Fax 96 351 17 32 – www.eltimonel.com
closed Monday **G3**
Rest – Carte 35/45 €
♦ Traditional ♦ Family ♦
A family-run eatery with the owner working the dining room and his son in the kitchen. Welcoming maritime décor and reasonably extensive menu.

XX **Alghero** Smokers rest.

Burriana 52 ✉ 46005 – Ⓜ Colón – ✆ 96 333 35 79 – correo@restaurantealghero.com – www.restaurante-alghero.com **H3**
Rest – Carte 30/35 €
♦ Mediterranean ♦ Formal ♦
An attractive setting and elegant furnishings. Creative, Mediterranean-influenced cuisine with an Italian slant.

X **Palace Fesol**

Hernán Cortés 7 ✉ 46004 – Ⓜ Colón – ✆ 96 352 93 23 – palacefesol@palacefesol.com – Fax 96 353 00 68 – www.palacefesol.com
closed Holy Week, 11 to 24 August, Saturday and Sunday in Summer, Sunday dinner and Monday for rest of the year **G3**
Rest – Carte 30/47 €
♦ Regional ♦ Family ♦
A restaurant with a great family tradition. Bar for a pre-dinner drink, a neo-rustic dining room decorated with azulejos on the walls, plus an attractive private room on the first floor. Traditional menu including rice dishes.

Montes Smokers rest.

pl. Obispo Amigó 5 ✉ 46007 – Ⓜ Pl. Espanya – ✆ 96 385 50 25
closed Holy Week, August, Sunday dinner, Monday and Tuesday dinner **E3**
Rest – Carte 22/33 €
◆ Traditional ◆ Family ◆
Pleasantly decorated main dining room with excellent service. The entrance is via an attractive hall with bar which leads to an elongated dining room.

Mey Mey Smokers rest.

Historiador Diago 19 ✉ 46007 – Ⓜ Pl. Espanya – ✆ 96 384 07 47 – Fax 96 185 71 76 – www.mey-mey.com
closed Holy Week and last 3 weeks in August **E3**
Rest – Carte 18/32 €
◆ Chinese ◆ Exotic ◆
Attractive décor in keeping with that of a traditional Chinese restaurant – note the circular fountain full of colourful fish. Cantonese menu, including a selection of steamed dishes.

CIUDAD DE LAS ARTES, HARBOURS AND BEACHES *Plan III*

The Westin Valencia No smokers rest.

Amadeo de Saboya 16 ✉ 46010 – Ⓜ Alameda – ✆ 96 362 59 00 – hotel.westinvalencia@westin.com – Fax 96 362 59 09 **J1**
130 rm – ††195/455 €, ☕ 20 € – 5 suites
Rest *Oscar Torrijos* – *(closed Sunday)* Carte 52/64 €
◆ Luxury ◆ Classic ◆
Located in a pretty historic building with a large interior patio complete with pergolas. Very spacious classico-elegant style rooms that are excellently equipped. The gastronomic restaurant is run by a chef who is renowned in the town.

Meliá Valencia Palace

paseo de la Alameda 32 ✉ 46023 – ✆ 96 337 50 37 – melia.valencia.palace@solmelia.com – Fax 96 337 55 32 – www.solmelia.com **J2**
243 rm – ††95/285 €, ☕ 15 € – 5 suites
Rest – Menu 32 €
◆ Business ◆ Chain hotel ◆ Classic ◆
The hotel offers its guests a high standard of comfort and facilities, including the spectacular entrance hall, reflecting the latest trends in interior design, and the bedrooms, furnished with impeccable taste. A mix of modern and traditional cuisine in the restaurant, decorated in functional minimalist style.

Las Arenas No smokers rest.

Eugenia Viñes 22 ✉ 46011 – Ⓜ Neptú – ✆ 96 312 06 00 – reservas@hotel-lasarenas.com – Fax 96 312 06 16 – www.hotel-lasarenas.com **K2**
243 rm – †160/270 € ††160/310 €, ☕ 19 € – 10 suites
Rest – Carte approx. 51 €
◆ Business ◆ Chain hotel ◆ Classic ◆
A luxury beachfront hotel spread around three buildings with welcoming lounge areas, superb meeting rooms and fully-equipped guestrooms. Restaurant serving Mediterranean cuisine.

NH Las Artes I No smokers rest.

av. Instituto Obrero 28 ✉ 46013 – ✆ 96 335 13 10 – nhlasartes@nh-hotels.com – Fax 96 374 86 22 – www.nh-hotels.com **J2**
172 rm – †63/255 € ††79/315 €, ☕ 13 € – 2 suites
Rest – Menu 25 €
◆ Business ◆ Chain hotel ◆ Functional ◆
A contemporary hotel offering excellent facilities and refined comfort. Great attention to detail in the bedrooms, plus an extensive range of guest services.

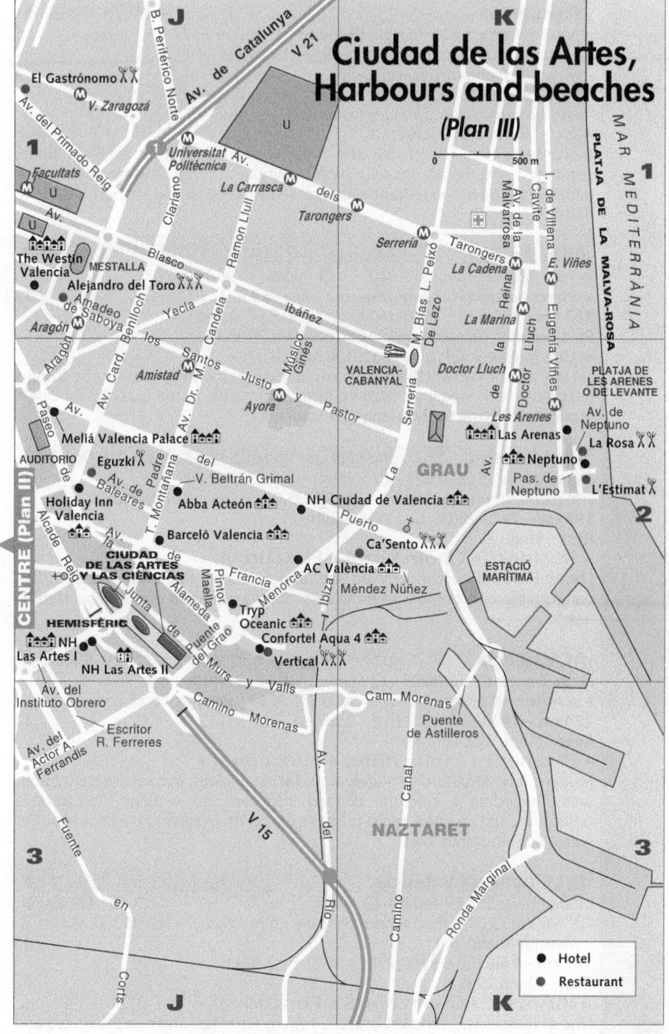

Holiday Inn Valencia

paseo de la Alameda 38 ✉ 46023 – ✆ 96 303 21 00 – reservas@holidayinnvalencia.com – Fax 96 303 21 26 – www.holidayinn.es

200 rm – †70/250 € ††80/260 €, ☕ 15 € J2

Rest – Menu 10 €

♦ Business ♦ Chain hotel ♦ Functional ♦

A modern hotel geared towards business travellers with the standards and comforts associated with this international chain. Terrace-bar with fine views and a restaurant connected to the hall-cafeteria.

Neptuno VISA

paseo de Neptuno 2 46011 – Neptú – 96 356 77 77
– reservas@hotelneptunovalencia.com – Fax 96 356 04 30
– www.hotelneptunovalencia.com **K2**

48 rm – 103/363 €, 16 €

Rest ***Tridente*** – *(closed Sunday in Winter)* Carte 44/56 €

♦ Business ♦ Modern ♦

A contemporary hotel by the beach offering guests well-equipped, minimalist-style bedrooms with high-quality furnishings, and hydro-massage bath tubs. Modern restaurant with a glazed wine cellar and kitchens visible to diners.

Abba Acteón No smokers rest. VISA

Vicente Beltrán Grimal 2 46023 – Ayora – 96 331 07 07
– reservas-acteon@abbahoteles.com – Fax 96 330 22 30 **J2**

182 rm – 63/230 € 63/260 €, 12.50 € – 5 suites

Rest ***Amalur*** – *(closed Sunday)* Carte approx. 35 €

♦ Business ♦ Chain hotel ♦ Modern ♦

Quality and design are the buzzwords in this hotel, with its spacious bedrooms decorated with elegant materials, including marble in the bathrooms. Open, modern and attractively arranged restaurant.

Tryp Oceanic No smokers rest. VISA

Pintor Maella 35 46023 – Serrería – 96 335 03 00
– tryp.oceanic@solmelia.com – Fax 96 335 03 11 – www.solmelia.com

195 rm – 70/200 €, 14 € – 2 suites **J2**

Rest – Menu 28 €

♦ Business ♦ Chain hotel ♦ Functional ♦

Located closed to the City of Arts and Sciences. Adequate public areas, comfortable bedrooms with armchairs, and a swimming pool surrounded by lawns.

AC València No smokers rest. VISA

av. de Francia 67 46023 – Serrería – 96 331 70 00
– acvalencia@ac-hotels.com – Fax 96 331 70 01 – www.ac-hotels.com

174 rm – 70/400 €, 15 € – 2 suites **J2**

Rest – Menu 21 €

♦ Business ♦ Chain hotel ♦ Functional ♦

Modern, functional and resolutely aimed at the business market. Pleasant public areas, including a cafeteria divided into separate sections. Comfortable bedrooms, and an open, multi-purpose dining room serving traditional dishes with a contemporary twist.

NH Ciudad de Valencia No smokers rest.

av. del Puerto 214 46023 – Ayora VISA
– 96 330 75 00 – nhciudaddevalencia@nh-hotels.com – Fax 96 330 98 64
– www.nh-hotels.com **J2**

147 rm – 68/180 € 68/250 €, 11 € – 2 suites

Rest – Menu 19 €

♦ Business ♦ Chain hotel ♦ Functional ♦

One of the chain's standard-bearers, with its large hall and reception area and lounge-bar. The fully-equipped bedrooms include details such as wood floors and triple glazing. Sizeable dining room with functional yet warm décor.

Barceló Valencia No smokers rest.

av. de Francia 11 46009 – Amistat VISA
– 96 330 63 44 – valencia@barcelovalencia.com – Fax 96 335 07 99
– www.barcelovalencia.com **J2**

185 rm – 105/230 €, 16 € – 2 suites

Rest – Menu 19 €

♦ Business ♦ Chain hotel ♦ Modern ♦

Boasts a privileged location with beautiful views of the City of Arts and Sciences. The rooms are very spacious and there is a spa on the roof terrace.

Confortel Aqua 4 No smokers rest.

Luis García Berlanga 19-21 ✉ 46023 – ✆ 96 318 71 00 – reservasagua4@confortel.com – Fax 96 318 71 67 – www.confortelhoteles.com J2

176 rm – ††70/300 €, ☕ 12 € – 8 suites

Rest – Menu 17 €

♦ Business ♦ Chain hotel ♦ Modern ♦

Combined with two hotels that share services and lounges. Located over a shopping centre, and of note for its interesting combination of design and functionality.

NH Las Artes II without rest

av. Instituto Obrero 26 ✉ 46013 – ✆ 96 335 60 62 – exlasartes@nh-hotels.com – Fax 96 333 46 83 – www.nh-hotels.com J2

121 rm – †55/205 € ††60/255 €, ☕ 10 €

♦ Business ♦ Chain hotel ♦ Functional ♦

A functional chain hotel with the expected level of facilities but limited public areas. Simply furnished yet colourful guestrooms.

Ca'Sento (Raúl Alexandre) Smokers rest.

Méndez Núñez 17 ✉ 46024 – Ⓜ Ayora – ✆ 96 330 17 75 closed Holy Week, August, Sunday and Monday K2

Rest – *(booking essential)* Menu 110 € – Carte 86/95 €

Spec. Ensalada de trufa de Benasal con alcachofas marinadas (December-March). Rosejat de fideos a la plancha con espardenyes. Ravioli de chocolate con helado de caramelo y especias.

♦ Inventive ♦ Family ♦

A family-run restaurant with a surprisingly modern design, where the emphasis is on fish and seafood dishes influenced by contemporary trends.

Alejandro del Toro Smokers rest.

Amadeo de Saboya 15 ✉ 46010 – Ⓜ Aragón – ✆ 96 393 40 46 – info@restaurantealejandrodeltoro.com – Fax 96 369 84 86 – www.restaurantealejandrodeltoro.com closed Saturday lunch and Sunday J1

Rest – Menu 85 € – Carte 55/73 €

Spec. Ensalada templada de pichón de Bresse con garbanzos de Vegasaúco. Gelatina caliente de titaina con centro de bacalao confitado. Chuleta de vaca limpia con terrina de patata trufada (winter).

♦ Inventive ♦ Friendly ♦

The owner-chef is known for his creative cuisine, served in a spacious, minimalist-style restaurant with a glass-fronted wine cellar giving diners a full view of the kitchens.

Vertical

Luis García Berlanga 19 ✉ 46013 – ✆ 96 330 38 00 – info@restaurantevertical.com – Fax 96 330 38 00 – www.resturantevertical.com closed 10 to 25 August J2

Rest – Carte 48/58 €

♦ Inventive ♦ Design ♦

On the roof terrace of the Confortel Aqua 4 hotel, it can only be accessed via the hotel. The modern-design dining room boasts a beautiful panoramic view.

El Gastrónomo Smokers rest.

av. Primado Reig 149 ✉ 46020 – Ⓜ Benimaclet – ✆ 96 369 70 36 – elgastronomo@gmail.com – www.elgastronomorestaurante.com closed Holy Week, August, Sunday, Monday dinner and Tuesday dinner J1

Rest – Carte 30/41 €

♦ International ♦ Formal ♦

A resolutely old-style restaurant both in terms of the way it's run and the nutritious cuisine on offer here.

XX **La Rosa**
av. de Neptuno 70 ✉ 46011 – Ⓜ Neptú – ✆ 96 371 20 76 – Fax 96 371 25 65
closed Holy Week and 15 August-15 September **K2**
Rest – *(lunch only in Winter)* Carte approx. 45 €
♦ Rice specialities ♦ Family ♦
Dining rooms adorned with a profusion of wood and America's Cup-inspired décor. Pleasant glass-enclosed terrace. Culinary emphasis on fish and seafood, including delicious rice dishes.

X **Eguzki** Smokers rest.
av. Baleares 1 ✉ 46023 – Ⓜ Alameda – ✆ 96 337 50 33 – Fax 96 337 50 33
closed Holy Week, August, Sunday and Bank Holidays **J2**
Rest – Carte 45/54 €
♦ Basque ♦ Family ♦
This Basque restaurant with an attractive stone façade is run with great enthusiasm by the family that owns it. A hall-bar on the ground floor and a pleasant dining room one floor up.

X **L'Estimat**
av. de Neptuno 16 ✉ 46011 – Ⓜ Neptú – ✆ 96 371 10 18 – info@lestimat.com
– Fax 96 372 73 85 – www.lestimat.com
closed 15 August-15 September, Sunday dinner,
Monday dinner and Tuesday **K2**
Rest – Carte 30/52 €
♦ Traditional ♦ Family ♦
Two aquariums in the entrance hall, a kitchen visible to diners, and a spacious, maritime-influenced dining room. Regional menu, with a fine selection of rice dishes.

AT PALACIO DE CONGRESOS *Plan I*

Hilton Valencia
av. Cortes Valencianas 52 ✉ 46015 – ✆ 96 303 00 00 – info.valencia@hilton.com – Fax 96 303 00 01 – www.valencia.hilton.com **B1**
269 rm – †120/340 € ††120/370 €, ☐ 18 € – 35 suites
Rest – Carte approx. 42 €
♦ Business ♦ Modern ♦
Located opposite the Palacio de Congresos (Parliament building) and extremely focused on a business clientele, offering spacious common areas, meeting rooms and very comfortable bedrooms. In the restaurant you can enjoy traditional cuisine with modern touches.

Sorolla Palace
av. Cortes Valencianas 58 ✉ 46015 – Ⓜ Burjassot – ✆ 96 186 87 00
– reservas@hotelsorollapalace.com – Fax 96 186 87 05
– www.hotelsorollapalace.com **B1**
246 rm – †250 € ††305 €, ☐ 19 € – 25 suites
Rest – Carte approx. 50 €
♦ Business ♦ Functional ♦
Boasts a regular business clientele thanks to its modern appearance and respective proximity to the Palacio de Congresos (Parliament building). Rooms along modern-functional lines. The restaurant has a pleasant layout, complemented by various private dining rooms.

Novotel Valencia Palacio de Congresos No smokers rest.
Valle de Ayora 1 ✉ 46015
– Ⓜ Beniferri – ✆ 96 399 74 00 – H3315@accor.com – Fax 96 340 12 94
– www.novotel.com **B1**
148 rm – ††72/199 €, ☐ 16 € – 3 suites
Rest – Menu 25 €
♦ Business ♦ Chain hotel ♦ Functional ♦
Boasts a pretty entrance hall, a varied common area and suitably equipped rooms, with pleasant work stations and full bathrooms, The restaurant, with its modern décor, has its kitchen visible to its customers.

SWEDEN
SVERIGE

PROFILE

→ **Area:**
449 964 km²
(173 731 sq mi).

→ **Population:**
9 003 000 inhabitants (est. 2006), density = 20 per km².

→ **Capital:**
Stockholm 781 000 (conurbation 1 912 000 inhabitants).

→ **Currency:**
Swedish Kronor (Skr or SEK); rate of exchange:
SEK 1 = € 0.10 = US$ 0.15 (Dec 2007).

→ **Government:**
Constitutional parliamentary monarchy (since 1950). Member of European Union since 1995.

→ **Language:**
Swedish; many Swedes also speak good English.

→ **Specific public holidays:**
Epiphany (6 January), Good Friday (Friday before Easter), National Day, 6 June, Midsummer's Day (Saturday between June 20-26), Halloween (Saturday between Oct 31-Nov 6), Christmas Day (25 December), Boxing Day (26 December).

→ **Local Time:**
GMT + 1 hour in winter and GMT + 2 hours in summer.

→ **Climate:**
Temperate continental with cold winters and mild summers (Stockholm: January: -3°C, July: 16°C).

→ **International dialling Code:**
00 46 followed by area code without the initial **0** and then the local number. International Directory Enquiries: ✆ **079 77**.

→ **Emergency:**
Dial ✆ **112** for Police, Fire Brigade, Ambulance, Poison hot-line, on-call doctors and 24hr Roadside breakdown service.

→ **Electricity:**
220 volts AC, 50 Hz; 2-pin round-shaped continental plugs.

→ **Formalities**
Travellers from the European Union (EU), Switzerland, Iceland and the main countries of North and South America need a national identity card or passport (America: passport required) to visit Sweden for less than three months (tourism or business purpose). For visitors from other countries a visa may be required, in addition to a passport, especially for those wishing to stay for longer than three months. We advise you to check with your embassy before travelling.

STOCKHOLM

STOCKHOLM

Population: 782 000 (conurbation 1 912 000) – Altitude: sea level

. Ryan/Stockholm Visitors Board/www.imagebank.swe

Stockholm is the place to go for clean air, big skies and handsome architecture. And water. One of the great beauties of the city, possibly *the* great beauty, is the amount of water that runs through and around it. It's built on fourteen islands, and looks out on twenty four thousand of them. Ferries glide out to the larger ones, and some, such as Vaxholm and Grinda, are great for swimming, others for picnicking, cycling and walking. An astounding two-thirds of the area within the city limits is made up of water, parks and woodland, and there are dozens of little bridges to cross to get from one part of town to another. No wonder Swedes appear so calm and relaxed.

It's in Stockholm that the salty waters of the Baltic meet head-on the fresh waters of Lake Mälaren, reflecting the broad boulevards and elegant buildings that shimmer along their edge. Truly, this is 'The City That Floats On Water'. Chain stores that seem so unavoidable in other European cities seem to have given Stockholm a wide berth, while domes, spires and turrets dot a skyline that in the summertime never truly darkens. It wasn't too long ago that this was a city with practically no nightlife, but now it rivals other European capitals for its after dark attractions. Admirers call Stockholm the most beautiful city in the world – day or night, you can see their point.

LIVING THE CITY

The city of Stockholm is enough to give you double vision. Alongside the important looking buildings is an almost rural quality of open space and water. The heart of the city is the Old Town, **Gamla Stan**, full of alleyways and lanes little changed from their medieval origins. Just to the north is the modern centre, **Norrmalm**, the part of the city with the least pastoral appeal: a buzzing quarter of shopping malls, restaurants and bars. East of Gamla Stan you reach the small island of **Skeppsholmen**, which boasts fine views of the waterfront. Directly north from here is **Östermalm**, an area full of grand residences, while south-east is the lovely park island of Djurgården, where you can find two of the city's most popular attractions. South and west of Gamla Stan are the two areas where Stockholmers like to hang out, the trendy (and hilly) Södermalm, and Kungsholmen.

PRACTICAL INFORMATION

ARRIVAL-DEPARTURE

Stockholm Arlanda Airport is 40km northwest of the city. The Arlanda Expresso train takes 20min to Centralstation and departs every 15min. The airport bus (Flygbuss) to Cityterminalen takes 40min. A taxi will cost around SEK 375.

TRANSPORT

Invest in a Stockholm Card, available from tourist offices. It is valid for one, two or three days and offers free travel on public transport, including sightseeing boats, and free entry to over 70 attractions (museums, galleries and castles).

If you're using public transport, it's best to go by metro, as it offers a more direct route than the buses. The No 7 tram, which runs throughout the summer, takes in quite a few of the main attractions.

You can buy single tickets for the bus, tram and metro, but if you're planning to do lots of travelling about the city, you can also get passes which cover a whole day or three whole days.

EXPLORING STOCKHOLM

Stockholm's old town, Gamla Stan, is the focal point of any visit, and that's as true now as it was in the thirteenth century, when its naturally fortuitous position between two channels of water made it the ideal setting for a fortress and the foundations of the city. It's a wonderfully enticing tangle of cobbled streets, small squares and gabled roofs. Remarkably, over eight hundred years it's been untouched by war or even the merest rumblings of local dissent. Its most imposing building is the Royal Palace, which has 600 rooms and good accessibility for the public. What it doesn't have is any royalty: they upped sticks and moved away to Drottningholm further along Lake Mälaren. What it retains is a

museum dedicated to the Nobel Prize, art shops, galleries, antique shops, and the joyous feeling that although you might get lost in its maze of medieval stone streets, you'll reach water before too long. Near the opulent German Church (Tyska Kyrkan) try and find Marten Trotzigs Grand, the narrowest street in Stockholm. It's little more than a yard wide and has a beguiling lamp-lit atmosphere (it's also pretty steep).

➜ QUAY MOMENTS

To escape any feelings of claustrophobia, head to the adjacent island of **Riddarholmen**, stand on its quay, breathe in its blasts of fresh air, and take in awesome views of **Lake Mälaren**, as well as the green heights of Southern Stockholm, and the vertical red-brick surprise of the City Hall, which seems to thrust straight out of the water. This is a graceful and imposing building, made up of eight million bricks, black granite reliefs, topped by three golden crowns; its first floor Golden Hall is decorated with nearly 20lb of gold leaf and eighteen million pieces of mosaic. If you're here in the summer, a great way of appreciating the visual splendour of the City Hall is to get to Riddarholmen at 3am (yes, three in the morning) and marvel at the changing hues of the early-hour light, from pastel blue to misty salmon, taking in the subtly changing shades of the brickwork. Catch up on your sleep later.

➜ GET SKEPPTICAL

With all this light, shade and water, the last thing you might feel like doing is submerging yourself indoors, but if you miss the museums of Stockholm, you miss an essential part of the city's character. Actually, most of them are conveniently located on the city's 'museum island', **Skeppsholmen**. As you approach it, you see its most striking edifice, the **National Museum of Fine Arts**, over 200 years old, with a superb old masters collection, including works by Rembrandt, El Greco and Canaletto, and more recent paintings by Gauguin, Cézanne and Renoir. Further along the island are three more intriguing museums: the Museum of Modern Art, with works by Matisse, Klee and Modigliani; the Architecture Museum, which showcases one thousand years of Scandinavian design; and the Museum of Far Eastern Antiquities, a former stable with an enormous collection of Asian art. The two most popular attractions, though, are just to the east in the 'National City Park' of **Djurgården**. This unspoiled island of natural beauty contains miles of trails, grand oaks, handy restaurants and coffee shops, and two world-famous museums. The first of these, the **Vasa Museum**, is commonly considered the very best Stockholm has to offer, even though it only features one exhibit! The *Vasa* warship sank on its maiden voyage in Stockholm harbour in 1628, and was preserved for 300 years beneath the Baltic. Raised in 1961, it now stands magnificently complete in its vast 'hangar' by the water. See it, and prepare to gasp…

Inland from here is the world's most famous open-air museum, **Skansen**, located perfectly atop a hill and covering seventy-four wondrous acres. Skansen's over a hundred years old, and contains over a hundred and fifty reconstructed buildings depicting the lives of Swedes over different eras. You can see everything from windmills and farms to an entire township. It's beautifully put together, with not an ounce of tackiness, and even serves you delicious traditional food. In winter, warm up with a big bowl of soup.

➜ DANCING QUEEN TO DRAMA QUEENS

Culture lovers can get a double hit in the smartly affluent area of **Östermalm**, 'over the water' northwest of Skansen. The Music Museum not only charts the history of music in Sweden but also allows visitors to experiment with the different instruments they find there. And yes, there's a section given over to ABBA. Leave here, and just in front of you is the suitably dramatic looking Royal Theatre of Drama, the place where Garbo, both Bergmans and Von Sydow cut their teeth. It's a great place to get your own canines into a bit of Swedish angst, though obviously, if you haven't mastered the language, then actions may speak louder than words.

One part of the Swedish capital not so easy to negotiate for the cycling fraternity is the southern island of **Södermalm**, which has steeply craggy cliffs plunging down into the sea and the lake. Buildings look a bit perilous as they perch on the edge, but venture into their midst and come across a green and pleasant land. As in other European cities, this is a working class area that's been 'gentrified' to the extent that it contains some strikingly trendy bars, fashion boutiques and cafés, along with a number of charming small parks. And, of course, some of the views from these dizzy heights looking towards the city centre are spectacular.

→ WEST END IS NIGH

The western island of Stockholm, **Kungsholmen**, is where you'll find the previously mentioned City Hall; apart from that it has a rather sedate, neighbourhood feel, but one that's gradually acquiring a real buzz as swish little restaurants, bars and bistros start to pop up all over it. There was a bit of a 'big bang' around here a few years ago with the opening of a particularly smart boutique mall, and since then it's been rivalling Södermalm as the hippest place in town. It also boasts a promenade much loved by Stockholmers. The landscaped Norr Mälarstrand runs for a mile or so all the way along the water's edge from the City Hall, giving lovely lake views to the south, and proving once again that in this city the urban is always likely to play second fiddle to the pastoral.

CALENDAR HIGHLIGHTS

The Swedes may be modern in outlook, but culturally speaking they like to look to their past. Celebrations can tend towards the traditional, and they don't come much more traditional than the January Viking Run, a skiing race, starting in the town of Uppsala and finishing in Stockholm. Viking influence is to the fore again on Walpurgis Night, at the end of April, when bonfires light up the night sky in celebration of the arrival of Spring: various city venues reflect the night's activities. In June, the Stockholm Marathon begins and ends at the Olympic Stadium, while Gamla Stan provides a fitting

STOCKHOLM IN...

→ ONE DAY

Gamla Stan, City Hall, Vasa or Skansen museums, meal on Södermalm

→ TWO DAYS

Coffee in Kungsholmen, museums in Skeppsholmen, Djurgården stroll, another evening in Södermalm

→ THREE DAYS

Shopping in Norrmalm, boat trip round the archipelago

backdrop for the Early Music Festival, featuring music of pre-1750. Everyone heads over to Skansen Museum on Midsummer Eve to dance and drink the night (which looks like day, of course) away...there's no guarantee that the drinks are any cheaper than usual, though. July's Jazz Festival also includes blues, soul and reggae, while in the run-up to Christmas there's the world-famous Nobel Prize Day, around 10th December, and St Lucia Day (13th) when candles burn in coffee shops and restaurants, and young girls are crowned with wreaths of lighted candles: it's all to signify the light that will eventually break through winter's gloom.

EATING OUT

Everyone thinks that eating out in Stockholm is invariably expensive, but with a little forward planning it doesn't have to be. In the middle of the day, most restaurants and cafés offer very good value set menus. Keep in mind that, unlike in Southern Europe, the Swedes like to get their eating done early. Lunch is considered fair game from 11am (until 2pm), while dinner is on the go from 6pm, and they might want to start putting chairs on the tables sometime after 9pm. Don't nip out for breakfast: there are few places open in the early morning. Picking wild food is a birthright of Swedes, and there's no law to stop you going into forest or field to pick blueberries, cloudberries, cranberries, strawberries, mushrooms and the like. This love of outdoor, natural fare means that Stockholmers have a special bond with menus which relate to the seasons: keep your eyes open for restaurants that feature *husmanskost,* or traditional Swedish dishes. Try and find somewhere with a good **smörgåsbord**: if you're lucky, this should include soup, herring, warm potatoes and gravlax, followed by salads, cold meats, meatballs, beef and chicken, washed down with beer. As for tipping, well, the service charge is included in the bill, but charming service (common in Stockholm) might make you add on a bit more for the waiting staff.

→ FULL STEAM AHEAD

More memorable than a trip on a motorised launch - why not head out from Stockholm's waterfront on a full-blown steamship? There are about ten plying the archipelago and Lake Mälaren. There used to be hundreds, but the introduction of car travel put paid to most of them. One blast from the funnel and you'll be smitten.

Apart from Södermalm, Stockholm's a pretty flat city that is ideal for cycling around. Alternatively, see its natural wonders from above – this is a rare example of a world capital that allows hot-air balloons to fly over.

Catching the metro (or tunnelbana, to be precise) in Stockholm is less of a chore than in other cities. That's because it's the world's longest art gallery! It displays artwork by the city's most creative talents along its underground system – so watch out for paintings, mosaics, sculptures and murals where you wouldn't normally expect to find them.

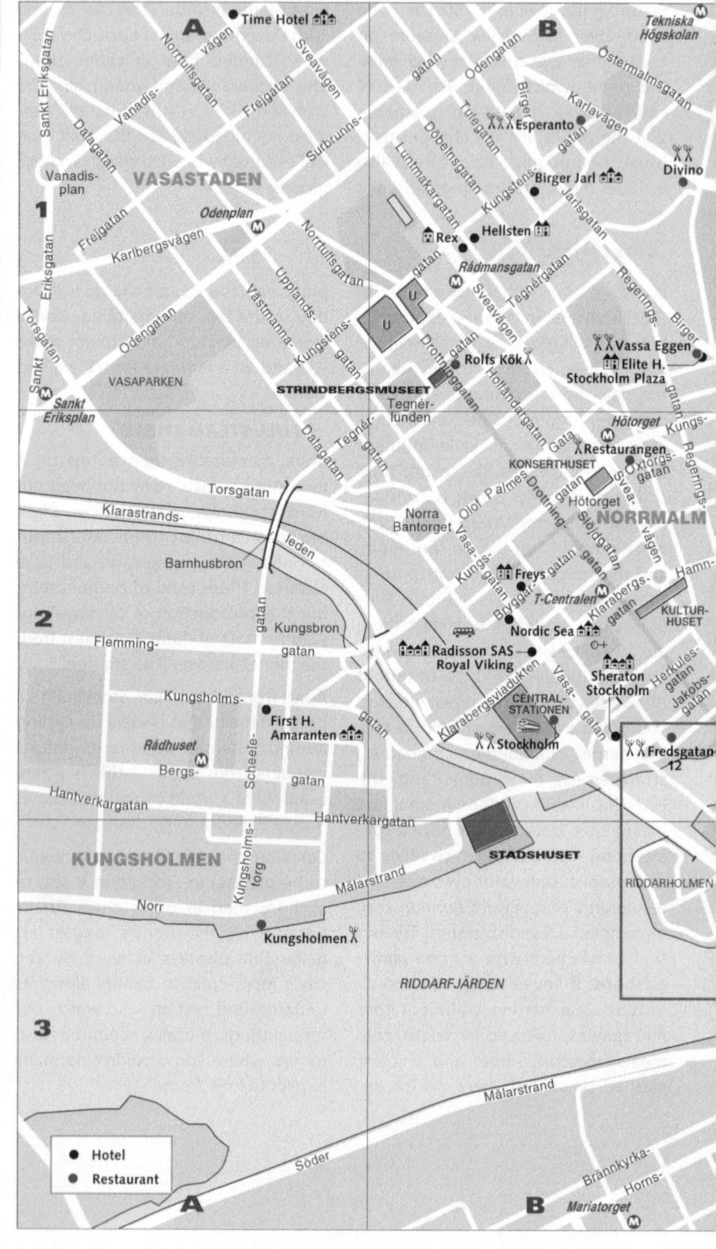
Time Hotel
Tekniska Högskolan
VASASTADEN
Odenplan
Esperanto
Divino
Birger Jarl
Hellsten
Rex
Rådmansgatan
Vassa Eggen
Rolfs Kök
Elite H. Stockholm Plaza
STRINDBERGSMUSEET
VASAPARKEN
Sankt Eriksplan
Hötorget
Restaurangen
KONSERTHUSET
NORRMALM
Freys
T-Centralen
Nordic Sea
KULTURHUSET
Radisson SAS Royal Viking
Sheraton Stockholm
CENTRALSTATIONEN
Stockholm
Fredsgatan 12
First H. Amaranten
Rådhuset
KUNGSHOLMEN
STADSHUSET
RIDDARHOLMEN
Kungsholmen
RIDDARFJÄRDEN
Mariatorget
Hotel
Restaurant

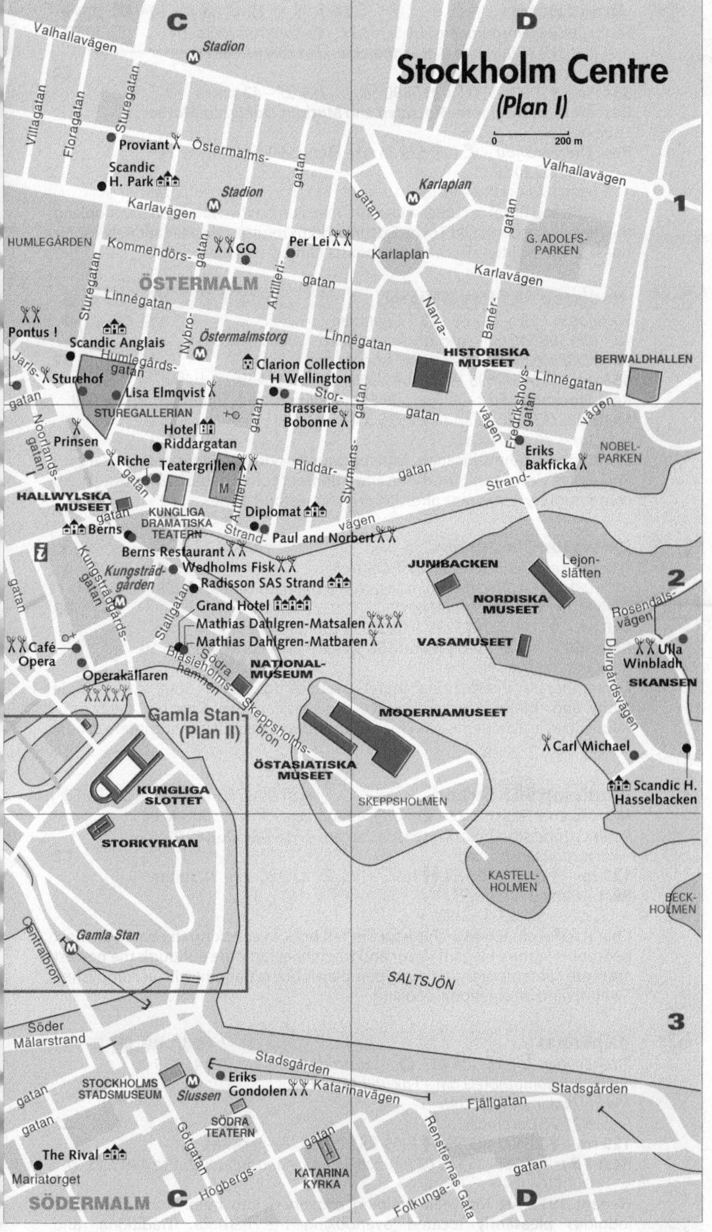
Stockholm Centre
(Plan I)
0
200 m
C
D
1
2
3
Valhallavägen
Stadion
Villagatan
Floragatan
Sturegatan
Proviant
Östermalms-
Scandic
H. Park
Stadion
Karlavägen
Karlaplan
HUMLEGÅRDEN
Kommendörs-
gatan
GQ
Per Lei
Karlaplan
G. ADOLFS-
PARKEN
Karlavägen
ÖSTERMALM
Artilleri-
Linnégatan
Pontus !
Scandic Anglais
Nybro-
Östermalmstorg
Linnégatan
Narva-
Banér-
HISTORISKA
MUSEET
BERWALDHALLEN
Humlegårds-
gatan
Jarls-
Sturehof
Clarion Collection
H Wellington
Fredrikshovs-
gatan
Linnégatan
Lisa Elmqvist
Stor-
gatan
STUREGALLERIAN
Brasserie
Bobonne
vägen
NOBEL-
PARKEN
Noorlands-
gatan
Prinsen
Hotel
Riddargatan
Eriks
Bakficka
Riche
Teatergrillen
Riddar-
Styrmans-
gatan
Strand-
M
HALLWYLSKA
MUSEET
KUNGLIGA
DRAMATISKA
TEATERN
Diplomat
Berns
Strand-
Paul and Norbert
vägen
Berns Restaurant
Wedholms Fisk
JUNIBACKEN
Lejon-
slätten
Kungsträd-
gården
Kungsträdgårds-
gatan
Radisson SAS Strand
NORDISKA
MUSEET
Stallgatan
Grand Hotel
Mathias Dahlgren-Matsalen
Mathias Dahlgren-Matbaren
VASAMUSEET
Rosendals-
vägen
Ulla
Winbladh
Café
Opera
Blasieholms-
hamnen
Södra
NATIONAL-
MUSEUM
SKANSEN
Operakällaren
Djurgårdsvägen
Gamla Stan
(Plan II)
Skeppsholms-
bron
MODERNAMUSEET
Carl Michael
ÖSTASIATISKA
MUSEET
KUNGLIGA
SLOTTET
SKEPPSHOLMEN
Scandic H.
Hasselbacken
STORKYRKAN
KASTELL-
HOLMEN
BECK-
HOLMEN
Centralbron
Gamla Stan
SALTSJÖN
Söder
Mälarstrand
Stadsgården
STOCKHOLMS
STADSMUSEUM
Slussen
Eriks
Gondolen
Katarinavägen
Stadsgården
Fjällgatan
gatan
SÖDRA
TEATERN
Götgatan
Renstiernas Gata
The Rival
Mariatorget
KATARINA
KYRKA
Högbergs-
Folkunga-
SÖDERMALM

Grand Hôtel

Södra Blasieholmshamnen 8 ✉ S-103 27 – Ⓜ Kungsträdgården – ✆ (08) 679 35 00 – info@grandhotel.se – Fax (08) 611 86 86 – www.grandhotel.se **C2**

334 rm – †2990/5590 SEK ††5890 SEK, ☕ 245 SEK – 42 suites

Rest *Mathias Dahlgren-Matsalen* and ***Mathias Dahlgren-Matbaren*** – see below

Rest *The Veranda* – *✆ (08) 679 35 86* – Menu 550 SEK (dinner) – Carte 425/720 SEK

♦ Grand Luxury ♦ Classic ♦

Sweden's top hotel occupies a late 19C mansion on the waterfront overlooking the Royal Palace and Old Town. Existing rooms refurbished; elegant new rooms boast latest facilities. The Veranda boasts famous smörgåsbord.

Radisson SAS Royal Viking

Vasagatan 1 ✉ S-101 24 – Ⓜ T-Centralen – ✆ (08) 506 540 00 – sales.royal.stockholm@radissonsas.com – Fax (08) 506 540 02 – www.radissonsas.com **B2**

456 rm – †1695/2695 SEK ††1695/2695 SEK, ☕ 125 SEK – 3 suites

Rest *Stockholm Fisk* – *✆ (08) 506 541 02 (Closed lunch Saturday and Sunday)* Menu 295/375 SEK – Carte 218/575 SEK

♦ Business ♦ Modern ♦

Large hotel in central location, with spacious, busy lobby. Panoramic Sky Bar with impressive views over Stockholm and 9 floors of comfortable bedrooms. Stylish contemporary restaurant offers an array of seafood dishes.

Sheraton Stockholm

Tegelbacken 6 ✉ S-101 23 – Ⓜ T-Centralen – ✆ (08) 412 34 00 – stockholm.sheraton@sheraton.com – Fax (08) 412 34 09 – www.sheraton.com/stockholm **B2**

448 rm – †3295 SEK ††3295 SEK, ☕ 225 SEK – 17 suites

Rest *360°* – *(buffet lunch)* Menu 550 SEK (dinner) – Carte 510/695 SEK

♦ Business ♦ Modern ♦

Contemporary international hotel overlooking Gamla Stan, with ample lobby and offering comprehensive business facilities. Spacious bedrooms, refurbished in a modern style. Open-plan all day restaurant serving international dishes.

Radisson SAS Strand

Nybrokajen 9 ✉ S-103 27 – Ⓜ Kungsträdgården – ✆ (08) 506 640 00 – sales.strand.stockholm@radissonsas.com – Fax (08) 506 640 01 – www.radissonsas.com **C2**

132 rm – †1395/3195 SEK ††1695/3195 SEK, ☕ 180 SEK – 20 suites

Rest – Carte 340/505 SEK

♦ Business ♦ Classic ♦

Characterful old world architecture in red brick overlooking the harbour. Most bedrooms feature elegant décor and traditional furniture although the newest are more contemporary in style. Open-plan lobby restaurant with accomplished Swedish and international cooking.

Diplomat

Strandvägen 7c ✉ S-104 40 – Ⓜ Kungsträdgården – ✆ (08) 459 68 00 – info@diplomathotel.com – Fax (08) 459 68 20 – www.diplomathotel.com

Closed 21-28 December **C2**

129 rm – †2095/2495 SEK ††2995 SEK, ☕ 185 SEK – 4 suites

Rest *T Bar* – *✆ (08) 459 68 02 (brunch Saturday and Sunday)* Carte 445/520 SEK

♦ Traditional ♦ Classic ♦

Elegant 1911 Art Nouveau building converted into hotel from diplomatic lodgings pleasantly located overlooking the harbour. Traditional and contemporary bedrooms. A popular terrace adjoins contemporary-style hotel restaurant offering traditional Swedish cooking.

Berns

Näckströmsgatan 8, Berzelii Park ✉ S-111 47 – Ⓜ Kungsträdgården – ✆ (08) 566 322 00 – frontoffice@berns.se – Fax (08) 566 322 01 – www.berns.se **C2**

61 rm – †2030/2950 SEK ††2360/2950 SEK – 4 suites

Rest *Berns Restaurant* – see below

♦ Business ♦ Stylish ♦

Boutique hotel with a modern minimalist interior décor verging on trendy; details in cherry wood and marble. Modern facilities in bedrooms, some have balconies.

Nordic Light

Vasaplan ✉ S-101 37 – Ⓜ T-Centralen – ✆ (08) 505 630 00 – info@nordichotels.se – Fax (08) 505 630 30 – www.nordiclighthotel.com **B2**

175 rm – †1530/3200 SEK ††1970/4000 SEK

Rest – Carte 255/450 SEK

♦ Business ♦ Design ♦

Stylish, modern hotel, whose harmonious black and white designer décor features a symphony of lights on the Nordic Lights theme. Cool bar and lounge. Comfortable bedrooms. Modern restaurant in the main hall: modish international cooking.

First H. Amaranten

Kungsholmsgatan 31 ✉ S-104 20 – Ⓜ Rådhuset – ✆ (08) 692 52 00 – amaranten@firsthotels.se – Fax (08) 652 62 48 – www.firsthotels.com/amaranten **A2**

423 rm – †950/2150 SEK ††1250/2350 SEK

Rest *Amaranten* – *(Closed Saturday lunch and Sunday)* Menu 265/337 SEK – Carte 271/585 SEK

♦ Business ♦ Modern ♦

Modernised, commercial hotel conveniently located with easy access to subway. Stylish, quiet public areas with American Bar; compact but up-to-date bedrooms. Stylish modern eating area with a large menu of modern Swedish cooking.

Scandic H. Park

Karlavägen 43 ✉ S-102 46 – Ⓜ Stadion – ✆ (08) 517 348 00 – park@scandic-hotels.com – Fax (08) 517 348 11 – www.scandic-hotels.com/park **C1**

193 rm – †990/2590 SEK ††1090/2690 SEK – 8 suites

Rest *Park Village* – *(Closed Bank Holiday lunch)* Carte 249/570 SEK

♦ Business ♦ Functional ♦

Convenient location by one of the city's prettiest parks (view from suites). All rooms a good size, modern and comfortable with good range of facilities. Contemporary lounge. Modern restaurant with small summer terrace; traditional Swedish and international fare.

Birger Jarl

Tulegatan 8 ✉ S-104 32 – Ⓜ Rådmansgatan – ✆ (08) 674 18 00 – info@birgerjarl.se – Fax (08) 673 73 66 – www.birgerjarl.se **B1**

230 rm – †890/2170 SEK ††2900 SEK – 5 suites

Rest – *(Closed lunch Saturday and Sunday)* Carte 259/392 SEK

♦ Business ♦ Modern ♦

Modern hotel in quieter part of city. Lobby features art and sculpture displays. Individually styled bedrooms; 17 of them decorated by Swedish artists of international repute. Simple and stylish restaurant with unfussy Swedish cooking.

Time Hotel without rest

Vanadisvägen 12 ✉ 113 46 – Ⓜ Odenplan – ✆ (08) 545 47 300 – info@timehotel.se – Fax (08) 54 54 73 01 – www.timehotel.se **A1**

144 rm – †1575/1745 ††2445/2995

♦ Business ♦ Modern ♦

Brand new business hotel in residential area, featuring spacious, functional rooms in warm colours. Contemporary breakfast room with buffet. Popular lounge bar.

Scandic Anglais

Humlegardsgatan 23 ✉ 102 44 – Ⓜ Östermalmstorg – ✆ (08) 517 340 00 – anglais@scandic-hotels.com – Fax (08) 517 340 11 – www.scandic-hotels.com **C1**

220 rm – 1700/2600 1800/2600 – 13 suites

Rest – Menu 595 (dinner) – Carte 405/640

◆ Chain hotel ◆ Modern ◆

Recently refurbished hotel featuring large, stylishly-furnished lobby, popular ground floor bar and contemporary bedrooms, ideal for the business traveller. Modern open plan restaurant serves international cuisine.

Elite H. Stockholm Plaza

Birger Jarlsgatan 29 ✉ S-103 95 – Ⓜ Östermalmstorg – ✆ (08) 566 220 00 – info.stoplaza@elite.se – Fax (08) 566 220 20 – www.elite.se

Closed 23-26 December **B1**

139 rm – 1050/2300 SEK 1450/2500 SEK – 4 suites

Rest *Vassa Eggen* – see below

◆ Business ◆ Functional ◆

Well preserved 1884 building with up-to-date comforts. Compact, well-run commercial hotel with conference rooms and basement sauna. Some rooms refurbished in a modish style.

Freys

Bryggargatan 12 ✉ S-101 31 – Ⓜ T-Centralen – ✆ (08) 506 213 00 – freys@freyshotels.com – Fax (08) 506 213 13 – www.freyshotels.com

Closed 22-28 December **B2**

123 rm – 1090/1950 SEK 1390/2050 SEK – 1 suite

Rest *Belgobaren* – *(Closed Sunday lunch)* Menu 295 SEK (dinner) – Carte 348/460 SEK

◆ Business ◆ Functional ◆

Located near Central station with good conference facilities and first-floor terrace. Fairly compact rooms with informal furnishings; superior rooms with balconies. Belgian specialities, including more than 100 different beers, on exclusive menu.

Hotel Riddargatan without rest

Riddargatan 14 ✉ S-114 35 – Ⓜ Östermalmstorg – ✆ (08) 555 730 00 – hotelriddargatan@profilhotels.se – Fax (08) 555 730 11 – www.profilhotels.se

Closed 20 December-4 January **C2**

75 rm – 1225/2150 SEK 1425/2350 SEK – 3 suites

◆ Business ◆ Modern ◆

Modern, boutique-style hotel in quiet location behind the Royal Dramatik Theatre, near shops and restaurants. Functional, modern bedrooms; 20 new rooms boast designer styling.

Hellsten without rest

Luntmakargatan 68 ✉ 113 51 – Ⓜ Rådmannsgatan – ✆ (08) 661 86 00 – hotel@hellsten.se – Fax (08) 6 61 86 01 – www.hellsten.se

Closed 19 December-5 January **B1**

78 rm – 1190/2890 1490/3090

◆ Townhouse ◆ Personalised ◆

Unique hotel in residential area, with warm atmosphere, filled with trinkets and antiques picked up by its globetrotting owner. Individually-styled rooms with modern bathrooms.

Clarion Collection H. Wellington without rest

Storgatan 6 ✉ S-114 51 – Ⓜ Östermalmstorg – ✆ (08) 667 09 10 – cc.wellington@choice.se – Fax (08) 667 12 54 – www.wellington.se

Closed 23 December-5 January **C1**

59 rm – 1295/2895 SEK 1695/3195 SEK – 1 suite

◆ Business ◆ Functional ◆

Apartment block converted to hotel in 1960s, well placed for shopping. Compact, well-equipped rooms; good city views from upper floor balconies. Complimentary dinner buffet.

Rex without rest

Luntmakargatan 73 ✉ 113 51 – Ⓜ Rådmannsgatan – ✆ (08) 16 00 40 – reception@rexhotel.se – Fax (08) 6 61 86 01 – www.rexhotel.se

Closed 19 December-5 January **B1**

32 rm – 990/2090 1190/2290

♦ Townhouse ♦ Modern ♦

Building dating from 1866, set in a residential area not far from metro station. Functional, modern bedrooms; grey slate bathrooms. Owner's black and white photos decorate.

Operakällaren (Stefano Catenacci)

Operahuset, Karl XII's Torg ✉ S-111 86 – Ⓜ Kungsträdgården – ✆ (08) 676 58 01 – matsal@operakallaren.se – Fax (08) 676 58 72 – www.operakallaren.se

Closed mid July-mid August, 25 December-7 January, Sunday and Monday **C2**

Rest – *(dinner only)* Carte 580/980 SEK

Spec. Half a Scottish lobster, caramelised salsify in sweet and sour reduction, cucumber and celeriac salad. Ginger glazed pork with fried scallop and white bean purée. Tea fondant with fig chips and grapefruit sorbet.

♦ Classic ♦ Formal ♦

Magnificent dining room with original 19C carved wood décor and fresco paintings situated in the historic Opera House. Classically based menu of gourmet dishes. Modern bar.

Mathias Dahlgren - Matsalen – at Grand Hotel

Södra Blasieholmshamnen 6 ✉ 103 27 – Ⓜ Kungsträdgården – ✆ (08) 679 35 84 – info@mdghs.com – Fax (08) 611 86 86 – www.mdghs.com

Closed 14 July-3 August, Christmas and Sunday **C2**

Rest – *(booking essential) (dinner only)* Menu 1300 SEK – Carte 670/940 SEK

Spec. Terrine of organic goose liver, truffle and white mushrooms. Cauliflower and langoustine with brown butter, lemon and crown dill. Pumpkin-vanilla-liquorice.

♦ Modern ♦ Elegant ♦

Fine dining in classically comfortable Matsalen. Tasty and inventive modern Swedish cooking makes vibrant use of high quality ingredients. Charming and professional service. Formal yet relaxed atmosphere.

Esperanto (Daniel Höglander/Sayan Isaksson)

Kungstensgatan 2 ✉ 114 25 – Ⓜ Tekniska Högskolan – ✆ 696 2323 – esperanto@sollevi.se – www.esperantorestaurant.se

Closed July, 3 weeks Christmas-New Year, first week August, Sunday and Monday **B1**

Rest – *(dinner only) (set menu only)* Menu 825/1075 SEK

Spec. Lobster with dehydrated peas and bacon. Complete pigeon with slow cooked corn. Apricots in chocolate with chestnut crèpes and frozen apricot kernels.

♦ Innovative ♦ Formal ♦

On first floor of a converted theatre. Candlelight adds warmth to the understated décor. Structured, well-organised service; original, innovative cooking, precisely prepared.

Fredsgatan 12 (Danyel Couet)

Fredsgatan 12 ✉ S-111 52 – Ⓜ T-Centralen – ✆ (08) 24 80 52 – info@fredsgatan12.com – Fax (08) 23 76 05 – www.fredsgatan12.com

Closed mid July-mid August, 1 week Christmas-New Year, Saturday lunch and Sunday **B2**

Rest – *(booking essential)* Menu 350 SEK (lunch) – Carte 440/820 SEK

Spec. Octopus "en tranche" with burritana onions and dehydrated lime. Lemon sole "fish 'n' chips" with vinegar and curry aroma. Grapefruit "ice" with caramelised sugar and olives.

♦ Innovative ♦ Fashionable ♦

A strikingly redesigned restaurant in a wing of the Academy of Arts. Divided into two rooms, both with a modern and stylish feel. Creative and original modern cuisine. Charming service.

XX **Pontus!**

Brunnsgatan 1 ✉ 111 38 – Ⓜ Östermalmstorg – ✆ (08) 54 52 73 00
– info@pontusfrithiof.com – Fax (08) 7 96 60 69 – www.pontusfrithiof.com
Closed 24 December, 1 January and Sunday **C1**
Rest – *(booking essential)* Carte 595/1025

◆ Inventive ◆ Fashionable ◆

Stylish restaurant with three separate areas; the oyster bar; the food bar and the dining room, which serves flavoursome and inventive modern cooking. Efficient service.

XX **GQ**

Kommendörsgatan 23 ✉ S-114 48 – Ⓜ Stadion
– ✆ (08) 545 674 30 – upplev@gqrestaurang.se – Fax (08) 662 25 06
– www.gqrestaurang.se
Closed 3 weeks July, Christmas-7 January and Sunday **C1**
Rest – *(dinner only)* Menu 625 SEK – Carte 435/740 SEK

◆ Modern ◆ Fashionable ◆

"Gastronomic intelligence" in a trendy, eye-catching restaurant with its own cookery school. Specially chosen wines complement seriously considered and ambitious dishes.

XX **Divino**

Karlavägen 28 ✉ 114 31 – Ⓜ Tekniska Högskolan – ✆ (08) 611 02 69
– info@divino.se – Fax (08) 611 12 04 – www.divino.se
Closed 24-25 December, 1 January and Sunday **B1**
Rest – *(dinner only)* Menu 450 – Carte 430/600

◆ Italian ◆ Elegant ◆

19C townhouse with elegant, intimate dining room. Seasonal menus offer flavourful, Italian cooking. Wine cellar and deli. Attentive, friendly service and warm atmosphere.

XX **Paul and Norbert**

Strandvägen 9 ✉ S-114 56 – Ⓜ Kungsträdgården – ✆ (08) 663 81 83
– restaurang.paul.norbert@telia.se – Fax (08) 661 72 36
– www.paulochnorbert.se
Closed Christmas-New Year, Monday lunch and Sunday **C2**
Rest – *(booking essential)* Menu 350 SEK (lunch) – Carte 570/755 SEK

◆ Classic ◆ Formal ◆

Small, sophisticated, well-run restaurant on harbour, with stylish, modern décor and artwork. Some tables in booths. Numerous menus feature classic dishes made with seasonal produce.

XX **Stockholm**

Centralplan/Entrance from Vasagatan ✉ 101 35 – Ⓜ T-Centralen
– ✆ 20 20 49 – Fax 613 62 55 – www.restaurangstockholm.se
Closed 7-13 July, 23 December-2 January,
Saturday lunch and Sunday **B2**
Rest – Menu 265 SEK – Carte dinner 440/660 SEK

◆ Swedish ◆ Fashionable ◆

Restaurant within a glass cube in front of the central station. Stylish and retro-style decoration, with lounge bar. Friendly and organised service; modern Swedish cuisine with some classic touches.

XX **Berns Restaurant** – at Berns H.

Näckströmsgatan 8, Berzelii Park ✉ S-111 47 – Ⓜ Kungsträdgården
– ✆ (08) 566 322 22 – info@berns.se – Fax (08) 566 323 23
– www.berns.se **C2**
Rest – Carte 255/485 SEK

◆ Asian influences ◆ Fashionable ◆

A stunningly-restored 19C rococo ballroom with galleries overlooking the dining room. Modern cuisine with strong Asian influences. Live music. The place to be seen.

XX **Teatergrillen**

Nybrogatan 3 ✉ S-111 48 – Ⓜ Östermalmstorg – ✆ (08) 545 035 65 – riche@riche.se – Fax (08) 545 035 69 – www.teatergrillen.se
Closed Sunday **C2**
Rest – Menu 500/900 SEK – Carte 355/830 SEK
♦ Traditional ♦ Intimate ♦
Intimate, traditional city institution, most pleasant in the evening. Menus are more expensive than its sister Riche. Expect traditional cooking of Scandinavian classics.

XX **Wedholms Fisk**

Nybrokajen 17 ✉ S-111 48 – Ⓜ Kungsträdgården – ✆ (08) 611 78 74 – info@wedholmsfisk.se – Fax (08) 678 60 11 – www.wedholmsfisk.se
Closed Christmas-New Year, Saturday lunch, Sunday and Bank Holidays **C2**
Rest – *(booking essential)* Carte 445/925 SEK
♦ Seafood ♦ Formal ♦
Classic 19-20C building near harbour. Busy, elegant restaurant serving a good choice of fish and shellfish, simply but accurately prepared; similar dishes in the bar.

XX **Café Opera**

Operahuset, Karl XII's Torg ✉ S-111 86 – Ⓜ Kungsträdgården – ✆ (08) 676 58 09 – info@cafeopera.se – Fax (08) 676 58 71 – www.cafeopera.se
Closed Monday in Winter **C2**
Rest – *(booking essential) (dinner only - music and dancing after 12am)* Carte 354/677 SEK
♦ International ♦ Brasserie ♦
Characterful rotunda-style historic restaurant with ceiling painted in 1895, Corinthian pillars, fine mouldings and covered terrace. Swedish-influenced, international menu.

XX **Per Lei**

Artillerigatan 56 ✉ S-114 45 – Ⓜ Karlaplan – ✆ (08) 411 38 11 – info@perlei.se – Fax (08) 662 64 45 – www.perlei.se
Closed July, 2 days Christmas, Sunday and Monday **C1**
Rest – *(booking essential) (light lunch)* Menu 320/445 SEK – Carte 315/505 SEK
♦ Italian influences ♦ Cosy ♦
Popular neighbourhood restaurant in converted boutique; elegant décor with Murano chandelier. Modern Italian-influenced menu, refined, flavourful cooking and attentive service.

XX **Vassa Eggen** – at Elite H. Stockholm Plaza

Birger Jarlsgatan 29 ✉ S-103 25 – Ⓜ Östermalmstorg – ✆ (08) 21 61 69 – info@vassaeggen.com – Fax (08) 20 34 46 – www.vassaeggen.com
Closed July, Christmas-New Year Saturday lunch and Sunday **B1**
Rest – *(light luch)* Menu 380/635 SEK (lunch) – Carte 635/665 SEK
♦ Inventive ♦ Fashionable ♦
Refined, well run restaurant popular with those in the know. Modern, fashionable styling and friendly service. Ambitious, innovative cooking.

X **Restaurangen**

Oxtorgsgatan 14 ✉ S-111 57 – Ⓜ Hötorget – ✆ (08) 22 09 52 – reservation@restaurangentm.com – Fax (08) 22 09 54 – www.restaurangentm.com
Closed 7 July-7 August, 22 December-5 January, Saturday lunch and Sunday **B2**
Rest – *(booking essential) (light lunch)* Menu 500 SEK (dinner) – Carte 300/700 SEK
♦ Innovative ♦ Trendy ♦
Contemporary interior with clean-cut minimalist décor and stylish furnishings. Unusual, modern menu concept based on a tasting of several small dishes. Lively atmosphere.

Kungsholmen
< Södermalm,

Norr Mälarstrand, Kajplats 464 ✉ 112 20 – Ⓜ Rådhuset – ✆ (08) 50 52 44 53 – info@kungsholmen.com – Fax (08) 50 52 44 55 – www.kungsholmen.com
Closed 24-26 & 30 December and 1 January **A3**
Rest – *(dinner only)* Carte 300/620
◆ International ◆ Trendy ◆
Trendy restaurant on the waterfront. Comfy furnishings; lounge feel. 7 open kitchens separately themed: sushi, bistro, grill, soup, bread, salad and ice cream. Friendly service.

Mathias Dahlgren - Matbaren – at Grand Hotel

Södra Blasieholmshamnen 6 ✉ 103 27 – Ⓜ Kungsträdgården – ✆ (08) 679 35 00 – info@mdghs.com – Fax (08) 611 86 86 – www.mdghs.com
Closed 4-24 August, Saturday lunch and Sunday **C2**
Rest – Carte 335/685 SEK
◆ Modern ◆ Trendy ◆
Matbaren means 'the food bar,' which translates as quick service in an informal atmosphere; order one dish at a time - all come in medium-sized portions. Flavourful, modern cooking is prepared with simplicity and finesse, using top quality produce.

Brasserie Bobonne

Storegatan 12 ✉ 114 44 – Ⓜ Östermalmstorg – ✆ (08) 660 03 18 – bobonne@telia.com – brasseriebobonne.se
Closed 5 weeks in Summer and Sunday **C1**
Rest – *(booking essential) (dinner only)* Menu 498 – Carte 355/545
◆ Bistro ◆ Cosy ◆
Small, busy French-style brasserie located in a residential area, serving flavourful French and Swedish dishes. Relaxing, welcoming atmosphere.

Proviant

Sturegatan 19 ✉ 114 36 – Ⓜ Stadion – ✆ (08) 22 60 50 – info@proviant.se – www.proviant.se
Closed 3 weeks July, 22 December-3 January, Saturday lunch and Sunday **C1**
Rest – *(light lunch)* Menu 435 (dinner) – Carte 353/565
◆ Swedish ◆ Bistro ◆
Simply furnished, professionally run restaurant near Humlegärden Park. Accomplished Swedish cooking. Friendly, efficient service.

Paus Bar & Kök

Rörstrandsgatan 18 (West : 2 km by Torsgatan and Odengatan) ✉ 116 40 – Ⓜ Sankt Eriksplan – ✆ (08) 34 44 05 – paus.mail@telia.com – www.restaurangpaus.se
Closed Christmas and Midsummer
Rest – *(dinner only)* Carte 375/565
◆ Modern ◆ Minimalist ◆
Small, simply furnished restaurant with tiled walls and a minimalist feel. Ambitious, modern cooking with innovative touches. Popular bar area boasts snug, cosy atmosphere.

Rolfs Kök

Tegnérgatan 41 ✉ S-111 61 – Ⓜ Rådmansgatan – ✆ (08) 10 16 96 – info@rolfskok.se – Fax (08) 789 88 80 – www.rolfskok.se
Closed July, 24-25 & 31 December, 1 January, Midsummer day, lunch Saturday and Sunday **B1**
Rest – *(booking essential) (light lunch)* Carte 325/550 SEK
◆ Modern ◆ Bistro ◆
Compact, trendy bar-restaurant; buzzy atmosphere guaranteed. Mix of modern and traditional international cooking. Home made bread and ice cream and up to 750 wines by the glass! Efficient service.

Lisa Elmqvist

Östermalms Saluhall ✉ 114 39 – Ⓜ Östermalmstorg – ✆ (08) 553 40410 – info@lisaelmqvist.se – Fax (08) 553 4 04 24 – www.lisaemlqvist.se
Closed Easter, Christmas-New Year, Sunday and Bank Holidays **C1**
Rest – *(booking essential-not taken on Saturday) (lunch only) (communal dining)* Carte 440/810 SEK
♦ Seafood ♦ Friendly ♦
A fourth generation family affair where shared tables and fresh seafood combine to create a contented and lively atmosphere. Open kitchen with seasonal fish display and deli.

BRASSERIES AND BISTRO *Plan I*

Prinsen

Mäster Samuelsgatan 4 ✉ S-111 44 – Ⓜ Östermalmstorg – ✆ (08) 611 13 31 – kontoret@restaurangprinsen.se – Fax (08) 611 70 79 – www.restaurangprinsen.se
Closed 24-26 & 31 December, 1 January, 20-21 June and Sunday lunch **C2**
Rest – *(booking essential)* Carte 393/629 SEK
♦ Traditional ♦ Brasserie ♦
Long-standing, busy and well-run brasserie with literary associations. Spread over ground and lower floor with traditional décor and well-priced Swedish and French classics.

Eriks Bakficka

Fredrikshovsgatan 4 ✉ S-115 23 – ✆ (08) 660 15 99 – info.bakfickan@eriks.se – Fax (08) 663 25 67 – www.eriks.se
Closed 20-23 March, Saturday lunch and Sunday **D2**
Rest – Menu 475 SEK (dinner) – Carte 405/560 SEK
♦ Modern ♦ Bistro ♦
Quiet residential setting and well-run bistro and bar-counter with small terrace. Cosy dining rooms in the basement. Traditional Swedish dishes with modern global twists.

Sturehof

Stureplan 2-4 ✉ S-114 46 – Ⓜ Östermalmstorg – ✆ (08) 440 57 30 – info@sturehof.com – Fax (08) 678 11 01 – www.sturehof.com **C1**
Rest – Carte 345/610 SEK
♦ Traditional ♦ Brasserie ♦
Very popular classic café-brasserie with closely packed tables and a busy atmosphere due to the steady stream of local business clientele. Good choice of seafood dishes.

Riche

Birger Jarlsgatan 4 ✉ S-114 53 – Ⓜ Östermalmstorg – ✆ (08) 545 035 60 – riche@riche.se – Fax (08) 545 035 69 – www.riche.se
closed Sunday **C2**
Rest – *(brunch Saturday)* Carte 360/605 SEK
♦ Traditional ♦ Brasserie ♦
Lively bar and friendly, bustling brasserie; very different from, but with same menu as, its sister Teatergrillen. Serves classic Scandinavian as well as international dishes.

at Gamla Stan (Old Stockholm) *Plan II*

First H. Reisen

Skeppsbron 12 ✉ S-111 30 – Ⓜ Gamla Stan – ✆ (08) 22 32 60 – reisen@firsthotels.se – Fax (08) 20 15 59 – www.firsthotels.com/reisen **F1**
137 rm – †1350/2750 SEK ††1750/2950 SEK, ☕ 165 SEK – 7 suites
Rest *Reisen Bar and Dining Room* – *(light lunch)* Carte 315/485 SEK
♦ Business ♦ Classic ♦
19C hotel on waterfront with original maritime décor. Popular piano bar. Sauna in 17C vault. Classically-styled rooms; de luxe and superior offer quayside view and small balconies. Modern, airy brasserie-style restaurant with a welcoming atmosphere. Traditional Swedish and international menu.

Victory
Lilla Nygatan 5 ✉ S-111 28 – Ⓜ Gamla Stan – ✆ (08) 506 400 00
– info@victoryhotel.se – Fax (08) 506 400 10 – www.victoryhotel.se
Closed 19 December-4 January **E1**
45 rm – 1190/3450 SEK 1850/3450 SEK, 195 SEK – 3 suites
Rest ***Leijontornet*** – see below
◆ Historic ◆ Classic ◆
Pleasant 17C hotel with Swedish rural furnishings and maritime antiques. Rooms named after sea captains with individually-styled fittings, mixing modern and antique.

Rica H. Gamla Stan without rest
Lilla Nygatan 25 ✉ S-111 28 – Ⓜ Gamla Stan – ✆ (08) 723 72 50
– info.gamlastan@rica.se – Fax (08) 723 72 59 – www.rica.se **F1**
50 rm – 1895 SEK 1960 SEK – 1 suite
◆ Business ◆ Classic ◆
Conveniently located 17C house with welcoming style. Well-furnished rooms with traditional décor and antique-style furniture. Pleasant top-floor terrace with rooftop outlook.

Lady Hamilton without rest
Storkyrkobrinken 5 ✉ S-111 28 – Ⓜ Gamla Stan – ✆ (08) 506 401 00
– info@ladyhamiltonhotel.se – Fax (08) 506 401 10
– www.ladyhamiltonhotel.se **E-F1**
34 rm – 990/2650 SEK 1850/2650 SEK, 150 SEK
◆ Historic ◆ Cosy ◆
15C houses of character full of fine Swedish rural furnishings. Rooms boast antique pieces and modern facilities. Sauna and 14C well plunge pool in basement.

Leijontornet – at Victory H.
Lilla Nygatan 5 ✉ S-111 28 – Ⓜ Gamla Stan – ✆ (08) 506 400 80
– info@leijontornet.se – Fax (08) 506 400 85 – www.leijontornet.se
Closed July, 21 December-4 January, Saturday lunch and Sunday **E1**
Rest – *(booking essential) (light lunch)* Menu 350/895 SEK
Spec. Scallop from Trondheim, cured halibut. Saddle of Lamb, smoked sausage. Woodruff ice cream, dried raspberries.
◆ Innovative ◆ Fashionable ◆
Fashionable cellar restaurant built around the remains of a 14C fortified tower. Modern, flavourful, inventive cooking makes vibrant use of high quality ingredients. Excellent wine list. Knowledgeable service.

Le Rouge
Brunnsgränd 2-4 ✉ 111 30 – Ⓜ Gamla Stan – ✆ (08) 505 244 30
– info@lerouge.se – Fax (08) 505 244 35 – www.lerouge.se
Closed mid July-mid August and 22 December-1 January **F1**
Rest – *(dinner only)* Menu 300/550 SEK – Carte 375/560 SEK
Rest ***Le Bar Rouge*** – Menu 650 SEK – Carte 245/415 SEK
◆ French traditional ◆ Intimate ◆
Intimate cellar restaurant with striking red décor creating a tented effect. Traditional French menu. Long bar and banquette booths in Le Bar Rouge, where simpler lunch and tapas style dinner are served.

Fem Små Hus
Nygränd 10 ✉ S-111 30 – Ⓜ Gamla Stan – ✆ (08) 10 87 75
– info@femsmahus.se – Fax (08) 14 96 95 – www.femsmahus.se
Closed 22-26 December and 1 January **F1**
Rest – *(dinner only)* Menu 415 SEK – Carte approx. 665 SEK
◆ Traditional ◆ Rustic ◆
Lively, characterful restaurant set in 9 rooms located in the 17C cellars of 'five small houses.' Popular with tourists. Several menus available offering traditional cuisine.

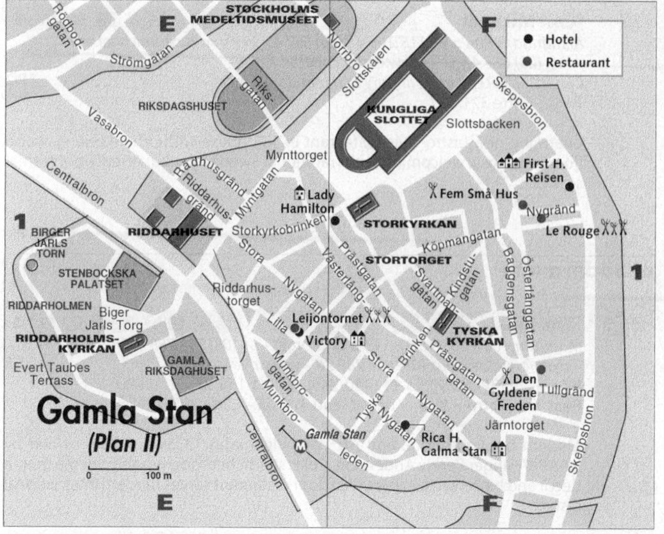

Den Gyldene Freden

Österlånggatan 51 ✉ S-103 17 – Ⓜ Gamla Stan – ☎ (08) 24 97 60 – info@gyldenefreden.se – Fax (08) 21 38 70 – www.gyldenefreden.se
Closed 24-26 & 31 December, 1 January, Midsummer, Sunday and Bank Holidays **F1**

Rest – *(booking essential) (light lunch)* Menu 325/520 SEK – Carte 405/735 SEK

◆ Traditional ◆ Rustic ◆

Popular restaurant in attractive early 18C inn, divided into assorted rooms including vaulted cellar. Friendly service and robust cooking incorporating plenty of flavours.

at Djurgården *Plan I*

Scandic H. Hasselbacken

Hazeliusbacken 20 ✉ S-102 74 – ☎ (08) 517 343 00 – hasselbacken@scandic-hotels.com – Fax (08) 517 343 11 – www.scandic-hotels.com/hasselbacken **D2**

111 rm – †1890/2290 SEK ††1990/2390 SEK – 1 suite

Rest *Restaurang Hasselbacken* – *(buffet lunch Monday-Saturday)* Menu 220/395 SEK

◆ Business ◆ Modern ◆

Modern hotel situated on island in former Royal park, close to the Vasa Museum. Comfortable, contemporary bedrooms; some refurbished, some with views. Regular musical events. Restaurant with ornate mirrored ceilings, attractive terrace and pleasant outlook; traditional Swedish cooking.

Ulla Winbladh

Rosendalsvägen 8 ✉ S-115 21 – ☎ (08) 534 897 01 – info@ullawinbladh.se – Fax (08) 545 001 67 – www.ullawinbladh.se **D2**

Rest – *(booking essential)* Menu 255 SEK (lunch) – Carte 183/665 SEK

◆ Traditional Swedish ◆ Formal ◆

Late 19C pavilion in former Royal hunting ground houses several welcoming dining rooms with terraces. Mix of traditional and modern Swedish cuisine, with international influences.

Carl Michael VISA MC AE
Allmänna Gränd 6 ✉ 115 21 – ✆ (08) 667 45 96 – info@carlmichael.se – Fax (08) 662 43 61 – www.carlmichael.se
Closed 22 December-6 January and Monday dinner **D2**
Rest – Carte 321/567
◆ Swedish ◆ Cosy ◆
Charming new bistro-style restaurant in 18C house with ornate ceiling, wood floors and cosy, welcoming feel. Traditional Swedish menu. Attentive, informal service.

at Södermalm *Plan I*

The Rival VISA MC AE
Mariatorget 3 ✉ S-118 91 – Ⓜ Mariatorget – ✆ (08) 545 789 00 – rival@rival.se – Fax (08) 545 789 24 – www.rival.se **C3**
97 rm – †1390/2290 SEK ††1490/2490 SEK, ☕ 165 SEK – 2 suites
Rest *The Bistro* – *(dinner only)* Menu 375 SEK – Carte 295/479 SEK
◆ Business ◆ Stylish ◆
Modern boutique hotel and Art Deco cinema in 1930s building, owned by ex-ABBA singer Benny Andersson. Cosy, stylish bedroooms with cinema theme décor and high-tech facilities. First floor restaurant serves modern international dishes.

Clarion H. Stockholm VISA MC AE
Ring Vägen 98 ✉ 104 60 – Ⓜ Skanstull – ✆ 462 1000 – cl.stockholm@choice.se – Fax 08462 10 99 – www.clarionstockholm.se
531 rm ☕ – †2195 SEK ††2695 SEK – 1 suite
Rest *Greta's Kok* – *(Closed Sunday) (dinner only)* Carte 300/515 SEK
◆ Business ◆ Modern ◆
Displaying more character than most modern, purpose built hotels, with impressive collection of Nordic art. Comfortable lounge, functional bedrooms and good conference facilities. Restaurant named after Greta Garbo who was born locally; international menu.

Eriks Gondolen ≤ Stockholm and water, VISA MC AE
Stadsgården 6 (11th floor) ✉ S-104 56 – Ⓜ Slussen – ✆ (08) 641 70 90 – info@eriks.se – Fax (08) 641 11 40 – www.eriks.se
Closed 1 July-13 August, 24-26 December, 1 January, Saturday lunch and Sunday **C3**
Rest – Menu 375/490 SEK – Carte 390/575 SEK
◆ Traditional ◆ Brasserie ◆
Glass-enclosed suspended passageway, renowned for stunning panoramic view of city and water. Open-air dining and barbecue terraces on 12th floor. Traditional Swedish fare.

at Arlanda Airport

Radisson SAS Sky City VISA MC AE
at Terminals 4-5, 2nd floor above street level (Stockholm-Arlanda, Sky City) ✉ 190 45 – ✆ (08) 506 740 00 – reservations.skycity.stockholm@radissonsas.com – Fax (08) 506 740 01 – www.radissonsas.com
229 rm – †2595 SEK ††2595 SEK, ☕ 135 SEK – 1 suite
Rest *Stockholm Fish* – Carte approx. 350 SEK
◆ Business ◆ Modern ◆
The perfect place not to miss your plane: modern, corporate airport hotel. Refurbished bedrooms in Scandinavian style or with maritime décor. Balcony restaurant overlooking airport terminal offering fish-based menu.

ENVIRONS OF STOCKHOLM

to the North 2 km by Sveavägen (at beginning of E 4)

Stallmästaregården

Nortull (North : 2 km by Sveavägen (at beginning of E 4)) ✉ S-113 47 – ✆ (08) 610 13 00 – info@stallmastaregarden.se – Fax (08) 610 13 40 – www.stallmastaregarden.se
Closed 25-30 December
46 rm – 1150/2095 SEK 1350/2395 SEK – 3 suites
Rest – Menu 495 SEK – Carte 510/635 SEK
♦ Inn ♦ Cosy ♦
Attractive 17C inn with central courtyard and modern bedroom wing. Quieter rooms overlook waterside and park. 18C-style rustic Swedish décor with modern comforts. Restaurant serves modern swedish cuisine.

at Ladugårdsgärdet

Villa Källhagen

Djurgårdsbrunnsvägen 10 (East: 3 km by Strandvägen) ✉ S-115 27 – ✆ (08) 665 03 00 – villa@kallhagen.se – Fax (08) 665 03 99 – www.kallhagen.se
Closed 22-27 December
36 rm – 2250 SEK 2450 SEK – 2 suites
Rest *Villa Källhagen* – see below
Rest *Bistro* – Carte 350/40 SEK
♦ Inn ♦ Modern ♦
A relaxing hotel in a lovely waterside setting with extensive open-air terraces among the trees. Contemporary bedrooms, some brand new; some with views. Simple bistro with international menu.

XX **Villa Källhagen** – at Villa Källhagen

Djurgårdsbrunnsvägen 10 (East: 3 km by Strandvägen) ✉ S-115 27 – ✆ (08) 665 03 00 – villa@kallhagen.se – Fax (08) 665 03 99 – www.kallhagen.se
Closed 22-27 December and Sunday dinner
Rest – Carte 500/695 SEK
♦ Traditional ♦ Brasserie ♦
Busy restaurant with terrace in great spot overlooking lake. Popular lunch with mostly traditional fare; more international influences at dinner. Raised area the best place to sit.

at Fjäderholmarna Island

XX **Fjäderholmarnas Krog** — neighbouring islands and sea,

Stora Fjäderholmen ✉ S-100 05 – ✆ (08) 718 33 55 – fjaderholmarna@atv.se – Fax (08) 716 39 89 – www.fjaderholmarnaskrog.se
Closed 15 September-30 April except December
Rest – *(booking essential)* Carte 480/670 SEK
♦ Seafood ♦ Friendly ♦
Delightful waterside setting on archipelago island with fine view. Fresh produce, mainly fish, delivered daily by boat. Wide selection of traditional Swedish dishes.

at Nacka Strand Southeast : 10 km by Stadsgården or 20 mins by boat from Nybrokajen

Hotel J — Sea,

Ellensviksvägen 1 ✉ S-131 28 – ✆ (08) 601 30 00 – nackastrand@hotelj.com – Fax (08) 601 30 09 – www.hotelj.com
Closed 23-31 December
40 rm – 1895 SEK 2995 SEK – 5 suites
Rest *Restaurant J* – see below
♦ Historic ♦ Design ♦
Former politician's early 20C summer residence in quiet waterside setting. 'Boutique'- style hotel with maritime theme. Stylish spacious rooms, some with sea view.

X

Restaurant J ← Sea, VISA

Augustendalsvägen 52 ✉ S-131 28 – ☎ (08) 601 30 25 – info@restaurantj.com – Fax (08) 601 30 09 – www.restaurantj.com

Rest – Carte 339/587 SEK

♦ Traditional ♦ Brasserie ♦

Bright, informal restaurant with sleek maritime décor and attractive terrace beside marina. Selective menu of Swedish and international dishes.

at Lilla Essingen West : 5.5 km by Norr Mälarstrand

XX ✿

Lux Stockholm (Henrik Norström) VISA

Primusgatan 116 ✉ S-112 67 – ☎ (08) 619 01 90 – info@luxstockholm.com – Fax (08) 619 04 47 – www.luxstockholm.com

Closed 13 July-11 August, 2 weeks Christmas-New Year, Saturday lunch, Sunday and Monday

Rest – *(booking essential) (light lunch)* Menu 705 SEK (dinner) – Carte 675/765 SEK

Spec. Fried perch with carrot juice, sugar crisp and crayfish "snifter". Crispy fried turkey, Swedish truffle, apple oil and curry spices. Sea buckthorn sorbet, surprise juice, candy floss and Swedish arrack punch.

♦ Innovative ♦ Fashionable ♦

Former Electrolux factory overlooking waterways, with light, airy feel and delightful terrace. Innovative Swedish cooking makes good use of regional products. Attentive service.

at Bromma West : 5.5 km by Norr Mälarstrand and Drottningholmsvägen

X

Sjöpaviljongen VISA

Traneberg Strand 4, Alvik (East : 1.5 km) ✉ 167 40 – Ⓜ Alvik – ☎ (08) 704 04 24 – info@sjopaviljongen.se – Fax (08) 704 82 40 – www.sjopaviljongen.se

Closed 23 December-6 January and Sunday dinner

Rest – *(booking essential)* Menu 395 SEK (dinner) – Carte 278/465 SEK

♦ Traditional ♦ Friendly ♦

Modern pavilion in attractive lakeside setting, with pleasant waterfront terrace. Swedish-style décor with busy, friendly atmosphere. Good value classic Swedish cuisine.

to the Northwest 8 km by Sveavägen and E 18 towards Norrtälje

XX

Ulriksdals Wärdshus P VISA

(take first junction for Ulriksdals Slott) ✉ 170 79 Solna – ☎ (08) 85 08 15 – info@ulriksdalswardshus.se – Fax (08) 85 08 58 – www.ulriksdalswardshus.se

Closed 2 weeks July, 1 week February, 26-30 December, Monday September-April and Tuesday dinner except December

Rest – *(booking essential)* Menu 300/375 SEK (lunch) – Carte 230/710 SEK

♦ Traditional ♦ Inn ♦

19C former inn in Royal Park with classic winter garden-style décor, delightful summer terrace and wine cellar. Traditional Swedish cooking; extensive smörgåsbord at weekends.

at Sollentuna Northwest : 15 km by Sveavägen and E 4, (exit Sollentuna c)

XXXX ✿✿

Edsbacka Krog (Christer Lingström) P VISA

Sollentunavägen 220 ✉ 191 35 – ☎ (08) 96 33 00 – info@edsbackakrog.se – Fax (08) 96 40 19 – www.edsbackakrog.se

Closed Midsummer weekend, 6-31 July, 23 December-2 January, Sunday and Bank Holidays

Rest – *(dinner only and Saturday lunch)* Menu 875 SEK – Carte 810/940 SEK

Spec. Cured salmon and Swedish caviar. Saddle of venison with pears, mushrooms and blackcurrant sauce. Seasonal Swedish berries and fruits.

♦ Classic ♦ Inn ♦

Charming part 17C inn in small park with elegantly understated décor, divided into 5 rooms. Attention to detail in service and menus. Precisely prepared, classic cooking with modern influences.

Edsbacka Bistro

Sollentunavägen 223 ✉ 191 35 – ✆ (08) 631 00 34 – bistro@edsbackakrog.se – Fax (08) 96 40 14 – www.edsbacka.se

Closed Midsummer weekend, 14 July-3 August, 23-26 & 31 December and 1 January

Rest – *(booking essential)* Menu 385 SEK – Carte 320/475 SEK

♦ Traditional ♦ Bistro ♦

Simple modern bistro with black and white décor. Smart rear terrace shielded from traffic. Good value menu of tasty classic Swedish dishes. Friendly, informal service.

WE 58
FLAX

GOTHENBURG
GÖTEBORG

Population: 489 500 (conurbation 872 200) - Altitude: sea level

ell Holmner/Göteborg & Co/www.imagebank.sweden.se

It's not everywhere you find a cook's face on a postage stamp, but Gothenburg's Leif Mannerström has achieved this curious honour, as good an indication as any that in this attractive west coast city, cuisine is a major priority, and seafood its *cause célèbre*. Gothenburg is universally considered to be Sweden's friendliest town, a throwback to its days as a leading trading centre and seaport, a cosmospolitan place where you're as likely to strike up a conversation with a local as come face-to-face with a restaurant – and there are over 650 of those.

This is a compact, pretty city whose roots go back four hundred years. It has trams, broad avenues and canals – the Dutch designed it all. Its centre is boisterous but never feels tourist heavy and overcrowded; Gothenburgers take life at a more leisurely pace than their Stockholm cousins over on the east coast. The mighty shipyards that once dominated the shoreline are now quiet. Go to the centre, though, and you find the good-time ambience of Avenyn, a vivacious thoroughfare full of places to eat and drink. But for those still itching for a feel of the heavy industry that once defined the place, there's a Volvo museum sparkling with chrome and shiny steel. Truly, a city for all comers.

LIVING THE CITY

Unless you really do fancy the visit to the Volvo museum (which is north of the Göta river) there's not much point in crossing from the southern side of Gothenburg. The Old Town is the historic heart: its tight grid of streets has grand façades and a fascinating waterfront. Southeast of here is the commercial and retail hub of **Avenyn**, where the pretty people like to be seen. Just west is the **Vasastan** quarter, full of fine National Romantic buildings. Further west again is **Haga**, an old working-class district which – you've guessed it – has been gentrified, its cobbled streets sprawling with cafes and boutiques. Adjacent to Haga is the district of **Linné**, a racy and vibrant area that has catapulted itself into the same league as Avenyn – its elegantly tall nineteenth-century Dutch-inspired buildings perhaps giving it the edge.

PRACTICAL INFORMATION

ARRIVAL-DEPARTURE

Landvetter Airport is 25km east of the city although City Airport in the northwest is increasingly popular. A taxi from either airport will cost approximately SEK350, although there are also bus connections. There are regular ferry services from Kiel.

TRANSPORT

The Gothenburg Pass gives you unlimited bus, tram and boat travel within the city. It will also guarantee you a sightseeing tour, admission to the Liseberg amusement park, entry to all museums, and discounts in certain shops and restaurants. They are valid for either one or two days, and are available from Tourist Information offices, the amusement park, newspaper kiosks, hotels and campsites.

Doing a fair amount of bus and tram travel? Then get a 10-trip carnet of tickets from the driver, or from Travel Information Centres. Single tickets are also available.

Punts – flat Paddan boats - are a pleasant way to explore this maritime city, gliding past stately canalside buildings. They pass under 20 bridges; you're advised to duck on numerous occasions, as a lot of them were built for the vertically challenged.

EXPLORING GOTHENBURG

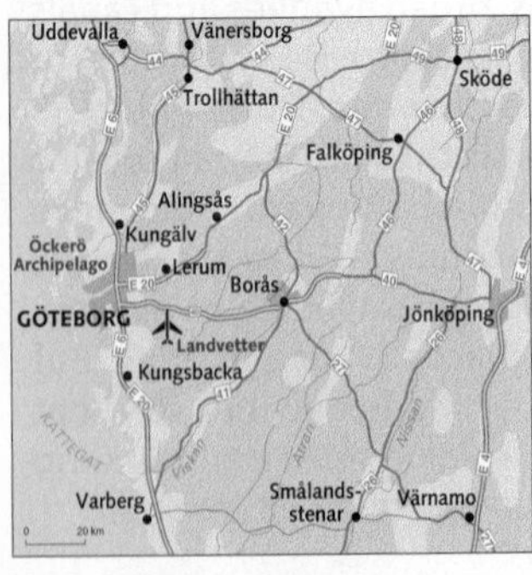

If you've been to San Francisco and liked what you saw, then you'll probably be partial to Gothenburg. It's often compared to the hip US city: it occupies a breezy west coast location, has plenty of bridges, hills, water and trams, and, as with Fisherman's Wharf, it boasts an abundance of seafood restaurants. Like San Francisco, there's a welcoming spirit about the place, and a true cosmopolitan air. Canals, silently ringing the city, bring the emphasis back to Europe, as does the grand Neoclassical architecture, a product of Gothenburg's spirited history of trading, as merchants from around the continent stayed on and built grand houses in which to live.

➜ CRANE SUPREME

As this is a maritime town, down along the quayside is as good a place to get your bearings as any. There is much character here, as the grandly decaying shipyards sadly eye your progress along the waterfront. Here, at Lilla Bommen harbour, the sombre glory of the rusting, arching cranes are juxtaposed against temples of modernism, such as the iconic **Utkiken Tower** from the late 1980s, better known as 'The Lipstick Tower' because of its lusty scarlet tip, offering a great viewing platform over Gothenburg. And just along the blustery waterfront, competing with it in the iconic stakes, is another relatively recent arrival, 1994's strikingly modern **Opera House,** designed with its location uppermost, to resemble a fine ship. It puts on not just opera, but ballet and musicals, too. The salty location meets its match two minutes' stroll further along at the **Maritiman**, a truly floating maritime museum which can rightly label itself the 'largest ship museum in the world'. It's a retirement home for twenty boats – a cross-section of Sweden's naval heritage. These include a lightship, a fire-fighting vessel, a vast destroyer and a submarine that should be avoided by claustrophobia sufferers at all costs.

➜ MAKING HIS POINT

It won't take you long to turn inland and reach the heart of the Old Town. You'll know when you're there, because you'll see a big copper statue of Gustav II Adolf pointing down to the spot where he allegedly declared he would build his city. This is **Gustav Adolf's Torg**, the stately main square, and close by are two buildings worth visiting. The **Kronhuset** was built by the Dutch over 350 years ago and is the city's oldest secular building, while the **Stadsmuseum** is a cultural powerhouse, boasting exhibits of Gothenburg's rich history all the way back to the days of the Vikings and including a very impressive long-boat. All around this area are 17C streets, canals and buildings; and the Stadsmuseum itself is housed inside the former auction house of the Swedish East India Company, richly endowed with stone pillars, frescoes and stained glass.

Both these buildings are dwarfed by a monstrous interloper, one which owes its origins to twenty first century consumerism. The gigantic **Nordstan** is Sweden's biggest shopping centre and it has some eye-catching modern Nordic design amongst its sparkly boutiques and chain stores. It should satisfy any shopping itch you were waiting to scratch, but if not then head due south to the main thoroughfare of Kungsportsavenyn, more elegantly known as **Avenyn**, which, to be more accurate, is actually a place to be seen rather than to shop. It's adorned with grand nineteenth century houses, and their ground floors have been transformed into swish cafés, bars or restaurants, for this is the avenue with the highest density of places to eat in Sweden. In the summer, tables spill out, a chrome carnival shimmering along Avenyn's spacious, cobbled length, the young and the wish-they-were-still-young adding their own lustre. One of the city's abiding delights is that the centre, though lively, never feels over-crowded or in a rush: the sense of harmony and space is never strained.

➜ NORTHERN LIGHT

At the southern end of Avenyn stands one of the city's best attractions, the **Art Museum**, housed in a massive building, which, rather impressively, claims the finest collection of Nordic art in Scandinavia. Head for the sixth floor where the Furstenberg Galleries are full of work by revered early 20C century artists which brings to life the landscapes, shades and nuances of the Nordic countries. On other floors there are also works by the French Impressionists, Munch, Van Gogh and Gauguin. Half-way down Avenyn, just over in the adjoining area of Vasastan, can be found the Röhsska Museum of Design and Applied Art, which takes you on an excellent trip through the centuries and continents, looking at aesthetic glories from ancient Asian ceramics to 21C mod cons.

Gothenburg boasts another 'biggest in Scandinavia' if you meander southeast from Avenyn. It's **Liseberg** - a magical name to those in the know, conjuring up roller coaster rides, shocking pink paintwork, fairy lights and sweet-scented waffles. Opened in 1923, it's Scandinavia's biggest amusement park, bigger even than Copenhagen's Tivoli, and reaches the parts of adults other amusement parks fail to reach, as it boasts trees, fountains and flowers to give it the authentic feel of a 'proper' park. There's another reason to go to Liseberg now: it's right next door to a museum, opened only in 2004, that's won a host of plaudits including Sweden's most prestigious architecture award, plus worldwide praise for its refreshing exhibitions. This is the **Museum of World Culture**, which apart from its startling four-storey glass atrium, also offers a clear-sighted angle on the diverse variety of world cultures through a series of changing exhibitions. The café/restaurant here is pretty good, too.

➔ HAGA SAGA

Gothenburg's most remarkably transformed quarter is **Haga**, its south-western suburb. Not so long ago it was so run-down that it was on the verge of demolition, but the nineteenth-century artisan houses were replenished in the 1980s and now some of the coolest of the city's cool hang out here. During the daytime it can be a delightful place to visit with its village-like ambience – sip a coffee at an outside table on a cobbled street, or wander round the stylish boutiques. Carry on a bit further west and you're in **Linné**, the smart area named after famed Swedish scientist Carl von Linné (whose 300th birthday was celebrated in style in the country in 2007. Linné has a rash of trendy places to eat and drink, and is now considered a second Avenyn, but without the tourist gloss. There are nineteenth century buildings in the Dutch style, atmospheric antique shops and sex stores, all melding together to create a quarter very much with its own style and patina.

➔ STOCK COMMENT

If you hear a Gothenburger making a dismissive remark about an 08-er, it's not some kind of Swedish rhyming slang. 08 is the telephone code for Stockholm, and saying something not

GOTHENBURG IN...

➔ ONE DAY

The old town, the harbour, a meal in Haga, a stroll around Linné

➔ TWO DAYS

Liseburg, The Museum of World Culture, Art Museum

➔ THREE DAYS

A trip on a Pattan boat, a night at the Opera House (or a boat trip around the archipelago)

so nice about Stockholm is par for the course in Gothenburg.

→ STATUESQUE

At the southern end of Avenyn, in Götaplatsen square, stands the unmissable bronze statue of the nude Poseidon. In 1931, when he first appeared, the outlandish size of his male member caused outrage amongst the citizenry, so it was chopped painfully short, leaving modern onlookers to wonder at the somewhat out of proportion 7m high statue staring at them.

CALENDAR HIGHLIGHTS

Gothenburg is a serious party city, and the stress is on the serious side of things in May when the International Science Festival hits town. This is closely followed by the party element when, the same month, the Gothenburg Jazz Festival explodes into life. A sporting and musical dimension is much to the fore in June and July: June's Nokia Oops Cup is a well-established yachting event, with spectators close to the action as the trimarans race near to shore; blues fans should head to Slottsparken zoo the same month for the Gothenburg Blues Party. Then in July, the Gothia Cup at the Ullevi Stadium is a massively important youth cup for footballers from around the world, established for over thirty years with representations from over a hundred countries, and, yes, boasting more wins for Swedish teams than any other. August's Gothenburg Party is the biggest city festival in Sweden, taking up every inch the town has to offer, with more than six hundred concerts, cultural events and fireworks. Culture vultures can gorge themselves on the Art Biennial from September to November – a contemporary art smorgasbord with seminars and workshops at various city locations. As the nights get darker in October, Kulturnatta brings much light relief with events ranging from poetry readings to theatrical productions.

EATING OUT

No wonder Gothenburg's oldest food market is called Feskekörka or 'Fish Church'. Locals will always give thanks for the humble herring and the Fish Church does indeed look like a place of worship, but its pews are stalls of oysters, prawns and salmon, and where you might expect to find an organ loft, you'll find a restaurant instead. There are more than 650 of them in the city, a bewildering total for a population of around half a million. Food – and in particular the piscine variety - is a big reason for visiting Gothenburg. Its restaurants have earned a plethora of Michelin stars which are dotted all over the compact city. As a general rule of thumb, it's best to steer clear of Avenyn, where prices leap higher than salmon in spring, and instead head for Haga or Linné, where the dining scene has come on tremendously over the last decade. As is often the case in Scandinavia, best practice is to eat your main meal at lunchtime, when fixed price specials are such good value. Restaurants with a European base are worth trying out: there are a lot of them here and often they use a Swedish fishy staple as a starting point. If you're in town in the summer, don't miss out on the delicious local fruits for dessert: soft and juicy, they're a must. Gothenburgers also love coffee and cake, a combination they twin under the umbrella term 'fika', and ideal after a glass of traditional brannvin (vodka) and marinated herring. You're not expected to tip in Gothenburg's eateries, though it is customary to round the bill up to the nearest 10-20kr.

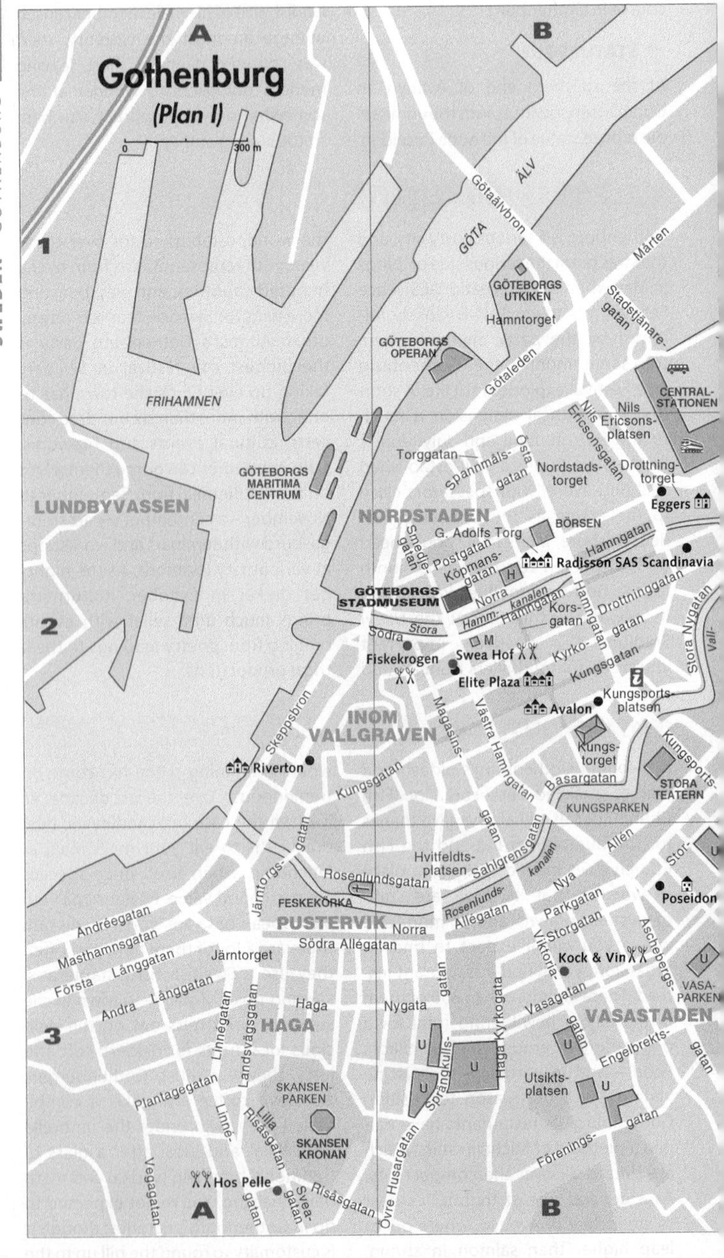
Gothenburg
(Plan I)
0
300 m
A
B
1
2
3
GÖTA ÄLV
Götaälvbron
Mårten
GÖTEBORGS UTKIKEN
Hamntorget
Stadstjänare-gatan
GÖTEBORGS OPERAN
Götaleden
FRIHAMNEN
CENTRAL-STATIONEN
Nils Ericsons-platsen
Nils Ericsonsgatan
Torggatan
Spannmåls-gatan
Östa
Nordstads-torget
Drottning-torget
Eggers
GÖTEBORGS MARITIMA CENTRUM
LUNDBYVASSEN
NORDSTADEN
BÖRSEN
G. Adolfs Torg
Smedie-gatan
Postgatan
Köpmans-gatan
Hamngatan
Radisson SAS Scandinavia
GÖTEBORGS STADMUSEUM
Norra Hamngatan
Hamm-kanalen
Stora
Södra
Kors-gatan
Drottninggatan
Hamngatan
Stora Nygatan
Vall-
M
Fiskekrogen
Swea Hof
Kyrko-gatan
Elite Plaza
Kungsgatan
Kungsports-platsen
Avalon
Magasins-gatan
Västra Hamngatan
INOM VALLGRAVEN
Skeppsbron
Riverton
Kungs-torget
Kungsports-
Basargatan
STORA TEATERN
KUNGSPARKEN
Kungsgatan
Järntorgs-gatan
Sahlgrensgatan
kanalen
Allén
Hvitfeldts-platsen
Rosenlundsgatan
Stor-
Nya
Poseidon
FESKEKÖRKA
Rosenlunds-
Allégatan
Parkgatan
Storgatan
PUSTERVIK
Norra
Andréegatan
Masthamnsgatan
Södra Allégatan
Järntorget
Första Långgatan
Viktoria-
Kock & Vin
Aschebergs-gatan
Andra Långgatan
Linnégatan
Landsvägsgatan
Haga
Nygata
gatan
Haga Kyrkogata
Vasagatan
VASA-PARKEN
VASASTADEN
HAGA
U
gatan
Engelbrekts-gatan
Plantagegatan
SKANSEN-PARKEN
Sprängkulls-
Utsikts-platsen
Linné-
Lilla Risåsgatan
SKANSEN KRONAN
Förenings-gatan
Vegagatan
Hos Pelle
Svea-gatan
Risåsgatan
Övre Husargatan

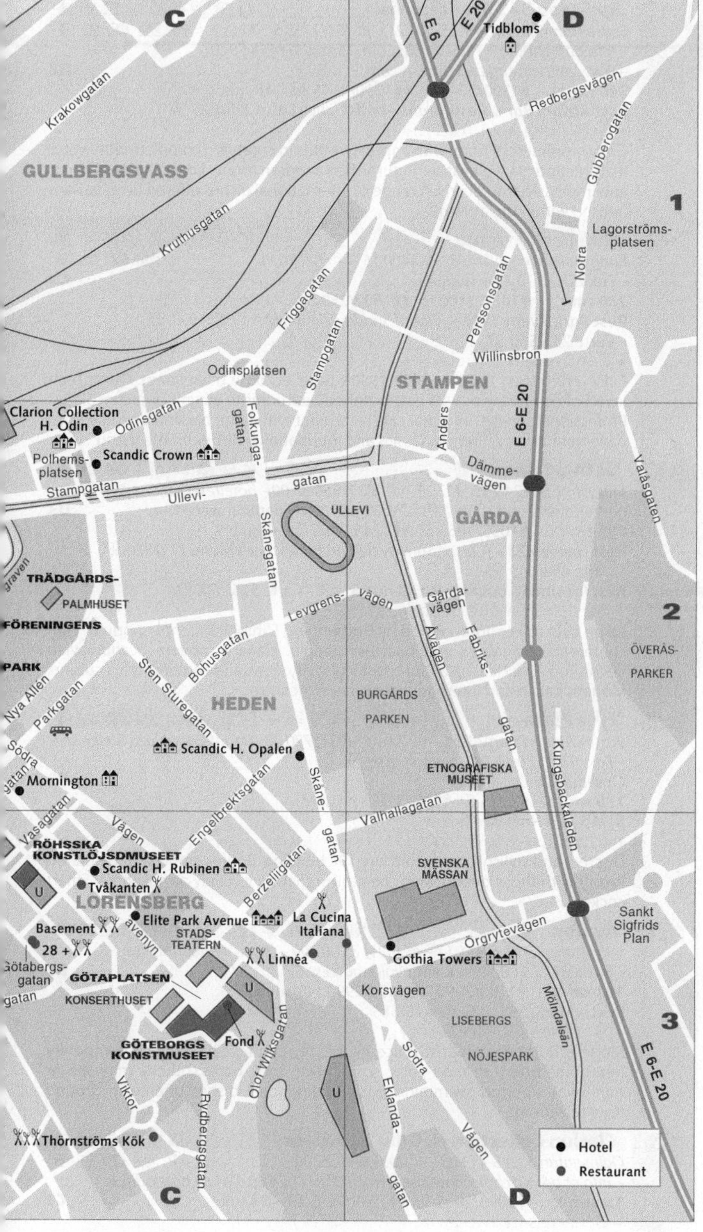

C
D
1
2
3
GULLBERGSVASS
STAMPEN
GÅRDA
HEDEN
LORENSBERG
Krakowgatan
Kruthusgatan
Friggagatan
Stampgatan
Odinsplatsen
Odinsgatan
Folkungagatan
Stampgatan
Ullevigatan
ULLEVI
Skånegatan
Levgrensvägen
Gårdavägen
Åvägen
Fabriksgatan
Bohusgatan
Sten Sturegatan
Nya Allén
Parkgatan
Södra vägen
Vasagatan
Engelbrektsgatan
Valhallagatan
Berzeliigatan
Olof Wijksgatan
Viktor Rydbergsgatan
Korsvägen
Södra Vägen
Eklandagatan
Örgrytevägen
Mölndalsån
Kungsbackaleden
Redbergsvägen
Gubberogatan
Notra
Lagorströmsplatsen
Perssonsgatan
Willinsbron
Anders
Dämmevägen
Valåsgatan
E 6
E 20
E 6-E 20
Tidbloms
Clarion Collection H. Odin
Polhemsplatsen
Scandic Crown
TRÄDGÅRDSFÖRENINGENS PARK
PALMHUSET
BURGÅRDS PARKEN
ÖVERÅS-PARKER
ETNOGRAFISKA MUSEET
SVENSKA MÄSSAN
Sankt Sigfrids Plan
Scandic H. Opalen
Mornington
RÖHSSKA KONSTLÖJSDMUSEET
Scandic H. Rubinen
Tvåkanten
Basement
28 +
Elite Park Avenue
La Cucina Italiana
STADSTEATERN
Linnéa
Gothia Towers
Götabergsgatan
GÖTAPLATSEN
KONSERTHUSET
GÖTEBORGS KONSTMUSEET
Fond
LISEBERGS NÖJESPARK
Thörnströms Kök
Hotel
Restaurant

Radisson SAS Scandinavia
Södra Hamngatan 59 ✉ S-401 24 – ✆ (031) 758 50 00 – info.gothenburg@radissonsas.com – Fax (031) 758 50 01 – www.gothenburg.radissonsas.com **B2**
349 rm – 1290/2045 SEK 1390/2145 SEK – 18 suites
Rest *Atrium Bar & Restaurant* – *buffet lunch* Carte 255/625 SEK
♦ Business ♦ Modern ♦
Grand commercial hotel with impressive atrium courtyard complete with water features and glass elevators. Refurbished, modern rooms boast choice of décor and impressive mod cons. A range of international dishes offered in restaurant housed within the atrium.

Elite Park Avenue
Kungsportsavenyn 36-38 ✉ S-400 15 – ✆ 727 1000 – Fax 727 10 10 – www.elite.se **C3**
280 rm – 1000/2100 SEK 1600/2500 SEK – 11 suites
Rest *Park Aveny Cafe* – *(Closed Sunday dinner)* Menu 325/695 SEK – Carte 265/569 SEK
♦ Business ♦ Modern ♦
Fully refurbished purpose-built 1950's hotel on busy main street. Offers high levels of comfort with well proportioned bedrooms in creams and chocolates. Professional service. Informal café restaurant with large bar and opening onto pavement terrace; French classics and international dishes on the menu.

Gothia Towers
Mässans Gata 24 ✉ S-402 26 – ✆ (031) 750 88 00 – hotelreservations@gothiatowers.com – Fax (031) 750 88 82 – www.gothiatowers.com **D3**
695 rm – 1095/1865 SEK 1245/2065 SEK – 9 suites
Rest *Heaven 23* – *(Closed Sunday dinner) buffet lunch* Menu 272/526 SEK – Carte 498/649 SEK
Rest *Incontro* – *buffet lunch* Menu 451 SEK – Carte 395/677 SEK
♦ Business ♦ Modern ♦
Large twin tower hotel owned by Gothenburg Exhibition Centre, popular with conference delegates and business people. Elegant modern Scandinavian décor. Top floor Heaven 23, for spectacular city views and contemporary cuisine. Modern Italian and international dishes in Incontro.

Elite Plaza
Västra Hamngatan 3 ✉ S-402 22 – ✆ (031) 720 40 40 – info.gbgplaza@elite.se – Fax (031) 720 40 10 – www.elite.se
Closed 24-26 December **B2**
130 rm – 2925 SEK 2925 SEK – 4 suites
Rest *Swea Hof* – see below
♦ Luxury ♦ Modern ♦
Discreet and stylishly converted late 19C building. Rooms embody understated luxury with those overlooking the atrium sharing its lively atmosphere. Smart cocktail bar.

Avalon
Kungstorget 9 ✉ S-411 17 – ✆ (031) 751 02 00 – info@avalonhotel.se – Fax (031) 7 51 02 08 – www.avalonhotel.se **B2**
101 rm – 1290/2990 1390/2990 – 3 suites
Rest – Menu 595 – Carte 445/585
♦ Business ♦ Modern ♦
Modern hotel near tourist office in the city centre. Spacious, contemporary bedrooms boast all mod cons; some have open baths; others, mini-spa or mini-gym. Rooftop swimming pool. International dishes offered in ground floor restaurant.

Clarion Collection H. Odin without rest
Odinsgatan 6 ✉ S-411 03 – ✆ (031) 745 22 00 – info.cc.odin@choicehotels.se – Fax (031) 711 24 60 – www.hotelodin.se
156 rm – 1095/2095 SEK 1295/2295 SEK – 24 suites **C2**
♦ Business ♦ Modern ♦
Central location near railway station. Smart, Scandic-style, well-equipped, serviced apartments with mini-kitchen; also spacious and appealing suites.

Scandic H. Rubinen

Kungsportsavenyn 24 ✉ *S-400 14 – ✆ (031) 751 54 00 – rubinen@scandic-hotels.com – Fax (031) 751 54 11 – www.scandic-hotels.com/rubinen* **C3**

191 rm – 🛉950/2150 SEK 🛉🛉1250/2250 SEK – 1 suite

Rest – Carte 299/409 SEK

◆ Business ◆ Modern ◆

Well-located central hotel with smart, modern style and international atmosphere. Comfy, modern bedrooms in warm shades. Top-floor suites boast delightful roof terraces. Modish restaurant with dominant bar; trendy "New Latino" style cuisine.

Riverton

Stora Badhusgatan 26 ✉ *S-411 21 – ✆ (031) 750 10 00 – riverton@riverton.se – Fax (031) 750 10 01 – www.riverton.se* **A2**

191 rm – 🛉1095/1885 SEK 🛉🛉1195/2155 SEK – 9 suites

Rest – *(Closed Sunday) (dinner only)* Menu 275 SEK – Carte 490/550 SEK

◆ Business ◆ Modern ◆

Modern hotel offering fine view of city and docks from upper floors. Some rooms redecorated in a contemporary style; others have sleek Swedish décor. Good business facilities. 12th floor restaurant, overlooking Göta Älv river and docks. Local and international cuisine.

Scandic Crown

Polhemsplatsen 3 ✉ *S-411 11 – ✆ (031) 751 51 00 – crown@scandic-hotels.com – Fax (031) 751 51 11 – www.scandic-hotels.se*

Closed 24-25 December and 1-2 January **C2**

338 rm – 🛉1950 SEK 🛉🛉1950 SEK – 4 suites

Rest – *(Closed Sunday) buffet lunch* Menu 345 SEK – Carte 355/425 SEK

◆ Business ◆ Modern ◆

Modern group hotel in good location for transport connections. Fresh, bright, functional rooms with wood floors and colourful fabrics. Executive rooms with balconies. Top floor gym and sauna. Pleasant atrium restaurant with a wide range of Swedish and international cuisine.

Scandic H. Opalen

Engelbrektsgatan 73 ✉ *S-412 52 – ✆ (031) 751 53 00 – opalen@scandic-hotels.com – Fax (031) 751 53 11 – www.scandic-hotels.com* **C2**

241 rm – 🛉690/1250 SEK 🛉🛉790/1850 SEK – 2 suites

Rest – *(Closed Sunday)* Menu 199 SEK (lunch) – Carte 350/389 SEK

◆ Business ◆ Modern ◆

Corporate hotel near the business centre and stadium. Classical style bedrooms vary in size but all have same good level of facilities. Relaxation zone with single-sex saunas. Large restaurant, varied choice of Swedish and international dishes. Popular weekend entertainment with dancing several nights a week.

Eggers

Drottningtorget ✉ *S-404 24 – ✆ (031) 333 44 40 – hotel.eggers@telia.com – Fax (031) 333 44 49 – www.hoteleggers.se*

Closed 23-26 December **B2**

69 rm – 🛉1230/1835 SEK 🛉🛉1230/2380 SEK

Rest – *(Closed July, 23-26 December and Bank Holidays)* Menu 190/400 SEK – Carte 395/549 SEK

◆ Traditional ◆ Classic ◆

Charming 1850s hotel, one of Sweden's oldest: wrought iron and stained glass on staircase, Gothenburg's oldest lift. Rooms feature period furniture and fittings. Ornate restaurant busy during day, more elegant in evening. Traditional Swedish and international cuisine.

Novotel Göteborg

Klippan 1 (Southwest : 3.5 km by Andréeg taking Kiel-Klippan Ö exit, or boat from Rosenlund) ✉ *S-414 51 – ☎ (031) 720 22 00 – info@novotel.se – Fax (031) 720 22 99 – www.novotel.se*

151 rm – 🚹1490/1590 SEK 🚹🚹1590/1690 SEK – 4 suites

Rest *Carnegie Kaj* – *buffet lunch* Carte 260/535 SEK

♦ Chain hotel ♦ Business ♦ Functional ♦

Converted brewery on waterfront with view of Göta Älv. Central atrium-style lobby. Spacious rooms with international-style décor and sofabeds. Restaurant overlooking the harbour. International cooking to appeal to all tastes.

Mornington

Kungsportsavenyn 6 ✉ *S-411 36 – ☎ (031) 767 34 00 – goteborg@mornington.se – Fax (031) 711 34 39 – www.mornington.se* **C2**

91 rm – 🚹795/2550 SEK 🚹🚹1195/2550 SEK

Rest *Brasserie Lipp* – Menu 465 SEK (dinner) – Carte 327/497 SEK

♦ Business ♦ Modern ♦

Modern office block-style façade conceals hotel on famous shopping street. Compact rooms of dark brown, comfortable functional furniture with slightly English "feel" to them. Pleasant brasserie-style restaurant, hearty home cooking and international fare.

Tidbloms

Olskroksgatan 23 ✉ *S-416 66 – ☎ (031) 707 50 00 – info@tidbloms.se – Fax (031) 707 50 99 – www.tidbloms.se*

Closed 2 weeks Christmas **D1**

42 rm – 🚹795/1535 SEK 🚹🚹995/1535 SEK

Rest – *(closed lunch Saturday and Sunday)* Menu 155 SEK

♦ Business ♦ Functional ♦

Old red brick hotel in quiet residential area. Quaint turret and semi-circular veranda-cum-conservatory. Sunny, refurbished rooms with standard comforts. Rustic restaurant in the round, serving modern international cuisine.

Poseidon without rest

Storgatan 33 ✉ *S-411 38 – ☎ (031) 10 05 50 – info@hotelposeidon.com – Fax (031) 13 83 91 – www.hotelposeidon.com* **B3**

49 rm – 🚹745/1200 SEK 🚹🚹975/1690 SEK

♦ Family ♦ Functional ♦

Informal hotel in residential area not far from main shopping street. Comfortable neutral décor and functional furnishings in rooms. Accommodation for families available.

Sjömagasinet (Leif Mannerström)

Klippans Kulturreservat 5 (Southwest : 3.5 km by Andréeg taking Kiel-Klippan Ö exit, or boat from Rosenlund. Also evenings and weekends in summer from Lilla Bommens Hamn) ✉ *S-414 51 – ☎ (031) 775 59 20 – info@sjomagasinet.se – Fax (031) 24 55 39 – www.sjomagasinet.se*

Closed 24-25 & 31 December, 1 January, lunch Saturday, Sunday & Bank Holidays and Sunday January-April

Rest – *(booking essential) (buffet lunch also in summer)* Menu 395/525 SEK (lunch) – Carte 675/925 SEK

Spec. Kalix bleak roe with red onions, chives, sour cream and fried toast. Pan-fried angler fish with citrus sauce, scallops and bleak roe. Rosemary crème brûlée, lingonberry foam and vodka jelly.

♦ Seafood ♦ Rustic ♦

Delightful 18C former warehouse on the waterfront. Busy restaurant on two floors with ship's mast and charming terrace. Accomplished, flavourful seafood cooking uses quality ingredients.

XXX

Thörnströms Kök

Teknologgatan 3 ✉ S-411 32 – ✆ (031) 16 20 66 – info@thornstromskok.com – Fax (031) 16 40 17 – www.thornstromskok.com
Closed 1 July-12 August, Sunday, Monday and Bank Holidays **C3**
Rest – *(booking essential) (dinner only)* Menu 530 SEK – Carte 505/550 SEK
♦ Seasonal cuisine ♦ Neighbourhood ♦
Professionally run, popular and stylishly elegant restaurant, set in a quiet area near university. Accomplished and flavourful modern Swedish dishes with European influences; very good service.

XX ✿

Basement (Ulf Wagner)

Götabergsgatan 28 ✉ S-411 34 – ✆ (031) 28 27 29 – bokning@restbasement.com – Fax (031) 28 27 37 – www.restbasement.com
Closed July, Christmas-New Year and Sunday **C3**
Rest – *dinner only (set menu only)* Menu 660/1050 SEK
Spec. Lobster and Jerusalem artichoke with white truffle spaghetti. Fillet of venison, braised endives and thyme honey. Arctic bramble mousse and cloudberry consommé.
♦ Modern ♦ Fashionable ♦
Centrally located restaurant serving imaginative, modern cooking which makes vibrant use of quality Swedish produce. Relaxed atmosphere and friendly service. Special events on Fridays.

XX ✿

28 +

Götabergsgatan 28 ✉ S-411 34 – ✆ (031) 20 21 61 – 28plus@telia.com – Fax (031) 81 97 57 – www.28plus.se
Closed 29 June-23 August, 23-26 & 31 December, 2 & 4-7 January and Sunday
Rest – *(dinner only)* Carte 685/805 SEK **C3**
Spec. Smoked king scallops with Jerusalem artichoke soup and pancetta. Saddle of roe deer with chanterelles, tonka bean sauce. Lemon mousse with liquorice fudge, pistachio and molasses ice cream.
♦ Modern ♦ Cosy ♦
Popular three-roomed restaurant in one of Sweden's finest wine cellars. Imaginative, accomplished cooking uses fresh, quality produce. Well chosen wines. Professional, friendly service.

XX

Linnéa

Södra Vägen 32 ✉ S-412 52 – ✆ (031) 16 11 83 – info@restauranglinnea.com – Fax (031) 18 12 92 – www.restauranglinnea.com
Closed 15 July-20 August, 23 December-8 January, Sunday and Bank Holidays
Rest – *(dinner only)* Menu 465/500 SEK – Carte 495/645 SEK **C3**
♦ Modern ♦ Neighbourhood ♦
Smart, professionally run restaurant serving skillfully-prepared, seasonal Swedish cuisine. Stylish place settings, with plates of Swedish glass; wines served in splendid crystal glasses.

XX

Fiskekrogen

Lilla Torget 1 ✉ S-411 18 – ✆ (031) 10 10 05 – info@fiskekrogen.com – Fax (031) 10 10 06 – www.fiskekrogen.com
Closed July, Christmas-New Year, Sunday and Bank Holidays **B2**
Rest – *(buffet lunch)* Menu 295/625 SEK – Carte 499/625 SEK
♦ Seafood ♦ Brasserie ♦
Busy 1920s restaurant with reputation for its seafood. Striking room with high ceiling, wood panelling, columns and modern Scandinavian art. Good choice seafood buffet lunch. Wine list with over 300 bins.

XX

Hos Pelle

Djupedalsgatan 2 ✉ S-413 07 – ✆ (031) 12 10 31 – info@hospelle.com – Fax (031) 775 38 32 – www.hospelle.com
Closed July, 20-21 June, 24-26 December, 1 January, Sunday and lunch Saturday
Rest – Menu 250/350 SEK **A3**
♦ Traditional ♦ Neighbourhood ♦
Popular local restaurant with comfortable atmosphere, displaying Swedish art. Serves classic and modern Swedish cuisine prepared to high standard. Ground floor bistro.

Kock & Vin

Viktoriagatan 12 ✉ S-411 25 – ✆ (031) 701 79 79 – info@kockvin.se – www.kockvin.se

Closed 6 July-6 August and 21-28 December **B3**

Rest – *(dinner only)* Menu 595/795 SEK – Carte 495/595 SEK

Spec. Confit of rabbit with duck liver. Roast pigeon with chorizo and chestnuts. Coriander ice cream and turnip infused with sea buckthorn.

♦ Modern ♦ Friendly ♦

Attractive candlelit restaurant with ornate 19C ceiling and basement wine bar. Menu of the senses for refined, innovative cooking. À la carte offers classically-based dishes with a contemporary twist.

Swea Hof – at Elite Plaza H.

Västra Hamngatan 3 ✉ S-404 22 – ✆ (031) 720 40 40 – Fax (031) 720 40 10

Closed 20 December-7 January, Saturday lunch and Sunday **B2**

Rest – Menu 365/495 SEK – Carte 545/675 SEK

♦ Modern ♦ Formal ♦

Striking atrium-style restaurant in heart of hotel with glass roof on metal framework and open-plan kitchen. Dinner menu offers elaborate and accomplished modern cuisine.

Fond

Götaplatsen ✉ S-412 56 – ✆ (031) 81 25 80 – fond@fondrestaurang.com – Fax (031) 18 37 90 – www.fondrestaurang.com

closed 4 weeks Summer, 2 weeks Christmas, Sunday, Saturday lunch and Bank Holidays **C3**

Rest – Menu 700 SEK (dinner) – Carte 610/705 SEK

Spec. Langoustines with glazed carrots and orange flavoured butter cream sauce. Venison fillet with ceps and game jus. Lingonberry dessert.

♦ Modern ♦ Trendy ♦

Well located, contemporary glass restaurant by the Theatre and Art Museum. Interesting and unfussy modern cooking inspired by quality ingredients chosen from the Nordic landscape.

La Cucina Italiana

Skånegatan 33 ✉ S-412 52 – ✆ (031) 16 63 07 – pietro@swipnet.ie – Fax (031) 16 63 07 – www.lacucinaitaliana.nu

closed Easter, Midsummer, Christmas-New Year and Sunday **C3**

Rest – *(booking essential) (dinner only)* Menu 480 SEK – Carte 474/615 SEK

♦ Italian ♦ Friendly ♦

Snugly intimate and authentic Italian restaurant, away from the city centre, with a smart line in modern furnishings and a pleasant ambience. Good value modish menus change daily.

Tvåkanten

Kungsportsavenyn 27 ✉ S-411 36 – ✆ (031) 18 21 15 – info@tvakanten.se – Fax (031) 81 11 98 – www.tvakanten.se

Closed Sunday lunch **C3**

Rest – Carte 365/685 SEK

♦ Traditional ♦ Brasserie ♦

Busy characterful restaurant with simpler lunch and more extensive dinner menus. Dining rooms with brick walls, plus elegant first-floor private dining room. Rustic fare.

at Eriksberg West : 6 km by Götaälvbron and Lundbyleden, or boat from Rosenlund

Quality Hotel 11

Maskingatan 11 ✉ S-417 64 – ✆ (031) 779 11 11 – q.hotel11@choice.se – Fax (031) 779 11 10 – www.hotel11.se

260 rm – †1290/2074 SEK ††1290/3978 SEK

Rest *Kök & Bar 67* – *(dinner only)* Carte 298/379 SEK

♦ Business ♦ Functional ♦

Striking former shipbuilding warehouse, part see-through; there is so much glass! Rooms feature stylish modern Scandinavian interior design with pale wood and bright fabrics. Gym and sauna with a view. Upper floor restaurant with bar area, waterway views and international cooking.

River Café Göta Älv river and harbour,

Dockepiren ✉ S-417 64 – ✆ (031) 51 00 00 – info@rivercafe.se – Fax (31) 51 00 01 – www.rivercafe.se

Closed Sunday except in Summer

Rest – Menu 295 SEK (lunch) – Carte 295/450 SEK

♦ Seasonal cuisine ♦ Friendly ♦

Delightfully set on the pier in Eriksburg with fine view to harbour. Agreeable bar; elegant first-floor restaurant with panoramic glass frontage. Seasonal, international cooking.

at Landvetter Airport East : 30 km by Rd 40

Landvetter Airport H.

Flygets Hotellväg ✉ S-438 13 – ✆ (031) 97 75 50 – info@landvetterairporthotel.se – Fax (031) 94 64 70 – www.landvetterairporthotel.se

134 rm – †1445/1595 SEK ††1595 SEK – 1 suite

Rest – *(buffet lunch)* Menu 198 SEK – Carte 219/498 SEK

♦ Business ♦ Modern ♦

Adjacent to airport. Welcoming bedrooms; 'old' style rooms are bright and feature Swedish décor in bright colours; 'new' rooms are more contemporary. Modern and business facilities. Relaxed restaurant and terrace off the main lobby. Offers Swedish and global fare.

SWITZERLAND

SUISSE, SCHWEIZ, SVIZZERA

PROFILE

→ **Area:**
41 284 km²
(15 940 sq mi).

→ **Population:**
7 460 000 (est. 2006), density = 181 per km².

→ **Capital:**
Bern (Berne) (conurbation 349 100 inhabitants).

→ **Currency:**
Swiss Franc (CHF); rate of exchange CHF 1 = € 0.60 = US$ 0.88 (Dec 2007).

→ **Government:**
Federation of 26 cantons with 2 assemblies (National Council and Council of State) forming the Federal Assembly.

→ **Languages:**
German (64% of population), French (20%), Italian (7%) are spoken in all administrative departments, shops, hotels and restaurants. Romansh (1%) in the Grisons canton.

→ **Sepcific public holidays:**
Berchtold's Day (2 January); Good Friday (Friday before Easter); Swiss National Holiday (1 August); St. Stephen's Day (26 December). Thanksgiving (Jeûne Fédéral in French; Bettag in German) is observed in all cantons, except Geneva, on the third Sunday in September; the Geneva canton holds Thanksgiving on the second Thursday in September.

→ **Local Time:**
GMT + 1 hour in winter, GMT+ 2 hours in summer.

→ **Climate**
Temperate continental, varies with altitude – most of the country has cold winters and warm summers (Bern: January: 0°C, July: 19°C).

→ **International dialling Code**
00 41 followed by the area or city code (Geneva: **22**, Bern: **31**, Zurich: **44** or **43**) and then the local number.

→ **Emergency**
Police: ✆ **117**; Medical emergencies: ✆ **144**; Fire Brigade: ✆ **118**.

Anglo-Phone (24 hr information and helpline in English): ✆ **0900 576 444**.

→ **Electricity:**
220 volts AC, 50 Hz; 2-pin round-shaped continental plugs.

→ **Formalities**
Travellers from the European Union (EU), Iceland and the main countries of North and South America need a national identity card or passport (America: passport required) to visit Switzerland for less than three months (tourism or business purpose). For visitors from other countries a visa may be required, in addition to a passport, especially for those wishing to stay for longer than three months. We advise you to check with your embassy before travelling.

Bern
BERNE

Population: 122 300 (conurbation 349 100) – Altitude: 548m

Bern Tourisme

To look at Bern, you'd never believe it a capital city. Small and beautifully proportioned, its old town sits sedately on a spur overlooking the river Aare, at a point where the river bends back on itself, giving a graceful curve to the landscape. UNESCO was so impressed it gave Bern World Heritage status.

In fact, the little city is the best preserved medieval centre north of the Alps, and the layout of the streets has barely changed since the Duke of Zahringen chose the superbly defended site to found a city over eight hundred years ago. Most of the buildings date from the period between the 14 and 16C when Bern was at the height of its power – one good reason why it feels much more human than many other European cities. The cluster of cobbled lanes, surrounded by ornate sandstone arcaded buildings and numerous fountains and wells, give it the feel of a delightfully overgrown village. Albert Einstein felt so secure here that while ostensibly employed as a clerk in the Bern patent office he managed to find the time to work out his Theory of Relativity.

LIVING THE CITY

Bern is a wonderfully compact city. Its **Old Town** stretches eastwards over a narrow peninsula, and is surrounded by the curving **River Aare**. The eastern limit of the Old Town is the **Nydeggbrücke** (bridge); the western end is the **Käfigturm** tower, once a city gate and prison. On the southern side of the Aare lies the small **Kirchenfeld** quarter which houses some impressive museums. The capital's famous brown bears are over the river via the Nydeggbrücke.

PRACTICAL INFORMATION

ARRIVAL-DEPARTURE

Bern-Belp International Airport is 9km southeast of the city. There's a shuttle bus every 30 minutes which takes 20 minutes to the city centre. A taxi will cost around 50CHF.

TRANSPORT

The Bern Card is well worth investing in. It gives unlimited travel, free admission to museums and gardens, and various reductions around the city. It's available from the Tourist Office, museums and hotels, and is valid for 24hr, 48hr or 72hr.

As Bern is small enough to walk around, it requires no more than a super-efficient bus and tram network. A short cable-railway links the Marzili quarter to the Bundeshaus. You can buy your ticket at the bus or tram stop.

EXPLORING BERN

It might sound like a cliché, but Bern is the secret jewel of the Alps. Its spectacular setting takes newcomers aback. Perched aloft on its precipice, surrounded by steep, wooded hills and mountains, who could resist a visit to one of the city's fifty-foot high bridges to watch the gushing grey-green foaming glacier waters of the Aare below? It's not hard to see why UNESCO bestowed its seal of approval upon Bern in 1983. Its perfectly preserved ancient centre comprises superb five-storey red-roofed houses, many of which date back to the 15C, separated by broad, cobbled streets enlivened by equally ancient, brightly coloured fountains. From springtime onwards, the rich sandstone of the buildings is shocked into life by dazzlingly-hued hanging baskets and the heraldic pennants of the Swiss cantons. It's an easy place to explore on foot, and even easier to get your bearings. With dominant landmarks all around your eyes would have to be closed to miss either the river, the Prison Tower, the **Clock Tower**, or the spiralling splendour of the Gothic **Cathedral.**

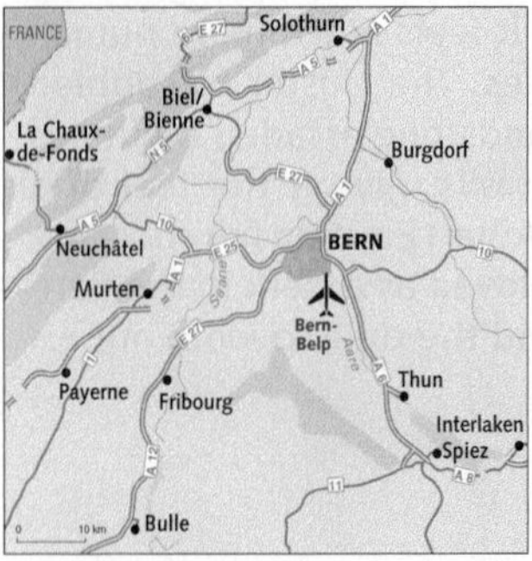

→ TOWERING ACHIEVEMENT

Bern's dramatic Cathedral is the tallest church in Switzerland. It was a long time in creation: over four hundred and fifty years, from 1421 until 1893, when the spire was finally added. The least you can do is pay it a visit, and when you do, don't miss the dramatic 15C stained glass windows in the choir. The tower is unusual in that it still has tower-keepers to look after it. If you're feeling energetic, you can climb to the top yourself, and take in a fine view of the city's curves. There's barely a straight line to be seen as cobbled streets wind every which way, forming fascinating parabolas. Back down at *gasse* level, a little way west from the Cathedral, is the central landmark of Bern, the Clock Tower. Its beautiful astronomical clockface has been keeping time here since 1530 and its elaborate chimes start at four minutes before the hour, when mechanical bears and a crowing cock start their regular procession in front of captivated visitors.

➜ SHOPPING? IT'S COVERED

Appearances can deceive. On first acquaintance, the Swiss capital may hardly seem like a retail hot-spot. But rather surprisingly, this is a city beloved for its shopping opportunities. Not for Bern the antiseptic malls or cloned high streets of less fortunate towns. Instead, it boasts the longest covered shopping promenade in Europe. Sheltering underneath arcades with medieval vaulted roofs covering the pavement below, these dainty shops take the form of small boutiques selling a bewildering assortment of things. And they're entwined with charming cafés and restaurants, many within atmospheric vaulted cellars. Most of these arcades are along an east-west axis running from the Nydeggbrücke ; at its western end a sprinkling of colourful markets brings you back out into the open air.

➜ FEAT OF KLEE

The world of art has a picture-perfect setting here. Until 2005, the main attraction was based at the **Museum of Fine Arts** (on the old town's north side), and with good reason: its globally renowned collection spans the 14C to 20C and includes everything from early Renaissance to Old Master to French Impressionist, not forgetting a broad representation of Switzerland's finest, including Albert Anker and Ferdinand Hodler. Since 2005, many visitors to Bern have been beating a path to the easterly **Schöngrün** quarter, to an audacious and extraordinary wave-shaped museum which emerges from a hillside: The **Zentrum Paul Klee**. This holds a mind-bogglingly amount of paintings (shown in rotation) by Bern's most famous artist, including four thousand works donated by a couple of collectors alone. The building was designed by Renzo Piano, creator of Paris's Pompidou Centre, and also includes a chamber concert hall.

Cross the **Kirchenfeldbrücke** to the southern side of the Aare, and you're in a museum wonderland. There's the **Bern Museum of History** in a building like a grand medieval castle; the **Art Gallery** with its rolling programme of modern art exhibitions; the **Swiss Alpine Museum**, which offers an engrossing look at environmental issues as well as the history, flora and fauna of the Alps; and three other museums with an eclectic focus ranging from human communications, to Swiss rifles to natural history.

Being out of doors is the real clue to getting the most out of Bern. A top walk is beside the Aare through the former artisans' quarter of **Matte**, or, in the eastern section of the main axis through the old town, the streets of **Postgasse** and **Gerechtigkeitsgasse**. Some of the oldest and most appealing of Bern's arcaded buildings are here: many were built as guild houses, and sport decorative motifs proudly pointing out the relevant trade.

→ A FINE TOWN, RELATIVELY SPEAKING

Albert Einstein was a man who loved the outdoors: he would famously shuffle around the streets of Bern, often in green slippers, carrying a net bag for his shopping. He lived on **Kramgasse** for two years from 1903, and it was while here that he began to develop his Theory of Relativity. His small apartment is now a little museum, hung with documents and photos, and containing his writing desk. There's not much doubt the great man would have related strongly to the street in which he lived: in an earlier decade, the poet Goethe called Kramgasse "the most beautiful street in the world".

→ FRINGE BENEFITS

Adding to the beauty and beguilement of Bern's streets are a warren of fringe theatres, many of them tucked comfortably away in the cellars of houses along the thoroughfares of the old town. More conventionally, performance lovers can head for the very visible Stadttheater on centrally located Kornhausplatz, to get a more mainstream dramatic fix. This is Bern's most beautiful theatre, the primary venue for the city's resident opera company and contemporary dance troupe. Another fine show is offered at the Bundesplatz, home of the Swiss Federal Parliament. The fountain in the square has twenty-six jets, each one representing a canton. In the summer months, these shoot skywards every thirty minutes, stopping passers-by in their tracks, and enhancing the centuries-old feeling that in its modest way Bern is just a delightful place to be.

CALENDAR HIGHLIGHTS

It's not often that deepest November plays host to a city's biggest annual bash; even less so when onions are involved. But Bern's November Onion Market takes pride of place in the events calendar. Taking over the old town between the railway station and the Bundesplatz, over fifty tons of onions from all over Switzerland guarantee a tear-jerking celebration. Incongruously, jazz is the other big-hitter in the city. There are four annual festivals, two of which take place in January and February (the Jazz Weekend and the Be-Jazz Winterfestival). The biggest is the week-long International Jazz Festival in May, which features top stars from the worlds of jazz, blues, gospel and Latin. Costumed parades light up the streets at the Fasnacht Carnival in February, while the summer's two top events are the Gurtenfestival (July), a high-powered rock music event in Gurtenpark, over the river to the south of the old town, and Altstadtsommer,

BERN IN…

→ ONE DAY

River walk, Old Town (Cathedral, Clock Tower, arcades), Museum of Fine Arts, cellar fringe theatre

→ TWO DAYS

Zentrum Paul Klee, Einstein's house, Stadttheater

→ THREE DAYS

Repeat some of the delights of the first two days…but more slowly!

a series of concerts in the magical setting of the old town itself. There's also an absorbing Bern Dance Festival in June, in which people arrive from all over the world to give displays of their country's dance styles. You can check it out in bars, restaurants, concert halls and theatres.

EATING OUT

Bern is a great place to sit and enjoy a meal. Pride of place must go to the good range of al fresco venues in the squares of the old town, invariably popular spots to enjoy coffee and cake. Hiding away in the arcades are many delightful dining choices; some of the best for location alone are in vaulted cellars that breathe historic ambience. There's no shortage of international restaurants, either, but if you want to feel what a real Swiss restaurant is like, head for a traditional old-style rustic eatery complete with cow-bells, and sample local dishes like the Berner Platte - a heaving plate of hot and cold meats, served with beans and sauerkraut – or treberwurst, a sausage poached with fermented grape skins. Along with German restaurants, French and Italian Switzerland each has its own distinctive cuisine well represented here, so it's not difficult to go from rösti to risotto and gnocchi, raclette and fondue. And, of course, there's always cheese and chocolate waiting in the wings. A fifteen percent service charge is always added, but it's customary to round the bill up.

→ BEAR NECESSITIES

For good or bad, there are bears in Bern, in the bear pits, just across from the Nydeggbrücke. The city is named after bears, and they've been kept in the city since the early sixteenth century. Despite constant protests from animal rights activists, the bears are a very popular tourist attraction.

→ MOUNTAIN CLIMB

If you fancy a memorable day trip from Bern, the city is handily placed for excursions to the dramatic mountain ranges of the Bernese Oberland. It's only twenty minutes by train to Thun, where lake cruise boats leave from outside the station. You can easily get to Interlaken, but best of all, perhaps, is the unforgettable journey to Europe's highest railway station at Jungfraujoch, an easy day trip.

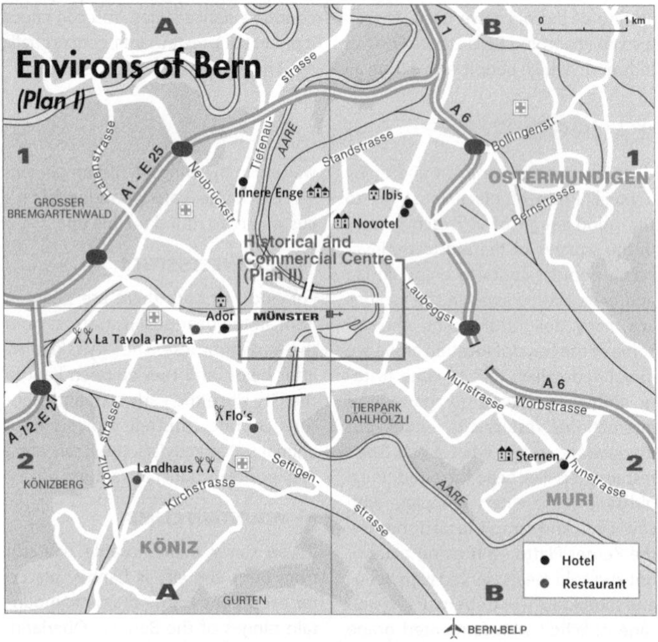

Environs of Bern
(Plan I)

HISTORICAL AND COMMERCIAL CENTRE *Plan II*

Bellevue Palace
Kochergasse 3 ✉ 3001 – ✆ 031 320 45 45
– info@bellevue-palace.ch – Fax 031 311 47 43
– www.bellevue-palace.ch **D2**
115 rm – †360/450 CHF ††470/560 CHF, ☕ 32 CHF – 15 suites
Rest *Bellevue Grill / Bellevue Terrasse* – Menu 72 CHF (lunch)/132 CHF
– Carte 83/166 CHF
♦ Palace ♦ Classic ♦
A touch of elegance pervades the luxury hotel now open again following renovation. The combination of modern and classic make this establishment an exclusive place to stay. Enjoy a beautiful view of the Aare from the terrace of the restaurant.

Allegro
Kornhausstr. 3 ✉ 3013 – ✆ 031 339 55 00
– info@kursaal-bern.ch – Fax 031 339 55 10
– www.kursaal-bern.ch **D1**
171 rm – †169/600 CHF ††209/600 CHF, ☕ 28 CHF
Rest *Meridiano* – see below
Rest *Yù* – *(closed 31 March - 14 April, 28 July - 18 August, 5 - 12 October, 1 - 7 January, Monday and Tuesday)* Menu 28 CHF (lunch)/98 CHF
– Carte 63/133 CHF
Rest *Allegretto* – Carte 48/101 CHF
♦ Business ♦ Modern ♦
A chic hotel providing ultramodern, functional rooms ideal for business guests. In-house casino. Chinese specialities are served in Yù. Friendly atmosphere and contemporary cuisine in the Allegretto.

Hotelbern

Zeughausgasse 9 ✉ 3011 – ✆ 031 329 22 22 – hotelbern@hotelbern.ch – Fax 031 329 22 99 – www.hotelbern.ch **D1**

95 rm – 🛉175/295 CHF 🛉🛉230/340 CHF

Rest *Kurierstube* – *(closed 7 July - 10 August and Sunday)* Menu 35 CHF (lunch)/78 CHF – Carte 57/114 CHF

Rest *7-Stube* – Carte 41/90 CHF

♦ Business ♦ Modern ♦

This centrally located hotel named after the town and canton, is in an old townhouse offering modern, colourful rooms and seminar facilities. The Kurierstube is classic and elegant. The 7-Stube : a rustic restaurant.

Savoy without rest

Neuengasse 26 ✉ 3011 – ✆ 031 311 44 05 – reservation-sar@zghotels.ch – Fax 031 312 19 78 – www.zghotels.ch **C1**

56 rm – 🛉205/320 CHF 🛉🛉275/400 CHF, 25 CHF

♦ Business ♦ Classic ♦

This old townhouse is in Bern's pedestrian zone. The rooms are spacious, clean, tastefully decorated and feature the latest technology.

Belle Epoque

Gerechtigkeitsgasse 18 ✉ 3011 – ✆ 031 311 43 36 – info@belle-epoque.ch – Fax 031 311 39 36 – www.belle-epoque.ch **E1**

17 rm – 🛉195/280 CHF 🛉🛉280/340 CHF, 19 CHF

Rest – *(only snacks at lunch)* Carte 54/91 CHF

♦ Business ♦ Cosy ♦

Touches of art deco accompany you from the lovely reception area through to the tastefully decorated rooms at this charming residence amidst the UNESCO world heritage site. The restaurant serves snacks at midday and roasted specialities from the cart in the evening.

Bristol without rest

Schauplatzgasse 10 ✉ 3011 – ✆ 031 311 01 01 – reception@bristolbern.ch – Fax 031 311 94 79 – www.bristolbern.ch **C2**

92 rm – 🛉200/265 CHF 🛉🛉270/320 CHF

♦ Business ♦ Modern ♦

The old, renovated townhouse has modern rooms with light-coloured solid wood furniture. The small sauna is shared with the Hotel Bern.

Bären without rest

Schauplatzgasse 4 ✉ 3011 – ✆ 031 311 33 67 – reception@baerenbern.ch – Fax 031 311 69 83 – www.baerenbern.ch **C2**

57 rm – 🛉200/265 CHF 🛉🛉270/320 CHF

♦ Business ♦ Modern ♦

Just a stone's throw from the Bundesplatz: hotel rooms with modern furnishings and every facility for the business traveller.

Kreuz

Zeughausgasse 41 ✉ 3011 – ✆ 031 329 95 95 – info@hotelkreuz-bern.ch – Fax 031 329 95 96 – www.hotelkreuz-bern.ch **D1**

100 rm – 🛉125/150 CHF 🛉🛉180/210 CHF

Rest – *(closed 28 June - 4 August, Saturday and Sunday)* Carte 32/71 CHF

♦ Business ♦ Modern ♦

The Kreuz conference hotel offers functional rooms outfitted with grey built-in furnishings. Various meeting rooms are also available.

City am Bahnhof without rest

Bubenbergplatz 7 ✉ 3011 – ✆ 031 311 53 77 – cityab@fhotels.ch – Fax 031 311 06 36 – www.fhotels.ch **C2**

58 rm – 🛉116/180 CHF 🛉🛉148/220 CHF, 18 CHF

♦ Business ♦ Functional ♦

This city hotel is centrally located across from the train station (under renovation until early summer 2008). Contemporary, functional guest rooms.

Meridiano – Hotel Allegro
< Bern and mountains,

Kornhausstr. 3 ✉ 3013 – ✆ 031 339 52 45
– info@kursaal-bern.ch – Fax 031 339 55 10 – www.kursaal-bern.ch
closed 6 - 28 July, 1 - 14 January, 3 - 18 February, Saturday lunch, Sunday and Monday
Rest – Menu 54 CHF (lunch)/165 CHF – Carte 92/161 CHF **D1**
◆ Modern ◆ Elegant ◆
Modern design and the unique terrace with panoramic views distinguish this restaurant, located on the 6th floor of the Hotel Allegro. Contemporary cuisine.

Mille Sens

Bubenbergplatz 9 (in the market hall) ✉ 3011 – ✆ 031 329 29 29
– info@millesens.ch – Fax 031 329 29 91 – www.millesens.ch
closed 3 weeks July, Sunday and Bank Holidays **C2**
Rest – *(closed dinner from June - August except on Saturday) (set menu only at lunch)* Menu 64 CHF (lunch)/98 CHF – Carte 78/118 CHF
Rest *Marktplatz* – Menu 70 CHF (dinner) – Carte 53/98 CHF
◆ Modern ◆ Fashionable ◆
In a centre with numerous shops is this restaurant with its modern decor and contemporary cuisine. The simple Bistro Marktplatz with a small, reasonably priced menu.

Kirchenfeld

Thunstr. 5 ✉ 3005 – ✆ 031 351 02 78 – restaurant@kirchenfeld.ch
– Fax 031 351 84 16 – www.kirchenfeld.ch
closed Sunday and Monday **E2**
Rest – Menu 56 CHF (lunch)/62 CHF – Carte 50/90 CHF
◆ Modern ◆ Brasserie ◆
Stucco and antiques provide a stylish atmosphere to this restaurant serving delicious cuisine ranging from traditional to modern.

Wein & Sein (Beat Blum)

Münstergasse 50 ✉ 3011 – ✆ 031 311 98 44 – blum@weinundsein.ch
– www.weinundsein.ch
closed 20 July - 11 August, Sunday and Monday **E2**
Rest – *(dinner only) (booking essential) (set menu only)* Menu 92 CHF
Spec. Sommerwild (June - July). Sauerbraten vom Kalbstafelspitz mit luftigem Härdöpfelstock. Marillenknödel (spring).
◆ Modern ◆ Trendy ◆
This lovely restaurant, with its vaulted ceiling, offers a 4-course menu. The extensive wine list offers options to complement all meals. Pleasant outdoor dining area on Münstergasse.

Flo's

Weissenbühlweg 40 ✉ 3007 – ✆ 031 372 05 55 – info@flos-restaurant.ch
– Fax 031 372 05 54 – www.flos-restaurant.ch
closed 29 June - 10 August, 23 December - 13 January, Sunday, Monday and Tuesday **A2**
Rest – *(booking advisable) (dinner only)* Carte 59/86 CHF
◆ Modern ◆Fashionable ◆
A modern restaurant offering the atmosphere of a culinary class, located away from the city centre. Two siblings prepare fresh dishes from fresh market ingredients. Midday cooking classes offered.

Schwellenmätteli - Terrasse

Dalmaziquai 11 ✉ 3005 – ✆ 031 350 50 01 – info@schwellenmaetteli.ch
– Fax 031 350 50 02 – www.schwellenmaetteli.ch **D2**
Rest – *(booking advisable)* Carte 47/91 CHF
Rest *Casa* – *(closed Monday)* Menu 33 CHF (lunch) – Carte 49/92 CHF
◆ Modern ◆ Trendy ◆
This modern restaurant with modern cuisine has a beautiful setting on the Aare. The restaurant's terrace, which extends over the river, offers unparalleled views. The Casa is a fashionable Italian restaurant.

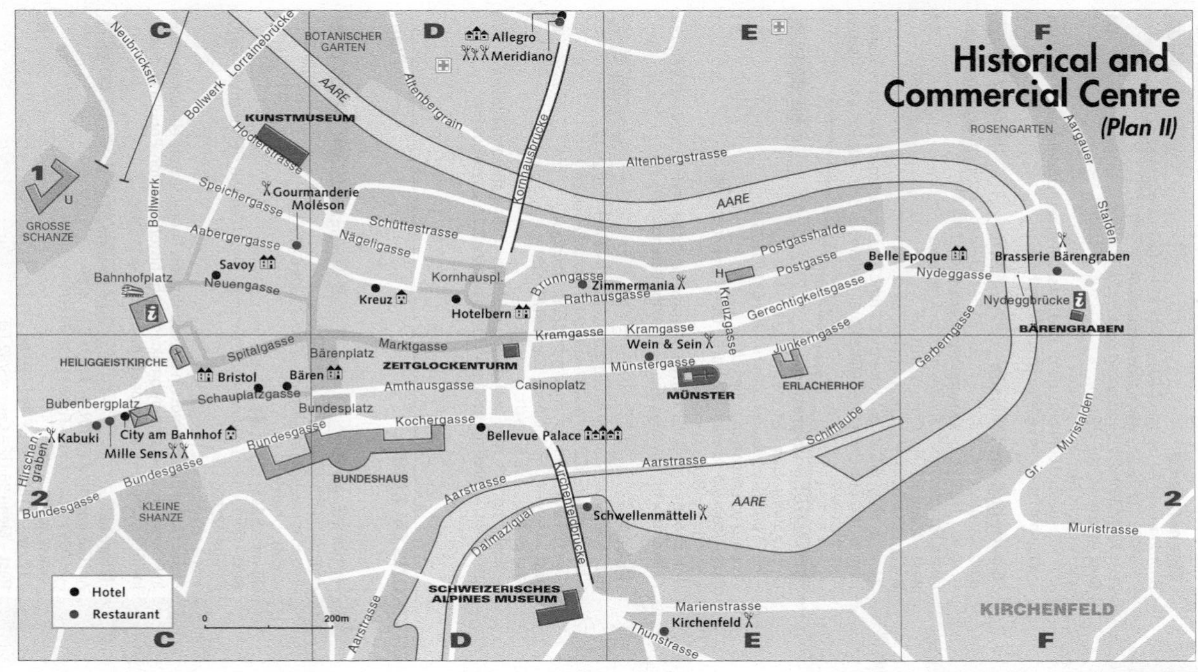
Historical and Commercial Centre
(Plan II)
C
D
E
F
1
2
Allegro
Meridiano
BOTANISCHER GARTEN
Neubrückstr.
Lorrainebrücke
Bollwerk
AARE
Altenbergrain
Kornhausbrücke
KUNSTMUSEUM
Hodlerstrasse
Altenbergstrasse
ROSENGARTEN
Aargauer
Stalden
GROSSE SCHANZE
Speichergasse
Gourmanderie Moléson
Schüttestrasse
Aabergergasse
Nägeligasse
Postgasshalde
Belle Epoque
Brasserie Bärengraben
Savoy
Bahnhofplatz
Neuengasse
Kornhauspl.
Brunngasse
Zimmermania
Rathausgasse
Postgasse
Nydeggasse
Kreuz
Hotelbern
Kreuzgasse
Gerechtigkeitsgasse
Nydeggbrücke
BÄRENGRABEN
Kramgasse
Wein & Sein
Marktgasse
Spitalgasse
Bärenplatz
Junkerngasse
Gerberngasse
HEILIGGEISTKIRCHE
ZEITGLOCKENTURM
Münstergasse
Bristol
Bären
Amthausgasse
Casinoplatz
MÜNSTER
ERLACHERHOF
Schauplatzgasse
Bubenbergplatz
Bundesplatz
Kochergasse
Bundesgasse
Kabuki
City am Bahnhof
Bellevue Palace
Schifflaube
Gr. Muristalden
Hirschengraben
Mille Sens
Aarstrasse
BUNDESHAUS
KLEINE SCHANZE
Dalmaziquai
Kirchenfeldbrücke
Schwellenmätteli
Muristrasse
Hotel
Restaurant
0
200m
SCHWEIZERISCHES ALPINES MUSEUM
Marienstrasse
Kirchenfeld
Thunstrasse
KIRCHENFELD

Zimmermania

VISA MC

Brunngasse 19 ✉ 3011 – ✆ 031 311 15 42 – info@zimmermania.ch – Fax 031 312 28 22 – www.zimmermania.net
closed July, Monday, Sunday and Bank Holidays **D1**
Rest – Carte 44/101 CHF
♦ Traditional ♦ Bistro ♦
This 150 year-old Bern bistro is located in a small street in the old part of the town. Traditional fare is served in a cosy atmosphere.

Gourmanderie Moléson

VISA MC

Aarbergergasse 24 ✉ 3011 – ✆ 031 311 44 63 – info@moleson-bern.ch – Fax 031 312 01 45 – www.moleson-bern.ch
closed Saturday lunch, Sunday and Bank Holidays **C1**
Rest – Menu 59 CHF – Carte 62/101 CHF
♦ Traditional ♦ Brasserie ♦
"Dine as they did in grandmother's time" is the motto of this cosy restaurant in the old town. Specialities are traditional Bern cuisine and Alsatian Flammkuchen.

Brasserie Bärengraben

VISA MC AE

Grosser Muristalden 1 ✉ 3006 – ✆ 031 331 42 18 – info@brasseriebaerengraben.ch – Fax 031 331 25 60 – www.brasseriebaerengraben.ch **F1**
Rest – *(booking advisable)* Menu 60 CHF – Carte 40/85 CHF
♦ Bistro ♦ Brasserie ♦
One of the most popular and typical brasseries in the city is located in the historic tollhouse on the Nydegg Bridge, near the Bärengraben.

Kabuki

A/C VISA MC AE

Bubenbergplatz 9 (in the market hall) ✉ 3011 – ✆ 031 329 29 19 – kabuki@kabuki.ch – Fax 031 329 29 17 – www.kabuki.ch
closed 28 July - 3 August, Sunday and Bank Holidays **C2**
Rest – Menu 85 CHF (dinner) – Carte 41/99 CHF
♦ Japanese ♦ Exotic ♦
A sleek, modern style and a long sushi bar define the atmosphere in this restaurant, located downstairs in the market hall. Japanese cuisine.

ENVIRONS OF BERN *Plan I*

Innere Enge

rm P VISA MC AE

Engestr. 54 ✉ 3012 – ✆ 031 309 61 11 – reservation-ieb@zghotels.ch – Fax 031 309 61 12 – www.zghotels.ch **A1**
26 rm – †245/320 CHF ††310/400 CHF, ☐ 25 CHF
Rest – *(closed Sunday dinner from October - May)* Menu 50 CHF (lunch)/85 CHF – Carte 48/106 CHF
♦ Business ♦ Classic ♦
A quiet hotel that is almost in the countryside. Rooms feature elegant furniture in Provençal colours. Enjoy breakfast in the historic pavilion. Popular jazz cellar. Inviting : Café and restaurant in bistro-brasserie style.

Novotel

rm A/C rm VISA MC AE

Am Guisanplatz 2 ✉ 3014 – ✆ 031 339 09 09 – h5009@accor.com – Fax 031 339 09 10 – www.novotel.com **B1**
112 rm – †185/280 CHF ††199/280 CHF, ☐ 25 CHF
Rest – Menu 36 CHF – Carte 46/82 CHF
♦ Chain hotel ♦ Modern ♦
Next to the Bern Expo site and not far from the new Wankdorf Stadium, this hotel offers modern, well-equipped rooms. Bright, modern restaurant. The bar, decorated in its original style, celebrates the 1954 world champions.

Sternen

Thunstr. 80 ✉ 3074 Muri – ☎ 031 950 71 11 – info@sternenmuri.ch – Fax 031 950 71 00 – www.sternenmuri.ch **B2**

44 rm – 140/240 CHF 190/300 CHF

Rest – *(closed 19 July - 3 August and 22 December - 6 January)* Menu 45 CHF (lunch)/50 CHF – Carte 50/88 CHF

◆ Traditional ◆ Functional ◆

This traditional Bern guesthouse offers modern, functional rooms in both the main building and the extension. Läubli and restaurant offer contemporary cuisine.

Ador

Laupenstr. 15 ✉ 3001 – ☎ 031 388 01 11 – info@hotelador.ch – Fax 031 388 01 10 – www.hotelador.ch

closed 21 December - 3 January **A2**

52 rm – 125/219 CHF 170/308 CHF

Rest – *(closed Saturday, Sunday and Bank Holidays)* Carte 35/70 CHF

◆ Business ◆ Modern ◆

This hotel near the train station caters specifically to business travellers and offers modern, technologically functional rooms.

Ibis without rest

Guisanplatz 4 ✉ 3014 – ☎ 031 335 12 00 – h5007@accor.com – Fax 031 335 12 10 – www.ibishotel.com **B1**

96 rm – 101/165 CHF 101/165 CHF, 15 CHF

◆ Chain hotel ◆ Minimalist ◆

A hotel offering simple, practical and reasonably-priced accommodation with brightly furnished, clean rooms. 24-hour snack service at the bar.

Landhaus - Rôtisserie with rm

Schwarzenburgstr. 134 ✉ 3097 Liebefeld – ☎ 031 971 07 58 – info@landhaus-liebefeld.ch – Fax 031 972 02 49 – www.landhaus-liebefeld.ch **A2**

6 rm – 170 CHF 240 CHF

Rest – *(closed Sunday) (booking advisable)* Menu 56 CHF (lunch)/116 CHF – Carte 57/115 CHF

Rest *Gaststube* – *(closed Sunday)* Menu 50 CHF (dinner) – Carte 51/94 CHF

◆ Modern ◆ Formal ◆

This lovely rotisserie is located in a former country bailiwick. Contemporary cuisine is served. A cosy garden terrace. This restaurant serves both classic and seasonal cuisine in tasteful, light, modern rooms. Tasteful, bright and modern guest rooms.

La Tavola Pronta

Laupenstr. 57 ✉ 3008 – ☎ 031 382 66 33 – Fax 031 381 56 93 – www.latavolapronta.ch

closed August, Saturday lunch and Sunday **A2**

Rest – *(booking advisable)* Menu 55 CHF (lunch)/90 CHF – Carte 59/111 CHF

◆ Italian ◆ Cosy ◆

This small restaurant, tucked away in a cosy cellar, has a lovely dining room with a fireplace and serves Italian specialities in a charming atmosphere.

GENEVA

GENEVE

Population (est. 2005): 198 500 (conurbation 698 000) - Altitude: 375m

P. Wysocki/HEMIS.fr

In just about every detail except efficiency, Geneva exudes a distinctly Latin feel. It boasts a proud cosmopolitanism, with about one in three of its residents being non-Swiss, drawn here by the presence of the largest UN office outside New York, as well as a whole swathe of international organisations dealing with every human concern under the – frequently dazzling - sun. Its renowned *savoir-vivre* challenges that of equally swishy Zurich, while it also enjoys cultural ties with Paris, and is often called 'the twenty first arrondissement'.

It could hardly have a better setting. It's strung around the sparkling shores of Europe's largest alpine lake. Enter the city on that lake and you have mountains to either side – take your pick from Jura or Alps. There are manicured city parks and the world's tallest fountain, the bisecting River Rhone and the world's longest bench on which to sit and take it all in. Geneva is renowned for its orderliness: the Reformation was born here under the austere preachings of Calvin, and the city has been a place of refuge to Europeans for at least five centuries, providing sanctuary for religious dissidents, revolutionaries and elopers. Hell-raising poets, too, in the shape of Byron and Shelley. Nowadays, new arrivals tend to be of a more conservative persuasion, as they go their elegant way balancing international affairs alongside *la belle vie.*

LIVING THE CITY

Geneva may be in Switzerland, but it's almost totally surrounded by France. The **River Rhône** snakes through the centre, dividing the city into **the right bank** (north side, the **'international quarter'**), and the **left bank** (south side, the **old town**). To the east of Geneva is **Lake Léman** (Lake Geneva in English), while the **Jura** mountains dominate the right bank, and the **Alps** form a backdrop to the left bank. Geneva's **international airport** is to the north-west of the city, while the popular suburb of **Carouge** is to the south.

PRACTICAL INFORMATION

ARRIVAL-DEPARTURE

Geneva International Airport is just 4km from the city centre and a taxi will cost around 35CHF. Trains depart every 15min and take just 6min. Bus 10 runs every 10min.

TRANSPORT

Geneva is served by an efficient public transport network which, true to the cliché, runs like clockwork. There are various timed cards depending on how much travelling you intend to do: for one hour, one day, or 9am-midnight.

A useful alternative: if you're making several trips, pick up a 48- or 72-hour Geneva Transport Card from the tourist office for unlimited use of the city's trams, trains, buses and boats. It also offers free admission to many top museums and attractions, plus reductions in some restaurants and shops.

There's nothing better than a cycle ride along the long quaysides by the lake. The city encourages pedal power, and from May to October bikes can be borrowed for free. More information from Geneva Tourism on Rue du Mont-Blanc.

EXPLORING GENEVA

It may be one of the most famous cities in the world, in one of the world's most beautiful locations, but Geneva is actually pretty small, not much bigger than a medium-sized town. The fame that goes before it stems mostly from all those organisations based here whose tentacles embrace the world. And, of course, everyone knows about the Lake. This is what makes Geneva extra special, giving it that sense of a bygone seaside resort. The huge expanse of water is a perfect foil for the majesty of the surrounding mountains. Its mirror-like surface is as flat as a pancake, save for an iconic landmark that has first-time visitors drawing breath before the search for superlatives. The **Jet d'Eau** is a stirring sight from the aeroplane window coming in to land. The world's tallest fountain, it shoots water with incredible force 140m into the air, and when the sun shines creates a shimmering rainbow. Watch out, though: spectators on the adjacent pier get a regular spraying.

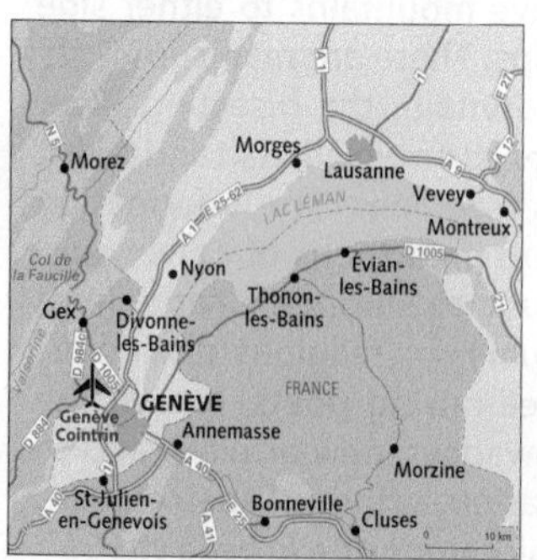

Its forceful presence is at odds with the quiet and measured calm of the medieval old town, which lies nearby along the left bank. Here, the cobbled streets invariably lead to the dominant **St Peter's Cathedral**, sitting proudly atop its hill. This medieval monolith has Romanesque and Gothic origins hidden behind a neoclassical façade; its huge rose window is a glowing gem in the sunlight. You can go from the highs (via steep spiral steps for a look at the bell tower and awesome views of the lake and mountains) to the subterranean lows (an underground archaeological site that traces the cathedral's early foundations).

→ SEEDS OF TIME

Back up at lake level, and standing in an enviable position close to the water's edge, is a permanent tribute to 'Swiss timing' - the **Floral Clock**. This is a favourite spot for clicking cameras. It's certainly colourful: over six thousand dazzling flowers and plants are arranged in new displays each spring and autumn in celebration of local watch-making. You won't need to check your timepiece to get to one of the old town's most fascinating attractions – **Maison Tavel** is just a short stroll south. This is the place to visit to get an idea of what Geneva looked like in the Middle Ages. Set in the city's oldest house, dating back to the fourteenth century, there are displays of antique furniture, silverware and tapestries spanning six hundred years. Highlight is a seven-metre-long model of Geneva pre-1850. It took the very patient Auguste Magnin eighteen years to make it out of zinc and copper.

→ WALL OF DEFIANCE

Magnin's honest endeavours would have met with the approval of Jean Calvin, the father of the 16C Protestant movement who lived and lectured in Geneva, and set in stone the city's 'work ethic' image that lives on to this day. There are two lasting memorials to him: one is the recently opened **International Museum of the Reformation,** near the Cathedral, which is chock-full of objects, books and paintings about the religious upheavals of the time; and then there's the breathtaking, hundred-yard long **Reformation Wall** in the **Parc des Bastions**, a dazzlingly white construction, a century old, with a fifteen-foot high statue of Calvin at its heart. If all this earnestness has left you feeling the need to chill out a bit, then the park itself is an ideal place. Its wide, tree-lined avenues are tailor-made for strolling, stopping off to watch chess being played on giant boards, while locals jog along trying to decide which of the thousand restaurants in town will play host to their expense account tonight.

For the ultimate Genevan chill-out, the coolest place in town in the summer months is **Bains des Paquis** on the Right Bank – just look for the soaring white lighthouse. Some forty years ago, this area had a bad boy reputation forged by its proximity to the dodgy Paquis district. Today, not only is Paquis the multicultural buzzword for boho chic, but the Bains itself is now a fun-filled pier and beach zone that entices a veritable league of nations to sample its charms. This is where, whether Rastafarian or restaurateur, the world comes to hang around, to graze on a lazy lunchtime picnic, read a paperback, swim in the lake, or just enjoy the sun. Beaches, boardwalk or rocks – take your pick of where you want to flop down. When it gets chilly, a big draw is the state-of-the-art spa complex on the pier, where you can steam in the hammams, sauna or solarium.

→ DRAWN AWAY

There comes a time when everyone has to forego the delights of the Lake, and Geneva has a sprinkling of top museums to investigate.

Modernists should head for **MAMCO – the Museum of Contemporary Art** – which, suitably enough, is housed in a refitted industrial factory from the 1950s. It puts on a whole raft of fresh, cutting edge exhibitions that cover a range of mediums. Across town is the more conservative but equally riveting **Art & History Museum**, a cavernous place that makes the most of its space with paintings, sculpture, arty room interiors and medieval weaponry. Roman pottery and Egyptian antiquities are popular attractions, as are masterpieces from the likes of Van Gogh, Rembrandt and Monet, but the highlight is a fifteenth century altarpiece by Konrad Witz. Meanwhile, right in the centre of the old town, on **Place Neuve**, the **Rath Museum** is dedicated to fine arts and is well known for putting on excellent temporary exhibitions. For something completely different, the **International Red Cross Museum**, way up north on the right bank near the massive HQ of the United Nations, is a thought-provoking museum with multimedia displays that highlights the work through the decades of the world's largest humanitarian network, started by Genevan philanthropist Henri Dunant in 1864. The soundtracks, photos and films that accompany this sometimes-harrowing exhibition enhance the Red Cross's compelling story. That other Swiss speciality, timekeeping, is celebrated in a treasure trove of ticks and tocks at **Patek Philippe Museum**, next to the Museum of Contemporary Art. On show is everything from exquisite seventeenth century pocket watches to stylish art nouveau creations.

→ THE GENEVA UNCONVENTION

When Genevans seek a musical fix, their natural port of call is the **Grand Theatre**, in the heart of Place Neuve, which is internationally famous for its world-class theatre, ballet, dance and opera. Those looking for more edgy material have a pretty impressive choice: **Salle Centrale** puts on everything from art-house movies to improvised plays; **Theatre du Grütli** takes the term 'experimental' to new levels in its theatre and comedy productions; and **L'Usine** – an old gold-roughing factory – contributes art happenings, dance nights and weird cabaret to Geneva's cultural map.

CALENDAR HIGHLIGHTS

One event stands head and shoulders above any other here: the Escalade. This atmospheric procession through the old town over the weekend closest to 12 December commemorates the battle to defend the Protestant city against the Catholic House of Savoy. The attack, in 1602, was repulsed, and Geneva's celebratory costumed procession takes place by the light of

GENEVA IN…

→ ONE DAY

St Peter's Cathedral, Maison Tavel, Jet d'Eau. Reformation Wall

→ TWO DAYS

MAMCO (or Art & History Museum), a stroll along the edge of the lake, a trip to Carouge

→ THREE DAYS

A day in Paquis, with a lazy time at the Bains des Paquis

torches to the sound of drums, fifes, trumpets and musketeers opening fire on horseback. It can get quite noisy. The volume's pretty high in August, too, when another big event, The Geneva Fête, kicks off. Days of music, shows, dancing and gastronomy are concluded with a firework display that lights up the lakeside. Other summer highlights include June's Bol d'Or Race, when the peace of Lake Geneva succumbs to over six hundred boats and yachts contesting the Golden Cup; the Fête de la Musique, also in June, which sees open-air stages in many streets and squares for a riot of concerts featuring every kind of musical form; and August's Fêtes de Geneve, when the streets are again awash with colour for fireworks, parties and parades (and it's all free!). There's more of a 'Protestant friendly' air about the Antiques and Bric-A-Brac Fair (October) in the Plaine de Plainpalais, an immense showcase of dealers' stalls by the Rhône. But the temperature rises again in October for the Flamenco Festival, a week-long celebration that brings the spirit of Seville to the Swiss Alps.

EATING OUT

One thing's for sure: you won't be hard pressed to find an eating establishment in Geneva. All those big international organisations take a bit of feeding, and so you'll find over a thousand dining establishments in the city and its surrounds. If you're looking for elegance, then head to a restaurant overlooking the lake; if your tastes are more for the 'nonna' style of home-cooked Sardinian fare, make tracks for the charming Italianate suburb of Carouge just to the south, where little cafés serve up delicious antipasti, risotto and fresh fish. If you haven't an expense account to blow, but fancy something with an international accent, then Paquis has it all, and at a fair price. This trendy part of Geneva offers flavours on a truly global scale from Moroccan to Mexican, from Jordanian to Japanese. The old town is the place for Swiss staples, packed as it is with delightful brasseries and alpine-style chalets: you can't go wrong here if your fancy is for fondue, or a heartily rustic papet vaudois (cream-leek casserole). Longeole (pork sausage enlivened with cumin and fennel) is a popular choice for meat eaters. Rösti, of course, is ubiquitous. For a bit of extra atmosphere, head downstairs to dine in a vaulted cellar with flickering candles. Though restaurants include a service charge of fifteen per cent, it's customary to leave a tip if you were happy with the service – round up the bill or give the waiter a tip between five and ten per cent.

→ CAROUSE IN CAROUGE

For Geneva with a true Latin heart, take a tram to Carouge. From 1754 till 1816, this now hip suburb was part of the kingdom of Sardinia. Designed by Piedmontese architects, its chessboard pattern of blocks enclosing courtyard gardens provides a wonderfully understated charm, enhanced by funky bars, boutiques, Italian cafés and artists' workshops.

→ CHILLON OUT

Byron and Shelley visited Geneva in 1816, and the Lord wrote a poem afterwards about the four-year imprisonment of Prior Bonivard in the fabulous castle of Chillon overlooking Lake Geneva. You can see the castle, and others, on an idyllic lake cruise. Vessels – some of them paddlesteamers – serve forty-two piers, and are a delightfully relaxing way of getting to see many of the places around the lake.

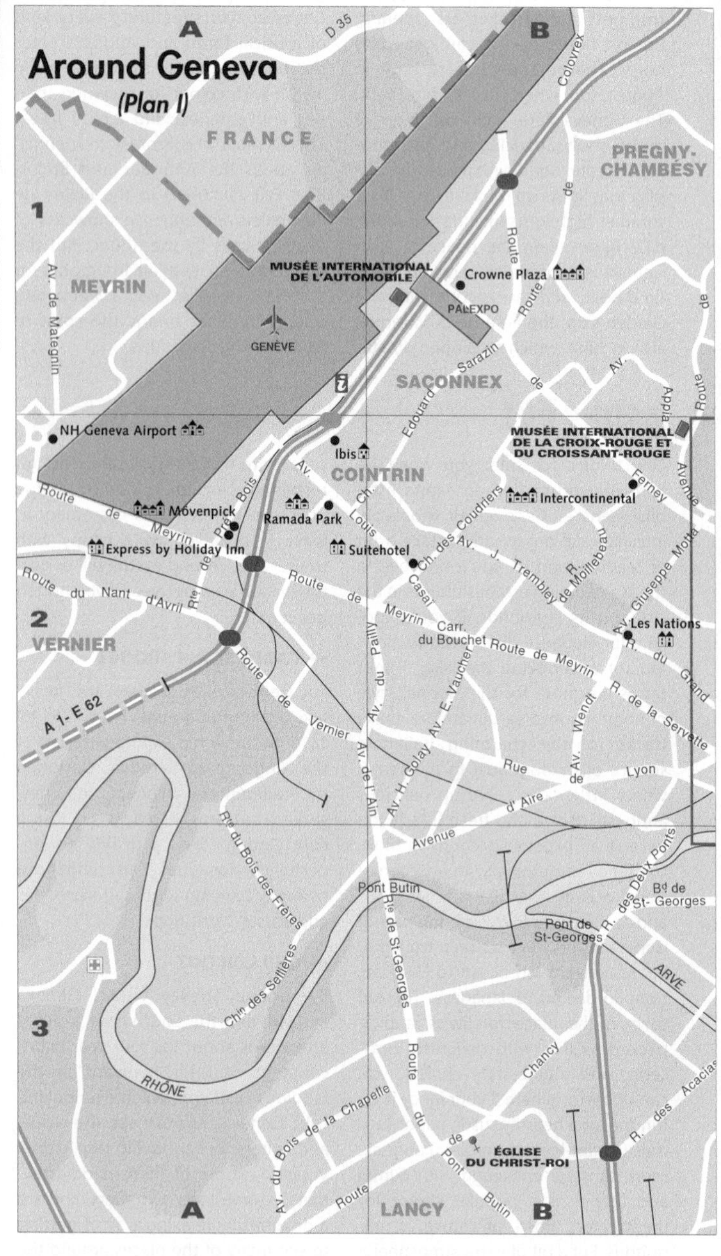

Around Geneva
(Plan I)
A
B
1
2
3
FRANCE
MEYRIN
PREGNY-CHAMBÉSY
SACONNEX
COINTRIN
VERNIER
LANCY
MUSÉE INTERNATIONAL DE L'AUTOMOBILE
GENÈVE
PALEXPO
Crowne Plaza
NH Geneva Airport
Ibis
Mövenpick
Ramada Park
Express by Holiday Inn
Suitehotel
Intercontinental
Les Nations
MUSÉE INTERNATIONAL DE LA CROIX-ROUGE ET DU CROISSANT-ROUGE
ÉGLISE DU CHRIST-ROI
D 35
Colovrex
A 1- E 62
Av. de Mategnin
Route de Meyrin
Route du Nant d'Avril
Route de Vernier
Rte. de Pré Bois
Av. Louis Casaï
Ch. Edouard Sarazin
Ch. des Coudriers
Av. J. Trembley
R. de Moillebeau
Av. Giuseppe Motta
Avenue de France
Ferney
Av. Appia
Carr. du Bouchet
Av. du Pailly
Av. E. Vaucher
Av. H. Golay
Av. de l'Ain
Av. Wendt
R. du Grand
R. de la Servette
Rue de Lyon
Avenue d'Aire
Rte du Bois des Frères
Pont Butin
Rte de St-Georges
Pont de St-Georges
R. des Deux Ponts
Bd de St- Georges
ARVE
Chin des Sellières
RHÔNE
Route du Pont Butin
Route de Chancy
Av. du Bois de la Chapelle
R. des Acacias

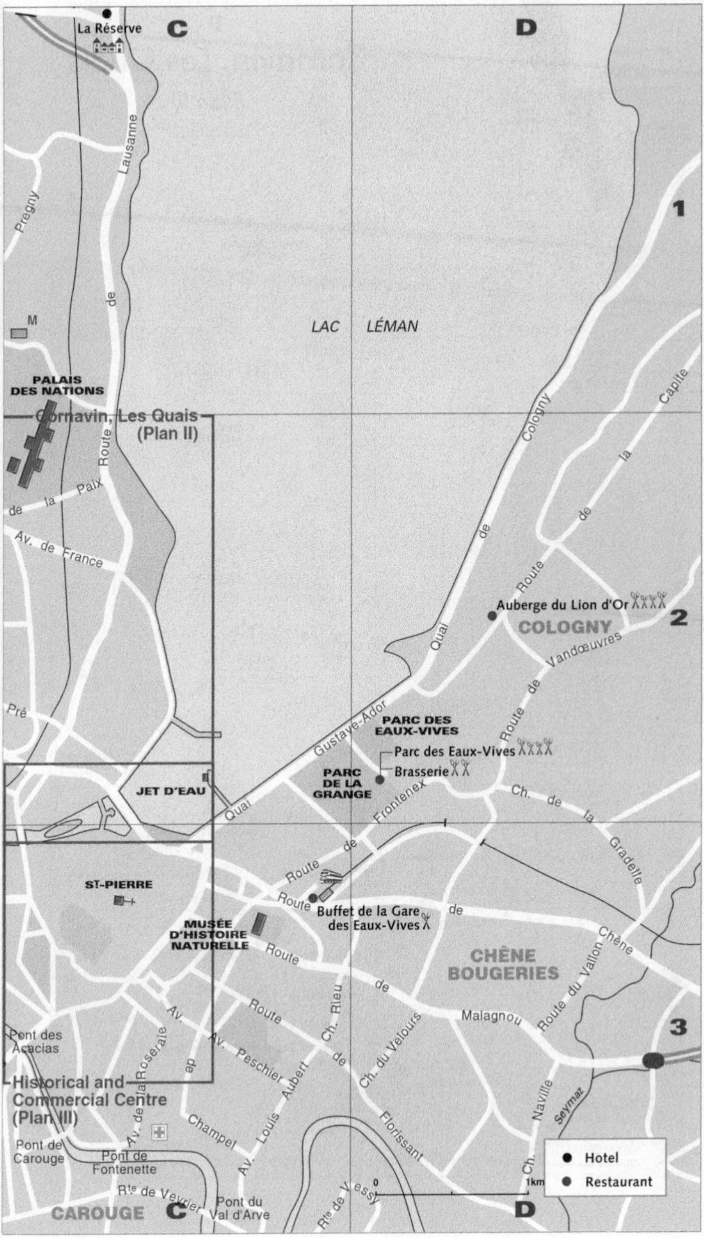

C
D
La Réserve
Route de Lausanne
Pregny
M
LAC LÉMAN
PALAIS DES NATIONS
Cornavin, Les Quais (Plan II)
Route de la Paix
Av. de France
Pré
JET D'EAU
Quai Gustave-Ador
Quai de Cologny
Route de la Capite
Auberge du Lion d'Or XXXX
COLOGNY
Route de Vandœuvres
PARC DES EAUX-VIVES
Parc des Eaux-Vives XXXX
Brasserie XX
PARC DE LA GRANGE
Route de Frontenex
Ch. de la Gradelle
ST-PIERRE
Buffet de la Gare des Eaux-Vives X
Route de Chêne
MUSÉE D'HISTOIRE NATURELLE
Route de Malagnou
CHÊNE BOUGERIES
Route du Vallon
Route de Florissant
Ch. Rieu
Ch. du Velours
Av. Peschier
Av. Louis Aubert
Av. de la Roseraie
Pont des Acacias
Historical and Commercial Centre (Plan III)
Champel
Ch. Naville
Seymaz
Pont de Carouge
Pont de Fontenette
Rte de Veyrier
Pont du Val d'Arve
Rte de Vessy
CAROUGE
1
2
3
0
1km
● Hotel
● Restaurant

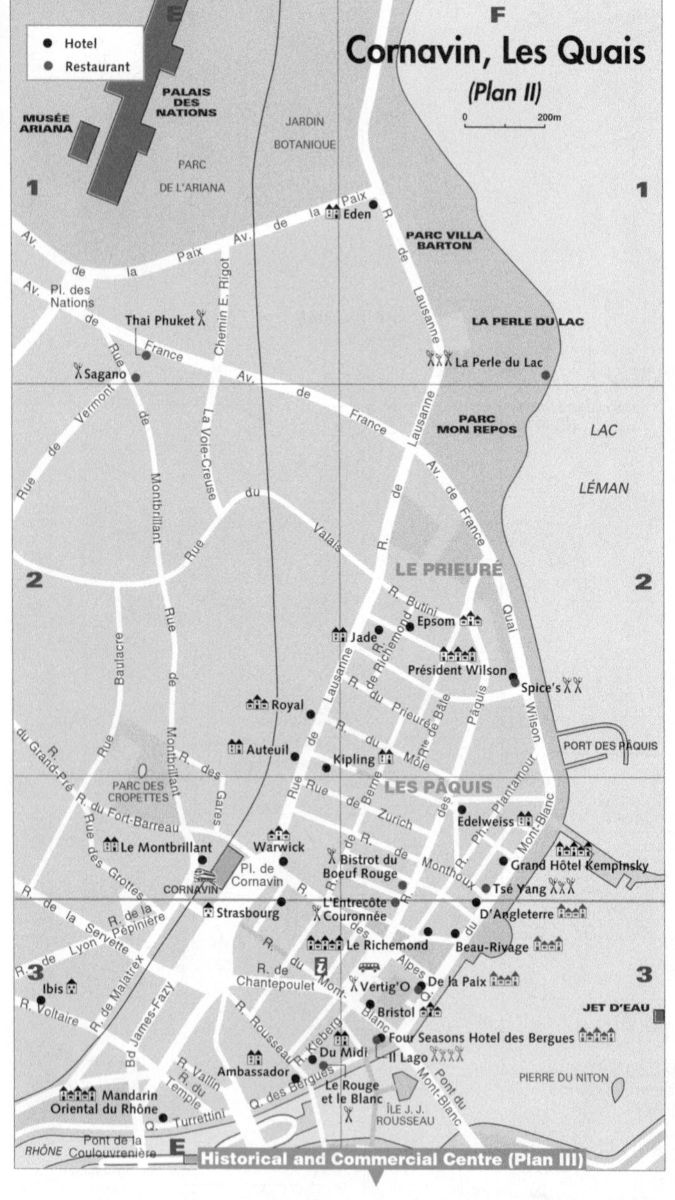
Cornavin, Les Quais
(Plan II)
Hotel
Restaurant
0
200m
PALAIS DES NATIONS
MUSÉE ARIANA
JARDIN BOTANIQUE
PARC DE L'ARIANA
PARC VILLA BARTON
LA PERLE DU LAC
PARC MON REPOS
LAC LÉMAN
LE PRIEURÉ
LES PÂQUIS
PORT DES PÂQUIS
PARC DES CROPETTES
CORNAVIN
JET D'EAU
PIERRE DU NITON
ÎLE J. J. ROUSSEAU
RHÔNE
Eden
Thai Phuket
Sagano
La Perle du Lac
Epsom
Jade
Président Wilson
Spice's
Royal
Auteuil
Kipling
Edelweiss
Le Montbrillant
Warwick
Bistrot du Boeuf Rouge
Grand Hôtel Kempinsky
Tsé Yang
Strasbourg
L'Entrecôte Couronnée
D'Angleterre
Le Richemond
Beau-Rivage
Ibis
Vertig'O
De la Paix
Bristol
Four Seasons Hotel des Bergues
Du Midi
Il Lago
Ambassador
Le Rouge et le Blanc
Mandarin Oriental du Rhône
Av. de la Paix
Pl. des Nations
Av. de France
Chemin E. Rigot
R. de Lausanne
Rue de Vermont
Rue de Montbrillant
La Voie-Creuse
Rue du Valais
R. Butini
R. de Richemond
R. du Prieuré
Rte de Bâle
R. du Môle
Quai Wilson
Pâquis
Rue Baulacre
R. des Gares
Rue de Berne
Rue de Zurich
R. de Monthoux
R. Ph. Plantamour
Quai du Mont-Blanc
R. du Grand-Pré
R. du Fort-Barreau
Rue des Grottes
Pl. de Cornavin
R. de la Servette
R. de la Pépinière
R. de Lyon
R. Voltaire
R. de Malatrex
Bd James-Fazy
R. de Chantepoulet
R. du Mont-Blanc
R. des Alpes
R. Rousseau
R. Kleberg
R. Vallin
R. du Temple
Q. des Bergues
Q. Turrettini
Pont de la Coulouvrenière
Pont du Mont-Blanc
Historical and Commercial Centre (Plan III)

Four Seasons Hôtel des Bergues

33 quai des Bergues ✉ 1201 – ✆ 022 908 70 00
– info.gen@fourseasons.com – Fax 022 908 74 00
– www.fourseasons.com/geneva **F3**
83 rm – †575/895 CHF ††635/945 CHF, ☕ 40 CHF – 20 suites
Rest *Il Lago* – see below

◆ Palace ◆ Stylish ◆

Recently renovated, the oldest and most luxurious hotel in Geneva (1834) offers lounges adorned with gleaming marble, an elegant bar, guestrooms and suites decorated in Empire style. Excellent service.

Mandarin Oriental du Rhône

1 quai Turrettini ✉ 1201 – ✆ 022 909 00 00
– mogva-enquiry@mohg.com – Fax 022 909 00 10
– www.mandarinoriental.com **E3**
180 rm – †570/1150 CHF ††790/1150 CHF, ☕ 41 CHF – 10 suites
Rest *Café Rafael* – ✆ 022 909 00 05 – Menu 61 CHF – Carte 69/118 CHF

◆ Grand Luxury ◆ Art Deco ◆

This centrally located hotel is situated on the right bank of the River Rhône, the course of which is attractively depicted here. Magnificent rooms adorned with Art Deco furnishings and smart marble bathrooms. A pretty riverside terrace at the Café Rafael.

Le Richemond

Jardin Brunswick ✉ 1201 – ✆ 022 715 70 00
– reservations.lerichemond@roccofortecollection.com – Fax 022 715 70 01
– www.roccofortecollection.com **F3**
99 rm – †695/1140 CHF ††695/1140 CHF, ☕ 42 CHF – 10 suites
Rest *Sapori* – Menu 65 CHF (lunch) – Carte 106/169 CHF

◆ Grand Luxury ◆ Modern ◆

Opened in 1863 and completely renovated in 2007, this hotel offers a choice of standard rooms, junior suites and suites decorated in chic, contemporary style. Those on the upper floors have a view of the lake and the Jet d'Eau. Italian specialities, a smart, modern decor and an attractive terrace overlooking the Brunswick Garden are the highlights of the Sapori.

Président Wilson

47 quai Wilson ✉ 1201 – ✆ 022 906 66 66
– sales@hotelpwilson.com – Fax 022 906 66 67
– www.hotelpwilson.com **F2**
219 rm – †730/890 CHF ††730/890 CHF, ☕ 42 CHF – 11 suites
Rest *Spice's* – see below
Rest *L'Arabesque* – Menu 56 CHF (lunch)/105 CHF – Carte 60/114 CHF
Rest *Pool Garden* – *(closed mid September - May)* Menu 55 CHF (lunch)/80 CHF – Carte 82/163 CHF

◆ Grand Luxury ◆ Stylish ◆

Overlooking the lake, this hotel is adorned with marble decor, fine wood furnishings and attractive flower arrangements. Enjoy the subtle flavours of Lebanese cuisine amid the enchanting decor (goldleaf mosaics) of L'Arabesque. The Pool Garden is ideal for summer dining, with tables set around the swimming pool.

Grand Hôtel Kempinski

19 quai du Mont-Blanc ✉ 1201 – ✆ 022 908 90 81
– reservations.grandhotelgeneva@kempinski.com – Fax 022 908 90 90
– www.kempinski-geneva.com **F3**
409 rm – †331/890 CHF ††331/990 CHF, ☕ 45 CHF – 14 suites
Rest – Carte 57/117 CHF

◆ Grand Luxury ◆ Classic ◆

Total renovation for this lakeside hotel. Contemporary public areas, guestrooms and suites. Conference centre, impressive fitness and spa facilities. There's something for everyone at the Kempinski, which offers four dining areas and four different types of cuisine.

Beau-Rivage

13 quai du Mont-Blanc ✉ 1201 – ✆ 022 716 66 66
– info@beau-rivage.ch – Fax 022 716 60 60
– www.beau-rivage.ch **F3**
80 rm – †790/1100 CHF ††890/1200 CHF, ☕ 43 CHF – 11 suites
Rest *Le Chat Botté* – Menu 65 CHF (lunch)/180 CHF – Carte 109/223 CHF
Rest *Patara* – *✆ 022 731 55 66 (closed 21 - 24 March, 22 December - 6 January, Saturday lunch and Sunday lunch)* Menu 39 CHF (lunch)/126 CHF – Carte 67/106 CHF

♦ Grand Luxury ♦ Stylish ♦

The same family has run this hotel facing the lake since 1865. The stylish guestrooms have an elegant atmosphere and the hotel has a fine atrium adorned with colonnades and a fountain. Modern cuisine in a cosy atmosphere in Le Chat Botté. The Patara specialises in Thai cuisine.

D'Angleterre

17 quai du Mont-Blanc ✉ 1201 – ✆ 022 906 55 55
– angleterre@rchmail.com – Fax 022 906 55 56
– www.hoteldangleterre.ch **F3**
45 rm – †450/980 CHF ††450/980 CHF, ☕ 45 CHF
Rest *Windows* – Menu 49 CHF (lunch)/190 CHF – Carte 98/157 CHF

♦ Luxury ♦ Classic ♦

Dating from 1872, this elegant neo-Classical building overlooks Lake Geneva. Excellent service, tastefully decorated rooms with individual touches, and a cosy colonial decor in the Leopard Lounge. This exclusive restaurant-veranda overlooking the lake serves traditional French cuisine.

De la Paix

11 quai du Mont-Blanc ✉ 1201 – ✆ 022 909 60 00
– info-hdlp@concorde-hotels.com – Fax 022 909 60 01
– www.hoteldelapaix.ch **F3**
84 rm – †370/750 CHF ††370/750 CHF, ☕ 40 CHF
Rest *Vertig'O* – see below

♦ Luxury ♦ Classic ♦

Luxury hotel (1865), renovated in 2005. Exuberant public areas with a vertiginous, gold-covered atrium. Personalised guestrooms decorated in "water droplet" or "rose petal" themes.

Intercontinental

7 ch. du Petit-Saconnex ✉ 1209 – ✆ 022 919 39 39
– inter-geneva@intercontinental-geneva.ch – Fax 022 919 38 38
– www.intercontinental.com/geneva *Plan I* **B2**
266 rm – †314/650 CHF ††314/700 CHF, ☕ 42 CHF – 62 suites
Rest *Woods* – Menu 59 CHF (lunch)/98 CHF – Carte 73/127 CHF

♦ Chain hotel ♦ Classic ♦

This hotel is located in a 1960s building near the Palais des Nations. Renovated public areas, excellent conference facilities and rooms awaiting renovation. A spacious and comfortable restaurant serving modern cuisine in a contemporary setting.

Bristol

10 r. du Mont-Blanc ✉ 1201 – ✆ 022 716 57 00
– reservations@bristol.ch – Fax 022 738 90 39
– www.bristol.ch **F3**
95 rm – †310/610 CHF ††345/650 CHF, ☕ 34 CHF – 5 suites
Rest *Relais Bristol* – Menu 50 CHF (lunch)/85 CHF – Carte 72/111 CHF

♦ Business ♦ Classic ♦

Situated near the lakeside, the Bristol has a luxurious lobby, vertiginous winding staircase and spacious guestrooms (ask for one overlooking the square). Fitness room, sauna and hammam. Modern meals served in a fine, standard restaurant atmosphere. Piano bar.

Epsom

18 r. Richemont ✉ 1202 – ✆ 022 544 66 66 – epsom@manotel.com – Fax 022 544 66 99 – www.manotel.com **F2**

153 rm – 🚹350/590 CHF 🚹🚹350/590 CHF, ☕ 30 CHF

Rest *Portobello* – *(closed 23 December - 2 January)* Menu 40 CHF (lunch)/61 CHF – Carte 63/113 CHF

♦ Business ♦ Classic ♦

Contemporary-style hotel situated in a quiet road in the city centre. Relaxing atmosphere and pleasant guestrooms. Conference rooms also available. Contemporary dishes and international wines served in an exotic setting (parquet, woven furniture, plants) under a modern glass canopy.

Royal

41 r. de Lausanne ✉ 1201 – ✆ 022 906 14 14 – royal@manotel.com – Fax 022 906 14 99 – www.manotel.com/royal **E2**

197 rm – 🚹350/590 CHF 🚹🚹350/590 CHF, ☕ 30 CHF – 5 suites

Rest *Rive Droite* – Menu 56 CHF – Carte 49/96 CHF

♦ Business ♦ Classic ♦

A modern hotel located on a busy road between the lake and the railway station. The moderately sized rooms are designed with business travellers in mind. Conference centre. Decorated in chic brasserie style, this restaurant specialises in contemporary cuisine, with a simplified menu served on the terrace under the arches.

Warwick

14 r. de Lausanne ✉ 1201 – ✆ 022 716 80 00 – res.geneva@warwickhotels.com – Fax 022 716 80 01 – www.warwickgeneva.com **E3**

167 rm – 🚹430/550 CHF 🚹🚹470/650 CHF, ☕ 28 CHF

Rest *Teseo* – Menu 30 CHF (lunch)/45 CHF – Carte 65/114 CHF

♦ Business ♦ Functional ♦

This hotel in front of the station is a popular choice for tourist groups and business seminars. Contemporary, functional guestrooms. Restaurant with a Parisian brasserie-style atmosphere and typical bistro cuisine.

Le Montbrillant

2 r. de Montbrillant ✉ 1201 – ✆ 022 733 77 84 – contact@montbrillant.ch – Fax 022 733 25 11 – www.montbrillant.ch **E3**

82 rm ☕ – 🚹170/275 CHF 🚹🚹255/360 CHF

Rest – Carte 46/92 CHF

♦ Family ♦ Personalised ♦

Reliable hotel close to the station. Alpine-style public areas, rooms of various sizes and studios with kitchenette. Massage available. This Parisian brasserie and friendly restaurant combines traditional and Italian cuisine (pizzas cooked on an open fire).

Les Nations without rest

62 r. du Grand-Pré ✉ 1202 – ✆ 022 748 08 08 – info@hotel-les-nations.com – Fax 022 734 38 84 – www.hotel-les-nations.com Plan I **B2**

71 rm ☕ – 🚹175/280 CHF 🚹🚹220/350 CHF

♦ Business ♦ Classic ♦

Corridors adorned with antiques, guestrooms with individual touches, and attractive junior suites on the 7th floor. A mural depicting the theme of the transhumance decorates the back façade of the building.

Jade without rest

55 r. Rothschild ✉ 1202 – ✆ 022 544 38 38 – jade@manotel.com – Fax 022 544 38 99 – www.manotel.com **F2**

47 rm – 🚹290/390 CHF 🚹🚹290/390 CHF, ☕ 18 CHF

♦ Business ♦ Modern ♦

This hotel has been redecorated in ultra modern style according to the principles of Feng Shui. Harmony and serenity in a refined, modern environment.

Kipling without rest

27 r. de la Navigation ✉ 1201 – ☎ 022 544 40 40 – kipling@manotel.com – Fax 022 544 40 99 – www.manotel.com **E-F2**

62 rm – 290/390 CHF 290/390 CHF, ☕ 18 CHF

♦ Business ♦ Modern ♦

This pleasant hotel with a colonial-style decor pays tribute to the famous author of the "Jungle Book". Aroma of incense in the entrance hall.

Auteuil without rest

33 r. de Lausanne ✉ 1201 – ☎ 022 544 22 22 – auteuil@manotel.com – Fax 022 544 22 99 – www.manotel.com **E2**

104 rm – 320/490 CHF 320/490 CHF, ☕ 28 CHF

♦ Business ♦ Classic ♦

A modern lobby adorned with portraits of film stars, guestrooms with dark wooden furniture brightened with velvet fabrics, and a trendy breakfast area.

Edelweiss

2 pl. de la Navigation ✉ 1201 – ☎ 022 544 51 51 – edelweiss@manotel.com – Fax 022 544 51 99 – www.manotel.com **F3**

42 rm – 290/390 CHF 290/390 CHF, ☕ 18 CHF

Rest – *(closed 1 - 15 January) (dinner only)* Menu 55 CHF – Carte 48/91 CHF

♦ Business ♦ Cosy ♦

Decorated inside and out in the style of a typical Swiss chalet, this hotel offers cosy, comfortable guestrooms. Welcoming dining room with a mezzanine level. Traditional regional dishes, including fondue and raclette, are served in this typical Swiss setting.

Du Midi

4 pl. Chevelu ✉ 1201 – ☎ 022 544 15 00 – info@hotel-du-midi.ch – Fax 022 544 15 20 – www.hotel-du-midi.ch **E-F3**

78 rm – 260/400 CHF 280/450 CHF, ☕ 26 CHF

Rest – *(closed Saturday and Sunday)* Menu 38 CHF (lunch)/100 CHF – Carte 47/85 CHF

♦ Business ♦ Functional ♦

This family-run hotel stands on a small square overlooking the Rhône. Features include an elegant lobby adorned with colonnades, a cosy lounge, a modern art collection and renovated rooms with contemporary decor. Modern, cosy restaurant and an outdoor terrace for summer dining.

Ambassador

21 quai des Bergues ✉ 1201 – ☎ 022 908 05 30 – info@hotel-ambassador.ch – Fax 022 738 90 80 – www.hotel-ambassador.ch **E3**

73 rm – 300/450 CHF 400/550 CHF, ☕ 24 CHF

Rest – *(closed Sunday lunch, Saturday and Bank Holidays)* Menu 41 CHF (lunch)/64 CHF – Carte 47/93 CHF

♦ Business ♦ Classic ♦

Hotel on a busy road overlooking the Rhône. Ask for one of the recently refurbished rooms which have been decorated in a modern style. Traditional dishes served in a wood-panelled dining room or on the summer terrace.

Eden

135 r. de Lausanne ✉ 1202 – ☎ 022 716 37 00 – eden@eden.ch – Fax 022 731 52 60 – www.eden.ch **F1**

54 rm ☕ – 175/280 CHF 235/330 CHF

Rest – *(closed 19 July - 10 August, 21 December - 6 January, Saturday and Sunday)* Menu 32/47 CHF – Carte 42/74 CHF

♦ Business ♦ Classic ♦

Regularly refurbished hotel opposite the Palais des Nations. The classic rooms are bright and functional. A traditional restaurant which is popular with locals and visitors alike.

Strasbourg without rest
10 r. Pradier ✉ 1201 – ✆ 022 906 58 00 – info@hotelstrasbourg.ch – Fax 022 738 42 08 – www.hotelstrasbourg.ch **E3**
51 rm – †170/210 CHF ††220/270 CHF
◆ Business ◆ Functional ◆
A traditional hotel with rather small, but functional rooms, just a stone's throw from the station and Cornavin car park. Welcoming wood-panelled reception area.

Ibis without rest
10 r. Voltaire ✉ 1201 – ✆ 022 338 20 20 – h2154@accor.com – Fax 022 338 20 30 – www.ibishotel.com **E3**
65 rm – †142 CHF ††142 CHF, 14 CHF
◆ Chain hotel ◆ Minimalist ◆
This non-smoking chain hotel is situated in a rather dull part of Geneva. Functional guestrooms, some of which are family rooms.

Il Lago – Four Seasons Hôtel des Bergues
33 quai des Bergues ✉ 1201 – ✆ 022 908 70 00 – info.gen@fourseasons.com – Fax 022 908 74 00 – www.fourseasons.com/geneva **F3**
Rest – Menu 80 CHF (lunch)/180 CHF – Carte 110/188 CHF
◆ Italian ◆ Classic ◆
This restaurant specialising in fine Italian cuisine has a classical, opulent decor, including exquisite hand-painted wallpaper in the dining room. Ask for one of the tables overlooking the lake.

La Perle du Lac lake,
126 r. de Lausanne ✉ 1202 – ✆ 022 909 10 20 – info@laperledulac.ch – Fax 022 909 10 30 – www.laperledulac.ch
closed 24 December - 20 January and Monday **F1**
Rest – Menu 65 CHF (lunch)/120 CHF – Carte 102/148 CHF
◆ Traditional ◆ Classic ◆
This hundred-year-old chalet, surrounded by a large outdoor dining area, enjoys an attractive location in the middle of a park facing the lake. Bright tones in the more modern of the two dining rooms.

Spice's – Hôtel Président Wilson
47 quai Wilson ✉ 1201 – ✆ 022 906 66 66 – sales@hotelpwilson.com – Fax 022 906 66 67 – www.hotelpwilson.com **F2**
closed 1 July - 15 August, 2 - 14 January, Saturday lunch and Sunday
Rest – Menu 59 CHF (lunch)/140 CHF – Carte 103/185 CHF
◆ Euro-asiatic ◆ Fashionable ◆
A cosmopolitan menu, fashionable decor and trendy atmosphere are the order of the day in this restaurant, which also has a boutique selling a range of products from around the world.

Tsé Yang
19 quai du Mont-Blanc (1st floor) ✉ 1201 – ✆ 022 732 50 81 – Fax 022 731 05 82
Rest – Menu 45 CHF (lunch)/139 CHF – Carte 60/144 CHF **F3**
◆ Chinese ◆ Exotic ◆
Elegant dining room with a Far Eastern decor, separated into alcoves by carved wood partitions. Savour Chinese specialities while enjoying the view of Lake Geneva.

Vertig'O – Hôtel de la Paix
11 quai du Mont-Blanc ✉ 1201 – ✆ 022 909 60 00 – info-hdlp@concorde-hotels.com – Fax 022 909 60 01 – www.hoteldelapaix.ch **F3**
closed 14 July - 17 August, 22 December - 6 January, Saturday, Sunday and Bank Holidays
Rest – Menu 55 CHF (lunch)/120 CHF – Carte 85/129 CHF
◆ Traditional ◆ Fashionable ◆
Hotel restaurant serving updated traditional cooking in a fashionable, modern bistro setting (orange, grey and blue tones).

Thai Phuket

33 av. de France ✉ *1202 –* ✆ *022 734 41 00 – Fax 022 734 42 40*
closed Saturday lunch **E1**
Rest – Menu 36 CHF (lunch)/90 CHF – Carte 39/82 CHF
◆ Asian ◆ Exotic ◆
Good Thai restaurant where waitresses in Thai costume provide attentive service. Fine wines, including vintage Bordeaux. Superb aquarium with exotic fish.

Bistrot du Boeuf Rouge

17 r. Alfred-Vincent ✉ *1201 –* ✆ *022 732 75 37 – Fax 022 731 46 84 – www.boeufrouge.ch*
closed 14 July - 13 August, Saturday, Sunday and Bank Holidays **F3**
Rest – Menu 37/54 CHF – Carte 50/92 CHF
◆ Lyons cuisine ◆ Brasserie ◆
A French-style bistro with a bar, benches, old advertisements and mirrors on the walls. Specialities from Lyon, local dishes and gourmet specials.

Sagano

86 r. de Montbrillant ✉ *1202 –* ✆ *022 733 11 50 – Fax 022 733 27 50*
closed Saturday lunch and Sunday **E1**
Rest – Menu 40 CHF (lunch)/90 CHF – Carte 49/102 CHF
◆ Japanese ◆ Exotic ◆
This restaurant offers a good introduction to Japanese cuisine, with decor typical of Japan, including tatamis (Japanese floor cushions) and low tables.

L'Entrecôte Couronnée

5 r. des Pâquis ✉ *1201 –* ✆ *022 732 84 45 – Fax 022 732 84 46*
closed Christmas - New Year, Saturday lunch and Sunday **F3**
Rest – Menu 60 CHF – Carte 57/84 CHF
◆ Modern ◆ Bistro ◆
Attractive residence housing a small bistro with a typical local atmosphere. Retro decor and specialities made with regional produce and served by the chefs themselves.

Le Rouge et le Blanc

27 quai des Bergues ✉ *1201 –* ✆ *022 731 15 50*
closed 21 December - 3 January and Sunday **E3**
Rest – Carte 50/66 CHF
◆ Modern ◆ Wine bar ◆
This friendly wine-bar-cum-restaurant serves contemporary dishes at lunchtime (the waiter will tell you what's available) and a more traditional menu in the evening. Home-made charcuterie and excellent wines.

LEFT BANK *Plan III*

Swissôtel Métropole Geneva

34 quai Général-Guisan ✉ *1204 –* ✆ *022 318 32 00 – geneva@swissotel.com – Fax 022 318 33 00 – www.geneva.swissotel.com*
118 rm – †330/810 CHF ††360/880 CHF, ☕ 39 CHF – 9 suites **H1**
Rest *Le Grand Quai* – Carte 69/138 CHF
◆ Luxury ◆ Classic ◆
This hotel facing the famous Jet d'Eau dates from 1854. Traditional rooms (those overlooking the lake are the most spacious), pleasant piano bar, panoramic terrace and fitness room. Le Grand Quai specialises in French cuisine.

Les Armures

1 r. du Puits-Saint-Pierre ✉ *1204 –* ✆ *022 310 91 72 – armures@span.ch – Fax 022 310 98 46 – www.hotel-les-armures.ch* **H2**
32 rm ☕ – †370/490 CHF ††485/615 CHF
Rest – *(closed Christmas and New Year)* Menu 58 CHF – Carte 52/90 CHF
◆ Traditional ◆ Historic ◆
Elegant 17C residence nestling in the heart of old Geneva and decorated with a pleasing mix of old and new. The hotel owner was born in the property. Choose between the rustic-style dining room or the outdoor terrace of this restaurant, which serves traditional Swiss cuisine. Fondue and raclette at the carnotzet.

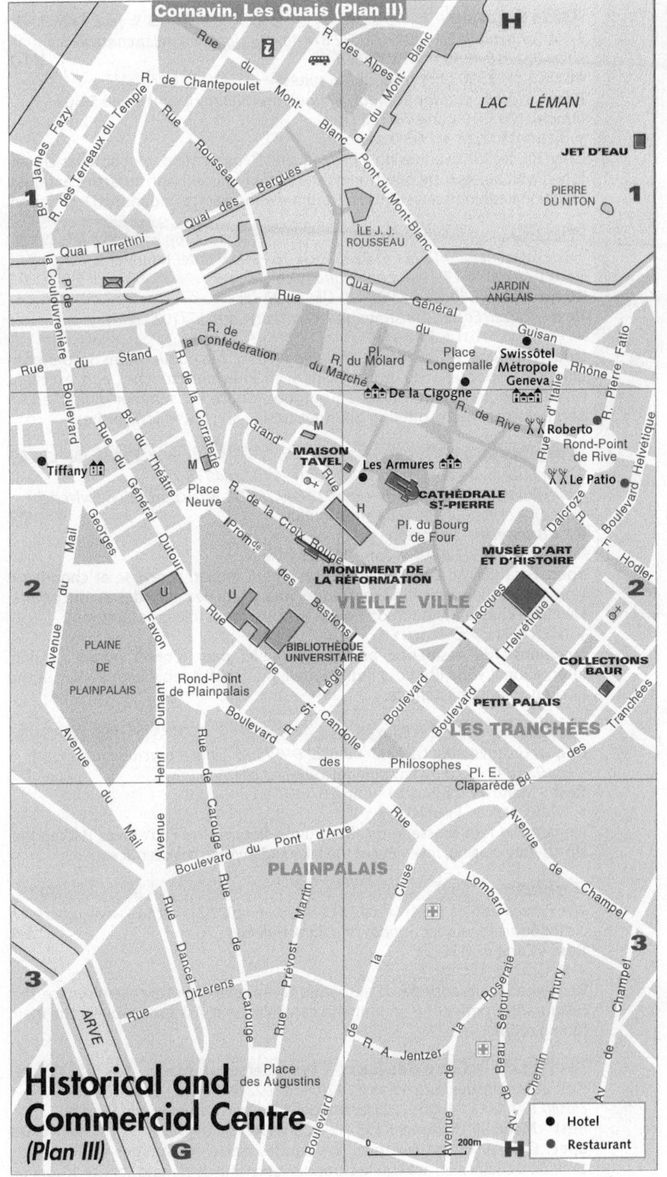
Cornavin, Les Quais (Plan II)
LAC LÉMAN
JET D'EAU
PIERRE DU NITON
ÎLE J. J. ROUSSEAU
JARDIN ANGLAIS
Pont du Mont-Blanc
Quai Turrettini
Quai des Bergues
Rue du Mont-Blanc
R. des Alpes
Q. du Mont-Blanc
R. de Chantepoulet
Rue Rousseau
Bd. James Fazy
R. des Terreaux du Temple
Pt de la Coulouvrenière
Quai Général Guisan
Rue du Rhône
R. de la Confédération
Rue du Stand
R. du Marché
Pl. du Molard
Place Longemalle
Swissôtel Métropole Geneva
De la Cigogne
R. de Rive
Roberto
Rond-Point de Rive
Le Patio
R. Pierre Fatio
Rue d'Italie
Boulevard Helvétique
Grand' Rue
MAISON TAVEL
Les Armures
CATHÉDRALE ST-PIERRE
Pl. du Bourg de Four
MUSÉE D'ART ET D'HISTOIRE
R. Dalcroze
Bd du Théâtre
Rue du Général Dufour
R. de la Corraterie
Place Neuve
Tiffany
Rue Georges Favon
R. de la Croix Rouge
Promde des Bastions
MONUMENT DE LA RÉFORMATION
VIEILLE VILLE
Jacques
Helvétique
F. Hodler
COLLECTIONS BAUR
PETIT PALAIS
LES TRANCHÉES
Bd des Tranchées
Avenue du Mail
PLAINE DE PLAINPALAIS
Rond-Point de Plainpalais
BIBLIOTHÈQUE UNIVERSITAIRE
Rue de Candolle
R. St. Léger
Boulevard des Philosophes
Pl. E. Claparède
Avenue Henri Dunant
Rue de Carouge
Boulevard du Pont d'Arve
PLAINPALAIS
Rue de la Cluse
Lombard
Avenue de Champel
Rue Prévost Martin
Rue Dancel
Rue Dizerens
ARVE
R. A. Jentzer
Avenue de la Roseraie
Av. de Beau Séjour
Chemin Thury
Av de Champel
Place des Augustins
Boulevard
Historical and Commercial Centre (Plan III)
0 200m
G
H
1
2
3
Hotel
Restaurant

De la Cigogne

17 pl. Longemalle ✉ 1204 – ✆ 022 818 40 40 – cigogne@relaischateaux.com – Fax 022 818 40 50 – www.cigogne.ch **H1-2**

46 rm – 🚹390 CHF 🚹🚹495 CHF – 6 suites

Rest – *(closed Saturday from July - August and Sunday lunch)* Menu 59 CHF (lunch)/120 CHF – Carte 78/122 CHF

♦ Traditional ♦ Historic ♦

Early-20C façade overlooking a busy square. Elegant fittings, public areas embellished with objets d'art, guestrooms and suites furnished with attractive antiques. Traditional cuisine is served in this restaurant with a glass ceiling and Art Deco design.

Tiffany

1 r. des Marbriers ✉ 1204 – ✆ 022 708 16 16 – info@hotel-tiffany.ch – Fax 022 708 16 17 – www.hotel-tiffany.ch **G2**

46 rm – 🚹260/340 CHF 🚹🚹360/420 CHF, ☕ 22 CHF

Rest – *(closed Easter, Christmas and New Year)* Carte 57/102 CHF

♦ Traditional ♦ Classic ♦

Housed in a late-19C residence, this elegant hotel has public rooms decorated in chic Belle Époque style, guestrooms with individual touches and excellent quality bedding. Retro decor, an outdoor terrace for summer dining, and a contemporary menu offering gourmet cuisine and low-calorie dishes.

Parc des Eaux-Vives

82 quai Gustave-Ador (1st floor) ✉ 1211 – ✆ 022 849 75 75 – info@parcdeseauxvives.ch – Fax 022 849 75 70 – www.parcdeseauxvives.ch

closed 1 - 21 January, Sunday and Monday *Plan I* **D2**

Rest *Brasserie* – see below

Rest – Menu 79/220 CHF – Carte 152/234 CHF

Spec. Féra du Lac Léman, vinaigrette d'oeuf mollet, écrevisse et chou-fleur. Homard breton, rafraîchi à la pastèque, vinaigrette de palourdes et concombre. Lièvre de chasse à la tradition Royale avec truffes et foie gras (autumn).

♦ Modern ♦ Design ♦

Luxurious 18C residence built in a public park. Contemporary cuisine, international wine list, cosy lounge area and "chef's" table with a view of the kitchen. Panoramic terrace.

Brasserie – Parc des Eaux-Vives

82 quai Gustave-Ador ✉ 1211 – ✆ 022 849 75 75 – info@parcdeseauxvives.ch – Fax 022 849 75 70 – www.parcdeseauxvives.ch *Plan I* **D2**

Rest – Menu 49 CHF (lunch) – Carte 67/107 CHF

♦ Modern ♦ Trendy ♦

Elegant modern brasserie on the ground floor of the Eaux-Vives Park lodge. Up-to-date cuisine, fine view of the lake and inviting teak terrace.

Roberto

10 r. Pierre-Fatio ✉ 1204 – ✆ 022 311 80 33 – Fax 022 311 84 66 – www.roberto.ch

closed Saturday dinner, Sunday and Bank Holidays **H2**

Rest – Carte 62/136 CHF

♦ Italian ♦ Cosy ♦

Renowned for its cosy decor, authentic Italian cuisine and excellent service, this restaurant is perfect for an intimate candlelit meal. Ask for a table in the main dining room.

Buffet de la Gare des Eaux-Vives (Serge Labrosse)

7 av. de la Gare des Eaux-Vives ✉ 1207 – ✆ 022 840 44 30 – Fax 022 840 44 31

closed 19 July - 11 August, 22 December - 7 January, Saturday and Sunday

Rest – Menu 59 CHF (lunch)/155 CHF – Carte 94/134 CHF *Plan I* **C-D3**

Spec. Croustillant de foie gras des Landes poêlé et asperges de Provence. Grillade de Saint-Pierre à l'huile citronnée et tartine de tomate confite. L'agneau de l'Adret en trois façons, caviar d'aubergine et ail rose confit.

♦ Inventive ♦ Classic ♦

A "station buffet" that stands out from the crowd, with its very modern interior, summer terrace next to the platforms, up-to-date cuisine and good selection of wines from Switzerland and the Rhone Valley.

Le Patio VISA AE

19 bd Helvétique ✉ 1207 – ✆ 022 736 66 75 – lepatio.ch@freesurf.ch – Fax 022 786 40 74

closed 24 December - 2 January, Saturday and Sunday **H2**

Rest – Menu 46 CHF (lunch) – Carte 66/104 CHF

♦ Traditional ♦ Neighbourhood ♦

Run by an art enthusiast, this neighbourhood restaurant features large paintings by a Cuban artist in the dining room. Traditional menu and daily seasonal specials.

ENVIRONS AND COINTRIN AIRPORT *Plan I*

La Réserve rm P

301 rte de Lausanne ✉ 1293 Bellevue VISA AE

– ✆ 022 959 59 59 – info@lareserve.ch – Fax 022 959 59 60

– www.lareserve.ch **C1**

87 rm – †430/990 CHF ††540/990 CHF – 15 suites

Rest *Le Loti* – Carte 76/173 CHF

Rest *Tsé-Fung* – Menu 70/150 CHF – Carte 65/237 CHF

♦ Grand Luxury ♦ Design ♦

This luxury hotel boasts modern rooms and suites with terraces, most of which overlook the park and swimming pool. Magnificent decor designed by Garcia, plus a superb spa. Italian-influenced menu and stylish exotic decor at Le Loti. Enjoy inventive Chinese cuisine in elegant surroundings at the Tsé-Fung.

Crowne Plaza rm

34 r. François-Peyrot ✉ 1218 Grand-Saconnex VISA AE

– ✆ 022 747 02 02 – sales@cpgeneva.ch – Fax 022 747 03 03

– www.crowneplazageneva.com **B1**

496 rm – †295/510 CHF ††295/570 CHF, 36 CHF

Rest *Carlights* – Carte 47/101 CHF

Rest *L'Olivo* – *(closed 20 December - 5 January, Saturday and Sunday)*

Carte 59/118 CHF

♦ Business ♦ Contemporary ♦

Business hotel near the airport specialising in conferences and congresses. Modern bedrooms, trendy public areas and a fitness club. The Carlights serves fusion cuisine in a modern and functional setting. Contemporary cuisine and a Mediterranean ambience at L'Olivo.

Mövenpick rest rm VISA AE

20 rte de Pré-Bois ✉ 1216 Cointrin – ✆ 022 717 11 11 – hotel.geneva.airport@moevenpick.com – Fax 022 717 11 22

– www.moevenpick-geneva-airport.com **A2**

344 rm – †220/590 CHF ††250/630 CHF, 36 CHF – 6 suites

Rest *Latitude* – Menu 58/61 CHF – Carte 48/101 CHF

Rest *Kamomé* – *(closed Monday lunch, Saturday lunch and Sunday)*

Menu 45 CHF (lunch)/110 CHF – Carte 52/109 CHF

♦ Chain hotel ♦ Modern ♦

Business hotel with lounge, bars, casino and various types of guestrooms, the newest of which are the executive rooms. Trendy decor and fusion cuisine at the Latitude. At the Kamomé, Japanese food is served in the sushi bar or around hotplates (teppanyaki).

Ramada Park rm VISA

75 av. Louis-Casaï ✉ 1216 Cointrin – ✆ 022 710 30 00 – info@ramadaparkhotel.ch – Fax 022 710 31 00 – www.ramadaparkhotel.ch

302 rm – †195/500 CHF ††195/500 CHF, 37 CHF – 6 suites **A2**

Rest *La Récolte* – Menu 35 CHF – Carte 49/107 CHF

♦ Chain hotel ♦ Modern ♦

Hotel near the airport offering a wide range of amenities, including a news-stand, hairdresser's, sauna, fitness centre and meeting rooms. Modern guestrooms. This contemporary-style restaurant organises weekly events based on different culinary themes.

NH Geneva Airport

21 av. de Mategnin ✉ 1217 Meyrin – ✆ 022 989 90 00 – nhgenevaairport@nh-hotels.ch – Fax 022 989 99 99 – www.nh-hotels.com **A2**

190 rm – 150/450 CHF 150/450 CHF, 27 CHF

Rest ***Le Pavillon*** – *(closed Saturday lunch and Sunday lunch)* Carte 52/98 CHF

◆ Chain hotel ◆ Design ◆

This hotel has a distinctive circular shape built in red brick, in keeping with its modern style interiors. Designer lobby, with an attractive bar and well-kept rooms. Modern cuisine served in a contemporary atmosphere under the dome of the Pavillon.

Suitehotel

28 av. Louis-Casaï ✉ 1216 Cointrin – ✆ 022 710 46 46 – h5654@accor.com – Fax 022 710 46 00 – www.suite-hotel.com **B2**

86 rm – 182/230 CHF 182/230 CHF, 10 CHF

Rest ***Swiss Bistro*** – *(closed Sunday lunch, Saturday and Bank Holidays)* Carte 37/67 CHF

◆ Chain hotel ◆ Modern ◆

Located between the airport and the town centre, this hotel offers contemporary-style rooms with an office separated by a sliding door. Modern and light public areas. Modern style bistro serving simple cuisine with a Swiss touch.

Express by Holiday Inn without rest

16 rte de Pré-Bois ✉ 1216 Cointrin – ✆ 022 939 39 39 – info@expressgeneva.com – Fax 022 939 39 30 – www.expressgeneva.com **A2**

154 rm – 165/240 CHF 165/240 CHF

◆ Chain hotel ◆ Modern ◆

This modern, mid-range chain hotel near the airport is designed with business travellers in mind. Functional guestrooms.

Ibis

10 ch. de la Violette ✉ 1216 Cointrin – ✆ 022 710 95 00 – h3535@accor.com – Fax 022 710 95 95 – www.ibishotel.com **A2**

109 rm – 106/166 CHF 106/166 CHF, 14 CHF

Rest – *(closed 22 December - 2 January) (dinner only)* Carte 45/72 CHF

◆ Chain hotel ◆ Minimalist ◆

Situated near the motorway and Geneva airport, this hotel has all the facilities you would expect of the Ibis chain. Functional rooms with bathrooms. This restaurant has a tavern-style decor and a menu featuring contemporary cuisine.

Auberge du Lion d'Or (Thomas Byrne et Gilles Dupont) ← lake,

5 pl. Pierre-Gautier ✉ 1223 Cologny – ✆ 022 736 44 32 – liondorcologny@bluewin.ch – Fax 022 786 74 62 – www.liondor.ch

closed 21 December - 13 January, Saturday and Sunday **D2**

Rest – Menu 70 CHF (lunch)/220 CHF – Carte 135/201 CHF

Rest ***Le Bistro de Cologny*** – Menu 48 CHF (lunch) – Carte 71/118 CHF

Spec. Pétales de thon rouge au sel de Maldon, gelée d'eau de tomate, tartine de copeaux de fenouil. Poitrine de pigeonneau rôtie en cocotte, étuvée de petits pois nouvelle saison (spring). Pavé de loup de mer clouté de citron, fumet de coquillages.

◆ Modern ◆ Luxury ◆

Enjoy superb views of the lake and mountains through the bay windows of this chic, modern dining room designed by Wilmotte. The building also features a contemporary-style bar and an elevated terrace. A modern bistro and an outdoor restaurant with a flower-filled garden for summer dining.

XXXX
✿✿

Domaine de Châteauvieux (Philippe Chevrier) with rm

16 ch. de Châteauvieux
1242 Satigny – 022 753 15 11 – info@chateauvieux.ch
– Fax 022 753 19 24 – www.chateauvieux.ch
closed 28 July - 12 August and 22 December - 8 January
13 rm – 225/365 CHF 275/415 CHF
Rest – *(closed Sunday and Monday)* Menu 88 CHF (lunch)/260 CHF
– Carte 190/256 CHF

Spec. Carpaccio de coquilles Saint-Jacques et tartare de langoustines. Bar de ligne au sel. Biscuit coulant au chocolat chaud.

♦ Innovative ♦ Luxury ♦

Former farm set in the heart of the vineyards. Exquisite cuisine, prestigious wines and all the trappings you expect from a truly great restaurant.

ZURICH
ZÜRICH

Population (est.2005): 345 300 (conurbation 1 081 700) – Altitude: 409m

M. Bauer/Zürich Tourismus

Zurich has a lot of things going for it. A lot of history (two thousand years' worth), a lot of water (two rivers and a huge lake), a lot of beauty (its old town is a visual feast), and, let's face it, a lot of wealth (it's Switzerland's richest city). It's an important financial and commercial centre, and has a well-earned reputation for good living with a rich cultural life, reflected in an abundance of smart restaurants and outdoor cafés.

The place strikes a nice balance – it's large enough to boast some world-class facilities but small enough to hold on to its charm and old-world ambience. The window-shopping here sets it apart from many other European cities – from tiny boutiques and specialist emporiums to a shopping boulevard that's famed across the globe. Although it's not Switzerland's political capital, it's the spiritual one because of its pulsing arts scene: for those who might think the Swiss a bit staid, think again – this is where the nihilistic, anti-art Dada movement began.

LIVING THE CITY

The attractive **Lake Zurich** flows northwards into the city, which forms a pleasingly symmetrical arc around it. From the lake, the river **Limmat** bisects Zurich, flowing north until it reaches another river, the narrower **Sihl.** On the Limmat's west bank lies the **Old Town**, the medieval hub, overlooked by two dominant churches. The stylishly vibrant **Bahnhofstrasse**, the smartest shopping street in town, follows the line of the former city walls. Across the Limmat on the east side, the unmissable landmark is the magnificent twin-towered **Grossmünster**, while just beyond is the charmingly historic district of **Niederdorf**. Way down south is the city's largest green space, the **Zürichhorn Park.**

PRACTICAL INFORMATION

ARRIVAL-DEPARTURE

Zurich International Airport (Kloten) is located 10km north of the city. Trains run every 10-15min and take 10min. A taxi will be about 50CHF. Zürich Hauptbahnhof is the main railway station for international and inter-city trains.

TRANSPORT

As this is Switzerland, you can guarantee that the public transport system runs like clockwork. The city operates an efficient system on bus, tram, metro, train and boat. You can buy a single ticket, day ticket, or 9 o'clock Pass. Tickets are available from ticket machines and tourist offices. Remember to validate your ticket at the ticket machine or special orange-coloured machine before boarding.

The Zurichcard grants unlimited travel on all public transport (including river and lake boats). It also gives you admission to more than forty museums and art collections. The card can be purchased for twenty-four or seventy-two hours.

Cycle riding is encouraged here. Hire bikes for free for the day from beside the main railway station. All you have to do is leave ID and a local currency deposit.

EXPLORING ZURICH

Mention Zurich and your first thoughts may turn to bankers and precision timing. But Zurich is a beautiful, medieval city that has been a respected base of European culture for centuries. To wander round and about the alleyways of its Old Town (the **Altstadt**) is to explore a fascinating labyrinth of cobbled streets, flower-filled squares and ancient pastel-shaded houses. Momentous events have happened here. In the cobbled **Münsterhof Square**, in the Old Town's heart, Winston Churchill delivered a famous speech after World War II, declaring "Europe Arise!" in praise of a postwar European union. These words are on a plaque set into the cobbles,

a reminder that this city has played a recognisable part in the continent's history. Further proof is just over the water at the imposing Grossmünster, where the zealous preaching of radical cleric Huldrych Zwingli set in motion the wheels of the sixteenth-century Reformation.

→ BAHN-STORMER

The plaque to Churchill is no more than a cuckoo's call from the Bahnhofstrasse, a mile-long, tram-packed avenue stretching south to the edge of Lake Zurich. The city's commercial centre, Bahnhoffstrasse is lined with upmarket shops and chic restaurants, its gravitas enhanced by the headquarters of several major Swiss banks. Between it and the river lies a warren of medieval lanes full of small, individual shops selling a range of quirky things. Act like a smart local, and get some respite from the bustle by ducking into the lanes that head up to the **Lindenhof.** This tree-covered hill is where Zurich began: the Romans founded a customs post here as early as the first century BC. It's a delightful spot to take a rest; an observation platform gives you views of the surrounding rooftops and the Limmat gliding along below. There's a giant chessboard on the hill-top where old boys wreathed in concentration search for checkmate underneath the lime trees.

On this west side of the Limmat there are two distinctive churches, less than two hundred metres apart. The **Church of St Peter**, whose main body is exactly three hundred years old, seems to be an ideal landmark for the punctual Swiss: its clockface, at twenty-eight feet in diameter, is the largest in Europe, so you'll know if you have the time to nip south a little way and pay a visit to **Fraumünster**. This is a graceful building whose history stretches back over a thousand years, but its main claim to fame is more recent. The breathtaking stained glass windows were added in 1970, and were the inspiration of Marc Chagall. They're a delicious fusion of ethereal light and colour.

→ SWISS ROLE

At the top end of Bahnhofstrasse, past the grand railway station, is the equally imposing **Swiss National Museum**. Ideal for a rainy day, this vast collection covers everything you'll need to know about Switzerland from prehistoric times to the21C. Its main highlight is a beautifully preserved 18C Benedictine pharmacy. Head across the river, though, for the top cultural attraction of the city: if you go on past the Grossmünster, you'll reach the **Kunsthaus**, Switzerland's premier art gallery. It's easy to get round, and its permanent art collection is outstanding. You can admire thrilling paintings by Swiss artists such as Giacometti and Fussli, plus a broad range of work that takes in medieval religious paintings, Dutch Old Masters, Impressionists and Surrealists. Dadaists are there too, of course, but it might be fun to see their actual birthplace before encountering them at the Kunsthaus. For this, stroll up through the pretty eastern section of the Altstadt – Niederdorf – till you come to the near-mystical **Cabaret Voltaire** on the corner of **Niederdorfstrasse** and **Spiegelgasse**. This updated café-bar and arts centre is where artist Tristan Tzara and like-minded refugees from World War I founded an avant-garde artistic movement in 1916 as an anarchic reaction against all the horrifying carnage – Dada.

→ LOOK WHO'S AT THE ODEON

At the same time as Tzara and his pals were in the process of revolutionising art, guess who was down the road killing time before the armistice? None other than James Joyce and Vladimir Ilyich Lenin. They'd both become devotees of another legendary Zurich watering hole, the **Café Odeon** (although, unfortunately, there's no record of them ever having met). What would have captivated the great writer and the great revolutionary was the wonderful atmosphere of this Viennese-style coffee house. Looking out over bustling **Bellevueplatz**, the Café Odeon had, and still has, all the grand trimmings, including plate-glass windows, polished red marble and deep leather armchairs.

→ GO WEST

The shock of the new has slammed into Zurich. Go north of the main station and you'll come to Zurich West. But this is no railway terminus; it's the evolutionary outcome of the city's vibrant cultural scene and its cutting-edge reputation in the worlds of fashion and design. Zurich West is set in a former industrial and red light area that's taken on a new life. It's now an arty warehouse zone with a funky, chic, up-and-coming feel. Full of clubs, cinemas and restaurants, it's centred round **Langstrasse**, a road crisscrossed by flyovers and railway bridges, and is the complete antithesis to the idea of Zurich as an icy financial centre.

→ LAKE ARRIVAL

Search out a more peaceful, relaxing vibe at the other end of the city. If you head south from Grossmünster, there's a delightful narrow strip of parkland running parallel to the lake's eastern shore alongside the arrow-straight **Utoquai**. It's full of trees and flowerbeds and ends up at the idyllically set Zürichhorn Park, which rubs verdant shoulders with the wide expanses of Lake Zurich. From here, watch the boats in and out of the Limmat: catch one yourself from the city's landing stage at **Bürkliplatz**. A trip on the water is a must here. The lovely forty-kilometre lake stretches in an arc from Zurich to the foot of the Alps. There's a good choice of trips, from short sorties to cruises of half a day, taking in a range of lakeshore towns and villages. The water is crystal clear and unpolluted, so if you fancy, you can take a dip, too.

On your walk down Utoquai, you might like to take a little detour at **Falkenstrasse** and check out the glorious **Opera House**. Better still, try and get some tickets for a performance. This is one of Europe's leading opera and ballet theatres, a neo-Baroque beauty, designed by nineteenth century Viennese architects who knew a thing or two about this kind of opulence.

CALENDAR HIGHLIGHTS

Zurich's renown as a cultural leader reaches its annual highpoint at the Zurich Festival, every June and July, during which much of the city resounds to

ZURICH IN…

→ ONE DAY
Old Town, Bahnhofstrasse, Zurich West, Grossmünster

→ TWO DAYS
Watch the chessplayers on Lindenhof, see Chagall's glorious windows at Fraumünster, Kunsthaus, Cabaret Voltaire, Café Odeon

→ THREE DAYS
Utoquai, Zürichhorn Park, a night at the Opera House

international music, opera, theatre and dance, and thousands pour in to visit the performances. Theatre lovers can indulge their habit for longer at August's Theatre Spectacle, where innovative productions take centre stage, while in September athletics fans flock to the Letzigrund Stadium – the 'magic track' – for the legendary Weltklasse, which in 2008 celebrates eighty years of the event. The Zurich International Art Fair at Kongresshaus in October features everything from painting to sculpture and photography to video, but by then many will be outdoors in training for December's Silvesterlauf, a festively decorated race through the Old Town in which ten thousand competitors select various distances to run. February's Art On Ice at Hallenstadium is a 'feelgood' mix of musical stars, ice skaters and dynamic lightshow, while the same month's Carnival Procession transforms the city centre into a garish float-fest, highlighted by guggen music, when groups of musicians and non-musicians bang out an impromptu blast of rhythms, culminating in the Guggen Monster Concert in Münsterhof Square.

EATING OUT

Zurich stands out in Switzerland (along with Geneva) for its top-class restaurants serving international cuisine. Zurich, though, takes the prize when it comes to trendy, cutting-edge places to dine, whether restaurant or bar, whether along the lakeside or in the converted loft of an old factory. In the middle of the day, most locals go for the cheaper daily lunchtime menus, saving themselves for the glories of the evening. The city is host to many traditional, longstanding Italian restaurants, but if you want to try something 'totally Zurcher', you can't do any better than tackle geschnetzeltes with rösti: sliced veal fried in butter, simmered with onions and mushrooms, with a dash of white wine and cream, served with hashed brown potatoes. A good place for simple restaurants and bars is Niederdorf, while Zurich West is coming on strong with its twenty first century zeitgeist diners. When you're happy with the service you usually round up a small bill or leave up to ten percent on a larger one.

→ PANORAMA

Take a 15-minute train journey from the main station for quite simply the very best view of Zurich. Known to Zurchers as the 'top of Zurich', Uetliberg is an 871m mountain with a forested mountain ridge, lush green meadows, tinkling cowbells and, best of all, fantastic 360-degree views of the city, the lake and the Alps. The train will take you to the summit, or you can walk up yourself: it should take a fit person about one and a half hours.

→ AN ARTY BREW

An old brewery is now the home of two of Zurich's very best contemporary art museums. The former home of Löwenbräu in Limmatstrasse has been converted into bright, white rooms which house the Migros Museum, with its huge permanent collection, and the Kunsthalle Zurich, which puts on temporary exhibitions for up-and-coming stars of the art world.

→ AND FINALLY...

In case anyone still thinks of Zurich as a staid place for intrepid clockwatchers: it has the highest density of pavement cafés in the world; its opera house has staged more premieres than any other; and its river and lake are home to no less than eighteen sandy beaches.

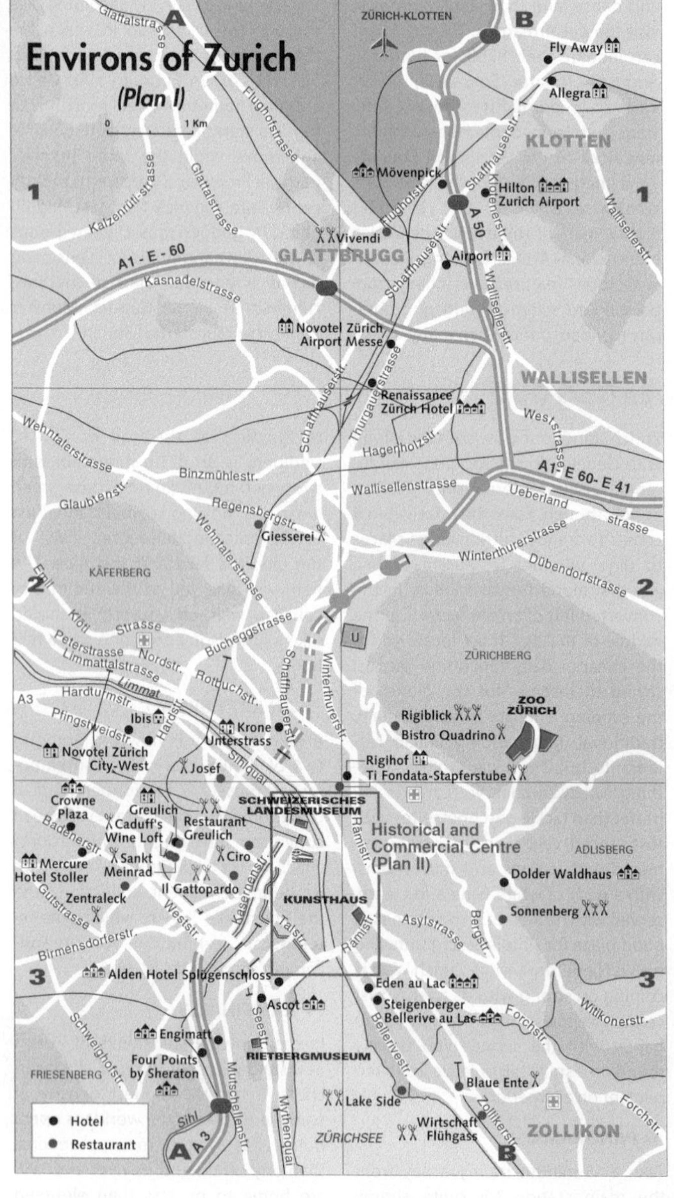

Environs of Zurich
(Plan I)
0
1 Km
A
B
1
2
3
ZÜRICH-KLOTTEN
Fly Away
Allegra
KLOTTEN
Mövenpick
Hilton Zurich Airport
Vivendi
GLATTBRUGG
Airport
A 50
A1 - E - 60
Novotel Zürich Airport Messe
WALLISELLEN
Renaissance Zürich Hotel
A1- E 60- E 41
Giesserei
KÄFERBERG
ZÜRICHBERG
Rigiblick
Bistro Quadrino
ZOO ZÜRICH
Ibis
Krone Unterstrass
Novotel Zürich City-West
Josef
Rigihof
Ti Fondata-Stapferstube
Crowne Plaza
Greulich
Restaurant Greulich
Caduff's Wine Loft
SCHWEIZERISCHES LANDESMUSEUM
Historical and Commercial Centre (Plan II)
ADLISBERG
Sankt Meinrad
Ciro
Mercure Hotel Stoller
Il Gattopardo
Dolder Waldhaus
Zentraleck
KUNSTHAUS
Sonnenberg
Alden Hotel Splügenschloss
Eden au Lac
Ascot
Steigenberger Bellerive au Lac
Engimatt
RIETBERGMUSEUM
Four Points by Sheraton
FRIESENBERG
Blaue Ente
Lake Side
Wirtschaft Flühgass
ZOLLIKON
ZÜRICHSEE
Hotel
Restaurant
A3
Glattalstrasse
Flughofstrasse
Kalzenrüti-strasse
Kasnadelstrasse
Flugholstr.
Schaffhauserstr.
Klotenerstr.
Wallisellerstr.
Thurgauerstrasse
Hagenholzstr.
Weststrasse
Wehntalerstrasse
Binzmühlestr.
Wallisellenstrasse
Ueberlandstrasse
Glaubtenstr.
Regensbergstr.
Winterthurerstrasse
Dübendorfstrasse
Emil Klöti Strasse
Bucheggstrasse
Peterstrasse
Nordstr.
Limmattalstrasse
Limmat
Rotbuchstr.
Hardturmstr.
Pfingstweidstr.
Hardstr.
Sihlquai
Winterthurerstr.
Rämistr.
Badenerstr.
Kasernenstr.
Weststr.
Gutstrasse
Talstr.
Asylstrasse
Bergstr.
Birmensdorferstr.
Witikonerstr.
Forchstr.
Seestr.
Bellerivestr.
Schweighofstr.
Zollikerstr.
Sihl
Mutschellenstr.
Mythenquai

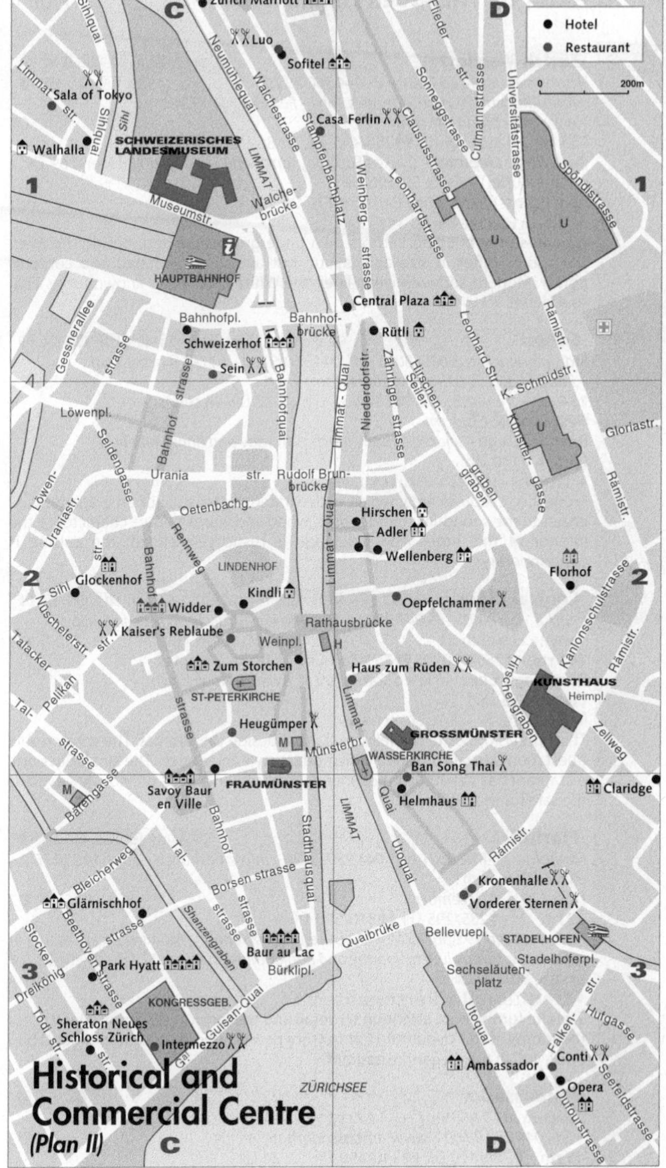
Hotel
Restaurant
0 200m
Zürich Marriott
Luo
Sofitel
Sala of Tokyo
Casa Ferlin
Walhalla
SCHWEIZERISCHES LANDESMUSEUM
HAUPTBAHNHOF
Central Plaza
Schweizerhof
Rütli
Sein
Hirschen
Adler
Wellenberg
Florhof
Glockenhof
Kindli
Widder
Oepfelchammer
Kaiser's Reblaube
Zum Storchen
Haus zum Rüden
KUNSTHAUS
ST-PETERKIRCHE
Heugümper
GROSSMÜNSTER
WASSERKIRCHE
Ban Song Thai
Savoy Baur en Ville
FRAUMÜNSTER
Helmhaus
Claridge
Kronenhalle
Vorderer Sternen
Glärnischhof
Baur au Lac
STADELHOFEN
Park Hyatt
KONGRESSGEB.
Sheraton Neues Schloss Zürich
Intermezzo
Ambassador
Conti
Opera
ZÜRICHSEE
LIMMAT
LINDENHOF
Bahnhofpl.
Bellevuepl.
Sechseläutenplatz
Bürklipl.
Quaibrüke

Historical and Commercial Centre
(Plan II)

Zürich Marriott

Neumühlequai 42 ✉ 8001 – ☎ 044 360 70 70 – marriott.zurich@marriotthotels.com – Fax 044 360 77 77 – www.zurichmarriott.com **C1**

255 rm – 🚹255/445 CHF 🚹🚹255/445 CHF, ☕ 36 CHF – 9 suites

Rest *White Elephant* – *(closed Saturday lunch and Sunday lunch)* Menu 69 CHF (dinner buffet) – Carte 50/106 CHF

Rest *Echo* – *(dinner only)* Carte 54/116 CHF

♦ Chain hotel ♦ Classic ♦

A multi-storey building with its own underground parking, beside the river. The rooms differ in size and layout, but are all comfortable and contemporary. Modern and with clean lines, the White Elephant is known for its Thai specialities.

Sofitel

Stampfenbachstr. 60 ✉ 8006 – ☎ 044 360 60 60 – h1196@accor.com – Fax 044 360 60 61 – www.sofitel.com **C1**

134 rm – 🚹210/535 CHF 🚹🚹230/535 CHF, ☕ 32 CHF – 4 suites

Rest *Luo* – see below

Rest *Bel Etage* – *(closed Sunday lunch, Saturday and Bank Holidays)* Carte 54/110 CHF

♦ Chain hotel ♦ Functional ♦

From the reception area, which is decorated in the style of an elegant Swiss chalet to the sound-insulated rooms, wood and warm colours characterise the interior of this hotel. The Bel Etage is rustic yet refined; the cuisine is contemporary.

Central Plaza

Central 1 ✉ 8001 – ☎ 044 256 56 56 – info@central.ch – Fax 044 256 56 57 – www.central.ch **D1**

101 rm – 🚹250/320 CHF 🚹🚹250/385 CHF, ☕ 18 CHF – 4 suites

Rest *King's Cave* – *(closed Saturday lunch and Sunday lunch)* Carte 44/95 CHF

♦ Business ♦ Modern ♦

This hotel is opposite the railway station, beside the Limmat. The comfortable guest rooms are all furnished with modern style and design. The King's Cave grill restaurant has beautiful atmosphere: the basement vaults previously served as the safe for the UBS bank.

Florhof

Florhofgasse 4 ✉ 8001 – ☎ 044 250 26 26 – info@florhof.ch – Fax 044 250 26 27 – www.florhof.ch

closed 21 - 28 December **D2**

35 rm ☕ – 🚹235/295 CHF 🚹🚹370/390 CHF

Rest – *(closed 19 April - 5 May, 22 December - 7 January, Monday except dinner in summer, Saturday lunch, Sunday and Bank Holidays)* Menu 47 CHF (lunch)/88 CHF – Carte 80/110 CHF

♦Traditional ♦ Personalised ♦

Tasteful furnishings, attention to detail and the latest technology characterise the rooms of this beautiful 16th century patrician house. Beautifully set tables await you in the elegant restaurant.

Ambassador

Falkenstr. 6 ✉ 8008 – ☎ 044 258 98 98 – welcome@ambassadorhotel.ch – Fax 044 258 98 00 – www.ambassadorhotel.ch **D3**

45 rm – 🚹220/410 CHF 🚹🚹340/490 CHF, ☕ 24 CHF

Rest *A l'Opera* – Menu 41 CHF (lunch)/65 CHF – Carte 52/111 CHF

♦ Business ♦ Modern ♦

This former patrician house is located on the edge of the city centre, very close to the opera house. It features modern, well equipped guest rooms. The restaurant A l'Opera is decorated with murals of operatic scenes.

Opera without rest

Dufourstr. 5 ✉ 8008 – ✆ 044 258 99 99 – welcome@operahotel.ch – Fax 044 258 99 00 – www.operahotel.ch **D3**

62 rm – †198/370 CHF ††310/470 CHF, ☕ 24 CHF

♦ Business ♦ Modern ♦

This business hotel faces the opera house which has given it its name. The rooms are modern and homey, decorated in warm colours.

Claridge

Steinwiesstr. 8 ✉ 8032 – ✆ 044 267 87 87 – info@claridge.ch – Fax 044 251 24 76 – www.claridge.ch

closed 21 December - 2 January **D3**

31 rm – †230/340 CHF ††260/490 CHF, ☕ 25 CHF

Rest *Orson's* – *(closed Sunday)* Menu 48 CHF (lunch) – Carte 55/107 CHF

Rest *Ace* – *(closed Sunday)* Menu 48 CHF (lunch) – Carte 43/73 CHF

♦ Traditional ♦ Classic ♦

This hotel, dating back to 1835, is located near the city centre. The individually designed rooms are beautifully furnished, some with Louis XV pieces. Orson's serves classical cuisine. L'Ace is a bistro/restaurant serving traditional dishes.

Wellenberg without rest

Niederdorfstr. 10 ✉ 8001 – ✆ 043 888 44 44 – reservation@hotel-wellenberg.ch – Fax 043 888 44 45 – www.hotel-wellenberg.ch **D2**

45 rm ☕ – †215/390 CHF ††275/450 CHF

♦ Business ♦ Functional ♦

This hotel is located right in the middle of the old town and offers modern rooms, some furnished in the Art Deco style. Elegant breakfast room with terrace under an arcade.

Adler

Rosengasse 10 (at Hirschenplatz) ✉ 8001 – ✆ 044 266 96 96 – info@hotel-adler.ch – Fax 044 266 96 69 – www.hotel-adler.ch **D2**

52 rm ☕ – †150/300 CHF ††230/330 CHF

Rest *Swiss Chuchi* – *(closed Christmas)* Carte 42/88 CHF

♦ Business ♦ Functional ♦

The rooms have light-coloured, functional wood furnishings and modern technology and also feature artwork depicting views of Zurich's old town by the painter Heinz Blum. A rustic atmosphere awaits you in the Swiss Chuchi, which looks out onto the street.

Helmhaus without rest

Schifflände 30 ✉ 8001 – ✆ 044 266 95 95 – info@helmhaus.ch – Fax 044 266 95 66 – www.helmhaus.ch **D3**

24 rm ☕ – †190/280 CHF ††270/390 CHF

♦ Business ♦ Functional ♦

This hotel, located in the heart of town, offers functional guest rooms, some of which have a particularly modern design. Pleasant breakfast room on the first floor.

Hirschen without rest

Niederdorfstr. 13 ✉ 8001 – ✆ 043 268 33 33 – info@hirschen-zuerich.ch – Fax 043 268 33 34 – www.hirschen-zuerich.ch **D2**

27 rm ☕ – †150/175 CHF ††175/210 CHF

♦ Family ♦ Functional ♦

A 300-year-old inn with functional and modern rooms and a wine tavern in the historic 16th century vaulted cellar. A beautiful roof terrace opens in the summer.

Rütli without rest

Zähringerstr. 43 ✉ 8001 – ✆ 044 254 58 00 – info@rutli.ch – Fax 044 254 58 01 – www.rutli.ch

closed 21 December - 6 January **D1**

62 rm ☕ – †175/220 CHF ††300/340 CHF

♦ Business ♦ Functional ♦

This hotel near the train station has a pleasant reception area and simple modern guest rooms. Of special interest are the graffiti rooms.

XX **Conti**

Dufourstr. 1 ✉ 8008 – ✆ 044 251 06 66 – ristorante.conti@bindella.ch – Fax 044 251 06 86 – www.bindella.ch **D3**

Rest – Carte 64/133 CHF

♦ Italian ♦ Formal ♦

This restaurant, just near the Opera, has a classic, refined interior with a beautiful, high stucco ceiling, display of artwork, and Italian cuisine.

XX **Kronenhalle**

Rämistr. 4 ✉ 8001 – ✆ 044 262 99 00 – kronenhalle@bluewin.ch – Fax 044 262 99 19 – www.kronenhalle.com **D3**

Rest – *(booking advisable)* Carte 74/136 CHF

♦ Traditional ♦ Formal ♦

This elegant, well-established Zurich institution has a long tradition and offers attentive service. Noteworthy art collection.

XX **Haus zum Rüden**

Limmatquai 42 ✉ 8001 – ✆ 044 261 95 66 – info@hauszumrueden.ch – Fax 044 261 18 04 – www.hauszumrueden.ch
closed Christmas, Saturday and Sunday **D2**

Rest – Menu 59 CHF (lunch)/138 CHF – Carte 73/140 CHF

♦ Classic ♦ Formal ♦

The Gothic ceiling of the restaurant in this lovely 13th century Guildhall is surprisingly made of wooden barrels. Refined historical ambiance and a classic menu.

XX **Ti-Fondata-Stapferstube**

Culmannstr. 45 ✉ 8006 – ✆ 044 350 11 00 – massimiliano@restauranti.ch – Fax 044 350 11 01 – www.restauranti.ch
closed 20 July - 4 August, Christmas, New Year, Monday from June - August, Saturday lunch, Sunday and Bank Holidays *Plan I* **A3**

Rest – Menu 39 CHF – Carte 55/92 CHF

♦ Italian ♦ Formal ♦

This traditional restaurant specialises in products from the Ticino region: fresh, typical cuisine as well as a large selection of Ticino wines and grappa.

XX **Luo** – Hotel Sofitel

Stampfenbachstr. 60 ✉ 8006 – ✆ 043 810 00 65 – Fax 043 322 58 18
closed 21 July - 10 August, 23 December - 6 January, Saturday lunch and Sunday **C1**

Rest – Menu 65/95 CHF – Carte 46/93 CHF

♦ Chinese ♦ Friendly ♦

Brick walls and a beautiful wood ceiling give this restaurant its refined, rustic character. Delicious Chinese cuisine is served.

XX **Casa Ferlin**

Stampfenbachstr. 38 ✉ 8006 – ✆ 044 362 35 09 – casaferlin@bluewin.ch – Fax 044 362 35 34 – www.casaferlin.ch
closed 12 July - 10 August, Saturday and Sunday **C-D1**

Rest – *(booking advisable)* Menu 52 CHF (lunch)/105 CHF – Carte 63/138 CHF

♦ Italian ♦ Family ♦

A traditional, family-run restaurant with a classically rustic atmosphere. The restaurant was opened in 1907 and offers Italian dishes.

X **Oepfelchammer**

Rindermarkt 12 (1st floor) ✉ 8001 – ✆ 044 251 23 36 – Fax 044 262 75 33 – www.oepfelchammer.ch
closed 13 July - 11 August, 22 December - 8 January, Monday, Sunday and Bank Holidays **D2**

Rest – Carte 53/95 CHF

♦ Modern ♦ Rustic ♦

The poet Gottfried Keller was a regular guest at the original wine tavern. Contemporary as well as traditional cuisine is served in this 19th century inn.

Vorderer Sternen

Theaterstr. 22 ✉ 8001 – ✆ 044 251 49 49 – info@vorderer-sternen.ch – Fax 044 252 90 63 – www.vorderer-sternen.ch **D3**

Rest – Carte 42/92 CHF

◆ Traditional ◆ Brasserie ◆

On the ground floor is a simple café, while upstairs there is a cosy restaurant decorated in dark wood, offering a traditional menu.

Ban Song Thai

Kirchgasse 6 ✉ 8001 – ✆ 044 252 33 31 – bansong@bluewin.ch – Fax 044 252 33 15 – www.bansongthai.ch

closed 21 July - 10 August, 24 December - 2 January, Saturday lunch and Sunday

Rest – *(booking advisable)* Menu 60 CHF – Carte 44/82 CHF **D2**

◆ Asian ◆ Exotic ◆

This restaurant is located near the Kunsthaus and the Grossmünster cathedral. The name says it all: the cuisine invites you on a trip to Thailand.

LEFT BANK OF THE RIVER LIMMAT — *Plan II*

Baur au Lac

Talstr. 1 ✉ 8001 – ✆ 044 220 50 20 – info@bauraulac.ch – Fax 044 220 50 44 – www.bauraulac.ch **C3**

107 rm – †520/820 CHF ††820 CHF, ☕ 42 CHF – 17 suites

Rest *Le Pavillon / Le Français* – Menu 90 CHF – Carte 81/182 CHF

Rest *Rive Gauche* – *(closed 20 July - 11 August and Sunday)* Carte 63/131 CHF

◆ Grand Luxury ◆ Stylish ◆

This traditional, stately 19th century hotel includes a spacious lobby, luxurious rooms and a beautiful garden. Mediterranean cuisine is served in the summer in Le Pavillon and in winter in Le Français. A stylish favourite: the Rive Gauche.

Park Hyatt

Beethovenstr. 21 ✉ 8002 – ✆ 043 883 12 34 – zurich.park@hyattintl.com – Fax 043 883 12 35 – www.zurich.park.hyatt.ch **C3**

138 rm – †460/1230 CHF ††610/1380 CHF, ☕ 40 CHF – 4 suites

Rest *Parkhuus* – *(closed Saturday lunch and Sunday)* Menu 59 CHF (lunch) – Carte 54/147 CHF

◆ Grand Luxury ◆ Stylish ◆

Behind a modern glass façade are tasteful, luxurious rooms outfitted with the latest technology, as well as professional service. Snacks available in the lounge. Onyx bar. Elegant : the Parkhuus restaurant occupies two stories and boasts floor-to-ceiling windows and a beautiful glass-front wine cellar.

Savoy Baur en Ville

at Paradeplatz ✉ 8001 – ✆ 044 215 25 25 – welcome@savoy-zuerich.ch – Fax 044 215 25 00 – www.savoy-zuerich.ch **C3**

104 rm ☕ – †510 CHF ††780 CHF – 8 suites

Rest *Baur* – (1st floor) *(closed Saturday, Sunday and Bank Holidays)* Menu 72 CHF (lunch) – Carte 72/140 CHF

Rest *Orsini* – *(in front of the cathedral) (booking advisable)* Menu 66 CHF (lunch) – Carte 74/137 CHF

◆ Grand Luxury ◆ Classic ◆

This hotel in the heart of town creates a stylish setting with its grand 19th century architecture. It is distinguished by its service and modern, elegant interior. Classic and elegant: the Baur on the first floor. The Italian alternative: the Orsini.

Widder

Rennweg 7 ✉ 8001 – ✆ 044 224 25 26 – home@widderhotel.ch – Fax 044 224 24 24 – www.widderhotel.ch **C2**

42 rm – †520/600 CHF ††770/900 CHF, ☕ 48 CHF – 7 suites

Rest – *(closed Sunday lunch)* Menu 72 CHF (lunch)/130 CHF – Carte 90/142 CHF

◆ Luxury ◆ Design ◆

This hotel is a group of 8 historic old townhouses which feature contemporary architectural elements. Tasteful, refined interior. Two beautiful restaurants, each with its own charm and character.

Schweizerhof
Bahnhofplatz 7 ✉ 8001 – ✆ 044 218 88 88 – info@hotelschweizerhof.com – Fax 044 218 81 81 – www.hotelschweizerhof.com **C1**
115 rm – 322/509 CHF 535/759 CHF
Rest *La Soupière* – *(closed 25 December - 2 January, Saturday from July - August and Sunday)* Menu 76 CHF (lunch) – Carte 90/134 CHF
♦ Luxury ♦ Classic ♦
In the centre of town, directly opposite the main railway station, you will find this hotel which is steeped in tradition. Behind its imposing façade lie modern elegance and comfort. The La Soupière restaurant is classic and refined.

Four Points by Sheraton
Kalandergasse 1 (Sihlcity) ✉ 8045 – ✆ 044 554 00 00 – sihlcity@fourpoints.com – Fax 044 554 00 01 – www.fourpoints.com/zurich *Plan I* **A3**
128 rm – 230/410 CHF 230/410 CHF, 30 CHF – 4 suites
Rest *Rampe Süd* – *(closed Sunday and Bank Holidays)* Menu 60/80 CHF – Carte 44/96 CHF
♦ Chain hotel ♦ Design ♦
In the Sihlcity, with a large shopping centre, is this large, comfortable hotel with well equipped rooms and modern design. This stylish restaurant serves international cuisine.

Zum Storchen
Am Weinplatz 2 ✉ 8001 – ✆ 044 227 27 27 – info@storchen.ch – Fax 044 227 27 00 – www.storchen.ch **C2**
70 rm – 410/470 CHF 560/780 CHF
Rest *Rôtisserie* – Menu 95 CHF – Carte 67/112 CHF
♦ Traditional ♦ Classic ♦
This traditional hotel, one of the oldest in town, is located directly on the Limmat. Tasteful Jouy fabrics adorn the elegant and comfortable rooms. A beautiful terrace by the river complements the restaurants and offers views over the old part of town.

Sheraton Neues Schloss Zürich
Stockerstr. 17 ✉ 8002 – ✆ 044 286 94 00 – neuesschloss@arabellasheraton.com – Fax 044 286 94 45 – www.arabellasheraton.com **C3**
60 rm – 240/490 CHF 240/490 CHF, 35 CHF
Rest *Le Jardin* – *(closed Saturday, Sunday and Bank Holidays)* Carte 51/97 CHF
♦ Business ♦ Classic ♦
This hotel is not far from the lake and is an excellent starting point for your activities. The guest rooms are furnished in an elegant, modern style. Ground-floor restaurant with contemporary cuisine.

Glärnischhof
Claridenstr. 30 ✉ 8002 – ✆ 044 286 22 22 – info@hotelglaernischhof.ch – Fax 044 286 22 86 – www.hotelglaernischhof.ch **C3**
62 rm – 240/430 CHF 290/490 CHF
Rest *Le Poisson* – *(closed Saturday, Sunday and Bank Holidays)* Menu 59 CHF (lunch)/78 CHF – Carte 65/114 CHF
Rest *Vivace* – Carte 44/99 CHF
♦ Business ♦ Modern ♦
This townhouse is on the edge of the city centre and offers large guest rooms with high ceilings and beautiful walnut furniture. Le Poisson features delicious fish specialities.

Glockenhof
Sihlstr. 31 ✉ 8001 – ✆ 044 225 91 91 – info@glockenhof.ch – Fax 044 225 92 92 – www.glockenhof.ch **C2**
95 rm – 200/410 CHF 300/540 CHF
Rest – Menu 45 CHF (lunch) – Carte 41/92 CHF
♦ Business ♦ Modern ♦
The central location is just one of the advantages of this well-run hotel. In addition to traditional rooms there are tastefully modern designer rooms. Glogge-Stube restaurant with a lovely, quiet terrace. Glogge-Egge Bistro.

Kindli

Pfalzgasse 1 ✉ 8001 – ✆ 043 888 76 76 – hotel@kindli.ch – Fax 043 888 76 77 – www.kindli.ch **C2**

17 rm ☕ – 🛉260/360 CHF 🛉🛉400/440 CHF

Rest *Zum Kindli* – *(closed Sunday and Bank Holidays except in winter)*

Carte 67/117 CHF

♦ Traditional ♦ Cosy ♦

This very traditional Zurich townhouse offers you a homey atmosphere and comfortable, individual rooms, most of which are in a classic Laura Ashley style and some of which are modern. A refined, elegant restaurant with contemporary cuisine.

Walhalla without rest

Limmatstr. 5 ✉ 8005 – ✆ 044 446 54 00 – walhalla-hotel@bluewin.ch – Fax 044 446 54 54 – www.walhalla-hotel.ch **C1**

48 rm – 🛉135/160 CHF 🛉🛉185/220 CHF, ☕ 16 CHF

♦ Business ♦ Functional ♦

Convenient to transportation, located at a tram station behind the train station. Beautiful painted scenes of the gods adorn the rooms, which are furnished in dark wood.

Sein

Schützengasse 5 ✉ 8001 – ✆ 044 221 10 65 – restaurantsein@bluewin.ch – Fax 044 212 65 80 – www.zürichsein.ch

closed 21 July - 10 August, 24 - 30 December, Saturday except dinner from mid November - Christmas, Sunday and Bank Holidays **C1**

Rest – Menu 68 CHF (lunch)/150 CHF – Carte 74/134 CHF

Rest *Tapas Bar* – Carte 53/96 CHF

♦ Modern ♦ Fashionable ♦

The Sein is a modern restaurant near the train station. A gourmet menu is served in the evening, with simpler fare on offer at lunch. Contemporary cuisine. Little delicious bites in the Tapas Bar.

Kaiser's Reblaube

Glockengasse 7 ✉ 8001 – ✆ 044 221 21 20 – rest.reblaube@bluewin.ch – Fax 044 221 21 55 – www.kaisers-reblaube.ch

closed 21 July - 10 August, Monday dinner from April - September, Saturday lunch and Sunday **C2**

Rest – *(booking advisable)* Menu 58 CHF (lunch)/130 CHF – Carte 69/129 CHF

♦ Modern ♦ Rustic ♦

In a historic old townhouse in the midst of old alleyways is the Goethe-Stübli. Located on the first floor and boasting a lively wine tavern with a garden. Contemporary cuisine.

Intermezzo

Beethovenstr. 2 (in the Kongresshaus) ✉ 8002 – ✆ 044 206 36 36 – intermezzo@kongresshaus.ch – Fax 044 206 36 59 – www.kongresshaus.ch

closed 14 July - 10 August, Saturday, Sunday and Bank Holidays **C3**

Rest – Menu 59 CHF (lunch) – Carte 75/133 CHF

♦ Modern ♦ Formal ♦

This restaurant in the Kongresshaus is pleasantly bright and elegant and serves a contemporary menu.

Sala of Tokyo

Limmatstr. 29 ✉ 8005 – ✆ 044 271 52 90 – sala@active.ch – Fax 044 271 78 07 – www.sala-of-tokyo.ch

closed 20 July - 11 August, 23 December - 7 January, Saturday lunch, Sunday and Monday **C1**

Rest – Menu 90/125 CHF – Carte 49/121 CHF

♦ Japanese ♦ Fashionable ♦

Along with the sushi bar and restaurant, authentic dishes are served here, prepared on special Sankaiyaki grill tables, in an atmosphere featuring clean lines and modern design.

Heugümper

Waaggasse 4 ✉ 8001 – ✆ 044 211 16 60 – info@restaurantheuguemper.ch – Fax 044 211 16 61 – www.restaurantheuguemper.ch
closed 12 July - 17 August, 22 December - 2 January, Saturday except dinner from October - December, Sunday and Bank Holidays **C2**
Rest – Menu 108 CHF – Carte 68/129 CHF
◆ Euro-asiatic ◆ Fashionable ◆
This restaurant, in the old part of town, next to the Fraumünster, has a stylish, modern bistro serving delicious Eurasian dishes.

NEAR THE AIRPORT *Plan I*

Renaissance Zürich Hotel

Thurgauerstr. 101 ✉ 8152 Glattbrugg – ✆ 044 874 50 00 – renaissance.zurich@renaissancehotels.com – Fax 044 874 50 01 – www.renaissancehotels.com **B2**
196 rm – †199/455 CHF ††199/455 CHF, ☕ 35 CHF – 8 suites
Rest *Asian Place* – *(closed 6 weeks July - August, 24 December - 2 January, Saturday lunch and Sunday)* Carte 47/117 CHF
Rest *Brasserie* – Menu 39 CHF (lunch) – Carte 43/94 CHF
◆ Business ◆ Functional ◆
The hotel boasts large, public leisure facilities in the basement and spacious rooms with dark-coloured, solid wood furnishings. Asian Place serves a range of Chinese, Thai, Japanese and Indonesian cuisine. Traditional: the Brasserie.

Hilton Zurich Airport

Hohenbühlstr. 10 ✉ 8152 Glattbrugg – ✆ 044 828 50 50 – zurich@hilton.ch – Fax 044 828 51 51 – www.hilton.de/zurich **B1**
310 rm – †199/584 CHF ††199/584 CHF, ☕ 35 CHF – 13 suites
Rest *Market Place* – Menu 55 CHF (buffet) – Carte 48/117 CHF
◆ Chain hotel ◆ Functional ◆
This hotel is located near the airport and offers welcoming rooms furnished in light-coloured wood. Two floors of executive rooms. The Market Place offers guests a view of the open kitchen.

Mövenpick

Walter Mittelholzerstr. 8 ✉ 8152 Glattbrugg – ✆ 044 808 88 88 – hotel.zurich.airport@moevenpick.com – Fax 044 808 88 77 – www.moevenpick-zurich.com **B1**
333 rm – †215/685 CHF ††215/685 CHF, ☕ 33 CHF
Rest *Appenzeller Stube* – *(closed 4 weeks July - August)* Menu 45 CHF (lunch)/85 CHF – Carte 59/121 CHF
Rest *Mövenpick* – Carte 40/112 CHF
Rest *Dim Sum* – *(closed 4 weeks July - August and Sunday)* Carte 41/112 CHF
◆ Chain hotel ◆ Modern ◆
This hotel is near the motorway and has modern, comfortable superior rooms as well as functional and spacious standard rooms. The Appenzeller Stube has a typical Swiss atmosphere. The Mövenpick Restaurant offers international dishes. Delicious Chinese cuisine is served in Dim Sum.

Novotel Zürich Airport Messe

Lindbergh - Platz 1 ✉ 8152 Glattbrugg – ✆ 044 829 90 00 – h0884@accor.com – Fax 044 829 99 99 – www.novotel.com **A-B1**
255 rm – †140/430 CHF ††140/455 CHF, ☕ 25 CHF
Rest – Carte 54/93 CHF
◆ Chain hotel ◆ Modern ◆
On the outskirts of the city centre, just a few minutes from the new exhibition site, this business hotel has spacious, modern rooms furnished in light-coloured, solid wood. Colourful art is displayed in this modern restaurant serving international cuisine.

Airport

Oberhauserstr. 30 ✉ 8152 Glattbrugg – ☎ 044 809 47 47 – reservation@hotel-airport.ch – Fax 044 809 47 74 – www.hotel-airport.ch **B1**

44 rm – 140/210 CHF 180/240 CHF, 20 CHF

Rest *Edo Garden* – *(closed Saturday lunch and Sunday lunch)* Menu 54 CHF – Carte 45/114 CHF

Rest *Fujiya of Japan* – *(closed Saturday lunch and Sunday lunch) (dinner only from 14 June - 17 August)* Menu 84/114 CHF – Carte 53/114 CHF

♦ Business ♦ Functional ♦

This hotel is particularly ideal for business travellers, from its functional, contemporary furnishings and its location only a few minutes from the airport. Edo Garden specializes in Japanese cuisine. Fujiya of Japan serves Teppanyaki specialities.

Allegra

Hamelirainstr. 3 ✉ 8302 Kloten – ☎ 044 804 44 44 – reservation@hotel-allegra.ch – Fax 044 804 41 41 – www.hotel-allegra.ch **B1**

132 rm – 130/180 CHF 150/220 CHF, 16 CHF

Rest – Carte 40/87 CHF

♦ Business ♦ Modern ♦

This modern business hotel offers spacious rooms with functional, colourful built-in furniture. The hotel offers a free shuttle service to and from the airport.

Fly away

Marktgasse 19 ✉ 8302 Kloten – ☎ 044 804 44 55 – reservation@hotel-flyaway.ch – Fax 044 804 44 50 – www.hotel-flyaway.ch **B1**

42 rm – 123/222 CHF 150/296 CHF, 15 CHF

Rest – Carte 46/107 CHF

♦ Business ♦ Functional ♦

Located near the train station, the rooms in this hotel are classic, functional and spacious. Italian cuisine at the restaurant.

Vivendi

Europastr. 2 ✉ 8152 Glattbrugg – ☎ 043 211 32 42 – info@restaurant-vivendi.ch – Fax 043 211 32 41 – www.restaurant-vivendi.ch

closed 22 December - 2 January, Saturday, Sunday and Bank Holidays

Rest – Carte 52/95 CHF **B1**

♦ Traditional ♦ Friendly ♦

A modern, refined restaurant, characterised by bold lines and subtle colours, serving traditional cuisine with contemporary touches.

ENVIRONS OF ZURICH *Plan I*

Eden au Lac

Utoquai 45 ✉ 8008 – ☎ 044 266 25 25 – info@edenaulac.ch – Fax 044 266 25 00 – www.edenaulac.ch **B3**

46 rm – 440/520 CHF 660/740 CHF, 40 CHF – 4 suites

Rest – Menu 65 CHF (lunch)/145 CHF – Carte 79/150 CHF

♦ Luxury ♦ Classic ♦

This new-baroque style hotel is a cultural monument, gracing the lakeside since 1909. Inside, you will find everything that you would expect from a luxury hotel. A classic gourmet restaurant with seasonal, contemporary cuisine.

Steigenberger Bellerive au Lac

Utoquai 47 ✉ 8008 – ☎ 044 254 40 00 – bellerive@steigenberger.ch – Fax 044 254 40 01 – www.zuerich.steigenberger.ch **B3**

51 rm – 290/500 CHF 340/580 CHF

Rest – Menu 55 CHF (lunch) – Carte 63/138 CHF

♦ Business ♦ Modern ♦

The hotel, modern yet elegantly decorated in the style of the 1920s, is located on the lakeside. The rooms are contemporary in design, technology and comfort. This restaurant offers perfectly executed 5-element cuisine made from regional products.

Alden Hotel Splügenschloss

Splügenstr. 2 ✉ 8002 – ✆ 044 289 99 99 – welcome@alden.ch – Fax 044 289 99 98 – www.alden.ch **A3**

10 rm – 700/1500 CHF 700/1500 CHF – **12 suites**

Rest *Gourmet* – *(closed Saturday lunch and Sunday)* Menu 65 CHF (lunch)/150 CHF – Carte 92/149 CHF

Rest *Bar / Bistro* – Carte 48/91 CHF

♦ Luxury ♦ Stylish ♦

Behind the grand façade of this building that dates from 1895 are very modern suites with elegant designer furnishings. Contemporary cuisine is served in the tasteful and refined Gourmet.

Crowne Plaza

Badenerstr. 420 ✉ 8040 – ✆ 044 404 44 44 – info@cpzurich.ch – Fax 044 404 44 40 – www.crowneplaza.com/zurich **A3**

364 rm – 230/550 CHF 230/550 CHF, 33 CHF

Rest *Relais des Arts* – *(closed Saturday and Sunday)* Menu 45 CHF (lunch) – Carte 50/101 CHF

♦ Business ♦ Retro ♦

The amenities of this hotel include comfortable rooms, furnished in a modern, functional style, and good connections to local area. Fitness area. The Relais des Arts offers bright, elegant surroundings.

Ascot

Tessinerplatz 9 ✉ 8002 – ✆ 044 208 14 14 – info@ascot.ch – Fax 044 208 14 20 – www.ascot.ch **A3**

74 rm – 290/460 CHF 350/580 CHF

Rest *Lawrence* – *(closed Saturday and Sunday)* Menu 62 CHF (lunch) – Carte 67/129 CHF

♦ Traditional ♦ Classic ♦

This hotel has a stylish interior with comfortable rooms that are either furnished in dark mahogany or pale whitewashed oak. The Lawrence features a beautiful Tudor style.

Dolder Waldhaus — Zurich and lake,

Kurhausstr. 20 ✉ 8032 – ✆ 044 269 10 00 – info@dolderwaldhaus.ch – Fax 044 269 10 01 – www.dolderwaldhaus.ch **B3**

70 rm – 230/330 CHF 340/480 CHF – 30 suites

Rest – Carte 56/110 CHF

♦ Business ♦ Functional ♦

A 9-story hotel in a quiet location offers modern rooms with balconies and a view over the city and the lake. Apartments are available for families and longer stays. Restaurant with a classic, refined ambiance and a beautiful terrace.

Engimatt

Engimattstr. 14 ✉ 8002 – ✆ 044 284 16 16 – info@engimatt.ch – Fax 044 201 25 16 – www.engimatt.ch **A3**

73 rm – 210/360 CHF 240/430 CHF

Rest – Menu 45 CHF (lunch)/79 CHF – Carte 53/86 CHF

♦ Business ♦ Modern ♦

The hotel is located near the centre of town and yet has a country-like setting. The rooms – each with its own balcony - are individually designed and feature solid, modern furnishings. The Orangerie has modern winter garden-style glass and steel construction and a pleasant garden terrace.

Greulich

Herman Greulich-Str. 56 ✉ 8004 – ✆ 043 243 42 43 – mail@greulich.ch – Fax 043 243 42 00 – www.greulich.ch **A3**

18 rm – 205/225 CHF 285/305 CHF, 25 CHF

Rest *Greulich* – see below

♦ Business ♦ Modern ♦

In an inner courtyard lined with birch trees are garden rooms and junior suites furnished in a clean, pure, modern design.

Krone Unterstrass

rest rm rm

Schaffhauserstr. 1 ✉ 8006 – ✆ 044 360 56 56 – info@hotel-krone.ch – Fax 044 360 56 00 – www.hotel-krone.ch **A2**

57 rm – 180/220 CHF 250/300 CHF, 19 CHF

Rest – Carte 52/86 CHF

◆ Business ◆ Modern ◆

The rooms in this hotel, which is a short distance from the city centre, are tastefully decorated in a contemporary style and offer modern comfort. An elegant a-la-carte restaurant and a simpler daytime restaurant facing the street.

Novotel Zürich City-West

rest

Schiffbaustr. 13 ✉ 8005 – ✆ 044 276 22 22 – h2731@accor.com – Fax 044 276 23 23 – www.novotel.com **A2**

142 rm – 160/299 CHF 160/299 CHF, 25 CHF

Rest – Carte 53/92 CHF

◆ Chain hotel ◆ Modern ◆

This hotel, with its black glass façade, offers uniformly outfitted modern and spacious rooms with white built-in furnishings.

Mercure Hotel Stoller

Badenerstr. 357 ✉ 8003 – ✆ 044 405 47 47 – h5488@accor.com – Fax 044 405 48 48 – www.mercure.com **A3**

79 rm – 135/315 CHF 135/335 CHF, 25 CHF

Rest *Ratatouille* – Menu 45 CHF – Carte 42/90 CHF

◆ Chain hotel ◆ Functional ◆

Located on the edge of the city centre near a tram station. Unique rooms with grey veneer furniture. Rooms at the back are quieter and have balconies. Ratatouille has two dining rooms, furnished in dark wood. Sidewalk café in summer.

Rigihof

Universitätstr. 101 ✉ 8006 – ✆ 044 360 12 00 – info@hotel-rigihof.ch – Fax 044 360 12 07 – www.hotel-rigihof.ch **B2**

67 rm – 190/310 CHF 270/390 CHF

Rest *Bauhaus* – Menu 42/55 CHF – Carte 50/91 CHF

◆ Business ◆ Functional ◆

A hotel in the Bauhaus style: each bright, modern room is artistically dedicated to a different Zurich personality and bears his or her name. Clean lines and colours set the Bauhaus restaurant apart.

Ibis

rm rest rm

Schiffbaustr. 11 ✉ 8005 – ✆ 044 276 21 00 – h2942@accor.com – Fax 044 276 21 01 – www.ibishotel.com **A2**

155 rm – 120/170 CHF 120/170 CHF, 14 CHF

Rest – *(closed Saturday lunch and Sunday lunch)* Carte 40/69 CHF

◆ Chain hotel ◆ Functional ◆

Located today on the site of an old ship building hall, this hotel, with is well-equipped rooms, offers all the essentials at reasonable prices.

Rigiblick - Spice (Felix Eppisser) with rm

≤ Zurich,

Germaniastr. 99 ✉ 8006 – ✆ 043 255 15 70 – eppisser@restaurantrigiblick.ch – Fax 043 255 15 80 – www.restaurantrigiblick.ch **B2**

7 rm – 350/700 CHF 350/700 CHF

Rest *Bistro Quadrino* – see below

Rest – *(closed Sunday and Monday) (booking advisable)* Menu 62 CHF (lunch)/152 CHF – Carte 105/138 CHF

Spec. Milchlamm mit Spargeln und Morcheln (spring). Ravioli von weissem Trüffel (autumn). Steinbutt auf Mungobohnen-Dahl mit Massamam-Curry-Espuma.

◆ Euro-asiatic ◆ Formal ◆

Clean, pure and elegant is the atmosphere in the Spice restaurant. Guests enjoy Eurasian cuisine and a beautiful view. The junior suites are furnished in the most modern style.

XXX **Sonnenberg** — < Zurich and lake, A/C P VISA MC AE

Hitziweg 15 ✉ 8032 – ✆ 044 266 97 97 – restaurant@sonnenberg-zh.ch – Fax 044 266 97 98 – www.sonnenberg-zh.ch **B3**

Rest – *(booking essential)* Carte 66/160 CHF

♦ Classic ♦ Formal ♦

Located high in the FIFA building with a magnificent view of the city, the lake and the mountains. Specialities of this panorama restaurant include veal and beef dishes.

XX **Wirtschaft Flühgass** — P VISA MC AE

Zollikerstr. 214 ✉ 8008 – ✆ 044 381 12 15 – info@fluehgass.ch – Fax 044 422 75 32 – www.fluehgass.ch

closed 12 July - 10 August, 21 December - 6 January, Saturday except dinner from November - December and Sunday **B3**

Rest – *(booking advisable)* Menu 65/140 CHF – Carte 57/126 CHF

♦ Classic ♦ Family ♦

This former 16th century wine tavern is now a cosy restaurant, offering classical French cuisine.

XX **Il Gattopardo** — A/C VISA MC AE

Rotwandstr. 48 ✉ 8004 – ✆ 043 443 48 48 – Fax 043 243 85 51 – www.ilgattopardo.ch

closed 14 July - 13 August, Saturday lunch and Sunday **A3**

Rest – Menu 48 CHF (lunch)/85 CHF – Carte 71/124 CHF

♦ Italian ♦ Trendy ♦

This restaurant offers attentive service and top-notch Italian cuisine. The setting is a successful mixture of classical and modern. Walk-in wine cellar (for groups).

XX **Restaurant Greulich** – Hotel Greulich — P VISA MC AE

Herman Greulich-Str. 56 ✉ 8004 – ✆ 043 243 42 43 – mail@greulich.ch – Fax 043 243 42 00 – www.greulich.ch

closed Saturday lunch and Sunday lunch **A3**

Rest – Menu 80 CHF – Carte 75/119 CHF

♦ Inventive ♦ Trendy ♦

Guests are greeted with a modern ambiance, clean lines and creative, Spanish-inspired cuisine in this restaurant, which also features a beautiful inner courtyard terrace.

XX **Lake Side** — < lake Zurich, A/C VISA MC AE

Bellerivestr. 170 ✉ 8008 – ✆ 044 385 86 00 – info@lake-side.ch – Fax 044 385 86 01 – www.lake-side.ch **B3**

Rest – Carte 57/122 CHF

♦ Modern ♦ Trendy ♦

Located in the Seepark Zürichhorn, this modern restaurant features contemporary cuisine and a sushi bar. A summer attraction is the large deck on the shore of the lake.

X **Sankt Meinrad** — A/C VISA MC AE

Stauffacherstr. 163 ✉ 8004 – ✆ 043 534 82 77 – restaurant@sanktmeinrad.ch – www.sanktmeinrad.ch

closed 20 July - 11 August, 23 December - 7 January, Saturday lunch, Sunday and Monday **A3**

Rest – Carte 64/110 CHF

♦ Inventive ♦ Fashionable ♦

The restaurant, near the Bäckeranlage, has an atmosphere that is modern yet cosy and warm and features creative cuisine.

X **Caduff's Wine Loft** — VISA MC AE

Kanzleistr. 126 ✉ 8004 – ✆ 044 240 22 55 – caduff@wineloft.ch – Fax 044 240 22 56 – www.wineloft.ch

closed 24 December - 3 January, Saturday lunch and Sunday **A3**

Rest – *(booking advisable)* Menu 52 CHF (lunch)/115 CHF – Carte 80/129 CHF

♦ Modern ♦ Trendy ♦

Fresh, delicious, choice specialities are served in this former flower warehouse or on the new terrace. Enjoy fine wines from the legendary wine cellar with your meal.

Bistro Quadrino – Restaurant Rigiblick

Germaniastr. 99 ✉ 8006 – ✆ 043 255 15 70 – eppisser@restaurantrigiblick.ch – Fax 043 255 15 80 – www.restaurantrigiblick.ch
closed Sunday and Monday **B2**
Rest – Carte 56/90 CHF
◆ Modern ◆ Trendy ◆
This bistro successfully combines sleek design, the Ess bar, lounge and walk-in showcase wine cellar along with contemporary cuisine. Beautiful views.

Blaue Ente

Seefeldstr. 223 (Tiefenbrunnen mill) ✉ 8008 – ✆ 044 388 68 40 – info@blaue-ente.ch – Fax 044 422 77 41 – www.blaue-ente.ch
closed Christmas and New Year **B3**
Rest – *(booking advisable)* Carte 66/111 CHF
◆ Modern ◆ Trendy ◆
The stylish restaurant, with lots of glass and tubes and a gigantic wheel mechanism, is in what was the Tiefenbrunnen mill. A lively atmosphere and a modern, homestyle menu.

Ciro

Militärstr. 16 ✉ 8004 – ✆ 044 241 78 41 – ciro@swissonline.ch – Fax 044 291 14 24
closed Sunday **A3**
Rest – Carte 50/85 CHF
◆ Italian ◆ Friendly ◆
This small restaurant near the train station serves typical Italian dishes and wines.

Zentraleck

Zentralstr. 161 ✉ 8003 – ✆ 044 461 08 00 – restaurant@zentraleck.ch – www.zentraleck.ch
closed 19 July - 10 August, 29 December - 6 January, Saturday and Sunday
Rest – Menu 78 CHF (dinner) – Carte 59/103 CHF **A3**
◆ Modern ◆ Bistro ◆
Located a bit beyond the city centre, near a tram station, is this modern restaurant, offering a small, changing selection of contemporary, fresh cuisine.

Josef

Gasometerstr. 24 ✉ 8005 – ✆ 044 271 65 95 – info@josef.ch – www.josef.ch
closed Saturday lunch and Sunday **A2**
Rest – Menu 66 CHF (dinner) – Carte 56/66 CHF
◆ Modern ◆ Friendly ◆
This restaurant and bar feature a relaxed atmosphere and are located in a lively district. Guests choose from many small dishes to build their meal.

Giesserei

Birchstr. 108 ✉ 8050 Zürich-Oerlikon – ✆ 043 205 10 10 – info@diegiesserei.ch – Fax 043 205 10 11 – www.diegiesserei.ch
closed 24 December - 6 January, Saturday from July - August, Sunday in summer and Bank Holidays **A2**
Rest – Carte 56/98 CHF
◆ Modern ◆ Trendy ◆
A restaurant with a homelike setting in two former manufacturing halls that feature industrial architecture. Contemporary cuisine served.

Clouds [illegible]

London

LONDON

Population: 2 914 000 (conurbation 9 332 000) – Altitude: sea level

R. Mattès/HEMIS.fr

The term 'world city' could have been invented for London. Time zones radiate from Greenwich, and global finances zap round the Square Mile, while a phalanx of international restaurants is the equal of anywhere on earth. A stunning diversity of population is testament to the city's famed tolerance; different lifestyles and languages are as much a part of the London scene as cockneys and black cabs. This mesmerising blur of life lures long-term visitors from abroad; recently, for example, many thousands of French and Polish workers have laid down roots within the M25.

Whereas Paris evolved through a grand design of formal planning, London grew over time in a pretty haphazard way, swallowing up surrounding villages, but retaining an enviable acreage of green 'lungs': a comforting 30 per cent of London's area is made up of open space. The drama of the city is reflected in its history. From Roman settlement to banking centre to capital of a 19C empire, the city's pulse has never missed a beat; it's no surprise that a dazzling array of theatres, restaurants, museums, markets and art galleries populate its streets. Plus, of course, over 3,500 pubs, the like of which you won't find anywhere else in the world.

LIVING THE CITY

London's piecemeal character has endowed it with distinctly different areas, often breathing down each other's necks. North of Piccadilly lie the playgrounds of Soho and Mayfair, while south is the classier gentleman's clubland of St James's. On the other side of town are Clerkenwell and Southwark, historically artisan areas that have been scrubbed down, freshened up and populated with hip offices and trendy places to eat and drink. The cool sophistication of Kensington and Knightsbridge is to the west, while a more touristy aesthetic is found in the heaving piazza zone of Covent Garden further east along the river.

PRACTICAL INFORMATION

ARRIVAL-DEPARTURE

Heathrow Express to Paddington is the quickest way of getting into the city from Heathrow Airport which is 20 miles west of London. A black cab will cost about £55. There are also bus and underground connections. From Gatwick Airport, take the Gatwick Express to Victoria station. Stansted Airport is 34 miles northeast of London and Luton 35 miles north and both are served by rail links.

TRANSPORT

If you're in London for a short period, get a Travelcard, which will take you all over the city's transport system. If you're around for the longer haul, invest in an Oyster Card, much beloved by locals: these are smartcards with electronically stored pre-pay credit, and they offer good savings on fares.

Just when everyone had got used to calling Waterloo the home of their Eurostar journey to the likes of Paris and Brussels, lo and behold the London terminus changed, and these days you should head for St Pancras.

EXPLORING LONDON

In a city that grew organically without planning committee, is there anywhere you'd call the centre? Instinctively, most locals would probably say **Piccadilly Circus** if only because all that neon advertising gives it the feel of a focal point. It can certainly make a claim as gateway to the West End: when you see the statue of Eros, you know you've 'arrived'. Along Piccadilly itself, the main attractions are a top end version of what draws people to London: culture (at the Royal Academy of Arts), retail (at Fortnum & Mason) and tradition (at The Ritz). From here, London sprawls out in all directions. To the south and west are the wide-open expanses of **Green Park** and **Hyde Park**. In the latter, riders trot their horses along Rotten Row and swimmers chill out in the cool waters of the snaking Serpentine. To the north, the

habitués of **Mayfair** tend towards the monied, their dark suits flitting round the environs of Bond Street (with its Premier League shops), Grosvenor Square and the swanky Dorchester hotel. Go east, meanwhile, and you're in **Soho**, home to a lively gay culture and a dazzling array of little eateries and hip lounge bars in an equally bewildering maze of narrow streets.

→ THE GHERKIN CLASSES

The engine-room of London is the **City**, where the bonus levels paid to bankers are almost as high as the vertiginous buildings in which they work. The skyline here is a blur of steel and glass, in recent years dominated by the highly distinctive Swiss Re building, affectionately known as The Gherkin. The City, and its upstream location, has been London's centre of commerce for nearly a thousand years. In the 11C, Edward The Confessor separated it from Westminster, where he concentrated royal power. But these days the area is not all about corporate finance. Flanking the City are Shoreditch, Hoxton, Finsbury and Clerkenwell, former run-down areas that have undergone a resurgence powered by a young(ish) and creatively-minded crowd.

→ MARKET FRESH

For those who prefer their retail establishments of a more traditional kind, smart **Knightsbridge** is a perennial choice. Harrods and Harvey Nichols have stood proudly along the road from each other for many decades, the epitome of SW1 sophistication, but one of the great things about London is that street markets hold (nearly) as much cachet as the consumerist shrines. There are a great many of them, and they're dotted around all over the place. Food lovers should head for **Borough market**, under the railway arches at London Bridge. It's a gourmet's paradise, offering top quality produce from all over Britain. A grander setting is **Leadenhall market** in the City, which boasts cobbled walkways, glass roof and rare meats. **Portobello Road** in Notting Hill is world famous for its bric-à-brac, fruit and veg, and East End favourites **Brick Lane** and Ridley Road markets will keep you well stocked with everything from cheap perfume to blackened smoked fish heads! A top destination for plant lovers is **Columbia Road** market in the East End, while Old Spitalfields in the City is a great place to go for stylish handicrafts from the area's young artists.

Your Oyster card will take you far and wide sussing out the markets, but if a musical's your thing after a day battling for bargains, then you probably won't even need to take the Tube since the Leicester Square/Piccadilly area in the heart of town crams in enough board-treading venues to overwhelm even the most voracious addict of stage extravaganzas. Fringe theatre tends to play on the, well, fringes of town, so if you're looking for something a bit more thought-provoking than Abba, Queen or Andrew Lloyd Webber, then you might be better served looking to the likes of the Royal Court in Chelsea, the Old Vic at Waterloo or Islington's Kings Head or Almeida.

→ POWER MAD

London's a great place to look at pictures. Who would have believed even a decade ago that the capital's leading tourist venue would be a disused old power station on the 'wrong' side of the Thames, but the **Tate Modern**, scrubbed up and, cocking a snook at St Paul's over the river, has proved itself a record-breaker and continues to draw the crowds. As ever, London's art galleries of an older vintage also attract visitors like bees to the honeypot, so prepare to stand a few tourists deep as you admire the world's greatest artists at the likes of The **National Gallery**, The **National Portrait**

Gallery and The **Royal Academy of Arts**. Museums – there are over 200 of them in London – are an institution here, and the Imperial War Museum in Lambeth is one of the best: first-rate exhibits on the First and Second World Wars offer fascinating and sobering perspectives on the realities of conflict.

→ CAPITAL ACTION

Despite all its other claims to fame, you'd lay short odds that most of London's headlines around the world revolve around sport. On the football front, Chelsea FC's recent successes have doused the Royal Borough in even more glamorous gold-dust (getting a ticket for a home game, though, can be challenging); the brand new, behind-schedule, wow-factor **Wembley** opened its doors in 2007 and looks set for an illustrious future; the London Marathon, run every April since 1981, was the first big-city 26 miler, and competitor numbers increase each year; there's the perennial newsworthiness of **Wimbledon** fortnight and the UniversitY; and, of course, the city will remain in the sporting spotlight as the 2012 Olympics edges closer by the day.

It's not hard to see London as a melding together of its constituent parts, its 'villages': Kensington and Chelsea, Hampstead and Highgate, Bayswater and Maida Vale, Richmond and Twickenham. Each of these boasts its own community feel and its own areas of treasured green space. Don't be afraid to jump on a bus or dive onto a tube and find out for yourself what each has to offer. There are nearly 4000 pubs around the city and each one offers a clue to the character of the area you're in. If you want to join the dots and link up lots of areas in one go, take a walk along the **Thames Path**, which covers the whole length of the river from source to sea – it's a stress-free way to take in some cracking views of a pulsating city.

CALENDAR HIGHLIGHTS

Some things never change. You can set your watch by some of London's calendar highlights: from the Boat Race in April to the Chelsea Flower Show in May, from Wimbledon Fortnight in June to the Great British Beer Festival in August, from the Notting Hill Carnival, also in August, to the London Film Festival in October. Other annual highlights are of more recent vintage. The New Year's Day Parade of extravagant floats starting from Parliament Square is settling in nicely, as is the St Patrick's Day Parade through Whitehall in March. The South Bank Beach, 'laid' in July to August, would have been considered a joke even 10 years ago, while ice rinks at the Natural History Museum, Hampton Court Palace, Tower of London, Somerset House and Kew Gardens now give an extra glow to Christmas revellers.

LONDON IN...

→ ONE DAY

British Museum, Tower of London, St Paul's Cathedral, Tate Modern

→ TWO DAYS

National Gallery, London Eye, Natural History Museum

→ THREE DAYS

Science Museum, Victoria and Albert Museum, National Portrait Gallery

EATING OUT

Some years ago you could dine out in London on anything from a bacon and egg sandwich to its cucumber variant. Or so popular memory has it. These days it's one of the food capitals of the world, and you really can eat Malay to Mediterranean, Latin American to Lebanese right across zones one to five. But those wishing to sample classic British dishes also have more choice these days as more and more chefs are rediscovering home-grown ingredients, regional classics and traditional recipes. Eating in the capital can be pricey, so check out good value pre- and post-theatre menus, or tuck into lunch at one of the many eateries that drop their prices, but not their standards, in the middle of the day.

With over 6,000 restaurants in London (to say nothing of its cafés), it's possible to eat at any time. But central London restaurants can get very busy from about 7.30pm; if you haven't booked well in advance you might have more luck trying somewhere a bit further out.

"Would I were in an alehouse in London! I would give all my fame for a pot of ale and safety," says Shakespeare's Henry V. Samuel Johnson tended to agree, waxing lyrical upon the happiness produced by a good tavern or inn. Two examples of the dewy-eyed love the Londoner (albeit one a monarch) has for beer. Pubs are often open these days from 11am to 11pm (and beyond) so this particular love now knows no bounds, and any tourist is welcome to come along and enjoy the romance. It is not just the cooking that has improved in pubs - wine, too, has gained in popularity in recent years: woe betide any establishment in this city that can't distinguish its Chardonnay from its Pinot Grigio. And with more Champagne being quaffed in London than any city outside France, it's fair to say the taste for a tipple offers up a wide range of opportunities to anyone within the M25.

→ THERE'S NO RHYME OR REASON...

...when it comes to a formal tipping procedure. Some restaurants leave the amount open, while others add on anything up to 15%. Leaving a cash tip on the table guarantees the tip goes to the people it's meant for, the waiters. If you're not sure whether it's heading for their pockets then just ask them.

HOTELS – ALPHABETIC LIST

RESTAURANTS – ALPHABETIC LIST

R

S

T

U

V

W

Y

Z

OPEN SATURDAY AND SUNDAY

Restaurant	Category	Page
Amaya	XXX ✿	894
Angelus	XX	912
Arbutus	X ✿	882
Atelier de Joël Robuchon (L')	X ✿	890
Awana	XXX	929
Benares	XXX ✿	876
Bentley's (Oyster Bar)	X	880
Bibendum	XXX	928
Bluebird	XX	930
Bombay Brasserie	XXX	935
Brasserie Roux	XX ☺	886
Butlers Wharf Chop House	X	920
Café du Jardin (Le)	X	890
Capital Restaurant (The)	XXX ✿✿	928
Caprice (Le)	XX	885
Chelsea Brasserie	XX	930
China Tang	XXXX	875
Chutney Mary	XXX	929
Cigala	X	906
Daphne's	XX	929
Deuxième (Le)	XX	890
Etranger (L')	XX	935
Foliage	XXX ✿	907
Galvin N	XX ☺	902
Gordon Ramsay at Claridge's	XXXX ✿	874
Imli	X	883
Inn the Park	X	886
Ivy (The)	XXX	889
J. Sheekey	XX	889
Kensington Place	X	938
Kiasu	X	913
Ledbury (The)	XXX ✿	939
Locanda Locatelli	XXX ✿	901
L Restaurant and Bar	XX	938
Malabar	X ☺	939
Mirabelle	XXX ✿	876
Mr Chow	XX	909
Narrow (The) N	🍺 ☺	922
Noura Central	XX	886
Nozomi	XX	930
Only Running Footman (The)	🍺	880
Ozer	XX	903
Papillon	XX	930
Pasha	XX	935
Phoenix Palace	XX	903
Porte des Indes (La)	XX	902
Poule au Pot (La)	X	897
Providores (The)	XX	902
Quaglino's	XX	885
Quilon N	XXX ✿	896
Racine	XX	930
Rhodes W1 Brasserie	XX	902
Roka	XX	903
Rules	XX	889
St Alban	XXX	885
Scott's	XXX	875
Tamarind	XXX ✿	877
Tom's Kitchen	X	931
Veeraswamy	XX	880
Wild Honey N	XX ✿	877
Zafferano	XXX ✿	894
Zuma	XX	908

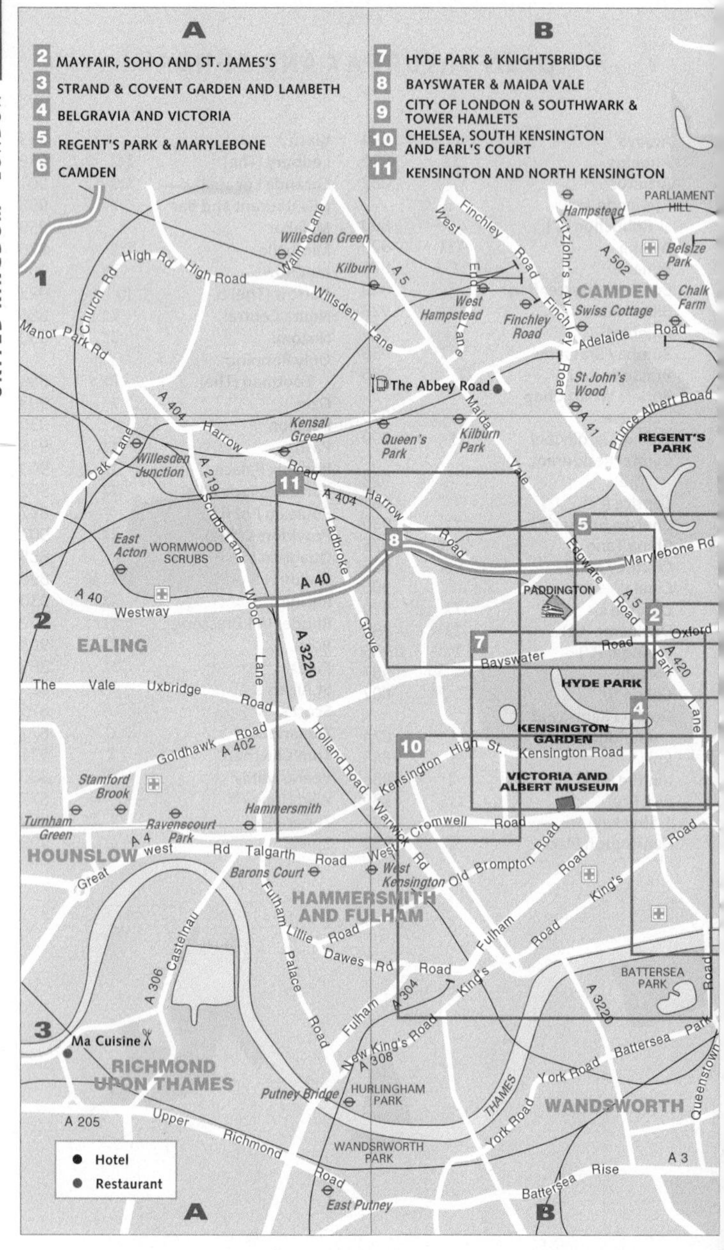
A
B
2 MAYFAIR, SOHO AND ST. JAMES'S
3 STRAND & COVENT GARDEN AND LAMBETH
4 BELGRAVIA AND VICTORIA
5 REGENT'S PARK & MARYLEBONE
6 CAMDEN
7 HYDE PARK & KNIGHTSBRIDGE
8 BAYSWATER & MAIDA VALE
9 CITY OF LONDON & SOUTHWARK & TOWER HAMLETS
10 CHELSEA, SOUTH KENSINGTON AND EARL'S COURT
11 KENSINGTON AND NORTH KENSINGTON
CAMDEN
REGENT'S PARK
PADDINGTON
HYDE PARK
KENSINGTON GARDEN
VICTORIA AND ALBERT MUSEUM
WORMWOOD SCRUBS
EALING
HOUNSLOW
HAMMERSMITH AND FULHAM
RICHMOND UPON THAMES
WANDSWORTH
BATTERSEA PARK
HURLINGHAM PARK
WANDSRWORTH PARK
PARLIAMENT HILL
The Abbey Road
Ma Cuisine
Hotel
Restaurant

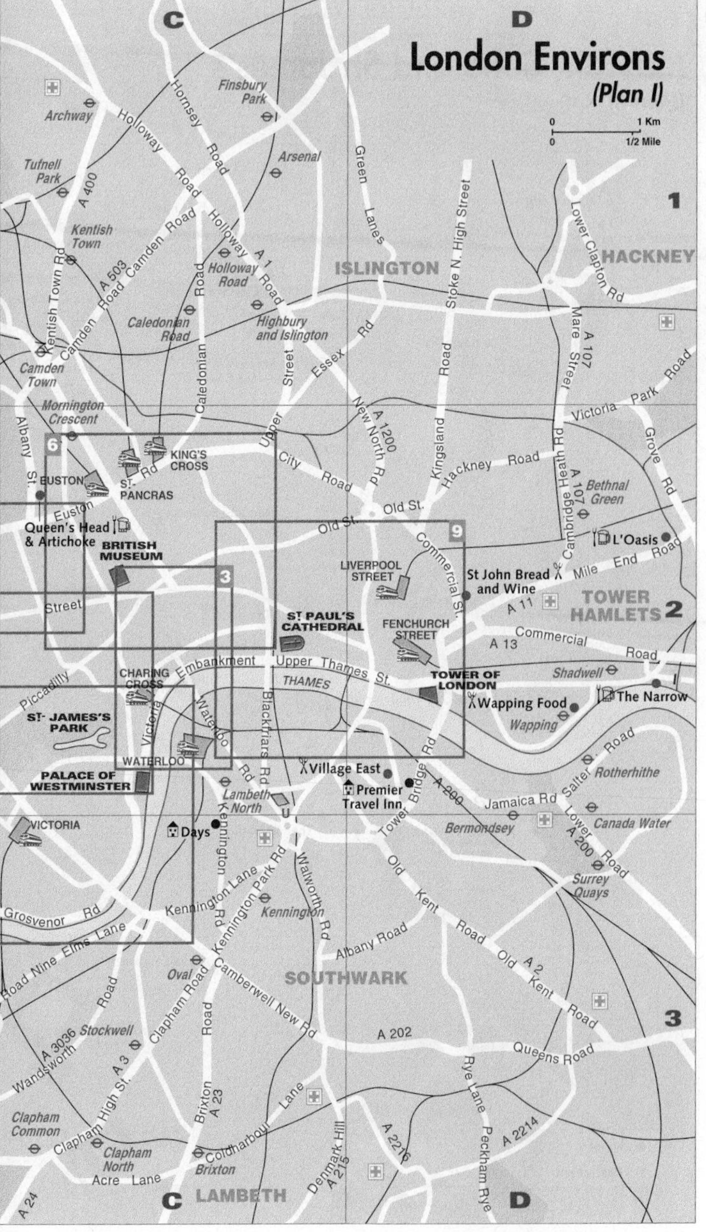
London Environs
(Plan I)
C
D
1
2
3
ISLINGTON
HACKNEY
TOWER HAMLETS
SOUTHWARK
LAMBETH
KING'S CROSS
ST. PANCRAS
EUSTON
BRITISH MUSEUM
ST. PAUL'S CATHEDRAL
LIVERPOOL STREET
FENCHURCH STREET
TOWER OF LONDON
CHARING CROSS
ST. JAMES'S PARK
PALACE OF WESTMINSTER
WATERLOO
VICTORIA
THAMES
Queen's Head & Artichoke
L'Oasis
St John Bread and Wine
Wapping Food
The Narrow
Village East
Premier Travel Inn
Days
Archway
Tufnell Park
Kentish Town
Camden Town
Mornington Crescent
Finsbury Park
Arsenal
Holloway Road
Caledonian Road
Highbury and Islington
Bethnal Green
Shadwell
Wapping
Rotherhithe
Canada Water
Bermondsey
Surrey Quays
Lambeth North
Kennington
Oval
Stockwell
Clapham Common
Clapham North
Brixton

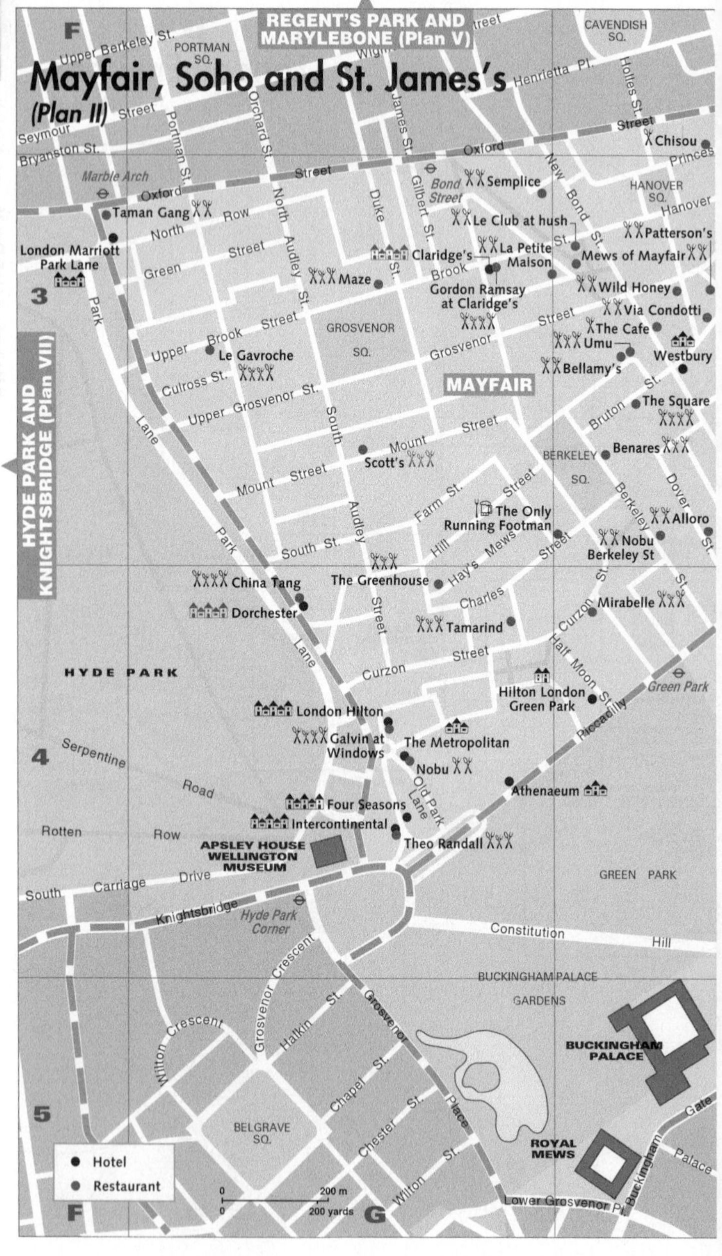
Mayfair, Soho and St. James's
(Plan II)
REGENT'S PARK AND MARYLEBONE (Plan V)
HYDE PARK AND KNIGHTSBRIDGE (Plan VII)
MAYFAIR
HYDE PARK
GREEN PARK
GROSVENOR SQ.
BERKELEY SQ.
HANOVER SQ.
CAVENDISH SQ.
PORTMAN SQ.
BELGRAVE SQ.
BUCKINGHAM PALACE GARDENS
BUCKINGHAM PALACE
ROYAL MEWS
APSLEY HOUSE WELLINGTON MUSEUM
Marble Arch
Bond Street
Green Park
Hyde Park Corner
Oxford Street
Piccadilly
Park Lane
Knightsbridge
Constitution Hill
Grosvenor Place
Serpentine Road
Rotten Row
South Carriage Drive
Taman Gang
London Marriott Park Lane
Le Gavroche
Maze
Claridge's
Gordon Ramsay at Claridge's
Semplice
Le Club at hush
La Petite Maison
Patterson's
Mews of Mayfair
Wild Honey
Via Condotti
The Cafe
Umu
Westbury
Bellamy's
Chisou
The Square
Benares
Scott's
The Only Running Footman
Alloro
Nobu Berkeley St
China Tang
Dorchester
The Greenhouse
Tamarind
Mirabelle
Hilton London Green Park
London Hilton
Galvin at Windows
The Metropolitan
Nobu
Athenaeum
Four Seasons
Intercontinental
Theo Randall
Hotel
Restaurant
0 200 m
0 200 yards
F
G
3
4
5

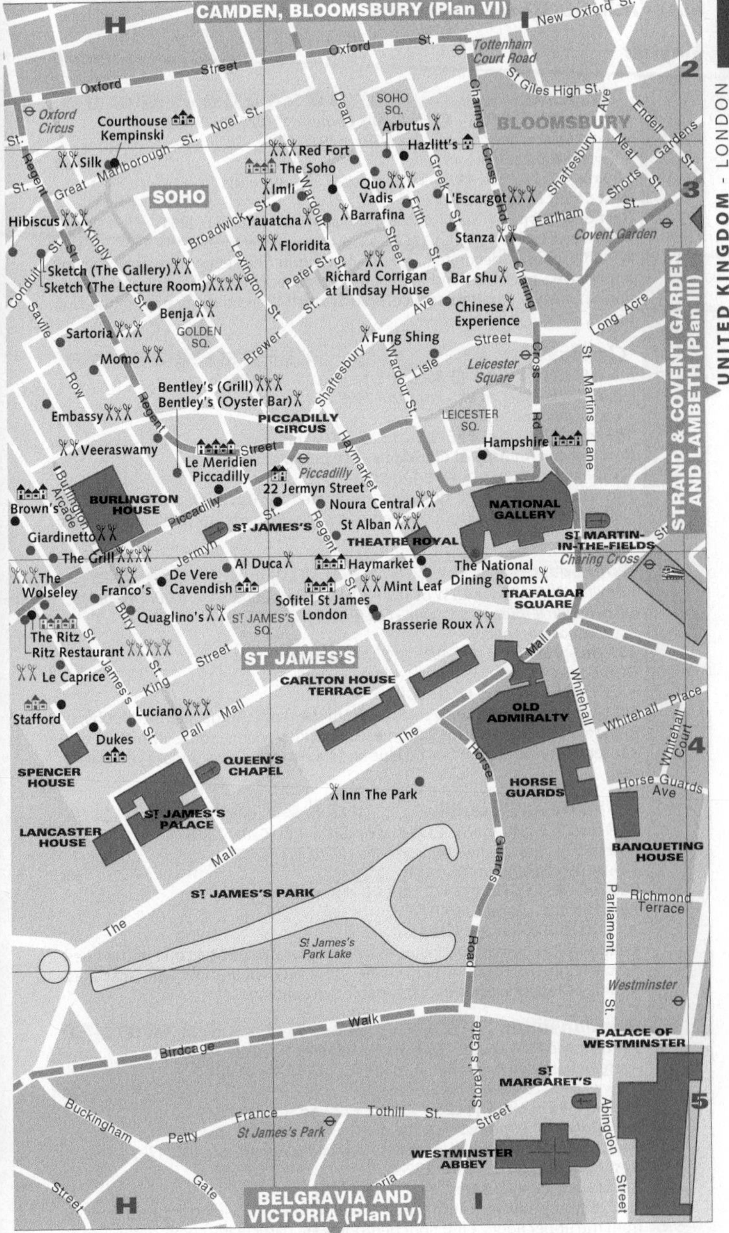
CAMDEN, BLOOMSBURY (Plan VI)
BELGRAVIA AND VICTORIA (Plan IV)
STRAND & COVENT GARDEN AND LAMBETH (Plan III)
SOHO
ST JAMES'S
BLOOMSBURY
PICCADILLY CIRCUS
BURLINGTON HOUSE
NATIONAL GALLERY
THEATRE ROYAL
ST MARTIN-IN-THE-FIELDS
TRAFALGAR SQUARE
CARLTON HOUSE TERRACE
OLD ADMIRALTY
QUEEN'S CHAPEL
SPENCER HOUSE
ST JAMES'S PALACE
LANCASTER HOUSE
HORSE GUARDS
BANQUETING HOUSE
ST JAMES'S PARK
St James's Park Lake
PALACE OF WESTMINSTER
ST MARGARET'S
WESTMINSTER ABBEY
Courthouse Kempinski
Silk
Hibiscus
Sketch (The Gallery)
Sketch (The Lecture Room)
Sartoria
Benja
Momo
Bentley's (Grill)
Bentley's (Oyster Bar)
Embassy
Veeraswamy
Le Meridien Piccadilly
Brown's
Giardinetto
The Grill
The Wolseley
Franco's
The Ritz
Ritz Restaurant
Le Caprice
Stafford
Dukes
Luciano
Quaglino's
De Vere Cavendish
Al Duca
22 Jermyn Street
Noura Central
St Alban
Haymarket
Mint Leaf
Sofitel St James London
Brasserie Roux
The National Dining Rooms
Inn The Park
Hampshire
Red Fort
The Soho
Imli
Yauatcha
Floridita
Arbutus
Hazlitt's
Quo Vadis
Barrafina
L'Escargot
Stanza
Richard Corrigan at Lindsay House
Bar Shu
Chinese Experience
Fung Shing
Oxford Circus
Tottenham Court Road
Covent Garden
Leicester Square
Piccadilly
Charing Cross
Westminster
St James's Park
New Oxford St.
Oxford Street
St Giles High St.
Shaftesbury Ave
Regent St.
Great Marlborough St.
Noel St.
Broadwick St.
Wardour St.
Dean St.
Greek St.
Frith St.
Charing Cross Rd
Lexington St.
Peter St.
Long Acre
Earlham St.
Shorts Gardens
Neal St.
Endell St.
St Martins Lane
Lisle St.
Brewer St.
Haymarket
Piccadilly
Jermyn St.
Bury St.
St James's St.
King St.
Pall Mall
The Mall
Whitehall
Whitehall Place
Whitehall Court
Horse Guards Ave
Horse Guards Road
Richmond Terrace
Parliament St.
Birdcage Walk
Storey's Gate
Tothill St.
Petty France
Buckingham Gate
Abingdon Street
Conduit St.
Savile Row
Kingly St.
Burlington Arcade
SOHO SQ.
GOLDEN SQ.
LEICESTER SQ.
ST JAMES'S SQ.
H
I
2
3
4
5

MAYFAIR, SOHO & ST JAMES'S

Mayfair

Plan II

Dorchester

Park Lane ✉ W1K 1QA – Ⓜ Hyde Park Corner – ☎ (020) 7629 8888 – info@thedorchester.com – Fax (020) 7629 80 80 – www.thedorchester.com **G4**

200 rm – †£323/664 ††£611/734, ☐ £25.50 – 49 suites

Rest *China Tang* – see below

Rest *Grill Room* – *☎ (020) 7317 6336* – Menu £28 – Carte £40/69

♦ Grand Luxury ♦ Classic ♦

A sumptuously decorated, luxury hotel offering every possible facility. Impressive marbled and pillared promenade. Rooms quintessentially English in style. Faultless service. Bold Scottish-themed decoration in the Grill Room.

Claridge's

Brook St ✉ W1K 4HR – Ⓜ Bond Street – ☎ (020) 7629 8860 – guest@claridges.co.uk – Fax (020) 7499 22 10 – www.claridges.co.uk **G3**

143 rm – †£563/633 ††£739, ☐ £26 – 60 suites

Rest *Gordon Ramsay at Claridge's* – see below

♦ Grand Luxury ♦ Art Deco ♦

The epitome of English grandeur, celebrated for its Art Deco. Exceptionally well-appointed and sumptuous bedrooms, all with butler service. Magnificently restored foyer.

Four Seasons

Hamilton Pl, Park Lane ✉ W1A 1AZ – Ⓜ Hyde Park Corner – ☎ (020) 7499 0888 – fsh.london@fourseasons.com – Fax (020) 7493 18 95 – www.fourseasons.com **G4**

193 rm – †£411/446 ††£493, ☐ £27 – 26 suites

Rest *Lanes* – Menu £38 (lunch) – Carte £50/65

♦ Grand Luxury ♦ Classic ♦

Set back from Park Lane so shielded from the traffic. Large, marbled lobby; its lounge a popular spot for light meals. Spacious rooms, some with their own conservatory. Restaurant's vivid blue and stained glass give modern yet relaxing feel.

Le Meridien Piccadilly

21 Piccadilly ✉ W1J 0BH – Ⓜ Piccadilly Circus – ☎ (020) 7734 8000 – piccadilly.sales@lemeridien.com – Fax (020) 7437 35 74 – www.lemeridien.com/piccadilly **H3**

249 rm – †£400/435 ††£470, ☐ £24 – 18 suites

Rest *Terrace* – Carte £24/49

♦ Grand Luxury ♦ Classic ♦

Comfortable international hotel, in a central location. Boasts one of the finest leisure clubs in London. Individually decorated bedrooms with first class facilities. Modern cuisine in comfortable surroundings.

London Hilton

< London,

22 Park Lane ✉ W1K 1BE – Ⓜ Hyde Park Corner – ☎ (020) 7493 8000 – reservations.parklane@hilton.com – Fax (020) 7208 41 42 – www.hilton.co.uk/londonparklane **G4**

395 rm – †£269/434 ††£269/434, ☐ £22 – 56 suites

Rest *Galvin at Windows* – see below

Rest *Trader Vics* – *(closed lunch Saturday and Sunday)* Carte £32/47

Rest *Park Brasserie* – Carte £29/40

♦ Business ♦ Classic ♦

This 28 storey tower is one of the city's tallest hotels, providing impressive views from the upper floors. Club floor bedrooms are particularly comfortable. Exotic Trader Vics with bamboo and plants. A harpist adds to the relaxed feel of Park Brasserie.

InterContinental
1 Hamilton Place, Park Lane ✉ W1J 7QY – Ⓜ Hyde Park Corner – ✆ (020) 7409 3131 – london@ihg.com – Fax (020) 7493 34 76 – www.intercontinental.com **G4**
399 rm – †£282/388 ††£282/388, ☕ £27 – 48 suites
Rest *Theo Randall* – see below
Rest *Cookbook Cafe* – Menu £25 – Carte £25/34
♦ Business ♦ Modern ♦
International hotel relaunched in 2007 after major refit. English style bedrooms with high tech equipment and large, open plan lobby. Cookbook Café invites visiting chefs to showcase their talents.

Brown's
Albemarle St ✉ W1S 4BP – Ⓜ Green Park – ✆ (020) 7493 6020 – reservations.browns@roccofortecollection.com – Fax (020) 7493 93 81 – www.roccofortecollection.com **H3**
105 rm – †£415/575 ††£540/725, ☕ £27 – 12 suites
♦ Luxury ♦ Stylish ♦
Rest *The Grill* – see below
After a major refit, this urbane hotel offers a swish bar featuring Terence Donovan prints, up-to-the minute rooms and, of course, a quintessentially English lounge for tea.

London Marriott H. Park Lane
140 Park Lane ✉ W1K 7AA – Ⓜ Marble Arch – ✆ (020) 7493 7000 – Fax (020) 7493 83 33 – www.marriott.com/lonpl **F3**
148 rm – †£347/370 ††£347/370, ☕ £20.95 – 9 suites
Rest *140 Park Lane* – *(bar lunch Saturday)* Carte £28/34
♦ Luxury ♦ Design ♦
Superbly located 'boutique' style hotel at intersection of Park Lane and Oxford Street. Attractive basement health club. Spacious, well-equipped rooms with luxurious elements. Attractive restaurant overlooking Marble Arch.

Westbury
Bond St ✉ W1S 2YF – Ⓜ Bond Street – ✆ (020) 7629 7755 – sales@westburymayfair.com – Fax (020) 7495 11 63 – www.westburymayfair.com **H3**
230 rm – †£468 ††£515, ☕ £20.95 – 19 suites
Rest – *(Closed Sunday and Saturday lunch)* Menu £30 – Carte £31/54
♦ Business ♦ Modern ♦
Surrounded by London's most fashionable shops; the renowned Polo bar and lounge provide soothing sanctuary. Some suites have their own terrace. Bright, fresh restaurant enhanced by modern art.

The Metropolitan
Old Park Lane ✉ W1K 1LB – Ⓜ Hyde Park Corner – ✆ (020) 7447 1000 – res.lon@metropolitan.como.bz – Fax (020) 7447 11 00 – www.metropolitan.como.bz **G4**
147 rm – †£440 ††£440/763, ☕ £25 – 3 suites
Rest *Nobu* – see below
♦ Luxury ♦ Minimalist ♦
Minimalist interior and a voguish reputation make this the favoured hotel of pop stars and celebrities. Innovative design and fashionably attired staff set it apart.

Athenaeum
116 Piccadilly ✉ W1J 7BJ – Ⓜ Hyde Park Corner – ✆ (020) 7499 3464 – info@athenaeumhotel.com – Fax (020) 7493 18 60 – www.athenaeumhotel.com **G4**
145 rm – †£347 ††£452, ☕ £22 – 12 suites
Rest *Damask* – Menu £21/24
♦ Luxury ♦ Classic ♦
Built in 1925 as a luxury apartment block. Comfortable bedrooms with video and CD players. Individually designed suites are in an adjacent Edwardian townhouse. Conservatory roofed dining room renowned for its mosaics and malt whiskies.

Hilton London Green Park

rm A/C SAT VISA MO AE D

Half Moon St ✉ *W1J 7BN* – Ⓜ *Green Park* – ✆ *(020) 7629 7522*
– reservations.greenpark@hilton.com – Fax (020) 7491 89 71
– www.hilton.co.uk/greenpark **H4**

162 rm – †£292/304 ††£304, ☐ £19.95

Rest – *(bar lunch)* Menu £28

♦ Business ♦ Functional ♦

A row of sympathetically adjoined townhouses, dating from the 1730s. Discreet marble lobby. Bedrooms share the same décor but vary in size and shape. Monet prints decorate light, airy dining room.

Le Gavroche (Michel Roux)

XXXX ✿✿

A/C VISA MO AE D

43 Upper Brook St ✉ *W1K 7QR* – Ⓜ *Marble Arch* – ✆ *(020) 7408 0881*
– bookings@le-gavroche.com – Fax (020) 7491 43 87
– www.le-gavroche.co.uk
closed Christmas-New Year, Sunday,
Saturday lunch and Bank Holidays **G3**

Rest – *(booking essential)* Menu £48 – Carte £60/130

Spec. Hot foie gras and crispy duck pancake flavoured with cinnamon. Roast saddle of rabbit with crispy potatoes and parmesan. Bitter chocolate and praline 'indulgence'.

♦ French ♦ Formal ♦

Long-standing, renowned restaurant with a clubby, formal atmosphere. Accomplished classical French cuisine, served by smartly attired and well-drilled staff.

Gordon Ramsay at Claridge's

XXXX ✿

A/C VISA MO AE D

Brook St ✉ *W1K 4HR* – Ⓜ *Bond Street* – ✆ *(020) 7499 0099*
– reservations@gordonramsay.com – Fax (020) 7499 30 99
– www.gordonramsay.com **G3**

Rest – *(booking essential)* Menu £30/65

Spec. Persillade of rabbit with vegetables à la grecque, grain mustard vinaigrette. Roast John Dory with sautéed langoustines with artichokes and fennel cream. Lemon meringue with mascarpone ice cream and summer berries.

♦ Modern ♦ Formal ♦

A thoroughly comfortable dining room with a charming and gracious atmosphere. Serves classically-inspired food executed with a high degree of finesse.

The Square (Philip Howard)

XXXX ✿✿

A/C VISA MO AE D

6-10 Bruton St ✉ *W1J 6PU* – Ⓜ *Green Park* – ✆ *(020) 7495 7100*
– info@squarerestaurant.com – Fax (020) 7495 71 50
– www.squarerestaurant.com
closed 25 December, 1 January and lunch Saturday, Sunday and Bank Holidays **H3**

Rest – Menu £30/65

Spec. Sautéed langoustines with parmesan gnocchi and truffle. Herb-crusted saddle of lamb with shallot purée and rosemary. Brillat-Savarin cheesecake with gooseberry and elderflower.

♦ Modern ♦ Formal ♦

Smart, popular restaurant; comfortable and never overformal. Cooking is thoughtful and honest, with a dextrous balance of flavours and textures. Prompt, efficient service.

The Grill – (at Brown's H.)

XXXX

A/C VISA MO AE D

Albemarle St ✉ *W1S 4BP* – ✆ *(020) 7518 4004 – reservations.browns@roccofortehotels.com – Fax (020) 7518 40 64* **H3-4**

Rest – Menu £25 – Carte £38/50

♦ English ♦ Formal ♦

Cavernous room decorated by Olga Polizzi to reflect hotel's heritage: dark wood panelling, lime green banquettes. Well executed and unashamedly traditional English cooking.

XXXX ✿

Sketch (The Lecture Room & Library)

First Floor, 9 Conduit St ✉ W1S 2XG – Ⓜ Oxford Street – ✆ (0870) 7774488 – Fax (0870) 7 77 44 00 – www.sketch.uk.com

closed 25-30 December, Sunday, Monday, Saturday lunch and Bank Holidays **H3**

Rest – *(booking essential)* Menu £35/65 – Carte £70/131

Spec. Langoustines 'addressed in five ways'. Lamb from Limousin. Pierre Gagnaire's Grand dessert.

♦ French ♦ Design ♦

A work of animated art, full of energy, vitality and colour; an experience of true sensory stimulation. Ambitious, highly elaborate and skilled cooking; try the tasting menu.

XXXX

China Tang – at Dorchester H.

Park Lane ✉ W1A 2HJ – Ⓜ Hyde Park Corner – ✆ (020) 7629 9988 – Fax (020) 7629 95 95

closed 25 December **G4**

Rest – Carte £40/120

♦ Chinese ♦ Fashionable ♦

A striking mix of Art Deco, Oriental motifs, hand-painted fabrics, mirrors and marbled table tops. Carefully prepared, traditional Cantonese dishes using quality ingredients.

XXXX

Galvin at Windows – at London Hilton H. ← City Styline

22 Park Lane ✉ W1K 1BE – Ⓜ Hyde Park Corner – ✆ (020) 7208 4021 – www.galvinatwindows.com

Closed Saturday lunch and Sunday dinner **G4**

Rest – Menu £29/75 – Carte £60/75

♦ Modern ♦ Formal ♦

On the 28th floor, so the views are spectacular. Contemporary makeover includes silk curtains and opulent gold leaf effect sculpture on ceiling. Intricate, thoughtful cooking.

XXX

Scott's

20 Mount St ✉ W1K 2HE – ✆ (020) 7495 7309 – Fax (020) 7647 63 27 – www.scotts-restaurant.com

Closed 25-26 December, 1 January and August Bank holiday **G3**

Rest – Carte £45/67

♦ Seafood ♦ Fashionable ♦

A landmark London institution reborn. Stylish yet traditional; oak panelling juxtaposed with vibrant artwork from young British artists. Top quality seafood, kept simple.

XXX ✿

Hibiscus (Claude Bosi)

29 Maddox St ✉ W1S 2PA – Ⓜ Oxford Circus – ✆ (020) 7629 2999 – www.hibiscusrestaurant.co.uk

closed 10 days Christmas - New Year, 1 week August, Saturday, Sunday and Bank Holiday Mondays **H3**

Rest – Menu £28 (lunch)/60

Spec. Foie gras ice cream with brioche emulsion, balsamic vinegar caramel. Roast rack of Shropshire veal with goat's cheese and anchovy jus. Iced sweet olive oil parfait, date sauce, caramelised chickpeas.

♦ Innovative ♦ Elegant ♦

Purpose built, with oak wood panelling and Welsh slate walls reminiscent of its previous incarnation in Ludlow. Shropshire ingredients feature; cooking is accomplished and original.

XXX ✿

The Greenhouse

27a Hay's Mews ✉ W1J 5NY – Ⓜ Hyde Park Corner – ✆ (020) 7499 3331 – reservations@greenhouserestaurant.co.uk – Fax (020) 7499 53 68 – www.greenhouserestaurant.co.uk
Closed 24 December-5 January, Saturday lunch, Sunday and Bank Holidays **G4**
Rest – Menu £29/60
Spec. Scottish langoustines with pea, coconut and Moroccan mint. Roast veal chop with baby carrots and rosemary honey. 'Carré Dubuffet' chocolate biscuit with paraline ice cream.
♦ Innovative ♦ Fashionable ♦
Smart, elegant restaurant broken up into sections by glass screens. Innovative selection of elaborately presented dishes, underpinned with sound French culinary techniques.

XXX ✿

Mirabelle

56 Curzon St ✉ W1J 8PA – Ⓜ Green Park – ✆ (020) 7499 4636 – sales@whitestarline.org.uk – Fax (020) 7499 54 49 – www.whitestarline.org.uk
Closed 26 December **H4**
Rest – Menu £23 (lunch) – Carte £33/55
Spec. Parfait of foie gras with truffles en gelée. Caramelised wing of skate with winkles and beurre noisette. Tarte Tatin with cinnamon.
♦ Modern ♦ Design ♦
Comfortable, elegant restaurant with long, stylish bar and resident pianist. Rich, indulgent French cooking, with plenty of classic dishes, perfected over time. Formal service.

XXX ✿

Maze

10-13 Grosvenor Sq ✉ W1K 6JP – Ⓜ Bond Street – ✆ (020) 7107 0000 – maze@gordonramsay.com – Fax (020) 7107 00 01 – www.gordonramsay.com **G3**
Rest – Carte £41/55
Spec. Cornish crab mayonnaise with avocado, sweetcorn sorbet and caviar. Butter poached chicken with maple skin and smoked mussel bread sauce. Coconut panna cotta with black olive caramel.
♦ Contemporary ♦ Fashionable ♦
Choose between a variety of small dishes at this sleek, contemporary restaurant. Innovative, balanced and precise, cooking has a French base and the occasional Asian influence.

XXX

Theo Randall – at InterContinental H.

1 Hamilton Place, Park Lane ✉ W1J 7QY – Ⓜ Hyde Park Corner – ✆ (020) 7318 8747 – www.theorandall.com
closed 25-26 December, Saturday lunch, Sunday dinner and Bank Holidays **G4**
Rest – Menu £23 (weekday lunch) – Carte £34/48
♦ Italian ♦ Fashionable ♦
Swanky ground floor restaurant with intimate lighting, stylistic flourishes and chatty service. Rustic, seasonal Italian dishes focus on the best ingredients available.

XXX ✿

Benares (Atul Kochhar)

12a Berkeley Square House ✉ W1J 6BS – Ⓜ Green Park – ✆ (020) 7629 8886 – reservations@benaresrestaurant.com – Fax (020) 7499 24 30 – www.benaresrestaurant.com
closed 25-26 December, 1 January, and Bank Holidays **H3**
Rest – Menu £30 (lunch) – Carte £34/68
Spec. Soft shell crab with squid salad. Seared sea bass in coconut milk and curry leaf sauce. Pistachio and star anise mousse with rum raisins.
♦ Indian ♦ Formal ♦
Indian restaurant where pools of water scattered with petals and candles compensate for lack of natural light. Original Indian dishes; particularly good value at lunch.

XXX

Embassy

29 Old Burlington St ✉ W1S 3AN – Ⓜ Green Park – ☎ (020) 7851 0956 – embassy@embassylondon.com – Fax (020) 7734 32 24 – www.embassylondon.com
closed Sunday, Monday and Bank Holidays **H3**
Rest – *(dinner only)* Menu £40 – Carte £27/58
♦ Modern ♦ Trendy ♦
Marble floors, ornate cornicing and a long bar create a characterful, moody dining room. Tables are smartly laid and menus offer accomplished, classic dishes.

XXX ✿

Tamarind

20 Queen St ✉ W1J 5PR – Ⓜ Green Park – ☎ (020) 7629 3561 – manager@tamarindrestaurant.com – Fax (020) 7499 50 34 – www.tamarindrestaurant.com
closed 25-26 December, 1 January and lunch Saturday and Bank Holidays
Rest – Menu £22/52 – Carte £35/59 **G4**
Spec. Salad leaves with melon, plums and kumquats in pine nut dressing. Grilled chicken in creamed tomatoes, fenugreek, ginger and honey. White chocolate and cardamom mousse with a ginger semi-freddo.
♦ Indian ♦ Fashionable ♦
Gold coloured pillars add to the opulence of this basement room. Windows allow diners the chance to watch the kitchen prepare original and accomplished Indian dishes.

XXX

Bentley's (Grill)

11-15 Swallow St ✉ W1B 4DG – Ⓜ Piccadilly Circus – ☎ (020) 7734 4756 – reservations@bentleys.org – www.bentleysoysterbarandgrill.co.uk
closed 25-26 December **H3**
Rest – Carte £34/49
♦ British ♦ Elegant ♦
Entrance into striking bar; panelled staircase to richly decorated restaurant. Carefully sourced seafood or meat dishes enhanced by clean, crisp cooking. Unruffled service.

XXX

Sartoria

20 Savile Row ✉ W1S 3PR – Ⓜ Green Park – ☎ (020) 7534 7000 – sartoriareservations@danddlondon.com – Fax (020) 7534 70 70 – www.danddlondon.com
closed 24-28 December, 1 January and Sunday **H3**
Rest – Menu £25 – Carte approx. £35
♦ Italian ♦ Formal ♦
In the street renowned for English tailoring, a coolly sophisticated restaurant to suit those looking for classic Italian cooking with modern touches.

XXX ✿

Umu

14-16 Bruton Pl ✉ W1J 6LX – Ⓜ Bond Street – ☎ (020) 7499 8881 – enquiries@umurestaurant.com – Fax (020) 7499 51 20 – www.umurestaurant.com
Closed Christmas, 2 weeks August, Saturday lunch, Sunday and Bank Holidays
Rest – Menu £21 (lunch) – Carte £34/73 **H3**
Spec. Sweet shrimp with sake jelly and caviar. Grilled toro teriyaki, yuzu citrus flavoured grated radish, wasabi. White miso ice cream.
♦ Japanese ♦ Fashionable ♦
Exclusive neighbourhood location: stylish, discreet interior with central sushi bar. Japanese dishes, specialising in Kyoto cuisine, employing highest quality ingredients.

XX ✿

Wild Honey

12 St George St ✉ W1S 2FB – Ⓜ Oxford Circus – ☎ (020) 7758 9160 – info@wildhoneyrestaurant.co.uk – Fax (020) 7493 45 49 – www.wildhoneyrestaurant.co.uk
Closed 25-26 December and 1 January **H3**
Rest – Menu £16 (lunch) – Carte £30/36
♦ Modern ♦ Fashionable ♦
Spec. Warm smoked eel with fig jam and raw vegetable salad. Shin of veal with tomato and carrots. Wild honey ice cream with crushed honeycomb.
High-ceilinged, oak-panelled restaurant, with banquette and booth seating; sister to Arbutus in Soho. Easy to eat, gimmick-free food with flavoursome and seasonal ingredients.

XX **Semplice**

10 Blenheim St ✉ W1S 1LJ – Ⓜ Bond Street – ✆ (020) 7495 1509 – info@ristorantesemplice.com – Fax (020) 7493 70 74 – www.ristorantesemplice.com
Closed Christmas, Easter, Saturday lunch, Sunday and Bank Holidays **G3**
Rest – Menu £18 (lunch) – Carte £28/38
◆ Italian ◆ Fashionable ◆
Comfortable and stylish with custom laquered ebony, wavy gold walls and leather seating. Delicately textured, confidently presented dishes run the gamut of Italian cooking.

XX **Bellamy's**

18 Bruton Pl ✉ W1J 6LY – Ⓜ Bond Street – ✆ (020) 7491 2727 – info@bellamysrestaurant.co.uk – Fax (020) 7491 99 90
closed Saturday lunch, Sunday, 25 December and Bank Holidays **H3**
Rest – Menu £29 – Carte £36/53
◆ Traditional ◆ Brasserie ◆
French deli/brasserie tucked down a smart mews. Go past the caviar and cheeses into the restaurant proper for a very traditional, but well-executed, range of Gallic classics.

XX **Giardinetto**

39-40 Albemarle St ✉ W1S 4TE – Ⓜ Green Park – ✆ (020) 7493 7091 – info@giardinetto.co.uk – Fax (020) 7493 70 96 – www.giardinetto.co.uk
closed 22 December-6 January, Saturday lunch, Sunday and Bank Holidays **H3**
Rest – Carte £17/49
◆ Italian ◆ Cosy ◆
Manages to mix a smart, stylish interior with a neighbourhood intimacy. Three dining areas, front being largest. Genoese chef/owner conjures up well-presented Ligurian dishes.

XX **Patterson's**

4 Mill St ✉ W1S 2AX – Ⓜ Oxford Street – ✆ (020) 7499 1308 – info@pattersonsrestaurant.com – Fax (020) 7491 21 22 – www.pattersonsrestaurant.com
Closed 25-26 December, Sunday, Saturday lunch and Bank Holidays **H3**
Rest – Menu £20/40 – Carte £40/44
◆ Contemporary ◆ Intimate ◆
Stylish modern interior in black and white. Elegant tables and attentive service. Modern British cooking with concise wine list and sensible prices.

XX **Alloro**

19-20 Dover St ✉ W1S 4LU – Ⓜ Green Park – ✆ (020) 7495 4768 – alloro@hotmail.co.uk – Fax (020) 7629 53 48 – www.alloro-restaurant.com
Closed Easter, 25 December, Saturday lunch, Sunday and Bank Holidays **H3**
Rest – Menu £29/34
◆ Italian ◆ Fashionable ◆
One of the new breed of stylish Italian restaurants with contemporary art and leather seating. A separate, bustling bar. Smoothly run with modern cooking.

XX **Hush**

8 Lancashire Court, Brook St ✉ W1S 1EY – Ⓜ Bond Street – ✆ (020) 7659 1500 – info@hush.co.uk – Fax (020) 7659 15 01 – www.hush.co.uk **H3**
Rest – *(Closed 25 December, 31 December, 1 January and Sunday except lunch in summer) (booking essential)* Carte £31/47
◆ Modern ◆ Fashionable ◆
Tucked away down a delightful mews courtyard, this brasserie - with sunny courtyard terrace - is an informal and lively little place to eat rustic Mediterranean fare.

XX ✿

Nobu – at The Metropolitan H.

19 Old Park Lane ✉ W1Y 1LB – Ⓜ Hyde Park Corner – ✆ (020) 7447 4747 – confirmations@noburestaurants.com – Fax (020) 7447 47 49 – www.noburestaurants.com

Closed 25-26 December and 1 January **G4**

Rest – *(booking essential)* Menu £25/70 – Carte £44/52

Spec. Lobster ceviche. Black cod with miso. Chocolate bento box, green tea ice cream.

♦ Japanese ♦ Fashionable ♦

Its celebrity clientele has made this one of the most glamorous spots. Staff are fully conversant in the unique menu that adds South American influences to Japanese cooking.

XX

Via Condotti

23 Conduit St ✉ W1S 2XS – Ⓜ Oxford Circus – ✆ (020) 7493 7050 – info@viacondotti.co.uk – Fax (020) 7409 79 85 – www.viacondotti.co.uk

Closed 25 December, Sunday and Bank Holidays **H3**

Rest – Menu £25/28

♦ Italian ♦ Fashionable ♦

Chic bar-room leads to restaurant with Italian prints and leather banquettes. Full-flavoured rustic dishes with most ingredients from Italy; chef/owner makes his own breads.

XX

Taman Gang

141 Park Lane ✉ W1K 7AA – Ⓜ Marble Arch – ✆ (020) 7518 3160 – info@tamangang.com – Fax (020) 7518 31 61 – www.tamangang.com

closed Sunday **F3**

Rest – *(dinner only)* Menu £55/75

♦ Asian ♦ Exotic ♦

Basement restaurant with largish bar and lounge area. Stylish but intimate décor. Informal and intelligent service. Pan-Asian dishes presented in exciting modern manner.

XX

Mews of Mayfair

10-11 Lancashire Court, New Bond St ✉ W1S 1EY – Ⓜ Bond Street – ✆ (020) 7518 9388 – Fax (020) 7518 93 89 – www.mewsofmayfair.com

closed Christmas and New Year and Sunday **H3**

Rest – Menu £26/40 – Carte £36/54

♦ Modern ♦ Friendly ♦

Converted mews houses once used as storage rooms for Savile Row. Ground floor bar with French windows. Pretty first floor restaurant where eclectic modern menus are served.

XX

Sketch (The Gallery)

9 Conduit St ✉ W1S 2XG – Ⓜ Oxford Street – ✆ (0870) 7774488 – info@sketch.uk.com – Fax (0870) 7 77 44 00 – www.sketch.uk.com

closed 25-26 December, 1 January, Sunday and Bank Holidays **H3**

Rest – *(dinner only) (booking essential)* Carte £34/53

♦ Modern ♦ Trendy ♦

On the ground floor of the Sketch building: daytime video art gallery metamorphoses into evening brasserie with ambient wall projections and light menus with eclectic range.

XX ✿

Nobu Berkeley St

15 Berkeley St ✉ W1J 8DY – Ⓜ Green Park – ✆ (020) 7290 9222 – nobuberkeley@noburestaurants.com – Fax (020) 7290 92 23 – www.noburestaurants.com

Closed 25-26 December, 1 January, lunch Saturday and Sunday **H3**

Rest – Menu £25/60 – Carte £33/49

Spec. Yellowtail sashimi with jalapeño. Anti-Cucho rib-eye beef. Yuzu tart.

♦ Japanese ♦ Fashionable ♦

In a prime position off Berkeley Square: downstairs 'destination' bar and above, a top quality, soft-hued restaurant. Innovative Japanese dishes with original combinations.

Momo

25 Heddon St ✉ W1B 4BH – Ⓜ Oxford Circus – ✆ (020) 7434 4040 – info@momoresto.com – Fax (020) 7287 04 04 – www.momoresto.com
closed 24-26 and 31 December, 1 January and Sunday **H3**
Rest – Menu £18/45 – Carte £29/52
♦ Moroccan ♦ Exotic ♦
Elaborate adornment of rugs, drapes and ornaments mixed with Arabic music lend an authentic feel to this busy Moroccan restaurant. Helpful service. Popular basement bar.

Veeraswamy

Victory House, 99 Regent St (entrance on Swallow St) ✉ W1B 4RS – Ⓜ Piccadilly Circus – ✆ (020) 7734 1401 – veeraswamy@realindianfood.com – Fax (020) 7439 84 34 – www.realindianfood.com
Closed dinner 25 December **H3**
Rest – Menu £20 (lunch) – Carte £29/52
♦ Indian ♦ Design ♦
The country's oldest Indian restaurant enlivened by vivid coloured walls and glass screens. The menu also combines the familiar with some modern twists.

Bentley's (Oyster Bar)

11-15 Swallow St ✉ W1B 4DG – Ⓜ Piccadilly Circus – ✆ (020) 7734 4756 – reservations@bentleys.org – Fax (020) 7758 41 40 – www.bentleysoysterbarand grill.co.uk
Closed 25 December and 1 January **H3**
Rest – Carte £27/39
♦ Seafood ♦ Bistro ♦
Ground floor location, behind the busy bar. White-jacketed staff open oysters by the bucket load. Interesting seafood menus feature tasty fish pies. Hearty Sunday roasts.

The Only Running Footman

5 Charles St. ✉ W1J 5DF – Ⓜ Green Park – ✆ (020) 7499 2988 – info@therunningfootman.biz – Fax (020) 7491 81 62 – www.therunningfootman.biz **H3**
Rest – Carte £22/30
♦ British ♦ Pub ♦
Charming, historic pub whose small, atmospheric ground floor is always busy, with a first-come-first-served rule. Upstairs you can book, it's plush and the menu more ambitious.

Soho

Plan II

The Soho

4 Richmond Mews ✉ W1D 3DH – Ⓜ Tottenham Court Road – ✆ (020) 7559 3000 – soho@firmdale.com – Fax (020) 7559 30 03 – www.sohohotel.com **I3**
83 rm – †£300 ††£370, ☕ £18.50 – 2 suites
Rest ***Refuel*** – Menu £20 – Carte £26/37
♦ Luxury ♦ Stylish ♦
Opened in autumn 2004: stylish hotel with two screening rooms, comfy drawing room and up-to-the-minute bedrooms, some vivid, others more muted, all boasting hi-tec extras. Contemporary bar and restaurant.

Hampshire

Leicester Sq ✉ WC2H 7LH – Ⓜ Leicester Square – ✆ (020) 7839 9399 – reshamp@radisson.com – Fax (020) 7930 81 22 – www.radissonedwardian.com **I3**
119 rm – †£407/436 ††£436, ☕ £19 – 5 suites
Rest ***The Apex*** – *(dinner only)* Menu £26 – Carte £22/33
♦ Luxury ♦ Classic ♦
The bright lights of the city are literally outside and many rooms overlook the bustling Square. Inside it is tranquil and comfortable with well-appointed bedrooms. Formal yet relaxing dining room with immaculately dressed tables.

Courthouse Kempinski
19-21 Great Marlborough St ✉ W1F 7HL – Ⓜ Oxford Circus – ✆ (020) 7297 5555 – info@courthouse-hotel.com – Fax (020) 7297 55 66 – www.courthouse-hotel.com **H3**
107 rm – †£199/352 ††£199/352, ☕ £22.50 – 5 suites
Rest *Silk* – see below – **Rest *The Carnaby*** – Menu £16/20 – Carte £23/34
♦ Business ♦ Classic ♦
Striking Grade II listed ex magistrates' court: interior fused imaginatively with original features; for example, the bar incorporates three former cells. Ultra stylish rooms. Informal Carnaby offers extensive French, modern and British menu.

Hazlitt's without rest
6 Frith St ✉ W1D 3JA – Ⓜ Tottenham Court Road – ✆ (020) 7434 1771 – reservations@hazlitts.co.uk – Fax (020) 7439 15 24 – www.hazlittshotel.com
22 rm – †£206 ††£241, ☕ £9.75 – 1 suite **I3**
♦ Townhouse ♦ Historic ♦
A row of three adjoining early 18C town houses and former home of the eponymous essayist. Individual and charming bedrooms, many with antique furniture and Victorian baths.

L'Escargot
48 Greek St ✉ W1D 4EF – Ⓜ Tottenham Court Road – ✆ (020) 7437 2679 – sales@whitestarline.org.uk – Fax (020) 7437 07 90 – www.lescargotrestaurant.co.uk
Rest – *(Closed 25-26 December, 1 January, Sunday and Saturday lunch)* **I3**
Menu £18 (lunch) – Carte £28/30
Rest *Picasso Room* – *(closed 2 weeks Christmas-New Year, August, Sunday, Monday and Saturday lunch)* Menu £26/42
Spec. Tian of crab with shrimp and avocado, citrus mayonnaise. Roast rump of lamb with an onion purée. Raspberry soufflé with raspberry and lime sauce.
♦ Modern ♦ Fashionable ♦
Soho institution. Ground Floor is chic, vibrant brasserie with early-evening buzz of theatre-goers. Finely judged modern dishes. Intimate and more formal upstairs Picasso Room famed for its limited edition art.

Quo Vadis
26-29 Dean St ✉ W1D 3LL – Ⓜ Tottenham Court Road – ✆ (020) 7437 9585 – sales@whitestarline.org.uk – Fax (020) 7734 75 93 – www.whitestarline.org.uk
Closed 24-25 December, 1 January, Saturday lunch and Sunday **I3**
Rest – Menu £18 (lunch) – Carte £25/31
♦ Italian ♦ Formal ♦
Stained glass windows and a neon sign hint at the smooth modernity of the interior. Modern artwork abounds. Contemporary cooking and a serious wine list.

Red Fort
77 Dean St ✉ W1D 3SH – Ⓜ Tottenham Court Road – ✆ (020) 7437 2525 – info@redfort.co.uk – Fax (020) 7434 07 21 – www.redfort.co.uk
Closed lunch Saturday, Sunday and Bank Holidays **I3**
Rest – Carte £35/45
♦ Indian ♦ Formal ♦
Smart, stylish restaurant with modern water feature and glass ceiling to rear. Seasonally changing menus of authentic dishes handed down over generations.

Richard Corrigan at Lindsay House
21 Romilly St ✉ W1D 5AF – Ⓜ Leicester Square – ✆ (020) 7439 0450 – richardcorrigan@lindsayhouse.co.uk – Fax (020) 7437 73 49 – www.lindsayhouse.co.uk
Closed 25, 26 December, 1 January, Saturday lunch and Sunday **I3**
Rest – Menu £56 (dinner) – Carte lunch £31/52
Spec. Ballotine of foie gras with parfait of liver, hazelnuts. Pan-roast halibut with langoustine ravioli and samphire. Peanut parfait with caramelised banana and praline ice cream.
♦ Contemporary ♦ Intimate ♦
Handsome four storey house; ring the doorbell before being welcomed into one of two cosy, fabric-clad dining rooms. Modern, confidently-presented cooking boasts bold flavours.

XX **Floridita**
100 Wardour St ✉ W1F 0TN – Ⓜ Tottenham Court Road – ✆ (020) 7314 4000 – Fax (020) 7314 40 40 – www.floriditalondon.com
Closed 24-26 December, 1 January and Sunday **I3**
Rest – *(dinner only and lunch mid November-December)* Carte £32/61
♦ Latin American ♦ Musical ♦
Buzzy destination where the Latino cuisine is a fiery accompaniment to the vivacious Cuban dancing. Slightly less frenetic upstairs in the Spanish tapas and cocktail bar.

XX **Silk** – at Courthouse Kempinksi H.
19-21 Great Marlborough St ✉ W1F 7HL – Ⓜ Oxford Circus – ✆ (020) 7297 5567 – Fax (020) 7297 55 66 – www.courthouse-hotel.com
Closed Sunday-Monday **H3**
Rest – *(dinner only)* Carte £24/36
♦ International ♦ Formal ♦
Stunningly unique former courtroom with original panelling, court benches and glass roof. Menu follows the journey of the Silk Route with Asian, Indian and Italian influences.

XX **Stanza**
97-107 Shaftesbury Ave ✉ W1D 5DY – Ⓜ Leicester Square – ✆ (020) 7494 3020 – reception@stanzalondon.com – Fax (020) 7494 30 50 – www.stanzalondon.com
Closed Easter, 25 December and Sunday **I3**
Rest – Menu £19 (dinner) – Carte £23/36
♦ British ♦ Fashionable ♦
Large bar with vibrant orange seats; open dining room has views of China town. Rustic seasonal cooking; the chef is from Northern England - as are many of the ingredients.

XX **Benja**
17 Beak St ✉ W1F 9RW – Ⓜ Oxford Circus – ✆ (020) 7287 0555 – info@krua.co.uk – Fax (020) 7287 00 56 – www.benjarestaurant.com
Closed 25 December, Sunday and lunch Bank Holidays **H3**
Rest – Carte £19/32
♦ Thai ♦ Intimate ♦
Named after the Thai word for 5, since there are 5 owners, 5 floors and 5 colours used to decorate. Authentic, vibrant Thai cooking. Best place to sit is spacious first floor.

X ✿ **Arbutus** (Anthony Demetre)
63-64 Frith St ✉ W1D 3JW – Ⓜ Tottenham Court Road – ✆ (020) 7734 4545 – info@arbutusrestaurant.co.uk – Fax (020) 7287 86 24 – www.arbutusrestaurant.co.uk
Closed 25-26 December and 1 January **I3**
Rest – Menu £16 (lunch) – Carte £29/35
Spec. Braised pig's head with potato purée and caramelised onions. Bavette of beef with gratin dauphinois, red wine and shallot sauce. Vanilla panna cotta with poached rhubarb.
♦ Modern European ♦ Bistro ♦
Dining room and bar that's bright and stylish without trying too hard. Bistro classics turned on their head: poised, carefully crafted cooking - but dishes still pack a punch.

X ✿ **Yauatcha**
15 Broadwick St ✉ W1F 0DL – Ⓜ Tottenham Court Road – ✆ (020) 7494 8888 – mail@yauatcha.com – Fax (020) 7494 88 89
Closed 24-25 December **I3**
Rest – Carte £20/48
Spec. Prawn cheung fun; scallop shumai. Szechuan tea smoked duck with Chinese pancake, kumquat and plum sauce. White chocolate with mandarin and kumquat rice pudding.
♦ Chinese ♦ Fashionable ♦
Converted 1960s post office in heart of Soho. Choose between darker, atmospheric basement or lighter, brighter ground floor. Refined Chinese dishes served on both levels.

Barrafina VISA MC AE

54 Frith St ✉ W1D 4SL – ✆ (020) 7813 8016 – info@barrafina.co.uk – Fax (020) 7813 80 11 – www.barrafina.co.uk

Closed Sunday I3

Rest – *(bookings not accepted)* Carte £19/35

♦ Spanish ♦ Tapas Bar ♦

Centred around a counter with seating for 20, come here if you want authentic Spanish tapas served in a buzzy atmosphere. Seafood is a speciality and the Jabugo ham a must.

Imli AC VISA MC AE

167-169 Wardour St ✉ W1F 8WR – Ⓜ Tottenham Court Road – ✆ (020) 7287 4243 – info@imli.co.uk – Fax (020) 7287 42 45 – www.imli.co.uk

Closed 25 December and 1 January I3

Rest – Menu £17 (dinner) – Carte £11/18

♦ Indian ♦ Bistro ♦

Long, spacious interior is a busy, buzzy place to be: not the venue to while away an evening! Good value, fresh and tasty Indian tapas style dishes prove a popular currency.

Bar Shu AC VISA MC AE

28 Frith St ✉ W1D 5LF – Ⓜ Leicester Square – ✆ (020) 7287 8822 – Fax (020) 7287 88 58

Closed 25-26 December I3

Rest – Carte £20/25

♦ Chinese ♦ Exotic ♦

Three floors decorated in carved wood and lanterns. Truly authentic Sichuan cooking typified by intense heat generated by peppers and chillies. Not for the faint hearted!

Chinese Experience AC VISA MC AE

118 Shaftesbury Ave ✉ W1D 5EP – Ⓜ Leicester Square – ✆ (020) 7437 0377 – info@chineseexperience.com – www.chineseexperience.com I3

Rest – Menu £15 – Carte approx. £19

♦ Chinese ♦ Fashionable ♦

Bright, airy restaurant: sit at long bench or chunky wood tables. Large, good value menus cover a wide range of Chinese dishes. Knowledgable service. A buzzy, informal place.

Fung Shing AC VISA MC AE

15 Lisle St ✉ WC2H 7BE – Ⓜ Leicester Square – ✆ (020) 7437 1539 – Fax (020) 7734 02 84 – www.fung.shing.co.uk

Closed 24-26 December and lunch Bank Holidays I3

Rest – Menu £17 – Carte £16/25

♦ Chinese ♦ Friendly ♦

A long-standing Chinese restaurant on the edge of Chinatown. Chatty and pleasant service. A mix of authentic, rustic dishes and the more adventurous chef's specials.

St James's *Plan II*

The Ritz AC VISA MC AE

150 Piccadilly ✉ W1J 9BR – Ⓜ Green Park – ✆ (020) 7493 8181 – enquire@theritzlondon.com – Fax (020) 7493 26 87 – www.theritzlondon.com H4

116 rm – †£306/494 ††£423/470, ☕ £30 – 17 suites

Rest ***The Ritz Restaurant*** – see below

♦ Grand Luxury ♦ Classic ♦

Opened 1906, a fine example of Louis XVI architecture and decoration. Elegant Palm Court famed for afternoon tea. Many of the lavishly appointed rooms overlook the park.

Sofitel St James London

6 Waterloo Pl ✉ SW1Y 4AN – Ⓜ Piccadilly Circus – ✆ (020) 7747 2200 – Fax (020) 7747 22 10 – www.sofitelstjames.com **I4**

179 rm – †£161/252 ††£280/400, ☕ £21 – 7 suites

Rest ***Brasserie Roux*** – see below

◆ Luxury ◆ Classic ◆

Grade II listed building in smart Pall Mall location. Classically English interiors include floral Rose Lounge and club-style St. James bar. Comfortable, well-fitted bedrooms.

Haymarket

1 Suffolk Place ✉ SW1Y 4BP – Ⓜ Piccadilly Circus – ✆ (020) 7470 4000 – haymarket@firmdale.com – Fax (020) 7470 40 04 – www.haymarkethotel.com **I4**

47 rm – †£288 ††£364, ☕ £18.50 – 3 suites

Rest ***Brumus*** – ✆ *(020) 7451 1012* – Carte £26/31

◆ Luxury ◆ Stylish ◆

Smart, spacious hotel next to Theatre Royal Haymarket with eclectic blend of modern and antique furnishings. Large, comfortable bedrooms in soothing colours. Impressive pool. Brumus bar and restaurant puts focus on Italian cooking.

Stafford

16-18 St James's Pl ✉ SW1A 1NJ – Ⓜ Green Park – ✆ (020) 7493 0111 – information@thestaffordhotel.co.uk – Fax (020) 7493 71 21 – www.thestaffordhotel.co.uk **H4**

73 rm – †£317/352 ††£411/440, ☕ £23 – 32 suites

Rest – *(Closed Saturday lunch)* Menu £30 (lunch) – Carte dinner £29/63

◆ Traditional ◆ Luxury ◆ Classic ◆

A genteel atmosphere prevails in this elegant and discreet country house in the city. Do not miss the famed American bar. Well-appointed rooms created from 18C stables. Refined, elegant, intimate dining room.

Dukes

35 St James's Pl ✉ SW1A 1NY – Ⓜ Green Park – ✆ (020) 7491 4840 – bookings@dukeshotel.com – Fax (020) 7493 12 64 – www.dukeshotel.com **H4**

83 rm – †£364/417 ††£505/523, ☕ £19.50 – 7 suites

Rest – Menu £17 – Carte £29/40

◆ Traditional ◆ Luxury ◆ Classic ◆

Privately owned, discreet and quiet hotel. Traditional bar, famous for its martinis and Cognac collection. Well-kept spacious rooms in a country house style. Refined dining.

The Cavendish

81 Jermyn St ✉ SW1Y 6JF – Ⓜ Piccadilly Circus – ✆ (020) 7930 2111 – reservations@thecavendishlondon.com – Fax (020) 7930 36 87 – www.thecavendishlondon.com **H4**

227 rm – †£152/275 ††£306, ☕ £21 – 3 suites

Rest – *(Closed lunch Saturday, Sunday and Bank Holidays)* Menu £20 (lunch) – Carte £26/35

◆ Business ◆ Design ◆

Modern hotel in heart of Piccadilly. Contemporary, minimalist style of rooms with moody prints of London; top five floors offer far-reaching views over and beyond the city. Classic-styled restaurant overlooks Jermyn Street.

22 Jermyn Street Without rest

22 Jermyn St ✉ SW1Y 6HL – Ⓜ Piccadilly Circus – ✆ (020) 7734 2353 – office@22jermyn.com – Fax (020) 7734 07 50 – www.22jermyn.com **I3**

5 rm – †£258 ††£258 – 13 suites

◆ Townhouse ◆ Classic ◆

Exclusive boutique hotel with entrance amid famous shirt-makers' shops. Stylishly decorated bedrooms more than compensate for the lack of lounge space. Room service available.

XXXXX **The Ritz Restaurant** – at The Ritz H.

150 Piccadilly ✉ W1V 9DG – Ⓜ Green Park – ✆ (020) 7493 8181 – Fax (020) 7493 26 87 **H4**

Rest – Menu £38/65 – Carte £47/74

♦ Traditional ♦ Formal ♦

The height of opulence: magnificent Louis XVI décor with trompe l'oeil and ornate gilding. Delightful terrace over Green Park. Refined service, classic and modern menu.

XXX **The Wolseley**

160 Piccadilly ✉ W1J 9EB – Ⓜ Green Park – ✆ (020) 7499 6996 – Fax (020) 7499 68 88 – www.thewolseley.com

Closed 25 December, 1 January, August Bank Holiday and dinner 24 and 31 December **H4**

Rest – *(booking essential)* Carte £26/70

♦ Modern ♦ Fashionable ♦

Has the feel of a grand European coffee house: pillars, high vaulted ceiling, mezzanine tables. Menus range from caviar to a hot dog. Also open for breakfasts and tea.

XXX **St Alban**

4-12 Regent St ✉ SW1Y 4PE – ✆ (020) 7499 8558 – info@stalban.net – Fax (020) 7499 68 88 – www.stalban.net

Closed 25-26 December and 1 January **I3**

Rest – Carte £29/41

♦ Modern ♦ Fashionable ♦

Light, airy restaurant with colourful booth seating and wonderful feeling of space. Weekly-changing modern European menu with global influences. Convenient for theatre dining.

XXX **Luciano**

72-73 St James's St ✉ SW1A 1PH – Ⓜ Green Park – ✆ (020) 7408 1440 – info@lucianorestaurant.co.uk – www.lucianorestaurant.co.uk

Closed Sunday **H4**

Rest – Menu £22 (lunch) – Carte £25/49

♦ Italian ♦ Brasserie ♦

Art Deco, David Collins styled bar leads to restaurant sympathetic to its early 19C heritage. Mix of Italian and English dishes cooked in rustic, wholesome and earthy manner.

XX **Le Caprice**

Arlington House, Arlington St ✉ SW1A 1RJ – Ⓜ Green Park – ✆ (020) 7629 2239 – reservation@le-caprice.co.uk – Fax (020) 7493 90 40 – www.le-caprice.co.uk

Closed 24-26 December, 1 January and August Bank Holiday **H4**

Rest – *(Sunday brunch)* Carte £35/50

♦ Modern ♦ Fashionable ♦

Still attracting a fashionable clientele and as busy as ever. Dine at the bar or in the smoothly run restaurant. Food combines timeless classics with modern dishes.

XX **Quaglino's**

16 Bury St ✉ SW1Y 6AL – Ⓜ Green Park – ✆ (020) 7930 6767 – quaglinos@danddlondon.com – Fax (020) 7930 27 32 – www.quaglinos.co.uk

Closed 25-26 December and 1 January **H4**

Rest – *(booking essential)* Carte £25/41

♦ Modern ♦ Design ♦

Descend the sweeping staircase into the capacious room where a busy and buzzy atmosphere prevails. Watch the chefs prepare everything from osso bucco to fish and chips.

XX **Mint Leaf** A/C VISA MC AE

Suffolk Pl ✉ SW1Y 4HX – Ⓜ Piccadilly Circus – ✆ (020) 7930 9020
– reservations@mintleafrestaurant.com – Fax (020) 7930 62 05
– www.mintleafrestaurant.com
Closed lunch Saturday and Sunday **I4**
Rest – Menu £15 – Carte £33/40
♦ Indian ♦ Design ♦
Basement restaurant in theatreland. Cavernous dining room incorporating busy, trendy bar with unique cocktail list and loud music. Helpful service. Contemporary Indian dishes.

XX **Brasserie Roux** A/C VISA MC AE

8 Pall Mall ✉ SW1Y 5NG – Ⓜ Piccadilly Circus – ✆ (020) 7968 2900
– h3144-fb4@accor.com – Fax (020) 7747 22 51
– www.sofitelstjames.com **I4**
Rest – Menu £20/25 – Carte £26/35
♦ French ♦ Brasserie ♦
Informal, smart, classic brasserie style with large windows making the most of the location. Large menu of French classics with many daily specials; comprehensive wine list.

XX **Franco's** A/C VISA MC AE

61 Jermyn St ✉ SW1Y 6LX – Ⓜ Green Park – ✆ (020) 7499 2211
– reserve@francoslondon.com – Fax (020) 7495 13 75
– www.francoslondon.com
Closed 24 December-2 January, Sunday and Bank Holidays **H4**
Rest – *(booking essential)* Menu £25 (lunch) – Carte £36/45
♦ Italian ♦ Brasserie ♦
Great all-day menu at 'the café'. Further in, regulars have taken to smart refurbishment. Classic/modern Italian cooking allows bold but refined flavours to shine through.

XX **Noura Central** A/C VISA MC AE

22 Lower Regent St ✉ SW1Y 4UJ – Ⓜ Piccadilly Circus – ✆ (020) 7839 2020
– Fax (020) 7839 77 00 – www.noura.co.uk **I3**
Rest – Menu £18/30 – Carte £20/39
♦ Lebanese ♦ Exotic ♦
Eye-catching Lebanese façade, matched by sleek interior design. Buzzy atmosphere enhanced by amplified background music. Large menus cover all aspects of Lebanese cuisine.

X **Al Duca** A/C VISA MC AE

4-5 Duke of York St ✉ SW1Y 6LA – Ⓜ Piccadilly Circus – ✆ (020) 7839 3090
– info@alduca-restaurants.co.uk – Fax (020) 7839 40 50
– www.alduca-restaurant.co.uk
Closed 25 December, Sunday and Bank Holidays **H4**
Rest – Menu £25/27
♦ Italian ♦ Friendly ♦
Relaxed, modern, stylish restaurant. Friendly and approachable service of robust and rustic Italian dishes. Set priced menu is good value.

X **Inn the Park** VISA MC AE

St James's Park ✉ SW1A 2BJ – Ⓜ Charing Cross – ✆ (020) 7451 9999
– info@innthepark.com – Fax (020) 7451 99 98 – www.innthepark.com
Closed 25 December **I4**
Rest – Carte £32/52
♦ British ♦ Design ♦
Eco-friendly restaurant with grass covered roof; pleasant views across park and lakes. Super-heated dining terrace. Modern British menus of tasty, wholesome dishes.

Portrait

3rd Floor, National Portrait Gallery, St Martin's Pl ✉ WC2H 0HE – Ⓜ Charing Cross – ✆ (020) 7312 2490 – portrait.restaurant@searcys.co.uk – Fax (020) 7925 02 44 – www.searcys.co.uk
Closed 25-26 December *Plan III* **I3**
Rest – *(lunch only and dinner Thursday and Friday) (booking essential)*
Carte £25/46
♦ Modern ♦ Brasserie ♦
On the top floor of National Portrait Gallery with rooftop local landmark views: a charming spot for lunch. Modern British/European dishes find favour with hungry tourists.

The National Dining Rooms

Sainsbury Wing, The National Gallery, Trafalgar Sq ✉ WC2N 5DN – Ⓜ Charing Cross – ✆ (020) 7747 2525 – enquiries@thenationaldiningrooms.co.uk – www.thenationaldiningrooms.co.uk
Closed Christmas **I3/4**
Rest – *(lunch only and dinner Wednesday)* Menu £30
♦ Design ♦ British ♦
Set on the East Wing's first floor, you can tuck into cakes in the bakery or grab a prime corner table in the restaurant for great views and proudly seasonal British menus.

STRAND, COVENT GARDEN & LAMBETH

Strand and Covent Garden *Plan III*

Swissôtel The Howard

Temple Pl ✉ WC2R 2PR – Ⓜ Temple – ✆ (020) 7836 3555 – reservations.london@swissotel.com – Fax (020) 7379 45 47 – www.london.swissotel.com **J3**
177 rm – †£188/316 ††£723, ☐ £23.50 – 12 suites
Rest *Jaan* – see below
♦ Luxury ♦ Modern ♦
Cool elegance is the order of the day at this handsomely appointed hotel. Many of the comfortable rooms enjoy balcony views of the Thames. Attentive service.

The Waldorf Hilton

Aldwych ✉ WC2B 4DD – Ⓜ Covent Garden – ✆ (020) 7836 2400 – enquiry.waldorflondon@hilton.com – Fax (020) 7836 46 48 – www.hilton.co.uk/waldorf **J3**
289 rm – †£198/421 ††£198/421, ☐ £22 – 10 suites
Rest *Homage* – *(Closed lunch Saturday and Sunday)* Menu £20 – Carte £29/44
♦ Luxury ♦ Modern ♦
Impressive curved and columned façade: an Edwardian landmark. Basement leisure club. Ornate meeting rooms. Two bedroom styles: one contemporary, one more traditional. Large, modish brasserie with extensive range of modern menus.

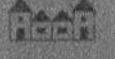

One Aldwych

1 Aldwych ✉ WC2B 4RH – Ⓜ Covent Garden – ✆ (020) 7300 1000 – sales@onealdwych.com – Fax (020) 7300 10 01 – www.onealdwych.com **J3**
96 rm – †£447 ††£447, ☐ £29.50 – 9 suites
Rest *Axis* – see below
Rest *Indigo* – *(Closed Sunday, Easter and Christmas)* Menu £18 – Carte £28/51
♦ Luxury ♦ Stylish ♦
Decorative Edwardian building, former home to the Morning Post newspaper. Now a stylish and contemporary address with modern artwork, a screening room and hi-tech bedrooms. All-day restaurant looks down on fashionable bar.

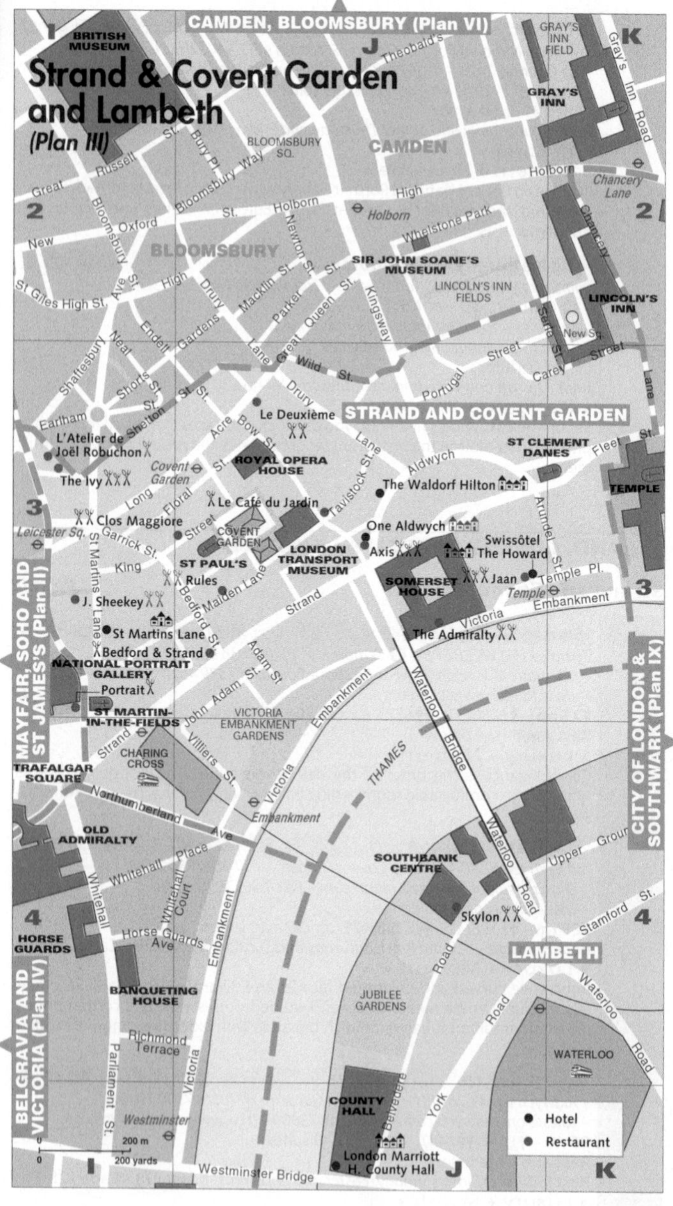
Strand & Covent Garden and Lambeth
(Plan III)
CAMDEN, BLOOMSBURY (Plan VI)
STRAND AND COVENT GARDEN
LAMBETH
MAYFAIR, SOHO AND ST JAMES'S (Plan II)
CITY OF LONDON & SOUTHWARK (Plan IX)
BELGRAVIA AND VICTORIA (Plan IV)
BRITISH MUSEUM
BLOOMSBURY
CAMDEN
SIR JOHN SOANE'S MUSEUM
LINCOLN'S INN FIELDS
LINCOLN'S INN
GRAY'S INN
GRAY'S INN FIELD
ST CLEMENT DANES
TEMPLE
ROYAL OPERA HOUSE
COVENT GARDEN
ST PAUL'S
LONDON TRANSPORT MUSEUM
SOMERSET HOUSE
NATIONAL PORTRAIT GALLERY
ST MARTIN-IN-THE-FIELDS
TRAFALGAR SQUARE
CHARING CROSS
VICTORIA EMBANKMENT GARDENS
OLD ADMIRALTY
HORSE GUARDS
BANQUETING HOUSE
SOUTHBANK CENTRE
JUBILEE GARDENS
COUNTY HALL
WATERLOO
THAMES
Le Deuxième
L'Atelier de Joël Robuchon
The Ivy
Le Café du Jardin
Clos Maggiore
Rules
J. Sheekey
St Martins Lane
Bedford & Strand
Portrait
The Waldorf Hilton
One Aldwych
Axis
Swissôtel The Howard
Jaan
The Admiralty
Skylon
London Marriott H. County Hall
Hotel
Restaurant
200 m
200 yards

St Martins Lane

45 St Martin's Lane ✉ WC2N 4HX – Ⓜ Charing Cross – ✆ (020) 7300 5500 – sml@morganshotelgroup.com – Fax (020) 7300 55 01 – www.morganshotelgroup.com I3

202 rm – †£252/393 ††£276/417, ☕ £20.50 – 2 suites

Rest ***Asia de Cuba*** – Carte £53/83

♦ Luxury ♦ Design ♦

The unmistakable hand of Philippe Starck evident at this most contemporary of hotels. Unique and stylish, from the starkly modern lobby to the state-of-the-art rooms. 350 varieties of rum and tasty Asian dishes at fashionable Asia de Cuba.

The Ivy

1-5 West St ✉ WC2H 9NQ – Ⓜ Leicester Square – ✆ (020) 7836 4751 – Fax (020) 7240 93 33 – www.the-ivy.co.uk

Closed 24-26 December, 1 January and August Bank Holiday I3

Rest – Carte £30/54

♦ Modern ♦ Fashionable ♦

Wood panelling and stained glass combine with an unpretentious menu to create a veritable institution. A favourite of 'celebrities', so securing a table can be challenging.

Axis

1 Aldwych ✉ WC2B 4RH – Ⓜ Covent Garden – ✆ (020) 7300 0300 – axis@onealdwych.com – Fax (020) 7300 03 01 – www.onealdwych.com

Closed 24 December-4 January, Easter, Sunday, Saturday lunch and Bank Holidays J3

Rest – Menu £18 (lunch) – Carte £28/37

♦ Modern ♦ Design ♦

Lower-level room overlooked by gallery bar. Muted tones, black leather chairs and vast futuristic mural appeal to the fashion cognoscenti. Globally-influenced menu.

Jaan – at Swissôtel The Howard

Temple Pl ✉ WC2R 2PR – Ⓜ Temple – ✆ (020) 7300 1700 – jaan.london@swissotel.com – Fax (020) 7240 78 16 – www.swissotel-london.com

Closed Saturday lunch and Sunday and bank holidays J3

Rest – Menu £24/38 – Carte £33/49

♦ Innovative ♦ Design ♦

Bright room on the ground floor of the hotel with large windows overlooking an attractive terrace. Original cooking - modern French with Cambodian flavours and ingredients.

J. Sheekey

28-32 St Martin's Court ✉ WC2 4AL – Ⓜ Leicester Square – ✆ (020) 7240 2565 – reservations@j-sheekey.co.uk – Fax (020) 7497 08 91 – www.j-sheeky.co.uk

Closed 25-26 December, 1 January and August Bank Holiday I3

Rest – *(booking essential)* Carte £25/51

♦ Seafood ♦ Fashionable ♦

Festooned with photographs of actors and linked to the theatrical world since opening in 1890. Wood panels and alcove tables add famed intimacy. Accomplished seafood cooking.

Rules

35 Maiden Lane ✉ WC2E 7LB – Ⓜ Leicester Square – ✆ (020) 7836 5314 – info@rules.co.uk – Fax (020) 7497 10 81 – www.rules.co.uk

closed 4 days Christmas J3

Rest – *(booking essential)* Carte £35/53

♦ British ♦ Formal ♦

London's oldest restaurant boasts a fine collection of antique cartoons, drawings and paintings. Tradition continues in the menu, specialising in game from its own estate.

XX **Clos Maggiore**

33 King St ✉ WC2E 8JD – Ⓜ Leicester Square – ✆ (020) 7379 9696 – enquiries@closmaggiore.com – Fax (020) 7379 67 67 – www.closmaggiore.com
Closed 25-26 December, Saturday and Sunday lunch and Bank Holidays **IJ3**
Rest – Menu £20 (lunch) – Carte £46/56
♦ French ♦ Formal ♦
Walls covered with flowering branches create delightful woodland feel to rear dining area with retractable glass roof. Seriously accomplished, original, rustic French cooking.

XX **Admiralty**

Somerset House, The Strand ✉ WC2R 1LA – Ⓜ Temple – ✆ (020) 7845 4646 – info@theadmiraltyrestaurant.com – Fax (020) 7845 46 58 – www.theadmiraltyrestaurant.com
Closed 24-27 December, dinner Sunday and Bank Holiday Mondays **J3**
Rest – Menu £16 (lunch) – Carte £26/37
♦ French ♦ Brasserie ♦
Interconnecting rooms with bold colours and informal service contrast with its setting within the restored Georgian splendour of Somerset House. 'Cuisine de terroir'.

XX **Le Deuxième**

65a Long Acre ✉ WC2E 9JH – Ⓜ Covent Garden – ✆ (020) 7379 0033 – Fax (020) 7379 00 66 – www.ledeuxieme.com
Closed 24-25 December **J3**
Rest – Menu £16 – Carte £29/30
♦ Modern ♦ Brasserie ♦
Caters well for theatregoers: opens early, closes late. Buzzy eatery, quietly decorated in white with subtle lighting. Varied international menu: Japanese to Mediterranean.

X ✿ **L'Atelier de Joël Robuchon**

13-15 West St ✉ WC2H 9NE – Ⓜ Leicester Square – ✆ (020) 7010 8600 – info@joelrobuchon.co.uk – Fax (020) 7010 86 01 – www.joel-robuchon.com
Rest – *(Closed 24-26 December and 1-2 January)* Carte £33/75 **I3**
Rest *La Cuisine* – *(Closed 24-26 December, 1-2 January and Saturday lunch)* Carte £33/100
Spec. Fresh mackerel tart with parmesan shavings and olives. Free range quail stuffed with foie gras, truffled mashed potatoes. Araguani chocolate, white chocolate ice cream and Oreo cookie.
♦ French ♦ Fashionable ♦
Entrance into trendy atelier with counter seating; upstairs the more structured La Cuisine has wonderfully delicate, precise modern French cooking. Cool top floor lounge bar.

X **Le Café du Jardin**

28 Wellington St ✉ WC2E 7BD – Ⓜ Covent Garden – ✆ (020) 7836 8769 – info@lecafedujardin.com – Fax (020) 7836 41 23 – www.lecafedujardin.com
Closed 25-26 December **J3**
Rest – Menu £16 – Carte £28/34
♦ Modern ♦ Bistro ♦
Divided into two floors with the downstairs slightly more comfortable. Light and contemporary interior with European-influenced cooking. Ideally placed for the Opera House.

X **Bedford & Strand**

1a Bedford St ✉ WC2E 9HH – Ⓜ Charing Cross – ✆ (020) 7836 3033 – www.bedford-strand.com
Closed 25-26 and 31 December, 1 January, Saturday lunch, Sunday and Bank Holidays **J3**
Rest – *(booking essential)* Menu £16 – Carte £24/53
♦ Traditional ♦ Wine bar ♦
Basement bistro/wine bar with simple décor and easy-going atmosphere; kitchen sources well and has a light touch with Italian, French and British dishes.

Lambeth

Plan III

London Marriott H. County Hall

Westminster Bridge Rd ✉ SE1 7PB – Ⓜ Westminster – ✆ (020) 7928 5200 – mhrs.lonch.salesadmin@marriotthotels.com – Fax (020) 7928 53 00 – www.marriott.countyhall.com **J5**

195 rm – †£328 ††£363, ☕ £21.95 – 5 suites

Rest *County Hall* – Menu £23 – Carte £29/42

♦ Luxury ♦ Classic ♦

Occupying the historic County Hall building. Many of the spacious and comfortable bedrooms enjoy river and Parliament outlook. Impressive leisure facilities. World famous views from restaurant.

Skylon

< River Thames and Hungerford Bridge,

1 Southbank Centre, Belvedere Rd ✉ SE1 8XX – Ⓜ Waterloo – ✆ (020) 7654 7800 – skylon@danddlondon.com – Fax (020) 7654 78 01 – www.skylonrestaurant.co.uk **J4**

Rest – Menu £22/30 – Carte £27/38

♦ Modern ♦ Design ♦

1950s style dining flagship in Royal Festival Hall. Grill with bar, river views and easy-to-eat menu. Restaurant offers more ambitious dishes, which means higher prices.

BELGRAVIA & VICTORIA

Belgravia

Plan IV

The Berkeley

Wilton Pl ✉ SW1X 7RL – Ⓜ Knightsbridge – ✆ (020) 7235 6000 – info@the-berkeley.co.uk – Fax (020) 7235 43 30 – www.the-berkeley.co.uk **G4**

189 rm – †£539 ††£598, ☕ £29 – 25 suites

Rest *Pétrus* – see below

Rest *Boxwood Café* – Carte £28/36

♦ Grand Luxury ♦ Stylish ♦

A gracious and discreet hotel. Relax in the gilded and panelled Lutyens lounge or enjoy a swim in the roof-top pool with its retracting roof. Opulent bedrooms.

The Lanesborough

Hyde Park Corner ✉ SW1X 7TA – Ⓜ Hyde Park Corner – ✆ (020) 7259 5599 – info@lanesborough.com – Fax (020) 7259 56 06 – www.lanesborough.com **G4**

86 rm – †£393/417 ††£652/675, ☕ £28 – 9 suites

Rest *The Lanesborough* – Menu £24/38 – Carte £52/76

♦ Grand Luxury ♦ Classic ♦

Converted in the 1990s from 18C St George's Hospital. A grand and traditional atmosphere prevails. Butler service offered. Regency-era decorated, lavishly appointed rooms. Ornate, glass-roofed dining room with palm trees and fountains.

The Halkin

5 Halkin St ✉ SW1X 7DJ – Ⓜ Hyde Park Corner – ✆ (020) 7333 1000 – res@halkin.como.bz – Fax (020) 7333 11 00 – www.halkin.como.bz **G5**

35 rm – †£458 ††£558, ☕ £25 – 6 suites

Rest *Nahm* – see below

♦ Luxury ♦ Stylish ♦

One of London's first minimalist hotels. The cool, marbled reception and bar have an understated charm. Spacious rooms have every conceivable facility.

Sheraton Belgravia

20 Chesham Pl ✉ SW1X 8HQ – Ⓜ Knightsbridge – ✆ (020) 7235 6040 – reservations.sheratonbelgravia@sheraton.com – Fax (020) 7259 62 43 – www.sheraton.com/belgravia **FG5**

82 rm – †£233/257 ††£233/257, ☕ £21 – 7 suites

Rest *The Dining Room* – Menu £20 – Carte £31/40

♦ Business ♦ Classic ♦

Modern corporate hotel overlooking Chesham Place. Comfortable and well-equipped for the tourist and business traveller alike. A few minutes' walk from Harrods. Modern, international menus.

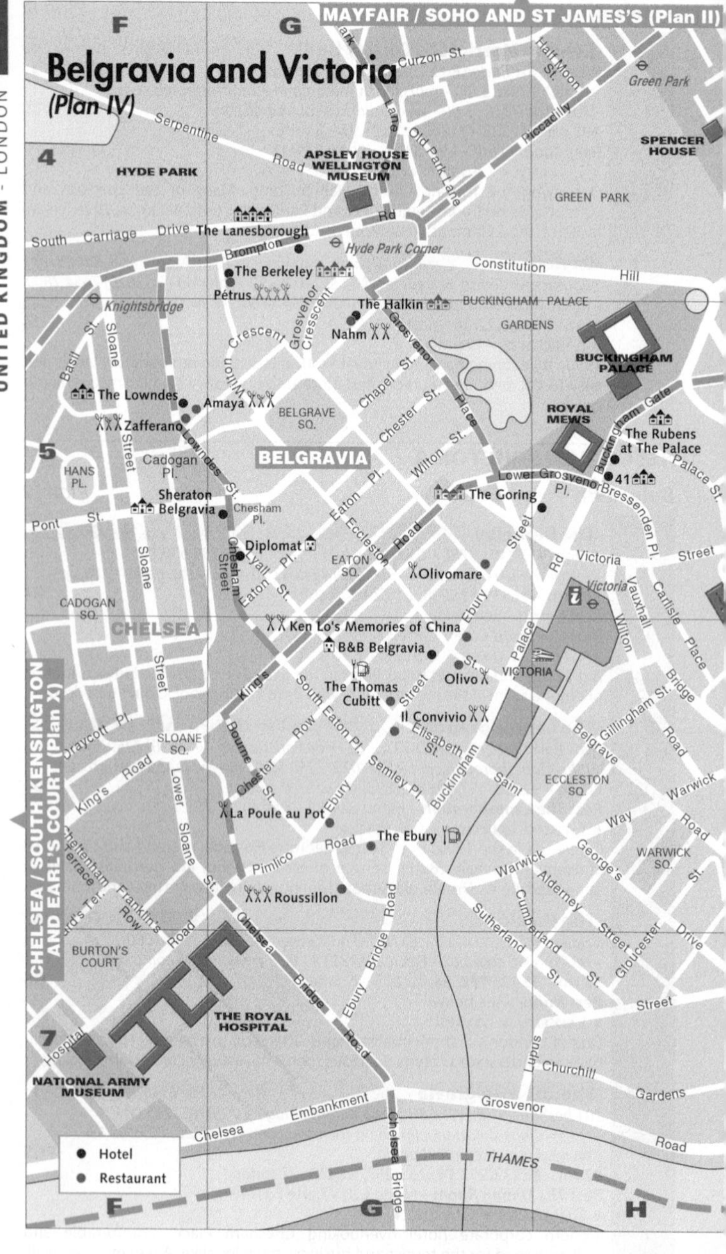

Belgravia and Victoria
(Plan IV)
MAYFAIR / SOHO AND ST JAMES'S (Plan II)
CHELSEA / SOUTH KENSINGTON AND EARL'S COURT (Plan X)
HYDE PARK
APSLEY HOUSE WELLINGTON MUSEUM
GREEN PARK
SPENCER HOUSE
BUCKINGHAM PALACE GARDENS
BUCKINGHAM PALACE
ROYAL MEWS
BELGRAVIA
BELGRAVE SQ.
EATON SQ.
CHELSEA
CADOGAN SQ.
HANS PL.
SLOANE SQ.
ECCLESTON SQ.
WARWICK SQ.
VICTORIA
BURTON'S COURT
THE ROYAL HOSPITAL
NATIONAL ARMY MUSEUM
THAMES
The Lanesborough
The Berkeley
Pétrus
The Halkin
Nahm
The Lowndes
Amaya
Zafferano
Sheraton Belgravia
Diplomat
Olivomare
Ken Lo's Memories of China
B&B Belgravia
The Thomas Cubitt
Olivo
Il Convivio
La Poule au Pot
The Ebury
Roussillon
The Goring
The Rubens at The Palace
41
Hyde Park Corner
Knightsbridge
Green Park
Victoria
Hotel
Restaurant
F
G
H
4
5
7

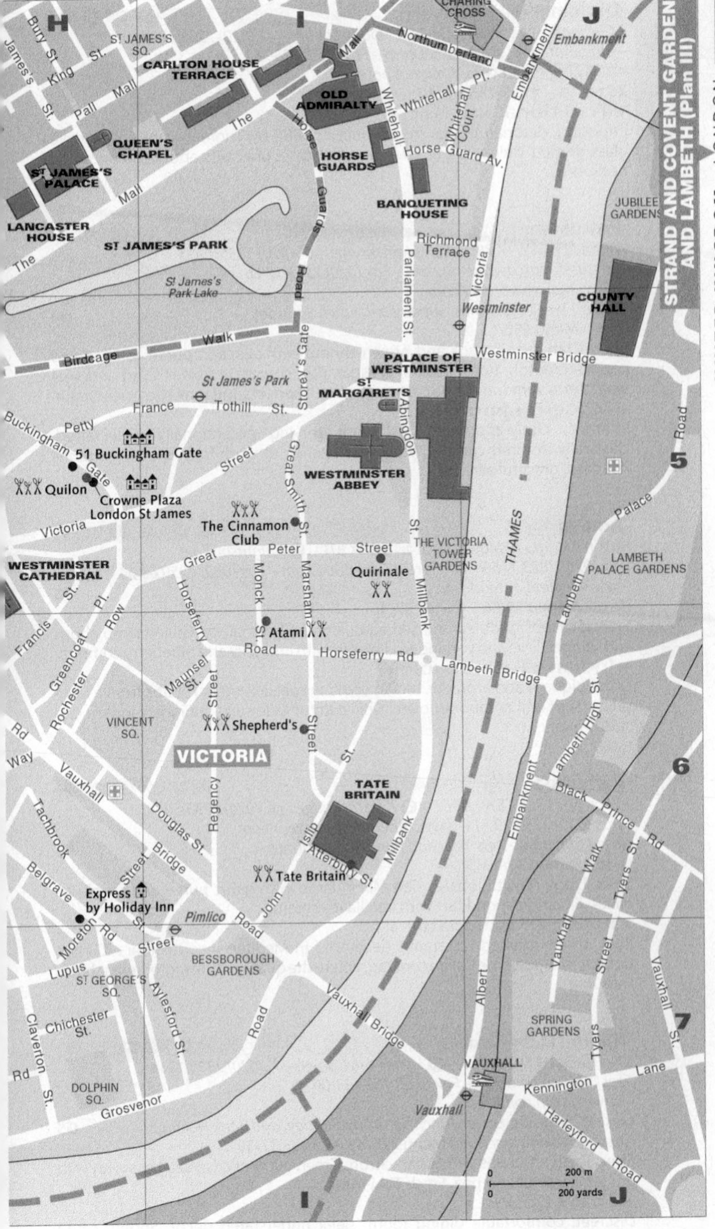
CHARING CROSS
Embankment
STRAND AND COVENT GARDEN AND LAMBETH (Plan III)
ST JAMES'S SQ.
CARLTON HOUSE TERRACE
OLD ADMIRALTY
QUEEN'S CHAPEL
ST JAMES'S PALACE
HORSE GUARDS
BANQUETING HOUSE
LANCASTER HOUSE
ST JAMES'S PARK
St James's Park Lake
JUBILEE GARDENS
COUNTY HALL
Westminster
PALACE OF WESTMINSTER
ST MARGARET'S
St James's Park
51 Buckingham Gate
Quilon
Crowne Plaza London St James
WESTMINSTER ABBEY
The Cinnamon Club
THE VICTORIA TOWER GARDENS
WESTMINSTER CATHEDRAL
Quirinale
THAMES
LAMBETH PALACE GARDENS
Atami
VINCENT SQ.
Shepherd's
VICTORIA
TATE BRITAIN
Tate Britain
Express by Holiday Inn
Pimlico
BESSBOROUGH GARDENS
ST GEORGE'S SQ.
SPRING GARDENS
VAUXHALL
Vauxhall
DOLPHIN SQ.
200 m
200 yards

Diplomat without rest
2 Chesham St ✉ SW1X 8DT – Ⓜ Sloane Square – ✆ (020) 7235 1544 – diplomat.hotel@btinternet.com – Fax (020) 7259 61 53 – www.btinternet.com/diplomat.hotel **G5**
26 rm – ♦£95/115 ♦♦£175
♦ Traditional ♦ Classic ♦
Imposing Victorian corner house built in 1882 by Thomas Cubitt. Attractive glass-domed stairwell and sweeping staircase. Spacious and well-appointed bedrooms.

Pétrus (Marcus Wareing) – at The Berkeley H.
Wilton Pl ✉ SW1X 7RL – Ⓜ Knightsbridge – ✆ (020) 7235 1200 – petrus@marcuswareing.com – Fax (020) 7235 12 66 – www.marcuswareing.com
Closed 1 week Christmas, Sunday and lunch Saturday **G4**
Rest – Menu £30/65
Spec. Crab, langoustine and brown shrimp with avocado purée and smoked paprika crouton. Roast veal with asparagus, courgette flower salad and veal vinaigrette. Almond panna cotta with glazed apricots and tonka bean ice cream.
♦ Modern ♦ Formal ♦
Intimate, richly-appointed restaurant serving exceptionally well-crafted, classically-inspired cuisine. Watch the kitchen at work from the chef's table. Polished, graceful service.

Amaya
Halkin Arcade, 19 Motcomb St ✉ SW1X 8JT – Ⓜ Knightsbridge – ✆ (020) 7823 1166 – info@realindianfood.com – Fax (020) 7259 64 64 – www.realindianfood.com **F5**
Rest – Menu £16/36 – Carte £37/46
Spec. Scallops griddled and served in a green herb sauce. Grilled lamb chops with ginger, lime and coriander. Lime tart with lime jelly and blueberry compote
♦ Indian ♦ Fashionable ♦
Light, piquant and aromatic Indian cooking specialising in kebabs from a tawa skillet, sigri grill or tandoor oven. Chic comfortable surroundings, modern and subtly exotic.

Zafferano
15 Lowndes St ✉ SW1X 9EY – Ⓜ Knightsbridge – ✆ (020) 7235 5800 – Fax (020) 7235 19 71 – www.zafferanorestaurant.com
closed Christmas-New Year and Bank Holiday lunches **F5**
Rest – Menu £30/40
Spec. Linguini with lobster. Salt Marsh lamb with garlic purée and taggiasca olives. Fig and almond tart with vanilla ice cream.
♦ Italian ♦ Fashionable ♦
Busy, three-roomed restaurant decorated in Mediterranean colours. Classic, unfussy, flavoursome Italian cooking, where the quality of the ingredients shines through.

Nahm – at The Halkin H.
5 Halkin St ✉ SW1X 7DJ – Ⓜ Hyde Park Corner – ✆ (020) 7333 1234 – res@nahm.como.bz – Fax (020) 7333 11 00 – www.halkin.como.bz
Closed Christmas, Easter, lunch Saturday-Sunday, and Bank Holidays **G5**
Rest – *(booking essential)* Menu £26/55 – Carte £37/39
Spec. Crispy noodles with Asian citron. Green curry of crisp sea bass with wild ginger, coconut and pea. Fresh Thai fruits.
♦ Thai ♦ Design ♦
Discreet, comfortable dining room; sleek understated décor. Sophisticated cooking showcases the harmony of Thai cooking achieved through careful combinations of textures and flavours.

Victoria

Plan IV

The Goring

15 Beeston Pl, Grosvenor Gdns ✉ SW1W 0JW – Ⓜ Victoria – ✆ (020) 7396 9000 – reception@goringhotel.co.uk – Fax (020) 7834 43 93 – www.goringhotel.co.uk **H5**

65 rm – 🚹£327/393 🚹🚹£386/434, ☕ £23 – 6 suites

Rest – *(Closed Saturday lunch)* Menu £33/44

◆ Traditional ◆ Luxury ◆ Classic ◆

Opened in 1910 as a quintessentially English hotel. The fourth generation of Goring is now at the helm. Many of the attractive rooms overlook a peaceful garden. Elegantly appointed restaurant provides memorable dining experience.

Crowne Plaza London - St James

45 Buckingham Gate ✉ SW1E 6AF – Ⓜ St James's Park – ✆ (020) 7834 6655 – sales@cplonsj.co.uk – Fax (020) 7630 75 87 – www.london.crowneplaza.com **H5**

323 rm – 🚹£323 🚹🚹£388, ☕ £16 – 19 suites

Rest Quilon and **Bank** – see below

Rest *Bistro 51* – Menu £18/22 – Carte £30/36

◆ Luxury ◆ Classic ◆

Built in 1897 as serviced accommodation for visiting aristocrats. Behind the impressive Edwardian façade lies an equally elegant interior. Quietest rooms overlook courtyard. Bright and informal café-style restaurant.

51 Buckingham Gate without rest

51 Buckingham Gate ✉ SW1E 6AF – Ⓜ St James's Park – ✆ (020) 7769 7766 – info@51-buckinghamgate.co.uk – Fax (020) 7828 59 09 – www.51-buckinghamgate.com **H5**

86 suites – 🚹🚹£423/628, ☕ £21.75

Rest Quilon and **Bank** – see below

◆ Luxury ◆ Classic ◆

Canopied entrance leads to luxurious suites: every detail considered, every mod con provided. Colour schemes echoed in plants and paintings. Butler and nanny service.

41 without rest

41 Buckingham Palace Rd ✉ SW1W 0PS – Ⓜ Victoria – ✆ (020) 7300 0041 – book41@rchmail.com – Fax (020) 7300 01 41 – www.41hotel.com **H5**

27 rm – 🚹£264/382 🚹🚹£288/415, ☕ £25 – 1 suite

◆ Luxury ◆ Classic ◆

Discreet appearance; exudes exclusive air. Leather armchairs; bookcases line the walls. Intimate service. State-of-the-art rooms where hi-tec and fireplace merge appealingly.

The Rubens at The Palace

39 Buckingham Palace Rd ✉ SW1W 0PS – Ⓜ Victoria – ✆ (020) 7834 6600 – bookrb@rchmail.com – Fax (020) 7828 54 01 – www.rubenshotel.com **H5**

170 rm – 🚹£155/300 🚹🚹£172/320, ☕ £18.50 – 2 suites

Rest – *(dinner only)* Menu £35 – Carte £35/47

◆ Traditional ◆ Classic ◆

Traditional hotel with an air of understated elegance. Tastefully furnished rooms: the Royal Wing, themed after Kings and Queens, features TVs in bathrooms. Smart carvery restaurant.

B + B Belgravia without rest

64-66 Ebury St ✉ SW1W 9QD – Ⓜ Victoria – ✆ (020) 7259 8570 – info@bb-belgravia.com – Fax (020) 7259 85 91 – www.bb-belgravia.com **G6**

17 rm ☕ – 🚹£97/107 🚹🚹£107

◆ Townhouse ◆ Personalised ◆

Two houses, three floors, and, considering the location, some of the best value accommodation in town. Sleek, clean-lined rooms. Breakfast overlooking little garden terrace.

XXX

The Cinnamon Club

30-32 Great Smith St ✉ SW1P 3BU – Ⓜ St James's Park – ✆ (020) 7222 2555 – info@cinnamonclub.com – Fax (020) 7222 13 33 – www.cinnamonclub.com
Closed Sunday **I5**
Rest – Menu £22 (lunch) – Carte £35/48
♦ Indian ♦ Formal ♦
Housed in former Westminster Library: exterior has ornate detail, interior is stylish and modern. Walls are lined with books. New Wave Indian cooking with plenty of choice.

XXX ✿

Quilon – at Crowne Plaza London - St James H.

41 Buckingham Gate ✉ SW1 6AF – Ⓜ St James's Park – ✆ (020) 7821 1899 – info@quilonrestaurant.co.uk – Fax (020) 7233 95 97 – www.quilon.co.uk
Closed 25 December and Saturday lunch **H5**
Rest – Menu £18 – Carte £34/47
Spec. Crab cakes with curry leaves, ginger and green chillies. Char-grilled lobster, prawn, fish and scallops with a mild sauce. Spiced chocolate dessert.
♦ Indian ♦ Formal ♦
Original, vibrant and well balanced Indian dishes, many of which originate from the South West coast. Excellent use of spices, appealing seafood specialities and graceful service.

XXX

Shepherd's

Marsham Court, Marsham St ✉ SW1P 4LA – Ⓜ Pimlico – ✆ (020) 7834 9552 – admin@langansrestaurants.co.uk – Fax (020) 7233 60 47 – www.langansrestaurants.co.uk
Closed Saturday, Sunday and Bank Holidays **I6**
Rest – *(booking essential)* Menu £33
♦ British ♦ Formal ♦
A truly English restaurant where game and traditional puddings are a highlight. Popular with those from Westminster - the booths offer a degree of privacy.

XXX ✿

Roussillon (Alex Gauthier)

16 St Barnabas St ✉ SW1W 8PE – Ⓜ Sloane Square – ✆ (020) 7730 5550 – alexis@roussillon.co.uk – Fax (020) 7824 86 17 – www.roussillon.co.uk
Closed Saturday lunch and Sunday **G6**
Rest – Menu £35/55
Spec. Black truffle risotto, veal jus. Highland venison with pumpkin, poached pear and celeriac, tuffle purée. Louis XV, crunchy praline and chocolate.
♦ French ♦ Neighbourhood ♦
Tucked away in a smart residential area. Cooking clearly focuses on the quality of the ingredients. Seasonal menu with inventive elements and a French base.

XX

Atami

37 Monck St (entrance on Great Peter St) ✉ SW1P 2BL – Ⓜ Pimlico – ✆ (020) 7222 2218 – mail@atami-restaurant.com – Fax (020) 7222 27 88 – www.atami-restaurant.com
Closed Saturday lunch and Sunday **I6**
Rest – Menu £23 (lunch) – Carte £25/37
♦ Japanese ♦ Design ♦
Clean, modern lines illuminated by vast ceiling orbs induce a sense of calm. Menus true to Japanese roots feature sushi and sashimi turning down interesting modern highways.

XX

Il Convivio

143 Ebury St ✉ SW1W 9QN – Ⓜ Sloane Square – ✆ (020) 7730 4099 – comments@etruscarestaurants.com – Fax (020) 7730 41 03 – www.etruscarestaurants.com
closed 25 December and Sunday **G6**
Rest – Menu £22 (lunch) – Carte approx. £34
♦ Italian ♦ Design ♦
A retractable roof provides alfresco dining to part of this comfortable and modern restaurant. Contemporary and traditional Italian menu with home-made pasta specialities.

Ken Lo's Memories of China

65-69 Ebury St ✉ SW1W 0NZ – Ⓜ Victoria – ✆ (020) 7730 7734 – Fax (020) 7730 29 92 – www.memories-of-china.co.uk
Closed 25-26 December, Sunday lunch and Bank Holidays **G6**
Rest – Menu £19/30 – Carte £29/35
♦ Chinese ♦ Neighbourhood ♦
An air of tranquillity pervades this traditionally furnished room. Lattice screens add extra privacy. Extensive Chinese menu: bold flavours with a clean, fresh style.

Quirinale

North Court, 1 Great Peter St ✉ SW1P 3LL – Ⓜ Westminster – ✆ (020) 7222 7080 – info@quirinale.co.uk – www.quirinale.co.uk
Closed August, 1week Christmas, Saturday and Sunday **I3**
Rest – Carte 28/38
♦ Italian ♦ Neighbourhood ♦
Light and bright Italian restaurant with contemporary, minimalist feel typified by cream leather banquettes. Seasonally-changing menu encompasses all things Italian.

Olivo

21 Eccleston St ✉ SW1W 9LX – Ⓜ Victoria – ✆ (020) 7730 2505 – maurosanna@oliveto.fsnet.co.uk – Fax (020) 7823 53 77
Closed Bank Holidays, lunch Saturday and Sunday **G6**
Rest – Menu £21 (lunch) – Carte £26/30
♦ Italian ♦ Neighbourhood ♦
Rustic, informal Italian restaurant. Relaxed atmosphere provided by the friendly staff. Simple, non-fussy cuisine with emphasis on best available fresh produce.

La Poule au Pot

231 Ebury St ✉ SW1W 8UT – Ⓜ Sloane Square – ✆ (020) 7730 7763 – Fax (020) 7259 96 51 – Closed 25-26 December **G6**
Rest – Menu £17 – Carte £27/41
♦ French ♦ Bistro ♦
The subdued lighting and friendly informality make this one of London's more romantic restaurants. Classic French menu with extensive plats du jour.

Olivomare

10 Lower Belgrave St ✉ SW1W 0LJ – Ⓜ Victoria – ✆ (020) 7730 9022 – maurosanna@oliveto.fsnet.co.uk – Fax (020) 7823 53 77
Closed Sunday and Bank Holidays **G5**
Rest – Carte £29/36
♦ Seafood ♦ Design ♦
Chic minimalist décor with magic-eye mural of intertwined fish. The food is robust and full-flavoured; seafood is the theme, with a subtle Sardinian subtext. Assured service.

The Ebury

11 Pimlico Rd ✉ SW1W 8NA – Ⓜ Sloane Square – ✆ (020) 7730 6784 – info@theebury.co.uk – Fax (020) 7730 61 49 – www.theebury.co.uk
Closed 25-26 December **G6**
Rest – Carte £25/30
♦ Modern ♦ Pub ♦
Victorian corner pub restaurant with walnut bar, simple tables and large seafood bar. Friendly service. Wide-ranging menu from snacks to full meals.

The Thomas Cubitt

44 Elizabeth Street ✉ SW1W 9PA – Ⓜ Sloane Square – ✆ (020) 7730 6060 – reservations@thethomascubitt.co.uk – Fax (020) 7730 60 55 – www.thethomascubitt.co.uk
Closed 24 December-1 January **G6**
Rest – *(booking essential)* Menu £25 – Carte £23/40
♦ Modern ♦ Pub ♦
Georgian pub refurbished and renamed after master builder. He'd approve of elegant, formal dining room. Carefully supplied ingredients underpin tasty, seasonal English dishes.

Landmark London

222 Marylebone Rd ✉ NW1 6JQ – Ⓜ Edgware Rd – ✆ (020) 7631 8000 – reservations@thelandmark.co.uk – Fax (020) 7631 80 80 – www.landmarklondon.co.uk **F1**

290 rm – †£211/340 ††£246/376, ☕ £28 – 9 suites

Rest *Winter Garden* – Menu £35 (lunch) – Carte £30/46

♦ Grand Luxury ♦ Classic ♦

Imposing Victorian Gothic building with a vast glass enclosed atrium, overlooked by many of the modern, well-equipped bedrooms. Winter Garden popular for afternoon tea.

Langham

1c Portland Pl, Regent St ✉ W1B 1JA – Ⓜ Oxford Circus – ✆ (020) 7636 1000 – loninfo@langhamhotels.com – Fax (020) 7323 23 40 – www.langhamhotels.com **H2**

368 rm – †£411 ††£411, ☕ £24.95 – 20 suites

Rest – Menu £37.50/45 – Carte £39/47

♦ Luxury ♦ Classic ♦

Opposite the BBC, with traditional bedrooms and impressive infinity suite. Designer-styled bar with oriental edge is named after 360ft well under hotel and specialises in rum.

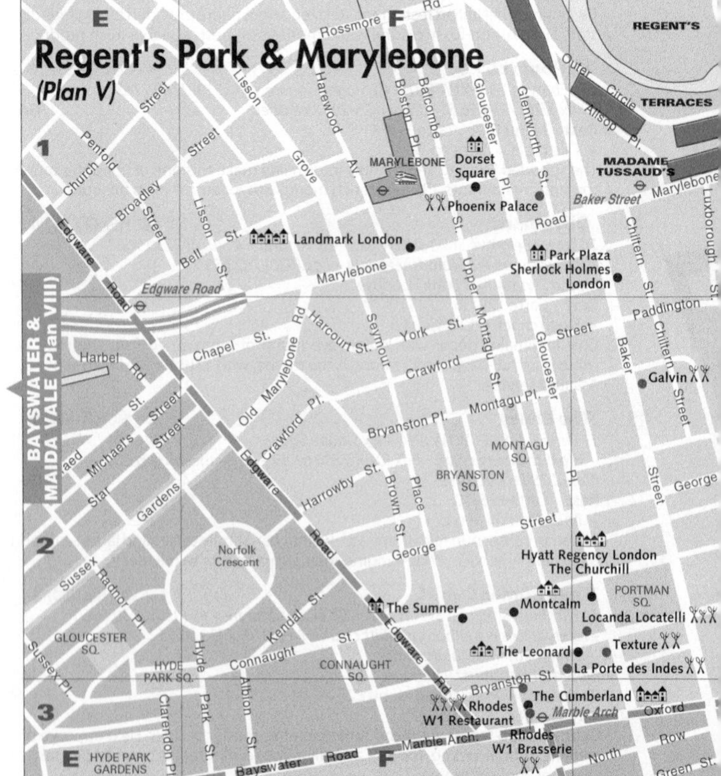

The Cumberland

Great Cumberland Place ✉ W1A 4RF – Ⓜ Marble Arch – ☎ (0870) 3339280 – enquiries@thecumberland.co.uk – Fax (0870) 3 33 92 81 – www.guoman.com **FG3**

1010 rm – †£358 ††£366

Rest *Rhodes W1 Restaurant* and *Rhodes W1 Brasserie* – see below

♦ Business ♦ Design ♦

Fully refurbished, conference oriented hotel whose vast lobby boasts modern art, sculpture and running water panels. Distinctive bedrooms with a host of impressive extras.

Hyatt Regency London-The Churchill

30 Portman Sq ✉ W1A 4ZX – Ⓜ Marble Arch – ☎ (020) 7486 5800 – london.churchill@hyattintl.com – Fax (020) 7486 12 55 – www.london-churchill.hyatt.com **G2**

396 rm – †£194/447 ††£217/470, £25 – 40 suites

Rest *The Montagu* – Menu £23 (lunch) – Carte £35/47

♦ Luxury ♦ Classic ♦

Modern property overlooking attractive square. Elegant marbled lobby. Cigar bar open until 2am for members. Well-appointed rooms have the international traveller in mind. Restaurant provides popular Sunday brunch entertainment.

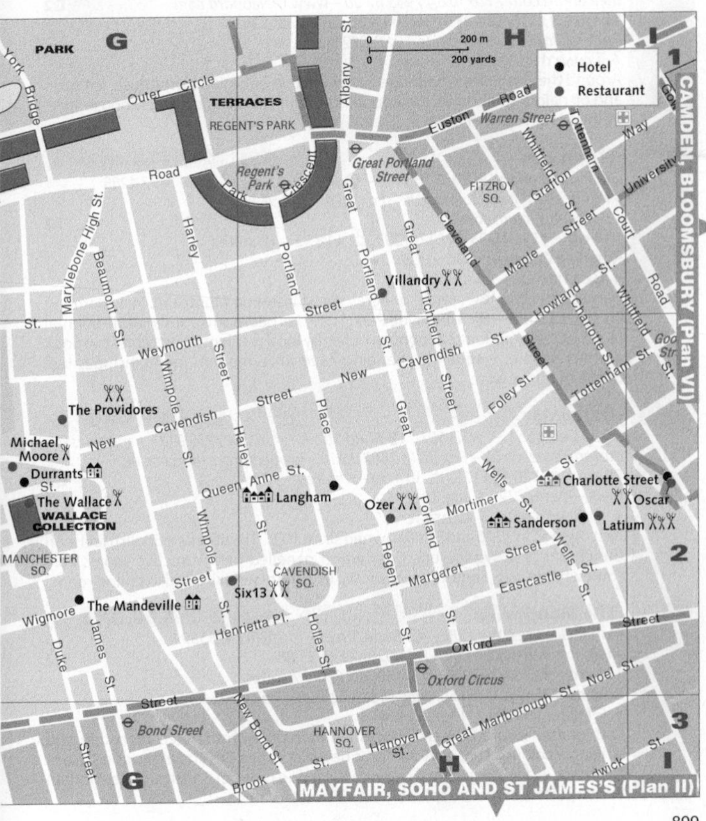

Charlotte Street

15 Charlotte St ✉ W1T 1RJ – Ⓜ Goodge Street – ✆ (020) 7806 2000 – charlotte@firmdale.com – Fax (020) 7806 20 02 – www.charlottestreethotel.co.uk

44 rm – †£247/282 ††£347, ☕ £19 – 8 suites **I2**

Rest *Oscar* – see below

◆ Luxury ◆ Stylish ◆

Interior designed with a charming and understated English feel. Welcoming lobby laden with floral displays. Individually decorated rooms with CDs and mobile phones.

Sanderson

50 Berners St ✉ W1T 3NG – Ⓜ Oxford Circus – ✆ (020) 7300 1400 – sanderson@morganshotelgroup.com – Fax (020) 7300 14 01 – www.morganshotelgroup.com **H2**

150 rm – †£264/441 ††£294/499, ☕ £21.50

Rest *Suka* – Carte £36/84

◆ Luxury ◆ Minimalist ◆

Designed by Philipe Starck: the height of contemporary design. Bar is the place to see and be seen. Bedrooms with minimalistic white décor have DVDs and striking bathrooms. Stylish Spoon+ allows diners to construct own dishes.

The Leonard

15 Seymour St ✉ W1H 7JW – Ⓜ Marble Arch – ✆ (020) 7935 2010 – reservations@theleonard.com – Fax (020) 7935 67 00 – www.theleonard.com **G2**

19 rm – †£116/194 ††£164/194 – 20 suites, ☕ £19.50

Rest – *(Closed Sunday dinner)* Carte £21/27

◆ Townhouse ◆ Classic ◆

Around the corner from Selfridges, an attractive Georgian townhouse: antiques and oil paintings abound. Well-appointed rooms in classic country house style. Intimate front dining room.

Montcalm

Great Cumberland Pl ✉ W1H 7TW – Ⓜ Marble Arch – ✆ (020) 7402 4288 – montcalm@montcalm.co.uk – Fax (020) 7724 91 80 – www.montcalm.co.uk **F2**

110 rm – †£164/293 ††£176/293, ☕ £18.95 – 10 suites

Rest *The Crescent* – Menu £26/29.50

◆ Business ◆ Classic ◆

Named after the 18C French general, the Marquis de Montcalm. In a charming crescent a short walk from Hyde Park. Spacious bedrooms with a subtle oriental feel. Discreetly appointed room favoured by local residents. Best tables overlook a pretty square. Frequently changing fixed price modern menu includes half bottle of house wine.

Durrants

26-32 George St ✉ W1H 5BJ – Ⓜ Bond Street – ✆ (020) 7935 8131 – enquiries@durrantshotel.co.uk – Fax (020) 7487 35 10 – www.durrantshotel.co.uk

89 rm – †£120 ††£175, ☕ £14.50 – 3 suites **G2**

Rest – Menu £22 – Carte £30/43

◆ Traditional ◆ Classic ◆

First opened in 1790 and family owned since 1921. Traditionally English feel with the charm of a bygone era. Cosy wood panelled bar. Attractive rooms vary somewhat in size. Semi-private booths in quintessentially British dining room.

The Mandeville

Mandeville Pl ✉ W1V 2BE – Ⓜ Bond Street – ✆ (020) 79355599 – info@mandeville.co.uk – Fax (020) 79 35 95 88 **G2**

135 rm – †£250/275 ††£275/450, ☕ £20 – 7 suites

Rest *de Ville* – *(Closed Sunday)* Menu £20/25 – Carte £25/37

◆ Chain hotel ◆ Design ◆

Fashionably located hotel, refurbished in 2005 with marbled reception and strikingly colourful bar. Stylish rooms have flatscreen TVs and make good use of the space available. Informal restaurant serving modern British cuisine. Modern British cuisine served in splendid de Ville restaurant.

Dorset Square

39-40 Dorset Sq ✉ NW1 6QN – Ⓜ Marylebone – ✆ (020) 7723 7874
– reservations@dorsetsquare.co.uk – Fax (020) 7724 33 28
– www.dorsetsquare.co.uk
Closed 1 week Christmas **F1**
37 rm – †£176 ††£282, ☕ £14
Rest *The Potting Shed* – *(Closed Saturday lunch and Sunday dinner) (booking essential)* Menu £23/25 – Carte £23/35

♦ Townhouse ♦ Classic ♦

Converted Regency townhouses in a charming square and the site of the original Lord's cricket ground. A relaxed country house in the city. Individually decorated rooms. The Potting Shed features modern cuisine and a set business menu.

The Sumner without rest

54 Upper Berkeley St ✉ W1H 7QR – Ⓜ Marble Arch
– ✆ (020) 7723 2244 – hotel@thesumner.com – Fax (0870) 705 87 67
– www.thesumner.com **F2**
20 rm ☕ – †£153 ††£165

♦ Townhouse ♦ Personalised ♦

Two Georgian terrace houses in developing area of town. Comfy, stylish sitting room; basement breakfast room. Largest bedrooms, 101 and 201, have sunny, full-length windows.

Rhodes W1 Restaurant – at The Cumberland H.

Great Cumberland Place ✉ W1A 4RF – Ⓜ Marble Arch
– ✆ (020) 7479 3737 – restaurant@rhodesw1.com – Fax (020) 7479 38 88
– www.rhodesw1.com
Closed 28 December-5 January, Easter, Sunday, Monday and lunch Saturday **F3**
Rest – Menu £28/48

Spec. Double oyster ragoût with samphire and fresh herbs. Salt roast pigeon with asparagus, cabbage hearts and lemon cumin gravy. Caramel chocolate mousse millefeuille with lemon sorbet.

♦ French ♦ Design ♦

Flamboyant in feel, with purples, blacks, velvets, mirrors and enormous Swarovski chandeliers à la Kelly Hoppen. Precise, polished cooking, with French flavours to the fore.

Locanda Locatelli

8 Seymour St ✉ W1H 7JZ – Ⓜ Marble Arch – ✆ (020) 7935 9088
– info@locandalocatelli.com – Fax (020) 7935 11 49
– www.locandalocatelli.com
Closed Bank Holidays **G2**
Rest – Carte £35/56

Spec. Pan-fried scallops with a saffron viniagrette and celeriac purée. Roast monkfish with a walnut and caper sauce. Amarelli liquorice, coffee and mascarpone.

♦ Italian ♦ Fashionable ♦

Forever popular restaurant serving authentic, seasonal Italian cooking of outstanding quality, complemented by a comprehensive wine list. Best tables are the corner booths.

Latium

21 Berners St, Fitzrovia ✉ W1T 3LP – Ⓜ Oxford Circus – ✆ (020) 7323 9123
– info@latiumrestaurant.com – Fax (020) 7323 32 05
– www.latiumrestaurant.com
Closed 25 December, Saturday lunch, Sunday, and Bank Holidays **H2**
Rest – Menu £20/29

♦ Italian ♦ Neighbourhood ♦

Welcoming restaurant owned by affable chef. Smart feel with well-spaced linen-clad tables, tiled floors and rural pictures. Italian country cooking in the heart of town.

XX **Rhodes W1 Brasserie** – at The Cumberland H.
Great Cumberland Pl ✉ W1A 4RF – Ⓜ Marble Arch
– ✆ (020) 7479 3838 – rhodesw1@thecumberland.co.uk – Fax (020) 7479 38 88
– www.garyrhodes.com **FG3**
Rest – Carte £25/42
♦ Modern ♦ Brasserie ♦
In the heart of the Cumberland Hotel, a very stylish dining experience with impressively high ceiling and classical Gary Rhodes dishes bringing out the best of the seasons.

XX **Galvin**
66 Baker St ✉ W1U 7DH – Ⓜ Baker Street – ✆ (020) 7935 4007
– info@galvinuk.com – Fax (020) 7486 17 35 – www.galvinuk.com
Closed 25-26 December and 1 January **G2**
Rest – Menu £16 – Carte £24/35
♦ French ♦ Bistro ♦
A modern take on the classic Gallic bistro with ceiling fans, globe lights, rich wood panelled walls and French influenced dishes where precision and good value are paramount.

XX **Six13**
19 Wigmore St ✉ W1H 9LA – Ⓜ Bond Street – ✆ (020) 7629 6133
– inquiries@six13.com – Fax (020) 7629 61 35 – www.six13.com
Closed Jewish Holidays, Friday and Saturday **G2**
Rest – Menu £28 – Carte £28/45
♦ Kosher ♦ Friendly ♦
Stylish and immaculate with banquette seating. Strictly kosher menu supervised by the Shama offering interesting cooking with a modern slant.

XX **Oscar** – at Charlotte Street H.
15 Charlotte St ✉ W1T 1RJ – Ⓜ Goodge Street – ✆ (020) 7907 4005
– charlotte@firmdale.com – Fax (020) 7806 20 02
– www.charlottestreethotel.co.uk
Closed Sunday lunch **I2**
Rest – *(booking essential)* Carte £29/44
♦ Modern ♦ Trendy ♦
Adjacent to hotel lobby and dominated by a large, vivid mural of contemporary London life. Sophisticated dishes served by attentive staff: oysters, wasabi and soya dressing.

XX **The Providores**
109 Marylebone High St ✉ W1U 4RX – Ⓜ Bond Street – ✆ (020) 7935 6175
– anyone@theprovidores.co.uk – Fax (020) 7935 68 77
– www.theprovidores.co.uk
Closed Easter and Christmas **G2**
Rest – Carte £26/46
♦ Innovative ♦ Trendy ♦
Swish, stylish restaurant on first floor; unusual dishes with New World base and fusion of Asian, Mediterranean influences. Tapas and light meals in downstairs Tapa Room.

XX **La Porte des Indes**
32 Bryanston St ✉ W1H 7EG – Ⓜ Marble Arch – ✆ (020) 7224 0055
– london.reservation@laportedesindes.com – Fax (020) 7224 11 44
– www.laportedesindes.com
Closed 25-28 December and Saturday lunch **F2**
Rest – Menu £15/29 – Carte £28/42
♦ Indian ♦ Exotic ♦
Don't be fooled by the discreet entrance: inside there is a spectacularly unrestrained display of palm trees, murals and waterfalls. French influenced Indian cuisine.

XX **Ozer** AC VISA MC AE

4-5 Langham Pl, Regent St ✉ W1B 3DG – Ⓜ Oxford Circus – ✆ (020) 7323 0505 – info@sofra.co.uk – Fax (020) 7323 01 11 – www.sofra.co.uk **H2**

Rest – Menu £21 – Carte £15/29

♦ Turkish ♦ Design ♦

Behind the busy and vibrantly decorated bar you'll find a smart modern restaurant. Lively atmosphere and efficient service of modern, light and aromatic Turkish cooking.

XX **Roka** AC VISA MC AE ①

37 Charlotte St ✉ W1T 1RR – Ⓜ Tottenham Court Road – ✆ (020) 7580 6464 – info@rokarestaurant.com – Fax (020) 7580 02 20 – www.rokarestaurant.com

Closed 25 December *Plan VI* **I2**

Rest – Carte £29/36

♦ Japanese ♦ Fashionable ♦

Striking glass and steel frontage. Airy, atmospheric interior of teak, oak and paper wall screens. Authentic, flavoursome Japanese cuisine with variety of grill dishes.

XX **Phoenix Palace** AC ⇔ VISA MC AE

3-5 Glentworth St ✉ NW1 5PG – Ⓜ Baker Street – ✆ (020) 7486 3515 – info@phoenixpalace.uk.com – Fax (020) 7486 34 01 – www.phoenixpalace.uk.com **F1**

Rest – Menu £18 – Carte £18/26

♦ Chinese ♦ Friendly ♦

Tucked away near Baker Street; lots of photos of celebrities who've eaten here. Huge room for 200 diners where authentic, fresh, well prepared Chinese dishes are served.

XX **Villandry** AC VISA MC AE ①

170 Great Portland St ✉ W1W 5QB – Ⓜ Regent's Park – ✆ (020) 7631 3131 – contactus@villandry.com – Fax (020) 7631 30 30 – www.villandry.com

Closed 25, 31 December, 1 January and Sunday dinner **H1**

Rest – Carte £29/40

♦ Modern ♦ Rustic ♦

The senses are heightened by passing through the well-stocked deli to the dining room behind. Bare walls, wooden tables and a menu offering simple, tasty dishes.

X **The Wallace** ⅟ VISA MC AE

Hertford House, Manchester Sq ✉ W1U 3BN – Ⓜ Bond St – ✆ (020) 7563 9505 – reservations@thewallacerestaurant.com – www.thewallacerestaurant.com **G2**

Rest – *(lunch only and dinner Friday-Saturday)* Menu £25 – Carte £29/36

♦ French ♦ Friendly ♦

Situated in the Wallace Collection's delightful glass-roofed courtyard, divided by Japanese maple trees. Comprehensive selection of classic French fare; terrines a speciality.

The Salt House VISA MC AE ①

63 Abbey Road, St John's Wood ✉ NW8 0AE – Ⓜ St John's Wood – ✆ (020) 7328 6626 – salthousemail@majol.co.uk – www.thesalthouse.co.uk

closed 25 December *Plan I* **B1**

Rest – Carte £20/45

♦ Modern ♦ Pub ♦

Grand Victorian pub appearance in bottle green. Busy bar at the front; main dining room, in calm duck egg blue, to the rear. Modern menus boast a distinct Mediterranean style.

Queen's Head & Artichoke AC VISA MC AE

30-32 Albany St ✉ NW1 4EA – Ⓜ Great Portland Street – ✆ (020) 7916 6206 – info@theartichoke.net – www.theartichoke.net

Closed 24 December-2 January **G2**

Rest – Carte £19/25

♦ Modern ♦ Pub ♦

Busy, wood-panelled bar and eccentrially-styled upstairs restaurant. Modern, European influenced food mixed with a large selection of all-day international 'tapas.'

CAMDEN

Bloomsbury

Plan VI

Covent Garden

10 Monmouth St ✉ WC2H 9HB – Ⓜ Covent Garden – ✆ (020) 7806 1000 – covent@firmdale.com – Fax (020) 7806 11 00 – www.coventgardenhotel.co.uk

56 rm – ♦£264/323 ♦♦£376, ☕ £19.50 – 2 suites I3

Rest *Brasserie Max* – *(closed Sunday lunch) (booking essential)* Carte £28/50

♦ Luxury ♦ Stylish ♦

Individually designed and stylish bedrooms, with CDs and VCRs discreetly concealed. Boasts a very relaxing first floor oak-panelled drawing room with its own honesty bar. Informal restaurant.

Mountbatten

20 Monmouth St ✉ WC2H 9HD – Ⓜ Covent Garden – ✆ (020) 7836 4300 – dial@radisson.com – Fax (020) 7240 35 40 – www.radissonedwardian.com

149 rm ☕ – ♦£140/180 ♦♦£160/180 – 2 suites I3

Rest *Dial* – *(Closed Saturday lunch, Sunday and Bank Holidays)* Menu £25 – Carte £28/34

♦ Business ♦ Classic ♦

Photographs and memorabilia of the eponymous Lord Louis adorn the walls and corridors. Ideally located in the heart of Covent Garden. Compact but comfortable bedrooms. Bright, stylish restaurant.

Myhotel Bloomsbury

11-13 Bayley St, Bedford Sq ✉ WC1B 3HD – Ⓜ Tottenham Court Road – ✆ (020) 7667 6000 – bloomsbury@myhotels.co.uk – Fax (020) 7667 60 01 – www.myhotels.com I2

78 rm – ♦£240/276 ♦♦£276/417, ☕ £18

Rest *Yo! Sushi* – Menu £15 (lunch) – Carte £26/35

♦ Business ♦ Minimalist ♦

The minimalist interior is designed on the principles of feng shui; even the smaller bedrooms are stylish and uncluttered. Mybar is a fashionable meeting point. Diners can enjoy Japanese food from conveyor belt.

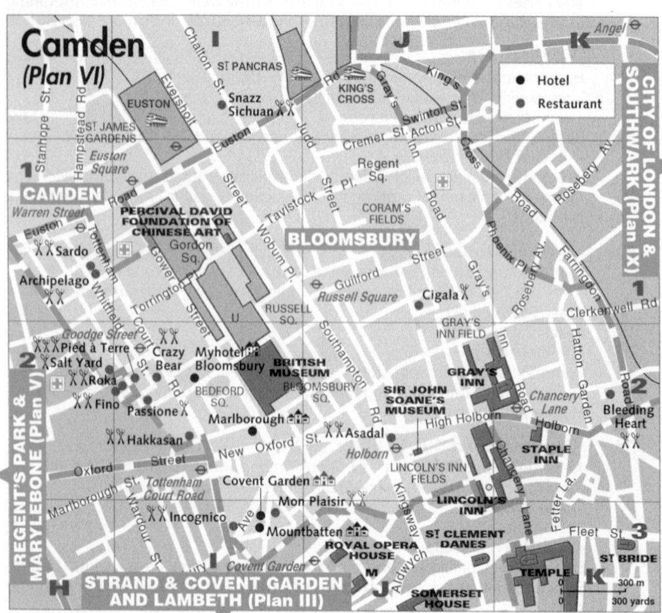

XXX ✿✿

Pied à Terre (Shane Osborn)

34 Charlotte St ✉ W1T 2NH – Ⓜ Goodge Street – ✆ (020) 7636 1178 – info@pied-a-terre.co.uk – Fax (020) 7916 11 71 – www.pied-a-terre.co.uk
closed last week December-first week January, Saturday lunch and Sunday
Rest – Menu £30/62 I2
Spec. Seared and poached foie gras with borlotti beans and girolles. Steamed halibut with tomato fondue and courgette flower beignet. Bitter chocolate tart with stout ice cream and macadamia nut cream.
◆ Innovative ◆ Fashionable ◆
Smart, low-key exterior; stylish interior with intimately-set tables; ask for a table in rear room. Elaborate, expertly-crafted classical dishes incorporate unusual combinations.

XX

Mon Plaisir

21 Monmouth St ✉ WC2H 9DD – Ⓜ Covent Garden – ✆ (020) 7836 7243 – eatafrog@mail.com – Fax (020) 7240 47 74 – www.monplaisir.co.uk
closed 25 December-2 January, Saturday lunch, Sunday and Bank Holidays
Rest – Menu £17 – Carte £28/34 I3
◆ French ◆ Family ◆
London's oldest French restaurant and family-run for over fifty years. Divided into four rooms, all with a different feel but all proudly Gallic in their decoration.

XX

Incognico

117 Shaftesbury Ave ✉ WC2H 8AD – Ⓜ Tottenham Court Road – ✆ (020) 7836 8866 – incognicorestaurant@gmail.com – Fax (020) 7240 95 25 – www.incognico.com
Closed 1 week Christmas, Sunday and Bank Holidays I3
Rest – Menu £25 – Carte £30/38
◆ Modern ◆ Brasserie ◆
Firmly established with robust décor of wood panelling and brown leather chairs. Downstairs bar has a window into the kitchen, from where French and English classics derive.

XX

Sardo

45 Grafton Way ✉ W1T 5DQ – Ⓜ Warren Street – ✆ (020) 7387 2521 – info@sardo-restaurant.com – Fax (020) 7387 25 59 – www.sardo-restaurant.com
Closed Saturday lunch and Sunday H1
Rest – Carte £23/32
◆ Italian ◆ Family ◆
Simple, stylish interior run in a very warm and welcoming manner with very efficient service. Rustic Italian cooking with a Sardinian character and a modern tone.

XX ✿

Hakkasan

8 Hanway Place ✉ W1T 1HD – Ⓜ Tottenham Court Road – ✆ (020) 7927 7000 – mail@hakkasan.com – Fax (020) 7907 18 89
closed 24-25 December I2
Rest – Menu £40/55 – Carte £27/90
Spec. Crispy duck salad with pomelo, pine nut and shallot. Silver cod with Chinese honey and champagne. Chocolate fondant with passion fruit sorbet.
◆ Chinese ◆ Fashionable ◆
Contemporary basement restaurant, with 'Ling Ling' room opulently styled in black and gold. Seriously trained staff serve expertly crafted and innovative Chinese cooking.

XX

Fino

33 Charlotte St (entrance on Rathbone St) ✉ W1T 1RR – Ⓜ Goodge Street – ✆ (020) 7813 8010 – info@finorestaurant.com – Fax (020) 7813 80 11 – www.finorestaurant.com
closed Saturday lunch and Sunday I2
Rest – Carte £45/55
◆ Spanish ◆ Fashionable ◆
Spanish-run basement bar with modern style décor and banquette seating. Wide-ranging menu of authentic dishes; 2 set-price selections offering an introduction to tapas.

XX **Crazy Bear** A/C VISA MC AE

26-28 Whitfield St ✉ W1T 2RG – Ⓜ Goodge Street – ✆ (020) 7631 0088 – enquiries@crazybear-london.co.uk – Fax (020) 7631 11 88 – www.crazybeargroup.co.uk

Closed Christmas, Saturday lunch, Sunday and Bank Holidays **I2**

Rest – Carte £30/40

♦ Asian ♦ Trendy ♦

Exotic destination: downstairs bar geared to fashionable set; ground floor dining room is art deco inspired. Asian flavoured menus, with predominance towards Thai dishes.

XX **Archipelago** VISA MC AE

110 Whitfield St ✉ W1T 5ED – Ⓜ Goodge Street – ✆ (020) 7383 3346 – archipelago@onetel.com – Fax (020) 7383 71 81 – www.archipelago-restaurant.co.uk

closed Christmas -New Year,Bank Holidays, Saturday lunch and Sunday **H1**

Rest – Menu £39 – Carte £26/37

♦ Innovative ♦ Exotic ♦

Eccentric in both menu and décor and not for the faint hearted. Crammed with knick-knacks from cages to Buddhas. Menu an eclectic mix of influences from around the world.

X **Passione** VISA MC AE

10 Charlotte St ✉ W1T 2LT – Ⓜ Tottenham Court Road – ✆ (020) 7636 2833 – liz@passione.co.uk – Fax (020) 7636 28 89 – www.passione.co.uk

Closed Christmas-New Year, Bank Holidays, Saturday lunch and Sunday **I2**

Rest – *(booking essential)* Carte £40/47

♦ Italian ♦ Friendly ♦

Compact but light and airy. Modern Italian cooking served in informal surroundings, with friendly and affable service. Particularly busy at lunchtime.

X **Cigala** VISA MC AE

54 Lamb's Conduit St ✉ WC1N 3LW – Ⓜ Holborn – ✆ (020) 7405 1717 – tasty@cigala.co.uk – Fax (020) 7242 99 49 – www.cigala.co.uk

Closed 24-26 December, 1 January and Easter **J1**

Rest – Menu £18 (lunch) – Carte £24/37

♦ Spanish ♦ Rustic ♦

Spanish restaurant on the corner of attractive street. Simply furnished with large windows and open-plan kitchen. Robust Iberian cooking. Informal tapas bar downstairs.

X **Salt Yard** A/C VISA MC AE

54 Goodge St ✉ W1T 4NA – Ⓜ Goodge Street – ✆ (020) 7637 0657 – info@saltyard.co.uk – Fax (020) 7580 74 35 – www.saltyard.co.uk

closed Sunday, Saturday lunch and Bank Holidays **H2**

Rest – Carte £18/40

♦ Mediterranean ♦ Tapas bar ♦

Vogue destination with buzzy downstairs restaurant specialising in inexpensive sharing plates of tasty Italian and Spanish dishes: try the freshly cut hams. Super wine list.

Euston *Plan VI*

XX **Snazz Sichuan** VISA MC

37 Chalton St ✉ NW1 1JD – Ⓜ Euston – ✆ (020) 7388 0808 – www.newchinaclub.co.uk **H2**

Rest – Carte £10/50

♦ Chinese ♦ Fashionable ♦

Authentic Sichuan atmosphere and cooking, with gallery and traditional tea room. Menu split into hot and cold dishes; the fiery Sichuan pepper helps heat you from inside out.

Hatton Garden — Plan VI

Bleeding Heart
Bleeding Heart Yard (off Greville St) ✉ EC1N 8SJ – Ⓜ Farringdon – ✆ (020) 7242 8238 – bookings@bleedingheart.co.uk – Fax (020) 7831 14 02 – www.bleedingheart.co.uk
closed Christmas-New Year, Saturday, Sunday and Bank Holidays **K2**
Rest – *(booking essential)* Carte £28/37
◆ French ◆ Romantic ◆
Busy downstairs restaurant, popular with City suits. Fast-paced service, terrific wine list and well-practised cooking. Seasonally-changing French menu with traditional core.

Holborn — Plan VI

Asadal
227 High Holborn ✉ WC1V 7DA – Ⓜ Holborn – ✆ (020) 7430 9006 – info@asadal.co.uk – www.asadal.co.uk
closed Sunday lunch **J2**
Rest – Menu £10 (lunch) – Carte £18/30
◆ Korean ◆ Friendly ◆
A hectic, unprepossessing location, but delivers the authenticity of a modest Korean café with the comfort and service of a proper restaurant. Good quality Korean cooking.

HYDE PARK & KNIGHTSBRIDGE — Plan VII

Mandarin Oriental Hyde Park
66 Knightsbridge ✉ SW1X 7LA – Ⓜ Knightsbridge – ✆ (020) 7235 2000 – molon-info@mohg.com – Fax (020) 7235 20 01 – www.mandarinoriental.com/london **F4**
173 rm – †£417 ††£476, ☕ £28 – 25 suites
Rest *Foliage* – see below
Rest *The Park* – Menu £33 – Carte £20/47
◆ Grand Luxury ◆ Classic ◆
Built in 1889 this classic hotel, with striking façade, remains one of London's grandest. Many of the luxurious bedrooms enjoy Park views. Immaculate and detailed service. Smart ambience in The Park.

Knightsbridge Green without rest
159 Knightsbridge ✉ SW1X 7PD – Ⓜ Knightsbridge – ✆ (020) 7584 6274 – reservations@thekghotel.com – Fax (020) 7225 16 35 – www.thekghotel.com
Closed Christmas **F4**
16 rm – †£135/206 ††£176/206, ☕ £12 – 12 suites
◆ Traditional ◆ Classic ◆
Privately owned hotel, boasting peaceful sitting room with writing desk. Breakfast - sausage and bacon from Harrods! - served in the generously proportioned bedrooms.

Foliage – at Mandarin Oriental Hyde Park H.
66 Knightsbridge ✉ SW1X 7LA – Ⓜ Knightsbridge – ✆ (020) 7201 3723 – molon-dine@mohg – Fax (020) 7235 45 52 – www.mandarinoriental.com **F4**
Rest – Menu £29/60
Spec. Foie gras jelly rolls with smoked duck salad and foie gras ice cream. Lamb with girolles, haricot blanc and jus gras. Guava sorbet with raspberry tuile and exotic fruits.
◆ Inventive ◆ Formal ◆
Sophisticated, modern cooking features experimental combinations and unexpected flavours. View of the park through the windows reflected by earthy colours and foliage motif.

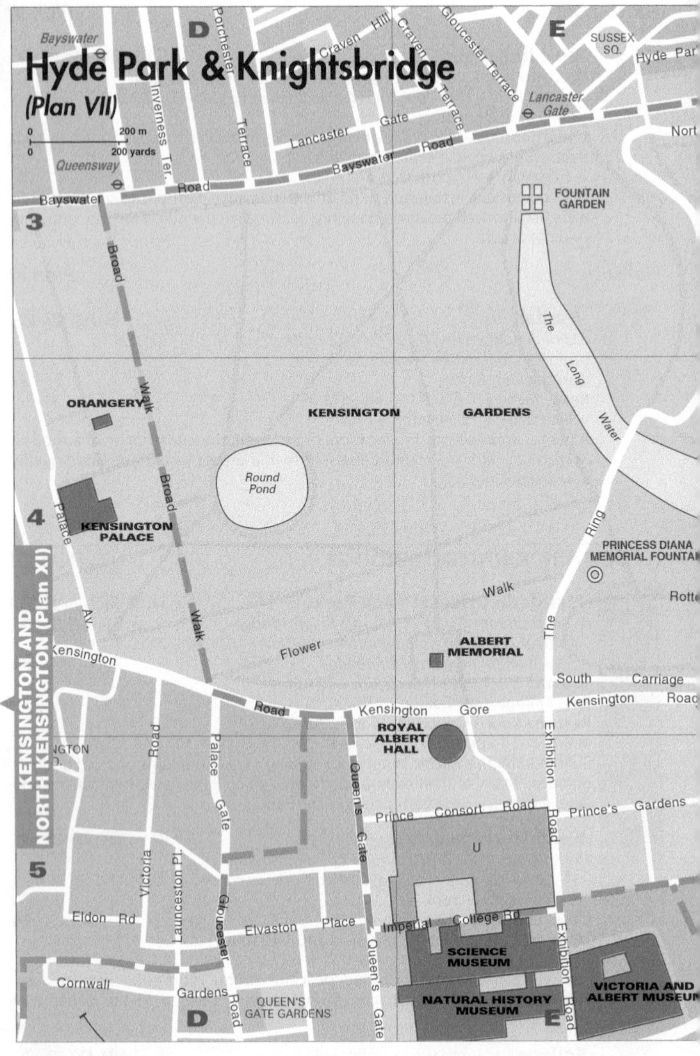

Zuma

5 Raphael St ✉ SW7 1DL – Ⓜ Knightsbridge – ✆ (020) 7584 1010
– info@zumarestaurant.com – Fax (020) 7584 50 05 – www.zumarestaurant.com
Closed 25 December and 1 January **F5**

Rest – Carte £30/96

◆ Japanese ◆ Fashionable ◆

Strong modern feel with exposed pipes, modern lighting and granite flooring. A theatrical atmosphere around the Sushi bar and a varied and interesting modern Japanese menu.

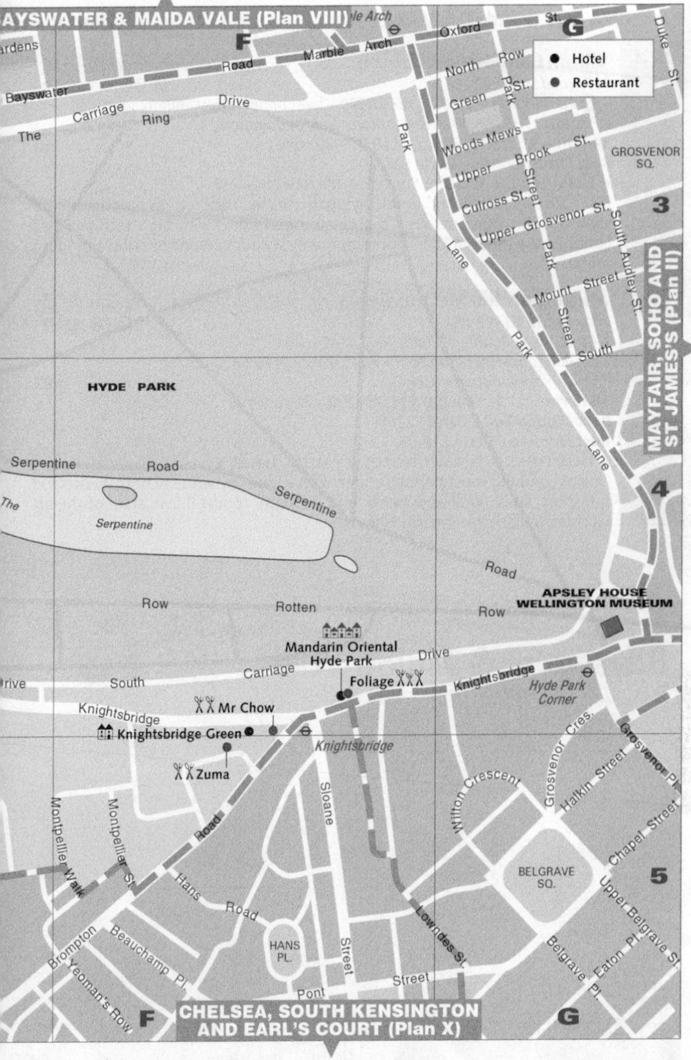

XX	**Mr Chow**

151 Knightsbridge ✉ SW1X 7PA – Ⓜ Knightsbridge – ✆ (020) 7589 7347 – mrchowuk@aol.com – Fax (020) 7584 57 80 – www.mrchow.com
closed 24-26 December, 1 January and Easter Monday **F4**
Rest – Menu £25/40 – Carte £38/57
◆ Chinese ◆ Friendly ◆
Cosmopolitan Chinese restaurant with branches in New York and L.A. Well established ambience. Walls covered with mirrors and modern art. House specialities worth opting for.

Hilton London Paddington

146 Praed St ✉ W2 1EE
– Ⓜ Paddington – ✆ (020) 7850 0500 – sales.paddington@hilton.com
– Fax (020) 7850 06 00 – www.hilton.co.uk/paddington
344 rm – †£328 ††£328, ☕ £19.95 – 20 suites **E2**
Rest *The Brasserie* – Carte £27/40

♦ Business ♦ Chain hotel ♦ Modern ♦

Early Victorian railway hotel, sympathetically restored in contemporary style with Art Deco details. Co-ordinated bedrooms with high tech facilities continue the modern style. Contemporarily styled brasserie offering a modern menu.

Hilton London Metropole

Edgware Rd ✉ W2 1JU
– Ⓜ Edgware Road – ✆ (020) 7402 4141
– cbs-londonmet@hilton.com – Fax (020) 7724 88 66
– www.hiltonlondonmet.com **E2**
1033 rm ☕ – †£140/200 ††£140/200 – 21 suites
Rest *Nippon Tuk* – Carte £22/41
Rest *Fiamma* – Carte £17/28

♦ Business ♦ Chain hotel ♦ Functional ♦

One of London's most popular convention venues by virtue of both its size and transport links. Well-appointed and modern rooms have state-of-the-art facilities. Italian favourites at Fiamma.

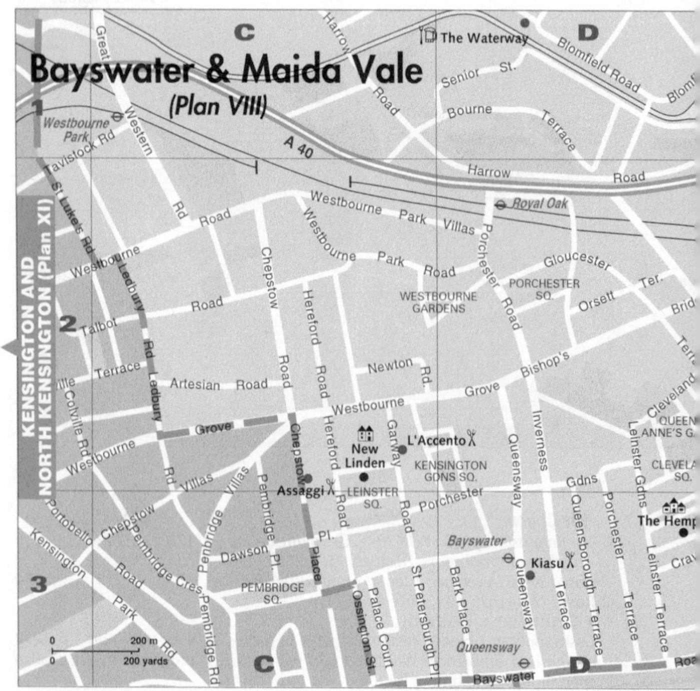

Royal Lancaster

Lancaster Terrace ✉ W2 2TY
– Ⓜ Lancaster Gate – ✆ (020) 7262 6737
– sales@royallancaster.com – Fax (020) 7724 31 91
– www.royallancaster.com **E3**

394 rm – †£304 ††£304, ☕ £19 – 22 suites
Rest Island and **Nipa** – see below
♦ Business ♦ Classic ♦

Imposing 1960s purpose-built hotel overlooking Hyde Park. Some of London's most extensive conference facilities. Well-equipped bedrooms are decorated in traditional style.

The Hempel

31-35 Craven Hill Gdns ✉ W2 3EA
– Ⓜ Queensway – ✆ (020) 7298 9000
– hotel@the-hempel.co.uk – Fax (020) 7402 46 66
– www.the-hempel.co.uk
closed 25 December **D3**

42 rm – †£346/370 ††£370, ☕ £19.75 – 5 suites
Rest *I-Thai* – *(closed Sunday and Bank Holidays)* Carte £35/41
♦ Luxury ♦ Minimalist ♦

A striking example of minimalist design. Individually appointed bedrooms are understated yet very comfortable. Relaxed ambience. Modern basement restaurant.

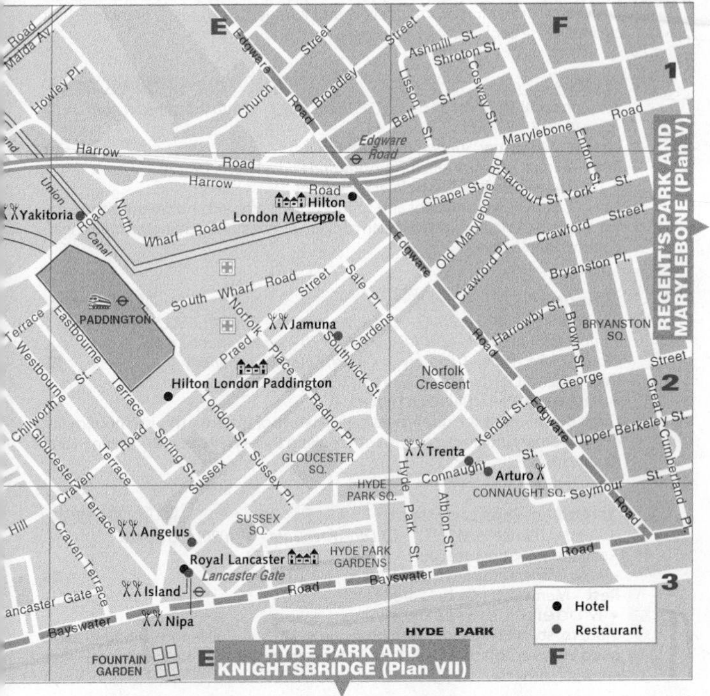

Colonnade Town House without rest

2 Warrington Crescent ✉ W9 1ER – Ⓜ Warwick Avenue – ✆ (020) 7286 1052 – rescolonnade@theetoncollection.com – Fax (020) 7286 10 57 – www.theetoncollection.com Plan XI **D1**

43 rm – †£164/211 ††£188/211, ☐ £15

◆ Townhouse ◆ Classic ◆

Two Victorian townhouses with comfortable well-furnished communal rooms decorated with fresh flowers. Stylish and comfortable bedrooms with many extra touches.

New Linden without rest

58-60 Leinster Sq ✉ W2 4PS – Ⓜ Bayswater – ✆ (020) 7221 4321 – newlindenhotel@mayflower-group.co.uk – Fax (020) 7727 31 56 – www.newlinden.co.uk **C2**

50 rm – †£79/89 ††£89/120, ☐ £9

◆ Family ◆ Functional ◆

Smart four storey white stucco façade. Basement breakfast room with sunny aspect. Bedrooms are its strength: flat screen TVs and wooden floors; two split level family rooms.

Angelus

4 Bathurst St ✉ W2 2SD – Ⓜ Lancaster Gate – ✆ (020) 7402 0083 – info@angelusrestaurant.co.uk – Fax (020) 7402 53 83 – www.angelusrestaurant.co.uk

Closed 25-26 and 31 December, 1 January and Monday **E3**

Rest – Carte £27/44

◆ French ◆ Brasserie ◆

In the style of a French brasserie, with studded leather banquettes, huge art nouveau mirror, Murano chandeliers and lounge bar. Unfussy, French dishes; clean, precise cooking.

Trenta

30 Connaught St ✉ W2 2AF – ✆ (020) 7262 9623 – trenta@btconnect.com – Fax (020) 7262 96 36

closed 1-14 January, Sunday, and Bank Holidays **F2**

Rest – *(dinner only and lunch Thursday and Friday)* Carte £21/26

◆ Italian ◆ Neighbourhood ◆

Only 7 tables on ground floor and 5 more downstairs; red and cream with comfy leather seats. Uncomplicated Italian cooking on constantly changing menu, with commendable prices.

Jamuna

38A Southwick St ✉ W2 1JQ – Ⓜ Edgware Road – ✆ (020) 7723 5056 – info@jamuna.co.uk – Fax (020) 7706 18 70 – www.jamuna.co.uk

Closed 25 December-1 January and lunch Saturday to Sunday **E2**

Rest – Menu £20 (lunch) – Carte £35/63

◆ Indian ◆ Neighbourhood ◆

Don't be put off by the unprepossessing nature of the area: this is a modern out of the ordinary Indian restaurant with cooking that's well presented, refined and flavoursome.

Island – at Royal Lancaster H.

Lancaster Terrace ✉ W2 2TY – Ⓜ Lancaster Gate – ✆ (020) 7551 6070 – eat@islandrestaurant.co.uk – Fax (020) 7551 60 71 – www.islandrestaurant.co.uk **E3**

Rest – Menu £21 – Carte £24/36

◆ Modern ◆ Brasserie ◆

Modern, stylish restaurant with buzzy open kitchen. Full length windows allow good views of adjacent Hyde Park. Seasonally based, modern menus with wide range of dishes.

XX **Yakitoria**

25 Sheldon Sq ✉ W2 6EY – Ⓜ Paddington – ✆ (020) 3214 3000 – info@yakitoria.co.uk – Fax (020) 3214 30 01 – www.yakitoria.co.uk

Closed 24-26 December, 1-2 January, Saturday lunch and Sunday **E2**

Rest – Menu £35 – Carte £29/43

♦ Japanese ♦ Design ♦

Funky, sleek interior accessible from platform 8 at Paddington. Appealing blend of old and new Japanese menus with a distinctive American edge. Bento boxes to take away.

XX **Nipa** – at Royal Lancaster H.

Lancaster Terrace ✉ W2 2TY – Ⓜ Lancaster Gate – ✆ (020) 7551 6039 – Fax (020) 7724 31 91 – www.niparestaurant.co.uk

Closed Saturday lunch, Sunday and Bank Holidays **E3**

Rest – Menu £27/32 – Carte £21/47

♦ Thai ♦ Exotic ♦

On the 1st floor and overlooking Hyde Park. Authentic and ornately decorated restaurant offers subtly spiced Thai cuisine. Keen to please staff in traditional silk costumes.

X **Assaggi** (Nino Sassu)

39 Chepstow Pl, (above Chepstow pub) ✉ W2 4TS – Ⓜ Bayswater – ✆ (020) 7792 5501 – nipi@assaggi.demon.co.uk – www.assaggi.com

closed 2 weeks Christmas, Sunday and Bank Holidays **C2**

Rest – *(booking essential)* Carte £36/48

Spec. Tonno alla tartara. Pan-fried calf's liver with sage and onions. Dark chocolate flourless cake, white chocolate ice cream.

♦ Italian ♦ Rustic ♦

Tall windows and modern artwork provide the bright surroundings, while high quality ingredients are used to create appetisingly rustic dishes with more than a hint of Sardinia.

X **L'Accento**

16 Garway Rd ✉ W2 4NH – Ⓜ Bayswater – ✆ (020) 7243 2201 – laccentorest@aol.com – Fax (020) 7243 22 01

Closed Sunday and Bank Holidays **C2**

Rest – Menu £22 – Carte £22/31

♦ Italian ♦ Rustic ♦

Rustic surroundings and provincial, well priced, Italian cooking. Menu specialises in tasty pasta, made on the premises, and shellfish. Rear conservatory for the summer.

X **Arturo**

23 Connaught St ✉ W2 2AY – Ⓜ Marble Arch – ✆ (020) 7706 3388 – enquiries@arturorestaurant.co.uk – Fax (020) 7402 91 95 – www.arturorestaurant.co.uk

Closed 25-26 December, 1 January, Good Friday and Easter Sunday **F2**

Rest – Menu £17 (lunch) – Carte £24/33

♦ Italian ♦ Friendly ♦

On a smart street near Hyde Park: sleek, modish feel imbues interior with intimate, elegant informality. Tuscan and Sicilian dishes cooked with confidence and originality.

X **Kiasu**

48 Queensway ✉ W2 3RY – Ⓜ Bayswater – ✆ (020) 7727 8810 – info@kiasu.co.uk – Fax (020) 7727 72 20 – www.kiasu.co.uk **D3**

Rest – Carte £11/24

♦ Asian ♦ Friendly ♦

Its name means 'afraid to be second best.' Malaysian owner; some dishes are hot and spicy, others light and fragrant; all designed for sharing. Brightly decorated; good fun.

The Waterway
54 Formosa St ✉ W9 2JU – Ⓜ Warwick Avenue – ✆ (020) 7266 3557 – info@thewaterway.co.uk – Fax (020) 7266 35 47 – www.thewaterway.co.uk
Rest – Carte £28/38 **D1**
◆ Modern ◆ Pub ◆
Pub with a thoroughly modern, metropolitan ambience. Spacious bar and large decked terrace overlooking canal. Concise, well-balanced menu served in open plan dining room.

CITY OF LONDON, SOUTHWARK & TOWER HAMLETS

City of London *Plan IX*

Andaz Liverpool Street
Liverpool St ✉ EC2M 7QN – Ⓜ Liverpool Street – ✆ (020) 7961 1234 – info.londonliv@andaz.com – Fax (020) 7961 12 35 – www.london.liverpoolstreet.andaz.com **M2**
264 rm – †£487/511 ††£546 – 3 suites
Rest *Aurora* – see below
Rest *Catch* – *✆ (020) 7618 7200 (closed Saturday, Sunday and Bank Holidays)* Carte £34/54
Rest *Miyako* – *✆ (020) 7618 5000 (closed Saturday lunch, Sunday and Bank Holidays) (booking essential)* Carte approx. £20
◆ Luxury ◆ Modern ◆
A contemporary and stylish interior hides behind the classic Victorian façade of this railway hotel. Bright and spacious bedrooms with state-of-the-art facilities. Seafood at Catch, based within original hotel lobby. Miyako is compact Japanese restaurant.

Crowne Plaza London - The City
19 New Bridge St ✉ EC4V 6DB – Ⓜ Blackfriars – ✆ (0870) 4009190 – loncy.info@ihg.com – Fax (020) 7438 80 80 – www.crowneplaza.com **K3**
201 rm – †£347/423 ††£347/423, ☕ £19.50 – 2 suites
Rest *Refettorio* – *✆ (020) 7438 8052 (Closed Saturday lunch, Sunday and Bank Holidays)* Menu £45 (dinner) – Carte £24/39
Rest *Spicers* – *✆ (020) 7438 8051 (lunch only Monday - Saturday)* Carte £20/26
◆ Business ◆ Chain hotel ◆ Modern ◆
Art deco façade by the river; interior enhanced by funky chocolate, cream and brown palette. Compact meeting room; well equipped fitness centre. Sizable, stylish rooms. Modish Refettorio for Italian cuisine. British dishes with a modern twist at Spicers.

Threadneedles
5 Threadneedle St ✉ EC2R 8AY – Ⓜ Bank – ✆ (020) 7657 8080 – resthreadneedles@theetoncollection.com – Fax (020) 7657 81 00 – www.theetoncollection.com **M3**
68 rm – †£370/392 ††£370/392, ☕ £19 – 1 suite
Rest *Bonds* – see below
◆ Business ◆ Modern ◆
A converted bank, dating from 1856, with a stunning stained-glass cupola in the lounge. Rooms are very stylish and individual featuring CD players and Egyptian cotton sheets.

Apex City of London
No 1, Seething Lane ✉ EC3N 4AX – Ⓜ Fenchurch Street – ✆ (020) 7702 2020 – Fax (020) 7702 20 20 – www.apexhotels.co.uk **N3**
129 rm – †£287 ††£287, ☕ £10 – 1 suite
Rest *Addendum* – see below
Rest *Addendum Bar* – No 1, Seething Hill, – Carte £17/27
◆ Business ◆ Modern ◆
Tucked away behind Tower of London, overlooking leafy square. Smart meeting facilities, well-equipped gym and treatment rooms. Bedrooms are super sleek with bespoke extras.

Novotel London Tower Bridge

10 Pepys St ✉ EC3N 2NR – Ⓜ Tower Hill – ✆ (020) 7265 6000 – h3107@accor.com – Fax (020) 7265 60 60 – www.accorhotels.com **N3**

199 rm – ♦£190/215 ♦♦£210/235, ☕ £13.50 – 4 suites

Rest *The Garden Brasserie* – *(buffet lunch, bar lunch Saturday-Sunday)* Menu £20 (buffet lunch)/25 – Carte £18/44

♦ Business ♦ Chain hotel ♦ Functional ♦

Modern, purpose-built hotel with carefully planned, comfortable bedrooms. Useful City location and close to Tower of London which is visible from some of the higher rooms. Informally styled brasserie.

Aurora – at Andaz Liverpool Street H.

Liverpool St ✉ EC2M 7QN – Ⓜ Liverpool Street – ✆ (020) 7618 7000 – aurora.londonliv@andaz.com – Fax (020) 7618 50 35 – www.london.liverpoolstreet.andaz.com

closed Saturday, Sunday and Bank Holidays **M2**

Rest – Menu £28 (lunch) – Carte £38/54

♦ Modern ♦ Formal ♦

Vast columns, ornate plasterwork and a striking glass dome feature in this imposing dining room. Polished and attentive service of an elaborate and modern menu.

Rhodes Twenty Four

< London,

24th floor, Tower 42, 25 Old Broad St ✉ EC2N 1HQ – Ⓜ Liverpool Street – ✆ (020) 7877 7703 – reservations@rhodes24.co.uk – Fax (020) 7877 77 88 – www.rhodes24.co.uk

closed Christmas-New Year, Saturday, Sunday and Bank Holidays **M3**

Rest – Carte £32/58

Spec. Seared scallops with mashed potato and shallot mustard sauce. Steamed mutton and onion suet pudding with buttered carrots. Bread and butter pudding.

♦ British ♦ Formal ♦

Panoramic views are afforded from this contemporary restaurant, set on the 24th floor of Tower 42; the former Natwest building. Well balanced British dishes, appetisingly presented.

Coq d'Argent

No.1 Poultry ✉ EC2R 8EJ – Ⓜ Bank – ✆ (020) 7395 5000 – coqdargent@danddlondon.com – Fax (020) 7395 50 50 – www.danddlondon.com

closed Christmas, Easter, Saturday lunch, Sunday dinner and Bank Holidays **M3**

Rest – *(booking essential)* Menu £29 – Carte £31/47

♦ French ♦ Design ♦

Take the dedicated lift to the top of this modern office block. Tables on the rooftop terrace have city views; busy bar. Gallic menus highlighted by popular shellfish dishes.

1 Lombard Street (Restaurant)

1 Lombard St ✉ EC3V 9AA – Ⓜ Bank – ✆ (020) 7929 6611 – hb@1lombardstreet.com – Fax (020) 7929 66 22 – www.1lombardstreet.com

closed 22 December- 3 January, Saturday, Sunday and Bank Holidays **M3**

Rest – *(booking essential at lunch)* Menu £39/45 – Carte £54/62

Spec. Carpaccio of tuna with Oriental spices, ginger and lime vinaigrette. Trio of lamb with sorrel velouté and tomato compote, lamb jus. Warm strawberries in Sauternes with crème fraîche sorbet.

♦ Modern ♦ Formal ♦

Skilfully prepared, elaborately presented classical cooking uses luxury ingredients. Attractively priced nine course dégustation menu. Changes to the layout are imminent.

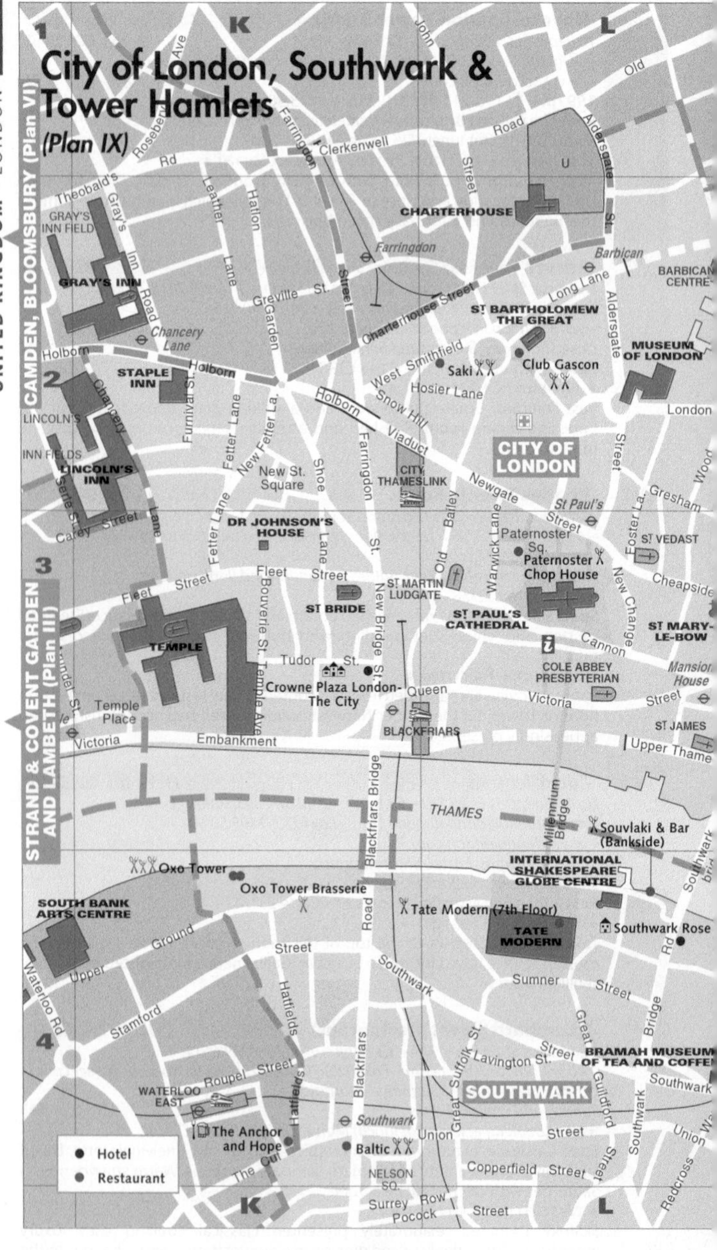
City of London, Southwark & Tower Hamlets
(Plan IX)
CAMDEN, BLOOMSBURY (Plan VI)
STRAND & COVENT GARDEN AND LAMBETH (Plan III)
CHARTERHOUSE
GRAY'S INN
STAPLE INN
LINCOLN'S INN
ST BARTHOLOMEW THE GREAT
MUSEUM OF LONDON
BARBICAN CENTRE
Saki
Club Gascon
CITY OF LONDON
CITY THAMESLINK
DR JOHNSON'S HOUSE
Paternoster Chop House
ST VEDAST
ST MARTIN LUDGATE
ST BRIDE
ST PAUL'S CATHEDRAL
ST MARY-LE-BOW
TEMPLE
COLE ABBEY PRESBYTERIAN
Crowne Plaza London-The City
BLACKFRIARS
ST JAMES
THAMES
Souvlaki & Bar (Bankside)
INTERNATIONAL SHAKESPEARE GLOBE CENTRE
Oxo Tower
Oxo Tower Brasserie
SOUTH BANK ARTS CENTRE
Tate Modern (7th Floor)
TATE MODERN
Southwark Rose
BRAMAH MUSEUM OF TEA AND COFFEE
SOUTHWARK
WATERLOO EAST
The Anchor and Hope
Baltic
NELSON SQ.
Hotel
Restaurant

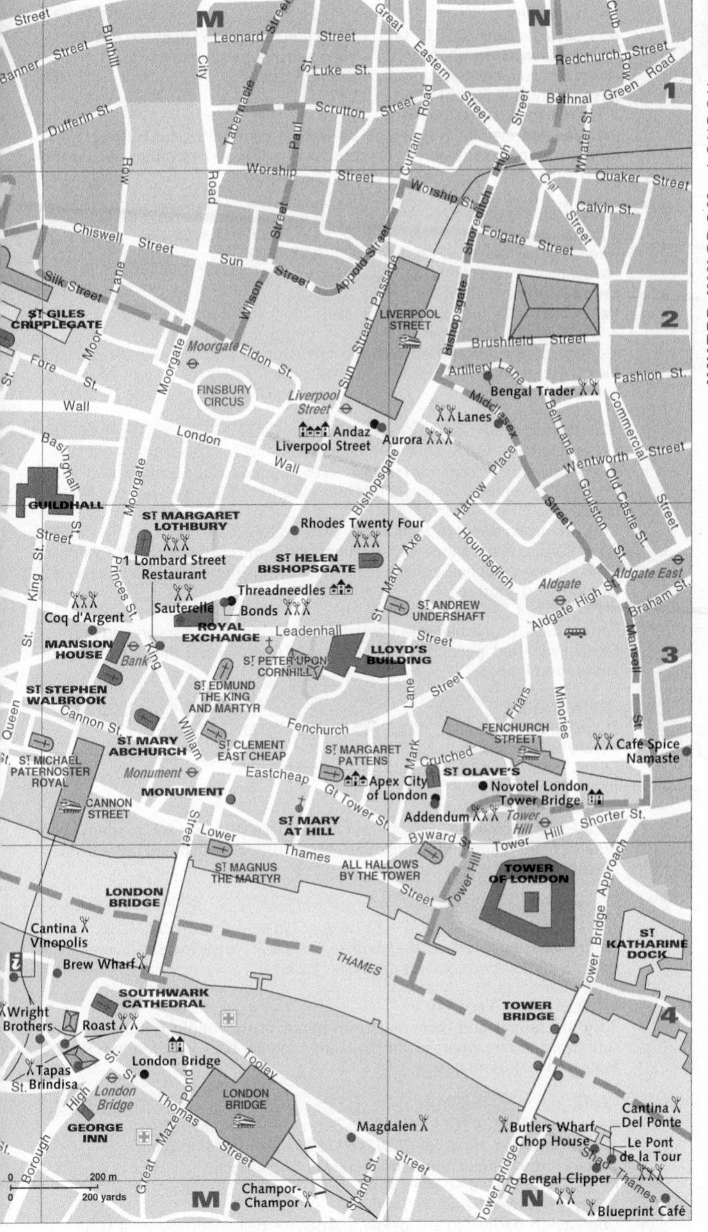

ST GILES CRIPPLEGATE
GUILDHALL
ST MARGARET LOTHBURY
LIVERPOOL STREET
FINSBURY CIRCUS
Andaz Liverpool Street
Aurora
Bengal Trader
Lanes
Rhodes Twenty Four
ST HELEN BISHOPSGATE
1 Lombard Street Restaurant
Threadneedles
Sauterelle
Bonds
Coq d'Argent
ROYAL EXCHANGE
ST ANDREW UNDERSHAFT
MANSION HOUSE
LLOYD'S BUILDING
ST PETER UPON CORNHILL
ST STEPHEN WALBROOK
ST EDMUND THE KING AND MARTYR
ST MARY ABCHURCH
ST CLEMENT EAST CHEAP
FENCHURCH STREET
Café Spice Namaste
ST MICHAEL PATERNOSTER ROYAL
ST MARGARET PATTENS
ST OLAVE'S
Apex City of London
Novotel London Tower Bridge
MONUMENT
CANNON STREET
Addendum
ST MARY AT HILL
ST MAGNUS THE MARTYR
ALL HALLOWS BY THE TOWER
TOWER OF LONDON
LONDON BRIDGE
ST KATHARINE DOCK
Cantina Vinopolis
Brew Wharf
THAMES
SOUTHWARK CATHEDRAL
TOWER BRIDGE
Wright Brothers
Roast
Tapas Brindisa
London Bridge
GEORGE INN
Magdalen
Cantina Del Ponte
Butlers Wharf Chop House
Le Pont de la Tour
Bengal Clipper
Champor-Champor
Blueprint Café
200 m
200 yards
M
N
1
2
3
4

XXX **Addendum** AC VISA MC AE D

No 1, Seething Lane ✉ EC3N 4AX – Ⓜ Fenchurch Street – ✆ (020) 7977 9500 – londonevents@apexhotels.co.uk – www.addendumrestaurant.co.uk
closed 20 December -5 January and Bank Holidays **N3**
Rest – Menu £27 (lunch) – Carte £33/37
♦ Modern ♦ Elegant ♦
Intimate and elegant with chocolate leather banquettes, fresh flowers and modern mirrors. Precise service of robust, earthy dishes which often rejoice in the use of offal.

XXX **Bonds** – at Threadneedles H. AC VISA MC AE D

5 Threadneedle St ✉ EC2R 8AY – Ⓜ Bank – ✆ (020) 7657 8088 – bonds@theetongroup.com – Fax (020) 7657 80 89 – www.theetoncollection.com
closed Saturday and Sunday **M3**
Rest – Menu £25 (lunch) – Carte £31/48
♦ Modern ♦ Retro ♦
Modern interior juxtaposed with the grandeur of a listed city building. Vast dining room with high ceiling and tall pillars. Attentive service of hearty, contemporary food.

XX ✿ **Club Gascon** (Pascal Aussignac) AC VISA MC AE

57 West Smithfield ✉ EC1A 9DS – Ⓜ Barbican – ✆ (020) 7796 0600 – info@clubgascon.com – Fax (020) 7796 06 01 – www.clubgascon.com
closed 22 December-6 January, 21-24 March, Sunday, Saturday lunch and Bank Holidays **L2**
Rest – *(booking essential)* Menu £42 – Carte £38/72
Spec. Carpaccio of venison with summer truffle and crispy artichoke. Pyrenean lamb on vine shoot embers with blinis and trevise. Cherries with yoghurt coulis, almonds and griottes.
♦ French ♦ Fashionable ♦
Former bank; its marble walls now softened by big floral displays and mirrors. Elegantly crafted 'petits plats' are a paean to Gascony and the gastronomy of South West France.

XX **Sauterelle** AC VISA MC AE D

The Royal Exchange ✉ EC3V 3LR – Ⓜ Bank – ✆ (020) 7618 2483 – www.conran.com
Closed Saturday and Sunday **M3**
Rest – Carte £32/49
♦ French ♦ Design ♦
Located on mezzanine level of Royal Exchange, a stunning 16C property with ornate columns and pillars. Typically Conran rustic French menus attract smart lunchtime diners.

XX **Lanes** AC VISA MC AE D

109-117 Middlesex St ✉ E1 7JF – Ⓜ Liverpool Street – ✆ (020) 7247 5050 – info@lanesrestaurant.co.uk – Fax (020) 7247 80 71 – www.lanesrestaurant.co.uk
closed Saturday lunch, Sunday and Bank Holidays **N2**
Rest – Carte £33/41
♦ Modern ♦ Trendy ♦
Busy lunchtimes and more sedate evenings at this bright destination with subterranean bar, where art displays are a regular backdrop. Modern British/ European menus hold sway.

XX **Saki** AC VISA MC AE

4 West Smithfield ✉ EC1A 9JX – Ⓜ Barbican – ✆ (020) 7489 7033 – info@saki-food.com – Fax (020) 7489 16 58 – www.saki-food.com
closed Christmas-New Year, Sunday and Bank Holidays **L2**
Rest – Menu £17/58 – Carte £17/45
♦ Japanese ♦ Fashionable ♦
Uber-stylish bar/restaurant below a Japanese deli. Incorporates a sushi bar, communal 'garden table' and impressive Japanese dishes based on seasonality and healthy eating.

Paternoster Chop House

Warwick Court, Paternoster Square ✉ EC4N 7DX – Ⓜ St Paul's – ☎ (020) 7029 9400 – paternosterr@conran-restaurants.co.uk – Fax (020) 7029 94 09 – www.conran.com
closed Sunday dinner and Saturday **L3**
Rest – Carte approx. £30
◆ British ◆ Brasserie ◆
A modern ambience holds sway, while there's a reassuringly resolute British classic style to the dishes. Back to basics menu relies on seasonality and sourcing of ingredients.

Southwark

Plan IX

Bermondsey

London Bridge

8-18 London Bridge St ✉ SE1 9SG – Ⓜ London Bridge – ☎ (020) 7855 2200 – sales@londonbridgehotel.com – Fax (020) 7855 22 33 – www.londonbridgehotel.com **M4**
135 rm – †£219 ††£219, ☕ £14.95 – 3 suites
Rest *Georgetown* – *(dinner only)* Carte £26/34
◆ Business ◆ Classic ◆
In one of the oldest parts of London, independently owned with an ornate façade dating from 1915. Modern interior with classically decorated bedrooms and an impressive gym. Restaurant echoing the colonial style serving Malaysian dishes.

Bengal Clipper

Cardamom Building, Shad Thames, Butlers Wharf ✉ SE1 2YR – Ⓜ London Bridge – ☎ (020) 7357 9001 – mail@bengalclipper.co.uk – Fax (020) 7357 90 02 – www.bengalclipper.co.uk **N4**
Rest – Carte £13/27
◆ Indian ◆ Friendly ◆
Housed in a Thames-side converted warehouse, a smart Indian restaurant with original brickwork and steel supports. Menu features Bengali and Goan dishes. Evening pianist.

Magdalen

152 Tooley St ✉ SE1 2TU – Ⓜ London Bridge – ☎ (020) 7403 1342 – info@magdalenrestaurant.co.uk – Fax (020) 7403 99 50 – www.magdalenrestaurant.co.uk
closed 17-31 August, 24-31 December, Saturday lunch, Sunday and Bank Holidays
Rest – Carte £25/44 **M4**
◆ British ◆ Bistro ◆
Appealing bistro style restaurant set over two floors, with aubergine-coloured walls and chandeliers. Seasonal menus offer precise, well-executed and simply presented cooking.

Village East

171 Bermondsey St ✉ SE1 3UW – Ⓜ London Bridge – ☎ (020) 7357 6082 – info@villageeast.co.uk – Fax (020) 7403 33 60 – www.villageeast.co.uk
closed 25-26 December, and 1 January **D2**
Rest – Menu £15 (lunch) – Carte £24/34
◆ Modern ◆ Trendy ◆
In a glass fronted block sandwiched by Georgian townhouses, this trendy restaurant has two loud, buzzy bars and dining areas serving ample portions of modern British fare.

Cantina Del Ponte

36c Shad Thames, Butlers Wharf ✉ SE1 2YE – Ⓜ London Bridge – ☎ (020) 7403 5403 – Fax (020) 7940 18 45 – www.conran.com
closed 25-26 December **N4**
Rest – Menu £14/15 – Carte approx. £25
◆ Italian ◆ Bistro ◆
Quayside setting with a large canopied terrace. Terracotta flooring; modern rustic style décor, simple and unfussy. Tasty, refreshing Mediterranean-influenced cooking.

Butlers Wharf Chop House ≤ Tower Bridge, VISA MO AE

36e Shad Thames, Butlers Wharf ✉ SE1 2YE – Ⓜ London Bridge – ✆ (020) 7403 3403 – bwchophouse@dandddlondon.com – Fax (020) 7940 18 55 – www.danddlondon.com

closed 1-3 January **N4**

Rest – Menu £26 – Carte £26/38

◆ British ◆ Rustic ◆

Book the terrace in summer and dine in the shadow of Tower Bridge. Rustic feel to the interior, with obliging service. Menu focuses on traditional English dishes.

Southwark

Southwark Rose &rm AC P VISA MO AE

43-47 Southwark Bridge Rd ✉ SE1 9HH – Ⓜ London Bridge – ✆ (020) 7015 1480 – info@southwarkrosehotel.co.uk – Fax (020) 7015 14 81 – www.southwarkrosehotel.co.uk **L4**

78 rm – †£180 ††£180, ☐ £12.95 – 6 suites

Rest – *(dinner only)* Carte £16/22

◆ Business ◆ Functional ◆

Purpose built budget hotel south of the City, near the Globe Theatre. Top floor dining room with bar. Uniform style, reasonably spacious bedrooms with writing desks.

Oxo Tower ≤ London Skyline and River Thames, AC VISA MO AE

(8th Floor) Oxo Tower Wharf, Barge House St ✉ SE1 9PH – Ⓜ Southwark – ✆ (020) 7803 3888 – oxo.reservations@harveynichols.co.uk – Fax (020) 7803 38 38 – www.harveynichols.com

closed 25-26 December **K4**

Rest *Oxo Tower Brasserie* – see below

Rest – Menu £30 – Carte dinner £42/57

◆ Modern ◆ Formal ◆

Top of a converted factory, providing stunning views of the Thames and beyond. Stylish, minimalist interior with huge windows. Smooth service of modern cuisine.

Roast AC VISA MO AE

The Floral Hall, Borough Market ✉ SE1 1TL – Ⓜ London Bridge – ✆ (020) 7940 1300 – info@roast-restaurant.com – Fax (020) 7655 20 79 – www.roast-restaurant.com

closed Sunday dinner **M4**

Rest – Carte £32/50

◆ British ◆ Modern ◆

Set into the roof of Borough Market's Floral Hall. Extensive cocktail list in bar; split-level restaurant has views to St. Paul's. Robust English cooking using market produce.

Baltic VISA MO AE

74 Blackfriars Rd ✉ SE1 8HA – Ⓜ Southwark – ✆ (020) 7928 1111 – info@balticrestaurant.co.uk – Fax (020) 7928 84 87 – www.balticrestaurant.co.uk

Rest – Menu £14 – Carte £23/28 **K4**

◆ Eastern European ◆ Brasserie ◆

Set in a Grade II listed 18C former coach house. Enjoy authentic and hearty east European and Baltic influenced food. Interesting vodka selection and live jazz on Sundays.

Oxo Tower Brasserie ≤ London Skyline and River Thames, AC VISA MO AE

(8th Floor) Oxo Tower Wharf,Barge House St ✉ SE1 9PH – Ⓜ Southwark – ✆ (020) 7803 3888 – oxo.reservations@harveynichols.co.uk – Fax (020) 7803 38 38 – www.harveynichols.com

closed 25-26 December **K4**

Rest – Menu £22 – Carte £30/41

◆ Modern ◆ Brasserie ◆

Same views but less formal than the restaurant. Open-plan kitchen, relaxed service, the modern menu is slightly lighter. In summer, try to secure a table on the terrace.

Cantina Vinopolis

No 1 Bank End ✉ SE1 9BU – Ⓜ London Bridge – ☎ (020) 7940 8333 – cantina@vinopolis.co.uk – Fax (020) 7940 83 34 – www.cantinavinopolis.com **L4**
closed Christmas, New Year and Sunday dinner
Rest – Menu £18 – Carte £20/28
◆ Modern ◆ Bistro ◆
Large, solid brick vaulted room under Victorian railway arches, with an adjacent wine museum. Modern menu with a huge selection of wines by the glass.

Tate Modern

London Skyline and River Thames,
Tate Modern, Bankside ✉ SE1 9TG – Ⓜ Southwark – ☎ (020) 7401 5020 – Fax (020) 7401 51 71 – www.tate.org.uk **L4**
closed 24-26 December
Rest – Carte £20/32
◆ Innovative ◆ Design ◆
Modernity to match the museum, with vast murals and huge windows affording stunning views. Canteen-style menu at a sensible price with obliging service.

Wright Brothers

11 Stoney St, Borough Market ✉ SE1 9AD – Ⓜ London Bridge – ☎ (020) 7403 9554 – reservations@wrightbros.eu.com – Fax (020) 7403 95 58 – www.wrightbros.eu.com **L4**
closed 25-26 December and Sunday
Rest – Carte £23/43
◆ Seafood ◆ Wine bar ◆
Classic style oyster and porter house - a large number of porter ales on offer. Simple settings afford a welcoming ambience to enjoy huge range of oysters and prime shellfish.

Anchor and Hope

36 The Cut ✉ SE1 8LP – Ⓜ Southwark – ☎ (020) 7928 9898 – Fax (020) 7928 45 95
closed Christmas-New Year, 2 weeks August, Sunday, Monday lunch and Bank Holidays **K4**
Rest – Carte £20/30
◆ Modern ◆ Pub ◆
Close to Waterloo, the distinctive dark green exterior lures visitors in droves. Bare floorboards, simple wooden furniture. Seriously original cooking with rustic French base.

Tower Hamlets

Bow

The Morgan Arms

43 Morgan St ✉ E3 5AA – Ⓜ Bow Road – ☎ (020) 8980 6389 – themorgan@geronimo-inns.co.uk – www.geronimo-inns.co.uk **L3**
Closed 25-26 December and 1 January
Rest – *(closed Sunday dinner) (bookings not accepted)* Carte £22/35
◆ Modern ◆ Pub ◆
Characterful pub with mismatch of furniture and shabby chic appeal. Constantly evolving menu offers robust cooking with some unusual ingredients to fill your Auntie Nelly.

Canary Wharf

Four Seasons

Westferry Circus ✉ E14 8RS – Ⓜ Canary Wharf – ☎ (020) 7510 1999 – sales.caw@fourseasons.com – Fax (020) 7510 19 98 – www.fourseasons.com/canarywharf
128 rm – †£411/434 ††£411/494, ☕ £22.50 – 14 suites
Rest *Quadrato* – see below
◆ Grand Luxury ◆ Classic ◆
Sleek and stylish with striking river and city views. Atrium lobby leading to modern bedrooms boasting every conceivable extra. Detailed service.

XX

Ubon by Nobu

River Thames and city skyline,

39 Westferry Circus ✉ *E14 8RR – Ⓜ Canary Wharf (DLR) – ✆ (020) 7719 7800 – ubon@noburestaurants.com – Fax (020) 7719 78 01 – www.noburestaurants.com*

Rest – Menu £45/70

◆ Japanese ◆ Trendy ◆

Light, airy, open-plan restaurant, with floor to ceiling glass and great Thames views. Informal atmosphere. Large menu with wide selection of modern Japanese dishes.

XX

Quadrato – at Four Seasons H.

Westferry Circus ✉ *E14 8RS – Ⓜ Canary Wharf (DLR) – ✆ (020) 7510 1999 – Fax (020) 7510 19 98 – www.fourseasons.com/canarywharf*

Rest – Menu £27/33 – Carte £27/41

◆ Italian ◆ Design ◆

Striking, modern restaurant with terrace overlooking river. Sleek, stylish dining room with glass-fronted open-plan kitchen. Menu of northern Italian dishes; swift service.

XX

Plateau

Canada Place, Canada Square ✉ *E14 5ER – Ⓜ Canary Wharf (DLR) – ✆ (020) 7715 7100 – Fax (020) 7715 71 10 – www.conran.com*

Rest – Menu £20/35 – Carte £24/35

◆ Modern ◆ Design ◆

Situated on fourth floor of 21C building; adjacent to Plateau Restaurant, with simpler table settings. Classical dishes, with seasonal base, employing grill specialities.

The Gun

27 Coldharbour ✉ *E14 9NS – Ⓜ Blackwall (DLR) – ✆ (020) 7515 5222 – info@thegundocklands.com – www.thegundocklands.com*

Rest – Carte £20/33

◆ Modern ◆ Pub ◆

Restored historic pub with a terrace facing the Dome: tasty dishes, including Billingsgate market fish, balance bold simplicity and a bit of French finesse. Efficient service.

Limehouse

The Narrow

Narrow Street ✉ *E14 8DP – Ⓜ Limehouse (DLR) – ✆ (020) 7592 7950 – thenarrow@gordonramsay.com – Fax (020) 7592 16 03 – www.gordonramsay.com*

Plan I **D2**

Rest – *(booking essential)* Carte £17/26

◆ British ◆ Pub ◆

Gordon Ramsay's Grade II listed former dockmaster's house on the edge of the Thames, sympathetically restyled and serving good value old school British favourites. Spacious terrace.

Mile End

L'Oasis

237 Mile End Rd ✉ *E1 4AA – Ⓜ Stepney Green – ✆ (020) 7702 7051 – info@loasisstepney.co.uk – Fax (020) 7265 98 50 – www.loasisstepney.co.uk*

Closed 2 weeks August, 25 December-first Monday in the New Year and Monday

Plan I **D2**

Rest – Carte £25/38

◆ Modern ◆ Pub ◆

Narrow, cavernous and bright, its original features include ornamental Victorian ceiling. Concise menus offer hearty, rustic cooking with influences from all over the world.

Spitalfields

Bengal Trader

44 Artillery Lane ✉ E1 7NA – Ⓜ Liverpool Street – ✆ (020) 7375 0072 – mail@bengalclipper.co.uk – Fax (020) 7247 10 02 – www.bengalclipper.co.uk **N2**

Rest – Carte £13/25

◆ Indian ◆ Brasserie ◆

Contemporary Indian paintings feature in this stylish basement room beneath a ground floor bar. Menu provides ample choice of Indian dishes.

St John Bread and Wine

94-96 Commercial St ✉ E1 6LZ – Ⓜ Shoreditch – ✆ (020) 7247 8724 – Fax (020) 7247 89 24 – www.stjohnbreadandwine.com *Plan I* **D2**

Rest – Carte £25/29

◆ Innovative ◆ Bistro ◆

Very popular neighbourhood bakery providing wide variety of home-made breads. Appealing, intimate dining section: all day menus that offer continually changing dishes.

Wapping

Wapping Food

Wapping Wall ✉ E1W 3ST – Ⓜ Wapping – ✆ (020) 7680 2080 – info@wapping-wpt.com – www.thewappingproject.com *Plan I* **D2**

Rest – Carte £26/42

◆ Modern ◆ Design ◆

Something a little unusual; a combination of restaurant and gallery in a converted hydraulic power station. Enjoy the modern menu surrounded by turbines and TV screens.

Whitechapel

Cafe Spice Namaste

16 Prescot St ✉ E1 8AZ – Ⓜ Tower Hill – ✆ (020) 7488 9242 – info@cafespice.co.uk – Fax (020) 7481 05 08 – www.cafespice.co.uk **N3**

Rest – Menu £30 – Carte £17/29

◆ Indian ◆ Neighbourhood ◆

A riot of colour from the brightly painted walls to the flowing drapes. Sweet-natured service adds to the engaging feel. Fragrant and competitively priced Indian cooking.

CHELSEA, SOUTH KENSINGTON & EARL'S COURT

Chelsea

Plan X

Jumeirah Carlton Tower

Cadogan Pl ✉ SW1X 9PY – Ⓜ Knightsbridge – ✆ (020) 7235 1234 – jctinfo@jumeirah.com – Fax (020) 7235 91 29 – www.jumeirah.com **F5**

190 rm – †£293 ††£640, ☕ £30 – 30 suites

Rest *Rib Room* – Carte £51/66

◆ Grand Luxury ◆ Classic ◆

Imposing international hotel overlooking a leafy square. Well-equipped roof-top health club has funky views. Generously proportioned rooms boast every conceivable facility. Rib Room restaurant has a clubby atmosphere.

Wyndham Grand

Chelsea Harbour ✉ SW10 0XG – Ⓜ Fulham Broadway – ✆ (020) 7823 3000 – Fax (020) 7352 81 74 – www.wyndhamlondon.com **D8**

160 suites – ††£558, ☕ £22.50

Rest *Aquasia* – see below

Rest *Aquasia* – Carte £25/45

◆ Luxury ◆ Modern ◆

Modern, all-suite hotel within an exclusive marina and retail development. Many of the spacious and well-appointed rooms have balconies and views across the Thames.

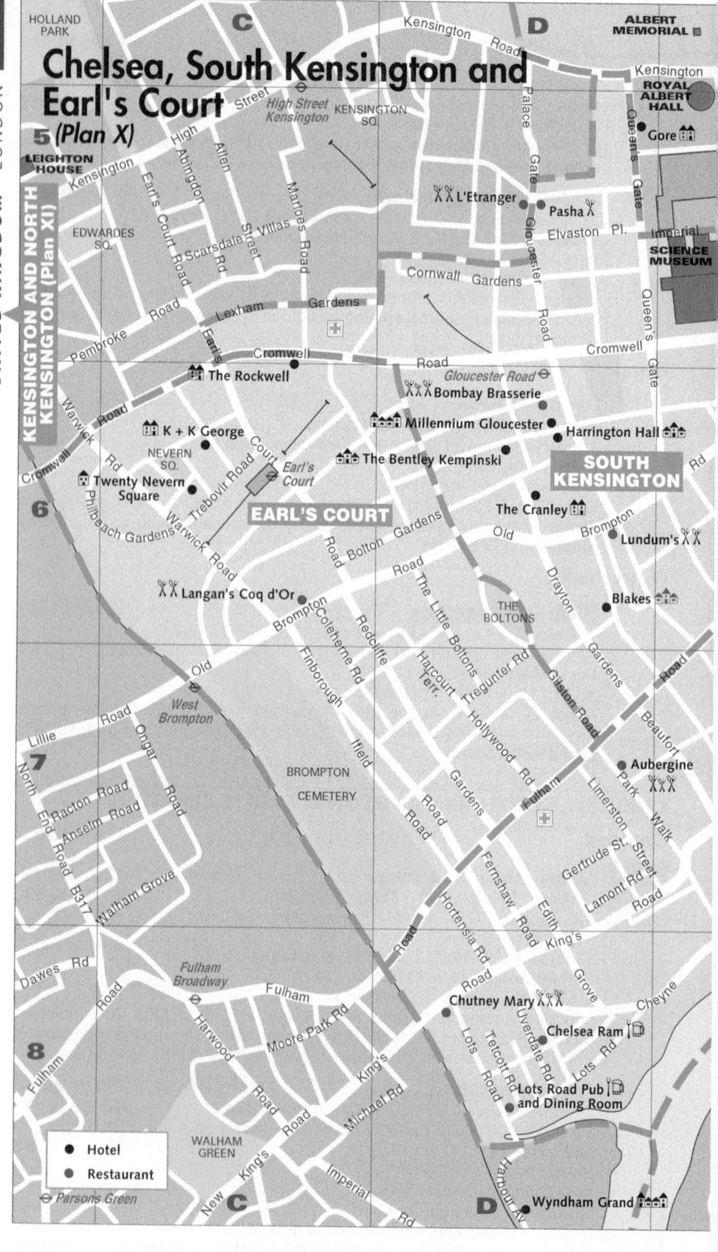
Chelsea, South Kensington and Earl's Court
(Plan X)
KENSINGTON AND NORTH KENSINGTON (Plan XI)
HOLLAND PARK
LEIGHTON HOUSE
ALBERT MEMORIAL
ROYAL ALBERT HALL
SCIENCE MUSEUM
High Street Kensington
KENSINGTON SQ.
EDWARDES SQ.
NEVERN SQ.
Earl's Court
EARL'S COURT
Gloucester Road
SOUTH KENSINGTON
THE BOLTONS
West Brompton
BROMPTON CEMETERY
Fulham Broadway
WALHAM GREEN
Parsons Green
Gore
L'Etranger
Pasha
The Rockwell
Bombay Brasserie
Millennium Gloucester
Harrington Hall
K + K George
The Bentley Kempinski
Twenty Nevern Square
The Cranley
Lundum's
Langan's Coq d'Or
Blakes
Aubergine
Chutney Mary
Chelsea Ram
Lots Road Pub and Dining Room
Wyndham Grand
Hotel
Restaurant

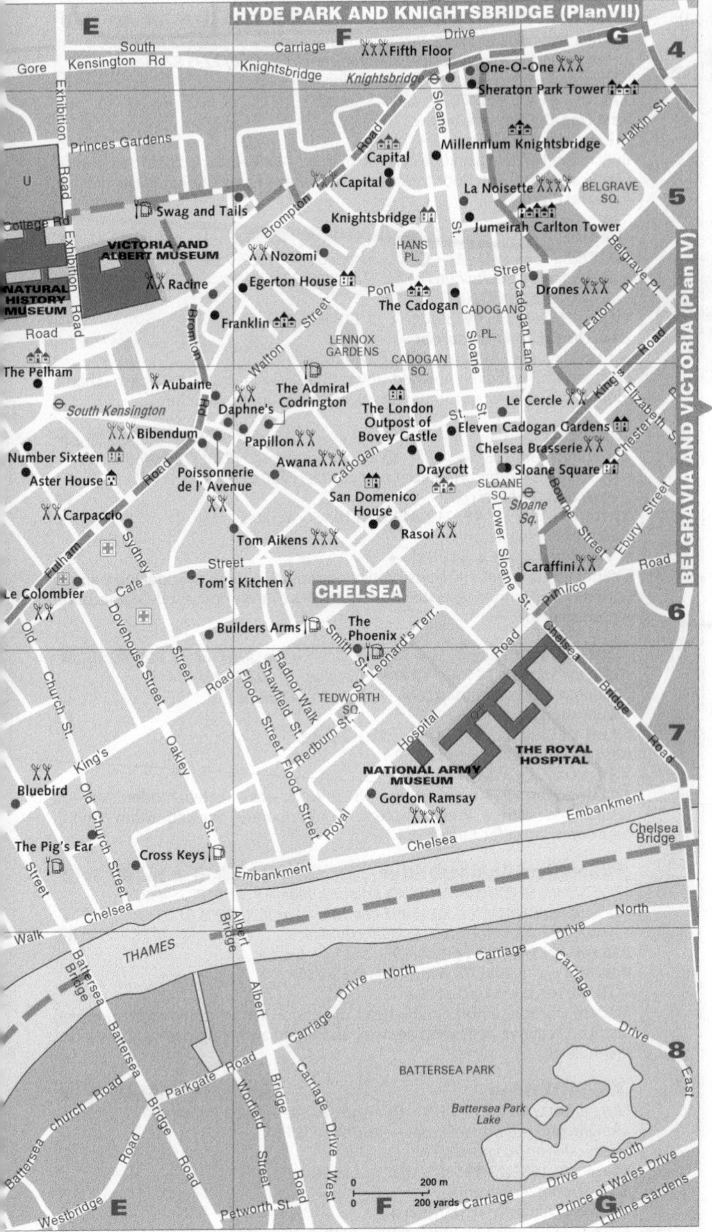

HYDE PARK AND KNIGHTSBRIDGE (Plan VII)
BELGRAVIA AND VICTORIA (Plan IV)
Fifth Floor
One-O-One
Sheraton Park Tower
Millennium Knightsbridge
Capital
La Noisette
Swag and Tails
Knightsbridge
Jumeirah Carlton Tower
Nozomi
Racine
Egerton House
The Cadogan
Drones
Franklin
The Pelham
Aubaine
The Admiral Codrington
Daphne's
The London Outpost of Bovey Castle
Le Cercle
Eleven Cadogan Gardens
Bibendum
Papillon
Number Sixteen
Chelsea Brasserie
Awana
Draycott
Sloane Square
Aster House
Poissonnerie de l' Avenue
San Domenico House
Carpaccio
Rasoi
Tom Aikens
Caraffini
Tom's Kitchen
Le Colombier
CHELSEA
Builders Arms
The Phoenix
THE ROYAL HOSPITAL
NATIONAL ARMY MUSEUM
Gordon Ramsay
Bluebird
The Pig's Ear
Cross Keys
VICTORIA AND ALBERT MUSEUM
NATURAL HISTORY MUSEUM
South Kensington
Sloane Sq.
Knightsbridge
HANS PL.
LENNOX GARDENS
CADOGAN SQ.
CADOGAN PL.
BELGRAVE SQ.
SLOANE SQ.
TEDWORTH SQ.
THAMES
BATTERSEA PARK
Battersea Park Lake
0 200 m
0 200 yards

Sheraton Park Tower

101 Knightsbridge ✉ SW1X 7RN – Ⓜ Knightsbridge – ✆ (020) 7235 8050
– central.london.reservations@sheraton.com – Fax (020) 7235 82 31
– www.luxurycollection.com/parktowerlondon **F4**

275 rm – †£470 ††£470, ☕ £25 – 5 suites

Rest *One-O-One* – see below

◆ Luxury ◆ Business ◆

Built in the 1970s in a unique cylindrical shape. Well-equipped bedrooms are all identical in size. Top floor executive rooms have commanding views of Hyde Park and City.

Capital

22-24 Basil St ✉ SW3 1AT – Ⓜ Knightsbridge – ✆ (020) 7589 5171
– reservations@capitalhotel.co.uk – Fax (020) 7225 00 11
– www.capitalhotel.co.uk **F5**

49 rm – †£206/335 ††£394/429, ☕ £18.50

Rest *The Capital Restaurant* – see below

◆ Luxury ◆ Traditional ◆ Classic ◆

Discreet and privately owned town house with distinct English charm. Individually decorated rooms with plenty of thoughtful touches.

Draycott

26 Cadogan Gdns ✉ SW3 2RP – Ⓜ Sloane Square – ✆ (020) 7730 6466
– reservations@draycotthotel.com – Fax (020) 7730 02 36
– www.draycotthotel.com **F6**

31 rm – †£159/347 ††£219/347, ☕ £19.95 – 4 suites

Rest – *(room service only)*

◆ Townhouse ◆ Stylish ◆

Charmingly discreet 19C house with elegant sitting room overlooking tranquil garden, for afternoon tea. Individual rooms in a country house style, named after writers or actors.

The Cadogan

75 Sloane St ✉ SW1X 9SG – Ⓜ Knightsbridge – ✆ (020) 7235 7141
– cadogan@thesteingroup.com – Fax (020) 7245 09 94
– www.cadogan.com **F5**

63 rm – †£300/347 ††£347, ☕ £20 – 2 suites

Rest – Menu £23 – Carte £38/50

◆ Luxury ◆ Cosy ◆

An Edwardian town house, where Oscar Wilde was arrested; modernised and refurbished with a French accent. Contemporary drawing room. Stylish bedrooms; latest facilities.

Millennium Knightsbridge

17-25 Sloane St ✉ SW1X 9NU – Ⓜ Knightsbridge – ✆ (020) 7235 4377
– reservations.knightsbridge@mill-cop.com – Fax (020) 7235 37 05
– www.millenniumhotels.co.uk/knightsbridge **F5**

218 rm – †£176/323 ††£265/393, ☕ £15 – 4 suites

Rest *Mju* – ✆ (020) 7201 6330 – Menu £24/36

◆ Business ◆ Modern ◆

Modern, corporate hotel in the heart of London's most fashionable shopping district. Executive bedrooms are well-appointed and equipped with the latest technology.

Knightsbridge

10 Beaufort Gdns ✉ SW3 1PT – Ⓜ Knightsbridge – ✆ (020) 7584 6300
– knightsbridge@firmdale.com – Fax (020) 7584 63 55
– www.knightsbridgehotel.com **F5**

44 rm – †£188/229 ††£280/329, ☕ £16.50

Rest – *(room service only)*

◆ Townhouse ◆ Stylish ◆

Attractively furnished town house with a very stylish, discreet feel. Every bedroom is immaculately appointed and has an individuality of its own; fine detailing throughout.

The Sloane Square H.

Sloane Sq ✉ SW1W 8EG – Ⓜ Sloane Square – ☎ (020) 7896 9988 – reservations@sloanesquarehotel.co.uk – Fax (020) 7751 42 11 – www.sloanesquarehotel.co.uk F6

102 rm – 🚹£160/230 🚹🚹£198/230, ☕ £9.50

Rest Chelsea Brasserie – see below

♦ Business ♦ Modern ♦

Redbrick hotel opened in 2007, boasts bright, contemporary décor. Suprisingly spacious bedrooms boast sumptuous beds with crisp white linen, window seats and all mod cons.

The Levin

28 Basil St ✉ SW3 1AS – ☎ (020) 7589 6286 – reservations@thelevinhotel.co.uk – Fax (020) 7823 78 26 – www.thelevinhotel.co.uk F5

12 rm ☕ – 🚹£229/311 🚹🚹£229/511

Rest *Le Metro* – *(Closed Sunday)* Carte £20/26

♦ Townhouse ♦ Classic ♦

Impressive façade, contemporary interior and comfortable bedrooms in subtle art deco style, boasting marvellous champagne mini bars. Superb junior suite on top floor. Informal brasserie offers classic bistro fare; includes blackboard menu and pies of the week.

San Domenico House

29-31 Draycott Pl ✉ SW3 2SH – Ⓜ Sloane Square – ☎ (020) 7581 5757 – info@sandomenicohouse.com – Fax (020) 7584 13 48 – www.sandomenicohouse.com F6

15 rm – 🚹£247/270 🚹🚹£276/300, ☕ £22.35

Rest – *(room service only)*

♦ Townhouse ♦ Classic ♦

Intimate and discreet Victorian town house with an attractive rooftop terrace. Individually styled and generally spacious rooms with antique furniture and rich fabrics.

The London Outpost without rest

69 Cadogan Gdns ✉ SW3 2RB – Ⓜ Sloane Square – ☎ (020) 7589 7333 – info@londonoutpost.co.uk – Fax (020) 7581 49 58 – www.londonoutpost.co.uk F6

closed 23-27 December

11 rm – 🚹£235 🚹🚹£273/387, ☕ £16.95

♦ Townhouse ♦ Cosy ♦

Classic town house in a most fashionable area. Relaxed and comfy lounges full of English charm. Bedrooms, named after local artists and writers, full of thoughtful touches.

Egerton House

17-19 Egerton Terrace ✉ SW3 2BX – Ⓜ South Kensington – ☎ (020) 7589 2412 – bookeg@rchmail.com – Fax (020) 7584 65 40 – www.egertonhousehotel.com F5

29 rm – 🚹£276 🚹🚹£347/582, ☕ £24.50

Rest – *(room service only)*

♦ Townhouse ♦ Classic ♦

Stylish redbrick Victorian town house close to the exclusive shops. Relaxed drawing room. Antique furnished and individually decorated rooms.

Gordon Ramsay

68-69 Royal Hospital Rd ✉ SW3 4HP – Ⓜ Sloane Square – ☎ (020) 7352 4441 – Fax (020) 7352 33 34 – www.gordonramsay.com

Closed 1 week Christmas, Saturday and Sunday F7

Rest – *(booking essential)* Menu £40/85 ✿

Spec. Pan-fried Scottish scallops with millefeuille of potato, parmesan velouté. Roast Bresse pigeon with grilled polenta, baby golden beetroot and date sauce. Bitter chocolate cylinder with coffee granité and ginger mousse.

♦ Modern ♦ Formal ♦

Discreetly located, with meticulous service; its best tables by the windows. Luxury ingredients employed in perfectly balanced classical dishes. Book 2 months in advance.

XXXX ✿

La Noisette A/C VISA MC AE ①

164 Sloane St ✉ SW1X 9QB – Ⓜ Knightsbridge – ✆ (020) 7750 5000 – lanoisette@gordonramsay.com – Fax (020) 7750 50 01 – www.gordonramsay.com

closed Saturday lunch and Sunday **F5**

Rest – Menu £21/55

Spec. Seared foie gras with coffee syrup and amaretto foam. Spit-roasted chicken from Bresse for two. White peach soufflé, verbena sorbet and palmito.

♦ Innovative ♦ Formal ♦

From the Ramsay portfolio, with Art Deco and hazelnut meeting at the top of the stairs. Confident service of highly accomplished original/classical dishes with bold flavours.

XXX ✿✿

The Capital Restaurant – at Capital H. A/C ⊕ VISA MC AE ①

22-24 Basil St ✉ SW3 1AT – Ⓜ Knightsbridge – ✆ (020) 7589 5171 – caprest@capitalhotel.co.uk – Fax (020) 7225 00 11 **F5**

Rest – *(booking essential)* Menu £30/55 ❀

Spec. Assiette 'Landaise.' Saddle of rabbit with seared calamari and tomato risotto. Iced coffee parfait with chocolate fondant.

♦ Modern ♦ Formal ♦

Hotel restaurant imbued with an understated elegance. Confident, precise cooking; classical dishes come with impishly ingenious touches. Enthusiastic and knowledgeable staff.

XXX

Bibendum A/C VISA MC AE ①

Michelin House, 81 Fulham Rd ✉ SW3 6RD – Ⓜ South Kensington – ✆ (020) 7581 5817 – reservations@bibendum.co.uk – Fax (020) 7823 79 25 – www.bibendum.co.uk

Closed 25-26 December and 1 January **E6**

Rest – Menu £29 (lunch) – Carte £37/60 ❀

♦ Modern ♦ Design ♦

A fine example of Art Nouveau architecture; a London landmark. 1st floor restaurant with striking stained glass 'Michelin Man'. Attentive service of modern British cooking.

XXX ✿

Tom Aikens A/C VISA MC AE

43 Elystan St ✉ SW3 3NT – Ⓜ South Kensington – ✆ (020) 7584 2003 – info@tomaikens.co.uk – Fax (020) 7584 20 01 – www.tomaikens.co.uk

closed two weeks August, 10 days Christmas-New Year, Saturday, Sunday and Bank Holidays **E6**

Rest – Menu £29/65 ❀

Spec. Hen's egg with truffled scambled egg, foie gras mousse and cured duck breast. Roast pork cutlet with apple purée, baby squid and pork lasagna. Apple toasted in honey with saffron ice cream.

♦ Innovative ♦ Fashionable ♦

Minimalist in style, with a warm feel. Classically based French cooking features original touches, with the focus firmly on seasonal, traceable ingredients. Attentive service.

XXX ✿

Aubergine (Billy Drabble) A/C VISA MC AE ①

11 Park Walk ✉ SW10 0AJ – Ⓜ South Kensington – ✆ (020) 7352 3449 – info@auberginerestaurant.co.uk – Fax (020) 7351 17 70 – www.auberginerestaurant.co.uk

closed 2 weeks Christmas, Easter, Saturday lunch, Sunday and Bank Holidays **D7**

Rest – *(booking essential)* Menu £34 (lunch)/64

Spec. Seared scallops with smoked salmon, potatoes and peas. Best end of lamb with braised sweetbreads, tomato and basil. Poached peach jelly and crumble, lemon verbena sorbet.

♦ Modern ♦ Formal ♦

Longstanding restaurant in heart of Chelsea, serving classic French cooking which shows off the kitchen's considerable skill. Elegant, intimate feel; immaculately laid tables.

XXX

One-O-One – at Sheraton Park Tower H.
William St ✉ SW1X 7RN – Ⓜ Knightsbridge – ✆ (020) 7290 7101 – Fax (020) 7235 61 96 F4
Rest – Menu £19/30 – Carte £35/55
♦ Seafood ♦ Design ♦
Spacious, refurbished ground floor restaurant. Brittany-born chef focuses primarily on seafood; served in 'petits plats' for a lighter and more flexible eating experience.

XXX

Drones
1 Pont St ✉ SW1X 9EJ – Ⓜ Knightsbridge – ✆ (020) 7235 9555 – sales@whitestarline.org.uk – Fax (020) 7235 95 66 – www.whitestarline.org.uk
closed 26 December, 1 January, Saturday lunch and Sunday dinner G5
Rest – Menu £19 (lunch) – Carte £32/45
♦ Modern ♦ Formal ♦
Smart exterior with etched plate-glass window. U-shaped interior with moody film star photos on walls. French and classically inspired tone to dishes.

XXX

Fifth Floor – at Harvey Nichols
Knightsbridge ✉ SW1X 7RJ – Ⓜ Knightsbridge – ✆ (020) 7235 5250 – www.harveynichols.com
closed Christmas and Sunday dinner F4
Rest – Menu £20/40 – Carte £28/44
♦ Modern ♦ Fashionable ♦
On Harvey Nichols' top floor; elevated style sporting a pink-hued oval shaped interior with green frosted glass. Chic surroundings with food to match and smooth service.

XXX

Awana
85 Sloane Ave ✉ SW3 3DX – Ⓜ South Kensington – ✆ (020) 7584 8880 – info@awana.co.uk – Fax (020) 7584 61 88 – www.awana.co.uk
Closed 25-26 December and 1 January F6
Rest – Menu £15/40 – Carte £29/41
♦ Malaysian ♦ Exotic ♦
Enter into stylish cocktail bar. Traditional Malay elements adorn restaurant. Satay chef cooks to order. Malaysian dishes authentically prepared and smartly presented.

XXX

Chutney Mary
535 King's Rd ✉ SW10 0SZ – Ⓜ Fulham Broadway – ✆ (020) 7351 3113 – chutneymary@realindianfood.com – Fax (020) 7351 76 94 – www.realindianfood D8
Rest – *(dinner only and lunch Saturday and Sunday)* Carte £34/43
♦ Indian ♦ Exotic ♦
Soft lighting and sepia etchings hold sway at this forever popular restaurant. Extensive menu of specialities from all corners of India. Complementary wine list.

XX

Daphne's
112 Draycott Ave ✉ SW3 3AE – Ⓜ South Kensington – ✆ (020) 7589 4257 – reservations@daphnes-restaurant.co.uk – Fax (020) 7225 27 66 – www.daphnes-restaurant.co.uk
closed 25-26 December E6
Rest – *(booking essential)* Menu £19 (lunch) – Carte £33/47
♦ Italian ♦ Fashionable ♦
Positively buzzes in the evening, the Chelsea set gelling smoothly and seamlessly with the welcoming Tuscan interior ambience. A modern twist updates classic Italian dishes.

XX ✿ **Rasoi** (Vineet Bhatia) AC VISA MC AE DC
10 Lincoln St ✉ SW3 2TS – Ⓜ Sloane Square – ✆ (020) 7225 1881 – info@rasoirestaurant.co.uk – Fax (020) 7581 02 20 – www.rasoirestaurant.co.uk
closed 25 -26 December, 1 January, Saturday lunch, Sunday and Bank Holidays **F6**
Rest – Menu £24 (lunch) – Carte £38/73
Spec. Grilled scallops with asparagus, curry leaf and spinach. Ginger and and chilli lobster with curry leaf and spiced cocoa powder. Chocolate samosa with Bailey's ice cream.
♦ Indian ♦ Neighbourhood ♦
L-shaped dining room and conservatory decorated with Indian trinkets; intimate upstairs rooms. Contemporary Indian cooking with subtle spicing and innovative flavour combinations.

XX **Racine** AC VISA MC AE
239 Brompton Rd ✉ SW3 2EP – Ⓜ South Kensington – ✆ (020) 7584 4477 – Fax (020) 7584 49 00
closed 25 December **E5**
Rest – Menu £18/20 – Carte £26/37
♦ French ♦ Brasserie ♦
Dark leather banquettes, large mirrors and wood floors create the atmosphere of a genuine Parisienne brasserie. Good value, well crafted, regional French fare.

XX **Chelsea Brasserie** – at The Sloane Square H. AC VISA MC AE DC
7-12 Sloane Sq. ✉ SW1W 8EG – Ⓜ Sloane Square – ✆ (020) 7881 5999 – robert@chelsea-brasserie.co.uk – www.sloanesquarehotel.co.uk
closed 25 December **F6**
Rest – Carte £27/37
♦ Modern ♦ Brasserie ♦
Glass doors open into roomy brasserie-style restaurant, with smoky green lamps and brick walls inlaid with mirror tiles. A European menu includes some classic French dishes.

XX **Papillon** AC ⇔ VISA MC AE
96 Draycott Ave ✉ SW3 3AD – Ⓜ South Kensington – ✆ (020) 7225 2555 – info@papillonchelsea.co.uk – Fax (020) 7225 25 54 – www.papillonchelsea.co.uk
closed 24-27 December, 1-4 January **F6**
Rest – Menu £17 (lunch) – Carte £26/46
♦ French ♦ Brasserie ♦
Feels like a Parisian brasserie: large arched windows, brown décor, fleur-de-lys green banquettes and leather chairs. Classic French menus please the smart Chelsea set.

XX **Nozomi** AC ⇔ VISA MC AE
15 Beauchamp Pl ✉ SW3 1NQ – Ⓜ Knightsbridge – ✆ (020) 7838 1500 – info@nazomi.co.uk – Fax (020) 7838 10 01 – www.nazomi.co.uk **F5**
Rest – Carte £50/65
♦ Japanese ♦ Minimalist ♦
DJ mixes lounge music at the front bar; up the stairs in the restaurant the feeling is minimal with soft lighting. Innovative Japanese menus provide an interesting choice.

XX **Bluebird** AC ⇔ VISA MC AE DC
350 King's Rd ✉ SW3 5UU – Ⓜ Sloane Square – ✆ (020) 7559 1000 – enquiries@bluebird-store.co.uk – Fax (020) 7559 11 15 – www.danddlondon.com **E7**
Rest – Carte £29/44
♦ Modern ♦ Design ♦
A foodstore, café and homeware shop also feature at this impressive skylit restaurant. Much of the modern British food is cooked in wood-fired ovens. Lively atmosphere.

XX **Poissonnerie de l'Avenue**

82 Sloane Ave ✉ SW3 3DZ – Ⓜ South Kensington – ☎ (020) 7589 2457 – info@poissonnerie.co.uk – Fax (020) 7581 33 60 – www.poissonneriedel'avenue.co.uk
closed 24-26 December and Sunday **E6**
Rest – Menu £24 (lunch) – Carte £27/40
♦ French ♦ Formal ♦
Long-established and under the same ownership since 1965. Spacious and traditional French restaurant offering an extensive seafood menu. An institution favoured by locals.

XX **Le Cercle**

1 Wilbraham Pl ✉ SW1X 9AE – Ⓜ Sloane Square – ☎ (020) 7901 9999 – info@lecercle.co.uk – Fax (020) 7901 91 11
closed 24 December-5 January, Sunday and Monday **F6**
Rest – Menu £15 (lunch) – Carte £20/32
♦ French ♦ Fashionable ♦
Discreetly signed basement restaurant down residential side street. High, spacious room with chocolate banquettes. Tapas style French menus; accomplished cooking.

XX **Le Colombier**

145 Dovehouse St ✉ SW3 6LB – Ⓜ South Kensington – ☎ (020) 7351 1155 – lecolombier1998@aol.com – Fax (020) 7351 51 24 – www.lecolombier-sw3.co.uk **E6**
Rest – Menu £16/19 – Carte £28/39
♦ French ♦ Neighbourhood ♦
Proudly Gallic corner restaurant in an affluent residential area. Attractive enclosed terrace. Bright and cheerful surroundings and service of traditional French cooking.

XX **Caraffini**

61-63 Lower Sloane St ✉ SW1W 8DH – Ⓜ Sloane Square – ☎ (020) 7259 0235 – info@caraffini.co.uk – Fax (020) 7259 02 36 – www.caraffini.co.uk
closed 25 December, Easter, Sunday and Bank Holidays **F6**
Rest – *(booking essential)* Carte £24/33
♦ Italian ♦ Friendly ♦
The omnipresent and ebullient owner oversees the friendly service in this attractive neighbourhood restaurant. Authentic and robust Italian cooking; informal atmosphere.

XX **Carpaccio**

4 Sydney St ✉ SW3 6PP – Ⓜ South Kensington – ☎ (020) 7352 3435 – carpacciorest@aol.com – Fax (020) 7622 83 04 – www.carpacciorestaurant.co.uk
closed 25 December, Easter, last 2 weeks August, Sunday and Bank Holidays **E6**
Rest – Carte £27/33
♦ Italian ♦ Neighbourhood ♦
Fine Georgian exterior housing James Bond stills, 1920s silent Italian comedies, Ayrton Senna's Honda cockpit, witty waiters, and enjoyable, classical Trattoria style cooking.

X **Tom's Kitchen**

27 Cale St ✉ SW3 3QP – Ⓜ South Kensington – ☎ (020) 7349 0202 – info@tomskitchen.co.uk – Fax (020) 7823 36 52 – www.tomskitchen.co.uk
Closed 4 days Christmas **E6**
Rest – Carte 37/49
♦ Modern ♦ Neighbourhood ♦
A converted pub, whose white tiles and mirrors help to give it an industrial feel. Appealing and wholesome dishes come in man-sized portions. The eponymous Tom is Tom Aikens.

The Admiral Codrington

A/C VISA MC AE

17 Mossop St ✉ SW3 2LY – Ⓜ South Kensington – ✆ (020) 7581 4005 – admiral-codrington@333holdingsltd.com – Fax (020) 7589 24 52 – www.theadmiralcodrington.com

Closed 24-27 December **F6**

Rest – Carte £24/31

♦ Modern ♦ Pub ♦

Aproned staff offer attentive, relaxed service in this busy gastropub. A retractable roof provides alfresco dining in the modern back room. Cosmopolitan menu of modern dishes.

Chelsea Ram

VISA MC

32 Burnaby St ✉ SW10 0PL – Ⓜ Gloucester Road – ✆ (020) 7351 4008 – bookings@chelsearam.co.uk **D8**

Rest – Carte £18/24

♦ Modern ♦ Pub ♦

Wooden floors, modern artwork and books galore feature in this forever popular pub. Concise menu of modern British cooking with daily changing specials. Friendly atmosphere.

Swag and Tails

VISA MC AE

10-11 Fairholt St, Knightsbridge ✉ SW7 1EG – Ⓜ Knightsbridge – ✆ (020) 7584 6926 – theswag@swagandtails.com – Fax (020) 7581 99 35 – www.swagandtails.com

Closed Christmas-New Year **EF5**

Rest – Carte £22/33

♦ Modern ♦ Pub ♦

Attractive Victorian pub close to Harrods and the fashionable Knightsbridge shops. Polite and approachable service of a blackboard menu of light snacks and seasonal dishes.

Builders Arms

A/C VISA MC AE

13 Britten St ✉ SW3 3TY – Ⓜ South Kensington – ✆ (020) 7349 9040 – buildersarms@geronimo-inns.co.uk – www.geronimo-inns.co.uk

Closed 25-26 December **E6**

Rest – *(bookings not accepted)* Carte £20/35

♦ Modern ♦ Pub ♦

Extremely busy modern 'gastropub' favoured by the locals. Eclectic menu of contemporary dishes with blackboard specials. Polite service from a young and eager team.

The Pig's Ear

VISA MC AE

35 Old Church St ✉ SW3 5BS – Ⓜ Sloane Square – ✆ 020 7352 2908 – thepigsear@hotmail.co.uk – Fax 020 7352 93 21 – www.thepigsear.co.uk

Closed 25-26 December, 31 December, 1 January **E7**

Rest – Carte £25/30

♦ Modern ♦ Pub ♦

Corner pub that gets very busy, particularly for downstairs bar dining. Upstairs, more sedate wood panelled dining room. Both menus are rustic, robust and seasonal in nature.

The Phoenix

A/C VISA MC AE

23 Smith St ✉ SW3 4EE – Ⓜ Sloane Square – ✆ 020 7730 9182 – thephoenix@geronimo-inns.co.uk – www.geronimo-inns.co.uk

closed 25-26 December **F67**

Rest – Carte £22/28

♦ Modern ♦ Pub ♦

Tile-fronted pub with al fresco seating area, very popular in summer. Shabby chic décor that's been modernised but feels retro. Modern British repertoire on extensive menus.

The Cross Keys

1 Lawrence St ✉ SW3 5NB – Ⓜ South Kensington – ✆ (020) 7349 9111 – xkeys.nicole@hotmail.co.uk – Fax (020) 7349 93 33 – www.thexkeys.co.uk
Closed Bank Holidays **E7**
Rest – Carte £21/30
♦ Modern ♦ Pub ♦
Hidden away near the Embankment, this 18C pub has period furniture and impressive carved stone fireplaces. Interesting, modern menus include blackboard of daily specials.

Lots Road Pub & Dining Room

114 Lots Rd ✉ SW10 0RJ – Ⓜ Fulham Broadway – ✆ (020) 7352 6645 – lotsroad@foodandfuel.co.uk – Fax (020) 7376 49 75 – www.lotsroadpub.com **D8**
Rest – Carte £35/60
♦ Modern ♦ Pub ♦
Traditional corner pub with an open-plan kitchen, flowers at each table and large modern pictures on the walls. Contemporary menus change daily.

South Kensington *Plan X*

The Pelham

15 Cromwell Pl ✉ SW7 2LA – Ⓜ South Kensington – ✆ (020) 7589 8288 – pelham@firmdale.com – Fax (020) 7584 84 44 – www.pelhamhotel.co.uk **E6**
50 rm – †£200/223 ††£305, ☕ £21 – 2 suites
Rest *Kemps* – Menu £18 – Carte £25/33
♦ Luxury ♦ Stylish ♦
Attractive Victorian town house with a discreet and comfortable feel. Wood panelled drawing room and individually decorated bedrooms with marble bathrooms. Detailed service. Warm basement dining room.

Blakes

33 Roland Gdns ✉ SW7 3PF – Ⓜ Gloucester Road – ✆ (020) 7370 6701 – blakes@blakeshotels.com – Fax (020) 7373 04 42 – www.blakeshotels.com **D6**
40 rm – †£205/315 ††£440, ☕ £25 – 12 suites
Rest – Carte approx. £80
♦ Luxury ♦ Design ♦
Behind the Victorian façade lies one of London's first 'boutique' hotels. Dramatic, bold and eclectic décor, with oriental influences and antiques from around the globe. Fashionable restaurant with bamboo and black walls.

The Bentley Kempinski

27-33 Harrington Gdns ✉ SW7 4JX – Ⓜ Gloucester Road – ✆ (020) 7244 5555 – info@thebentley-hotel.com – Fax (020) 7244 55 66 – www.thebentley-hotel.com **D6**
52 rm – †£353 ††£470, ☕ £22.50 – 12 suites
Rest *1880* – *(closed Sunday-Monday) (dinner only)* Menu £26/32 – Carte £34/53
♦ Grand Luxury ♦ Classic ♦
A number of stucco-fronted 19C houses were joined to create this opulent, lavish hotel decorated with marble, mosaics and ornate gold leaf. Bedrooms with gorgeous silk fabrics. 1880 for formal dining and ambitious cooking.

NH Harrington Hall

5-25 Harrington Gdns ✉ SW7 4JB – Ⓜ Gloucester Road – ✆ (020) 7396 9696 – book.london@nh-hotels.com – Fax (020) 7396 17 19 – www.nh-hotels.com **D6**
200 rm ☕ – †£115/210 ††£127/227
Rest *Wetherby's* – Menu £20 – Carte £21/33
♦ Business ♦ Functional ♦
A series of adjoined terraced houses, with an attractive period façade that belies the size. Tastefully furnished bedrooms, with an extensive array of facilities. Classically decorated dining room.

Number Sixteen without rest

16 Sumner Pl ✉ SW7 3EG
– Ⓜ South Kensington – ✆ (020) 7589 5232
– sixteen@firmdale.com – Fax (020) 7584 86 15
– www.numbersixteenhotel.co.uk **E6**
42 rm – †£130/217 ††£311, ☕ £19.50
♦ Townhouse ♦ Stylish ♦
Enticingly refurbished 19C town houses in smart area. Discreet entrance, comfy sitting room and charming breakfast terrace. Bedrooms in English country house style.

The Cranley

10 Bina Gardens ✉ SW5 0LA
– Ⓜ Gloucester Road – ✆ (020) 7373 0123
– info@thecranley.com – Fax (020) 7373 94 97
– www.thecranley.com **D6**
38 rm – †£265 ††£295/325, ☕ £29.50
1 suite
Rest – *(room service only)*
♦ Townhouse ♦ Stylish ♦
Delightful Regency town house combines charm and period details with modern comforts and technology. Individually styled bedrooms; some with four-posters. Room service available.

The Gore

190 Queen's Gate ✉ SW7 5EX
– Ⓜ Gloucester Road – ✆ (020) 7584 6601
– reservations@gorehotel.com – Fax (020) 7589 81 27
– www.gorehotel.com **D5**
50 rm – †£330 ††£340/520, ☕ £16.95
Rest *190 Queensgate* – *(booking essential)* Menu £16 (lunch)
– Carte £31/51
♦ Townhouse ♦ Personalised ♦
Opened its doors in 1892; has retained its individual charm. Richly decorated with antiques, rugs and over 4,000 pictures that cover every inch of wall. 190 Queensgate boasts French-inspired décor.

The Rockwell

181-183 Cromwell Rd ✉ SW5 0SF – ✆ (020) 7244 2000
– enquiries@therockwell.com – Fax (020) 7244 20 01
– www.therockwell.com **C5**
40 rm – †£120/160 ††£180/200, ☕ £12.50
Rest – Carte £21/32
♦ Townhouse ♦ Design ♦
Two Victorian houses with open, modern lobby and secluded, south-facing garden terrace. Bedrooms come in bold warm colours; 'Garden rooms' come with their own patios. Small dining room offers easy menu of modern European staples.

Aster House without rest

3 Sumner Pl ✉ SW7 3EE
– Ⓜ South Kensington – ✆ (020) 7581 5888
– asterhouse@btinternet.com – Fax (020) 7584 49 25
– www.asterhouse.com **E6**
13 rm – †£146 ††£177/211
♦ Townhouse ♦ Cosy ♦
End of terrace Victorian house with a pretty little rear garden and first floor conservatory. Ground floor rooms available. A wholly non-smoking establishment.

XXX **Bombay Brasserie**

Courtfield Rd ✉ SW7 4QH – Ⓜ Gloucester Road – ☎ (020) 7370 4040 – bombay1brasserie@aol.com – Fax (020) 7835 16 69 – www.bombaybrasserielondon.com
closed 25-26 December **D6**
Rest – *(buffet lunch)* Menu £19 (weekday lunch) – Carte £42/52
♦ Indian ♦ Exotic ♦
Something of a London institution: an ever busy Indian restaurant with Raj-style décor. Ask to sit in the brighter plant-filled conservatory. Popular lunchtime buffet.

XX **L'Etranger**

36 Gloucester Rd ✉ SW7 4QT – Ⓜ Gloucester Road – ☎ (020) 7584 1118 – etranger@etranger.co.uk – Fax (020) 7584 88 86 – www.circagroupltd.co.uk
closed 25-26 December, 1 January, Saturday lunch **D5**
Rest – *(booking essential)* Menu £16.50 (lunch) – Carte £31/82
♦ Innovative ♦ Neighbourhood ♦
Corner restaurant with mosaic entrance floor and bay window. Modern décor. Tables extend into adjoining wine shop. French based cooking with Asian influences.

XX **Pasha**

1 Gloucester Rd ✉ SW7 4PP – Ⓜ Gloucester Road – ☎ (020) 7589 7969 – info@pasha-restaurant.co.uk – Fax (020) 7581 99 96 – www.pasha-restaurant.co.uk
closed 25-26 December, and 1 January **D5**
Rest – Menu £15/30 – Carte £22/33
♦ Moroccan ♦ Exotic ♦
Relax over ground floor cocktails, then descend to mosaic floored restaurant where the rose-petal strewn tables are the ideal accompaniment to tasty Moroccan home cooking.

Earl's Court *Plan X*

K + K George

1-15 Templeton Pl ✉ SW5 9NB – Ⓜ Earl's Court – ☎ (020) 7598 8700 – hotelgeorge@kkhotels.co.uk – Fax (020) 7370 22 85 – www.kkhotels.com **C6**
154 rm – †£200 ††£235
Rest – Carte £20/31
♦ Business ♦ Modern ♦
Five converted 19C houses overlooking large rear garden. Scandinavian style to rooms with low beds, white walls and light wood furniture. Breakfast room has the garden view. Informal dining in the bar.

Twenty Nevern Square without rest

Nevern Sq ✉ SW5 9PD – Ⓜ Earl's Court – ☎ (020) 7565 9555 – hotel@twentynevernsquare.co.uk – Fax (020) 7565 94 44 – www.twentynevernsquare.co.uk **C6**
20 rm – †£89/140 ††£110/175, £13
♦ Townhouse ♦ Functional ♦
In an attractive Victorian garden square, an individually designed, privately owned town house. Original pieces of furniture and some rooms with their own terrace.

XX **Langan's Coq d'Or**

254-260 Old Brompton Rd ✉ SW5 9HR – Ⓜ Earl's Court – ☎ (020) 7259 2599 – admin@langansrestaurant.co.uk – Fax (020) 7370 77 35 – www.langansrestaurants.co.uk
closed Bank Holidays **C6**
Rest – Menu £23 – Carte approx. £27
♦ Traditional ♦ Brasserie ♦
Classic, buzzy brasserie and excellent-value menu to match. Walls adorned with pictures of celebrities: look out for more from the enclosed pavement terrace. Smooth service.

KENSINGTON, NORTH KENSINGTON & NOTTING HILL

Kensington

Plan XI

Royal Garden

2-24 Kensington High St ✉ *W8 4PT* – Ⓜ *High Street Kensington*
– ✆ *(020) 7937 8000* – *sales@royalgardenhotel.co.uk* – *Fax (020) 7361 19 91*
– *www.royalgardenhotel.co.uk* **D4**

376 rm – 🚹£317/387 🚹🚹£387, ☕ £19.50 – 20 suites

Rest *Park Terrace* – Carte approx. £23

Rest *The Tenth* – ✆ *(020) 7361 1910* – Menu £23/65 – Carte £36/45

◆ Luxury ◆ Classic ◆

A tall, modern hotel with many of its rooms enjoying enviable views over the adjacent Kensington Gardens. All the modern amenities and services, with well-drilled staff. Bright, spacious Park Terrace offers British, Asian and modern European cuisine. The Tenth reopening mid-2008. Modern menu and commanding views from the top floor Tenth restaurant.

The Milestone

1-2 Kensington Court ✉ *W8 5DL* – Ⓜ *High Street Kensington*
– ✆ *(020) 7917 1000* – *bookms@rchmail.com* – *Fax (020) 7917 10 10*
– *www.milestonehotel.com* **D4**

52 rm – 🚹£376 🚹🚹£376, ☕ £25 – 5 suites

Rest – *(booking essential for non-residents)* Menu £27 – Carte £43/56

◆ Luxury ◆ Stylish ◆

Elegant 'boutique' hotel with decorative Victorian façade and English feel. Charming oak panelled lounge and snug bar. Meticulously decorated bedrooms with period detail. Panelled dining room with charming little oratory for privacy seekers.

Baglioni

60 Hyde Park Gate ✉ *SW7 5BB* – Ⓜ *High Street Kensington* – ✆ *(020) 7368 5700*
– *info@baglionihotellondon.com* – *Fax (020) 7368 57 01*
– *www.baglionihotels.com* **D4**

53 rm – 🚹£452 🚹🚹£452, ☕ £25 – 15 suites

Rest *Brunello* – ✆ *(020) 7368 5711* – Menu £24 (lunch) – Carte £52/70

◆ Luxury ◆ Stylish ◆

Opposite Kensington Palace: ornate interior, trendy basement bar. Impressively high levels of service. Small gym/sauna. Superb rooms in cool shades boast striking facilities. Restaurant specialises in rustic Italian cooking.

Belvedere

Holland House, off Abbotsbury Rd ✉ *W8 6LU*
– Ⓜ *Holland Park* – ✆ *(020) 7602 1238*
– *info@belvedererestaurant.co.uk* – *Fax (020) 7610 43 82*
– *www.belvedererestaurant.co.uk*
closed 26 December, 1 January and Sunday dinner **B4**

Rest – Menu £18/25 (lunch) – Carte £25/45

◆ Modern ◆ Romantic ◆

Former 19C orangery in a delightful position in the middle of the Park. On two floors with a bar and balcony terrace. Huge vases of flowers. Modern take on classic dishes.

Clarke's

124 Kensington Church St ✉ *W8 4BH* – Ⓜ *Notting Hill Gate*
– ✆ *(020) 7221 9225* – *restaurant@sallyclarke.com* – *Fax (020) 7229 45 64*
– *www.sallyclarke.com*
closed 23 December-8 January, 1 week August, Sunday, Monday dinner and Bank Holidays **C4**

Rest – Menu £43 (dinner) – Carte lunch approx. £29

◆ Modern ◆ Neighbourhood ◆

Forever popular restaurant, now serving a choice of dishes boasting trademark fresh, seasonal ingredients and famed lightness of touch. Loyal following for over 20 years.

XX **Zaika**

1 Kensington High St ✉ W8 5NP
– Ⓜ High Street Kensington – ✆ (020) 7795 6533
– info@zaika-restaurant.co.uk – Fax (020) 7937 88 54
– www.zaika-restaurant.co.uk
closed 25- December and Sunday lunch **D4**
Rest – Menu £20 – Carte £20/33
♦ Indian ♦ Exotic ♦
A converted bank, sympathetically restored, with original features and Indian artefacts. Well organised service of modern Indian dishes.

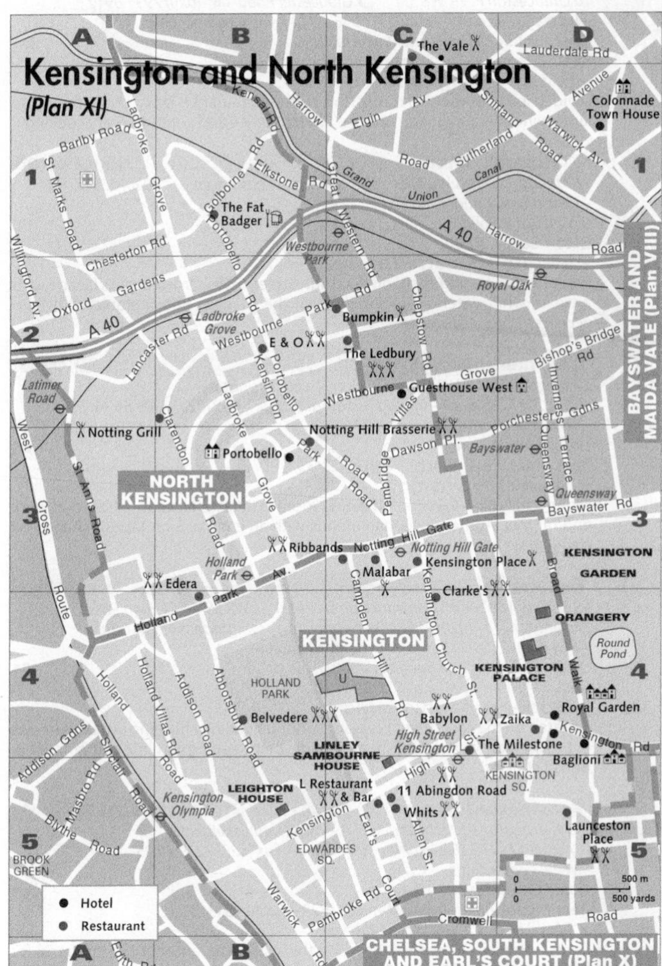

XX **Whits**

AC VISA MC AE

21 Abingdon Rd ✉ W8 6AH – Ⓜ High Street Kensington – ✆ (020) 7938 1122 – eva@whits.co.uk – Fax (020) 7937 61 21 – www.whits.co.uk

closed last 2 weeks August, 24-31 December, Sunday dinner and Monday **C5**

Rest – *(dinner only and Sunday lunch)* Menu £19/24 – Carte £28/37

♦ Modern ♦ Neighbourhood ♦

Buzzy destination: bar runs length of lower level. Most diners migrate upstairs with its modish art work, intimate tables and modern dishes: do check out the souffles!

XX **Launceston Place**

AC VISA MC AE

1a Launceston Pl ✉ W8 5RL – Ⓜ Gloucester Road – ✆ (020) 7937 6912 – lpr@egami.co.uk – Fax (020) 7938 24 12 – www.egami.co.uk

Closed Saturday lunch and Bank Holidays **D5**

Rest – Menu £15/19 – Carte £25/45

♦ British ♦ Neighbourhood ♦

Divided into a number of rooms, this corner restaurant is lent a bright feel by its large windows and gilded mirrors. Chatty service and contemporary cooking.

XX **11 Abingdon Road**

AC VISA MC AE

11 Abingdon Rd ✉ W8 6AH – Ⓜ High Street Kensington – ✆ (020) 7937 0120 – eleven@abingdonroad.co.uk

Closed Bank Holidays **C5**

Rest – Carte £20/30

♦ Mediterranean ♦ Brasserie ♦

Part of a little 'eating oasis' off Ken High Street. Stylish frosted glass façade with a clean, white interior. Cooking's from the modern British stable with Euro accents.

XX **L Restaurant & Bar**

AC VISA MC AE

2 Abingdon Rd ✉ W8 6AF – Ⓜ High Street Kensington – ✆ (020) 7795 6969 – info@l-restaurant.co.uk – Fax (020) 7795 66 99 – www.l-restaurant.co.uk

closed Monday lunch **C5**

Rest – Menu £16 (lunch) – Carte £23/33

♦ Spanish ♦ Design ♦

Wonderfully airy glass-roofed dining room with tastefully designed wood work and mirrors. Authentic Iberian menus with an emphasis on tapas matched by good-value wine list.

XX **Babylon** – at The Roof Gardens

AC VISA MC AE

99 Kensington High St (entrance on Derry St) ✉ W8 5SA – Ⓜ High Street Kensington – ✆ (020) 7368 3993 – babylon@roofgardens.virgin.co.uk – Fax (020) 7368 39 95 – www.roofgardens.com

closed Christmas and Sunday dinner **C4**

Rest – Menu £18 – Carte £33/54

♦ Modern ♦ Fashionable ♦

Situated on the roof of this pleasant London building affording attractive views of the London skyline. Stylish modern décor in keeping with the contemporary, British cooking.

X **Kensington Place**

AC VISA MC AE

201 Kensington Church St ✉ W8 7LX – Ⓜ Notting Hill Gate – ✆ (020) 7727 3184 – kpr@egami.co.uk – Fax (020) 7229 20 25 – www.egami.co.uk

closed Christmas and 1 January **C3**

Rest – *(booking essential)* Menu £19/25 – Carte £31/40

♦ Modern ♦ Fashionable ♦

A cosmopolitan crowd still head for this establishment that set the trend for large, bustling and informal restaurants. Professionally run with skilled modern cooking.

Malabar

27 Uxbridge St ✉ W8 7TQ – Ⓜ Notting Hill Gate – ✆ (020) 7727 8800 – feedback@malabar-restaurant.co.uk – www.malabar-restaurant.co.uk **C3**

Rest – *(buffet lunch Sunday)* Menu £21 – Carte £20/36

◆ Indian ◆ Neighbourhood ◆

Indian restaurant in a residential street. Three rooms with individual personalities and informal service. Extensive range of good value dishes, particularly vegetarian.

North Kensington

Plan XI

The Portobello without rest

22 Stanley Gdns ✉ W11 2NG – Ⓜ Notting Hill Gate – ✆ (020) 7727 2777 – info@portobello-hotel.co.uk – Fax (020) 7792 96 41 – www.portobello-hotel.co.uk

closed 23-29 December **B3**

23 rm – †£142/180 ††£310, ☕ £15

◆ Townhouse ◆ Personalised ◆

An attractive Victorian town house in an elegant terrace. Original and theatrical décor. Circular beds, half-testers, Victorian baths: no two bedrooms are the same.

Guesthouse West

163-165 Westbourne Grove ✉ W11 2RS – Ⓜ Notting Hill Gate – ✆ (020) 7792 9800 – reception@guesthousewest.com – Fax (020) 7792 97 97 – www.guesthousewest.com **C2**

20 rm – †£183 ††£183

Rest – Carte approx. £35

◆ Townhouse ◆ Stylish ◆

Attractive Edwardian house in the heart of Notting Hill, close to its shops and restaurants. Contemporary bedrooms boast the latest in audio visual gadgetry. Chic Parlour Bar for all-day light dishes in a tapas style.

The Ledbury

127 Ledbury Rd ✉ W11 2AQ – Ⓜ Notting Hill Gate – ✆ (020) 7792 9090 – info@theledbury.com – Fax (020) 7792 91 91 – www.theledbury.com **C2**

Rest – Menu £25/50 – Carte £34/47

Spec. Flame-grilled mackerel with a mackerel tartare, avocado and shiso. Suckling pig with spring onions, mangosteen, salsify and ham beignet. Date and vanilla tart with cardamom and orange ice cream.

◆ Modern ◆ Neighbourhood ◆

Former pub with elegant, minimalist décor. Seasonal menu with innovative edge; flavours are pronounced and well judged; ingredients are superbly sourced.

Notting Hill Brasserie

92 Kensington Park Rd ✉ W11 2PN – Ⓜ Notting Hill Gate – ✆ (020) 7229 4481 – enquiries@nottinghillbrasserie.com – Fax (020) 7221 12 46

closed Sunday dinner **B3**

Rest – Menu £23/30 – Carte £35/45

◆ Modern ◆ Neighbourhood ◆

Modern, comfortable restaurant with quiet, formal atmosphere set over four small rooms. Authentic African artwork on walls. Contemporary dishes with European influence.

Edera

148 Holland Park Ave ✉ W11 4UE – Ⓜ Holland Park – ☎ (020) 7221 6090
– Fax (020) 7313 97 00 – Closed Bank Holidays **B4**

Rest – Carte £32/49

♦ Italian ♦ Neighbourhood ♦

Split level restaurant with outdoor tables. Modern Italian cooking with some unusual ingredients and combinations. Sardinian specialities include Bottarga and homemade pastas.

E&O

14 Blenheim Crescent ✉ W11 1NN – Ⓜ Ladbroke Grove – ☎ (020) 7229 5454
– eando@rickerrestaurants.com – Fax (020) 7229 55 22
– www.rickerrestaurants.com
closed 24-26 and 31 December, Sunday and Bank Holidays **B2**

Rest – Carte £24/38

♦ Asian ♦ Minimalist ♦

Mean, dark and moody: never mind the exterior, we're talking about the A-list diners. Minimalist chic meets high sound levels. Menus scour Far East: cutlery/chopstick choice.

Notting Grill

123A Clarendon Rd ✉ W11 4JG – Ⓜ Holland Park – ☎ (020) 7229 1500
– nottinggrill@aol.com – Fax (020) 7229 88 89
closed 24 December-3 January and Monday lunch **B2**

Rest – Menu £19 (dinner) – Carte approx. £30

♦ Beef specialities ♦ Neighbourhood ♦

Converted pub that retains a rustic feel, with bare brick walls and wooden tables. Specialises in well sourced, quality meats.

Bumpkin

209 Westbourne Park Rd ✉ W11 1EA – ☎ (020) 7243 9818 – www.bumpkinuk.com

Rest – *(dinner only Tuesday-Saturday)* Carte £25/40 **C2**

Rest *Brasserie* – *(closed Monday lunch)* Carte £24/39

♦ Mediterranean ♦ Family ♦

Converted pea-green pub with casual, clubby feel and wholesome philosophy of cooking seasonal, carefully-sourced and organic food. Whisky tasting and private dining on top floors. First floor restaurant offers modern Mediterranean menu.

The Fat Badger

310 Portobello Road ✉ W10 5TA – Ⓜ Ladbroke Grove – ☎ (020) 8969 4500
– info@thefatbadger.com – Fax (020) 8969 67 14 – www.thefatbadger.com
Closed 25-26 December **B1**

Rest – Carte £20/28

♦ British ♦ Pub ♦

Large rustic pub with old sofas, chandeliers, upstairs dining room and some intriguing wallpaper. Seasonal and earthy British food, with whole beasts delivered to the kitchen.

LONDON AIRPORTS

Heathrow Airport West : 17 m. by A 4 and M 4

London Heathrow Marriott

Bath Rd, Hayes ✉ UB3 5AN – ☎ (0870) 400 7250
– salesadmin.heathrow@marriotthotels.com – Fax (0870) 400 73 50
– www.londonheathrowmarriott.co.uk

391 rm – †£182 ††£182, ☕ £16.95 – 2 suites

Rest *Tuscany* – *(Closed Sunday) (dinner only)* Menu £39 – Carte £30/44

Rest *Allie's grille* – Carte £27/39

♦ Chain hotel ♦ Business ♦ Functional ♦

Built at the end of 20C, this modern, comfortable hotel is centred around a large atrium, with comprehensive business facilities: there is an exclusive Executive floor. Italian cuisine at bright and convivial Tuscany. Grill favourites at Allie's.

Crowne Plaza London - Heathrow

Stockley Rd, West Drayton ✉ UB7 9NA
– ✆ (0870) 400 9140 – reservations.cplhr@ichotelsgroup.com
– Fax (01895) 44 51 22 – www.crowneplaza.com/lon-heathrow
460 rm – †£247 ††£247, ☕ £17.95 – 3 suites
Rest ***Simply Nico Heathrow*** – see below – **Rest** ***Orwell's Brasserie*** – Menu £15/20
♦ Chain hotel ♦ Business ♦ Functional ♦
Extensive leisure, aromatherapy and beauty salons make this large hotel a popular stop-over for travellers. Club bedrooms are particularly well-equipped. Bright, breezy Concha Grill with juice bar.

Sheraton Skyline

Bath Rd, Hayes ✉ UB3 5BP – ✆ (020) 8759 2535 – res268-skyline@sheraton.com
– Fax (020) 8750 91 50 – www.sheraton.com/skyline
348 rm – †£93/280 ††£145/334, ☕ £17 – 2 suites
Rest ***Sage*** – Menu £20/45 – Carte £32/49
♦ Chain hotel ♦ Business ♦ Functional ♦
Well known for its unique indoor swimming pool surrounded by a tropical garden which is overlooked by many of the bedrooms. Business centre available. Classically decorated dining room.

Hilton London Heathrow Airport

Terminal 4 ✉ TW6 3AF – ✆ (020) 8759 7755
– sales.heathrow@hilton.com – Fax (020) 8759 75 79 – www.hilton.co.uk/heathrow
390 rm – †£292 ††£292, ☕ £20.50 – 5 suites
Rest ***Brasserie*** – *(closed lunch Saturday and Sunday) (buffet lunch)*
Menu £28/34 – Carte £30/54
Rest ***Zen Oriental*** – Menu £29/39
♦ Chain hotel ♦ Business ♦ Functional ♦
Group hotel with a striking modern exterior and linked to Terminal 4 by a covered walkway. Good sized bedrooms, with contemporary styled suites. Spacious Brasserie in vast atrium. Zen Oriental offers formal Chinese experience.

Simply Nico Heathrow – at Crowne Plaza London - Heathrow H.

Stockley Rd, West Drayton ✉ UB7 9NA
– ✆ (01895) 437564 – heathrow.simplynico@corushotels.com
– Fax (01895) 43 75 65 – www.simplyrestaurants.com – closed Sunday
Rest – *(dinner only)* Carte £23/44
♦ French ♦ Brasserie ♦
Located within the hotel but with its own personality. Mixes modern with more classically French dishes. Professional service in comfortable surroundings.

Gatwick Airport South : 28 m. by A 23 and M 23

Hilton London Gatwick Airport

South Terminal ✉ RH6 0LL – ✆ (01293) 518080
– londongatwick@hilton.com – Fax (01293) 52 89 80 – www.hilton.co.uk/gatwick
823 rm – †£195/285 ††£195/285, ☕ £18.50
Rest – Menu £18 – Carte £35/40
♦ Chain hotel ♦ Business ♦ Functional ♦
Large, well-established hotel, popular with business travellers. Two ground floor bars, lounge and leisure facilities. Older rooms co-ordinated, newer in minimalist style. Restaurant enlivened by floral profusions.

Renaissance London Gatwick

Povey Cross Rd ✉ RH6 0BE – ✆ (01293) 820169
– rhi.lgwbr.dos@renaissancehotels.com – Fax (01293) 82 69 34
– www.renaissancelondongatwick.co.uk
253 rm – †£119/145 ††£149/175, ☕ £16.50 – 1 suite
Rest – *(bar lunch)* Carte £21/38
♦ Chain hotel ♦ Business ♦ Functional ♦
Large red-brick hotel. Good recreational facilities including indoor pool, solarium. Bedrooms are spacious and decorated in smart, chintzy style. Small brasserie area open all day serving popular meals.

UNITED KINGDOM - LONDON

Stansted Airport North : 37 m. by M 11 and A 120

Radisson SAS

Waltham Close ✉ CM24 1PP – ✆ (01279) 661012 – info.stansted@radissonsas.com – Fax (01279) 66 10 13 – www.stansted.radissonsas.com

484 rm – 🚹£140 🚹🚹£140, ☕ £14.95 – 16 suites

Rest *New York Grill Bar* – Carte £28/40

Rest *Wine Tower* – Carte £18/30

Rest *Filini* – Carte £17/28

♦ Chain hotel ♦ Business ♦ Functional ♦

Impressive hotel just two minutes from main terminal; vast open atrium housing 40 foot wine cellar. Extensive meeting facilities. Very stylish bedrooms in three themes. Small, formal New York Grill Bar. Impressive Wine Tower. Filini for Italian dishes.

Hilton London Stansted Airport

Round Coppice Rd ✉ CM24 1SF – ✆ (01279) 680800 – reservations.stansted@hilton.com – Fax (01279) 68 08 90 – www.hilton.co.uk

237 rm – 🚹£99/145 🚹🚹£99/145, ☕ £17.95 – 2 suites

Rest – *(closed lunch Saturday, Sunday and Bank Holidays)* Menu £21 (dinner) – Carte £33/41

♦ Chain hotel ♦ Business ♦ Functional ♦

Bustling hotel whose facilities include leisure club, hairdressers and beauty salon. Modern rooms, with two of executive style. Transport can be arranged to and from terminal. Restaurant/bar has popular menu; sometimes carvery lunch as well.

Birmingham

BIRMINGHAM

Population: 889 000 (conurbation 2 371 000) – Altitude: 98m

Duclerc/COLORISE

It takes a pretty big backwards leap of the imagination to visualise Birmingham as an insignificant market town, but England's second city was just such a place through much of its history. Then came the boom times of the Industrial Revolution, the town fattening up on the back of the local iron and coal trades. In many people's minds that legacy lives on, the city seen as a rather dour place with shoddy Victorian housing, but 21C Brum has swept away much of its factory grime and polished up its civic face.

Its first 'makeover' was nearly a century ago when Neville Chamberlain's dad Joseph, the then mayor, enlarged the city's boundaries to make it the second largest in the country. Today it's feeling the benefits of a second modernist surge - a multi-million pound regeneration, typified by a fusion of appealing squares and modern shopping arcades: the 'armadillo' shaped Selfridges store became a fashion icon and city symbol when it opened a few years ago. Being pretty much in the centre of England, Birmingham is easily accessible from all areas and is within a curtain call of Shakespeare's Stratford while the charming Cotswolds are practically in its southern suburbs (if you stretch the imagination a bit more). To add to its impressive credentials, it can boast more canal miles than Venice and more trees than it has inhabitants.

LIVING THE CITY

Birmingham is surrounded by towns of all shapes and sizes, from the glories of Stratford-on-Avon in the south and Bridgnorth and Ironbridge in the west, to the more 'subtle' attractions of Wolverhampton and Coventry in its hinterland. Birmingham's landscape inspired a certain resident, JRR Tolkien, to write 'Lord of the Rings', but he'd be lost nowadays, what with the undulating contours of the flyovers, the self-important muscle of the adjoining National Indoor Arena and International Convention Centre, and the nearby trendy makeover of the Gas Street Basin. To say nothing with what they've done to the Bullring ...he wouldn't know where he was in the Balti Triangle (south of the centre) but perhaps would feel more at home in the elegant Jewellery Quarter further north.

PRACTICAL INFORMATION

ARRIVAL-DEPARTURE

Birmingham International Airport is 8 miles east of the city. There's free Air-Rail connection to Birmingham International Station every 2mins. From there, frequent trains to New St Station take 20min.

TRANSPORT

Three miles an hour might seem like a slow way to get round the city, but canal travel by narrowboat is stress-free and relaxing. Alternatively, take a cycle ride or walk along the towpaths. Stop off at Brindleyplace's floating café, or take a short summer trip from there.

Birmingham has eight local rail lines for travel to anywhere in the country. A recent addition, Midland Metro, is a light railway linking Snow Hill station with Wolverhampton.

Centro provides a regular service around the city. Give the exact fare to your driver as you board or purchase day or off-peak weekly Centrocards.

EXPLORING BIRMINGHAM

A sassy blend of refined arcades, stylish malls, well-stocked markets and the world-famous Jewellery Quarter just up the road, not to mention miles of canal pathways and impressive galleries... strolling round Brum has a lot going for it. In the past, you'd have thought 'coal' or 'cars', even 'great key locks' when you thought of this city, but now a more likely reaction would be "Oh, let's go there for our shopping." Historically, there's no reason why this shouldn't be the case. Many world famous British brands were created here, ranging from Bakelite to Cadbury's, HP Sauce and Typhoo Tea to Brylcreem.

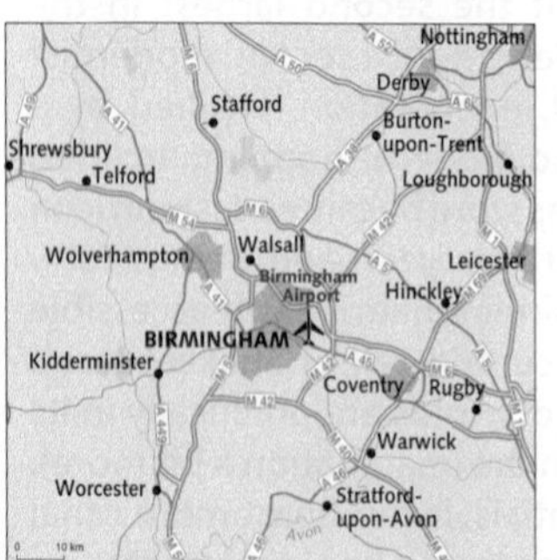

➔ RAG TO A BULL (RING)

Much of the action takes place in the **Bullring** mega-complex, overseen by the shimmering ego of the Selfridges building, less a department store, more a self-assured statement of intent from Future Systems, who designed it. Slightly more down-to-earth, and a mere stone's throw from the Bullring, is the flea market in Saint Martin's Market, known affectionately for 50 years as The Rag. Its 350 stalls complement the Bullring's grandeur rather well, and the antiques' and collectors' fairs it puts on are renowned amongst in-the-know locals. One less salubrious claim to fame...it also has a bit of a risqué reputation for early morning 'business transactions' before the stallholders arrive.

On the other side of the city, in the northern area of Hockley, is the **Jewellery Quarter**, the place to head for if you're after a quality piece of body adornment or silverware. Also known as 'The Golden Triangle', it's an area of smart Victorian buildings between Warstone Lane and Vyse Street, and it's steeped in 19C folklore: it democratized writing by supplying the world with cheap pen nibs for 130 years; it was where Joseph Hudson invented the police whistle, borrowing £20 from the Metropolitan Police so that he could get his hands on enough brass for 21,000 of them to be produced; and it's where the same man made the doomed whistles for the Titanic lifeboats (Kate Winslet used a 'rescued' one in the movie!). There are fascinating museums in the area too, such as the Jewellery Quarter Discovery Centre, which does pretty much what it says on the label.

➜ A POSTING TO THE MAILBOX

You feel like you've moved forward a century or two when you step into the **Mailbox** area, not a half-mile from the main New Street railway station. It has a distinct noughties feel to it, proudly referring to itself as the UK's 'largest mixed use building'. What that actually means is that it incorporates penthouse style apartments, health clubs, office space, hotels, restaurants and shops... not a bad refit for a former mail sorting office. It's the West Midlands' answer to Bond Street, and it's where you'll find Britain's biggest Malmaison Hotel. But it's not the only area laying claim to being Brum's coolest. Just a waterbus ride away along the quaintly named Gas Street Basin sits **Brindleyplace**, an impressive and vibrant canalside destination, boasting tree-lined streets, eye-catching water features, striking architecture and a good few clear open spaces. It's got the Sea Life Centre, too, complete with a fully transparent underwater tube letting you walk, suspended in mid-'ocean', completely surrounded by sharks, skate, rays and all manner of marine life. One final conversion that's of interest: about 700 paces from the Bullring, southeast in the area of Digbeth, stands another icon of Birmingham's branded past: the Bird's custard factory. They don't make yellow gooey stuff there anymore though: The **Custard Factory** is now an arts and media quarter with a trendy pub, The Medicine Bar, and a host of urban style shops, green spaces, fountains and sculpture. It's in a smart square too.

➜ ART ATTACK

Not everything in England's second city is rebranded, spruced up or brand new. There's still a reverence for old-fashioned style and taste embodied in a variety of esteemed establishments around the city. Take the **Barber Institute of Fine Art,** on the University of Birmingham campus in Edgbaston. This impressive art deco building, opened by Queen Mary in 1939, contains one of the finest small collections of European art in the UK, including Botticelli, Holbein, Rembrandt, Rubens, Van Gogh, Turner and Monet. Go up to the central Chamberlain Square to be equally impressed by the **Museum & Art Gallery**, which boasts a renowned collection of Pre-Raphaelite paintings, as well as works by Degas, Renoir and Canaletto. It also houses popular natural and local history sections, and the archaeology department is highly acclaimed. The Edwardian tearoom's not a bad place to relax for a spot of cultural reflection. Further north is Aston Hall, a fine Jacobean mansion built between 1618 and 1635 with friezes and plaster ceilings, a 40m long panelled gallery, gables and turrets, and with a collection that features textiles, furniture and paintings from the Birmingham Museum.

The world of science comes to life at **Millennium Point**, 10 minutes walk from the centre, its public areas dominated by an awesome central Hub with soaring atrium. This is where you'll find two visitor attractions, Thinktank, the city's science museum, and IMAX cinema. If you're more at home outdoors, then The Birmingham Botanical Gardens and Glasshouses is probably more your style. Based in Edgbaston, they opened in 1832, and today their 15 acres are an ideal place to wind down and find tranquility.

Of course, the city is only some 20 miles from the birthplace of William Shakespeare, **Stratford-upon-Avon**, and it's not unknown for visitors to forego even the delights of Birmingham in order to breathe in a bit of the Bard's magic. If you're lucky enough to be around on a summer Sunday (between July and September) there's really only one way to do the trip, and that's on the Shakespeare Express, a wonderful steam locomotive which starts from Snow Hill station, picks up passengers at Moor Street, and chugs its way through leafy Warwickshire countryside to Stratford. There's Pullman class dining if you're feeling extravagant: you can take breakfast on the way out, and high tea on the return journey.

CALENDAR HIGHLIGHTS

They like a party in Birmingham. There's a St George's Day Celebration every April, while in Handsworth the Caribbean-style Birmingham International Carnival takes place in August every second year, and winds its way to Perry Barr Park. Birmingham Pride attracts 100,000 visitors each year to the Hurst Street 'gay village' location. The largest single-day event, though, is the St. Patrick's Day Parade, which can claim to be the second biggest in Europe, after the one held in Dublin.

BIRMINGHAM IN...

→ ONE DAY

The Rag, The Bullring, a museum

→ TWO DAYS

Brindleyplace, a trip on the waterbus to The Mailbox, and a cycle ride round the canals.

→ THREE DAYS

If you're around on a summer Sunday, take the Shakespeare Express to Stratford. Or visit Bridgnorth and Ironbridge, cradle of the Industrial Revolution. Venture south to the idyllic Cotswolds.

EATING OUT

Temptation isn't far away from students at the city's main centre of learning, the University of Birmingham, to the south-west of the city, and not a million miles away from Cadbury World, the UK's only purpose-built visitor centre devoted entirely to chocolate. Located in the evocative sounding Bourneville area, staff are on hand to tell visitors the history of chocolate and how it's made, but, let's face it, most people go along to get a face full of the stuff in fresh liquid form straight from the vat.

More conventionally, many people who come to Birmingham make for the now legendary area of Sparkbrook, Balsall Heath and Moseley. In itself that may not sound too funky, but over the last 30 years it's become the area known as the Balti Triangle. The balti was 'officially' discovered in Birmingham in 1976, a full-on dish of aromatic spices, fresh herbs and rich curries, and The Triangle now boasts over 50 establishments dedicated to the dish.

For those after something a little more subtle, the city offers a growing number of lively and fashionable restaurants, offering assured and contemporary cuisine.

CENTRAL BIRMINGHAM

Plan II

Hyatt Regency

2 Bridge St ✉ B1 2JZ – ✆ (0121) 643 1234 – birmingham@hyattintl.com – Fax (0121) 616 23 23 – www.birmingham.regency.hyatt.com
closed 25-30 September **D2**
315 rm – †£199 ††£199, ☕ £15.25 – 4 suites
Rest *Aria* – Menu £14/17 – Carte £25/41
♦ Luxury ♦ Modern ♦
Striking mirrored exterior. Glass enclosed lifts offer panoramic views. Sizeable rooms with floor to ceiling windows. Covered link with International Convention Centre. Contemporary style restaurant in central atrium; modish cooking.

Radisson SAS

12 Holloway Circus ✉ B1 1BT – ✆ (0121) 654 6000 – info.birmingham@radissonsas.com – Fax (0161) 654 60 01 – www.birmingham.radissonsas.com
204 rm – †£135/205 ††£135/205, ☕ £14.95 – 7 suites
Rest *Filini* – *(Closed Saturday lunch and Sunday)* Carte £20/48
♦ Business ♦ Modern ♦
Occupies 18 uber-modern floors of a city centre skyscraper. Well-equipped business facilities; ultra stylish bedrooms in three distinctly slinky themes. Modern bar leads to airy, easy-going Italian restaurant, Filini.

Malmaison

Mailbox, 1 Wharfside St ✉ B1 1RD – ✆ (0121) 246 5000 – Fax (0121) 246 50 02 – www.malmaison.com **E2**
184 rm – †£150 ††£150, ☕ £13.95 – 5 suites
Rest *Brasserie* – Menu £16 – Carte approx. £26
♦ Luxury ♦ Stylish ♦
Stylish, modern boutique hotel, forms centrepiece of Mailbox development. Stylish bar. Spacious contemporary bedrooms with every modern facility; superb petit spa. Brasserie serving contemporary French influenced cooking at reasonable prices.

Hotel Du Vin

25 Church St ✉ B3 2NR – ✆ (0121) 200 0600 – info.birmingham@hotelduvin.com – Fax (0121) 236 08 89 – www.hotelduvin.com **E2**
66 rm – †£150/185 ††£150/185, ☕ £13.50
Rest *Bistro* – Menu £18 (lunch) – Carte £25/33
♦ Business ♦ Design ♦
Former 19C eye hospital in heart of shopping centre; has relaxed, individual, boutique style. Low lighting in rooms of muted tones: Egyptian cotton and superb bathrooms. Champagne in "bubble lounge"; Parisian style brasserie.

The Burlington

Burlington Arcade, 126 New St ✉ B2 4JQ – ✆ (0121) 643 9191 – general.burlington@macdonald-hotels.co.uk – Fax (0121) 628 50 05 – www.macdonaldhotels.co.uk
Closed 25-26 December **E2**
110 rm ☕ – †£175 ††£195 – 2 suites
Rest *Berlioz* – *(dinner only)* Menu £29 – Carte £30/43
♦ Traditional ♦ Classic ♦
Approached by a period arcade. Restored Victorian former railway hotel retains much of its original charm. Period décor to bedrooms yet with fax, modem and voice mail. Elegant dining room: ornate ceiling, chandeliers and vast mirrors.

Copthorne

Paradise Circus ✉ B3 3HJ – ✆ (0121) 200 2727 – reservations.birmingham@mill-cop.com – Fax (0121) 200 11 97 – www.milleniumhotels.com **E2**
209 rm – †£165 ††£165, ☕ £15.75 – 3 suites
Rest *Turners Grill* – *(closed Saturday lunch and Sunday)* Menu £14 (lunch) – Carte £23/29
Rest *Goldie' s Brasserie* – Menu £11/19 – Carte £21/34
♦ Business ♦ Functional ♦
Overlooking Centenary Square. Corporate hotel with extensive leisure club and cardiovascular gym. Cricket themed bar. Connoisseur rooms offer additional comforts. Flambé dishes offered in intimate Turner's Grill.

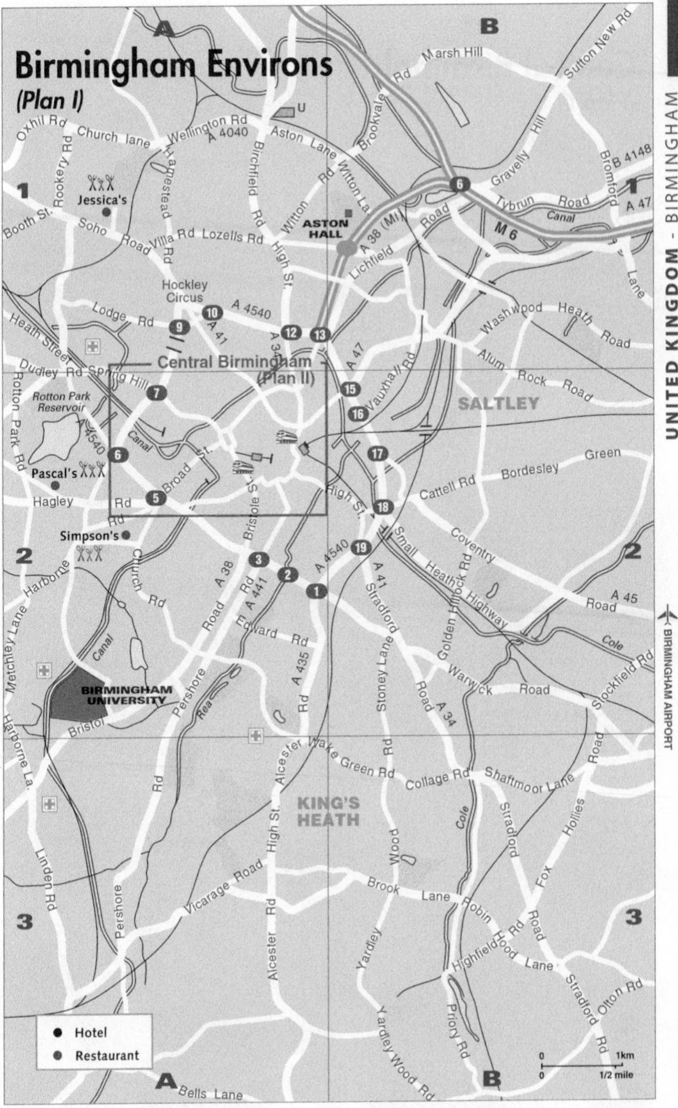
Birmingham Environs
(Plan I)
Central Birmingham
(Plan II)
ASTON HALL
BIRMINGHAM UNIVERSITY
SALTLEY
KING'S HEATH
Hockley Circus
Rotton Park Reservoir
Jessica's
Pascal's
Simpson's
Hotel
Restaurant
BIRMINGHAM AIRPORT
1km
1/2 mile

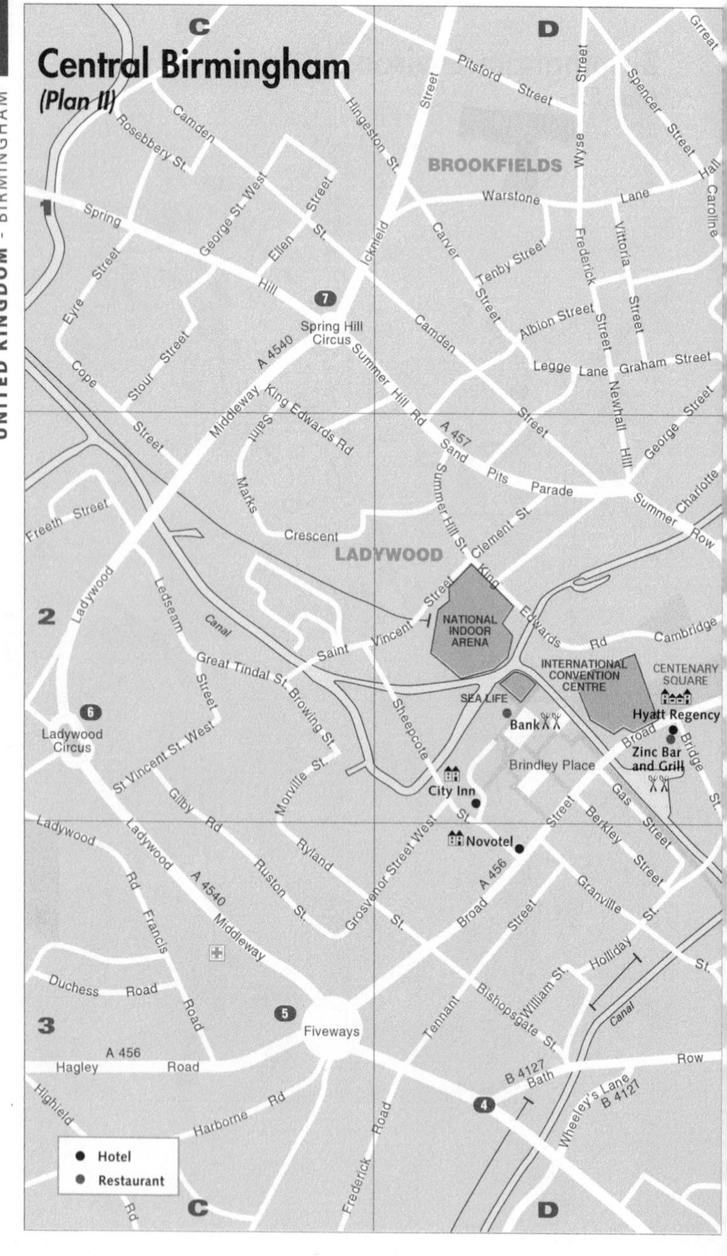
Central Birmingham
(Plan II)
BROOKFIELDS
LADYWOOD
NATIONAL INDOOR ARENA
INTERNATIONAL CONVENTION CENTRE
CENTENARY SQUARE
SEA LIFE
Bank
Hyatt Regency
Zinc Bar and Grill
Brindley Place
City Inn
Novotel
Spring Hill Circus
Ladywood Circus
Fiveways
Hotel
Restaurant

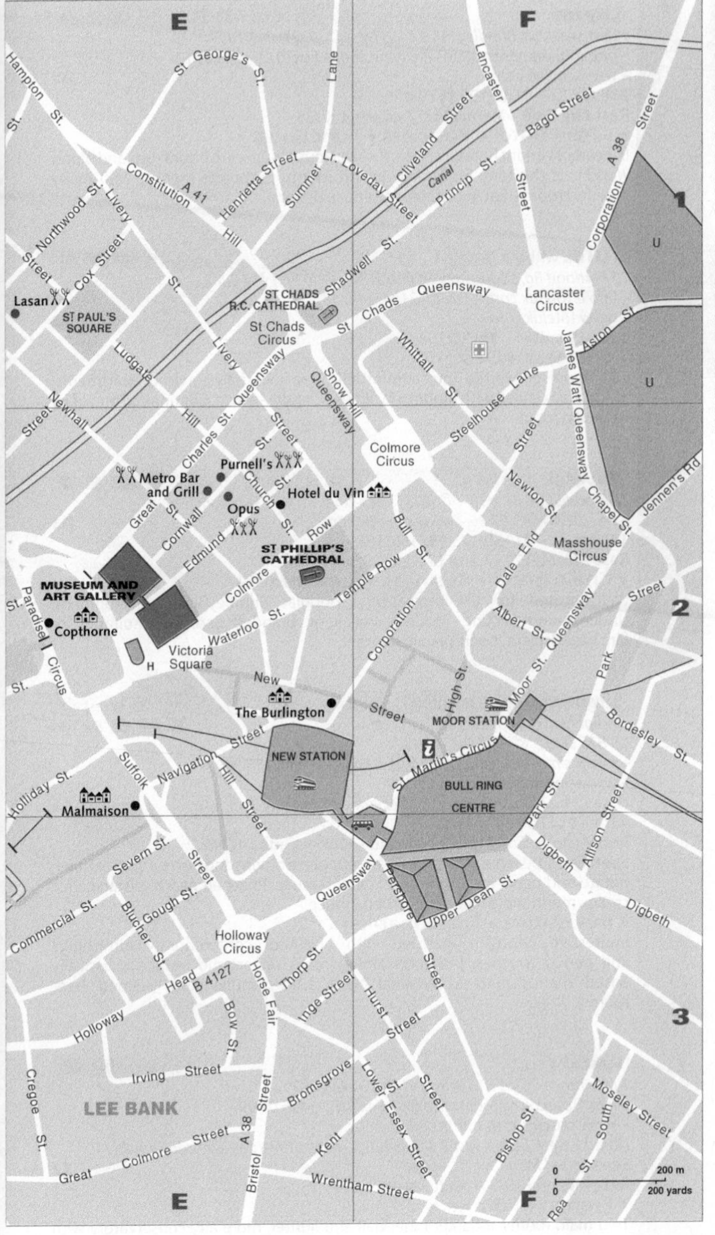
E
F
1
2
3
MUSEUM AND ART GALLERY
ST PHILLIP'S CATHEDRAL
ST CHADS R.C. CATHEDRAL
St Chads Circus
Colmore Circus
Lancaster Circus
Masshouse Circus
Victoria Square
Holloway Circus
NEW STATION
MOOR STATION
BULL RING CENTRE
ST PAUL'S SQUARE
LEE BANK
Lasan
Metro Bar and Grill
Purnell's
Opus
Hotel du Vin
Copthorne
The Burlington
Malmaison
200 m
200 yards

City Inn

1 Brunswick Sq, Brindley Pl ✉ B1 2HW – ✆ (0121) 643 1003 – birmingham.reservations@cityinn.com – Fax (0121) 643 10 05 – www.cityinn.com

D2

238 rm – £89/195 £99/205

Rest *City Café* – Menu £13/17 – Carte £17/35

◆ Chain hotel ◆ Business ◆ Functional ◆

In heart of vibrant Brindley Place; the spacious atrium with bright rugs and blond wood sets the tone for equally stylish rooms. Corporate friendly with many meeting rooms. Eat in restaurant, terrace or bar.

TOTEL without rest

19 Portland Rd, Edgbaston ✉ B16 9HN – ✆ (0121) 454 5282 – info@toteluk.com – Fax (0121) 456 46 68 – www.toteluk.com

Plan I **A2**

1 rm – 9 suites – £75/105

◆ Business ◆ Design ◆

19C house converted into comfortable, spacious fully-serviced apartments, individually styled with modern facilities. Friendly service. Continental breakfast served in room.

Novotel

70 Broad St ✉ B1 2HT – ✆ (0121) 643 2000 – h1077@accor.com – Fax (0121) 643 97 86 – www.novotel.com

D3

148 rm – £155/175 £165/185

Rest – Menu £20 – Carte £21/28

◆ Chain hotel ◆ Business ◆ Functional ◆

Well located for the increasingly popular Brindleyplace development. Underground parking. Modern, well-kept, branded bedrooms suitable for families. Modern, open-plan restaurant.

Simpsons (Andreas Antona) with rm

20 Highfield Rd, Edgbaston ✉ B15 3DU – ✆ (0121) 454 3434 – info@simpsonsrestaurant.co.uk – Fax (0121) 454 33 99 – www.simpsonsrestaurant.co.uk

closed 24-27 December and 31 December-1 January

Plan I **A2**

4 rm – £110 £160/225

Rest – *(closed Sunday dinner)* Menu £20/65 – Carte £42/49

Spec. Quail, pear purée with vanilla, compote of onions and port syrup. Beef fillet, potato and pancetta terrine and Madeira sauce. Poached peach, pistachio ice cream, meringue and lemon verbena sauce.

◆ Innovative ◆ Fashionable ◆

Impressive Georgian mansion with blend of contemporary furnishings and period touches. L-shaped dining room set around terrace. Classically based menus with a personal twist. Large, individually themed bedrooms.

Pascal's

1 Montague Rd ✉ B16 9HN – ✆ (0121) 455 0999 – info@pascalsrestaurant.co.uk – Fax (0121) 455 09 99 – www.pascalsrestaurant.co.uk

closed 1 week Easter, last 2 weeks July, 1 week Christmas, Saturday lunch, Sunday and Monday

Plan I **A2**

Rest – Menu £19/26 – Carte approx. £29

◆ French ◆ Formal ◆

Two main rooms; a darker inner hall and lighter, more airy conservatory with views of the small rear garden. Classical, carefully priced cooking with strong French overtones.

XXX **Purnell's** VISA AE
55 Cornwall St ✉ B3 2DH – ☎ (0121) 212 9799
– www.purnellsrestaurant.com
closed 1 week Easter, last week July, 1st week August, 1 week Christmas, Saturday lunch, Sunday and Monday **E2**
Rest – Menu £26/54
♦ Innovative ♦ Design ♦
Red brick Victorian building in heart of city, boasting large arched floor to ceiling windows and central bar. Well-priced, modern and innovative food uses quality ingredients.

XXX **Opus** AC VISA AE
54 Cornwall St ✉ B3 2DE – ☎ (0121) 200 2323
– restaurant@opusrestaurant.co.uk – Fax (0121) 200 20 90
– www.opusrestaurant.co.uk
closed 25 December-4 January, Saturday lunch, Sunday and Bank Holidays **E2**
Rest – Menu £18 – Carte £28/39
♦ Modern ♦ Design ♦
Restaurant of floor-to-ceiling glass in evolving area of city. Seafood and shellfish bar for diners on the move. Assured cooking underpins modern menus with traditional base.

XX **Lasan** VISA AE
3-4 Dakota Buildings, James St ✉ B3 1SD – ☎ (0121) 212 3664
– info@lasan.co.uk – Fax (0121) 212 36 65 – www.lasan.co.uk
closed 25-26 December **E1**
Rest – Carte £28/36
♦ Indian ♦ Design ♦
Jewellery quarter restaurant of sophistication and style; good quality ingredients allow the clarity of the spices to shine through in this well-run Indian establishment.

XX **Bank** AC VISA AE
4 Brindleyplace ✉ B1 2JB – ☎ (0121) 633 4466 – birmres@bankrestaurants.com
– Fax (0121) 633 44 65 – www.bankrestaurants.com
closed 26 December and 1 January **D2**
Rest – Menu £15 – Carte £31/37
♦ Modern ♦ Brasserie ♦
Capacious, modern and busy bar-restaurant where chefs can be watched through a glass wall preparing the tasty modern dishes. Pleasant terrace area.

XX **Metro Bar and Grill** AC VISA AE
73 Cornwall St ✉ B3 2DF – ☎ (0121) 200 1911 – Fax (0121) 200 16 11
– www.metrobarandgrill.co.uk
closed 25 December-2 January, Sunday and Bank Holidays **E2**
Rest – *(booking essential)* Carte £21/29
♦ Modern ♦ Brasserie ♦
Gleaming chrome and mirrors in a bright, contemporary basement restaurant. Modern cooking with rotisserie specialities. Spacious, ever-lively bar serves lighter meals.

XX **Zinc Bar and Grill** AC VISA AE
Regency Wharf, Broad St ✉ B1 2DS – ☎ (0121) 200 0620
– zinc.birmingham@irpic.co.uk – Fax (0121) 200 06 30
– www.zincbar.co.uk
closed 24-26 December, 1 January, Sunday and Monday **D2**
Rest – Menu £13 – Carte £23/30
♦ Modern ♦ Brasserie ♦
Purpose-built restaurant in lively pub and club area of city. Spiral staircase leads to dining area, including terrace overlooking canal. Modern, classically toned, dishes.

at Birmingham Airport

Novotel Birmingham Airport

Terminal 1 ✉ *B26 3QL* – ✆ *(0121) 782 7000 – h1158@accor.com – Fax (0121) 782 04 45 – www.novotel.com*
195 rm – £135 ££135, £13.95
Rest – *(bar lunch Saturday, Sunday and Bank Holidays)* Menu £18 (lunch) – Carte £20/34

• Chain hotel • Business • Functional •

Opposite main terminal building: modern hotel benefits from sound proofed doors and double glazing. Mini bars and power showers provided in spacious rooms with sofa beds. Open-plan garden brasserie.

at National Exhibition Centre

Crowne Plaza

Pendigo Way ✉ *B40 1PS* – ✆ *(0870) 400 9160 – necroomsales@ihg.com – Fax (0121) 781 43 21 – www.crowneplaza.co.uk*
242 rm – £99/259 £119/279, £15.95
Rest – *(bar lunch Saturday)* Carte £29/32

• Business • Modern •

Modern hotel adjacent to NEC. Small terrace area overlooks lake. Extensive conference facilities. State-of-the-art bedrooms with a host of extras.

EDINBURGH

EDINBURGH

Population: 430 082 (conurbation 452 194 – Altitude: 50m

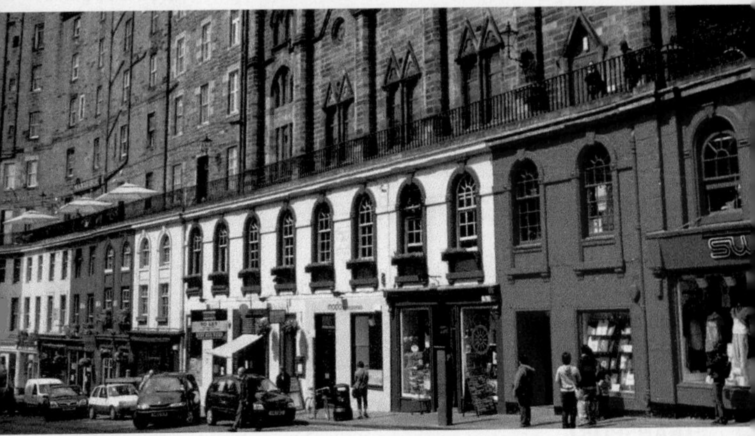

T. Bognar/PHOTONONSTOP

Edinburgh is often called 'the Athens of the North', but the beautiful Scottish capital can also bear comparison with Rome: like the Italian capital, it's laid out on seven hills. These were once of a volcanic nature, in contrast to the modern city, which is elegant, cool and sophisticated. It's essentially two cities in one, the medieval Old Town, huddled around and beneath the crags and battlements of the castle, and the smart Georgian terraces of the New Town, overseen by the eighteenth century architect Robert Adam. You could say there's a third element to the equation: the port of Leith, two miles from the centre, which has undergone a revamp over the last decade to take its place as Edinburgh's proud little relative.

This is a city that's been attracting tourists since the nineteenth century. You could even make a claim for Edinburgh being one of the places where the tourist industry came of age. That's why it sits so easily with the annual August invasion of the Edinburgh Festival. Since 1999 it's also been the home of the Scottish Parliament, adding a new dimension to its world-wide reputation. It accepts its plaudits with the same ease that it accepts an extra half million visitors at the height of summer. Its status as a UNESCO World Heritage site confirms it as a city that knows how to be both ancient and modern.

LIVING THE CITY

In the middle is the **castle**; to the south is the **old town;** to the north is the **new town**. There, in a nutshell, you have Edinburgh. But within that briefest of outlines lies so much life and colour you could find a new facet to interest you each day for a week. There's a natural boundary to the north at the Firth of Forth, while to the south lie the rolling Pentland Hills. Unless you've had a few too many drams, it's just about impossible to get lost here, as prominent landmarks like the Castle, Arthur's Seat and Calton Hill access all areas. Filleting the centre of town is the main artery of Princes Street, one side of which invites you to shop, the other to sit and relax in your own space.

PRACTICAL INFORMATION

ARRIVAL-DEPARTURE

8 miles to the west of the city is Edinburgh International Airport. There is an Airlink Bus Service to Waveley Bridge every 10min. A taxi to the city centre will cost around £17.

TRANSPORT

A great way of gaining access to many of Edinburgh's top sights is by getting an Edinburgh Pass. It gives you free entry to over 30 of the city's attractions and includes loads of great offers.

There's no underground or tram system in the city, so it might be wise to invest in a Daysaver ticket for the buses. For £2.50 you'll have the freedom of Edinburgh for 24 hours.

There are plenty of guided options for showing you around. Choose from an open-top bus, a walking or cycling tour, or, slightly more off the wall, a ghost tour of the old town. All city bus tours leave from Waverley Bridge and the hop-on, hop-off nature of the ticket will last you 24 hours.

EXPLORING EDINBURGH

The Castle Rock, epicentre of the Scottish capital, has been an elevated and indomitable refuge for over a thousand years, and it's from here that the city grew, abetted by Stuart kings who favoured Edinburgh as their royal residence. Breathe in its air and pick up its scent. Wherever you are, its ancient geography seeps into your pores. Whether it's from the extinct volcanic mound of Arthur's Seat in Holyrood Park, or the pivotal lump of rock upon which the castle hovers; whether you're atop the craggy splendour of Calton Hill or down in the mysterious dank of a medieval wynd, this is a city scraped from the work of primeval forces.

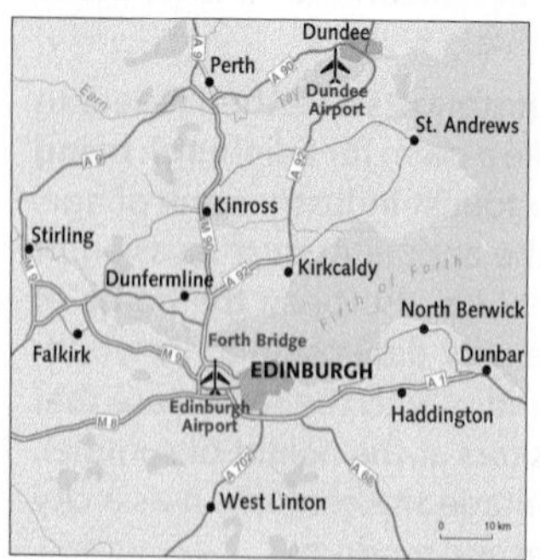

The old town is hued from stone, with tightly packed, granite grey houses, each having their own story to tell. **The Royal Mile** is the main spine of the area, running downhill from the castle through Lawnmarket past St Giles' Cathedral, through Canongate to Holyroodhouse and the Scottish Parliament building. The bottom section is far quieter than the tourist-oriented upper part, but all the way down, every narrow wynd (stone staircase) and (nearly) every building withholds ancient secrets, bound up in wondrous gables, turrets and towering chimneys. Two places to seek out in this vicinity: one is the **Writers' Museum** in Lady Stair's Close off Lawnmarket. This is full of the paraphernalia of three of Scotland's most famous writers – Robert Burns, Sir Walter Scott and Robert Louis Stevenson. The latter got his inspiration for Dr. Jekyll and Mr. Hyde from a notorious local schizophrenic who was a respectable councillor and cabinet-maker by day, burglar and thief by night. The man was eventually caught and hanged, but his name lives on at Deacon Brodie's Tavern further along Lawnmarket.

Try and avoid the crowds for a while by wandering off into a charming little close, or exploring the tunnels and wynds that connect streets on different levels - these can be the most fascinating elements of the Royal Mile. Gladstone's Land in Lawnmarket will enhance this feel for the sixteenth century: it's a six-storey former merchant's home and shop, and it's been restored to its former glory. You can actually partake in this yourself, as four of the apartments are available to rent. Any stroll down the Royal Mile wouldn't be complete without coming under the lowering glare of **St Giles Cathedral**, or to give it its proper Scottish name, The High Kirk. It's a magnificently sombre place dating from 1120, but don't expect the interior to be too ornate: Calvinist zealots during the Reformation saw to that. This deep, dark landmark acts as a kind of focal point for Festival revellers, but of more relevance it's where ghost-tour companies pitch up and lead you off to spooky cellars and shabby arches.

→ SO WHAT'S NEW?

A different feel pervades the New Town, which you reach via a pleasant walk over the Waverley railway bridge and across Princes Street. 'New' in this case is a relative term. This part of town was pastureland known as The Long Dikes and architect Robert Adam transformed it in the latter part of the 18C, when union with England was bringing the city new prosperity. It's an area with wide, spacious streets, open grassy squares and classical lines: essentially it's the diametric opposite of the Old Town. Its rectangle of streets and terraces is one of the first and finest examples of town planning in Europe. The elegant Georgian architecture you find here now acts as the backdrop to a yummy collection of equally stylish shops, restaurants and bars; rather out of the ordinary in a stylistic sense is the distinctive neo-Gothic **Scottish National Portrait Gallery**, a great place to spend a wet afternoon, taking in the visual history of the country's rebels, philosophers, heroes and villains. Contemporary portraits include the likes of novelist Irvine Welsh, actor Sean Connery and ex-footballer Danny McGrain, possibly a surprise inclusion since he made his name playing for a Glasgow club...

Edinburgh never really takes on an 'industrial' aspect; with the likes of **Princes Street Gardens** right there in the heart of things, it's easy to feel green here. Nevertheless, there's a wonderful place to go if you want to take things to a more rural plane. It's The Water of Leith, a short bus ride out of the centre; it starts close to the entrance to Murrayfield Rugby Stadium and meanders along a walkway for all of 21 miles, taking in the delightful Dean Village, a former grain-milling centre dating from the twelfth century, plunged down a valley 30 metres deep. The village's old buildings have been restored and converted into apartments and houses: there's a famous view here looking downstream beneath the thrusting arches of Thomas Telford's Dean Bridge (close by you can get a cultural hit at the Scottish National Gallery of Modern Art, which includes works by Vuillard, Matisse, Lichtenstein and Giacometti, as well as Scottish painters of the vibrant Colourist school).

The Water of Leith Walkway is one of the city's most tranquil strolls, with a pleasant mix of village and woodland along the way. An ideal end point for many is the **Royal Botanic Garden**, which boasts the world's largest collection of rhododendrons, plus rock gardens with a waterfall and redwoods in a mini-forest.

→ KEEPING YOU PAGED

Per capita head, Edinburgh boasts more booksellers than any other city in Britain. In 2004 it became the first city in the world to be named City of Literature by UNESCO.

→ TAKE IT OR LEITH IT

At the end of the engaging Walkway, **Leith** is a very agreeable place to pitch up. The former dockland area staring out onto the Firth of Forth was a typical run-down port of aching infrastructure and rough-and-ready seamen's bars until the late 80s, when it experienced a renaissance. Nineteenth century warehouses were converted into loft apartments and a coterie of stylish bars and restaurants opened their doors. Proof of their impact came when two eating establishments in the area earned Michelin stars: Martin Wishart and The Kitchin. Both are located in old dockside conversions. There's also the smart Ocean Terminal shopping complex adding a retail landmark to the serene waterfront ambience.

Edinburgh is a superb city to explore. Its topography and its architecture give it varied nuance and colour. It can also be a pretty cool city, and not just in the cultural sense. Summer temperatures are unlikely to climb much above 18 Celsius, but in a place as fascinating as this, wrap up warm and you'll hardly notice.

→ REEL LIFE

Edinburgh's a popular place with filmmakers. Movies shot in and around the city include Trainspotting, The Prime of Miss Jean Brodie, The Da Vinci Code, The 39 Steps, and Mary Reilly.

EDINBURGH IN...

→ ONE DAY

Calton Hill, Royal Mile, Edinburgh Castle, New Town café, Old town pub

→ TWO DAYS

Water of Leith, Scottish National Gallery of Modern Art, Leith and one of its smart restaurants, Forth Rail Bridge

→ THREE DAYS

Arthur's Seat, National Museum of Scotland, Holyrood Park, a trip to the Pentland Hills

CALENDAR HIGHLIGHTS

Festivals are a part and parcel of Edinburgh life, and not just the famous jamboree every August. In the spring, the Ceilidh Culture Festival highlights local performers as well as others from around the world, and takes place over three weeks in 30 different venues. Mary King's Ghost Fest is a 10-day bonanza for anyone interested in the city's haunted sites, and includes overnight vigils and experiments. December is a special time of year here. There are all kinds of markets and fun fairs at Christmas, while Hogmanay is a four day sporrans-up with a torchlight procession on the 29th, a carnival on George Street on the 30th, a street party (to end all street parties) on New Year's Eve, plus a host of events to detox and energise on the first day of the year. The Summer Festival, the one that the world not only knows about but appears to attend en masse, is in fact an umbrella term for many distinct cultural events taking place, including an international festival and others for film, fringe, art, books, jazz and blues.

EATING OUT

Food and drink in Edinburgh takes on many forms. It can range from the 'tartan menus' fodder for tourists to the very best, via the smart conversions of Leith or the exquisite central hotels, as in the case of the landmark Balmoral, at the head of Princes Street with its immaculate basement restaurant, Number One. Edinburgh is said to have more restaurants per head of population than anywhere else in the UK, and you can admire the city from a rooftop table, or dine with ghosts in a basement eatery. There are some good pubs in the old town, such as the tiny but hip Black Bo's in Blackfriars Street, or the authentically atmospheric Ensign Ewart on Lawnmarket. Drinking dens also abound in Cowgate and Grassmarket. Further away, in West End, you'll find enticing late-night bars, while the stylish variety, serving cocktails, are more in order in the George Street area of new town. What to drink in Scotland's capital? Any beer by Deuchar's gets the thumbs-up, or a pint of Dark Island from Orkney. Peaty flavoured Laphroaig is a highly recommended dram of whisky. For those who might want to buy their grub and take it away to eat, then a visit to Valvona & Crolla is a must. It's in Elm Row near Calton Hill, and is a great Italian deli: a weekly van from Italy brings wonderful cheeses, olive oils, wine and salamis, and if the temptation's too strong, you can try them at once in the café at the back. The nineteenth century Cadenhead's on the Royal Mile is the place to go for whiskies: it sells a mind-boggling range of rare distillations.

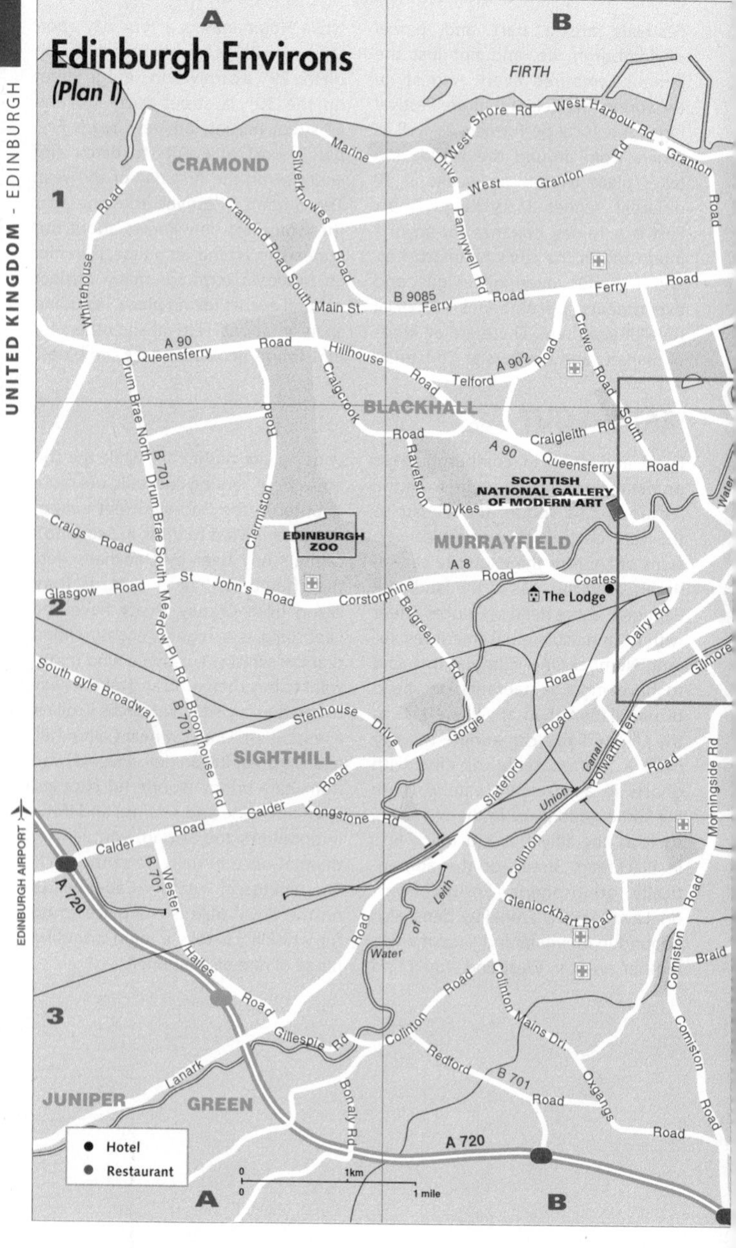
Edinburgh Environs
(Plan I)
A
B
1
2
3
FIRTH
CRAMOND
BLACKHALL
MURRAYFIELD
SIGHTHILL
JUNIPER
GREEN
SCOTTISH NATIONAL GALLERY OF MODERN ART
EDINBURGH ZOO
The Lodge
West Shore Rd
West Harbour Rd
Granton
Marine
West Drive
West Granton Rd
Silverknowes Road
Cramond Road South
Pannywell Rd
Whitehouse Road
B 9085 Ferry Road
Ferry Road
Main St.
A 90 Queensferry Road
Hillhouse Road
Telford A 902 Road
Crewe Road South
Craigcrook Road
Craigleith Rd
A 90 Queensferry Road
Drum Brae North
B 701 Drum Brae South
Clermiston Road
Ravelston Dykes
Craigs Road
A 8 Road
Coates
Glasgow Road
St John's Road
Corstorphine
Balgreen Rd
Dairy Rd
Gilmore
Water
Meadow Pl. Rd
South gyle Broadway
B 701 Broomhouse Rd
Stenhouse Drive
Gorgie Road
Slateford Road
Polwarth Terr.
Union Canal
Road
Morningside Rd
Calder Road
Longstone Rd
Colinton
Gleniockhart Road
Road
Braid
B 701 Wester Hailes Road
A 720
Water of Leith
Colinton Road
Comiston
Comiston Road
Colinton Mains Dri.
Gillespie Rd
Lanark
Redford B 701 Road
Oxgangs Road
Bonaly Rd
A 720
EDINBURGH AIRPORT
Hotel
Restaurant
0
1km
0
1 mile

C
D
OF
FORTH
1
2
3
TRINITY
Lindsay Rd
901
Craighall Rd
Newhaven Rd
Ferry Rd
The Kitchin
Malmaison
Kings Wark
Martin Wishart
The Vintners Rooms
The Plumed Horse
A 199
Seafield Road
LEITH
ROYAL BOTANIC GARDENS
Broughton Rd
Pilrig St.
Leith Walk
Easter Road
Lockend Rd
Restalrig Rd
Edinburgh Centre (Plan II)
Sleigh Drive
Craigentimy Rd
Seafield Road East
Marionville Rd
Restalrig Rd S.
RESTALRIG
London Road
York Pl.
Queen St.
George St.
WAVERLEY
Regent Rd
ABBEY AND PALACE OF HOLYROODHOUSE
A 1140
Portobello Road
Portobello High St.
Willowbrae Road
CASTLE
Holyrood Rd
Queen's Drive
West Port
Nicolson St.
HOLYROOD PARK
MEADOW PARK
Melville Drive
West Milton Rd
Milton Road West
Queen's Drive
DUDDINGSTON
Grange Rd
Mainto St.
Dalkeith Road
Prestonfield
Duddingston
Grange Loan
Mayfield Road
A 6095
Niddrie Mains Rd
Peffermill Road
Kildonan Lodge
Lady Rd
A 6106
Craigmillar Castle Road
Old Dalkeith Road
RAID
U
Braid Burn
Liberton Brae
Gilmerton
The Wisp
Millerhill Road
Hills Drive
Kirk Brea
Kirkgate
CRAIGMILLAR CASTLE
Liberton Drive
NORTHFIELD
Liberton Gdns
Lasswade Road
Ferniehill Drive
DRUM WOOD
FAIRMILEHEAD
B 701
Drum St.
GILMERTON
Howden Hall Rd
Captain's Rd
Gilmerton Rd
Frogston Rd West
Frogston Rd East
Lasswade Rd

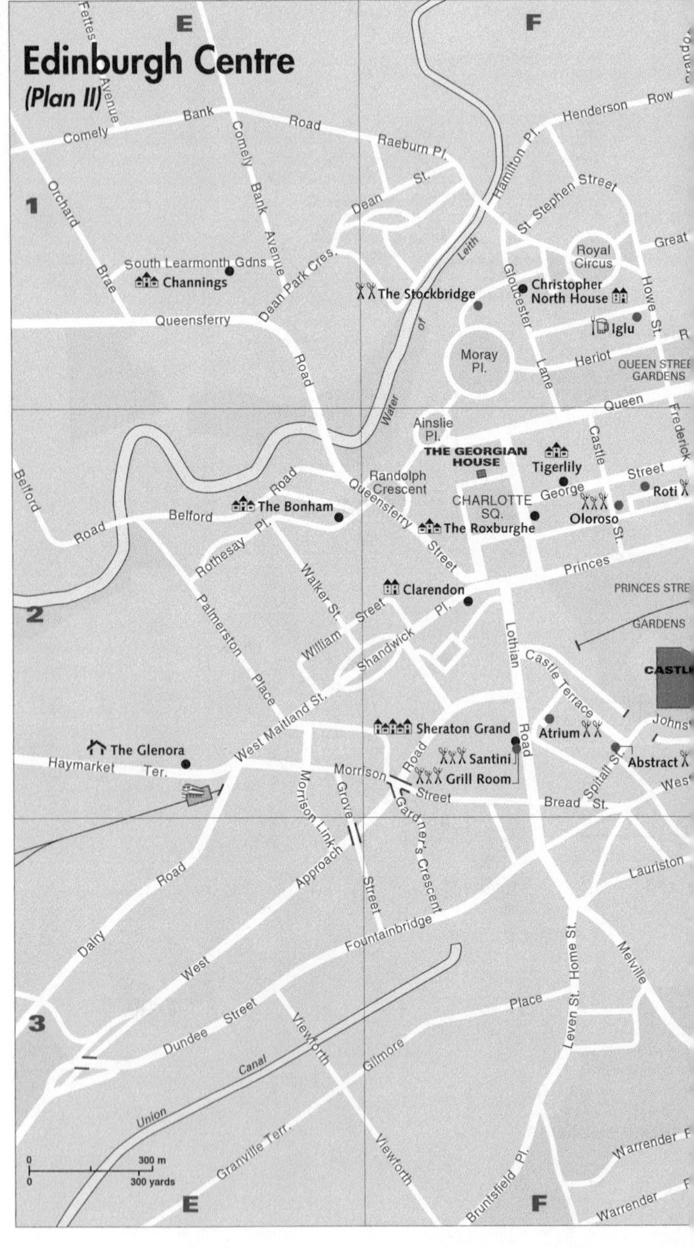

Edinburgh Centre
(Plan II)
E
F
1
2
3
Channings
The Stockbridge
Christopher North House
Iglu
THE GEORGIAN HOUSE
Tigerlily
The Bonham
The Roxburghe
Oloroso
Roti
Clarendon
Sheraton Grand
Atrium
The Glenora
Santini
Grill Room
Abstract
Royal Circus
Moray Pl.
CHARLOTTE SQ.
Randolph Crescent
Ainslie Pl.
QUEEN STREET GARDENS
PRINCES STREET GARDENS
CASTLE
Queensferry Road
Queensferry Street
Princes Street
George Street
Queen Street
Haymarket Ter.
West Maitland St.
Lothian Road
Fountainbridge
Union Canal
Water of Leith
300 m
300 yards

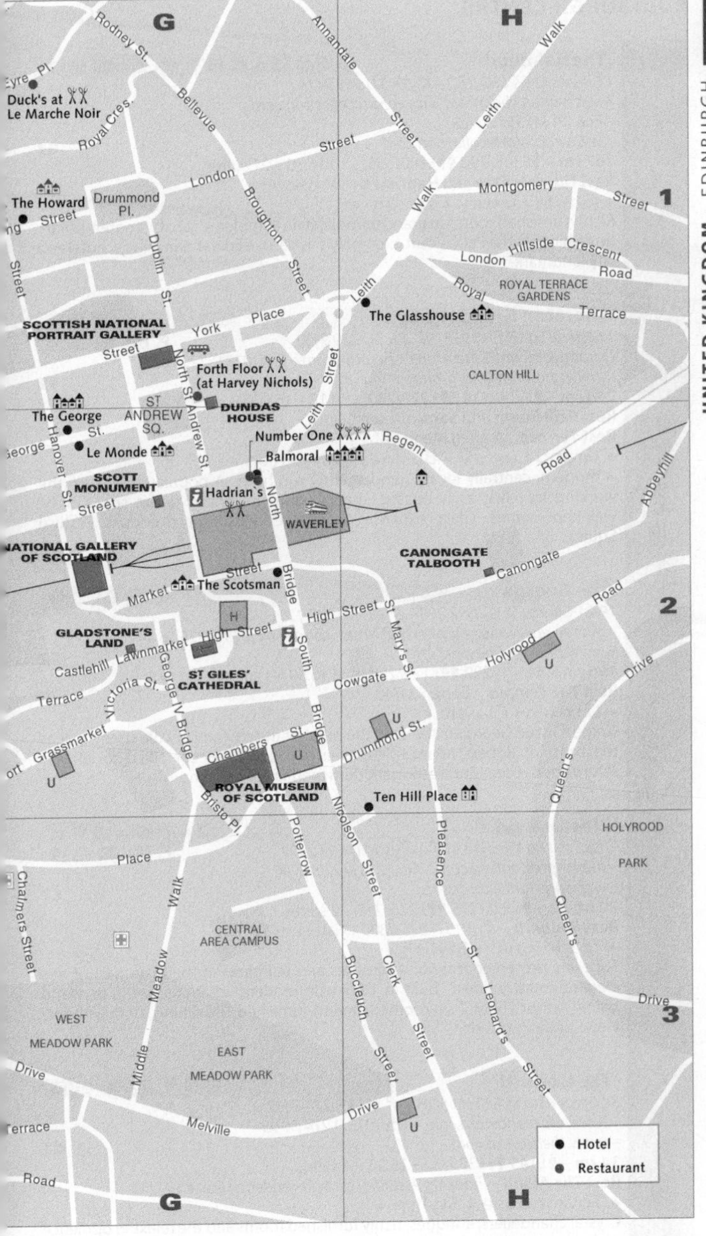
G
H
1
2
3
Duck's at Le Marche Noir
The Howard
The Glasshouse
SCOTTISH NATIONAL PORTRAIT GALLERY
Forth Floor (at Harvey Nichols)
DUNDAS HOUSE
The George
Le Monde
Number One
Balmoral
SCOTT MONUMENT
Hadrian's
WAVERLEY
NATIONAL GALLERY OF SCOTLAND
CANONGATE TALBOOTH
The Scotsman
GLADSTONE'S LAND
ST GILES' CATHEDRAL
ROYAL MUSEUM OF SCOTLAND
Ten Hill Place
CALTON HILL
ROYAL TERRACE GARDENS
HOLYROOD PARK
CENTRAL AREA CAMPUS
WEST MEADOW PARK
EAST MEADOW PARK
ST ANDREW SQ.
Hotel
Restaurant

The Balmoral

1 Princes St ✉ EH2 2EQ – ✆ (0131) 556 2414
– reservations.balmoral@roccofortecollection.com
– Fax (0131) 557 87 40
– www.roccofortecollection.com **G2**
167 rm – ♀£305/490 ♀♀£360/555, ☕ £18.50 – 21 suites
Rest Number One and **Hadrian's** – see below
◆ Grand Luxury ◆ Classic ◆
Richly furnished rooms in grand baronial style complemented by contemporary furnishings in the Palm Court exemplify this de luxe Edwardian railway hotel and city landmark.

Sheraton Grand H & Spa

1 Festival Sq ✉ EH3 9SR – ✆ (0131) 229 9131
– grandedinburgh.sheraton@sheraton.com – Fax (0131) 229 96 31
– www.sheraton.com/grandedinburgh **F2**
244 rm – ♀£209/219 ♀♀£229/239, ☕ £18 – 16 suites
Rest Grill Room and **Santini** – see below
Rest *Terrace* – *(buffet)* Menu £21/22
◆ Grand Luxury ◆ Business ◆ Modern ◆
A modern, centrally located and smartly run hotel. A popular choice for the working traveller, as it boasts Europe's most advanced urban spa. Comfy, well-kept rooms. Glass expanse of Terrace restaurant overlooks Festival Square.

The George

19-21 George St ✉ EH2 2PB – ✆ (0131) 225 1251
– george.reservations@principal-hotels.com – Fax (0131) 226 56 44
– www.principal-hayley.com **G2**
196 rm – ♀£129/299 ♀♀£129/299, ☕ £16.50 – 1 suite
Rest *The Tempus* – Carte £24/40
◆ Luxury ◆ Classic ◆
Grade II listed Georgian classic in the heart of the city's most chic street; makes the most of Robert Adam's listed design. Modern decor allied to smartly refurbished rooms. Interesting modern menus at The Tempus.

Prestonfield

Priestfield Rd ✉ EH16 5UT – ✆ (0131) 662 2300
– mail@prestonfield.com – Fax (0131) 220 43 92
– www.prestonfield.com *Plan I* **C2**
20 rm ☕ – ♀£225/275 ♀♀£225/275 – 2 suites
Rest *Rhubarb* – ✆ *(0131) 225 7800* – Carte £36/52
◆ Traditional ◆ Stylish ◆
Superbly preserved interior, tapestries and paintings in the main part of this elegant country house, built in 1687 with modern additions. Set in parkland below Arthur's Seat. Two-roomed, period-furnished 18C dining room with fine views of the grounds.

The Howard

34 Great King St ✉ EH3 6QH – ✆ (0131) 274 7402
– reserve@thehoward.com – Fax (0131) 274 74 05
– www.thehoward.com **G1**
14 rm – ♀£145 ♀♀£275, ☕ £16.50 – 4 suites
Rest *The Atholl* – *(booking essential for non-residents)* Carte £27/36
◆ Townhouse ◆ Stylish ◆
Crystal chandeliers, antiques, richly furnished rooms and the relaxing opulence of the drawing room set off a fine Georgian interior. An inviting "boutique" hotel. Elegant, linen-clad tables for sumptuous dining.

The Scotsman

20 North Bridge ✉ EH1 1YT – ✆ (0131) 556 5565 – reservations@thescotsmanhotelgroup.co.uk – Fax (0131) 652 36 52 – www.thescotsmanhotel.co.uk G2

57 rm – 🛉£200/260 🛉🛉£210/270, ☕ £17.50 – 12 suites

Rest *Vermilion* – *(closed Monday-Tuesday) (dinner only)* Carte £32/47

Rest *North Bridge Brasserie* – Carte £20/45

♦ Luxury ♦ Classic ♦

Imposing former offices of "The Scotsman" newspaper, with marble reception hall and historic prints. Notably impressive leisure facilities. Well-equipped modern bedrooms. Vibrant, richly red Vermilion. North Bridge Brasserie boasts original marble pillars.

Channings

15 South Learmonth Gdns ✉ EH4 1EZ – ✆ (0131) 315 2226 – reserve@channings.co.uk – Fax (0131) 332 96 31 – www.channings.co.uk E1

38 rm ☕ – 🛉£135/155 🛉🛉£175/185 – 3 suites

Rest – Menu £17 (lunch) – Carte £22/40

♦ Townhouse ♦ Stylish ♦

Sensitively refurbished rooms and fire-lit lounges blend an easy country house elegance with original Edwardian character. Individually appointed bedrooms. A warm, contemporary design doesn't detract from the formal ambience pervading this basement restaurant in which classic Gallic flavours hold sway.

The Bonham

35 Drumsheugh Gdns ✉ EH3 7RN – ✆ (0131) 274 7400 – reserve@thebonham.com – Fax (0131) 274 74 05 – www.thebonham.com E2

46 rm – 🛉£145/165 🛉🛉£195 – 2 suites

Rest – Carte £30/36

♦ Townhouse ♦ Stylish ♦

A striking synthesis of Victorian architecture, eclectic fittings and bold, rich colours of a contemporary décor. Numerous pictures by "up-and-coming" local artists. Chic dining room with massive mirrors and "catwalk" in spotlights.

The Glasshouse without rest

2 Greenside Pl ✉ EH1 3AA – ✆ (0131) 525 8200 – resglasshouse@theetoncollection.com – Fax (0131) 525 82 05 – www.theetoncollection.com H1

65 rm ☕ – 🛉£180/295 🛉🛉£180/295

♦ Business ♦ Modern ♦

Glass themes dominate the discreet style. Modern bedrooms, with floor to ceiling windows, have views of spacious roof garden or the city below. Breakfast room to the rear.

The Roxburghe

38 Charlotte Sq ✉ EH2 4HG – ✆ (0131) 240 5500 – roxburghe@macdonald-hotels.co.uk – Fax (0131) 240 55 55 – www.macdonaldhotels.co.uk/roxburghe F2

196 rm ☕ – 🛉£95/200 🛉🛉£95/255 – 1 suite

Rest *The Melrose* – *(closed Saturday lunch) (dinner only and Sunday lunch)* Menu £21.50/26.50 – Carte £25/32

♦ Business ♦ Classic ♦

Attentive service, understated period-inspired charm and individuality in the British style. Part modern, part Georgian but roomy throughout; welcoming bar. Restaurant reflects the grandeur of architect Robert Adam's exterior.

Tigerlily

125 George St ✉ EH2 4JN – ✆ (0131) 225 5005 – info@tigerlilyedinburgh.co.uk – Fax (0131) 225 70 46 – www.tigerlilyedinburgh.co.uk

closed Christmas Day F2

33 rm – 🛉£175 🛉🛉£175

Rest – Carte £20/34

♦ Townhouse ♦ Design ♦

Coverted Georgian townhouse boasting hip interior, including pink furnished bar, buzzy basement nightclub and glamourous, well-appointed bedrooms. Busy dining room offers wide choice of dishes, with Asian tendencies.

Le Monde &rm A/C SAT VISA MC AE

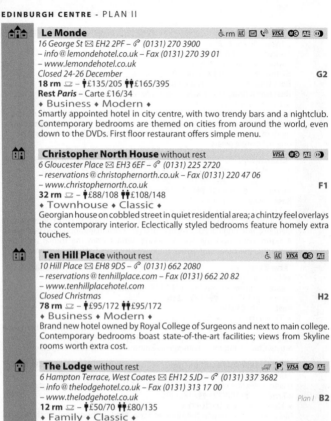

16 George St ✉ EH2 2PF – ✆ (0131) 270 3900
– info@lemondehotel.co.uk – Fax (0131) 270 39 01
– www.lemondehotel.co.uk
Closed 24-26 December **G2**

18 rm – £135/205 £165/395
Rest *Paris* – Carte £16/34

♦ Business ♦ Modern ♦

Smartly appointed hotel in city centre, with two trendy bars and a nightclub. Contemporary bedrooms are themed on cities from around the world, even down to the DVDs. First floor restaurant offers simple menu.

Christopher North House without rest VISA MC AE

6 Gloucester Place ✉ EH3 6EF – ✆ (0131) 225 2720
– reservations@christophernorth.co.uk – Fax (0131) 220 47 06
– www.christophernorth.co.uk **F1**

32 rm – £88/108 £108/148

♦ Townhouse ♦ Classic ♦

Georgian house on cobbled street in quiet residential area; a chintzy feel overlays the contemporary interior. Eclectically styled bedrooms feature homely extra touches.

Ten Hill Place without rest & A/C VISA MC AE

10 Hill Place ✉ EH8 9DS – ✆ (0131) 662 2080
– reservations@tenhillplace.com – Fax (0131) 662 20 82
– www.tenhillplacehotel.com
Closed Christmas **H2**

78 rm – £95/172 £95/172

♦ Business ♦ Modern ♦

Brand new hotel owned by Royal College of Surgeons and next to main college. Contemporary bedrooms boast state-of-the-art facilities; views from Skyline rooms worth extra cost.

The Lodge without rest P VISA MC AE

6 Hampton Terrace, West Coates ✉ EH12 5JD – ✆ (0131) 337 3682
– info@thelodgehotel.co.uk – Fax (0131) 313 17 00
– www.thelodgehotel.co.uk *Plan I* **B2**

12 rm – £50/70 £80/135

♦ Family ♦ Classic ♦

A converted Georgian manse, family owned and immaculately kept. Individually designed bedrooms and lounge decorated with taste and care; close to Murrayfield rugby stadium.

Kildonan Lodge without rest P VISA MC AE

27 Craigmillar Park ✉ EH16 5PE – ✆ (0131) 667 2793
– info@kildonanlodgehotel.co.uk – Fax (0131) 667 97 77
– www.kildonanlodgehotel.co.uk
closed one week Christmas *Plan I* **C3**

15 rm – £69/78 £78/149

♦ Family ♦ Cosy ♦

Privately managed, with a cosy, firelit drawing room which feels true to the Lodge's origins as a 19C family house. One room has a four-poster bed and a fine bay window.

The Glenora without rest SAT VISA MC

14 Rosebery Crescent ✉ EH12 5JY – ✆ (0131) 337 1186
– enquiries@glenorahotel.co.uk – Fax (0131) 337 11 19
– www.theglenorahotel.co.uk **E2**

11 rm – 45/85 80/130

♦ Family ♦ Modern ♦

Capacious Georgian house split over three floors with modern, stylish décor and generously sized bedrooms. Exclusively organic produce served at breakfast.

XXXX ✿

Number One – at The Balmoral H.

1 Princes St ✉ EH2 2EQ – ✆ (0131) 622 8831 – numberone@roccofortecollection.com – Fax (0131) 557 87 40 – www.roccofortecollection.com **G2**

Rest – *(dinner only)* Menu £63

Spec. Seared scallops, caramelized cauliflower risotto, spiced squid. Hazelnut crusted pork loin, belly parmentier, sauce Robert. Millefeuille of raspberries, peach coulis, raspberry sorbet.

♦ Modern ♦ Formal ♦

Opulently-appointed basement restaurant offering fine dining in grand railway hotel. Luxurious feel. Complex and elaborate cooking showcases Scottish produce.

XXX

Oloroso

33 Castle St ✉ EH2 3DN – ✆ (0131) 226 7614 – info@oloroso.co.uk – Fax (0131) 226 76 08 – www.oloroso.co.uk

closed first week January and 25-26 December **F2**

Rest – Carte £34/50

♦ Innovative ♦ Design ♦

Modish third floor restaurant in heart of city. Busy, atmospheric bar. Lovely terrace with good castle views to the west. Stylish, modern cooking with Asian influence.

XXX

Grill Room – at Sheraton Grand H & Spa.

1 Festival Sq ✉ EH3 9SR – ✆ (0131) 221 6422 – Fax (0131) 229 62 54

closed Saturday lunch, Sunday and Monday **F2**

Rest – Carte £29/50

♦ Modern ♦ Formal ♦

Ornate ceilings, wood panels and modern glass make an ideal setting for imaginative, well presented cooking. Local ingredients with a few European and Pacific Rim elements.

XXX

Abstract

33-35 Castle Terrace ✉ EH1 2EL – ✆ (0131) 229 1222 – reservations@abstractrestaurant.com – www.abstractrestaurant.com

Closed Sunday **F2**

Rest – Menu £17 (lunch) – Carte £30/43

♦ French ♦ Formal ♦

Tucked away behind the castle, all mock snakeskin furniture and vibrant wallpaper. Seasonal French cooking is balanced and thoughtful; formal service by a well-versed team.

XX

Santini – at Sheraton Grand H & Spa.

8 Conference Sq ✉ EH3 8AN – ✆ (0131) 221 7788 – Fax (0131) 221 77 89 **F2**

Rest – Menu £21/22 – Carte £27.50/46.50

♦ Italian ♦ Formal ♦

The personal touch is predominant in this stylish restaurant appealingly situated under a superb spa. Charming service heightens the enjoyment of tasty, modern Italian food.

XX

Atrium

10 Cambridge St ✉ EH1 2ED – ✆ (0131) 228 8882 – eat@atriumrestaurant.co.uk – Fax (0131) 228 88 08 – www.atriumrestaurant.co.uk

closed 25-26 December, 1 January, Sunday and Saturday lunch except during Edinburgh Festival **F2**

Rest – Menu £20/27 – Carte £37/47

♦ Modern ♦ Design ♦

Located inside the Traverse Theatre, an adventurous repertoire enjoyed on tables made of wooden railway sleepers. Twisted copper lamps subtly light the ultra-modern interior.

XX **Hadrian's** – at The Balmoral H. AC VISA MC AE

2 North Bridge ✉ EH1 1TR – ✆ (0131) 557 5000
– hadrians@roccofortecollection.com – Fax (0131) 557 37 47 **G2**
Rest – Carte £33/48
♦ Modern ♦ Brasserie ♦
Drawing on light, clean-lined styling, reminiscent of Art Deco, and a "British new wave" approach; an extensive range of contemporary brasserie classics and smart service.

XX **Forth Floor - Restaurant (at Harvey Nichols)**

30-34 St Andrew Sq ≤ Castle and city skyline, AC VISA MC AE
✉ EH2 2AD – ✆ (0131) 524 8350
– fourthfloorreservations@harveynichols.com
– Fax (0131) 524 83 51 – www.harveynichols.com
closed 25 December, 1 January and dinner Sunday-Monday **G1**
Rest – Menu £18 – Carte £20/38
♦ Modern ♦ Brasserie ♦
Stylish restaurant with delightful outside terrace affording views over the city. Half the room in informal brasserie-style and the other more formal. Modern, Scottish menus.

XX **The Stockbridge** VISA MC AE

54 St Stephens St ✉ EH3 5AL – ✆ (0131) 226 6766
– www.thestockbridgerestaurant.com
closed 2 weeks January, 25 December, Monday **CY**
Rest – *(dinner only Wednesday - Friday)* Menu £15/22 – Carte £24/43
♦ Modern ♦ Intimate ♦
Intimate neighbourhood restaurant, its black walls hung with colourful Scottish art. Professional staff serve a mix of classical and more modern dishes, precisely prepared.

XX **Duck's at Le Marche Noir** VISA MC AE

14 Eyre Pl ✉ EH3 5EP – ✆ (0131) 558 1608 – enquiries@ducks.co.uk
– Fax (0131) 556 07 98 – www.ducks.co.uk
Closed 25-26 December and lunch Sunday-Monday **G1**
Rest – Menu £16/28
♦ Innovative ♦ Bistro ♦
Confident, inventive cuisine with a modern, discreetly French character, served with friendly efficiency in bistro-style surroundings - intimate and very personally run.

XX **Roti** VISA MC AE

73 Morrison St ✉ EH3 8BU
– ✆ (0131) 221 9998 – info@roti.uk.com
– Fax (0131) 225 53 74 – www.roti.uk.com
Closed Saturday lunch, Sunday and Monday **F2**
Rest – Carte £23/27
♦ Indian ♦ Friendly ♦
Modern Indian restaurant in central location; traditional carved wood meets funky new fittings. Accomplished kitchen serves authentic dishes; tasting menus a highlight.

Iglu VISA MC AE

2B Jamaica Street ✉ EH3 6HH – ✆ (0131) 476 5333 – mail@theiglu.com
– www.theiglu.com
Closed 25 December and Monday-Thursday lunch **F1**
Rest – *(booking essential)* Menu £13/15 – Carte £22/35
♦ Modern ♦ Pub ♦
Vivid blue façade. Plasma screens, low tub chairs and funky music; fish tanks and potted plants upstairs. Their ethos is ethical eating; their motto 'wild, organic and local.'

Malmaison

1 Tower Pl ✉ EH6 7DB – ✆ (0131) 468 5000 – edinburgh@malmaison.com – Fax (0131) 468 50 02 – www.malmaison.com C1

95 rm – †£145/235 ††£145/235, ☕ £13.95 – 5 suites

Rest *Brasserie* – Menu £14/15 – Carte £26/41

♦ Business ♦ Stylish ♦

Imposing quayside sailors' mission converted in strikingly elegant style. Good-sized rooms, thoughtfully appointed, combine more traditional comfort with up-to-date overtones. Sophisticated brasserie with finely wrought iron.

Martin Wishart

54 The Shore ✉ EH6 6RA – ✆ (0131) 553 3557 – info@martin-wishart.co.uk – Fax (0131) 467 70 91 – www.martin-wishart.co.uk

closed 2 weeks January, Sunday and Monday C1

Rest – *(booking essential)* Menu £23/50

Spec. Lobster and smoked haddock soufflé, Poached Anjou pigeon, calamari risotto. Saint Felician and apple cannelloni.

♦ Innovative ♦ Formal ♦

Simply decorated dockside conversion with a fully formed reputation. Modern French-accented menus characterised by clear, intelligently combined flavours. Formal service.

The Kitchin

78 Commercial Quay ✉ EH6 6LX – ✆ (0131) 555 1755 – info@thekitchin.com – Fax (0131) 553 06 08 – www.thekitchin.com

closed 1-22 January, 1-16 July, Sunday and Monday C1

Rest – Menu £20 (lunch) – Carte £40/51

Spec. Roast langoustine, boned and rolled pig's head, crispy ear salad. Saddle of rabbit filled with spinach and foie gras, girolles and roasted beetroot. Cocktail of Valrhona chocolate, raspberry and praline sundae.

♦ Contemporary ♦ Design ♦

Former dockside warehouse, the industrial feel enhanced by original metal supports and battleship grey décor. Well-priced menus offering skilful, accomplished, modern cooking.

Plumed Horse

50-54 Henderson St ✉ EH6 6DE – ✆ (0131) 554 5556 – plumedhorse@aol.com – www.plumedhorse.co.uk

closed 2 weeks July, 1 week March, 1week July, 25-26 December, 1 Janaury, Sunday and Monday C1

Rest – Menu £21 (lunch) – Carte £31/38

♦ Modern ♦ Neighbourhood ♦

Homely, personally run restaurant with ornate ceiling, vivid paintings, an intimate feel and formal service. Classic cooking makes good use of seasonal Scottish ingredients.

The Vintners Rooms

The Vaults, 87 Giles St ✉ EH6 6BZ – ✆ (0131) 554 6767 – enquiries@thevintnersrooms.com – Fax (0131) 555 56 53 – www.thevintnersrooms.com/

closed 23 December-7 January, Sunday and Monday C1

Rest – Menu £20 (lunch) – Carte £33/42

♦ Mediterranean ♦ Rustic ♦

Atmospheric 18C bonded spirits warehouse with high ceilings, stone floor, rug-covered walls and candlelit side-room with ornate plasterwork. French/Mediterranean cooking.

The Kings Wark

36 The Shore ✉ EH6 6QU – ✆ (0131) 554 9260

Closed 25 December and 1 January C1

Rest – Carte £18/28

♦ Modern ♦ Pub ♦

Distinctive blue façade and cosy, characterful interior with exposed stone and beams. Hearty, unpretentious Scottish cooking. Well known for its all day weekend breakfasts.

GLASGOW

GLASGOW

Population: 616 000 (conurbation 1 228 000) – Altitude: 8m

J. Fife/Zefa/CORBIS

Rising like the proverbial phoenix from the ashes, Glasgow can claim to be one of the great urban success stories of the past 20 years. Like a punch-drunk boxer, Scotland's second city was slumped against the ropes throughout much of the post-World War II era, its shipbuilding industry in tatters, its troubled, drink-fuelled reputation a byword for the poverty endemic to its inner areas. But the place that Daniel Defoe once called "the cleanest and beautifullest and best built city in Britain, London excepted" had an ace up its sleeve: the 1990 City of Culture award that turned its PR image upside down. From that time on, Glasgow has grown immensely as an arts, business and retail centre, and tourists have discovered for themselves its grand Victorian façade and eye-catching riverside milieu.

The Clyde played a pivotal role in the original growth of Glasgow: in the 18C as a source of trade with the Americas, and in the 19th as the centre for one of the world's major shipbuilding industries. During this period many of the imposing buildings on show today were constructed, a testament to the wealth of the city. Enlightened patrons held sway, and the world of art benefited handsomely from their endowments. Now Glasgow reaps a rich cultural harvest, a dynamic image hard to imagine in the debris of a generation ago.

LIVING THE CITY

Look at a map of Glasgow and see just how the centre is laid out, Manhattan style, in a neat grid system that makes getting around town a piece of cake. Cocooned within the curving arm of the M8 motorway, the area is home to most of Glasgow's main cultural venues. "Old Glasgow", just to the east, was the original medieval centre, but is now a thriving arts quarter, and also incorporates a large part of the city's gay scene. The West End, in a kind of hinterland away from the grid system, has practically invented itself as a town in its own right. It's a bohemian district filled with cafés, bars and restaurants, a million miles from the old image of a rough, tough city, and it's where you'll also find the main art gallery and museum at Kelvingrove. Go across the Clyde, to the south, and amongst the sprawling suburbs you come across gems like The Burrell Collection and Charles Rennie Mackintosh's Scotland Street School Museum and House for an Art Lover.

PRACTICAL INFORMATION

ARRIVAL-DEPARTURE

Glasgow International Airport is 8 miles west. A taxi costs approximately £20 or there are buses that stop close to Central Station.

TRANSPORT

Glasgow has a circular underground system covering the centre and west of the city – to go right round it only takes 24 minutes! Adult single fares are £1, returns £2. 10 and 20 multi-journey tickets are available, as are seven-day passes and day passes (the Discovery ticket).

Black cabs are easy to hail all over the city: expect your driver to have a smile on his face as Glasgow cabbies are some of the friendliest in the world.

A good idea on the buses is to buy a FirstDay ticket from your driver; this will let you hop on or off buses all day until midnight.

EXPLORING GLASGOW

If you'd been bold enough to take a walk around Glasgow in its days of great industrial output, you'd have been forgiven for thinking the buildings had been constructed of black slate, such was the soot and pollutant grime that attached itself to them. Actually, many of those buildings were things of beauty constructed with red or blond sandstone, and in more recent times they've been restored to their striking original appearance. **George Square** - the heart of the city - typifies all this. It's an inspiring place to stand, its splendidly ornate nineteenth century buildings confidently reflecting the era in which they were built; in the City Chambers to this day sits the City Council. But Glasgow wouldn't be Glasgow if there weren't a temple of culture nearby, and round

the corner in Queen Street stands the **Gallery of Modern Art**, housed in a stunning neo-classical building. Outside London, it's the UK's second most visited contemporary art gallery; this is a city that knows how to put on a show.

→ BIG MACK

In the relentless days of heavy industry around the Clyde, one man's aesthetic vision helped raise people's sights above the back-breaking level of the shipyard and steel furnace. Charles Rennie Mackintosh kept alive the idea of architectural creativity with his stunning Art Nouveau 'Glasgow Style' designs. Go to Renfrew Street at the northern end of the central grid to find his elegant and unmistakable masterpiece, the **Glasgow School of Art**, started in 1899 and finished a decade later. Its stunning façade has been compared in scale and majesty to Michelangelo. On a slightly lesser scale, Mackintosh's distinctive lines are also evident at The Willow Tea Rooms in Sauchiehall Street and Buchanan Street (they're a great place to admire his work over a cuppa). Across the river, House For an Art Lover pretty much sums up its appeal. The legacy of CRM lives on: in 1999 Glasgow was the UK's City of Architecture and Design, and one of Mackintosh's buildings, the Glasgow Herald newspaper office, began a new life as **The Lighthouse**, Scotland's national centre for architecture and design. Since it opened its doors, The Lighthouse has attracted over three quarters of a million visitors making the most of attractions such as the Mackintosh Centre and The Mackintosh Tower with its spectacular views of the city.

→ WE NEED TO TALK ABOUT KELVIN

It's quite handy that it rains so much in Glasgow. It's a very good excuse for visiting any of the thirteen museums and galleries that scatter themselves around the city, which, through its teeming industrial and cultural heritage, owns one of the richest collections in Europe. There's the **People's Palace** on Glasgow Green, for instance, which lives up to its name by telling the social history of the city from 1750 to the present day, including the rise of the tobacco lords, the poverty of the 'single end' tenement house families of the 1930s...and the eye-catching banana boots Billy Connolly wore on stage in the 1970s. A trip down to the Clyde brings you to the Science Centre and IMAX theatre, a state-of-the-art attraction setting a benchmark for scientific discovery, and most definitely not the place for visitors with a creationist slant on life. Carry on down into the depths of the southern suburbs for **The Burrell Collection**, quite simply a magnificent display of works of art from all periods and all continents, or head eastwards to the eerie shadow of the Necropolis (where Glasgow's industrial barons keep silent watch over their one-time nest-egg) where you'll find Provand's Lordship, the medieval city's only surviving house, now extensively restored to give a real fifteenth century feel. It's in the West End of the city, though, that arguably Glasgow's favourite landmark can be found: **The Kelvingrove** Art Gallery and Museum was reopened two years ago after renovations, and it houses one of the finest civic collections in Europe, including fine art, archaeology and exhibits from the natural world. And if that's not enough to sate your appetite, the impressive Hunterian Museum and Art Gallery is just across Kelvingrove Park.

→ TOPS FOR SHOPS

You might not be surprised to find that the shopping's rather good in Glasgow; in fact it's second only to London for retail power in the UK. In the central grid are no fewer than three precincts, in Argyle, Sauchiehall and Buchanan Streets. There are shopping malls (Buchanan Galleries and St. Enoch Centre), and boutique designer malls (Princes Square and the Italian Centre). Out in the slightly more rarefied air of the West End, you'll find a treasure trove of antiques and rare books, while back in the heart of town, the art galleries of West Regent Street highlight the contemporary works of both up-and-coming and established artists.

➔ CLYDE VIBES

If you want to have a good time in this city it's almost impossible to fail in your quest. There's a vibrant music scene: in fact, Time Magazine not so long ago likened Glasgow to Detroit during its 1960s Motown heyday. Certainly the city has a happy knack of throwing up talented bands – of recent vintage are, for example, Franz Ferdinand, Belle & Sebastian and The Fratellis. And it was at the now legendary venue King Tut's Wah Wah Hut that Oasis were discovered by Glasgow's most famous record mogul Alan McGee. There are lots of venues to watch live music, from small pubs to landmark spaces such as the Glasgow Royal Concert Hall, the Scottish Exhibition Centre (impressively modernistic next to the Clyde), and the Barrowlands, a byword for musical excellence in the east end of the city.

Glasgow's legendary drinking culture does still live on, albeit in a noticeably more laidback 'European' style than of old, and nowhere more so than the cobbled Ashton Lane off trendy Byres Road in the West End. Jinty McGinty's bar is a favourite here, along with the locally renowned Chip. Beware strolling here on weekend evenings, as the cobbles disappear beneath the ever-burgeoning wave of humanity. Another establishment that will impress is Babbity Bowster, set in a carefully renovated townhouse in Blackfriars Street in the city centre, where the ale is invariably top-notch and the surroundings impressively informal.

If you should tire of this endlessly inspiring city, you'd be amazed at how close you are to the rugged Scottish countryside. Grab a seat on a West Highland line train out of Queen Street and you're staring at the wondrous hills within minutes…

CALENDAR HIGHLIGHTS

Glasgow's never short of a festival or two, and Glaswegians flock to them in their thousands. Celtic Connections, in January, is a widely acclaimed celebration of international roots music, while the Comedy Festival, each March, is the biggest in Europe, with the likes of Russell Brand and Joan Rivers doing a turn. Each June, The West End Festival, around Byres Road, is the

GLASGOW IN…

➔ ONE DAY

Kelvingrove Art Gallery, the West End, Glasgow School of Art

➔ TWO DAYS

Sauchiehall Street (including Willow Tea Rooms), Provand's Lordship and Necropolis, Glasgow Green, a trip on the Clyde, Science Centre

➔ THREE DAYS

A train journey to the rolling hills of the Clyde Valley, a concert at one of Glasgow's top ranking venues city's biggest, featuring a wide range of street bands and costume groups. The same month, the International Jazz Festival does exactly what it says on the label. There's a Merchant City Festival in September, in which that part of Glasgow plays host to a wide variety of cultural shows, but it's the event in chilly November that many locals keep a weather eye open for. Whisky Live, at the Exhibition Centre, is, quite simply, the world's greatest celebration of Scotland's (arguably) finest export.

EATING OUT

The dreaded legend of the deep-fried Mars bar did no favours for the reputation of the Scottish diet. Don't mention it in Glasgow, though. In the last decade, the place has undergone a gourmet revolution, and these days you can enjoy good food in restaurants from all areas of the world. There are now many establishments specializing in modern Scottish cooking and fish menus have come of age. Go to the trendy West End or Merchant City quarters to find bistros and brasseries that wouldn't be out of place in France or Italy. Glasgow has made the most of the glorious natural larder on its doorstep: spring lamb from the Borders, Perthshire venison, fresh fish and shellfish from the Western Highlands and Aberdeen Angus beef. It's always had a lot of respect for its liquid refreshment: if you want beer, you can't go far wrong with a pint of Deuchar's, the award-winning Bitter & Twisted, or an 'imported' Dark Island from the Orkneys: locals have taken to real ale from the Scottish regions in a big way.

CENTRE

Plan II

Hotel du Vin at One Devonshire Gardens

1 Devonshire Gardens ✉ G12 0UX – ✆ (0141) 339 2001 – Fax (0141) 337 16 63 – www.onedevonshiregardens.com

Plan I **A1**

45 rm – †£140/305 ††£140/305, ☐ £17 – 4 suites

Rest *Bistro* – *(Closed Saturday lunch)* Menu £18 (lunch) – Carte £36/53

♦ Townhouse ♦ Stylish ♦

Collection of adjoining 19C houses in terrace, refurbished with attention to detail. Warm, intimate and comfortable bedrooms are named after wines. High levels of service. Smart Bistro offers classic grill menu as well as more innovative carte.

Radisson SAS

301 Argyle St ✉ G2 8DL – ✆ (0141) 204 3333 – reservations.glasgow@radissonsas.com – Fax (0141) 204 33 44 – www.glasgow.radissonsas.com

D2

246 rm – †£149/200 ††£149/200, ☐ £16 – 1 suite

Rest *Collage* – *(Closed Sunday lunch)* Menu £15 – Carte £23/34

Rest *TaPaell'Ya* – *(Closed Sunday)* Carte £21/31

♦ Business ♦ Modern ♦

A stunning, angular, modish exterior greets visitors to this consummate, modern commercial hotel. Large, stylish, eclectically furnished bedrooms. Collage is a bright modern restaurant. Ta Paell'Ya serves tapas.

Hilton Glasgow

1 William St ✉ G3 8HT – ✆ (0141) 204 5555 – reservations.glasgow@hilton.com – Fax (0141) 204 50 04 – www.hilton.co.uk/glasgow

C2

317 rm – †£97/210 ††£97/210, ☐ £17.95 – 2 suites

Rest *Camerons* – *(Closed Saturday lunch and Sunday)* Carte £29/40

Rest *Minsky's* – Menu £15/25

♦ Luxury ♦ Business ♦ Modern ♦

A city centre tower with impressive views on every side. Comfortable, comprehensively fitted rooms. Extensive leisure and conference facilities. Spacious, modern Minsky's has the style of a New York deli. Contemporary cuisine served in formal Camerons.

Malmaison

278 West George St ✉ G2 4LL – ✆ (0141) 572 1000 – glasgow@malmaison.com – Fax (0141) 572 10 02 – www.malmaison.com

C2

68 rm – †£180 ††£240, ☐ £13.95 – 4 suites

Rest *The Brasserie* – Menu £15 – Carte £32/41

♦ Business ♦ Stylish ♦

Visually arresting former Masonic chapel. Comfortable, well-proportioned rooms seem effortlessly stylish with bold patterns and colours and thoughtful extra attentions. Informal Brasserie with French themed menu and Champagne bar.

Glasgow Marriott

500 Argyle St, Anderston ✉ G3 8RR – ✆ (0141) 226 5577 – frontdesk.glasgow@marriotthotels.co.uk – Fax (0141) 221 92 02 – www.marriott.co.uk/gladt

C2

302 rm – †£119/175 ††£119/245, ☐ £14.95

Rest *Mediterrano* – Carte £17/23

♦ Business ♦ Functional ♦

Internationally owned city centre hotel with every necessary convenience for working travellers and an extensive lounge and café-bar. Upper floors have views of the city.

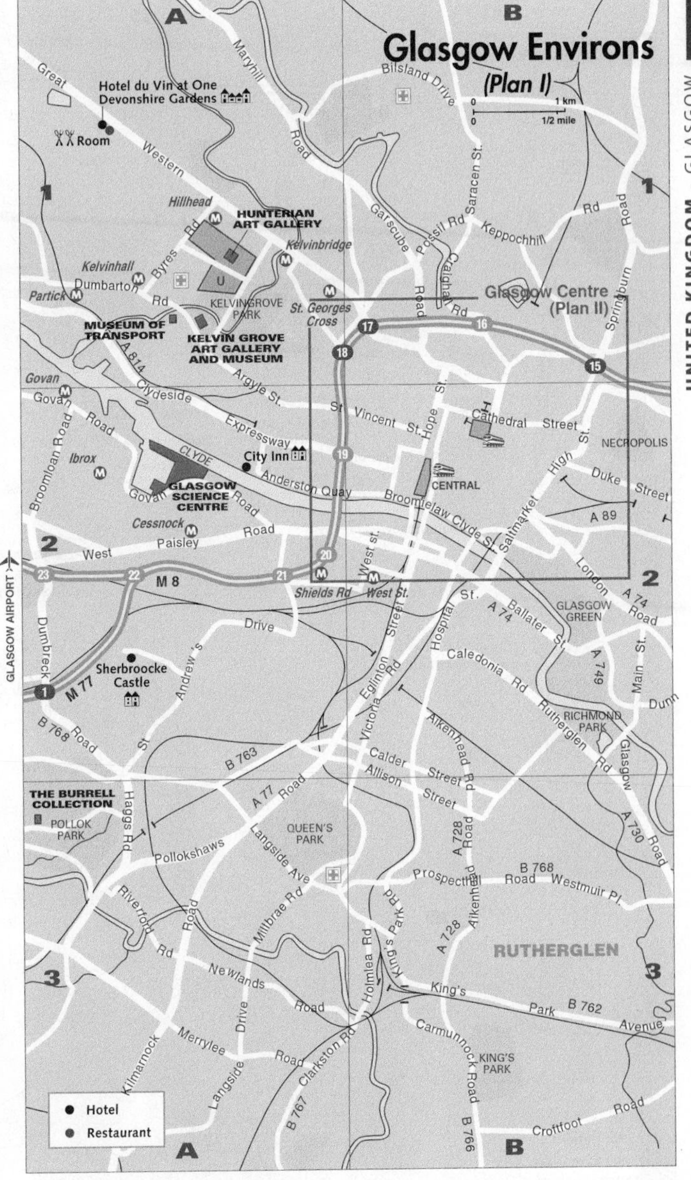
Glasgow Environs
(Plan I)
0 1 km
0 1/2 mile
A
B
1
2
3
Hotel du Vin at One Devonshire Gardens
Room
Great Western
Maryhill Road
Bilsland Drive
Hillhead
HUNTERIAN ART GALLERY
Kelvinbridge
Kelvinhall
Byres Rd
Partick
Dumbarton Rd
KELVINGROVE PARK
St. Georges Cross
Garscube Road
Possil Rd
Saracen St.
Keppochhill Rd
Craighall Rd
Springburn Road
Glasgow Centre (Plan II)
MUSEUM OF TRANSPORT
KELVIN GROVE ART GALLERY AND MUSEUM
A 814
Govan
Clydeside Expressway
Argyle St.
St Vincent St.
Hope St.
Cathedral Street
NECROPOLIS
Govan Road
Broomloan Road
Ibrox
CLYDE
City Inn
Anderston Quay
GLASGOW SCIENCE CENTRE
Govan Road
CENTRAL
High St.
Duke Street
Broomielaw
Clyde St.
Saltmarket
A 89
Cessnock
West Paisley Road
M 8
GLASGOW AIRPORT
Shields Rd
West St.
London Road
A 74
Ballater St.
GLASGOW GREEN
Main St.
Dumbreck Road
Drive
Andrew's St
Sherbroocke Castle
M 77
Eglinton Street
Victoria Rd
Hospital St.
Caledonia Rd
A 749
Dunn
Aikenhead Rd
Rutherglen Rd
RICHMOND PARK
Glasgow Road
B 768 Road
B 763
Calder Street
Allison Street
A 77 Road
THE BURRELL COLLECTION
POLLOK PARK
Haggs Rd
Pollokshaws Road
Langside Ave
QUEEN'S PARK
A 728 Road
A 730
Prospecthill Road
B 768
Westmuir Pl.
Riverford Rd
Millbrae Rd
King's Park Rd
Holmlea Rd
RUTHERGLEN
Newlands Road
King's Park Avenue
B 762
Carmunnock Road
Kilmarnock
Merrylee Road
Langside Drive
Clarkston Rd
B 767
KING'S PARK
B 766
Croftfoot Road
Hotel
Restaurant

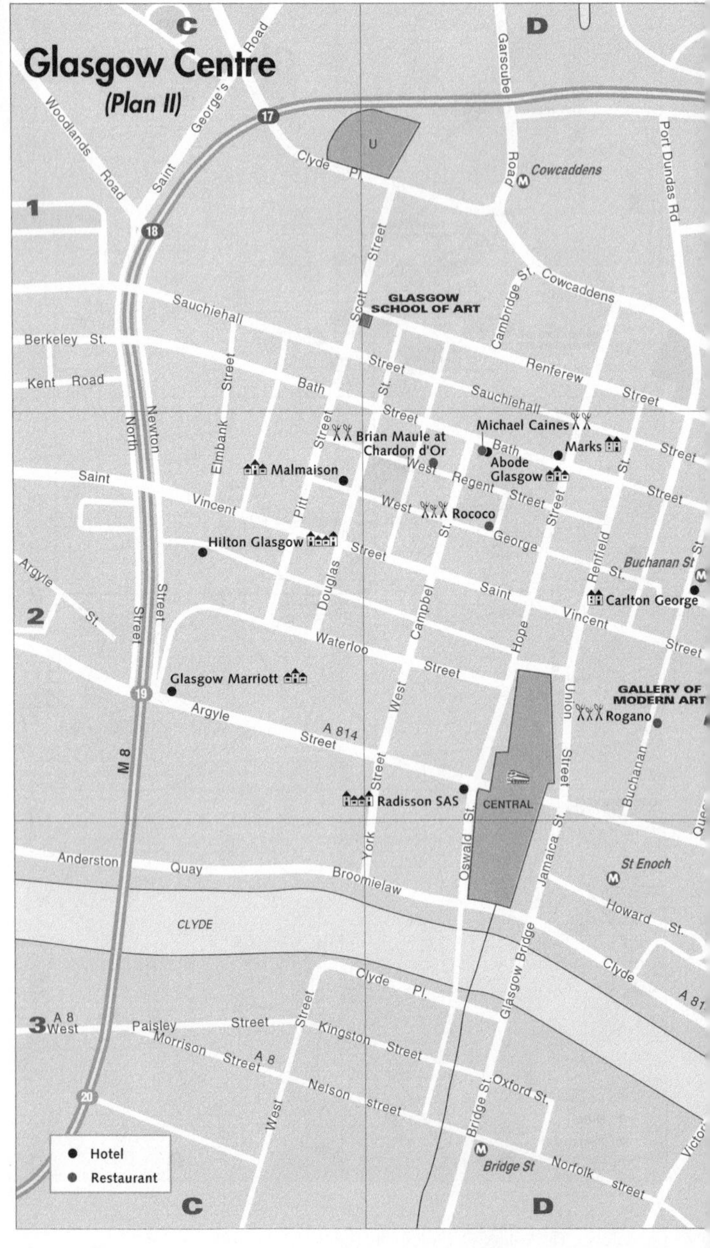
Glasgow Centre
(Plan II)
C
D
1
2
3
Woodlands Road
Saint George's Road
Clyde Pl.
Garscube Road
Cowcaddens
Port Dundas Rd
Scott Street
Cowcaddens
GLASGOW SCHOOL OF ART
Cambridge St.
Sauchiehall Street
Berkeley St.
Kent Road
Renferew Street
Bath Street
Sauchiehall Street
North Street
Newton Street
Elmbank Street
Pitt Street
Brian Maule at Chardon d'Or
Michael Caines
Marks
Abode Glasgow
Malmaison
West Regent Street
Saint Vincent Street
West George Street
Rococo
Hilton Glasgow
Douglas
Buchanan St
Carlton George
Argyle St.
Campbel St.
Hope Street
Renfield St.
Waterloo Street
Glasgow Marriott
Argyle Street
A 814
West Street
Union Street
GALLERY OF MODERN ART
Rogano
M 8
Radisson SAS
CENTRAL
Buchanan
York Street
Oswald St.
Jamaica St.
Anderston Quay
Broomielaw
St Enoch
Howard St.
CLYDE
Clyde
A 8 West
Clyde Pl.
Glasgow Bridge
Paisley Street
Morrison Street
A 8
Kingston Street
Street
Nelson street
Oxford St.
West Street
Bridge St.
Bridge St
Norfolk street
Hotel
Restaurant